Tax Formula for Individuals

Income (broadly defined)	$xx,xxx
Less: Exclusions	(x,xxx)
Gross income	$xx,xxx
Less: Deductions *for* adjusted gross income	(x,xxx)
Adjusted gross income	$xx,xxx
Less: The greater of—	
Total itemized deductions	
or standard deduction	(x,xxx)
Less: Personal and dependency exemptions	(x,xxx)
Taxable income	$xx,xxx
Tax on taxable income	$ x,xxx
Less: Tax credits (including Federal income tax	
withheld and prepaid)	(xxx)
Tax due (or refund)	$ xxx

Basic Standard Deduction Amounts

	Standard Deduction Amount	
Filing Status	**2015**	**2016**
Single	$ 6,300	$ 6,300
Married, filing jointly	12,600	12,600
Surviving spouse	12,600	12,600
Head of household	9,250	9,300
Married, filing separately	6,300	6,300

Amount of Each Additional Standard Deduction

Filing Status	**2015**	**2016**
Single	$1,550	$1,550
Married, filing jointly	1,250	1,250
Surviving spouse	1,250	1,250
Head of household	1,550	1,550
Married, filing separately	1,250	1,250

Personal and Dependency Exemption

2015	**2016**
$4,000	$4,050

South-Western Federal Taxation

Individual Income Taxes

2017

Hoffman | Young | Raabe | Maloney | Nellen

CENGAGE
Learning

Australia • Brazil • Japan • Korea • Mexico • Singapore • Spain • United Kingdom • United States

South-Western Federal Taxation: Individual Income Taxes, 2017 Edition

South-Western Federal Taxation 2017: Individual Income Taxes, 40th Edition
William H. Hoffman, Jr. | James C. Young | William A. Raabe | David M. Maloney | Annette Nellen

For product information and technology assistance, contact us at
Cengage Learning Customer & Sales Support, 1-800-354-9706

For permission to use material from this text or product,
submit all requests online at **cengage.com/permissions**
Further permissions questions can be emailed to
permissionrequest@cengage.com

This book contains select works from existing Cengage Learning resources and was produced by Cengage Learning Custom Solutions for collegiate use. As such, those adopting and/or contributing to this work are responsible for editorial content accuracy, continuity and completeness.

Compilation © 2016 Cengage Learning

ISBN: 978-1-337-05823-0

Cengage Learning
20 Channel Center Street
Boston, MA 02210
USA

Cengage Learning is a leading provider of customized learning solutions with office locations around the globe, including Singapore, the United Kingdom, Australia, Mexico, Brazil, and Japan. Locate your local office at:
www.international.cengage.com/region.

Cengage Learning products are represented in Canada by Nelson Education, Ltd.

For your lifelong learning solutions, visit **www.cengage.com/custom.**

Visit our corporate website at **www.cengage.com.**

Brief Contents

Contents

Part 3: Deductions

APPENDIXES

Online Appendixes

DEPRECIATION AND THE ACCELERATED COST RECOVERY SYSTEM (ACRS)

AFFORDABLE CARE ACT PROVISIONS

PART 1

INTRODUCTION AND BASIC TAX MODEL

CHAPTER **1**

An Introduction to Taxation and Understanding the Federal Tax Law

CHAPTER **2**

Working with the Tax Law

CHAPTER **3**

Tax Formula and Tax Determination; An Overview of Property Transactions

Part 1 provides an introduction to taxation in the United States. Although the primary orientation of this text is income taxation, other types of taxes are also briefly discussed. The purposes of the Federal tax law are examined, and the legislative, administrative, and judicial sources of Federal tax law, including their application to the tax research process, are analyzed. Part 1 concludes by introducing the basic tax model for the individual taxpayer and providing an overview of property transactions.

CHAPTER 1

An Introduction to Taxation and Understanding the Federal Tax Law

LEARNING OBJECTIVES: *After completing Chapter 1, you should be able to:*

LO.1 Demonstrate why taxation is important.

LO.2 Describe some of the history and trends of the Federal income tax.

LO.3 Assess some of the criteria for selecting a tax structure; recognize the components of a tax structure.

LO.4 Identify the different taxes imposed in the United States at the Federal, state, and local levels.

LO.5 Explain the administration of the tax law, including the audit process utilized by the IRS.

LO.6 Evaluate some of the ethical guidelines involved in tax practice.

LO.7 Recognize the economic, social, equity, and political considerations that justify various aspects of the tax law.

LO.8 Describe the role played by the IRS and the courts in the evolution of the Federal tax system.

CHAPTER OUTLINE

FAMILY AND TAXES—A TYPICAL YEAR

Travis and Betty Carter are married and live in a state that imposes both a sales tax and an income tax. They have two children, April (age 17) and Martin (age 18). Travis is a mining engineer who specializes in land reclamation. After several years with a mining corporation, Travis established a consulting practice that involves a considerable amount of travel. Betty is a registered nurse who, until recently, was a homemaker. In November of this year, she decided to reenter the job market and accepted a position with a medical clinic. The Carters live only a few blocks from Ernest and Mary Walker, Betty Carter's parents. The Walkers are retired and live on interest, dividends, and Social Security benefits.

Various developments occurring during the year with possible tax ramifications are summarized below.

- The ad valorem property taxes on the Carters' residence are increased, while those on the Walkers' residence are lowered.
- When Travis registers an automobile purchased last year in another state, he is forced to pay a sales tax to his home state.
- As an anniversary present, the Carters gave the Walkers a recreational vehicle (RV).
- When Travis made a consulting trip to Chicago, the client withheld Illinois state income tax from the payment made to Travis for his services.
- Travis employs his children to draft blueprints and prepare scale models for use in his work. Both April and Martin have had training in drafting and topography.
- Early in the year, the Carters are audited by the state on an income tax return filed several years ago. Later in the year, they are audited by the IRS on a Form 1040 they filed for the same year. In each case, a tax deficiency and interest were assessed.
- The Walkers are audited by the IRS. Unlike the Carters, they did not have to deal with an agent, but settled the matter by mail.

Explain these developments and resolve the issues raised.

Read the chapter and formulate your response.

The primary objective of this chapter is to provide an overview of the Federal tax system. Among the topics discussed are the following:

- The importance and relevance of taxation.
- A brief history of the Federal income tax.
- The types of taxes imposed at the Federal, state, and local levels.
- Some highlights of tax law administration.
- Tax concepts that help explain the reasons for various tax provisions.
- The influence the Internal Revenue Service (IRS) and the courts have had in the evolution of current tax law.

1-1 LEARNING AND COPING WITH TAXATION

LO.1

Demonstrate why taxation is important.

The study of taxation is important because taxes permeate our society. Even the simplest of decisions can carry tax implications. Does it matter, for example, which son or daughter pays the medical bills when all four adult children contribute to the support of their widowed mother? Or when you buy a new car, does it matter whether you finance the purchase through the dealership or with a home equity loan arranged by a bank?

Effectively coping with taxes often involves making decisions based on timing considerations. Does the employee who is trying to decide between a traditional Individual Retirement Account (IRA) and a Roth IRA want the tax benefit up front (i.e., traditional) or at retirement (i.e., Roth)? Timing considerations are paramount when it is deemed desirable to accelerate (or defer) income or accelerate (or defer) deductions for any one year.

Taxation is anything but stagnant. As circumstances change, so does the tax result. Consider, for example, what happens when an investor becomes a dealer—capital gains and losses on the disposition of property now convert to ordinary income and losses. Or consider an employee who becomes self-employed—the safe harbor of withholdings is lost, and new quarterly payments on income and self-employment taxes must be made. Even the purchase of a home can result in significant change—new mortgage interest and property tax deductions cause the standard deduction to be replaced by itemization on Schedule A of Form 1040.

One of the most common changes in circumstance that can affect the tax position of an individual is marital status. Getting married, although usually favorable, can sometimes have negative tax results. Even more diverse and pronounced, however, are the effects of a divorce. Are the payments from one ex-spouse to another ex-spouse deductible? From the standpoint of the recipient, are such payments taxable? Who can claim the children as dependents? Do these issues carry over to same-sex unions and divorces?

The study of taxation teaches us not to overlook the less obvious taxes that can block our intended objective. A grandson inherits his grandmother's personal residence. He has heard that rental property can generate significant income tax benefits. But does he realize that a change of ownership may unlock an appraised-value freeze on the property or that conversion from residential to income-producing use will cause an increase in ad valorem taxes on realty? Thus, an attractive income tax result could be materially diminished by adverse property tax consequences.

It is essential in working with taxation to maintain a balanced perspective. A corporation that is deciding where to locate a new factory does not automatically select the city or state that offers the most generous tax benefits. Nor does the person who is retiring to a warmer climate pick Belize over Arizona because the former has no income tax while the latter does. Tax considerations should not control decisions, but they remain one of many factors to be considered.

The study of taxation involves reviewing a multitude of rules and exceptions and, when possible, trying to understand the justification for them. But the desired goal of this learning process is the ability to recognize issues that carry tax implications. Suppose, for example, that you come upon a situation that involves a discharge of indebtedness. If you know that forgiveness of debt results in income but there are exceptions to this rule, the battle is won! The issue has been identified, and the outcome (i.e., when an exception applies) can easily be resolved by additional research.

1-2 A BRIEF HISTORY OF U.S. TAXATION

LO.2

Describe some of the history and trends of the Federal income tax.

1-2a Early Periods

An income tax was first enacted in 1634 by the English colonists in the Massachusetts Bay Colony, but the Federal government did not adopt this form of taxation until 1861. In fact, both the Federal Union and the Confederate States of America used the income tax to raise funds to finance the Civil War.

When the Civil War ended, the need for additional revenue disappeared and the income tax was repealed. Once again the Federal government was able to finance its operations almost exclusively from customs duties (tariffs). It is interesting to note that the courts held that the Civil War income tax was not contrary to the Constitution.

When a new Federal income tax on individuals was enacted in 1894, its opponents were prepared and were able to successfully challenge its constitutionality. In *Pollock v. Farmers' Loan and Trust Co.*, the U.S. Supreme Court found that taxes on the income of real and personal property were the legal equivalent of a tax on the property involved and, therefore, required apportionment.[1]

A Federal corporate income tax, enacted by Congress in 1909, fared better in the judicial system. The U.S. Supreme Court found this tax to be constitutional because it was treated as an excise tax.[2] In essence, it was a tax on the right to do business in the corporate form. As such, it was likened to a form of the franchise tax.[3] Since the corporate form of doing business had been developed in the late nineteenth century, it was an unfamiliar concept to the framers of the U.S. Constitution. Because a corporation is an entity created under law, jurisdictions possess the right to tax its creation and operation. Using this rationale, many states still impose franchise taxes on corporations.

The ratification of the Sixteenth Amendment to the U.S. Constitution in 1913 sanctioned both the Federal individual and corporate income taxes and, as a consequence, neutralized the continuing effect of the *Pollock* decision.

1-2b Revenue Acts

Following ratification of the Sixteenth Amendment, Congress enacted the Revenue Act of 1913. Under this Act, the first Form 1040 was due on March 1, 1914. The law allowed various deductions and personal exemptions of $3,000 for a single individual and $4,000 for married taxpayers. For those times, these were large exemptions that excluded all but the more wealthy taxpayers from the new income tax. Rates ranged from a low of 2 percent to a high of 6 percent. The 6 percent rate applied only to taxable income in excess of $500,000![4]

Various revenue acts were passed between 1913 and 1939. In 1939, all of these revenue laws were codified into the Internal Revenue Code of 1939. In 1954, a similar codification of the revenue law took place. The current law is entitled the Internal Revenue Code of 1986, which largely carries over the provisions of the 1954 Code. To date, the Code has been amended numerous times since 1986. This matter is discussed further in Chapter 2 under Origin of the Internal Revenue Code.

---

[1]3 AFTR 2602, 15 S.Ct. 912 (USSC, 1895). See Chapter 2 for an explanation of the citations of judicial decisions.

[2]*Flint v. Stone Tracy Co.*, 3 AFTR 2834, 31 S.Ct. 342 (USSC, 1911).

[3]See the discussion of state franchise taxes later in the chapter.

[4]This should be contrasted with the highest 2016 tax rate of 39.6%, which applies once taxable income exceeds $415,050 for single taxpayers and $466,950 for married taxpayers filing a joint return.

1-2c **Historical Trends**

The income tax has proved to be a major source of revenue for the Federal government. Exhibit 1.1, which contains a breakdown of the primary sources,[5] demonstrates the importance of the income tax. *Estimated* income tax collections from individuals and corporations amount to 60 percent of the total receipts.

The need for revenues to finance the war effort during World War II converted the income tax into a *mass tax*. For example, in 1939, less than 6 percent of the U.S. population was subject to the Federal income tax. In 1945, more than 74 percent of the population was subject to the Federal income tax.[6]

Certain changes in the income tax law are of particular significance in understanding the Federal income tax. In 1943, Congress passed the Current Tax Payment Act, which provided for the first pay-as-you-go tax system. A pay-as-you-go income tax system requires employers to withhold for taxes a specified portion of an employee's wages. Persons with income from other than wages may have to make quarterly payments to the IRS for estimated taxes due for the year.

One trend that has caused considerable concern is the increasing complexity of the Federal income tax laws. In the name of tax reform, Congress has added to this complexity by frequently changing the tax laws. Most recent legislation continues this trend. Increasingly, this complexity forces many taxpayers to seek assistance. According to estimates, more than one-half of individual taxpayers who file a return pay a preparer, and one-third purchase tax software. At this time, therefore, substantial support exists for tax law simplification.

LO.3

Assess some of the criteria for selecting a tax structure; recognize the components of a tax structure.

1-3 **CRITERIA USED IN THE SELECTION OF A TAX STRUCTURE**

In the eighteenth century, Adam Smith identified the following *canons of taxation*, which are still considered when evaluating a particular tax structure:[7]

- *Equality*. Each taxpayer enjoys fair or equitable treatment by paying taxes in proportion to his or her income level. Ability to pay a tax is one of the measures of how equitably a tax is distributed among taxpayers.

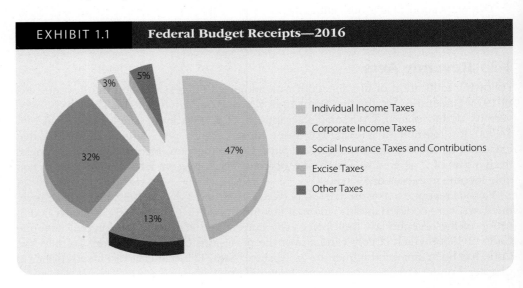

EXHIBIT 1.1   **Federal Budget Receipts—2016**

- Individual Income Taxes
- Corporate Income Taxes
- Social Insurance Taxes and Contributions
- Excise Taxes
- Other Taxes

47%, 32%, 13%, 5%, 3%

---

[5]**www.whitehouse.gov/omb**.

[6]Richard Goode, *The Individual Income Tax* (Washington, D.C.: The Brookings Institution, 1964), pp. 2–4.

[7]*The Wealth of Nations* (New York: Dutton, 1910), Book V, Chapter II, Part II.

TAX IN THE NEWS **Adam Smith Stopped Too Soon**

The American Institute of Certified Public Accountants (AICPA) has issued suggestions for Federal tax policy. Titled *Guiding Principles of Good Tax Policy: A Framework for Evaluating Tax Proposals*, the monograph sets forth 10 tax principles that are commonly used as indicators of desirable tax policy.

The first four principles are adapted from Adam Smith's *The Wealth of Nations*. The other six are summarized as follows:

- The tax system should be simple.

- The tax should be neutral in terms of its effect on business decisions.

- The tax system should not reduce economic growth and efficiency.

- The tax should be clear and readily understood so that taxpayers know about it and know when it applies.

- The tax should be structured so as to minimize non-compliance.

- The tax system should enable the IRS to predict the amount and timing of revenue production.

Source: Based on a Tax Policy Concept Statement issued by the Tax Division of the AICPA.

- *Convenience.* Administrative simplicity has long been valued in formulating tax policy. If a tax is easily assessed and collected and its administrative costs are low, it should be favored. An advantage of the existing withholding system (pay-as-you-go) is its convenience for taxpayers.

- *Certainty.* A tax structure is *good* if the taxpayer can readily predict when, where, and how a tax will be levied. Individuals and businesses need to know the likely tax consequences of a particular type of transaction.

- *Economy.* A *good* tax system involves only nominal collection costs by the government and minimal compliance costs on the part of the taxpayer.

By these canons, the Federal income tax is a contentious product. *Equality* is present as long as one accepts ability to pay as an ingredient of this component. *Convenience* exists due to a heavy reliance on pay-as-you-go procedures. *Certainty* probably generates the greatest controversy. In one sense, certainty is present because a mass of administrative and judicial guidelines exists to aid in interpreting the tax law. In another sense, however, certainty does not exist because many questions remain unanswered and frequent changes in the tax law by Congress lessen stability. Particularly troublesome in this regard are tax provisions that are given a limited life (e.g., only one year). If not extended by Congress, the provisions expire. All too often, Congress does not give the necessary approval in time, and the extension has to be applied retroactively. *Economy* is present if only the collection procedure of the IRS is considered. Although the government's cost of collecting Federal taxes amounts to less than one-half of 1 percent of the revenue collected, the complexity of our current tax structure imposes substantial taxpayer compliance costs.

1-4 THE TAX STRUCTURE

1-4a Tax Base

A tax base is the amount to which the tax rate is applied. In the case of the Federal income tax, the tax base is *taxable income.* As noted later in the chapter (Exhibit 1.2), taxable income is gross income reduced by certain deductions (both business and personal).

1-4b Tax Rates

Tax rates are applied to the tax base to determine a taxpayer's liability. The tax rates may be proportional or progressive. A tax is *proportional* if the rate of tax remains constant for any given income level. Examples of proportional taxes include most excise taxes, general sales taxes, and employment taxes (FICA and FUTA).

Assume that a jurisdiction applies a 30% tax rate to all taxable income. If Bill has $10,000 of taxable income, he will pay a tax of $3,000. If Sam has taxable income of $50,000, he will pay a tax of $15,000. If this constant rate is applied throughout the rate structure, the tax is *proportional*.

A tax is *progressive* if a higher rate of tax applies as the tax base increases. The Federal income tax, Federal gift and estate taxes, and most state income tax rate structures are progressive.

If Cora, a married individual filing jointly, has taxable income of $10,000, her Federal income tax for 2016 is $1,000 for an average tax rate of 10%. If, however, Cora's taxable income is $50,000, her Federal income tax will be $6,573 for an average tax rate of 13.1%. The tax is *progressive* because higher rates are applied to greater amounts of taxable income (see Appendix A to confirm these calculations and note how progressivity is built into the Federal income tax).

1-4c **Incidence of Taxation**

The degree to which various segments of society share the total tax burden is difficult to assess. Assumptions must be made concerning who absorbs the burden of paying the tax. For example, because dividend payments to shareholders are not deductible by a corporation and are generally taxable to shareholders, the same income is subject to a form of double taxation. Concern over double taxation is valid to the extent that corporations are *not* able to shift the corporate tax to the consumer through higher commodity prices. Many research studies have shown a high degree of shifting of the corporate income tax, converting it into a consumption tax that is borne by the ultimate purchasers of goods.

The progressiveness of the Federal income tax rate structure for individuals has varied over the years. As late as 1986, for example, there were 15 rates, ranging from 0 to 50 percent. These later were reduced to two rates of 15 and 28 percent. Currently, there are seven rates ranging from 10 to 39.6 percent.

1-5 **MAJOR TYPES OF TAXES**

LO.4

Identify the different taxes imposed in the United States at the Federal, state, and local levels.

Why does a text devoted primarily to the Federal individual income tax discuss state and local taxes? A simple illustration shows the importance of non-Federal taxes.

Rick is employed by Flamingo Corporation in San Antonio, Texas, at a salary of $74,000. Rick's employer offers him a chance to transfer to its New York City office at a salary of $94,000.

Although Rick must consider many nontax factors before he decides on a job change, he should also evaluate the tax climate. How do state and local taxes compare? For example, neither Texas nor San Antonio imposes an income tax, but New York State and New York City do. A quick computation indicates that the additional income taxes (Federal, state, and local) involve approximately $12,000.

Consequently, what appears to be a $20,000 pay increase is actually only about $8,000 when the additional $12,000 of income taxes are taken into account. Other taxes and costs (e.g., sales taxes, property taxes, food, utilities, transportation) will also have to be factored into a decision.

1-5a **Property Taxes**

Correctly referred to as **ad valorem taxes** because they are based on value, property taxes are a tax on wealth, or capital. In this regard, they have much in common with estate taxes and gift taxes discussed later in the chapter. Although property taxes do not tax income, the income actually derived (or the potential for any income) may be relevant insofar as it affects the value of the property being taxed.

Property taxes fall into *two* categories: those imposed on realty and those imposed on personalty, or assets other than land and buildings. Both have added importance because they usually generate a deduction for Federal income tax purposes (see Chapter 10).

Ad Valorem Taxes on Realty

Property taxes on realty are used exclusively by states and their local political subdivisions, such as cities, counties, and school districts. They represent a major source of revenue for *local* governments, but their importance at the *state* level has waned over the past few years. Some states, for example, have imposed freezes on upward revaluations of residential housing.

How realty is defined can have an important bearing on which assets are subject to tax. This is especially true in jurisdictions that do not impose ad valorem taxes on personalty. Primarily a question of state property law, **realty** generally includes real estate and any capital improvements that are classified as fixtures. Simply stated, a *fixture* is something so permanently attached to the real estate that its removal will cause irreparable damage. A built-in bookcase might well be a fixture, whereas a movable bookcase would not be a fixture. Certain items such as electrical wiring and plumbing cease to be personalty when installed in a building and become realty.

The following are some of the characteristics of ad valorem taxes on realty:

- Property owned by the Federal government is exempt from tax. Similar immunity usually is extended to property owned by state and local governments and by certain charitable organizations.

- Some states provide for lower valuations on property dedicated to agricultural use or other special uses (e.g., wildlife sanctuaries). Reductions in appraised valuations may also be available when the property is subject to a conservation easement (e.g., a limitation on further development).

- Some states partially exempt the homestead, or personal residence, portion of property from taxation.

- Lower taxes may apply to a residence owned by a taxpayer aged 65 or older.

- When non-income-producing property (e.g., a personal residence) is converted to income-producing property (e.g., a rental house), typically the appraised value increases.

- Some jurisdictions extend immunity from tax for a specified period of time (a *tax holiday*) to new or relocated businesses. A tax holiday can backfire, however, and cause more harm than good. If it is too generous, it can damage the local infrastructure (e.g., less funding for public works and education).

The Big Picture

EXAMPLE 4

Return to the facts of *The Big Picture* on p. 1-1. Why did the Walkers' property taxes decrease while those of the Carters increased?

A likely explanation is that one (or both) of the Walkers achieved senior citizen status. In the case of the Carters, the assessed value of their property was probably increased (see the following discussion). Perhaps they made significant home improvements (e.g., kitchen/bathroom renovation or addition of a sundeck).

Unlike the ad valorem tax on personalty (see the next section), the tax on realty is difficult to avoid. Because real estate is impossible to hide, a high degree of taxpayer compliance is not surprising. The only avoidance possibility that is generally available is associated with the assessed value of the property. For this reason, the assessed value of the property—particularly, a value that is reassessed upward—may be subject to controversy and litigation.

The history of the ad valorem tax on realty has been marked by inconsistent application due to a lack of competent tax administration and definitive guidelines for assessment procedures. In recent years, however, some significant improvements have occurred. Many jurisdictions, for example, have computerized their reassessment procedures so that they immediately affect all property located within the jurisdiction.

Several jurisdictions provide homeowners with a measure of protection from increased property taxes by "freezing" existing assessments and limiting future upward adjustments. Such restrictions on reassessments, however, do not carry over to the new owner when the property is sold. Thus, such measures tend to lock in ownership and restrict the mobility of those who might otherwise change residences.

Ad Valorem Taxes on Personalty

Personalty can be defined as all assets that are not realty. It may be helpful to distinguish between the *classification* of an asset (realty or personalty) and the *use* to which it is put. Both realty and personalty can be either business use or personal use property. Examples include a residence (realty that is personal use), an office building (realty that is business use), surgical instruments (personalty that is business use), and regular wearing apparel (personalty that is personal use).[8]

Personalty can also be classified as tangible property or intangible property. For ad valorem tax purposes, intangible personalty includes stocks, bonds, and various other securities (e.g., bank shares).

The following generalizations may be made concerning the ad valorem taxes on personalty:

- Particularly with personalty devoted to personal use (e.g., jewelry and household furnishings), taxpayer compliance ranges from poor to zero. Some jurisdictions do not even attempt to enforce the tax on these items. For automobiles devoted to personal use, many jurisdictions have converted from value as the tax base to arbitrary license fees based on the weight of the vehicle. Some jurisdictions also consider the vehicle's age (e.g., automobiles six years or older are not subject to the ad valorem tax because they are presumed to have little, if any, value).

- For personalty devoted to business use (e.g., inventories, trucks, machinery, equipment), taxpayer compliance and enforcement procedures are measurably better.

- Which jurisdiction possesses the authority to tax movable personalty (e.g., railroad rolling stock) always has been and continues to be a troublesome issue.

- A few states levy an ad valorem tax on intangibles such as stocks and bonds. Taxpayer compliance may be negligible if the state lacks a means of verifying security transactions and ownership.

1-5b Transaction Taxes

Transaction taxes, which characteristically are imposed at the manufacturer's, wholesaler's, or retailer's level, cover a wide range of transfers. Like many other types of taxes (e.g., income taxes, estate taxes, and gift taxes), transaction taxes usually are not within the exclusive province of any one level of taxing authority (Federal, state, or local government). As the description implies, these levies place a tax on transfers of property and normally are determined by multiplying the value involved by a percentage rate.

Federal Excise Taxes

Long one of the mainstays of the Federal tax system, Federal **excise taxes** had declined in relative importance until recently. In recent years, Congress substantially increased the Federal excise taxes on items such as tobacco products, fuel and gasoline sales, and air travel. Other Federal excise taxes include the following:

- Manufacturers' excise taxes on trucks, trailers, tires, firearms, sporting equipment, and coal and the gas guzzler tax on automobiles.[9]

- Alcohol taxes.

- Miscellaneous taxes (e.g., the tax on wagering).

---

[8]The distinction, important for ad valorem and for Federal income tax purposes, often becomes confused when personalty is referred to as "personal" property to distinguish it from "real" property. This designation does not give a complete picture of what is involved. The description "personal" residence, however, is clearer, because a residence can be identified as being realty. What is meant in this case is realty that is personal use property.

[9]The gas guzzler tax is imposed on the manufacturers of automobiles (both domestic and foreign) and increases in amount as the mileage ratings per gallon of gas decrease. For example, a 2015 Bentley Continental GTC manages 17 miles per gallon in combined city/highway driving and starts at $215,225. The gas guzzler tax is $3,000.

The list of transactions covered, although seemingly impressive, has diminished over the years. At one time, for example, there was a Federal excise tax on admission to amusement facilities (e.g., theaters) and on the sale of items such as leather goods, jewelry, furs, and cosmetics.

When reviewing the list of both Federal and state excise taxes, one should recognize the possibility that the tax laws may be trying to influence social behavior. For example, the gas guzzler tax is intended as an incentive for the automobile companies to build fuel-efficient cars.

State and Local Excise Taxes

Many state and local excise taxes parallel the Federal version. Thus, all states tax the sale of gasoline, liquor, and tobacco products; however, unlike the Federal version, the rates vary significantly. For gasoline products, for example, compare the 42.5 cents per gallon imposed by the state of California with the 17.3 cents per gallon levied by the state of Missouri. For tobacco sales, contrast the 17 cents per pack of 20 cigarettes in effect in Missouri with the $4.35 per pack applicable in the state of New York. Given the latter situation, is it surprising that the smuggling of cigarettes for resale elsewhere is so widespread?

Other excise taxes found at some state and local levels include those on admission to amusement facilities, on the sale of playing cards, and on prepared foods. Most states impose a transaction tax on the transfer of property that requires the recording of documents (e.g., real estate sales).[10] Some extend the tax to the transfer of stocks and other securities.

Over the last few years, two types of excise taxes imposed at the local level have become increasingly popular: the hotel occupancy tax and the rental car "surcharge." Because they tax the visitor who cannot vote, they are a political windfall and are often used to finance special projects that generate civic pride (e.g., convention centers and state-of-the-art sports arenas). These levies can be significant, as demonstrated by Houston's hotel tax of 17 percent [6 percent (state) + 7 percent (city) + 2 percent (county) + 2 percent (sports authority)].

General Sales Taxes

The distinction between an excise tax and a general sales tax is easy to make. One is restricted to a particular transaction (e.g., the 18.4 cents per gallon Federal excise tax on the sale of gasoline), while the other covers a multitude of transactions (e.g., a 5 percent tax on *all* retail sales). In actual practice, however, the distinction is not always that clear. Some state statutes exempt certain transactions from the application of the general sales taxes (e.g., sales of food to be consumed off the premises and sales of certain medicines and drugs). Also, it is not uncommon to find that rates vary depending on the commodity involved. Many states, for example, allow preferential rates for the sale of agricultural equipment or apply different rates (either higher or lower than the general rate) to the sale of automobiles. With many of these special exceptions and classifications of rates, a general sales tax can take on the appearance of a collection of individual excise taxes.

A use tax is an ad valorem tax, usually at the same rate as the sales tax, on the use, consumption, or storage of tangible property purchased outside the state but used in the state. The purpose of a use tax is to prevent the avoidance of a sales tax. Every state that imposes a general sales tax levied on the consumer also has a use tax. Alaska, Delaware, Montana, New Hampshire, and Oregon have neither tax. There is no Federal general sales or use tax.

---

[10]This type of tax has much in common with the stamp tax levied by Great Britain on the American colonies during the pre-Revolutionary War period in U.S. history.

The Big Picture

EXAMPLE 5

Return to the facts of *The Big Picture* on p. 1-1. The payment Travis made when he registered the car is probably a use tax.

When the car was purchased in another state, likely no (or a lesser) sales tax was levied. The current payment makes up for the amount of sales tax he would have paid had the car been purchased in his home state.

The use tax is difficult to enforce for many purchases; therefore, the purchaser often does not pay it. In some cases, for example, it may be worthwhile to make purchases through an out-of-state mail-order business or the websites of certain vendors. In spite of shipping costs, the avoidance of the local sales tax that otherwise might be incurred can lower the cost of such products as computer components. Some states are taking steps to curtail this loss of revenue. For items such as automobiles (refer to Example 5), the use tax probably will be collected when the purchaser registers the item in his or her home state.

ETHICS & EQUITY **Making Good Use of Out-of-State Relatives**

Marcus, a resident of Texas, has found the ideal gift for his wife in celebration of their upcoming wedding anniversary—a $22,000 diamond tennis bracelet. However, Marcus is appalled at the prospect of paying the state and local sales tax of $1,815 (combined rate of 8.25 percent). He, therefore, asks his aunt, a resident of Montana, to purchase the bracelet. The jewelry store lists the aunt as the buyer and ships the bracelet to her. Prior to the anniversary, Marcus receives the bracelet from his aunt. Is Marcus able to save $1,815 on the present for his wife? What can go wrong?

Local general sales taxes, over and above those levied by the state, are common. It is not unusual to find taxpayers living in the same state but paying different general sales taxes due to the location of their residence.

EXAMPLE 6

Pete and Sam both live in a state that has a general sales tax of 3%. Sam, however, resides in a city that imposes an additional general sales tax of 2%. Even though Pete and Sam live in the same state, one is subject to a rate of 3%, while the other pays a tax of 5%.

For various reasons, some jurisdictions will suspend the application of a general sales tax. Frequently, the "sales tax holiday" occurs in late summer when it applies to back-to-school clothing and supplies. Some states use sales tax holidays to encourage the purchase of energy-conserving appliances and hurricane preparedness items.

Severance Taxes

Severance taxes are transaction taxes that are based on the notion that the state has an interest in its natural resources (e.g., oil, gas, iron ore, or coal). Therefore, a tax is imposed when the natural resources are extracted.

For some states, severance taxes can be a significant source of revenue. Due to the severance tax on oil production, Alaska has been able to avoid both a state income tax and a state general sales tax.

1-5c **Taxes on Transfers at Death**

The right to transfer property or to receive property upon the death of the owner may be subject to estate and/or inheritance taxes. Consequently, such taxes fall into the category of excise taxes. If the tax is imposed on the right to pass property at death, it is classified as an **estate tax**. If it taxes the right to receive property from a decedent, it is termed an **inheritance tax**. As is typical of other types of excise taxes, the value of the property transferred provides the base for determining the amount of the tax.

The Federal government imposes only an estate tax. Many state governments, however, levy inheritance taxes, estate taxes, or both. Some states (e.g., Florida and Texas) levy neither tax. An estate tax is levied on the estate of the decedent, whereas an inheritance tax is paid from the property received by the heir.

At the time of her death, Wilma lived in a state that imposes an inheritance tax but not an estate tax. Mary, one of Wilma's heirs, lives in the same state. Wilma's estate is subject to the Federal estate tax, and Mary is subject to the state inheritance tax.

The Federal Estate Tax

The Revenue Act of 1916 incorporated the estate tax into the tax law. The tax was originally intended to prevent large concentrations of wealth from being kept in a family for many generations. Whether this objective has been accomplished is debatable. Like the income tax, estate taxes can be reduced through various planning procedures.

The gross estate includes property the decedent owned at the time of death. It also includes property interests, such as life insurance proceeds paid to the estate or to a beneficiary other than the estate if the deceased-insured had any ownership rights in the policy. Quite simply, the gross estate represents property interests subject to Federal estate taxation.[11] All property included in the gross estate is valued as of the date of death or, if the alternate valuation date is elected, six months later.[12]

Deductions from the gross estate in arriving at the taxable estate include funeral and administration expenses; certain taxes; debts of the decedent; casualty losses[13] incurred during the administration of the estate; transfers to charitable organizations; and, in some cases, the marital deduction. The *marital deduction* is available for amounts actually passing to a surviving spouse (a widow or widower).

Once the taxable estate has been determined and certain taxable gifts made by the decedent during life have been added to it, the estate tax can be computed. From the amount derived from the appropriate tax rate schedules, various credits should be subtracted to arrive at the tax, if any, that is due.[14] Although many other credits are also available, probably the most significant is the *unified transfer tax credit*. The main reason for this credit is to eliminate or reduce the estate tax liability for certain estates. For 2016, the amount of the credit is $2,125,800. Based on the estate tax rates, the credit exempts a tax base of up to $5.45 million.

Ned made no taxable gifts before his death in 2016. If Ned's taxable estate amounts to $5.45 million or less, no Federal estate tax is due because of the application of the unified transfer tax credit. Under the tax law, the estate tax on a taxable estate of $5.45 million is $2,125,800.

State Taxes on Transfers at Death

As noted earlier, some states levy an inheritance tax, an estate tax, or both. The two forms of taxes on transfers at death differ according to whether the tax is imposed on the heirs or on the estate.

---

[11]For further information on these matters, see *South-Western Federal Taxation: Corporations, Partnerships, Estates & Trusts*.

[12]See the discussion of the alternate valuation date in Chapter 14.

[13]For a definition of *casualty losses*, see the Glossary in Appendix C.

[14]For tax purposes, it is crucial to appreciate the difference between a deduction and a credit. A *credit* is a dollar-for-dollar reduction of tax liability. A *deduction*, however, benefits the taxpayer only to the extent of his or her tax bracket. A taxpayer in a 50% tax bracket, for example, would need $2 of deductions to prevent $1 of tax liability. In contrast, $1 of credit neutralizes $1 of tax liability.

Characteristically, an inheritance tax divides the heirs into classes based on their relationship to the decedent. The more closely related the heir, the lower the rates imposed and the greater the exemption allowed. Some states completely exempt from taxation amounts passing to a surviving spouse.

1-5d Gift Taxes

Like taxes on transfers at death, a **gift tax** is an excise tax levied on the right to transfer property. In this case, however, the tax is imposed on transfers made during the owner's life and not at death. A gift tax applies only to transfers that are not offset by full and adequate consideration.

Carl sells property worth $50,000 to his daughter for $1,000. Although property worth $50,000 has been transferred, only $49,000 represents a gift, because this is the portion not supported by full and adequate consideration.

The Federal Gift Tax

First enacted in 1932, the Federal gift tax was intended to complement the estate tax. If lifetime transfers by gift were not taxed, it would be possible to avoid the estate tax and escape taxation entirely.

Only taxable gifts are subject to the gift tax. For this purpose, a taxable gift is measured by the fair market value of the property on the date of transfer less the *annual exclusion per donee* and, in some cases, less the *marital deduction*, which allows tax-free transfers between spouses. In 2015 and 2016, each donor is allowed an annual exclusion of $14,000 for each donee.[15]

On December 31, 2015, Louise (a widow) gives $14,000 to each of her four married children, their spouses, and her eight grandchildren. On January 2, 2016, she repeats the procedure, again giving $14,000 to each recipient.

Due to the annual exclusion, Louise has not made a taxable gift, although she transferred $224,000 [$14,000 (annual exclusion) × 16 (donees)] in 2015 and $224,000 [$14,000 (annual exclusion) × 16 (donees)] in 2016, for a total of $448,000 ($224,000 + $224,000).

A married couple may make a special election that allows one-half of the gift made by the donor-spouse to a third party to be treated as being made by the nondonor-spouse. This *gift splitting* effectively allows the annual exclusion to double. Also, it allows the use of the nondonor-spouse's unified transfer tax credit and may lower the tax rates that will apply.

The Big Picture

Return to the facts of *The Big Picture* on p. 1-1. Although the value of the RV is not stated, it is highly likely to exceed the annual exclusion allowed of $56,000 [$14,000 (annual exclusion) × two donees (the Walkers) × two donors (the Carters)].

As a result, a taxable gift results, and a Form 709 (Gift Tax Return) must be filed. Whether any gift tax is due depends on what past taxable gifts the Carters have made and how much of their unified transfer tax credit (see the following discussion) is still available.

The gift tax rate schedule is the same as that applicable to the estate tax. The schedule is commonly referred to as the *unified transfer tax rate schedule*.

The Federal gift tax is *cumulative* in effect. What this means is that the tax base for current taxable gifts includes past taxable gifts. Although a credit is allowed for prior gift

---

[15]The purpose of the annual exclusion is to avoid the need to report and pay a tax on *modest* gifts. Without the exclusion, the IRS could face a real problem of taxpayer noncompliance. The annual exclusion is indexed as the level of inflation warrants. The exclusion was $13,000 from 2009 through 2012.

taxes, the result of adding past taxable gifts to current taxable gifts could be to force the donor into a higher tax bracket.[16] Like the Federal estate tax rates, the Federal gift tax rates are progressive (see Example 2 earlier in this chapter).

The unified transfer tax credit is available for all taxable gifts. As was the case with the Federal estate tax, the credit for 2016 is $2,125,800 (which covers taxable gifts up to $5,450,000) and for 2015 is $2,117,800 (which covers taxable gifts up to $5,430,000). There is, however, only one unified transfer tax credit, and it applies to both taxable gifts and the Federal estate tax. In a manner of speaking, therefore, once the unified transfer tax credit has been exhausted for Federal gift tax purposes, it is no longer available to insulate a decedent's transfers from the Federal estate tax, except to the extent of the excess of the credit amount for estate tax purposes over that for gift tax purposes.

Making lifetime gifts of property carries several tax advantages over passing the property at death. If income-producing property is involved (e.g., marketable securities and rental real estate), a gift may reduce income taxes for the family unit by shifting subsequent income to lower-bracket donees. If the gift involves property that is expected to appreciate in value (e.g., life insurance policies, real estate, and artwork), future increases in value will be assigned to the donee and will not be included in the donor's estate. Also important is that due to the annual exclusion ($14,000 per donee in 2016), some of the gift is not subject to any gift tax. Recall that the gift-splitting election enables married donors to double up on the annual exclusion.

Neither the receipt of a gift nor an inheritance will cause income tax consequences to the donee or heir.

1-5e Income Taxes

Income taxes are levied by the Federal government, most states, and some local governments. The trend in recent years has been to place greater reliance on this method of taxation. This trend is not consistent with what is happening in other countries, and in this sense, our system of taxation is somewhat different.

Income taxes generally are imposed on individuals, corporations, and certain fiduciaries (estates and trusts). Most jurisdictions attempt to ensure the collection of income taxes by requiring pay-as-you-go procedures, including withholding requirements for employees and estimated tax prepayments for all taxpayers.

Federal Income Taxes

The Federal income tax imposed on individuals follows the formula set forth in Exhibit 1.2. The formula for the individual income tax establishes the framework followed in the text. Beginning with Chapter 3, each component of the formula is illustrated and explained. In large part, the text coverage of individual taxpayers follows the same order as the components in the formula.

Like its individual counterpart, the Federal corporate income tax is progressive in nature. But its application does not require the computation of adjusted gross income (AGI) and does not provide for the standard deduction and personal and dependency exemptions. All allowable deductions of a corporation fall into the business-expense category. In effect, therefore, the taxable income of a corporation is the difference between gross income and deductions. While Chapters 3 through 19 cover the Federal income tax applicable to individuals, Chapter 20 summarizes the rules relating to corporations and partnerships.[17]

---

[16]For further information on the Federal gift tax, see *South-Western Federal Taxation: Corporations, Partnerships, Estates & Trusts*, Chapter 18.

[17]For an in-depth treatment of the Federal income tax as it affects corporations, partnerships, estates, and trusts, see *South-Western Federal Taxation: Corporations, Partnerships, Estates & Trusts*, Chapters 2 through 9, 12, and 20.

EXHIBIT 1.2	**Formula for Federal Income Tax on Individuals**

Income (broadly defined)	$xx,xxx
Less: Exclusions (income that is not subject to tax)	(x,xxx)
Gross income (income that is subject to tax)	$xx,xxx
Less: Certain deductions (usually referred to as deductions *for* adjusted gross income)	(x,xxx)
Adjusted gross income	$xx,xxx
Less: The greater of certain personal and employee deductions (usually referred to as *itemized deductions*)	
or	
The standard deduction (including any additional standard deduction)	(x,xxx)
and	
Less: Personal and dependency exemptions	(x,xxx)
Taxable income	$xx,xxx
Tax on taxable income (see the Tax Tables and Tax Rate Schedules in Appendix A)	$ x,xxx
Less: Tax credits (including Federal income tax withheld and other prepayments of Federal income taxes)	(xxx)
Tax due (or refund)	$ xxx

State Income Taxes

All but the following states impose an income tax on individuals: Alaska, Florida, Nevada, South Dakota, Texas, Washington, and Wyoming. New Hampshire and Tennessee impose an individual income tax only on interest and dividends.

Some of the characteristics of state income taxes are summarized as follows:

- With few exceptions, all states require some form of withholding procedures.

- Most states use as the tax base the income determination made for Federal income tax purposes.

- A minority of states go even further and impose a flat rate on AGI as computed for Federal income tax purposes. Several apply a rate to the Federal income tax liability. This is often referred to as the piggyback approach to state income taxation. Although the term *piggyback* does not lend itself to a precise definition, in this context, it means making use, for state income tax purposes, of what was done for Federal income tax purposes.

- Some states are somewhat eroding the piggyback approach by "decoupling" from selected recent tax reductions passed by Congress. The purpose of the decoupling is to retain state revenue that would otherwise be lost. In other words, the state cannot afford to allow its taxpayers the same deductions for state purposes that are allowed for Federal purposes.

- Because of the tie-ins to the Federal return, a state may be notified of any changes made by the IRS upon audit of a Federal return. In recent years, the exchange of information between the IRS and state taxing authorities has increased. Lately, some states (e.g., California) are playing a major role in revealing tax shelter abuses to the IRS.

- Most states allow a deduction for personal and dependency exemptions. Some states substitute a tax credit for a deduction.

- A diminishing minority of states allow a deduction for Federal income taxes.

- Virtually all state income tax returns provide checkoff boxes for donations to various causes. Many are dedicated to medical research and wildlife programs, but special projects are not uncommon. For example, Oklahoma had one to retire the debt incurred for its new capitol dome, while Wisconsin uses one for maintenance and operating costs of Lambeau Field (home of the Green Bay Packers). These checkoff boxes have been criticized as adding complexity to the returns and misleading taxpayers.[18]

- Most states allow their residents some form of tax credit for income taxes paid to other states.

The Big Picture

Return to the facts of *The Big Picture* on p. 1-1. Because the income earned by Travis on his Chicago trip will be subject to tax by his home state, he probably will be able to claim an offsetting tax credit. Whether this negates the double taxation of the same income depends on the amount of credit allowed.

EXAMPLE 12

- The objective of most states is to tax the income of residents and those who regularly conduct business in the state (e.g., nonresidents who commute to work). These states also purport to tax the income of nonresidents who earn income in the state on an itinerant basis. Usually, however, the only visitors actually taxed are highly paid athletes and entertainers. This so-called *jock tax* has been much criticized as being discriminatory due to its selective imposition.

- The due date for filing generally is the same as for the Federal income tax (the fifteenth day of the fourth month following the close of the tax year).

- Some states have occasionally instituted amnesty programs that allow taxpayers to pay back taxes (and interest) on unreported income with no (or reduced) penalty. In many cases, the tax amnesty has generated enough revenue to warrant the authorization of follow-up programs covering future years.[19] Amnesties usually include other taxes as well (e.g., sales, franchise, and severance). One major advantage of amnesty programs is that they uncover taxpayers who were previously unknown to the taxing authority.

- Because many consumers do not pay state and local sales taxes on out-of-state purchases, state income tax returns often contain a separate line for the reporting of the use tax that is due. The instructions to the form may provide tables of suggested amounts based on income levels for those who lack records on the purchases not previously taxed. Thus, the income tax return serves as a means of collecting use taxes.

Nearly all states have an income tax applicable to corporations. It is difficult to determine those that do not because a state franchise tax (discussed later in the chapter) sometimes is based in part on the income earned by the corporation.

Local Income Taxes

Cities imposing an income tax include, but are not limited to, Baltimore, Cincinnati, Cleveland, Detroit, Kansas City (Missouri), New York, Philadelphia, and St. Louis. The application of a city income tax is not limited to local residents.

1-5f Employment Taxes

Classification as an employee usually leads to the imposition of **employment taxes** and to the requirement that the employer withhold specified amounts for income taxes. The rules governing the withholding for income taxes are discussed in Chapter 13. The

---

[18]Many taxpayers do not realize that they are paying for the checkoff donation (usually with some of their income tax refund). Unlike the presidential election campaign fund available for Federal income tax purposes ($3 in this case), the contribution is *not made* by the government.

[19]Although the suggestion has been made, no comparable amnesty program has been offered for the Federal income tax. The IRS has, however, offered exemption from certain penalties for taxpayers who disclose offshore bank accounts and participation in certain tax shelters.

material that follows concentrates on the two major employment taxes: FICA (Federal Insurance Contributions Act—commonly referred to as the Social Security tax) and FUTA (Federal Unemployment Tax Act). Both taxes can be justified by social and public welfare considerations: FICA offers some measure of retirement security, and FUTA provides a modest source of income in the event of loss of employment.

Employment taxes come into play only if two conditions are satisfied. First, is the individual involved an *employee* (as opposed to *self-employed*)? The differences between an employee and a self-employed person are discussed in Chapter 9. Second, if the individual involved is an employee, is he or she covered under FICA or FUTA or both?[20]

FICA Taxes

The **FICA tax** rates and wage base have increased steadily over the years. It is difficult to imagine that the initial rate in 1937 was only 1 percent of the first $3,000 of covered wages. Thus, the maximum tax due was only $30.

The FICA tax has two components: Social Security tax (old age, survivors, and disability insurance) *and* Medicare tax (hospital insurance). The Social Security tax rate is 6.2 percent for 2016 and generally does not change each year. The base amount does vary but did not increase in 2016 and remains at $118,500.

The Medicare portion of FICA is applied at a rate of 1.45 percent and, unlike Social Security, is not subject to any dollar limitation. An additional .9 percent is imposed on earned income (including self-employment income) *above* $200,000 (single filers) or $250,000 (married filing jointly). Unlike the Social Security tax of 6.2 percent and the regular Medicare portion of 1.45 percent, an employer does not have to match the employees' .9 percent.

A spouse employed by another spouse is subject to FICA. However, children under the age of 18 who are employed in a parent's unincorporated trade or business are exempted.

The Big Picture

EXAMPLE 13

Return to the facts of *The Big Picture* on p. 1-1. Presuming that April and Martin perform meaningful services for Travis (which the facts seem to imply), they are legitimate employees. April is not subject to Social Security tax because she is under the age of 18. However, Martin is 18 and needs to be covered. Furthermore, recall that Betty Carter is now working at a medical clinic and will likewise be subject to Social Security tax. Travis, as an independent contractor, is subject to self-employment tax.

Taxpayers who are not employees (e.g., sole proprietors and independent contractors) may also be subject to Social Security taxes. Known as the self-employment tax, the rates are 12.4 percent for Social Security and 2.9 percent for Medicare, or twice that applicable to an employee. The additional .9 percent Medicare tax also covers situations involving high net income from self-employment. The Social Security tax is imposed on net self-employment income up to a base amount of $118,500 for 2016. The Medicare portion of the self-employment tax is not subject to any dollar limitation.

To defray the cost of extended medical care, Congress enacted a special tax on investment income.[21] For this purpose, "investment income" is often referred to as "unearned income" because it is not generated by the performance of services. A tax of 3.8 percent is imposed on investment income when a taxpayer's modified adjusted gross income (MAGI) exceeds certain threshold amounts.[22] The threshold amounts, which are not adjusted for inflation each year, are $250,000 for married taxpayers and

---

[20]Chapter 13 includes coverage of the self-employment tax (the Social Security and Medicare taxes for self-employed persons). See also Circular E, *Employer's Tax Guide*, issued by the IRS as Publication 15.

[21]Enacted as part of the Health Care and Education Reconciliation Act of 2010.

[22]MAGI is adjusted gross income (see Exhibit 1.2 and the bottom of page 1 of Form 1040) plus any foreign income or excluded foreign housing costs.

$200,000 for single taxpayers. Investment income generally includes passive income (e.g., taxable interest, dividends, and capital gains). For an in-depth discussion, see Chapter 13.

FUTA Taxes

The purpose of the **FUTA tax** is to provide funds the states can use to administer unemployment benefits. This leads to the somewhat unusual situation of one tax being handled by both Federal and state governments. The end result of such joint administration is to compel the employer to observe two sets of rules. Thus, state and Federal returns must be filed and payments made to both governmental units.

In 2016, FUTA is 6 percent on the first $7,000 of covered wages paid during the year to each employee. The Federal government allows a credit for FUTA paid (or allowed under a merit rating system) to the state. The credit cannot exceed 5.4 percent of the covered wages. Thus, the amount required to be paid to the IRS could be as low as .6 percent (6.0% − 5.4%).

States follow a policy of reducing the unemployment tax on employers who experience stable employment. Thus, an employer with little or no employee turnover might find that the state rate drops to as low as .1 percent or, in some states, even to zero. The reason for the merit rating credit is that the state has to pay fewer unemployment benefits when employment is steady.

FUTA, unlike FICA, is paid entirely by the employer. A few states, however, levy a special tax on employees to provide either disability benefits or supplemental unemployment compensation or both.

1-5g Other U.S. Taxes

To complete the overview of the U.S. tax system, some missing links need to be covered that do not fit into the classifications discussed elsewhere in this chapter.

Federal Customs Duties

One tax that has not yet been mentioned is the tariff on certain imported goods.[23] Generally referred to as customs duties or levies, this tax, together with selective excise taxes, provided most of the revenues needed by the Federal government during the nineteenth century. In view of present times, it is remarkable that tariffs and excise taxes alone paid off the national debt in 1835 and enabled the U.S. Treasury to pay a surplus of $28 million to the states.

In recent years, tariffs have served the nation more as an instrument for carrying out protectionist policies than as a means of generating revenue. Thus, a particular U.S. industry might be saved from economic disaster, so the argument goes, by imposing customs duties on the importation of foreign goods that can be sold at lower prices. Protectionists contend that the tariff thereby neutralizes the competitive edge held by the producer of the foreign goods. History shows that tariffs often lead to retaliatory action on the part of the nation or nations affected.

Miscellaneous State and Local Taxes

Most states impose a franchise tax on corporations. Basically, a **franchise tax** is levied on the right to do business in the state. The base used for the determination of the tax varies from state to state. Although corporate income considerations may come into play, this tax most often is based on the capitalization of the corporation (either with or without certain long-term indebtedness).

Closely akin to the franchise tax are **occupational fees** applicable to various trades or businesses (e.g., a liquor store license; a taxicab permit; or a fee to practice a profession such as law, medicine, or accounting). Most of these are not significant revenue

---

[23]Less-developed countries that rely principally on one or more major commodities (e.g., oil or coffee) are prone to favor *export* duties as well.

producers and fall more into the category of licenses than taxes. The revenue derived is used to defray the cost incurred by the jurisdiction in regulating the business or profession in the interest of the public good.

The Big Picture

Return to the facts of *The Big Picture* on p. 1-1. Although the facts do not mention the matter, both Travis and Betty will almost certainly pay occupational fees—Travis for engineering and Betty for nursing.

Concept Summary 1.1 provides an overview of the major taxes existing in the United States and specifies which political jurisdiction imposes them.

Concept Summary 1.1

Overview of Taxes in the United States

Type of Tax	Imposed by Jurisdiction		
	Federal	**State**	**Local**
Property taxes:			
Ad valorem on realty	No	Yes	Yes
Ad valorem on personalty	No	Yes	Yes
Transaction taxes:			
Excise	Yes	Yes	Few*
General sales	No	Most	Some
Severance	Yes**	Most	No
Estate	Yes	Some	No
Inheritance	No	Some	No
Gift	Yes	Few	No
Income taxes:			
Corporations	Yes	Most	Few
Individuals	Yes	Most	Few
Employment taxes:			
FICA	Yes	No	No
FUTA	Yes	Yes	No
Customs duties	Yes	No	No
Franchise taxes	No	Yes	No
Occupational taxes or fees***	Yes	Yes	Yes

  *An example of a local excise tax might be a tax on hotel occupancy.
 **For Federal public lands and continental-shelf areas.
***An example is a fee to operate a beauty salon or barbershop.

1-5h **Proposed U.S. Taxes**

Considerable dissatisfaction with the U.S. Federal income tax has led to several recent proposals that, to say the least, are rather drastic in nature. One proposal, the flat tax, would retain the income tax but with substantial change. Two other proposals, the value added tax and the national sales tax, would replace the Federal income tax with an entirely different system of taxation.

The Flat Tax

One proposal is for a **flat tax** that would replace the current graduated income tax with a single rate of 17 percent. Large personal exemptions (e.g., approximately $30,000 for a family of four) would allow many low- and middle-income taxpayers to pay no tax. All other deductions would be eliminated, and no tax would be imposed on income from investments.

Various other versions of the flat tax have been suggested that would retain selected deductions (e.g., interest on home mortgages and charitable contributions) and not exclude all investment income from taxation.

The major advantage of the flat tax is its simplicity. Everyone agrees that the current Federal income tax is inappropriately complex. Consequently, compliance costs are disproportionately high. Proponents of the flat tax further believe that simplifying the income tax will significantly reduce the current "tax gap" (i.e., the difference between the amount of taxes that *should be paid* and what is *actually paid*).

Political considerations are a major obstacle to the enactment of a flat tax in its pure form. Special interest groups, such as charitable organizations and mortgage companies, are likely to strongly oppose the elimination of a tax deduction that benefits their industry. In addition, there is uncertainty as to the economic effects of a flat tax.

Value Added Tax

The **value added tax (VAT)** is one of two proposals that would replace the Federal income tax. Under the VAT, a business would pay the tax (approximately 17 percent) on all of the materials and services required to manufacture its product. In effect, the VAT taxes the increment in value as goods move through production and manufacturing stages to the marketplace. Moreover, the VAT paid by the producer will be reflected in the selling price of the goods. Thus, the VAT is a tax on consumption. In fact, the VAT has been described by some as a "layered sales tax."

In spite of its extensive use by other countries (including Canada), the adoption of a VAT by the United States appears doubtful (see comments under "Global Tax Issues" above).

National Sales Tax

A **national sales tax** differs from a VAT in that it would be collected on the final sale of goods and services. Consequently, it is collected from the consumer, not from businesses that add value to the product. Like the VAT, the national sales tax is intended to replace the Federal income tax.

A current proposal for a national sales tax, called the "Fair Tax," would tax all purchases, including food and medicine, at approximately 23 percent. Exempt items include business expenses, used goods, and the costs of education. The "Fair Tax" would replace not only the income tax (both individual and corporate) but also payroll taxes (including the self-employment tax) and the gift and estate taxes.

Critics contend that both forms of consumption taxes, a VAT and a national sales tax, are regressive. They impose more of a burden on low-income taxpayers who must spend larger proportions of their incomes on essential purchases. The proposals attempt to remedy this inequity by granting some sort of credit, rebate, or exemption to low-income taxpayers.

In terms of taxpayer compliance, a VAT is preferable to a national sales tax. Without significant collection efforts, a national sales tax could easily be circumvented by resorting to a barter system of doing business. Its high rate would also encourage smuggling and black market activities.

LO.5

Explain the administration of the tax law, including the audit process utilized by the IRS.

1-6 TAX ADMINISTRATION

1-6a Internal Revenue Service

The responsibility for administering the Federal tax laws rests with the Treasury Department. The IRS is part of the Department of the Treasury and is responsible for enforcing the tax laws. The Commissioner of Internal Revenue is appointed by the President and is responsible for establishing policy and supervising the activities of the IRS.

1-6b The Audit Process

Selection of Returns for Audit

Due to budgetary limitations, only a small number of tax returns are audited. The overall audit rate for individuals in 2014 dropped to .86 percent, the lowest percentage since 2005. Personnel cutbacks within the IRS can be expected to further reduce this rate for 2015. Keep in mind, however, that the chance for audit increases for higher-income taxpayers.

The IRS utilizes mathematical formulas and statistical sampling techniques to select tax returns that are most likely to contain errors and to yield substantial amounts of additional tax revenues upon audit. The mathematical formula yields what is called a Discriminant Index Formula (DIF) score. It is the DIF score given to a particular return that may lead to its selection for audit. Periodically, the IRS updates the DIF components by auditing a cross section of returns to determine the most likely areas of taxpayer noncompliance.

Although the IRS does not openly disclose all of its audit selection techniques, the following observations may be made concerning the probability of selection for audit:

- Certain groups of taxpayers are subject to audit much more frequently than others. These groups include individuals with large amounts of gross income, self-employed individuals with substantial business income and deductions, and taxpayers with prior tax deficiencies. Also vulnerable are businesses that receive a large proportion of their receipts in cash (e.g., cafés and small service businesses) and thus have a high potential for tax avoidance.

EXAMPLE 15

Jack owns and operates a liquor store on a cash-and-carry basis. Because all of Jack's sales are for cash, he might well be a prime candidate for an audit by the IRS. Cash transactions are easier to conceal than those made on credit.

- If information returns (e.g., Form 1099 or Form W–2) are not in substantial agreement with reported income, an audit can be anticipated.
- If an individual's itemized deductions are in excess of norms established for various income levels, the probability of an audit is increased.
- Filing of a refund claim by the taxpayer may prompt an audit of the return.
- Information obtained from other sources (e.g., informants and news items) may lead to an audit. Recently, for example, the IRS advised its agents to be on the alert for newspaper accounts of large civil court judgments. The advice was based on the assumption that many successful plaintiffs were not reporting as income the taxable punitive damages portion of awards.

TAX IN THE NEWS **Pay or Shame!**

States and local jurisdictions are learning that the threat of public humiliation can be rewarding. When someone owes taxes but does not pay, the prospect of having his or her name listed on a public website may make a difference. Often payment is made to avoid the cybershame that comes from being exposed as a tax deadbeat. Numerous states are publishing the names of tax delinquents online. Some taxing jurisdictions have found the shaming procedure so productive that they maintain separate lists for different types of taxes (e.g., sales taxes and income taxes) or different types of delinquents (e.g., personal and business). As of yet, the IRS has not considered this approach for Federal tax scofflaws. Perhaps the length of the list would be too overwhelming!

The tax law permits the IRS to pay rewards to persons who provide information that leads to the detection and punishment of those who violate the tax laws. The rewards may not exceed 30 percent of the taxes, fines, and penalties recovered as a result of such information.

Information Leading to an IRS Audit

After 15 years of service, Rita is discharged by her employer, Dr. Benjamin Smith. Shortly thereafter, the IRS receives an anonymous letter stating that Dr. Smith keeps two separate sets of books and that the one used for tax reporting substantially understates his cash receipts.

EXAMPLE 16

During a divorce proceeding, it is revealed that Leo, a public official, kept large amounts of cash in a shoe box at home. This information is widely disseminated by the news media and comes to the attention of the IRS. Needless to say, the IRS is interested in knowing whether these funds originated from a taxable source and, if so, whether they were reported on Leo's income tax returns.

EXAMPLE 17

Types of Audits

Once a return is selected for audit, the taxpayer is notified. If the issue involved is minor, the matter often can be resolved simply by correspondence (a **correspondence audit**) between the IRS and the taxpayer.

Other examinations are generally classified as either office audits or field audits. An **office audit** usually is restricted in scope and is conducted in the facilities of the IRS. In contrast, a **field audit** involves an examination of numerous items reported on the return and is conducted on the premises of the taxpayer or the taxpayer's representative.

The Big Picture

Return to the facts of *The Big Picture* on p. 1-1. The audit of the Walkers by the IRS obviously was a correspondence type. The reason for the audit was probably triggered by a minor oversight by the Walkers, such as the omission of some interest or dividend income. The audit of the Carters, however, was more serious—probably a field or office type. Because the Federal audit followed a state audit that was productive (i.e., led to the assessment of a deficiency), there may have been an exchange of information between the two taxing authorities—see p. 1-14 in this chapter.

EXAMPLE 18

Upon the conclusion of the audit, the examining agent issues a Revenue Agent's Report (RAR) that summarizes the findings. The RAR will result in a refund (the tax was overpaid), a deficiency (the tax was underpaid), or a no change (the tax was correct) finding. If, during the course of an audit, a special agent accompanies (or takes over from) the regular auditor, this means the IRS suspects fraud. If the matter has progressed to an investigation for fraud, the taxpayer should retain competent counsel.

Settlement Procedures

If an audit results in an assessment of additional tax and no settlement is reached with the IRS agent, the taxpayer may attempt to negotiate a settlement with a higher level of the IRS. If an appeal is desired, an appropriate request must be made to the Appeals Division of the IRS. The Appeals Division is authorized to settle all disputes based on the *hazard of litigation* (the probability of favorable resolution of the disputed issue or issues if litigated). In some cases, a taxpayer may be able to obtain a percentage settlement or a favorable settlement of one or more disputed issues.

If a satisfactory settlement is not reached in the administrative appeal process, the taxpayer can litigate the case in the Tax Court, a Federal District Court, or the Court of Federal Claims. However, litigation is recommended only as a last resort because of the legal costs involved and the uncertainty of the final outcome. Tax litigation considerations are discussed more fully in Chapter 2.

1-6c Statute of Limitations

A **statute of limitations** is a provision in the law that offers a party a defense against a suit brought by another party after the expiration of a specified period of time. The purpose of a statute of limitations is to preclude parties from prosecuting stale claims. The passage of time makes the defense of such claims difficult because witnesses may no longer be available or evidence may have been lost or destroyed. Found at the state and Federal levels, such statutes cover a multitude of suits, both civil and criminal.

For our purposes, the relevant statutes deal with the Federal income tax. The two categories involved cover both the period of limitations applicable to the assessment of additional tax deficiencies by the IRS and the period applicable to claims for refunds by taxpayers.

Assessment by the IRS

Under the general rule, the IRS may assess an additional tax liability against a taxpayer within *three years* of the filing of the income tax return. If the return is filed early, the three-year period begins to run from the due date of the return (usually April 15 for a calendar year individual taxpayer). If the taxpayer files the return late (i.e., beyond the due date), the three-year period begins to run on the date filed.

If a taxpayer omits an amount of gross income in excess of 25 percent of the gross income reported on the return, the statute of limitations is increased to six years.

EXAMPLE 19

For 2016, Mark, a calendar year taxpayer, reported gross income of $400,000 on a timely filed income tax return. If Mark omitted more than $100,000 (25% × $400,000), the six-year statute of limitations would apply to the 2016 tax year.

The six-year provision on assessments by the IRS applies only to the omission of income and does not cover other factors that might lead to an understatement of tax liability, such as overstatement of deductions and credits.

There is *no* statute of limitations on assessments of tax if *no return* is filed or if a *fraudulent* return is filed.

Limitations on Refunds

If a taxpayer believes that an overpayment of Federal income tax was made, a claim for refund should be filed with the IRS. A *claim for refund,* therefore, is a request to the IRS that it return to the taxpayer excessive income taxes paid.[24]

A claim for refund generally must be filed within *three years* from the date the return was filed *or* within *two years* from the date the tax was paid, whichever is later. Income tax returns that are filed early are deemed to have been filed on the date the return was due.

---

[24]Generally, an individual filing a claim for refund should use Form 1040X.

1-6d Interest and Penalties

Interest rates are determined quarterly by the IRS based on the existing Federal short-term rate. Currently, the rates for tax refunds (overpayments) for individual taxpayers are the same as those applicable to assessments (underpayments). For the first quarter (January 1–March 31) of 2016, the rates are 3 percent for refunds and assessments.[25]

For assessments of additional taxes, the interest begins running on the unextended due date of the return. With refunds, however, no interest is allowed if the overpayment is refunded to the taxpayer within 45 days of the date the return is filed. For this purpose, returns filed early are deemed to have been filed on the due date.

In addition to interest, the tax law provides various penalties for lack of compliance by taxpayers. Some of these penalties are summarized as follows:

- For *failure to file* a tax return by the due date (including extension—see Chapter 3), a penalty of 5 percent per month up to a maximum of 25 percent is imposed on the amount of tax shown as due on the return. Any fraction of a month counts as a full month.

- A penalty for *failure to pay* the tax due as shown on the return is imposed in the amount of .5 percent per month up to a maximum of 25 percent. Again, any fraction of a month counts as a full month. During any month in which both the failure to file penalty and the failure to pay penalty apply, the failure to file penalty is reduced by the amount of the failure to pay penalty.

EXAMPLE 20

Adam files his tax return 18 days after the due date of the return. Along with the return, he remits a check for $1,000, which is the balance of the tax he owed. Disregarding the interest element, Adam's total penalties are as follows:

Failure to pay penalty (.5% × $1,000)		$ 5
Plus:		
Failure to file penalty (5% × $1,000)	$50	
Less failure to pay penalty for the same period	(5)	
Failure to file penalty		45
Total penalties		$50

Note that the penalties for one full month are imposed even though Adam was delinquent by only 18 days. Unlike the method used to compute interest, any part of a month is treated as a whole month.

- A *negligence* penalty of 20 percent is imposed if any of the underpayment was for intentional disregard of rules and regulations without intent to defraud. The penalty applies to just that portion attributable to the negligence.

EXAMPLE 21

Cindy underpaid her taxes in the amount of $20,000, of which $15,000 is attributable to negligence. Cindy's negligence penalty is $3,000 (20% × $15,000).

- Various penalties may be imposed in the case of *fraud*. Fraud involves specific intent on the part of the taxpayer to evade a tax. In the case of *civil* fraud, the penalty is 75 percent of the underpayment attributable to fraud. In the case of *criminal* fraud, the penalties can include large fines as well as prison sentences. The difference between civil and criminal fraud is one of degree. Criminal fraud involves the presence of willfulness on the part of the taxpayer. Also, the burden of proof, which is on the IRS in both situations, is more stringent for criminal fraud than for civil fraud. The negligence penalty is not imposed when the fraud penalty applies. For possible fraud situations, refer to Examples 16 and 17.

---

[25]The rates applicable after March 31, 2016, were not available when this text went to press.

1-6e **Tax Practice**

If a practitioner is a member of a profession such as law or public accounting, he or she must abide by certain ethical standards. Furthermore, the Internal Revenue Code imposes penalties upon the preparers of Federal tax returns who violate proscribed acts and procedures.

Ethical Guidelines

The American Institute of CPAs has issued numerous pronouncements, called the "Statements on Standards for Tax Services," dealing with CPAs engaged in tax practice. These pronouncements are *enforceable* as part of its Code of Professional Conduct. They include the following summarized provisions:

- Do not take questionable positions on a client's tax return in the hope that the return will not be selected for audit by the IRS. Any positions taken should be supported by a good-faith belief that they have a realistic possibility of being sustained if challenged. The client should be fully advised of the risks involved and of the penalties that will result if the position taken is not successful.

- A practitioner can use a client's estimates if they are reasonable under the circumstances. If the tax law requires receipts or other verification, the client should be so advised. In no event should an estimate be given the appearance of greater accuracy than is the case. For example, an estimate of $1,000 should not be deducted on a return as $999.

- Every effort should be made to answer questions appearing on tax returns. A question need not be answered if the information requested is not readily available, the answer is voluminous, or the question's meaning is uncertain. The failure to answer a question on a return cannot be justified on the grounds that the answer could prove disadvantageous to the taxpayer.

- Upon learning of an error on a past tax return, advise the client to correct it. Do not, however, inform the IRS of the error. If the error is material and the client refuses to correct it, consider withdrawing from the engagement. This will be necessary if the error has a carryover effect and prevents the current year's tax liability from being determined correctly.

Statutory Penalties Imposed on Tax Return Preparers

In addition to ethical constraints, a tax return preparer may be subject to certain statutorily sanctioned penalties, including the following:

- Various penalties involving procedural matters. Examples include failing to furnish the taxpayer with a copy of the return, endorsing a taxpayer's refund check, failing to sign the return as a preparer, failing to furnish one's identification number, and failing to keep copies of returns or maintain a client list.

- Penalty for understatement of a tax liability based on a position that lacks any realistic possibility of being sustained. If the position is not frivolous, the penalty can be avoided by disclosing it on the return.

- Penalty for any willful attempt to understate taxes. This usually results when a preparer disregards or makes no effort to obtain pertinent information from a client.

- Penalty for failure to exercise due diligence in determining eligibility for, or the amount of, an earned income tax credit.

GLOBAL TAX ISSUES Outsourcing of Tax Return Preparation

The use of foreign nationals to carry out certain job assignments for U.S. businesses is an increasingly popular practice. Outsourcing such activities as telemarketing to India, for example, usually produces the same satisfactory result as having the work done in the United States but at a much lower cost.

Outsourcing is also being applied to the preparation of tax returns. Not only can this practice be expected to continue, but it probably will increase in volume. Outsourcing tax return preparation does not violate Federal law and is compatible with accounting ethical guidelines as long as three safeguards are followed: First, the practitioner must make sure client confidentiality is maintained. Second, the practitioner must verify the accuracy of the work that has been outsourced. Third, the practitioner must inform clients, preferably in writing, when any third-party contractor is used to provide professional services.

Practitioners justify outsourcing as a means of conserving time and effort that can be applied toward more meaningful tax planning on behalf of their clients.

1-7 UNDERSTANDING THE FEDERAL TAX LAW

LO.7

Recognize the economic, social, equity, and political considerations that justify various aspects of the tax law.

The Federal tax law is a mosaic of statutory provisions, administrative pronouncements, and court decisions. Anyone who has attempted to work with this body of knowledge would have to admit to its complexity. For the person who has to trudge through a mass of rules to find the solution to a tax problem, it may be of some consolation to know that the law's complexity can generally be explained. Whether sound or not, there is a reason for the formulation of every rule. Knowing these reasons, therefore, is a considerable step toward understanding the Federal tax law.

The Federal tax law has as its *major objective* the raising of revenue. But although the fiscal needs of the government are important, other considerations explain certain portions of the law. Economic, social, equity, and political factors also play a significant role. Added to these factors is the marked impact the IRS and the courts have had and will continue to have on the evolution of Federal tax law. These matters are treated in the remainder of the chapter, and wherever appropriate, the discussion is referenced to subjects covered later in the text.

1-7a Revenue Needs

The foundation of any tax system has to be the raising of revenue to cover the cost of government operations. Ideally, annual outlays should not exceed anticipated revenues, thereby leading to a balanced budget with no resulting deficit.

When enacting tax legislation, a deficit-conscious Congress often has been guided by the concept of **revenue neutrality**. Also referred to as "pay-as-you-go" ("paygo"), the concept means that every new tax law that lowers taxes must include a revenue offset that makes up for the loss. Revenue neutrality does not mean that any one taxpayer's tax liability will remain the same. Because the circumstances involved will differ, one taxpayer's increased tax liability could be another's tax savings. Although revenue-neutral tax reform does not reduce deficits, at least it does not aggravate the problem.

In addition to making revenue-neutral changes in the tax law, several other procedures can be taken to mitigate any revenue loss. When tax reductions are involved, the full impact of the legislation can be phased in over a period of years. Or as an alternative, the tax reduction can be limited to a period of years. When the period expires, the prior law is reinstated through a **sunset provision**. Most of the major tax bills recently passed by Congress have contained numerous sunset provisions. They provide some semblance of revenue neutrality as some of the bills include tax cuts that were not offset by new sources of revenue. It remains to be seen, however, whether Congress will allow the sunset provisions to take effect and, thereby, kill the tax cuts that were enacted.

1-7b **Economic Considerations**

Using the tax system in an effort to accomplish economic objectives has become increasingly popular in recent years. Generally, proponents of this goal use tax legislation to amend the Internal Revenue Code in ways designed to help control the economy or encourage certain activities and businesses.

Control of the Economy

Congress has used depreciation write-offs as a means of controlling the economy. Theoretically, shorter asset lives and accelerated methods should encourage additional investment in depreciable property acquired for business use. Conversely, longer asset lives and the required use of the straight-line method of depreciation dampen the tax incentive for capital outlays.

Another approach that utilizes depreciation as a means of controlling capital investment is the amount of write-off allowed upon the acquisition of assets. This is the approach followed by the § 179 election to expense assets.

A change in the tax rate structure has a more immediate impact on the economy. With lower tax rates, taxpayers are able to retain additional spendable funds. If lower tax rates are accompanied by the elimination of certain deductions, exclusions, and credits, however, the overall result may not be lower tax liabilities.

Encouragement of Certain Activities

Without passing judgment on the wisdom of any such choices, it is quite clear that the tax law encourages certain types of economic activity or segments of the economy. For example, providing favorable treatment for research and development expenditures can be explained by the desire to foster technological progress. Under the tax law, these expenditures can be either deducted in the year incurred or capitalized and amortized over a period of 60 months or more. Given the time value of money, the tax savings from a current deduction usually is preferable to capitalizing the cost with a write-off over the estimated useful life of the asset created. If the asset developed has an indefinite useful life, no write-off would be available without the two options allowed by the tax law.

Part of the tax law addresses the nation's energy policy—in terms of both our reliance on foreign oil and the need to ease the problem of climate change. For example, a tax credit is allowed for installation of solar and small wind energy equipment. In addition, tax credits are available to those who purchase new plug-in electric drive motor vehicles. Residential energy credits are allowed for home improvements that conserve energy or make its use more efficient (e.g., solar hot water and geothermal heat pumps). Ecological considerations justify a tax provision that permits a more rapid expensing of the costs of installing pollution control facilities. Measures such as these that aid in maintaining a clean air environment and conserving energy resources can also be justified under social considerations.

Is it wise to stimulate U.S. exports of services? Along this line, Congress has deemed it advisable to establish incentives for U.S. citizens who accept employment overseas. Such persons receive generous tax breaks through special treatment of their foreign-source income.

Is saving desirable for the economy? Saving leads to capital formation and thereby makes funds available to finance home construction and industrial expansion. The tax law encourages saving by according preferential treatment to private retirement plans. Besides contributions to Keogh (H.R. 10) plans and certain IRAs being deductible, income from the contributions accumulates free of tax. The encouragement of private-sector pension plans can also be justified under social considerations.

Encouragement of Certain Industries

Because a sound agricultural base is necessary for a well-balanced national economy, farmers are accorded special treatment under the Federal tax system. Among the benefits are the election to expense rather than capitalize certain soil and water conservation expenditures and fertilizers and the election to defer the recognition of gain on the receipt of crop insurance proceeds.

To stimulate the manufacturing industry, Congress enacted a domestic production activities deduction. The provision provides a tax benefit in the form of a deduction for profits derived from manufacturing activities conducted in the United States. By restricting the deduction to manufacturing income attributable to wages reportable to the IRS, new U.S. jobs will result and the outsourcing of labor is discouraged. Thus, the tax system is used to encourage both domestic manufacturing and job growth.

Encouragement of Small Business

At least in the United States, a consensus exists that what is good for small business is good for the economy as a whole. Whether valid or not, this assumption has led to a definite bias in the tax law favoring small business.

In the corporate tax area, several provisions can be explained by the desire to benefit small business. One provision permits the shareholders of a small business corporation to make a special election that generally avoids the imposition of the corporate income tax.[26] Furthermore, such an election enables the corporation to pass through its operating losses to its shareholders.

1-7c Social Considerations

Some provisions of the Federal tax law, particularly those dealing with the income tax of individuals, can be explained by social considerations. Some notable examples and their rationales include the following:

- Certain benefits provided to employees through accident and health plans financed by employers are nontaxable to employees. Encouraging such plans is considered socially desirable because they provide medical benefits in the event of an employee's illness or injury.

- Most premiums paid by an employer for group term insurance covering the life of the employee are nontaxable to the employee. These arrangements can be justified on social grounds in that they provide funds for the family unit to help it adjust to the loss of wages caused by the employee's death.

- A contribution made by an employer to a qualified pension or profit sharing plan for an employee may receive special treatment. The contribution and any income it generates are not taxed to the employee until the funds are distributed. Such an arrangement also benefits the employer by allowing a tax deduction when the contribution is made to the qualified plan. Private retirement plans are encouraged to supplement the subsistence income level the employee otherwise would have under the Social Security system.[27]

- A deduction is allowed for contributions to qualified charitable organizations. The deduction attempts to shift some of the financial and administrative burden of socially desirable programs from the public (the government) to the private (the citizens) sector.

- A tax credit is allowed for amounts spent to furnish care for certain minor or disabled dependents to enable the taxpayer to seek or maintain gainful employment. For those employees who do not choose home care for their children, employers are allowed a credit for child care provided at the workplace. Who could deny the social desirability of encouraging taxpayers to provide care for their children while they work?

- To encourage taxpayers to join the workforce even though their wages may be marginal, an earned income tax credit can be claimed. The credit varies depending

---

[26]Known as the S election, it is discussed in Chapter 20.

[27]The same rationale explains the availability of similar arrangements for self-employed persons (e.g., the H.R. 10, or Keogh, plan). See Chapter 19.

on the number of qualifying children being claimed and the level of wages earned. Because it stimulates employment, the earned income tax credit can also be justified on economic grounds.

- Due to the usual impairment in earning potential, certain credits are made available to elderly and disabled persons. Credits also are allowed to businesses that incur expenditures to make their facilities more accessible to the disabled.

- Various tax credits, deductions, and exclusions are designed to encourage taxpayers to obtain additional education.[28]

- A tax deduction is not allowed for certain expenditures deemed to be contrary to public policy. This disallowance extends to such items as fines, penalties, illegal kickbacks, bribes to government officials, and gambling losses in excess of gains. Social considerations dictate that the tax law should not encourage these activities by permitting a deduction.

Although many other examples could be identified, these examples demonstrate that social considerations do explain a significant part of the Federal tax law.

1-7d Equity Considerations

The concept of equity is relative. Reasonable persons can, and often do, disagree about what is fair or unfair. In the tax area, moreover, equity is most often tied to a particular taxpayer's personal situation. To illustrate, compare the tax positions of those who rent their personal residences with those who own their homes. Renters receive no Federal income tax benefit from the rent they pay. For homeowners, however, a large portion of the house payments they make may qualify for the Federal interest and property tax deductions. Although renters may have difficulty understanding this difference in tax treatment, the encouragement of home ownership can be justified on both economic and social grounds.

In the same vein, compare the tax treatment of a corporation with that of a partnership. Although the two businesses may be equal in size, similarly situated, and competitors in the production of goods or services, they are not treated comparably under the tax law. The corporation is subject to a separate Federal income tax; the partnership is not. Whether the differences in tax treatment can be justified logically in terms of equity is beside the point. The point is that the tax law can and does make a distinction between these business forms.

Equity, then, is not what appears fair or unfair to any one taxpayer or group of taxpayers. Some recognition of equity does exist, however, and explains part of the law. The concept of equity appears in tax provisions that alleviate the effect of multiple taxation and postpone the recognition of gain when the taxpayer lacks the ability or wherewithal to pay the tax. Provisions that mitigate the effect of the application of the annual accounting period concept and help taxpayers cope with the eroding results of inflation also reflect equity considerations.

Alleviating the Effect of Multiple Taxation

The income earned by a taxpayer may be subject to taxes imposed by different taxing authorities. If, for example, the taxpayer is a resident of New York City, income might generate Federal, state of New York, and city of New York income taxes. To compensate for this apparent inequity, the Federal tax law allows a taxpayer to claim a deduction for state and local income taxes. The deduction does not, however, neutralize the effect of multiple taxation because the benefit derived depends on the taxpayer's Federal income tax rate. Only a tax credit, not a deduction, would eliminate the effects of multiple taxation on the same income.

---

[28]These provisions can also be justified under the category of economic considerations because a better-educated workforce carries a positive economic impact.

Equity considerations can explain the Federal tax treatment of certain income from foreign sources. Because double taxation results when the same income is subject to both foreign and U.S. income taxes, the tax law permits the taxpayer to choose between a credit and a deduction for the foreign taxes paid.

The Wherewithal to Pay Concept

The `wherewithal to pay` concept recognizes the inequity of taxing a transaction when the taxpayer lacks the means with which to pay the tax. It is particularly suited to situations in which the taxpayer's economic position has not changed significantly as a result of the transaction.

An illustration of the wherewithal to pay concept is the provision of the tax law dealing with the treatment of gain resulting from an involuntary conversion. An involuntary conversion occurs when property is destroyed by a casualty or taken by a public authority through condemnation. If gain results from the conversion, it need not be recognized if the taxpayer replaces the property within a specified period of time. The replacement property must be similar or related in service or use to that involuntarily converted.

Some of the pasture land belonging to Ron, a rancher, is condemned by the state for use as a game preserve. The condemned pasture land cost Ron $120,000, but the state pays him $150,000 (its fair market value). Shortly thereafter, Ron buys more pasture land for $150,000.

In Example 22, Ron has a realized gain of $30,000 [$150,000 (condemnation award) − $120,000 (cost of land)]. It would be inequitable to force Ron to pay a tax on this gain for two reasons. First, without disposing of the property acquired (the new land), Ron would be hard-pressed to pay the tax. Second, his economic position has not changed.

A warning is in order regarding the application of the wherewithal to pay concept. If the taxpayer's economic position changes in any way, tax consequences may result.

Assume the same facts as in Example 22, except that Ron reinvests only $140,000 of the award in new pasture land. Now Ron has a taxable gain of $10,000. Instead of ending up with only replacement property, Ron has $10,000 in cash.

Mitigating the Effect of the Annual Accounting Period Concept

For purposes of effective administration of the tax law, all taxpayers must report to and settle with the Federal government at periodic intervals. Otherwise, taxpayers would remain uncertain as to their tax liabilities, and the government would have difficulty judging revenues and budgeting expenditures. The period selected for final settlement of most tax liabilities, in any event an arbitrary determination, is one year. At the close of each year, therefore, a taxpayer's position becomes complete for that particular year. Referred to as the annual accounting period concept, its effect is to divide each taxpayer's life, for tax purposes, into equal annual intervals.

The finality of the annual accounting period concept could lead to dissimilar tax treatment for taxpayers who are, from a long-range standpoint, in the same economic position.

José and Alicia, both sole proprietors, have experienced the following results during the past three years:

	Profit (or Loss)	
Year	José	Alicia
2014	$50,000	$150,000
2015	60,000	60,000
2016	60,000	(40,000)

continued

Although José and Alicia have the same total profit of $170,000 over the period from 2014 to 2016, the finality of the annual accounting period concept places Alicia at a definite disadvantage for tax purposes. The net operating loss procedure offers Alicia some relief by allowing her to apply some or all of her 2016 loss to the earlier profitable years (in this case, 2014). Thus, with a net operating loss carryback, Alicia is in a position to obtain a refund for some of the taxes she paid on the $150,000 profit reported for 2014.

The same reasoning used to support the deduction of net operating losses can explain the special treatment the tax law accords to excess capital losses and excess charitable contributions.[29] Carryback and carryover procedures help mitigate the effect of limiting a loss or a deduction to the accounting period in which it was realized. With such procedures, a taxpayer may be able to salvage a loss or a deduction that might otherwise be lost.

The installment method of recognizing gain on the sale of property allows a taxpayer to spread tax consequences over the payout period.[30] The harsh effect of taxing all of the gain in the year of sale is thereby avoided. The installment method can also be explained by the wherewithal to pay concept because recognition of gain is tied to the collection of the installment notes received from the sale of the property. Tax consequences, then, tend to correspond to the seller's ability to pay the tax.

Coping with Inflation

Because of the progressive nature of the income tax, a wage adjustment to compensate for inflation can increase the income tax bracket of the recipient. Known as *bracket creep*, its overall impact is an erosion of purchasing power. Congress recognized this problem and began to adjust various income tax components, such as tax brackets, standard deduction amounts, and personal and dependency exemptions, through an indexation procedure. **Indexation** is based on the rise in the consumer price index over the prior year.

1-7e Political Considerations

A large segment of the Federal tax law is made up of statutory provisions. Because these statutes are enacted by Congress, is it any surprise that political considerations influence tax law? For purposes of discussion, the effect of political considerations on the tax law is divided into the following topics: special interest legislation, political expediency situations, and state and local government influences.

Special Interest Legislation

There is no doubt that certain provisions of the tax law can largely be explained by the political influence some pressure groups have had on Congress. Is there any other realistic reason that, for example, prepaid subscription and dues income is not taxed until earned while prepaid rents are taxed to the landlord in the year received?

For example, a provision, sponsored by a senator from Georgia, suspended the import duties on ceiling fans. The nation's largest seller of ceiling fans is Home Depot, which is based in Atlanta, Georgia. Another provision, sponsored by a member of Congress from Illinois, reduced the excise taxes on fishing tackle boxes. The representative's district includes Plano Molding, a major manufacturer of tackle boxes. The justification for this change was that it placed tackle boxes on a more level playing field with toolboxes (which are not subject to tax). Allegedly, anglers had been buying and converting toolboxes to avoid the excise tax.

Special interest legislation is not necessarily to be condemned if it can be justified on economic, social, or some other utilitarian grounds. In most cases, however, it is

---

[29]The tax treatment of these items is discussed in Chapters 7, 10, and 16.

[30]Under the installment method, each payment received by the seller represents both a recovery of capital (the nontaxable portion) and profit from the sale (the taxable portion). The tax rules governing the installment method are discussed in Chapter 18.

objectionable in that it adds further complexity to an already cluttered tax law. It is, however, an inevitable product of our political system.

Political Expediency Situations

Various tax reform proposals rise and fall in favor with the shifting moods of the American public. That Congress is sensitive to popular feeling is an accepted fact. Therefore, certain provisions of the tax law can be explained by the political climate at the time they were enacted.

Measures that deter more affluent taxpayers from obtaining so-called preferential tax treatment have always had popular appeal and, consequently, the support of Congress. A direct approach bars the benefit completely and explains such provisions as the imputed interest rules and the limitations on the deductibility of interest on investment indebtedness. More subtle are provisions that phase out tax breaks as income rises. Because taxpayers may be unaware of what is causing the shift to higher marginal tax rates, these phaseouts are often called "stealth taxes." The tax law contains several dozen such phaseout provisions. Examples include the earned income credit, the child tax credit, the lifetime learning credit, and personal and dependency exemptions. At least for the immediate future, the use of these stealth taxes can be expected to increase.

Other changes, explained at least partially by political expediency, include the lowering of individual income tax rates, the increase in the personal and dependency exemptions, and the increase in the amount of the earned income credit.

State and Local Government Influences

Political considerations have played a major role in the nontaxability of interest received on state and local obligations. In view of the furor that state and local political figures have raised every time any modification of this tax provision has been proposed, one might well regard it as next to sacred.

Somewhat less apparent has been the influence that state law has had in shaping our present Federal tax law. Such was the case with community property systems. The nine states with community property systems are Louisiana, Texas, New Mexico, Arizona, California, Washington, Idaho, Nevada, and Wisconsin. The rest of the states are classified as common law jurisdictions.[31] The difference between common law and community property systems centers around the property rights possessed by married persons. In a common law system, each spouse owns whatever he or she earns. Under a community property system, one-half of the earnings of each spouse is considered owned by the other spouse.

Al and Fran are husband and wife, and their only income is the $80,000 annual salary Al receives. If they live in New Jersey (a common law state), the $80,000 salary belongs to Al. If, however, they live in Arizona (a community property state), the $80,000 is divided equally, in terms of ownership, between Al and Fran.

EXAMPLE 25

At one time, the tax position of the residents of community property states was so advantageous that many common law states adopted community property systems. Needless to say, the political pressure placed on Congress to correct the disparity in tax treatment was considerable. To a large extent, this was accomplished in the Revenue Act of 1948, which extended many of the community property tax advantages to residents of common law jurisdictions.

The major advantage extended was the provision allowing married taxpayers to file joint returns and compute their tax liability as if one-half of the income had been earned

---

[31]In Alaska, spouses can choose to have the community property rules apply. Otherwise, property rights are determined under common law rules.

by each spouse. This result is automatic in a community property state, because half of the income earned by one spouse belongs to the other spouse. The income-splitting benefits of a joint return are now incorporated as part of the tax rates applicable to married taxpayers. See Chapter 3.

1-7f Influence of the Internal Revenue Service

The influence of the IRS is apparent in many areas beyond its role in issuing the administrative pronouncements that make up a considerable portion of our tax law. In its capacity as the protector of the national revenue, the IRS has been instrumental in securing the passage of much legislation designed to curtail the most flagrant tax avoidance practices (to close *tax loopholes*). As the administrator of the tax law, the IRS has sought and obtained legislation to make its job easier (to attain administrative feasibility).

The IRS as Protector of the Revenue

Innumerable examples can be given of provisions in the tax law that stem from the direct influence of the IRS. Usually, such provisions are intended to prevent a loophole from being used to avoid the tax consequences intended by Congress. Working within the letter of existing law, ingenious taxpayers and their advisers devise techniques that accomplish indirectly what cannot be accomplished directly. As a consequence, legislation is enacted to close the loopholes that taxpayers have located and exploited. Some tax law can be explained in this fashion and is discussed in the chapters to follow.

In addition, the IRS has secured from Congress legislation of a more general nature that enables it to make adjustments based on the substance, rather than the formal construction, of what a taxpayer has done. For example, one such provision permits the IRS to make adjustments to a taxpayer's method of accounting when the method used by the taxpayer does not clearly reflect income.[32]

EXAMPLE 26

Tina, a cash basis taxpayer, owns and operates a pharmacy. All drugs and other items acquired for resale, such as cosmetics, are charged to the purchases account and written off (expensed) for tax purposes in the year of acquisition. As this procedure does not clearly reflect income, it would be appropriate for the IRS to require that Tina establish and maintain an ending inventory account.

Administrative Feasibility

Some tax law is justified on the grounds that it simplifies the task of the IRS in collecting the revenue and administering the law. With regard to collecting the revenue, the IRS long ago realized the importance of placing taxpayers on a pay-as-you-go basis. Elaborate withholding procedures apply to wages, while the tax on other types of income may be paid at periodic intervals throughout the year. The IRS has been instrumental in convincing the courts that accrual basis taxpayers should, in most cases, pay taxes on prepaid income in the year received and not when earned. The approach may be contrary to generally accepted accounting principles, but it is consistent with the wherewithal to pay concept.

Of considerable aid to the IRS in collecting revenue are the numerous provisions that impose interest and penalties on taxpayers for noncompliance with the tax law. Provisions such as the penalties for failure to pay a tax or to file a return that is due, the negligence penalty for intentional disregard of rules and regulations, and various penalties for civil and criminal fraud serve as deterrents to taxpayer noncompliance.

One of the keys to an effective administration of our tax system is the audit process conducted by the IRS. To carry out this function, the IRS is aided by provisions that reduce the chance of taxpayer error or manipulation and therefore simplify the audit effort that is necessary. An increase in the amount of the standard deduction, for example, reduces the number of individual taxpayers who will choose the alternative of

---

[32]See Chapter 18.

itemizing their personal deductions.[33] With fewer deductions to check, the audit function is simplified.[34]

1-7g **Influence of the Courts**

In addition to interpreting statutory provisions and the administrative pronouncements issued by the IRS, the Federal courts have influenced tax law in two other respects.[35] First, the courts have formulated certain judicial concepts that serve as guides in the application of various tax provisions. Second, certain key decisions have led to changes in the Internal Revenue Code.

Judicial Concepts Relating to Tax

A leading tax concept developed by the courts deals with the interpretation of statutory tax provisions that operate to benefit taxpayers. The courts have established the rule that these relief provisions are to be narrowly construed if there is any doubt about their application.

Important in this area is the *arm's length* concept. Particularly in dealings between related parties, transactions may be tested by looking to whether the taxpayers acted in an arm's length manner. The question to be asked is: Would unrelated parties have handled the transaction in the same way?

Rex, the sole shareholder of Silver Corporation, leases property to the corporation for a yearly rent of $60,000. To test whether the corporation should be allowed a rent deduction for this amount, the IRS and the courts will apply the arm's length concept. Would Silver Corporation have paid $60,000 a year in rent if it had leased the same property from an unrelated party (rather than from Rex)? Suppose it is determined that an unrelated third party would have charged an annual rent for the property of only $50,000. Under these circumstances, Silver Corporation will be allowed a deduction of only $50,000. The other $10,000 it paid for the use of the property represents a non-deductible dividend. Accordingly, Rex will be treated as having received rent income of $50,000 and dividend income of $10,000.

Judicial Influence on Statutory Provisions

Some court decisions have been of such consequence that Congress has incorporated them into statutory tax law. For example, many years ago the courts found that stock dividends distributed to the shareholders of a corporation were not taxable as income. This result was largely accepted by Congress, and a provision in the tax statutes now covers the issue.

On occasion, however, Congress has reacted negatively to judicial interpretations of the tax law.

Nora leases unimproved real estate to Wade for 20 years. At a cost of $400,000, Wade erects a building on the land. The building is worth $150,000 when the lease terminates and Nora takes possession of the property. Does Nora have any income either when the improvements are made or when the lease terminates? In a landmark decision, a court held that Nora must recognize income of $150,000 upon the termination of the lease.

Congress believed that the result reached in Example 28 was inequitable in that it was not consistent with the wherewithal to pay concept. Consequently, the tax law was amended to provide that a landlord does not recognize any income either when the improvements are made (unless made in lieu of rent) or when the lease terminates.

---

[33]For a discussion of the standard deduction, see Chapter 3.

[34]The same justification was given by the IRS when it proposed to Congress the $100 limitation on personal casualty and theft losses. Imposition of the limitation eliminated many casualty and theft loss deductions and, as a consequence, saved the IRS considerable audit time. Later legislation, in addition to retaining the $100 feature, limits deductible losses to those in excess of 10% of a taxpayer's adjusted gross income. See Chapter 7.

[35]A great deal of case law is devoted to ascertaining congressional intent. The courts, in effect, ask: What did Congress have in mind when it enacted a particular tax provision?

1-8 **SUMMARY**

In addition to its necessary revenue-raising objective, the Federal tax law has developed in response to several other factors:

- *Economic considerations.* The emphasis here is on tax provisions that help regulate the economy and encourage certain activities and types of businesses.

- *Social considerations.* Some tax provisions are designed to encourage (or discourage) certain socially desirable (or undesirable) practices.

- *Equity considerations.* Of principal concern in this area are tax provisions that alleviate the effect of multiple taxation, recognize the wherewithal to pay concept, mitigate the effect of the annual accounting period concept, and recognize the eroding effect of inflation.

- *Political considerations.* Of significance in this regard are tax provisions that represent special interest legislation, reflect political expediency, and exhibit the effect of state and local law.

- *Influence of the IRS.* Many tax provisions are intended to aid the IRS in the collection of revenue and the administration of the tax law.

- *Influence of the courts.* Court decisions have established a body of judicial concepts relating to tax law and have, on occasion, led Congress to enact statutory provisions to either clarify or negate their effect.

These factors explain various tax provisions and thereby help in understanding why the tax law developed to its present state. The next step involves learning to work with the tax law, which is the subject of Chapter 2.

REFOCUS ON THE BIG PICTURE

FAMILY AND TAXES—A TYPICAL YEAR

The explanation given for the difference in the ad valorem property taxes—the Carters' increase and the Walkers' decrease—seems reasonable (see Example 4). It is not likely that the Carters' increase was due to a *general* upward assessment in valuation, as the Walkers' taxes on their residence (located nearby) dropped. More business use of the Carters' residence (presuming that Travis conducts his consulting practice from his home) might be responsible for the increase, but capital improvements appear to be a more likely cause.

The imposition of the use tax when Travis registered the new automobile illustrates one of the means by which a state can preclude the avoidance of its sales tax (see Example 5).

When gifts between family members are material in amount (e.g., an RV) and exceed the annual exclusion, a gift tax return needs to be filed (see Example 11). Even though no gift tax may be due because of the availability of the unified transfer tax credit, the filing of a return starts the running of the statute of limitations.

The imposition of the "jock tax" on nonathletes is unusual but not improper. The Carters must recognize that some of their income is subject to income taxes in two states and take advantage of whatever relief is available to mitigate the result (see Example 12).

Employment within and by the family group (e.g., children, other relatives, and domestics) has become a priority item in the enforcement of Social Security tax and income tax withholdings. Thus, the Carters must be aware of the need to cover their son, Martin (see Example 13).

Because of the double audit (i.e., both state and Federal) and the deficiency assessed, the Carters need to make sure that future returns do not contain similar errors (see Example 18). As the text suggests, taxpayers with prior deficiencies are among those whose returns may be selected for audit.

Key Terms

Ad valorem taxes, 1-6
Correspondence audit, 1-21
Employment taxes, 1-15
Estate tax, 1-11
Excise taxes, 1-8
FICA tax, 1-16
Field audit, 1-21
Flat tax, 1-18
Franchise tax, 1-17

FUTA tax, 1-17
Gift tax, 1-12
Indexation, 1-30
Inheritance tax, 1-11
National sales tax, 1-19
Occupational fees, 1-17
Office audit, 1-21
Personalty, 1-8
Realty, 1-7

Revenue neutrality, 1-25
Sales tax, 1-9
Severance taxes, 1-10
Statute of limitations, 1-22
Sunset provision, 1-25
Use tax, 1-9
Value added tax (VAT), 1-19
Wherewithal to pay, 1-29

Discussion Questions

1. **LO.1** In the following independent situations, is the tax position of the taxpayer likely to change? Explain why or why not.
   a. John used to make casual purchases and sales of real estate as an investor. Currently, he does so on a regular basis and has obtained a license as a dealer.
   b. Theresa quit her job as a staff accountant and has established her own practice as a CPA.
   c. After saving enough for a down payment, Paul has purchased a personal residence.

2. **LO.1** Marvin is the executor and sole heir of his aunt's estate. The estate includes her furnished home, which Marvin is considering converting to rental property to generate additional cash flow. What are some of the tax problems Marvin may confront? — Issue ID

3. **LO.2** The Sixteenth Amendment to the U.S. Constitution was passed to overturn a Supreme Court decision that had invalidated the Federal income tax. Do you agree? Why or why not?

4. **LO.2** World War II converted the Federal income tax into a *mass tax*. Explain.

5. **LO.2** How does the pay-as-you-go procedure apply to wage earners? To persons who have income from sources other than wages?

6. **LO.3** Using Adam Smith's canon on *economy*, evaluate the Federal income tax.

7. **LO.3** Distinguish between taxes that are *proportional* and those that are *progressive*.

8. **LO.4** Several years ago Ethan purchased the former parsonage of St. James Church to use as a personal residence. To date, Ethan has not received any ad valorem property tax bills from either the city or the county tax authorities. — Issue ID
   a. What is a reasonable explanation for this oversight?
   b. What should Ethan do?

9. **LO.4** The Adams Independent School District wants to sell a parcel of unimproved land that it does not need. Its three best offers are as follows: from the state's Department of Public Safety (DPS), $2.3 million; from the Second Baptist Church, $2.2 million; and from Baker Motors, $2.1 million. DPS would use the property for a new state highway patrol barracks, Second Baptist would start a church school, and Baker would open a car dealership. If you are the financial adviser for the school district, which offer would you prefer? Why? — Issue ID

10. **LO.4** The commissioners for Walker County are actively negotiating with Falcon Industries regarding the location of a new manufacturing plant in the area. As Falcon is considering several other sites, a "generous tax holiday" may be needed to influence the final choice. The local school district is opposed to any "generous tax holiday."
    a. What would probably be involved in a generous tax holiday?
    b. Why would the school district be opposed?

11. **LO.4** Sophia lives several blocks from her parents in the same residential subdivision. Sophia is surprised to learn that her ad valorem property taxes for the year were raised, while those of her parents were lowered. What is a possible explanation for the difference?

12. **LO.4** The Morgan family lives in Massachusetts. They moor their sailboat in Rhode Island. What might be a plausible reason for the possible inconvenience?

13. **LO.4** Is the breadth and number of Federal excise taxes increasing or decreasing? Explain.

14. **LO.4** After his first business trip to a major city, Herman is alarmed when he reviews his credit card receipts. Both the hotel bill and the car rental charge are in excess of the price he was quoted. Was Herman overcharged, or is there an explanation for the excess amounts?

15. **LO.4** What is the difference between an excise tax and a general sales tax?
    a. Do all states impose a general sales tax?
    b. Does the Federal government impose a general sales tax?

16. **LO.4** The Grays live in Clay County, which is adjacent to Jackson County. Although the retail stores in both counties are comparable, the Grays usually drive a few extra miles to shop in Jackson County. As to why the Grays might do this, consider the following:
    a. Clay County is in a different state than Jackson County.
    b. Clay County and Jackson County are in the same state.

Issue ID   17. **LO.4** During a social event, Muriel and Earl are discussing the home computer each recently purchased. Although the computers are identical makes and models, Muriel is surprised to learn that she paid a sales tax, while Earl did not. Comment as to why this could happen.

18. **LO.4** Distinguish between an estate tax and an inheritance tax.
    a. Do some states impose both? Neither?
    b. Which, if either, does the Federal government impose?

Issue ID   19. **LO.4** Jake (age 72) and Jessica (age 28) were recently married. To avoid any transfer taxes, Jake has promised to leave Jessica all of his wealth when he dies. Is Jake under some misconception about the operation of the Federal gift and estate taxes? Explain.

20. **LO.4** Address the following issues:
    a. What is the purpose of the unified transfer tax credit?
    b. Is the same amount available for both the Federal gift tax and the estate tax? Explain.
    c. Does the use of the credit for a gift affect the amount of credit available for the estate tax? Explain.

21. **LO.4** Elijah and Anastasia are husband and wife who have five married children and nine minor grandchildren. For 2016, what is the maximum amount they can give to their family (including the sons- and daughters-in-law) without using any of their unified transfer tax credit?

22. **LO.4** What is the difference between the Federal income tax on individuals and that imposed on corporations?

23. **LO.4** As to those states that impose an income tax, comment on the following:
    a.   "Piggyback" approach and possible "decoupling" from this approach.
    b.   Deductibility of Federal income taxes.
    c.   Credit for taxes paid to other states.

24. **LO.4** In May 2016, Hernando, a resident of California, has his 2014 Federal income tax return audited by the IRS. An assessment of additional tax is made because he had inadvertently omitted some rental income. In October 2016, California audits his state return for the same year. Explain the coincidence.

25. **LO.4** Mike Barr was an outstanding football player in college and expects to be drafted by the NFL in the first few rounds. Mike has let it be known that he would prefer to sign with a club located in Florida, Texas, or Washington. Mike sees no reason why he should have to pay state income tax on his player's salary. Is Mike under any delusions? Explain.   Issue ID

26. **LO.4, 5** A question on a state income tax return asks the taxpayer if he or she made any out-of-state Internet or mail-order catalog purchases during the year. The question requires a yes or no answer, and if the taxpayer answers yes, the amount of such purchases is to be listed.   Issue ID
    a.   Does such an inquiry have any relevance to the state income tax? If not, why is it being asked?
    b.   Your client, Harriet, wants to leave the question unanswered. As the preparer of her return, how do you respond?

27. **LO.4** Many state income tax returns contain checkoff boxes that allow taxpayers to make donations to a multitude of local charitable causes. On what grounds has this procedure been criticized?

28. **LO.4** Many states have occasionally adopted amnesty programs that allow taxpayers to pay back taxes with reduced penalties.
    a.   Besides the revenue generated, how are these programs advantageous?
    b.   Could an amnesty program be used by a state that does not levy an income tax?
    c.   Does the IRS utilize this approach?

29. **LO.4** Contrast FICA and FUTA as to the following:
    a.   Purpose of the tax.
    b.   Upon whom imposed.
    c.   Governmental administration of the tax.
    d.   Reduction of tax based on a merit rating system.

30. **LO.4** In connection with the Medicare component of FICA, comment on the following:
    a.   Any dollar limitation imposed.
    b.   The applicability of the .9% increase in the 1.45% regular tax rate.

31. **LO.4** One of the tax advantages of hiring family members to work in your business is that FICA taxes are avoided. Do you agree with this statement? Explain.

32. **LO.4** Describe the nature and purpose of the following taxes:
    a.   Severance taxes.
    b.   Franchise taxes.
    c.   Occupational fees.
    d.   Customs duties.
    e.   Export duties.

33. **LO.4** Regarding the value added tax (VAT), comment on the following:
    a. Popularity of this type of tax.
    b. Nature of the tax.
    c. Effect on government spending.

34. **LO.4** Both a value added tax (VAT) and a national sales tax have been criticized as being *regressive* in their effect.
    a. Explain.
    b. How could this shortcoming be remedied in the case of a national sales tax?

35. **LO.4, 5** Serena operates a lawn maintenance service in Southern California. As most of her employees are itinerant, they are paid on a day-to-day basis. Because of cash-flow problems, Serena requires her customers to pay cash for the services she provides.
    a. What are some of the tax problems Serena might have?
    b. Assess Serena's chances of audit by the IRS.

36. **LO.5** With regard to the IRS audit process, comment on the following:
    a. The audit is resolved by mail.
    b. The audit is conducted at the office of the IRS.
    c. A "no change" RAR results.
    d. A special agent joins the audit team.

37. **LO.5** Aldo has just been audited by the IRS. He does not agree with the agent's findings but believes that he has only two choices: pay the proposed deficiency or resort to the courts. Do you agree with Aldo's conclusion? Why or why not?

38. **LO.5** What purpose is served by a statute of limitations? How is it relevant in the case of tax controversies?

39. **LO.5** Regarding the statute of limitations on additional assessments of tax by the IRS, determine the applicable period in each of the following situations. Assume a calendar year individual with no fraud or substantial omission involved.
    a. The income tax return for 2015 was filed on February 19, 2016.
    b. The income tax return for 2015 was filed on June 25, 2016.
    c. The income tax return for 2015 was prepared on April 4, 2016, but was never filed. Through some misunderstanding between the preparer and the taxpayer, each expected the other to file the return.
    d. The income tax return for 2015 was never filed because the taxpayer thought no additional tax was due.

40. **LO.5** Brianna, a calendar year taxpayer, files her income tax return for 2015 on February 3, 2016. Although she makes repeated inquiries, she does not receive her refund from the IRS until May 28, 2016. Is Brianna entitled to interest on the refund? Explain.

41. **LO.5, 6** On a Federal income tax return filed five years ago, Andy inadvertently omitted a large amount of gross income.
    a. Andy seeks your advice as to whether the IRS is barred from assessing additional income tax in the event he is audited. What is your advice?
    b. Would your advice differ if you were the person who prepared the return in question? Explain.
    c. Suppose Andy asks you to prepare his current year's return. Would you do so? Explain.

42. **LO.5** Isabella files her income tax return 35 days after the due date of the return without obtaining an extension from the IRS. Along with the return, she remits a check for $40,000, which is the balance of the tax she owes. Disregarding the interest element, what are Isabella's penalties for failure to file and for failure to pay?

43. **LO.5** For tax year 2013, the IRS assesses a deficiency against David for $500,000. Disregarding the interest component, what is David's penalty if the deficiency is attributable to:
    a. Negligence?
    b. Fraud?

44. **LO.5, 6** In March 2016, Jim asks you to prepare his Federal income tax returns for tax years 2013, 2014, and 2015. In discussing this matter with him, you discover that he also has not filed for tax year 2012. When you mention this fact, Jim tells you that the statute of limitations precludes the IRS from taking any action as to this year.
    a. Is Jim correct about the application of the statute of limitations? Why or why not?
    b. If Jim refuses to file for 2012, should you prepare returns for 2013 through 2015? Explain.

45. **LO.5, 6** The Benson CPA firm is considering utilizing an offshore service provider to prepare many of its tax returns. In this regard, what ethical considerations must be taken into account?

46. **LO.7** In terms of tax policy, what do the following mean?
    a. Revenue neutrality.
    b. Pay-as-you-go, or "paygo."
    c. Sunset provision.
    d. Indexation.

47. **LO.7** Some tax rules can be justified on multiple grounds (e.g., economic and social). In this connection, comment on the possible justification for the rules governing the following:
    a. Pension plans.
    b. Education.
    c. Home ownership.

48. **LO.7, 8** Discuss the probable justification for each of the following aspects of the tax law:
    a. A tax credit is allowed for amounts spent to furnish care for minor children while the parent works.
    b. Deductions for interest on home mortgage and property taxes on a personal residence.
    c. The income-splitting benefits of filing a joint return.
    d. Gambling losses in excess of gambling gains.
    e. Net operating losses of a current year can be carried back to profitable years.
    f. A taxpayer who sells property on an installment basis can recognize gain on the sale over the period the payments are received.
    g. The exclusion from Federal tax of certain interest income from state and local bonds.
    h. Prepaid income is taxed to the recipient in the year received and not in the year earned.

49. **LO.7** Mia owns a warehouse that has a cost basis to her of $80,000. The city condemns the warehouse to make room for a new fire station. It pays Mia $400,000 for the property, its agreed-to fair market value. Shortly after the condemnation, Mia purchases another warehouse as a replacement. What is her recognized gain if the new property cost:

    a. $280,000?

    b. $444,000?

    c. $80,000?

    d. What, if any, is the justification for deferring the recognition of gain on the involuntary conversion?

50. **LO.8** A mother sells a valuable collection of antiques to her daughter for $1,000. What judicial concept might the IRS invoke to question this transaction?

Working with the Tax Law

LEARNING OBJECTIVES: *After completing Chapter 2, you should be able to:*

LO.1 Distinguish between the statutory, administrative, and judicial sources of the tax law and understand the purpose of each source.

LO.2 Locate and work with the appropriate tax law sources.

LO.3 Develop an awareness of tax research tools.

LO.4 Describe the tax research process.

LO.5 Communicate the results of the tax research process in a client letter and a tax file memorandum.

LO.6 Apply tax research techniques and planning procedures.

LO.7 Be aware of taxation on the CPA examination.

CHAPTER OUTLINE

© MORGAN BUSINESS IMAGES/SHUTTERSTOCK.COM

IMPORTANCE OF TAX RESEARCH

Early in December 2016, Fred and Megan Samuels review their financial and tax situation with their son, Sam, and daughter-in-law, Dana, who live with them. Fred and Megan are in the 28 percent tax bracket in 2016. Both Sam and Dana are age 21. Sam, a student at a nearby university, owns some publicly traded stock that he inherited from his grandmother. A current sale would result in $8,000 of gross income ($19,000 amount realized − $11,000 basis). At this point, Fred and Megan provide about 55 percent of Sam and Dana's support. Although neither is now employed, Sam has earned $960 and Dana has earned $900 during the year. The problem: Should the stock be sold? If the stock was sold, would the sale prohibit Fred and Megan from claiming Sam and Dana as dependents? Would the stock sale in 2016 result in a tax liability for Sam and Dana?

Read the chapter and formulate your responses.

F ederal tax law is a mixture of statutory provisions, administrative pronouncements, and court decisions. Anyone who has attempted to work with this body of knowledge is familiar with its complexity. Tax research provides the vehicle by which one makes sense out of this complexity.

2-1 TAX SOURCES

Understanding taxation requires a mastery of the sources of the *rules of tax law*. These sources include not only legislative provisions in the form of the Internal Revenue Code but also congressional Committee Reports, Treasury Department Regulations, other Treasury Department pronouncements, and court decisions. Thus, the *primary sources* of tax information include pronouncements from all three branches of government: legislative, executive, and judicial.

In addition to being able to locate and interpret the sources of the tax law, a tax professional must understand the relative weight of authority that each source carries. The tax law is of little significance, however, until it is applied to a set of facts and circumstances. This chapter, therefore, both introduces the statutory, administrative, and judicial sources of tax law and explains how the law is applied to individual and business transactions. It also explains how to apply research techniques and use planning procedures effectively. A large part of tax research focuses on determining the intent of Congress.

Frequently, uncertainty in the tax law causes disputes between the Internal Revenue Service (IRS) and taxpayers. Due to these *gray areas* and the complexity of the tax law, a taxpayer may have more than one alternative for structuring a financial transaction. In structuring financial transactions and engaging in other tax planning activities, the tax adviser must be cognizant that the objective of tax planning is not necessarily to minimize the tax liability. Instead, a taxpayer should maximize his or her after-tax return, which may include maximizing nontax as well as noneconomic benefits.

2-1a Statutory Sources of the Tax Law

Statutory sources of law include the Constitution (Article I, Sections 7, 8, and 10), tax treaties (agreements between countries to mitigate the double taxation of taxpayers subject to the tax laws of those countries), and the Internal Revenue Code. The Constitution grants Congress the power to impose and collect taxes and authorizes the creation of treaties with other countries. The power of Congress to implement and collect taxes is reflected in the Internal Revenue Code, the official title of U.S. tax law, and it is the basis for arriving at solutions to all tax questions.

Origin of the Internal Revenue Code

Before 1939, the statutory provisions relating to Federal taxation were contained in the individual revenue acts enacted by Congress. Because dealing with many separate acts was inconvenient and confusing, Congress codified all of the Federal tax laws in 1939. Known as the Internal Revenue Code of 1939, the codification arranged all Federal tax provisions in a logical sequence and placed them in a separate part of the Federal statutes. A further rearrangement took place in 1954 and resulted in the Internal Revenue Code of 1954, which continued in effect until 1986, when it was replaced by the Internal Revenue Code of 1986. Although Congress did not recodify the law in the Tax Reform Act (TRA) of 1986, the magnitude of the changes made by TRA of 1986 did provide some rationale for renaming the Federal tax law the Internal Revenue Code of 1986.

The following observations help clarify the codification procedure:

- Neither the 1939 nor the 1954 Code substantially changed the tax law existing on the date of its enactment. Much of the 1939 Code, for example, was incorporated into the 1954 Code; the major change was the reorganization and renumbering of the tax provisions.

In income tax history, 1913 was an important year. In that year, the Sixteenth Amendment to the Constitution was ratified:

The Congress shall have power to tax and collect taxes on incomes, from whatever source derived, without apportionment among the several States, and without regard to any census or enumeration.

The first income tax legislation was passed that same year.

According to the Tax Foundation, in 2015, Tax Freedom Day fell on April 24, the 114th day of the year and one day later than in 2014. Tax Freedom Day is the date on which an average taxpayer through working has paid off his or her taxes for the year. If annual Federal borrowing is included, Tax Freedom Day occurred on May 8, 14 days later.

Americans work the longest to pay Federal, state, and local individual income taxes (43 days). Payroll taxes take 26 days to pay, followed by sales and excise taxes (15 days), corporate income taxes (12 days), and property taxes (11 days). The remaining 7 days are spent paying estate and inheritance taxes, customs duties, and other taxes. As in prior years, Americans paid more in taxes in 2015 than they spent on food, clothing, and shelter combined. As you might suspect, Tax Freedom Day differs based on the state where you live. If you lived in Connecticut and New Jersey, the states with the heaviest total tax burden, Tax Freedom Day fell on May 13. Louisiana celebrated Tax Freedom Day the earliest—on April 2, the 92nd day of the year.

Source: Tax Foundation, "America Celebrates Tax Freedom Day," **taxfoundation.org/tax-topics/tax-freedom-day**.

- Although the 1986 Code resulted in substantial changes, only a minority of the statutory provisions were affected.[1]
- Statutory amendments to the tax law are integrated into the Code. For example, over the past few years, the American Taxpayer Relief Act of 2012 and the Protecting Americans from Tax Hikes Act of 2015 became part of the Internal Revenue Code of 1986. Given the current political environment, it appears that the tax law will continue to be amended frequently.

The Legislative Process

Federal tax legislation generally originates in the House of Representatives, where it is first considered by the House Ways and Means Committee. Tax bills also can originate in the Senate when they are attached as riders to other legislative proposals.[2] If acceptable to the House Ways and Means Committee, the proposed bill is referred to the entire House of Representatives for approval or disapproval. Approved bills are sent to the Senate, where they are considered by the Senate Finance Committee.

The next step is referral from the Senate Finance Committee to the entire Senate. Assuming no disagreement between the House and Senate, passage by the Senate results in referral to the President for approval or veto. If the bill is approved or if the President's veto is overridden, the bill becomes law and part of the Internal Revenue Code of 1986.

House and Senate versions of major tax bills frequently differ. One reason bills are often changed in the Senate is that each senator has considerable latitude to make amendments when the Senate as a whole is voting on a bill referred to it by the Senate Finance Committee.[3] In contrast, the entire House of Representatives either accepts or rejects what is proposed by the House Ways and Means Committee, and changes from the floor are rare. When the Senate version of the bill differs from that passed by the House, the Joint Conference Committee, which includes members of both the House Ways and Means

---

[1]This point is important in assessing judicial decisions interpreting provisions of the Internal Revenue Code of 1939 and the Internal Revenue Code of 1954. If the same provision was included in the Internal Revenue Code of 1986 and has not been subsequently amended, the provision and the related judicial decisions have continuing validity.

[2]The Tax Equity and Fiscal Responsibility Act of 1982 originated in the Senate, and its constitutionality was unsuccessfully challenged in the courts.

The Senate version of the Deficit Reduction Act of 1984 was attached as an amendment to the Federal Boat Safety Act.

[3]During the passage of the Tax Reform Act of 1986, Senate leaders tried to make the bill *amendment proof* to avoid the normal amendment process.

Committee and the Senate Finance Committee, is called upon to resolve the differences. The deliberations of the Joint Conference Committee usually produce a compromise between the two versions, which then is voted on by both the House and the Senate. If both bodies accept the bill, it is referred to the President for approval or veto. Former Senator Daniel Patrick Moynihan observed that in the last hours of Congress, the White House and lawmakers often agree on a "1,200-page monster, we vote for it; nobody knows what is in it." Exhibit 2.1 summarizes the typical legislative process for tax bills.

The role of the Joint Conference Committee indicates the importance of compromise in the legislative process. As an example of the practical effect of the compromise process, consider Exhibit 2.2, which shows what happened with amendments to the earned income threshold for determining when the child tax credit becomes refundable.

Referrals from the House Ways and Means Committee, the Senate Finance Committee, and the Joint Conference Committee are usually accompanied by Committee Reports. These Committee Reports often explain the provisions of the proposed legislation and are a valuable source for ascertaining the *intent of Congress*. What Congress had in mind when it considered and enacted tax legislation is, of course, the key to interpreting such legislation by taxpayers, the IRS, and the courts. Because Regulations normally are not issued immediately after a statute is enacted, tax researchers often look to Committee Reports to determine congressional intent.

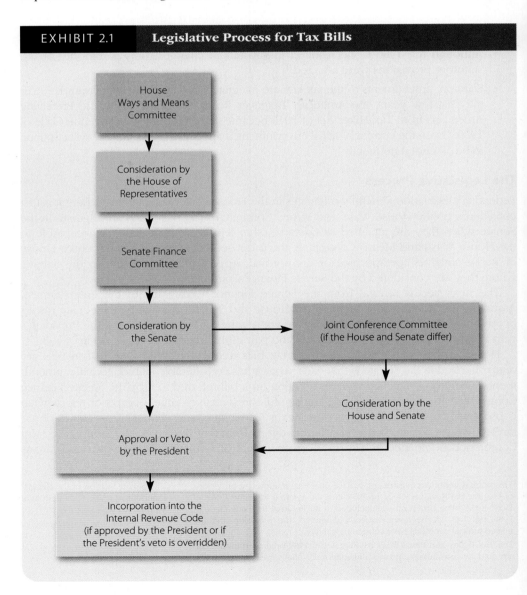

EXHIBIT 2.1   **Legislative Process for Tax Bills**

EXHIBIT 2.2	Example of Compromise in the Joint Conference Committee

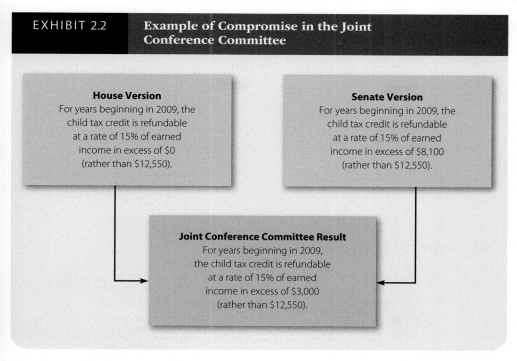

House Version
For years beginning in 2009, the child tax credit is refundable at a rate of 15% of earned income in excess of $0 (rather than $12,550).

Senate Version
For years beginning in 2009, the child tax credit is refundable at a rate of 15% of earned income in excess of $8,100 (rather than $12,550).

Joint Conference Committee Result
For years beginning in 2009, the child tax credit is refundable at a rate of 15% of earned income in excess of $3,000 (rather than $12,550).

Arrangement of the Internal Revenue Code

The Internal Revenue Code of 1986 is found in Title 26 of the U.S. Code. In working with the Internal Revenue Code, it helps to understand the format. Note, for example, the following partial table of contents:

Subtitle A. Income Taxes
  Chapter 11. Normal Taxes and Surtaxes
    Subchapter A. Determination of Tax Liability
      Part I. Tax on Individuals
        Sections 1–5
      Part II. Tax on Corporations
        Sections 11–12

In referring to a provision of the Code, the *key* is usually the Section number. In citing Section 2(a) (dealing with the status of a surviving spouse), for example, it is unnecessary to include Subtitle A, Chapter 1, Subchapter A, Part I. Merely mentioning Section 2(a) will suffice, because the Section numbers run consecutively and do not begin again with each new Subtitle, Chapter, Subchapter, or Part. Not all Code Section numbers are used, however. Notice that Part I ends with Section 5 and Part II starts with Section 11 (at present, there are no Sections 6, 7, 8, 9, and 10).[4]

Tax researchers commonly refer to some specific areas of income tax law by their Subchapters. Some of the more common Subchapter designations include Subchapter C ("Corporate Distributions and Adjustments"), Subchapter K ("Partners and Partnerships"), and Subchapter S ("Tax Treatment of S Corporations and Their Shareholders"). In the last situation in particular, it is much more convenient to describe the subject of the applicable Code provisions (Sections 1361–1379) as S corporation status rather than as the "Tax Treatment of S Corporations and Their Shareholders."

---

[4]When the 1954 Code was drafted, some Section numbers were intentionally omitted so that later changes could be incorporated into the Code without disrupting its organization. When Congress does not leave enough space, subsequent Code Sections are given A, B, C, etc., designations. A good example is the treatment of §§ 280A through 280H.

Citing the Code

Code Sections often are broken down into subparts.[5] Section 2(a)(1)(A) serves as an example.

Broken down by content, § 2(a)(1)(A) becomes:

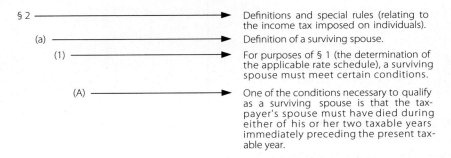

§ 2	Definitions and special rules (relating to the income tax imposed on individuals).
(a)	Definition of a surviving spouse.
(1)	For purposes of § 1 (the determination of the applicable rate schedule), a surviving spouse must meet certain conditions.
(A)	One of the conditions necessary to qualify as a surviving spouse is that the tax-payer's spouse must have died during either of his or her two taxable years immediately preceding the present taxable year.

Throughout the text, references to the Code Sections are in the form given above. The symbols "§" and "§§" are used in place of "Section" and "Sections," respectively. Unless otherwise stated, all Code references are to the Internal Revenue Code of 1986. The following table summarizes the format that will be used:

Complete Reference	Text Reference
Section 2(a)(1)(A) of the Internal Revenue Code of 1986	§ 2(a)(1)(A)
Sections 1 and 2 of the Internal Revenue Code of 1986	§§ 1 and 2
Section 2 of the Internal Revenue Code of 1954	§ 2 of the Internal Revenue Code of 1954
Section 12(d) of the Internal Revenue Code of 1939[7]	§ 12(d) of the Internal Revenue Code of 1939

2-1b Administrative Sources of the Tax Law

The administrative sources of the Federal tax law can be grouped as follows: Treasury Department Regulations, Revenue Rulings and Revenue Procedures, and various other administrative pronouncements (see Exhibit 2.3). All are issued by either the U.S. Treasury Department or the IRS.

---

[5]Some Code Sections do not require subparts. See, for example, §§ 211 and 241.

[6]Some Code Sections omit the subsection designation and use the paragraph designation as the first subpart. See, for example, §§ 212(1) and 1222(1).

[7]Section 12(d) of the Internal Revenue Code of 1939 is the predecessor to § 2 of the Internal Revenue Code of 1954 and the Internal Revenue Code of 1986. Keep in mind that the 1954 Code superseded the 1939 Code and the 1986 Code has superseded the 1954 Code. Footnote 1 of this chapter explains why references to the 1939 or 1954 Code are included.

EXHIBIT 2.3	**Administrative Sources**	

Source	Location	Authority
Regulations	*Federal Register*	Force and effect of law.
Temporary Regulations	*Federal Register* *Internal Revenue Bulletin* *Cumulative Bulletin*	May be cited as a precedent.
Proposed Regulations	*Federal Register* *Internal Revenue Bulletin* *Cumulative Bulletin*	Preview of final Regulations.
Revenue Rulings Revenue Procedures Treasury Decisions Actions on Decisions	*Internal Revenue Bulletin* *Cumulative Bulletin*	Do not have the force and effect of law.

General Counsel Memoranda
Technical Advice Memoranda
	Tax Analysts' *Tax Notes;* Thomson Reuters
	   Checkpoint*; Commerce Clearing House
	   IntelliConnect
		May not be cited as a precedent.

Letter Rulings	Thomson Reuters and Commerce Clearing
	   House tax services
		Applicable only to taxpayer addressed.
		   No precedential force.

* Thomson Reuters *Checkpoint* includes a wide variety of tax resources. The most significant are materials produced by the Research Institute of America (RIA), including the *Federal Tax Coordinator 2d.*

Treasury Department Regulations

Regulations are issued by the U.S. Treasury Department under authority granted by Congress.[8] Interpretive by nature, they provide taxpayers with considerable guidance on the meaning and application of the Code. Regulations, which may be issued in *proposed, temporary,* or *final* form, carry considerable authority as the official interpretation of tax statutes. They are an important factor to consider in complying with the tax law.

Because Regulations interpret the Code, they are arranged in the same sequence as the Code. A number is added at the beginning, however, to indicate the type of tax or administrative, procedural, or definitional matter to which they relate. For example, the prefix 1 designates the Regulations under the income tax law. Thus, the Regulations under Code § 2 are cited as Reg. § 1.2, with subparts added for further identification. The numbering patterns of these subparts often have no correlation with the Code subsections. The prefix 20 designates estate tax Regulations, 25 covers gift tax Regulations, 31 relates to employment taxes, and 301 refers to procedure and administration. This list is not all-inclusive.

ETHICS & EQUITY   **Reporting Tax Fraud**

Maybe it is someone in your extended family who is driving a luxury car and comments that only fools pay all their taxes. Or maybe it is a contractor who demands payment in cash. Or perhaps it is someone at work who is not reporting all of his or her income. If cheating on taxes bothers you, the IRS wants to hear from you (and may make it worthwhile). The IRS has two whistleblower programs: The small-awards program is for cases involving less than $2 million of tax, and the award can be as high as 15% of collections, although it often is less. The large-awards program is more generous: For cases involving $2 million or more of tax, the reward can go as high as 30%. The IRS's tip line is 1-800-829-0433, and the appropriate form to report tax fraud is Form 3949–A (Information Referral). Would you turn in someone?

---

[8]§ 7805.

New Regulations and changes to existing Regulations are usually issued in proposed form before they are finalized. The interval between the proposal of a Regulation and its finalization permits taxpayers and other interested parties to comment on the propriety of the proposal. **Proposed Regulations** under Code § 2, for example, are cited as Prop.Reg. § 1.2. The Tax Court indicates that Proposed Regulations carry little weight. **Finalized Regulations** have the force and effect of law.[9]

Sometimes the Treasury Department issues **Temporary Regulations** relating to matters where immediate guidance is important. These Regulations are issued without the comment period required for Proposed Regulations. Temporary Regulations have the same authoritative value as final Regulations and may be cited as precedents. However, Temporary Regulations must also be issued as Proposed Regulations and automatically expire within three years after the date of issuance.[10] Temporary Regulations and the simultaneously issued Proposed Regulations carry more weight than traditional Proposed Regulations. An example of a Temporary Regulation is Temp.Reg. § 1.6081–8T, which allows only a single 30-day, non-automatic extension of time to file certain information returns.

Proposed, Temporary, and final Regulations are published in the *Federal Register*, in the *Internal Revenue Bulletin* (I.R.B.), and by major tax services. Final Regulations are issued as Treasury Decisions (TDs).

Regulations may also be classified as *legislative, interpretive*, or *procedural*. This classification scheme is discussed under Assessing the Validity of a Treasury Regulation later in the chapter.

Revenue Rulings and Revenue Procedures

Revenue Rulings are official pronouncements of the National Office of the IRS.[11] They typically provide one or more examples of how the IRS would apply a law to specific fact situations. Like Regulations, Revenue Rulings are designed to provide interpretation of the tax law. However, they do not carry the same legal force and effect as Regulations and usually deal with more restricted problems. Regulations are approved by the Secretary of the Treasury, whereas Revenue Rulings generally are not.

Although letter rulings (discussed in the next section) are not the same as Revenue Rulings, a Revenue Ruling often results from a specific taxpayer's request for a letter ruling. If the IRS believes that a taxpayer's request for a letter ruling deserves official publication because of its widespread impact, the letter ruling will be converted into a Revenue Ruling and issued for the information and guidance of taxpayers, tax professionals, and IRS personnel. Names, identifying descriptions, and money amounts are changed to conceal the identity of the requesting taxpayer. Revenue Rulings also arise from technical advice to District Offices of the IRS, court decisions, suggestions from tax practitioner groups, and various tax publications.

Revenue Procedures are issued in the same manner as Revenue Rulings but deal with the internal management practices and procedures of the IRS. Familiarity with these procedures can increase taxpayer compliance and help the IRS administer the tax laws more efficiently. A taxpayer's failure to follow a Revenue Procedure can result in unnecessary delay or, in a discretionary situation, can cause the IRS to decline to act.

Both Revenue Rulings and Revenue Procedures serve an important function by providing *guidance* to IRS personnel and taxpayers in handling routine tax matters. For example, one recent Revenue Procedure provided inflation-adjusted amounts for various Code provisions. Revenue Rulings and Revenue Procedures generally apply retroactively and may be revoked or modified by subsequent rulings or procedures, Regulations, legislation, or court decisions.

Revenue Rulings and Revenue Procedures are published weekly by the U.S. Government in the *Internal Revenue Bulletin* (I.R.B.).

---

[9]*F. W. Woolworth Co.*, 54 T.C. 1233 (1970); *Harris M. Miller*, 70 T.C. 448 (1978); and *James O. Tomerlin Trust*, 87 T.C. 876 (1986).

[10]§ 7805(e).

[11]§ 7805(a).

TAX IN THE NEWS **Origin of the April 15 Tax Day**

April 15 has not always been the tax return due date in the United States. Congress originally established March 15 as the due date of personal income tax returns. This date selection was apparently based upon the date of the Sixteenth Amendment. According to Jessica Sung, "when the Sixteenth Amendment, which allows Congress to institute the income tax, was adopted on Feb. 3, 1913, Congress chose March 1—one year and a few dozen days later—as the deadline for filing returns."

In order to give taxpayers more time to deal with the complexity of the tax laws, the Internal Revenue Code of 1954 changed the deadline to April 15.

Sources: Based on Jessica Sung, Tax Clinic, "Why Is Tax Day April 15?" *Fortune*, April 15, 2002, available at **archive.fortune.com/magazines/fortune/fortune_ archive/2002/04/15/321414/index.htm**; J. J. Thorndike, "Why Is Tax Day April 15?" *Tax Notes*, April 16, 2012, pp. 247–248.

The proper form for citing Revenue Rulings is as follows. Revenue Procedures are cited in the same manner, except that "Rev.Proc." is substituted for "Rev.Rul."

Rev.Rul. 2015–9, 2015–21 I.R.B. 972.

Explanation: Revenue Ruling Number 9, appearing on page 972 of the 21st weekly issue of the *Internal Revenue Bulletin* for 2015.

Revenue Rulings and other tax resources may be found at the IRS website: **www.irs.gov**.[12]

Letter Rulings

Letter rulings are issued for a fee upon a taxpayer's request and describe how the IRS will treat a *proposed* transaction for tax purposes. They apply only to the taxpayer who asks for and obtains the ruling, but post-1984 letter rulings may be substantial authority for purposes of the accuracy-related penalty.[13] Letter rulings can be useful to taxpayers who want to be certain of how a transaction will be taxed before proceeding with it. Letter rulings also allow taxpayers to avoid unexpected tax costs. Although the procedure for requesting a ruling can be quite cumbersome, sometimes requesting a ruling is the most effective way to carry out tax planning. Nevertheless, the IRS limits the issuance of individual rulings to restricted, preannounced areas of taxation. The main reason the IRS will not rule in certain areas is that they involve fact-oriented situations. Thus, a ruling may not be obtained on many of the problems that are particularly troublesome for taxpayers.[14] The IRS issues more than 2,500 letter rulings each year.

The law now requires the IRS to make individual rulings available for public inspection after identifying details are deleted.[15] Published digests of private letter rulings can be found in *IRS Letter Rulings Reports* (published by CCH), Bloomberg BNA's *Daily Tax Reports,* and Tax Analysts' *Tax Notes*. In addition, computerized databases of letter rulings are available through several private publishers.

Letter rulings are issued multidigit file numbers that indicate the year and week of issuance as well as the number of the ruling during that week. Consider, for example, Ltr.Rul. 201503010, requesting whether an entity is a real estate investment trust.

---

[12]Commercial sources for Revenue Rulings and Revenue Procedures are available, usually requiring a subscription fee. Older Revenue Rulings and Revenue Procedures are often cited as being published in the *Cumulative Bulletin* (C.B.) rather than in the *Internal Revenue Bulletin* (I.R.B.).

[13]See pp. 2-27 and 2-29; Notice 90–20, 1990–1 C.B. 328. In this regard, letter rulings differ from Revenue Rulings, which are applicable to *all* taxpayers. A letter ruling may later lead to the issuance of a Revenue Ruling if the holding affects many taxpayers. In its Agents' Manual, the IRS indicates that letter

rulings may be used as a guide with other research materials in formulating a District Office position on an issue. The IRS is required to charge a taxpayer a fee for letter rulings, determination letters, etc.

[14]Rev.Proc. 2016–3, 2016–1 I.R.B. 126 contains a list of areas in which the IRS will not issue advance rulings. From time to time, subsequent Revenue Procedures are issued that modify or amplify Rev.Proc. 2016–3.

[15]§ 6110.

2015	03	010
Year 2015	3rd week of 2015	10th ruling issued during the 3rd week

Other Administrative Pronouncements

Treasury Decisions (TDs) are issued by the Treasury Department to promulgate new Regulations, amend or otherwise change existing Regulations, or announce the position of the Government on selected court decisions. Like Revenue Rulings and Revenue Procedures, TDs are published in the *Internal Revenue Bulletin* and subsequently transferred to the *Cumulative Bulletin*.

The IRS also publishes other administrative communications in the *Internal Revenue Bulletin*, such as Announcements, Notices, IRs (News Releases), Internal Legal Memoranda (ILMs), Chief Counsel Notices (CC), and Prohibited Transaction Exemptions.

Like letter rulings, **determination letters** are issued at the request of taxpayers and provide guidance on the application of the tax law. They differ from letter rulings in that the issuing source is the Area Director rather than the National Office of the IRS. Also, determination letters usually involve *completed* (as opposed to proposed) transactions. Determination letters are not published and are made known only to the party making the request.

The following examples illustrate the distinction between letter rulings and determination letters:

Difference between Letter Rulings and Determination Letters

EXAMPLE 1

The shareholders of Red Corporation and Green Corporation want assurance that the consolidation of the corporations into Blue Corporation will be a nontaxable reorganization. The proper approach is to request that the National Office of the IRS issue a letter ruling concerning the income tax effect of the proposed transaction.

EXAMPLE 2

Chris operates a barbershop in which he employs eight barbers. To comply with the rules governing income tax and payroll tax withholdings, Chris wants to know whether the barbers working for him are employees or independent contractors. The proper procedure is to request a determination letter on their status from the appropriate Area Director.

A variety of internal memoranda that constitute the working law of the IRS also are released. These General Counsel Memoranda (GCMs), Technical Advice Memoranda (TAMs), Internal Legal Memoranda (ILMs), and Field Service Advice Memoranda (FSAs) are not officially published, and the IRS indicates that they may not be cited as precedents by taxpayers.[16] However, these working documents do explain the IRS's position on various issues.

The National Office of the IRS releases **Technical Advice Memoranda (TAMs)** weekly. TAMs resemble letter rulings in that they give the IRS's determination of an issue. However, they differ in several respects. Letter rulings deal with proposed transactions and are issued to taxpayers at their request. In contrast, TAMs deal with completed transactions. Furthermore, TAMs arise from questions raised by IRS personnel during audits and are issued by the National Office of the IRS to its field personnel. TAMs are often requested for questions relating to exempt organizations and employee plans. TAMs are not officially published and may not be cited or used as precedent.[17] They are assigned file numbers according to the same procedure used for letter rulings. For example, TAM 201532034 refers to the 34th TAM issued during the 32nd week of 2015.

---

[16]These are unofficially published by the publishers listed in Exhibit 2.3. Such internal memoranda for post-1984 transactions may be substantial authority for purposes of the accuracy-related penalty (see pp. 2-27 and 2-29; Notice 90–20, 1990–1 C.B. 328).

[17]§ 6110(j)(3). Post-1984 TAMs may be substantial authority for purposes of avoiding the accuracy-related penalty. Notice 90–20, 1990–1 C.B. 328.

The Office of Chief Counsel prepares Field Service Advice Memoranda to help IRS employees. These are issued in response to requests for advice, guidance, and analysis on difficult or significant tax issues. FSAs are not binding on either the taxpayer to whom they pertain or the IRS. For example, FSA 200233016 states that § 269 may be used to disallow foreign tax credits and deductions that arise from a series of reorganizations if the underlying transaction's principal purpose is to secure tax benefits.

Field Service Advice Memoranda are being replaced by another form of field guidance called Technical Expedited Advice Memoranda (TEAMs). The purpose of TEAMs is to expedite legal guidance to field agents as disputes are developing. FSAs are reverting to their original purpose of case-specific development of facts.

A TEAM guidance differs from a TAM in several ways, including a mandatory presubmission conference involving the taxpayer. In the event of a tentatively adverse conclusion for the taxpayer or the field agent, a conference of right is offered to the taxpayer and to the field agent; once the conference of right is held, no further conferences are offered.

2-1c Judicial Sources of the Tax Law

Five Federal courts have jurisdiction over tax disputes between the IRS and taxpayers: the U.S. Tax Court, the U.S. District Court, the U.S. Court of Federal Claims, the U.S. Court of Appeals, and the U.S. Supreme Court.

The Judicial Process in General

After a taxpayer has exhausted some or all of the remedies available within the IRS (i.e., no satisfactory settlement has been reached at the agent or at the Appeals Division level), the dispute can be taken to the Federal courts. The dispute is first considered by a **court of original jurisdiction** (known as a trial court) with any appeal (either by the taxpayer or the IRS) taken to the appropriate appellate court. In most situations, the taxpayer has a choice of any of *four trial courts:* a **Federal District Court**, the **U.S. Court of Federal Claims**, the **U.S. Tax Court**, or the **Small Cases Division** of the U.S. Tax Court. The trial and appellate court system for Federal tax litigation is illustrated in Exhibit 2.4.

EXHIBIT 2.4	Federal Judicial System

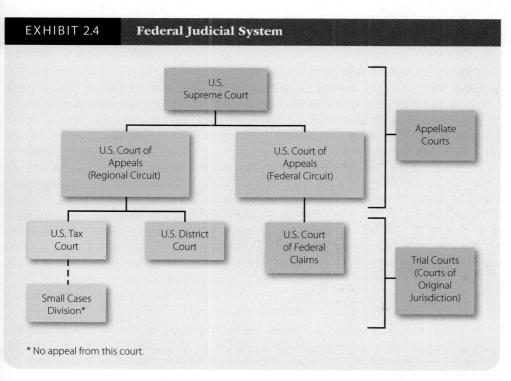

* No appeal from this court.

The broken line between the U.S. Tax Court and the Small Cases Division indicates that there is no appeal from the Small Cases Division. The jurisdiction of the Small Cases Division is limited to cases involving amounts of $50,000 or less. The proceedings of the Small Cases Division are informal (e.g., no necessity for the taxpayer to be represented by a lawyer or other tax adviser). Special trial judges rather than Tax Court judges preside over these proceedings. The decisions of the Small Cases Division are not precedents for any other court decision and are not reviewable by any higher court. Proceedings can be more timely and less expensive in the Small Cases Division. Some of these cases can now be found on the U.S. Tax Court website.

American law, following English law, is frequently *created* by judicial decisions. Under the doctrine of *stare decisis*, each case (except in the Small Cases Division) has precedential value for future cases with the same controlling set of facts. Most Federal and state appellate court decisions and some decisions of trial courts are published. Published court decisions are organized by jurisdiction (Federal or state) and level of court (trial or appellate).

A decision of a particular court is called its holding. Sometimes a decision includes *dicta* or incidental opinions beyond the current facts. Such passing remarks, illustrations, or analogies are not essential to the current holding. Although the holding has precedential value under *stare decisis*, dicta are not binding on a future court.

Knowledge of several terms is important in understanding court decisions. The term *plaintiff* refers to the party requesting action in a court, and the *defendant* is the party against whom the suit is brought. Sometimes a court uses the terms *petitioner* and *respondent*. In general, *petitioner* is a synonym for *plaintiff*, and *respondent* is a synonym for *defendant*. At the trial court level, a taxpayer is normally the plaintiff (or petitioner), and the Government is the defendant (or respondent). If the taxpayer wins and the Government appeals as the new petitioner (or appellant), the taxpayer becomes the new respondent.

Trial Courts

The differences among the various trial courts (courts of original jurisdiction) can be summarized as follows:

- *Number of courts.* There is only one Court of Federal Claims and only one Tax Court, but there are many Federal District Courts. The taxpayer does not select the District Court that will hear the dispute, but must sue in the one that has jurisdiction where the taxpayer resides.

- *Number of judges.* District Courts have various numbers of judges, but only one judge hears a case. The Court of Federal Claims has 16 judges, and the Tax Court has 19 regular judges. The entire Tax Court, however, reviews a case (the case is sent to court conference) only when more important or novel tax issues are involved. Many cases will be heard and decided by one of the 19 regular judges. If a case is reviewed by the full Tax Court, such an *en banc* decision has compelling authority.

- *Location.* The Court of Federal Claims meets most often in Washington, D.C., whereas a District Court meets at a prescribed seat for the particular district. Each state has at least one District Court, and many of the more populous states have more than one. Choosing the District Court usually minimizes the inconvenience and expense of traveling for the taxpayer and his or her counsel. Although the Tax Court is officially based in Washington, D.C., the various judges travel to different parts of the country and hear cases at predetermined locations and dates. This procedure eases the distance problem for the taxpayer, but it can mean a delay before the case comes to trial and is decided.

- *Jurisdiction of the Court of Federal Claims.* The Court of Federal Claims has jurisdiction over any claim against the United States that is based upon the Constitution, any Act of Congress, or any regulation of an executive department. Thus, the Court of Federal Claims hears nontax litigation as well as tax cases. This forum

TAX IN THE NEWS **Dispute Alternatives within the IRS**

If a taxpayer disagrees with the findings of a Revenue Agent, the taxpayer may appeal to the Appeals Division. This Appeals Division is an independent division within the IRS that provides a forum for a taxpayer to contest a compliance action by any part of the IRS.

If the taxpayer decides not to go to the Appeals Division, the taxpayer may take advantage of several arbitration and mediation alternatives. Under a Fast Track Mediation option,

an Appeals Officer or team case leader trained in mediation techniques will help speed up the IRS settlement process. A Fast Track Settlement attempts to resolve disputes through a mediated settlement within 170 days.

Source: Based on Leeah Fontaine, Tax Clinic, "Overview of IRS Pre-Appeals Alternative Dispute Resolution Methods," *The Tax Adviser*, April 2012, pp. 229–231.

appears to be more favorable for issues having an equitable or pro-business orientation (as opposed to purely technical issues) and for those requiring extensive discovery of evidence.[18]

- *Jurisdiction of the Tax Court and District Courts.* The Tax Court hears only tax cases and is the most popular forum. The District Courts hear a wide variety of nontax cases, including drug crimes and other Federal violations, as well as tax cases. Some Tax Court judges have been appointed from IRS or Treasury Department positions. For these reasons, some people suggest that the Tax Court has more expertise in tax matters.

- *Jury trial.* The only court in which a taxpayer can obtain a jury trial is a District Court. But because juries can decide only questions of fact and not questions of law, even taxpayers who choose the District Court route often do not request a jury trial. In that event, the judge will decide all issues. Note that a District Court decision applies only in the district in which the court has jurisdiction.

- *Payment of deficiency.* For the Court of Federal Claims or a District Court to have jurisdiction, the taxpayer must pay the tax deficiency assessed by the IRS and sue for a refund. A taxpayer who wins (assuming no successful appeal by the Government) recovers the tax paid plus appropriate interest. For the Tax Court, however, jurisdiction is usually obtained without first paying the assessed tax deficiency. In the event the taxpayer loses in the Tax Court (and does not appeal or an appeal is unsuccessful), the deficiency must be paid with appropriate interest. With the elimination of the deduction for personal (consumer) interest (see Chapter 10), the Tax Court route of delaying payment of the deficiency can become expensive. By paying the tax, a taxpayer limits underpayment interest and penalties on the underpayment.

- *Termination of running of interest.* A taxpayer who selects the Tax Court may deposit a cash bond to stop the running of interest. The taxpayer must deposit both the amount of the tax and any accrued interest. If the taxpayer wins and the deposited amount is returned, the Government does not pay interest on the deposit.

- *Appeals.* Appeals from a District Court or a Tax Court decision are to the U.S. Court of Appeals for the circuit in which the taxpayer resides. Appeals from the Court of Federal Claims go to the Court of Appeals for the Federal Circuit. Few Tax Court cases are appealed, and when appeals are made, most are filed by the taxpayer rather than the IRS.

- *Bankruptcy.* When a taxpayer files a bankruptcy petition, the IRS, like other creditors, is prevented from taking action against the taxpayer. Sometimes a bankruptcy court may settle a tax claim.

For a summary of various attributes of the Federal trial courts, see Concept Summary 2.1.

---

[18]T. D. Peyser, "The Case for Selecting the Claims Court to Litigate a Federal Tax Liability," *The Tax Executive* (Winter 1988): 149.

Concept Summary 2.1

Federal Judicial System: Trial Courts

Issue	U.S. Tax Court	U.S. District Court	U.S. Court of Federal Claims
Number of judges per court	19*	Varies	16
Payment of deficiency before trial	No	Yes	Yes
Jury trial available	No	Yes	No
Types of disputes	Tax cases only	Most criminal and civil issues	Claims against the United States
Jurisdiction	Nationwide	Location of taxpayer	Nationwide
IRS acquiescence policy	Yes	Yes	Yes
Appeal route	U.S. Court of Appeals	U.S. Court of Appeals	U.S. Court of Appeals for the Federal Circuit

*Currently, there are also 4 special trial judges and 13 senior judges.

Appellate Courts

The losing party can appeal a trial court decision to a **Circuit Court of Appeals**. The 11 geographic circuits, the circuit for the District of Columbia, and the Federal Circuit[19] appear in Exhibit 2.5. The appropriate circuit for an appeal depends on where the litigation originated. For example, an appeal from New York goes to the Second Circuit.

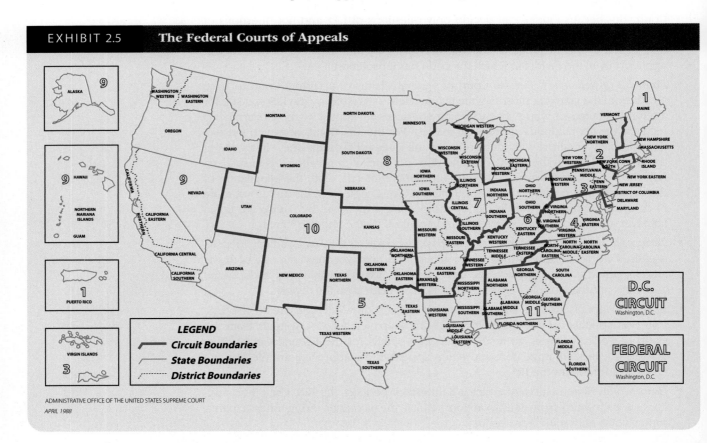

EXHIBIT 2.5   The Federal Courts of Appeals

LEGEND
Circuit Boundaries
State Boundaries
District Boundaries

ADMINISTRATIVE OFFICE OF THE UNITED STATES SUPREME COURT
APRIL 1988

---

[19]The Court of Appeals for the Federal Circuit was created, effective October 1, 1982, by P.L. No. 97–64 (4/2/82) to hear decisions appealed from the Claims Court (now the Court of Federal Claims).

If the Government loses at the trial court level (District Court, Tax Court, or Court of Federal Claims), it need not (frequently does not) appeal. The fact that an appeal is not made, however, does not indicate that the IRS agrees with the result and will not litigate similar issues in the future. The IRS may decide not to appeal for a number of reasons. First, if the current litigation load is heavy, the IRS may decide that available personnel should be assigned to other more important cases. Second, the IRS may determine that this case is not a good one to appeal. Perhaps the taxpayer is in a sympathetic position or the facts are particularly strong in his or her favor. In that event, the IRS may wait to test the legal issues involved with a taxpayer who has a much weaker case. Third, if the appeal is from a District Court or the Tax Court, the Court of Appeals of jurisdiction could have some bearing on whether the IRS chooses to go forward with an appeal. Based on past experience and precedent, the IRS may conclude that the chance for success on a particular issue might be more promising in another Court of Appeals. If so, the IRS will wait for a similar case to arise in a different jurisdiction.

The Federal Circuit at the appellate level provides the taxpayer with an alternative forum to the Court of Appeals for his or her home circuit. Appeals from both the Tax Court and the District Court go to a taxpayer's home circuit. When a particular circuit has issued an adverse decision in a similar case, the taxpayer may prefer the Court of Federal Claims route, because any appeal will be to the Federal Circuit.

The Appellate Process

The *role* of the appellate court is limited to a review of the trial record compiled by the trial court. Thus, the appellate process usually involves a determination of whether the trial court applied the proper law in arriving at its decision. Rarely will an appellate court question a lower court's fact-finding determination.

Both the Code and the Supreme Court indicate that Federal appellate courts are bound by findings of facts unless they are clearly erroneous.[20] This aspect of the appellate process is illustrated by a decision of the Court of Appeals for the District of Columbia involving whether a taxpayer was engaged in an activity for profit under § 183.[21] This appeals court specifically held that the "Tax Court's findings of facts are binding on Federal courts of appeals unless clearly erroneous." The court applauded the Tax Court for the thoroughness of its factual inquiry but could "not place the stamp of approval upon its eventual legal outcome." In reversing and remanding the decision to the Tax Court, the appellate court said that "the language of § 183, its legislative history and the applicable Treasury Regulation combine to demonstrate that the court's (Tax Court's) standard is erroneous as a matter of law." The appeals court held that this taxpayer's claims of deductibility were to be evaluated by proper legal standards.

An appeal can have any of a number of possible outcomes. The appellate court may approve (affirm) or disapprove (reverse) the lower court's finding, or it may send the case back for further consideration (remand). When many issues are involved, a mixed result is not unusual. Thus, the lower court may be affirmed (*aff'd*) on Issue A and reversed (*rev'd*) on Issue B, while Issue C is remanded (*rem'd*) for additional fact finding.

When more than one judge is involved in the decision-making process, disagreements are not uncommon. In addition to the majority view, one or more judges may concur (agree with the result reached but not with some or all of the reasoning) or dissent (disagree with the result). In any one case, of course, the majority view controls. But concurring and dissenting views can have an influence on other courts or at some subsequent date when the composition of the court has changed.

Appellate Precedents and the Tax Court District Courts, the Tax Court, and the Court of Federal Claims must abide by the precedents set by the Court of Appeals of jurisdiction. A particular Court of Appeals need not follow the decisions of another Court of Appeals. All courts, however, must follow the decisions of the U.S. Supreme Court.

---

[20]§§ 7482(a) and (c). *Comm. v. Duberstein*, 60–2 USTC ¶9515, 5 AFTR 2d 1626, 80 S.Ct. 1190 (USSC, 1960). See Rule 52(a) of the Federal Rules of Civil Procedure.

[21]*Dreicer v. Comm.*, 81–2 USTC ¶9683, 48 AFTR 2d 5884, 665 F.2d 1292 (CA–DC, 1981).

This pattern of appellate precedents raises an issue for the Tax Court. Because the Tax Court is a national court, it decides cases from all parts of the country. For many years, the Tax Court followed a policy of deciding cases based on what it thought the result should be, even though its decision might be appealed to a Court of Appeals that had previously decided a similar case differently. A number of years ago, this policy was changed in the *Golsen*[22] decision. Now the Tax Court will decide a case as it believes the law should be applied *only* if the Court of Appeals of appropriate jurisdiction has not yet passed on the issue or has previously decided a similar case in accord with the Tax Court's decision. If the Court of Appeals of appropriate jurisdiction has previously held otherwise, the Tax Court will conform under the *Golsen* rule even though it disagrees with the holding.

EXAMPLE 3

Emily lives in Texas and sues in the Tax Court on Issue A. The Fifth Circuit Court of Appeals is the appellate court of appropriate jurisdiction. It has already decided, in a case involving similar facts but a different taxpayer, that Issue A should be resolved against the Government. Although the Tax Court believes that the Fifth Circuit Court of Appeals is wrong, under its *Golsen* policy, it will render judgment for Emily.

Shortly thereafter, Rashad, a resident of New York, in a comparable case, sues in the Tax Court on Issue A. Assume that the Second Circuit Court of Appeals, the appellate court of appropriate jurisdiction, has never expressed itself on Issue A. Presuming that the Tax Court has not reconsidered its position on Issue A, it will decide against Rashad.

Thus, it is entirely possible for two taxpayers suing in the same court to end up with opposite results merely because they live in different parts of the country.

Appeal to the U.S. Supreme Court Appeal to the U.S. Supreme Court is by **Writ of Certiorari**. If the Court agrees to hear the case, it will grant the Writ (*Cert. granted*). Most often, it will deny jurisdiction (*Cert. denied*). For whatever reason or reasons, the Supreme Court rarely hears tax cases. The Court usually grants certiorari to resolve a conflict among the Courts of Appeals (e.g., two or more appellate courts have assumed opposing positions on a particular issue) or where the tax issue is extremely important. The granting of a Writ of Certiorari indicates that at least four of the nine members of the Supreme Court believe that the issue is of sufficient importance to be heard by the full Court.

Judicial Citations

LO.2

Locate and work with the appropriate tax law sources.

Having briefly described the judicial process, it is appropriate to consider the more practical problem of the relationship of case law to tax research. As previously noted, court decisions are an important source of tax law. The ability to cite and locate a case is, therefore, a must in working with the tax law. Judicial citations usually follow a standard pattern: case name, volume number, reporter series, page or paragraph number, court (where necessary), and year of the decision (see Concept Summary 2.2).

Judicial Citations—The U.S. Tax Court A good starting point is with the Tax Court, which issues two types of decisions: Regular and Memorandum, based on the Chief Judge's determination. The distinction between the two involves both substance and form. In terms of substance, *Memorandum* decisions deal with situations necessitating only the application of already established principles of law. *Regular* decisions involve novel issues not previously resolved by the court. In actual practice, however, this distinction is not always preserved. Not infrequently, Memorandum decisions will be encountered that appear to warrant Regular status and vice versa. At any rate, do not conclude that Memorandum decisions possess no value as precedents. Both represent the position of the Tax Court and, as such, can be relied on.

The Regular and Memorandum decisions issued by the Tax Court also differ in form. Memorandum decisions are made available but are not published by the government. Regular decisions are published by the U.S. Government in a series entitled *Tax Court*

---

[22]*Jack E. Golsen*, 54 T.C. 742 (1970).

Concept Summary 2.2

Judicial Sources

Court	Location	Authority
U.S. Supreme Court	S.Ct. Series (West) U.S. Series (U.S. Gov't.) L.Ed.2d (Lawyer's Co-op.) AFTR (RIA) USTC (CCH)	Highest authority
U.S. Courts of Appeal	Federal 3d (West) AFTR (RIA) USTC (CCH)	Next highest appellate court
Tax Court (Regular decisions)	U.S. Gov't. Printing Office RIA/CCH separate services	Highest trial court*
Tax Court (Memorandum decisions)	RIA T.C.Memo. (RIA) TCM (CCH)	Less authority than Regular T.C. decision
U.S. Court of Federal Claims**	Federal Claims Reporter (West) AFTR (RIA) USTC (CCH)	Similar authority as Tax Court
U.S. District Courts	F.Supp.2d Series (West) AFTR (RIA) USTC (CCH)	Lowest trial court
Small Cases Division of Tax Court	U.S. Tax Court website***	No precedent value

*Theoretically, the Tax Court, Court of Federal Claims, and District Courts are on the same level of authority. But some people believe that because the Tax Court hears and decides tax cases from all parts of the country (i.e., it is a national court), its decisions may be more authoritative than a Court of Federal Claims or District Court decision.

**Before October 29, 1992, the U.S. Claims Court.

***Starting in 2001.

of the United States Reports (T.C.). Each volume of these *Reports* covers a six-month period (January 1 through June 30 and July 1 through December 31) and is given a succeeding volume number. But there is usually a time lag between the date a decision is rendered and the date it appears in bound form. A temporary citation may be necessary to help the researcher locate a recent Regular decision. Consider, for example, the temporary and permanent citations for *MoneyGram International, Inc. and Subsidiaries*, a decision filed on January 7, 2015:

Temporary Citation
{ *MoneyGram International, Inc. and Subsidiaries*, 144 T.C.
  ___, No. 1 (2015).
  Explanation: Page number left blank because not yet known.

Permanent Citation
{ *MoneyGram International, Inc. and Subsidiaries*, 144 T.C. 1
  (2015).
  Explanation: Page number now available.

Both citations tell us that the case will ultimately appear in Volume 144 of the *Tax Court of the United States Reports*. But until this volume is bound and made available to the general public, the page number must be left blank. Instead, the temporary citation identifies the case as being the 1st Regular decision issued by the Tax Court since Volume 143 ended. With this information, the decision can easily be located in either of the special Tax Court services published by Commerce Clearing House (CCH) or Research Institute of America

(RIA). Once Volume 144 is released, the permanent citation can be substituted and the number of the case dropped. Starting in 1999, both Regular decisions and Memorandum decisions are published on the U.S. Tax Court website (**www.ustaxcourt.gov**).

Before 1943, the Tax Court was called the Board of Tax Appeals, and its decisions were published as the *United States Board of Tax Appeals Reports* (B.T.A.). These 47 volumes cover the period from 1924 to 1942. For example, the citation *Karl Pauli*, 11 B.T.A. 784 (1928), refers to the 11th volume of the *Board of Tax Appeals Reports*, page 784, issued in 1928.

If the IRS loses in a decision, it may indicate whether it agrees or disagrees with the results reached by the court by publishing an acquiescence ("A" or "*Acq.*") or nonacquiescence ("NA" or "*Nonacq.*"), respectively. Until 1991, acquiescences and nonacquiescences were published only for certain Regular decisions of the Tax Court, but the IRS has expanded its acquiescence program to include other civil tax cases where guidance is helpful. The acquiescence or nonacquiescence is published in the *Internal Revenue Bulletin* and the *Cumulative Bulletin* as an *Action on Decision*. The IRS can retroactively revoke an acquiescence.

Most often, the IRS issues nonacquiescences to adverse decisions that are not appealed. In this manner, the Government indicates that it disagrees with the result reached, despite its decision not to seek review of the matter in an appellate court. A nonacquiescence provides a warning to taxpayers that a similar case cannot be settled administratively. A taxpayer will incur fees and expenses while the case moves through the IRS even though the IRS may be unwilling to litigate a fact pattern similar to a nonacquiescence decision.[23]

Although Memorandum decisions were not published by the U.S. Government until recently, they have been and are published by CCH and RIA. Consider, for example, the three different ways the *Nick R. Hughes* case can be cited:

> *Nick R. Hughes*, T.C.Memo. 2009–94
>> *Explanation:* The 94th Memorandum decision issued by the Tax Court in 2009.

> *Nick R. Hughes*, 97 TCM 1488
>> *Explanation:* Page 1488 of Vol. 97 of the CCH *Tax Court Memorandum Decisions.*

> *Nick R. Hughes*, 2009 RIA T.C.Memo. ¶2009,094
>> *Explanation:* Paragraph 2009,094 of the RIA *T.C. Memorandum Decisions.*

Note that the third citation contains the same information as the first. Thus, ¶2009,094 indicates the following information about the case: year 2009, 94th T.C.Memo. decision.[24]

U.S. Tax Court Summary Opinions relate to decisions of the Tax Court's Small Cases Division.[25] These opinions are published commercially, and on the U.S. Tax Court website, with the warning that they may not be treated as precedent for any other case. For example, *Darrel W. Wyatt*, filed on April 20, 2015, is cited as follows:

> *Darrel W. Wyatt*, T.C. Summary Opinion 2015–31.

Judicial Citations—The U.S. District Court, Court of Federal Claims, and Courts of Appeals District Court, Court of Federal Claims, Court of Appeals, and Supreme Court decisions dealing with Federal tax matters are reported in both the CCH *U.S. Tax Cases* (USTC) and the RIA *American Federal Tax Reports* (AFTR) series. Federal District Court decisions, dealing with *both* tax and nontax issues, also are published by West in its *Federal Supplement Series* (F.Supp.). Volume 999, published in 1998, is the last volume of the *Federal Supplement Series*. It is followed by the *Federal*

---

[23]G. W. Carter, "Nonacquiescence: Winning by Losing," *Tax Notes* (September 19, 1988): 1301–1307.

[24]In this text, the RIA citation for Memorandum decisions of the U.S. Tax Court is omitted. Thus, *Nick R. Hughes* will be cited as 97 TCM 1488, T.C. Memo. 2009–94.

[25]In 2005, the U.S. Supreme Court held that decisions of the Small Cases Division must be made public.

Supplement Second Series (F.Supp.2d). The following examples illustrate three different ways of citing a District Court case:

> *Turner v. U.S.*, 2004–1 USTC ¶60,478 (D.Ct. Tex., 2004).
>
>> *Explanation:* Reported in the first volume of the *U.S. Tax Cases* published by Commerce Clearing House for calendar year 2004 (2004–1) and located at paragraph 60,478 (¶60,478).
>
> *Turner v. U.S.*, 93 AFTR 2d 2004–686 (D.Ct. Tex., 2004).
>
>> *Explanation:* Reported in the 93rd volume of the second series of the *American Federal Tax Reports* (AFTR 2d) published by RIA and beginning on page 686.
>
> *Turner v. U.S.*, 306 F.Supp.2d 668 (D.Ct. Tex., 2004).
>
>> *Explanation:* Reported in the 306th volume of the *Federal Supplement Second Series* (F.Supp.2d) published by West and beginning on page 668.

In all of the preceding citations, note that the name of the case is the same (Turner being the taxpayer), as is the reference to the Federal District Court of Texas (D.Ct. Tex.) and the year the decision was rendered (2004).[26]

Decisions of the Court of Federal Claims[27] and the Courts of Appeals are published in the USTCs, the AFTRs, and a West reporter called the *Federal Second Series* (F.2d). Volume 999, published in 1993, is the last volume of the *Federal Second Series*. It is followed by the *Federal Third Series* (F.3d). Beginning with October 1982, the Court of Federal Claims decisions are published in another West reporter entitled the *Claims Court Reporter* (abbreviated Cl.Ct.). Beginning with Volume 27 on October 30, 1992, the name of the reporter changed to the *Federal Claims Reporter* (abbreviated as Fed.Cl.). The following examples illustrate the different forms:

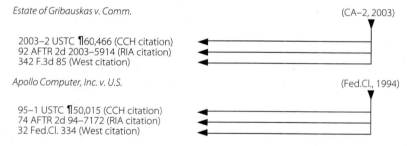

Note that *Estate of Gribauskas v. Comm.* is a decision rendered by the Second Circuit Court of Appeals in 2003 (CA–2, 2003), while *Apollo Computer, Inc.* was issued by the Court of Federal Claims in 1994 (Fed.Cl., 1994).

Judicial Citations—The U.S. Supreme Court Like all other Federal tax decisions (except those rendered by the Tax Court), Supreme Court decisions are published by CCH in the USTCs and by RIA in the AFTRs. The U.S. Government Printing Office also publishes these decisions in the *United States Supreme Court Reports* (U.S.) as does West in its *Supreme Court Reporter* (S.Ct.) and the Lawyer's Co-operative Publishing Company in its *United States Reports, Lawyer's Edition* (L.Ed.). The following illustrates the different ways the same decision can be cited:

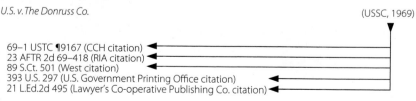

---

[26]In this text, the case would be cited in the following form: *Turner v. U.S.*, 2004–1 USTC ¶60,478, 93 AFTR 2d 2004–686, 306 F.Supp.2d 668 (D.Ct. Tex., 2004).

[27]Before October 29, 1992, the Court of Federal Claims was called the Claims Court. Before October 1, 1982, the Court of Federal Claims was called the Court of Claims.

The parenthetical reference (USSC, 1969) identifies the decision as having been rendered by the U.S. Supreme Court in 1969. In this text, the citations of Supreme Court decisions will be limited to the CCH (USTC), RIA (AFTR), and West (S.Ct.) versions.

2-1d Other Sources of the Tax Law

Other sources of tax information that a tax professional may need to consult include tax treaties and tax periodicals.

Tax Treaties

The United States signs certain tax treaties (sometimes called tax conventions) with foreign countries to render mutual assistance in tax enforcement and to avoid double taxation. Tax legislation enacted in 1988 provided that neither a tax law nor a tax treaty takes general precedence. Thus, when there is a direct conflict between the Code and a treaty, the most recent item takes precedence. A taxpayer must disclose on the tax return any position where a treaty overrides a tax law.[28] There is a $1,000 penalty per failure to disclose for individuals and a $10,000 per failure penalty for corporations.[29]

Tax Periodicals

The use of tax periodicals can often shorten the research time needed to resolve a tax issue. If the article is relevant to the issue at hand, it may provide the references needed to locate the primary sources of the tax law that apply (e.g., citations to judicial decisions, Regulations, and other IRS pronouncements). Thus, the researcher obtains a "running start" in arriving at a solution to the problem.

Among the many indexes available for locating tax articles pertinent to a tax problem is CCH's *Federal Tax Articles*. This multivolume service includes a subject index, a Code Section number index, and an author's index. Another is the *Index to Federal Tax Articles* (published by Thomson Reuters). Both of these indexes are updated periodically, but are available only in print form.

The following are some of the more useful tax periodicals:

Journal of Taxation
Journal of International Taxation
Practical Tax Strategies
Estate Planning
Corporate Taxation
Business Entities
Taxation of Exempts
Real Estate Taxation
ria.thomsonreuters.com/journals

The Tax Executive
www.tei.org

The Tax Adviser
aicpa.org/pubs/taxadv

Tax Law Review
**www.law.nyu.edu/tax
/taxlawreview/**

*Journal of the American Taxation
Association*
aaajournals.org/loi/atax

The ATA Journal of Legal Tax Research
aaajournals.org/loi/jltr

Oil, Gas & Energy Quarterly
**www.bus.lsu.edu/accounting
/faculty/lcrumbley/oilgas.html**

Trusts and Estates
wealthmanagement.com/te-home

Journal of Passthrough Entities
TAXES—The Tax Magazine
tax.cchgroup.com/books

Tax Notes
taxanalysts.com

---

[28]§ 7852(d).

[29]Reg. §§ 301.6114–1, 301.6712–1, and 301.7701(b)(7).

2-2 WORKING WITH THE TAX LAW— TAX RESEARCH TOOLS

Tax law consists of a body of legislative (e.g., Code Sections and tax treaties), administrative (e.g., Regulations and Rulings), and judicial (e.g., court cases) pronouncements. Working with the tax law requires being able to locate and use these sources effectively. A key consideration is the time required to find relevant information related to the issues identified.

Unless the problem is simple (e.g., the Code Section is known and there is a Regulation on point), the research process should begin with a tax service.

2-2a Commercial Tax Services

Due to various changes, categorizing tax services has become an almost impossible task. Previously, services could be classified as *annotated* (i.e., organized by Internal Revenue Code) or *topical* (i.e., organized by major topics), but this classification system is no longer appropriate for many tax services as their format has been modified. Often, the change is due to the acquisition of what was a competing tax service. For example, Thomson Reuters *Checkpoint* includes both the *Federal Tax Coordinator 2d* (topical) and the *United States Tax Reporter* (annotated).

Tax services also can no longer be distinguished based on whether they are available only in hard copy or online versions. Previously, for example, *Tax Management Portfolios* was solely a print publication. Now, like most other tax services, it is also accessible online.

A partial list of the available commercial tax services includes:

- *Standard Federal Tax Reporter*, Commerce Clearing House.
- *CCH IntelliConnect*, Commerce Clearing House. The online version of the *Standard Federal Tax Reporter* (along with other CCH materials).
- *United States Tax Reporter*, Research Institute of America.
- Thomson Reuters *Checkpoint*, Research Institute of America. The online versions of RIA's *Federal Tax Coordinator 2d* and *United States Tax Reporter*.
- ATX/Kleinrock *Practical Tax Expert*, CCH/Wolters Kluwer.
- *Tax Management Portfolios*, Bloomberg BNA.
- *Mertens Law of Federal Income Taxation*, Thomson Reuters.
- Thomson Reuters *Westlaw* and *WestlawNext*—compilations include access to *Tax Management Portfolios*, *Federal Tax Coordinator 2d*, and *Mertens*.
- LexisNexis *TaxCenter*. A compilation of primary sources and various materials taken from CCH, Matthew Bender, Kleinrock, and Bloomberg BNA.
- *Federal Research Library*, Tax Analysts (a nonprofit organization) databases dealing with explanations and commentaries on primary source materials.

2-2b Using Online Tax Services

Instructions on how to use a tax service are not particularly worthwhile unless a specific service is involved. Even here, instructions need to be followed by hands-on experience to be effective. For online versions of a tax service, however, following certain procedures can simplify the research process. Because a tax professional's time is valuable and several research services base usage charges on time spent, time is of the essence.

When the principal emphasis is on time, every shortcut helps. The following suggestions (most of which are familiar to any user of the Internet) may be helpful:[30]

---

[30]For a more complete discussion of the use of Thomson Reuters *Checkpoint* and CCH *IntelliConnect* and Internet research in taxation, see Sawyers, Raabe, Whittenburg, and Gill, *Federal Tax Research*, 10th ed. (Cengage Learning, 2015), Chapters 6 and 7.

- Choose keywords for the search carefully. Words with a broad usage, such as *income*, are worthless when standing alone. If the researcher is interested in qualified dividend income, even *dividend income* is too broad because it will call up stock dividends, constructive dividends, liquidating dividends, and more. By using *qualified dividend income* at the outset, the search is considerably narrowed. In CCH *IntelliConnect*, for example, these two modifications narrowed the search from over 2.7 million items to 30,188 and finally to 1,921. From that point, further contraction will be needed.

- Take advantage of *connectors*, such as "+" and quotation marks, to place parameters on the search and further restrict the output. Although each service has its own set of connectors, many are used by several services. Thus, quotation marks around a phrase mean "exact phrase" in both Thomson Reuters *Checkpoint* and CCH *IntelliConnect* (e.g., "personal service corporation").

- Be selective in choosing a database. For example, if the research project does not involve case law, there is no point in including the judicial decision component in the search database. Doing so just adds to the output items and will necessitate further screening through a search modification.

- Use a table of contents, index, or citation approach when appropriate. Although the keyword approach is most frequently used, databases can be searched in other ways. Using the table of contents or index is the usual approach with print versions of a tax service. With the citation route, access may be through a statutory (e.g., Code Section), administrative (e.g., Rev.Rul.), or judicial citation (e.g., Tax Court), depending on the tax service. Using just a Code Section number or the taxpayer's last name, however, can require a significant amount of screening to narrow the information.

2-2c **Noncommercial Online Tax Services**

The Internet provides a wealth of tax information in several popular forms, sometimes at no direct cost to the researcher. Using so-called browser software that often is distributed with new computer systems and their communication devices, the tax professional can access information provided around the world that aids the research process.

- *Home pages (sites) on the Web* are provided by accounting and consulting firms, publishers, tax academics and libraries, and governmental bodies as a means of making information widely available or of soliciting subscriptions or consulting engagements. The best sites offer links to other sites and direct contact to the site providers. One of the best sites available to the tax professional is the Internal Revenue Service's home page, illustrated in Exhibit 2.6. This site offers downloadable forms and instructions, "plain English" versions of Regulations, and news update items. Exhibit 2.7 lists some of the websites and their Internet addresses as of press date that may be most useful to tax researchers. Particularly useful is the directory at **taxsites.com**, which provides links to accounting and tax sources (including international, state, and payroll tax sources).

- *Newsgroups* provide a means by which information related to the tax law can be exchanged among taxpayers, tax professionals, and others who subscribe to the group's services. Newsgroup members can read the exchanges among other members and offer replies and suggestions to inquiries as desired. Discussions address the interpretation and application of existing law, analysis of proposals and new pronouncements, and reviews of tax software.

EXHIBIT 2.6	The IRS's Home Page

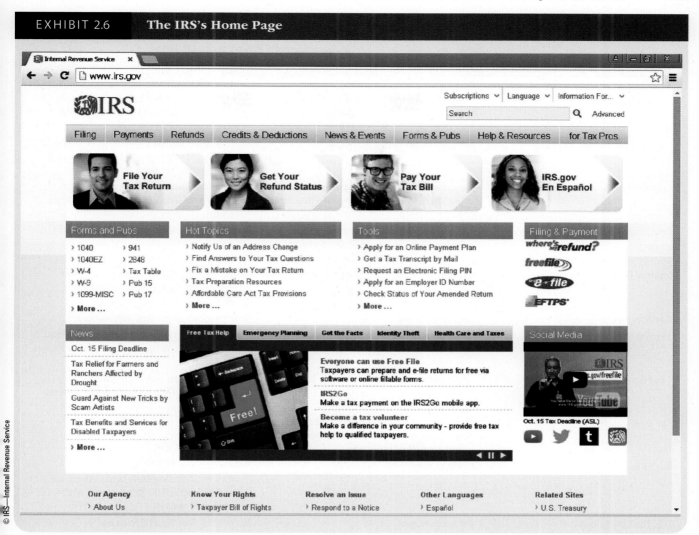

In many situations, solutions to research problems benefit from or require the use of various electronic tax research tools. A competent tax professional must become familiar and proficient with these tools and be able to use them to meet the expectations of clients and the necessities of work in the modern world.[31]

2-3 WORKING WITH THE TAX LAW— TAX RESEARCH

LO.4

Describe the tax research process.

Tax research is the method used to determine the best available solution to a situation that possesses tax consequences. In other words, it is the process of finding a competent and professional conclusion to a tax problem. The problem may originate from completed or proposed transactions. In the case of a completed transaction,

---

[31]For a more detailed discussion of the use of electronic tax research in tax practice, see Sawyers, Raabe, Whittenburg, and Gill, *Federal Tax Research*, 10th ed. (Cengage Learning, 2015).

EXHIBIT 2.7	Tax-Related Websites	

Website	Web Address	Description
Accounting firms and professional organizations	For instance, the AICPA's page is at **aicpa.org**, Ernst & Young is at **ey.com**, and KPMG is at **kpmg.com**	Tax planning newsletters, descriptions of services offered and career opportunities, and exchange of data with clients and subscribers
Cengage Learning	**cengagebrain.com**	Informational updates, newsletters, support materials for students and adopters, and continuing education
Commercial tax publishers	For instance, **tax.com**, **cchgroup.com**, **tax.thomsonreuters.com**, and **bna.com**	Information about products and services available for subscription and newsletter excerpts
Court opinions	The site at **law.justia.com** covers state, Federal, and Supreme Court decisions but not the Tax Court	A synopsis of results reached by the court
Internal Revenue Service	**irs.gov**	News releases, downloadable forms and instructions, tables, Circular 230, and e-mail
Tax Almanac	**taxalmanac.org**	Smorgasbord of tax research resources
Tax Analysts	**taxanalysts.com**	Policy-oriented readings on the tax law and proposals to change it, moderated bulletins on various tax subjects
Tax Foundation	**taxfoundation.org**	Nonprofit educational organization that promotes sound tax policy and measures tax burdens
Tax laws online	Regulations are at **law.cornell.edu/cfr**, and the Code is at **uscode.house.gov** and **law.cornell.edu/uscode**	
Tax Sites Directory	**taxsites.com**	References and links to tax sites on the Internet, including state and Federal tax sites, academic and professional pages, tax forms, and software
U.S. Tax Court decisions	**ustaxcourt.gov**	Recent U.S. Tax Court decisions

Caution: Web addresses change frequently.

the objective of the research is to determine the tax result of what has already taken place. For example, was the expenditure incurred by the taxpayer deductible or not deductible for tax purposes? When dealing with proposed transactions, the tax research process is directed toward the determination of possible alternative tax consequences. To the extent that tax research leads to a choice of alternatives or otherwise influences the future actions of the taxpayer, it becomes the key to effective tax planning.

Tax research involves the following procedures:

- Identifying and refining the problem.
- Locating the appropriate tax law sources.
- Assessing the validity of the tax law sources.
- Arriving at the solution or at alternative solutions with due consideration given to nontax factors.
- Effectively communicating the solution to the taxpayer or the taxpayer's representative.
- Following up on the solution (where appropriate) in light of new developments.

This process is depicted schematically in Exhibit 2.8. The broken lines reflect the steps of particular interest when tax research is directed toward proposed, rather than completed, transactions.

2-3a **Identifying the Problem**

Problem identification must start with a compilation of the relevant facts involved.[32] In this regard, *all* of the facts that may have a bearing on the problem must be gathered because any omission could modify the solution reached. To illustrate, return to the facts of *The Big Picture* on p. 2-1 and consider what appears to be a very simple problem: Can Fred and Megan claim Sam and Dana as dependents?

2-3b **Refining the Problem**

Returning to the facts of *The Big Picture* on p. 2-1, the simple question of whether Fred and Megan can claim Sam and Dana as dependents becomes more complicated with the potential stock sale. Initially, it appears that Fred and Megan could *not* claim Sam and Dana as dependents if the stock was sold, because Sam would then have gross income of more than the exemption amount under § 151(d).[33] However, after 2004, the test for whether a child qualifies for dependency status is first conducted under the *qualifying child* requirements. Only if these requirements cannot be satisfied is the test for dependency status conducted under the *qualifying relative* requirements. The gross income test is applicable only under

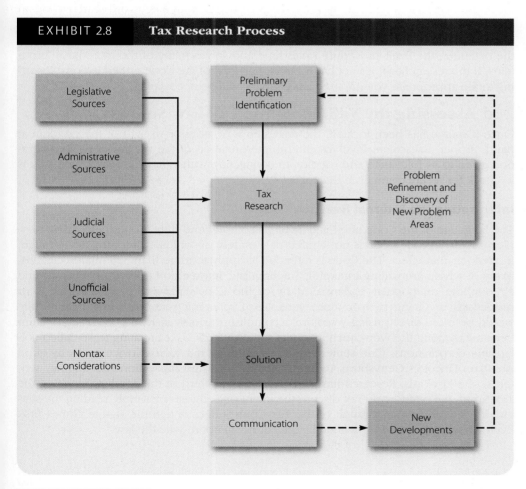

EXHIBIT 2.8   **Tax Research Process**

---

[32]For an excellent discussion of the critical role of facts in carrying out tax research, see Gardner, Stewart, and Worsham, *Tax Research Techniques*, 9th ed. (New York: The American Institute of Certified Public Accountants, 2012), Chapter 2.

[33]§ 152(d)(2). See the related discussion in Chapter 3.

the qualifying relative status.[34] Thus, Sam could sell the stock without penalizing the parents with respect to the gross income test. Under the qualifying child provision, however, Sam must not have provided more than one-half of his own support.[35] Hence, the $19,000 of proceeds from the sale of the stock might lead to the failure of the "not self-supporting" requirement, depending on how much Sam spends for his support.

Assume, however, that further fact gathering reveals the following additional information:

- Sam does not really need to spend the proceeds from the sale of the stock.
- Sam receives a sizable portion of his own support from a scholarship.

With these new facts, additional research leads to § 152(f)(5) and Regulation § 1.152–1(c), which indicate that a scholarship received by a student is not included for purposes of computing whether Sam is self-supporting under the qualifying child provision. Further, if Sam does not spend the proceeds from the sale of the stock, the unexpended amount is not counted for purposes of the "not self-supporting" test. Thus, in contrast to the initial conclusion, it appears that the parents will be allowed the dependency exemptions for Sam and Dana, as the qualifying child requirements appear to be satisfied for Sam and the qualifying relative requirements appear to be satisfied for Dana.

2-3c Locating the Appropriate Tax Law Sources

Once the problem is clearly defined, what is the next step? Although the next step is a matter of individual judgment, most tax research begins with a keyword search using an online tax service. If the problem is not complex, the researcher may bypass the tax service and turn directly to the Internal Revenue Code and Treasury Regulations. For the beginner, the latter procedure saves time and solves many of the more basic problems. If the researcher does not have a personal copy of the Code or Regulations, resorting to the appropriate volume(s) of a tax service will be necessary.[36]

2-3d Assessing the Validity of the Tax Law Sources

Once a source has been located, the next step is to assess it in light of the problem at hand. Proper assessment involves careful interpretation of the tax law with consideration given to its relevance and validity. In connection with validity, an important step is to check for recent changes in the tax law.

Interpreting the Internal Revenue Code

The language of the Code often is difficult to comprehend fully. Contrary to many people's suspicions, the Code is not written deliberately to confuse. Unfortunately, though, it often has that effect. The Code is intended to apply to more than 320 million citizens, many of whom are willing to exploit any linguistic imprecision to their benefit—to find a "loophole" in popular parlance. Many of the Code's provisions are limitations or restrictions involving two or more variables. Expressing such concepts algebraically would be more direct; using words to accomplish this task instead is often quite cumbersome. Among the worst such attempts was former § 341(e) relating to so-called collapsible corporations. One sentence had more than 450 words (twice as many as in Abraham Lincoln's Gettysburg Address). Within this same subsection was another sentence of 300 words. Research has shown that in one-third of the conflicts reaching the Tax Court, the court could not discern the intent of Congress by simply reading the statute. Yet the overriding attitude of the Tax Court judges is that the statute comes first. Even when the statute is unworkable, the court will not rewrite the law.[37]

---

[34]Compare § 152(c) for qualifying child with § 152(d) for qualifying relative.

[35]§ 152(c)(1)(D).

[36]Several of the major tax services publish paperback editions of the Code and Treasury Regulations that can be purchased at modest prices. These editions are usually revised twice each year. For an annotated and abridged version of the Code and Regulations that is published annually,

see James E. Smith and Mark Altieri, *South-Western Federal Taxation: Internal Revenue Code of 1986 and Treasury Regulations: Annotated and Selected* (Cengage Learning, 2017).

[37]T. L. Kirkpatrick and W. B. Pollard, "Reliance by the Tax Court on the Legislative Intent of Congress," *The Tax Executive* (Summer 1986): 358–359.

Assessing the Validity of a Treasury Regulation

Treasury Regulations are the official interpretation of the Code and are entitled to great deference. Occasionally, however, a court will invalidate a Regulation or a portion thereof on the grounds that the Regulation is contrary to the intent of Congress. Usually, the courts do not question the validity of Regulations because of the belief that "the first administrative interpretation of a provision as it appears in a new act often expresses the general understanding of the times or the actual understanding of those who played an important part when the statute was drafted."[38]

Keep the following observations in mind when assessing the validity of a Regulation:

- IRS agents must give the Code and any related Regulations equal weight when dealing with taxpayers and their representatives.

- Proposed Regulations provide a preview of future final Regulations, but they are not binding on the IRS or taxpayers.

- In a challenge, the burden of proof is on the taxpayer to show that the Regulation varies from the language of the statute and has no support in the Committee Reports.

- If the taxpayer loses the challenge, a 20 percent negligence penalty may be imposed.[39] This accuracy-related penalty applies to any failure to make a reasonable attempt to comply with the tax law and any disregard of rules and Regulations.[40]

- Final Regulations can be classified as procedural, interpretive, or legislative. **Procedural Regulations** neither establish tax laws nor attempt to explain tax laws. Procedural Regulations are *housekeeping-type instructions* indicating information that taxpayers should provide the IRS, as well as information about the internal management and conduct of the IRS itself.

- Some **interpretive Regulations** rephrase and elaborate what Congress stated in the Committee Reports that were issued when the tax legislation was enacted. Such Regulations are *hard* and *solid* and almost impossible to overturn because they clearly reflect the intent of Congress. An interpretive Regulation is given less deference than a legislative Regulation, however. The Supreme Court has told lower courts to analyze Treasury Regulations carefully before accepting the Treasury's interpretation.[41]

- In some Code Sections, Congress has given the *Treasury Secretary or his delegate* the authority to prescribe Regulations to carry out the details of administration or to otherwise complete the operating rules. Under such circumstances, Congress effectively is delegating its legislative powers to the Treasury Department. Regulations issued pursuant to this type of authority possess the force and effect of law and are often called **legislative Regulations** (e.g., consolidated return Regulations).

- Courts tend to apply a legislative reenactment doctrine. A particular Regulation is assumed to have received congressional approval if the Regulation was finalized many years earlier and Congress has not amended the Code Section pertaining to that Regulation.

Assessing the Validity of Other Administrative Sources of the Tax Law

Revenue Rulings issued by the IRS carry less weight than Treasury Department Regulations. Revenue Rulings are important, however, in that they reflect the position of the IRS on tax

---

[38]*Augustus v. Comm.*, 41–1 USTC ¶9255, 26 AFTR 612, 118 F.2d 38 (CA–6, 1941).

[39]§§ 6662(a) and (b)(1).

[40]§ 6662(c). The term *reasonable* is not defined in the Code; the IRS looks at all the facts and circumstances surrounding the effort of the taxpayer to report the correct tax liability.

[41]*U.S. v. Vogel Fertilizer Co.*, 82–1 USTC ¶9134, 49 AFTR 2d 82–491, 102 S.Ct. 821 (USSC, 1982); *National Muffler Dealers Assn., Inc.*, 79–1 USTC ¶9264, 43 AFTR 2d 79–828, 99 S.Ct. 1304 (USSC, 1979).

matters. In any dispute with the IRS on the interpretation of tax law, therefore, taxpayers should expect agents to follow the results reached in any applicable Revenue Rulings. A 1986 Tax Court decision, however, indicated that Revenue Rulings "typically do not constitute substantive authority for a position."[42] Most Revenue Rulings apply retroactively unless a specific statement indicates the extent to which a ruling is to be applied without retroactive effect.[43]

Actions on Decisions further tell the taxpayer the IRS's reaction to certain court decisions. Recall that the IRS follows a practice of either acquiescing (agreeing) or nonacquiescing (not agreeing) with selected judicial decisions. A nonacquiescence does not mean that a particular court decision is of no value, but it does indicate that the IRS may continue to litigate the issue involved.

Assessing the Validity of Judicial Sources of the Tax Law

The judicial process as it relates to the formulation of tax law has already been described. How much reliance can be placed on a particular decision depends upon the following variables:

- The higher the level of the court that issued a decision, the greater the weight accorded to that decision. A decision rendered by a trial court (e.g., a Federal District Court) carries less weight than one issued by an appellate court (e.g., the Fifth Circuit Court of Appeals). Unless Congress changes the Code, decisions by the U.S. Supreme Court represent the last word on any tax issue.

- More reliance is placed on decisions of courts that have jurisdiction in the area where the taxpayer's legal residence is located. If, for example, a taxpayer lives in Texas, a decision of the Fifth Circuit Court of Appeals (which would hear an appeal from a Texas trial court) means more than one rendered by the Second Circuit Court of Appeals.[44]

- A Tax Court Regular decision carries more weight than a Memorandum decision because the Tax Court does not consider Memorandum decisions to be binding precedents.[45] Furthermore, a Tax Court *reviewed* decision (where *all* of the Tax Court judges participate) carries even more weight.

- A Circuit Court decision where certiorari has been requested and denied by the U.S. Supreme Court carries more weight than a Circuit Court decision that was not appealed. A Circuit Court decision heard *en banc* (all of the judges participate) carries more weight than a normal Circuit Court case.

- A decision that is supported by cases from other courts carries more weight than a decision that is not supported by other cases.

- The weight of a decision also can be affected by its status on appeal. For example, was the decision affirmed or overruled?

In connection with the last two variables, the use of a citator is invaluable to tax research.[46] A **citator** provides the history of a case, including the authority relied on (e.g., other judicial decisions) in reaching the result. Reviewing the references listed in the citator discloses whether the decision was appealed and, if so, with what result (e.g., affirmed, reversed, or remanded). It also reveals other cases with the same or similar issues and how they were decided. Thus, a citator reflects on the validity of a case and may lead to other relevant judicial material.[47] If one intends to rely on a judicial decision to any significant degree, "running" the case through a citator is imperative.

---

[42]*Nelda C. Stark*, 86 T.C. 243 (1986). See also *Ann R. Neuhoff*, 75 T.C. 36 (1980). For a different opinion, however, see *Industrial Valley Bank & Trust Co.*, 66 T.C. 272 (1976).

[43]Rev.Proc. 87–1, 1987–1 C.B. 503.

[44]Before October 1, 1982, an appeal from the then-named U.S. Court of Claims (the other trial court) was directly to the U.S. Supreme Court.

[45]*Severino R. Nico, Jr.*, 67 T.C. 647 (1977).

[46]The major citators are published by CCH; RIA; Westlaw; and Shepard's Citations, Inc.

[47]The CCH version is available online through the CCH *IntelliConnect* service; for RIA, use Thomson Reuters *Checkpoint*. Shepard's Internet version is part of LexisNexis.

FINANCIAL DISCLOSURE INSIGHTS **Where Does GAAP Come From?**

As this chapter has described, the tax law is developed by many entities, including Congress, and the legislators of other countries, the courts, and the IRS. Accounting principles also have many sources. Consequently, in reconciling the tax and financial accounting reporting of a transaction, the tax professional will need to know the hierarchy of authority of accounting principles—in particular, the level of importance to assign to a specific GAAP document. The diagram below presents the sources of GAAP arranged in a general order of authority from highest to lowest.

Professional research is conducted to find and analyze the sources of accounting reporting standards in much the same way a tax professional conducts research on an open tax question. In fact, many of the publishers that provide tax research materials also can be used to find GAAP and International Financial Reporting Standards (IFRS) documents. The Financial Accounting Standards Board (FASB) also makes its standards and interpretations available by subscription.

Highest Authority	• Financial Accounting Standards and Interpretations of the FASB. • Pronouncements of bodies that preceded the FASB, such as the Accounting Principles Board (APB).
	• FASB Technical Bulletins. • Audit and Accounting Guides, prepared by the American Institute of CPAs (AICPA) and cleared by the FASB. • Practice Bulletins, prepared by the American Institute of CPAs (AICPA) and cleared by the FASB.
	• Interpretation Guides of the FASB Staff. • Accounting Interpretations of the AICPA. • IASB Accounting Standards. • FASB Concepts Standards. • Widely accepted accounting practices, professional journals, accounting textbooks, and treatises.

Assessing the Validity of Other Sources

Primary sources of tax law include the Constitution, legislative history materials, statutes, treaties, Treasury Regulations, IRS pronouncements, and judicial decisions. In general, the IRS considers only primary sources to constitute substantial authority. However, a researcher might want to refer to *secondary materials* such as legal periodicals, treatises, legal opinions, General Counsel Memoranda, and written determinations. In general, secondary sources are not authority.

Although the statement that the IRS regards only primary sources as substantial authority generally is true, there is one exception. In Notice 90–20,[48] the IRS expanded the list of substantial authority *for purposes of* the accuracy-related penalty in § 6662 to include a number of secondary materials (e.g., letter rulings, General Counsel Memoranda, and the Bluebook). "Authority" does not include conclusions reached in treatises, legal periodicals, and opinions rendered by tax professionals.

A letter ruling or determination letter is substantial authority *only* for the taxpayer to whom it is issued, except as noted previously with respect to the accuracy-related penalty.

Upon the completion of major tax legislation, the staff of the Joint Committee on Taxation (in consultation with the staffs of the House Ways and Means and Senate Finance Committees) often will prepare a General Explanation of the Act, commonly known as the Bluebook because of the color of its cover. The IRS will not accept this detailed

---

[48]1990–1 C.B. 328; see also Reg. § 1.6661–3(b)(2).

explanation as having legal effect, except as noted previously with respect to the accuracy-related penalty. The Bluebook does, however, provide valuable guidance to tax advisers and taxpayers until Regulations are issued. Some letter rulings and General Counsel Memoranda of the IRS cite Bluebook explanations.

2-3e **Arriving at the Solution or at Alternative Solutions**

The Big Picture on p. 2-1 raised the question of whether a taxpayer would be denied dependency exemptions for a son and a daughter-in-law if the son sold some stock near the end of the year. A refinement of the problem supplies additional information:

- Sam and Dana anticipate filing a joint return.

Section 152(b)(2) indicates that a taxpayer is not permitted a dependency exemption for a married dependent if the married individual files a joint return. An initial reaction is that a joint return by Sam and Dana would be problematic to the parents. However, more research uncovers two Revenue Rulings that provide an exception if neither the dependent nor the dependent's spouse is required to file a return but does so solely to claim a refund of tax withheld. The IRS asserts that each spouse must have gross income of less than the exemption amount.[49] Therefore, if Sam sells the stock and he and Dana file a joint return, the parents will lose the dependency exemption for both Sam and Dana.

If the stock is not sold until January 2017, both dependency exemptions are available to the parents in 2016 even if Sam and Dana file a joint return. However, under § 151(d)(2), a personal exemption is not available to a taxpayer who can be claimed as a dependent by another taxpayer (whether actually claimed). Thus, if the parents can claim Sam and Dana as dependents, Sam and Dana would lose their personal exemptions on their tax return.

2-3f **Communicating Tax Research**

LO.5

Communicate the results of the tax research process in a client letter and a tax file memorandum.

Once the problem has been researched adequately, the researcher may need to prepare a memo, a letter, or an oral presentation setting forth the result. The form such a communication takes could depend on a number of considerations. For example, does the employer or professor recommend a particular procedure or format for tax research memos? Is the memo to be given directly to the client, or will it first go to the researcher's employer? Who is the audience for the oral presentation? How long should you talk? Whatever form it takes, a good tax research communication should contain the following elements:

- A clear statement of the issue.
- In more complex situations, a short review of the facts that raise the issue.
- A review of the pertinent tax law sources (e.g., Code, Regulations, Revenue Rulings, and judicial authority).
- Any assumptions made in arriving at the solution.
- The solution recommended and the logic or reasoning supporting it.
- The references consulted in the research process.

In short, a good tax research communication should tell the audience what was researched, the results of that research, and the justification for the recommendation made.[50]

Illustrations of the memos for the tax file and the client letter associated with the facts of *The Big Picture* appear in Exhibit 2.9, Exhibit 2.10, and Exhibit 2.11.

---

[49]Rev.Rul. 54–567, 1954–2 C.B. 108; Rev.Rul. 65–34, 1965–1 C.B. 86.

[50]See Chapter 6 of the publication cited in Footnote 32. For oral presentations, see W. A. Raabe and G. E. Whittenburg, "Talking Tax: How to Make a Tax Presentation," *The Tax Adviser* (March 1997): 179–182.

EXHIBIT 2.9	Tax File Memorandum

December 16, 2016

TAX FILE MEMORANDUM

FROM: John J. Jones
SUBJECT: Fred and Megan Samuels
                Engagement: Issues

Today I talked to Fred Samuels about his December 10, 2016 letter requesting tax assistance. He wants to know if his son, Sam, can sell stock worth $19,000 (with an $11,000 basis) without the parents losing the dependency exemptions for Sam and Sam's wife, Dana. Fred would also like to know the effect on Sam and Dana's 2016 tax liability if the stock is sold.

Fred Samuels is married to Megan, and Sam is a full-time student at a local university. Sam inherited the stock from his grandmother about five years ago. If he sells the stock, he will save the proceeds from the sale rather than spend them because he receives a $5,500 scholarship that he uses for his own support (i.e., to pay for tuition, books, and fees). Although neither Sam nor Dana is currently employed, Sam has earned income of $960 and Dana has earned income of $900 during the current year. Fred and Megan are in the 28% tax bracket and furnish approximately 55% of Sam and Dana's support.

ISSUES: If the stock is sold, would the sale prohibit Fred and Megan from claiming Sam and Dana as dependents? What is the effect on Sam and Dana's tax liability if the stock is sold in 2016? Fred would like an answer within two weeks.

EXHIBIT 2.10	Tax File Memorandum

December 18, 2016

TAX FILE MEMORANDUM

FROM: John J. Jones
SUBJECT: Fred and Megan Samuels
                Engagement: Conclusions

See the Tax File Memorandum dated December 16, 2016, which contains the facts and identifies the tax issues.

Section 152(a) provides that for a taxpayer to take a dependency exemption, the potential dependent must satisfy either the qualifying child requirements or the qualifying relative requirements (see Chapter 3). Fred and Megan provide about 55% of the support of their son, Sam, and their daughter-in-law, Dana. If Sam should sell the stock in 2016, he would not need to spend the proceeds for support purposes (i.e., would save the proceeds). Thus, the stock sale would not affect his qualifying as not self-supporting under § 152(c)(1)(D). In calculating the percentage of support provided by Fred and Megan, a $5,500 scholarship received by Sam is not counted in determining the amount of support Sam provides for himself [see § 152(f)(5) and Reg. § 1.152–1(c)]. Note, however, that if the $5,500 had been provided by student loans, it would have been included in calculating support [*Philip J. McCauley*, 56 T.C. 48 (1971)].

Section 152(d)(1)(B) provides that to qualify for a dependency exemption as a qualifying relative, the potential dependent's gross income must be less than the exemption amount (i.e., $4,050 in 2016). Without the stock sale, the gross income of both Sam ($960) and Dana ($900) will be below the exemption amount in 2016. The $5,500 Sam receives as a scholarship is excluded from his gross income under § 117(a) because he uses the entire amount to pay for his tuition, books, and fees at a local university.

Although the gross income test is not applicable to Sam (he is a qualifying child), it is applicable to Dana, the daughter-in-law (she is a qualifying relative; see Concept Summary 3.3). A key issue is whether the stock sale that produces $8,000 of recognized gain for Sam and Dana will cause the gross income test to be violated for Dana. Because the $8,000 recognized gain is from the sale of Sam's separately owned asset and they do not live in a community property state, Dana should qualify as a dependent because her gross income would be only $900.

The stock sale would result in the parents' loss of the dependency exemptions for Sam and Dana if they file a joint return for 2016 [see § 152(b)(2)]. The joint return requirement does not apply, however, if the dependent files a joint return solely to claim a refund and neither spouse had a tax liability on a separate return (Rev.Rul. 65–34, 1965–1 C.B. 86). However, sale of the stock would keep this exception from applying.

From a tax planning perspective, Sam can choose to sell the stock in 2016. However, if this choice is made, Sam and Dana need to file separate returns so as not to violate the absence of a joint return provision. Under these circumstances, the sale will not interfere with Fred and Megan's ability to claim dependency exemptions for Sam and Dana on their 2016 return. Note, however, that neither Sam nor Dana will be permitted to take a personal exemption deduction on their 2016 tax return because they are claimed as dependents on someone else's return [see § 151(d)(2)]. This disallowance of the personal exemption deduction will not produce any significant negative tax consequences for Dana because her tax liability would be $0. However, Sam's tax liability would now be $885 (see the kiddie tax discussion in Chapter 3; Sam's net unearned income is $5,900 and is a long-term capital gain taxed at a rate of 15% given his parent's marginal tax bracket). Alternatively, Sam could delay the sale of the stock until 2017. In this case, Sam and Dana's tax liability in 2016 would be $0. The disallowance of the personal exemption deductions by Sam and Dana will not produce any negative tax consequences because both Sam and Dana's tax liability would be $0.

EXHIBIT 2.11	**Client Letter**

Hoffman, Young, Raabe, Maloney, & Nellen, CPAs
5191 Natorp Boulevard
Mason, OH 45040

December 21, 2016

Mr. and Mrs. Fred Samuels
111 Boulevard
Williamsburg, VA 23185

Dear Mr. and Mrs. Samuels:

This letter is in response to your request for us to review your family's financial and tax situation. Our conclusions are based upon the facts as outlined in your December 10 letter. Any change in the facts may affect our conclusions.

You provide over 50% of the support for your son, Sam, and his wife, Dana. The scholarship Sam receives is not included in determining support. If the stock is not sold, you will qualify for a dependency exemption for both Sam and Dana.

If the stock is sold in 2016, a gain of approximately $8,000 will result. If Sam and Dana then file a joint return, you will lose the dependency exemption for Sam as a qualifying child and will lose the dependency exemption for Dana as a qualifying relative. You can avoid the loss of these two dependency exemptions if Sam and Dana file separate returns. This would result in a tax liability of $0 for Dana and $885 for Sam.

From a family tax planning and tax avoidance perspective, Sam should not sell the stock in 2016. Delaying the stock sale will enable you to claim dependency exemptions for both Sam and Dana and will enable Sam and Dana to have a $0 tax liability for 2016.

Should you need more information or need to clarify our conclusions, do not hesitate to contact me.

Sincerely yours,

John J. Jones, CPA
Partner

LO.6

Apply tax research techniques and planning procedures.

2-4 WORKING WITH THE TAX LAW— TAX PLANNING

Tax research and tax planning are inseparable. The *primary* purpose of effective *tax planning* is to reduce the taxpayer's total tax bill. This statement does not mean that the course of action selected must produce the lowest possible tax under the circumstances. The minimization of tax liability must be considered in context with the legitimate business goals of the taxpayer.

A *secondary* objective of effective tax planning is to reduce or defer the tax in the current tax year. Specifically, this objective aims to accomplish one or more of the following: eradicating the tax entirely; eliminating the tax in the current year; deferring the receipt of income; converting ordinary income into capital gains; converting active income to passive activity income; converting passive activity expense to active expense; proliferating taxpayers (i.e., forming partnerships and corporations or making lifetime gifts to family members); eluding double taxation; avoiding ordinary income; or creating, increasing, or accelerating deductions. However, this second objective should be approached with considerable reservation and moderation. For example, a tax election in one year may reduce taxes currently but saddle future years with a disadvantageous tax position.

2-4a Nontax Considerations

There is an honest danger that tax motivations may take on a significance that does not correspond to the true values involved. In other words, tax considerations may impair the exercise of sound business judgment by the taxpayer. Thus, the tax planning process can become a medium through which to accomplish ends that are socially and economically objectionable. All too often, planning seems to lean toward the opposing extremes of placing either too little or too much emphasis on tax considerations. The goal should be a balance that recognizes the significance of taxes, but not beyond the point where planning detracts from the exercise of good business judgment.

The remark is often made that a good rule is to refrain from pursuing any course of action that would not be followed were it not for certain tax considerations. This statement is not entirely correct, but it does illustrate the desirability of preventing business logic from being *sacrificed at the altar of tax planning.*

2-4b **Components of Tax Planning**

The popular perception of tax planning often is restricted to the adage "defer income and accelerate deductions." Although this timing approach does hold true and is important, meaningful tax planning involves considerably more.

Preferable to deferring income is complete *avoidance.* Consider, for example, the corporate employee who chooses nontaxable fringe benefits (e.g., group term life insurance and health insurance) over a fully taxable future pay increase.[51] Complete avoidance of gain recognition also occurs when the owner of appreciated property transfers it by death. If this "step-up" in basis to fair market value occurs, the built-in appreciation escapes the income tax forever.[52]

If the recognition of income cannot be avoided, its deferral will postpone income tax consequences. *Deferral* of income can take many forms. Besides like-kind exchanges and involuntary conversions, most retirement plans put off income tax consequences until the payout period. Deferral of gain recognition also can occur when appreciated property is transferred to a newly formed corporation or partnership.[53]

A corollary to the deferral of income is the acceleration of deductions. For example, an accrual basis, calendar year corporation wants an additional charitable deduction for 2016 but has a cash-flow problem. If the corporation authorizes the contribution in 2016 and pays it on or before April 15, 2017, the deduction can be claimed for 2016.[54] Taxes can be saved by *shifting* income to lower-bracket taxpayers. Gifts of appreciated property to lower-bracket family members can reduce the applicable capital gain rate on a later sale by 15 percentage points (from 15 percent to 0 percent).[55] For certain high-income taxpayers, the reduction is 20 percentage points (from 20 percent to 0 percent).

If income cannot be avoided, deferred, or shifted, the nature of the gain can be *converted.* By changing the classification of property, income taxes can be reduced. Thus, a taxpayer who transfers appreciated inventory to a controlled corporation has converted ordinary income property to a capital asset. When the taxpayer's stock is later sold, preferential capital gain rates apply.

The conversion approach also can work in tax planning for losses. Properly structured, a loan to a corporation that becomes worthless can be an ordinary loss rather than the less desirable capital loss. Likewise, planning with § 1244 permits an investor in qualified small business stock to convert what would be a capital loss into an ordinary loss.[56]

Effective tax planning requires that careful consideration be given to the *choice of entity* used for conducting a business. The corporate form results in double taxation but permits shareholder-employees to be covered by fringe benefit programs. Partnerships and S corporations allow a pass-through of losses and other tax attributes, but transferring ownership interests as gifts to family members may be difficult.[57]

Although the substance of a transaction, rather than its form, generally controls, this rule is not always the case with tax planning. *Preserving formalities*, particularly clear

---

[51]See text Sections 5-6 and 5-8 and Examples 19 and 38 in Chapter 5.

[52]See Example 19 in Chapter 14.

[53]See Examples 22 and 41 in Chapter 20, and Chapter 19 in general.

[54]See Example 7 in Chapter 20.

[55]See text Section 14-3b in Chapter 14.

[56]See Example 9 in Chapter 7.

[57]See text Sections 20-4 and 20-6c in Chapter 20.

documentation, often is crucial to the result. Is an advance to a corporation a loan or a contribution to capital? The answer may well depend on the existence of a note. Along with preserving formalities, the taxpayer should keep records that support a transaction. Returning to the issue of loan versus contribution to capital, how is the advance listed on the books of the borrower? What do the corporate minutes say about the advance?

Finally, effective tax planning requires *consistency* on the part of taxpayers. A shareholder who treats a corporate distribution as a return of capital cannot later avoid a stock basis adjustment by contending that the distribution was really a dividend.

In summary, the key components of tax planning include the following:

- *Avoid* the recognition of income (usually by resorting to a nontaxable source or nontaxable event).
- *Defer* the recognition of income (or accelerate deductions).
- *Convert* the classification of income (or deductions) to a more advantageous form (e.g., ordinary income into capital gain).
- *Choose* the business *entity* with the desired tax attributes.
- Preserve *formalities* by generating and maintaining supporting documentation.
- Act in a manner *consistent* with the intended objective.

2-4c **Tax Avoidance and Tax Evasion**

A fine line exists between legal tax planning and illegal tax planning—tax avoidance versus tax evasion. **Tax avoidance** is merely tax minimization through legal techniques. In this sense, tax avoidance is the proper objective of all tax planning. Tax evasion, while also aimed at the elimination or reduction of taxes, connotes the use of subterfuge and fraud as a means to an end. Popular usage—probably because of the common goals involved—has so linked these two concepts that many individuals are no longer aware of the true distinctions between them. Consequently, some taxpayers have been deterred from properly taking advantage of planning possibilities. The now classic words of Judge Learned Hand in *Commissioner v. Newman* reflect the true values the taxpayer should have:

> Over and over again courts have said that there is nothing sinister in so arranging one's affairs as to keep taxes as low as possible. Everybody does so, rich or poor; and all do right, for nobody owes any public duty to pay more than the law demands: taxes are enforced extractions, not voluntary contributions. To demand more in the name of morals is mere cant.[58]

As Denis Healy, a former British Chancellor, once said, "The difference between tax avoidance and tax evasion is the thickness of a prison wall."

The Government Accountability Office estimates that U.S. taxpayers spend at least $107 billion each year on tax compliance costs. The Treasury Department estimates that individuals spend at least 6.4 billion hours preparing Federal income tax returns. Small businesses, self-employed persons, and taxpayers with the highest marginal tax rates have the highest levels of tax evasion.[59]

2-4d **Follow-Up Procedures**

Because tax planning usually involves a proposed (as opposed to a completed) transaction, it is predicated upon the continuing validity of the advice based upon the tax research. A change in the tax law (legislative, administrative, or judicial) could alter the

---

[58]*Comm. v. Newman*, 47–1 USTC ¶9175, 35 AFTR 857, 159 F.2d 848 (CA–2, 1947).

[59]Adapted from J. A. Tackett, Joe Antenucci, and Fran Wolf, "A Criminological Perspective of Tax Evasion," *Tax Notes* (February 6, 2006): 654–658; L. E.

Burman, "Tax Evasion, IRS Priorities, and the EITC," *Statement before the United States House of Representatives Committee on the Budget; On Waste, Fraud, and Abuse in Federal Mandatory Programs* (July 9, 2003).

original conclusion. Additional research may be necessary to test the solution in light of current developments (refer to the broken lines at the right in Exhibit 2.8).

2-4e **Tax Planning—A Practical Application**

Returning to the facts of *The Big Picture* on p. 2-1, what could be done to protect the dependency exemptions for the parents? If Sam and Dana refrain from filing a joint return, both could be claimed by the parents.

Another tax planning tool is the installment method. Could the securities be sold using the installment method so that most of the gain is deferred into the next year? Under the installment method (§ 453), certain gains may be postponed and recognized as the cash proceeds are received. The problem is that the installment method is not available for stock traded on an established securities market.[60]

A little more research, however, indicates that Sam might be able to sell the stock and postpone the recognition of gain until the following year by selling short an equal number of substantially identical shares and covering the short sale in the subsequent year with the shares originally held. Selling short means that Sam sells borrowed stock (substantially identical) and repays the lender with the stock held on the date of the short sale. This *short against the box* technique would allow Sam to protect his $8,000 profit and defer the closing of the sale until the following year.[61] However, additional research indicates that 1997 tax legislation provides that the short against the box technique will no longer produce the desired postponement of recognized gain. That is, at the time of the short sale, Sam will have a recognized gain of $8,000 from a constructive sale. Note the critical role of obtaining the correct facts in attempting to resolve the proper strategy for the taxpayers.

Throughout this text, most chapters include observations on tax planning. Such observations are not all-inclusive, but are intended to illustrate some of the ways in which the material covered can be effectively utilized to minimize taxes.

2-5 **TAXATION ON THE CPA EXAMINATION**

Be aware of taxation on the CPA examination.

The CPA examination has changed from a paper-and-pencil exam to a computer-based exam with increased emphasis on information technology and general business knowledge. The exam has four sections, and taxation is included in the Regulations section.

In January 2011, the CPA examination was reorganized, with all written communication tasks now concentrated in the Business Environment & Concepts (BEC) section. Shorter simulations have replaced the longer simulations.

Each exam section includes multiple-choice questions and two other sections that have short task-based simulation (TBS) questions. The Regulations section is 60 percent Taxation and 40 percent Law & Professional Responsibilities (all areas other than Business Structure). The three-hour Regulations section contains:

- Three multiple-choice question (MCQ) testlets consisting of 72 questions.
- One testlet (i.e., a group of questions prepared to appear together) containing six short task-based simulations with the research question in a new format.

A candidate may review and change answers within each testlet but cannot go back after exiting a testlet. Candidates take different but equivalent exams.

Simulations are small case studies designed to test a candidate's tax knowledge and skills using real-life work-related situations. Simulations include a four-function, pop-up calculator, a blank spreadsheet with some elementary functionality, and authoritative literature appropriate to the subject matter. The taxation database includes authoritative

---

[60]See Chapter 18 for a discussion of installment sales.

[61]§§ 1233(a) and 1233(b)(2). See Chapter 16 for a discussion of short sales.

excerpts that are necessary to complete the tax case study simulations (e.g., Internal Revenue Code, Regulations, IRS publications, and Federal tax forms). Examples of such simulations follow.

CPA Exam Simulation Examples

EXAMPLE 4

The *tax citation type* simulation requires the candidate to research the Internal Revenue Code and enter a Code Section and subsection.

For example, Amber Company is considering using the simplified dollar-value method of pricing its inventory for purposes of the LIFO method that is available to certain small businesses. What Code Section is the relevant authority in the Internal Revenue Code to which you should turn to determine whether the taxpayer is eligible to use this method? To be successful, the candidate needs to find § 474.

EXAMPLE 5

A *tax form completion* simulation requires the candidate to fill out a portion of a tax form. For example, Red Company is a limited liability company (LLC) for tax purposes. Complete the income section of the IRS Form 1065 for Red Company using the values found and calculated on previous tabs along with the following data:

Ordinary income from other partnerships	$ 5,200
Net gain (loss) from Form 4797	2,400
Management fee income	12,000

The candidate is provided with page 1 of Form 1065 on which to record the appropriate amounts.

Any field that requires an entry is a shaded rectangular cell. Some white rectangular cells will automatically calculate based on the entries in the shaded cell.

Candidates can learn more about the CPA examination at **www.cpa-exam.org**. This online tutorial site's topics include:

- Common tools.
- Navigation.
- Form completion.
- Numeric entry.
- Research questions.
- Authoritative literature search.
- Written communication.

The common tools are a calculator, a spreadsheet, reminder flags, and an examination clock. A 30- to 60-minute sample exam will familiarize a candidate with the types of questions on the examination.

The AICPA is proposing changes to the CPA exam that will take effect during 2017. Although the four existing sections would be retained, a number of changes will be implemented:

- The exam will be designed to enhance the testing of higher-order cognitive skills that include critical thinking, problem solving, analytical ability, and professional skepticism.
- Each section will have a "*blueprint*" illustrating the knowledge and skills that will be tested on the CPA exam and are linked directly to tasks that are representative of the work of a newly licensed CPA. The blueprints will be available to candidates to aid in preparation for the exam.
- To test a combination of content knowledge and higher-order skills, more task-based simulations are planned.
- Task-based simulations will be added to the BEC section for the first time.
- Microsoft Excel will be added as a tool for candidates beginning in 2018 (but candidates will not be tested on their ability to use Excel).
- Total exam testing time will increase from 14 to 16 hours—four sections of four hours each.

Key Terms

Discussion Questions

1. **LO.1** A large part of tax research consists of determining what?

2. **LO.1** Why do taxpayers often have more than one alternative for structuring a business transaction?

3. **LO.1** Where does the Federal tax legislation generally originate?

4. **LO.2, 5** Butch Bishop operates a small international firm named Tile, Inc. A new   Communications
treaty between the United States and Spain conflicts with a Section of the Internal Revenue Code. Butch asks you for advice. If he follows the treaty position, does he need to disclose this on his tax return? If he is required to disclose, are there any penalties for failure to disclose? Prepare a letter in which you respond to Butch. Tile's address is 100 International Drive, Tampa, FL 33620.

5. **LO.1, 2** Interpret this Regulation citation: Reg. § 1.163–10(a)(2).

6. **LO.1** In the citation Notice 90–20, 1990–1 C.B. 328, to what do the 20 and the 328 refer?

7. **LO.1, 4** Rank the following items from the lowest to highest authority in the Federal tax law system:
   a. Interpretive Regulation.
   b. Legislative Regulation.
   c. Letter ruling.
   d. Revenue Ruling.
   e. Internal Revenue Code.
   f. Proposed Regulation.

8. **LO.1** Interpret each of the following citations:
   a. Temp.Reg. § 1.956–2T.
   b. Rev.Rul. 2012–15, 2012–23 I.R.B. 975.
   c. Ltr.Rul. 200204051.

9. **LO.1, 5** Sally Andrews calls you on the phone. She says that she has found a 2007   Communications
letter ruling that agrees with a position she wants to take on her tax return. She asks you about the precedential value of a letter ruling. Draft a memo for the tax files outlining what you told Sally.

10. **LO.1** Sri is considering writing the IRS to find out whether a possible stock redemp-   Issue ID
tion would be a qualified stock redemption. Outline some relevant tax issues Sri faces in determining whether to request a letter ruling.

11. **LO.1** Where may private letter rulings be found?

12. **LO.1** What are the differences between Technical Advice Memoranda (TAMs) and Technical Expedited Advice Memoranda (TEAMs)?

Issue ID   13. **LO.1** Dwain receives a 90-day letter after his discussion with an appeals officer. He is not satisfied with the $101,000 settlement offer. Identify the relevant tax research issues facing Dwain.

14. **LO.1** List an advantage and a disadvantage of using the U.S. Court of Federal Claims as the trial court for Federal tax litigation.

Communications   15. **LO.1, 5** Eddy Falls is considering litigating a tax deficiency of approximately $229,030 in the court system. He asks you to provide him with a short description of his alternatives, indicating the advantages and disadvantages of each. Prepare your response to Eddy in the form of a letter. His address is 200 Mesa Drive, Tucson, AZ 85714.

16. **LO.1** List an advantage and a disadvantage of using the U.S. Tax Court as the trial court for Federal tax litigation.

17. **LO.1** A taxpayer lives in Michigan. In a controversy with the IRS, the taxpayer loses at the trial court level. Describe the appeal procedure under the following different assumptions:
    a. The trial court was the Small Cases Division of the U.S. Tax Court.
    b. The trial court was the U.S. Tax Court.
    c. The trial court was a U.S. District Court.
    d. The trial court was the U.S. Court of Federal Claims.

18. **LO.1** What is meant by the term *petitioner*?

19. **LO.1** An appellate court will often become involved in fact-finding determination. Discuss the validity of this statement.

20. **LO.1** For the U.S. Tax Court, U.S. District Court, and U.S. Court of Federal Claims, indicate the following:
    a. Number of regular judges per court.
    b. Availability of a jury trial.
    c. Whether the deficiency must be paid before the trial.

21. **LO.1** A taxpayer living in the following states would appeal a decision of the U.S. District Court to which Court of Appeals?
    a. Wyoming.
    b. Nebraska.
    c. Idaho.
    d. Louisiana.
    e. Illinois.

22. **LO.1** What precedents must each of these courts follow?
    a. U.S. Tax Court.
    b. U.S. Court of Federal Claims.
    c. U.S. District Court.

23. **LO.1** What determines the appropriate Circuit Court of Appeals for a particular taxpayer?

24. **LO.1, 4** In assessing the validity of a prior court decision, discuss the significance of the following on the taxpayer's issue:
    a. The decision was rendered by the U.S. District Court of Wyoming. Taxpayer lives in Wyoming.
    b. The decision was rendered by the U.S. Court of Federal Claims. Taxpayer lives in Wyoming.

c.   The decision was rendered by the Second Circuit Court of Appeals. Taxpayer lives in California.

d.   The decision was rendered by the U.S. Supreme Court.

e.   The decision was rendered by the U.S. Tax Court. The IRS has acquiesced in the result.

f.   Same as (e) except that the IRS has issued a nonacquiescence as to the result.

25. **LO.2** In the citation *Schuster's Express, Inc.*, 66 T.C. 588 (1976), *aff'd* 562 F.2d 39 (CA–2, 1977), *nonacq.*, to what do the 66, 39, and *nonacq.* refer?

26. **LO.2** Is there an automatic right to appeal to the U.S. Supreme Court? If so, what is the process?

27. **LO.2** Referring to the citation only, determine which court issued these decisions.

a.   716 F.2d 693 (CA–9, 1983).

b.   92 T.C. 400 (1998).

c.   70 U.S. 224 (1935).

d.   3 B.T.A. 1042 (1926).

e.   T.C.Memo. 1957–169.

f.   50 AFTR2d 92–6000 (Ct. Cl., 1992).

g.   Ltr.Rul. 9046036.

h.   111 F.Supp.2d 1294 (S.D.N.Y., 2000).

i.   98–50, 1998–1 C.B. 10.

28. **LO.2** Interpret each of the following citations:

a.   14 T.C. 74 (1950).

b.   592 F.2d 1251 (CA–5, 1979).

c.   95–1 USTC ¶50,104 (CA–6, 1995).

d.   75 AFTR2d 95–110 (CA–6, 1995).

e.   223 F.Supp. 663 (W.D. Tex., 1963).

29. **LO.2** Give the Commerce Clearing House citation for the following courts:

a.   Small Cases Division of the Tax Court.

b.   Federal District Court.

c.   U.S. Supreme Court.

d.   U.S. Court of Federal Claims.

e.   Tax Court Memorandum decision.

30. **LO.2** Where can you locate a published decision of the U.S. Court of Federal Claims?

31. **LO.1, 2** Which of the following items can probably be found in the *Internal Revenue Bulletin*?

a.   Action on Decision.

b.   Small Cases Division of the U.S. Tax Court decision.

c.   Letter ruling.

d.   Revenue Procedure.

e.   Finalized Regulation.

f.   U.S. Court of Federal Claims decision.

g.   Acquiescences to Tax Court decisions.

h.   U.S. Circuit Court of Appeals decision.

32. **LO.3** For her tax class, Yvonne has to prepare a research paper discussing the tax   Issue ID
aspects of child support payments. Explain to Yvonne how she can research
this topic using various tax research resources.

33. **LO.4** Where can a researcher find the current Internal Revenue Code of 1986?

Decision Making   34. **LO.2, 4** You inherit a tax problem that was researched five months ago. You believe the answer is correct, but you are unfamiliar with the general area. How would you find recent articles dealing with the subject area? How do you evaluate the reliability of the authority cited in the research report? How do you determine the latest developments pertaining to the research problem?

35. **LO.6** What is the primary purpose of effective tax planning? Explain.

36. **LO.7** Describe simulation questions on the CPA exam.

Problems

37. **LO.1** In which Subchapter of the Internal Revenue Code would one find information about corporate distributions?
    a. Subchapter S.
    b. Subchapter C.
    c. Subchapter P.
    d. Subchapter K.
    e. Subchapter M.

38. **LO.1** To locate an IRS Revenue Procedure that was issued during the past week, which source would you consult?
    a. *Federal Register*.
    b. *Internal Revenue Bulletin*.
    c. Internal Revenue Code.
    d. Some other source.

39. **LO.1** Which of the following items can be found in the *Federal Register*?
    a. Letter Ruling.
    b. Action on Decision.
    c. Revenue Procedure.
    d. Temporary Regulation.
    e. Technical Advice Memorandum.

40. **LO.1, 4** Rank the items below from most reliable to least reliable:
    a. Letter Ruling.
    b. Legislative Regulation.
    c. Code Section.
    d. Revenue Ruling.
    e. Proposed Regulation.
    f. Interpretive Regulation.
    g. Recent Temporary Regulation.

41. **LO.4** Using the legend provided, classify each of the following tax sources:

Legend
P = Primary tax source
S = Secondary tax source
B = Both
N = Neither

a.   Sixteenth Amendment to the U.S. Constitution.

b.   Tax treaty between the United States and India.

c.   Revenue Procedure.

d.   General Counsel Memoranda (1989).

e.   U.S. District Court decision.

f.   *Yale Law Journal* article.

g.   Temporary Regulations (issued 2014).

h.   U.S. Tax Court Memorandum decision.

i.   Small Cases Division of the U.S. Tax Court decision.

j.   House Ways and Means Committee report.

42. **LO.1, 2** Using the legend provided, classify each of the following citations as to publisher:

Legend
RIA = Research Institute of America
CCH = Commerce Clearing House
W = West
U.S. = U.S. Government
O = Others

a.   83–2 USTC ¶9600.

b.   52 AFTR 2d 83–5954.

c.   67 T.C. 293 (1976).

d.   39 TCM 32 (1979).

e.   416 U.S. 938.

f.   RIA T.C. Memo. ¶80,582.

g.   89 S.Ct. 501.

h.   2 Cl.Ct. 600.

i.   415 F.2d 488.

j.   592 F.Supp. 18.

k.   77–37, 1977–2 C.B. 568.

l.   S. Rep. No. 1622, 83rd Cong., 2d Sess. 42 (1954).

43. **LO.6** Using the legend provided, classify each of the following statements:

Legend
A = Tax avoidance
E = Tax evasion
N = Neither

a.   Sue writes a $707 check for a charitable contribution on December 28, 2016, but does not mail the check to the charitable organization until January 10, 2017. She takes a deduction in 2016.

b.   Sam decides not to report interest income from a bank because the amount is only $19.75.

c.   Harry pays property taxes on his home in December 2016 rather than waiting until February 2017.

d.   Variet switches her investments from taxable corporate bonds to tax-exempt municipal bonds.

e.   Mel encourages his mother to save most of her Social Security benefits so that he will be able to claim her as a dependent.

Research Problems

THOMSON REUTERS
CHECKPOINT®
Student Edition

**Note: Solutions to Research Problems can be prepared by using the Checkpoint®
Student Edition online research product, which is available to accompany this text. It
is also possible to prepare solutions to the Research Problems by using tax research
materials found in a standard tax library.**

Research Problem 1. Determine the missing data in these court decisions and rulings.

    a. *Higgens v. Comm.*, 312 U.S._____ (1941).

    b. *Talen v. U.S.*, 355 F.Supp.2d 22 (D.Ct. D.C., _____).

    c. Rev.Rul. 2008–18, 2008–13 I.R.B._____.

    d. *Pahl v. Comm.*, 150 F.3d 1124 (CA–9, _____).

    e. *Veterinary Surgical Consultants PC*, 117 T.C._____ (2001).

    f. *Yeagle Drywall Co.*, T.C.Memo. 2001_____.

Research Problem 2. Can a Tax Court Small Case Decision be treated as a precedent
for other cases? Explain.

Partial list of research aids:
IRC § 7463(b).
Maria Antionette Walton Mitchell, T.C. Summ. 2004–160.

Decision Making

Research Problem 3. When Oprah gave away Pontiac G6 sedans to her TV audience,
was the value of the cars taxable? On Labor Day weekend in 2006, World Furniture
Mall in Plano, Illinois, gave away $275,000 of furniture because the Chicago Bears
shut out the Green Bay Packers in the team's football season opener at Lambeau
Field in Green Bay (26–0). Was the free furniture in the form of a discount or rebate
taxable, or should the furniture company have handed the customers a Form 1099–
MISC?

Decision Making

Research Problem 4. You are interviewing a client before preparing his tax return. He
indicates that he did not list as income $96,000 received as a recovery for false
imprisonment. What should you do with respect to this significant recovery?

Partial list of research aids:
CCA 200809001.
Daniel and Brenda Stadnyk, T.C.Memo. 2008–289.
Rev.Rul. 2007–14, 2007–1 C.B. 747.
§ 104.

Internet
Activity

**Use the tax resources of the Internet to address the following questions. Do not
restrict your search to the Web, but include a review of newsgroups and general
reference materials, practitioner sites and resources, primary sources of the tax law,
chat rooms and discussion groups, and other opportunities.**

Research Problem 5. (1) Go to **www.taxalmanac.org**, and use the website to find
§ 61(a). What is defined in this Code Section? Is the definition broad or narrow? (2) Go to
www.legalbitstream.com, and find the case in which Mark Spitz, the former Olympic
gold medalist, is the petitioner. Answer the following questions about the case:

    a. What tax years are at issue in the case?

    b. In what year was the case decided?

    c. Did the court decide in favor of Mr. Spitz or the IRS?

    d. Were any penalties imposed on Mr. Spitz? Why or why not?

Research Problem 6. Go to the U.S. Tax Court website (**www.ustaxcourt.gov**).

    a. What different types of cases can be found on the site?

    b. What is a Summary Opinion? Find one.

    c. What is a Memorandum Opinion? Find one.

    d. Find the "Rules of Practice and Procedure."

CHAPTER

3

Tax Formula and Tax Determination; An Overview of Property Transactions

LEARNING OBJECTIVES: *After completing Chapter 3, you should be able to:*

LO.1 Recognize and apply the components of the Federal income tax formula.

LO.2 Explain the standard deduction and evaluate its choice in arriving at taxable income.

LO.3 Apply the rules for arriving at personal exemptions.

LO.4 Explain the rules for determining dependency exemptions.

LO.5 Choose the proper filing status and identify the related filing requirements.

LO.6 Demonstrate the proper procedures for determining the tax liability.

LO.7 Identify and report kiddie tax situations.

LO.8 Formulate the fundamentals of property transactions.

LO.9 Evaluate tax planning opportunities associated with the individual tax formula.

CHAPTER OUTLINE

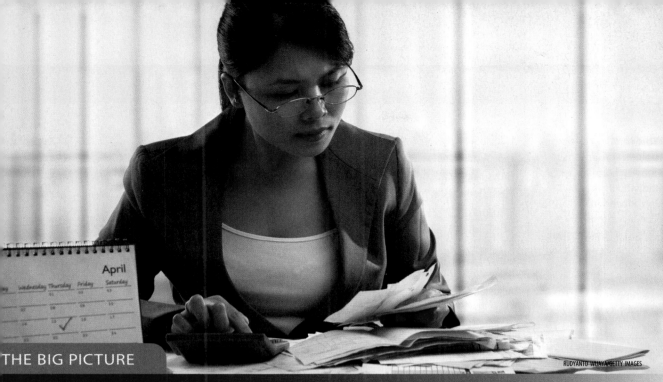

THE BIG PICTURE

A DIVIDED HOUSEHOLD

Polly maintains a household in which she lives with her unemployed husband (Nick), stepdaughter (Paige), and a family friend (Maude). She provides more than one-half of the support for both Paige and Maude. Maude was fatally injured in an automobile accident in February, and Polly paid for her hospitalization and funeral expenses. Paige, an accomplished gymnast, graduated from high school last year. Paige has a part-time job but spends most of her time training and looking for an athletic scholarship to the "right" college. In March, Nick left for parts unknown and has not been seen or heard from since. Polly was more surprised than distressed over Nick's unexpected departure. One reaction, however, was to sell her wedding rings to a cousin who was getting married. The rings cost $11,800 and were sold for their approximate value of $9,000.

Based on these facts, what are Polly's income tax concerns for the current year?

Read the chapter and formulate your response.

FRAMEWORK 1040. **Tax Formula for Individuals**

This chapter covers the boldfaced portions of the Tax Formula for Individuals that is introduced in Concept Summary 3.1 on p. 3-3. Below those portions are the sections of Form 1040 where the results are reported.

Income *(broadly defined)*	$xx,xxx
Less: Exclusions	(x,xxx)
Gross income	$xx,xxx
Less: **Deductions** *for* adjusted gross income	(x,xxx)

FORM 1040 (p.1)

1 ☐ Single
2 ☐ Married filing jointly (even if only one had income)
3 ☐ Married filing separately. Enter spouse's SSN above and full name here. ▶

4 ☐ Head of household (with qualifying person). (See instructions.) If the qualifying person is a child but not your dependent, enter this child's name here. ▶ _____
5 ☐ Qualifying widow(er) with dependent child

Adjusted gross income	$xx,xxx
Less: The greater of total **itemized deductions** *or* the standard deduction	(x,xxx)

FORM 1040 (p. 2)

39a Check if: ☐ **You** were born before January 2, 1951,   ☐ Blind.   **Total boxes**
☐ **Spouse** was born before January 2, 1951,   ☐ Blind.   **checked ▶ 39a** ☐

b If your spouse itemizes on a separate return or you were a dual-status alien, check here ▶   **39b** ☐

40 **Itemized deductions** (from Schedule A) **or** your **standard deduction** . . . .

42 **Exemptions.** If line 38 is $154,950 or less, multiply $4,000 by the number on line 6d. Otherwise, see instructions

Personal and dependency exemptions	(x,xxx)
Taxable income	$xx,xxx
Tax on taxable income *(see Tax Tables or Tax Rate Schedules)*	$ x,xxx
Less: Tax credits *(including income taxes withheld and prepaid)*	(xxx)
Tax due (or refund)	$ xxx

The framework for the application of the Federal income tax to individuals is the tax formula. As Chapter 1 mentioned, the tax formula is an integral part of our U.S. tax system (i.e., local, state, and Federal), and Chapter 3 provides a summary of its components. In addition, several of its key components—the standard deduction, personal and dependency exemptions, and tax determination—are discussed at length in Chapter 3.

By introducing the tax formula, therefore, Chapter 3 establishes the framework for almost all of the rest of the text (i.e., Chapters 4 through 19). The formula and its impact on the chapters to follow are reflected in Concept Summary 3.1. In integrating the formula with the chapters in the text, however, some liberties were taken. In the interest of simplicity, Concept Summary 3.1 omits references to several chapters for the following reasons:

- Chapter 18 deals with the more advanced aspects of accounting periods and methods. The main consideration in this area is the distinction between the cash and accrual methods of accounting. The method used affects the timing of *income* and *deductions* and, therefore, is discussed in Chapters 4 and 6.

- Chapter 19 deals with deferred compensation and cuts across several parts of the tax formula. Depending on the type of arrangement involved, gross income may be recognized (or deferred) or a deduction can materialize.

Chapter 3 also provides an overview of property transactions. When property is sold or otherwise disposed of, a gain or loss results, which can affect the

Concept Summary 3.1

Tax Formula for Individuals (Components Integrated into the Text)

		Text Discussion
Income (broadly defined)	$xx,xxx	Chs. 3, 4
Less: **Exclusions**	(x,xxx)	Ch. 5
Gross income	$xx,xxx	Chs. 4, 16, 17
Less: **Deductions** *for* adjusted gross income	(x,xxx)	Chs. 6–9, 11, 16, 17
Adjusted gross income	$xx,xxx	
Less: The greater of—		
Total **itemized deductions** *or* **standard deduction**	(x,xxx)	Chs. 6, 9, 10, 11 / Ch. 3
Less: **Personal** and **dependency exemptions**	(x,xxx)	Ch. 3
Taxable income	$xx,xxx	Chs. 3, 12, 13
Tax on taxable income	$ x,xxx	Chs. 3, 12, 13
Less: **Tax credits**	(xxx)	Ch. 13
Tax due (or refund)	$ xxx	Chs. 3, 12, 13

determination of taxable income. Although property transactions are covered in detail in Chapters 14 through 17, an understanding of certain basic concepts helps in working with some of the materials to follow. The chapter concludes by addressing the difference between realized and recognized gain or loss and the classification of such gain or loss (ordinary or capital) for income tax purposes.

3-1 TAX FORMULA

LO.1

Recognize and apply the components of the Federal income tax formula.

Given that the tax formula establishes the framework for the Federal income tax on individuals, a brief review of its components is helpful in understanding the in-depth discussion that follows in this and subsequent chapters.

3-1a Components of the Tax Formula

Income (Broadly Defined)

In the tax formula, "income" is broadly defined and includes all of the taxpayer's income, both taxable and nontaxable. In general, the courts have defined "income" as any increase in wealth.[1] As a result, it does not include a return of capital or receipt of borrowed funds.

EXAMPLE 1

Dan decides to quit renting and move into a new house. Consequently, the owner of the apartment building returns to Dan the $600 damage deposit he previously made. To make a down payment on the house, Dan sells stock for $20,000 (original cost of $8,000) and borrows $50,000 from a bank.

Only the $12,000 gain from the sale of the stock is income to Dan. The $600 damage deposit and the $8,000 cost of the stock are a return of capital. The $50,000 bank loan is not income as Dan has an obligation to repay that amount (and it does not increase his wealth).

---

[1]*Comm. v. Glenshaw Glass Co.*, 55–1 USTC ¶9308, 47 AFTR 162, 348 U.S. 426 (USSC, 1955).

Exclusions

For various reasons, Congress has chosen to exclude certain types of income from the income tax base. The principal income exclusions are discussed in Chapter 5. A partial list of these exclusions is shown in Exhibit 3.1.

Gross Income

The Internal Revenue Code defines gross income broadly as "except as otherwise provided ..., all income from whatever source derived."[2] The "except as otherwise provided" phrase refers to exclusions. Gross income includes, but is not limited to, the items in the partial list in Exhibit 3.2. It does not include unrealized gains. Gross income is discussed in Chapters 4 and 5.

EXAMPLE
2

Beth received the following amounts during the year:

Salary	$30,000
Interest on savings account	900
Gift from her aunt	10,000
Prize won in state lottery	1,000
Alimony from ex-husband	12,000
Child support from ex-husband	6,000
Damages for injury in auto accident	25,000
Ten $50 bills in an unmarked envelope found in an airport lounge (airport authorities could not locate anyone who claimed ownership)	500
Federal income tax refund for last year's tax overpayment	120
Increase in the value of stock held for investment	5,000

Review Exhibits 3.1 and 3.2 to determine the amount Beth must include in the computation of taxable income and the amount she may exclude.[3]

EXHIBIT 3.1	**Partial List of Exclusions from Gross Income**

Accident insurance proceeds	Life insurance paid upon death
Annuities (cost element)	Meals and lodging (if furnished for employer's convenience)
Bequests	
Child support payments	Military allowances
Cost-of-living allowance (for military)	Minister's dwelling rental value allowance
Damages for personal injury or sickness	Railroad retirement benefits (to a limited extent)
Gifts received	
Group term life insurance, premium paid by employer (for coverage up to $50,000)	Scholarship grants (to a limited extent)
	Social Security benefits (to a limited extent)
Inheritances	Veterans' benefits
Interest from state and local (i.e., municipal) bonds	Welfare payments
	Workers' compensation benefits

---

[2]§ 61(a).

[3]Beth must include $44,400 in computing taxable income ($30,000 salary + $900 interest + $1,000 lottery prize + $12,000 alimony + $500 found property). She can exclude $41,000 ($10,000 gift from aunt + $6,000 child support + $25,000 damages). The $120 Federal income tax refund is excluded because it represents an adjustment (i.e., overpayment) of a non-deductible expenditure made in the previous year. The unrealized gain on the stock held for investment also is not included in gross income. Such gain will be included in gross income only when realized upon disposition of the stock; see text Sections 3–8 and 3–9.

EXHIBIT 3.2	**Partial List of Gross Income Items**

Alimony	Group term life insurance, premium paid by employer (for coverage over $50,000)
Annuities (income element)	
Awards	Hobby income
Back pay	Interest
Bargain purchase from employer	Jury duty fees
Bonuses	Living quarters, meals (unless furnished for employer's convenience)
Breach of contract damages	
Business income	Mileage allowance (in certain cases)
Clergy fees	Military pay (unless combat pay)
Commissions	Notary fees
Compensation for services	Partnership income
Death benefits	Pension distributions
Debts forgiven	Prizes
Director's fees	Professional fees
Dividends	Punitive damages
Embezzled funds	Rents
Employee awards (in certain cases)	Rewards
	Royalties
Employee benefits (except certain fringe benefits)	Salaries
	Severance pay
Estate and trust income	Strike and lockout benefits
Farm income	Supplemental unemployment benefits
Fees	Tips and gratuities
Gains from illegal activities	Travel allowance (in certain cases)
Gains from sale of property	Treasure trove (found property)
Gambling winnings	Wages

Deductions for Adjusted Gross Income

Individual taxpayers have two categories of deductions: (1) deductions *for* adjusted gross income (deductions from gross income to arrive at adjusted gross income) and (2) deductions *from* adjusted gross income.

Deductions *for* adjusted gross income (AGI) are sometimes known as *above-the-line* deductions because on the tax return they are taken before the "line" designating AGI. They are also referred to as *page 1 deductions* because they are claimed, either directly or indirectly (i.e., through supporting schedules), on page 1 of Form 1040. Deductions *for* AGI include, but are not limited to, the following:[4]

- Expenses incurred in a trade or business.
- Part of the self-employment tax.
- Unreimbursed moving expenses.
- Certain contributions to traditional Individual Retirement Accounts (IRAs) and other retirement plans.
- Fees for college tuition and related expenses.
- Contributions to Health Savings Accounts (HSAs).
- Penalty for early withdrawal from savings.
- Interest on student loans.
- Excess capital losses.
- Alimony payments.

---

[4]§ 62; many of these deductions are limited by statute.

The effect on AGI of deductions *for* AGI is illustrated below.

Mason, age 45, earned a salary of $78,000 in the current year. He contributed $4,000 to his traditional Individual Retirement Account (IRA), sold stock held as an investment for a short-term capital loss of $2,000, and paid $4,600 in alimony to his ex-wife. His AGI is determined as follows:

Gross income		
Salary		$ 78,000
Less: Deductions *for* AGI		
IRA contribution	$4,000	
Capital loss	2,000	
Alimony paid	4,600	(10,600)
AGI		$ 67,400

The principal deductions *for* AGI are discussed in Chapters 6, 7, 8, 9, 11, 16, and 17.

Deductions from Adjusted Gross Income

As a general rule, personal expenditures are disallowed as deductions in arriving at taxable income. However, Congress allows specified personal expenses as deductions *from* AGI (commonly referred to as **itemized deductions**).

AGI is an important subtotal that serves as the basis for computing percentage limitations on certain itemized deductions such as medical expenses, charitable contributions, and certain casualty losses. For example, in 2016, medical expenses are deductible only to the extent they exceed 10 percent of AGI (7.5 percent if the taxpayer is at least age 65), and charitable contribution deductions may not exceed 50 percent of AGI. These limitations might be described as a 10 percent (or 7.5 percent) *floor* under the medical expense deduction and a 50 percent *ceiling* on the charitable contribution deduction.

Assume the same facts as in Example 3, and assume that Mason had medical expenses of $8,000. Medical expenses are included in itemized deductions to the extent they exceed 10% of AGI. In computing his itemized deductions, Mason includes medical expenses of $1,260 [$8,000 medical expenses—$6,740 (10% × $67,400 AGI)].

In addition to these personal expenses, taxpayers are allowed itemized deductions for expenses related to (1) the production or collection of income and (2) the management of property held for the production of income.[5] These expenses, sometimes referred to as *nonbusiness expenses*, differ from trade or business expenses (which are deductions *for* AGI). Nonbusiness expenses are expenses incurred in connection with an income-producing activity that does not qualify as a trade or business. These expenses are itemized deductions.

Leo is the owner and operator of a video game arcade. All allowable expenses that he incurs in connection with the arcade business are deductions *for* AGI. In addition, Leo has an extensive portfolio of stocks and bonds. Leo's investment activity is not treated as a trade or business. All allowable expenses that Leo incurs in connection with these investments are itemized deductions.

Itemized deductions include, but are not limited to, the expenses listed in Exhibit 3.3. See Chapters 9 and 10 for a detailed discussion of itemized deductions.

---

[5]§ 212.

EXHIBIT 3.3	Partial List of Itemized Deductions

Medical expenses in excess of 10% of AGI (through 2016, 7.5% if at least age 65)

State and local income or sales taxes

Real estate taxes

Personal property taxes

Interest on home mortgage (subject to certain limitations)

Investment interest (up to the amount of net investment income)

Charitable contributions (within specified percentage limitations)

Casualty and theft losses in excess of 10% of AGI

Miscellaneous expenses (to the extent such expenses in aggregate exceed 2% of AGI)

    Union dues

    Professional dues and subscriptions

    Certain educational expenses

    Tax return preparation fee

    Investment counsel fees

    Unreimbursed employee business expenses (after a percentage reduction for meals
      and entertainment)

Nondeductible Expenditures

Many expenditures are not deductible and, therefore, provide no tax benefit. Examples include, but are not limited to, the following:

- Personal living expenses.
- Losses on the sale of personal use property.
- Hobby losses.
- Life insurance premiums.
- Gambling losses (in excess of gains).
- Child support payments.
- Fines and penalties.
- Political contributions.
- Funeral expenses.
- Expenses paid on another's behalf.
- Capital expenditures.

If an expenditure is classified as nondeductible, the component of the tax formula affected is either the deduction *for* AGI or the deduction *from* AGI. Thus, a traffic fine for speeding is nondeductible whether the taxpayer was using the automobile while on a business trip for his or her sole proprietorship (normally a deduction *for* AGI) or participating in a Habitat for Humanity project (normally a deduction *from* AGI).[6] Most of the nondeductible items in the preceding list are discussed in Chapter 6.

Standard Deduction

Instead of claiming itemized deductions, taxpayers use the **standard deduction** . As discussed later in the chapter, the standard deduction varies depending on filing status, age, and blindness. The standard deduction is adjusted (i.e., indexed) each year for inflation.

---

[6]The use of a personal automobile in connection with a charitable activity would probably qualify for the charitable contribution deduction—a deduction *from* AGI.

Personal and Dependency Exemptions

Exemptions, another type of deduction, are allowed for the taxpayer, the taxpayer's spouse, and each dependent of the taxpayer. Like the standard deduction, personal and dependency exemptions (discussed later) are adjusted each year for inflation. The exemption amount for 2016 is $4,050 (up from $4,000 in 2015).

Taxable Income

The determination of taxable income is illustrated in Example 6.

EXAMPLE
6

Grace, age 25, is single and has her disabled and dependent mother living with her. This qualifies Grace for head-of-household filing status and a standard deduction of $9,300 in 2016. In 2016, Grace earned a $42,000 salary as a high school teacher. Her other income consisted of $1,100 interest on a certificate of deposit (CD) and $500 interest on nontaxable municipal bonds that she had received as a graduation gift in 2011. During 2016, she sustained a deductible capital loss of $1,000 from the sale of stock. Her itemized deductions are $9,500. Grace's taxable income for the year is computed as follows:

Income (broadly defined)	
Salary	$42,000
Interest on a CD	1,100
Interest on municipal bonds	500
	$43,600
Less: Exclusion—Interest on municipal bonds	(500)
Gross income	$43,100
Less: Deduction *for* adjusted gross income—capital loss	(1,000)
Adjusted gross income	$42,100
Less: The greater of total itemized deductions ($9,500) *or* the standard deduction for head of household ($9,300)	(9,500)
Personal and dependency exemptions (2 × $4,050)	(8,100)
Taxable income	$24,500

Note that the exclusion of $500 (i.e., interest from municipal bonds) is subtracted in determining gross income. The capital loss of $1,000 from a property transaction is classified as a deduction *for* AGI. Grace chose to itemize her deductions *from* AGI as they exceed the standard deduction (see Exhibit 3.4). Grace's income tax is determined later in this chapter in Example 42.

Tax Due (or Refund)

The last step in applying the tax formula is the determination of tax due (or refund). Ascertain the appropriate filing status (e.g., single, head of household), and then apply the

EXHIBIT 3.4	**Basic Standard Deduction Amounts**	
	Standard Deduction Amount	
Filing Status	**2015**	**2016**
Single	$ 6,300	$ 6,300
Married, filing jointly	12,600	12,600
Surviving spouse	12,600	12,600
Head of household	9,250	9,300
Married, filing separately	6,300	6,300

appropriate set of tax rates (i.e., Tax Rate Schedules or Tax Tables) to taxable income. Once the tax is computed, reduce this amount by any tax credits allowed (e.g., withholdings, earned income, research, or foreign) to arrive at the additional tax due or any overpayment (i.e., refund) involved. Filing status and the use of the tax rates are discussed later in this chapter; tax credits are the subject of Chapter 13.

3-1b Tax Formula—Correlation with Form 1040

The structure of individual income tax returns (Forms 1040, 1040A, or 1040EZ) parallels the tax formula in Concept Summary 3.1. Like the formula, the tax return places major emphasis on adjusted gross income (AGI), which appears on the bottom of page 1 and at the top of page 2 of Form 1040. In arriving at gross income (referred to as *total income*), *most* exclusions are not reported on the tax return. Deductions *for* AGI are summarized on page 1 of Form 1040.

Deductions *from* AGI (referred to as "itemized deductions") are carried over from Schedule A to page 2 of Form 1040. The choice between the standard deduction and itemized deductions is made on page 2. This is followed by the deduction for personal and dependency exemptions to arrive at taxable income. Page 2 contains the tax determination aspects of the tax formula, including any reduction allowed for available tax credits. The format of Form 1040 and its tie-in to the various supporting schedules containing components of the tax formula is graphically illustrated in Exhibit 6.1 of Chapter 6.

3-2 STANDARD DEDUCTION

LO.2

Explain the standard deduction and evaluate its choice in arriving at taxable income.

A major component of the tax formula is the standard deduction. The effect of the standard deduction is to exempt part of a taxpayer's income from Federal income tax liability. In the past, Congress has attempted to set the tax-free amount represented by the standard deduction approximately equal to an estimated poverty level,[7] but it has not always been consistent in doing so.

3-2a Basic and Additional Standard Deduction

The standard deduction is the sum of two components: the *basic* standard deduction and the *additional* standard deduction.[8] Exhibit 3.4 lists the basic standard deduction allowed for taxpayers in each filing status. The standard deduction amounts are subject to adjustment for inflation each year.

Certain taxpayers are not allowed to claim *any* standard deduction, and the standard deduction is *limited* for others. These provisions are discussed later in the chapter.

A taxpayer who is age 65 or over *or* blind in 2016 qualifies for an *additional standard deduction* of $1,250 or $1,550, depending on filing status (see amounts in Exhibit 3.5). Two additional standard deductions are allowed for a taxpayer who is age 65 or over *and* blind. The additional standard deduction provisions also apply for a qualifying spouse who is age 65 or over or blind, but a taxpayer may not claim an additional standard deduction for a dependent.

To determine whether to itemize, the taxpayer compares the *total* standard deduction (the sum of the basic standard deduction and any additional standard deductions) with total itemized deductions. Taxpayers are allowed to deduct the *greater* of itemized deductions or the standard deduction. The choice is elective. About two-thirds of individual tax returns filed use the standard deduction (rather than itemized deductions).

Undoubtedly, some taxpayers claim the standard deduction because they do not want to bother completing the additional tax form (Schedule A) required for itemizing deductions *from* AGI. Likewise, the choice is an annual one, and a taxpayer is not bound by choices made in prior years. For example, many taxpayers who have

---

[7]S.Rep. No. 92–437, 92nd Cong., 1st Sess., 1971, p. 54. Another purpose of the standard deduction, discussed in Chapter 1, is to reduce the number of taxpayers who itemize their deductions. Reducing the number of taxpayers who itemize also reduces the audit effort required from the IRS.

[8]§ 63(c)(1).

EXHIBIT 3.5	Amount of Each Additional Standard Deduction		
Filing Status		**2015**	**2016**
Single		$1,550	$1,550
Married, filing jointly		1,250	1,250
Surviving spouse		1,250	1,250
Head of household		1,550	1,550
Married, filing separately		1,250	1,250

previously claimed the standard deduction will switch to itemizing after purchasing a home (because of the mortgage interest and property tax deductions). In other circumstances, the reverse could be true—the taxpayer will switch from itemizing to the standard deduction. As illustrated in the next example, age can make a difference.

Prior to 2016, Sara, who is single, had always chosen to itemize. In 2016, however, she reaches age 65. Her itemized deductions for 2016 are $6,500, but her total standard deduction is $7,850 [$6,300 (basic standard deduction) + $1,550 (additional standard deduction)].

Sara should compute her taxable income for 2016 using the standard deduction ($7,850), because it exceeds her itemized deductions ($6,500).

3-2b Individuals Not Eligible for the Standard Deduction

Some individuals are not allowed to use the standard deduction. The following individual taxpayers must itemize:[9]

- A married individual filing a separate return where either spouse itemizes deductions.
- A nonresident alien (an individual who is neither a U.S. citizen nor a U.S. resident).

The death of an individual does not eliminate the standard deduction for the year of death; nor does the deduction have to be allocated to the pre-death portion of the year. If, for example, Sandy (age 80 and single) died on January 14, 2016, his executor would be able to claim a standard deduction of $7,850 [$6,300 (basic standard deduction) + $1,550 (additional standard deduction for age)] on his final income tax return (covering the period from January 1 to January 14, 2016). This presumes, of course, that the standard deduction is preferable to itemizing.

3-2c Special Limitations on the Standard Deduction for Dependents

Special rules apply to the standard deduction and personal exemption of an individual who can be claimed as a dependent on another person's tax return.

When filing his or her own tax return, a *dependent's* basic standard deduction in 2016 is limited to the greater of $1,050 or the sum of the individual's earned income for the year plus $350.[10] However, if the sum of the individual's earned income plus $350 exceeds the normal standard deduction, the standard deduction is limited to the appropriate amount shown in Exhibit 3.4. These limitations apply only to the basic standard deduction. A dependent who is 65 or over or blind or both is also allowed the

---

[9]§ 63(c)(6); also ineligible is an individual filing a return for a period of less than 12 months because of a change in the annual accounting period.

[10]§ 63(c)(5). Both the $1,050 amount and the $350 amount are subject to adjustment for inflation each year. In 2015, the amounts were $1,050 and $350; in 2014, the amounts were $1,000 and $350.

additional standard deduction amount on his or her own return (refer to Exhibit 3.5). These provisions are illustrated in Examples 8 through 11.

Dependent Standard Deduction

Susan, who is 17 years old and single, is claimed as a dependent on her parents' tax return. During 2016, she received $1,200 interest (unearned income) on a savings account. She also earned $400 from a part-time job. When Susan files her own tax return, her standard deduction is $1,050 [the greater of $1,050 or $750 (the sum of earned income of $400 plus $350)].

EXAMPLE
8

Assume the same facts as in Example 8, except that Susan is 67 years old and is claimed as a dependent on her son's tax return. In this case, when Susan files her own tax return, her standard deduction is $2,600 [$1,050 (see Example 8) + $1,550 (the additional standard deduction allowed because Susan is 65 or over)].

EXAMPLE
9

Peggy, who is 16 years old and single, earned $800 from a summer job and had no unearned income during 2016. She is claimed as a dependent on her parents' tax return. Her standard deduction is $1,150 [the greater of $1,050 or $1,150 (the sum of $800 earned income plus $350)].

EXAMPLE
10

Jack, who is a 20-year-old, single, full-time college student, is claimed as a dependent on his parents' tax return. He worked as a musician during the summer of 2016, earning $6,500. Jack's standard deduction is $6,300 [the greater of $1,050 or $6,300 (the sum of $6,500 earned income plus $350, but limited to the $6,300 standard deduction for a single taxpayer)].

EXAMPLE
11

3-3 PERSONAL EXEMPTIONS

LO.3

Apply the rules for arriving at personal exemptions.

The use of exemptions in the tax system is based in part on the idea that a taxpayer with a small amount of income should be exempt from income taxation. An exemption frees a specified amount of income from tax ($4,050 in 2016 and $4,000 in 2015). The exemption amount is adjusted (i.e., indexed) annually for inflation.

Exemptions that are allowed for the taxpayer and spouse are designated as **personal exemptions**. Those exemptions allowed for the care and maintenance of other persons are called dependency exemptions and are discussed in the next section.

An individual cannot claim a personal exemption if he or she is claimed as a dependent by another.

Assume the same facts as in Example 11. On his own income tax return,[11] Jack's taxable income is determined as follows:

Gross income	$ 6,500
Less: Standard deduction	(6,300)
Personal exemption	(–0–)
Taxable income	$ 200

EXAMPLE
12

Note that Jack is not allowed a personal exemption because he is claimed as a dependent by his parents.

When a married couple files a joint return, they may claim two personal exemptions. However, when separate returns are filed, a married taxpayer cannot claim an

---

[11]As noted on p. 3-26 (Filing Requirements for Dependents), Jack will be required to file an income tax return.

exemption for his or her spouse *unless* the spouse has no gross income and is not claimed as the dependent of another taxpayer.[12]

The determination of marital status generally is made at the end of the taxable year, except when a spouse dies during the year. Spouses who enter into a legal separation under a decree of divorce or separate maintenance before the end of the year are considered to be unmarried at the end of the taxable year.

The amount of the exemption is not reduced due to the taxpayer's death. The same rule applies to dependency exemptions. As long as an individual qualified as a dependent at the time of death, the full amount of the exemption can be claimed.

LO.4

Explain the rules for determining dependency exemptions.

3-4 DEPENDENCY EXEMPTIONS

As is the case with personal exemptions, a taxpayer is permitted to claim an exemption of $4,050 in 2016 ($4,000 in 2015) for each person who qualifies as a dependent. A **dependency exemption** is available for either a qualifying child or a qualifying relative and must not run afoul of certain other rules (i.e., joint return or nonresident alien prohibitions).

3-4a Qualifying Child

In the interest of uniformity and simplicity, Congress has tried to establish a uniform definition of a qualifying child. The qualifying child definition applies to the following tax provisions:

- Dependency exemption.
- Head-of-household filing status.
- Earned income tax credit.
- Child tax credit.
- Credit for child and dependent care expenses.

A **qualifying child** must meet the relationship, abode, age, and support tests.[13] For dependency exemption purposes, a qualifying child must also satisfy the joint return test and the citizenship or residency test.

Relationship Test

The relationship test includes a taxpayer's child (son or daughter), adopted child, stepchild, eligible foster child, brother, sister, half brother, half sister, stepbrother, stepsister, or a *descendant* of any of these parties (e.g., grandchild, nephew, niece). Note that *ancestors* of any of these parties (e.g., uncles and aunts) and in-laws (e.g., son-in-law and brother-in-law) *are not included*.

An adopted child includes a child lawfully placed with the taxpayer for legal adoption even though the adoption is not final. An eligible foster child is a child who is placed with the taxpayer by an authorized placement agency or by a court order.

EXAMPLE 13

Maureen's household includes her mother, grandson, stepbrother, stepbrother's daughter, uncle, and sister. All meet the relationship test for a qualifying child except the mother and uncle.

Abode Test

A qualifying child must live with the taxpayer for more than half of the year. For this purpose, temporary absences (e.g., school, vacation, medical care, military service,

---

[12]§ 151(b).   [13]§ 152(c).

detention in a juvenile facility) are disregarded. Special rules apply in the case of certain kidnapped children.[14]

Age Test

A qualifying child must, by the end of the tax year, be under age 19 or under age 24 in the case of a student. A student is a child who, during any part of five months of the year, is enrolled full-time at a school or government-sponsored on-farm training course.[15] The age test does not apply to a child who is disabled during any part of the year.[16] Also, an individual cannot be older than the taxpayer claiming him or her as a qualifying child (e.g., a brother cannot claim his older sister as a qualifying child).

The Big Picture

EXAMPLE 14

Return to the facts of *The Big Picture* on p. 3-1. Does Paige meet the requirements of a qualifying child as to Polly? Paige satisfies the relationship and abode tests, but the answer to the age test remains unclear. Because she is not a full-time student or disabled, she must be under 19 to meet the age test.

Support Test

To be a qualifying child, the individual must not be self-supporting (i.e., provide more than one-half of his or her own support). In the case of a child who is a full-time student, scholarships are not considered to be support.[17]

EXAMPLE 15

Shawn, age 23, is a full-time student and lives with his parents and an older cousin. During 2016, Shawn receives his support from the following sources: 30% from a part-time job, 30% from a scholarship, 20% from his parents, and 20% from the cousin.

Shawn is not self-supporting and can be claimed by his parents as a dependent even though his parents contribute only 20% of his support. (Note: Shawn cannot be a qualifying child as to his cousin due to the relationship test.)

Tiebreaker Rules

In some situations, a child may be a qualifying child to more than one person. In this event, the tax law specifies which person has priority in claiming the dependency exemption.[18] Called "tiebreaker rules," these rules are summarized in Concept Summary 3.2 and are illustrated in the examples that follow.

Concept Summary 3.2

Tiebreaker Rules for Claiming Qualified Child

Persons Eligible to Claim Exemption	Person Prevailing
One of the persons is the parent.	Parent
Both persons are the parents, and the child lives longer with one parent.	Parent with the longer period of residence
Both persons are the parents, and the child lives with each the same period of time.	Parent with the higher adjusted gross income (AGI)
None of the persons is the parent.	Person with highest AGI

---

[14]§ 152(f)(6).

[15]§ 152(f)(2).

[16]Within the meaning of § 22(e)(3). See the discussion of the credit for the elderly or disabled in Chapter 13.

[17]§ 152(f)(5).

[18]§ 152(c)(4).

ETHICS & EQUITY   Whose Qualifying Child Is He?

The Rands are successful professionals and have combined AGI of approximately $400,000. Their household includes two children: Henry (age 16) and Belinda (age 22). Belinda is not a student and has a job where she earns $15,000 a year. After a short family meeting in early April 2016, the parties decide that Belinda should claim Henry as her qualifying child. As a result, Belinda is able to deduct a full dependency exemption and claim a child tax credit and an earned income tax credit for a tax savings of more than $3,000. Had the Rands claimed Henry on their joint return, no child tax credit or earned income credit would have been available. As noted in Chapter 13, these credits are phased out for higher-bracket taxpayers. Further, only a partial dependency exemption would have been allowed. Has the Rand family acted properly?

Qualified Child—Tiebreaker Rules

EXAMPLE 16

Tim, age 15, lives in the same household with his mother and grandmother. As the parent, the mother has priority as to the dependency exemption.

EXAMPLE 17

Jennifer, age 17, lives in the same household with her parents during the entire year. If her parents file separate returns, the one with the higher AGI has priority as to the dependency exemption.

EXAMPLE 18

Assume the same facts as in Example 17, except that the father moves into an apartment in November (Jennifer remains with her mother). The mother has priority as to the dependency exemption (see Concept Summary 3.2).

3-4b Qualifying Relative

In addition to the category of a qualifying child, there is a second category of dependency exemption designated as the **qualifying relative** .

A qualifying relative must meet the relationship, gross income, and support tests.[19] As in the case of the qualifying child category, qualifying relative status also requires that the joint return and nonresident alien restrictions be avoided (see Other Rules for Dependency Exemptions later in the chapter).

Relationship Test

The relationship test for a qualifying relative is more expansive than for a qualifying child. Also included are the following relatives:

- Lineal ascendants (e.g., parents and grandparents).
- Collateral ascendants (e.g., uncles and aunts).
- Certain in-laws (e.g., son-, daughter-, father-, mother-, brother-, and sister-in-law).[20]

Children who do not satisfy the qualifying child definition may meet the qualifying relative criteria.

The relationship test also includes individuals who are "members of the household" (i.e., live with the taxpayer for the entire year). These individuals can be related or unrelated. For example, cousins are not "qualifying relatives" (cousins are not included in the list above). But a cousin can meet the relationship test if he or she is a "member of the household." Member-of-the-household status is not available for anyone whose

---

[19]§ 152(d).

[20]Once established by marriage, in-law status continues to exist and survives divorce.

relationship with the taxpayer violates local law or anyone who was a spouse during any part of the year.[21] However, an ex-spouse can qualify as a member of the household in a year following that of the divorce.

As the relationship test indicates, the category designation of "qualifying relative" is somewhat misleading, as persons other than relatives can qualify as dependents. And, not all relatives will qualify (although relatives that are not listed could be a "member of the household").

The Big Picture

Return to the facts of *The Big Picture* on p. 3-1. Although Maude is unrelated to Polly, she qualifies as Polly's dependent by being a member of the household. Because Maude is a dependent, Polly can also claim the medical expenses she paid on Maude's behalf. The funeral expenses are not deductible. Although Maude lived for only two months, the full amount of the dependency exemption is allowed and does not have to be apportioned.

EXAMPLE 19

Gross Income Test

A dependent's gross income must be *less* than the exemption amount—$4,050 in 2016 and $4,000 in 2015. Gross income is determined by the income that is taxable. In the case of scholarships, for example, include the taxable portion (e.g., amounts received for room and board) and exclude the nontaxable portion (e.g., amounts received for books and tuition).

Gross Income Test

Elsie provides more than half of the support of her son, Tom, who does not live with her. Tom, age 26, is a full-time student in medical school, earns $3,000 from a part-time job, and receives a $12,000 scholarship covering his tuition.

Elsie may claim Tom as a dependent because he meets the gross income test and is a qualifying relative. (Note: Tom is *not* a qualifying child; he fails both the abode and the age test.)

EXAMPLE 20

Aaron provides more than half of the support of his widowed aunt, Myrtle, who does not live with him. Myrtle's income for the year is as follows: dividend income of $1,100, earnings from pet sitting of $1,200, nontaxable Social Security benefits of $6,000, and nontaxable interest from City of Milwaukee bonds of $8,000.

Because Myrtle's gross income is only $2,300 ($1,100 + $1,200), she meets the gross income test and can be claimed as Aaron's dependent.

EXAMPLE 21

The Big Picture

Return to the facts of *The Big Picture* on p. 3-1. Assuming that Paige is not a qualifying child (see Example 14), can she be a qualifying relative for dependency exemption purposes? She meets the relationship and support tests, but what about the gross income test?

If her income from her part-time job is less than $4,050 (the 2016 exemption amount), she does qualify and can be claimed by Polly as a dependent.

EXAMPLE 22

Support Test

Over one-half of the support of the qualifying relative must be furnished by the taxpayer. Support includes food, shelter, clothing, toys, medical and dental care, education, and the like.[22] However, a scholarship (both taxable and nontaxable portions) received

---

[21]§§ 152(d)(2)(H) and (f)(3).

[22]A worksheet for determining support is provided in IRS Publication 501 (*Exemptions, Standard Deduction, and Filing Information*).

by a student is not included for purposes of computing whether the taxpayer furnished more than half of the child's support.

EXAMPLE 23

Hal contributed $3,400 (consisting of food, clothing, and medical care) toward the support of his nephew, Sam, who lives with him. Sam earned $1,300 from a part-time job and received $2,000 from a student loan to attend a local university. Assuming that the other dependency tests are met, Hal can claim Sam as a dependent because Hal has contributed more than half of Sam's support.

If the individual does not spend funds that have been received from any source, the unexpended amounts are not counted for purposes of the support test.

EXAMPLE 24

Emily contributed $3,000 to her father's support during the year. In addition, her father received $2,400 in Social Security benefits, $200 of interest, and wages of $600. Her father deposited the Social Security benefits, interest, and wages in his own savings account and did not use any of the funds for his support. Thus, the Social Security benefits, interest, and wages are not considered as support provided by Emily's father. Emily may claim her father as a dependent if the other tests are met.

An individual's own funds, however, must be taken into account if applied toward support. In this regard, the source of the funds so used is not relevant.

EXAMPLE 25

Frank contributes $8,000 toward his parents' total support of $20,000. The parents, who do not live with Frank, obtain the other $12,000 from savings and a home equity loan on their residence. Although the parents have no income, their use of savings and borrowed funds are counted as part of their support. Because Frank does not satisfy the support test, he cannot claim his parents as dependents.

Capital expenditures for items such as furniture, appliances, and automobiles are included in total support if the item does, in fact, constitute support.

EXAMPLE 26

Norm purchased a television set costing $950 and gave it to his mother who lives with him. The television set was placed in the mother's bedroom and was used exclusively by her. Norm should include the cost of the television set in determining the support of his mother.

Multiple Support Agreements An exception to the support test involves a **multiple support agreement** . A multiple support agreement permits one of a group of taxpayers who furnish support for a qualifying relative to claim a dependency exemption for that individual even if no one person provides more than 50 percent of the support.[23] The group together must provide more than 50 percent of the support. Any person who contributed *more than 10 percent* of the support is entitled to claim the exemption if each person in the group who contributed more than 10 percent files a written consent. This provision frequently enables one of the children of aged dependent parents to claim an exemption when none of the children meet the 50 percent support test.

Each person who is a party to the multiple support agreement must meet all other requirements (except the support requirement) for claiming the exemption. A person who does not meet the relationship or member-of-the-household requirement, for instance, cannot claim the dependency exemption under a multiple support agreement. It does not matter if he or she contributes more than 10 percent of the individual's support.

---

[23]§ 152(d)(3).

Wanda, who resides with her son, Adam, received $12,000 from various sources during the year. This constituted her entire support for the year. She received support from the following:

EXAMPLE

27

	Amount	Percentage of Total
Adam, a son	$ 5,760	48%
Bob, a son	1,200	10
Carol, a daughter	3,600	30
Diane, a friend	1,440	12
	$12,000	100%

If Adam and Carol file a multiple support agreement, either may claim the dependency exemption for Wanda. Bob may not claim Wanda because he did not contribute *more than 10%* of her support. Bob's consent is not required for Adam and Carol to file a multiple support agreement. Diane does not meet the relationship or member-of-the-household test and cannot be a party to the agreement. The decision as to who claims Wanda rests with Adam and Carol. It is possible for Carol to claim Wanda, even though Adam furnished more of Wanda's support.

The individual claiming the exemption must complete Form 2120 (Multiple Support Declaration) and file it with his or her tax return. In addition, each person who qualifies under the more-than-10% rule (except for the person claiming the exemption) must submit a signed statement waiving his or her right to the exemption to the person who is claiming the exemption.

ETHICS & EQUITY   **Discovering Lost Dependency Exemptions**

For the six years prior to his death in late 2016, Jesse lived with his daughter, Hannah. Because he had no source of income, Jesse was supported by equal contributions from Hannah and his two sons, Bill and Bob. At Jesse's funeral, his surviving children are amazed to discover that none of them has been claiming Jesse as a dependent. Upon the advice of the director of the funeral home, they decide to divide among themselves the dependency exemptions for the past six years. Multiple Forms 2120 are executed, and each of the three children files amended returns for different past years. As Jesse died before the end of the current year, no deduction is planned for 2016.

Comment on the tax expectations of the parties involved.

Children of Divorced or Separated Parents Another exception to the support test applies when parents with children are divorced or separated under a decree of separate maintenance. For unmarried parents, living apart (for the last six months of the year) will suffice. Special rules apply if the parents meet the following conditions:

- They would have been entitled to the dependency exemption(s) had they been married and filed a joint return.
- They have custody (either jointly or singly) of the child (or children) for more than half of the year.

Under the general rule, the parent having custody of the child (children) for the greater part of the year (i.e., the custodial parent) is entitled to the dependency exemption(s).[24] The general rule does not apply if a multiple support agreement is in effect. It also does not apply if the custodial parent signs a waiver in favor of the noncustodial parent.[25]

---

[24]Reg. § 1.152–4.

[25]§§ 152(e)(2) and (5).

The waiver, Form 8332 (Release/Revocation of Release of Claim to Exemption for Child by Custodial Parent), can apply to a single year, a number of specified years, or all future years. The noncustodial parent must attach a Form 8332 to his or her return.

3-4c Other Rules for Dependency Exemptions

In addition to fitting into either the qualifying child or the qualifying relative category, a dependent must meet the joint return and the citizenship or residency tests.

Joint Return Test

If a dependent is married, the supporting taxpayer (e.g., the parent of a married child) generally is not permitted a dependency exemption if the married individual files a joint return with his or her spouse.[26] The joint return rule does not apply, however, if the following conditions are met:

- The reason for filing is to claim a refund for tax withheld.
- No tax liability would exist for either spouse on separate returns.
- Neither spouse is required to file a return (tested using the married, filing separately rules).

See Exhibit 3.6 later in the chapter and the related discussion concerning income level requirements for filing a return.

EXAMPLE 28

Paul provides over half of the support of his son, Quinn. He also provides over half of the support of Vera, who is Quinn's wife. During the year, both Quinn and Vera had part-time jobs. To recover the taxes withheld, they file a joint return. If Quinn and Vera are not required to file a return, Paul is allowed to claim both as dependents.

Citizenship or Residency Test

To be a dependent, the individual must be a U.S. citizen, a U.S. resident, or a resident of Canada or Mexico for some part of the calendar year in which the taxpayer's tax year begins.[27]

Under an exception, an adopted child need not be a citizen or resident of the United States (or a contiguous country) as long as his or her principal abode is with a U.S. citizen.

EXAMPLE 29

Esther is a U.S. citizen who lives and works in Spain. She has adopted Benito, a 4-year-old Italian national, who lives with her and is a member of her household.

Although Benito does not meet the usual citizenship or residency test, he is covered by the exception. Benito is a qualifying child, and Esther can claim him as a dependent.

3-4d Comparison of Categories for Dependency Exemptions

Concept Summary 3.3 identifies the tests for the two categories of dependency exemptions. In contrasting the two categories, the following observations are in order:

- As to the relationship tests, the qualifying relative category is considerably more expansive. Besides including those prescribed under the qualifying child grouping, other relatives are added. Nonrelated persons who are members of the household are also included.

---

[26]§ 152(b)(2).

[27]§ 152(b)(3).

- The support tests are entirely different. In the case of a qualifying child, support is not necessary. What is required is that the child not be self-supporting.
- The qualifying child category has no gross income limitation, whereas the qualifying relative category has no age restriction.

Concept Summary 3.3

Tests for Dependency Exemption

Test	Qualifying Child	Qualifying Relative
Relationship:		
• Children (natural, step, or adopted) and their *descendants*, and siblings and stepsiblings and their *descendants*.	X	
• Children (natural, step, or adopted) and their *descendants*, siblings and their children, parents and their *ascendants*, uncles and aunts, stepparents and stepsiblings, and certain in-laws.		X
• Member of the household (live with taxpayer for *entire* year; relative or non-relative)		X
Abode	X	
Age	X	
Support:		
• Not self-supporting ("child" furnishes one-half or less of his or her support)	X	
• Taxpayer furnishes over one-half of the support of potential dependent		X
Gross income *less* than the exemption amount		X
Joint return (potential dependent cannot file joint return)	X	X
Citizenship or residency (potential dependent must meet test)	X	X

3-4e Phaseout of Exemptions

Several provisions of the tax law are intended to increase the tax liability of more affluent taxpayers who might otherwise enjoy some benefit of certain deductions and credits. One such provision phases out certain itemized deductions and is discussed in Chapter 10. Another provision phases out personal and dependency exemptions.[28] The exemption phaseout occurs as AGI exceeds specified threshold amounts (indexed annually for inflation). The phaseout begins when AGI exceeds the following amounts:

Filing Status	2015	2016
Married, filing jointly	$309,900	$311,300
Head of household	284,050	285,350
Single	258,250	259,400
Married, filing separately	154,950	155,650

---

[28]§ 151(d)(3).

TAX IN THE NEWS How to Subtly Pluck the Chicken

No government likes to admit that it is enacting new taxes or even raising the rates on existing taxes. Needless to say, this is particularly true of the U.S. Congress. But there are more subtle ways to raise revenue (or to curtail revenue loss). The most popular way is to use a so-called *stealth tax*. A stealth tax is not really a tax at all. Instead, it is a means of reducing the benefits of certain tax provisions to higher-income taxpayers.

The heart and soul of the stealth tax is the phaseout approach. As income increases, the tax benefit thought to be derived from a particular provision decreases. Because the phaseout usually is gradual and not drastic, many affected taxpayers are unaware of what has happened.

The tax law is rampant with phaseouts. The two most prominent phaseouts limit the deductibility of personal and dependency exemptions (discussed in this chapter) and itemized deductions (discussed in Chapter 10). In addition to these, here are some other examples of these stealth taxes, along with where each is discussed in the text:

- Earned income credit (Chapter 13).
- Spousal IRA deduction (Chapter 19).
- Child tax credit (Chapter 13).
- College tuition deduction (Chapter 9).
- Interest deduction on student loans (Chapter 10).
- American Opportunity college credit (Chapter 13).
- Social Security benefits (Chapter 4).
- Premium tax credit (Chapter 13).

Exemptions (both personal and dependency) are phased out by 2 percent for each $2,500 (or fraction thereof) by which the taxpayer's AGI exceeds the threshold amounts. For a married taxpayer filing separately, the phaseout is 2 percent for each $1,250 (or fraction thereof). The allowable exemption amount can be determined with the following steps:

1. AGI − threshold amount = excess amount.
2. Excess amount ÷ $2,500 = reduction factor [rounded up to the next whole number (e.g., 18.1 = 19)] × 2 = phaseout percentage.
3. Phaseout percentage × exemption amount = phaseout amount.
4. Exemption amount − phaseout amount = allowable exemption deduction.

EXAMPLE 30

Brad files as a single individual in 2016. His AGI is $292,050. He is entitled to one personal exemption. Brad's allowable exemption amount is determined as follows:

1. $292,050 − $259,400 = $32,650 excess amount.
2. [($32,650 ÷ $2,500) = 13.06; rounded to 14]; 14 × 2 = 28% (phaseout percentage).
3. 28% × $4,050 = $1,134 phaseout amount.
4. $4,050 − $1,134 = $2,916 allowable exemption deduction.

Note that the exemption amount is completely phased out when the taxpayer's AGI exceeds the threshold amount by more than $122,500 ($61,250 for a married taxpayer filing a separate return). With an excess amount of $122,501, the phaseout percentage is 100 percent, calculated as follows:

$$\$122,501 \div \$2,500 = 49.0004, \text{ rounded to 50 and multiplied by } 2 = 100\%$$

EXAMPLE 31

Bill and Carol file a joint return in 2016 claiming two personal exemptions and two dependency exemptions for their children. Their AGI equals $443,500.

$$\$443,450 − \$311,300 = \$132,150 \text{ excess amount}$$

Since the excess amount exceeds $122,500, their exemptions are completely phased out. The loss of the full deduction for personal and dependency exemptions effectively increases Bill and Carol's tax liability by increasing their tax base—taxable income—rather than their tax rate. This is why phaseouts are sometimes referred to as "stealth taxes."

3-4f Child Tax Credit

In addition to providing a dependency exemption, a taxpayer's child may also provide a child tax credit . A $1,000 credit is allowed for each dependent child (including step-children and eligible foster children) under the age of 17.[29] For a more complete discussion of the child tax credit, see Chapter 13.

3-5 FILING STATUS AND FILING REQUIREMENTS

Once taxable income has been ascertained, a two-step process is used in determining income tax due (or refund available). First, the taxpayer's filing status must be determined and then whether a tax return must be filed. Second, the tax has to be computed and adjusted for available tax credits—see Concept Summary 3.1 and the tax formula. This section deals with filing status and filing requirements. Text Section 3-6 covers the tax computation procedures. Text Section 3-7 covers tax return filing procedures (including selecting the right form and determining when and how the tax return should be filed).

LO.5

Choose the proper filing status and identify the related filing requirements.

3-5a Filing Status

Every year, taxpayers must determine their filing status . The taxpayer's filing status is used to determine:

- The taxpayer's standard deduction;
- Whether the taxpayer must file a tax return;
- The taxpayer's tax liability;
- Reductions of exemptions, itemized deductions, and certain tax credits; and
- Eligibility for certain provisions (e.g., some credits are not available when the married, filing separately status is used).

There are five filing statuses, and all taxpayers will file a return based on the filing status selected.

- Single
- Married, filing jointly
- Married, filing separately
- Surviving spouse (qualifying widow or widower)
- Head of household

The amount of tax will vary considerably depending on which filing status is used. Consider the following example.

EXAMPLE

32

The following amounts of tax are computed using the 2016 Tax Rate Schedules for a taxpayer (or taxpayers in the case of a joint return) with $60,000 of taxable income (see Appendix A).

Filing Status	Amount of Tax
Single	$10,771
Married, filing jointly	8,073
Married, filing separately	10,771
Head of household	9,298

Besides the effect on the tax rates that will apply, filing status also has an impact on the amount of the standard deduction that is allowed—see Exhibits 3.4 and 3.5 earlier in the chapter.

---

[29]§ 24(a).

GLOBAL TAX ISSUES **Filing a Joint Return**

John Garth is a U.S. citizen and resident, but he spends much of his time in London, where his employer sends him on frequent assignments. John is married to Victoria, a citizen and resident of the United Kingdom.

Can John and Victoria file a joint return for U.S. Federal income tax purposes? Although § 6013(a)(1) specifically precludes the filing of a joint return if one spouse is a nonresident alien, another Code provision permits an exception. Under § 6013(g), the parties can elect to treat the nonqualifying spouse as a "resident" of the United States. This election would allow John and Victoria to file jointly.

But should John and Victoria make this election? If Victoria has considerable income of her own (from non-U.S. sources), the election could be ill-advised. As a nonresident alien, Victoria's non-U.S. source income *would not* be subject to the U.S. income tax. If she is treated as a U.S. resident, however, her non-U.S. source income *will be subject to U.S. tax.* Under the U.S. global approach to taxation, all income (regardless of where earned) of anyone who is a *resident* or *citizen* of the United States is subject to tax.

Single Taxpayers

A taxpayer who is unmarried or separated from his or her spouse by a decree of divorce or separate maintenance and does not qualify for another filing status must use the rates for single taxpayers. Marital status is determined as of the last day of the tax year, except when a spouse dies during the year. In that case, marital status is determined as of the date of death.

Married Individuals

The joint return [Tax Rate Schedule Y, Code § 1(a)] was originally enacted in 1948 to establish equity between married taxpayers in common law states and those in community property states. Before the joint return rates were enacted, taxpayers in community property states were in an advantageous position relative to taxpayers in common law states because they could split their income. For instance, in a community property state, if one spouse earned $100,000 and the other spouse was not employed, each spouse could report $50,000 of income. Splitting the income in this manner caused the total income to be subject to lower marginal tax rates. Each spouse would start at the bottom of the rate structure.

Taxpayers in common law states did not have this income-splitting option, so their taxable income was subject to higher marginal rates. This inconsistency in treatment was remedied by the joint return provisions. The progressive rates in the joint return Tax Rate Schedule are constructed based on the assumption that income is earned equally by the two spouses.

A legally married same-sex couple is treated as married for Federal tax purposes no matter where they live. Registered domestic partners, however, are not "spouses" under Federal law. Therefore, they cannot file Federal tax returns using married filing jointly or married filing separately status. The same rule applies to same-sex partners in civil unions.[30]

If married individuals elect to file separate returns, each reports only his or her own income, exemptions, deductions, and credits, and each must use the Tax Rate Schedule applicable to married taxpayers filing separately. In a community property state, each individual must report his or her half of the community property income.[31] It is generally advantageous for married individuals to file a joint return, because the combined amount of tax is lower. However, special circumstances (e.g., significant medical expenses incurred by one spouse subject to the 10 percent limitation) may

---

[30]Rev.Rul. 2013–17, 2013–38 I.R.B. 201 and *U.S. v. Windsor*, 111 AFTR 2d 2013–2385, 133 S.Ct. 2675; **www.irs.gov/uac/Answers-to-Frequently-Asked-Questions-for-Registered-Domestic-Partners-and-Individuals-in-Civil-Unions**.

[31]Form 8958 (Allocation of Tax Amounts Between Certain Individuals in Community Property States) is used for this purpose.

In *U.S. v. Windsor*, the Supreme Court struck down portions of the Defense of Marriage Act. Specifically, this decision invalidated a Federal definition of marriage as between one man and one woman. Guidance from the IRS (Rev.Rul. 2013–17) provides that a same-sex couple possessing a marriage license from any U.S. state or other jurisdiction will be considered married for Federal income tax purposes (no matter where they live). However, this interpretation of marriage does not extend to "domestic partnerships" or "civil unions." Couples in these relationships are still regarded as *single* by the IRS.

As far as income taxes are concerned, have these rules resolved the prior difficulties of same-sex couples? The answer depends on where they live and whether such location imposes an income tax. Consider the following possibilities as to residence.

1. No state or local income taxes imposed.
2. State and local income taxes imposed and jurisdiction recognizes same-sex marriages.
3. State and local income taxes imposed but jurisdiction does not recognize same-sex marriages.

Category (1) was never a problem and Category (2) was resolved via *U.S. v. Windsor*. Thus, the filing status used for state and local purposes (e.g., married filing jointly) will also be available for Federal purposes. With the 2015 Supreme Court decision in *Obergefell v. Hodges* (135 S.Ct. 2584), Category (3) has been resolved as each state must now accept same-sex marriages (no matter where licensed).

However, challenges remain for persons in a domestic partnership or civil union. They could be treated as married for state purposes but single for Federal tax law.

---

warrant the election to file separate returns. It may be necessary to compute the tax under both assumptions to determine the most advantageous filing status.

The Internal Revenue Code places some limitations on married persons who file separate returns. Here are some examples:

- If either spouse itemizes deductions, the other spouse must also itemize.
- The earned income credit and the credit for child and dependent care expenses cannot be claimed (see Chapter 13).
- No deduction is allowed for interest paid on qualified education loans (see Chapter 10).
- Only $1,500 of excess capital losses can be claimed by each spouse (see Chapter 16).

In these cases, being single would be preferable to being married and filing separately.

Filing a joint return carries the potential disadvantage of joint and several liability.[32] This means that the IRS can pursue the collection of the tax due for that year against either spouse.

Once a joint return has been filed and the due date has passed, the spouses cannot switch to separate returns for that year. However, if married persons file separately, they can change later to a joint return.

Marriage Penalty When Congress enacted the rate structure available to those filing joint returns, it generally favored married taxpayers. In certain situations, however, the parties would incur less tax if they were not married and filed separate returns. The additional tax that a joint return caused, commonly called the **marriage penalty**, usually developed when *both* spouses had large taxable incomes. Long aware of the inequity of the marriage penalty, Congress reduced (but did not eliminate) the effect of the problem for some couples by increasing the standard deduction available to married filers to 200 percent of that applicable to single persons and increasing the 15 percent bracket for joint filers to 200 percent of the size of that bracket applicable to single filers. However, the marriage penalty still exists for couples who itemize their deductions and have substantial amounts of income beyond the 15 percent tax bracket.

---

[32]§ 6013(d)(3).

Surviving Spouse The joint return rates also apply for two years following the death of one spouse if the surviving spouse maintains a household for a dependent child. The child must be a son, stepson, daughter, or stepdaughter who qualifies as a dependent of the taxpayer. This is referred to as **surviving spouse** status.[33]

Fred dies in 2015, leaving Ethel with a dependent child. For the year of Fred's death (2015), Ethel files a joint return with Fred (presuming that the consent of Fred's executor is obtained). For the next two years (2016 and 2017), Ethel, as a surviving spouse, may use the joint return rates. In subsequent years, Ethel may use the head-of-household rates if she continues to maintain a household as her home that is the domicile of the child.

Keep in mind, however, that for the year of death, the surviving spouse is treated as being married. Thus, a joint return can be filed if the deceased spouse's executor agrees. If not, the surviving spouse is forced into the status of married, filing separately.

Head of Household

Unmarried individuals who maintain a household for a dependent (or dependents) are generally entitled to use the **head-of-household** rates.[34] The tax liability using the head-of-household rates falls between the liability using the joint return Tax Rate Schedule and the liability using the Tax Rate Schedule for single taxpayers.

To qualify for head-of-household rates, a taxpayer must pay more than half the cost of maintaining a household as his or her home. The household must also be the principal home of a dependent. Except for temporary absences (e.g., school, hospitalization), the dependent must live in the taxpayer's household for over half the year.

A dependent must be either a qualifying child or a qualifying relative who meets the relationship test (other than a member-of-the-household test).

The Big Picture

Return to the facts of *The Big Picture* on p. 3-1. Assuming that Polly can be treated as single (i.e., not married), can Maude qualify Polly for head-of-household filing status? The answer is no. Even though Maude can be claimed as Polly's dependent (see Example 19), she does not meet the relationship test.

Emma, a widow, maintains a household in which she and her aunt live. If the aunt qualifies as a dependent, Emma may file as head of household. Note that an aunt meets the relationship test.

A special rule allows taxpayers to avoid having to live with their parents. Head-of-household status still may be claimed if the taxpayer maintains a *separate home* for his or her *parent or parents* if at least one parent qualifies as a dependent of the taxpayer.[35]

Rick, an unmarried individual, lives in New York City and maintains a household in Detroit for his dependent parents. Rick may use the head-of-household rates even though his parents do not reside in his New York home.

Head-of-household status is not changed during the year by the death of the dependent. As long as the taxpayer provided more than half of the cost of maintaining the household prior to the dependent's death, head-of-household status is preserved.

---

[33]§ 2(a). The IRS term for surviving spouse status is "qualifying widow(er) with dependent child."

[34]§ 2(b).

[35]§ 2(b)(1)(B).

Abandoned Spouse Rules

As discussed earlier, when married persons file separate returns, several unfavorable tax consequences result. For example, the taxpayer must use the Tax Rate Schedule for married taxpayers filing separately. To mitigate such harsh treatment for some taxpayers, Congress enacted provisions commonly referred to as the **abandoned spouse** rules. The IRS does not use the "abandoned spouse" terminology but considers the taxpayer to be treated as *not married* if the following conditions are satisfied:[36]

- The taxpayer does not file a joint return.
- The taxpayer paid more than one-half the cost of maintaining his or her home for the tax year.
- The taxpayer's spouse did not live in the home during the last six months of the tax year.
- The home was the principal residence of the taxpayer's son, daughter, stepson, stepdaughter, foster child, or adopted child for more than half the year, and the child can be claimed as a dependent.[37]

Thus, the net effect of being treated as unmarried and having the specified dependents is that the abandoned spouse qualifies for head-of-household filing status.

ETHICS & EQUITY Abandoned Spouse?

Bob and Carol have been in and out of marital counseling for the past few years. Early in 2016, they decide to separate. However, because they are barely able to get by on their current incomes, they cannot afford separate housing or the legal costs of a divorce. So Bob moves out of their house in March and takes up residence in their detached garage (which has an enclosed workshop and bathroom). Carol stays in the house with their two children and pays more than half of the costs of maintaining their residence. Bob does not enter the house for the remainder of the year. Can Carol qualify as an abandoned spouse?

The Big Picture

EXAMPLE 37

Return to the facts of *The Big Picture* on p. 3-1. Can Polly qualify as an abandoned spouse? Yes, if she can claim Paige as a dependent—either as a qualifying child (see Example 14) or as a qualifying relative (see Example 22). If so, Polly can use head-of-household filing status. If not, her filing status is married filing separately.

3-5b Filing Requirements

General Rules

An individual must file a tax return if certain minimum amounts of gross income have been received. The general rule is that a tax return is required for every individual who has gross income that equals or exceeds the sum of the exemption amount plus the applicable standard deduction. Because the exemption and standard deduction amounts are subject to an annual inflation adjustment, the gross income amounts for determining whether a tax return must be filed normally change each year.[38] For example, a single taxpayer under age 65 must file a tax return in 2016 if gross income equals or exceeds

---

[36]§ 7703(b).

[37]§ 152(f)(1). The dependency requirement does not apply, however, if the taxpayer could have claimed a dependency exemption except for the fact

that the exemption was claimed by the noncustodial parent under a written agreement.

[38]See §§ 1(f), 63(c)(4), and 151(d)(3).

EXHIBIT 3.6	Filing Requirements for Most Taxpayers	

Filing Status	2015 Gross Income	2016 Gross Income
Single		
Under 65	$10,300	$10,350
65 or older	11,850	11,900
Married, filing jointly		
Both spouses under 65	$20,600	$20,700
One spouse 65 or older	21,850	21,950
Both spouses 65 or older	23,100	23,200
Married, filing separately		
All	$ 4,000	$ 4,050
Head of household		
Under 65	$13,250	$13,350
65 or older	14,800	14,900
Qualifying widow(er)		
Under 65	$16,600	$16,650
65 or older	17,850	17,900

$10,350 ($4,050 exemption plus $6,300 standard deduction). Exhibit 3.6 lists the income levels[39] that require tax returns under the general rule and under certain special rules.

The additional standard deduction for being age 65 or older is considered in determining the gross income filing requirements. For example, note in Exhibit 3.6 that the 2016 filing requirement for a single taxpayer age 65 or older is $11,900 ($6,300 basic standard deduction + $1,550 additional standard deduction + $4,050 exemption). Except in the case of dependents, the additional standard deduction for blindness is not taken into account in determining whether a taxpayer must file a tax return (see Filing Requirements for Dependents below).

A self-employed individual with net earnings of $400 or more from a business or profession must file a tax return regardless of the amount of gross income.

Even though an individual has gross income below the filing level amounts and therefore does not owe any tax, he or she must file a return to obtain a tax refund of amounts withheld. A return is also necessary to obtain the benefits of the earned income credit allowed to taxpayers with little or no tax liability. Chapter 13 discusses the earned income credit.

Filing Requirements for Dependents

Computation of the gross income filing requirement for an individual who can be claimed as a dependent on another person's tax return is subject to more complex rules. Such an individual must file a return if he or she has *any* of the following:

- Earned income only and gross income that is more than the total standard deduction (including any additional standard deduction) the individual is allowed for the year.

- Unearned income only and gross income of more than $1,050 plus any additional standard deduction the individual is allowed for the year.

- Both earned and unearned income and gross income of more than the larger of $1,050 or the sum of earned income plus $350 (but limited to the applicable basic standard deduction) plus any additional standard deduction the individual is allowed for the year.

[39]§ 6012(a)(1).

Thus, the filing requirement for a dependent who has no unearned income is the total of the *basic* standard deduction plus any *additional* standard deduction, which includes *both* the additional deduction for blindness and the deduction for being age 65 or older. For example, the 2016 filing requirement for a single dependent who is under age 65 and not blind is $6,300, the amount of the basic standard deduction. The filing requirement for a single dependent under age 65 and blind is $7,850 ($6,300 basic standard deduction + $1,550 additional standard deduction).

3-6 TAX DETERMINATION

LO.6

Demonstrate the proper procedures for determining the tax liability.

The computation of income tax due (or refund) involves applying the proper set of tax rates to taxable income and then adjusting for available credits. In certain cases, however, the application of the kiddie tax will change how the tax is determined (see text Section 3-6c).

3-6a Tax Rates

The basic tax rate structure is progressive, with current rates ranging from 10 percent to 39.6 percent.[40] By way of comparison, the lowest rate structure, which was in effect in 1913–1915, ranged from 1 to 7 percent, and the highest, in effect during 1944–1945, ranged from 23 to 94 percent.

Tax Table Method

The tax liability is computed using either the Tax Table method or the Tax Rate Schedule method. Most taxpayers compute their tax using the **Tax Table**. Eligible taxpayers compute taxable income (as shown in Concept Summary 3.1) and *must* determine their tax by reference to the Tax Table. The following taxpayers, however, may not use the Tax Table method:

- Individuals whose taxable income exceeds the maximum (ceiling) amount in the Tax Table. The 2015 Tax Table applies to taxable income below $100,000 for Form 1040.

- An estate or a trust.

The IRS does not release the Tax Tables until late in the year to which they apply. However, the Tax Rate Schedules for any given year are released at the end of the preceding year. So, the 2016 Tax Tables will be available at the end of 2016. The 2016 Tax Rate Schedules, however, were released at the end of 2015.[41] For purposes of estimating tax liability and making quarterly prepayments, the Tax Rate Schedules usually need to be consulted. Based on its availability, the 2015 Tax Table is used to illustrate the tax computation using the Tax Table method.

Although the Tax Table is derived by using the Tax Rate Schedules (discussed next), the tax calculated using the two methods may vary slightly. This variation occurs because the tax for a particular income range in the Tax Table is based on the midpoint amount.

Linda is single and has taxable income of $30,000 for calendar year 2015. To determine Linda's tax using the Tax Table (see Appendix A), find the $30,000 to $30,050 income line. The tax of $4,043 is actually the tax the Tax Rate Schedule for 2015 would yield on taxable income of $30,025 (i.e., the midpoint amount between $30,000 and $30,050).

EXAMPLE

38

---

[40]The Tax Relief Reconciliation Act of 2001 as amended by the American Taxpayer Relief Act of 2012.

[41]Rev.Proc. 2015–53, 2015–44 I.R.B. 615. The 2015 Tax Tables and the 2016 and 2015 Tax Rate Schedules are reproduced in Appendix A. For

quick reference, the rate schedules are also reproduced inside the front cover of this text.

Tax Rate Schedule Method

Taxpayers who do not use the Tax Tables use the Tax Rate Schedules . The 2016 tax rate schedule for single taxpayers is reproduced in Exhibit 3.7.[42] This schedule is used to illustrate the tax computations in Examples 39 and 40.

EXAMPLE 39

Pat is single and had $5,870 of taxable income in 2016. His tax is $587 ($5,870 × 10%).

Several terms are used to describe tax rates. The rates in the Tax Rate Schedules are often referred to as *statutory* (or nominal) rates. The *marginal* rate is the tax rate that would be assessed on the next dollar of income for a particular taxpayer. In Example 39, the statutory rate and the marginal rate are both 10 percent.

EXAMPLE 40

Chris is single and had taxable income of $92,000 in 2016. Her tax is $18,796.75 [$18,558.75 + 28%($92,000 − $91,150)].

The *average* rate is equal to the tax liability divided by taxable income. In Example 40, Chris has statutory rates of 10 percent, 15 percent, 25 percent, and 28 percent and a marginal rate of 28 percent. Chris's average rate is 20.4 percent ($18,796.75 tax liability ÷ $92,000 taxable income).

A tax is *progressive* (or graduated) if a higher rate of tax applies as the tax base increases. The progressive nature of the Federal income tax on individuals is illustrated by computing the tax in Example 40 utilizing each rate bracket.

Tax on first $9,275 at 10%	$ 927.50
Tax on $37,650 − $9,275 at 15%	4,256.25
Tax on $91,150 − $37,650 at 25%	13,375.00
Tax on $92,000 − $91,150 at 28%	238.00
Total tax on taxable income of $92,000	$18,796.75

A special computation limits the effective tax rate on qualified dividends (see Chapter 4) and net long-term capital gain (see Chapter 16).

EXHIBIT 3.7	2016 Tax Rate Schedule for Single Taxpayers

If Taxable Income Is		The Tax Is:	Of the Amount Over
Over	**But Not Over**		
$ –0–	$ 9,275	10%	$ –0–
9,275	37,650	$ 927.50 + 15%	9,275
37,650	91,150	5,183.75 + 25%	37,650
91,150	190,150	18,558.75 + 28%	91,150
190,150	413,350	46,278.75 + 33%	190,150
413,350	415,050	119,934.75 + 35%	413,350
415,050		120,529.75 + 39.6%	415,050

---

[42]§ 1(i).

3-6b Computation of Net Taxes Payable or Refund Due

The pay-as-you-go feature of the Federal income tax system requires payment of all or part of the taxpayer's income tax liability during the year. These payments take the form of Federal income tax withheld by employers or estimated tax paid by the taxpayer or both.[43] The payments are applied against the tax from the Tax Table or Tax Rate Schedules to determine whether the taxpayer will get a refund or pay additional tax.

Employers are required to withhold income tax on compensation paid to their employees and to pay this tax to the government. The employer notifies the employee of the amount of income and income tax withheld on Form W–2 (Wage and Tax Statement). The employee should receive this form by January 31 after the year in which the income tax is withheld.

If taxpayers receive income that is not subject to withholding or income from which not enough tax is withheld, they may have to pay estimated tax. These individuals must file Form 1040–ES (Estimated Tax for Individuals) and pay in quarterly installments the income tax and self-employment tax estimated to be due (see Chapter 13 for a thorough discussion).

The income tax from the Tax Table or the Tax Rate Schedules is reduced first by the individual's tax credits. There is an important distinction between tax credits and tax deductions. Tax credits reduce the tax liability dollar for dollar. Tax deductions reduce taxable income on which the tax liability is based.

EXAMPLE 41

Gail is a taxpayer in the 25% tax bracket. As a result of incurring $1,000 in child care expenses (see Chapter 13 for details), she is entitled to a $200 child care credit ($1,000 child care expenses × 20% credit rate). She also contributed $1,000 to the American Cancer Society and included this amount in her itemized deductions.

The child care credit results in a $200 reduction of Gail's tax liability for the year. The contribution to the American Cancer Society reduces taxable income by $1,000 and results in a $250 reduction in Gail's tax liability ($1,000 reduction in taxable income × 25% tax rate).

Tax credits are discussed in Chapter 13. Some of the more common credits include:

- Earned income credit.
- Credit for child and dependent care expenses.
- Credit for the elderly.
- Foreign tax credit.
- Child tax credit.
- Premium tax credit.

The computation of net taxes payable or refund due can be illustrated by returning to the facts of Example 6.

EXAMPLE 42

Grace is single and has her disabled and dependent mother living with her. Recall that Example 6 established that Grace has taxable income of $24,500. Further assume that she has the following: income tax withheld, $2,500; estimated tax payments, $600; and credit for dependent care expenses, $200. Grace's net taxes payable is computed as follows:

Income tax (from 2016 Tax Rate Schedule, for head of household, Appendix A)		$ 3,013 (rounded)
Less: Tax credits and prepayments—		
Credit for dependent care expenses	$ 200	
Income tax withheld	2,500	
Estimated tax payments	600	(3,300)
Net taxes payable or (refund due, if negative)		$ (287)

---

[43]§ 3402 for withholding; § 6654 for estimated payments.

Because Grace maintains a home for a qualifying dependent relative, she can utilize head-of-household filing status. Her tax was computed using the Tax Rate Schedules rather than the Tax Tables (footnote 41 explains why the Tax Rate Schedules were used).

LO.7

Identify and report kiddie tax situations.

3-6c Kiddie Tax—Unearned Income of Children Taxed at Parents' Rate

At one time, a dependent child could claim an exemption on his or her own return even if claimed as a dependent by the parents. This enabled a parent to shift investment income (such as interest and dividends) to a child by transferring ownership of the assets producing the income. The child would pay no tax on the income to the extent that it was sheltered by the child's exemption and standard deduction amounts.

Also, an additional tax motivation existed for shifting income from parents to children. Although a child's unearned income in excess of the exemption and standard deduction amounts was subject to tax, it was taxed at the child's rate, rather than the parents' rate.

To reduce the tax savings that result from shifting income from parents to children, the net **unearned income** (commonly called investment income) of certain children is taxed as if it were the parents' income. Unearned income includes taxable interest, dividends, capital gains, rents, royalties, the taxable portion of scholarships, pension and annuity income, and income (other than earned income) received as the beneficiary of a trust. This provision, commonly referred to as the **kiddie tax**, applies to any child who is under age 19 (or under age 24 if a full-time student) and has unearned income of more than $2,100 (the same as in 2015).[44] The kiddie tax does not apply if the child has earned income that exceeds half of his or her support, if the child is married and files a joint return, or if both parents are deceased.

Net Unearned Income

In 2016, net unearned income of a dependent child is computed as follows:

Unearned income
Less: $1,050
Less: The greater of
- $1,050 of the standard deduction *or*
- The amount of allowable itemized deductions directly connected with the production of the unearned income

Equals: Net unearned income

If net unearned income is zero (or negative), the child's tax is computed without using the parents' rate. If the amount of net unearned income (regardless of source) is positive, the net unearned income is taxed at the parents' rate. The child's remaining taxable income (known as nonparental source income) is taxed at the child's rate. The $1,050 amounts in the preceding formula are subject to adjustment for inflation each year (these amounts were $1,050 in 2015 and $1,000 in 2014).

Tax Determination

If a child is subject to the kiddie tax, there are two options for computing the tax on the income. A separate return may be filed for the child, or the parents may elect to report the child's income on their own return. If a separate return is filed for the child,

---

[44]§ 1(g)(2).

the tax on net unearned income (referred to as the *allocable parental tax*) is computed as though the income had been included on the parents' return. Form 8615 is used to compute the tax. The steps required in this computation are illustrated in Example 43.

Olaf and Olga have a child, Hans (age 10). In 2016, Hans received $3,200 of interest income and paid investment-related fees of $200. Olaf and Olga had $70,000 of taxable income, not including their child's investment income. The parents have no qualified dividends or capital gains. Olaf and Olga do not make the parental election (discussed below).

EXAMPLE 43

1. Determine Hans's net unearned income

Gross income (unearned)	$ 3,200
Less: $1,050	(1,050)
Less: The greater of	
• $1,050 or	
• Investment expense ($200)	(1,050)
Equals: Net unearned income	$ 1,100

2. Determine allocable parental tax

Parents' taxable income	$70,000
Plus: Hans's net unearned income	1,100
Equals: Revised taxable income	$71,100
Tax on revised taxable income	$ 9,738
Less: Tax on parents' taxable income	(9,573)
Allocable parental tax	$ 165

3. Determine Hans's nonparental source tax

Hans's AGI	$ 3,200
Less: Standard deduction	(1,050)
Less: Personal exemption	(–0–)
Equals: Taxable income	$ 2,150
Less: Net unearned income	(1,100)
Nonparental source taxable income	$ 1,050
Equals: Tax ($1,050 × 10% rate)	$ 105

4. Determine Hans's total tax liability

Nonparental source tax (step 3)	$ 105
Allocable parental tax (step 2)	165
Total tax	$ 270

Election to Claim Certain Unearned Income on Parent's Return

In 2016, if a child who is subject to the kiddie tax is required to file a tax return and meets all of the following requirements, the parent may elect to report the child's unearned income that exceeds $2,100 (the same in 2015) on the parent's own tax return.

- Gross income is from interest and dividends only.
- Gross income is more than $1,050 but less than $10,500 (for 2015, these amounts are the same).
- No estimated tax has been paid in the name and Social Security number of the child, and the child is not subject to backup withholding (see Chapter 13).

If the parental election is made, the child is treated as having no gross income and is not required to file a tax return. In this case, Form 8814 (Parents' Election to Report Child's Interest and Dividends) must be filed as part of the parents' tax return.

The parent(s) must also pay an additional tax equal to the smaller of $105 or 10 percent of the child's gross income over $1,050. Parents who have substantial itemized deductions based on AGI (see Chapter 10) may find that making the parental election increases total taxes for the family unit. Taxes should be calculated both with and without the parental election to determine the appropriate choice.

Other Provisions

If parents have more than one child subject to the tax on net unearned income, the tax for the children is computed as shown in Example 43 and then allocated to the children based on their relative amounts of income. For children of divorced parents, the taxable income of the custodial parent is used to determine the allocable parental tax. This parent is the one who may elect to report the child's unearned income. For married individuals filing separate returns, the individual with the greater taxable income is the applicable parent.[45]

3-7 TAX RETURN FILING PROCEDURES

3-7a Selecting the Proper Form

As the 2016 tax forms had not been released when this text was published, the following comments apply to the 2015 forms. It is possible that some items will change on the 2016 forms.

Although a variety of forms are available to individual taxpayers, the use of some of these forms is restricted. For example, Form 1040EZ cannot be used if:

- Taxpayer claims any dependents;
- Taxpayer (or spouse) is 65 or older or blind;
- Taxable income is $100,000 or more; or
- Taxpayer claims the Premium tax credit.

Taxpayers who want to itemize deductions *from* AGI cannot use Form 1040A, but must file Form 1040.

3-7b The E-File Approach

The e-file program is used by the vast majority of individual taxpayers (and is mandatory for most tax return preparers). The required tax information is transmitted to the IRS electronically either directly from the taxpayer (i.e., an "e-file online return") or indirectly through an electronic return originator (ERO). EROs are tax professionals who have been accepted into the electronic filing program by the IRS. Such parties hold themselves out to the general public as "authorized IRS e-file providers." Providers often are the preparers of the return as well.

Through arrangements with the IRS, a number of software providers offer free e-filing services. These services are generally available only to taxpayers who have AGI of $60,000 or less. A list of these providers and their eligibility requirements can be obtained through the IRS website.

All taxpayers and tax return preparers must attest to the returns they file. For most taxpayers, this attesting can be done through an electronic return signature using a personal identification number (a Self-Select PIN). Information on establishing a

---

[45]See Chapter 31 of *Your Federal Income Tax* (IRS Publication 17) and Form 8615 (Tax for Certain Children Who Have Unearned Income).

Self-Select PIN can be found in the instructions to Form 1040, Form 1040A, or Form 1040EZ or at **www.irs.gov/Filing/E-File-Options**. If certain paper documents must be submitted, a one-page form must be completed and filed when the return is e-filed. Form 8453 (U.S. Individual Income Tax Transmittal for an IRS *e-file* Return) is used to submit required attachments for both self- and practitioner-prepared electronic returns. Or a practitioner PIN method may be used whereby the taxpayer authorizes a tax preparer to generate a PIN by signing Form 8879 (IRS e-file Signature Authorization).

The e-file approach has two major advantages over paper filing. First, compliance with the format required by the IRS eliminates many errors that would otherwise occur. Second, the time required for processing a refund usually is reduced to three weeks or less.

3-7c **When and Where to File**

Tax returns of individuals are due on or before the fifteenth day of the fourth month following the close of the tax year. For the calendar year taxpayer, the usual filing date is on or before April 15 of the following year.[46] When the due date falls on a Saturday, Sunday, or legal holiday, the last day for filing falls on the next business day. If the return is mailed to the proper address with sufficient postage and is postmarked on or before the due date, it is deemed timely filed. The Code enables the IRS to prescribe rules governing the filing of returns using various private parcel delivery services (e.g., FedEx, UPS).[47]

If a taxpayer is unable to file the return by the specified due date, a six-month extension of time can be obtained by filing Form 4868 (Application for Automatic Extension of Time to File U.S. Individual Income Tax Return) on or before the specified due date. Certain taxpayers who are members of the U.S. Armed Forces are allowed additional time for filing their Federal income tax returns.[48]

Although obtaining an extension excuses a taxpayer from a penalty for failure to file, it does not insulate against the penalty for failure to pay. If more tax is owed, the filing of Form 4868 should be accompanied by an additional payment to cover the balance due. The failure to file and failure to pay penalties are discussed in Chapter 1.

The return should be sent or delivered to the IRS Regional Service Center listed in the instructions for each type of return or contained in software applications.[49] If an individual taxpayer needs to file an amended return (e.g., because of a failure to report income or to claim a deduction or tax credit), Form 1040X is filed. The form generally must be filed within three years of the filing date of the original return or within two years from the time the tax was paid, whichever is later.

3-7d **Modes of Payment**

Payments of any taxes due can be made in a variety of ways, including check or money order (with payment made to "United States Treasury"), IRS Direct Pay (electronic funds withdrawal from a bank account), or the Electronic Federal Tax Payment System (EFTPS). Information about the electronic options is available on the IRS website. In addition, the IRS has approved the use of MasterCard, American Express, Discover, and Visa to pay Federal taxes using a payment processor. The use of a credit card or debit

---

[46]§ 6072(a); Rev.Rul. 2015–13 (2015–22 I.R.B. 1011) provides filling deadline guidance when there are unique state holidays.

[47]§ 7502(f); see Notice 2015–38 (2015–21 I.R.B. 984) for the current list of "designated private delivery services" that, if used, will meet the timely filed rules.

[48]Reg. § 1.6081–4. See also *Your Federal Income Tax* (IRS Publication 17), Chapter 1.

[49]The appropriate IRS Regional Service Center address can be found at **www.irs.gov/uac/Where-To-File-Addresses-for-Tax-Professionals**.

card to pay taxes results in a charge to the taxpayer by the payment processor (in addition to any fees that may be charged by the debit/credit card company).

LO.8

Formulate the fundamentals of property transactions.

3-8 GAINS AND LOSSES FROM PROPERTY TRANSACTIONS—IN GENERAL

Gains and losses from property transactions are discussed in detail in Chapters 14 through 17. Because of their importance in the tax system, however, they are introduced briefly at this point.

When property is sold or otherwise disposed of, a gain or loss results. This gain or loss has an effect on the income tax position of the party making the sale or other disposition when the *realized* gain or loss is *recognized* for tax purposes. Without realized gain or loss, there generally can be no recognized gain or loss. The concept of realized gain or loss is expressed as follows:

$$\begin{array}{ccc} \text{Amount realized} & & \text{Adjusted basis of} & & \text{Realized gain} \\ \text{from the sale} & - & \text{the property} & = & \text{(or loss)} \end{array}$$

The amount realized is the selling price of the property less any costs of disposition (e.g., brokerage commissions) incurred by the seller. The adjusted basis of the property is determined as follows:

Cost (or other original basis) at date of acquisition[50]
Add: Capital additions
Subtract: Depreciation (if appropriate) and other capital recoveries (see Chapter 8)
Equals: Adjusted basis at date of sale or other disposition

All realized gains are recognized (taxable) unless some specific part of the tax law provides otherwise (see Chapter 15 dealing with certain nontaxable exchanges). Realized losses may or may not be recognized (deductible) for tax purposes, depending on the circumstances involved. Generally, losses realized from the disposition of personal use property (property neither held for investment nor used in a trade or business) are not recognized.

EXAMPLE 44

During the current year, Ted sells his sailboat (adjusted basis of $4,000) for $5,500. Ted also sells one of his personal automobiles (adjusted basis of $8,000) for $5,000.

Ted's realized gain of $1,500 from the sale of the sailboat is recognized. On the other hand, the $3,000 realized loss on the sale of the automobile is not recognized and will not provide Ted with any deductible tax benefit.

In terms of the tax formula, net gains from property transactions that are recognized will affect gross income. If the gain is deferred (e.g., like-kind exchanges or involuntary conversions—see Chapter 15) or not recognized (e.g., sale of a residence—see Chapter 15), there is no immediate tax effect. Recognized losses from property transactions are treated as deductions *for* adjusted gross income (AGI).

Once it has been determined that the disposition of property results in a recognized gain or loss, the next step is to classify the gain or loss as capital or ordinary. Although ordinary gain is fully taxable and ordinary loss is fully deductible, the same may not hold true for capital gains and capital losses.

---

[50]Cost usually means purchase price plus expenses related to the acquisition of the property and incurred by the purchaser (e.g., brokerage commissions). For the basis of property acquired by gift or inheritance and other basis rules, see Chapter 14.

3-9 GAINS AND LOSSES FROM PROPERTY TRANSACTIONS—CAPITAL GAINS AND LOSSES

To obtain a good perspective on how the Federal income tax functions, an overview of property transactions is needed. Capital gains and losses are treated uniquely in the Federal income tax system. Capital gains are included in the determination of taxable income and may be taxed at lower (preferential) tax rates. Capital losses, on the other hand, may not be fully deductible when determining taxable income (if limited, the amount not allowed can be carried over and used in subsequent years).

3-9a Definition of a Capital Asset

Capital assets are defined in the Code as any property held by the taxpayer *other than* property listed in § 1221. The list in § 1221 includes inventory, accounts receivable, and depreciable property or real estate used in a business. Thus, the sale or exchange of assets in these categories usually results in ordinary income or loss treatment (see Chapter 17).

Kelly owns a pizza parlor. During the current year, he sells an automobile that had been used as a pizza delivery car for three years. The sale resulted in a loss of $1,000. Because this automobile is property used in his business, Kelly has an ordinary loss deduction of $1,000, rather than a capital loss deduction.

The principal capital assets held by an individual taxpayer include (1) assets held for personal (rather than business) use (e.g., a personal residence or an automobile), and (2) assets held for investment purposes (e.g., corporate securities or land). Capital assets generally include collectibles, which are subject to somewhat unique tax treatment. **Collectibles** include art, antiques, gems, metals, stamps, some coins and bullion, and alcoholic beverages that are held as investments.

3-9b Determination of Net Capital Gain

To arrive at a net capital gain, capital losses must be taken into account. The capital losses are aggregated by holding period (short-term and long-term) and applied against the gains in that category. If excess losses result, they are then shifted to the category carrying the *highest* tax rate. A *net capital gain* will occur if the net long-term capital gain (NLTCG) exceeds the net short-term capital loss (NSTCL).

In the current year, Colin is in the 35% tax bracket and has the following capital transactions and resulting gains (losses):

Penguin Corporation stock (held for 8 months)	$ 1,000
Owl Corporation stock (held for 10 months)	(3,000)
Stamp collection (held for 5 years)	2,000
Land (held as an investment for 3 years)	4,000

The Penguin Corporation short-term capital gain (STCG) of $1,000 is offset by the Owl Corporation short-term capital loss (STCL) of $3,000, resulting in a net STCL of $2,000. This $2,000 net STCL is then applied against the stamp collection gain—a collectible long-term capital gain (LTCG) with the *highest* tax rate (28%). Because there is no remaining STCL, Colin has a net LTCG of $4,000 from the land sale. This is Colin's net capital gain, and it is taxed at a 15% rate.

3-9c **Treatment of Net Capital Loss**

For individual taxpayers, net capital loss can be used to offset ordinary income of up to $3,000 ($1,500 for married persons filing separate returns). If a taxpayer has both short- and long-term capital losses, the short-term category is used first to arrive at the $3,000. Any remaining net capital loss is carried over indefinitely until used up (subject to the annual $3,000 limit). When carried over, the excess capital loss retains its classification as short- or long-term.

EXAMPLE 47

In 2016, Tina has a short-term capital loss of $2,000, a long-term capital loss of $2,500, and no capital gains. She can deduct $3,000 ($2,000 short-term + $1,000 long-term) of this amount as an ordinary loss. The remaining $1,500 is carried over to 2017 as a long-term capital loss.

The Big Picture

EXAMPLE 48

Return to the facts of *The Big Picture* on p. 3-1. Polly's sale of her wedding rings resulted in a realized capital loss of $2,800 [$9,000 (selling price) − $11,800 (cost basis)]. However, because they were personal use property, Polly cannot deduct the loss.

3-9d **Taxation of Net Capital Gain**

Net capital gains are classified and taxed as follows:

Classification	Maximum Rate
Short-term gains (held for one year or less)	39.6%
Long-term gains (held for more than one year)—	
Collectibles	28%
Certain depreciable property used in a trade or business (known as unrecaptured § 1250 gain and discussed in Chapter 17)	25%
All other long-term capital gains	20%, 15%, or 0%

The special tax rate applicable to long-term capital gains (called the alternative tax computation) is used when the taxpayer's regular tax rate *exceeds* the alternative tax rate. When tax liability is determined, long-term capital gains are taxed last. As a result, the tax rate applied to a long-term capital gain will depend on the taxpayer's regular tax rate on other income and the size of the long-term capital gain (a large long-term capital gain may cross marginal rates brackets and, theoretically, could be taxed at 0%, 15%, and 20% rates). The 0 percent rate applies only when the taxpayer's regular tax rate is 15 percent or less. The 20 percent rate applies only when the taxpayer's regular tax rate is 39.6 percent.[51]

Net Capital Gain Tax Computation

EXAMPLE 49

During 2016, Polly is in the 15% tax bracket and has the following capital gains for the year:

Robin Corporation stock (held for 6 months)	$1,000
Crow Corporation stock (held for 13 months)	1,000

Although both transactions yield a $1,000 capital gain, the tax effects are quite different. Polly pays a tax of $150 ($1,000 × 15%) on the Robin stock gain but $0 ($1,000 × 0%) on the Crow stock gain.

---

[51]§ 1(h)(1); as noted in the table, special rates apply to collectibles and certain types of depreciable realty.

Net Capital Gain Tax Computation

Assume the same facts as in Example 49, except that Polly's regular tax bracket for the year is 33% (not 15%).

Polly now pays a tax of $330 ($1,000 × 33%) on the Robin stock gain and $150 ($1,000 × 15%) on the Crow stock gain.

EXAMPLE 50

This brief discussion of property transactions provides insight into the complexities that exist in this area. Chapters 14 through 17 provide an in-depth discussion of this topic (including more detail on capital gains and losses).

3-10 TAX PLANNING

LO.9

Evaluate tax planning opportunities associated with the individual tax formula.

3-10a Maximizing the Use of the Standard Deduction

In most cases, the choice between using the standard deduction and itemizing deductions *from* AGI is a simple matter—pick whichever yields the larger tax benefit. Families in the initial stages of home ownership, for example, will invariably make the itemization choice due to the substantial mortgage interest and property tax payments involved. Older taxpayers, however, may have repaid the mortgage debt on their homes and, in some states, may have reduced property taxes due to senior exemptions. For them, the more attractive benefit may be the additional standard deduction that can accompany the standard deduction choice.

In some cases, the difference between using the standard deduction and itemizing may not be a significant amount. Here, taxes might be saved by alternating between the two options. The taxpayer does this by using the cash method to concentrate multiple years' deductions in a single year (e.g., church pledges for several years can be paid in one year). Then the standard deduction is used in alternate years.

3-10b Dependency Exemptions

The Joint Return Test

A married person can be claimed as a dependent only if that individual does not file a joint return with his or her spouse. If a joint return has been filed, the damage may be undone if separate returns are substituted on a timely basis (on or before the due date of the return).

While preparing a client's 2015 income tax return on April 2, 2016, the tax professional discovered that the client's daughter had filed a joint return with her husband in late January 2016. Presuming that the daughter otherwise qualifies as the client's dependent, the exemption is not lost if she and her husband file separate returns on or before April 15, 2016.

EXAMPLE 51

An initial election to file a joint return must be considered carefully in any situation in which the taxpayers might later decide to amend their return and file separately. As indicated previously, separate returns may be substituted for a joint return only if the amended returns are filed on or before the normal (unextended) due date of the return. If the taxpayers in Example 51 attempt to file separate returns after April 15, 2016, the returns will not be accepted and the joint return election is binding.[52]

Keep in mind that the filing of a joint return is not fatal to the dependency exemption if the parties are filing solely to recover all income tax withholdings, they are not required to file a return, and no tax liability would exist on separate returns.

---

[52]Reg. § 1.6013–1(a)(1).

Support Considerations

The support of a qualifying child becomes relevant only if the child is self-supporting. In cases where the child has an independent source of funds, planning could help prevent an undesirable result. When a qualifying relative is involved, meeting the support test is essential, as the dependency exemption is not otherwise available.

In 2016, Cheryl maintains a household that she shares with her son and mother. The son, Barry, is 23 years of age and a full-time student in law school. The mother, Gladys, is 68 years of age and active in charitable causes. Barry works part-time for a local law firm, while Gladys has income from investments. In resolving the support issue (or self-support in the case of Barry), one must compare Cheryl's contribution with that made by Barry and Gladys.[53]

In this connection, what Barry and Gladys do with their funds becomes crucial. Funds that are used for nonsupport purposes (e.g., purchase of investments) or not used at all (e.g., deposited in a bank) are not considered. Limiting how much Barry and Gladys contribute to their own support enhances Cheryl's chances of claiming them as dependents. Records should be maintained showing the amount of support and its source.

Example 52 does not mention the possible application of the gross income test. Presuming that Barry is a qualifying child, the amount he earns does not matter, as the gross income test does not apply. Gladys, however, comes under the qualifying relative category, where the gross income test applies. Therefore, for her to be claimed as a dependent, her income that is taxable will have to be less than $4,050.

Community Property Ramifications

In certain cases, state law can have an effect on the availability of a dependency exemption.

Dependency Exemptions: State Law Implications

During the year, Mitch provides more than half of the support of his son, Ross, and daughter-in-law, Connie, who live with him. Ross, age 22, is a full-time student, while Connie earns $5,000 from a part-time job. Ross and Connie do not file a joint return. All parties live in New York, a common law state. Mitch can claim Ross as a dependent, as he is a qualifying child. Connie is not a dependent because she does not meet the gross income test under the qualifying relative category.

Assume the same facts as in Example 53, except that all parties live in Arizona, a community property state. Now Connie also qualifies as a dependent. Because Connie's gross income is only $2,500 (one-half of the community income), she satisfies the gross income test.

Relationship to the Deduction for Medical Expenses

Generally, medical expenses are deductible only if they are paid on behalf of the taxpayer, his or her spouse, and their dependents. Because deductibility may rest on dependency status, planning is important in arranging multiple support agreements.

During the upcoming year, Zelda will be supported by her two sons (Vern and Vito) and her daughter (Maria). Each will furnish approximately one-third of the required support. If the parties decide that the dependency exemption should be claimed by the daughter under a multiple support agreement, any medical expenses incurred by Zelda should be paid by Maria.

In planning a multiple support agreement, take into account which of the parties is most likely to exceed the 10 percent (7.5 percent if at least age 65 through 2016) limitation

---

[53]As part of her support contribution to Barry and Gladys, Cheryl can count the fair market value of the meals and lodging she provides.

(see Chapter 10). In Example 55, for instance, Maria might be a poor choice if she and her family do not expect to incur many medical and drug expenses of their own.

One exception permits the deduction of medical expenses paid on behalf of someone who is not a spouse or a dependent. If the person could be claimed as a dependent *except* for the gross income or joint return test, the medical expenses are, nevertheless, deductible. For additional discussion, see Chapter 10.

3-10c **Taking Advantage of Tax Rate Differentials**

It is natural for taxpayers to be concerned about the taxes they are paying. How does a tax professional communicate information about tax rates to clients? There are several possibilities.

The *marginal rate* (refer to Examples 39 and 40) provides information that can help a taxpayer evaluate a particular course of action or structure a transaction in the most advantageous manner. For example, a taxpayer who is in the 15 percent bracket this year and expects to be in the 28 percent bracket next year should, if possible, defer payment of deductible expenses until next year to maximize the tax benefit of the deduction.

A note of caution is in order with respect to shifting income and expenses between years. Congress has recognized the tax planning possibilities of such shifting and has enacted many provisions to limit a taxpayer's ability to do so. Some of these limitations on the shifting of income are discussed in Chapters 4, 5, and 18. Limitations that affect a taxpayer's ability to shift deductions are discussed in Chapters 6 through 11 and in Chapter 18.

A taxpayer's *effective rate* can be an informative measure of the effectiveness of tax planning. The effective rate is computed by dividing the taxpayer's tax liability by the total amount of income. A low effective rate can be considered an indication of effective tax planning.

One way of lowering the effective rate is to exclude income from the tax base. For example, a taxpayer might consider investing in tax-free municipal bonds rather than taxable corporate bonds. Although pre-tax income from corporate bonds is usually higher, after-tax income may be higher if the taxpayer invests in tax-free municipals.[54]

Another way of lowering the effective rate is to make sure the taxpayer's expenses and losses are deductible. For example, losses on investments in passive activities may not be deductible (see Chapter 11). Therefore, a taxpayer who plans to invest in an activity that will produce a loss in the early years should take steps to ensure that the business is treated as active rather than passive. Active losses are deductible, while passive activity losses are not.

3-10d **Income of Certain Children**

Taxpayers can use several strategies to avoid or minimize the effect of the rules that tax the unearned income of certain children at the parents' rate. With the cutoff age being 19 (under 24 for full-time students), many children are vulnerable to the application of the kiddie tax. Parents should consider giving a younger child assets that defer taxable income until the child reaches a nonvulnerable age. For example, U.S. government Series EE savings bonds can be used to defer income until the bonds are cashed in (see Chapter 4).

Growth stocks typically pay little in the way of dividends. However, the profit on an astute investment may more than offset the lack of dividends. The child can hold the stock until he or she reaches a safe age. If the stock is sold then at a profit, the profit is taxed at the child's low rates.

Taxpayers in a position to do so can employ their children in their business and pay them a reasonable wage for the work they actually perform (e.g., light office help such as filing). The child's earned income is sheltered by the standard deduction, and the parents' business is allowed a deduction for the wages. The kiddie tax rules have no effect on earned income, even if it is earned from the parents' business.

---

[54]Investment in tax-free bonds will also reduce the net investment income tax (§ 1411) if the individual is subject to this additional tax (see Chapter 13).

REFOCUS ON THE BIG PICTURE

A Divided Household

Of major concern to Polly is her filing status. If she qualifies as an abandoned spouse, she is entitled to file as head of household. If not, she is considered to be a married person filing separately. Moreover, to be an abandoned spouse, Polly must be able to claim Paige as a dependent. To be a dependent, Paige must meet the requirements of a qualifying child *or* a qualifying relative.

For qualifying child purposes, Paige must meet either the age (i.e., under age 19) or the full-time student (under age 24) test. (A disabled child exception seems highly unlikely.) Because Paige currently is not a full-time student, is she under age 19? If so, she is a qualifying child (see Example 14). If Paige is not a qualifying child, is she a qualifying relative? Here, the answer depends on meeting the gross income test (see Example 22). How much did Paige earn from her part-time job? If her earnings are under $4,050, she satisfies the gross income test. Thus, if Paige can be claimed as a dependent under either the qualifying child or the qualifying relative category, Polly is an abandoned spouse entitled to head-of-household filing status (see Example 37). If not, she is a married person filing separately.

Maude can be claimed as Polly's dependent because she is a member of the household. It does not matter that she died in February, and the dependency exemption amount need not be apportioned and is allowed in full. Because Maude is her dependent, Polly can claim the medical expenses she paid on Maude's behalf. The funeral expenses, however, are not deductible (see Example 19).

Does Maude qualify Polly for head-of-household filing status? No—although she is a dependent, Maude does not meet the relationship test (see Example 34).

The sale of the wedding rings results in a capital loss of $2,800 ($9,000 − $11,800). Because the loss is for personal use property, it cannot be claimed for tax purposes (see Example 50).

What If?

Assume that Nick left for parts unknown in *August* (not March). Now Polly cannot qualify as an abandoned spouse. Her spouse lived in the home during part of the last six months of the year. As Polly is married, she cannot qualify for head-of-household filing status. She must file as a married person filing separately. The change in when Nick left will not affect the dependency issue regarding Paige, however.

Key Terms

Abandoned spouse, 3-25

Child tax credit, 3-21

Collectibles, 3-35

Dependency exemption, 3-12

E-file, 3-32

Filing status, 3-21

Head-of-household, 3-24

Itemized deductions, 3-6

Kiddie tax, 3-30

Marriage penalty, 3-23

Multiple support agreement, 3-16

Personal exemptions, 3-11

Qualifying child, 3-12

Qualifying relative, 3-14

Standard deduction, 3-7

Surviving spouse, 3-24

Tax Rate Schedules, 3-28

Tax Table, 3-27

Unearned income, 3-30

Discussion Questions

1. **LO.1, 5, 8, 9** During the year, Addison is involved in the following transactions: Issue ID

   - Lost money gambling on a recent trip to a casino.
   - Helped pay for her neighbor's dental bills. The neighbor is a good friend who is unemployed.
   - Received from the IRS a tax refund due to Addison's overpayment of last year's Federal income taxes.
   - Paid a traffic ticket received while double parking to attend a business meeting.
   - Contributed to the mayor's reelection campaign. The mayor had promised Addison to have some of her land rezoned. The mayor was reelected and got Addison's land rezoned.
   - Borrowed money from a bank to make a down payment on an automobile.
   - Sold a houseboat and a camper on eBay. Both were personal use items, and the gain from one offset the loss from the other.
   - Her dependent grandfather died on June 3 of the year.
   - Paid for dependent grandfather's funeral expenses.
   - Paid premiums on her dependent son's life insurance policy.

   What are the possible income tax ramifications of these transactions?

2. **LO.1** Which of the following items are *inclusions* in gross income?
   a. During the year, stock that the taxpayer purchased as an investment doubled in value.
   b. Amount an off-duty motorcycle police officer received for escorting a funeral procession.
   c. While his mother was in the hospital, the taxpayer sold her jewelry and gave the money to his girlfriend.
   d. Child support payments received.
   e. A damage deposit the taxpayer recovered when he vacated the apartment he had rented.
   f. Interest received by the taxpayer on an investment in general purpose bonds issued by IBM.
   g. Amounts received by the taxpayer, a baseball "Hall of Famer," for autographing sports equipment (e.g., balls and gloves).
   h. Tips received by a bartender from patrons. (Taxpayer is paid a regular salary by the cocktail lounge that employs him.)
   i. Taxpayer sells his Super Bowl tickets for three times what he paid for them.
   j. Taxpayer receives a new BMW from his grandmother when he passes the CPA exam.

3. **LO.1** Which of the following items are *exclusions* from gross income?
   a. Alimony payments received.
   b. Damages award received by the taxpayer for personal physical injury—none were for punitive damages.
   c. A new golf cart won in a church raffle.
   d. Amount collected on a loan previously made to a college friend.
   e. Insurance proceeds paid to the taxpayer on the death of her uncle—she was the designated beneficiary under the policy.
   f. Interest income on City of Chicago bonds.

g.   Jury duty fees.

h.   Stolen funds the taxpayer had collected for a local food bank drive.

i.   Reward paid by the IRS for information provided that led to the conviction of the taxpayer's former employer for tax evasion.

j.   An envelope containing $8,000 found (and unclaimed) by the taxpayer in a bus station.

Decision Making   4.   **LO.1, 8, 9** In late 2016, the Polks come to you for tax advice. They are considering selling some stock investments for a loss and making a contribution to a traditional IRA. In reviewing their situation, you note that they have large medical expenses and a casualty loss, neither of which is covered by insurance. What advice would you give the Polks?

Issue ID   5.   **LO.2** In choosing between the standard deduction and itemizing deductions *from* AGI, what effect, if any, does each of the following have?

a.   The age of the taxpayer(s).

b.   The health (i.e., physical condition) of the taxpayer.

c.   Whether taxpayers rent or own their residence.

d.   Taxpayer's filing status (e.g., single, married, filing jointly).

e.   Whether married taxpayers decide to file separate returns.

f.   The taxpayer's uninsured personal residence was recently destroyed by fire.

g.   The number of personal and dependency exemptions the taxpayer can claim.

6.   **LO.2, 3, 5** David is age 78, is a widower, and is being claimed as a dependent by his son. How does this situation affect the following?

a.   David's own individual filing requirement.

b.   David's personal exemption.

c.   The standard deduction allowed to David.

d.   The availability of any additional standard deduction.

Issue ID   7.   **LO.4** Patsy maintains a household that includes a son (age 30) and a cousin (age 28). She can claim the cousin as a dependent but not her son. Explain.

8.   **LO.4** Heather, age 12, lives in the same household with her mother, grandmother, and uncle.

a.   Who can qualify for the dependency exemption?

b.   Who takes precedence?

9.   **LO.4** Caden and Lily are divorced on March 3, 2015. For financial reasons, however, Lily continues to live in Caden's apartment and receives her support from him. Caden does not claim Lily as a dependent on his 2015 Federal income tax return but does so on his 2016 return. Explain.

10.   **LO.4** Isabella, Emma, and Jacob share equally in the support of their parents. Jacob tells his sisters to split the dependency exemptions between the two of them. Explain what Jacob means.

Issue ID   11.   **LO.4** Mark and Lisa were divorced in 2015. In 2016, Mark has custody of their children, but Lisa provides nearly all of their support. Who is entitled to claim the children as dependents?

Issue ID   12.   **LO.4** Mario, who is single, is a U.S. citizen and resident. He provides almost all of the support of his parents and two aunts, who are citizens and residents of Guatemala. Mario's parents and aunts are seriously considering moving to and becoming residents of Mexico. Would such a move have any impact on Mario? Why or why not?

13.   **LO.3, 4** What are stealth taxes? What purpose do they serve, and why are they used?

14. **LO.5** Oliver is a U.S. citizen employed by a multinational corporation at its London office. Oliver is married to Regina, a British citizen, and they reside in England. Regina receives substantial rent income from real estate she owns in western Europe.   Issue ID
    a. Must Oliver file a U.S. income tax return?
    b. Under what circumstances might Regina be considered a resident of the United States? Would such a classification be advantageous? Disadvantageous? Explain.

15. **LO.4, 5** Comment on the availability of head-of-household filing status for 2016 in each of the following independent situations:
    a. Taxpayer lives alone but maintains the household of his parents. In July 2016, the parents use their savings to purchase a new BMW for $62,000.
    b. Taxpayer maintains a home in which she and her dependent father live. The father enters a nursing facility for treatment of a mental disorder.
    c. Taxpayer, a single parent, maintains a home in which she and her unmarried son live. The son, age 18, earns $5,000 from a part-time job.
    d. Assume the same facts as in (c), except that the son is age 19, not 18.
    e. Taxpayer is married and maintains a household in which he and his dependent stepson live.
    f. Taxpayer lives alone but maintains the household where her dependent daughter lives.
    g. Taxpayer maintains a household that includes an unrelated friend who qualifies as his dependent.

16. **LO.5** In many cases, a surviving spouse ultimately becomes a head of household for filing status purposes. Explain this statement.

17. **LO.6** Jayden calculates his 2016 income tax by using both the Tax Tables and the Tax Rate Schedules. Because the Tax Rate Schedules yield a slightly lower tax liability, he plans to pay this amount.
    a. Why is there a difference?
    b. Is Jayden's approach permissible? Why or why not?

18. **LO.7** In connection with the application of the kiddie tax, comment on the following:
    a. The child has only earned income.
    b. The child has a modest amount of unearned income.
    c. The child is age 20, not a student, and not disabled.
    d. The child is married.
    e. Effect of the parental election.
    f. The result when the parental election is made and the married parents file separate returns.

19. **LO.8** During the year, Hernando has the following transactions:
    - Gain on the sale of stock held as an investment for 10 months.
    - Gain on the sale of land held as an investment for 4 years.
    - Gain on the sale of a houseboat owned for 2 years and used for family vacations.
    - Loss on the sale of a reconditioned motorcycle owned for 3 years and used for recreational purposes.

    How should Hernando treat these transactions for income tax purposes?

20. **LO.8** During the year, Brandi had the following transactions: a long-term capital gain from the sale of land, a short-term capital loss from the sale of stock, and a long-term capital gain from the sale of a gun collection.

    a. How are these transactions treated for income tax purposes?

    b. Does this treatment favor the taxpayer or the IRS? Explain.

Computational Exercises

Issue ID   21. **LO.2** Sam and Abby are dependents of their parents, and each has income of $2,100 for the year. Sam's standard deduction for the year is $1,050, while Abby's is $2,450. As their income is the same, what causes the difference in the amount of the standard deduction?

22. **LO.2** Compute the 2016 standard deduction for the following taxpayers.

    a. Margie is 15 and claimed as a dependent by her parents. She has $800 in dividends income and $1,400 in wages from a part-time job.

    b. Ruby and Woody are married and file a joint tax return. Ruby is age 66, and Woody is 69. Their taxable retirement income is $10,000.

    c. Shonda is age 68 and single. She is claimed by her daughter as a dependent. Her earned income is $500, and her interest income is $125.

    d. Frazier, age 55, is married but is filing a separate return. His wife itemizes her deductions.

23. **LO.4** In 2016, Dominique and Felix are married and file a joint tax return. Their AGI is $314,050, and they claim three exemptions. Determine their total exemption amount for 2016.

Issue ID   24. **LO.5, 9** Paul and Sonja, who are married, had itemized deductions of $8,200 and $400, respectively, during 2016. Paul suggests that they file separately—he will itemize his deductions *from* AGI, and she will claim the standard deduction.

    a. Evaluate Paul's suggestion.

    b. What should they do?

25. **LO.6** Compute the 2016 tax liability and the marginal and average tax rates for the following taxpayers (use the 2016 tax rate schedules in Appendix A for this purpose).

    a. Chandler, who files as a single taxpayer, has taxable income of $93,000.

    b. Lazare, who files as a head of household, has taxable income of $56,000.

26. **LO.7** In 2016, Simon, age 12, has interest income of $800 and dividend income of $4,000. He has no investment expenses. His parents have taxable income of $80,200 and file a joint tax return. Assume that no parental election is made. Determine Simon's net unearned income, allocable parental tax, and total tax liability.

27. **LO.8** Rebecca sells her personal scooter for $550. She purchased the scooter for $700 three years ago. She also sells a painting for $1,200 that she acquired five years ago for $900. What are the tax implications of these sales?

28. **LO.8** During the year, Tamara had capital transactions resulting in gains (losses) as follows:

Sold stock in ABC Company (acquired two years ago)	($1,500)
Sold collectible coins (held for more than one year)	$2,000
Sold stock in XYZ Company (acquired six months ago)	($4,100)
Sold stock in LMN Company (acquired three years ago)	$500

Determine Tamara's net capital gain or loss as a result of these transactions.

Problems

29. **LO.1** Compute the taxable income for 2016 in each of the following independent situations:

    a. Drew and Meg, ages 40 and 41, respectively, are married and file a joint return. In addition to four dependent children, they have AGI of $65,000 and itemized deductions of $15,000.

    b. Sybil, age 40, is single and supports her dependent parents who live with her, as well as her grandfather who is in a nursing home. She has AGI of $80,000 and itemized deductions of $8,000.

    c. Scott, age 49, is a surviving spouse. His household includes two unmarried stepsons who qualify as his dependents. He has AGI of $75,000 and itemized deductions of $10,100.

    d. Amelia, age 33, is an abandoned spouse who maintains a household for her three dependent children. She has AGI of $58,000 and itemized deductions of $9,500.

    e. Dale, age 42, is divorced but maintains the home in which he and his daughter, Jill, live. Jill is single and qualifies as Dale's dependent. Dale has AGI of $64,000 and itemized deductions of $9,900.

    Note: Problems 30 and 31 can be solved by referring to Concept Summary 3.1, Exhibits 3.1 through 3.5, and the discussion under Deductions for Adjusted Gross Income in this chapter.

30. **LO.1, 8** Compute the taxable income for 2016 for Emily on the basis of the following information. Her filing status is single.

Salary	$85,000
Interest income from bonds issued by Xerox	1,100
Alimony payments received	6,000
Contribution to traditional IRA	5,500
Gift from parents	25,000
Short-term capital gain from stock investment	2,000
Amount lost in football office pool	500
Number of potential dependents (two cousins, who live in Canada)	?
Age	40

31. **LO.1** Compute the taxable income for 2016 for Aiden on the basis of the following information. Aiden is married but has not seen or heard from his wife since 2014.

Salary	$ 80,000
Interest on bonds issued by City of Boston	3,000
Interest on CD issued by Wells Fargo Bank	2,000
Cash dividend received on Chevron common stock	2,200
Life insurance proceeds paid upon death of aunt (Aiden was the designated beneficiary of the policy)	200,000
Inheritance received upon death of aunt	100,000
Jackson (a cousin) repaid a loan Aiden made to him in 2010 (no interest was provided for)	5,000
Itemized deductions (state income tax, property taxes on residence, interest on home mortgage, and charitable contributions)	9,700
Number of dependents (children, ages 17 and 18, and mother-in-law, age 70)	3
Age	43

32. **LO.2** Determine the amount of the standard deduction allowed for 2016 in the following independent situations. In each case, assume that the taxpayer is claimed as another person's dependent.

   a. Curtis, age 18, has income as follows: $700 interest from a certificate of deposit and $6,100 from repairing cars.

   b. Mattie, age 18, has income as follows: $600 cash dividends from a stock investment and $4,700 from handling a paper route.

   c. Mel, age 16, has income as follows: $675 interest on a bank savings account and $800 for painting a neighbor's fence.

   d. Lucy, age 15, has income as follows: $400 cash dividends from a stock investment and $500 from grooming pets.

   e. Sarah, age 67 and a widow, has income as follows: $500 from a bank savings account and $3,200 from babysitting.

33. **LO.4** Using the legend provided below, classify each statement as to the taxpayer for dependency exemption purposes.

Legend
QC = Could be a qualifying child
QR = Could be a qualifying relative
B = Could satisfy the definition of *both* a qualifying child *and* a qualifying relative
N = Could not satisfy the definition of *either* a qualifying child *or* a qualifying relative

   a. Taxpayer's son has gross income of $7,000.

   b. Taxpayer's niece has gross income of $3,000.

   c. Taxpayer's uncle lives with him.

   d. Taxpayer's daughter is age 25 and disabled.

   e. Taxpayer's daughter is age 18, has gross income of $8,000, and does not live with him.

   f. Taxpayer's cousin does not live with her.

   g. Taxpayer's brother does not live with her.

   h. Taxpayer's sister has dropped out of school, is age 17, and lives with him.

   i. Taxpayer's older nephew is age 23 and a full-time student.

   j. Taxpayer's grandson lives with her and has gross income of $7,000.

34. **LO.3, 4** For tax year 2016, determine the number of personal and dependency exemptions in each of the following independent situations:

   a. Leo and Amanda (ages 48 and 46, respectively) are husband and wife and furnish more than 50% of the support of their two children, Elton (age 18) and Trista (age 24). During the year, Elton earns $4,500 providing transportation for elderly persons with disabilities, and Trista receives a $5,000 scholarship for tuition at the law school she attends.

   b. Audry (age 45) was divorced this year. She maintains a household in which she, her ex-husband (Clint), and his mother (Olive) live and furnishes more than 50% of their support. Olive is age 91 and blind.

   c. Crystal, age 45, furnishes more than 50% of the support of her married son, Andy (age 18), and his wife, Paige (age 19) who live with her. During the year, Andy earned $8,200 from a part-time job. All parties live in Iowa (a common law state).

   d. Assume the same facts as in (c), except that all parties live in Washington (a community property state).

35. **LO.3, 4** Compute the number of personal and dependency exemptions in each of the following independent situations:

   a. Reginald, a U.S. citizen and resident, contributes 100% of the support of his parents who are citizens of Canada and live there.

b. Pablo, a U.S. citizen and resident, contributes 100% of the support of his parents, who are citizens of Panama. Pablo's father is a resident of Panama, and his mother is a legal resident of the United States.

c. Gretchen, a U.S. citizen and resident, contributes 100% of the support of her parents, who are U.S. citizens but residents of Germany.

d. Elena is a U.S. citizen and a resident of Italy. Her household includes Carlos, a 4-year-old adopted son who is a citizen of Spain.

36. **LO.3, 4** Determine how many personal and dependency exemptions would be available in each of the following independent situations. Specify whether any such exemptions would come under the qualifying child or the qualifying relative category.

a. Andy maintains a household that includes a cousin (age 12), a niece (age 18), and a son (age 26). All are full-time students. Andy furnishes all of their support.

b. Minerva provides all of the support of a family friend's son (age 20) who lives with her. She also furnishes most of the support of her stepmother, who does not live with her.

c. Raul, a U.S. citizen, lives in Costa Rica. Raul's household includes a friend, Helena, who is age 19 and a citizen of Costa Rica. Raul provides all of Helena's support.

d. Karen maintains a household that includes her ex-husband, her mother-in-law, and her brother-in-law (age 23 and not a full-time student). Karen provides more than half of all of their support. Karen is single and was divorced last year.

37. **LO.4** During 2016, Jenny, age 14, lives in a household with her father, uncle, and grandmother. The household is maintained by the uncle. The parties, all of whom file separate returns, have AGI as follows: father ($30,000), uncle ($50,000), and grandmother ($40,000).

a. Who is eligible to claim Jenny as a dependent?

b. Who has precedence as to the exemption?

38. **LO.3, 4** Sam and Elizabeth Jefferson file a joint return and have three children—all of whom qualify as dependents. If the Jeffersons have AGI of $333,400, what is their allowable deduction for personal and dependency exemptions for 2016?

39. **LO.4, 9** Wesley and Myrtle (ages 90 and 88, respectively) live in an assisted care facility and for 2015 and 2016 received their support from the following sources:

	Percentage of Support
Social Security benefits	16%
Son	20
Niece	29
Cousin	12
Brother	11
Family friend (not related)	12

a. Which persons are eligible to claim the dependency exemptions under a multiple support agreement?

b. Must Wesley and Myrtle be claimed by the same person(s) for both 2015 and 2016? Explain.

c. Who, if anyone, can claim their medical expenses?

40. **LO.3, 7** Taylor, age 18, is claimed as a dependent by her parents. For 2016, she has the following income: $4,000 wages from a summer job, $1,800 interest from a money market account, and $2,000 interest from City of Boston bonds.

   a. What is Taylor's taxable income for 2016?

   b. What is Taylor's tax for 2016? [Her parents file a joint return and have taxable income of $130,000 (no dividends or capital gains).]

Issue ID

Decision Making

41. **LO.4, 9** Walter and Nancy provide 60% of the support of their daughter (age 18) and son-in-law (age 22). The son-in-law (John) is a full-time student at a local university, while the daughter (Irene) holds various part-time jobs from which she earns $11,000. Walter and Nancy engage you to prepare their tax return for 2016. During a meeting with them in late March 2017, you learn that John and Irene have filed a joint return. What tax advice would you give based on the following assumptions:

   a. All parties live in Louisiana (a community property state).

   b. All parties live in New Jersey (a common law state).

42. **LO.1, 2, 3, 4, 5, 6** Charlotte (age 40) is a surviving spouse and provides all of the support of her four minor children who live with her. She also maintains the household in which her parents live and furnished 60% of their support. Besides interest on City of Miami bonds in the amount of $5,500, Charlotte's father received $2,400 from a part-time job. Charlotte has a salary of $80,000, a short-term capital loss of $2,000, a cash prize of $4,000 from a church raffle, and itemized deductions of $10,500. Using the Tax Rate Schedules, compute the 2016 tax liability for Charlotte.

43. **LO.1, 2, 3, 4, 5, 6** Morgan (age 45) is single and provides more than 50% of the support of Rosalyn (a family friend), Flo (a niece, age 18), and Jerold (a nephew, age 18). Both Rosalyn and Flo live with Morgan, but Jerold (a French citizen) lives in Canada. Morgan earns a salary of $95,000, contributes $5,000 to a traditional IRA, and receives sales proceeds of $15,000 for an RV that cost $60,000 and was used for vacations. She has $8,200 in itemized deductions. Using the Tax Rate Schedules, compute the 2016 tax liability for Morgan.

44. **LO.5** Which of the following individuals are required to file a tax return for 2016? Should any of these individuals file a return even if filing is not required? Why or why not?

   a. Patricia, age 19, is a self-employed single individual with gross income of $5,200 from an unincorporated business. Business expenses amounted to $4,900.

   b. Mike is single and is 67 years old. His gross income from wages was $10,800.

   c. Ronald is a dependent child under age 19 who received $6,500 in wages from a part-time job.

   d. Sam is married and files a joint return with his spouse, Lana. Both Sam and Lana are 67 years old. Their combined gross income was $24,250.

   e. Quinn, age 20, is a full-time college student who is claimed as a dependent by his parents. For 2016, Quinn has taxable interest and dividends of $2,500.

Decision Making

45. **LO.5, 6, 9** Roy and Brandi are engaged and plan to get married. During 2016, Roy is a full-time student and earns $9,000 from a part-time job. With this income, student loans, savings, and nontaxable scholarships, he is self-supporting. For the year, Brandi is employed and has wages of $61,000. How much income tax, if any, can Brandi save if she and Roy marry in 2016 and file a joint return?

46. **LO.5** In each of the following independent situations, determine Winston's filing status for 2016. Winston is not married.

    a. Winston lives alone, but he maintains a household in which his parents live. The mother qualifies as Winston's dependent, but the father does not.

    b. Winston lives alone but maintains a household in which his married daughter, Karin, lives. Both Karin and her husband (Winston's son-in-law) qualify as Winston's dependents.

    c. Winston maintains a household in which he and a family friend, Ward, live. Ward qualifies as Winston's dependent.

    d. Winston maintains a household in which he and his mother-in-law live. Winston's wife died in 2015.

    e. Same as (d), except that Winston's wife disappeared (i.e., she did not die) in 2014.

47. **LO.4, 5** Christopher died in 2014 and is survived by his wife, Chloe, and their 18-year-old son, Dylan. Chloe is the executor of Christopher's estate and maintains the household in which she and Dylan live. All of their support is furnished by Chloe while Dylan saves his earnings. Dylan's status for 2014 to 2016 is as follows:

Year	Earnings	Student Status
2014	$5,000	Yes
2015	7,000	No
2016	6,000	Yes

    What is Chloe's filing status for:

    a. 2014?

    b. 2015?

    c. 2016?

48. **LO.3, 4, 5** Nadia died in 2015 and is survived by her husband, Jerold (age 44); her married son, Travis (age 22); and her daughter-in-law, Macy (age 18). Jerold is the executor of his wife's estate. He maintains the household where he, Travis, and Macy live and furnishes all of their support. During 2015 and 2016, Travis is a full-time student, while Macy earns $7,000 each year from a part-time job. Travis and Macy do not file jointly during either year. What is Jerold's filing status for 2015 and 2016 if all parties reside in:

    a. Idaho (a community property state)?

    b. Kansas (a common law state)?

49. **LO.1, 3, 7** Paige, age 17, is claimed as a dependent on her parents' 2016 return, on which they report taxable income of $120,000 (no qualified dividends or capital gains). Paige earned $3,900 pet sitting and $4,100 in interest on a savings account. What are Paige's taxable income and tax liability for 2016?

50. **LO.1, 3, 7** Terri, age 16, is claimed as a dependent on her parents' 2016 return. During the year, Terri earned $5,000 in interest income and $3,000 from part-time jobs.

    a. What is Terri's taxable income?

    b. How much of Terri's income is taxed at her rate? At her parents' rate?

    c. Can the parental election be made? Why or why not?

51. **LO.8** During 2016, Inez had the following transactions involving capital assets:

Gain on the sale of unimproved land (held as an investment for 3 years)	$ 3,000
Loss on the sale of a camper (purchased 2 years ago and used for family vacations)	(5,000)
Gain on the sale of ADM stock (purchased 9 months ago as an investment)	4,000
Gain on the sale of a fishing boat and trailer (acquired 18 months ago at an auction and used for recreational purposes)	1,000

    a.   If Inez is in the 35% bracket, how much income tax results?

    b.   If Inez is in the 15% bracket, how much income tax results?

52. **LO.8** During 2016, Chester had the following transactions involving capital assets:

Gain on the sale of an arrowhead collection (acquired as an investment at different times but all pieces have been held for more than one year)	$ 6,000
Loss on the sale of IBM Corporation stock (purchased 11 months ago as an investment)	(4,000)
Gain on the sale of a city lot (acquired 5 years ago as an investment)	2,000

    a.   If Chester is in the 33% bracket, how much income tax results?

    b.   If Chester is in the 15% bracket, how much income tax results?

Decision Making

Communications

53. **LO.9** Each year, Tom and Cindy Bates normally have itemized deductions of $10,000, including a $4,000 pledge payment to their church. Upon the advice of a friend, they do the following: in early January 2016, they pay their pledge for 2015; during 2016, they pay the pledge for 2016; and in late December 2016, they prepay their pledge for 2017.

    a.   Explain what the Bateses are trying to accomplish.

    b.   What will be the tax saving if their marginal tax bracket is 25% for all three years? (Assume that the standard deduction amounts for 2016 and 2017 are the same.)

    c.   Write a letter to Tom and Cindy Bates (8212 Bridle Court, Reston, VA 20194) summarizing your analysis.

Cumulative Problems

Tax Return Problem

54. Lance H. and Wanda B. Dean are married and live at 431 Yucca Drive, Santa Fe, NM 87501. Lance works for the convention bureau of the local Chamber of Commerce, while Wanda is employed part-time as a paralegal for a law firm.

    During 2015, the Deans had the following receipts:

Salaries ($60,000 for Lance, $41,000 for Wanda)		$101,000
Interest income—		
City of Albuquerque general purpose bonds	$1,000	
Ford Motor company bonds	1,100	
Ally Bank certificate of deposit	400	2,500
Child support payments from John Allen		7,200
Annual gifts from parents		26,000
Settlement from Roadrunner Touring Company		90,000
Lottery winnings		600
Federal income tax refund (for tax year 2014)		400

    Wanda was previously married to John Allen. When they divorced several years ago, Wanda was awarded custody of their two children, Penny and Kyle. (Note: Wanda has never issued a Form 8332 waiver.) Under the divorce decree, John was obligated to pay alimony and child support—the alimony payments were to terminate if Wanda remarried.

    In July, while going to lunch in downtown Santa Fe, Wanda was injured by a tour bus. As the driver was clearly at fault, the owner of the bus, Roadrunner Touring Company, paid her medical expenses (including a one-week stay in a hospital). To avoid a lawsuit, Roadrunner also transferred $90,000 to her in settlement of the personal injuries she sustained.

The Deans had the following expenditures for 2015:

Medical expenses (not covered by insurance)		$7,200
Taxes—		
Property taxes on personal residence	$3,600	
State of New Mexico income tax (includes amount withheld from wages during 2015)	4,200	7,800
Interest on home mortgage		6,000
Paid church pledge		3,600
Life insurance premiums (policy on Lance's life)		1,200
Contribution to traditional IRA (on Wanda's behalf)		5,000
Traffic fines		300
Contribution to the reelection campaign fund of the mayor of Santa Fe		500
Funeral expenses for Wayne Boyle		6,300

The life insurance policy was taken out by Lance several years ago and designates Wanda as the beneficiary. As a part-time employee, Wanda is excluded from coverage under her employer's pension plan. Consequently, she provides for her own retirement with a traditional IRA obtained at a local trust company. Because the mayor is a member of the local Chamber of Commerce, Lance felt compelled to make the political contribution.

The Deans' household includes the following, for whom they provide more than half of the support:

	Social Security Number	Birth Date
Lance Dean (age 42)	123-45-6786	12/16/1973
Wanda Dean (age 40)	123-45-6787	08/08/1975
Penny Allen (age 19)	123-45-6788	10/09/1996
Kyle Allen (age 17)	123-45-6789	05/03/1998
Wayne Boyle (age 75)	123-45-6785	06/15/1940

Penny graduated from high school on May 9, 2015, and is undecided about college. During 2015, she earned $8,500 (placed in a savings account) playing a harp in the lobby of a local hotel. Wayne is Wanda's widower father who died on January 20, 2015. For the past few years, Wayne qualified as a dependent of the Deans.

Federal income tax withheld is $5,200 (Lance) and $3,100 (Wanda). The proper amount of Social Security and Medicare tax was withheld.

Determine the Federal income tax for 2015 for the Deans on a joint return by completing the appropriate forms. They do not want to contribute to the Presidential Election Campaign Fund. All members of the family had health care coverage for all of 2015. If an overpayment results, it is to be refunded to them. Suggested software: H&R BLOCK Tax Software.

55. Logan B. Taylor is a widower whose wife, Sara, died on June 6, 2013. He lives at 4680 Dogwood Lane, Springfield, MO 65801. He is employed as a paralegal by a local law firm. During 2015, he had the following receipts:

Tax Return Problem

Decision Making

Communications

Salary		$ 80,000
Interest income—		
Money market account at Omni Bank	$ 300	
Savings account at Boone State Bank	1,100	
City of Springfield general purpose bonds	3,000	4,400
Inheritance from Daniel		60,000
Life insurance proceeds		200,000
Amount from sale of St. Louis lot		80,000
Proceeds from estate sale		9,000
Federal income tax refund (for 2014 tax overpayment)		700

Logan inherited securities worth $60,000 from his uncle, Daniel, who died in 2015. Logan also was the designated beneficiary of an insurance policy on Daniel's life with a maturity value of $200,000. The lot in St. Louis was purchased on May 2, 2010, for $85,000 and held as an investment. As the neighborhood has deteriorated, Logan decided to cut his losses and sold the lot on January 5, 2015, for $80,000. The estate sale consisted largely of items belonging to Sara and Daniel (e.g., camper, boat, furniture, and fishing and hunting equipment). Logan estimates that the property sold originally cost at least twice the $9,000 he received and has declined or stayed the same in value since Sara and Daniel died.

Logan's expenditures for 2015 include the following:

Medical expenses (including $10,500 for dental)		$11,500
Taxes—		
State of Missouri income tax (includes withholdings during 2015)	$3,200	
Property taxes on personal residence	4,500	7,700
Interest on home mortgage		4,600
Contribution to church (paid pledges for 2015 and 2016)		4,800

Logan and his dependents are covered by his employer's health insurance policy for all of 2015. However, he is subject to a deductible, and dental care is not included. The $10,500 dental charge was for Helen's implants. Helen is Logan's widowed mother, who lives with him (see below). Logan normally pledges $2,400 ($200 per month) each year to his church. On December 5, 2015, upon the advice of his pastor, he prepaid his pledge for 2016.

Logan's household, all of whom he supports, includes the following:

	Social Security Number	**Birth Date**
Logan Taylor (age 48)	123-45-6787	08/30/1967
Helen Taylor (age 70)	123-45-6780	01/13/1945
Asher Taylor (age 23)	123-45-6783	07/18/1992
Mia Taylor (age 22)	123-45-6784	02/16/1993

Helen receives a modest Social Security benefit. Asher, a son, is a full-time student in dental school and earns $4,500 as a part-time dental assistant. Mia, a daughter, does not work and is engaged to be married.

Part 1—Tax Computation
Using the appropriate forms and schedules, compute Logan's income tax for 2015. Federal income tax of $5,500 was withheld from his wages. If Logan has any overpayment on his income tax, he wants the refund sent to him. Assume that the proper amounts of Social Security and Medicare taxes were withheld. Logan does not want to contribute to the Presidential Election Campaign Fund. Suggested software: H&R BLOCK Tax Software.

Part 2—Follow-Up Advice
In early 2016, the following take place:

- Helen decides that she wants to live with one of her daughters and moves to Arizona.
- Asher graduates from dental school and joins an existing practice in St. Louis.
- Mia marries, and she and her husband move in with his parents.
- Using the insurance proceeds he received on Daniel's death, Logan pays off the mortgage on his personal residence.

Logan believes that these events may have an effect on his tax position for 2016. Therefore, he requests your advice.

Write a letter to Logan explaining in general terms the changes that will occur for tax purposes. Assume that Logan's salary and other factors not mentioned (e.g., property and state income taxes) will remain the same. Use the Tax Rate Schedules in projecting Logan's tax for 2016.

Research Problems

Note: Solutions to Research Problems can be prepared by using the Checkpoint® Student Edition online research product, which is available to accompany this text. It is also possible to prepare solutions to the Research Problems by using tax research materials found in a standard tax library.

THOMSON REUTERS
CHECKPOINT
Student Edition

Research Problem 1. Kathy and Brett Ouray married in 1998. They began to experience marital difficulties in 2012 and, in the current year, although they are not legally separated, consider themselves completely estranged. They have contemplated getting a divorce. However, because of financial concerns and because they both want to remain involved in the lives of their three sons, they have not yet filed for divorce. In addition, their financial difficulties have meant that Kathy and Brett cannot afford to live in separate residences. So although they consider themselves emotionally estranged, they and their three sons all reside in a single-family home in Chicago, Illinois.

Although Brett earns significantly more than Kathy, both contribute financially to maintaining their home and supporting their teenage sons. In one of their few and brief conversations this year, they determined that Brett had contributed far more than Kathy to the maintenance of their home and the support of their sons. Thus, Brett has decided that for the current tax year, they will file separate Federal income tax returns and that he will claim head-of-household filing status. While they live under the same roof, Brett believes that he and Kathy should maintain separate households. Given this fact and the fact that he provides significantly more for the support of their sons, he believes that he is eligible for head-of-household filing status. Advise Brett on which filing status is most appropriate for him in the current year. His address is 16 Lahinch, Chicago, IL 60608.

Communications

Research Problem 2. John and Janet Baker are husband and wife and maintain a household in which the following persons live: Calvin and Florence Carter and Darin, Andrea, and Morgan Baker.

Decision Making

- Calvin and Florence are Janet's parents, who are retired. During the year, they receive $19,000 in nontaxable funds (e.g., disability income, interest on municipal bonds, and Social Security benefits). Of this amount, $8,000 is spent equally between them for clothing, transportation, and recreation (e.g., vacation) and the balance of $11,000 is invested in tax-exempt securities. Janet paid $1,000 for her mother's dental work and paid the $1,200 premium on an insurance policy her father owned on his own life. Calvin also had medical expenses, but he insisted on paying for them with his own funds.
- Darin is the Bakers' 18-year-old son who is not a student but operates a pool-cleaning service on a part-time basis. During the year, he earns $14,000 from the business, which he places in a savings account for later college expenses.
- Andrea is the Bakers' 19-year-old daughter who does not work or go to school. Tired of the inconvenience of borrowing and sharing the family car, during the year, she purchased a Camaro for $21,000. Andrea used funds from a savings account she had established several years ago with an inheritance from her paternal grandfather.
- Morgan is the Bakers' 23-year-old daughter. To attend graduate school at a local university, she applied for and obtained a student loan of $20,000. She uses the full amount to pay her college tuition.

The Bakers' fair rental value of their residence, including utilities, is $14,000, while their total food expense for the household is $10,500.

a. How many dependency exemptions are the Bakers entitled to claim for the year? Explain your answer.

b. From a planning standpoint, how might the Bakers have improved the tax result?

Partial list of research aids:
Reg. §§ 1.152–1(a) and –1(c).
Your Federal Income Tax (IRS Publication 17), Chapter 3.

Internet Activity

Use the tax resources of the Internet to address the following questions. Do not restrict your search to the Web, but include a review of newsgroups and general reference materials, practitioner sites and resources, primary sources of the tax law, chat rooms and discussion groups, and other opportunities.

Research Problem 3. Locate IRS Form 2120 (at **www.irs.gov**), and answer the following questions.

a. Who must sign the form?

b. Who must file the form?

c. Can it be used for someone who is not related to the taxpayer? Explain.

Research Problem 4. What purpose is served by Form 8857? Read the directions for the form, and see IRS Publication 971 for additional information.

Research Problem 5. A nonresident alien earns money in the United States that is subject to Federal income tax. What guidance does the IRS provide about what tax form needs to be used and when it should be filed? In terms of the proper filing date, does it matter whether the earnings were subject to income tax withholding? Explain.

Roger CPA Review Questions

1. Slaton served 10 days on jury duty in 2016, for which Slaton was paid $25 per day by the county. Slaton's employer requires employees to remit to it all pay received by the county during jury duty, because Slaton's employer pays employees their normal compensation for the duration of jury duty. Slaton's W–2 income for 2016 is $40,000. What should Slaton's adjusted gross income be for 2016?

   a. $40,250   c. $39,750
   b. $40,000   d. $40,125

2. For "qualifying widow(er)" filing status, which of the following requirements must be met?

   I.   The surviving spouse does not remarry before the end of the current year
   II. The surviving spouse was eligible to file a joint tax return in the year of the spouse's death
   III. The surviving spouse maintains the cost of the principal residence for six months.

   a. I, II, and III   c. I and III, but not II
   b. I and II, but not III   d. I only

3. Which of the following prevents a husband and wife from filing a joint tax return?

   I.   The spouses have different accounting methods
   II. The spouses have different tax years, provided that both spouses are alive at the end of the year
   III. One spouse was a nonresident alien for three months during the year, and no proper election was made

a. I and II only

b. II and III only

c. I and III only

d. II only

4. Parker and his wife Marie would have been filing a joint tax return for 2014, however Marie died in October 2014. Parker has not remarried and continues to maintain a home for himself and his two children during 2014, 2015, 2016, and 2017. Parker's filing statuses for 2014, 2015, 2016, and 2017 are as follows:

	2014	2015	2016	2017
a.	Qualifying widower	Married filing joint return	Qualifying widower	Head of household
b.	Married filing joint return	Married filing joint return	Head of household	Qualifying widower
c.	Married filing joint return	Qualifying widower	Qualifying widower	Head of household
d.	Qualifying widower	Qualifying widower	Head of household	Qualifying widower

5. Which of the following items are included in determining the total support of a dependent?

I. Medical expenditures paid on behalf of the dependent

II. Life insurance premiums paid on behalf of the dependent

III. Fair rental value of dependent's lodging

a. All of the above

b. I and II only

c. I and III only

d. I only

6. Kyle and Elena Smith contributed to the support of their two children, Alexandra and Matthew, and Elena's divorced father, Nick. For 2016, Alexandra, a 22-year-old full-time college student, earned $1,700 from a part-time job. Matthew, a 27-year-old full-time graduate student, earned $23,000 from his job as a teaching assistant. Nick received $12,000 in capital gains income and $7,000 in nontaxable Social Security benefits. Alexandra, Matthew, and Nick are U.S. citizens and were over one-half supported by Kyle and Elena. How many exemptions can Kyle and Elena claim on their 2016 joint income tax return?

a. 2

b. 3

c. 4

d. 5

PART 2

GROSS INCOME

CHAPTER **4**
Gross Income: Concepts and Inclusions

CHAPTER **5**
Gross Income: Exclusions

Part 2 presents the income component of the basic tax model. Included here are the determination of what is income and the statutory exclusions that are permitted in calculating gross income. Because the taxpayer's accounting method and accounting period affect when income is reported, an introductory discussion of these topics is also included.

CHAPTER

4

Gross Income: Concepts and Inclusions

LEARNING OBJECTIVES: *After completing Chapter 4, you should be able to:*

LO.1 Explain the concepts of gross income and realization and distinguish between the economic, accounting, and tax concepts of gross income.

LO.2 Describe the cash and accrual methods of accounting and the related effects of the choice of taxable year.

LO.3 Identify who should pay the tax on a particular item of income in various situations.

LO.4 Apply the Internal Revenue Code provisions on alimony, loans made at below-market interest rates, annuities, prizes and awards, group term life insurance, unemployment compensation, and Social Security benefits.

LO.5 Identify tax planning strategies for minimizing gross income.

CHAPTER OUTLINE

CALCULATION OF GROSS INCOME

In 2016, Dr. Cliff Payne, age 27, opened his dental practice as a sole proprietorship with a December 31 year-end. By the beginning of February, construction on his medical building was completed. He also leased an office building and entered into a contract to make improvements. In addition, early in the year, he used $12,000 of extra money to purchase some stock.

The following financial information shows the results of Dr. Payne's first year of operation. The accounts receivable represent the amounts billed to patients.

Revenues (amounts billed patients for dental services)	$385,000
Accounts receivable: January 1	–0–
Accounts receivable: December 31	52,000

During the year, Sam Jones, a contractor who owed Dr. Payne $4,000 for dental services, satisfied the account by installing solar panels on the roof of Dr. Payne's new medical building.

As an undergraduate student, Cliff took an accounting course in which he learned that the accrual method of accounting provides a better measure of the income and expenses of a business. Therefore, based on the above financial information, Cliff concludes that the gross income for Federal income tax purposes is the $385,000 he billed his patients for the dental services rendered.

Has Dr. Payne correctly calculated the gross income of this dental practice?

Read the chapter and formulate your response.

FRAMEWORK 1040 **Tax Formula for Individuals**

This chapter covers the boldfaced portions of the Tax Formula for Individuals that was introduced in Concept Summary 3.1 on p. 3-3. Below those portions are the sections of Form 1040 where the results are reported.

Income *(broadly defined)*	$xx,xxx
Less: Exclusions	(x,xxx)
Gross income	$xx,xxx

FORM 1040 (p. 1)

7	Wages, salaries, tips, etc. Attach Form(s) W-2	
8a	**Taxable** interest. Attach Schedule B if required	
b	**Tax-exempt** interest. **Do not** include on line 8a . . . **8b**	
9a	Ordinary dividends. Attach Schedule B if required	
b	Qualified dividends **9b**	
11	Alimony received	
12	Business income or (loss). Attach Schedule C or C-EZ	
20a	Social security benefits **20a**	**b** Taxable amount . . .
21	Other income. List type and amount _____	

Less: Deductions *for* adjusted gross income	(x,xxx)
Adjusted gross income	$xx,xxx
Less: The greater of total **itemized deductions** *or* the standard deduction	(x,xxx)
Personal and dependency exemptions	(x,xxx)
Taxable income	$xx,xxx
Tax on taxable income *(see Tax Tables or Tax Rate Schedules)*	$ x,xxx
Less: Tax credits *(including income taxes withheld and prepaid)*	(xxx)
Tax due (or refund)	$ xxx

This chapter addresses the first step in the computation of taxable income—the determination of gross income. Questions that are addressed include the following:

- What is income?
- When is the income recognized?
- Who must include the gross income?

The Code provides an all-inclusive definition of gross income in § 61. Chapter 5 presents items of income that are specifically excluded from gross income (exclusions).

LO.1

Explain the concepts of gross income and realization and distinguish between the economic, accounting, and tax concepts of gross income.

4-1 GROSS INCOME—WHAT IS IT?

4-1a **Definition**

Section 61(a) of the Internal Revenue Code defines the term **gross income** as follows:

> Except as otherwise provided in this subtitle, gross income means all income from whatever source derived.

Unless you can find an exception

This definition is based on the language of the Sixteenth Amendment to the Constitution.

Supreme Court decisions have made it clear that all sources of income are subject to tax unless Congress specifically excludes a type of income.[1]

---

[1] *James v. U.S.*, 61–1 USTC ¶9449, 7 AFTR 2d 1361, 81 S.Ct. 1052 (USSC, 1961).

When § 61 refers to "income from whatever source derived," the taxing authorities are reaching far beyond the borders of the United States. Although one interpretation of "source" in this context is type of income (wages, interest, etc.), a broader interpretation revolves around the place where the income is generated. In this context, citizens and residents of the United States are subject to taxation on income earned from sources both inside and outside the country. This "worldwide income" tax base can cause potential double taxation problems, with other countries also taxing income earned within their borders, but mechanisms such as the foreign tax credit can alleviate these tax burdens.

Recently, some U.S. corporations have relocated to other countries to avoid the higher U.S. tax rates on income earned abroad. In the first nine months of 2014, 2,353 Americans renounced their U.S. citizenship to avoid taxes. Congress is considering ways of stopping this "flight of capital and tax base." See "Record Number of Americans Renouncing Citizenship Because of Overseas Tax Burden," by Ali Weinberg, ABC News, October 28, 2014, **http://abcnews.go. com/International/record-number-americans-renouncing-citizenship-overseas-tax-burdens/story?id=26496154**. Once per quarter, the Department of State publishes the names of U.S. citizens who have renounced their citizenship. Some of these individuals may owe Federal taxes upon renouncing. See § 877A.

Congress left it to the judicial and administrative branches to specifically determine the meaning of *income*.

4-1b Recovery of Capital Doctrine

While the Constitution grants Congress the power to tax income, it does not define the term. Thus, it would seem that Congress could simply tax gross receipts. Although Congress does allow certain deductions, none are constitutionally required. On the other hand, the Supreme Court has held that there is no income subject to tax until the taxpayer has recovered the capital invested.[2] This concept is known as the **recovery of capital doctrine**.

In its simplest application, this doctrine means that sellers can reduce their gross receipts (selling price) by the adjusted basis of the property sold to determine the amount of gross income.[3]

[handwritten margin note:] Gross Receipts − COGS ――――― Gross Income

The Big Picture

Return to the facts of *The Big Picture* on p. 4-1. Assume that Dr. Payne receives $15,000 when he sells the common stock he had purchased for $12,000. His gross receipts are $15,000, which consist of a $12,000 recovery of capital and $3,000 of gross income.

EXAMPLE 1

4-1c Economic and Accounting Concepts

The term **income** is used in the Code but is not separately defined. Thus, the courts were required to interpret "the commonly understood meaning of the term which must have been in the minds of the people when they adopted the Sixteenth Amendment to the Constitution."[4] Early in the development of the income tax law, a choice had to be made between two competing models: economic income and accounting income. In determining the definition of income, the Supreme Court rejected the economic concept of income.

Economists measure income (**economic income**) by first determining the fair market value of the individual's net assets (assets minus liabilities) at the beginning and end of the year (change in net worth). Then to arrive at economic income, this change in net

---

[2]*Doyle v. Mitchell Bros. Co.*, 1 USTC ¶17, 3 AFTR 2979, 38 S.Ct. 467 (USSC, 1916).
[3]Reg. § 1.61–3. For a definition of *adjusted basis*, see the Glossary in Appendix C.

[4]*Merchants Loan and Trust Co. v. Smietanka*, 1 USTC ¶42, 3 AFTR 3102, 41 S.Ct. 386 (USSC, 1921).

worth is increased by the value of the goods and services that person actually consumed during the period. Economic income also includes imputed values for such items as the rental value of an owner-occupied home and the value of food a taxpayer might grow for personal consumption.[5]

EXAMPLE 2

Helen has economic income as follows:

Fair market value of Helen's assets on December 31, 2016	$220,000	
Less liabilities on December 31, 2016	(40,000)	
Net worth on December 31, 2016		$ 180,000
Fair market value of Helen's assets on January 1, 2016	$200,000	
Less liabilities on January 1, 2016	(80,000)	
Net worth on January 1, 2016		(120,000)
Increase in net worth		$ 60,000
Consumption		
Food, clothing, and other personal expenditures		25,000
Imputed rental value of the home Helen owns and occupies		12,000
Economic income		$ 97,000

The need to value assets annually would make compliance with the tax law burdensome and would cause numerous controversies between the taxpayer and the IRS over valuation. In addition, using market values to determine income for tax purposes could result in liquidity problems. The taxpayer's assets may increase in value even though they are not readily convertible into the cash needed to pay the tax (e.g., commercial real estate). Thus, the IRS, Congress, and the courts have rejected the economic concept of income as impractical.

In contrast, the accounting concept of income is founded on the realization principle.[6] According to this principle, income (**accounting income**) is not recognized until it is realized. For realization to occur, (1) an exchange of goods or services must take place between the accounting entity and some independent, external party and (2) in the exchange, the accounting entity must receive assets that are capable of being objectively valued. Thus, income is recognized when an employee embezzles his or her employer's funds, when the income from an illegal business is realized, and when a person discovers buried treasure.[7] On the other hand, the appreciation in the market value of an asset owned is not realized and thus is not included in gross income until the asset is sold. Income is not realized when an individual creates assets for his or her own use (e.g., vegetables grown in a personal garden) because there is no exchange transaction with another party.

The Supreme Court expressed an inclination toward the accounting concept of income when it adopted the realization requirement in *Eisner v. Macomber*.[8]

In summary, *income* represents an increase in wealth recognized for tax purposes only upon realization.[9]

4-1d Comparison of the Timing of Income Rules for Tax and Accounting

Although income tax rules frequently parallel financial accounting measurement concepts, differences do exist. Of major significance, for example, is the fact that unearned

[5]See Henry C. Simons, *Personal Income Taxation* (Chicago: University of Chicago Press, 1933), Chapters 2–3.

[6]See the American Accounting Association Committee Report on the "Realization Concept," *The Accounting Review* (April 1965): 312–322.

[7]*Rutkin v. U.S.*, 52–1 USTC ¶9260, 41 AFTR 2d 596, 72 S.Ct. 571 (USSC, 1952); Rev.Rul. 61, 1953–1 C.B. 17.

[8]1 USTC ¶32, 3 AFTR 3020, 40 S.Ct. 189 (USSC, 1920).

[9]*Glenshaw Glass Co.*, 348 U.S. 426, 429–430, 75 S.Ct. 473, 99 L.Ed. 483 (1955).

TAX IN THE NEWS   **Bartering Gets Organized**

Bartering was the only way to conduct commerce before money was invented. But bartering has experienced a revival as a result of the creation of "barter trade exchanges." Advertisements appear on the Internet encouraging individuals to form "barter trade exchanges," which operate like a local eBay, except that services are exchanged (rather than sold for cash) among members.

Bartering may be a part of the "underground economy." The individuals who exchange services informally often do not report their income from these transactions, and it is very difficult for the IRS to discover the unreported income. However, the organized exchanges should provide the IRS with a source for discovering the taxable income from bartering. Brokers in the trade or business of facilitating barter exchanges are required to use Form 1099-B to provide the IRS and participants with information regarding the exchange.

Source: See, for example, "Start Your Own Barter Trade Exchange Using Tom McDowell's Proven Barter System," **www.bartertrainer.com/clubs.asp**.

(prepaid) income received by an accrual basis taxpayer often is taxed in the year of receipt. For financial accounting purposes, such prepayments are not treated as income until earned.[10] Because of this and other differences, many corporations report financial accounting income that is substantially different from the amounts reported for tax purposes (see Reconciliation of Corporate Taxable Income and Accounting Income in Chapter 20).

The Supreme Court provided an explanation for some of the variations between accounting and taxable income in a decision involving inventory and bad debt adjustments:

> The primary goal of financial accounting is to provide useful information to management, shareholders, creditors, and others properly interested; the major responsibility of the accountant is to protect these parties from being misled. The primary goal of the income tax system, in contrast, is the equitable collection of revenue.... Consistently with its goals and responsibilities, financial accounting has as its foundation the principle of conservatism, with its corollary that 'possible errors in measurement [should] be in the direction of understatement rather than overstatement of net income and net assets.' In view of the Treasury's markedly different goals and responsibilities, understatement of income is not destined to be its guiding light.
>
> ... Financial accounting, in short, is hospitable to estimates, probabilities, and reasonable certainties; the tax law, with its mandate to preserve the revenue, can give no quarter to uncertainty.[11]

4-1e **Form of Receipt**

Gross income is not limited to cash received. "It includes income realized in any form, whether in money, property, or services. Income may be realized [and recognized], therefore, in the form of services, meals, accommodations, stock or other property, as well as in cash."[12]

Form of Receipt

Ostrich Corporation allows Bill, an employee, to use a company car for his vacation. Bill realizes income equal to the rental value of the car for the time and mileage.

EXAMPLE

3

---

[10]Similar differences exist in the deduction area.

[11]*Thor Power Tool Co. v. Comm.*, 79–1 USTC ¶9139, 43 AFTR 2d 79–362, 99 S.Ct. 773 (USSC, 1979).

[12]Reg. § 1.61–1(a).

Form of Receipt

EXAMPLE 4

Terry owes $10,000 on a mortgage. The creditor accepts $8,000 in full satisfaction of the debt. Terry realizes income of $2,000 from retiring the debt.[13]

EXAMPLE 5

Sam began his law practice in a building in need of repairs. Sam decided to list his services on a barter exchange. He offered to provide an hour of legal services in exchange for building repairs. A qualified carpenter performed the repairs in eight hours. The carpenter normally charges $50 an hour. Sam formed a corporation for the carpenter in exchange for the carpenter's services. Sam realized $400 (8 hours × $50) in gross income for his services.

4-2 YEAR OF INCLUSION

LO.2

Describe the cash and accrual methods of accounting and the related effects of the choice of taxable year.

4-2a Taxable Year

The annual accounting period, or **taxable year**, is a basic component of our tax system.[14] Generally, an entity must use the *calendar year* to report its income. However, a *fiscal year* (a period of 12 months ending on the last day of any month other than December) can be elected if the taxpayer maintains adequate books and records. This fiscal year option generally is not available to partnerships, S corporations, and personal service corporations, as discussed in Chapter 18.[15]

In determining a person's tax liability, it is important that the income be placed in the correct tax year. The tax on the income is dependent on the applicable tax rates. The applicable rates can change between years for the following reasons:

- With a progressive rate system, a taxpayer's marginal tax rate can change from year to year.
- Congress may change the tax rates.
- The relevant rates may change because of a change in the entity's status (e.g., a person may marry or a business may be incorporated).
- Several provisions in the Code are dependent on the taxpayer's gross income for the year (e.g., whether the person can be claimed as a dependent, as discussed in Chapter 3).

Even when the rates do not change between tax years, the longer payment of the tax can be postponed, the lower the present value of the tax.

4-2b Accounting Methods

The year an item of income is subject to tax often depends upon which acceptable **accounting method** the taxpayer regularly employs.[16] The three primary methods of accounting are (1) the cash receipts and disbursements method, (2) the accrual method, and (3) the hybrid method. Most individuals use the cash receipts and disbursements method of accounting, while large corporations use the accrual method. The Regulations require the accrual method for determining purchases and sales when inventory is an income-producing factor.[17] Some businesses use a hybrid method that is a combination of the cash and accrual methods of accounting.

In addition to these overall accounting methods, a taxpayer may choose to spread the gain from an installment sale of eligible property over the collection periods by

---

[13]Reg. § 1.61–12. See *U.S. v. Kirby Lumber Co.*, 2 USTC ¶814, 10 AFTR 458, 52 S.Ct. 4 (USSC, 1931). Exceptions to this general rule are discussed in Chapter 5.

[14]See Accounting Periods in Chapter 18.

[15]§§ 441(a) and (d).

[16]See Accounting Methods in Chapter 18.

[17]Reg. § 1.446–1(c)(2)(i). Other circumstances in which the accrual method must be used are presented in Chapter 18. For the small business exception to the inventory requirement, see Rev.Proc. 2002–28, 2002–1 C.B. 815.

using the *installment method* of income recognition. Contractors may either spread profits from contracts over the periods in which the work is done (the *percentage of completion method*) or defer all profit until the year in which the project is completed (the *completed contract method*, which can be used only in limited circumstances).[18]

The IRS has the power to prescribe the accounting method to be used by the taxpayer. Section 446(b) grants the IRS broad powers to determine whether the accounting method used *clearly reflects income*:

> If no method of accounting has been regularly used by the taxpayer, or *if the method used does not clearly reflect income, the computation of taxable income shall be made under such method as, in the opinion of the Secretary ... does clearly reflect income.*

A change in method of accounting requires the consent of the IRS.[19]

Cash Receipts Method

Under the **cash receipts method**, property or services received are included in the taxpayer's gross income in the year of actual or constructive receipt by the taxpayer or agent, regardless of whether the income was earned in that year.[20] The income received need not be reduced to cash in the same year. All that is necessary for income recognition is that property or services received have a fair market value—a cash equivalent.[21] Thus, a cash basis taxpayer who receives a note in payment for services has income in the year of receipt equal to the fair market value of the note. However, a creditor's mere promise to pay (e.g., an account receivable), with no supporting note, usually is not considered to have a fair market value.[22] Thus, the cash basis taxpayer defers income recognition until the account receivable is collected.

EXAMPLE

6

Dana, an accountant, reports her income using the cash method. In 2016, she performed an audit for Orange Corporation and billed the client for $5,000, which was collected in 2017. In 2016, Dana also performed an audit for Blue Corporation. Because of Blue's precarious financial position, Dana required Blue to issue an $8,000 secured negotiable note in payment of the fee. The note had a fair market value of $6,000. Dana collected $8,000 on the note in 2017. Dana's gross income for the two years is as follows:

	2016	2017
Fair market value of note received from Blue	$6,000	
Cash received		
From Orange on account receivable		$ 5,000
From Blue on note receivable		8,000
Less: Recovery of capital		(6,000)
Total gross income	$6,000	$ 7,000

Generally, a check received is considered a cash equivalent and, upon receipt, must be recognized as income by a cash basis taxpayer. An exception to this rule is if the person paying with the check requests that the check not be cashed until a subsequent date, the income is deferred until that later date.[23]

Accrual Method

Under the **accrual method**, an item is generally included in gross income for the year in which it is earned, regardless of when it is collected. The income is earned when (1) all

---

[18]§§ 453 and 460. See Chapter 18 for limitations on the use of the installment method and the completed contract method.

[19]§ 446(e).

[20]*Julia A. Strauss*, 2 B.T.A. 598 (1925). See the Glossary in Appendix C for a discussion of the terms *cash equivalent doctrine* and *constructive receipt*.

[21]Reg. §§ 1.446–1(a)(3) and (c)(1)(i).

[22]*Bedell v. Comm.*, 1 USTC ¶359, 7 AFTR 8469, 30 F.2d 622 (CA–2, 1929).

[23]*Charles F. Kahler*, 18 T.C. 31 (1952); *Bright v. U.S.*, 91–1 USTC ¶50, 142, 67 AFTR 2d 91–673, 926 F.2d 383 (CA–5, 1991).

events have occurred that fix the right to receive such income and (2) the amount to be received can be determined with reasonable accuracy.[24]

Generally, the taxpayer's rights to the income accrue when title to property passes to the buyer or the services are performed for the customer or client.[25] If the rights to the income have accrued but are subject to a potential refund claim (e.g., under a product warranty), the income is reported in the year of sale and a deduction is allowed in subsequent years when actual claims accrue.[26]

warranty →

Where the taxpayer's right to the income is contested (e.g., when a contractor fails to meet specifications), the year in which the income is subject to tax depends upon whether payment has been received. If payment has not been received, no income is recognized until the claim is settled. Only then is the right to the income established.[27] However, if the payment is received before the dispute is settled, a **claim of right doctrine** requires the taxpayer to recognize the income in the year of receipt.[28]

> **The Big Picture**
>
> **EXAMPLE 7**
>
> Return to the facts of *The Big Picture* on p. 4-1. On completing the construction improvements to Dr. Payne's medical office building in 2016, assume that the contractor, who uses the accrual method, submitted a bill. Dr. Payne refused to pay the bill, however, claiming that the contractor had not met specifications. The contractor did not reach a settlement with Dr. Payne until 2017. No income accrues to the contractor until 2017. If Dr. Payne had paid for the work and then filed suit for damages, the contractor could not defer the income (the income would be taxable in 2016).

Goods ⇒ Accrual (required)
Services ⇒ Cash (general)
Goods + Services/other ⇒ Hybrid

The measure of accrual basis income is generally the amount the taxpayer has a right to receive. Unlike the cash basis, the fair market value of the customer's obligation is irrelevant in measuring accrual basis income. The ability to defer income is a distinct advantage over the accrual method; therefore, service businesses usually use the cash method. However, the accrual method must be used when inventories are an income-producing factor to the business.[29]

> **EXAMPLE 8**
>
> Assume the same facts as in Example 6, except that Dana is an accrual basis taxpayer. Dana must recognize $13,000 ($8,000 + $5,000) of gross income in 2016, the year her rights to the income accrued.

Hybrid Method

The **hybrid method** is a combination of the accrual method and the cash method. Generally, when the hybrid method is used, inventory is an income-producing factor. The Regulations require use of the accrual method for determining sales of inventory and cost of goods sold. Thus, the taxpayer accounts for inventory using the accrual method and uses the cash method for all other income and expense items (e.g., services and interest income). The hybrid method is primarily used by small businesses.

4-2c Special Rules Applicable to Cash Basis Taxpayers

Constructive Receipt

Income that has not actually been received by the taxpayer is taxed as though it had been received—the income is constructively received—under the following conditions:

[24]Reg. § 1.451–1(a).

[25]*Lucas v. North Texas Lumber Co.*, 2 USTC ¶484, 8 AFTR 10276, 50 S.Ct. 184 (USSC, 1930). See also Rev.Rul. 84–31, 1984–1 C.B. 127.

[26]*Brown v. Helvering*, 4 USTC ¶1222, 13 AFTR 851, 54 S.Ct. 356 (USSC, 1933).

[27]*Burnet v. Sanford and Brooks*, 2 USTC ¶636, 9 AFTR 603, 51 S.Ct. 150 (USSC, 1931).

[28]*North American Oil Consolidated Co. v. Burnet*, 3 USTC ¶943, 11 AFTR 16, 52 S.Ct. 613 (USSC, 1932).

[29]Reg. § 1.446–1(c)(2).

- The amount is made readily available to the taxpayer.   *Available*
- The taxpayer's actual receipt is not subject to substantial limitations or restrictions.[30]   *Has right to it*

The rationale for the constructive receipt doctrine is that if the income is available, the taxpayer should not be allowed to postpone the income recognition. For instance, a taxpayer is not permitted to defer income for December services by refusing to accept payment until January. However, determining whether the income is *readily available* and whether *substantial limitations or restrictions exist* necessitates a factual inquiry.[31] Following are some examples of the application of the constructive receipt doctrine.

EXAMPLE 9

Ted is a member of a barter club. In 2016, Ted performed services for other club members and earned 1,000 points. Each point entitles him to $1 in goods and services sold by other members of the club; the points can be used at any time. In 2017, Ted exchanged his points for a new high-definition TV. Ted must recognize $1,000 gross income in 2016 when the 1,000 points were credited to his account.[32]

The Big Picture

EXAMPLE 10

Return to the facts of *The Big Picture* on p. 4-1. On December 31, Dr. Payne has $10,000 in patients' checks that have not been deposited. They include a check for $3,000 from a patient who asked Dr. Payne not to deposit the check until after January 4 of next year because her account did not contain sufficient funds to pay the debt.

Under the cash method, Dr. Payne must recognize $7,000 income from the $7,000 in checks on hand in the current year because the checks are a cash equivalent that is actually received. The income from the $3,000 check is neither actually nor constructively received in the current year because an insufficient account means that the funds are not available.[33]

EXAMPLE 11

Rick has a savings account with Eagle Savings and Loan Association. Under the terms of the account, interest accrues monthly and the depositor can withdraw the funds (including accrued interest) at any time. The interest for the year is constructively received by Rick even though he does not withdraw the funds.[34]

The constructive receipt doctrine does not reach income the taxpayer is not yet entitled to receive even though the taxpayer could have contracted to receive the income at an earlier date.[35]

The Big Picture

EXAMPLE 12

Return to the facts of *The Big Picture* on p. 4-1. Assume that Dr. Payne adopted the cash basis of accounting. If he allowed patients to pay by credit card, Dr. Payne would receive immediate credit in his bank account for 96% of the charge. The other 4% would be retained by the credit card issuer. To avoid the 4% charge, Dr. Payne chose not to accept credit card payments. Instead, he established a policy of requiring all bills to be paid within 30 days after the dental services were provided. He communicated this policy to patients before he performed the services. At the end of the year, several patients who owed a combined $2,000 offered to pay with credit cards, but his office rejected their offers.

The $2,000 was not constructively received at the end of the year. Although Dr. Payne could have received payment by credit card in the current year before the dental services were performed, he contracted to receive payment at a later date. Moreover, the 4% charge by the credit card company would be a "substantial limitation." [36]

---

[30]Reg. § 1.451–2(a).

[31]*Baxter v. Comm.*, 87–1 USTC ¶9315, 59 AFTR 2d 87–1068, 816 F.2d 493 (CA–9, 1987).

[32]Rev.Rul. 80–52, 1980–1 C.B. 100.

[33]*L. M. Fischer*, 14 T.C. 792 (1950).

[34]Reg. § 1.451–2(a).

[35]*Baxter v. Comm.*, 816 F.2d 493, 59 AFTR 2d 87–1068, 87–1 USTC ¶9315 (CA–9, 1997).

[36]*Cowden v. Comm.*, 61–1 USTC ¶9382, 7 AFTR 2d 1160, 289 F.2d 20 (CA–5, 1961).

Income set apart or made available is not constructively received if its actual receipt is subject to *substantial restrictions*. The life insurance industry has used substantial restrictions as a cornerstone for designing life insurance contracts with favorable tax features. Ordinary life insurance policies provide (1) current protection—an amount payable in the event of death—and (2) a savings feature—a cash surrender value payable to the policyholder if the policy is terminated during the policyholder's life. The annual increase in cash surrender value is not taxable because the policyholder must cancel the policy to actually receive the increase in value. Because the cancellation requirement is a substantial restriction, the policyholder does not constructively receive the annual increase in cash surrender value.[37] Employees often receive from their employers property subject to substantial restrictions. Generally, no income is recognized until the restrictions lapse.[38]

Carlos is a key employee of Red, Inc. The corporation gives stock with a value of $10,000 to Carlos. The stock cannot be sold, however, for five years. Carlos is not required to recognize income until the restrictions lapse at the end of five years.

Original Issue Discount

Lenders frequently make loans that require a payment at maturity of more than the amount of the original loan. The difference between the amount due at maturity is actually interest but is referred to as **original issue discount**. In such an arrangement, the Code requires the original issue discount to be reported when it is earned, regardless of the taxpayer's accounting method.[39] The interest "earned" is calculated by the effective interest rate method.

On January 1, 2016, Mark, a cash basis taxpayer, pays $82,645 for a 24-month certificate. The certificate is priced to yield 10% (the effective interest rate) with interest compounded annually. No interest is paid until maturity, when Mark receives $100,000. Thus, Mark's gross income from the certificate is $17,355 ($100,000 − $82,645). Mark's income earned each year is calculated as follows:

2016 (.10 × $82,645) =	$ 8,265
2017 [.10 × ($82,645 + $8,265)] =	9,090
	$17,355

The original issue discount rules do not apply to U.S. savings bonds (discussed in the following paragraphs) or to obligations with a maturity date of one year or less from the date of issue.[40] See Chapter 16 for additional discussion of the tax treatment of original issue discount.

Series E and Series EE Bonds

Certain U.S. government savings bonds (Series E before 1980 and Series EE after 1979) are issued at a discount and are redeemable for fixed amounts that increase at stated intervals. No interest payments are actually made. The difference between the purchase price and the amount received on redemption is the bondholder's interest income from the investment.

The income from these savings bonds is generally deferred until the bonds are redeemed or mature. Thus, U.S. savings bonds have attractive income deferral features not available with corporate bonds and certificates of deposit issued by financial institutions.

Of course, the deferral feature of government bonds issued at a discount is not an advantage if the investor has insufficient income to be subject to tax as the income

---

[37] *Theodore H. Cohen*, 39 T.C. 1055 (1963).

[38] § 83(a). See also Restricted Property Plans in Chapter 19.

[39] §§ 1272(a)(3) and 1273(a).

[40] § 1272(a)(2).

accrues. In fact, the deferral may work to the investor's disadvantage if the investor has other income in the year the bonds mature or the bunching of the bond interest into one tax year creates a tax liability. Fortunately, U.S. government bonds have a provision for these investors. A cash basis taxpayer can elect to include in gross income the annual increment in redemption value.[41] These savings bond features can be relevant in planning with respect to reducing the kiddie tax (see Chapter 3).

Kate purchases Series EE U.S. savings bonds for $500 (face value of $1,000) on January 2 of the current year. If the bonds are redeemed during the first six months, no interest is paid. At December 31, the redemption value is $519.60.

If Kate elects to report the interest income annually, she must report interest income of $19.60 for the current year. If she does not make the election, she will report no interest income for the current year. When the bond matures, Kate may receive a Form 1099 from the bank for all of the interest. She should keep good records to prove that she paid the tax on the interest income over the life of the bond.

When a taxpayer elects to report the income from the bonds on an annual basis, the election applies to all such bonds the taxpayer owns at the time of the election and to all such securities acquired subsequent to the election. A change in the method of reporting the income from the bonds requires permission from the IRS.

ETHICS & EQUITY   Should the Tax Treatment of Government Bonds and Corporate Bonds Be Different?

Taxpayers are permitted to defer the original issue discount earned on U.S. Government Series EE bonds until the bonds mature, but the original issue discount on a corporate bond must be taken into gross income each year the bond is held. Is this difference in the tax treatment of income earned on government and corporate bonds defensible in terms of equity? Why or why not?

Amounts Received under an Obligation to Repay

The receipt of funds with an obligation to repay that amount in the future is the essence of borrowing. Because the taxpayer's assets and liabilities increase by the same amount, no income is realized when the borrowed funds are received. Thus, if an obligation to repay the funds exists, the receipt of deposited or borrowed funds is not a taxable event.

A landlord receives a damage deposit from a tenant. The landlord does not recognize income until the deposit is forfeited because the landlord has an obligation to repay the deposit if no damage occurs.[42] However, if the deposit is in fact a prepayment of rent, it is taxed in the year of receipt.

4-2d Exceptions Applicable to Accrual Basis Taxpayers

Prepaid Income

For financial reporting purposes under accrual accounting, advance payments received from customers are reflected as prepaid income and as a liability of the seller. However, for tax purposes, the prepaid income often is taxed in the year of receipt.

---

[41]§ 454(a).

[42]*John Mantell*, 17 T.C. 1143 (1952).

GLOBAL TAX ISSUES   **Tax Credit Neutralizes Foreign Income Taxes**

When a U.S. taxpayer invests in a foreign country, that investment income is subject to tax in the United States and may also be subject to tax in the foreign country. However, the taxpayer is allowed a credit on his or her U.S. Federal income tax return for income taxes paid to the foreign country. The credit system allows the taxpayer to treat the taxes paid to the foreign country as though they were paid to the United States.

If the foreign taxes paid are less than the U.S. tax on the income, the foreign taxes have cost the taxpayer nothing. On the other hand, if the foreign taxes are greater than the U.S. tax on the income, the credit is limited to the amount of the U.S. tax on the income. In this case, the taxes paid by the taxpayer will exceed what they would have been if the income had been earned in the United States.

EXAMPLE 17

In December 2016, a tenant pays his January 2017 rent of $1,000. The accrual basis landlord must include the $1,000 in her 2016 gross income for tax purposes, although the unearned rent income is reported as a liability on the landlord's December 31, 2016 financial accounting balance sheet.

Taxpayers have repeatedly argued that deferral of income until it is actually earned properly matches revenues and expenses. Moreover, a proper matching of income with the expenses of earning the income is necessary to clearly reflect income, as required by the Code. The IRS responds that § 446(b) grants it broad powers to determine whether an accounting method clearly reflects income. The IRS further argues that generally accepted financial accounting principles should not dictate tax accounting for prepaid income because of the practical problems of collecting Federal revenues. Collection of the tax is simplest in the year the taxpayer receives the cash from the customer or client.

After a number of years of continual disputes between the IRS and taxpayers, the IRS relented and modified its rules on the prepaid income issue in some situations, as explained below.

Deferral of Advance Payments for Goods

Generally, a taxpayer can elect to defer recognition of income from *advance payments for goods* if the method of accounting for the sale is the same for tax and financial reporting purposes.[43]

EXAMPLE 18

Brown Company will ship goods only after payment for the goods has been received. In December 2016, Brown received $10,000 for goods that were not shipped until January 2017. Brown can elect to report the income for tax purposes in 2017, assuming that the company reports the income in 2017 for financial reporting purposes.

Deferral of Advance Payments for Services

Revenue Procedure 2004–34[44] permits an accrual basis taxpayer to defer recognition of income for *advance payments for services* to be performed after the end of the tax year of receipt. The portion of the advance payment that relates to services performed in the tax year of receipt is included in gross income in the tax year of receipt, matching what was reported in the taxpayer's financial statements. The portion of the advance payment that relates to services to be performed after the tax year of receipt is included in gross income in the subsequent tax year. This method of accounting may also be used for advance payments received for goods, as well as licensing of intellectual property, and the sale, lease, or license of software.

---

[43]Reg. § 1.451–5(b). See Reg. § 1.451–5(c) for exceptions to this deferral opportunity. The financial accounting conformity requirement is not applicable to contractors who use the completed contract method.

[44]2004–1 C.B. 991.

> **EXAMPLE**
>
> 19 ✳
>
> Yellow Corporation, an accrual basis calendar year taxpayer, sells its services under 12-month, 24-month, and 36-month contracts. The corporation provides services to each customer every month. On May 1, 2016, Yellow Corporation sold the following customer contracts:
>
> | Length of Contract | Total Proceeds |
> | --- | --- |
> | 12 months | $3,000 |
> | 24 months | 4,800 |
> | 36 months | 7,200 |
>
> Yellow may defer until 2017 all of the income that will be earned after 2016.
>
> | Length of Contract | Income Recorded in 2016 | Income Recorded in 2017 |
> | --- | --- | --- |
> | 12 months | $2,000 ($3,000 × 8/12) | $1,000 ($3,000 × 4/12) |
> | 24 months | 1,600 ($4,800 × 8/24) | 3,200 ($4,800 × 16/24) |
> | 36 months | 1,600 ($7,200 × 8/36) | 5,600 ($7,200 × 28/36) |

Revenue Procedure 2004–34 *does not* apply to prepaid rent or prepaid interest. Advance payments for these items are always taxed in the year of receipt.

Lucas v. Earl does NOT apply to property income

4-3 INCOME SOURCES

LO.3

Identify who should pay the tax on a particular item of income in various situations.

4-3a Personal Services

It is a well-established principle of taxation that income from personal services must be included in the gross income of the person who performs the services. This principle was first established in a Supreme Court decision, *Lucas v. Earl*.[45] Mr. Earl entered into a binding agreement with his wife under which Mrs. Earl was to receive one-half of Mr. Earl's salary. Justice Holmes used the celebrated **fruit and tree metaphor** to explain that the fruit (income) must be attributed to the tree from which it came (Mr. Earl). A mere **assignment of income** does not shift the liability for the tax.

Services of an Employee

Services performed by an employee for the employer's customers are considered performed by the employer. Thus, the employer is taxed on the income from the services provided to the customer, and the employee is taxed on any compensation received from the employer.[46]

> **The Big Picture**
>
> **EXAMPLE**
>
> 20
>
> Return to the facts of *The Big Picture* on p. 4-1. Assume that instead of operating his dental practice as a sole proprietorship, Dr. Payne incorporated his dental practice in an attempt to limit his liability. He entered into an employment contract with his corporation and was to receive a salary. All patients contract to receive their services from the corporation, and those services are provided through the corporation's employee, Dr. Payne. Thus, the corporation earned the income from patients' services and must include the patients' fees in its gross income. Dr. Payne must include his salary in his gross income. The corporation is allowed a deduction for the reasonable salary paid to Dr. Payne. (See the discussion of unreasonable compensation in Chapter 6.)

---

[45]2 USTC ¶496, 8 AFTR 10287, 50 S.Ct. 241 (USSC, 1930).

[46]*Sargent v. Comm.*, 91–1 USTC ¶50,168, 67 AFTR 2d 91–718, 929 F.2d 1252 (CA–8, 1991).

Services of a Child

In the case of a child, the Code specifically provides that amounts earned from personal services must be included in the child's gross income. This result applies even though the income is paid to other persons (e.g., the parents).[47]

4-3b Income from Property

The courts have used the fruit and tree metaphor to determine who should pay the tax on the income from property. The "tree" is the property, and income is its "fruit." The owner of the tree has control over the fruit; therefore, the owner of the property should pay tax on the income the property produces. Thus, if a father clips interest coupons associated with corporate bonds shortly before the interest payment date and gives the coupons to his son, the interest will still be taxed to the father. And a father who assigns to his daughter the right to collect the rent from his rental property will be taxed on the rent because he retains ownership of the property.[48]

Interest

According to the IRS, interest accrues daily. Therefore, the interest for the period that includes the date of the transfer is allocated between the transferor and transferee based on the number of days during the period that each owned the property.

Floyd, a cash basis taxpayer, gave his son, Ethan, corporate bonds with a face amount of $12,000 and a 5% stated annual interest rate. The gift was made on February 28, 2016, and the interest was paid on the last day of each quarter. Floyd must recognize $100 of interest income (5% × $12,000 × 3/12 × 2/3) accrued at the time of the gift.

For the transferor, the timing of the recognition of the income from the property depends upon the accounting method and the manner in which the property was transferred. In the case of a gift of income-producing property, the donor must recognize his or her share of the accrued income at the time it would have been recognized had the donor continued to own the property.[49] However, if the transfer is a sale, the transferor must recognize the accrued income at the time of the sale. This results because the accrued interest will be included in the sales proceeds.

Mia purchased a corporate bond at its face amount of $10,000 on January 1, 2016. The bond pays 5% interest on each December 31. On March 31, 2016, Mia sold the bond for $10,600. Mia must recognize $125 interest income in 2016 (5% × $10,000 × 3/12). She must also recognize a $475 capital gain from the sale of the bond:

Amount received from sale	$ 10,600
Less accrued interest income	(125)
Selling price of bond less interest	$ 10,475
Less cost of the bond	(10,000)
Gain on sale	$ 475

Dividends

A corporation is taxed on its earnings, and the shareholders are taxed on the dividends paid to them from the corporation's after-tax earnings.

Double Taxation

---

[47]§ 73. For circumstances in which the child's unearned income is taxed at the parents' rate, see Kiddie Tax—Unearned Income of Children Taxed at Parents' Rate in Chapter 3.

[48]*Galt v. Comm.*, 54–2 USTC ¶9457, 46 AFTR 633, 216 F.2d 41 (CA–7, 1954); *Helvering v. Horst*, 40–2 USTC ¶9787, 24 AFTR 1058, 61 S.Ct. 144 (USSC, 1940).

[49]Rev.Rul. 72–312, 1972–1 C.B. 22.

GLOBAL TAX ISSUES Do Dividends from Foreign Corporations Warrant Special Treatment?

The special rates on dividends are intended to mitigate the double-tax burden—taxing income at the corporate level then taxing the dividends to the shareholder. The United States taxes foreign corporations only on the income the corporation earns in this country. Therefore, if the corporation does no business in the United States but pays dividends to shareholders subject to U.S. taxes, the corporation's income is only taxed once.

Nevertheless, special rates apply to the foreign corporation's dividends if (1) the foreign corporation's stock is traded on an established U.S. securities market or (2) the foreign corporation is eligible for the benefits of an income tax treaty between its country of incorporation and the United States. The apparent reason for the first exception is that if the corporation is listed on an established U.S. securities market, it probably does enough business in the United States to be subject to its tax. The second exception is a reciprocal arrangement: the United States confers a benefit to corporations formed in countries that exempt U.S. corporations from taxes.

Corporations are permitted a dividend received deduction of from 70 percent to 100 percent of the dividends received from another domestic corporation. This is discussed in Chapter 20.

Partial relief from double taxation is provided by taxing qualified dividends received by individuals at the same rate as capital gains.[50] Individuals otherwise subject to the 10 or 15 percent marginal tax rate are eligible for a 0 percent tax on qualified dividends received. Individuals subject to the 25, 28, 33, or 35 percent marginal tax rate pay a 15 percent tax on qualified dividends received. Beginning in 2013, the maximum tax rate that applies to qualified dividends increased from 15 percent to 20 percent for high-income taxpayers—those subject to the 39.6 percent marginal tax rate.

A holding period requirement must be satisfied for the special rates to apply: the stock must have been held for more than 60 days during the 121-day period beginning 60 days before the ex-dividend date.[51] The purpose of this requirement is to prevent the taxpayer from buying the stock shortly before the dividend is paid, receiving the dividend, and then selling the stock at a loss (a short-term capital loss) after the stock goes ex-dividend. A stock's price often declines after the stock goes ex-dividend.

Note that qualified dividends are not included as capital gains in the gains and losses netting process; thus, they are *not* reduced by capital losses. Qualified dividend income is merely taxed at the rates that would apply to the taxpayer if he or she had an excess of net long-term capital gain over net short-term capital loss.

Stock Holding Period

EXAMPLE 23

In June 2016, Green Corporation pays a dividend of $1.50 on each share of its common stock. Madison and Daniel, two unrelated shareholders, each own 1,000 shares of the stock. Consequently, each receives a dividend of $1,500 (1,000 shares × $1.50). Assume that Daniel satisfies the 60/121-day holding period rule but Madison does not.

The $1,500 that Daniel receives is subject to preferential 0%/15%/20% treatment in 2016. The $1,500 that Madison receives, however, is not. Because Madison did not comply with the holding period rule, her dividend is not a *qualified dividend* and is taxed at ordinary income rates.

---

[50]§ 1(h)(11).

[51]The ex-dividend date is the date before the record date on which the corporation finalizes the list of shareholders who will receive the dividends.

Stock Holding Period

EXAMPLE 24

Assume that both Madison and Daniel in Example 23 are in the 35% tax bracket. Consequently, Madison pays a tax of $525 (35% × $1,500) on her dividend, while Daniel pays a tax of $225 (15% × $1,500) on his. The $300 saving that Daniel enjoys underscores the advantages of qualified dividend treatment.

Unlike interest, dividends do not accrue on a daily basis because the declaration of a dividend is at the discretion of the corporation's board of directors. Generally, dividends are taxed to the person who is entitled to receive them—the shareholder of record as of the corporation's record date.[52] Thus, if a taxpayer sells stock after a dividend has been declared but before the record date, the dividend generally will be taxed to the purchaser.

This rule differs in the case of a gift of stock. If a donor makes a gift of stock to someone (e.g., a family member) after the declaration date but before the record date, the Tax Court has held that the donor does not shift the dividend income to the donee. The *fruit* has sufficiently ripened as of the declaration date to tax the dividend income to the donor of the stock.[53] In a similar set of facts, the Fifth Circuit Court of Appeals concluded that the dividend income should be included in the gross income of the donee (the owner at the record date). In this case, the taxpayer gave stock to a qualified charity (a charitable contribution) after the declaration date and before the record date.[54] Thus, gifts to charities and gifts to family members are treated differently.

EXAMPLE 25

On June 20, the board of directors of Black Corporation declares a $10 per share dividend. The dividend is payable on June 30 to shareholders of record on June 25. As of June 20, Maria owned 200 shares of Black Corporation's stock. On June 21, Maria sold 100 of the shares to Norm for their fair market value and gave 100 of the shares to Sam (her son). Both Norm and Sam are shareholders of record as of June 25.

Norm (the purchaser) will be taxed on $1,000 because he is entitled to receive the dividend. However, Maria (the donor) will be taxed on the $1,000 received by Sam (the donee) because the gift was made after the declaration date but before the record date of the dividend.

4-3c Income Received by an Agent

Income received by the taxpayer's agent is considered to be received by the taxpayer. A cash basis principal must recognize the income at the time it is received by the agent.[55]

EXAMPLE 26

Jack, a cash basis taxpayer, delivered cattle to the auction barn in late December. The auctioneer, acting as the farmer's agent, sold the cattle and collected the proceeds in December. The auctioneer did not pay Jack until the following January. Jack must include the sales proceeds in his gross income for the year the auctioneer received the funds.

4-3d Income from Partnerships, S Corporations, Trusts, and Estates

A **partnership** is not a separate taxable entity. Rather, the partnership merely files an information return (Form 1065), which serves to provide the data necessary for determining the character and amount of each partner's distributive share of the partnership's income and deductions. Each partner must then report his or her distributive share of the partnership's income and deductions for the partnership's tax year ending in or with the partner's tax year. The income must be reported by each partner in the year it is earned,

---

[52]Reg. § 1.61–9(c). The record date is the cutoff for determining the shareholders who are entitled to receive the dividend.

[53]*M. G. Anton*, 34 T.C. 842 (1960).

[54]*Caruth Corp. v. U.S.*, 89–1 USTC ¶9172, 63 AFTR 2d 89–716, 865 F.2d 644 (CA–5, 1989).

[55]Rev.Rul. 79–379, 1979–2 C.B. 204.

TAX IN THE NEWS   **The Attorney's Fee Was the Plaintiff's Income**

Mr. Banks sued his employer for employment discrimination and received a settlement. Banks's attorney received approximately one-third of the settlement, and Banks reasoned that he should include only the remaining amount in his gross income.

The U.S. Supreme Court disagreed. The Court applied "assignment of income" and "principal-agent" reasoning to conclude that Banks was required to include the entire settlement amount in his gross income. The Court considered the lawsuit a property interest. Banks controlled the lawsuit and diverted some of the proceeds to the attorney; that is, Banks assigned a portion of his income to the attorney. The Court rejected Banks's argument that he and the attorney were partners pursuing the lawsuit. Instead, the Court concluded that Banks and his attorney maintained a

"quintessential principal-agent relationship," with the attorney-agent pursuing the rights of his principal, Banks. Under well-settled principles of tax law, the amount received as a result of the agent's efforts nevertheless belonged to Banks, the principal. According to the Court, the tax treatment of the amount due the attorney would have to be addressed through the tax deduction rules. For Mr. Banks, this deduction was classified as a miscellaneous itemized deduction subject to the 2%-of-AGI floor under § 67. Because of the rather harsh result, § 67 was modified. Under the modification, Mr. Banks could have claimed a deduction *for* AGI as to the attorney's portion and thereby avoided the need to itemize. As noted in Chapter 1 (Example 28), Congress can and does sometimes intervene to rectify an undesirable Supreme Court holding.

even if such amounts are not actually distributed to the partners. Because a partner pays tax on income as the partnership earns it, a distribution by the partnership to the partner is treated under the recovery of capital rules.[56]

> **EXAMPLE 27**
>
> Tara owns a one-half interest in the capital and profits of T & S Company (a calendar year partnership). For tax year 2016, the partnership earned revenue of $150,000 and had operating expenses of $80,000. During the year, Tara withdrew from her capital account $2,500 per month (for a total of $30,000).
>
> For 2016, Tara must report $35,000 as her share of the partnership's profits [$\frac{1}{2} \times$ ($150,000 − $80,000)] even though she received distributions of only $30,000.

Contrary to the general provision that a corporation must pay tax on its income, a *small business corporation* may elect to be taxed similarly to a partnership. Thus, the shareholders rather than the corporation pay the tax on the corporation's income.[57] The electing corporation is referred to as an **S corporation**. The shareholders report their proportionate shares of the corporation's income and deductions for the year, regardless of whether the corporation actually makes any distributions to the shareholders.

The *beneficiaries of estates and trusts* generally are taxed on the income earned by the estates or trusts that is actually distributed or required to be distributed to them.[58] Any income not taxed to the beneficiaries is taxable to the estate or trust.

The taxation of income and distributions of partnerships, S corporations, and estates and trusts are compared in Concept Summary 4.1.

Concept Summary 4.1

Taxation of Income and Distributions

	Partnership	S Corporation	Estate or Trust
Share of the income for the year	Partner's share taxed when earned by the partnership.	Stockholder's share taxed when earned by the S corporation.	Undistributed income taxed to the estate or trust.
Distributions	Recovery of capital, which reduces basis in the partnership.	Recovery of capital, which reduces basis in the stock.	Beneficiary's income taxed when distributed.

---

[56]§ 706(a) and Reg. § 1.706–1(a)(1). For further discussion, see Chapter 20.

[57]§§ 1361(a) and 1366. For further discussion, see Chapter 20.

[58]§§ 652(a) and 662(a). For further discussion of the taxation of income from partnerships, S corporations, trusts, and estates, see *South-Western Federal*

Taxation: Corporations, Partnerships, Estates & Trusts, Chapters 10, 11, 12, and 20.

4-3e **Income in Community Property States**

General

State law in Louisiana, Texas, New Mexico, Arizona, California, Washington, Idaho, Nevada, and Wisconsin is based upon a community property system. In Alaska, spouses can choose to have the community property rules apply. All other states have a common law property system. The basic difference between common law and community property systems centers around the property rights of married persons. Questions about community property income most frequently arise when the husband and wife file separate returns.

Under a community property system, all property is deemed either to be separately owned by the spouse or to belong to the marital community. Property may be held separately by a spouse if it was acquired before marriage or received by gift or inheritance following marriage. Otherwise, any property is deemed to be community property. For Federal tax purposes, each spouse is taxed on one-half of the income from property belonging to the community.

The laws of Texas, Louisiana, Wisconsin, and Idaho distinguish between separate property and the income it produces. In these states, the income from separate property belongs to the community. Accordingly, for Federal income tax purposes, each spouse is taxed on one-half of the income. In the remaining community property states, separate property produces separate income that the owner-spouse must report on his or her Federal income tax return.

What appears to be income, however, may really represent a recovery of capital. A recovery of capital and gain realized on separate property retain their identity as separate property. Items such as nontaxable stock dividends, royalties from mineral interests, and gains and losses from the sale of property take on the same classification as the assets to which they relate.

EXAMPLE 28

Bob and Jane are are married and reside in California. Among other transactions during the year, the following occurred:

- Nontaxable stock dividend received by Jane on stock that was given to her by her mother after Jane's marriage.
- Gain of $10,000 on the sale of unimproved land purchased by Bob before his marriage.
- Oil royalties of $15,000 from a lease Jane acquired with her separate funds after marriage.

Because the stock dividend was distributed on stock held by Jane as separate property, it also is her separate property. The same result occurs for the oil royalties Jane receives. All of the proceeds from the sale of the unimproved land (including the gain of $10,000) are Bob's separate property.

In all community property states, income from personal services (e.g., salaries, wages, and income from a professional partnership) is generally treated as if one-half is earned by each spouse.

EXAMPLE 29

Fred and Wilma are married but file separate returns. Fred received $25,000 of salary and $300 of taxable interest on a savings account he established in his name. All deposits to the savings account were made from Fred's salary that he earned since the marriage. Wilma collected $2,000 taxable dividends on stock she inherited from her father. Wilma's gross income is computed as follows under three assumptions as to the state of residency of the couple:

	California	Texas	Common Law States
Dividends	$ 2,000	$ 1,000	$2,000
Salary	12,500	12,500	–0–
Interest	150	150	–0–
	$14,650	$13,650	$2,000

Note that the savings account is a community asset because it was created with community funds (i.e., Fred's salary).

Do not confuse community property with jointly owned property, as a number of differences can exist.

- Jointly owned property (i.e., tenants in common, joint tenants) is not limited to married couples.
- More than two owners can be involved. Thus, three brothers or two or more unrelated individuals can be joint owners of a tract of land.

Ownership interests need not be equal. Of three brothers who own a tract of land, one can hold a one-half interest, while each of the other two brothers owns a one-quarter interest.

Community Property Spouses Living Apart

The general rules for taxing the income from services performed by residents of community property states can create complications and even inequities for spouses who are living apart.

Mason and Lily, a married couple, have always lived in a community property state. After a bitter argument in December 2015, Lily moves in with her parents, where she remains for all of 2016. When Lily files her separate return for 2016, must she include one-half of Mason's salary? No, if she meets the requirements set forth below.

EXAMPLE
30

Congress has developed a simple solution to this problem. A spouse (or former spouse) is taxed only on his or her actual earnings from personal services if the following conditions are met:[59]

- The individuals live apart for the entire year.
- They do not file a joint return with each other.
- No portion of the earned income is transferred between the individuals.

4-4 ITEMS SPECIFICALLY INCLUDED IN GROSS INCOME

LO.4

Apply the Internal Revenue Code provisions on alimony, loans made at below-market interest rates, annuities, prizes and awards, group term life insurance, unemployment compensation, and Social Security benefits.

As discussed earlier, the general principles of gross income determination have occasionally yielded results that Congress found unacceptable. Thus, Congress has provided more specific rules for determining the gross income from certain sources. Some of these special rules appear in §§ 71–90 of the Code.

4-4a Alimony and Separate Maintenance Payments

When a married couple divorce or become legally separated, state law generally requires a division of the property accumulated during the marriage. In addition, one spouse may have a legal obligation to support the other spouse. The Code distinguishes between the support payments (alimony or separate maintenance) and the property division in terms of the tax consequences.

Alimony and separate maintenance payments are *deductible* by the party making the payments and are *includible* in the gross income of the party receiving the payments.[60] Thus, income is shifted from the income earner to the income beneficiary, who is better able to pay the tax on the amount received.

---

[59]§ 66. See Form 8958.   [60]§§ 71 and 215.

Pete and Tina are divorced, and Pete is required to pay Tina $15,000 of alimony each year. Pete earns $61,000 a year. The tax law presumes that because Tina receives the $15,000, she is better able than Pete to pay the tax on that amount. Therefore, Tina must include the $15,000 in her gross income, and Pete is allowed to deduct $15,000 from his gross income.

Property Settlements

A transfer of property *other than cash* to a former spouse under a divorce decree or agreement is not a taxable event. The transferor is not entitled to a deduction and does not recognize gain or loss on the transfer. The transferee does not recognize income and has a basis equal to the transferor's basis.[61]

Paul transfers stock to Rosa as part of a divorce settlement. The cost of the stock to Paul is $12,000, and the stock's value at the time of the transfer is $15,000. Rosa later sells the stock for $16,000. Paul is not required to recognize gain from the transfer of the stock to Rosa, and Rosa has a realized and recognized gain of $4,000 ($16,000 − $12,000) when she sells the stock.

Requirements for Alimony

To clarify whether payments are classified as support obligations (alimony) or as property of the other spouse (property settlements), Congress developed the following objective rules. Payments made under agreements and decrees are *classified as alimony* only if the following conditions are satisfied:

- The payments are in cash. (This clearly distinguishes alimony from a property division.)
- The agreement or decree does not specify that the payments are not alimony. (This allows the parties to determine by agreement whether the payments will be alimony.)
- The payor and payee are not members of the same household at the time the payments are made. (This ensures that the payments are for maintaining two households.)
- There is no liability to make the payments for any period after the death of the payee.

Front-Loading

As a further safeguard against a property settlement being disguised as alimony, special rules apply if payments in the first or second year exceed $15,000. If the change in the amount of the payments exceeds statutory limits, alimony recapture results to the extent of the excess alimony payments. In the *third* year, the payor must include the excess alimony payments for the first and second years in gross income, and the payee is allowed a deduction for these excess alimony payments. The mechanics involved in computing recapture are complex and beyond the scope of this text. Worksheets for computing the recapture are provided in *Divorced or Separated Individuals* (IRS Publication 504).

Child Support

A taxpayer does not realize income from the receipt of child support payments made by his or her former spouse. This result occurs because the money is received subject to

---

[61]§ 1041, added to the Code in 1984 to repeal the rule of *U.S. v. Davis*, 62–2 USTC ¶9509, 9 AFTR 2d 1625, 82 S.Ct. 1190 (USSC, 1962). Under the *Davis* rule, which applied to pre-1985 divorces, a property transfer incident to divorce was a taxable event.

the duty to use the money for the child's benefit. The payor is not allowed to deduct the child support payments because the payments are made to satisfy the payor's legal obligation to support the child.

In many cases, it may be difficult to determine whether the payments are intended to be alimony or child support. The tax law resolves this issue in many cases with the following rule: if the amount of the payments would be reduced upon the happening of a contingency related to a child (e.g., the child attains age 21 or dies), the amount of the future reduction in the payment is deemed child support.[62] The rule is applied even though the divorce agreement specifies other amounts for the support of the child.[63]

EXAMPLE

33

Under the divorce agreement, Matt is required to make periodic alimony payments of $500 per month to Grace. However, when Matt and Grace's child reaches age 21, marries, or dies (whichever occurs first), the payments will be reduced to $300 per month. Grace has custody of the child. Because the required contingency is the cause for the reduction in the payments, from $500 to $300, child support payments are $200 per month and alimony is $300 per month.

The tax rules relating to marital disputes are reviewed in Concept Summary 4.2.

Concept Summary 4.2

Tax Treatment of Payments and Transfers Pursuant to Divorce Agreements and Decrees

	Payor	Recipient
Alimony	Deduction from gross income.	Included in gross income.
Alimony recapture	Included in gross income of the third year.	Deducted from gross income of the third year.
Child support	Not deductible.	Not includible in gross income.
Property settlement	No income or deduction.	No income or deduction; basis for the property is the same as the transferor's basis.

4-4b Imputed Interest on Below-Market Loans

As discussed earlier in the chapter, generally no income is recognized unless it is realized. Realization usually occurs when the taxpayer performs services or sells goods, thus becoming entitled to a payment from the other party. It follows that no income is realized if the goods or services are provided at no charge (i.e., not in exchange for property or services). Under this interpretation of the realization requirement, before 1984, interest-free loans were used to shift income between taxpayers.

EXAMPLE

34

Kareem (father) is in the 50% marginal tax bracket, and Veneia (daughter) is in the 20% marginal tax bracket. Kareem has $400,000 that he does not need, and Veneia could use the income from Kareem's excess cash. Before 1984, Kareem could transfer the cash to Veneia in exchange for a non-interest bearing demand note. Veneia could invest the cash, and the income would be taxed at her 20% tax rate. Thus, the income that Kareem could have earned and that could be taxed at 50% became Veneia's income taxed at 20%. Furthermore, Kareem retained control over the principal because he could demand payment on the note at any time.

---

[62]§ 71(c)(2).

[63]*Johnson v. Commissioner*, T.C.Memo. 2014–67.

Kareem in Example 34 is required to recognize **imputed interest** income.[64] Veneia is deemed to have incurred interest expense equal to Kareem's imputed interest income. Veneia's interest may be deductible on her return as investment interest if she itemizes deductions (see Chapter 10). In addition, Kareem is then deemed to have given Veneia the amount of the imputed interest she did not pay. The gift received by Veneia is not subject to income tax (see Chapter 5), although Kareem may be subject to the gift tax on the amount deemed given to Veneia (refer to Chapter 1).

Imputed interest is calculated using the rate the Federal government pays on new borrowings and is compounded semiannually. This Federal rate is adjusted monthly and is published by the IRS.[65] There are three Federal rates: short-term (not over three years and including demand loans), mid-term (over three years but not over nine years), and long-term (over nine years).[66]

Assume that the Federal rate applicable to the loan in Example 34 is 3.5% through June 30 and 4% from July 1 through December 31. Kareem made the loan on January 1, and the loan is still outstanding on December 31. Kareem must recognize interest income of $15,140, and Veneia has interest expense of $15,140. Kareem is deemed to have made a gift of $15,140 to Veneia.

Imputed interest calculations:

January 1–June 30—.035($400,000) (½ year)	$ 7,000
July 1–December 31—.04($400,000 + $7,000) (½ year)	8,140
	$15,140

If interest is charged on the loan but is less than the Federal rate, the imputed interest is the difference between the amount that would have been charged at the Federal rate and the amount actually charged.

Assume the same facts as in Example 35, except that Kareem charged 3% interest, compounded annually.

Interest at the Federal rate	$ 15,140
Less interest charged (.03 × $400,000)	(12,000)
Imputed interest	$ 3,140

The imputed interest rules apply to the following *types* of below-market loans:[67]

- Gift loans (made out of love, affection, or generosity, as in Example 34).
- Compensation-related loans (employer loans to employees).
- Corporation-shareholder loans (a corporation's loans to its shareholders).

The effects of these loans on the borrower and lender are summarized in Concept Summary 4.3.

Exceptions and Limitations

No interest is imputed on total outstanding *gift loans* of $10,000 or less between individuals, unless the loan proceeds are used to purchase income-producing property.[68] This exemption eliminates immaterial amounts that do not result in apparent shifts of income. However, if the proceeds of such a loan are used to purchase income-producing property, the limitations discussed in the following paragraphs apply instead.

On loans of $100,000 or less between individuals, the imputed interest cannot exceed the borrower's net investment income for the year (gross income from all investments less the related expenses).[69] Thus, the income imputed to the lender is limited to the

---

[64]§ 7872(a)(1).
[65]§§ 7872(b)(2) and (f)(2).
[66]§ 1274(d).

[67]§ 7872(c).
[68]§ 7872(c)(2).
[69]§ 7872(d).

Concept Summary 4.3

Effect of Certain Below-Market Loans on the Lender and Borrower

Type of Loan	Lender	Borrower
Gift	Interest income	Interest expense
	Gift made	Gift received
Compensation-related	Interest income	Interest expense
	Compensation expense	Compensation income
Corporation to shareholder	Interest income	Interest expense
	Dividend paid	Dividend income

borrower's net investment income. In addition, if the borrower's net investment income for the year does not exceed $1,000, no interest is imputed on loans of $100,000 or less. However, these limitations for loans of $100,000 or less do not apply if a principal purpose of a loan is tax avoidance.[70]

Vicki made interest-free gift loans as follows:

EXAMPLE

37

Borrower	Amount	Borrower's Net Investment Income	Purpose
Susan	$ 8,000	$ –0–	Education
Dan	9,000	500	Purchase of stock
Bonnie	25,000	–0–	Purchase of a business
Megan	90,000	15,000	Purchase of a residence
Olaf	120,000	–0–	Purchase of a residence

Assume that tax avoidance is not a principal purpose of any of the loans. The loan to Susan is not subject to the imputed interest rules because the $10,000 exception applies. The $10,000 exception does not apply to the loan to Dan because the proceeds were used to purchase income-producing assets. However, under the $100,000 exception, the imputed interest is limited to Dan's investment income ($500). Because the $1,000 exception also applies to this loan, no interest is imputed.

No interest is imputed on the loan to Bonnie because the $100,000 exception applies. Interest is imputed on the loan to Megan based on the lesser of (1) the borrower's $15,000 net investment income or (2) the interest as calculated by applying the Federal rate to the outstanding loan. None of the exceptions apply to the loan to Olaf because the loan was for more than $100,000.

Assume that the relevant Federal rate is 10% and that the loans were outstanding for the entire year. Vicki would recognize interest income, compounded semiannually, as follows:

Loan to Megan:	
First 6 months (.10 × $90,000 × ½ year)	$ 4,500
Second 6 months (.10 × $94,500 × ½ year)	4,725
	$ 9,225
Loan to Olaf:	
First 6 months (.10 × $120,000 × ½ year)	$ 6,000
Second 6 months (.10 × $126,000 × ½ year)	6,300
	$12,300
Total imputed interest ($9,225 + $12,300)	$21,525

---

[70]*Deficit Reduction Tax Bill of 1984: Explanation of the Senate Finance Committee* (April 2, 1984), p. 484.

As with gift loans, there is a $10,000 exemption for *compensation-related loans* and *corporation-shareholder loans*. However, the $10,000 exception does not apply if tax avoidance is one of the principal purposes of a loan.[71] This vague tax avoidance standard makes practically all compensation-related and corporation-shareholder loans suspect. Nevertheless, the $10,000 exception should apply when an employee's borrowing was necessitated by personal needs (e.g., to meet unexpected expenses) rather than tax considerations.

These exceptions to the imputed interest rules are summarized in Concept Summary 4.4.

Concept Summary 4.4

Exceptions to the Imputed Interest Rules for Below-Market Loans

Exception	Eligible Loans	Ineligible Loans and Limitations
De minimis—aggregate loans of $10,000 or less	Gift loans	Proceeds are used to purchase income-producing assets.
	Employer-employee	Principal purpose is tax avoidance.
	Corporation-shareholder	Principal purpose is tax avoidance.
Aggregate loans of $100,000 or less	Between individuals	Principal purpose is tax avoidance. For all other loans, interest is imputed to the extent of the borrower's net investment income if that income exceeds $1,000.

ETHICS & EQUITY   Taxing "Made-Up" Income

Under the imputed interest rules, the taxpayer who makes a below-market loan may be required to recognize income he or she did not actually receive. For example, assume that Christian loans $200,000 to Mia, his daughter, to start a business (income-producing property).

Christian does not charge interest because Mia needs the funds to operate a struggling startup business. Why should Christian be required to pay tax on a "made-up" number (i.e., the interest he did not charge)? This type of income is sometimes referred to as "phantom" income.

4-4c Income from Annuities

Read this again → (handwritten margin note)

Annuity contracts generally require the purchaser (the annuitant) to pay a fixed amount for the right to receive a future stream of payments. Typically, the issuer of the contract is an insurance company and will pay the annuitant a cash value if the annuitant cancels the contract. The insurance company invests the amounts received from the annuitant, and the income earned serves to increase the cash value of the annuity. No income is recognized by the annuitant at the time the cash value of the annuity increases because the taxpayer has not actually received any income. The income is not constructively received because, generally, the taxpayer must cancel the policy to receive the increase in value (the increase in value is subject to substantial restrictions).

---

[71]§ 7872(c)(3).

Jean, age 50, pays $30,000 for an annuity contract that is to pay her $500 per month beginning when she reaches age 65 and continuing until her death. If Jean should cancel the policy after one year, she would receive $30,200 and would include $200 ($30,200 − $30,000) in her gross income. However, if she does not cancel the policy, the $200 increase in value is not includible in her gross income, as long as she does not actually receive the $200.

EXAMPLE 38

The tax accounting problem associated with receiving payments under an annuity contract is one of apportioning the amounts received between recovery of capital and income. The statutory solution to this problem depends upon whether the payments began before or after the annuity starting date and upon when the policy was acquired.

Computing the Exclusion Amount

The annuitant can exclude from income (as a recovery of capital) the proportion of each payment that the investment in the contract bears to the expected return under the contract. The *exclusion amount* is calculated as follows:

$$\frac{\text{Investment}}{\text{Expected return}} \quad \textbf{X} \quad \text{Annuity payment} \quad \textbf{=} \quad \text{Exclusion amount}$$

The *expected return* is the annual amount to be paid to the annuitant multiplied by the number of years the payments will be received. The payment period may be fixed (a *term certain*) or for the life of one or more individuals. When payments are for life, the taxpayer generally must use the annuity table published by the IRS to determine the expected return (see Exhibit 4.1). This is an actuarial table that contains life expectancies.[72] The expected return is calculated by multiplying the appropriate multiple (life expectancy) by the annual payment.

A taxpayer, age 60, purchases an annuity from an insurance company for $90,000. She is to receive $500 per month for life. Her life expectancy (from Exhibit 4.1) is 24.2 years from the annuity starting date. Thus, her expected return is $500 × 12 × 24.2 = $145,200, and the exclusion amount is $3,719 [($90,000 investment/$145,200 expected return) × $6,000 annual payment]. The $3,719 is a nontaxable return of capital, and $2,281 ($6,000 − $3,719) is included in gross income.

EXAMPLE 39

The *exclusion ratio* (investment ÷ expected return) applies until the annuitant has recovered his or her investment in the contract. Once the investment is recovered, the entire amount of subsequent payments is taxable. If the annuitant dies before recovering the investment, the unrecovered cost (adjusted basis) is deductible in the year the payments cease (usually the year of death).[73]

Assume that the taxpayer in Example 39 receives annuity payments for 25.2 years (302 months). For the last 12 months [302 − (12 × 24.2) = 12], the taxpayer will include $500 each month in gross income. If instead the taxpayer dies after 36 months, she is eligible for a $78,843 deduction on her final tax return.

EXAMPLE 40

Cost of the contract	$ 90,000
Cost previously recovered $90,000/$145,200 × 36($500) =	(11,157)
Deduction	$ 78,843

---

[72] The life expectancies in Exhibit 4.1 apply for annuity investments made on or after July 1, 1986. See *General Rules for Pensions and Annuities*, IRS Publication 939 (Rev. April 2003), p. 25. See also *Pension and Annuity Income*, IRS Publication 575.

[73] § 72(b).

EXHIBIT 4.1		Ordinary Life Annuities: One Life—Expected Return Multiples			
Age	**Multiple**	**Age**	**Multiple**	**Age**	**Multiple**
5	76.6	42	40.6	79	10.0
6	75.6	43	39.6	80	9.5
7	74.7	44	38.7	81	8.9
8	73.7	45	37.7	82	8.4
9	72.7	46	36.8	83	7.9
10	71.7	47	35.9	84	7.4
11	70.7	48	34.9	85	6.9
12	69.7	49	34.0	86	6.5
13	68.8	50	33.1	87	6.1
14	67.8	51	32.2	88	5.7
15	66.8	52	31.3	89	5.3
16	65.8	53	30.4	90	5.0
17	64.8	54	29.5	91	4.7
18	63.9	55	28.6	92	4.4
19	62.9	56	27.7	93	4.1
20	61.9	57	26.8	94	3.9
21	60.9	58	25.9	95	3.7
22	59.9	59	25.0	96	3.4
23	59.0	60	24.2	97	3.2
24	58.0	61	23.3	98	3.0
25	57.0	62	22.5	99	2.8
26	56.0	63	21.6	100	2.7
27	55.1	64	20.8	101	2.5
28	54.1	65	20.0	102	2.3
29	53.1	66	19.2	103	2.1
30	52.2	67	18.4	104	1.9
31	51.2	68	17.6	105	1.8
32	50.2	69	16.8	106	1.6
33	49.3	70	16.0	107	1.4
34	48.3	71	15.3	108	1.3
35	47.3	72	14.6	109	1.1
36	46.4	73	13.9	110	1.0
37	45.4	74	13.2	111	.9
38	44.4	75	12.5	112	.8
39	43.5	76	11.9	113	.7
40	42.5	77	11.2	114	.6
41	41.5	78	10.6	115	.5

Simplified Method for Annuity Distributions from Qualified Retirement Plans

A simplified method is required for allocating basis to the annuity payments received under a qualified retirement plan.[74] The portion of each annuity payment that is excluded as a return of capital is the employee's investment in the contract divided by the number of anticipated monthly payments determined in accordance with Exhibit 4.2.[75]

---

[74]See Chapter 19.   [75]§ 72(d).

EXHIBIT 4.2	Number of Anticipated Monthly Annuity Payments under the Simplified Method	
Age		**Number of Anticipated Monthly Payments**
55 and under		360
56–60		310
61–65		260
66–70		210
71 and over		160

EXAMPLE 41

Andrea, age 62, receives an annuity distribution of $500 per month for life from her qualified retirement plan beginning in January 2016. Her investment in the contract is $100,100. The excludible amount of each payment is $385 ($100,100 investment/260 monthly payments). Thus, $115 ($500 − $385) of each annuity payment is included in Andrea's gross income.

The rules for annuity payments received after the basis has been recovered by the annuitant and for the annuitant who dies before the basis is recovered are the same as under the exclusion ratio method discussed earlier.

4-4d Prizes and Awards

The fair market value of prizes and awards (other than scholarships exempted under § 117, to be discussed subsequently) must be included in gross income.[76] Therefore, TV giveaway prizes, magazine publisher prizes, door prizes, and awards from an employer to an employee in recognition of performance are fully taxable to the recipient.

A narrow exception permits a prize or an award to be excluded from gross income if *all* of the following requirements are satisfied:

- The prize or award is received in recognition of religious, charitable, scientific, educational, artistic, literary, or civic achievement (e.g., Nobel Prize, Pulitzer Prize, or faculty teaching award).
- The recipient transfers the prize or award to a qualified governmental unit or nonprofit organization.
- The recipient was selected without any action on his or her part to enter the contest or proceeding.
- The recipient is not required to render substantial future services as a condition for receiving the prize or award.[77]

Because the transfer of the property to a qualified governmental unit or nonprofit organization ordinarily would be a charitable contribution (an itemized deduction as presented in Chapter 10), the exclusion produces beneficial tax consequences in the following situations:

- The taxpayer does not itemize deductions and thus would receive no tax benefit from the charitable contribution.
- The taxpayer's charitable contributions exceed the annual statutory ceiling on the deduction.

---

[76]§ 74.   [77]§ 74(b).

- Including the prize or award in gross income would reduce the amount of deductions the taxpayer otherwise would qualify for because of gross income limitations (e.g., the gross income test for a dependency exemption or the adjusted gross income limitation in calculating the medical expense deduction).

The taxpayer can avoid including prizes and awards in gross income by refusing to accept the prize or award.[78]

Another exception is provided for certain *employee achievement awards* in the form of tangible personal property (e.g., a gold watch). The awards must be made in recognition of length of service or safety achievement. Generally, the ceiling on the excludible amount for an employee is $400 per taxable year. However, if the award is a qualified plan award, the ceiling on the exclusion is $1,600 per taxable year.[79]

4-4e Group Term Life Insurance

For many years, the IRS did not attempt to tax the value of life insurance protection provided to an employee by the employer. Some companies took undue advantage of the exclusion by providing large amounts of insurance protection for executives. Therefore, Congress enacted § 79, which created a limited exclusion for **group term life insurance**. The premiums on the first $50,000 of group term life insurance protection are excludible from the employee's gross income.

The benefits of this exclusion are available only to employees. Proprietors and partners are not considered employees. The Regulations generally require broad-scale coverage of employees to satisfy the *group* requirement (e.g., shareholder-employees would not constitute a qualified group). The exclusion applies only to term insurance (protection for a period of time but with no cash surrender value) and not to ordinary life insurance (lifetime protection plus a cash surrender value that can be drawn upon before death).

As mentioned, the exclusion applies to the first $50,000 of group term life insurance protection. For each $1,000 of coverage in excess of $50,000, the employee must include the amounts indicated in Exhibit 4.3 in gross income.[80]

EXAMPLE 42

Finch Corporation has a group term life insurance policy with coverage equal to the employee's annual salary. Keith, age 52, is president of the corporation and receives an annual salary of $350,000. Keith must include $828 in gross income from the insurance protection for the year.

$$\frac{\$350{,}000 - \$50{,}000}{\$1{,}000} \times \$.23 \times 12 \text{ months} = \$828$$

Generally, the amount that must be included in gross income, computed from Exhibit 4.3, is much less than the price an individual would pay an insurance company for the same amount of protection. Thus, even the excess coverage provides some tax-favored income for employees when group term life insurance coverage in excess of $50,000 is desirable.

If the plan discriminates in favor of certain key employees (e.g., officers), the key employees are not eligible for the exclusion. In such a case, the key employees must include in gross income the *greater* of actual premiums paid by the employer or the amount calculated from the Uniform Premiums in Exhibit 4.3. The other employees are still eligible for the $50,000 exclusion and continue to use the Uniform Premiums table to compute the income from excess insurance protection.[81]

---

[78]See Rev.Rul. 57–374, 1957–2 C.B. 69 and Rev.Proc. 87–54, 1987–2 C.B. 669.

[79]§ 74(c). Qualified plan awards are defined in § 274(j) and explained in *Business Expenses*, Chapter 2 (IRS Publication 535).

[80]Reg. § 1.79–3(d)(2).

[81]§ 79(d).

EXHIBIT 4.3	Uniform Premiums for $1,000 of Group Term Life Insurance Protection

Attained Age on Last Day of Employee's Tax Year	Cost per $1,000 of Protection for One-Month Period*
Under 25	$ .05
25–29	.06
30–34	.08
35–39	.09
40–44	.10
45–49	.15
50–54	.23
55–59	.43
60–64	.66
65–69	1.27
70 and above	2.06

*Reg. § 1.79–3, effective for coverage after June 30, 1999.

4-4f Unemployment Compensation

The unemployment compensation program is sponsored and operated by the states and Federal government to provide a source of income for people who have been employed and are temporarily (hopefully) out of work. In a series of rulings over a period of 40 years, the IRS exempted unemployment benefits from tax. These payments were considered social benefit programs for the promotion of the general welfare. After experiencing dissatisfaction with the IRS's treatment of unemployment compensation, Congress amended the Code to make the benefits taxable.[82]

4-4g Social Security Benefits — Not on Exam

If a taxpayer's income exceeds a specified base amount, as much as 85 percent of Social Security retirement benefits must be included in gross income. The taxable amount of benefits is determined through the application of one of two formulas that utilize a unique measure of income—*modified adjusted gross income (MAGI)*.[83] MAGI is, for this purpose, the taxpayer's adjusted gross income from all sources (other than Social Security) plus the foreign earned income exclusion and any tax-exempt interest income.

In the formulas, two sets of base amounts are established. The first set is as follows:

- $32,000 for married taxpayers who file a joint return.
- $0 for married taxpayers who do not live apart for the entire year but file separate returns.
- $25,000 for all other taxpayers.

The second set of base amounts is as follows:

- $44,000 for married taxpayers who file a joint return.
- $0 for married taxpayers who do not live apart for the entire year but file separate returns.
- $34,000 for all other taxpayers.

[82]§ 85.

[83]§ 86. The rationale for taxing 85% of the Social Security benefits is as follows: for the average Social Security recipient, 15% of the amount received is a recovery of amounts that the individual paid into the program, and the remainder of the benefits is financed by the employer's contribution and interest earned by the Social Security trust fund.

TAX IN THE NEWS   Social Security Benefits as a Source of Federal Revenue

Recipients' Social Security benefits are indexed for inflation, but the base amounts used in the formula to calculate the taxable portion of the benefits are not indexed. The $25,000 and $32,000 base amounts were established in 1984. If they were indexed for inflation, these nontaxable amounts would have doubled by 2010. Thus, as income and Social Security benefits rise with inflation, taxable income increases more than the related increase in "real" benefits.

If the sum of MAGI and 50 percent of Social Security benefits is less than or equal to the base amount from the first set of such amounts (using the applicable filing status), then none of the benefits are taxable. If MAGI plus one-half of Social Security benefits exceeds the first set of base amounts but not the second set, the taxable amount of Social Security benefits is the *lesser* of the following:

- .50(Social Security benefits).
- .50[MAGI + .50(Social Security benefits) − first base amount].

EXAMPLE 43

A married couple with adjusted gross income of $30,000, no tax-exempt interest, and $11,000 of Social Security benefits who file jointly must include $1,750 of the benefits in gross income. This works out as the lesser of the following:

1. .50($11,000) = $5,500.
2. .50[$30,000 + .50($11,000) − $32,000] = .50($3,500) = $1,750.

If instead the couple had adjusted gross income of $15,000 and their Social Security benefits totaled $5,000, none of the benefits would be taxable because .50[$15,000 + .50($5,000) − $32,000] is not a positive number.

If MAGI plus one-half of Social Security benefits exceeds the second set of base amounts, the taxable amount of Social Security benefits is the *lesser* of 1 or 2 below:

1. .85(Social Security benefits).
2. Sum of:
    a. .85[MAGI + .50(Social Security benefits) − second base amount], and
    b. Lesser of:
        - Amount included through application of the first formula.
        - $4,500 ($6,000 for married filing jointly).

EXAMPLE 44

A married couple who file jointly have adjusted gross income of $72,000, no tax-exempt interest, and $12,000 of Social Security benefits. Their includible Social Security benefits will be $10,200. Include the lesser of the following:

1. .85($12,000) = $10,200.
2. Sum of:
    a. .85[$72,000 + .50($12,000) − $44,000] = $28,900, and
    b. Lesser of:
        - Amount calculated by the first formula, which is the lesser of:
            - .50($12,000) = $6,000.
            - .50[$72,000 + .50($12,000) − $32,000] = $23,000.
        - $6,000.
        The sum equals $34,900 ($28,900 + $6,000).

Because 85% of the Social Security benefits received is less than this amount, $10,200 is included in the couple's gross income.[84]

---

[84]To compute taxable benefits, a worksheet is provided in the instructions to Form 1040 at lines 20a and 20b and to Form 1040A at lines 14a and 14b, as well as in *Social Security and Railroad Retirement Benefits* (IRS Publication 915).

4-5 TAX PLANNING

The materials in this chapter have focused on the following questions:

- What is income?
- When is the income recognized?
- Who is the taxpayer?

Planning strategies suggested by these materials include the following:

- Maximize economic benefits that are not included in gross income.
- Defer the recognition of income.
- Shift income to taxpayers who are in a lower marginal tax bracket.

Some specific techniques for accomplishing these strategies are discussed in the following paragraphs.

4-5a **Tax Deferral**

General

Because deferred taxes are tantamount to interest-free loans from the government, the deferral of taxes is a worthy goal of the tax planner. However, the tax planner must also consider the tax rates for the years the income is shifted from and to. For example, a one-year deferral of income from a year in which the taxpayer's tax rate was 28 percent to a year in which the tax rate will be 35 percent would not be advisable if the taxpayer expects to earn less than a 7 percent after-tax return on the deferred tax dollars.

The taxpayer can often defer the recognition of income from appreciated property by postponing the event triggering realization (the final closing on a sale or exchange of property). If the taxpayer needs cash, obtaining a loan by using the appreciated property as collateral may be a less costly alternative than selling the property.

Ira owns 100 shares of Pigeon Company common stock with a cost of $20,000 and a fair market value of $50,000. Although the stock's value has increased substantially in the past three years, Ira thinks the growth days are over. If he sells the Pigeon stock, Ira will invest the proceeds from the sale in other common stock. Assuming that Ira's marginal tax rate on the sale is 15%, he will have only $45,500 [$50,000 − .15($50,000 − $20,000)] to reinvest. The alternative investment must substantially outperform Pigeon in the future for the sale to be beneficial.

EXAMPLE 45

Selection of Investments

Because no tax is due until a gain has been recognized, the law favors investments that yield appreciation rather than annual income.

Vera can buy a corporate bond or an acre of land for $10,000. The bond pays $1,000 of interest (10%) each year, and Vera expects the land to increase in value 10% each year for the next 10 years. She is in the 40% (combined Federal and state) tax bracket for ordinary income and 26% for qualifying capital gains. Assuming that the bond would mature or the land would be sold in 10 years and Vera would reinvest the interest at a 10% before-tax return, she would accumulate the following amount at the end of 10 years:

EXAMPLE 46

continued

		Bond	Land
Original investment		$10,000	$10,000
Annual income	$ 1,000		
Less tax	(400)		
	$ 600		
Compound amount reinvested for 10 years at 6% after-tax	×13.18	7,908	
		$17,908	
Compound amount, 10 years at 10%			× 2.59
			$25,900
Less tax on sale: 26%($25,900 − $10,000)			(4,134)
			$21,766

Therefore, the value of the deferral that results from investing in the land rather than in the bond is $3,858 ($21,766 − $17,908).

Series EE bonds can also be purchased for long-term deferrals of income. In situations where the taxpayer's goal is merely to shift income one year into the future, bank certificates of deposit are useful tools. If the maturity period is one year or less, all interest is reported in the year of maturity. Bank certificates of deposit are especially useful for a taxpayer who realizes an unusually large gain from the sale of property in one year (and thus is in a high tax bracket) but expects his or her gross income to be less the following year.

Cash Basis

The timing of income from services can often be controlled through the use of the cash method of accounting. Although taxpayers are somewhat constrained by the constructive receipt doctrine (they cannot turn their backs on income), seldom will customers and clients offer to pay before they are asked. The usual lag between billings and collections (e.g., December's billings collected in January) will result in a continuous deferring of some income until the last year of operations. A salaried individual approaching retirement may contract with the employer before the services are rendered to receive a portion of compensation in the lower tax bracket retirement years.

Prepaid Income

For the accrual basis taxpayer who receives advance payments from customers, the transactions should be structured to avoid payment of tax on income before the time the income is actually earned. Revenue Procedure 2004–34 provides the guidelines for deferring the tax on prepayments for services and licensing of software and certain other items, and Regulation § 1.451–5 provides the guidelines for deferrals on sales of goods. In addition, both cash and accrual basis taxpayers can sometimes defer income by structuring the payments as deposits rather than prepaid income. For example, a landlord should require an equivalent damage deposit rather than prepayment of the last month's rent under the lease. Of course, the arrangement must meet the definition of a deposit for Federal tax purposes.[85]

---

[85]See *Commissioner v. Indianapolis Power and Light*, 494 U.S. 203 (1990).

4-5b **Reporting Conflicts**

The IRS relies upon businesses to report the amounts they paid to individuals for services. Employees receive a Form W–2, and independent contractors receive a Form 1099–MISC. The IRS attempts to match the forms they receive to the individual's income tax return. If the form submitted by the business and the individual's tax return are not in agreement, the individual has a problem, but innocent differences can occur.

Dr. Anders, a college professor on a cash basis, performs consulting services for Dove Corporation in early December 2016. In late December, Dove mailed a check in payment, but Anders did not receive the check until early January 2017. Dove sent Anders a Form 1099–MISC showing the payment date as 2016. If Anders did not report the income on his 2016 return, he could have a problem. Dr. Anders should include the income shown on the Form 1099–MISC and then subtract the same amount, noting that it should be properly included in 2017 income.

4-5c **Shifting Income to Relatives**

The tax liability of a family can be minimized by shifting income from higher- to lower-bracket family members. This can be accomplished through gifts of income-producing property. Furthermore, in many cases, income can be shifted with no negative effect on the family's investment plans.

Adam, who is in the 28% tax bracket, would like to save for his children's education. All of the children are under 19 years of age and are dependents of Adam. Adam could transfer income-producing properties to the children, and the children could each receive up to $1,050 of income each year (refer to Chapter 3) with no tax liability. The next $1,050 would be taxed at the child's tax rate. After a child has more than $2,100 of unearned income, there is no tax advantage to shifting more income to the child (because the income will be taxed at the parents' rate) until the child is 19 years old (or age 24 if a full-time student), when all income will be taxed according to the child's tax rate.

The Uniform Gifts to Minors Act, a model law adopted by all states (but with some variations among the states), facilitates income shifting. Under the Act, a gift of intangibles (e.g., bank accounts, stocks, bonds, and life insurance contracts) can be made to a minor but with an adult serving as custodian. Usually, a parent who makes the gift is also named as custodian. The state laws allow the custodian to sell or redeem and reinvest the principal and to accumulate or distribute the income, practically at the custodian's discretion provided there is no commingling of the child's income with the parent's property. Thus, the parent can give appreciated securities to the child, and the donor custodian can then sell the securities and reinvest the proceeds, thereby shifting both the gain and the annual income to the child. Such planning is limited by the tax liability calculation provision for a child under the age of 19 (or age 24 if a full-time student) (refer to Chapter 3).

U.S. government bonds (Series EE) can be purchased by parents for their children. When this is done, the children generally should file a return and elect to report the income on the accrual basis.

Abby pays $7,500 for Series EE bonds in 2016 and registers them in her son's name. The son, Wade, will enter college the year of original maturity of the bonds. The bonds have a maturity value of $10,000. Wade elects to report the annual increment in redemption value as income for each year the bonds are held. The first year the increase is $250, and Wade includes that amount in his gross income. If Wade has no other income, no tax will be due on the $250 bond interest because such an amount will be more than offset by his available standard deduction. The following year, the increment is $260, and Wade includes this amount in income. Thus, over the life of the bonds, Wade will include $2,500 in income ($10,000 − $7,500), none of which will result in a tax liability, assuming that he has no other income. However, if the election had not been made, Wade would have been required to include $2,500 in income on the bonds in the year of original maturity, if they had been redeemed as planned. This amount of income might result in a tax liability.

In some cases, it may be advantageous for the child not to make the accrual election. For example, a child under age 19 (or age 24 if a full-time student) with investment income of more than $2,100 each year and parents in the 25, 28, 33, 35, or 39.6 percent tax bracket would probably benefit from deferring the tax on the savings bond interest. The child would also benefit from the use of the usually lower tax rate (rather than subjecting the income to the parents' tax rate) if the bonds mature after the child is age 19 or older (or age 24 or older if a full-time student).

4-5d Accounting for Community Property

The classification of income as community or separate property becomes important when either of two events occurs:

- A married couple files separate income tax returns for the year.
- A married couple obtains a divorce and therefore must file separate returns for the year (refer to Chapter 3).

For planning purposes, it behooves married persons to keep track of the source of income (community or separate). To be in a position to do this effectively when income-producing assets are involved, it may be necessary to distinguish between separate and community property.[86]

4-5e Alimony

The person making the alimony payments favors a divorce settlement that includes a provision for deductible alimony payments. On the other hand, the recipient prefers that the payments not qualify as alimony. If the payor is in a higher tax bracket than the recipient, both parties may benefit by increasing the payments and structuring them so that they qualify as alimony.

EXAMPLE 50

Carl and Polly are negotiating a divorce settlement. Carl has offered to pay Polly $10,000 each year for 10 years, but payments would cease upon Polly's death. Polly is willing to accept the offer if the agreement will specify that the cash payments are not alimony. Carl is in the 35% tax bracket, and Polly's marginal rate is 15%.

If Carl and Polly agree that Carl will pay Polly $12,000 of alimony each year, both will have improved after-tax cash flows.

	Annual Cash Flows	
	Carl	**Polly**
Nonalimony payments	($10,000)	$10,000
Alimony payments	($12,000)	$12,000
Tax effects		
Tax savings [.35($12,000)]	4,200	
Tax cost [.15($12,000)]		(1,800)
After-tax cash flows	($ 7,800)	$10,200
Benefit of alimony option	$ 2,200	$ 200

Both parties benefit at the government's expense if the $12,000 alimony option is used.

---

[86]Being able to distinguish between separate and community property is crucial to the determination of a property settlement incident to a divorce. It also is vital in the estate tax area (refer to Chapter 1) because the surviving spouse's share of the community property is not included in the gross estate of the deceased spouse.

REFOCUS ON THE BIG PICTURE

CALCULATION OF GROSS INCOME

Using the accrual method of accounting, Dr. Cliff Payne has correctly calculated the gross income of his sole proprietorship. He will report the $385,000 amount on his tax return (Schedule C of Form 1040).

What If?

From a tax planning perspective, what can Dr. Payne do to decrease his gross income from the first year of operating his dental practice and thereby produce better financial results for him?

Rather than adopt the accrual method of accounting, Dr. Payne should adopt the cash method of accounting because his dental practice is a service entity rather than a merchandising entity. His gross income for Federal income tax purposes under the cash method is calculated as follows:

Revenues	$385,000
Plus: Accounts receivable: January 1	–0–
Less: Accounts receivable: December 31	(52,000)
Gross income	$333,000

The cash method of accounting enables Dr. Payne to defer paying Federal income taxes on the unpaid accounts receivable. Furthermore, each year that Dr. Payne has accounts receivable at the end of the tax year, that income is continuously deferred. Thus, if his accounts receivable remain at $52,000 at the end of each tax year, by using the cash method of accounting rather than the accrual method, he will defer that amount of income until he terminates his practice.

Key Terms

Accounting income, 4-4

Accounting method, 4-6

Accrual method, 4-7

Alimony and separate maintenance payments, 4-19

Alimony recapture, 4-20

Annuity, 4-24

Assignment of income, 4-13

Cash receipts method, 4-7

Claim of right doctrine, 4-8

Community property, 4-18

Constructive receipt, 4-9

Economic income, 4-3

Fruit and tree metaphor, 4-13

Gross income, 4-2

Group term life insurance, 4-28

Hybrid method, 4-8

Imputed interest, 4-22

Income, 4-3

Original issue discount, 4-10

Partnership, 4-16

Recovery of capital doctrine, 4-3

S corporation, 4-17

Taxable year, 4-6

Discussion Questions

1. **LO.1** According to the Supreme Court, would it be good tax policy to use income as computed by financial accounting principles as the correct measure of income for Federal income tax purposes? Explain.

2. **LO.1** Compare and contrast the economist's concept used to recognize income with the concept employed in measuring taxable income.

Issue ID   3.   **LO.1** Allen visits Reno, Nevada, once a year to gamble. This year his gambling loss was $25,000. He commented to you, "At least I didn't have to pay for my airfare and hotel room. The casino paid that because I am such a good customer. That was worth at least $3,000." What are the relevant tax issues for Allen?

4.   **LO.1** Ben lost his job when his employer moved its plant. During the year, he collected unemployment benefits for three months, a total of $1,800. While he was waiting to hear from prospective employers, he painted his house. If Ben had paid someone else to paint his house, the cost would have been $3,000. The cost of the paint Ben used was $800. What is Ben's gross income for tax purposes from the above events?

Issue ID   5.   **LO.1** Howard buys wrecked cars and stores them on his property. Recently, he purchased a 1990 Ford Taurus for $400. If he can sell all of the usable parts, his total proceeds from the Taurus will be over $2,500. As of the end of the year, he has sold only the radio for $75 and he does not know how many, if any, of the remaining parts will ever be sold. What are Howard's income recognition issues?

6.   **LO.2, 3** On December 29, 2016, an employee received a $5,000 check from her employer's client. The check was payable to the employer. The employee did not remit the funds to the employer until December 30, 2016. The employer deposited the check on December 31, 2016, but the bank did not credit the employer's bank account until January 2, 2017. When is the cash basis employer required to include the $5,000 in gross income?

7.   **LO.2** What is the purpose of the constructive receipt doctrine?

8.   **LO.2** A Series EE U.S. government savings bond accrues 3.5% interest each year. The bond matures in three years, at which time the principal and interest will be paid. The bank will pay the taxpayer at a 3.5% interest rate each year if he agrees to leave money on deposit for three years. What tax advantage does the Series EE bond offer that is not available with the bank deposit?

9.   **LO.2** The taxpayer performs services with payment due from the customer within 30 days. All customers pay within the time limit. What would be the benefit to the taxpayer using the cash method of accounting rather than the accrual method?

10.   **LO.3, 5** Wade paid $7,000 for an automobile that needed substantial repairs. He worked nights and weekends to restore the car and spent $2,400 on parts for it. He knows that he can sell the car for $13,000, but he is very wealthy and does not need the money. On the other hand, his daughter, who has very little income, needs money to make the down payment on a house.

     a.   Would it matter, after taxes, whether Wade sells the car and gives the money to his daughter or whether he gives the car to his daughter and she sells it for $13,000? Explain.

     b.   Assume that Wade gave the car to his daughter after he had arranged for another person to buy it from his daughter. The daughter then transferred the car to the buyer and received $13,000. Who is taxed on the gain?

11.   **LO.3** Anita, a cash basis taxpayer, sued her former employer for wage discrimination. Her attorney agreed to pursue the case on a contingent fee basis—the attorney would receive one-third of any settlement or court award. The parties reached a settlement, and the attorney for Anita's former employer wrote a check payable to Anita for $320,000 and a check payable to her attorney for $160,000. Anita reasons that she and the attorney were partners in the lawsuit who shared profits two-thirds and one-third, respectively. Therefore, she includes $320,000 in her gross income. Is Anita's analysis correct? Explain.

12.   **LO.3** Rex became a partner with a 30% interest in the partnership profits when he invested $200,000. In 2016, the partnership generated $400,000 of taxable

income, and Rex withdrew $100,000. In 2017, the partnership had $600,000 of taxable income, and Rex withdrew $200,000. What is Rex's gross income from the partnership in 2016 and 2017?

13. **LO.4** The divorce agreement requires Alice to pay her former spouse $50,000 a year for the next ten years. Will the payments qualify as alimony? Why or why not?

14. **LO.4, 5** William and Abigail, who live in San Francisco, have been experiencing problems with their marriage. They have a 3-year-old daughter, April, who stays with William's parents during the day because both William and Abigail are employed. Abigail worked to support William while he attended medical school, and now she has been accepted by a medical school in Mexico. Abigail has decided to divorce William and attend medical school. April will stay in San Francisco because of her strong attachment to her grandparents and because they can provide her with excellent day care. Abigail knows that William will expect her to contribute to the cost of raising April. Abigail also believes that to finance her education, she must receive cash for her share of the property they accumulated during their marriage. In addition, she believes that she should receive some reimbursement for her contribution to William's support while he was in medical school. She expects the divorce proceedings to take several months. Identify the relevant tax issues for Abigail.

Issue ID

15. **LO.4, 5** Patrick and Eva are planning to divorce. Patrick has offered to pay Eva $12,000 each year until their 11-year-old daughter reaches age 21. Alternatively, Patrick will transfer to Eva common stock that he owns with a fair market value of $100,000. What factors should Eva and Patrick consider in deciding between these two options?

Decision Making

16. **LO.4** In the current year, the Rose Corporation made a $400,000 interest-free loan to John Rose, the corporation's controlling shareholder. Mr. Rose is also the corporation's chief executive officer and receives a salary of $300,000 a year. What are the tax consequences of classifying the loan as a compensation-related loan rather than as a corporation-shareholder loan?

17. **LO.4** Connor purchased an annuity that was to pay him a fixed amount each month for the remainder of his life. He began receiving payments in 2000, when he was 65 years old. In 2016, Connor was killed in an automobile accident. What are the effects of the annuity on Connor's final tax return?

18. **LO.4** An employer provides all of his employees with life insurance protection equal to twice the employee's annual salary. Melba, age 42, has an annual salary of $70,000. Is Melba required to recognize income even though she is still alive at the end of the year and thus nothing has been collected on the life insurance policy? Explain.

19. **LO.4** For a person who receives Social Security benefits, what effect, if any, can an increase in other income have on that person's taxable income?

Issue ID

Computational Exercises

20. **LO.2** On January 1, 2016, Kunto, a cash basis taxpayer, pays $46,228 for a 24-month certificate. The certificate is priced to yield 4% (the effective interest rate) with interest compounded annually. No interest is paid until maturity, when Kunto receives $50,000. In your computations:

a. Compute Kunto's gross income from the certificate for 2016.

b. Compute Kunto's gross income from the certificate for 2017.

Round any amounts to the nearest dollar.

21. **LO.2** Bigham Corporation, an accrual basis calendar year taxpayer, sells its services under 12-month and 24-month contracts. The corporation provides services to each customer every month. On July 1, 2016, Bigham sold the following customer contracts:

Length of Contract	Total Proceeds
12 months	$14,000
24 months	$24,000

Determine the income to be recognized in taxable income in 2016 and 2017.

Length of Contract	2015 Income	2016 Income
12 months	a. _____	c. _____
24 months	b. _____	d. _____

22. **LO.3** Simba and Zola are married but file separate returns. Simba received $80,000 of salary and $1,200 of taxable dividends on stock he purchased in his name and paid from the salary that he earned since the marriage. Zola collected $900 in taxable interest on certificate of deposit that she inherited from her aunt. Compute Zola's gross income under two assumptions as to the state of residency of the couple. If an amount is zero, enter "$0."

	Idaho (Community Property State)	South Carolina (Common Law State)
Dividends	a. _____	d. _____
Interest	b. _____	e. _____
Salary	c. _____	f. _____

23. **LO.4** Casper and Cecile are divorced this year. As part of the divorce settlement, Casper transferred stock to Cecile. Casper purchased the stock for $25,000, and it had a market value of $43,000 on the date of the transfer. Cecile sold the stock for $40,000 a month after receiving it. In addition, Casper is required to pay Cecile $1,500 a month in alimony. He made five payments to her during the year.

What are the tax consequences for Casper and Cecile regarding these transactions?

a. How much gain or loss does Casper recognize on the transfer of the stock?

b. Does Casper receive a deduction for the $7,500 alimony paid?

c. How much income does Cecile have from the $7,500 alimony received?

d. When Cecile sells the stock, how much does she report?

24. **LO.4** Elizabeth made the following interest-free loans during the year. Assume that tax avoidance is not a principal purpose of any of the loans. Assume that the relevant Federal rate is 5% and that the loans were outstanding for the last six months of the year.

Borrower	Amount	Borrower's Net Investment Income	Purpose of Loan
Richard	$ 5,000	$800	Gift
Woody	8,000	600	Purchase stock
Irene	105,000	–0–	Purchase residence

What are the effects of the imputed interest rules on these transactions? Compute Elizabeth's gross income from each loan:

a. Richard

b. Woody

c. Irene

25. **LO.4** A taxpayer, age 64, purchases an annuity from an insurance company for $50,000. She is to receive $300 per month for life. Her life expectancy is 20.8 years from the annuity starting date. Assuming that she receives $3,600 this year, what is the exclusion percentage and how much is included in her gross income? Round the exclusion percentage to two decimal places. Round the final answer for the income to the nearest dollar.

26. **LO.4** Compute the taxable Social Security benefits in each of the following situations:

a. Erwin and Eleanor are married and file a joint tax return. They have adjusted gross income of $46,000, no tax-exempt interest, and $12,400 of Social Security benefits.

b. Erwin and Eleanor have adjusted gross income of $12,000, no tax-exempt interest, and $16,000 of Social Security benefits.

c. Erwin and Eleanor have adjusted gross income of $85,000, no tax-exempt interest, and $15,000 of Social Security benefits.

Problems

27. **LO.1** Determine the taxpayer's current-year (1) economic income and (2) gross income for tax purposes from the following events:

a. Sam's employment contract as chief executive of a large corporation was terminated, and he was paid $500,000 not to work for a competitor of the corporation for five years.

b. Elliot, a 6-year-old child, was paid $5,000 for appearing in a television commercial. His parents put the funds in a savings account for the child's education.

c. Valery found a suitcase that contained $100,000. She could not determine who the owner was.

d. Winn purchased a lottery ticket for $5 and won $750,000.

e. Larry spent $1,000 to raise vegetables that he and his family consumed. The cost of the vegetables in a store would have been $2,400.

f. Dawn purchased an automobile for $1,500 that was worth $3,500. The seller was in desperate need of cash.

28. **LO.1, 2, 5** Harper is considering three alternative investments of $10,000. Assume that the taxpayer is in the 25% marginal tax bracket for ordinary income and 15% for qualifying capital gains in all tax years. The selected investment will be liquidated at the end of five years. The alternatives are:

Decision Making

• A taxable corporate bond yielding 5.333% before tax and the interest can be reinvested at 5.333% before tax.

• A Series EE bond that will have a maturity value of $12,200 (a 4% before-tax rate of return).

• Land that will increase in value.

The gain on the land is classified and taxed as a long-term capital gain. The income from the bonds is taxed as ordinary income. How much must the land increase in value to yield a greater after-tax return than either of the bonds?

Use the future value tables in Appendix H as needed for your calculations and comparisons.

29. **LO.1** Determine the taxpayer's gross income for tax purposes in each of the following situations:

   a. Deb, a cash basis taxpayer, traded a corporate bond with accrued interest of $300 for corporate stock with a fair market value of $12,000 at the time of the exchange. Deb's cost of the bond was $10,000. The value of the stock had decreased to $11,000 by the end of the year.

   b. Deb needed $10,000 to make a down payment on her house. She instructed her broker to sell some stock to raise the $10,000. Deb's cost of the stock was $3,000. Based on her broker's advice, instead of selling the stock, she borrowed the $10,000 using the stock as collateral for the debt.

   c. Deb's boss gave her two tickets to the Rabid Rabbits rock concert because she met her sales quota. At the time she received the tickets, each ticket had a face price of $200 and was selling on eBay for $300. On the date of the concert, the tickets were selling for $250 each. Deb and her son attended the concert.

30. **LO.1, 2** Determine Amos's gross income in each of the following cases:

   a. In the current year, Amos purchased an automobile for $25,000. As part of the transaction, Amos received a $1,500 rebate from the manufacturer.

   b. Amos sold his business. In addition to the selling price of the stock, he received $50,000 for a covenant not to compete—an agreement that he will not compete with his former business for five years.

   c. Amos owned some land he held as an investment. As a result of a change in the zoning rules, the property increased in value by $20,000.

Decision Making   31. **LO.2, 5** Al is a medical doctor who conducts his practice as a sole proprietor. During 2016, he received cash of $280,000 for medical services. Of the amount collected, $40,000 was for services provided in 2015. At the end of 2016, Al had accounts receivable of $60,000, all for services rendered in 2016. In addition, at the end of the year, Al received $12,000 as an advance payment from a health maintenance organization (HMO) for services to be rendered in 2017. Compute Al's gross income for 2016:

   a. Using the cash basis of accounting.

   b. Using the accrual basis of accounting.

   c. Advise Al on which method of accounting he should use.

32. **LO.2** Selma operates a contractor's supply store. She maintains her books using the cash method. At the end of the year, her accountant computes her accrual basis income that is used on her tax return. For 2016, Selma had cash receipts of $1.4 million, which included $200,000 collected on accounts receivable from 2015 sales. It also included the proceeds of a $100,000 bank loan. At the end of 2016, she had $250,000 in accounts receivable from customers, all from 2016 sales.

   a. Compute Selma's accrual basis gross receipts for 2016.

   b. Selma paid cash for all of the purchases. The total amount paid for merchandise in 2016 was $1.3 million. At the end of 2015, she had merchandise on hand with a cost of $150,000. At the end of 2016, the cost of merchandise on hand was $300,000. Compute Selma's gross income from merchandise sales for 2016.

33. **LO.2, 3, 5** Your client is a partnership, ARP Associates, which is an engineering consulting firm. Generally, ARP bills clients for services at the end of each month. Client billings are about $50,000 each month. On average, it takes 45 days to collect the receivables. ARP's expenses are primarily for salary and rent. Salaries are paid on the last day of each month, and rent is paid on the first day of each month. The partnership has a line of credit with a bank, which requires monthly financial statements. These must be prepared using the accrual method. ARP's managing partner, Amanda Sims, has suggested that the firm also use the accrual method for tax purposes and thus reduce accounting fees by $600. Assume that the partners are in the 35% (combined Federal and state) marginal tax bracket. Write a letter to your client explaining why you believe it would be worthwhile for ARP to file its tax return on the cash basis even though its financial statements are prepared on the accrual basis. ARP's address is 100 James Tower, Denver, CO 80208.

Decision Making

Communications

34. **LO.2** Trip Garage, Inc. (459 Ellis Avenue, Harrisburg, PA 17111), is an accrual basis taxpayer that repairs automobiles. In late December 2016, the company repaired Samuel Mosley's car and charged him $1,000. Samuel did not think the problem had been fixed and refused to pay; thus, Trip refused to release the automobile. In early January 2017, Trip made a few adjustments and convinced Samuel that the automobile was working properly. At that time, Samuel agreed to pay only $900 because he did not have the use of the car for a week. Trip said "fine," accepted the $900, and released the automobile to Samuel. An IRS agent thinks Trip, as an accrual basis taxpayer, should report $1,000 of income in 2016, when the work was done, and then deduct a $100 loss in 2017. Prepare a memo to Susan Apple, the treasurer of Trip, with the recommended treatment for the disputed income.

Communications

35. **LO.2** Determine the effects of the following on a <u>cash basis</u> taxpayer's gross income for 2016 and 2017.

    a. On the morning of December 31, 2016, the taxpayer received a $1,500 check from a customer. The taxpayer did not cash the check until January 3, 2017.

    b. The same as part (a), except the customer asked the taxpayer not to cash the check until January 3, 2017, after the customer's salary check could be deposited.

    c. The same as part (a), except that the check was not received until after the bank had closed on December 31, 2016.

36. **LO.2** Marlene, a <u>cash basis</u> taxpayer, invests in Series EE U.S. government savings bonds and bank certificates of deposit (CDs). Determine the tax consequences of the following on her 2016 gross income:

    a. On September 30, 2016, she cashed in Series EE bonds for $10,000. She purchased the bonds in 2006 for $7,090. The yield to maturity on the bonds was 3.5%.

    b. On July 1, 2015, she purchased a CD for $10,000. The CD matures on June 30, 2017, and will pay $10,816, thus yielding a 4% annual return.

    c. On July 1, 2016, she purchased a CD for $10,000. The maturity date on the CD was June 30, 2017, when Marlene would receive $10,300.

37. **LO.2** Drake Appliance Company, an <u>accrual basis</u> taxpayer, sells home appliances and service contracts. Determine the effect of each of the following transactions on the company's 2016 gross income assuming that the company uses any available options to defer its taxes.

    a. In December 2015, the company received a $1,200 advance payment from a customer for an appliance that Drake special ordered from the manufacturer. The appliance did not arrive from the manufacturer until January 2016, and Drake immediately delivered it to the customer. The sale was reported in 2016 for financial accounting purposes.

    b. In October 2016, the company sold a 6-month service contract for $240. The company also sold a 36-month service contract for $1,260 in July 2016.

WWW For the latest in changes to tax legislation, visit www.cengagebrain.com.

c. On December 31, 2016, the company sold an appliance for $1,200. The company received $500 cash and a note from the customer for $700 and $260 interest, to be paid at the rate of $40 a month for 24 months. Because of the customer's poor credit record, the fair market value of the note was only $600. The cost of the appliance was $750.

38. **LO.2, 5** Freda is a cash basis taxpayer. In 2016, she negotiated her salary for 2017. Her employer offered to pay her $21,000 per month in 2017 for a total of $252,000. Freda countered that she would accept $10,000 each month for the 12 months in 2017 and the remaining $132,000 in January 2018. The employer accepted Freda's terms for 2017 and 2018.

a. Did Freda actually or constructively receive $252,000 in 2017?

b. What could explain Freda's willingness to spread her salary over a longer period of time?

c. In December 2017, after Freda had earned the right to collect the $132,000 in 2018, the employer offered $133,000 to Freda at that time, rather than $132,000 in January 2018. The employer wanted to make the early payment so as to deduct the expense in 2017. Freda rejected the employer's offer. Was Freda in constructive receipt of the income in 2017? Explain.

Decision Making   39. **LO.2, 5** The Bluejay Apartments, a new development, is in the process of structuring its lease agreements. The company would like to set the damage deposits high enough that tenants will keep the apartments in good condition. The company is actually more concerned about damage than about tenants not paying their rent.

a. Discuss the tax effects of the following alternatives:
   - $1,000 damage deposit with no rent prepayment.
   - $500 damage deposit and $500 rent for the final month of the lease.
   - $1,000 rent for the final two months of the lease and no damage deposit.

b. Which option do you recommend? Why?

40. **LO.3** Rusty has been experiencing serious financial problems. His annual salary was $100,000, but a creditor garnished his salary for $20,000; so the employer paid the creditor (rather than Rusty) the $20,000. To prevent creditors from attaching his investments, Rusty gave his investments to his 21-year-old daughter, Rebecca. Rebecca received $5,000 in dividends and interest from the investments during the year. Rusty transferred some cash to a Swiss bank account that paid him $6,000 interest during the year. Rusty did not withdraw the interest from the Swiss bank account. Rusty also hid some of his assets in his wholly owned corporation that received $150,000 rent income but had $160,000 in related expenses, including a $20,000 salary paid to Rusty. Rusty reasons that his gross income should be computed as follows:

Salary received	$ 80,000
Loss from rental property ($150,000 − $160,000)	(10,000)
Gross income	$ 70,000

Compute Rusty's correct gross income for the year, and explain any differences between your calculation and Rusty's.

41. **LO.2, 3** Troy, a cash basis taxpayer, is employed by Eagle Corporation, also a cash basis taxpayer. Troy is a full-time employee of the corporation and receives a salary of $60,000 per year. He also receives a bonus equal to 10% of all collections from clients he serviced during the year. Determine the tax consequences of the following events to the corporation and to Troy:

a. On December 31, 2016, Troy was visiting a customer. The customer gave Troy a $10,000 check payable to the corporation for appraisal services Troy performed during 2016. Troy did not deliver the check to the corporation until January 2017.

b. The facts are the same as in (a), except that the corporation is an accrual basis taxpayer and Troy deposited the check on December 31, but the bank did not add the deposit to the corporation's account until January 2017.

c. The facts are the same as in (a), except that the customer told Troy to hold the check until January 2017 when the customer could make a bank deposit that would cover the check.

42. **LO.3, 4** Faye, Gary, and Heidi each have a one-third interest in the capital and profits of the FGH Partnership. Each partner had a capital account of $50,000 at the beginning of the tax year. The partnership profits for the tax year were $270,000. Changes in their capital accounts during the tax year were as follows:

	Faye	Gary	Heidi	Total
Beginning balance	$ 50,000	$ 50,000	$ 50,000	$150,000
Withdrawals	(20,000)	(35,000)	(10,000)	(65,000)
Additional contributions	–0–	–0–	5,000	5,000
Allocation of profits	90,000	90,000	90,000	270,000
Ending balance	$120,000	$105,000	$135,000	$360,000

In arriving at the $270,000 of partnership profits, the partnership deducted $2,400 ($800 for each partner) in premiums paid for group term life insurance on the partners. Faye and Gary are 39 years old, and Heidi is 35 years old. Other employees are also eligible for group term life insurance equal to their annual salary. These premiums of $10,000 have been deducted in calculating the partnership profits of $270,000. Compute each partner's gross income from the partnership for the tax year.

43. **LO.3, 5** In 2016, Alva received dividends on her stocks as follows:

Amur Corporation (a French corporation whose stock is traded on an established U.S. securities market)	$60,000
Blaze, Inc., a Delaware corporation	40,000
Grape, Inc., a Virginia corporation	22,000

a. Alva purchased the Grape stock three years ago, and she purchased the Amur stock two years ago. She purchased the Blaze stock 18 days before it went ex-dividend and sold it 20 days later at a $5,000 loss. Alva had no other capital gains and losses for the year. She is in the 35% marginal tax bracket. Compute Alva's tax on her dividend income for 2016.

b. Alva's daughter, who is 25 and not Alva's dependent, had taxable income of $6,000, which included $1,000 of dividends on Grape, Inc. stock. The daughter had purchased the stock two years ago. Compute the daughter's tax liability on the dividends.

c. Alva can earn 5% before-tax interest on a corporate bond or a 4% dividend on a preferred stock. Assuming that the appreciation in value is the same, which investment produces the greater after-tax income?

d. The same as part (c), except that Alva's daughter is to make the investment.

44. **LO.3** Liz and Doug were divorced on December 31 of the current year after 10 years of marriage. Their current year's income received before the divorce was as follows:

Doug's salary	$41,000
Liz's salary	55,000
Rent on apartments purchased by Liz 15 years ago	8,000
Dividends on stock Doug inherited from his mother 4 years ago	1,900
Interest on a savings account in Liz's name funded with her salary	2,400

Allocate the income to Liz and Doug assuming that they live in:

a.   California.

b.   Texas.

45.   **LO.4** Nell and Kirby are in the process of negotiating their divorce agreement. What should be the tax consequences to Nell and Kirby if the following, considered individually, became part of the agreement?

a.   In consideration for her one-half interest in their personal residence, Kirby will transfer to Nell stock with a value of $200,000 and $50,000 of cash. Kirby's cost of the stock was $150,000, and the value of the personal residence is $500,000. They purchased the residence three years ago for $300,000.

b.   Nell will receive $1,000 per month for 120 months. If she dies before receiving all 120 payments, the remaining payments will be made to her estate.

c.   Nell is to have custody of their 12-year-old son, Bobby. She is to receive $1,200 per month until Bobby (1) dies or (2) attains age 21 (whichever occurs first). After either of these events occurs, Nell will receive only $300 per month for the remainder of her life.

Decision Making   46.   **LO.4** Alicia and Rafel are in the process of negotiating a divorce agreement. They both worked during the marriage and contributed an equal amount to the marital assets. They own a home with a fair market value of $400,000 (cost of $300,000) that is subject to a mortgage of $250,000. They have lived in the home for 12 years. They also have investment assets with a cost of $160,000 and a fair market value of $410,000. Thus, the net worth of the couple is $560,000 ($400,000 − $250,000 + $410,000). The holding period for the investments is longer than one year. Alicia would like to continue to live in the house. Therefore, she has proposed that she receive the residence subject to the mortgage, a net value of $150,000. In addition, she would receive $17,600 each year for the next 10 years, which has a present value (at 6% interest) of $130,000. Rafel would receive the investment assets. If Rafel accepts this plan, he must sell one-half of the investments so that he can purchase a home. Assume that you are counseling Alicia. Explain to Alicia whether the proposed agreement would be "fair" on an after-tax basis.

Decision Making   47.   **LO.4, 5** Roy decides to buy a personal residence and goes to the bank for a $150,000 loan. The bank tells him that he can borrow the funds at 4% if his father will guarantee the debt. Roy's father, Hal, owns a $150,000 CD currently yielding 3.5%. The Federal rate is 3%. Hal agrees to either of the following:

•   Roy borrows from the bank with Hal's guarantee to the bank.

•   Cash in the CD (with no penalty) and lend Roy the funds at 2% interest.

Hal is in the 33% marginal tax bracket. Roy, whose only source of income is his salary, is in the 15% marginal tax bracket. The interest Roy pays on the mortgage will be deductible by him. Which option will maximize the family's after-tax wealth?

48.   **LO.2, 4** Ridge is a generous individual. During the year, he made interest-free loans to various family members when the Federal rate was 3%. What are the tax consequences of the following loans by Ridge:

a.   On June 30, 2015, Ridge loaned $12,000 to his cousin, Jim, to buy a used truck. Jim's only source of income was his wages on various construction jobs during the year.

b.   On August 1, 2015, Ridge loaned $8,000 to his niece, Sonja. The loan was to enable her to pay her college tuition. Sonja had $1,200 interest income from CDs her parents had given her.

c.   On September 1, 2015, Ridge loaned $25,000 to his brother, Al, to start a business. Al had $220 of dividends and interest for the year.

d. On September 30, 2015, Ridge loaned $150,000 to his mother so that she could enter a nursing home. His mother's only income was $9,000 of Social Security benefits and $500 of interest income.

49. **LO.4** Indicate whether the imputed interest rules should apply in the following situations. Assume that all of the loans were made at the beginning of the tax year unless otherwise indicated.

a. Mike loaned his sister $90,000 to buy a new home. Mike did not charge interest on the loan. The Federal rate was 5%. Mike's sister had $900 of investment income for the year.

b. Sam's employer maintains an emergency loan fund for its employees. During the year, Sam's wife was very ill, and he incurred unusually large medical expenses. He borrowed $8,500 from his employer's emergency loan fund for six months. The Federal rate was 5.5%. Sam and his wife had no investment income for the year.

c. Jody borrowed $25,000 from her controlled corporation for six months. She used the funds to pay her daughter's college tuition. The corporation charged Jody 4% interest. The Federal rate was 5%. Jody had $3,500 of investment income for the year.

d. Kait loaned her son, Jake, $60,000 for six months. Jake used the $60,000 to pay off college loans. The Federal rate was 5%, and Kait did not charge Jake any interest. Jake had dividend and interest income of $2,100 for the tax year.

50. **LO.4** Vito is the sole shareholder of Vito, Inc. He is also employed by the corporation. On June 30, 2016 Vito borrowed $8,000 from Vito, Inc., and on July 1, 2017, he borrowed an additional $10,000. Both loans were due on demand. No interest was charged on the loans, and the Federal rate was 4% for all relevant dates. Vito used the money to purchase a boat, and he had $2,500 of investment income. Determine the tax consequences to Vito and Vito, Inc., in each of the following situations:

a. The loans are considered employer-employee loans.

b. The loans are considered corporation-shareholder loans.

51. **LO.4** Pam retires after 28 years of service with her employer. She is 66 years old and has contributed $42,000 to her employer's qualified pension fund. She elects to receive her retirement benefits as an annuity of $3,000 per month for the remainder of her life.

a. Assume that Pam retires in June 2016 and collects six annuity payments this year. What is her gross income from the annuity payments in the first year?

b. Assume that Pam lives 25 years after retiring. What is her gross income from the annuity payments in the twenty-fourth year?

c. Assume that Pam dies after collecting 160 payments. She collected eight payments in the year of her death. What are Pam's gross income and deductions from the annuity contract in the year of her death?

52. **LO.4** For each of the following, determine the amount that should be included in gross income:

a. Peyton was selected the most valuable player in the Super Bowl. In recognition of this, he was awarded an automobile with a value of $60,000. Peyton did not need the automobile, so he asked that the title be put in his parents' names.

b. Jacob was awarded the Nobel Peace Prize. When he was presented the check for $1.4 million, Jacob said, "I do not need the money. Give it to the United Nations to use toward the goal of world peace."

c. Linda won the Craig County Fair beauty pageant. She received a $10,000 scholarship that paid her $6,000 for tuition and $4,000 for meals and housing for the academic year.

53. **LO.4** The LMN Partnership has a group term life insurance plan. Each partner has $150,000 of protection, and each employee has protection equal to twice his or her annual salary. Employee Alice (age 32) has $90,000 of insurance under the plan, and partner Kay (age 47) has $150,000 of coverage. Because the plan is a "group plan," it is impossible to determine the cost of coverage for an individual employee or partner.

    a.   Assuming that the plan is nondiscriminatory, how much must Alice and Kay each include in gross income as a result of the partnership paying the insurance premiums?

    b.   Assume that the partnership is incorporated. Kay becomes a shareholder and an employee who receives a $75,000 annual salary. The corporation provides Kay with $150,000 of group term life insurance coverage under a nondiscriminatory plan. What is Kay's gross income as a result of the corporation paying the insurance premiums?

54. **LO.2, 4** Herbert was employed for the first six months of 2016 and earned $90,000 in salary. During the next six months, he collected $8,800 of unemployment compensation, borrowed $12,000 (using his personal residence as collateral), and withdrew $2,000 from his savings account (including $60 of interest). He received dividends of $550. His luck was not all bad, for in December, he won $1,500 in the lottery on a $5 ticket. Calculate Herbert's gross income.

Decision Making   55. **LO.4, 5** Linda and Don are married and file a joint return. In 2016, they received $12,000 in Social Security benefits and $35,000 in taxable pension benefits and interest.

    a.   Compute the couple's adjusted gross income on a joint return.

    b.   Don would like to know whether they should sell for $100,000 (at no gain or loss) a corporate bond that pays 8% in interest each year and use the proceeds to buy a $100,000 nontaxable State of Virginia bond that will pay $6,000 in interest each year.

    c.   If Linda in (a) works part-time and earns $30,000, how much will Linda and Don's adjusted gross income increase?

56. **LO.4** Melissa, who is 70 years old, is unmarried and has no dependents. Her annual income consists of a taxable pension of $17,000, $14,000 in Social Security benefits, and $3,000 of dividend income. She does not itemize her deductions. She is in the 15% marginal income tax bracket. She is considering getting a part-time job that would pay her $5,000 a year.

    a.   What would be Melissa's after-tax income from the part-time job, considering Social Security and Medicare tax (7.65%) as well as Federal income tax on the earnings of $5,000?

    b.   What would be the effective tax rate (increase in tax/increase in income) on the additional income from the part-time job?

57. **LO.3, 4** Donna does not think she has an income tax problem but would like to discuss her situation with you just to make sure there is no unexpected tax liability. Base your suggestions on the following relevant financial information:

    a.   Donna's share of the SAT Partnership income is $150,000, but none of the income can be distributed because the partnership needs the cash for operations.

    b.   Donna's Social Security benefits totaled $8,400, but Donna loaned the cash received to her nephew.

    c.   Donna assigned to a creditor the right to collect $1,200 of interest on some bonds she owned.

    d.   Donna and her husband lived together in California until September, when they separated. Donna has heard rumors that her husband had substantial gambling winnings since they separated.

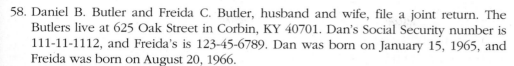

Cumulative Problems

Tax Return Problem

Decision Making

Communications

TAX SOFTWARE

58. Daniel B. Butler and Freida C. Butler, husband and wife, file a joint return. The Butlers live at 625 Oak Street in Corbin, KY 40701. Dan's Social Security number is 111-11-1112, and Freida's is 123-45-6789. Dan was born on January 15, 1965, and Freida was born on August 20, 1966.

During 2015, Dan and Freida furnished over half of the total support of each of the following individuals, all of whom still live at home:

a. Gina, their daughter, age 22, a full-time student, who married on December 21, 2015, has no income of her own and for 2015 did not file a joint return with her husband, Casey, who earned $10,600 during 2015. Gina's Social Security number is 123-45-6788.

b. Sam, their son, age 20, who had gross income of $6,300 in 2015, dropped out of college in October 2015. He had graduated from high school in May 2015. Sam's Social Security number is 123-45-6787.

c. Ben, their oldest son, age 26, is a full-time graduate student with gross income of $5,200. Ben's Social Security number is 123-45-6786.

Dan was employed as a manager by WJJJ, Inc. (employer identification number 11-1111111, 604 Franklin Street, Corbin, KY 40702), and Freida was employed as a salesperson for Corbin Realty, Inc. (employer identification number 98-7654321, 899 Central Street, Corbin, Ky 40701). Selected information from the W–2 Forms provided by the employers is presented below. Dan and Freida use the cash method.

Line	Description	Dan	Freida
1	Wages, tips, other compensation	$74,000	$86,000
2	Federal income tax withheld	11,000	12,400
17	State income tax withheld	2,960	3,440

Freida sold a house on December 30, 2015, and will be paid a commission of $3,100 (not included in the $86,000 reported on the W–2) on the January 10, 2016 closing date.

Other income (as reported on 1099 Forms) for 2015 consisted of the following:

Dividends on CSX stock (qualified)	$4,200
Interest on savings at Second Bank	1,600
Interest on City of Corbin bonds	900
Interest on First Bank CD	382

The $382 from First Bank was original issue discount. Dan and Freida collected $16,000 on the First Bank CD that matured on September 30, 2015. The CD was purchased on October 1, 2013, for $14,995, and the yield to maturity was 3.3%.

Dan received a Schedule K–1 from the Falcon Partnership, which showed his distributive share of income as $7,000. In addition to the above information, Dan and Freida's itemized deductions included the following:

Paid on 2015 Kentucky income tax	$ 700
Personal property tax paid	600
Real estate taxes paid	1,800
Interest on home mortgage (Corbin S&L)	4,900
Cash contributions to the Boy Scouts	800

Sales tax from the sales tax table is $1,860. Dan and Freida made Federal estimated tax payments of $8,000. All members of the family had health insurance coverage for all of 2015. Dan and Freida do not wish to contribute to the Presidential Election Campaign. The Kentucky income tax rate is 4%.

Part 1—Tax Computation

Compute Dan and Freida's 2015 Federal income tax payable (or refund due). If you use tax forms for your computations, you will need Form 1040 and Schedules A, B, and E. Suggested software: H&R BLOCK Tax Software.

Part 2—Tax Planning

Dan plans to reduce his work schedule and work only half-time for WJJJ in 2016. He has been writing songs for several years and wants to devote more time to developing a career as a songwriter. Because of the uncertainty in the music business, however, he would like you to make all computations assuming that he will have no income from songwriting in 2016. To make up for the loss of income, Freida plans to increase the amount of time she spends selling real estate. She estimates that she will be able to earn $90,000 in 2016. Assume that all other income and expense items will be approximately the same as they were in 2015. Assume that Sam will be enrolled in college as a full-time student for the summer and fall semesters. Will the Butlers have more or less disposable income (after Federal income tax) in 2016? Write a letter to the Butlers that contains your advice, and prepare a memo for the tax files.

Tax Computation Problem   59. Cecil C. Seymour is a 64-year-old widower. He had income for 2016 as follows:

Pension from former employer	$39,850
Interest income from Alto National Bank	5,500
Interest income on City of Alto bonds	4,500
Dividends received from IBM stock held for over one year	2,000
Collections on annuity contract he purchased from Great Life Insurance	5,400
Social Security benefits	14,000
Rent income on townhouse	9,000

The cost of the annuity was $46,800, and Cecil was expected to receive a total of 260 monthly payments of $450. Cecil has received 22 payments through 2016.

Cecil's 40-year-old daughter, Sarah C. Seymour, borrowed $60,000 from Cecil on January 2, 2016. She used the money to start a new business. Cecil does not charge her interest because she could not afford to pay it, but he does expect to collect the principal eventually. Sarah is living with Cecil until the business becomes profitable. Except for housing, Sarah provides her own support from her business and $1,600 in dividends on stocks that she inherited from her mother.

Other relevant information is presented below:

- Cecil's Social Security number: 123-45-6785
- Address: 3840 Springfield Blvd., Alto, GA 30510
- Sarah's Social Security number: 123-45-6784
- Expenses on rental townhouse:

Utilities	$2,800
Maintenance	1,000
Depreciation	2,000
Real estate taxes	750
Insurance	700

- State income taxes paid: $3,500
- County personal property taxes paid: $2,100
- Payments on estimated 2015 Federal income tax: $5,900
- Charitable contributions of cash to Alto Baptist Church: $6,400
- Federal interest rate: 6%
- Sales taxes paid: $912

Compute Cecil's 2016 Federal income tax payable (or refund due).

Research Problems

Note: Solutions to Research Problems can be prepared by using the Checkpoint® Student Edition online research product, which is available to accompany this text. It is also possible to prepare solutions to the Research Problems by using tax research materials found in a standard tax library.

Research Problem 1. Tranquility Funeral Home, Inc., your client, is an accrual basis taxpayer that sells preneed funeral contracts. Under these contracts, the customer pays in advance for goods and services to be provided at the contract beneficiary's death. These payments are refundable at the contract purchaser's request, pursuant to state law, anytime until the goods and services are furnished. Tranquility, consistent with its financial accounting reporting, includes the payments in income for the year the funeral service is provided. The IRS agent insists that the payments be prepaid income subject to tax in the year of receipt. Your client believes that the amounts involved are customer deposits. Write a letter to Tranquility that contains your advice about how the issue should be resolved. The client's address is 400 Rock Street, Memphis, TN 38152.

Communications

Research Problem 2. Your client was the beneficiary of an annuity contract purchased by her stepmother. When the stepmother died, the insurance company paid the client $400,000 and sent her a Form 1099 indicating that the taxable portion (i.e., the amount in excess of the investment in the contract) was $50,000. However, according to the client, her father fraudulently convinced her that he was the intended beneficiary. She gave her father a check equal to the amount she had received from the insurance company. She did not report any of the annuity proceeds in her income tax return. She later discovered the fraud and filed a lawsuit to collect from her father. The IRS has examined your client's return and has taken the position that she must include the $50,000 in her gross income.

Evaluate the IRS's position.

Research Problem 3. Your client owns a life insurance policy on his life. He has paid $6,800 in premiums, and the cash surrender value of the policy is $30,000. He borrowed $30,000 from the insurance company, using the cash surrender value as collateral. He is considering canceling the policy in payment of the loan. He would like to know the tax consequences of canceling his policy.

Research Problem 4. Your client is a new retailer who often issues store gift (debit) cards to customers in lieu of a cash refund. You recall that the IRS issued a Revenue Procedure that provided that the prepaid income rules in Revenue Procedure 2004–34 could be applied to the income from the gift cards. Locate the Revenue Procedure authorizing the deferral of the income from gift cards.

Use the tax resources of the Internet to address the following questions. Do not restrict your search to the Web, but include a review of newsgroups and general reference materials, practitioner sites and resources, primary sources of the tax law, chat rooms and discussion groups, and other opportunities.

Internet Activity

Research Problem 5. Lottery winnings are taxable for Federal income tax purposes. What many lottery hopefuls forget to factor into their tax considerations are that lottery winnings are also taxable in many states. Search the Internet to see whether you can determine if lottery winnings are taxable for California residents.

Research Problem 6. Go to the web page of a consulting firm that offers counseling services to individuals as they negotiate the terms of a divorce. What specific tax-related services do these firms offer? Suggest a new tax-related service the consulting firm could offer.

Communications

Roger CPA Review Questions

1. Smith, an individual, is required to pay Goode yearly alimony of $6,000 and yearly child support of $18,000. Smith paid Goode $20,000 in 2016. Smith's 2016 W–2 income was $50,000. Considering only the foregoing facts, what should Smith's adjusted gross income be for 2016?

   a. $30,000   c. $48,000
   b. $45,000   d. $50,000

2. Which of the following is excluded from gross income on an individual's 2016 tax return?

   a. January 2017 rent received in December 2016
   b. Value arising from personal use of company vehicle in 2016
   c. Dividends announced by a C corporation in December 2015 and received in January 2016
   d. Refundable security deposit received in January 2016 for a lease ending in July 2017

3. Walters, an individual, received the following in 2016:

W–2 income	$10,000
Federal tax refund for 2015	1,250
Scholarship stipend, in return for teaching assistant duties performed	25,000
Cash inheritance from deceased great-uncle	5,000

   Considering only the above, what is Walters' 2016 gross income?

   a. $35,000   c. $15,000
   b. $36,250   d. $16,250

4. Doran, a single individual, received $20,000 in Social Security benefits in 2016. Doran's 2016 provisional income was $65,000. Considering only these facts, what should Doran report as gross income on Doran's 2016 tax return?

   a. $75,000   c. $57,000
   b. $72,000   d. $65,000

5. On October 1, 2016, Cruz purchased an annuity for $90,000 in post-tax dollars, effective immediately, that pays Cruz $500 a month until death. At the date of purchase, Cruz's official life expectancy was 25 years. How much of Cruz's 2016 annuity payments should be included in Cruz's gross income for 2016?

   a. $0   c. $600
   b. $900   d. $1,500

Gross Income: Exclusions

LEARNING OBJECTIVES: *After completing Chapter 5, you should be able to:*

LO.1 Be aware that statutory authority is required to exclude an item from gross income.

LO.2 Identify the circumstances under which various items are excludible from gross income.

LO.3 Determine the extent to which receipts can be excluded under the tax benefit rule.

LO.4 Describe the circumstances under which income must be reported from the discharge of indebtedness.

LO.5 Identify tax planning strategies for obtaining the maximum benefit from allowable exclusions.

CHAPTER OUTLINE

EXCLUSIONS

Paul is a graduate student in the last semester of an accounting program at State University. This past summer he was an intern with a CPA firm, working in the compliance area. Paul was paid well enough for his work as an intern that he was able to pay for his meals and lodging and to save some for school. The CPA firm was so pleased with Paul's work that at the conclusion of his internship, he was given a bonus of $1,500 more than the firm had agreed to pay him. The extra amount was intended to help with his graduate school expenses. The CPA firm has offered him a full-time job after he completes his graduate program in December.

Because of his excellent academic record, the university awarded Paul a graduate assistantship that waives his tuition of $6,000 per semester and pays him $400 per month. Paul is required to teach a principles of accounting course each semester. Paul has used the $400 per month for books and for room and board.

In November, Paul was crossing a street in the pedestrian crosswalk when a delivery van struck him. The driver of the truck had a blood alcohol level of .12. Paul suffered a severe injury to his right arm that delayed his starting date for work by three months. The delivery company's insurance company settled the case by paying damages, itemized as follows:

Compensatory damages:	
Medical expenses	$ 30,000
Injury to Paul's right arm	100,000
Pain and suffering	50,000
Loss of income	15,000
Legal fees	25,000
Punitive damages	160,000
	$380,000

Paul's mother was with him in the crosswalk. Fortunately, the van did not hit her, and she was not physically injured. But she did suffer emotional distress and received $25,000 in the settlement.

Besides being Paul's friend, you also are a senior accounting major and have a keen interest in taxation. You tell Paul that you will look into the tax consequences of the settlement.

Read the chapter and formulate your response.

FRAMEWORK 1040 **Tax Formula for Individuals**

This chapter covers the boldfaced portions of the Tax Formula for Individuals that was introduced in Concept Summary 3.1 on p. 3-3. Below those portions are the sections of Form 1040 where the results are reported.

Income *(broadly defined)*	$xx,xxx
Less: Exclusions	(x,xxx)

> **FORM 1040 (p. 1)**
>
> **8b**   **Tax-exempt** interest. **Do not** include on line 8a . . . | **8b** | | |

Gross income...	$xx,xxx

> **FORM 1040 (p. 1)**
>
> **10**   Taxable refunds, credits, or offsets of state and local income taxes . . . .
> **19**   Unemployment compensation . . . .
> **21**   Other income. List type and amount   _____

Less: Deductions *for* adjusted gross income	(x,xxx)
Adjusted gross income...	$xx,xxx
Less: The greater of total itemized deductions *or* the standard deduction.............................	(x,xxx)
Personal and dependency exemptions	(x,xxx)
Taxable income	$xx,xxx
Tax on taxable income *(see Tax Tables or Tax Rate Schedules)*	$ x,xxx
Less: Tax credits *(including income taxes withheld and prepaid)*.................................	(xxx)
Tax due (or refund)	$ xxx

C hapter 4 discussed the concepts and judicial doctrines that affect the determination of gross income. If an income item is within the all-inclusive definition of gross income, the item can be excluded only if the taxpayer can locate specific authority for doing so. Chapter 5 focuses on the exclusions Congress has authorized.

5-1 **STATUTORY AUTHORITY**

Sections 101 through 150 provide the authority for excluding specific items from gross income. Each exclusion has its own legislative history and reason for enactment. Certain exclusions are intended as a form of indirect welfare payments. Other exclusions prevent double taxation of income or provide incentives for socially desirable activities (e.g., nontaxable interest on certain U.S. government bonds where the owner uses the funds for educational expenses).

In some cases, Congress has enacted exclusions to rectify the effects of judicial decisions or IRS pronouncements.[1] For example, in the past, the IRS and some courts interpreted gross income to include payments the taxpayer received from his or her insurance policy to cover temporary living expenses after the person's residence was destroyed by fire. Although the IRS's and the courts' reasoning may have been a sound interpretation of the meaning of gross income, Congress determined that taxing the person under such dire circumstances was bad policy. Therefore, in 1969, Congress enacted § 123, which exempts from tax the insurance proceeds received for extraordinary living expenses when the taxpayer's home has been destroyed by fire or other casualty.[2]

---

[1]See Chapter 1, Example 28.

[2]P.L. 91–172, Tax Reform Act of 1969, Senate Report No. 91–552.

At times, Congress responds to specific events. For example, in 2001, Congress enacted § 139, Disaster Relief Payment, to ensure that victims of a *qualified disaster* (disaster resulting from a terrorist attack, Presidentially declared disaster, or common carrier accident of a catastrophic nature) would not be required to include in gross income payments received for living expenses, funeral expenses, and property damage resulting from the disaster.

5-2 GIFTS AND INHERITANCES

LO.2

Identify the circumstances under which various items are excludible from gross income.

5-2a Legislative Intent

Beginning with the Income Tax Act of 1913 and continuing to the present, Congress has allowed the recipient of a gift to exclude the value of the property from gross income. The exclusion applies to gifts made during the life of the donor (*inter vivos* gifts) and transfers that take effect upon the death of the donor (bequests and inheritances).[3] However, as discussed in Chapter 4, the recipient of a gift of income-producing property is subject to tax on the income subsequently earned from the property. Also, as discussed in Chapter 1, the donor or the decedent's estate may be subject to gift or estate taxes on the transfer.

In numerous cases, gifts are made in a business setting. For example, a salesperson gives a purchasing agent free samples, an employee receives cash from his or her employer upon retirement, or a corporation makes payments to employees who were victims of a natural disaster. In these and similar instances, it is frequently unclear whether the payment was a gift or represents compensation for past, present, or future services.

The courts have defined a gift as "a voluntary transfer of property by one to another without adequate [valuable] consideration or compensation therefrom."[4] If the payment is intended to be for services rendered, it is not a gift, even though the payment is made without legal or moral obligation and the payor receives no economic benefit from the transfer. To qualify as a gift, the payment must be made "out of affection, respect, admiration, charity or like impulses."[5] Thus, the cases on this issue have been decided on the basis of the donor's intent.

In a landmark case, *Comm. v. Duberstein*,[6] the taxpayer (Duberstein) received a Cadillac from a business acquaintance. Duberstein had supplied the businessman with the names of potential customers with no expectation of compensation. The Supreme Court concluded:

> … despite the characterization of the transfer of the Cadillac by the parties [as a gift] and the absence of any obligation, even of a moral nature, to make it, it was at the bottom a recompense for Duberstein's past service, or an inducement for him to be of further service in the future.

Duberstein was therefore required to include the fair market value of the automobile in gross income.

5-2b Employer Payments to Employees

In the case of cash or other property *received by an employee* from his or her employer, Congress has eliminated any ambiguity. Transfers from an employer to an employee cannot be excluded as a gift.[7]

---

[3]§ 102.

[4]*Estate of D. R. Daly*, 3 B.T.A. 1042 (1926).

[5]*Robertson v. U.S.*, 52–1 USTC ¶9343, 41 AFTR 1053, 72 S.Ct. 994 (USSC, 1952).

[6]60–2 USTC ¶9515, 5 AFTR 2d 1626, 80 S.Ct. 1190 (USSC, 1960).

[7]§ 102(c). But see § 139 for qualified disaster situations.

The Big Picture

EXAMPLE 1

Return to the facts of *The Big Picture* on p. 5-1. The $1,500 bonus paid to Paul by his summer employer was compensation for his services rather than a gift, even though the employer had not contracted to pay this additional amount. This results because the payment was most likely not motivated by the employer's generosity, but rather was made as a result of business considerations. Even if the payment had been made out of generosity, because the payment was received from his employer, Paul could not exclude the "gift."

5-2c Employee Death Benefits

Frequently, an employer makes payments (**death benefits**) to a deceased employee's surviving spouse, children, or other beneficiaries. If the decedent had a nonforfeitable right to the payments (e.g., the decedent's accrued salary), the amounts are generally taxable to the recipient as if the employee had lived and collected the payments. But when the employer makes voluntary payments, the gift issue arises. Generally, the IRS considers such payments to be compensation for prior services rendered by the deceased employee.[8] However, some courts have held that payments to an employee's surviving spouse or other beneficiaries are gifts if the following are true:[9]

- The payments were made to the surviving spouse and children rather than to the employee's estate.
- The employer derived no benefit from the payments.
- The surviving spouse and children performed no services for the employer.
- The decedent had been fully compensated for services rendered.
- Payments were made pursuant to a board of directors' resolution that followed a general company policy of providing payments for families of deceased employees (but not exclusively for families of shareholder-employees).

When all of the above conditions are satisfied, the payment is presumed to have been made *as an act of affection or charity.* When one or more of these conditions is not satisfied, the surviving spouse and children may still be deemed the recipients of a gift if the payment is made in light of the survivors' financial needs.[10]

Income earned by an employee that was not received by the employee prior to his or her death is not an employee death benefit. These earnings are referred to as "income in respect of a decedent"[11] and are generally taxable income to the decedent's beneficiary. This is another rare instance (see Alimony in Chapter 4) where the beneficiary of the income, rather than the person who earned the income, is subject to tax.

---

[8]Rev.Rul. 62–102, 1962–2 C.B. 37.

[9]*Estate of Sydney J. Carter v. Comm.*, 72–1 USTC ¶9129, 29 AFTR 2d 332, 453 F.2d 61 (CA–2, 1972), and the cases cited there.

[10]*Simpson v. U.S.*, 58–2 USTC ¶9923, 2 AFTR 2d 6036, 261 F.2d 497 (CA–7, 1958), *cert. denied* 79 S.Ct. 724 (USSC, 1958).

[11]§ 691.

5-3 LIFE INSURANCE PROCEEDS

5-3a General Rule

Life insurance proceeds paid to the beneficiary because of the death of the insured are exempt from income tax.[12]

Mark purchases an insurance policy on his life and names his wife, Linda, as the beneficiary. Mark pays $45,000 in premiums. When he dies, Linda collects the insurance proceeds of $200,000. The $200,000 is exempt from Federal income tax.

Congress chose to exempt life insurance proceeds for the following reasons:

• For family members, life insurance proceeds serve much the same purpose as a nontaxable inheritance.

• In a business context (as well as in a family situation), life insurance proceeds replace an economic loss suffered by the beneficiary.

Gold Corporation purchases a life insurance policy to cover its key employee. If the proceeds were taxable, the corporation would require more insurance coverage to pay the tax as well as to cover the economic loss of the employee.

Thus, in general, Congress concluded that making life insurance proceeds exempt from income tax was a good policy.

5-3b Accelerated Death Benefits

Generally, if the owner of a life insurance policy cancels the policy and receives the cash surrender value, the taxpayer must recognize gain equal to the excess of the amount received over premiums paid on the policy (a loss is not deductible). The gain is recognized because the general exclusion provision for life insurance proceeds applies only to life insurance proceeds paid upon the death of the insured. If the taxpayer cancels the policy and receives the cash surrender value, the life insurance policy is treated as an investment by the insured.

In a limited circumstance, however, the insured is permitted to receive the benefits of the life insurance contract without having to include the gain in gross income. Under the **accelerated death benefits** provisions, exclusion treatment is available for insured taxpayers who are either terminally ill or chronically ill.[13] A terminally ill taxpayer can collect the cash surrender value of the policy from the insurance company or assign the policy proceeds to a qualified third party. The resultant gain, if any, is excluded from the insured's gross income. A *terminally ill* individual is a person whom a medical doctor certifies as having an illness that is reasonably expected to cause death within 24 months.

---

[12]§ 101(a). [13]§ 101(g).

In the case of a chronically ill patient, no gain is recognized if the proceeds of the policy are used for the long-term care of the insured. A person is *chronically ill* if he or she is certified as being unable to perform without assistance certain activities of daily living. These exclusions for the terminally ill and the chronically ill are available only to the insured. Thus, a person who purchases a life insurance policy from the insured does not qualify.

Accelerated Death Benefits

EXAMPLE 4

Tom owned a term life insurance policy at the time he was diagnosed as having a terminal illness. After paying $5,200 in premiums, he sold the policy to Amber Benefits, Inc., a company that is authorized by the state of Virginia to purchase such policies. Amber paid Tom $50,000. When Tom died six months later, Amber collected the face amount of the policy, $75,000. Tom is not required to include the $44,800 gain ($50,000 − $5,200) on the sale of the policy in his gross income.

EXAMPLE 5

Assume that Amber in Example 4 paid additional premiums of $4,000 during the six months it owned the policy. When Amber collects the life insurance proceeds of $75,000, it must include the $21,000 gain [$75,000 proceeds − ($50,000 cost + $4,000 additional premiums paid)] in gross income.

ETHICS & EQUITY **Should the Terminally Ill Pay Social Security Taxes?**

The rationale for excluding accelerated death benefits from the gross income of the terminally ill is that they often use the funds to pay medical expenses and other costs associated with dying and do not have the ability to pay tax on the gain from the accelerated receipt of the life insurance proceeds. Yet the wages of a terminally ill person who is employed (or profits of a self-employed person) are subject to Social Security taxes. The Social Security taxes are intended to pay for retirement benefits, but a terminally ill person is unlikely to collect any Social Security benefits.

Several bills have been introduced in Congress to exempt the terminally ill from the Social Security tax. Evaluate the equity of the current tax treatment versus that in the proposed legislation.

5-3c Transfer for Valuable Consideration

A life insurance policy (other than one associated with accelerated death benefits) may be transferred after it is issued by the insurance company. If the policy is *transferred for valuable consideration*, the insurance proceeds are includible in the gross income of the transferee to the extent the proceeds received exceed the amount paid for the policy by the transferee plus any subsequent premiums paid.

EXAMPLE 6

Adam pays premiums of $4,000 for an insurance policy in the face amount of $10,000 upon the life of Beth and subsequently transfers the policy to Carol for $6,000. Upon Beth's death, Carol receives the proceeds of $10,000. The amount Carol can exclude from gross income is limited to $6,000 plus any premiums she paid subsequent to the transfer.

The Code, however, provides five exceptions to the rule illustrated in the preceding example. These exceptions permit exclusion treatment for transfers to the following:

1. The insured under the policy.
2. A partner of the insured.
3. A partnership in which the insured is a partner.
4. A corporation in which the insured is an officer or a shareholder.
5. A transferee whose basis in the policy is determined by reference to the transferor's basis.

When Logan's daughter Emily was born, he purchased an insurance policy on her life. Twenty-four years later after Emily graduated from college and married, Logan sold her the policy for its fair value. When Emily dies, the transfer for consideration rules will not apply.

Because the transfer was to the insured, the policy proceeds will be excluded from the recipient's gross income. The results would be the same if Logan gave (rather than sold) the policy to Emily.

The fifth exception applies to policies that were transferred pursuant to a tax-free exchange or were received by gift.[14]

Investment earnings arising from the reinvestment of life insurance proceeds are generally subject to income tax. Often the beneficiary will elect to collect the insurance proceeds in installments. The annuity rules (discussed in Chapter 4) are used to apportion the installment payment between the principal element (excludible) and the interest element (includible).[15]

5-4 SCHOLARSHIPS

5-4a General Information

Payments or benefits received by a student at an educational institution may be (1) compensation for services, (2) a gift, or (3) a scholarship. If the payments or benefits are received as compensation for services (past or present), the fact that the recipient is a student generally does not render the amounts received nontaxable.[16] Thus, a university teaching or research assistant is generally considered an employee, and his or her stipend is taxable compensation for services rendered. On the other hand, athletic scholarships generally are nontaxable when the individual is not required to participate in the sport.[17] In general, amounts received to be used for educational purposes (other than amounts received from family members) cannot be excluded as gifts because conditions attached to the receipt of the funds mean that the payments were not made out of "detached generosity."

The scholarship rules are intended to provide exclusion treatment for education-related benefits that cannot qualify as gifts but are not compensation for services. According to the Regulations, "a scholarship is an amount paid or allowed to, or for the benefit of, an individual to aid such individual in the pursuit of study or research."[18] The recipient must be a candidate for a degree at an educational institution.[19]

Terry enters a contest sponsored by a local newspaper. Each contestant is required to submit an essay on local environmental issues. The prize is one year's tuition at State University. Terry wins the contest. The newspaper has a legal obligation to Terry (as contest winner). Thus, the benefits are not a gift. However, because the tuition payment aids Terry in pursuing her studies, the payment is a scholarship.

As an exception to the compensation for services, nonprofit educational institutions can provide qualified tuition reduction plans for their employees and the employees can exclude the tuition from their gross income. The exclusion also applies to tuition reductions granted to the employee's spouse and the employee's dependent children.[20]

A scholarship recipient may exclude from gross income the amount used for tuition and related expenses (fees, books, supplies, and equipment required for courses), provided the conditions of the grant do not require that the funds be used for other purposes.[21]

---

[14]See the discussion of gifts in Chapter 14 and tax-free exchanges in Chapters 15 and 20. In the case of a gift, the donor's basis becomes the donee's basis.

[15]Reg. §§ 1.72–7(c)(1) and 1.101–7T.

[16]Reg. § 1.117–2(a). See *C. P. Bhalla*, 35 T.C. 13 (1960), for a discussion of the distinction between a scholarship and compensation. See also *Bingler v. Johnson*, 69–1 USTC ¶9348, 23 AFTR 2d 1212, 89 S.Ct. 1439 (USSC, 1969). For potential exclusion treatment, see the subsequent discussion of qualified tuition reductions.

[17]Rev.Rul. 77–263, 1977–2 C.B. 47.

[18]Prop.Reg. § 117–6(c)(3)(i).

[19]§ 117(a).

[20]§ 117(d).

[21]§ 117(b).

TAX IN THE NEWS   **NCAA Change Results in Taxable Scholarship Amounts**

In 2015, the NCAA began permitting athletic scholarships to include a "cost of attendance" amount. Now, in addition to tuition, fees, books, and room and board, the scholarship can include expenses such as academic-related supplies, transportation, and other similar items. The value of these benefits may differ from campus to campus. Only the amounts received for tuition, books, and supplies can be excluded from gross income. The IRS treats taxable scholarship amounts as unearned income for kiddie tax purposes (see instructions to Form 8615).

EXAMPLE
9

Kelly received an athletic scholarship from State University. The scholarship pays her tuition, $9,000, and books and supplies, $2,400. She also received $4,500 a year for costs of attendance, which she uses to pay for housing, food, laundry, and transportation.

The tuition and the cost of books and supplies are excluded from gross income as a scholarship. The $4,500 received as costs of attendance does not qualify for the scholarship exclusion; therefore, Kelly must include that amount in her gross income.

Some employers make scholarships available solely to the children of key employees. The tax objective of these plans is to provide a nontaxable fringe benefit to the executives by making the payment to the child in the form of an excludible scholarship. However, the IRS has ruled that the payments are generally includible in the gross income of the parent-employee.[22]

5-4b Timing Issues

Frequently, the scholarship recipient is a cash basis taxpayer who receives the money in one tax year but pays the educational expenses in a subsequent year. The amount eligible for exclusion may not be known at the time the money is received. In that case, the transaction is held *open* until the educational expenses are paid.[23]

EXAMPLE
10

In August 2016, Sanjay received $10,000 as a scholarship for the academic year 2016–2017. Sanjay's expenditures for tuition, books, and supplies were as follows:

August–December 2016	$3,000
January–May 2017	4,500
	$7,500

Sanjay's gross income for 2017 includes $2,500 ($10,000 − $7,500) that is not excludible as a scholarship. None of the scholarship is included in his gross income in 2016.

The Big Picture

EXAMPLE
11

Return to the facts of *The Big Picture* on p. 5-1. Paul was paid $400 a month by the university for teaching. This is reasonable compensation for his services. Although he received the assistantship because of his excellent academic record, the monthly pay of $400 must be included in his gross income because it is compensation for his services. However, the $6,000 graduate tuition reduction can be excluded from gross income.

5-5 COMPENSATION FOR INJURIES AND SICKNESS

5-5a Damages

A person who suffers harm caused by another is often entitled to compensatory damages. The tax consequences of the receipt of damages depend on the type of harm

[22]Rev.Rul. 75–448, 1975–2 C.B. 55; *Richard T. Armantrout*, 67 T.C. 996 (1977).

[23]Prop.Reg. § 1.117–6(b)(2).

TAX IN THE NEWS **Damages Cannot Be Agreed to in Advance**

In a 2015 Tax Court decision, the taxpayer was paid for undergoing a series of procedures to retrieve her unfertilized eggs for transfer to an infertile woman. Under the contract, the compensation was for her pain and suffering and her "good faith and compliance with the donor egg procedure." Possibly, for tax purposes, the events could be characterized as a sale of body parts, compensation for services, or compensation for physical damages.

According to the Tax Court, the issue was whether a taxpayer suffering physical pain or injury while performing a contract for personal services may exclude the amounts received as "damages received on account of physical pain or injury." The court concluded that the physical pain was a by-product of performing a service contract to which she had agreed to the

suffering. The Tax Court ruled that "the payments were made not to compensate her for some unwanted invasion against her bodily integrity but to compensate her for services rendered." Thus, the court held that the payment received could not be excluded from income. The court found that the exclusion for damages received for personal injury did not cover situations where an individual agrees in advance to be injured, even analogizing the situation to compensation contracts of professional athletes. As summarized by the court: "We don't doubt that some portion of the compensation paid all these people reflects the risk that they will feel pain and suffering, but it's a risk of pain and suffering that they agree to before they begin their work. And that makes it taxable compensation and not excludable damages" *Perez*, 144 T.C. 51 (2015).

the taxpayer has experienced. The taxpayer may seek recovery for (1) a loss of income, (2) expenses incurred, (3) property destroyed, or (4) personal injury.

Generally, reimbursement for a loss of income is taxed the same as the income replaced (see the exception under Personal Injury below). The recovery of an expense is not income unless the expense was deducted. Damages that are a recovery of the taxpayer's previously deducted expenses are generally taxable under the tax benefit rule, discussed later in this chapter.

A payment for damaged or destroyed property is treated as an amount received in a sale or exchange of the property. Thus, the taxpayer has a realized gain if the damages received exceed the property's basis. Damages for personal injuries receive special treatment under the Code.

Personal Injury

The legal theory of personal injury damages is that the amount received is intended "to make the plaintiff [the injured party] whole as before the injury."[24] It follows that if the damages payments received were subject to tax, the after-tax amount received would be less than the actual damages incurred and the injured party would not be "whole as before the injury." In terms of personal injury damages, a distinction is made between compensatory damages and punitive damages.

ETHICS & EQUITY **Tax Treatment of Damages Not Related to Physical Personal Injury**

An individual who prevails in a personal injury claim for something other than a physical injury or sickness must include the amount of the award or a settlement in gross income. In contrast, an award or a settlement for a physical personal injury or sickness can be excluded (except for

punitive damages) from gross income. Should damages awarded for a physical personal injury or sickness be treated more favorably than damages awarded for emotional distress or other nonphysical personal injuries such as age and sex discrimination?

Compensatory damages are intended to compensate the taxpayer for the damages incurred. Only those compensatory damages received on account of *physical personal injury or physical sickness* can be excluded from gross income.[25] Such exclusion treatment includes amounts received for loss of income associated with the physical personal injury or physical sickness. Compensatory damages awarded on account of

---

[24] *C. A. Hawkins*, 6 B.T.A. 1023 (1928).   [25] § 104(a)(2).

emotional distress are not received on account of physical injury or physical sickness and thus cannot be excluded (except to the extent of any amount received for medical care) from gross income. Likewise, any amounts received for age discrimination or injury to one's reputation cannot be excluded.

Punitive damages are amounts the person who caused the harm must pay to the victim as punishment for outrageous conduct. Punitive damages are not intended to compensate the victim, but rather to punish the party who caused the harm. Thus, it follows that amounts received as punitive damages may actually place the victim in a better economic position than before the harm was experienced. Thus, punitive damages are included in gross income.

These rules are set forth in Concept Summary 5.1.

Concept Summary 5.1

Taxation of Damages

Type of Claim	Taxation of Award or Settlement
Breach of contract (generally loss of income)	Taxable.
Property damages	Gain to the extent damages received exceed basis. A loss is deductible for business property and investment property to the extent of basis over the amount realized. A loss may be deductible for personal use property (see discussion of casualty losses in Chapter 7).
Personal injury	
Physical	All compensatory amounts are excluded unless previously deducted (e.g., medical expenses). Amounts received as punitive damages are included in gross income.
Nonphysical	Compensatory damages and punitive damages are included in gross income.

The Big Picture

EXAMPLE 12

Return to the facts of *The Big Picture* on p. 5-1. The damages Paul received were awarded as a result of a physical personal injury. Therefore, all of the compensatory damages can be excluded. Note that even the compensation for the loss of income of $15,000 can be excluded. The punitive damages Paul received, however, must be included in his gross income.

Paul's mother did not suffer a personal physical injury or sickness. Therefore, the $25,000 she received must be included in her gross income.

ETHICS & EQUITY Classifying the Amount of the Claim

Lee was injured in an automobile accident caused by a negligent driver of a commercial vehicle. Lee threatened to file a lawsuit against the company for $100,000 in damages for his physical injury and $100,000 for punitive damages. The company's insurer would not pay punitive damages. Therefore, the company advised Lee to revise his claim for $150,000 in physical damages and no punitive damages. Should Lee accept the offer?

5-5b Workers' Compensation

State workers' compensation laws require the employer to pay fixed amounts for specific job-related injuries. The state laws were enacted so that the employee will not have to go through the ordeal of a lawsuit (and possibly not collect damages because of some defense available to the employer) to recover the damages. Although the payments are intended, in part, to compensate for a loss of future income, Congress has specifically exempted workers' compensation benefits from inclusion in gross income.[26]

---

[26]§ 104(a)(1).

5-5c **Accident and Health Insurance Benefits**

The income tax treatment of accident and health insurance benefits depends on whether the policy providing the benefits was purchased by the taxpayer or the taxpayer's employer. Benefits collected under an accident and health insurance policy *purchased by the taxpayer* are excludible even though the payments are a substitute for income.[27]

Exempt Benefits

Bonnie purchases a medical and disability insurance policy. The insurance company pays Bonnie $1,000 per week to replace wages she loses while in the hospital. Although the payments serve as a substitute for income, the amounts received are tax-exempt benefits collected under Bonnie's insurance policy.

EXAMPLE
13

Joe's injury results in a partial paralysis of his left foot. He receives $20,000 for the injury from his accident insurance company under a policy he had purchased. The $20,000 accident insurance proceeds are tax-exempt.

EXAMPLE
14

A different set of rules applies if the accident and health insurance protection was *purchased by the individual's employer*, as discussed in the following section.

5-6 **EMPLOYER-SPONSORED ACCIDENT AND HEALTH PLANS**

Congress encourages employers to provide employees, retired former employees, and their dependents with **accident and health benefits**, disability insurance, and long-term care plans. The *premiums* are deductible by the employer and excluded from the employee's income.[28] Although § 105(a) provides the general rule that the employee has includible income when he or she collects the insurance *benefits,* two exceptions are provided.

Section 105(b) generally excludes payments received for medical care of the employee, spouse, and dependents. However, if the payments are for expenses that do not meet the Code's definition of medical care,[29] the amount received must be included in gross income. In addition, the taxpayer must include in gross income any amounts received for medical expenses that were deducted by the taxpayer on a prior return.

In 2016, Tab's employer-sponsored health insurance plan pays $4,000 for hair transplants that do not meet the Code's definition of medical care. Tab must include the $4,000 in his gross income for 2016.

EXAMPLE
15

Section 105(c) excludes payments for the permanent loss or the loss of the use of a member or function of the body or the permanent disfigurement of the employee, the spouse, or a dependent. Payments that are a substitute for salary (e.g., related to the period of time absent) are includible.

---

[27]§ 104(a)(3).

[28]§ 106, Reg. § 1.106–1, and Rev.Rul. 82–196, 1982–1 C.B. 106.

[29]See the discussion of medical care in Chapter 10.

EXAMPLE
16

Jill loses an eye in an automobile accident unrelated to her work. As a result of the accident, Jill incurs $2,000 of medical expenses, which she deducts on her return. She collects $10,000 from an accident insurance policy carried by her employer. The benefits are paid according to a schedule of amounts that vary with the part of the body injured (e.g., $10,000 for loss of an eye and $20,000 for loss of a hand). Because the payment is for loss of a *member or function of the body*, the $10,000 is excluded from gross income. Jill is absent from work for a week as a result of the accident. Her employer provides her with insurance for the loss of income due to illness or injury. Jill collects $500, which is includible in gross income.

5-6a Medical Reimbursement Plans

In lieu of providing the employee with insurance coverage for hospital and medical expenses, the employer may agree to reimburse the employee for these expenses. The amounts received through the insurance coverage (insured plan benefits) are excluded from income under § 105 (as previously discussed). Unfortunately, in terms of cost considerations, the insurance companies that issue this type of policy usually require a broad coverage of employees. An alternative is to have a plan that is not funded with insurance (a self-insured arrangement). The benefits received under a self-insured plan can be excluded from the employee's income if the plan does not discriminate in favor of highly compensated employees.[30]

There is also an alternative means of accomplishing a medical reimbursement plan. The employer can purchase a medical insurance plan with a high deductible (e.g., the employee is responsible for the first $2,600 of the family's medical expenses) and then make contributions to the employee's **Health Savings Account (HSA)**.[31] The employer can make contributions each month up to the maximum contribution of 100 percent of the deductible amount. The monthly deductible amount is limited to one-twelfth of $3,350 under a high-deductible plan for self-only coverage. The monthly amount for an individual who has family coverage is limited to one-twelfth of $6,750 under a high-deductible plan. Withdrawals from the HSA must be used to reimburse the employee for the medical expenses paid by the employee that are not covered under the high-deductible plan. The employee is not taxed on the employer's contributions to the HSA, the earnings on the funds in the account, or the withdrawals made for medical expenses.[32]

5-6b Long-Term Care Insurance Benefits

Generally, **long-term care insurance**, which covers expenses such as the cost of care in a nursing home, is treated the same as accident and health insurance benefits. Thus, the employee does not recognize income when the employer pays the premiums. Also, the individual who purchases his or her own policy can exclude the benefits from gross income. However, statutory limitations (indexed for inflation) exist for the following amounts:

- Premiums paid by the employer.
- Benefits collected under the employer's plan.
- Benefits collected from the individual's policy.

The employer or insurance company generally provides the employee with information on the amount of his or her taxable benefits.

The maximum amount excluded must be reduced by any amount received from third parties (e.g., Medicare, Medicaid).[33]

---

[30]§ 105(h). Also see § 106 and Rev.Rul. 61–146, 1961–2 C.B. 25. Employers should make sure such reimbursement plans fall within the requirements of the Affordable Care Act to avoid an excise tax. See § 4980D, Notice 2013–54, 2013–40 I.R.B. 287, and Notice 2015–17, 2015–10 I.R.B. 845.

[31]§§ 106(d) and 223. See additional coverage in Chapter 10.

[32]§§ 106(d), 223(b), and 223(d). The amounts for 2015 were $3,350 and $6,650.

[33]§§ 7702B and § 213(d)(10). See IRS Publication 525 for the taxable and nontaxable amounts that the employer is required to report on the employee's W–2.

Hazel, who suffers from Alzheimer's disease, is a patient in a nursing home for the last 30 days of 2016. While in the nursing home, she incurs total costs of $7,600. Medicare pays $3,500 of the costs. Hazel receives $7,000 from her long-term care insurance policy, which pays while she is in the facility.

The amount Hazel may exclude is calculated as follows:

Greater of:		
Daily statutory amount in 2016 ($340 × 30 days)	$10,200	
Actual cost of the care	7,600	$10,200
Less: Amount received from Medicare		(3,500)
Amount of exclusion		$ 6,700

Therefore, Hazel must include $300 ($7,000 − $6,700) of the long-term care benefits received in her gross income.

The exclusion for long-term care insurance is not available if it is provided as part of a cafeteria plan or a flexible spending plan (explained later in the chapter).

5-7 MEALS AND LODGING

5-7a General Rules for the Exclusion

As discussed in Chapter 4, income can take any form, including meals and lodging. However, § 119 excludes from income the value of meals and lodging provided to the employee and the employee's spouse and dependents under the following conditions:[34]

- The meals and/or lodging are *furnished* by the employer on the employer's *business premises* for the *convenience of the employer*.

- In the case of lodging, the *employee is required* to accept the lodging as a condition of employment.

The courts have interpreted these requirements strictly.

Furnished by the Employer

The following two questions have been raised with regard to the *furnished by the employer* requirement:

- Who is considered an *employee*?
- What is meant by *furnished*?

The IRS and some courts have reasoned that because a partner is not an employee, the exclusion does not apply to a partner. However, the Tax Court and the Fifth Circuit Court of Appeals have ruled in favor of the taxpayer on this issue.[35]

The Supreme Court held that a cash meal allowance was ineligible for the exclusion because the employer did not actually furnish the meals.[36] Similarly, one court denied the exclusion where the employer paid for the food and supplied the cooking facilities but the employee prepared the meal.[37]

---

[34]§ 119(a). The meals and lodging are also excluded from FICA and FUTA tax. *Rowan Companies, Inc. v. U.S.*, 81–1 USTC ¶9479, 48 AFTR 2d 81–5115, 101 S.Ct. 2288 (USSC, 1981).

[35]Rev.Rul. 80, 1953–1 C.B. 62; *Comm. v. Doak*, 56–2 USTC ¶9708, 49 AFTR 1491, 234 F.2d 704 (CA–4, 1956); but see *G. A. Papineau*, 16 T.C. 130 (1951); *Armstrong v. Phinney*, 68–1 USTC ¶9355, 21 AFTR 2d 1260, 394 F.2d 661 (CA–5, 1968).

[36]*Comm. v. Kowalski*, 77–2 USTC ¶9748, 40 AFTR 2d 6128, 98 S.Ct. 315 (USSC, 1977).

[37]*Tougher v. Comm.*, 71–1 USTC ¶9398, 27 AFTR 2d 1301, 441 F.2d 1148 (CA–9, 1971).

On the Employer's Business Premises

The *on the employer's business premises* requirement, applicable to both meals and lodging, has resulted in much litigation. The Regulations define business premises as simply "the place of employment of the employee."[38] Thus, the Sixth Circuit Court of Appeals held that a residence, owned by the employer and occupied by an employee, two blocks from the motel that the employee managed was not part of the business premises.[39] However, the Tax Court considered an employer-owned house across the street from the hotel that was managed by the taxpayer to be on the business premises of the employer.[40] Apparently, the closer the lodging is to the business operations, the more likely the convenience of the employer is served.

For the Convenience of the Employer

The *convenience of the employer* test is intended to focus on the employer's motivation for furnishing the meals and lodging rather than on the benefits received by the employee. If the employer furnishes the meals and lodging primarily to enable the employee to perform his or her duties properly, it does not matter that the employee considers these benefits to be a part of his or her compensation.

The Regulations give the following examples in which the tests for excluding meals are satisfied:[41]

- A restaurant requires its service staff to eat their meals on the premises during the busy lunch and breakfast hours.
- A bank furnishes meals on the premises for its tellers to limit the time the employees are away from their booths during the busy hours.
- A worker is employed at a construction site in a remote part of Alaska. The employer must furnish meals and lodging due to the inaccessibility of other facilities.

Required as a Condition of Employment

The *employee is required to accept* test applies only to lodging. If the employee's use of the housing would serve the convenience of the employer but the employee is not required to use the housing, the exclusion is not available.

EXAMPLE 18

Khalid is the manager of a large apartment complex. The employer requires Khalid to live on the premises but does not charge him rent. The rental value of his apartment is $9,600 a year. Although Khalid considers the rent-free housing a significant benefit, he is not required to include the value of the housing in his gross income.

ETHICS & EQUITY Employee Meals

Some companies famous for their products, such as Google, Facebook, and Twitter, are also famous for the perks they offer their employees. One of these benefits is free meals on the business premises. Part of the rationale for providing the food is that employees may not have food alternatives close by and business discussions may be more likely to happen when employees do not have to leave the premises. Such reasoning is intended to allow the meals to fit within the statutory exclusion of being "for the convenience of the employer." Whether excluding these meals from the employees' income will survive IRS and congressional scrutiny is uncertain. If these employees are allowed to exclude their meals from gross income, should employees whose employers do not provide meals be permitted to deduct the cost of their meals?

---

[38]Reg. § 1.119–1(c)(1).

[39]*Comm. v. Anderson*, 67–1 USTC ¶9136, 19 AFTR 2d 318, 371 F.2d 59 (CA–6, 1966).

[40]*J. B. Lindeman*, 60 T.C. 609 (1973).

[41]Reg. § 1.119–1(f).

A minister of the gospel who receives a housing allowance may be living in a home being purchased. The funds received as a housing allowance and excluded from gross income may be used to pay on the home mortgage, and the minister may deduct the mortgage interest as an itemized deduction. This was blessed by Congress when it enacted § 265(a)(6) permitting the minister to deduct his or her home mortgage interest even though the payments are financed from tax-exempt income.

5-7b Other Housing Exclusions

An employee of an educational institution may be able to exclude the value of campus housing provided by the employer. Generally, the employee does not recognize income if he or she pays annual rents equal to or greater than 5 percent of the appraised value of the facility. If the rent payments are less than 5 percent of the value of the facility, the deficiency must be included in gross income.[42]

Ministers of the gospel and other religious leaders can exclude (1) the rental value of a home furnished as compensation, (2) a rental allowance paid to them as compensation, to the extent the allowance is used to rent, buy, or provide a home; or (3) the rental value of a home owned by the minister.[43] The housing or housing allowance must be provided as compensation for the conduct of religious worship, the administration and maintenance of religious organizations, or the performance of teaching and administrative duties at theological seminaries.

Military personnel are allowed housing exclusions under various circumstances. Authority for these exclusions generally is found in Federal laws that are not part of the Internal Revenue Code.[44]

5-8 EMPLOYEE FRINGE BENEFITS

Benefits other than wages and salary that are provided to employees by the employer are often referred to as **fringe benefits**. Generally, Congress decided that the availability of these benefits serve social goals. Moreover, the income tax exclusion will provide an incentive for employees to bargain for these fringe benefits in lieu of cash, thus increasing the use of this form of compensation. For example, if the employee is in the 25 percent marginal tax bracket, $1.00 of nontaxable fringe benefits is equivalent to $1.33 ($1.00/(1 − .25) = $1.33) in taxable compensation. From the employer's perspective then, it costs only $1.00 to provide $1.33 in value to that employee in the form of a tax-favored fringe benefit.

In Chapter 4 and earlier in this chapter, various fringe benefits were discussed (e.g., group term life insurance, accident and health insurance, and meals and lodging). Other employee benefits are discussed below.

5-8a Specific Benefits

Congress has dealt specifically with some other fringe benefits, which are summarized below.

- The employee does not have to include in gross income the value of child and dependent care services paid for by the employer and incurred to enable the employee to work. The exclusion cannot exceed $5,000 per year ($2,500 if married and filing separately). For a married couple, the annual exclusion cannot exceed the earned income of the spouse who has the lesser amount of earned income. For an unmarried taxpayer, the exclusion cannot exceed the taxpayer's earned income.[45]

---

[42]§ 119(d).

[43]§ 107 and Reg. § 1.107–1.

[44]H. Rep. No. 99–841, 99th Cong., 2d Sess., p. 548 (1986). See § 134 and *Armed Forces Tax Guide* (IRS Publication 3).

[45]§ 129. The exclusion applies to the same types of expenses that, if paid by the employee (and not reimbursed by the employer), would be eligible for the credit for child and dependent care expense discussed in Chapter 13.

- The value of the use of a gymnasium or other athletic facilities by employees, their spouses, and their dependent children may be excluded from an employee's gross income. The facilities must be on the employer's premises, and substantially all of the use of the facilities must be by employees and their family members.[46]

- Qualified employer-provided educational assistance (tuition, fees, books, and supplies) at the undergraduate and graduate level is excludible from gross income. The exclusion does not cover meals, lodging, and transportation costs. In addition, it does not cover educational payments for courses involving sports, games, or hobbies. The exclusion is subject to an annual employee statutory ceiling of $5,250.[47]

- The employee can exclude from gross income up to $13,460 of expenses incurred to adopt a child where the adoption expenses are paid or reimbursed by the employer under a qualified adoption assistance program.[48] The limit on the exclusion is the same even if the child has special needs (is not physically or mentally capable of caring for himself or herself). However, for a child with special needs, the $13,460 exclusion from gross income applies even if the actual adoption expenses are less than that amount. For 2016, the exclusion is phased out as adjusted gross income increases from $201,920 to $241,920.

5-8b Cafeteria Plans

Generally, if an employee is offered a choice between cash and some other form of compensation, the employee is deemed to have constructively received the cash even when the noncash option is elected. Thus, the employee has gross income regardless of the option chosen.

An exception to this constructive receipt treatment is provided under the **cafeteria plan** rules. Under such a plan, the employee is permitted to choose between cash and nontaxable benefits (e.g., group term life insurance, health and accident protection, child care). If the employee chooses the otherwise nontaxable benefits, the cafeteria plan rules enable the benefits to remain nontaxable.[49] Cafeteria plans provide tremendous flexibility in tailoring the employee pay package to fit individual needs. Some employees (usually the younger group) prefer cash, while others (usually the older group) will opt for the fringe benefit program.

EXAMPLE 19

Hawk Corporation offers its employees (on a nondiscriminatory basis) a choice of any one or all of the following benefits:

Benefit	Cost
Group term life insurance	$ 200
Hospitalization insurance for family members	2,400
Child care payments	1,800
	$4,400

If a benefit is not selected, the employee receives cash equal to the cost of the benefit. Kay, an employee, has a spouse who works for another employer that provides hospitalization insurance but no child care payments. Kay elects to receive the group term life insurance, the child care payments, and $2,400 of cash. Only the $2,400 must be included in Kay's gross income.

5-8c Flexible Spending Plans

Flexible spending plans (often referred to as flexible benefit plans) operate much like cafeteria plans. Under these plans, the employee accepts lower cash compensation (as much as $2,550) in return for the employer agreeing to pay certain costs that the employer can pay without the employee recognizing gross income. For example, assume that the employer's health insurance policy does not cover dental expenses.

---

[46]§ 132(j)(4).

[47]§ 127.

[48]§ 137. A credit is also available under § 23, as discussed in Chapter 13.

[49]§ 125.

The employee could estimate his or her dental expenses for the upcoming year and agree to a salary reduction equal to the estimated dental expenses. The employer then pays or reimburses the employee for the actual dental expenses incurred, with a ceiling of the amount of the salary reduction. If the employee's actual dental expenses are less than the reduction in cash compensation, the employee cannot recover the difference. Hence, these plans are often referred to as *use or lose* plans. To avoid forfeiture of unpaid amounts, the IRS allows a payment until March 15 of the following year to count. As is the case for cafeteria plans, flexible spending plans cannot be used to pay long-term care insurance premiums.

5-8d General Classes of Excluded Benefits

An employer can confer numerous forms and types of economic benefits on employees. Under the all-inclusive concept of income, the benefits are taxable unless one of the provisions previously discussed specifically excludes the item from gross income. The amount of the income is the fair market value of the benefit.

Ryan is employed in New York as a ticket clerk for Trans National Airlines. He has a sick mother in Miami, Florida, but has no money for plane tickets. Trans National has daily flights from New York to Miami that often leave with empty seats. The cost of a round-trip ticket is $400. If Trans National allows Ryan to fly without charge to Miami, under the general gross income rules, Ryan has income equal to the value of a ticket. Therefore, Ryan must include $400 in gross income on a trip to Miami.

Because Congress believed that taxing fringe benefits often yielded harsh results, § 132 was enacted to provide exclusion treatment. This provision established seven broad classes of nontaxable employee benefits:[50]

- No-additional-cost services.
- Qualified employee discounts.
- Working condition fringes.
- *De minimis* fringes.
- Qualified transportation fringes.
- Qualified moving expense reimbursements.
- Qualified retirement planning services.

The value of the services that the employer provides its employees are nontaxable under certain circumstances.

No-Additional-Cost Services

Return to Example 20 above. This illustrates the reason for the **no-additional-cost service** type of fringe benefit. The services will be nontaxable if all of the following conditions are satisfied:

- The employee receives services, as opposed to property.
- The employer does not incur substantial additional cost, including forgone revenue, in providing the services to the employee.
- The services are offered to customers in the ordinary course of the business in which the employee works.[51]

In Example 20, although the airplane may burn slightly more fuel because Ryan is on board and he may receive the same snacks and meals as paying customers, the additional costs to the airline would not be substantial. Thus, the trip could qualify as a no-additional-cost service, and the value of Ryan's flight can be excluded from his gross income.

---

[50]See, generally, § 132. Section 132 also excludes "qualified military base realignment and closure fringe," which is not discussed here.

[51]Reg. § 1.132–2.

The no-additional-cost exclusion extends to the employee's spouse and dependent children and to retired and disabled former employees.[52] However, the exclusion is not allowed to highly compensated employees unless the benefit is available on a nondiscriminatory basis.

Qualified Employee Discounts

When the employer sells goods or services (other than no-additional-cost benefits just discussed) to the employee for a price that is less than the price charged regular customers, the employee realizes income equal to the discount. However, the discount, referred to as a **qualified employee discount**, can be excluded from the gross income of the employee, subject to the following conditions and limitations:

- The exclusion is not available for real property (e.g., a house) or for personal property of the type commonly held for investment (e.g., common stocks).
- The property or services must be from the same line of business in which the employee works.
- In the case of *property*, the exclusion is limited to the *gross profit component* of the price to customers.
- In the case of *services*, the exclusion is limited to 20 percent of the customer price.

EXAMPLE 22

Silver Corporation, which operates a department store, sells a television set to a store employee for $300. The regular customer price is $500, and the gross profit rate is 25%. The corporation also sells the employee a service contract for $120. The regular customer price for the contract is $150. The employee must include $75 in gross income.

Customer price for property	$ 500
Less: Gross profit (25%)	(125)
	$ 375
Employee price	(300)
Income	$ 75
Customer price for service	$ 150
Less: 20%	(30)
	$ 120
Employee price	(120)
Income	$ –0–

As in the case of no-additional-cost benefits, the exclusion applies to employees (including service partners), employees' spouses and dependent children, and retired and disabled former employees.

Working Condition Fringes

Generally, an employee is not required to include in gross income the cost of property or services provided by the employer if the employee could deduct the cost of those items if he or she had actually paid for them. These benefits are called **working condition fringes**.

EXAMPLE 23

Mitch is a CPA employed by an accounting firm. The employer pays Mitch's annual dues to professional organizations. Mitch is not required to include the payment of the dues in gross income because if he had paid the dues, he would have been allowed to deduct the amount as an employee business expense (as discussed in Chapter 9).[53]

Unlike the other fringe benefits discussed previously, working condition fringes can be made available on a discriminatory basis and still qualify for the exclusion.

---

[52]Reg. § 1.132–1(b).

[53]In many cases, this exclusion merely avoids reporting income and an offsetting deduction.

De Minimis **Fringes**

As the term suggests, **de minimis fringe** benefits are so small that accounting for them is impractical. The House Report contains the following examples of *de minimis* fringes:

- Occasional personal use of a company copying machine, occasional company cocktail parties or picnics for employees, occasional supper money or taxi fare for employees because of overtime work, and certain holiday gifts of property with a low fair market value are excluded.

- Subsidized eating facilities (e.g., an employees' cafeteria) operated by the employer are excluded if located on or near the employer's business premises, if revenue equals or exceeds direct operating costs, and if nondiscrimination requirements are met.

When taxpayers venture beyond the specific examples contained in the House Report and the Regulations, there is obviously much room for disagreement as to what is *de minimis*. According to the IRS, cash or gift cards are not considered *de minimis*.[54]

In Notice 2011–72, the IRS addressed the question of whether cell phones provided by the employer could be excluded from gross income as a working condition fringe benefit. Generally, the value of the cell phone can be excluded if it is provided for business reasons such as to enable the employee to be in contact with clients when the employee is away from the office. When the primary purpose test is satisfied, any personal use of the employer-provided cell phone will be excluded as a *de minimis* fringe benefit.

Qualified Transportation Fringes

The intent of the exclusion for **qualified transportation fringes** is to encourage the use of mass transit for commuting to and from work. Qualified transportation fringes encompass the following transportation benefits provided by the employer to the employee:

1. Transportation in a commuter highway vehicle between the employee's residence and the place of employment.
2. A transit pass.
3. Qualified parking.
4. Qualified bicycle commuting reimbursement.

Statutory dollar limits are placed on the amount of the exclusion. Categories (1) and (2) above are combined for purposes of applying the limit. For 2016, the inflation adjusted limit for categories (1) and (2) combined, as well as for category (3), is $255 per month ($250 in 2015). The bicycle benefit is $20 per month and is not adjusted annually for inflation.

A *commuter highway vehicle* is any highway vehicle with a seating capacity of at least six adults (excluding the driver). In addition, at least 80 percent of the vehicle's use must be for transporting employees between their residences and place of employment.

Qualified parking includes the following:

- Parking provided to an employee on or near the employer's business premises.
- Parking provided to an employee on or near a location from which the employee commutes to work via mass transit, in a commuter highway vehicle, or in a carpool.

The *qualified bicycle commuting reimbursement* enables an employee to exclude up to $20 per month received from an employer as reimbursement for the cost of commuting by bicycle (i.e., bicycle purchase, improvement, repair, and storage).

Qualified transportation fringes may be provided directly by the employer or may be in the form of cash reimbursements.

EXAMPLE
24

Gray Corporation's offices are located in the center of a large city. The company pays for parking spaces to be used by the company officers. Steve, a vice president, receives $300 of such benefits each month during 2016. The parking space rental qualifies as a qualified transportation fringe. Of the $300 benefit received each month by Steve, $255 is excludible from gross income. The balance of $45 is included in his gross income. The same result would occur if Steve paid for the parking and was reimbursed by his employer.

---

[54]TAM 200437030 (9/10/04) and IRS Publication 15B (2015), *Employer's Tax Guide to Fringe Benefits*, p. 8.

Qualified Moving Expense Reimbursements

Qualified moving expenses that are reimbursed or paid by the employer are excludible from gross income. A qualified moving expense is an expense that would be deductible under § 217. See the discussion of moving expenses in Chapter 9.

Qualified Retirement Planning Services

Qualified retirement planning services include any retirement planning advice or information that an employer who maintains a qualified retirement plan provides to an employee or the employee's spouse. Congress decided to exclude the value of such services from gross income because they are a key part of retirement income planning. Such an exclusion should motivate more employers to provide retirement planning services to their employees.

Nondiscrimination Provisions

For no-additional-cost services, qualified employee discounts, and qualified retirement planning services that are discriminatory in favor of highly compensated employees, exclusion treatment is denied. However, for the discriminatory plans, the exclusion treatment for non-highly compensated employees remains.[55]

EXAMPLE 25

Dove Company's officers are allowed to purchase goods from the company at a 25% discount. All other employees are allowed only a 15% discount. The company's gross profit margin on these goods is 30%. Because the officers receive more favorable discounts, the plan is discriminatory in favor of the officers. In regard to all other employees, the discount is "qualified" because it is available to all employees (other than the officers who receive a more favorable discount) and the discount is less than the company's gross profit.

Peggy, an officer in the company, purchased goods from the company for $750 when the price charged to customers was $1,000. Peggy must include $250 in gross income because the plan is discriminatory.

Mason, an employee of the company who is not an officer, purchased goods for $850 when the customer price was $1,000. Mason is not required to recognize gross income because he received a qualified employee discount.

De minimis (except in the case of subsidized eating facilities) and working condition fringe benefits can be provided on a discriminatory basis. The *de minimis* benefits are not subject to tax because the accounting problems that would be created are out of proportion to the amount of additional tax that would result.

A review of employee fringe benefits is set forth in Concept Summary 5.2.

5-9 FOREIGN EARNED INCOME

The United States uses a global tax system as opposed to a territorial system. Under this global system, a U.S. citizen is generally subject to tax on his or her income regardless of its economic origin. Some other countries use a territorial system; that is, a person's income is taxed only in the country in which the income was earned. Under this global system, a U.S. citizen who earns income in another country could experience double taxation: the same income would be taxed in the United States and in the foreign country. Out of a sense of fairness and to encourage U.S. citizens to work abroad (so that exports might be increased), Congress has provided alternative forms of relief from taxes on foreign earned income. The taxpayer can elect *either* (1) to include the foreign earned income in his or her taxable income and then claim a credit for foreign taxes paid or (2) to exclude up to $101,300 in foreign earned income from his or her U.S. gross income (the **foreign earned income exclusion**).[56] The foreign tax credit option is discussed in Chapter 13, but as is apparent from the following discussion, most taxpayers choose the exclusion.

---

[55] §§ 132(j)(1) and 132(m)(2).

[56] § 911(a). The exclusion for 2015 was $100,800.

Concept Summary 5.2

Employee Fringe Benefits

Type of Benefit	Exclusion
Group term life insurance (§ 79)	Premiums on up to $50,000 protection
Employee achievement awards (§ 74)	Up to $1,600 in a year
Accident, health, and long-term care insurance and medical reimbursement (§§ 105 and 106)	Insurance premiums paid by the employer and benefits collected
High-deductible health insurance and contributions to employee's Health Savings Account (§§ 106 and 223)	Employer premiums on high-deductible medical insurance plus contributions to Health Savings Account (statutory limits, indexed for inflation).
Meals and lodging furnished for the convenience of the employer (§ 119)	Value of meals and lodging on the employer's premises
Child care provided by the employer or reimbursement for employee's cost (§ 129)	Services provided or reimbursement of expenses up to $5,000 a year
Athletic facilities on the employer's premises (§ 132)	Value of services
Educational assistance for tuition, fees, books, and supplies (§ 127)	Limited to $5,250 per year
No-additional-cost services [e.g., use of employer's facilities (§ 132)]	Value of the use
Employee discount on purchase of goods from employer at employer's cost (§ 132)	Employer's normal profit margin
Employee discount for purchases of employer's services (§ 132)	Maximum of 20% of employer's normal price
Working condition fringes [e.g., the mechanic's tools (§ 132)]	Employer's cost
De minimis items so small that the accounting effort is not warranted [e.g., use of employer telephone (§ 132)]	Value of the goods or services
Qualified transportation [e.g, transit passes and parking (§ 132)]	Statutory amounts, adjusted for inflation
Moving expense reimbursement (§ 132)	Reimbursement to the extent otherwise deductible by employee
Retirement planning services (§ 132)	Reasonable cost of services

Foreign earned income consists of the earnings from the individual's personal services rendered in a foreign country (other than as an employee of the U.S. government). To qualify for the exclusion, the taxpayer must be either of the following:

- A bona fide resident of the foreign country (or countries).
- Present in a foreign country (or countries) for at least 330 days during any 12 consecutive months.[57]

Calculating the Exclusion

Sandra's trip to and from a foreign country in connection with her work were as follows:

EXAMPLE 26

Arrived in Foreign Country	Returned to United States
March 10, 2015	February 15, 2016

During the 12 consecutive months ending on March 10, 2016, Sandra was present in the foreign country for at least 330 days (366 days less 14 days in February 2016 and 10 days in March 2016). Therefore, all income earned in the foreign country through March 10, 2016, is eligible for the exclusion.

---

[57]§ 911(d). For the definition of *resident*, see Reg. § 1.871–2(b). Under the Regulations, a taxpayer is not a resident if he or she is there for a definite period (e.g., until completion of a construction contract).

Calculating the Exclusion

EXAMPLE 27

Keith qualifies for the foreign earned income exclusion. He was present in France for all of 2016. Keith's salary for 2016 is $120,000. Because all of the days in 2016 are qualifying days, Keith can exclude $101,300 of his $120,000 salary.

Assume instead that only 339 days were qualifying days. Then Keith's exclusion is limited to $93,827, computed as follows:

$$\$101{,}300 \times \frac{339 \text{ days in foreign country}}{366 \text{ days in the year}} = \$93{,}827$$

EXAMPLE 28

In 2016, Carol, who is not married, had taxable income of $30,000 after excluding $101,300 of foreign earned income. Without the benefit of the exclusion, Carol's taxable income would have been $131,300 ($30,000 + $101,300). The tax on the taxable income of $30,000 is calculated using the marginal rate applicable to income between $101,300 and $131,300, which is 28%. Therefore, Carol's tax liability is $8,400 (.28 × $30,000).

As previously mentioned, the taxpayer may elect to include the foreign earned income in gross income and claim a credit (an offset against U.S. tax) for the foreign tax paid. The credit alternative may be advantageous if the individual's foreign earned income far exceeds the excludible amount so that the foreign taxes paid exceed the U.S. tax on the amount excluded. However, once an election is made, it applies to all subsequent years unless affirmatively revoked. A revocation is effective for the year of the change and the four subsequent years.

5-10 INTEREST ON CERTAIN STATE AND LOCAL GOVERNMENT OBLIGATIONS

At the time the Sixteenth Amendment was ratified by the states, there was some question as to whether the Federal government possessed the constitutional authority to tax interest on state and local government obligations. Taxing such interest was thought to violate the doctrine of intergovernmental immunity in that the tax would impair the state and local governments' ability to finance their operations.[58] Thus, interest on state and local government obligations was specifically exempted from Federal income taxation.[59] However, the Supreme Court has concluded that there is no constitutional prohibition against levying a nondiscriminatory Federal income tax on state and local government obligations.[60] Nevertheless, currently, the statutory exclusion still exists.

GLOBAL TAX ISSUES   **Benefits of the Earned Income Exclusion Are Questioned**

The foreign earned income exclusion is intended to be a means to increase exports. But a recent GAO questioned whether the $6 billion of lost revenue is money well spent. The report was inconclusive. It is clear that repealing the exclusion would make it more costly for U.S. companies to send their employees abroad, but there is no evidence that the benefits to the U.S., in general, are worth the cost.

Source: Economic Benefits of Income Exclusion for U.S. Citizens Working Abroad Are Uncertain GAO-14-387: Published: May 20, 2014, available at **www.gao .gov/products/GAO-14-387**.

---

[58]*Pollock v. Farmer's Loan & Trust Co.*, 3 AFTR 2602, 15 S.Ct. 912 (USSC, 1895).

[59]§ 103(a).

[60]*South Carolina v. Baker III*, 88–1 USTC ¶9284, 61 AFTR 2d 88–995, 108 S.Ct. 1355 (USSC, 1988).

Obviously, the exclusion of the interest reduces the cost of borrowing for state and local governments. A taxpayer in the 35 percent tax bracket requires only a 5.2 percent yield on a tax-exempt bond to obtain the same after-tax income as a taxable bond paying 8 percent interest [5.2% ÷ (1 − .35) = 8%].

The current exempt status applies solely to state and local government bonds. Thus, income received from the accrual of interest on a condemnation award or an overpayment of state income tax is fully taxable.[61] Nor does the exemption apply to gains on the sale of tax-exempt securities.

EXAMPLE 29

Megan purchases State of Virginia bonds for $10,000 on July 1, 2015. The bonds pay $400 interest each June 30 and December 31. On March 31, 2016, Megan sells the bonds for $10,500 plus $200 for accrued interest. Megan must recognize a $500 gain ($10,500 − $10,000), but the $200 accrued interest is exempt from taxation.

Although the Internal Revenue Code excludes from Federal gross income the interest on state and local government bonds, the interest on U.S. government bonds is not excluded from the Federal tax base. Congress has decided, however, that if the Federal government is not to tax state and local bond interest, the state and local governments are prohibited from taxing interest on U.S. government bonds.[62] While this parity between the Federal and state and local governments exists in regard to taxing each other's obligations, the states are free to tax one another's obligations. Thus, some states exempt the interest on the bonds they issue, but tax the interest on bonds issued by other states.[63]

5-11 CORPORATE DISTRIBUTIONS TO SHAREHOLDERS

5-11a General Information

A corporate distribution is a payment to a shareholder with respect to his or her stock (see Chapter 4). Distributions are taxed as dividends to shareholders only to the extent the payments are made from *either* the corporation's *current earnings and profits* (similar to net income per books) or its *accumulated earnings and profits* (similar to retained earnings per books).[64] Distributions that exceed earnings and profits are treated as a nontaxable recovery of capital and reduce the shareholder's basis in the stock. Once the shareholder's basis is reduced to zero, any subsequent distributions are taxed as capital gains (see Chapters 14 and 20).[65]

Some payments are frequently referred to as dividends but are not considered dividends for tax purposes:

- Dividends received on deposits with savings and loan associations, credit unions, and banks are actually interest (a contractual rate paid for the use of money).

- Patronage dividends paid by cooperatives (e.g., for farmers) are rebates made to the users and are considered reductions in the cost of items purchased from the association. The rebates are usually made after year-end (after the cooperative has determined whether it has met its expenses) and are apportioned among members on the basis of their purchases.

- Mutual insurance companies pay dividends on unmatured life insurance policies that are considered rebates of premiums.

[61]*Kieselbach v. Comm.*, 43–1 USTC ¶9220, 30 AFTR 370, 63 S.Ct. 303 (USSC, 1943); *U.S. Trust Co. of New York v. Anderson*, 3 USTC ¶1125, 12 AFTR 836, 65 F.2d 575 (CA–2, 1933).

[62]31 U.S.C.A. § 742.

[63]The practice of a state exempting interest on its bonds from tax but taxing the interest on bonds issued by other states has been upheld by the Supreme Court. See *Department of Revenue of Kentucky v. Davis*, 128 S.Ct. 1801 (USSC, 2008).

[64]§ 316(a). Refer to the discussion of the beneficial tax rates for qualified dividends in Chapter 4.

[65]§ 301(c). See Chapter 5, *South-Western Federal Taxation: Corporations, Partnerships, Estates & Trusts*, for a detailed discussion of corporate distributions.

- Shareholders in a mutual investment fund are allowed to report as capital gains their proportionate share of the fund's gains realized and distributed. The capital gain and ordinary income portions are reported on the Form 1099 that the fund supplies its shareholders each year.

5-11b Stock Dividends

When a corporation issues a simple stock dividend (e.g., common stock issued to common shareholders), the shareholder has merely received additional shares that represent the same total investment. Thus, the shareholder does not realize income.[66] However, if the shareholder has the *option* of receiving either cash or stock in the corporation, the individual realizes gross income whether he or she receives stock or cash.[67] A taxpayer who elects to receive the stock could be deemed to be in constructive receipt of the cash he or she has rejected.[68] However, the amount of the income in this case is the value of the stock received, rather than the cash the shareholder has rejected. See Chapter 14 for a detailed discussion of stock dividends.

5-12 EDUCATIONAL SAVINGS BONDS

The cost of a college education has risen dramatically during the past few decades. According to U.S. Department of Education estimates, the cost of attending a publicly supported university for four years now commonly exceeds $60,000. For a private university, the cost often exceeds $200,000. Consequently, Congress has attempted to assist low- to middle-income parents in saving for their children's college education.

One of the ways Congress assists such families is through an interest income exclusion on **educational savings bonds**.[69] The interest on Series EE U.S. government savings bonds may be excluded from gross income if the bond proceeds are used to pay qualified higher education expenses.

Qualified higher education expenses consist of tuition and fees paid to an eligible educational institution for the taxpayer, spouse, or dependent. If the redemption proceeds (both principal and interest) exceed the qualified higher education expenses, only a pro rata portion of the interest will qualify for exclusion treatment.

EXAMPLE 30

Tracy's redemption proceeds from qualified savings bonds during the taxable year are $6,000 (principal of $4,000 and interest of $2,000). Tracy's qualified higher education expenses are $5,000. Because the redemption proceeds exceed the qualified higher education expenses, only $1,667 [($5,000/$6,000) × $2,000] of the interest is excludible.

The exclusion is limited by the application of the wherewithal to pay concept. That is, once the modified adjusted gross income exceeds a threshold amount, the phaseout of the exclusion begins. *Modified adjusted gross income (MAGI)* is adjusted gross income prior to the foreign earned income exclusion and the educational savings bond exclusion. The threshold amounts are adjusted for inflation each year. For 2016, the phaseout begins at $77,550 ($116,300 on a joint return).[70] The phaseout is completed when MAGI exceeds the threshold amount by more than $15,000 ($30,000 on a joint return). The otherwise excludible interest is reduced by the amount calculated as follows:

$$\frac{\text{MAGI} - \$77,550}{\$15,000} \times \frac{\text{Excludible interest}}{\text{before phaseout}} = \frac{\text{Reduction in}}{\text{excludible interest}}$$

On a joint return, $116,300 is substituted for $77,550 (in 2016), and $30,000 is substituted for $15,000.

---

[66]*Eisner v. Macomber*, 1 USTC ¶32, 3 AFTR 3020, 40 S.Ct. 189 (USSC, 1920); § 305(a).

[67]§ 305(b).

[68]Refer to the discussion of constructive receipt in Chapter 4.

[69]§ 135.

[70]The indexed amounts for 2015 were $77,200 and $115,750.

Assume the same facts as in Example 30, except that Tracy's MAGI for 2016 is $80,000. The phase-out results in Tracy's interest exclusion being reduced by $272 {[($80,000 − $77,550)/$15,000] × $1,667}. Therefore, Tracy's exclusion is $1,395 ($1,667 − $272).

EXAMPLE 31

5-13 EDUCATION SAVINGS PROGRAMS (§ 529 AND § 530 PLANS)

The Federal tax law provides two types of programs to help families save for education costs. These savings programs are referred to as the Qualified Tuition Program (§ 529 plans) and Coverdell Education Savings Accounts (§ 530 plans). Similarities between the two plans are that earnings in the accounts are not taxable if distributions are used for qualified education expenses. Also, rules govern the type of account that can be used for these savings programs, and specific rules exist regarding contributions, distributions, rollovers, and other transfers. In addition, the benefits of these plans must be coordinated with other educational tax provisions, such as nontaxable scholarships. Distributions from these accounts are reported on Form 1099–Q, Payments from Qualified Education Programs. Taxable distributions (generally those not used for qualified purposes) may be subject to an additional 10 percent tax [reported on Form 5329, Additional Taxes on Qualified Plans (Including IRAs) and Other Tax-Favored Accounts].

Significant differences between § 529 and § 530 plans are that in addition to specified higher education expenses, a Coverdell Account can also be used for specified K–12 expenses. Also, there are income limits on contributions to Coverdell Accounts as well as a dollar limit on the annual contribution per beneficiary. A beneficiary may have both § 529 and § 530 plans.

5-13a Qualified Tuition Program

Nearly all, if not all, states have created programs whereby parents can in effect prepay their child's college tuition. The prepayment serves as a hedge against future increases in tuition. Generally, if the child does not attend college, the parents are refunded their payments plus interest. Upon first impressions, these prepaid tuition programs resemble the below-market loans discussed in Chapter 4. That is, assuming that the tuition increases, the parent receives a reduction in the child's tuition in exchange for the use of the funds. However, Congress has created an exclusion provision for these programs.

Under a **qualified tuition program (§ 529 plan)**, the amounts contributed must be used for qualified higher education expenses. These expenses include tuition, fees, books, supplies, room and board, and equipment required for enrollment or attendance at a college, a university, or certain vocational schools. Allowable expenses also include computers and peripheral equipment, software, and Internet access used primarily by the beneficiary while enrolled at an eligible educational institution. Qualified higher education expenses also include the expenses for special needs services that are incurred in connection with the enrollment and attendance of special needs students.

The earnings of the contributed funds, including the discount on tuition charged to participants, are not included in Federal gross income provided the contributions and earnings are used for qualified higher education expenses. Some states also exclude these educational benefits from state gross income.

Agnes paid $20,000 into a qualified tuition program to be used for her son's college tuition. When her son graduated from high school, the fund balance had increased to $30,000 as a result of interest credited to the account. The interest was not included in Agnes's gross income. During the current year, $7,500 of the balance in the fund was used to pay the son's tuition and fees. None of this amount is included in either Agnes's or the son's gross income.

EXAMPLE 32

If the parent receives a refund (e.g., child does not attend college), the excess of the amount refunded over the amount contributed by the parent is included in the parent's gross income. A special rule applies to refunded amounts recontributed to a qualified tuition program of the beneficiary.

5-13b Coverdell Education Savings Account

A **Coverdell education savings account (§ 530 plan)**, may be used to save for K–12 education as well as postsecondary education expenses. The contributions to the plan are limited to $2,000 in any year, and the beneficiary must be under 18 or must be a special needs beneficiary in the year the contribution is made. As with the § 529 plan, contributions are nondeductible, but the income to the beneficiary is nontaxable provided the funds are used for qualified education expenses.

5-14 QUALIFIED ABLE PROGRAMS (§ 529A PLANS)

In 2014, a law change created a new type of program to assist individuals who became blind or disabled before age 26. The **qualified ABLE program** allows for § 529A plans, or ABLE (Achieving a Better Life Experience) plans, similar in concept to § 529 plans described earlier. The program must be established by a state. The ABLE account must be for the benefit of a designated beneficiary's disability expenses, and the beneficiary must have a disability certification from the government.

Contributions to the account must be in cash and may not in aggregate exceed the annual gift tax exclusion for the year ($14,000 for 2015 and 2016). Contributions to the account are not deductible. The tax benefit of an ABLE account is that its earnings are not taxable. Distributions from the account also are not taxable provided they do not exceed the qualified disability expenses of the designated beneficiary.

5-15 TAX BENEFIT RULE

LO.3

Determine the extent to which receipts can be excluded under the tax benefit rule.

Generally, if a taxpayer claims a deduction for an item in one year and in a later year recovers all or a portion of the prior deduction, the recovery is included in gross income in the year received.[71]

EXAMPLE 33

An accrual basis taxpayer deducted as a loss a $1,000 receivable from a customer when it appeared the amount would never be collected. The following year, the customer paid $800 on the receivable. The taxpayer must report the $800 as gross income in the year it is received.

However, the § 111 **tax benefit rule** provides that no income is recognized upon the recovery of a deduction, or the portion of a deduction, that did not yield a tax benefit in the year it was taken. If the taxpayer in Example 33 had no tax liability in the year of the deduction (e.g., itemized deductions and personal exemptions exceeded adjusted gross income), the recovery would be partially or totally excluded from gross income in the year of the recovery.[72]

EXAMPLE 34

Ali filed his 2015 income tax return as a single individual. His AGI for 2015 was $48,000. He had $6,650 in itemized deductions, including $1,200 in state income tax. His personal exemption was $4,000. In 2016, he received a $700 refund of the state income taxes that he paid in 2015. Because the standard deduction in 2015 was $6,300, the $1,200 of state income taxes Ali paid in 2015 yielded a tax benefit of only $350 ($6,650 itemized deductions − $6,300 standard deduction) in 2015. Under the tax benefit rule, only $350 of the state income tax refund is included in gross income in 2016.

---

[71]§ 111(a).

[72]Itemized deductions are discussed in Chapter 10.

5-16 INCOME FROM DISCHARGE OF INDEBTEDNESS

LO.4

Describe the circumstances under which income must be reported from the discharge of indebtedness.

When a person is relieved of a debt for less than the amount owed, the debtor's net worth increases. This increase in net worth is taxable income, unless one of the exceptions discussed below applies.[73]

> Kayla is unable to make her credit card payments and has negotiated a settlement with the credit card issuer. Her $40,000 debt will be settled for $25,000. Kayla must recognize income of $15,000 from the discharge of debt.

EXAMPLE 35

When property serves as security for debt, the creditor may foreclose on the property. The foreclosure is treated as a sale.[74]

> Juan owns land that serves as security for a $60,000 mortgage held by State Bank. Juan does not have personal liability for the mortgage (it is non-recourse debt). When Juan's basis in the land is $20,000 and the land's fair market value is $50,000, the bank forecloses on the loan and takes title to the land. Juan must recognize a $40,000 gain on the foreclosure, as though he sold the land for $60,000 (the amount of the non-recourse debt). Juan has no income from discharge of indebtedness.

EXAMPLE 36

If property serves as security for the debt and the taxpayer is personally liable for the difference between the value of the property and the amount of the debt (i.e., the debt is "with recourse"), the taxpayer may have income from the discharge of the debt in addition to gain or loss from the foreclosure.

> Assume the same facts in Example 36, except that Juan's debt is recourse. Juan is treated as selling the property for its fair market value ($50,000) resulting in a gain or loss. His gain is $30,000 ($50,000 sales price less $20,000 basis). In addition, Juan has $10,000 of income from discharge of indebtedness because the lender accepted the $50,000 sales price in discharging the $60,000 debt. Juan will want to determine whether any exclusion applies to his income from discharge of indebtedness (discussed next).

EXAMPLE 37

The following discharge of indebtedness situations are subject to special exclusion treatment:[75]

1. Creditors' gifts.
2. Discharges under Federal bankruptcy law.
3. Discharges that occur when the debtor is insolvent (the exclusion is limited to the amount of insolvency).
4. Discharge of the farm debt of a solvent taxpayer.
5. Discharge of **qualified real property business indebtedness**.
6. A seller's cancellation of the buyer's indebtedness.
7. A shareholder's cancellation of the corporation's indebtedness.
8. Forgiveness of certain loans to students.
9. Discharge of indebtedness on the taxpayer's principal residence that occurs between January 1, 2007, and January 1, 2017, and is the result of the financial condition of the debtor.

If the creditor reduces the debt as an act of *love, affection,* or *generosity,* the debtor has simply received a nontaxable gift (situation 1). Rarely will a gift be found to have

---

[73]§ 61(a)(12) and Reg. § 1.1001–2(a).

[74]*Estate of Delman*, 73 T.C. 15 (1979).

[75]§§ 108 and 1017. See Rev.Proc. 2015–57, 2015–51 I.R.B. 863, for a special debt discharge exclusion under the U.S. Department of Education's "Defense to Repayment" program.

occurred in a business context. A businessperson may settle a debt for less than the amount due, but as a matter of business expediency (e.g., high collection costs or disputes as to contract terms) rather than generosity.[76]

In situations 2, 3, 4, 5, and 9, the Code allows the debtor to reduce his or her basis in the assets by the realized income from the discharge.[77] Thus, the realized income is merely deferred until the assets are sold (or depreciated). Similarly, in situation 6 (a price reduction), the debtor reduces the basis in the specific assets financed by the seller.[78]

A shareholder's cancellation of the corporation's indebtedness to him or her (situation 7) usually is considered a tax-free contribution of capital to the corporation by the shareholder. Thus, the corporation's paid-in capital is increased, and its liabilities are decreased by the same amount.[79]

Many states make loans to students on the condition that the loan will be forgiven if the student practices a profession in the state upon completing his or her studies. The amount of the loan that is forgiven (situation 8) is excluded from gross income.[80]

5-17 TAX PLANNING

LO.5

Identify tax planning strategies for obtaining the maximum benefit from allowable exclusions.

The present law excludes certain types of economic gains from taxation. Therefore, taxpayers may find tax planning techniques helpful in obtaining the maximum benefits from the exclusion of such gains. Following are some of the tax planning opportunities made available by the exclusions described in this chapter.

5-17a Life Insurance

Life insurance offers several favorable tax attributes. As discussed in Chapter 4, the annual increase in the cash surrender value of the policy is not taxable (because no income has been actually or constructively received). By borrowing on the policy's cash surrender value, the owner can actually receive the policy's increase in value in cash without recognizing income.

5-17b Employee Fringe Benefits

Generally, employees view accident and health insurance, as well as life insurance, as necessities. Employees can obtain group coverage at much lower rates than individuals would have to pay for the same protection. Premiums paid by the employer can be excluded from the employees' gross income. Because of the exclusion, employees will have a greater after-tax and after-insurance income if the employer pays a lower salary but also pays the insurance premiums.

EXAMPLE 38

Pat receives a salary of $30,000. The company has group insurance benefits, but Pat is required to pay his own premiums as follows:

Hospitalization and medical insurance	$1,400
Term life insurance ($30,000 coverage)	200
Disability insurance	400
	$2,000

continued

---

[76]*Comm. v. Jacobson*, 49–1 USTC ¶9133, 37 AFTR 516, 69 S.Ct. 358 (USSC, 1949).

[77]§§ 108(a), (c), (e), and (g). Note that § 108(b) provides that other tax attributes (e.g., net operating loss) will be reduced by the realized gain from the debt discharge prior to the basis adjustment unless the taxpayer elects to apply the basis adjustment first.

[78]§ 108(e)(5).

[79]§ 108(e)(6).

[80]§ 108(f).

To simplify the analysis, assume that Pat's tax rate on income is 25%. After paying taxes of $7,500 (.25 × $30,000) and $2,000 for insurance, Pat has $20,500 ($30,000 − $7,500 − $2,000) for his other living needs.

If Pat's employer reduced Pat's salary by $2,000 (to $28,000) but paid his insurance premiums, Pat's tax liability would be only $7,000 ($28,000 × .25). Thus, Pat would have $21,000 ($28,000 − $7,000) to meet his other living needs. The change in the compensation plan would save Pat $500 ($21,000 − $20,500), which is the marginal tax times the value of the insurance benefits, .25 × $2,000 = $500.

Similarly, employees must often incur expenses for child care and parking. The employee can have more income for other uses if the employer pays these costs for the employee but reduces the employee's salary by the cost of the benefits.

The use of cafeteria plans has increased dramatically in recent years. These plans allow employees to tailor their benefits to meet their individual situations. Thus, where both spouses in a married couple are working, duplications of benefits can be avoided and other needed benefits can often be added. If less than all of the employee's allowance is spent, the employee can receive cash.

The meals and lodging exclusion enables employees to receive from their employer what they ordinarily must purchase with after-tax dollars. Although the requirements that the employee live on the employer's premises to exclude the value of the lodging limits the tax planning opportunities, the exclusion is an important factor in the employee's compensation in certain situations (e.g., hotels, motels, restaurants, farms, and ranches). The meals and lodging are clearly a benefit to the employee but are for the convenience of the employer and thus are excluded from income.

The employees' discount provision is especially important for manufacturers and wholesalers. Employees of manufacturers can avoid tax on the manufacturer's, wholesaler's, and retailer's markups. The wholesaler's employees can avoid tax on an amount equal to the wholesale and retail markups.

It should be recognized that the exclusion of benefits is generally available only to employees. Proprietors and partners must pay tax on the same benefits their employees receive tax-free. By incorporating and becoming an employee of the corporation, the former proprietor or partner can also receive these tax-exempt benefits. Thus, the availability of employee benefits is a consideration in the decision to incorporate.

5-17c Investment Income

Tax-exempt state and local government bonds are almost irresistible investments for high-income taxpayers, who may be subject to a 39.6 percent regular tax rate plus a 3.8 percent rate on their net investment income. To realize the maximum benefit from the exemption, the investor can purchase zero-coupon bonds. Like Series EE U.S. government savings bonds, these investments pay interest only at maturity. The advantage of the zero-coupon feature for a tax-exempt bond is that the investor can earn tax-exempt interest on the accumulated principal and interest. If the investor purchases a bond that pays the interest each year, the interest received may be such a small amount that an additional tax-exempt investment cannot be made. In addition, reinvesting the interest may entail transaction costs (brokers' fees). The zero-coupon feature avoids these problems.

Series EE U.S. government savings bonds can earn tax-exempt interest if the bond proceeds are used for qualified higher education expenses. Many taxpayers can foresee these expenditures being made for their children's educations. In deciding whether to invest in the bonds, however, the investor must take into account the income limitations for excluding the interest from gross income.

REFOCUS ON THE BIG PICTURE

EXCLUSIONS

You have looked into Paul's tax situation and have the following information for him:

- *Compensation.* The amount Paul was paid for his internship is compensation for services rendered and must be included in his gross income. This includes both his base pay and the $1,500 bonus (Example 1).

- *Graduate assistantship.* The tuition waiver of $6,000 is excluded from Paul's gross income. The related payments of $400 per month are intended as a form of compensation. So Paul must include the $400 per month in his gross income (Example 11).

- *Damages.* Damages awards that relate to personal physical injury or sickness can be excluded from gross income if the payments are for compensatory damages. So all of the compensatory damages of $220,000 can be excluded from gross income. The punitive damages of $160,000 must be included in Paul's gross income. Likewise, the compensatory damages of $25,000 received by Paul's mother must be included in her gross income because emotional distress does not qualify as personal physical injury or sickness (Example 12).

What If?

From a tax planning perspective, can Paul do anything to reduce the amount of the punitive damages settlement that he must include in his gross income?

As things now stand (i.e., a completed settlement), Paul cannot reduce the $160,000 punitive damages amount he must include in gross income. However, proper tax planning might have enabled Paul to reduce the amount includible in gross income. Note that both the amount of the damages and the labels attached to the damages are negotiated. If a larger portion of the settlement had been assigned to compensatory damages rather than punitive damages, Paul could have reduced the amount he must include in his gross income.

Key Terms

Discussion Questions

1. **LO.2** Fred specified in his will that his nephew John should serve as executor of Fred's estate. John received $10,000 for serving as executor. Can John exclude the $10,000 from his gross income? Explain.

2. **LO.2** Leonard's home was damaged by a fire. He also had to be absent from work for several days to make his home habitable. Leonard's employer paid Leonard his regular salary, $2,500, while he was absent from work. In Leonard's pay envelope was the following note from the employer: To help you in your time of need. Leonard's fellow employees also took up a collection and gave him $900. Leonard spent over $4,000 repairing the fire damage.

    Based on the above information, how much is Leonard required to include in his gross income?

3. **LO.2** Dolly is a college student who works as a part-time server in a restaurant. Her usual tip is 20% of the price of the meal. A customer ordered a piece of pie and said that he would appreciate prompt service. Dolly abided with the customer's request. The customer's bill was $8, but the customer left a $100 bill on the table and did not ask for a receipt. Dolly gave the cashier $8 and pocketed the $100 bill. Dolly concludes that the customer thought that he had left a $10 bill, although the customer did not return to correct the apparent mistake. The customer had commented about how much he appreciated Dolly's prompt service. Dolly thinks that a $2 tip would be sufficient and that the other $98 is like "found money." How much should Dolly include in her gross income?

4. **LO.2** Carey is a waiter at a restaurant that pays a small hourly amount plus tips. Customers are not required to tip the waiter. Carey is especially attentive and friendly, and her tips average 25% of the restaurant charges. Is Carey required to include any of her tips in gross income when the customer has no legal obligation to make the payment? Explain the basis for your conclusion.

5. **LO.2** Lime Finance Company requires its customers to purchase a credit life insurance policy associated with the loans it makes. Lime is the beneficiary of the policy to the extent of the remaining balance on the loan at the time of the customer's death. In 2015, Lime wrote off as uncollectible a $5,000 account receivable from Wally, which included $1,500 of accrued interest. When Wally died in 2016, the life insurance policy was still in force and Lime received $3,500. Is the $3,500 of life insurance proceeds received by Lime included in its gross income? Explain.

6. **LO.2** Billy fell off a bar stool and hurt his back. As a result, he was unable to work for three months. He sued the bar owner and collected $100,000 for the physical injury and $50,000 for the loss of income. Billy also collected $15,000 from an income replacement insurance policy he purchased. Amber was away from work for three months following heart bypass surgery. Amber collected $30,000 under an income replacement insurance policy purchased by her employer. Are the amounts received by Billy and Amber treated the same under the tax law? Explain.

7. **LO.2** Wes was a major league baseball pitcher who earned $10 million for his 20 wins this year. Sam was also a major league baseball pitcher before a career-ending injury caused by a negligent driver. Sam sued the driver and collected $6 million as compensation for lost estimated future income as a pitcher and $4 million as punitive damages. Do the amounts that Wes and Sam receive have the same effect on their gross income? Explain.

8. **LO.2** Holly was injured while working in a factory and received $12,000 as workers' compensation while she was unable to work because of the injury. Jill, who was self-employed, was also injured and unable to work. Jill collected $12,000 on an

insurance policy she had purchased to replace her loss of income while she was unable to work. How much are Holly and Jill each required to include in their gross income?

Decision Making 9. **LO.2, 5** Casey is in the 15% marginal tax bracket, and Jean is in the 35% marginal tax bracket. Their employer is experiencing financial difficulties and cannot continue to pay for the company's health insurance plan. The annual premiums are approximately $8,000 per employee. The employer has proposed to either (1) require the employee to pay the premiums or (2) reduce each employee's pay by $10,000 per year with the employer paying the premium. Which option is less objectionable to Casey, and which is less objectionable to Jean?

10. **LO.2** What is the difference between a cafeteria plan and an employee flexible spending plan?

11. **LO.2** Ted works for Azure Motors, an automobile dealership. All employees can buy a car at the company's cost plus 2%. The company does not charge employees the $300 dealer preparation fee that nonemployees must pay. Ted purchased an automobile for $29,580 ($29,000 + $580). The company's cost was $29,000. The price for a nonemployee would have been $33,900 ($33,600 + $300 preparation fee). What is Ted's gross income from the purchase of the automobile?

12. **LO.2, 5** Wilbur has been offered a job at a salary that would put him in the 25% marginal tax bracket. In addition to his salary, he would receive health insurance coverage. Another potential employer does not offer health insurance but has agreed to match the first offer on an after-tax and insurance basis. The cost of health insurance comparable to that provided by the other potential employer is $9,000 per year. How much more in salary must the second potential employer pay so that Wilbur's financial status will be the same under both offers?

13. **LO.2, 5** Eagle Life Insurance Company pays its employees $.30 per mile for driving their personal automobiles to and from work. The company reimburses each employee who rides the bus $100 a month for the cost of a pass. Tom collected $100 for his automobile mileage, and Mason received $100 as reimbursement for the cost of a bus pass.
   a.   What are the effects of the above on Tom's and Mason's gross income?
   b.   Assume that Tom and Mason are in the 28% marginal tax bracket and the actual before-tax cost for Tom to drive to and from work is $.30 per mile. What are Tom's and Mason's after-tax costs of commuting to and from work?

Issue ID 14. **LO.2** Several of Egret Company's employees have asked the company to create a hiking trail that employees could use during their lunch hours. The company owns vacant land that is being held for future expansion but would have to spend approximately $50,000 if it were to make a trail. Nonemployees would be allowed to use the facility as part of the company's effort to build strong community support. What are the relevant tax issues for the employees?

15. **LO.2** The Sage Company has the opportunity to purchase a building located next to its office. Sage would use the building as a day care center for the children of its employees and an exercise facility for the employees. Occasionally, portions of the building could be used for employees' family events such as reunions, birthday parties, and anniversaries. The company would like to know if the planned uses of the building would fit into a beneficially taxed employee compensation plan.

Decision Making 16. **LO.2, 5** Tammy, a resident of Virginia, is considering purchasing a North Carolina bond that yields 4.6% before tax. She is in the 35% Federal marginal tax bracket and the 5% state marginal tax bracket. She is aware that State of Virginia bonds of comparable risk are yielding 4.5%. However, the Virginia bonds are exempt from Virginia tax, but the North Carolina bond interest is taxable in Virginia. Which of the two options will provide the greater after-tax return to Tammy? Tammy can deduct any state taxes paid on her Federal income tax return.

17. **LO.2** Andrea entered into a § 529 qualified tuition program for the benefit of her daughter, Joanna. Andrea contributed $15,000 to the fund. The fund balance had accumulated to $25,000 by the time Joanna was ready to enter college. However, Joanna received a scholarship that paid for her tuition, fees, books, supplies, and room and board. Therefore, Andrea withdrew the funds from the § 529 plan and bought Joanna a new car.

    a. What are the tax consequences to Andrea of withdrawing the funds?

    b. Assume instead that Joanna's scholarship did not cover her room and board, which cost $7,500 per academic year. During the current year, $7,500 of the fund balance was used to pay for Joanna's room and board. The remaining amount was left in the § 529 plan to cover her room and board for future academic years. What are the tax consequences to Andrea and to Joanna of using the $7,500 to pay for the room and board?

18. **LO.3** Dolly is a cash basis taxpayer. In 2016, she filed her 2015 South Carolina income tax return and received a $2,200 refund. Dolly took the standard deduction on her 2015 Federal income tax return, but will itemize her deductions in 2016. Molly, a cash basis taxpayer, also filed her 2015 South Carolina income tax return in 2016 and received a $600 refund. Molly had $12,000 in itemized deductions on her 2015 Federal income tax return, but will take the standard deduction in 2016. How does the tax benefit rule apply to Dolly's and Molly's situations? Explain.

19. **LO.4** Ralph has experienced financial difficulties as a result of his struggling business. He has been behind on his mortgage payments for the last six months. The mortgage holder, who is a friend of Ralph's, has offered to accept $80,000 in full payment of the $100,000 owed on the mortgage and payable over the next 10 years. The interest rate of the mortgage is 7%, and the market rate is now 8%. What tax issues are raised by the creditor's offer?

Issue ID

Computational Exercises

20. **LO.2** Valentino is a patient in a nursing home for 45 days of 2016. While in the nursing home, he incurs total costs of $13,500. Medicare pays $8,000 of the costs. Valentino receives $15,000 from his long-term care insurance policy, which pays while he is in the facility. Assume that the daily federal statutory amount for Valentino is $340.

    Of the $15,000, what amount may Valentino exclude from his gross income?

21. **LO.2** Mio was transferred from New York to Germany. He lived and worked in Germany for 340 days in 2016. Mio's salary for 2016 is $190,000. In your computation, round any division to four decimal places before converting to a percentage. For example, .473938 would be rounded to 47.39%.

    What is Mio's foreign earned income exclusion?

22. **LO.2** Ellie purchases an insurance policy on her life and names her brother, Jason, as the beneficiary. Ellie pays $32,000 in premiums for the policy during her life. When she dies, Jason collects the insurance proceeds of $500,000.

    As a result, how much gross income does Jason report?

23. **LO.2** Alfred owned a term life insurance policy at the time he was diagnosed with a terminal illness. After paying $18,300 in premiums, he sold the policy to a company that is authorized by the state of South Carolina to purchase such policies. The company paid Alfred $125,000. When Alfred died 18 months later, the company collected the face amount of the policy, $150,000.

    As a result of the sale of the policy, how much is Alfred required to include in his gross income?

24. **LO.2** Leland pays premiums of $5,000 for an insurance policy in the face amount of $25,000 upon the life of Caleb and subsequently transfers the policy to Tyler for $7,500. Over the years, Tyler pays subsequent premiums of $1,500 on the policy. Upon Caleb's death, Tyler receives the proceeds of $25,000.

    As a result, what amount is Tyler required to include in his gross income?

25. **LO.2** Jarrod receives a scholarship of $18,500 from Riggers University to be used to pursue a bachelor's degree. He spends $12,000 on tuition, $1,500 on books and supplies, $4,000 for room and board, and $1,000 for personal expenses.

    How much may Jarrod exclude from his gross income?

26. **LO.3** Myrna and Geoffrey filed a joint tax return in 2015. Their AGI was $85,000, and itemized deductions were $13,700, which included $4,000 in state income tax. In 2016, they received a $1,800 refund of the state income taxes they paid in 2015. The standard deduction for married filing jointly in 2015 was $12,600. Under the tax benefit rule, what amount of the state income tax refund is included in gross income in 2016?

Problems

27. **LO.2** Ed, an employee of the Natural Color Company, suffered from a rare disease that was very expensive to treat. The local media ran several stories about Ed's problems, and the family created a website that generated more than $10,000 in gifts from individuals to help pay the medical bills. Ed's employer provided hospital and medical insurance for its employees, but the policy did not cover Ed's illness. When it became apparent that Ed could not pay all of his medical expenses, the hospital canceled the $25,000 Ed owed at the time of his death. After Ed's death, his former employer paid Ed's widow $12,000 in "her time of need." Ed's widow also collected $50,000 on a group term life insurance policy paid for by Ed's employer. What are Ed's and his widow's gross income?

28. **LO.2** Determine the gross income of the beneficiaries in the following cases:

    a. Justin's employer was downsizing and offered employees an amount equal to one year's salary if the employee would voluntarily retire.

    b. Trina contracted a disease and was unable to work for six months. Because of her dire circumstances, her employer paid her one-half of her regular salary while she was away from work.

    c. Coral Corporation collected $1 million on a key person life insurance policy when its chief executive died. The corporation had paid the premiums on the policy of $77,000, which were not deductible by the corporation.

    d. Juan collected $40,000 on a life insurance policy when his wife, Leona, died in 2015. The insurance policy was provided by Leona's employer, and the premiums were excluded from Leona's gross income as group term life insurance. In 2016, Juan collected the $3,500 accrued salary owed to Leona at the time of her death.

Decision Making   29. **LO.2, 5** Laura was recently diagnosed with cancer and has begun chemotherapy treatments. A cancer specialist has stated that Laura has less than one year to live. She has incurred many medical bills and other general living expenses and is in need of cash. Therefore, she is considering selling stock that cost $35,000 and has a fair market value of $50,000. This amount would be sufficient to pay her medical bills. However, she has read about a company (the Vital Benefits Company) that would purchase her life insurance policy for $50,000. She has paid $30,000 in premiums on the policy.

a. Considering only the tax effects, would selling the stock or selling the life insurance policy result in more beneficial tax treatment?

b. Assume that Laura is a dependent child and that her mother owns the stock and the life insurance policy, which is on the mother's life. Which of the alternative means of raising the cash would result in more beneficial tax treatment?

30. **LO.2** What is the taxpayer's gross income in each of the following situations?

a. Darrin received a salary of $50,000 in 2016 from his employer, Green Construction.

b. In July 2016, Green gave Darrin an all-expense-paid trip to Las Vegas (value of $3,000) for exceeding his sales quota.

c. Megan received $10,000 from her employer to help her pay medical expenses not covered by insurance.

d. Blake received $15,000 from his deceased wife's employer "to help him in his time of greatest need."

e. Clint collected $50,000 as the beneficiary of a group term life insurance policy when his wife died. The premiums on the policy were paid by his deceased wife's employer.

31. **LO.2** Donald was killed in an accident while he was on the job in 2016. Darlene, Donald's wife, received several payments as a result of Donald's death. What is Darlene's gross income from the items listed below?

a. Donald's employer paid Darlene an amount equal to Donald's three months' salary ($60,000), which is what the employer does for all widows and widowers of deceased employees.

b. Donald had $20,000 in accrued salary that was paid to Darlene.

c. Donald's employer had provided Donald with group term life insurance of $480,000 (twice his annual salary), which was payable to his widow in a lump sum. Premiums on this policy totaling $12,500 had been included in Donald's gross income under § 79.

d. Donald had purchased a life insurance policy (premiums totaled $250,000) that paid $600,000 in the event of accidental death. The proceeds were payable to Darlene, who elected to receive installment payments as an annuity of $30,000 each year for a 25-year period. She received her first installment this year.

32. **LO.2** Ray and Carin are partners in an accounting firm. The partners have entered into an arm's length agreement requiring Ray to purchase Carin's partnership interest from Carin's estate if she dies before Ray. The price is set at 120% of the book value of Carin's partnership interest at the time of her death. Ray purchased an insurance policy on Carin's life to fund this agreement. After Ray had paid $45,000 in premiums, Carin was killed in an automobile accident and Ray collected $800,000 of life insurance proceeds. Ray used the life insurance proceeds to purchase Carin's partnership interest.

a. What amount should Ray include in his gross income from receiving the life insurance proceeds?

b. The insurance company paid Ray $16,000 interest on the life insurance proceeds during the period Carin's estate was in administration. During this period, Ray had left the insurance proceeds with the insurance company. Is this interest taxable?

c. When Ray paid $800,000 for Carin's partnership interest, priced as specified in the agreement, the fair market value of Carin's interest was $1 million. How much should Ray include in his gross income from this bargain purchase?

33. **LO.2** Sally was an all-state soccer player during her junior and senior years in high school. She accepted an athletic scholarship from State University. The scholarship provided the following:

Tuition and fees	$15,000
Housing and meals	6,000
Books and supplies	1,500
Transportation	1,200

a. Determine the effect of the scholarship on Sally's gross income.

b. Sally's brother, Willy, was not a gifted athlete, but he received $8,000 from their father's employer as a scholarship during the year. The employer grants the children of all executives a scholarship equal to one-half of annual tuition, fees, books, and supplies. Willy also received a $6,000 scholarship (to be used for tuition) as the winner of an essay contest related to bioengineering, his intended field of study. Determine the effect of the scholarships on Willy's and his father's gross income.

34. **LO.2** Adrian was awarded an academic scholarship to State University for the 2016–2017 academic year. He received $6,500 in August and $7,200 in December 2016. Adrian had enough personal savings to pay all expenses as they came due. Adrian's expenditures for the relevant period were as follows:

Tuition, August 2016	$3,700
Tuition, January 2017	3,750
Room and board	
August–December 2016	2,800
January–May 2017	2,500
Books and educational supplies	
August–December 2016	1,000
January–May 2017	1,200

Determine the effect on Adrian's gross income for 2016 and 2017.

35. **LO.2** Leigh sued an overzealous bill collector and received the following settlement:

Damage to her automobile that the collector attempted to repossess	$ 3,300
Physical damage to her arm caused by the collector	15,000
Loss of income while her arm was healing	6,000
Punitive damages	80,000

a. What effect does the settlement have on Leigh's gross income?

b. Assume that Leigh also collected $25,000 of damages for slander to her personal reputation caused by the bill collector misrepresenting the facts to Leigh's employer and other creditors. Is this $25,000 included in Leigh's gross income? Explain.

36. **LO.2** Determine the effect on gross income in each of the following cases:

a. Eloise received $150,000 in settlement of a sex discrimination case against her former employer.

b. Nell received $10,000 for damages to her personal reputation. She also received $40,000 in punitive damages.

c. Orange Corporation, an accrual basis taxpayer, received $50,000 from a lawsuit filed against its auditor who overcharged for services rendered in a previous year.

d. Beth received $10,000 in compensatory damages and $30,000 in punitive damages in a lawsuit she filed against a tanning parlor for severe burns she received from using its tanning equipment.

e. Joanne received compensatory damages of $75,000 and punitive damages of $300,000 from a cosmetic surgeon who botched her nose job.

37. **LO.2** Rex, age 55, is an officer of Blue Company, which provides him with the following nondiscriminatory fringe benefits in 2016:

    - Hospitalization insurance premiums for Rex and his dependents. The cost of the coverage for Rex is $2,900 per year, and the additional cost for his dependents is $3,800 per year. The plan has a $2,000 deductible, but his employer contributed $1,500 to Rex's Health Savings Account (HSA). Rex withdrew only $800 from the HSA, and the account earned $50 of interest during the year.

    - Insurance premiums of $840 for salary continuation payments. Under the plan, Rex will receive his regular salary in the event he is unable to work due to illness. Rex collected $4,500 on the policy to replace lost wages while he was ill during the year.

    - Rex is a part-time student working on his bachelor's degree in engineering. His employer reimbursed his $5,200 tuition under a plan available to all full-time employees.

    Determine the amount Rex must include in gross income.

38. **LO.2** The UVW Union and HON Corporation are negotiating contract terms. Assume that the union members are in the 25% marginal tax bracket and that all benefits are provided on a nondiscriminatory basis. Write a letter to the UVW Union members explaining the tax consequences of the options discussed below. The union's address is 905 Spruce Street, Washington, DC 20227.

    a. The company would eliminate the $250 deductible on medical insurance benefits. Most employees incur more than $250 each year in medical expenses.

    b. Employees would get an additional paid holiday with the same annual income (the same pay but less work).

    c. An employee who did not need health insurance (because the employee's spouse works and receives family coverage) would be allowed to receive the cash value of the coverage.

    Communications

39. **LO.2, 5** Mauve Corporation has a group hospitalization insurance plan that has a $200 deductible amount for hospital visits and a $15 deductible for doctor visits and prescriptions. The deductible portion paid by employees who have children has become substantial for some employees. The company is considering adopting a medical reimbursement plan or a flexible benefits plan to cover the deductible amounts. Either of these plans can be tailored to meet the needs of the employees. What are the cost considerations to the employer that should be considered in choosing between these plans?

    Decision Making

40. **LO.2** Belinda spent the last 60 days of 2016 in a nursing home. The cost of the services provided to her was $18,000 ($300 per day). Medicare paid $8,500 toward the cost of her stay. Belinda also received $5,500 of benefits under a long-term care insurance policy she purchased. What is the effect on Belinda's gross income?

41. **LO.2** Tim is the vice president of western operations for Maroon Oil Company and is stationed in San Francisco. He is required to live in an employer-owned home, which is three blocks from his company office. The company-provided home is equipped with high-speed Internet access and several telephone lines. Tim receives telephone calls and e-mails that require immediate attention any time of day or night because the company's business is spread all over the world. A full-time administrative assistant resides in the house to assist Tim with the urgent business matters. Tim often uses the home for entertaining customers, suppliers, and employees. The fair market value of comparable housing is $9,000 per month. Tim is also provided with free parking at his company's office. The value of the parking is $350 per month. Calculate the amount associated with the company-provided housing and free parking that Tim must include in his gross income for 2016.

42. **LO.2** Does the taxpayer recognize gross income in the following situations?

    a.   Ava is a filing clerk at a large insurance company. She is permitted to leave the premises for lunch, but she usually eats in the company's cafeteria because it is quick and she is on a tight schedule. On average, she pays $2 for a lunch that would cost $12 at a restaurant. However, if the prices in the cafeteria were not so low and the food was not so delicious, she would probably bring her lunch at a cost of $3 per day.

    b.   Scott is an executive for an international corporation located in New York City. Often he works late, taking telephone calls from the company's European branch. Scott often stays in a company-owned condominium when he has a late-night work session. The condominium is across the street from the company office.

    c.   Ira recently moved to take a job. For the first month on the new job, Ira was searching for a home to purchase or rent. During this time, his employer permitted Ira to live in an apartment the company maintains for customers during the buying season. The month that Ira occupied the apartment was not during the buying season, and the apartment would not otherwise have been occupied.

Decision Making 43. **LO.2, 5** Bertha is considering taking an early retirement offered by her employer. She would receive $3,000 per month, ~~indexed for inflation~~. However, she would no longer be able to use the company's health facilities, and she would be required to pay her hospitalization insurance premiums of $8,000 each year. Bertha and her husband will file a joint return and take the standard deduction. She currently receives a salary of $55,000 a year. If she retires, she will spend approximately $300 less each month for commuting and clothing. Bertha and her husband have other sources of income and are in and will remain in the 25% marginal tax bracket. ~~Her income tax for the current year was $8,875.~~ She currently pays Social Security and Medicare taxes of 7.65% on her salary, but her retirement pay would not be subject to this tax. According to Bertha, she and her husband could live ~~well if her after-tax retirement income was at least 50% of her current income.~~ Provide Bertha with information she will need to make her decision.

Communications 44. **LO.2, 5** Finch Construction Company provides the carpenters it employs with all of the required tools. However, the company believes that this practice has led to some employees not taking care of the tools and to the mysterious disappearance of some tools. The company is considering requiring all of its employees to provide their own tools. Each employee's salary would be increased by $1,500 to compensate for the additional cost. Write a letter to Finch's management explaining the tax consequences of this plan to the carpenters. Finch's address is 300 Harbor Drive, Vermillion, SD 57069.

45. **LO.2, 5** Bluebird, Inc., does not provide its employees with any tax-exempt fringe benefits. The company is considering adopting a hospital and medical benefits insurance plan that will cost approximately $9,000 per employee. To adopt this plan, the company may have to reduce salaries and/or lower future salary increases. Bluebird is in the 35% (combined Federal and state rates) bracket. Bluebird is also responsible for matching the Social Security and Medicare taxes withheld on employees' salaries (at the full 7.65% rate). The hospital and medical benefits insurance plan will not be subject to the Social Security and Medicare taxes, and the company is not eligible for the small business credit for health insurance. The employees generally fall into two marginal tax rate groups:

Income Tax	Social Security and Medicare Tax	Total
.15	.0765	.2265
.35	.0145	.3645

The company has asked you to assist in its financial planning for the hospital and medical benefits insurance plan by computing the following:

a. How much taxable compensation is the equivalent of $9,000 of exempt compensation for each of the two classes of employees?

b. What is the company's after-tax cost of the taxable compensation computed in part (a)?

c. What is the company's after-tax cost of the exempt compensation?

d. Briefly explain your conclusions from the preceding analysis.

46. **LO.2, 5** Rosa's employer has instituted a flexible benefits program. Rosa will use the plan to pay for her daughter's dental expenses and other medical expenses that are not covered by health insurance. Rosa is in the 28% marginal tax bracket and estimates that the medical and dental expenses not covered by health insurance will be within the range of $4,000 to $5,000. Her employer's plan permits her to set aside as much as $5,000 in the flexible benefits account. Rosa does not itemize her deductions.

Decision Making

a. Rosa puts $4,000 into her flexible benefits account, and her actual expenses are $5,000. What is her cost of underestimating the expenses?

b. Rosa puts $5,000 into her flexible benefits account, and her actual expenses are only $4,000. What is her cost of overestimating her expenses?

c. What is Rosa's cost of underfunding as compared with the cost of overfunding the flexible benefits account?

d. Does your answer in part (c) suggest that Rosa should fund the account closer to the low end or to the high end of her estimates?

47. **LO.2** Sparrow Corporation would like you to review its employee fringe benefits program with regard to the tax consequences of the plan for the company's president (Polly), who is also the majority shareholder.

a. The company has a qualified retirement plan. The company pays the cost of employees attending a retirement planning seminar. The employee must be within 10 years of retirement, and the cost of the seminar is $1,500 per attendee.

b. The company owns a parking garage that is used by customers, employees, and the general public. Only the general public is required to pay for parking. The charge to the general public for Polly's parking for the year would have been $3,600 (a $300 monthly rate).

c. All employees are allowed to use the company's fixed charge long-distance telephone services, as long as the privilege is not abused. Although no one has kept track of the actual calls, Polly's use of the telephone had a value (what she would have paid on her personal telephone) of approximately $600.

d. The company owns a condominium at the beach, which it uses to entertain customers. Employees are allowed to use the facility without charge when the company has no scheduled events. Polly used the facility 10 days during the year. Her use had a rental value of $1,000.

e. The company is in the household moving business. Employees are allowed to ship goods without charge whenever there is excess space on a truck. Polly purchased a dining room suite for her daughter. Company trucks delivered the furniture to the daughter. Normal freight charges would have been $750.

f. The company has a storage facility for household goods. Officers are allowed a 20% discount on charges for storing their goods. All other employees are allowed a 10% discount. Polly's discounts for the year totaled $900.

48. **LO.2** George is a U.S. citizen who is employed by Hawk Enterprises, a global company. Beginning on June 1, 2016, George began working in London. He worked there until January 31, 2017, when he transferred to Paris. He worked in

Paris the remainder of 2017. His salary for the first five months of 2016 was $100,000, and it was earned in the United States. His salary for the remainder of 2016 was $175,000, and it was earned in London. George's 2017 salary from Hawk was $300,000, with part being earned in London and part being earned in Paris. What is George's gross income in 2016 and 2017? (Assume that the 2017 indexed amount is the same as the 2016 indexed amount.)

49. **LO.2, 3** Determine Hazel's gross income from the following receipts for the year:

Gain on sale of Augusta County bonds	$800
Interest on U.S. government savings bonds	400
Interest on state income tax refund	200
Interest on Augusta County bonds	700
Patronage dividend from Potato Growers Cooperative	350

The patronage dividend was received in March of the current year for amounts paid for her (nondeductible) garden and lawn supplies.

50. **LO.2** In January 2016, Ezra purchased 2,000 shares of Gold Utility Mutual Fund for $20,000. In June, Ezra received an additional 100 shares as a dividend, in lieu of receiving $1,000 in cash dividends. In December, the company declared a two-for-one stock split. Ezra received an additional 2,100 shares, but there was no option to receive cash. At the time of the stock dividend in December and at the end of the year, the fund shares were trading for $5 per share. Also, at the end of the year, the fund offered to buy outstanding shares for $4.50. Ezra did not sell any shares during the year.

   a. What is Ezra's gross income from the 100 shares received in June?

   b. What is Ezra's gross income from the receipt of the 2,100 shares as a two-for-one stock split in December?

   c. Should Ezra be required to recognize gross income in 2016 even though the fair market value of his investment at the end of the year was less than the fair market value at the beginning of the year? Explain.

Decision Making   51. **LO.2** Tonya, who lives in California, inherited a $100,000 State of California bond in 2016. Her marginal Federal tax rate is 35%, and her marginal state tax rate is 5%. The California bond pays 3.3% interest, which is not subject to California income tax. She can purchase a corporate bond of comparable risk that will yield 5.2% or a U.S. government bond that pays 4.6% interest. Which investment will provide the greatest after-tax yield?

Decision Making   52. **LO.2** Lynn Swartz's husband died three years ago. Her parents have an income of
Communications   over $200,000 a year and want to ensure that funds will be available for the education of Lynn's 8-year-old son, Eric. Lynn is currently earning $45,000 a year. Lynn's parents have suggested that they start a savings account for Eric. They have calculated that if they invest $4,000 a year for the next 8 years, at the end of 10 years, sufficient funds will be available for Eric's college expenses. Lynn realizes that the tax treatment of the investments could significantly affect the amount of funds available for Eric's education. She asked you to write a letter to her advising about options available to her parents and to her for Eric's college education. Lynn's address is 100 Myrtle Cove, Fairfield, CT 06824.

53. **LO.2** Starting in 2005, Chuck and Luane have been purchasing Series EE bonds in their name to use for the higher education of their daughter Susie, who currently is age 18. During the year, they cash in $12,000 of the bonds to use for freshman year tuition, fees, and room and board. Of this amount, $5,000 represents interest. Of the $12,000, $8,000 is used for tuition and fees, and $4,000 is used for room and board. Chuck and Luane's AGI, before the educational savings bond exclusion, is $120,000. Review § 135, and answer the following questions.

   a. Determine the tax consequences for Chuck and Luane, who will file a joint return, and for Susie.

b. Assume that Chuck and Luane purchased the bonds in Susie's name. Determine the tax consequences for Chuck and Luane and for Susie.

c. How would your answer to (a) change if Chuck and Luane filed separate returns?

54. **LO.2** Albert established a qualified tuition program for each of his twins, Kim and Jim. He started each fund with $20,000 when the children were 5 years old. Albert made no further contributions to his children's plans. Thirteen years later, both children have graduated from high school. Kim's fund has accumulated to $45,000, while Jim's has accumulated to $42,000. Kim decides to attend a state university, which will cost $60,000 for four years (tuition, fees, room and board, and books). Jim decides to go to work instead of going to college. During the current year, $7,500 is used from Kim's plan to pay the cost of her first semester in college. Because Jim is not going to college now or in the future, Albert withdraws the $42,000 plan balance and gives it to Jim to start his new life after high school.

a. During the period since the plans were established, should Albert or the twins have been including the annual plan earnings in gross income? Explain.

b. What are the tax consequences to Kim and Albert of the $7,500 being used for the first semester's higher education costs?

c. Because of her participation in the qualified tuition program, Kim received a 10% reduction in tuition charges; so less than $7,500 was withdrawn from her account. Is either Albert or Kim required to include the value of this discount in gross income? Explain.

d. What are the tax consequences to Albert and Jim of Jim's qualified tuition program being closed?

55. **LO.3** How does the tax benefit rule apply in the following cases?

a. In 2014, the Orange Furniture Store, an accrual method taxpayer, sold furniture on credit for $1,000 to Sammy. The cost of the furniture was $600. In 2015, Orange took a bad debt deduction for the $1,000. In 2016, Sammy inherited some money and paid Orange the $1,000 he owed. Orange was in the 35% marginal tax bracket in 2014, the 15% marginal tax bracket in 2015, and the 35% marginal tax bracket in 2016.

b. In 2015, Marvin, a cash basis taxpayer, took a $2,000 itemized deduction for state income taxes paid. This increased his itemized deductions to a total that was $800 more than the standard deduction. In 2015, Marvin received a $1,600 refund when he filed his 2015 state income tax return. Marvin was in the 15% marginal tax bracket in 2015, but was in the 35% marginal tax bracket in 2016.

c. In 2015, Barb, a cash basis taxpayer, was in an accident and incurred $8,000 in medical expenses, which she claimed as an itemized deduction for medical expenses. Because of the 10%-of-AGI reduction, the expense reduced her taxable income by only $3,000. In 2016, Barb successfully sued the person who caused the physical injury and collected $8,000 to reimburse her for the cost of her medical expenses. Barb was in the 15% marginal tax bracket in both 2015 and 2016.

56. **LO.4, 5** Fran, who is in the 35% tax bracket, recently collected $100,000 on a life insurance policy she carried on her father. She currently owes $120,000 on her personal residence and $120,000 on business property. National Bank holds the mortgage on both pieces of property and has agreed to accept $100,000 in complete satisfaction of either mortgage. The interest rate on the mortgages is 8%, and both mortgages are payable over 10 years. What would be the tax consequences of each of the following alternatives assuming that Fran currently deducts the mortgage interest on her tax return?

Decision Making

a. Retire the mortgage on the residence.

b. Retire the mortgage on the business property.

Which alternative should Fran select?

57. **LO.4** Vic, who was experiencing financial difficulties, was able to adjust his debts as follows:

    a. Vic is an attorney. Vic owed his uncle $25,000. The uncle told Vic that if he serves as the executor of the uncle's estate, Vic's debt will be canceled in the uncle's will.

    b. Vic borrowed $80,000 from First Bank. The debt was secured by land that Vic purchased for $100,000. Vic was unable to pay, and the bank foreclosed when the liability was $80,000, which was also the fair market value of the property.

    c. The Land Company, which had sold land to Vic for $80,000, reduced the mortgage on the land by $12,000.

    Determine the tax consequences to Vic.

Cumulative Problems

Tax Return Problem

TAX SOFTWARE

58. Alfred E. Old and Beulah A. Crane, each age 42, married on September 7, 2013. Alfred and Beulah will file a joint return for 2015. Alfred's Social Security number is 111-11-1112. Beulah's Social Security number is 123-45-6789, and she adopted "Old" as her married name. They live at 211 Brickstone Drive, Atlanta, GA 30304.

    Alfred was divorced from Sarah Old in March 2013. Under the divorce agreement, Alfred is to pay Sarah $1,250 per month for the next 10 years or until Sarah's death, whichever occurs first. Alfred pays Sarah $15,000 in 2015. In addition, in January 2015, Alfred pays Sarah $50,000, which is designated as being for her share of the marital property. Also, Alfred is responsible for all prior years' income taxes. Sarah's Social Security number is 123-45-6788.

    Alfred's salary for 2015 is $150,000, and his employer, Cherry, Inc. (Federal I.D. No. 98-7654321), provides him with group term life insurance equal to twice his annual salary. His employer withheld $24,900 for Federal income taxes and $8,000 for state income taxes. The proper amounts were withheld for FICA taxes.

    Beulah recently graduated from law school and is employed by Legal Aid Society, Inc. (Federal I.D. No. 11-1111111), as a public defender. She receives a salary of $40,000 in 2015. Her employer withheld $7,500 for Federal income taxes and $2,400 for state income taxes. The proper amounts were withheld for FICA taxes.

    Beulah has $2,500 in qualified dividends on Yellow Corporation stock she inherited. Alfred and Beulah receive a $1,900 refund on their 2014 state income taxes. They itemized deductions on their 2014 Federal income tax return (total of $15,000). Alfred and Beulah pay $4,500 interest and $1,450 property taxes on their personal residence in 2015. Their charitable contributions total $2,400 (all to their church). They paid sales taxes of $1,400, for which they maintain the receipts. Both spouses had health insurance for all months of 2015 and do not want to contribute to the Presidential Election Campaign.

    Compute the Olds' net tax payable (or refund due) for 2015. If you use tax forms for your solution, you will need Form 1040 and Schedules A and B. Suggested software: H&R BLOCK Tax Software.

Tax Computation Problem
Decision Making
Communications

59. Martin S. Albert (Social Security number 111-11-1111) is 39 years old and is married to Michele R. Albert (Social Security number 123-45-6789). The Alberts live at 512 Ferry Road, Newport News, VA 23601. They file a joint return and have two dependent children, Charlene, age 17, and Jordan, age 18. Charlene's Social Security number is 123-45-6788, and Jordan's Social Security number is 123-45-6787. In 2016, Martin and Michele had the following transactions:

    a. Martin received $120,000 in salary from Red Steel Corporation, where he is a construction engineer. Withholding for Federal income tax was $10,750. The amounts withheld for FICA taxes were as follows: $7,049 ($113,700 × 6.2%) for

Social Security and $1,740 ($120,000 × 1.45%) for Medicare. Martin worked in Mexico from January 1, 2015, until February 15, 2016. His $120,000 salary for 2016 includes $18,000 he earned for January and one-half of February 2016 while working in Mexico.

b. Martin and Michele received $800 in qualified dividends on Green, Inc. stock and $400 interest on Montgomery County (Virginia) school bonds.

c. Martin received $2,300 interest from a Bahamian bank account.

d. Michele received 50 shares of Applegate Corporation common stock as a stock dividend. The shares had a fair market value of $2,500 at the time Michele received them, and she did not have the option of receiving cash.

e. Martin and Michele received a $1,200 refund on their 2015 Virginia income taxes. Their itemized deductions in 2015 totaled $14,000.

f. Martin paid $6,600 alimony to his former wife, Rose T. Morgan (Social Security number 123-45-6786).

g. Martin and Michele kept the receipts for their sales taxes paid of $1,100.

h. Martin and Michele's itemized deductions were as follows:

- State income tax paid and withheld totaled $5,100.

- Real estate taxes on their principal residence were $3,700.

- Mortgage interest on their principal residence was $2,500.

- Cash contributions to the church totaled $2,800.

Part 1—Tax Computation
Compute the Alberts's net tax payable (or refund due) for 2016.

Part 2—Tax Planning
The Alberts are considering buying another house. Their house mortgage payments would increase by $500 (to $1,500) per month, which includes a $250 increase in interest and a $100 increase in property tax. The Alberts would like to know how much the mortgage payments would increase net of any change in their income tax. Write a letter to the Alberts that contains your advice.

Research Problems

Note: Solutions to Research Problems can be prepared by using the Checkpoint® Student Edition online research product, which is available to accompany this text. It is also possible to prepare solutions to the Research Problems by using tax research materials found in a standard tax library.

THOMSON REUTERS
CHECKPOINT®
Student Edition

Research Problem 1. Murray reported to the Environmental Protection Agency that his employer was illegally dumping chemicals into a river. His charges were true, and Murray's employer was fined. In retaliation, Murray's employer fired him and made deliberate efforts to prevent Murray from obtaining other employment. Murray sued the employer, claiming that his reputation had been damaged. Murray won his lawsuit and received an award for "damages to his personal and professional reputation and for his mental suffering." Now he would like to know whether the award is taxable. He argues that he was awarded damages as a recovery of his human capital and that a recovery of capital is not income. Therefore, the Federal government does not have the power to tax the award.

Research Problem 2. The employees of the city of Greenville must make mandatory contributions to the city's postretirement health benefit plan. The employees' contributions are placed in a trust and are used exclusively for the employees' benefits. The employees believe that because they are required to make the contributions from their base salaries, the result should be the same as if the employer made the contribution and had reduced their salaries by the amount of the contributions. Therefore, the employees believe they should be permitted to exclude the payments from gross income. The employees have asked you to research the issue.

Research Problem 3. Your client, John Butler, is an avid Houston Astros fan. Last March at the Astros' home opener, as a result of a random drawing of those in attendance at the game, John won 300 Shipley Do-Nut coupons. Each coupon entitled him to a cup of coffee and a free doughnut or a dozen doughnut holes.

John used some of the coupons (approximately 20), but he found that eating so many doughnuts directly conflicted with his goal of losing weight. The unused coupons expired on January 1, 2016. Thus, John was surprised when he received a Form 1099 in February 2016 that valued his prize at $900. John would like to know whether the value of the doughnut coupons should be included in income and asks you to research his question. If you conclude that their value should be included in income, John also would like to know if he can reduce his gross income by including in income only the value of the coupons that he used. He has the unused coupons as documentation that neither he nor anyone else used them.

Research Problem 4. Aubrey Brown is a decorated veteran of the Vietnam War. As a result of his exposure to Agent Orange during the war, Aubrey developed lung cancer and is unable to work. He received $12,000 of Social Security disability payments in the current year. He reasons that the payments should be excluded from his gross income because the payments are compensation for the physical injury he suffered as a result of his service in the armed forces. Is Aubrey correct? Explain.

Partial list of research aids:
Rev.Rul. 77–318, 1977–2 C.B. 45.
Reimels v. Comm., 2006–1 USTC ¶50,147, 97 AFTR 2d 2006–820, 436 F.3d 344 (CA–2, 2006).

Research Problem 5. Your client works for a defense contractor and was assigned to work on a military base in Australia. As a condition of his employment, he was required to live in housing that was provided to military personnel. The housing provided was a condominium located in a civilian neighborhood that was 20 miles from the military base where he performed his services. The employer paid over $6,000 of rent while the employee was living there. Your client would like to know whether the value of the housing can be excluded from his gross income. He read an article that indicated that employees who are required to live in a "camp" in a foreign country can exclude the cost of the housing from gross income. What is the result of your research?

Internet
Activity

Use the tax resources of the Internet to address the following questions. Do not restrict your search to the Web, but include a review of newsgroups and general reference materials, practitioner sites and resources, primary sources of the tax law, chat rooms and discussion groups, and other opportunities.

Research Problem 6. Employers often use the Internet as a means of attracting applications from potential employees. Locate an Internet site offering employment opportunities, ideally one provided by a well-known corporation. How does the employer promote its fringe benefit and cafeteria plan packages? Compare and contrast several such sites.

Research Problem 7. One income exclusion that some states allow that the federal government does not is for lottery winnings. Does your state have an exclusion for lottery winnings? If so, how does it work? Why do you think a state might allow winnings from its own state lottery to be excluded from state income taxes?

Roger CPA Review Questions

1. In 2014 Randall suffered bodily injury while at work. On his 2014 tax return, Randall deducted related medical expenses of $10,000 and $5,000 in 2015. In 2016, Randall won a workers' compensation claim and prevailed in an injury lawsuit, both in connection with the 2014 injury. Randall received the following in 2016 as settlement:

Punitive damages	$150,000
Workers' compensation	50,000
Reimbursement for medical expenses	25,000
Compensation for emotional distress caused by the injury	15,000

What amount of the settlement should be excluded from Randall's 2016 gross income?

a. $ 75,000   c. $ 90,000
b. $ 60,000   d. $165,000

2. The following pertain to Joyce in 2016:

Medical insurance premiums paid by employer	$4,800
Teacher of the Year Award, in the form of gift cards redeemable at local businesses	500
Jewelry box, received from employer for 25 years of service (FMV)	100
2016 holiday bonus awarded in December 2016, to be paid in January 2017	250

What total amount from the above may be excluded from Joyce's 2016 gross income?

a. $5,650   c. $5,150
b. $350   d. $850

3. Pierce, a married individual, received the following in 2016:

Workers' compensation award	$25,000
W–2 income	20,000
Unemployment compensation	4,800
Damages awarded for emotional distress experienced as a result of workplace bodily injury	10,000

Considering only the above, what is Pierce's 2016 gross income?

a. $49,800   c. $30,000
b. $34,800   d. $24,800

4. Norbert works in a beauty salon. He receives a 50% employee discount for salon services. In 2016, he used his discount to buy $1,000 of services with a fair market value of $2,000. As a result of these bargain purchases, how much should Norbert include in 2016 gross income?

a. $1,000   c. $2,000
b. $600   d. $0

5. Cole, a 48-year-old married individual, received the following in 2016:

S corporation stock dividends	$5,000
Interest earned on federal Treasury bills	1,000
Interest earned on municipal bonds	2,500
Interest earned on state income tax refund	50
Interest earned on Series EE savings bonds, used to help pay for room and board for dependent in college	1,500
Common stock property dividend (FMV)	3,000

In addition, Cole spent $500 on lottery scratch-off cards in 2016. All of the cards were losers except for one, from which Cole won $1,000.

Given these facts, what total amount from the above should be included in gross income on Cole's 2016 tax return?

a. $ 4,550

b. $ 6,550

c. $11,050

d. $11,550

6. Manish is a student who began working part-time as a restaurant waiter in October of 2016. He earned the following tips in 2016, with each month's tips reported in a schedule submitted to the restaurant's management by the tenth of the following month:

October	$400
November	215
December	150

In addition, Manish received a scholarship in 2016 which provided $5,000 for tuition, $5,000 for room and board, $1,000 for travel to study abroad, and $1,000 for books.

What total amount from the above should be included in Manish's 2016 gross income?

a. $5,765

b. $5,615

c. $6,615

d. $6,765

PART 3

DEDUCTIONS

Part 3 presents the deduction component of the basic tax model. Deductions are classified as business versus nonbusiness, "for" AGI versus "from" AGI, employee versus employer, active versus passive, and reimbursed versus unreimbursed. The effect of each of these classifications is analyzed. The presentation includes not only the deductions that are permitted, but also limitations and disallowances associated with deductions. A separate chapter examines the special tax treatment accorded to losses resulting from investment activities.

CHAPTER 6

Deductions and Losses: In General

LEARNING OBJECTIVES: *After completing Chapter 6, you should be able to:*

LO.1 Differentiate between deductions *for* and *from* adjusted gross income and describe the relevance of the differentiation.

LO.2 Describe the cash and accrual methods of accounting with emphasis on the deduction aspects.

LO.3 Apply the Internal Revenue Code deduction disallowance provisions associated with the following: public policy limitations, political activities, excessive executive compensation, investigation of

business opportunities, hobby losses, vacation home rentals, payment of others' expenses, personal expenditures, capital expenditures, related-party transactions, and expenses related to tax-exempt income.

LO.4 Identify tax planning opportunities for maximizing deductions and minimizing the disallowance of deductions.

CHAPTER OUTLINE

THE BIG PICTURE

CALCULATION OF DEDUCTIBLE EXPENSES

Dr. Cliff Payne determines that his deductible expenses associated with his dental practice are as follows:

Salaries including FICA ($5,000 are unpaid at year-end)	$120,000
Building rent	24,000
Depreciation of dental equipment and office furnishings and equipment	52,000
Insurance (malpractice and of dental equipment and office furnishings and equipment)	22,000
Dental supplies	16,000
Office supplies	3,000
Investigation expenses	6,000
Contribution to the State Senate campaign fund of Tom Smith	1,000
Contribution to the State Senate campaign fund of Virginia White	1,000
Legal expenses associated with patient lawsuit	4,000
Fine imposed by city for improper disposal of medical waste	3,000
Dues paid to The Dental Society	10,000
Draw by Dr. Payne for living expenses ($5,000 monthly)	60,000

Has Dr. Payne correctly calculated the business expenses for his dental practice?

Read the chapter and formulate your response.

FRAMEWORK 1040 **Tax Formula for Individuals**

This chapter covers the boldfaced portions of the Tax Formula for Individuals that was introduced in Concept Summary 3.1 on p. 3-3. Below those portions are the sections of Form 1040 where the results are reported.

Income *(broadly defined)*	$xx,xxx
Less: Exclusions	(x,xxx)
Gross income..	$xx,xxx
Less: Deductions *for* adjusted gross income..	(x,xxx)

FORM 1040 (p. 1)

12	Business income or (loss). Attach Schedule C or C-EZ	

Adjusted gross income...	$xx,xxx
Less: The greater of total **itemized deductions** *or* **the standard deduction**............................	(x,xxx)

FORM 1040 (p. 2)

40	**Itemized deductions** (from Schedule A) **or** your **standard deduction**	

Personal and dependency exemptions	(x,xxx)
Taxable income	$xx,xxx
Tax on taxable income *(see Tax Tables or Tax Rate Schedules)*................................	$ x,xxx
Less: Tax credits *(including income taxes withheld and prepaid)*	(xxx)
Tax due (or refund)	$ xxx

The tax law has an all-inclusive definition of income; that is, income from whatever source derived is includible in gross income. Income cannot be excluded unless there is a specific statement to that effect in the Internal Revenue Code.

Similarly, deductions are disallowed unless a specific provision in the tax law permits them. The inclusive definition of income and the exclusive definition of deductions may not seem fair to taxpayers, but it is the structure of the tax law.

The courts have held that whether and to what extent deductions are allowed depends on legislative grace.[1] In other words, any exclusions from income and all deductions are gifts from Congress.

6-1 CLASSIFICATION OF DEDUCTIBLE EXPENSES

It is important to classify deductible expenses as **deductions *for* adjusted gross income** (AGI) or **deductions *from* adjusted gross income**. Deductions *for* AGI can be claimed whether or not the taxpayer itemizes. Deductions *from* AGI result in a tax benefit only if they exceed the taxpayer's standard deduction. If itemized deductions (*from* AGI) are less than the standard deduction, they provide no tax benefit. As Example 1 illustrates, whether a deduction is classified as *for* AGI or *from* AGI can affect the benefit the taxpayer receives from the deduction.

---

[1]*New Colonial Ice Co. v. Helvering*, 4 USTC ¶1292, 13 AFTR 1180, 54 S.Ct. 788 (USSC, 1934).

Steve is a self-employed CPA. Ralph is one of Steve's employees. During the year, Steve and Ralph incur the following expenses:

	Steve	Ralph
Dues to American Institute of CPAs and State Society of CPAs	$ 400	$ 300
Subscriptions to professional journals	500	200
Registration fees for tax conferences	800	800
	$1,700	$1,300

Steve does not reimburse any of his employees for dues, subscriptions, or educational programs.

Steve's expenses are classified as a deduction *for* AGI because they are considered business expenses since he is a sole proprietor. Therefore, he can deduct the $1,700 on his Federal income tax return. Ralph's unreimbursed employee business expenses are classified as deductions *from* AGI.

Ralph will be able to benefit from the $1,300 of expenses on his Federal income tax return only if his itemized deductions exceed his standard deduction. If, instead, he takes the standard deduction, the $1,300 of expenses will have no effect on the calculation of his taxable income. Even if Ralph does itemize deductions, he still may not benefit from the deduction because of the 2%-of-AGI phaseout rule for certain itemized deductions.

Concept Summary 6.4 later in the chapter shows the classification of deductions as deductions *for* AGI or as deductions *from* AGI.

It is important to understand that deductions *for* AGI may directly affect the *amount* of itemized deductions. The impact arises because many itemized deductions are limited to amounts in excess of specified percentages of AGI. Examples of such itemized deductions are medical expenses; personal casualty losses; and, as shown in Example 1, unreimbursed employee expenses.

Tina, age 36, earns a salary of $80,000 and has no other income. She itemizes her deductions during 2016. Unreimbursed medical expenses for the year are $12,000. Tina's medical expense deduction is $4,000, as computed below. Alternatively, assume that Tina receives a $10,000 bonus from her employer in 2016. Her AGI would then be $90,000 ($80,000 + $10,000), and her medical expense is reduced by $1,000 to $3,000.

	No Bonus	Bonus
Qualified medical expenses	$12,000	$12,000
Reduction: AGI × 10%	(8,000)	(9,000)
Deductible medical expenses	$ 4,000	$ 3,000

When Tina's income increased by $10,000, this reduced her medical expense deduction; so the total effect on taxable income is an increase of $11,000.[2]

6-1a **Classifying Deductions**

It is important to understand that two key issues must be resolved for any potential deduction. First, it must be determined whether the item is deductible, as discussed in text Section 6-1b. If the item is deductible, then the second issue is to determine if the deduction is classified as *for* AGI or *from* AGI. To understand how deductions of individual taxpayers are classified, it is necessary to examine the role of § 62. The purpose of § 62 is to classify various deductions as deductions *for* AGI. It does not provide the statutory authority for taking the deduction.

If a deduction is not listed in § 62, it is an itemized deduction, not a deduction *for* AGI. Exhibit 6.1 provides a partial list of the items classified as deductions *for* AGI by § 62.

---

[2]Example 4 in Chapter 3 illustrates this same point. See Chapter 10 for additional discussion of medical expenses.

EXHIBIT 6.1	Common Deductions *for* Adjusted Gross Income	
Deduction		**Chapter**
Alimony payments		4
Expenses attributable to property held for the production of rents and royalties		6
Expenses attributable to a trade or business		9
Employee business expenses		9
Moving expenses		9
Qualified tuition and related expenses		9
Professional development and supplies (up to $250) for elementary and secondary school teachers		9
Student loan interest		9 and 10
Contributions to retirement plans		9 and 19
Medical insurance premiums paid by a self-employed taxpayer		10
Self-employment taxes		13
Losses on the sale or exchange of property		14 and 16
Penalty on premature withdrawal of funds from time savings accounts		19

6-1b Authority for Deductions

The specific authority for deductions is provided in many different Code sections. However, two of the most important are § 212 and § 162. To determine the proper authority for claiming a deduction, first determine what type of activity the expenditure relates to. All activities can be divided into one of the following mutually exclusive categories:

1. Investment/production of income (§ 212)
2. Trade or business (§ 162)
3. Personal (various sections)

For example, are legal expenses deductible? To make that determination, first determine whether the legal expense relates to an investment or a trade or business or to personal activity.

Section 212 Expenses

Section 212 allows deductions for ordinary and necessary expenses paid or incurred for the following:

- The production or collection of income.
- The management, conservation, or maintenance of property held for the production of income.
- Expenses paid in connection with the determination, collection, or refund of any tax.

Section 212 expenses may be *for* AGI or *from* AGI. Common examples of deductions *for* AGI are expenses related to rent and royalty income (reported on Schedule E) and professional fees paid to determine tax liability for a sole proprietor (reported on Schedule C), a farmer (Schedule F), or one that has rent or royalties (Schedule E).

All other § 212 expenses are itemized deductions (deductions *from* AGI). For example, investment-related expenses (e.g., safe deposit box rentals) are deductible as itemized deductions attributable to the production of investment income.[3]

Section 162 Trade or Business Expenses

Section 162(a) permits a deduction for all ordinary and necessary expenses paid or incurred in carrying on a trade or business. These include reasonable salaries paid for services, expenses for the use of business property, and one-half of self-employment taxes paid (see Chapter 13). Such expenses are deducted *for* AGI.

---

[3]§ 62(a)(4) and Reg. § 1.212–1(g).

It is sometimes difficult to determine whether an expenditure is deductible as a trade or business expense. The term *trade or business* is not defined in the Code or Regulations, and the courts have not provided a satisfactory definition. It is usually necessary to ask one or more of the following questions to determine whether an item qualifies as a trade or business expense:

- Was the use of the particular item related to a business activity? For example, if funds are borrowed for use in a business, the interest is deductible as a business expense.
- Was the expenditure incurred with the intent to realize a profit or to produce income? For example, expenses in excess of the income from raising horses are not deductible if the activity is classified as a personal hobby rather than a trade or business.
- Were the taxpayer's operation and management activities extensive enough to indicate the carrying on of a trade or business?

Section 162 *excludes* the following items from classification as trade or business expenses:

- Charitable contributions or gifts.
- Illegal bribes and kickbacks and certain treble damage payments.
- Fines and penalties.

[handwritten: Not business expense]

6-1c **Deduction Criteria for § 162 and § 212**

The terms **ordinary and necessary** are found in both § 162 and § 212. To be deductible, any trade or business expense must be "ordinary and necessary." In addition, compensation for services must be "reasonable" in amount.

Many expenses that are necessary may not be ordinary. Neither "ordinary" nor "necessary" is defined in the Code or Regulations. The courts have held that an expense is *necessary* if a prudent businessperson would incur the same expense and the expense is expected to be appropriate and helpful in the taxpayer's business.[4] But as Example 3 shows, no deduction will be allowed unless the expense is also ordinary.

> Pat purchased a business that had just been adjudged bankrupt. Because the business had a poor financial rating, Pat wanted to restore its financial reputation. Consequently, he paid off some of the debts owed by the former owners that had been cancelled by the bankruptcy court.
>
> Because Pat had no legal obligation to make these payments, the U.S. Supreme Court found that he was trying to generate goodwill. Although the payments were necessary (i.e., appropriate and helpful), they were *not* ordinary and their deduction *was not* allowed.[5]

EXAMPLE 3

An expense is *ordinary* if it is normal, usual, or customary in the type of business conducted by the taxpayer and is not capital in nature.[6] However, an expense need not be recurring to be deductible as ordinary. For example, a business may be in a situation that is a very rare occurrence and incur an expense. If other businesses in a similar situation are likely to incur a similar expense, then the expense can be ordinary, even though it is not recurring.

> Albert engaged in a mail-order business. The post office judged that his advertisements were false and misleading. Under a fraud order, the post office stamped "fraudulent" on all letters addressed to Albert's business and returned them to the senders. Albert spent $30,000 on legal fees in an unsuccessful attempt to force the post office to stop.
>
> The legal fees (although not recurring) were ordinary business expenses because they were normal, usual, or customary in the circumstances.[7]

EXAMPLE 4

For § 212 deductions, the law requires that expenses bear a reasonable and proximate relationship to (1) the production or collection of income or to (2) the management, conservation, or maintenance of property held for the production of income.[8]

---

[4]*Welch v. Helvering,* 3 USTC ¶1164, 12 AFTR 1456, 54 S.Ct. 8 (USSC, 1933).

[5]*Welch v. Helvering,* cited in footnote 4.

[6]*Deputy v. DuPont,* 40–1 USTC ¶9161, 23 AFTR 808, 60 S.Ct. 363 (USSC, 1940).

[7]*Comm. v. Heininger,* 44–1 USTC ¶9109, 31 AFTR 783, 64 S.Ct. 249 (USSC, 1943).

[8]Reg. § 1.212–1(d).

EXAMPLE 5

Debbye is a retired pilot who owns a small portfolio of investments, including 10 shares of Robin, Inc., a publicly traded company, worth $1,000. She incurred $350 in travel expenses to attend the annual shareholders' meeting where she voted her 10 shares against the current management group.

No deduction is permitted because a 10-share investment is insignificant in value in relation to the travel expenses incurred.[9]

The Code refers to **reasonableness** solely with respect to salaries and other compensation for services.[10] But the courts have held that for any business expense to be ordinary and necessary, it must also be reasonable in amount.[11]

What constitutes reasonableness is a question of fact. If an expense is unreasonable, the excess amount is not allowed as a deduction. The question of reasonableness generally arises with respect to closely held corporations where there is no separation of ownership and management.

Transactions between the shareholders and the closely held company may result in the disallowance of deductions for excessive salaries and rent expense paid by the corporation to the shareholders. The courts will view an unusually large salary in light of all relevant circumstances and may find that the salary is reasonable despite its size.[12] If excessive payments for salaries and rents are closely related to the percentage of stock owned by the recipients, the payments are generally treated as dividends.[13] Because dividends are not deductible by the corporation, the disallowance results in an increase in the corporate taxable income. Deductions for reasonable salaries will not be disallowed *solely* because the corporation has paid insubstantial portions of its earnings as dividends to its shareholders.

EXAMPLE 6

Sparrow Corporation, a closely held corporation, is owned equally by Lupe, Carlos, and Ramon. The company has been highly profitable for several years and has not paid dividends. Lupe, Carlos, and Ramon are key officers of the company, and each receives a salary of $200,000. Salaries for similar positions in comparable companies average only $100,000.

Amounts paid to the owners in excess of $100,000 may be deemed unreasonable; if so, a total of $300,000 in salary deductions by Sparrow is disallowed. The disallowed amounts are treated as dividends rather than salary income to Lupe, Carlos, and Ramon because the payments are proportional to stock ownership. Salaries are deductible by the corporation, but dividends are not.

Note that the shareholders may benefit from this reclassification. Salaries would be taxed at ordinary income rates and are subject to payroll taxes. However, dividend income would be taxed at long-term capital rates if qualified.

6-1d Personal Expenses

Expenditures that are incurred in one's personal life are not deductible unless a specific Code section authorizes the deduction. These expenses, which generally are not related to the production of income, are usually deductions *from* AGI and, in some cases, must be less than (or greater than) a certain percentage of the AGI. Some of the more frequently encountered deductions in this category include the following:

- Contributions to qualified charitable organizations.
- Medical expenses.
- Certain state and local taxes.
- Personal casualty losses.
- Certain personal interest.
- Legal fees, but only if they relate to the determination of a tax liability.

Itemized deductions are discussed in detail in Chapter 10.

---

[9]*J. Raymond Dyer*, 36 T.C. 456 (1961).

[10]§ 162(a)(1).

[11]*Comm. v. Lincoln Electric Co.*, 49–2 USTC ¶9388, 38 AFTR 411, 176 F.2d 815 (CA–6, 1949).

[12]*Kennedy, Jr. v. Comm.*, 82–1 USTC ¶9186, 49 AFTR 2d 82–628, 671 F.2d 167 (CA–6, 1982), *rev'g* 72 T.C. 793 (1979).

[13]Reg. § 1.162–8.

6-1e **Business and Nonbusiness Losses**

Section 165 provides for a deduction for losses not compensated for by insurance. As a general rule, deductible losses of individual taxpayers are limited to those incurred in a trade or business or in a transaction entered into for profit. Individuals also are allowed to deduct losses that are the result of a casualty. Casualty losses include, but are not limited to, those caused by fire, storm, shipwreck, and theft. See Chapter 7 for a further discussion of this topic. A personal casualty loss is an itemized deduction (i.e., *from* AGI).

For profit + Tragedy

6-1f **Reporting Procedures**

All deductions *for* AGI are ultimately reported on page 1 of Form 1040. Most of the deductions *for* AGI originate on supporting schedules. Examples include business expenses (Schedule C); rent, royalty, partnership, and fiduciary deductions (Schedule E); and farming expenses (Schedule F). Other deductions *for* AGI, such as traditional IRAs, Keogh retirement plans, and alimony, are entered directly on page 1 of Form 1040.

Adjusted gross income appears on the last line of page 1 and again on the first line of page 2. The total of all itemized deductions, which is carried over from Schedule A, is then subtracted *from* AGI. After that, personal and dependency exemptions are deducted to arrive at taxable income.

As indicated in Exhibit 6.2, some Schedule A deductions originate on other forms. Form 1040 incorporates the deductible amounts for many expenses that are computed

---

EXHIBIT 6.2   Format of Form 1040

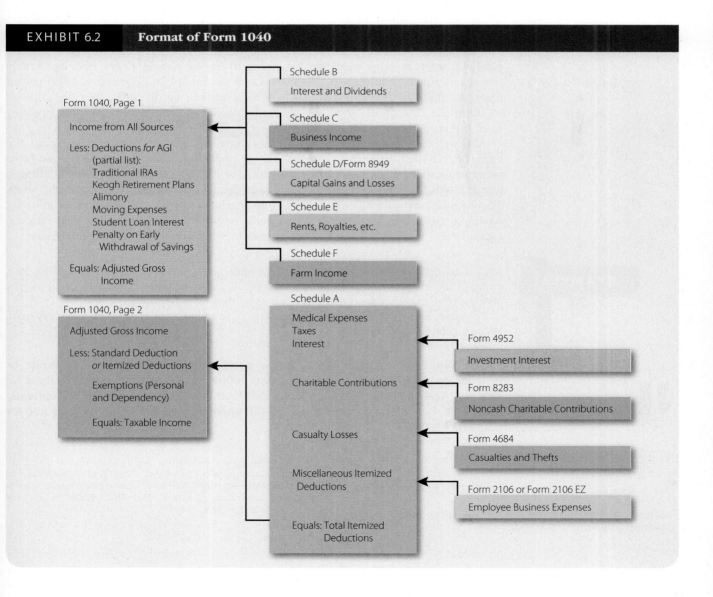

on other schedules and forms. Also, see Concept Summary 6.4 later in the chapter for the classification of deductions as *for* AGI or *from* AGI.

LO.2

Describe the cash and accrual methods of accounting with emphasis on the deduction aspects.

6-2 DEDUCTIONS AND LOSSES—TIMING OF EXPENSE RECOGNITION

6-2a Importance of Taxpayer's Method of Accounting

A taxpayer's <mark>accounting method</mark> is a major factor in determining taxable income. The method used determines when an item is includible in income and when an item is deductible on the tax return. Usually, the taxpayer's regular method of record keeping is used for income tax purposes.[14] The taxing authorities do not require uniformity among all taxpayers. They do require that the method used clearly reflect income and that items be handled consistently.[15] The most common methods of accounting are the cash method and the accrual method. If a taxpayer owns multiple businesses, it may be possible to use the cash method for some and the accrual method for others.

Throughout the portions of the Code dealing with deductions, the phrase *paid or incurred* is used. *Paid* refers to the cash basis taxpayer who gets a deduction only in the year of payment. *Incurred* concerns the accrual basis taxpayer who obtains the deduction in the year in which the liability for the expense becomes certain (refer to Chapter 4).

6-2b Cash Method Requirements

The expenses of cash basis taxpayers are deductible only when they are actually paid with cash or other property. Promising to pay or issuing a note does not satisfy the actually paid requirement.[16] However, the payment can be made with borrowed funds. At the time taxpayers charge expenses on their credit cards, they are allowed to claim the deduction. They are deemed to have simultaneously borrowed money from the credit card issuer and constructively paid the expenses.[17]

Although the cash basis taxpayer must have actually or constructively paid the expense, payment does not ensure a current deduction. Cash basis and accrual basis taxpayers cannot take a current deduction for capital expenditures except through amortization, depletion, or depreciation over the life (actual or statutory) of the asset. The Regulations set forth the general rule that an expenditure that creates an asset having a useful life that extends substantially beyond the end of the tax year must be capitalized.[18] Examples 7 and 8 illustrate how this rule applies to prepaid expenses.

EXAMPLE 7

John, a calendar year and cash basis taxpayer, rents property from Carl. On July 1, 2016, John pays $24,000 rent for the 24 months ending June 30, 2018. The prepaid rent extends 18 months after the close of the tax year—substantially beyond the year of payment.

Therefore, John must capitalize the prepaid rent and amortize the expense on a monthly basis. His deduction for 2016 is $6,000.

The Tax Court and the IRS took the position that an asset that will expire or be consumed by the end of the tax year following the year of payment must be prorated. The Ninth Circuit Court of Appeals held that such expenditures are currently deductible, however, and the Supreme Court apparently concurs (the one-year rule for prepaid expenses).[19]

---

[14]§ 446(a).

[15]§§ 446(b) and (e); Reg. § 1.446–1(a)(2).

[16]*Page v. Rhode Island Trust Co., Exr.*, 37–1 USTC ¶9138, 19 AFTR 105, 88 F.2d 192 (CA–1, 1937).

[17]Rev.Rul. 78–39, 1978–1 C.B. 73. See also Rev.Rul. 80–335, 1980–2 C.B. 170, which applies to pay-by-phone arrangements.

[18]Reg. § 1.461–1(a).

[19]*Zaninovich v. Comm.*, 80–1 USTC ¶9342, 45 AFTR 2d 80–1442, 616 F.2d 429 (CA–9, 1980), *rev'g* 69 T.C. 605 (1978). Cited by the Supreme Court in *Hillsboro National Bank v. Comm.*, 83–1 USTC ¶9229, 51 AFTR 2d 83–874, 103 S.Ct. 1134 (USSC, 1983).

Assume the same facts as in Example 7, except that John is required to pay only 12 months' rent in 2016. He pays $12,000 on July 1, 2016.

The entire $12,000 is deductible in 2016 as the benefit does not extend beyond the end of 2017.

The payment must be required, not a voluntary prepayment, to obtain the current deduction under the one-year rule.[20] The taxpayer must also demonstrate that allowing the current deduction will not result in a material distortion of income. Generally, the deduction will be allowed if the item is recurring or was made for a business purpose rather than to manipulate income.[21]

As Chapter 18 explains, not all taxpayers are allowed to use the cash method.[22] For example, in most cases, the taxpayer is required to use the accrual method for sales and cost of goods sold if inventories are an income-producing factor of the business.

6-2c Accrual Method Requirements

The period in which an accrual basis taxpayer can deduct an expense is determined by applying the *all events test* and the *economic performance test*. That is, a deduction cannot be claimed until (1) all of the events have occurred to create the taxpayer's liability and (2) the amount of the liability can be determined with reasonable accuracy. Once these requirements are satisfied, the deduction is permitted only if economic performance has occurred. The economic performance test is met only when the service, property, or use of property giving rise to the liability is actually performed for, provided to, or used by the taxpayer.[23]

Chris's entertainment business sponsored a jazz festival in a rented auditorium at a local college. His business is responsible for cleaning up after the festival, which took place on December 22, 2016, and reinstalling the auditorium seats. Because the college is closed over the Christmas holidays, the company hired by Chris to perform the work did not begin these activities until January 3, 2017. Chris's business cannot deduct its $1,200 labor cost until 2017, when the services are performed.

An exception to the economic performance requirements allows certain *recurring items* to be deducted if all of the following conditions are met:

- The item is recurring in nature and is treated consistently by the taxpayer.
- Either the accrued item is not material or accruing it results in better matching of income and expenses.
- All of the events have occurred that determine the fact of the liability, and the amount of the liability can be determined with reasonable accuracy.
- Economic performance occurs within a reasonable period (but not later than $8^1/_2$ months after the close of the taxable year).[24]

Exceptions to Economic Performance Rules

Rick, an accrual basis, calendar year taxpayer, entered into a monthly maintenance contract during the year. He makes a monthly accrual at the end of every month for this service and pays the fee sometime between the first and fifteenth of the following month when services are performed. The amount involved is immaterial, and all of the other tests are met.

The December 2016 accrual is deductible in 2016 even though the service is performed on January 12, 2017.

---

[20]*Bonaire Development Co. v. Comm.*, 82–2 USTC ¶9428, 50 AFTR 2d 82–5167, 679 F.2d 159 (CA–9, 1982).

[21]*Keller v. Comm.*, 84–1 USTC ¶9194, 53 AFTR 2d 84–663, 725 F.2d 1173 (CA–8, 1984), *aff'g* 79 T.C. 7 (1982).

[22]§ 448.

[23]§ 461(h).

[24]§ 461(h)(3)(A).

Exceptions to Economic Performance Rules

EXAMPLE 11

Rita, an accrual basis, calendar year taxpayer, shipped merchandise sold on December 30, 2016, via Greyhound Van Lines on January 3, 2017, and paid the freight charges at that time.

Because Rita reported the sale of the merchandise in 2016, the shipping charge should also be deductible in 2016. This procedure results in a better matching of income and expenses.

Reserves for estimated expenses (frequently employed for financial accounting purposes) generally are not allowed for tax purposes because the economic performance test cannot be satisfied.

EXAMPLE 12

Blackbird Airlines is required by Federal law to test its engines after 3,000 flying hours. Aircraft cannot return to flight until the tests have been conducted. An unrelated aircraft maintenance company does all of the company's tests for $1,500 per engine.

For financial reporting purposes, the company accrues an expense based upon $.50 per hour of flight and credits an allowance account. The actual amounts paid for maintenance are offset against the allowance account.

For tax purposes, the economic performance test is not satisfied until the work has been done. Therefore, the reserve method cannot be used for tax purposes.

6-2d Time Value of Tax Deductions

Cash basis taxpayers often have the ability to make early payments for their expenses at the end of the tax year. This may permit the payments to be deducted currently instead of in the following tax year. In view of the time value of money, a tax deduction this year may be worth more than the same deduction next year. Before employing this strategy, the taxpayer must consider what next year's expected income and tax rates will be and whether a cash-flow problem may develop from early payments. Thus, the time value of money as well as tax rate changes must be considered when an expense can be paid and deducted in either of two years.

EXAMPLE 13

Jena pledged $50,000 to her church's special building fund. She can make the contribution in December 2016 or January 2017. Jena is in the 35% tax bracket in 2016 and in the 28% bracket in 2017. She itemizes in both years. Assume that Jena's discount rate is 8%. If she takes the deduction in 2016, she saves $4,537 ($17,500 − $12,963) due to the decrease in the tax rates and the time value of money. See Table H-2 in Appendix H.

	2016	2017
Contribution	$50,000	$50,000
Tax bracket	× .35	× .28
Tax savings	$17,500	$14,000
Discounted @ 8%	× 1.0	× .9259
Savings in present value	$17,500	$12,963

If tax rates are changing between two years, there are several areas in which taxpayers may have discretion as to which year to make a payment to achieve tax savings. Examples include alimony payments (see Chapter 4), assets purchased to expense under § 179 (see Chapter 8), home mortgage interest, and charitable contributions (see Chapter 10). Always remember to consider the time value of money in the analysis.

6-3 DISALLOWANCE POSSIBILITIES

Apply the Internal Revenue Code deduction disallowance provisions associated with the following: public policy limitations, political activities, excessive executive compensation, investigation of business opportunities, hobby losses, vacation home rentals, payment of others' expenses, personal expenditures, capital expenditures, related-party transactions, and expenses related to tax-exempt income.

The tax law provides for the disallowance of certain types of expenses. Without specific restrictions in the tax law, taxpayers might attempt to deduct items that, in reality, are personal expenditures. For example, specific tax rules are provided to determine whether an expenditure is for trade or business purposes or is related to a personal hobby.

6-3a Public Policy Limitation

Certain disallowance provisions are a codification or extension of prior court decisions. For example, after the courts denied deductions for payments considered to be in violation of public policy, the tax law was changed to provide specific authority for the disallowance of these deductions.

Justification for Denying Deductions

The courts developed the principle that a payment in violation of public policy is not a necessary expense and is not deductible.[25] Although a bribe or fine may be helpful and may even contribute to the profitability of an activity, the courts held that to allow such expenses would be contrary to public policy. A deduction would, in effect, be indirectly subsidizing a taxpayer's wrongdoing.

Because tax law did not explain which actions violated public policy, the IRS and taxpayers had no clear guidance as to whether an expense was contrary to public policy. To solve these problems, Congress enacted legislation that attempts to better define the use of the public policy doctrine. Under the legislation, the following deductions are disallowed for certain specific types of expenditures that are considered contrary to public policy:

- Bribes and kickbacks, including those associated with Medicare or Medicaid. In the case of foreign bribes and kickbacks, only if the payments violate the U.S. Foreign Corrupt Practices Act of 1977.

- Fines and penalties paid to a government for violation of law.

The Big Picture

EXAMPLE
14

Refer to the facts of *The Big Picture* on p. 6-1. Dr. Payne had not instituted proper procedures for disposing of medical waste from his laboratory. During the current tax year, he was fined $3,000 by the city. Dr. Payne believes the fine should be deducted as an ordinary business expense.
  However, because the fine was due to a violation of public policy, the $3,000 is not deductible.

- Two-thirds of the treble damage payments made to claimants resulting from violation of the antitrust law.[26]

To be disallowed, the bribe or kickback must be illegal under either Federal or state law and must also subject the payor to a criminal penalty or the loss of a license or privilege to engage in a trade or business. For a bribe or kickback that is illegal under state law, a deduction is denied if the state law is generally enforced.

EXAMPLE
15

During the year, Keith, an insurance salesperson, paid $5,000 to Karen, a real estate broker. The payment represented 20% of the commissions Keith earned from customers referred by Karen. Under state law, the splitting of commissions by an insurance salesperson is an act of misconduct that could warrant a revocation of the salesperson's license.
  Keith's $5,000 payments to Karen are not deductible if the state law is generally enforced.

---

[25]*Tank Truck Rentals, Inc. v. Comm.*, 58–1 USTC ¶9366, 1 AFTR 2d 1154, 78 S.Ct. 507 (USSC, 1958).

[26]§§ 162(c), (f), and (g).

GLOBAL TAX ISSUES Overseas Gun Sales Result in Large Fines

The Foreign Corrupt Practices Act (FCPA) is intended to punish taxpayers who make illegal payments to foreign officials to obtain economic advantages. Not only are such payments (usually improperly recorded as business expenses) nondeductible for income tax purposes, but serious and consistent violations can lead to the imposition of fines. Severe consequences can result from violating the bribery provisions of the FCPA, as Smith & Wesson recently discovered.

Smith & Wesson is a Massachusetts-based firearms manufacturer that wanted to begin selling firearms in India, Pakistan, and other foreign countries. As a small player in this international market, company officials decided to provide gifts to government officials in these countries to encourage them to do business with Smith & Wesson. This turned out to be a costly mistake. Smith & Wesson had profits of only $100,000 from this scheme before it was uncovered, and in 2014, it agreed to pay the Securities and Exchange Commission fines of more than $2 million. Of course, the fines are not deductible because they are a violation of public policy.

Source: www.sec.gov/News/PressRelease/Detail/PressRelease/1370542384677#.

Legal Expenses Incurred in Defense of Civil or Criminal Penalties

To deduct legal expenses, the taxpayer must be able to show that the origin and character of the claim are directly related to a trade or business; an income-producing activity; or the determination, collection, or refund of a tax. Personal legal expenses are not deductible. Thus, legal fees incurred in connection with a criminal defense are deductible only if the crime is associated with the taxpayer's trade or business or income-producing activity.[27]

EXAMPLE 16

Debra, a financial officer of Blue Corporation, incurs legal expenses in connection with her defense in a criminal indictment for evasion of Blue's income taxes.

Debra may deduct her legal expenses because she is deemed to be in the trade or business of being an executive. The legal action impairs her ability to conduct this business activity.[28]

Deductible legal expenses associated with the following are deductible *for* AGI:

- Ordinary and necessary expenses incurred in connection with a trade or business.
- Ordinary and necessary expenses incurred in conjunction with rental or royalty property held for the production of income.

All other deductible legal expenses are deductible *from* AGI. For example, legal expenses generally are deductible *from* AGI if they are for fees for tax advice relative to the preparation of an individual's income tax return. Contrast this with the *for* AGI classification of legal fees for tax advice relative to the preparation of the portion of the tax return for a sole proprietor's trade or business (Schedule C) or an individual's rental or royalty income (Schedule E).

Expenses Relating to an Illegal Business

The usual expenses of operating an illegal business (e.g., a gambling operation) are deductible.[29] While allowing deductions for illegal activity may seem inappropriate, recall that the law taxes net income from a business operation, not gross revenue. However, § 162 disallows a deduction for fines, bribes to public officials, illegal kickbacks, and other illegal payments whether these payments are part of a legal or illegal business.

---

[27]*Comm. v. Tellier,* 66–1 USTC ¶9319, 17 AFTR 2d 633, 86 S.Ct. 1118 (USSC, 1966).

[28]Rev.Rul. 68–662, 1968–2 C.B. 69.

[29]*Comm. v. Sullivan,* 58–1 USTC ¶9368, 1 AFTR 2d 1158, 78 S.Ct. 512 (USSC, 1958).

EXAMPLE
17

Sam owns and operates an illegal gambling establishment. In connection with this activity, he has the following expenses during the year:

Rent	$ 60,000
Payoffs to the police	40,000
Depreciation on equipment	100,000
Wages	140,000
Interest	30,000
Criminal fines	50,000
Illegal kickbacks	10,000
Total	$430,000

All of the usual expenses (rent, depreciation, wages, and interest) are deductible; payoffs, fines, and kickbacks are not deductible. Of the $430,000 spent, $330,000 is deductible and $100,000 is not.

An exception applies to expenses incurred in illegal trafficking in drugs.[30] *Drug dealers* are not allowed a deduction for ordinary and necessary business expenses incurred in their business. In arriving at gross income from the business, however, dealers may reduce total sales by the cost of goods sold.[31]

ETHICS & EQUITY **Medical Marijuana: Trade or Business Activity or Illegal Operation?**

Cole England operates Herbal Medical Center in Sacramento, California, as a sole proprietorship. The distribution of marijuana for medical purposes is legal in California, as follows:

> Medical patients and their designated primary caregivers may legally possess and cultivate (but not distribute or sell) marijuana under Health and Safety Code 11362.5 (Prop 215) if they have a physician's recommendation or approval.

> This is Cole's first year of business operations. All of his patients have signed statements indicating that he

is their designated primary caregiver. He also has on file physician's recommendations for all marijuana that was provided to his patients. Tax information for this year is as follows:

Revenues	$200,000
Cost of goods sold	120,000
Other expenses	50,000

Cole reported $30,000 of net income on Schedule C this year for Herbal Medical Center. Is this position appropriate?

6-3b **Political Contributions and Lobbying Activities**

Generally, no business deduction is permitted for direct or indirect payments for political purposes.[32] Historically, the government has been reluctant to accord favorable tax treatment to business expenditures for political purposes. Allowing deductions might encourage abuses and enable businesses to have undue influence on the political process.

The Big Picture

EXAMPLE
18

Refer to the facts of *The Big Picture* on p. 6-1. Dr. Payne had made political contributions to the State Senate campaigns of Tom Smith and Virginia White. Dr. Payne made these contributions to encourage these senators to support a new bill that is beneficial to the state's dental profession. Therefore, he assumed that these would be deductible business expenses.

However, political contributions are not deductible, so he will receive no tax benefit from them.

---

[30]§ 280E.

[31]Reg. § 1.61–3(a). Gross income is defined as sales minus cost of goods sold. Thus, while § 280E prohibits any deductions for drug dealers, it does not modify the normal definition of gross income.

[32]§ 276.

Lobbying expenses incurred in attempting to influence state or Federal legislation or the actions of certain high-ranking public officials are not deductible.[33] The disallowance also applies to a pro rata portion of the membership dues of trade associations and other groups that are involved in lobbying activities.

The Big Picture

Refer to the facts of *The Big Picture* on p. 6-1. Dr. Payne had made contributions to The Dental Society, a trade association for dentists. The trade association estimates that 70% of its dues are allocated to lobbying activities. Thus, his deduction on Schedule C is limited to $3,000 ($10,000 × 30%).

There are three exceptions to the disallowance of lobbying expenses. First, an exception is provided for influencing local legislation (e.g., city and county governments). Second, the disallowance provision does not apply to activities devoted solely to monitoring legislation. Third, a *de minimis* exception is provided for annual in-house expenditures (lobbying expenses other than those paid to professional lobbyists or any portion of dues used by associations for lobbying) if such expenditures do not exceed $2,000. If the in-house expenditures exceed $2,000, none of the in-house expenditures can be deducted.

6-3c Excessive Executive Compensation

The deduction of executive compensation normally is subject to two limitations. As discussed earlier in this chapter, the compensation of shareholder-employees of closely held corporations is subject to the reasonableness requirement. The second limitation, the so-called millionaires' provision, applies to publicly held corporations (a corporation that has at least one class of stock registered under the Securities Exchange Act of 1934).[34]

The millionaires' provision does not limit the amount of compensation that can be paid to an employee. Instead, it limits the amount the employer can deduct for the taxable compensation of a covered executive to $1 million annually. Covered employees as defined by the SEC are the principal executive officer (PEO), the principal financial officer (PFO), and the three other most highly compensated executives.

This disallowance does not apply to commissions based on individual performance and performance-based compensation tied to overall company performance.

6-3d Investigation of a Business

Investigation expenses are expenses paid or incurred to determine the feasibility of entering a new business or expanding an existing business. They include such costs as travel, engineering and architectural surveys, marketing reports, and various legal and accounting services. How such expenses are treated for tax purposes depends on a number of variables, including the following:

- The current business, if any, of the taxpayer.
- The nature of the business being investigated.
- The extent to which the investigation has proceeded.
- Whether the acquisition actually takes place.

If the taxpayer is in a business that is the *same as or similar to* that being investigated, all investigation expenses are deductible in the year paid or incurred. The tax result is the same whether or not the taxpayer acquires the business being investigated.[35]

---

[33]§ 162(e).

[34]§ 162(m).

[35]§ 195. *York v. Comm.*, 58–2 USTC ¶9952, 2 AFTR 2d 6178, 261 F.2d 421 (CA–4, 1958).

TAX IN THE NEWS **Do Deduction Limits Affect Executive Compensation?**

Only $1 million of compensation can be deducted for the CEO, the CFO, and the three other highest-compensated executives of publicly traded companies. However, as noted previously, this limitation does not apply to *performance-based* compensation. One interesting issue is whether this exception is broad enough to allow publicly traded companies to pay substantial compensation to executives and still receive a tax deduction. The answer is clearly yes.

For example, in 2014, the CEO of Microsoft received a base salary of $918,917, which is just under the $1 million limitation. However, he received bonuses and stock incentives of over $80 million, which qualify to be deducted under the performance-based exception.

Fortune magazine recently reported that cash salaries account for only 10 percent of CEO compensation. The remaining 90 percent consists primarily of performance incentives. This indicates that the $1 million limit does have an influence on the base salary of CEOs. However, because of the performance-based exception, this tax law appears to have had very little impact on the escalation of executives' salaries.

Source: Based on Laura Lorenzetti, "Salaries for These CEOs Make Pay for Big Bank Bosses Look Modest," *Fortune,* September 2, 2015, **http://fortune.com/2015/09/02/pay-ratio-retail-ceos-banks/**.

The Big Picture

Refer to the facts of *The Big Picture* on p. 6-1. Dr. Payne believes that his administrative and business skills can be used to turn around dental practices whose revenues have been declining. He investigates Teeth Restoration LLC, a local dental practice that is for sale. Expenses paid to consultants and accountants as part of this investigation totaled $6,000. He determined that Teeth Restoration would not be a good investment, so he did not buy it.

The $6,000 spent to investigate this business is deductible as a business expense because Dr. Payne is already in the dental business. Investigating new business opportunities in one's current trade or business is an ordinary and necessary business expense.

EXAMPLE 20

When the taxpayer is *not* in a business that is the same as or similar to the one being investigated, the tax result depends on whether the new business is acquired. If the business is not acquired, all investigation expenses generally are nondeductible.[36]

Lynn, a retired merchant, incurs expenses in traveling from Rochester, New York, to California to investigate the feasibility of acquiring several auto care centers.

If no acquisition takes place, none of the expenses are deductible.

EXAMPLE 21

If the taxpayer is *not* in a business that is the same as or similar to the one being investigated and actually acquires the new business, the expenses must be capitalized as startup expenditures. Startup costs are not deductible under § 162 because they are incurred *before* a business begins rather than in the course of operating a trade or business. The first $5,000 of the expenses is immediately deducted. Any excess of expenses is amortized over a period of 180 months (15 years). In arriving at the $5,000 immediate deduction allowed, a dollar-for-dollar reduction must be made for those expenses in excess of $50,000.[37] An election can be made by the taxpayer not to deduct or amortize any portion of the startup costs. In that case, this intangible asset will remain on the balance sheet until the business is sold.

Complex Math Read again

Tina owns and operates 10 restaurants located in various cities throughout the Southeast. She travels to Atlanta to discuss the acquisition of an auto dealership. In addition, she incurs legal and accounting costs associated with the potential acquisition. After incurring total investigation costs of $52,000, she acquires the auto dealership on October 1, 2016.

Tina may immediately deduct $3,000 [$5,000 − ($52,000 − $50,000)] and amortize the balance of $49,000 ($52,000 − $3,000) over a period of 180 months. For calendar year 2016, therefore, Tina can deduct $3,817 [$3,000 + ($49,000 × 3/180)].

EXAMPLE 22

---

[36]Rev.Rul. 57–418, 1957–2 C.B. 143; *Morton Frank,* 20 T.C. 511 (1953); and *Dwight A. Ward,* 20 T.C. 332 (1953).

[37]§ 195(b).

Concept Summary 6.1 sets forth the tax rules applicable to the costs involved in investigating a business.

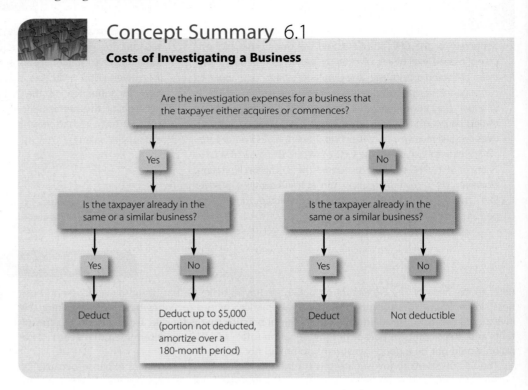

Concept Summary 6.1
Costs of Investigating a Business

Are the investigation expenses for a business that the taxpayer either acquires or commences?

Yes → Is the taxpayer already in the same or a similar business?

No → Is the taxpayer already in the same or a similar business?

(Yes) → Deduct

(No) → Deduct up to $5,000 (portion not deducted, amortize over a 180-month period)

(Yes) → Deduct

(No) → Not deductible

6-3e **Hobby Losses**

Business or investment expenses are deductible only if the taxpayer can show that the activity was entered into for the purpose of making a profit. Certain activities can have attributes that make it difficult to determine if the primary motivation for the activity is to make a profit or is for personal pleasure. Examples include raising horses and operating a farm used as a weekend residence. While personal losses are not deductible, losses attributable to profit-seeking activities may be deducted and used to offset a taxpayer's other income. Activities that have both personal and profit-seeking motives are classified as hobbies, and the tax law limits the deductibility of **hobby losses** .

The income and deductions from a hobby are reported separately on the tax return. Whether deductions related to a hobby generate a tax benefit, the revenue for the hobby is always reported as other income on page 1 of Form 1040. The reporting of deductions is discussed below.

General Rules

If an individual can show that an activity has been conducted with the intent to earn a profit, losses from the activity are fully deductible. The hobby loss rules apply only if the activity is not engaged in for profit. Hobby expenses are deductible only to the extent of hobby income.[38]

The Regulations stipulate that the following nine factors should be considered in determining whether an activity is profit-seeking or is a hobby:[39]

- Whether the activity is conducted in a businesslike manner.
- The expertise of the taxpayers or their advisers.
- The time and effort expended.

---

[38]§ 183(b)(2).

[39]Reg. §§ 1.183–2(b)(1) through (9).

TAX IN THE NEWS **IRS Doing Poorly in Policing Hobby Loss Deductions**

The Treasury Inspector General for Tax Administration (TIGTA) has issued a report on the number of taxpayers who file Schedule C of Form 1040 showing losses over several consecutive years. Many of the returns examined reported substantial income from other sources, and the majority of the individuals involved had their tax returns prepared by tax practitioners. By claiming the Schedule C losses, approximately 1.2 million taxpayers were able to save $2.8 billion in taxes for tax year 2005.

Because of the subjective nature of the hobby loss rules (i.e., whether a profit motive exists), these Schedule C losses

can be controlled only through thorough policing by the IRS. Unfortunately, the IRS has neither the time nor the resources to carry out the audit efforts required. The TIGTA report, therefore, suggests that § 183 be changed by legislation to establish a clear standard for determining whether an activity is a business or a hobby.

Source: "Significant Challenges Exist in Determining Whether Taxpayers with Schedule C Losses Are Engaged in Tax Abuse," *Treasury Inspector General for Tax Administration*, September 7, 2007 (Reference No. 2007-30-173).

- The expectation that the assets of the activity will appreciate in value.
- The taxpayer's previous success in conducting similar activities.
- The history of income or losses from the activity.
- The relationship of profits earned to losses incurred.
- The financial status of the taxpayer (e.g., if the taxpayer does not have substantial amounts of other income, this may indicate that the activity is engaged in for profit).
- Elements of personal pleasure or recreation in the activity.

The presence or absence of a factor is not by itself determinative of whether the activity is profit-seeking or is a hobby. Rather, the decision is a subjective one that is based on an analysis of the facts and circumstances. Exhibit 6.3 provides a list of the common activities that may be most likely to be treated as hobbies. Concept Summary 6.2 provides more details on the nature of the nine factors identified in the Regulations.

Presumptive Rule of § 183

The Code provides a rebuttable presumption that an activity is profit-seeking if the activity shows a profit in at least three of the previous five tax years.[40] If the activity involves horses, a profit in at least two of the previous seven tax years meets the presumptive rule. If these profitability tests are met, the activity is presumed to be a trade or business rather than a personal hobby. In this situation, the IRS bears the burden of proving that the activity is personal rather than trade or business-related. On the other hand, if the three-year test (two for horses) is not met, then the activity is presumed to be a hobby and the taxpayer has the burden to prove that it is profit-seeking.

Profitability Tests

EXHIBIT 6.3	**Common Activities Classified as Hobbies**	
Airplane Charter	Entertainers	Photography
Artists	Farming	Rentals
Auto Racing	Fishing	Stamp Collecting
Bowling	Gambling	Writing
Craft Sales	Horse Breeding	Yacht Charter
Direct Sales	Horse Racing	
Dog Breeding	Motorcross Racing	

Source: Internal Revenue Service Audit Technique Guide: IRC § 183: Activities Not Engaged in For Profit (Revised June 2009).

---

[40]§ 183(d).

Concept Summary 6.2

Common Questions from the IRS Concerning Hobbies/Business with Losses

Whether the activity is conducted in a businesslike manner.

- Is there a written business plan?
- Is there business insurance? Is it covered in the company name?
- Is there a business license to operate?

The expertise of the taxpayers or their advisers.

- Does the taxpayer have any relevant education?
- Did the taxpayer prepare for the activity by conducting research or an extensive study of its accepted business, economic, and scientific practices?

The time and effort expended.

- How many hours are spent on this activity per week? Per month? Per year? Per season?
- Who is involved with the day-to-day business operations?

The expectation that the assets of the activity will appreciate in value.

- Were the assets held prior to starting the business?
- Has anyone ever offered to buy any of the assets?

The taxpayer's previous success in conducting similar activities.

- In what other activities has the taxpayer had previous success?
- Was the business ultimately profitable?

The history of income or losses from the activity.

- Is there a trend toward profitability?
- Did the taxpayer change operating methods, adopt new techniques, or abandon nonprofitable methods in a manner consistent with intent to improve profitability?

The relationship of profits earned to losses incurred.

- Is this a highly speculative business?
- What amount of investment has the taxpayer made in the business?

The financial status of the taxpayer.

- Does the taxpayer have substantial income or capital (e.g., investments) from other sources?
- Are there other economic reasons for the taxpayer to be engaged in the activity (e.g., reduced property taxes for farmland, low-interest loans, or federal grants)?

Elements of personal pleasure or recreation in the activity.

- Are elements of fun or recreation generally associated with it by the taxpayer, by members of the taxpayer's family, or by the taxpayer's friends?
- If there are any personal benefits to being in this business, are they substantial?

Source: Internal Revenue Service Audit Technique Guide: IRC § 183: Activities Not Engaged in For Profit (Revised June 2009).

EXAMPLE 23

Camille and Walter are married taxpayers who enjoy a busy lifestyle. Camille, who is an executive for a large corporation, is paid a salary of $800,000. Walter is a collector of antiques. Several years ago he opened an antique shop in a local shopping center and spends most of his time buying and selling antiques. He occasionally earns a small profit from this activity but more frequently incurs substantial losses. If Walter's losses are business-related, they are fully deductible against Camille's salary income on a joint return. In resolving this issue, consider the following:

- Initially determine whether Walter's antique activity has met the three-out-of-five years profit test.
- If the presumption is not met, the activity may nevertheless qualify as a business if Walter can show that the intent is to engage in a profit-seeking activity. It is not necessary to show actual profits.
- Attempt to fit the operation within the nine criteria prescribed in the Regulations listed previously.

Determining the Amount of the Deduction

If an activity is deemed to be a hobby, the expenses are deductible only to the extent of the gross income from the hobby. These expenses must be deducted in the following order:

- Amounts deductible under other Code sections without regard to the nature of the activity, such as property taxes and home mortgage interest.
- Amounts deductible under other Code sections if the activity had been engaged in for profit, but only if those amounts do not affect adjusted basis. Examples include maintenance, utilities, and supplies.
- Amounts for depreciation, amortization, and depletion.[41]

The last two categories of deductions are deductible *from* AGI as itemized deductions to the extent they exceed 2 percent of AGI.[42] If the taxpayer uses the standard deduction rather than itemizing, the hobby loss deductions generate no tax benefit. Even if this is the case, the revenue from a hobby still must be reported on page 1 of Form 1040.

> **EXAMPLE**
> **24**
>
> Jim, the vice president of an oil company, has AGI of $80,000. He decides to pursue painting in his spare time. He uses a home studio comprising 10% of the home's square footage. During the current year, Jim incurs the following expenses:
>
> | | |
> |---|---:|
> | Frames | $ 1,800 |
> | Art supplies | 900 |
> | Fees paid to models | 4,000 |
> | Home studio expenses: | |
> | Total home property taxes | 2,000 |
> | Total home mortgage interest | 10,000 |
> | Total home maintenance and utilities | 4,600 |
> | Calculated depreciation on 10% of home | 500 |
>
> During the year, Jim sold paintings for a total of $8,660. If the activity is held to be a hobby, Jim is allowed deductions as follows:
>
> | | | |
> |---|---:|---:|
> | Gross income | | $ 8,660 |
> | Deduct: Taxes and interest (10% of $12,000) | | (1,200) |
> | Remainder | | $ 7,460. |
> | Deduct: Frames | $1,800 | |
> | Art supplies | 900 | |
> | Models' fees | 4,000 | |
> | Maintenance and utilities (10%) | 460 | (7,160) |
> | Remainder | | $ 300 |
> | Deduct: Depreciation ($500, but limited to $300) | | (300) |
> | Net income | | $ –0– |
>
> Jim includes the $8,660 of income in AGI, making his AGI $88,660. The taxes and interest are itemized deductions, deductible in full. The remaining $7,460 of expenses are reduced by 2% of his AGI (2% × $88,660 = $1,773), so the net deduction is $5,687. All of these deductions are reported as itemized deductions on Schedule A.
>
> Because the property taxes and home mortgage interest are deductible even without the hobby, the net effect is a $2,973 ($8,660 less $5,687) increase in taxable income.

6-3f **Rental of Vacation Homes**

Restrictions on the deductions allowed for part-year rentals of personal **vacation homes** were written into the law to prevent taxpayers from deducting essentially personal expenses as rental losses. Many taxpayers who own vacation homes use the property

---

[41]Reg. § 1.183–1(b)(1).

[42]Reg. § 1.67–1T(a)(1)(iv) and Rev.Rul. 75–14, 1975–1 C.B. 90.

for personal use during a portion of the year and rent the property at other times. For example, a summer cabin would be rented for 2 months per year, used for vacationing for 1 month, and left vacant the rest of the year. If the taxpayer could then deduct 11 months' depreciation, utilities, maintenance, etc., as rental expenses, resulting in a rental loss, the taxpayer would have converted into rental expenses personal expenses from the time the property was vacant. Section 280A eliminates this treatment by not allowing a loss for property that is not used primarily for rental purposes. Only a break-even situation is allowed; no losses can be deducted.

There are three possible tax treatments for residences used for both personal and rental purposes. The treatment depends upon the *relative time* the residence is used for personal purposes versus rental use. These rules are summarized in Concept Summary 6.3.

Concept Summary 6.3

Vacation/Rental Home

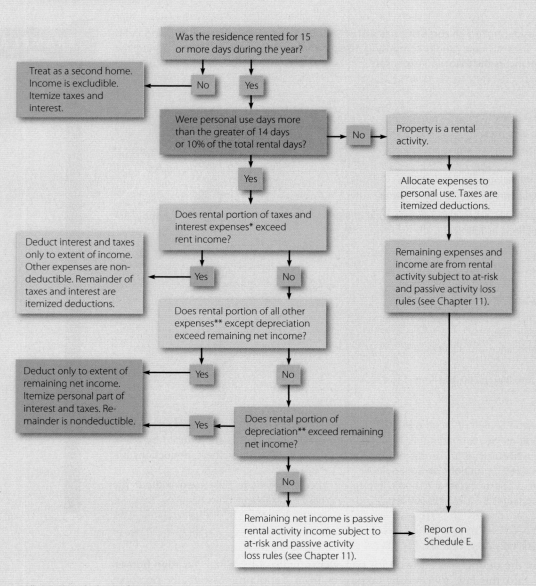

*Allocated on the basis of 365 (366 in a leap year) days (court decisions) or total days of use (IRS); see Examples 28 and 29.
**Allocated on the basis of total days of use.

Primarily Personal Use

If the residence is *rented* for *fewer than 15 days* in a year, it is treated as a personal residence. The rent income is excluded from gross income, and mortgage interest and real estate taxes are allowed as itemized deductions, as with any personal residence.[43] No other expenses (e.g., depreciation, utilities, and maintenance) are deductible.

EXAMPLE
25

Catherine owns a vacation cottage on the lake. During the current year, she rented it for $1,600 for two weeks, lived in it two months, and left it vacant the remainder of the year. The year's expenses amounted to $6,000 mortgage interest expense, $500 property taxes, $1,500 utilities and maintenance, and $2,400 depreciation.

Because the property was not rented for at least 15 days, the income is excluded, the mortgage interest and property tax expenses are itemized deductions, and the remaining expenses are nondeductible personal expenses.

Primarily Rental Use

If the residence is *rented* for 15 days or more in a year and is *not used* for personal purposes for more than the greater of (1) 14 days or (2) 10 percent of the total days rented, the residence is treated as rental property.[44] The expenses must be allocated between personal and rental days if there are any personal use days during the year. The real estate taxes allocated to the personal days are deductible as an itemized deduction. However, the mortgage interest allocated to the personal days cannot be deducted because the property is not a qualified residence. The deduction of the expenses allocated to rental days can exceed rent income and result in a rental loss. The loss may be deductible, subject to the at-risk and passive activity loss rules (discussed in Chapter 11).

EXAMPLE
26

Assume instead that Catherine in Example 25 used the cottage for 12 days and rented it for 48 days for $4,800. The threshold for personal use is 14 days—the greater of (1) 14 days or (2) 4.8 days (10% × 48 rental days). Because she rented the cottage for 15 days or more but did not use it for more than 14 days, the cottage is treated as rental property. The expenses must be allocated between personal and rental days.

	Percentage of Use	
	Rental 80%	Personal 20%
Income	$4,800	$ –0–
Expenses		
Mortgage interest ($6,000)	($4,800)	($1,200)
Property taxes ($500)	(400)	(100)
Utilities and maintenance ($1,500)	(1,200)	(300)
Depreciation ($2,400)	(1,920)	(480)
Total expenses	($8,320)	($2,080)
Rental loss	($3,520)	$ –0–

Catherine deducts the $3,520 rental loss *for* AGI on Schedule E (assuming that she satisfies the at-risk and passive activity loss rules, discussed in Chapter 11). She also has an itemized deduction for property taxes of $100 associated with the personal use. The mortgage interest of $1,200 associated with the personal use is not deductible as an itemized deduction because the cottage is not a qualified residence (qualified residence interest) for this purpose (see Chapter 10). The portion of utilities and maintenance and depreciation attributable to personal use is not deductible.

---

[43]§ 280A(g).

[44]§ 280A(d) and Prop.Reg. § 1.280A–3(c).

Personal/Rental Use

If the residence is rented for 15 days or more in a year *and* is used for personal purposes for more than the greater of (1) 14 days or (2) 10 percent of the total days rented, it is treated as a personal/rental use residence. The expenses must be allocated between personal days and rental days. Expenses are allowed only to the extent of rent income.[45]

EXAMPLE 27

Assume instead that Catherine in Example 25 rented the property for 30 days and lived in it for 30 days. The threshold for personal use is 14 days—the greater of (1) 14 days or (2) 3 days (10% × 30 rental days).

The residence is classified as personal/rental use property because she used it more than 14 days and rented it for 15 days or more. The expenses must be allocated between rental use and personal use, and the rental expenses are allowed only to the extent of rent income.

If a residence is classified as personal/rental use property, the expenses that are deductible anyway (e.g., real estate taxes and mortgage interest) must be deducted first. If a positive net income results, expenses, other than depreciation, that are deductible for rental property (e.g., maintenance, utilities, and insurance) are allowed next. Finally, if any positive balance remains, depreciation is allowed. Any disallowed expenses allocable to rental use are carried forward and used in future years subject to the same limitations. Note that these ordering rules for deductions are the same as for hobby expenses.

Expenses must be allocated between personal and rental days before the limits are applied. The courts have held that real estate taxes and mortgage interest, which accrue ratably over the year, are allocated on the basis of 365 days.[46] The IRS, however, disagrees and allocates real estate taxes and mortgage interest on the basis of total days of use.[47] Other expenses (e.g., utilities, maintenance, depreciation) are allocated on the basis of total days used.

Personal/Rental: IRS vs. Courts

EXAMPLE 28

Jason rents his vacation home for 60 days and lives in the home for 30 days. The property is classified as personal/rental because it is rented for 15 days or more, and personal use (30 days) is greater than 14 [greater of 14 days or 6 days (10% × 60 rental days)]. Jason's gross rent income is $10,000. For the entire year, the real estate taxes are $2,190, his mortgage interest expense is $10,220, utilities and maintenance expense equals $2,400, and depreciation is $9,000.

Using the IRS approach, these amounts are deductible in this specific order:

Days of use

Gross income	$10,000
Deduct: Taxes and interest ($^{60}/_{90}$ × $12,410$)	(8,273)
Remainder to apply to rental operating expenses and depreciation	$ 1,727
Deduct: Utilities and maintenance ($^{60}/_{90}$ × $2,400$)	(1,600)
Balance	$ 127
Deduct: Depreciation ($^{60}/_{90}$ × $9,000 = $6,000$ but limited to above balance)	(127)
Net rent income	$ –0–

The nonrental use portion of real estate taxes and mortgage interest ($4,137 in this case) is deductible if the taxpayer elects to itemize (see Chapter 10). The personal use portion of utilities, maintenance, and depreciation is not deductible in any case.

Jason has a carryover of $5,873 ($6,000 − $127) of the unused depreciation, which he may be able to deduct in future years. Also note that the basis of the property is only reduced by the $127 depreciation allowed because of the above limitation. (See Chapter 14 for a discussion of the reduction in basis for depreciation allowed or allowable.)

---

[45]A related issue is whether a taxpayer's primary residence is subject to the preceding rules if it is converted to rental property. If the vacation home rules apply, a taxpayer who converts a personal residence to rental property during the tax year, without any tax-avoidance motive, could have the allowable deductions limited to the rent income. To prevent this from occurring, the personal use days will not cause the property to be treated as personal/rental if once the rental period begins, the property is rented for at least 12 consecutive months at a fair rental price (a qualified rental period).

[46]*Bolton v. Comm.*, 82–2 USTC ¶9699, 51 AFTR 2d 83–305, 694 F.2d 556 (CA–9, 1982).

[47]Prop.Reg. § 1.280A–3(d)(4).

> **EXAMPLE**
> **29**
>
> Using the court's approach in allocating real estate taxes and mortgage interest, Jason, in Example 28, would have this result: *Pays of year* ↗
>
> | | |
> |---|---:|
> | Gross income | $10,000 |
> | Deduct: Taxes and interest ($60/365 \times \$12,410$) | (2,040) |
> | Remainder to apply to rental operating expenses and depreciation | $ 7,960 |
> | Deduct: Utilities and maintenance ($60/90 \times \$2,400$) | (1,600) |
> | Balance | $ 6,360 |
> | Deduct: Depreciation ($60/90 \times \$9,000$ but limited to above balance.) | (6,000) |
> | Net rent income | $ 360 |
>
> Jason can deduct $10,370 ($12,410 paid − $2,040 deducted as expense in computing net rent income) of personal use mortgage interest and real estate taxes as itemized deductions.

Note the contrasting results in Examples 28 and 29. The IRS's approach (Example 28) results in no rental gain or loss and an itemized deduction for real estate taxes and mortgage interest of $4,137. In Example 29, Jason has net rent income of $360 and $10,370 of itemized deductions. The court's approach decreases his taxable income by $10,010 ($10,370 itemized deductions less $360 net rent income). The IRS's approach reduces his taxable income by only $4,137.

IRS won't challenge in court, because they lose.

6-3g **Expenditures Incurred for Taxpayer's Benefit or Taxpayer's Obligation**

To be deductible, an expense must be incurred for the taxpayer's benefit or arise from the taxpayer's obligation. An individual cannot claim a tax deduction for the payment of the expenses of another individual.

> **EXAMPLE**
> **30**
>
> During the current year, Fred pays the property taxes on his son Jayden's home. Neither Fred nor Jayden can take a deduction for the amount paid for Jayden's property taxes. Fred is not entitled to a deduction because the property taxes are not his obligation. Jayden cannot claim a deduction because he did not pay the property taxes.
> The tax result would have been more favorable had Fred made a cash gift to Jayden and let him pay the property taxes. Then Jayden could have deducted the property taxes.

One exception to this disallowance rule is the payment of medical expenses for a dependent. Such expenses are deductible by the payor subject to the normal rules that limit the deductibility of medical expenses (see Chapters 3 and 10).[48]

6-3h **Disallowance of Personal Expenditures**

Section 262 states that "except as otherwise expressly provided in this chapter, no deduction shall be allowed for personal, living, or family expenses." To justify a deduction, an individual must be able to identify a particular section of the Code that sanctions the deduction (e.g., charitable contributions and medical expenses). Sometimes the character of a particular expenditure is not easily determined. For example, the legal fee associated with a property settlement that results in one party retaining ownership of a family business is not deductible.

The IRS has clarified the issue of the deduction of legal fees incurred in connection with a divorce.[49] To be deductible, an expense must relate solely to tax advice in a divorce proceeding. For example, legal fees attributable to the determination of dependency exemptions of children are deductible if the fees are distinguishable from the general legal fees incurred in obtaining a divorce. Therefore, it is advisable to request an itemization of attorney's fees to substantiate a deduction for the tax-related amounts.

← Divorce

---

[48]§ 213(a).   [49]Rev.Rul. 72–545, 1972–2 C.B. 179.

ETHICS & EQUITY Personal or Business Expenses?

For the last eight years, Jaynice and her family have lived in a large Victorian house in New England. In the current year, Jaynice and her husband decide to convert the home into a "bed-and-breakfast." The family (including the two children and the dog) moves into the basement, which accounts for 30 percent of the square footage of the house. The basement has two bedrooms, two baths, a den, and a small kitchen. The upper two floors of the house are used for the bed-and-breakfast, which is operated as a sole proprietorship.

Jaynice hires two employees to help her run the business. Total expenses for the first year of operation are as follows:

Mortgage interest	$18,000
Real estate taxes	3,000
Salaries for two employees	40,000
Groceries for breakfast and snacks	7,000
Depreciation	10,000

For breakfast, all of the family members eat the same food that is prepared for the guests. They usually also share in the homemade cookies and cakes in the evening.

On Jaynice's Schedule C for the business, she deducts $78,000 of expenses for the current tax year. Discuss whether these deductions are appropriate.

EXAMPLE 31

Terry and Jack are divorced near the end of the current tax year. They had been married for 28 years and have two dependent children, Pauline (age 17) and Neal (age 18). As part of the divorce agreement, Jack paid all of the legal fees, which amounted to $24,300. The invoice from the divorce lawyer listed the following charges:

Child custody agreement and determination of amount of monthly child support	$ 3,000
Divorce decree proceedings	10,000
County court filing costs	1,800
Property settlement determination	6,000
Tax consequences of property settlement	2,000
Tax consequences of child custody and child support payments and tax filing status	1,500

Only the $3,500 ($2,000 + $1,500) paid by Jack for the charges relating to tax advice is deductible.

6-3i Disallowance of Deductions for Capital Expenditures

The Code specifically disallows a deduction for "any amount paid out for new buildings or for permanent improvements or betterments made to increase the value of any property or estate."[50] Incidental repairs and maintenance of the property are not capital expenditures and can be deducted as ordinary and necessary business expenses. Repairing a roof is a deductible expense, but replacing a roof is a capital expenditure subject to depreciation deductions over its recovery period. The tune-up of a delivery truck is an expense; a complete overhaul probably is a capital expenditure. Adding new gravel to a gravel parking lot is a repair, but paving the parking lot is a capital expenditure because this is doing more than restoring the asset to its original condition.

For tax years beginning after 2013, all costs incurred in acquiring or producing a Unit of Property (UOP) are included in its cost, except for employee compensation and overhead costs. The taxpayer can elect to capitalize employee compensation and overhead costs (can elect separately or both). The cost includes all related expenditures incurred before the date the asset is placed in service, even if these expenditures would be repairs if incurred after the asset was placed in service. The cost of a UOP includes costs incurred to obtain a clean title and investigation costs.[51] Material or supplies that cost $200 or less can generally be deducted in the first tax year they are used or consumed.[52]

[50]§ 263(a)(1).
[51]Reg. § 1.263(a)–3(e)(1).
[52]Reg. § 1.162–3(a)(1).

Capitalize or Expense

EXAMPLE 32

In year 1, Corporation Biz purchases 100 cell phones for its employees to use, each phone costing $130. Each cell phone is considered to be a unit of property. During year 1, 60 of the phones are put into use. The remaining phones are not used until year 2.

Since the cell phones cost less than $200, they are considered to be material and supplies. Therefore, 60 of the phones can be expensed in year 1 ($7,800). The remaining 40 phones cannot be expensed until they are put into use in year 2.

EXAMPLE 33

Jared owns a building that has 10 apartments. During the current year, one of the apartments needed a new stove. Jared paid $800 for the stove, including $75 of sales tax. He also paid $50 for the stove to be delivered and an extra $60 for it to be installed.

The stove is considered to be a unit of property, and all of these costs are included in its basis. Therefore, $910 is capitalized for the stove and this amount will be depreciated.

A single UOP includes all components that are functionally interdependent. Thus, a building includes, for example, the walls, floors, ceilings, roof, windows, doors, electrical systems, plumbing, and heating and air systems. The major exception to this rule is that if a component is treated separately for depreciation purposes, it will not be grouped into another UOP.[53]

Taxpayers can elect under the *de minimis safe harbor election* to expense outlays for lower-cost items. The election is irrevocable. This safe harbor applies if the taxpayer:

- has written procedures in place at the beginning of the tax year that provide for the expensing of amounts below a specified dollar amount or that have a useful life of 12 months or less,
- also expenses the items for its accounting/book records, and
- ensures that items costing more than $5,000 are capitalized [$2,500 ($500 prior to 2016) if the company does not have acceptable (generally meaning audited) financial statements].

The *de minimis* safe harbor election cannot be made for inventory, land, and certain types of spare parts.[54]

Routine maintenance to keep UOPs operating efficiently is expensed, such as testing, cleaning, inspecting, and replacing parts. To be routine, the expectation is that the expenditure will be needed more than once during the asset's life. An expense cannot be treated as routine maintenance if it improves a UOP (treated as a betterment). A cost is treated as a betterment if it:

- enlarges or increases the capacity of a UOP, or
- materially increases the productivity, efficiency, or quality of the UOP.[55]

Qualifying small taxpayers (those with $10 million or less average annual gross receipts in the three preceding tax years) can deduct improvements made to an eligible building property (one with an unadjusted basis of $1 million or less). The new safe harbor election applies only if the total amount paid during the tax year for repairs, maintenance, improvements, and similar activities performed on the eligible building does not exceed the lesser of $10,000 or 2 percent of the building's unadjusted basis. In addition, qualifying small taxpayers (including businesses with less than $10 million in assets) may elect to make these changes in accounting methods on a cut-off basis. This allows the new accounting method to be used solely for amounts paid or incurred, and dispositions, in taxable years beginning after 2013. Since prior years are not affected, no adjustment to income is needed for the change. If elected, these taxpayers will not be required to file Form 3115, Application for Change in Accounting Method.[56]

---

[53]Reg. § 1.263(a)–3(e)(6).
[54]Reg. § 1.263(a)–1(f)(1).
[55]Reg. § 1.263(a)–3(i)(1).

Capitalization versus Expense

When an expenditure is capitalized rather than expensed, the deduction is at best deferred and at worst lost forever. Although an immediate tax benefit for a large cash expenditure is lost, the cost may be deductible in increments over a longer period of time as the asset is depreciated, amortized, or depleted.

If the expenditure is for a tangible asset that has an ascertainable life, it is capitalized and may be deducted as depreciation (or cost recovery) over its depreciable life. Land is not subject to depreciation (or cost recovery) because it does not have an ascertainable life. [See Chapter 8 for a discussion of depreciation (cost recovery).]

EXAMPLE 34

Stan purchased a prime piece of land located in an apartment-zoned area. Stan paid $500,000 for the property, which had an old but usable apartment building on it. He immediately had the building demolished at a cost of $100,000.

The $500,000 purchase price and the $100,000 demolition costs must be capitalized, and the basis of the land is $600,000. Because land is a nondepreciable asset, no deduction is allowed.

If the expenditure is for an intangible asset (e.g., copyright, patent, covenant not to compete, and goodwill), the capitalized expenditure can be amortized regardless of whether the intangible asset has an ascertainable life. Intangible assets, referred to as § 197 intangibles, are amortized over a 15-year statutory period using the straight-line method. See Chapter 8 for additional discussion of the amortization of intangibles.

6-3j Transactions between Related Parties

The Code places restrictions on the recognition of gains and losses from **related-party transactions**. Without these restrictions, relationships created by birth, marriage, and business would provide endless possibilities for engaging in financial transactions that produce tax savings with no real economic substance or change. For example, to create an artificial loss, a wife could sell investment property to her husband at a loss and deduct the loss on their joint return. Her husband could then hold the asset indefinitely, and the family would sustain no real economic loss. A complex set of laws has been designed to eliminate such possibilities.

Relationships and Constructive Ownership

Before reviewing the tax consequences of related party sales, it is important to know the individuals and business entities that are considered to be related parties. *Related parties* include the following:

- Brothers and sisters (whether whole, half, or adopted), spouse, ancestors (parents and grandparents), and lineal descendants (children and grandchildren) of the taxpayer.
- A corporation that is owned more than 50 percent (directly or indirectly) by the taxpayer.
- Two corporations that are members of a controlled group.
- A series of other complex relationships between trusts, corporations, and individual taxpayers.

Constructive ownership provisions are applied to determine whether the taxpayers are related. Under these provisions, stock owned by certain relatives or related entities is *deemed* to be owned by the taxpayer for purposes of applying the loss and expense deduction disallowance provisions. For example, a taxpayer is deemed to own not only his or her stock but also the stock owned by lineal descendants, ancestors, brothers and sisters or half-brothers and half-sisters, and spouse.

The stock of Sparrow Corporation is owned 20% by Ted, 30% by Ted's father, 30% by Ted's mother, and 20% by Ted's sister. Although Ted actually owns only 20% of Sparrow Corporation, he is *deemed* to own the stock owned by his father (30%), mother (30%), and sister (20%).

As a result, Ted directly and indirectly owns 100% of Sparrow Corporation, and Ted and Sparrow are related parties. The same outcome (100% direct and indirect ownership) results for all of the shareholders in this example.

Losses

The Code provides for the disallowance of any "losses from sales or exchanges of property ... directly or indirectly" between related parties.[57] A right of offset is created equal to the disallowed loss. When the property is subsequently sold to a nonrelated party, any gain recognized is reduced by the right of offset. However, the right of offset cannot create or increase a loss. Any right of offset is permanently lost if it is not used by the related-party buyer to offset some or all of the recognized gain on a subsequent sale or exchange to an unrelated party.

Use of Right of Offset

Freida sells common stock with a basis of $10,000 to her son, Bill, for its fair market value of $8,000. The $2,000 realized loss is not recognized, which creates a $2,000 right of offset. Bill sells the stock several years later for $11,000.

Freida's $2,000 loss is disallowed upon the sale to Bill, and only $1,000 of gain ($11,000 selling price − $8,000 basis − $2,000 right of offset) is taxable to him upon the subsequent sale.

Assume the same facts as in Example 36, except that Bill sells the stock for $9,000. Bill's gain of $1,000 ($9,000 selling price − $8,000 basis) is not recognized because of the right of offset of $2,000 from Freida's sale.

Note that the offset may result in only partial tax benefit upon the subsequent sale (as in this case). If Freida had sold the stock to an unrelated party rather than to Bill, she could have recognized a $2,000 loss. However, as a family unit, Freida and Bill recognized only $1,000 of loss.

A loss can also be disallowed even if the asset is sold to an unrelated party. This occurs if a related party repurchases the asset on or near the same day and the two sales were prearranged.[58]

Pete sells common stock with a basis of $10,000 to an unrelated third party for its fair market value of $8,000. Pete's son repurchased the same stock in the market on the same day for $8,000. The $2,000 loss is not allowed because the transaction is an indirect sale between related parties.

6-3k Substantiation Requirements

The tax law is built on a voluntary compliance system. Taxpayers file their tax returns, report income and take deductions to which they are entitled, and pay their taxes through withholding or estimated tax payments during the year. The taxpayer has the burden of proof for substantiating expenses deducted on the returns and must retain adequate records. Upon audit, the IRS can disallow any undocumented or unsubstantiated deductions. These requirements have resulted in numerous conflicts between taxpayers and the IRS.

---

[57]§ 267(a)(1).

[58]*McWilliams v. Comm.*, 47–1 USTC ¶9289, 35 AFTR 1184, 67 S.Ct. 1477 (USSC, 1947).

For example, *specific* and *more stringent* rules apply for deducting travel, entertainment, and gift expenses, which are discussed in Chapter 9. Certain mixed-use (both personal and business use) and listed property are also subject to the adequate records requirement (see Chapter 8).

Substantiation is also extremely important for establishing the basis of an asset (see Chapter 14). An asset's basis includes all costs incurred to place an asset in service, which includes transportation, sales tax, setup, testing, unpaid property taxes of the previous owner, and other purchase costs. Basis is used to determine gain or loss on a sale of the asset and to compute depreciation for depreciable assets. The taxpayer has the burden of substantiating all expenditures included in basis.

6-3l **Expenses and Interest Relating to Tax-Exempt Income**

Certain income, such as interest on municipal bonds, is tax-exempt.[59] The law also allows the taxpayer to deduct expenses incurred for the production of income.[60] However, the law does not permit a taxpayer to profit at the expense of the government by excluding interest income and deducting interest expense.[61] The Code specifically disallows as a deduction the expenses of producing tax-exempt income. Interest on any indebtedness used to purchase or hold tax-exempt obligations also is disallowed.

Sandy, a taxpayer in the 35% bracket, purchased $100,000 of 6% municipal bonds. At the same time, she used the bonds as collateral on a bank loan of $100,000 at 8% interest. A positive cash flow would result from the tax benefit as follows:

Cash paid out on loan	($8,000)
Cash received from bonds	6,000
Net negative cash flow	($2,000)

Had the deduction of $8,000 been allowed for interest expense, this would have resulted in a tax benefit of $2,800 (35% of $8,000). In that case, a positive cash flow of $800 ($6,000 + $2,800 − $8,000) would have resulted.

To eliminate the possibility illustrated in Example 39, the Code specifically disallows as a deduction the expenses of producing tax-exempt income. Interest on any indebtedness incurred or continued to purchase or carry tax-exempt obligations also is disallowed.

In January of the current year, Alan borrowed $100,000 at 8% interest. He used the loan proceeds to purchase 5,000 shares of stock in White Corporation. In July, he sold the stock for $120,000 and reinvested the proceeds in City of Denver bonds, the income from which is tax-exempt.

Assuming that the $100,000 loan remained outstanding throughout the entire year, Alan cannot deduct the interest attributable to the period in which he held the bonds.

The classification of various expenses in terms of their deductibility and nondeductibility is reflected in Concept Summary 6.4.

LO.4

Identify tax planning opportunities for maximizing deductions and minimizing the disallowance of deductions.

6-4 **TAX PLANNING**

6-4a **Vacation Homes**

As previously discussed in this chapter, homes that are used for both personal and rental use can fall into one of three categories, all of which have different tax consequences.

---

[59]§ 103.
[60]§ 212.

[61]§ 265.

Concept Summary 6.4

Classification of Expenses

Expense Item	Deductible		Not Deductible	Applicable Code Section
	For AGI	From AGI		
Investment expenses				
Rent and royalty	X			§ 62(a)(4)
All other investments		X[4]		§ 212
Employee expenses				
Commuting expenses			X	§ 262
Travel and transportation[1]		X[4,5]		§ 162(a)(2)
Reimbursed expenses[1]	X			§ 62(a)(2)(A)
Moving expenses	X			§ 62(a)(15)
Entertainment[1]		X[4,5]		§ 162(a)
Teacher professional development and supplies	X[11]	X[4]		§ 62(a)(2)(D)
All other employee expenses[1]		X[4,5]		§ 162(a)
Certain expenses of performing artists	X			§ 62(a)(2)(B)
Trade or business expenses	X			§§ 162 and 62(a)(1)
Casualty losses				
Business	X			§ 165(c)(1)
Personal		X[6]		§ 165(c)(3)
Tax determination				
Collection or refund expenses	X[8]	X		§§ 212 and 62(a)(1) or (4)
Bad debts	X			§§ 166 and 62(a)(1) or (3)
Medical expenses		X[7]		§ 213
Charitable contributions		X		§ 170
Taxes				
Trade or business	X			§§ 162, 164, and 62(a)(1)
Personal taxes				
Real property		X		§ 164(a)(1)
Personal property		X		§ 164(a)(2)
State and local income *or* sales tax		X		§§ 164(a)(3) and (b)(5)
Investigation of a business[2]	X			§§ 162 and 62(a)(1)
Interest				
Business	X			§§ 162, 163, and 62(a)(1)
Personal	X[9]	X[3]	X[10]	§§ 163(a), (d), and (h)
Qualified tuition and related expenses	X			§§ 62(a)(18) and 222
All other personal expenses			X	§ 262

[1]Deduction for AGI if reimbursed, an adequate accounting is made, and employee is required to repay excess reimbursements.
[2]Provided certain criteria are met.
[3]Subject to the excess investment interest and the qualified residence interest provisions.
[4]Subject (in the aggregate) to a 2%-of-AGI floor imposed by § 67.
[5]Only 50% of meals and entertainment are deductible.
[6]Subject to a $100 floor per event and a 10%-of-AGI floor per tax year.
[7]Subject to a 7.5%- or 10%-of-AGI floor.
[8]Only the portion relating to business, rental, or royalty income or losses.
[9]Only the portion relating to student loans.
[10]Other personal interest is disallowed.
[11]Subject to a statutory limit of $250.

Therefore, careful tax planning often ensures that the home is classified into the category that provides the optimal tax result. For example, if a taxpayer is planning to rent a home for 15 or more days, this will subject the net income from the rental activity to taxation. If the homeowner could rent the home for 14 days or less (possibly just one less day), then all of the rental income received would escape taxation. This strategy is particularly attractive to individuals who live in areas where major sporting or entertainment events are held if there is a lack of hotel accommodations in the area.

In addition, assume that a taxpayer intends to use a home for 150 rental days and 16 personal days. Because the personal days exceed 15 (the greater of 14 days or 10% × the number of rental days), the property will be classified as *rental/personal* and a rental loss will not be allowed. However, if the owner can reduce the personal use days by only one day to 15, then the property will be classified as *rental*, and a rental loss can be allowed (subject to the passive activity loss rules).

6-4b Hobby Losses

To demonstrate that an activity has been entered into for the purpose of making a profit, a taxpayer should treat the activity as a business. The business should engage in advertising, use business letterhead stationery, and maintain a business phone.

If a taxpayer's activity earns a profit in three out of five consecutive years, the presumption is that the activity is engaged in for profit. It may be possible for a cash basis taxpayer to meet these requirements by timing the payment of expenses or the receipt of revenues. The payment of certain expenses incurred before the end of the year might be made in the following year. The billing of year-end sales might be delayed so that collections are received in the following year.

Keep in mind that the three-out-of-five-years rule under § 183 is not absolute. All it does is shift the burden of proof. If a profit is not made in three out of five years, the losses may still be allowed if the taxpayer can show that they are due to the nature of the business. For example, success in artistic or literary endeavors can take a long time, so losses for several years in a row could occur even for a legitimate business. Also, depending on the state of the economy, full-time farmers and ranchers may have losses for several consecutive years.

Merely satisfying the three-out-of-five-years rule does not guarantee that a taxpayer is automatically home free. If the three years of profits are insignificant relative to the losses of other years or if the profits are not from the ordinary operation of the business, the taxpayer is vulnerable. The IRS may still be able to establish that the taxpayer is not engaged in an activity for profit.

EXAMPLE 41

Ashley had the following gains and losses in an artistic endeavor:

2012	($50,000)
2013	(65,000)
2014	400
2015	200
2016	125

Under these circumstances, the IRS might try to overcome the presumption that this is a business because it has profits in three of the last five years. To do this, the IRS would focus on the nine factors from the Regulations discussed in text Section 6-3e.

On the other hand, if Ashley could show conformity with the factors enumerated in the Regulations or could show evidence of business hardships (e.g., injury, death, or illness), the government might have difficulty overriding the presumption.[62]

---

[62]*Faulconer, Sr. v. Comm.*, 84–2 USTC ¶9955, 55 AFTR 2d 85–302, 748 F.2d 890 (CA–4, 1984), *rev'g* 45 TCM 1084, T.C.Memo. 1983–165.

CALCULATION OF DEDUCTIBLE BUSINESS EXPENSES AND TAX PLANNING

Of the expenses incurred by Dr. Payne, several comments need to be made. Being personal in nature, none of the $5,000 monthly draw is deductible. Nor is the amount involved subject to the reasonableness test (see Example 6). Dr. Payne is a sole proprietor and not in an employment relationship. The fine paid for violating waste control rules comes under the public policy limitations (see Example 14) and is specifically made nondeductible by Code § 162(f). Along the same line are the political contributions (Example 18) made nondeductible by § 162(e). However, Dr. Payne's investigation of the practice of another dental firm (Example 20) appears reasonable and the expense incurred deductible. The dues paid to The Dental Society are not 100 percent deductible because 70 percent of the Society's efforts relate to lobbying activities (Example 19). Although not specifically discussed in the text as to Dr. Payne, his legal fees incurred in connection with a lawsuit filed by a patient appear related to his practice (Example 16). As such, they are ordinary and necessary to his trade or business.

What If?

From a tax planning perspective, should Dr. Payne calculate his deductible business expenses using the accrual method of accounting or the cash method?

In Chapter 4, we concluded that Dr. Payne could minimize his Federal income tax liability if he used the cash method of accounting. If the cash method is used for reporting the gross income of a Schedule C business, the cash method must be used for reporting the deductible business expenses that will appear on Schedule C of Form 1040.

Key Terms

Accounting method, 6-8

Deductions *for* adjusted
gross income, 6-2

Deductions *from* adjusted
gross income, 6-2

Hobby losses, 6-16

Ordinary and necessary, 6-5

Reasonableness, 6-6

Related-party transactions, 6-26

Startup expenditures, 6-15

Vacation homes, 6-19

Discussion Questions

1. **LO.1** "All income must be reported, and all deductions are allowed unless specifically disallowed in the Code." Discuss.

2. **LO.1** Michael earned $20,000 at the K-M Resort Golf Club during the summer prior to his senior year in college. He wants to make a contribution to a traditional IRA, but the amount is dependent on whether it reduces his taxable income. If Michael is going to claim the standard deduction, will a contribution to a traditional IRA reduce his taxable income? Explain.

3. **LO.1** Classify each of the following expenditures as a deduction *for* AGI, a deduction *from* AGI, or not deductible:

   a. Sam gives cash to his father as a birthday gift.

   b. Sandra gives cash to her church.

   c. Albert pays Dr. Dafashy for medical services rendered.

   d. Mia pays alimony to Bill.

   e. Rex, who is self-employed, contributes to his pension plan.

   f. April pays expenses associated with her rental property.

4. **LO.1** Classify each of the following expenditures as a deduction *for* AGI, a deduction *from* AGI, or not deductible:

   a. Amos contributes to his H.R. 10 plan (i.e., a retirement plan for a self-employed individual).

   b. Keith pays child support to his former wife, Renee, for the support of their son, Chris.

   c. Judy pays professional dues that are reimbursed by her employer.

   d. Ted pays $500 as the monthly mortgage payment on his personal residence. Of this amount, $100 represents a payment on principal, and $400 represents an interest payment.

   e. Lynn pays a moving company for moving her household goods to Detroit, where she is starting a new job. She is not reimbursed by her employer.

   f. Ralph pays property taxes on his personal residence.

5. **LO.1** Larry and Susan each invest $10,000 in separate investment activities. They each incur deductible expenses of $800 associated with their respective investments. Explain why Larry's expenses might be properly classified as deductions *from* AGI (itemized deductions) and Susan's expenses might be appropriately classified as deductions *for* AGI.

6. **LO.1** Nanette is a first-grade teacher. Potential deductions are charitable contributions of $800, personal property taxes on her car of $240, and various supplies purchased for use in her classroom of $225 (none reimbursed by her school). How will these items affect Nanette's Federal income tax return for 2016?

7. **LO.1** In the determination of whether a business expense is deductible, the reasonableness requirement applies only to salaries. Evaluate this statement.

8. **LO.1** Dave uses the second floor of a building for his residence and the first floor for his business. The uninsured building is destroyed by fire. Are the tax consequences the same for each part of the building? Explain.

9. **LO.1** Mary Kate owns a building that she leases to an individual who operates a grocery store. Rent income is $10,000, and rental expenses are $6,000. On what Form 1040 schedule or schedules are the income and expenses reported?

10. **LO.2** What is the "actually paid" requirement for the deduction of an expense by a cash basis taxpayer? Does actual payment ensure a deduction? Explain.

11. **LO.2** Aubry, a cash basis and calendar year taxpayer, decides to reduce his taxable income for 2016 by buying $65,000 worth of supplies for his business on December 27, 2016. The supplies will be used up in 2017.

    a. Can Aubry deduct the expenditure for 2016? Explain.

    b. Would your answer in part (a) change if Aubry bought the supplies because the seller was going out of business and offered a large discount on the price? Explain.

12. **LO.3** Clear, Inc., is a bottled water distributor. Clear's delivery trucks frequently are required to park in no-parking zones to make their deliveries. If the trucks are occasionally ticketed, can Clear deduct the fines that it pays? Explain.

13. **LO.3** Ted, an agent for an airline manufacturer, is negotiating a sale with a repre-   Issue ID
sentative of the U.S. government and with a representative of a developing country. Ted's company has sufficient capacity to handle only one of the orders. Both orders will have the same contract price. Ted believes that if his employer authorizes a $500,000 payment to the representative of the foreign country, he can guarantee the sale. He is not sure that he can obtain the same result with the U.S. government. Identify the relevant tax issues for Ted.

14. **LO.3** Stuart, an insurance salesperson, is arrested for allegedly robbing a conven-
ience store. He hires an attorney who is successful in getting the charges dropped. Is the attorney's fee deductible? Explain.

15. **LO.3** Linda operates an illegal gambling operation. Which of the following expenses that she incurs can reduce taxable income?
a. Bribes paid to city employees.
b. Salaries to employees.
c. Security cameras.
d. Kickbacks to police.
e. Rent on an office.
f. Depreciation on office furniture and equipment.
g. Tenant's casualty insurance.
h. Utilities.

16. **LO.3** Gordon anticipates that being positively perceived by the individual who is elected mayor will be beneficial for his business. Therefore, he contributes to the campaigns of both the Democratic and the Republican candidates. The Republi-can candidate is elected mayor. Can Gordon deduct any of the political contribu-tions he made?

17. **LO.3** Melissa, the owner of a sole proprietorship, does not provide health insur-ance for her 20 employees. She plans to spend $1,500 lobbying in opposition to legislation that would require her to provide such insurance. Discuss the tax advantages and disadvantages of paying the $1,500 to a professional lobbyist rather than spending the $1,500 on in-house lobbying expenditures.

18. **LO.3** What limits exist on the deductibility of executive compensation? Do the limits apply to all types of business entities? Are there any exceptions to the limitations? Explain.

19. **LO.3** Paul operates a restaurant in Cleveland. He travels to Columbus to investigate acquiring a business. He incurs expenses as follows: $1,500 for travel, $2,000 for legal advice, and $3,500 for a market analysis. Based on the different tax conse-quences listed below, describe the circumstances that were involved in Paul's inves-tigation of the business.
a. Paul deducts the $7,000 of expenses.
b. Paul cannot deduct any of the $7,000 of expenses.
c. Paul deducts $5,000 of the expenses and amortizes the $2,000 balance over a period of 180 months.

20. **LO.3** Karen and Andy own a beach house. They have an agreement with a rental   Issue ID
agent to rent it up to 200 days per year. For the past three years, the agent has been successful in renting it for 200 days. Karen and Andy use the beach house for one week during the summer and one week during Thanksgiving. Their

daughter, Sarah, a college student, has asked if she and some friends can use the beach house for the week of spring break. Advise Karen and Andy on how they should respond, and identify any relevant tax issues.

21. **LO.3** Hank was transferred from Arizona to North Dakota on March 1 of the current year. He immediately put his home in Phoenix up for rent. The home was rented May 1 to November 30 and was vacant during the month of December. It was rented again on January 1 for six months. What expenses related to the home, if any, can Hank deduct on his return? Which deductions are *for* AGI, and which ones are *from* AGI?

Decision Making   22. **LO.3** Ray loses his job as a result of a corporate downsizing. Consequently, he falls behind on the mortgage payments on his personal residence. His friend Ted would like to make the delinquent mortgage payments for him.

a. Could the payments be structured so that Ray can deduct the mortgage interest?

b. Could the payment arrangement deny both Ray and Ted a mortgage interest deduction?

c. Could the payments be structured so that Ted can deduct the mortgage interest?

23. **LO.3** Edna incurs various legal fees in obtaining a divorce. Which types of expenses associated with the divorce are deductible by Edna, and which are not?

Issue ID   24. **LO.3** Ella owns 60% of the stock of Peach, Inc. The stock has declined in value since she purchased it five years ago. She is going to sell 5% of the stock to a relative. Ella is also going to make a gift of 10% of the stock to another relative. Identify the relevant tax issues for Ella.

25. **LO.3** Jarret owns City of Charleston bonds with an adjusted basis of $190,000. During the year, he receives interest payments of $3,800. Jarret partially financed the purchase of the bonds by borrowing $100,000 at 5% interest. Jarret's interest payments on the loan this year are $4,900, and his principal payments are $1,100.

a. Should Jarret report any interest income this year? Explain.

b. Can Jarret deduct any interest expense this year? Explain.

Computational Exercises

26. **LO.2** Glenda, a calendar year and cash basis taxpayer, rents property from Janice. As part of the rental agreement, Glenda pays $8,400 rent on April 1, 2016, for the 12 months ending March 31, 2017.

a. How much is Glenda's deduction for rent expense in 2016?

b. Assume the same facts, except that the $8,400 is for 24 months' rent ending March 31, 2018. How much is Glenda's deduction for rent expense in 2016?

27. **LO.2** Falcon, Inc., paid salaries of $500,000 to its employees during its first year of operations. At the end of the year, Falcon had unpaid salaries of $45,000.

a. Calculate the salary deduction if Falcon is a cash basis taxpayer.

b. Calculate the salary deduction if Falcon is an accrual basis taxpayer.

28. **LO.2** Maud, a calendar year taxpayer, is the owner of a sole proprietorship that uses the cash method. On February 1, 2016, she leases an office building to use in her business for $120,000 for an 18-month period. To obtain this favorable lease rate, she pays the $120,000 at the inception of the lease. How much rent expense may Maud deduct on her 2016 tax return?

29. **LO.3** Vella owns and operates an illegal gambling establishment. In connection with this activity, he has the following expenses during the year:

Rent	$ 24,000
Bribes	40,000
Travel expenses	4,000
Utilities	18,000
Wages	230,000
Payroll taxes	13,800
Property insurance	1,600
Illegal kickbacks	22,000

What are Vella's total deductible expenses for tax purposes?

30. **LO.3** Printer Company pays a $25,000 annual membership fee to a trade association for paper wholesalers. The trade association estimates that 60% of its dues are allocated to lobbying activities.
   a.   What are Printer's total deductible expenses for tax purposes?
   b.   Assume the same facts as above, except that the $25,000 was incurred for in-house lobbying expenses. What are Printer's total deductible expenses for tax purposes?

31. **LO.3** Stanford owns and operates two dry cleaning businesses. He travels to Boston to discuss acquiring a restaurant. Later in the month, he travels to New York to discuss acquiring a bakery. Stanford does not acquire the restaurant but does purchase the bakery on November 1, 2016.
   Stanford incurred the following expenses:

Total investigation costs related to the restaurant	$28,000
Total investigation costs related to the bakery	51,000

What is the maximum amount Stanford can deduct in 2016 for investigation expenses?

32. **LO.3** Murphy has a brokerage account and buys on the margin, which resulted in an interest expense of $20,000 during the year. Income generated through the brokerage account was as follows:

Municipal interest	$ 50,000
Taxable dividends and interest	350,000

How much investment interest can Murphy deduct?

Problems

33. **LO.1** Amos is a self-employed tax attorney. He and Monica, his employee, attend a conference in Dallas sponsored by the American Institute of CPAs. The following expenses are incurred during the trip:

	Amos	Monica
Conference registration	$ 900	$900
Airfare	1,200	700
Taxi fares	100	–0–
Lodging in Dallas	750	300

   a.   Amos pays for all of these expenses. Calculate the effect of these expenses on Amos's AGI.
   b.   Would your answer to part (a) change if the American Bar Association had sponsored the conference? Explain.

Decision Making   34. **LO.1** Daniel, age 38, is single and has the following income and expenses in 2016.

Salary income	$60,000
Net rent income	6,000
Dividend income	3,500
Payment of alimony	12,000
Mortgage interest on residence	4,900
Property tax on residence	1,200
Contribution to traditional IRA	5,000
Contribution to United Church	2,100
Loss on the sale of real estate (held for investment)	2,000
Medical expenses	3,250
State income tax	300
Federal income tax	7,000

a. Calculate Daniel's AGI.

b. Should Daniel itemize his deductions *from* AGI or take the standard deduction? Explain.

35. **LO.1** Janice, age 22, is a student who earns $10,000 working part-time at the college ice cream shop in 2016. She has no other income. Her medical expenses for the year total $3,000. During the year, she suffers a casualty loss of $3,500 when her apartment catches on fire. Janice contributes $2,500 to her church. On the advice of her parents, Janice is trying to decide whether to contribute $1,000 to the traditional IRA her parents set up for her. What effect would the IRA contribution have on Janice's itemized deductions?

36. **LO.1** A list of the items that Peggy sold and the losses she incurred during the current tax year is as follows:

Yellow, Inc. stock	$ 1,600
Peggy's personal use SUV	8,000
Peggy's personal residence	10,000
City of Newburyport bonds	900

She also had a theft loss of $1,500 on her uninsured business use car. Calculate Peggy's deductible losses.

37. **LO.2** Duck, an accrual basis corporation, sponsored a rock concert on December 29, 2016. Gross receipts were $300,000. The following expenses were incurred and paid as indicated:

Expense		Payment Date
Rental of coliseum	$ 25,000	December 21, 2016
Cost of goods sold:		
Food	30,000	December 30, 2016
Souvenirs	60,000	December 30, 2016
Performers	100,000	January 5, 2017
Cleaning of coliseum	10,000	February 1, 2017

Because the coliseum was not scheduled to be used again until January 15, the company with which Duck had contracted did not perform the cleanup until January 8–10, 2017.

Calculate Duck's net income from the concert for tax purposes for 2016.

38. **LO.3** Doug incurred and paid the following expenses during the year:

- $50 for a ticket for running a red light while he was commuting to work.
- $100 for a ticket for parking in a handicapped parking space.
- $200 to an attorney to represent him in traffic court as to the two tickets.

- $500 to an attorney to draft an agreement with a tenant for a one-year lease on an apartment that Doug owns.
- $1,000 to an attorney to negotiate a reduction in his child support payments.
- $2,500 to an attorney to negotiate a reduction in his qualified alimony payments to a former spouse.

Calculate the amount of Doug's deductible expenses.

39. **LO.3** Trevor, a friend of yours from high school, works as a server at the ST Café. He asks you to help him prepare his Federal income tax return. When you inquire about why his bank deposits substantially exceed his tip income, he confides to you that he is a bookie on the side. Trevor then provides you with the following documented income and expenses for the year:

Tip income	$16,000
Gambling income	52,000
Gambling expenses	
Payouts to winners	29,000
Employee compensation	8,000
Bribe to police officer who is aware of Trevor's bookie activity	7,500

a. How will these items affect Trevor's AGI (ignore the impact of self-employment taxes)?

b. His taxable income (ignore the impact of self-employment taxes)?

40. **LO.3, 4** Amber, a publicly held corporation, currently pays its president an annual salary of $900,000. In addition, it contributes $20,000 annually to a defined contribution pension plan for him. As a means of increasing company profitability, the board of directors decides to increase the president's compensation. Two proposals are being considered. Under the first proposal, the salary and pension contribution for the president would be increased by 30%. Under the second proposal, Amber would implement a performance-based compensation program that is projected to provide about the same amount of additional compensation and pension contribution for the president.

Decision Making

Communications

a. Evaluate the alternatives from the perspective of Amber.

b. Prepare a letter to Amber's board of directors that contains your recommendations. Address the letter to the board chairperson, Agnes Riddle, whose address is 100 James Tower, Cleveland, OH 44106.

41. **LO.3** Nancy, the owner of a very successful hotel chain in the Southeast, is exploring the possibility of expanding the chain into a city in the Northeast. She incurs $35,000 of expenses associated with this investigation. Based on the regulatory environment for hotels in the city, she decides not to expand. During the year, she also investigates opening a restaurant that will be part of a national restaurant chain. Her expenses for this are $53,000. The restaurant begins operations on September 1. Determine the amount that Nancy can deduct in the current year for investigating these two businesses.

42. **LO.3** Terry traveled to a neighboring state to investigate the purchase of two hardware stores. His expenses included travel, legal, accounting, and miscellaneous expenses. The total was $52,000. He incurred the expenses in June and July 2016. Under the following circumstances, what can Terry deduct in 2016?

a. Terry was in the hardware store business and did not acquire the two hardware stores.

b. Terry was in the hardware store business and acquired the two hardware stores and began operating them on October 1, 2016.

    c.   Terry did not acquire the two hardware stores and was not in the hardware store business.

    d.   Terry acquired the two hardware stores but was not in the hardware store business when he acquired them. Operations began on October 1, 2016.

43. **LO.3** Harold conducts a business with the following results for the year:

Revenue	$20,000
Depreciation on car	3,960
Operating expenses of car	3,100
Rent	6,000
Wages	8,200
Amortization of intangibles	680

Harold estimates that due to a depressed real estate market, the value of land owned by the business declined by $5,200.

    a.   Calculate the effect of Harold's business on his AGI.

    b.   How would your answer in part (a) change if the activity was a hobby?

44. **LO.3** Alex, who is single, conducts an activity in 2016 that is appropriately classified as a hobby. The activity produces the following revenues and expenses:

Revenue	$18,000
Property taxes	3,000
Materials and supplies	4,500
Utilities	2,000
Advertising	5,000
Insurance	750
Depreciation	4,000

Without regard to this activity, Alex's AGI is $42,000. Determine the amount of income Alex must report, the amount of the expenses he is permitted to deduct, and his taxable income.

45. **LO.3** Samantha, an executive, has AGI of $100,000 before considering income or loss from her miniature horse business. Her outside income comes from prizes for winning horse shows, stud fees, and sales of yearlings. Samantha's home is on 20 acres, half of which she uses for the horse activity (i.e., stables, paddocks, fences, tack houses, and other related improvements).

    Samantha's office in her home is 10% of the square footage of the house. She uses the office exclusively for maintaining files and records on the horse activities. Her books show the following income and expenses for the current year:

Income from fees, prizes, and sales		$22,000
Expenses		
Entry fees		1,000
Feed and veterinary bills		4,000
Supplies		900
Publications and dues		500
Travel to horse shows (no meals)		2,300
Salaries and wages of employees		8,000
Depreciation		
Horse equipment	$3,000	
Horse farm improvements	7,000	
On 10% of personal residence	1,000	11,000
Total home mortgage interest		24,000
Total property taxes on home		2,200
Total property taxes on horse farm improvements		800

The mortgage interest is only on her home because the horse farm improvements are not mortgaged.

a. What are Samantha's tax consequences if the miniature horse activity is a hobby?

b. If it is a business?

46. **LO.3** Sarah owns a vacation cabin in the Tennessee mountains. Without considering the cabin, she has gross income of $65,000. During the year, she rents the cabin for two weeks for $2,500 and uses it herself for four weeks. The total expenses for the year are $10,000 mortgage interest; $1,500 property tax; $2,000 utilities, insurance, and maintenance; and $3,200 depreciation.

a. What effect does the rental of the vacation cabin have on Sarah's AGI?

b. What expenses can Sarah deduct, and how are they classified (i.e., *for* or *from* AGI)?

47. **LO.3** Adelene, who lives in a winter resort area, rented her personal residence for 14 days while she was visiting Brussels. Rent income was $5,000. Related expenses for the year were as follows:

Real property taxes	$ 3,800
Mortgage interest	7,500
Utilities	3,700
Insurance	2,500
Repairs	2,100
Depreciation	15,000

Determine the effect on Adelene's AGI.

48. **LO.3** During the year (not a leap year), Anna rented her vacation home for 30 days, used it personally for 20 days, and left it vacant for 315 days. She had the following income and expenses:

Rent income	$ 7,000
Expenses	
Real estate taxes	2,500
Interest on mortgage	9,000
Utilities	2,400
Repairs	1,000
Roof replacement (a capital expenditure)	12,000
Depreciation	7,500

a. Compute Anna's net rent income or loss and the amounts she can itemize on her tax return, using the court's approach to allocating property taxes and interest.

b. How would your answer in part (a) differ using the IRS's method of allocating property taxes and interest?

49. **LO.3** How would your answer to Problem 48 differ if Anna had rented the house for 87 days and had used it personally for 13 days?

50. **LO.1, 3** Chee, single, age 40, had the following income and expenses during 2016:

Income	
Salary	$43,000
Rental of vacation home (rented 60 days, used personally 60 days, vacant 245 days)	4,000
Municipal bond interest	2,000
Dividend from General Electric	400
Expenses	
Interest on home mortgage	8,400
Interest on vacation home	4,758
Interest on loan used to buy municipal bonds	3,100

Property tax on home	$ 2,200
Property tax on vacation home	1,098
State income tax	3,300
State sales tax	900
Charitable contributions	1,100
Tax return preparation fee	300
Utilities and maintenance on vacation home	2,600
Depreciation on rental portion of vacation home	3,500

Calculate Chee's taxable income for the year before personal exemptions. If Chee has any options, choose the method that maximizes his deductions.

Decision Making   51. **LO.1, 3, 4** Elisa and Clyde operate a retail sports memorabilia shop. For the current year, sales revenue is $55,000 and expenses are as follows:

Cost of goods sold	$21,000
Advertising	1,000
Utilities	2,000
Rent	4,500
Insurance	1,500
Wages to Boyd	8,000

Elisa and Clyde pay $8,000 in wages to Boyd, a part-time employee. Because this amount is $1,000 below the minimum wage, Boyd threatens to file a complaint with the appropriate Federal agency. Although Elisa and Clyde pay no attention to Boyd's threat, Chelsie (Elisa's mother) gives Boyd a check for $1,000 for the disputed wages. Both Elisa and Clyde ridicule Chelsie for wasting money when they learn what she has done. The retail shop is the only source of income for Elisa and Clyde.

a.   Calculate Elisa and Clyde's AGI.

b.   Can Chelsie deduct the $1,000 payment on her tax return? Explain.

c.   How could the tax position of the parties be improved?

Decision Making   52. **LO.3, 4** Brittany Callihan sold stock (basis of $184,000) to her son, Ridge, for
Communications $160,000, the fair market value.

a.   What are the tax consequences to Brittany?

b.   What are the tax consequences to Ridge if he later sells the stock for $190,000? For $152,000? For $174,000?

c.   Write a letter to Brittany in which you inform her of the tax consequences if she sells the stock to Ridge for $160,000. Explain how a sales transaction could be structured that would produce better tax consequences for her. Brittany's address is 32 Country Lane, Lawrence, KS 66045.

53. **LO.3** The Robin Corporation is owned as follows:

Isabelle	26%
Peter, Isabelle's husband	19%
Sonya, Isabelle's mother	15%
Reggie, Isabelle's father	25%
Quinn, an unrelated party	15%

Robin is on the accrual basis, and Isabelle and Peter are on the cash basis. Isabelle and Peter each loaned the Robin Corporation $40,000 out of their separate funds. On December 31, 2016, Robin accrued interest at 7% on both loans. The interest was paid on February 4, 2017. What is the tax treatment of this interest expense/income to Isabelle, Peter, and Robin?

54. **LO.3** For each of the following independent transactions, calculate the recognized gain or loss to the seller and the adjusted basis to the buyer.

a.   Bonnie sells Parchment, Inc. stock (adjusted basis $17,000) to Phillip, her brother, for its fair market value of $12,000.

b.   Amos sells land (adjusted basis $85,000) to his nephew, Boyd, for its fair market value of $70,000.

c.   Susan sells a tax-exempt bond (adjusted basis $20,000) to her wholly owned corporation for its fair market value of $19,000.

d.   Ron sells a business truck (adjusted basis $20,000) that he uses in his sole pro-prietorship to his cousin, Agnes, for its fair market value of $18,500.

e.   Martha sells her partnership interest (adjusted basis $175,000) in Pearl Partner-ship to her adult daughter, Kim, for $220,000.

55. **LO.1, 3, 4** During the current year, Robert pays the following amounts associated with his own residence: Decision Making

Property taxes	$3,000
Mortgage interest	8,000
Repairs	1,200
Utilities	2,700
Replacement of roof	4,000

In addition, Robert paid $1,500 of property taxes on the home that is owned and used by Anne, his daughter.

a.   Which of these expenses can Robert deduct?

b.   Can Anne deduct the $1,500 of property taxes?

c.   Are the deductions *for* AGI or *from* AGI (itemized)?

d.   How could the tax consequences be improved?

Cumulative Problems

56. Roberta Santos, age 41, is single and lives at 120 Sanborne Avenue, Springfield, IL 60781. Her Social Security number is 123-45-6789. Roberta has been divorced from her former husband, Wayne, for three years. She has a son, Jason, who is 17, and a daughter, June, who is 18. Jason's Social Security number is 111-11-1112, and June's is 123-45-6788. Roberta does not want to contribute $3 to the Presidential Election Campaign Fund.   Tax Return Problem

Roberta, an advertising executive, earned a salary of $80,000 in 2015. Her employer withheld $9,000 in Federal income tax and $3,100 in state income tax.

Roberta has legal custody of Jason and June. The divorce decree provides that Roberta is to receive the dependency deductions for the children. Jason lives with his father during summer vacation. Wayne indicates that his expenses for Jason are $10,500. Roberta can document that she spent $6,500 for Jason's support during 2015. In prior years, Roberta gave a signed Form 8332 to Wayne regarding Jason. For 2015, she has decided not to do so. Roberta provides all of June's support.

Roberta's mother died on January 7, 2015. Roberta inherited assets worth $625,000 from her mother. As the sole beneficiary of her mother's life insurance policy, Roberta received insurance proceeds of $300,000. Her mother's cost basis for the life insurance policy was $120,000. Roberta's favorite aunt gave her $13,000 for her birthday in October.

On November 8, 2015, Roberta sells for $22,000 Amber stock that she had pur-chased for $24,000 from her first cousin, Walt, on December 5, 2010. Walt's cost basis for the stock was $26,000, and the stock was worth $23,000 on December 5,

2010. On December 1, 2015, Roberta sold Falcon stock for $13,500. She had acquired the stock on July 2, 2012, for $8,000.

An examination of Roberta's records reveals that she received the following:

- Interest income of $2,500 from First Savings Bank.
- Groceries valued at $750 from a local grocery store for being the 100,000th customer.
- Qualified dividend income of $1,800 from Amber.
- Interest income of $3,750 on City of Springfield school bonds.
- Alimony of $16,000 from Wayne.
- Distribution of $4,800 from ST Partnership. Her distributive share of the partnership passive taxable income was $5,300. She had no prior passive losses.

From her checkbook records, she determines that she made the following payments during 2015:

- Charitable contributions of $4,500 to First Presbyterian Church and $1,500 to the American Red Cross (proper receipts obtained).
- Mortgage interest on her residence of $7,800.
- Property taxes of $3,200 on her residence and $1,100 (ad valorem) on her car.
- Estimated Federal income taxes of $3,800 and estimated state income taxes of $1,000.
- Medical expenses of $5,000 for her and $800 for Jason. In December, her medical insurance policy reimbursed $1,500 of her medical expenses.
- A $1,000 ticket for parking in a handicapped space.
- Attorney's fees of $500 associated with unsuccessfully contesting the parking ticket.
- Contribution of $250 to the campaign of a candidate for governor.
- Because she did not maintain records of the sales tax she paid, she calculates the amount from the sales tax table to be $994.

Calculate Roberta's net tax payable or refund due for 2015. Use the appropriate forms and schedules. Suggested software: H&R BLOCK Tax Software.

Tax Computation Problem
Decision Making
Communications

57. John and Mary Jane Diaz are married, filing jointly. Their address is 204 Shoe Lane, Blacksburg, VA 24061. John is age 35, and Mary Jane is age 30. They are expecting their first child in early 2017. John's salary in 2016 was $105,000, from which $20,800 of Federal income tax and $4,700 of state income tax were withheld. Mary Jane made $52,000 and had $3,000 of Federal income tax and $3,100 of state income tax withheld. The appropriate amounts of FICA tax and Medicare tax were withheld for John and for Mary Jane. John's Social Security number is 111-11-1111, and Mary Jane's Social Security number is 123-45-6789.

John and Mary Jane are both covered by their employer's medical insurance policies with four-fifths of the premiums being paid by the employers. The total premiums were $10,000 for John and $6,200 for Mary Jane. Mary Jane received medical benefits of $7,300 under the plan. John was not ill during 2016. Mary Jane paid noncovered medical expenses of $1,300.

John makes child support payments of $15,000 for his son, Rod, who lives with June, John's former spouse, except for two months in the summer when he visits John and Mary Jane. At the time of the divorce, John worked for a Fortune 500 company and received a salary of $225,000. As a result of corporate downsizing, he lost his job.

Mary Jane's father lived with them until his death in November. His only sources of income were salary of $2,800, unemployment compensation benefits of $3,500, and Social Security benefits of $4,100. Of this amount, he deposited $6,000 in a savings account. The remainder of his support of $9,500, which included funeral expenses of $4,500, was provided by John and Mary Jane.

Other income received by the Diazes was as follows:

Interest on certificates of deposit	$3,500
Share of S corporation taxable income (distributions from the S corporation to Mary Jane were $1,100)	1,500
Award received by Mary Jane from employer for an outstanding suggestion for cutting costs	4,000

John has always wanted to operate his own business. In October 2016, he incurred expenses of $15,000 in investigating the establishment of a retail computer franchise. With the birth of their child expected next year, however, he decides to forgo self-employment for at least a couple of years.

John and Mary Jane made charitable contributions of $3,700 during the year and paid an additional $1,800 in state income taxes in 2016 upon filing their 2015 state income tax return. Their deductible home mortgage interest was $8,200, and their property taxes came to $4,800. They paid sales taxes of $2,000, for which they have receipts. They paid a ticket of $150 that Mary Jane received for running a red light (detected by a red light camera).

Part 1—Tax Computation
Calculate John and Mary Jane's tax (or refund) due for 2016.

Part 2—Tax Planning
Assume that the Diazes come to you for advice in December 2016. John has learned that he will receive a $30,000 bonus. He wants to know if he should take it in December 2016 or in January 2017. Mary Jane will quit work on December 31 to stay home with the baby. Their itemized deductions will decrease by $3,100 because Mary Jane will not have state income taxes withheld. Mary Jane will not receive the employee award in 2017. She expects the medical benefits received to be $9,000. The Diazes expect all of their other income items to remain the same in 2017. Write a letter to John and Mary Jane that contains your advice, and prepare a memo for the tax files.

Research Problems

Note: Solutions to Research Problems can be prepared by using the Checkpoint® Student Edition online research product, which is available to accompany this text. It is also possible to prepare solutions to the Research Problems by using tax research materials found in a standard tax library.

THOMSON REUTERS
CHECKPOINT®
Student Edition

Research Problem 1. Gray Chemical Company manufactured pesticides that were toxic. Over the course of several years, the toxic waste contaminated the air and water around the company's plant. Several employees suffered toxic poisoning, and the Environmental Protection Agency cited the company for violations. In court, the judge found Gray guilty and imposed fines of $15 million. The company voluntarily set up a charitable fund for the purpose of bettering the environment and funded it with $8 million. The company incurred legal expenses in setting up the foundation and defending itself in court. The court reduced the fine from $15 million to $7 million.

Communications

Gray Chemical Company deducted the $8 million paid to the foundation and the legal expenses incurred. The IRS disallowed both deductions on the grounds that the payment was, in fact, a fine and in violation of public policy.

Gray's president, Ted Jones, has contacted you regarding the deductibility of the $7 million fine, the $8 million payment to the foundation, and the legal fees. Write a letter to Mr. Jones that contains your advice, and prepare a memo for the tax files. Gray's address is 200 Lincoln Center, Omaha, NE 68182.

Partial list of research aids:
§§ 162(a) and (f).
Reg. § 1.162–21(b).

Research Problem 2. Rex and Agnes Harrell purchased a beach house at Duck, North Carolina, in early 2015. Although they intended to use the beach house occasionally for recreational purposes, to help pay the mortgage payments, property taxes, and maintenance costs, they also planned to rent it through the realty agency that had handled the purchase. Rex is a surgeon, and Agnes is a counselor.

The beach house was in need of substantial repairs. Rather than hiring a contractor, Rex and Agnes decided they would make the repairs themselves. During both high school and college, Rex had worked summers in construction. In addition, he had taken an advanced course in woodworking and related subjects from a local community college several years ago.

During 2015, according to a log maintained by the Harrells, they occupied the beach house 38 days and rented it 49 days. The log also indicated that on 24 of the 38 days they occupied the beach house, one or both of them were engaged in work on the beach house. Their two teenage children were with them on all of these days but did not help with the work being done. On their 2015 income tax return, Rex and Agnes, who filed a joint return, treated the beach house as a rental property and deducted a pro rata share of the property taxes, mortgage interest, utilities, maintenance and repairs, and depreciation in determining their net loss from the beach home. In the current year, after examining their return, an IRS agent has limited the deductions to the rent income. He contends that the 14-day personal use provision was exceeded and that many of the alleged repairs were capital expenditures. Advise the Harrells on how they should respond to the IRS.

Research Problem 3. Mona viewed herself as a creative individual who had chosen to go to law school for economic reasons. Mona's undergraduate majors were creative writing and American Indian studies.

Mona was very successful as an attorney and eventually was admitted to partnership in her law firm, having an expertise in negotiating settlements involving Indian water rights.

While practicing law, Mona continued her interest in the arts. She had directed plays in high school and maintained her involvement in the theater, even during law school. She belonged to local theater organizations while she practiced law. She took several courses in filmmaking and read extensively in the area. She even took several months off from her legal practice to enroll in NYU's filmmaking program. Her enrollment in the program provided her with hands-on experience and taught her about the technical aspects of filmmaking and allowed her to meet individuals who would later work with her on her documentary.

When she discovered that her husband had similar interests, she decided to create a documentary about Way to Sing America. After acquiring the rights to all of the archival footage of Way to Sing America, she hired a video production company to film interviews that she conducted with Way to Sing America alumni (over 400 hours of such interviews). She spent weekends and nights over a three-year period working on the documentary.

Once the documentary was completed, Mona began marketing it at film festivals. At some of these festivals, her documentary received awards. At the same time, she developed a business plan, hired a bookkeeper to manage the finances, and hired an accounting firm to provide tax advice.

During this three-year period, she reported the following losses:

2013	$ 30,000
2014	400,000
2015	200,000

On her tax returns for the three-year period, in each year, she offset these amounts against her law firm income of approximately $1 million.

Upon audit by the IRS, the agent concluded that her filmmaking activity is a hobby and therefore the losses cannot be deducted except to the extent of the income generated.

Who is correct? Explain.

Use the tax resources of the Internet to address the following questions. Do not restrict your search to the Web, but include a review of newsgroups and general reference materials, practitioner sites and resources, primary sources of the tax law, chat rooms and discussion groups, and other opportunities.

Internet
Activity

Research Problem 4. Sarah was contemplating making a contribution to her traditional IRA in 2015. She determined that she would contribute $5,000 in December 2015, but forgot about making the contribution until she was preparing her 2015 tax return in February 2016. Use the website of any well-known IRA provider (e.g., Fidelity, Vanguard, T. Rowe Price) to determine if Sarah can make a 2015 contribution to her IRA after the tax year has ended.

Research Problem 5. The $1 million maximum compensation deduction does not seem to have deterred large corporations from remunerating their executives at very high levels. What techniques are being used to work around the millionaires' provision? Are executives taking pay cuts, or are their salaries being deferred or changed in nature due to § 162(m)?

Roger CPA Review Questions

ROGER
CPA Review

1. Newton, a business owner, signed a ten-year lease beginning in July of 2016 and immediately paid rent for the remainder of 2016, all of 2017, and all of 2018. How much of the rent paid at the lease signing can be declared as a business expense on Schedule C of Newton's 2016 tax return?

   a. All of it

   b. The July 2016–June 2017 portion only

   c. None of it

   d. The 2016 portion only

2. Freddy, a sole proprietor, is one of several retail business owners competing to rent space in a desirable location that rents at a rate of $2,000 per month. Freddy pays the landlord 12 months' rent up front, even though only two months' advance rent is required. The lease term begins October 1, 2016. In addition, Freddy gives the landlord a $2,500 cash gift in order to sweeten the deal. Considering only these facts, what amount is deductible on Schedule C of Freddy's 2016 tax return?

   a. $4,000

   b. $6,000

   c. $6,500

   d. $8,500

3. Rebecca owns and runs an auto repair shop that is assessed an environmental fine of $2,500 by the state government for failing to properly dispose of used engine oil. Rebecca incurs $1,500 in legal fees to fight this assessment, but does not prevail. She also contributes $2,000 to the political campaign of a gubernatorial candidate who is a lawyer by profession and who specifically promises to simplify the

environmental ordinance under which Rebecca's fine was assessed. Considering the above facts, what total amount is deductible on Rebecca's business tax return?

a. $0
b. $1,500

c. $3,500
d. $6,000

4. Aman, a sole proprietor and rental property owner, had the following expenses in 2016:

Payment to tax lawyer for advice related to business tax liability	$1,000
Property taxes paid on rental home	2,000
Management fee for Aman's retirement portfolio	500

Specify whether each expense would be deducted *for* adjusted gross income (AGI) or *from* AGI on Aman's 2016 tax return.

	Tax Lawyer	Property Taxes	Management Fee
a.	For	From	From
b.	For	For	From
c.	From	For	For
d.	From	From	For

5. A sale between which of the following could trigger a gain or a loss for federal tax purposes?

a. Husband and wife
b. Cousin and cousin

c. Majority shareholder and corporation
d. Ancestor and descendent

Deductions and Losses: Certain Business Expenses and Losses

LEARNING OBJECTIVES: *After completing Chapter 7, you should be able to:*

LO.1 Determine the amount, classification, and timing of the bad debt deduction.

LO.2 State and illustrate the tax treatment of worthless securities, including § 1244 stock.

LO.3 Distinguish between deductible and nondeductible losses of individuals.

LO.4 Identify a casualty and determine the amount, classification, and timing of casualty and theft losses.

LO.5 State and apply the alternative tax treatments for research and experimental expenditures.

LO.6 Calculate the domestic production activities deduction.

LO.7 Determine the amount of the net operating loss and review the impact of the carryback and carryover provisions on previous and subsequent years' taxable income.

LO.8 Identify tax planning opportunities in deducting certain business expenses, business losses, and personal losses.

CHAPTER OUTLINE

© TETRA IMAGES/GETTY IMAGES

THE BIG PICTURE

LOSSES

Martha, a cash basis and calendar year taxpayer, is nearing the end of a year that she would like to forget. Several years ago, she loaned $25,000 to her friend Jamil to enable him to start a business. Jamil had made scheduled payments of $7,000 ($1,000 of this was interest) when he unexpectedly died in January. At the time of his death, he was insolvent. Martha's attempts to collect on the debt were fruitless.

Last October, Martha invested $50,000 in the stock of a pharmaceutical company that previously had been profitable. However, as a result of losing a patent infringement suit, the company declared bankruptcy in May of this year. The bankruptcy trustee has informed shareholders that they should not expect to receive anything from the company.

Martha has owned and operated a bookstore as a sole proprietorship for the past 10 years. The bookstore previously produced annual profits of about $75,000. Due to the growth of online vendors and e-books, Martha's bookstore sustained a net loss of $180,000 this year.

In September, a hurricane caused a large oak tree to blow over onto Martha's house. The cost of removing the tree and making repairs was $32,000. Martha received a check for $25,000 from her insurance company in final settlement of the claim. Her adjusted basis for the house was $280,000.

In March, Martha purchased from a friend, for $20,000, what she believed to be § 1244 stock. The stock's value began to decline significantly soon after its purchase. Several months after her purchase, Martha sold the stock for $12,000.

Can you help relieve Martha's feeling of despair by making her aware of beneficial loss provisions in the tax law?

Read the chapter and formulate your response.

FRAMEWORK 1040 **Tax Formula for Individuals**

This chapter covers the boldfaced portions of the Tax Formula for Individuals that was introduced in Concept Summary 3.1 on p. 3-3. Below those portions are the sections of Form 1040 where the results are reported.

Income *(broadly defined)*	$xx,xxx
Less: Exclusions	(x,xxx)
Gross income	$xx,xxx
Less: **Deductions** *for* adjusted gross income	(x,xxx)

FORM 1040 (p. 1)

12	Business income or (loss). Attach Schedule C or C-EZ	. . . .
35	Domestic production activities deduction. Attach Form 8903	. . . .

Adjusted gross income	$xx,xxx
Less: The greater of total **itemized deductions** *or* the standard deduction	(x,xxx)

FORM 1040 (p. 2)

40	**Itemized deductions** (from Schedule A) **or** your **standard deduction** . . . .

Personal and dependency exemptions	(x,xxx)
Taxable income	$xx,xxx
Tax on taxable income *(see Tax Tables or Tax Rate Schedules)*	$ x,xxx
Less: Tax credits *(including income taxes withheld and prepaid)*	(xxx)
Tax due (or refund)	$ xxx

Working with the tax formula for individuals requires the proper classification of items that are deductible *for* adjusted gross income (AGI) and items that are deductions *from* AGI (itemized deductions). Business expenses and losses, discussed in this chapter, are reductions of gross income to arrive at the taxpayer's AGI. Expenses and losses incurred in connection with a transaction entered into for profit and attributable to rents and royalties are deducted *for* AGI. All other expenses and losses incurred in connection with a transaction entered into for profit are deducted *from* AGI. The determination of the taxpayer's activity (i.e., whether the taxpayer is engaged in a trade or business, an investment, or a personal activity) is crucial in this classification process.[1]

Deductible losses on personal use property are deducted as an itemized deduction. Itemized deductions are deductions *from* AGI. While the general coverage of itemized deductions is in Chapter 10, casualty and theft losses on personal use property are discussed in this chapter.

In determining the amount and timing of the deduction for bad debts, proper classification is again important. A business bad debt is classified as a deduction *for* AGI, and a nonbusiness bad debt is classified as a short-term capital loss.

Other topics discussed in Chapter 7 are research and experimental expenditures, the domestic production activities deduction, and the net operating loss deduction.

7-1 BAD DEBTS

LO.1

Determine the amount, classification, and timing of the bad debt deduction.

If a taxpayer sells goods or provides services on credit and the account receivable subsequently becomes worthless, a **bad debt** deduction is permitted only if income arising from the creation of the account receivable was previously included in income.[2]

---

[1]See, for example, *Groetzinger v. Comm.*, 85–2 USTC ¶9622, 56 AFTR 2d 85–5683, 771 F.2d 269 (CA–7, 1985), aff'd in 87–1 USTC ¶ 9191, 59 AFTR 2d 87–532, 107 S.Ct. 980 (USSC, 1987).

[2]Reg. § 1.166–1(e).

No deduction is allowed, for example, for a bad debt arising from the sale of a product or service when the taxpayer is on the cash basis because no income is reported until the cash has been collected. Permitting a bad debt deduction for a cash basis taxpayer would amount to a double deduction because the expenses of the product or service rendered are deducted when payments are made to suppliers and to employees or at the time of the sale.

> ### EXAMPLE 1
>
> Tracy, a sole proprietor, operates a business named Executive Accounting and Tax Services. Last year, Pat hired Tracy to help him with the accounting for his small business. Tracy also prepared the S corporation income tax return for the business and Pat's personal income tax return. Tracy billed Pat $8,000 for the services she performed. Pat has never paid the bill, his business no longer exists, and his whereabouts are unknown.
>
> If Tracy is an *accrual basis taxpayer*, she includes the $8,000 in income when the services are performed. When she determines that Pat's account will not be collected, she deducts the $8,000 as a bad debt expense.
>
> If Tracy is a *cash basis taxpayer*, she does not include the $8,000 in income until payment is received. When she determines that Pat's account will not be collected, she cannot deduct the $8,000 as a bad debt expense because it was never recognized as income.

> ### The Big Picture
>
> ### EXAMPLE 2
>
> Return to the facts of *The Big Picture* on p. 7-1. Because Martha is a cash basis taxpayer, she cannot take as a bad debt deduction any unpaid accrued interest on the loan to her friend because it was never recognized as income.

A bad debt can also result from the nonrepayment of a loan made by the taxpayer or from purchased debt instruments.

7-1a Specific Charge-Off Method

Taxpayers (other than certain financial institutions) may use only the **specific charge-off method** in accounting for bad debts. Certain financial institutions are allowed to use the **reserve method** for computing deductions for bad debts.

A taxpayer using the specific charge-off method may claim a deduction when a specific business debt becomes either partially or wholly worthless or when a specific non-business debt becomes wholly worthless.[3] For the business debt, the taxpayer must have evidence that the debt is partially worthless and must demonstrate the amount of worthlessness.

If a business debt previously deducted as partially worthless becomes totally worthless in a future year, only the remainder not previously deducted can be deducted in the future year.

In the case of total worthlessness, a deduction is allowed for the entire amount in the year the debt becomes worthless. The amount of the deduction depends on the taxpayer's basis in the bad debt. If the debt arose from the sale of services or products and the face amount was previously included in income, that amount is deductible. If the taxpayer purchased the debt, the deduction is equal to the amount the taxpayer paid for the debt instrument.

One of the more difficult tasks is determining if and when a bad debt is worthless. The loss is deductible only in the year of partial or total worthlessness for business debts and only in the year of total worthlessness for nonbusiness debts. Legal proceedings need not be initiated against the debtor when the surrounding facts indicate that such action will not result in collection.

---

[3] § 166(a).

EXAMPLE 3

In 2014, Ross loaned $1,000 to Kay, who agreed to repay the loan in two years. In 2016, Kay disappeared after the note became delinquent. If a reasonable investigation by Ross indicates that he cannot find Kay or that a suit against Kay would not result in collection, Ross can deduct the $1,000 in 2016.

Bankruptcy is generally an indication of at least partial worthlessness of a debt. Bankruptcy may create worthlessness before the settlement date. If this is the case, the deduction may be taken in the year of worthlessness.

EXAMPLE 4

In Example 3, assume that Kay filed for personal bankruptcy in 2015 and that the debt is a business debt. At that time, Ross learned that unsecured creditors (including Ross) were ultimately expected to receive 20 cents on the dollar. In 2016, settlement is made, and Ross receives only $150. He should deduct $800 ($1,000 loan − $200 expected settlement) in 2015 and $50 in 2016 ($200 balance − $150 proceeds).

If a receivable has been written off as uncollectible during the current tax year and is subsequently collected during the current tax year, the write-off entry is reversed. If a receivable has been written off (deducted) as uncollectible, the collection of the receivable in a later tax year may result in income being recognized. Income will result if the deduction yielded a tax benefit in the year it was taken. See Examples 33 and 34 in Chapter 5.

Concept Summary 7.1 provides a summary of the tax treatment of bad debts using the specific charge-off method.

Concept Summary 7.1

The Tax Treatment of Bad Debts Using the Specific Charge-Off Method

	Business Bad Debts	Nonbusiness Bad Debts
Timing of deduction	A deduction is allowed when the debt becomes either partially or wholly worthless.	A deduction is allowed *only* when the debt becomes wholly worthless.
Character of deduction	The bad debt is deducted as an ordinary loss.	The bad debt is classified as a short-term capital loss, subject to the $3,000 capital loss limitation for individuals.
Recovery of amounts previously deducted	If the account recovered was written off during the current tax year, the write-off entry is reversed. If the account was written off in a previous tax year, income is created subject to the tax benefit rule.	If the account recovered was written off during the current tax year, the write-off entry is reversed. If the account was written off in a previous tax year, income is created subject to the tax benefit rule.

7-1b Business versus Nonbusiness Bad Debts

A **nonbusiness bad debt** is a debt unrelated to the taxpayer's trade or business either when it was created or when it became worthless. The nature of a debt depends upon whether the lender was engaged in the business of lending money or whether there is a proximate relationship between the creation of the debt and the lender's trade or business. The use to which the borrowed funds are put by the debtor is of no consequence. Loans to relatives or friends are the most common type of nonbusiness bad debt.

The Big Picture

EXAMPLE 5

Return to the facts of *The Big Picture* on p. 7-1. Martha loaned her friend Jamil $25,000. Jamil used the money to start a business, which subsequently failed. When Jamil died after having made payments of $7,000 on the loan, he was insolvent.

Even though the proceeds of the loan were used in a business, the loan is a nonbusiness bad debt because the business was Jamil's, not Martha's, and Martha is not in the business of lending money.

The distinction between a business bad debt and a nonbusiness bad debt is important. A **business bad debt** is deductible as an ordinary loss in the year incurred, whereas a nonbusiness bad debt is always treated as a short-term capital loss. Thus, regardless of the age of a nonbusiness bad debt, the deduction may be of limited benefit due to the limitations on capital loss deductibility in any one year. The maximum amount of a net short-term capital loss that an individual can deduct against ordinary income in any one year is $3,000 (see Chapter 16 for a detailed discussion). Although no deduction is allowed when a nonbusiness bad debt is partially worthless, the taxpayer is entitled to deduct the net amount of the loss upon final settlement.

The following example is an illustration of business bad debts adapted from the Regulations.[4]

In 2015, Leif sold his business but retained a claim (note or account receivable) against Bob. The claim became worthless in 2016.

Leif's loss is treated as a business bad debt because the debt was created in the conduct of his former trade or business. Leif is accorded business bad debt treatment even though he was holding the note as an investor and was no longer in a trade or business when the claim became worthless.

The nonbusiness bad debt provisions are *not* applicable to a business entity (e.g., a corporation or partnership). It is assumed that any loans made by a business are related to its trade or business. Therefore, any bad debts are business bad debts.

7-1c **Loans between Related Parties**

Loans between related parties (especially family members) raise the issue of whether the transaction was a *bona fide* loan or a gift. The Regulations state that a bona fide debt arises from a debtor-creditor relationship based on a valid and enforceable obligation to pay a fixed or determinable sum of money. Thus, individual circumstances must be examined to determine whether advances between related parties are gifts or loans. Some considerations are these:

- Was a note properly executed?
- Was there a reasonable rate of interest?
- Was collateral provided?
- What collection efforts were made?
- What was the intent of the parties?

Lana loans $2,000 to her widowed mother for an operation. Lana's mother owns no property and is not employed, and her only income consists of Social Security benefits. No note is issued for the loan, no provision for interest is made, and no repayment date is mentioned. In the current year, Lana's mother dies, leaving no estate.

Assuming that the loan is not repaid, Lana cannot take a deduction for a nonbusiness bad debt because the facts indicate that no debtor-creditor relationship existed.

See Concept Summary 7.2 for a review of the bad debt deduction rules.

7-2 **WORTHLESS SECURITIES AND SMALL BUSINESS STOCK LOSSES**

LO.2

State and illustrate the tax treatment of worthless securities, including § 1244 stock.

7-2a **Worthless Securities**

A loss is allowed for securities that become *completely* worthless during the year (**worthless securities**).[5] Such securities are shares of stock, bonds, notes, or other evidence of indebtedness issued by a corporation or government. The losses generated are treated as capital losses deemed to have occurred on the *last day* of the taxable year.

---

[4]Reg. § 1.166–5(d).   [5]§ 165(g).

Concept Summary 7.2

Bad Debt Deductions

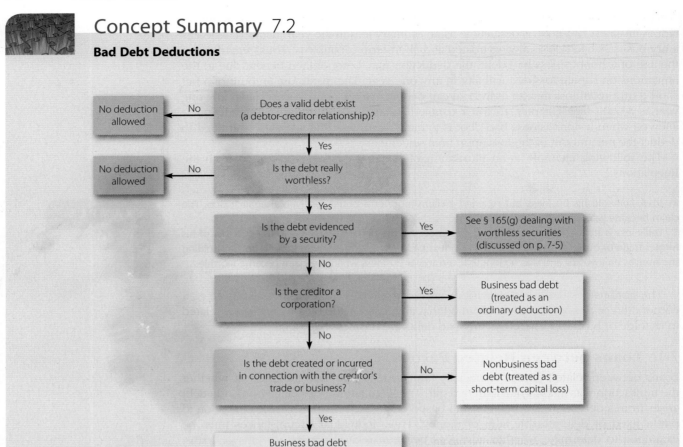

By treating the loss as having occurred on the last day of the taxable year, a loss that would otherwise have been classified as short term (if the date of worthlessness was used) may be classified as a long-term capital loss. Capital losses may be of limited benefit due to the $3,000 capital loss limitation.[6]

The Big Picture

EXAMPLE 8

Return to the facts of *The Big Picture* on p. 7-1. Martha owned stock in a pharmaceutical company that she acquired as an investment on October 1, 2015, at a cost of $50,000. On May 31, 2016, the stock became worthless when the company declared bankruptcy.

    Because the stock is deemed to have become worthless as of December 31, 2016, Martha has a capital loss from an asset held for 15 months (a long-term capital loss).

7-2b Small Business Stock (§ 1244 Stock) Losses

The general rule is that shareholders receive capital gain or loss treatment upon the sale or exchange of stock. However, it is possible to receive an ordinary loss deduction if the loss is sustained on **small business stock (§ 1244 stock)**. This loss could arise from a

---

[6]§ 1211(b).

sale of the stock or from the stock becoming worthless. Only *individuals*[7] who acquired the stock *from* the corporation are eligible to receive ordinary loss treatment under § 1244. The ordinary loss treatment is limited to $50,000 ($100,000 for married individuals filing jointly) per year. Losses on § 1244 stock in excess of the statutory limits receive capital loss treatment.

The corporation must meet certain requirements for the loss on § 1244 stock to be treated as an *ordinary*—rather than a capital—loss. The major requirement is that the total amount of money and other property received by the corporation for stock as a contribution to capital (or paid-in surplus) does not exceed $1 million. The $1 million test is made at the time the stock is issued. Section 1244 stock can be common or preferred stock. Section 1244 applies only to losses. If § 1244 stock is sold at a gain, the Section is not applicable and the gain is capital gain.

Iris, a single individual, was looking for an investment that would give some diversity to her stock portfolio. A friend suggested that she acquire some stock in Eagle Corporation, a new startup company. On July 1, 2014, Iris purchased 100 shares of Eagle Corporation for $100,000. At the time Iris acquired her stock from Eagle Corporation, the corporation had $700,000 of paid-in capital. As a result, the stock qualified as § 1244 stock. On June 20, 2016, Iris sold all of her Eagle stock for $20,000.

Because the Eagle stock is § 1244 stock, Iris has a $50,000 ordinary loss and a $30,000 long-term capital loss.

The Big Picture

Return to the facts of *The Big Picture* on p. 7-1. On March 8, 2016, Martha purchases what she believes is § 1244 stock from her friend Janice for $20,000. On November 2, 2016, she sells the stock in the marketplace for $12,000.

Because Martha purchases the stock from Janice and not the corporation, the stock is not § 1244 stock to Martha. As a result, Martha has an $8,000 short-term capital loss.

7-3 **LOSSES OF INDIVIDUALS**

LO.3

Distinguish between deductible and nondeductible losses of individuals.

An individual may deduct the following losses under § 165(c):

- Losses incurred in a trade or business.

- Losses incurred in a transaction entered into for profit.

- Losses caused by fire, storm, shipwreck, or other casualty or by theft.

Examples of losses in the first two categories include a loss on property used in a proprietorship or a loss on property held for rent. An individual taxpayer suffering losses from damage to *nonbusiness* property can deduct only those losses attributable to fire, storm, shipwreck, or other casualty or theft. Although the meaning of the terms *fire, storm, shipwreck*, and *theft* is relatively free from dispute, the term *other casualty* needs further clarification. It means casualties analogous to fire, storm, or shipwreck. The term also includes accidental loss of property provided the loss qualifies under the same rules as any other casualty. These rules are that the loss must result from an event that is (1) identifiable; (2) damaging to property; and (3) sudden, unexpected, and unusual in nature.

A *sudden event* is an event that is swift and precipitous and not gradual or progressive. An *unexpected event* is an event that is ordinarily unanticipated and occurs without the intent of the individual who suffers the loss. An *unusual event* is an event that is extraordinary and nonrecurring and does not commonly occur during the activity in which the taxpayer was engaged when the destruction occurred.[8] Examples include

---

[7]The term *individuals* for this purpose does not include a trust or an estate (but could include a partnership or an LLC).

[8]Rev.Rul. 72–592, 1972–2 C.B. 101.

auto accidents, mine cave-ins, sonic booms, and vandalism. Weather that causes damage (e.g., drought) must be unusual and severe for the particular region. Damage must be to the taxpayer's property to qualify as a casualty loss .

A taxpayer can take a deduction for a casualty loss from an automobile accident only if the damage was not caused by the taxpayer's willful act or willful negligence.

EXAMPLE 11

Ted parks his car on a hill and fails to set the brake properly and to curb the wheels. As a result of Ted's negligence, the car rolls down the hill and is damaged. The repairs to Ted's car should qualify for casualty loss treatment because Ted's act of negligence does not appear to be willful.

LO.4

Identify a casualty and determine the amount, classification, and timing of casualty and theft losses.

7-3a Events That Are Not Casualties

Not all acts of nature are treated as casualty losses for income tax purposes. Because a casualty must be sudden, unexpected, and unusual, progressive deterioration (such as erosion due to wind or rain) is not a casualty because it does not meet the suddenness test.

Examples of nonsudden events that generally do not qualify as casualties include disease and insect damage. When the damage was caused by termites over a period of several years, some courts have disallowed a casualty loss deduction.[9] On the other hand, some courts have held that termite damage over periods of up to 15 months after infestation constituted a sudden event and was, therefore, deductible as a casualty loss.[10] Despite the existence of some judicial support for the deductibility of termite damage as a casualty loss, the current position of the IRS is that termite damage is not deductible.[11]

Other examples of events that are not casualties are losses resulting from a decline in value rather than an actual loss of the property. No loss was allowed where the taxpayer's home declined in value as a result of a landslide that destroyed neighboring homes but did no actual damage to the taxpayer's home.[12] Similarly, a taxpayer was allowed a loss for the actual flood damage to his property but not for the decline in market value due to the property being flood-prone.[13]

7-3b Theft Losses

Theft includes, but is not necessarily limited to, larceny, embezzlement, and robbery.[14] Theft does not include misplaced items.[15]

Theft losses are computed like other casualty losses (discussed in the following section), but the *timing* for recognition of the loss differs. A theft loss is deducted in the year of discovery, which may not be the same as the year of the theft. If in the year of the discovery a claim exists (e.g., against an insurance company) and there is a reasonable expectation of recovering the adjusted basis of the asset from the insurance company, no deduction is permitted.[16] If in the year of settlement the recovery is less than the asset's adjusted basis, a partial deduction may be available. If the recovery is greater than the asset's adjusted basis, gain may be recognized.

Gains & Losses on Recovery

EXAMPLE 12

Keith's new sailboat, which he uses for personal purposes, was stolen from the storage marina in December 2015. He discovered the loss on June 3, 2016, and filed a claim with his insurance company that was settled on January 30, 2017.

Assuming that there is a reasonable expectation of full recovery, no deduction is allowed in 2016. A partial deduction may be available in 2017 if the actual insurance proceeds are less than the lower of the fair market value or the adjusted basis of the asset. (Loss measurement rules are discussed later in this chapter.)

[9]*Fay v. Helvering*, 41–2 USTC ¶9494, 27 AFTR 432, 120 F.2d 253 (CA–2, 1941); *U.S. v. Rogers*, 41–1 USTC ¶9442, 27 AFTR 423, 120 F.2d 244 (CA–9, 1941).

[10]*Rosenberg v. Comm.*, 52–2 USTC ¶9377, 42 AFTR 303, 198 F.2d 46 (CA–8, 1952); *Shopmaker v. U.S.*, 54–1 USTC ¶9195, 45 AFTR 758, 119 F.Supp. 705 (D.Ct. Mo., 1953).

[11]Rev.Rul. 63–232, 1963–2 C.B. 97.

[12]*H. Pulvers v. Comm.*, 69–1 USTC ¶9222, 23 AFTR 2d 69–678, 407 F.2d 838 (CA–9, 1969).

[13]*S. L. Solomon*, 39 TCM 1282, T.C.Memo. 1980–87.

[14]Reg. § 1.165–8(d).

[15]*Mary Francis Allen*, 16 T.C. 163 (1951).

[16]Reg. §§ 1.165–1(d)(2) and 1.165–8(a)(2).

7-3c **When to Deduct Casualty Losses**

General Rule

Generally, a casualty loss is deducted in the year the loss occurs. However, no casualty loss is permitted if a reimbursement claim with a *reasonable prospect of full recovery* exists.[17] If the taxpayer has a partial claim, only part of the loss can be claimed in the year of the casualty, and the remainder is deducted in the year the claim is settled.

Brian's new sailboat was completely destroyed by fire in 2016. Its cost and fair market value were $15,000. Brian's only claim against the insurance company was on a $10,000 policy, which was not settled by year-end. The following year, 2017, Brian settled with the insurance company for $8,000.

Brian is entitled to a $5,000 deduction in 2016 ($15,000 less $10,000) and a $2,000 deduction in 2017. If Brian held the sailboat for personal use, the $5,000 deduction in 2016 is reduced first by $100 and then by 10% of his 2016 AGI. The $2,000 deduction in 2017 is reduced by 10% of his 2017 AGI (see the following discussion on the $100 and 10% floors).

If a taxpayer receives reimbursement for a casualty loss sustained and deducted in a previous year, an amended return is not filed for that year. Instead, the taxpayer must include the reimbursement in gross income on the return for the year in which it is received to the extent the previous deduction resulted in a tax benefit.

Fran had a deductible casualty loss of $4,000 on her 2015 tax return. Fran's taxable income for 2015 was $60,000. In June 2016, Fran is reimbursed $2,750 for the prior year's casualty loss.

Fran includes the entire $2,750 in gross income for 2016 because the deduction in 2015 produced a tax benefit.

Disaster Area Losses

An exception to the general rule for the time of deduction is allowed for **disaster area losses**, which are casualties sustained in an area designated as a disaster area by the President of the United States.[18] In such cases, the taxpayer may *elect* to treat the loss as having occurred in the taxable year immediately *preceding* the taxable year in which the disaster actually occurred. The rationale for this exception is to provide immediate relief to disaster victims in the form of accelerated tax benefits.

If the due date, plus extensions, for the prior year's return has not passed, a taxpayer makes the election to claim the disaster area loss on the prior year's tax return. If the disaster occurs after the prior year's return has been filed, it is necessary to file either an amended return or a refund claim. In any case, the taxpayer must show clearly that such an election is being made.

Disaster loss treatment also applies in the case of a personal residence that has been rendered unsafe for use as a residence because of a disaster. This provision applies when, within 120 days after the President designates the area as a disaster area, the state or local government where the residence is located orders the taxpayer to demolish or relocate the residence.[19]

The Big Picture

EXAMPLE 15

Return to the facts of *The Big Picture* on p. 7-1. On September 28, 2016, Martha's personal residence was damaged when a hurricane caused an oak tree to fall onto the house. The amount of her uninsured loss was $7,000. Because of the extent of the damage in the area, the President of the United States designated the area a disaster area.

continued

---

[17]Reg. § 1.165–1(d)(2)(i).

[18]§ 165(h).

[19]§ 165(k).

Because Martha's loss is a disaster area loss, she may elect to file an amended return for 2015 and take the loss in that year.

If Martha elects this course of action, the amount of the loss will be reduced first by $100 (the materiality amount in 2015) and then by 10% of her 2015 AGI.

If Martha forgoes the election, she may take the loss on her 2016 income tax return. The amount of the loss will be reduced first by $100 (the materiality amount in 2016) and then by 10% of her 2016 AGI.

7-3d Measuring the Amount of Loss

Amount of Loss

The rules for determining the amount of a loss depend in part on whether business use, income-producing use, or personal use property was involved. Another factor that must be considered is whether the property was partially or completely destroyed.

If business property or property held for the production of income (e.g., rental property) is *completely destroyed*, the loss is equal to the adjusted basis of the property at the time of destruction.

EXAMPLE 16

Vicki's automobile, which was used only for business purposes, was destroyed by fire. Vicki had unintentionally allowed her insurance coverage to expire. The fair market value of the automobile was $9,000 at the time of the fire, and its adjusted basis was $10,000.

Vicki is allowed a loss deduction of $10,000 (the basis of the automobile). The $10,000 loss is a deduction *for* AGI.

A different measurement rule applies for *partial destruction* of business property and income-producing property and for *partial* or *complete destruction* of personal use property. In these situations, the loss is the *lesser* of the following:

- The adjusted basis of the property.
- The difference between the fair market value of the property before the event and the fair market value immediately after the event.

TAX IN THE NEWS   The Tax Consequences of Lost Bitcoins

In Notice 2014–21 (2014–16 I.R.B. 938), the Internal Revenue Service provided initial guidance on transactions involving virtual currency (including bitcoins). Specifically, the IRS indicates that bitcoin is *not* currency; rather, it is property. As such, gain and losses on the disposition of bitcoins will not be treated in a manner similar to other currencies (e.g., euros and British pounds). This is a disappointment to taxpayers who lost money in bitcoin investments and may have hoped that the losses would be classified as currency losses (and, as such, ordinary losses). Taxpayers who have disposed of appreciated investment positions in bitcoins may enjoy capital gains treatment. Taxpayers who hold bitcoin as inventory will be subject to ordinary gains and losses upon disposition.

But what happens if the hard drive on which bitcoins are stored crashes and the data are not recoverable? Is this a "sudden, unexpected, and unusual event" that could qualify for a casualty loss? One might argue that failure to back up the data on the hard drive might be deemed carelessness (and so none of the loss would be allowed). And, certainly, no loss would be allowed until the taxpayer could confirm that there was no chance of recovery.

What if the taxpayer inadvertently deletes keys to bitcoins he or she previously mined? In general, you cannot take a loss for lost or misplaced property. In this case, no loss would be allowed due to carelessness on the part of the taxpayer. So the bottom line is this: Always back up your digital files.

Kelly's uninsured automobile, which was used only for business purposes, was damaged in an accident. On the date of the accident, the fair market value of the automobile was $12,000, and its adjusted basis was $9,000. After the accident, the automobile was appraised at $4,000.

Kelly's loss deduction is $8,000 (the lesser of the adjusted basis or the decrease in fair market value). The $8,000 loss is a deduction *for* AGI.

The deduction for the loss of property that is part business and part personal must be computed separately for the business portion and the personal portion.

Any insurance recovery reduces the loss for business, production of income, and personal use losses. In fact, a taxpayer may realize a gain if the insurance proceeds exceed the amount of the loss. Chapter 17 discusses the treatment of net gains and losses on business property and income-producing property.

A taxpayer is not permitted to deduct a casualty loss for damage to insured personal use property unless a *timely insurance claim* is filed with respect to the damage to the property. This rule applies to the extent that any insurance policy provides for full or partial reimbursement for the loss.[20]

Generally, an appraisal before and after the casualty is needed to measure the amount of the loss. However, the *cost of repairs* to the damaged property is acceptable as a method of establishing the loss in value provided the following criteria are met:

- The repairs are necessary to restore the property to its condition immediately before the casualty.
- The amount spent for such repairs is not excessive.
- The repairs do not extend beyond the damage suffered.
- The value of the property after the repairs does not, as a result of the repairs, exceed the value of the property immediately before the casualty.[21]

Cost of Repairs Method

ETHICS & EQUITY   Is Policy Cancellation an Escape Hatch?

Noah's house is burglarized for the third time, and he knows that if he files a claim, the insurance company will cancel his homeowner's policy or impose a prohibitive premium. Noah does not file a claim, yet he deducts the loss on his tax return. Is his loss allowed?

Reduction for $100-per-Event and 10%-of-AGI Floors

The amount of the loss for personal use property must be further reduced by a $100-*per-event* floor and a 10%-of-AGI *aggregate* floor.[22] The $100 floor applies separately to each casualty and applies to the entire loss from each casualty (e.g., if a storm damages both a taxpayer's residence and automobile, only $100 is subtracted from the total amount of the loss). The losses are then added together, and the total is reduced by 10 percent of the taxpayer's AGI. The resulting loss is the taxpayer's itemized deduction for casualty and theft losses.

Rocky, who had AGI of $30,000, was involved in a motorcycle accident in 2016. His motorcycle, which was used only for personal use and had a fair market value of $12,000 and an adjusted basis of $9,000, was completely destroyed. He received $5,000 from his insurance company.

Rocky's casualty loss deduction is $900 [$9,000 basis − $5,000 insurance recovery − $100 floor − $3,000 (10% × $30,000 AGI)]. The $900 casualty loss is an itemized deduction (*from* AGI).

[20]§ 165(h)(5)(E).
[21]Reg. § 1.165–7(a)(2)(ii).

[22]§ 165(c)(3).

When a nonbusiness casualty loss is spread between two taxable years because of the *reasonable prospect of recovery* doctrine, the loss in the second year is not reduced by the $100 floor. This result occurs because this floor is imposed per event and has already reduced the amount of the loss in the first year. However, the loss in the second year is still subject to the 10 percent floor based upon the taxpayer's second-year AGI (refer to Example 13). For taxpayers who suffer qualified disaster area losses, the 10%-of-AGI floor is determined by using the AGI of the year for which the deduction is claimed.[23]

Multiple Losses

The rules for computing loss deductions where multiple losses have occurred are explained in Examples 19 and 20.

Multiple Casualty Losses

EXAMPLE 19

During the year, Tim had the following casualty losses:

| Asset | Adjusted Basis | Fair Market Value of Asset | | Insurance Recovery |
		Before the Casualty	After the Casualty	
A	$900	$600	$–0–	$400
B	300	800	250	100

Assets A and B were used in Tim's business at the time of the casualty. The following losses are allowed:

Asset A: $500. The complete destruction of a business asset results in a deduction of the adjusted basis of the property (reduced by any insurance recovery), regardless of the asset's fair market value.

Asset B: $200. The partial destruction of a business (or personal use) asset results in a deduction equal to the lesser of the adjusted basis ($300) or the decline in value ($550), reduced by any insurance recovery ($100).

Both the Asset A and Asset B losses are deductions *for* AGI. The $100 floor and the 10%-of-AGI floor do not apply because the assets are business assets.

EXAMPLE 20

In 2016, Emily had AGI of $20,000 and the following casualty losses:

| Asset | Adjusted Basis | Fair Market Value of Asset | | Insurance Recovery |
		Before the Casualty	After the Casualty	
A	$1,900	$1,400	$ –0–	$200
B	2,500	4,000	1,000	–0–
C	800	400	100	250

Assets A, B, and C were held for personal use, and the losses to these three assets are from three different casualties. The loss for each asset is computed as follows:

Asset A: $1,100. The lesser of the adjusted basis of $1,900 or the $1,400 decline in value, reduced by the insurance recovery of $200, minus the $100 floor.

Asset B: $2,400. The lesser of the adjusted basis of $2,500 or the $3,000 decline in value, minus the $100 floor.

Asset C: $0. The lesser of the adjusted basis of $800 or the $300 decline in value, reduced by the insurance recovery of $250, minus the $100 floor.

continued

---

[23]§ 165(i).

Emily's itemized casualty loss deduction for the year is $1,500:

Asset A loss	$ 1,100
Asset B loss	2,400
Asset C loss	–0–
Total loss	$ 3,500
Less: 10% of AGI (10% × $20,000)	(2,000)
Itemized casualty loss deduction	$ 1,500

7-3e **Statutory Framework for Deducting Losses of Individuals**

Concept Summary 7.3 provides a summary of the statutory framework of deducting losses of individuals.

Concept Summary 7.3

Statutory Framework for Deducting Losses of Individuals

	Personal Casualty/Theft Losses		Employee Casualty/Theft Losses	Production of Income Casualty/ Theft Losses	Trade or Business Casualty/Theft Losses
	$100-per-Event Rule	**10%-of-AGI Rule**	**2%-of-AGI Rule**		
General Application	Reduce each casualty or theft loss by $100 when figuring the potential casualty loss deduction. Apply this rule to personal use property after the amount of the loss has been determined.	Reduce the *total* casualty or theft loss by 10% of adjusted gross income. Apply this rule to personal use property after each loss is reduced by $100 (the "$100-per-event rule"). These personal losses are not subject to the 2%-of-AGI rule.	Casualty and theft losses incurred by an employee in connection with a trade or business are deductible *for* AGI if the loss is reimbursed by the employer (with the net loss being deductible). If the loss is not reimbursed, the loss is deductible *from* AGI as a miscellaneous itemized deduction subject to the 2%-of-AGI floor. These losses are not subject to the $100-per-event rule or the 10%-of-AGI rule.[24]	Casualty and theft losses incurred by an individual in a transaction entered into for profit are not subject to the $100-per-event and the 10%-of-AGI limitations. If these losses are attributable to rents or royalties, the deduction is *for* AGI.[25] If not, they are deductions *from* AGI.	Casualty and theft losses incurred by an individual in connection with a trade or business are deductible *for* AGI.[26] These losses are not subject to the $100-per-event and the 10%-of-AGI limitations.
Single Event	Apply this rule only once to each casualty or theft event, even if many pieces of property are affected by the event.	Apply this rule only once, even if many pieces of property are affected.	Apply this rule only once, even if many pieces of property are affected.		
More Than One Event	Apply to the loss from each event.	Apply to the total of all losses from all events.	Apply to the total of all losses from all events.		

---

[24]§ 67(b)(3).

[25]§ 62(a)(4).

[26]§ 62(a)(1).

7-3f **Personal Casualty Gains and Losses**

If a taxpayer has personal casualty and theft gains as well as losses, a special set of rules applies for determining the tax consequences. A **personal casualty gain** is the recognized gain from a casualty or theft of personal use property. A **personal casualty loss** for this purpose is a casualty or theft loss of personal use property after the application of the $100 floor. A taxpayer who has both gains and losses for the taxable year must first net (offset) the personal casualty gains and personal casualty losses. If the gains exceed the losses, the gains and losses are treated as gains and losses from the sale of capital assets. The capital gains and losses are short term or long term, depending on the period the taxpayer held each of the assets. In the netting process, personal casualty and theft gains and losses are not netted with the gains and losses on business and income-producing property.

During the year, Cliff had the following personal casualty gains and losses (after deducting the $100 floor):

Asset	Holding Period	Gain or (Loss)
A	Three months	($ 300)
B	Three years	(2,400)
C	Two years	3,200

Cliff computes the tax consequences as follows:

Personal casualty gain	$ 3,200
Personal casualty loss ($300 + $2,400)	(2,700)
Net personal casualty gain	$ 500

Cliff treats all of the gains and losses as capital gains and losses and has the following:

Short-term capital loss (Asset A)	$ 300
Long-term capital loss (Asset B)	2,400
Long-term capital gain (Asset C)	3,200

If personal casualty losses exceed personal casualty gains, all gains and losses are treated as ordinary items. The gains—and the losses to the extent of gains—are treated as ordinary income and ordinary loss in computing AGI. Losses in excess of gains are deducted as itemized deductions to the extent the losses exceed 10 percent of AGI.[27]

During the year, Hazel had AGI of $20,000 and the following personal casualty gain and loss (after deducting the $100 floor):

Asset	Holding Period	Gain or (Loss)
A	Three years	($2,700)
B	Four months	200

Hazel computes the tax consequences as follows:

Personal casualty loss	($2,700)
Personal casualty gain	200
Net personal casualty loss	($2,500)

Hazel treats the gain and the loss as ordinary items. The $200 gain and $200 of the loss are included in computing AGI. Hazel's itemized deduction for casualty losses is computed as follows:

Casualty loss in excess of gain ($2,700 − $200)	$ 2,500
Less: 10% of AGI (10% × $20,000)	(2,000)
Itemized deduction	$ 500

See Concept Summary 7.4 for a review of the tax treatment of casualty gains and losses.

---

[27]§ 165(h).

Concept Summary 7.4

Casualty Gains and Losses

	Business Use or Income-Producing Property	Personal Use Property
Event creating the loss	Any event.	Casualty or theft.
Amount	The lesser of the decline in fair market value or the adjusted basis, but always the adjusted basis if the property is totally destroyed.	The lesser of the decline in fair market value or the adjusted basis.
Insurance	Insurance proceeds received reduce the amount of the loss.	Insurance proceeds received (or for which there is an unfiled claim) reduce the amount of the loss.
$100 floor	Not applicable.	Applicable per event.
Gains and losses	Gains and losses are netted (see detailed discussion in Chapter 17).	Personal casualty and theft gains and losses are netted.
Gains exceeding losses	See Chapter 17.	The gains and losses are treated as gains and losses from the sale of capital assets.
Losses exceeding gains	See Chapter 17.	The gains—and the losses to the extent of gains—are treated as ordinary items in computing AGI. The losses in excess of gains, to the extent they exceed 10% of AGI, are itemized deductions.

7-4 RESEARCH AND EXPERIMENTAL EXPENDITURES

LO.5

State and apply the alternative tax treatments for research and experimental expenditures.

Section 174 covers the treatment of research and experimental expenditures. The Regulations define **research and experimental expenditures** as follows:

> all such costs incident to the development or improvement of a product (including an experimental or pilot model, a plant process, a product, a formula, an invention, or similar property). The term includes the costs of obtaining a patent, such as attorneys' fees expended in making and perfecting a patent application. Expenditures represent research and development costs in the experimental or laboratory sense if they are for activities intended to discover information that would eliminate uncertainty concerning the development or improvement of a product. The term does not include expenditures such as those for the ordinary testing or inspection of materials or products for quality control or those for efficiency surveys, management studies, consumer surveys, advertising, or promotions.[28]

Expenses in connection with the acquisition or improvement of land or depreciable property are not research and experimental expenditures. Rather, they increase the basis of the land or depreciable property. However, depreciation on a building used for research may be a research and experimental expense. Only the depreciation that is a research and experimental expense (not the cost of the asset) is subject to the three alternatives discussed below.

The law permits the following *three alternatives* for the handling of research and experimental expenditures:

- Expensed in the year paid or incurred.
- Deferred and amortized.
- Capitalized.

If the costs are capitalized, a deduction is not available until the research project is abandoned or is deemed worthless. Because many products resulting from research

---

[28]Reg. § 1.174–2(a)(1), (2), and (3).

projects do not have a definite and limited useful life, a taxpayer should ordinarily opt to write off the expenditures immediately or to defer and amortize them. It is generally preferable to elect an immediate write-off of the research expenditures because of the time value of the tax deduction.

The law also provides a credit for increasing research expenses over what the expense amount was in a base year or years. Two different formulas are available for computing the credit.[29]

7-4a **Expense Method**

A taxpayer can expense all of the research and experimental expenditures incurred in the current year and all subsequent years. The consent of the IRS is not required if the method is adopted for the first taxable year in which such expenditures were paid or incurred. Once this method is adopted, the taxpayer must continue to expense all qualifying expenditures unless a request for a change is made to, and approved by, the IRS. In certain instances, a taxpayer may incur research and experimental expenditures before actually engaging in any trade or business activity. In such instances, the Supreme Court has applied the liberal standard of deductibility crafted by Congress in § 174 and permitted a deduction in the year of incurrence.[30]

7-4b **Deferral and Amortization Method**

Alternatively, research and experimental expenditures may be deferred and amortized if the taxpayer makes an election.[31] Under the election, research and experimental expenditures are amortized ratably over a period of not less than 60 months. A deduction is allowed beginning with the month in which the taxpayer first realizes benefits from the experimental expenditure. The election is binding, and a change requires permission from the IRS.

EXAMPLE 23

Gold Corporation decides to develop a new line of adhesives. The project begins in 2016. Gold incurs the following expenses in 2016 and 2017 in connection with the project:

	2016	2017
Salaries	$25,000	$18,000
Materials	8,000	2,000
Depreciation on machinery	6,500	5,700

The benefits from the project will be realized starting in March 2018. If Gold Corporation elects a 60-month deferral and amortization period, there is no deduction prior to March 2018, the month benefits from the project begin to be realized. The deduction for 2018 is $10,867, computed as follows:

Salaries ($25,000 + $18,000)	$43,000
Materials ($8,000 + $2,000)	10,000
Depreciation ($6,500 + $5,700)	12,200
Total	$65,200
$65,200 × (10 months/60 months) =	$10,867

The option to treat research and experimental expenditures as deferred expense is usually employed when a company does not have sufficient income to offset the research and experimental expenses. Rather than create net operating loss carryovers that might not be utilized because of the 20-year limitation on such carryovers, the deferral and amortization method may be used.[32] The deferral of research and experimental expenditures should also be considered if the taxpayer expects higher tax rates in the future.

---

[29]§ 41. See Chapter 13 for a more detailed discussion of this credit.

[30]*Snow v. Comm.*, 74–1 USTC ¶9432, 33 AFTR 2d 74–1251, 94 S.Ct. 1876 (USSC, 1974).

[31]§ 174(b)(2).

[32]Another option is to deduct these expenses for regular tax purposes, but elect in any year where helpful, to capitalize and amortize the expenses over 10 years for both regular tax and alternative minimum tax purposes [§ 59(e)]. Chapter 12 includes a discussion of this option.

7-5 DOMESTIC PRODUCTION ACTIVITIES DEDUCTION

A number of years ago, Congress enacted changes to a variety of tax provisions that our world trading partners regarded as allowing unfair advantage to U.S. exports. Among other changes, Congress created a deduction based on the income from manufacturing activities (designated as *production activities*).[33] The **domestic production activities deduction (DPAD)** is contained in § 199. Form 8903 is used to report the calculation of the domestic production activities deduction.

7-5a Operational Rules

Calculation of the Domestic Production Activities Deduction

The DPAD is based on the following formula:[34]

$$9\% \times \text{Lesser of} \begin{cases} \text{Qualified production activities income (QPAI)} \\ \text{Taxable (or modified adjusted gross) income} \\ \text{or alternative minimum taxable income} \end{cases}$$

Taxable income is determined without regard to the DPAD. In the case of an individual (a sole proprietorship or an owner of a flow-through entity), **modified adjusted gross income** is substituted for taxable income.[35]

The taxable income limitation is determined after the application of any net operating loss (NOL) deduction for the tax year (NOLs are explained in detail later in the chapter). Thus, a company with an NOL carryforward for a tax year is ineligible for the DPAD if the carryforward eliminates current taxable income. Further, a taxpayer that has an NOL carryback may lose part or all of the DPAD benefit for that year. As taxable income is reduced by the NOL carryback, there is a corresponding reduction in the DPAD. If qualified production activities income (QPAI) cannot be used in a particular year due to the taxable income limitation (see the preceding formula), it is lost forever. (The calculation of QPAI is explained in the next section.)

DPAD: Calculation Using QPAI

> Opal, Inc., manufactures and sells costume jewelry. It also sells costume jewelry purchased from other manufacturers. During 2016, Opal had a *profit* of $200,000 (QPAI) from the sale of its own manufactured jewelry and a *loss* of $50,000 from the sale of the purchased jewelry.
>
> Based on this information, Opal's QPAI is $200,000 and its taxable income is $150,000 ($200,000 − $50,000). Opal's DPAD becomes $13,500 [9% of the lesser of $200,000 (QPAI) or $150,000 (taxable income)].

EXAMPLE 24

> Assume the same facts as in Example 24, except that Opal also has an NOL carryover from 2015 of $300,000.
>
> As taxable income for 2016 is zero ($200,000 − $50,000 − $300,000), there is no DPAD.

EXAMPLE 25

Another important limitation is that the amount of the DPAD cannot exceed 50 percent of certain **W–2 wages** paid by the taxpayer during the tax year.[36] If no W–2 wages are paid, no DPAD will be allowed. So part of the rationale behind this limitation is to preserve U.S. manufacturing jobs and to discourage their outsourcing. An employer's W–2 wages include the sum of the aggregate amount of wages and elective deferrals required to be included on the W–2 wage statements for certain employees during the employer's taxable year. Elective deferrals include those amounts deferred under § 457 plans and Roth contributions (see Chapter 19). An employer previously included wages paid to all workers during a tax

---

[33]Section 101 of the *American Jobs Creation Act of 2004*, Public Law No. 108-357 (October 22, 2004).

[34]§ 199(a). For tax years beginning in 2005 or 2006, the 9% rate was 3%. For tax years beginning in 2007, 2008, and 2009, the 9% rate was 6%.

[35]§ 199(d)(2). Generally, modified AGI is AGI before any DPAD.

[36]§ 199(b).

year and not just the wages of the employees engaged in qualified production activities. However, as a result of a subsequent statutory change, an employer is permitted to include only those W–2 wages paid to employees engaged in qualified production activities.

DPAD: W–2 Limitation

EXAMPLE 26

In 2016, Red, Inc., a calendar year taxpayer, has QPAI of $2 million and taxable income of $2.1 million. Because Red outsources much of its work to independent contractors, its W–2 wage base, which for Red is related entirely to production activities, is $80,000.

Although Red's DPAD normally would be $180,000 [9% of the lesser of $2 million (QPAI) or $2.1 million (taxable income)], it is limited to $40,000 [50% of $80,000 (W–2 wages)].

EXAMPLE 27

Assume the same facts as in Example 26, except that Red also pays salaries of $50,000 related to its *nonproduction* activities. Because these wages are not paid to employees engaged in production activities, the wage limitation on the DPAD remains at $40,000 [50% of $80,000 ($80,000 + $0)].

Calculation of Qualified Production Activities Income

Qualified production activities income (QPAI) is the excess of **domestic production gross receipts (DPGR)** over the sum of:

- The cost of goods sold allocated to such receipts.
- Other deductions, expenses, or losses directly allocated to such receipts.
- The ratable portion of deductions, expenses, and losses not directly allocable to such receipts or another class of income.[37]

QPAI is determined on an item-by-item basis—not on a division-by-division or a transaction-by-transaction basis. Because all items must be netted in the calculation, the final QPAI amount can be either positive or negative. The effect of the netting rule is to preclude taxpayers from selecting only profitable product lines or profitable transactions when calculating QPAI.

EXAMPLE 28

A taxpayer manufactures pants and shirts with the following QPAI results: $5 for one pair of pants and a negative $2 for one shirt. Because the two items are netted, the QPAI amount that controls is $3 ($5 − $2).

Five specific categories of DPGR qualify for the DPAD:[38]

- The lease, license, sale, exchange, or other disposition of qualified production property (QPP) that was manufactured, produced, grown, or extracted (MPGE) in the United States.
- Qualified films largely created in the United States.
- The production of electricity, natural gas, or potable water.
- Construction (but not self-construction) performed in the United States.
- Engineering and architectural services for domestic construction.

The sale of food and beverages prepared by a taxpayer at a retail establishment and the transmission or distribution of electricity, natural gas, or potable water are specifically excluded from the definition of DPGR.

7-5b Eligible Taxpayers

The deduction is available to a variety of taxpayers, including individuals, partnerships, S corporations, C corporations, cooperatives, estates, and trusts. For a pass-through entity (e.g., partnerships and S corporations), the deduction flows through to the individual

---

[37]§ 199(c).   [38]§ 199(c)(4).

owners. In the case of a sole proprietor, a deduction *for* AGI results and is claimed on Form 1040, line 35 on page 1. A Form 8903 must be attached to support the deduction.

In practice, the DPAD calculation is challenging (and complicated by numerous rules and definitions contained in the Code and Regulations). Further, the additional records needed to support the deduction, along with its computational complexities, increase the tax reporting burden. For additional information on the DPAD, see Chapter 3 in *South-Western Federal Taxation: Corporations, Partnerships, Estates & Trusts.*

7-6 NET OPERATING LOSSES

LO.7

Determine the amount of the net operating loss and review the impact of the carryback and carryover provisions on previous and subsequent years' taxable income.

The requirement that every taxpayer file an annual income tax return (whether on a calendar year or a fiscal year) may result in certain inequities for taxpayers who experience cyclical patterns of income or expense. Inequities result from the application of a progressive rate structure to taxable income determined on an annual basis. A **net operating loss (NOL)** in a particular tax year would produce no tax benefit if the Code did not provide for the carryback and carryforward of such losses to profitable years.

EXAMPLE 29

Juanita has a business and realizes the following taxable income or loss over a five-year period: year 1, $50,000; year 2, ($30,000); year 3, $100,000; year 4, ($200,000); and year 5, $380,000. She is married and files a joint return. Hubert also has a business and has a taxable income pattern of $60,000 every year. He, too, is married and files a joint return. Note that both Juanita and Hubert have total taxable income of $300,000 over the five-year period. Assume that there is no provision for carryback or carryover of NOLs. Juanita and Hubert would have the following five-year tax bills:

Year	Juanita's Tax	Hubert's Tax
1	$ 6,573	$ 8,073
2	–0–	8,073
3	16,543	8,073
4	–0–	8,073
5	100,813	8,073
	$123,929	$40,365

Note: The computation of tax is made without regard to any NOL benefit. The 2016 Tax Rate Schedules are used to compute the tax.

Even though Juanita and Hubert realized the same total taxable income ($300,000) over the five-year period, Juanita had to pay taxes of $123,929, while Hubert paid taxes of only $40,365.

To provide partial relief from this inequitable tax treatment, a deduction is allowed for NOLs.[39] This provision permits NOLs for any one year to be offset against taxable income of other years. The NOL provision is intended as a form of relief for business income and losses. Thus, only losses from the operation of a trade or business (or profession), casualty and theft losses, or losses from the confiscation of a business by a foreign government can create an NOL. In other words, a salaried individual with itemized deductions and personal exemptions in excess of gross income is not permitted to deduct the excess amounts as an NOL. On the other hand, a personal casualty loss is treated as a business loss and can therefore create (or increase) an NOL for an individual.

7-6a Carryback and Carryover Periods

General Rules

An NOL generally must be applied initially to the two taxable years preceding the year of the loss (unless an election is made not to carry the loss back at all). It is carried first

---

[39]§ 172.

to the second prior year and then to the immediately preceding tax year (or until used up). If the loss is not fully used in the carryback period, it must be carried forward to the first year after the loss year and then forward to the second, third, etc., year after the loss year. The carryover (i.e., carryforward) period is 20 years. A loss sustained in 2016 is used in this order: 2014, 2015, and then 2017 through 2036.

A three-year carryback period is available for any portion of an individual's NOL resulting from a casualty or theft loss. The three-year carryback rule also applies to NOLs that are attributable to Presidentially declared disasters that are incurred by a small business. A small business is a business whose average annual gross receipts for a three-year period are $5 million or less.

A 5-year carryback period and a 20-year carryover period are allowed for a farming loss. A taxpayer may elect to waive the special five-year carryback period. If this election is made, the general two-year carryback period applies. A farming loss is the amount of the NOL for the taxable year if only income and deductions attributable to the farming business are taken into account. However, the amount of the farming loss cannot exceed the amount of the taxpayer's NOL for the taxable year. To determine the amount of the carryback and carryover, a farming loss for any taxable year is treated as a separate NOL for such year and applied after the remaining portion of the NOL for the year is taken into account.

EXAMPLE 30

For 2016, the taxpayer and spouse have an NOL of $50,000. The $50,000 NOL includes a $40,000 loss that is attributable to a farming business.

Only the $40,000 loss attributable to the farming business can be carried back five years. The loss not attributable to the farming business can be carried back only two years.

If the loss is being carried to a preceding year, an amended return is filed on Form 1040X or a quick refund claim is filed on Form 1045. In either case, a refund of taxes previously paid is requested. Form 1045 is an application for a tentative refund. The IRS normally will process Form 1045 and pay the refund within 90 days of the date it is filed. When the loss is carried forward, the current return shows an NOL deduction for the prior year's loss.

Election to Forgo Carryback

A taxpayer can *irrevocably elect* not to carry back an NOL to any of the prior years. This election must be made by the due date (including extensions) for filing the taxpayer's return for the year in which the NOL occurred.[40] In that case, the loss is available as a carryover for 20 years. The election should be made if it is to the taxpayer's tax advantage. For example, a taxpayer might be in a low marginal tax bracket in the carryback years but expect to be in a high marginal tax bracket in future years. Therefore, it would be to the taxpayer's advantage to use the NOL to offset income in years when the tax rate is high rather than use it when the tax rate is relatively low.

EXAMPLE 31

For 2016, taxpayer and spouse have an NOL of $10,000. The NOL may be carried back and applied against taxable income first in 2014 and then in 2015. Any remaining NOL is carried forward to 2017 through 2036. If, however, the taxpayer and spouse elect to forgo the carryback period, the NOL initially is carried to 2017 and forward through 2036, until it's completely applied. The couple must maintain a record that notes when the NOL arose and how much is used in each year to ensure proper usage of the NOL carryover.

---

[40]§ 172(b)(3).

NOLs and Self-Employment Taxes

An NOL can be carried back to offset taxable income and, as a result, reduce the tax-payer's income tax liability. However, an NOL *cannot* be used to reduce self-employment income. As a result, a taxpayer's self-employment tax liability will not change as the result of an NOL.[41]

7-6b **Computation of the Net Operating Loss**

Because the NOL provisions apply solely to business-related losses, certain adjustments must be made so that the loss more closely resembles the taxpayer's *economic* loss. The required adjustments for corporate taxpayers are usually insignificant because a corporation's tax loss is generally similar to its economic loss. However, in computing taxable income, individual taxpayers are allowed deductions for such items as personal and dependency exemptions and itemized deductions that do not reflect actual business-related economic losses.

To arrive at the NOL for an individual, taxable income must be adjusted as follows:[42]

1. No deduction is allowed for personal and dependency exemptions. These amounts do not reflect economic, or business, outlays and hence must be added back.
2. The NOL carryover or carryback from another year is not allowed in the computation of the current year's NOL.
3. Capital losses and nonbusiness deductions are limited in determining the current year's NOL. These limits are as follows:
    a. The excess of nonbusiness capital losses over nonbusiness capital gains must be added back.
    b. The excess of nonbusiness deductions over the sum of nonbusiness income and *net* nonbusiness capital gains must be added back. *Net nonbusiness capital gains* are the excess of nonbusiness capital gains over nonbusiness capital losses. *Nonbusiness income* is income that is not attributable to, or derived from, a taxpayer's trade or business. It includes items such as dividends, investment interest, alimony received, and Social Security income. *Nonbusiness deductions* are those deductions that are not attributable to, or derived from, a taxpayer's trade or business. Examples are Individual Retirement Account (IRA) deductions, alimony paid deductions, most itemized deductions except for personal casualty and theft losses and losses incurred in a transaction entered into for profit, and employee business expense deductions.

         A taxpayer who does not itemize deductions computes the excess of non-business deductions over nonbusiness income by substituting the standard deduction for total itemized deductions.
    c. The excess of business capital losses over the sum of business capital gains and the excess of nonbusiness income and net nonbusiness capital gains over nonbusiness deductions must be added back.
    d. The add-back for net nonbusiness capital losses and excess business capital losses does not include net capital losses not included in the current-year computation of taxable income because of the capital loss limitation provisions (discussed in Chapter 16).

For a review of the computation of the net operating loss for individuals, see Concept Summary 7.5.

---

[41]§ 1402(a).

[42]§ 172(d); Reg. § 1.172–3(a). Also see *Net Operating Losses for Individuals* (IRS Publication 536) and Forms 1045 and 1139.

Concept Summary 7.5

Computation of Net Operating Loss

Taxable income shown on the return

Add back:

1. Personal and dependency exemptions.

2. Net operating loss carryover or carryback from another year.

3. The excess of nonbusiness capital losses over nonbusiness capital gains.

4. The excess of nonbusiness deductions over the sum of nonbusiness income plus *net* nonbusiness capital gains.

5. The excess of business capital losses over the sum of business capital gains plus the excess of nonbusiness income and *net* nonbusiness capital gains over nonbusiness deductions.

Note: The add-back from the total of items 3. and 5. will not exceed $3,000 because of the capital loss limitation rules.

Equals: The net operating loss

The capital loss and nonbusiness deduction limits are illustrated in Examples 32 through 35.

Capital Loss and Nonbusiness Deduction Limits

EXAMPLE 32

For 2016, taxpayer and spouse have $6,000 of nonbusiness capital losses and $4,000 of nonbusiness capital gains.

They must add back $2,000 to taxable income ($6,000 − $4,000), which is the excess of nonbusiness capital losses over nonbusiness capital gains.

EXAMPLE 33

For 2016, taxpayer and spouse have $2,600 of nonbusiness capital gains, $1,000 of nonbusiness capital losses, $2,000 of interest income, and no itemized deductions.

They must add back $9,000 to taxable income {$12,600 standard deduction − [$2,000 interest income + $1,600 ($2,600 − $1,000) net nonbusiness capital gains]}.

Note that in this example, there is no excess of nonbusiness capital losses over nonbusiness capital gains.

EXAMPLE 34

For 2016, taxpayer and spouse have $2,600 of nonbusiness capital gains, $1,000 of nonbusiness capital losses, $15,000 of interest income, $14,500 of itemized deductions (none of which are personal casualty and theft losses), $4,000 of business capital losses, and $1,000 of business capital gains.

They must add back $900 to taxable income {$4,000 business capital losses − [$1,000 business capital gains + ($15,000 nonbusiness income + $1,600 net nonbusiness capital gains − $14,500 nonbusiness deductions)]}.

Note that in this example, there is no excess of nonbusiness capital losses over nonbusiness capital gains, nor is there an excess of nonbusiness deductions over the sum of nonbusiness income and net nonbusiness capital gains.

EXAMPLE 35

For 2016, taxpayer and spouse have $2,600 of nonbusiness capital gains, $3,000 of nonbusiness capital losses, $13,000 of interest income, $15,000 of itemized deductions (none of which are personal casualty and theft losses), $8,000 of business capital losses, and $4,000 of business capital gains.

They must add back $5,000 to taxable income:

(1) $2,000 ($15,000 − $13,000), which is the excess of nonbusiness deductions over nonbusiness income, and

(2) $3,000, which is the excess of combined capital losses because the capital loss limitation caps the loss at $3,000 in computing taxable income for the year.

Example 36 illustrates the computation of an NOL.

EXAMPLE
36

James opened a retail store in 2015 and experienced an NOL of $185 for that year. James had no taxable income for 2013 or 2014. James is married, has no dependents, and files a joint return. For 2016, James and his wife have the following taxable income:

Gross income from the business	$ 67,000	
Less: Business expenses	(73,000)	($ 6,000)
Salary from a part-time job		875
Interest on savings account		525
Nonbusiness long-term capital gain		1,000
NOL carryover from 2015		(185)
Net loss on rental property		(100)
Adjusted gross income		($ 3,885)
Less: Itemized deductions		
Interest expense on home mortgage	$ 4,600	
Taxes	7,300	
Casualty loss	2,000	
Total itemized deductions		(13,900)
Exemptions (2 × $4,050)		(8,100)
Taxable income		($25,885)

James's 2016 NOL is computed as follows:

Taxable income				($25,885)
Add:				
Net operating loss from 2015			$ 185	
Personal exemptions (2)			8,100	
Excess of nonbusiness deductions				
over nonbusiness income				
Total itemized deductions		$13,900		
Less: Casualty loss		(2,000)		
		$11,900		
Less: Interest income	$ 525			
Less: Long-term capital gain	1,000	(1,525)	10,375	18,660
Net operating loss				($ 7,225)

The NOL can be thought of as follows:

Business loss	($6,000)
Rental loss	(100)
Casualty loss	(2,000)
Salary income	875
Net operating loss	($7,225)

7-6c Recomputation of Tax Liability for Year to Which Net Operating Loss Is Carried

When an NOL is carried back to a nonloss year, the taxable income and income tax for the carryback year must be recomputed by including the NOL as a deduction *for* AGI. Several deductions (such as medical expenses and charitable contributions) are based on the amount of AGI. When an NOL is carried back, all such deductions *except* the charitable contributions deduction must be recomputed on the basis of the new AGI after the NOL has been applied. The deduction for charitable contributions is determined without regard to any NOL carryback but with regard to any other modification affecting AGI. Furthermore, any tax credits limited by or based upon the tax must be recomputed, based on the recomputed tax.

EXAMPLE

37

Peggy sustains an NOL of $11,000 in 2016. Because Peggy had no taxable income in 2014, the loss is carried back to 2015. For 2015, the joint income tax return of Peggy and her husband was as follows:

Salary income		$ 15,000
Dividends (not qualified dividends)		4,000
Net short-term capital gain		1,700
Adjusted gross income		$ 20,700
Itemized deductions		
Charitable contributions	$3,810	
Medical [$2,140 − ($20,700 × 10%)]	70	
Interest expense on home mortgage	5,700	
Taxes	2,420	(12,000)
Exemptions (2 × $4,000)		(8,000)
Taxable income		$ 700
Tax (married filing jointly)		$ 70

Peggy's new tax liability for the carryback year is computed as follows:

Adjusted gross income		$ 20,700
Less: Net operating loss		(11,000)
Recomputed adjusted gross income		$ 9,700
Itemized deductions		
Charitable contributions	$3,810	
Medical [$2,140 − ($9,700 × 10%)]	1,170	
Interest expense on home mortgage	5,700	
Taxes	2,420	(13,100)
Exemptions (2 × $4,000)		(8,000)
Recomputed taxable income		($ 11,400)
Tax		$ –0–
Tax originally paid and refund claim		$ 70

7-6d Calculation of the Remaining Net Operating Loss

After computing the amount of the refund claim for the initial carryback year, it is then necessary to determine the extent to which any NOL remains to carry over to future years.[43] The amount of this carryover loss is the excess of the NOL over the taxable income of the year to which the loss is being applied. However, the taxable income of the year to which the loss is being applied must be determined with the following *modifications*:

• No deduction is allowed for excess capital losses over capital gains.

• No deduction is allowed for the NOL that is being carried back. However, deductions are allowed for NOLs occurring before the loss year.

• Any deductions claimed that are based on or limited by AGI must be determined after making the preceding adjustments. However, charitable contributions do not take into account any NOL carryback.

• No deduction is allowed for personal and dependency exemptions.

---

[43]Taxpayers with an NOL carryover must keep records to track its use in carryback and/or carryforward years.

Referring to the facts in Example 37, the NOL carryover from 2015 available for future years is ($2,300), computed as follows:

EXAMPLE

38

Salary income		$ 15,000
Dividends (not qualified dividends)		4,000
Net short-term capital gain		1,700
Adjusted gross income		$ 20,700
Itemized deductions		
Charitable contributions	$3,810	
Medical [$2,140 − ($20,700 × 10%)]	70	
Interest expense on home mortgage	5,700	
Taxes	2,420	(12,000)
Exemptions (not allowed)		–0–
Modified taxable income		$ 8,700
Net operating loss		($ 11,000)
Modified taxable income		8,700
Net operating loss to carry forward		($ 2,300)

Because the ending figure is negative, it represents the NOL remaining to carry over to 2017 or later years.

7-7 TAX PLANNING

LO.8

Identify tax planning opportunities in deducting certain business expenses, business losses, and personal losses.

7-7a Worthless Securities

To be deductible, a security must be completely worthless. To obtain the deduction, the taxpayer must prove that the security was not worthless in a prior year and that the security was worthless in the year claimed. Because of the subjectivity associated with this burden of proof, the only safe practice is to claim a loss for the earliest year when it may be allowed and to renew the claim in subsequent years if there is any reasonable chance that it will be applicable to the income for those years.[44] Fortunately, the statute of limitations for worthless securities is seven years.[45]

7-7b Small Business Stock (§ 1244 Stock) Losses

Because § 1244 limits the amount of loss classified as ordinary loss on a yearly basis, a taxpayer might maximize the benefits of § 1244 by selling the stock in more than one taxable year. The result could be that the losses in any one taxable year would not exceed the § 1244 limits on ordinary loss.

— Sell in multiple years

EXAMPLE

39

Mitch, a single individual, purchased small business stock in 2014 for $150,000 (150 shares at $1,000 per share). On December 20, 2016, the stock is worth $60,000 (150 shares at $400 per share). Mitch wants to sell the stock at this time. Mitch earns a salary of $80,000 a year, has no other capital transactions, and does not expect any in the future.

If Mitch sells all of the small business stock in 2016, his recognized loss will be $90,000 ($60,000 − $150,000). The loss will be characterized as a $50,000 ordinary loss and a $40,000 long-term capital loss. In computing taxable income for 2016, Mitch could deduct the $50,000 ordinary loss but could deduct only $3,000 of the capital loss. The remainder of the capital loss could be carried over and used in future years subject to the $3,000 limitation if Mitch has no capital gains.

If Mitch sells 82 shares in 2016, he will recognize an ordinary loss of $49,200 [82 × ($1,000 − $400)]. If Mitch then sells the remainder of the shares in 2017, he will recognize an ordinary loss of $40,800 [68 × ($1,000 − $400)]. Mitch could deduct the $49,200 ordinary loss in computing 2016 taxable income and the $40,800 ordinary loss in computing 2017 taxable income.

---

[44]*Young v. Comm.*, 41–2 USTC ¶9744, 28 AFTR 365, 123 F.2d 597 (CA–2, 1941).

[45]§ 6511(d)(1).

7-7c **Casualty Losses**

A special election is available for taxpayers who sustain casualty losses in an area designated by the President as a disaster area. This election affects only the *timing*, not the calculation, of the deduction. The deduction can be taken in the year before the year in which the loss occurred. Thus, for a loss occurring between January 1 and December 31, 2016, an individual can take the deduction on the 2015 return. The benefit, of course, is a faster refund (or reduction in tax). It will also be advantageous to carry the loss back if the taxpayer's tax rate in the carryback year is higher than the tax rate in the year of the loss.

To find out if an event qualifies as a disaster area loss, one can look in any of the major tax services, the Compilation of Presidential Documents (released by the U.S. Government Publishing Office), or the *Internal Revenue Bulletin*.

7-7d **Net Operating Losses**

In certain instances, it may be advisable for a taxpayer to elect *not* to carry back an NOL. For an individual, the benefits from the loss carryback could be scaled down or lost due to the economic adjustments that must be made to taxable income for the year to which the loss is carried. For example, a taxpayer should attempt to minimize the number of taxable years to which an NOL is carried. The more years to which the NOL is applied, the more benefits are lost from adjustments for items such as personal and dependency exemptions.

The election not to carry back the loss might also be advantageous if there is a disparity in marginal tax rates applicable to different tax years.

EXAMPLE 40

Abby sustained an NOL of $10,000 in year 3. Her marginal tax bracket in year 1 was 15%. In year 4, however, she expects her bracket to be 35% due to a large profit she will make on a business deal.

If Abby carries her loss back, her refund will be $1,500 (15% × $10,000). If she elects not to carry it back to year 1 but chooses, instead, to carry it forward, her savings will be $3,500 (35% × $10,000). Even considering the time value of an immediate tax refund, Abby appears to be better off using the carryover approach.

REFOCUS ON THE BIG PICTURE

LOSSES

Martha can receive tax benefits associated with her unfortunate occurrences during the current tax year. Some of the losses, however, will provide a greater tax benefit than others as a result of different tax provisions governing the amount and the classification of the losses.

Bad Debt

Based on the facts provided, it appears that Martha's loan to her friend was a bona fide debt. Otherwise, nothing would be deductible. The amount of the deduction is the unpaid principal balance of $19,000 ($25,000 − $6,000). Unfortunately, because the bad debt is a nonbusiness bad debt, it is classified as a short-term capital loss (see Example 5).

continued

Investment Losses

The $50,000 loss is deductible. However, it appears that the loss should be classified as a long-term capital loss rather than as a short-term capital loss. Although the actual holding period was not greater than one year (October through May), the disposal date for the stock (which qualifies as a worthless security) is deemed to be the last day of the tax year (October of last year through end of December of the current year). The loss does not appear to qualify for ordinary loss treatment under § 1244 (see Example 8). The stock she purchased from her friend results in an $8,000 short-term capital loss (and does not qualify under § 1244; see Example 10).

Loss from Bookstore

The $180,000 loss from the bookstore is reported on Schedule C of Form 1040. It is an ordinary loss, and it qualifies for NOL treatment. Therefore, Martha can carry any net loss back and offset it against taxable income of the past two years (starting with the earliest carryback year). Any amount not offset by carrying the loss back to the two previous taxable years can be carried forward for the next 20 years. Any carryback will produce a claim for a tax refund.

Casualty Loss

The loss on the damage to Martha's personal residence is classified as a personal casualty loss. Using the cost of repairs method, the amount of the casualty loss is $7,000 ($25,000 − $32,000). However, this amount must be reduced by the statutory materiality amounts of $100 and 10 percent of AGI.

If the President classified the area in which Martha's house is located as a disaster area, Martha has the option of deducting the casualty loss on the prior year's tax return (see Example 15).

Key Terms

Bad debt, 7-2

Business bad debt, 7-5

Casualty loss, 7-8

Disaster area losses, 7-9

Domestic production activities deduction (DPAD), 7-17

Domestic production gross receipts (DPGR), 7-18

Modified adjusted gross income, 7-17

Net operating loss (NOL), 7-19

Nonbusiness bad debt, 7-4

Personal casualty gain, 7-14

Personal casualty loss, 7-14

Qualified production activities income (QPAI), 7-18

Research and experimental expenditures, 7-15

Reserve method, 7-3

Small business stock (§ 1244 stock), 7-6

Specific charge-off method, 7-3

Theft losses, 7-8

W–2 wages, 7-17

Worthless securities, 7-5

Discussion Questions

1. **LO.1** Explain how an account receivable can give rise to a bad debt deduction.

2. **LO.1** Ron, a cash basis taxpayer, sells his business accounts receivable of $100,000 to Mike for $70,000 (70% of the actual accounts receivable). Discuss the amount and classification of Ron's bad debt deduction.

3. **LO.1** Discuss when a bad debt deduction can be taken for a nonbusiness debt.

WWW   **For the latest in changes to tax legislation, visit** www.cengagebrain.com.

4. **LO.1** Discuss the treatment of a business bad debt when the business also has long-term capital gains.

Issue ID 5. **LO.1** Many years ago, Jack purchased 400 shares of Canary stock. During the current year, the stock became worthless. It was determined that the company "went under" because several corporate officers embezzled a large amount of company funds. Identify the relevant tax issues for Jack.

6. **LO.2** Sean is in the business of buying and selling stocks and bonds. He has a bond of Green Corporation for which he paid $200,000. The bond is currently worth only $50,000. Discuss whether Sean can take a $150,000 loss for a business bad debt or for a worthless security.

7. **LO.2** Discuss the tax treatment of the sale of § 1244 stock at a gain.

8. **LO.3, 4** Jim discovers that his residence has extensive termite damage. Discuss whether he may take a deduction for the damage to his residence.

9. **LO.3, 4** The value of Mary's personal residence has declined significantly because of a recent forest fire in the area where she lives. Mary's house suffered no actual damage during the fire, but because much of the surrounding area was destroyed, the value of all of the homes in the area declined substantially. Discuss whether Mary can take a casualty loss for the decline in value of her residence caused by the fire.

10. **LO.4** Discuss at what point in time a theft loss generally is recognized.

11. **LO.4** Discuss the circumstances under which the cost of repairs to the damaged property can be used to measure the amount of a casualty loss.

12. **LO.4** Hazel sustained a loss on the theft of a painting. She had paid $20,000 for the painting, but it was worth $40,000 at the time of the theft. Evaluate the tax consequences of treating the painting as investment property or as personal use property.

Issue ID 13. **LO.4** Kelly decided to invest in Lime, Inc. common stock after reviewing Lime's public disclosures, including recent financial statements and a number of press releases issued by Lime. On August 7, 2014, Kelly purchased 60,000 shares of Lime for $210,000. In May 2015, Lime entered into a joint venture with Cherry, Inc. In November 2015, the joint venture failed, and Lime's stock began to decline in value. In December 2015, Cherry filed a lawsuit against Lime for theft of corporate opportunity and breach of fiduciary responsibility. In February 2016, Lime filed a countersuit against Cherry for fraud and misappropriation of funds. At the end of December 2016, Kelly's stock in Lime was worth $15,000. Identify the relevant tax issues for Kelly.

Issue ID 14. **LO.3, 4** In 2013, John opened an investment account with Randy Hansen, who held himself out to the public as an investment adviser and securities broker. John contributed $200,000 to the account in 2013. John provided Randy with a power of attorney to use the $200,000 to purchase and sell securities on John's behalf. John instructed Randy to reinvest any gains and income earned. In 2013, 2014, and 2015, John received statements of the amount of income earned by his account and included these amounts in his gross income for these years. In 2016, it was discovered that Randy's purported investment advisory and brokerage activity was in fact a fraudulent investment arrangement known as a Ponzi scheme. In reality, John's account balance was zero, the money having been used by Randy in his scheme. Identify the relevant tax issues for John.

15. **LO.5** Discuss under what circumstances a company would elect to amortize research and experimental expenditures rather than use the expense method.

Issue ID 16. **LO.6** Amos began a business, Silver, Inc., on July 1, 2013. The business extracts and processes silver ore. During 2016, Amos becomes aware of the domestic production activities deduction (DPAD) and would like to take advantage of this deduction. Identify the relevant tax issues for Silver, Inc.

17. **LO.6** The DPAD is unlike other deductions and is designed to provide a tax benefit in a somewhat unique manner. Explain this statement.

18. **LO.7** Discuss whether unreimbursed employee business expenses can create an NOL for an individual taxpayer.

19. **LO.7** Discuss whether deductions *for* AGI can be treated as nonbusiness deductions in computing an individual's NOL.

20. **LO.7** Thomas believes that he has an NOL for the current year and wants to carry it   Issue ID
    back to a previous year and receive a tax refund. In determining his NOL, Thomas offset his business income by alimony payments he made to his ex-wife, contributions he made to his traditional Individual Retirement Account (IRA), and moving expenses he incurred. His reason for using these items in the NOL computation is that each item is a deduction *for* AGI. Identify the relevant tax issues for Thomas.

Computational Exercises

21. **LO.1** Last year, Jane identified $50,000 as a nonbusiness bad debt. In that tax year, before considering the tax implications of the nonbusiness bad debt, Jane had $100,000 of taxable income, of which $5,000 consisted of short-term capital gains. This year, Jane collected $10,000 of the amount she had previously identified as a bad debt. Determine Jane's tax treatment of the $10,000 received in the current tax year.

22. **LO.1** Bob owns a collection agency. He purchases uncollected accounts receivable from other businesses at 60% of their face value and then attempts to collect these accounts. During the current year, Bob collected $60,000 on an account with a face value of $80,000. Determine the amount of Bob's bad debt deduction.

23. **LO.2** On May 9, 2014, Calvin acquired 250 shares of stock in Aero Corporation, a new startup company, for $68,750. Calvin acquired the stock directly from Aero, and it is classified as § 1244 stock (at the time Calvin acquired his stock, the corporation had $900,000 of paid-in capital). On January 15, 2016, Calvin sold all of his Aero stock for $7,000. Assuming that Calvin is single, determine his tax consequences as a result of this sale.

24. **LO.4** Mary's diamond ring was stolen in 2015. She originally paid $8,000 for the ring, but it was worth considerably more at the time of the theft. Mary filed an insurance claim for the stolen ring, but the claim was denied. Because the insurance claim was denied, Mary took a casualty loss for the stolen ring on her 2015 tax return. In 2015, Mary had AGI of $40,000. In 2016, the insurance company had a "change of heart" and sent Mary a check for $5,000 for the stolen ring. Determine the proper tax treatment of the $5,000 Mary received from the insurance company in 2016.

25. **LO.4** Determine the treatment of a loss on rental property under the following facts:

Basis	$650,000
FMV before the loss	800,000
FMV after the loss	200,000

26. **LO.4** Belinda was involved in a boating accident in 2016. Her speedboat, which was used only for personal use and had a fair market value of $28,000 and an adjusted basis of $14,000, was completely destroyed. She received $10,000 from her insurance company. Her AGI for 2016 is $37,000. What is Belinda's casualty loss deduction (after any limitations)?

27. **LO.4** During the year, Tucker had the following personal casualty gains and losses (after deducting the $100 floor):

Asset	Holding Period	Gain or (Loss)
Asset 1	18 months	($1,200)
Asset 2	2 months	750
Asset 3	3 years	1,500

What are the tax consequences of these items to Tucker?

28. **LO.5** Sandstorm Corporation decides to develop a new line of paints. The project begins in 2016. Sandstorm incurs the following expenses in 2016 in connection with the project:

Salaries	$85,000
Materials	30,000
Depreciation on equipment	12,500

The benefits from the project will be realized starting in July 2017. If Sandstorm Corporation chooses to defer and amortize its research and experimental expenditures over a period of 60 months, what are its related deductions in 2016 and 2017?

29. **LO.6** In 2016, Loftis, Inc., a calendar year taxpayer, has QPAI of $4.5 million and taxable income of $3.1 million. Because Loftis outsources much of its work to independent contractors, its W–2 wage base, which for Loftis is related entirely to production activities, is $214,000. What is Loftis, Inc.'s DPAD for 2016?

30. **LO.7** Phillis and Trey are married and file a joint tax return. For 2016, they have $4,800 of nonbusiness capital gains, $2,300 of nonbusiness capital losses, $500 of interest income, and no itemized deductions. The standard deduction for married filing jointly is $12,600.

Based on these transactions, to arrive at the NOL, Phillis and Trey's taxable income must be adjusted by what amount?

31. **LO.7** Emily, who is single, sustains an NOL of $7,800 in 2016. The loss is carried back to 2014. For 2014, Emily's income tax information was as follows:

Adjusted gross income		$ 38,200
Itemized deductions:		
Medical [$4,855 − (10% × $38,200)]	$ 1,035	
Taxes	6,100	
Interest expense on home mortgage	11,000	(18,135)
Personal exemption		(3,950)
Taxable income		$ 16,115

As a result of the carryback, what is Emily's recomputed adjusted gross income and her recomputed taxable income?

Problems

Communications   32. **LO.1** Several years ago, John Johnson, who is in the lending business, loaned Sara $30,000 to purchase an automobile to be used for personal purposes. In August of the current year, Sara filed for bankruptcy, and John was notified that he could not expect to receive more than $4,000. As of the end of the current year, John has received $1,000. John has contacted you about the possibility of taking a bad debt deduction for the current year.

Write a letter to John that contains your advice as to whether he can claim a bad debt deduction for the current year. Also prepare a memo for the tax files. John's address is 100 Tyler Lane, Erie, PA 16563.

33. **LO.1** Monty loaned his friend Ned $20,000 three years ago. Ned signed a note and made payments on the loan. Last year, when the remaining balance was $11,000, Ned filed for bankruptcy and notified Monty that he would be unable to pay the balance on the loan. Monty treated the $11,000 as a nonbusiness bad debt. Last year, before considering the tax implications of the nonbusiness bad debt, Monty had capital gains of $4,000 and taxable income of $20,000. During the current year, Ned paid Monty $10,000 in satisfaction of the debt. Determine Monty's tax treatment for the $10,000 received in the current year.

34. **LO.1** Sally is in the business of purchasing accounts receivable. Last year, Sally purchased an account receivable with a face value of $80,000 for $60,000. During the current year, Sally settled the account, receiving $65,000. Determine the maximum amount of the bad debt deduction for Sally for the current year.

35. **LO.1, 2** Mable and Jack file a joint return. For the current year, they had the following items:

Salaries	$120,000
Loss on sale of § 1244 stock acquired two years ago	105,000
Gain on sale of § 1244 stock acquired six months ago	20,000
Nonbusiness bad debt	19,000

Determine their AGI for the current year.

36. **LO.2, 8** Mary, a single taxpayer, purchased 10,000 shares of § 1244 stock several years ago at a cost of $20 per share. In November of the current year, Mary received an offer to sell the stock for $12 per share. She has the option of either selling all of the stock now or selling half of the stock now and half of the stock in January of next year. Mary will receive a salary of $80,000 for the current year and $90,000 next year. Mary will have long-term capital gains of $8,000 for the current year and $10,000 next year. If Mary's goal is to minimize her AGI for the two years, determine whether she should sell all of her stock this year or half of her stock this year and half next year.

Decision Making

37. **LO.3, 4, 8** Olaf lives in the state of Minnesota. A tornado hit the area and damaged his home and automobile. Applicable information is as follows:

Decision Making

Item	Adjusted Basis	FMV before	FMV after	Insurance Proceeds
Home	$350,000	$500,000	$100,000	$280,000
Auto	60,000	40,000	10,000	20,000

Because of the extensive damage caused by the tornado, the President designated the area a disaster area.

Olaf and his wife, Anna, always file a joint return. Their 2015 tax return shows AGI of $180,000 and taxable income of $140,000. In 2016, their return shows AGI of $300,000 and taxable income (exclusive of the casualty loss deduction) of $215,000.

Determine the amount of Olaf and Anna's loss and the year in which they should take the loss.

38. **LO.3, 4** Heather owns a two-story building. The building is used 40% for business use and 60% for personal use. During 2016, a fire caused major damage to the building and its contents. Heather purchased the building for $800,000 and has taken depreciation of $100,000 on the business portion. At the time of the fire, the building had a fair market value of $900,000. Immediately after the fire, the fair market value was $200,000. The insurance recovery on the building was $600,000. The contents of the building were insured for any loss at fair market value. The business assets had an adjusted basis of $220,000 and a fair market value of $175,000. These assets were totally destroyed. The personal use assets had an adjusted basis of $50,000 and a fair market value of $65,000. These assets were also totally destroyed.

If Heather's AGI is $100,000 before considering the effects of the fire, determine her itemized deduction as a result of the fire. Also determine Heather's AGI.

Decision Making

Communications

39. **LO.3, 4** On July 24 of the current year, Sam Smith was involved in an accident with his business use automobile. Sam had purchased the car for $30,000. The automobile had a fair market value of $20,000 before the accident and $8,000 immediately after the accident. Sam has taken $20,000 of depreciation on the car. The car is insured for the fair market value of any loss. Because of Sam's history, he is afraid that if he submits a claim, his policy will be canceled. Therefore, he is considering not filing a claim. Sam believes that the tax loss deduction will help mitigate the loss of the insurance reimbursement. Sam's current marginal tax rate is 35%.

    Write a letter to Sam that contains your advice with respect to the tax and cash-flow consequences of filing versus not filing a claim for the insurance reimbursement for the damage to his car. Also prepare a memo for the tax files. Sam's address is 450 Colonel's Way, Warrensburg, MO 64093.

40. **LO.5** Blue Corporation, a manufacturing company, decided to develop a new line of merchandise. The project began in 2016. Blue had the following expenses in connection with the project:

	2016	2017
Salaries	$500,000	$600,000
Materials	90,000	70,000
Insurance	8,000	11,000
Utilities	6,000	8,000
Cost of inspection of materials for quality control	7,000	6,000
Promotion expenses	11,000	18,000
Advertising	–0–	20,000
Equipment depreciation	15,000	14,000
Cost of market survey	8,000	–0–

The new product will be introduced for sale beginning in July 2018. Determine the amount of the deduction for research and experimental expenditures for 2016, 2017, and 2018 if:

a. Blue Corporation elects to expense the research and experimental expenditures.

b. Blue Corporation elects to amortize the research and experimental expenditures over 60 months.

41. **LO.6** Sarah Ham, operating as a sole proprietor, manufactures printers in the United States. For 2016, the proprietorship has QPAI of $400,000. Sarah's modified AGI was $350,000. The W–2 wages paid by the proprietorship to employees engaged in the qualified domestic production activity were $60,000. Calculate Sarah's DPAD for 2016.

42. **LO.6** Barbara, a calendar year taxpayer, owns and operates a company that manufactures toys. For 2016, she has modified AGI of $500,000 and QPAI of $550,000. Ignoring the W–2 wage limitation, calculate Barbara's DPAD.

43. **LO.6** Red Corporation manufactures hand tools in the United States. For the current year, the QPAI derived from the manufacture of hand tools was $1 million. Red's taxable income for the current year was $2.0 million. Last year, Red had an NOL of $800,000, which Red elected to carry forward. Calculate Red's DPAD for the current year.

44. **LO.6** Green Corporation manufactures skirts and blouses in the United States. The DPGR derived from the manufacture of one skirt is $12, and the DPGR from one blouse is $10. The cost of goods sold is $5 for one skirt and $6 for one blouse. Other allocated costs are $1 for one skirt and $5 for one blouse. What amount of QPAI is available to Green for calculating the DPAD?

45. **LO.6** In 2016, Rose, Inc., has QPAI of $4 million and taxable income of $3 million.   Decision Making
    Rose pays independent contractors $500,000. Rose's W–2 wages are $600,000, but only $400,000 of the wages are paid to employees engaged in qualified domestic production activities.

    a. Calculate the DPAD for Rose, Inc., for 2016.

    b. What suggestions could you make to enable Rose to increase its DPAD?

46. **LO.7** Sam, age 45, is single. For 2016, he has the following items:

Business income	$70,000
Business expenses	75,000
Alimony paid	12,000
Interest income	3,000
Itemized deductions	8,000

    a. Determine Sam's taxable income for 2016.

    b. Determine Sam's NOL for 2016.

47. **LO.7** Mary, a single taxpayer with two dependent children, has the following items of income and expense during 2016:

Gross receipts from business	$144,000
Business expenses	180,000
Alimony received	22,000
Interest income	3,000
Itemized deductions (no casualty or theft)	24,000

    a. Determine Mary's taxable income for 2016.

    b. Determine Mary's NOL for 2016.

48. **LO.7** Gus, who is married and files a joint return, owns a grocery store. In 2016, his gross sales were $276,000, and operating expenses were $320,000. Other items on his 2016 return were as follows:

Nonbusiness capital gains (short term)	$20,000
Nonbusiness capital losses (long term)	9,000
Itemized deductions (no casualty or theft)	18,000
Ordinary nonbusiness income	8,000
Salary from part-time job	10,000

    During 2014, Gus had no taxable income. In 2015, Gus had taxable income of $21,100 computed as follows:

Net business income		$ 60,000
Interest income		2,000
Adjusted gross income		$ 62,000
Less: Itemized deductions		
Charitable contributions of $40,000, limited to 50% of AGI	$31,000	
Medical expenses of $8,100, limited to the amount in excess of 10% of AGI ($8,100 − $6,200)	1,900	
Total itemized deductions		(32,900)
Exemptions (2 × $4,000)		(8,000)
Taxable income		$ 21,100

    a. What is Gus's 2016 NOL?

    b. Determine Gus's recomputed taxable income for 2015.

    c. Determine the amount of Gus's 2016 NOL to be carried forward to 2017.

49. **LO.7** During 2016, Rick and his wife, Sara, had the following items of income and expense to report:

Gross receipts from farming business	$400,000
Farming expenses	525,000
Interest income from bank savings accounts	8,000
Sara's salary	50,000
Long-term capital gain on stock held as an investment	4,000
Itemized deductions (no casualty or theft)	15,000

   a. Assuming that Rick and Sara file a joint return, what is their taxable income for 2016?

   b. What is the amount of Rick and Sara's farming loss for 2016?

   c. What is the amount of Rick and Sara's NOL for 2016?

   d. To what years can Rick and Sara's NOL be carried?

   e. Based on your computations, identify the components of their NOL. What is the rationale for excluding the items that do not affect the NOL computation?

50. **LO.7** Assume that in addition to the information in Problem 49, Rick and Sara had no taxable income for 2011, 2012, 2013, and 2014 and $3,700 of taxable income for 2015 computed as follows:

Salary		$ 25,000
Capital loss		(1,000)
Adjusted gross income		$ 24,000
Less: Itemized deductions		
Charitable contributions of $20,000, limited to 50% of AGI	$12,000	
Medical expenses of $2,700, limited to the amount in excess of 10% of AGI ($2,700 − $2,400)	300	
Total itemized deductions		(12,300)
Exemptions (2 × $4,000)		(8,000)
Taxable income		$ 3,700

   a. Determine Rick and Sara's recomputed taxable income for 2015.

   b. Determine the amount of Rick and Sara's 2016 NOL to be carried forward to 2017.

51. **LO.7** During 2016, Ron and his wife, Sue, had the following items of income and expense to report:

Farming income	$300,000
Farming expenses	350,000
Interest income	30,000
Taxes	15,000
Casualty loss (after $100 reduction and 10%-of-AGI reduction)	20,000

   a. Determine Ron and Sue's taxable income for 2016.

   b. Determine Ron and Sue's NOL for 2016.

   c. Determine Ron and Sue's farming loss for 2016.

   d. To what years can Ron and Sue's NOL be carried?

Communications   52. **LO.7** Robert and Susan Reid had an NOL of $30,000 in 2016. They had no taxable income for 2014 and $14,250 of taxable income for 2015 computed as follows:

Salary		$ 50,000
Capital loss		(4,000)
Adjusted gross income		$ 46,000
Less: Itemized deductions		
Charitable contributions of $24,000, limited to 50% of AGI	$23,000	
Medical expenses of $5,350, limited to the amount in excess of 10% of AGI ($5,350 − $4,600)	750	
Total itemized deductions		(23,750)
Exemptions (2 × $4,000)		(8,000)
Taxable income		$ 14,250

Write a letter to Robert and Susan informing them of the amount of the remaining NOL to be carried forward if the loss is applied against the 2015 taxable income. Also prepare a memo for the tax files. Their address is 201 Jerdone Avenue, Conway, SC 29526.

53. **LO.7** Pete and Polly are married and file a joint return. They had the following income and deductions for 2016:

Salary	$50,000
Interest from savings account	5,000
Itemized deductions (no casualty or theft)	15,000
2015 NOL carried to 2016	60,000

a. What is Pete and Polly's taxable income for 2016?
b. What is Pete and Polly's NOL for 2016?
c. What is Pete and Polly's NOL to be carried to 2017?

54. **LO.1, 2, 7** Soong, single and age 32, had the following items for the tax year 2016:
- Salary of $30,000.
- Interest income from U.S. government bonds of $2,000.
- Dividends from a foreign corporation of $500.
- Sale of small business § 1244 stock on October 20, 2016, for $20,000. The stock had been acquired two years earlier for $65,000.
- Business bad debt of $4,000.
- Nonbusiness bad debt of $5,000.
- Sale of small business § 1244 stock on November 12, 2016, for $4,000. The stock had been acquired on June 5, 2016, for $800.
- Sale of preferred stock on December 4, 2016, for $40,000. The stock was acquired four years ago for $18,000.
- Total itemized deductions of $25,000 (no casualty or theft).

a. Determine Soong's NOL for 2016.
b. Assuming that Soong had taxable income for each of the last five years, determine the carryback year to which the 2016 NOL should be applied.

55. **LO.1, 3** Nell, single and age 38, had the following income and expense items in 2016:

Nonbusiness bad debt	$ 6,000
Business bad debt	2,000
Nonbusiness long-term capital gain	4,000
Nonbusiness short-term capital loss	3,000
Salary	50,000
Interest income	3,000

Determine Nell's AGI for 2016.

56. **LO.1, 4** Assume that in addition to the information in Problem 55, Nell had the following items in 2016:

Personal casualty gain on an asset held for four months	$10,000
Personal casualty loss on an asset held for two years	1,000

Determine Nell's AGI for 2016.

57. **LO.1, 4, 7** Assume that in addition to the information in Problems 55 and 56, Nell had the following items in 2016:

Personal casualty loss on an asset held for five years	$60,000
Interest expense on home mortgage	15,000

Determine Nell's taxable income and NOL for 2016.

58. **LO.1, 2, 3, 4, 7** Jed, age 55, is married with no children. During 2016, Jed had the following income and expense items:

a.   Three years ago, Jed loaned a friend $10,000 to help him purchase a new car. In June of the current year, Jed learned that his friend had been declared bankrupt and had left the country. There is no possibility that Jed will ever collect any of the $10,000.

b.   In April of last year, Jed purchased some stock for $5,000. In March of the current year, the company was declared bankrupt, and Jed was notified that his shares of stock were worthless.

c.   Several years ago, Jed purchased some § 1244 stock for $120,000. This year, he sold the stock for $30,000.

d.   In July of this year, Jed sold some land that he had held for two years for $60,000. He had originally paid $42,000 for the land.

e.   Jed received $40,000 of interest income from State of Minnesota bonds.

f.   In September, Jed's home was damaged by an earthquake. Jed's basis in his home was $430,000. The value of the home immediately before the quake was $610,000. After the quake, the home was worth $540,000. Because earthquake damage was an exclusion on Jed's homeowner's insurance policy, he received no insurance recovery.

g.   Jed received a salary of $80,000.

h.   Jed paid home mortgage interest of $14,000.

If Jed files a joint return for 2016, determine his NOL for the year.

Cumulative Problems

Tax Return Problem

Decision Making

Communications

TAX SOFTWARE

59. Jane Smith, age 40, is single and has no dependents. She is employed as a legal secretary by Legal Services, Inc. She owns and operates Typing Services located near the campus of Florida Atlantic University at 1986 Campus Drive. Jane is a material participant in the business. She is a cash basis taxpayer. Jane lives at 2020 Oakcrest Road, Boca Raton, FL 33431. Jane's Social Security number is 123-45-6789. Jane indicates that she wants to designate $3 to the Presidential Election Campaign Fund. Jane had health insurance for all months of 2015. During 2015, Jane had the following income and expense items:

a. $100,000 salary from Legal Services, Inc.

b. $20,000 gross receipts from her typing services business.

c. $700 interest income from Acme National Bank.

d. $1,000 Christmas bonus from Legal Services, Inc.

e. $60,000 life insurance proceeds on the death of her sister.

f. $5,000 check given to her by her wealthy aunt.

g. $100 won in a bingo game.

h. Expenses connected with the typing service:

Office rent	$7,000
Supplies	4,400
Utilities and telephone	4,680
Wages to part-time typists	5,000
Payroll taxes	500
Equipment rentals	3,000

i. $9,500 interest expense on a home mortgage (paid to San Jose Savings and Loan).

j. $15,000 fair market value of silverware stolen from her home by a burglar on October 12, 2015. Jane had paid $14,000 for the silverware on July 1, 2006. She was reimbursed $1,500 by her insurance company.

k. Jane had loaned $2,100 to a friend, Joan Jensen, on June 3, 2012. Joan declared bankruptcy on August 14, 2015, and was unable to repay the loan. Assume that the loan is a bona fide debt.

l. Legal Services, Inc., withheld Federal income tax of $16,000 and the appropriate amount of FICA tax from her wages.

m. Alimony of $10,000 received from her former husband, Ted Smith.

n. Interest income of $800 on City of Boca Raton bonds.

o. Jane made estimated Federal tax payments of $1,000.

p. Sales taxes from the sales tax table of $946.

q. Property taxes on her residence of $1,100.

r. Charitable contributions of $2,500.

s. In November 2015, Jane was involved in an automobile accident. At the time of the accident, Jane's automobile had an FMV of $45,000. After the accident, the automobile's FMV was $38,000. Jane's basis in the car was $52,000. Jane's car was covered by insurance, but because the policy had a $5,000 deduction clause, Jane decided not to file a claim for the damage.

Part 1—Tax Computation
Compute Jane Smith's 2015 Federal income tax payable (or refund due). If you use tax forms for your computations, you will need Forms 1040 and 4684 and Schedules A, C, and D. Suggested software: H&R BLOCK Tax Software.

Part 2—Tax Planning
In 2016, Jane plans to continue her job with Legal Services, Inc. Therefore, items a, d, and l will recur in 2016. Jane plans to continue her typing services business (refer to item b) and expects gross receipts of $26,000. She projects that all business expenses (refer to item h) will increase by 10%, except for office rent, which, under the terms of her lease, will remain the same as in 2015. Items e, f, g, j, k, and s will not recur in 2016. Items c, i, m, n, p, q, and r will be approximately the same as in 2015.

Jane would like you to compute the minimum amount of estimated tax she will have to pay for 2016 so that she will not have to pay any additional tax upon filing her 2016 Federal income tax return. Write a letter to Jane that contains your advice, and prepare a memo for the tax files.

60. Mason Phillips, age 45, and his wife, Ruth, live at 230 Wood Lane, Salt Lake City, UT 84101. Mason's Social Security number is 111-11-1111. Ruth's Social Security number is 123-45-6789. Mason and Ruth are cash basis taxpayers and had the following items for 2016:

Tax Computation Problem

- Salary of $140,000.
- Bad debt of $30,000 from uncollected rent.

- Collection of unpaid rent from a prior year of $6,000.
- Sale of § 1244 stock resulting in a loss of $105,000. The stock was acquired eight months ago.
- Rental income of $60,000.
- Rental expenses of $33,000.
- Casualty loss on rental property of $10,000.
- Personal casualty loss (from one event) of $20,000.
- Theft loss of $5,000 on a computer used 100% associated with their jobs.
- Theft loss of $8,000 on a painting held for investment.
- Other itemized deductions of $18,000.
- Federal income tax withheld of $3,000.

Compute Mason and Ruth's 2016 Federal income tax payable (or refund due).

Research Problems

THOMSON REUTERS
CHECKPOINT
Student Edition

Note: Solutions to Research Problems can be prepared by using the Checkpoint® Student Edition online research product, which is available to accompany this text. It is also possible to prepare solutions to the Research Problems by using tax research materials found in a standard tax library.

Research Problem 1. During 2016, John was the chief executive officer and a shareholder of Maze, Inc. He owned 60% of the outstanding stock of Maze. In 2013, John and Maze, as co-borrowers, obtained a $100,000 loan from United National Bank. This loan was secured by John's personal residence. Although Maze was listed as a co-borrower, John repaid the loan in full in 2016. On Maze's Form 1120 tax returns, no loans from shareholders were reported. Discuss whether John is entitled to a bad debt deduction for the amount of the payment on the loan.

Partial list of research aids:
U.S. v. Generes, 405 U.S. 93 (1972).
Dale H. Sundby, T.C.Memo. 2003–204.
Arrigoni v. Comm., 73 T.C. 792 (1980).
Estate of Herbert M. Rapoport, T.C.Memo. 1982–584.
Clifford L. Brody and Barbara J. DeClerk, T.C. Summary Opinion, 2004–149.

Research Problem 2. Mary Marble took out a homeowner's insurance policy on her residence. One of the policy provisions listed the insured's duties with respect to a loss. This provision required the policyholder to give notice and required an inventory of damaged personal property within 60 days of the insurance company's request and to supply proof of loss.

   In November of the current year, Mary's home was damaged by a fire. Shortly after the fire, Mary reported the loss to the insurance company. In December, the insurance company generated a claim report sheet with a claim number and sent Mary a proof of loss form. Mary failed to provide the insurance company with the proof of loss form within the required 60-day period; hence, the insurance company denied Mary's claim for damages. Discuss whether Mary is entitled to a casualty loss deduction for the damage to her home caused by the fire.

Research Problem 3. Esther owns a large home on the East Coast. Her home is surrounded by large, mature oak trees that significantly increase the value of her home. In August 2015, a hurricane damaged many of the trees surrounding her home. In September 2015, Esther engaged a local arborist to evaluate and treat the trees, but five of the largest trees were seriously weakened by the storm. These trees died from disease in 2016. Esther has ascertained that the amount of the casualty loss from the death of the five trees is $25,000; however, she is uncertain in which year to deduct this loss. Discuss whether the casualty loss should be deducted in the calculation of Esther's 2015 or 2016 taxable income.

Partial list of research aids:
Reg. § 1.165–1.
Oregon Mesabi Corporation, 39 B.T.A. 1033 (1939).

Internet Activity

Use the tax resources of the Internet to address the following questions. Do not restrict your search to the Web, but include a review of newsgroups and general reference materials, practitioner sites and resources, primary sources of the tax law, chat rooms and discussion groups, and other opportunities.

Research Problem 4. Find a newspaper article that discusses tax planning for casualty losses when a disaster area designation is made. Does the article convey the pertinent tax rules correctly? Then list all of the locations identified by the President as Federal disaster areas in the last two years.

Research Problem 5. Many states that have corporate income taxes "piggyback" onto the Federal corporate income tax calculation. In other words, these states' corporate income tax calculations incorporate many of the Federal calculations and deductions to make both compliance and verification of tax liability easier. However, some state legislatures were concerned that the domestic production activities deduction, if allowed for state tax purposes, would result in significant revenue losses. Determine whether states with corporate income taxes allow or disallow the domestic production activities deduction in the calculation of the state's corporate income tax liability. Be sure to state the sources for your answer.

Communications

Roger CPA Review Questions

1. Glenn and Mary's house was damaged by a hurricane in 2016. The fair value of their home before the hurricane was $150,000. After the hurricane, the fair value of their home was $125,000. They received $10,000 from their homeowner's insurance policy. What is their casualty loss deduction for 2016 if their adjusted gross income was $40,000?

   a. $10,900
   b. $11,000
   c. $14,900
   d. $15,000

2. Hank's home is burglarized on December 22, 2016. Personal property with a fair market value of $40,000 and an adjusted basis to Hank of $25,000 is stolen. Hank paid an independent appraiser $700 on December 29 to determine the fair market value of the property at the time of the break-in. Hank's homeowner's insurance policy leads him to believe he is entitled to receive $15,000 in reimbursement for the event, but no settlement has been made with the insurance company by year-end. Hank's AGI in 2016 is $30,000. How much may Hank deduct from AGI as a result of these facts on his 2016 tax return? Assume Hank itemizes, and assume there has still been no settlement with the insurance company at the time of filing.

   a. $7,000
   b. $21,900
   c. $6,900
   d. $22,000

3. On the night of October 14, 2016, a hurricane caused serious damage to Paige's personal vehicle and to the roof of her personal residence, a townhome. Just prior to the hurricane, Paige had a $200,000 basis in her home and a $12,000 basis in her vehicle, which had a fair market value just prior to the hurricane of $10,000. The damage to the roof is appraised at $7,000, and the fair market value of the vehicle immediately after the hurricane is appraised at $5,000. Paige is uninsured and has a

2016 AGI of $40,000. What amount of casualty loss deduction may Paige claim on her 2016 tax return as a result of the hurricane?

a. $9,800

b. $7,900

c. $9,900

d. $7,800

4. Regarding the tax treatment of a business's research and experimental (R&E) expenditures, which of the following statements is true?

a. A common reason for electing tax deferral for such expenses is the expectation of lower tax rates in the future.

b. Expenses associated with the acquisition of land upon which a purpose-built R&E facility is constructed are considered R&E expenditures for tax purposes.

c. Companies generally prefer to expense R&E costs immediately, but may elect instead to defer and amortize such costs over a minimum of 60 months.

d. Companies may elect to immediately expense R&E costs incurred in the first applicable taxable year and all future years through an appropriate filing with the IRS.

5. Identify the correct statement below regarding the domestic production activities deduction (DPAD).

a. Qualified production activities income (QPAI) is calculated by applying a percentage to net income from an IRS rate table based on specific criteria.

b. The DPAD cannot exceed attributable W–2 wages paid.

c. A sole proprietorship cannot claim the DPAD, but a partnership or an S corporation with more than one shareholder can.

d. Taxable income for the purposes of calculating or amending the DPAD includes any net operating loss (NOL) deduction, such as an NOL carryforward or NOL carryback.

CHAPTER 8

Depreciation, Cost Recovery, Amortization, and Depletion

LEARNING OBJECTIVES: *After completing Chapter 8, you should be able to:*

LO.1 State the rationale for the cost consumption concept and identify the relevant time periods for depreciation, ACRS, and MACRS.

LO.2 Determine the amount of cost recovery under MACRS.

LO.3 Recognize when and how to make the § 179 expensing election, calculate the amount of the deduction, and apply the effect of the election in making the MACRS calculation.

LO.4 Identify listed property and apply the deduction limitations on listed property and on luxury automobiles.

LO.5 Determine when and how to use the alternative depreciation system (ADS).

LO.6 Report cost recovery deductions appropriately.

LO.7 Identify intangible assets that are eligible for amortization and calculate the amount of the deduction.

LO.8 Determine the amount of depletion expense, including being able to apply the alternative tax treatments for intangible drilling and development costs.

LO.9 Identify tax planning opportunities for cost recovery, amortization, and depletion.

CHAPTER OUTLINE

© ERSLER DMITRY/SHUTTERSTOCK.COM

CALCULATING COST RECOVERY DEDUCTIONS

Dr. Cliff Payne purchased and placed in service $612,085 of new fixed assets in his dental practice during the current year.

Office furniture and fixtures	$ 70,000
Computers and peripheral equipment	67,085
Dental equipment	475,000

Using his financial reporting system, he concludes that the depreciation expense on Schedule C of Form 1040 is $91,298.

Office furniture and fixtures ($70,000 × 14.29%)	$10,003
Computers and peripheral equipment ($67,085 × 20%)	13,417
Dental equipment ($475,000 × 14.29%)	67,878
	$91,298

In addition, this year Dr. Payne purchased another personal residence for $300,000 and converted his original residence to rental property. He also purchased a condo in the prior year for $170,000 near his office that he is going to rent to a third party.

Has Dr. Payne correctly calculated the depreciation expense for his dental practice? Will he be able to deduct any depreciation expense for his rental properties?

Read the chapter and formulate your response.

FRAMEWORK 1040 **Tax Formula for Individuals**

This chapter covers the boldfaced portions of the Tax Formula for Individuals that was introduced in Concept Summary 3.1 on p. 3-3. Below those portions are the sections of Form 1040 where the results are reported.

Income *(broadly defined)*	$xx,xxx
Less: Exclusions	(x,xxx)
Gross income	$xx,xxx
Less: Deductions *for* adjusted gross income	(x,xxx)

FORM 1040 (p. 1)

12	Business income or (loss). Attach Schedule C or C-EZ	. . . .

Adjusted gross income	$xx,xxx
Less: The greater of total itemized deductions *or* the standard deduction	(x,xxx)
Personal and dependency exemptions	(x,xxx)
Taxable income	$xx,xxx
Tax on taxable income *(see Tax Tables or Tax Rate Schedules)*	$ x,xxx
Less: Tax credits *(including income taxes withheld and prepaid)*	(xxx)
Tax due (or refund)	$ xxx

T he Internal Revenue Code allows a depreciation, cost recovery, amortization, or depletion deduction based on an asset's cost. These deductions are applications of the recovery of capital doctrine (discussed in Chapter 4). Cost recovery deductions are based on the premise that the asset acquired (or improvement made) benefits more than one accounting period. Otherwise, the expenditure is deducted in the year incurred.[1]

Congress completely overhauled the **depreciation** rules in 1981 by creating the **accelerated cost recovery system (ACRS)**, which shortened depreciable lives and allowed accelerated depreciation methods. In 1986, Congress made substantial modifications to ACRS, which resulted in the **modified accelerated cost recovery system (MACRS)**. Tax professionals use the terms *depreciation* and **cost recovery** interchangeably. Concept Summary 8.1 provides an overview of the various depreciation systems and the time frames involved.

Concept Summary 8.1

Depreciation and Cost Recovery: Relevant Time Periods

System	Date Property Is Placed in Service
Pre-1981 depreciation	Before January 1, 1981, and *certain* property placed in service after December 31, 1980.
Accelerated cost recovery system (ACRS)	After December 31, 1980, and before January 1, 1987.
Modified accelerated cost recovery system (MACRS)	After December 31, 1986.

---

[1]See Chapter 6 and the discussion of capitalization versus expense.

The statutory changes that have taken place since 1980 have widened the gap that exists between the accounting and tax versions of depreciation. The tax rules that existed prior to 1981 were much more compatible with generally accepted accounting principles.

This chapter focuses on the MACRS rules because they cover more recent property acquisitions (i.e., after 1986).[2] The chapter concludes with a discussion of the amortization of intangible property and startup expenditures and the depletion of natural resources.

Taxpayers may "write off" (deduct) the cost of certain assets that are used in a trade or business or held for the production of income. A write-off may take the form of depreciation (or cost recovery), depletion, or amortization. Tangible assets, other than natural resources, are *depreciated*. Natural resources, such as oil, gas, coal, and timber, are *depleted*. Intangible assets, such as copyrights and patents, are *amortized*. Generally, no write-off is allowed for an asset that does not have a determinable useful life.

8-1 DEPRECIATION AND COST RECOVERY

LO.1

State the rationale for the cost consumption concept and identify the relevant time periods for depreciation, ACRS, and MACRS.

8-1a **Nature of Property**

Property includes both realty (real property) and personalty (personal property). Realty generally includes land and buildings permanently affixed to the land. Personalty is defined as any asset that is not realty.[3] Do not confuse personalty (or personal property) with *personal use* property. Personal use property is any property (realty or personalty) that is held for personal use rather than for use in a trade or business or an income-producing activity. Cost recovery deductions are not allowed for personal use assets.

In summary, both realty and personalty can be either business use/income-producing property or personal use property. Examples include:

- A residence (realty that is personal use),
- An office building (realty that is business use),
- A dump truck (personalty that is business use), and
- Common wearing apparel (personalty that is personal use).

It is imperative that this distinction between the *classification* of an asset (realty or personalty) and the *use* to which the asset is put (business or personal) be understood.

Assets used in a trade or business or for the production of income are eligible for cost recovery if they are subject to wear and tear, decay or decline from natural causes, or obsolescence (e.g., an automobile that the taxpayer rents to third parties). Assets that do not decline in value on a predictable basis or that do not have a determinable useful life (e.g., land, stock, and antiques) are not eligible for cost recovery.

8-1b **Placed in Service Requirement**

The key date for the commencement of depreciation is the date an asset is placed in service. This date, and not the purchase date of an asset, is relevant. This distinction is particularly important for an asset that is purchased near the end of the tax year, but not placed in service until after the beginning of the following tax year.

8-1c **Cost Recovery Allowed or Allowable**

The basis of cost recovery property is reduced by the cost recovery allowed (and by not less than the allowable amount). The *allowed* cost recovery is the cost recovery actually deducted, whereas the *allowable* cost recovery is the amount that could have been taken under the applicable cost recovery method. If the taxpayer does not claim any cost recovery on property during a particular year, the basis of the property still is reduced by the amount of cost recovery that should have been deducted (the allowable cost recovery).

---

[2]§ 168. The terms *depreciation* and *cost recovery* are used interchangeably in the text and in § 168. The ACRS rules and the pre-1981 rules are covered in the online appendix *Depreciation and the Accelerated Cost Recovery System (ACRS)*.

[3]Refer to Chapter 1 (text Section 1-5a) for further discussion.

EXAMPLE 1

On March 15, year 1, Jack purchased a copier, to use in his business, for $10,000. The copier is 5-year property, and Jack elected to use the straight-line method of cost recovery. Jack made the election because the business was a new undertaking and he reasoned that in the first few years of the business, a large cost recovery deduction was not needed.

Because the business was doing poorly, Jack did not even claim any cost recovery deductions in years 3 and 4. In years 5 and 6, Jack deducted the proper amount of cost recovery. Therefore, the allowed cost recovery (cost recovery actually deducted) and the allowable cost recovery are computed as follows.

	Cost Recovery Allowed	Cost Recovery Allowable
Year 1	$1,000	$1,000
Year 2	2,000	2,000
Year 3	–0–	2,000
Year 4	–0–	2,000
Year 5	2,000	2,000
Year 6	1,000	1,000

If Jack sold the copier for $800 in year 7, he would recognize an $800 gain ($800 amount realized − $0 adjusted basis); the adjusted basis of the copier is zero ($10,000 cost − $10,000 total allowable cost recovery in years 1 through 6).

8-1d Cost Recovery Basis for Personal Use Assets Converted to Business or Income-Producing Use

If personal use assets are converted to business or income-producing use, the basis for cost recovery and for loss is the *lower* of the adjusted basis or the fair market value at the time the property was converted. As a result of this lower-of basis rule, losses that occurred while the property was personal use property are not recognized for tax purposes through the cost recovery of the property.

The Big Picture

EXAMPLE 2

Return to the facts of *The Big Picture* on p. 8-1. Five years ago, Dr. Payne purchased a personal residence for $250,000. In the current year, with the housing market down, Payne found a larger home that he acquired for his personal residence. Because of the downturn in the housing market, however, he was not able to sell his original residence and recover his purchase price of $250,000. The residence was appraised at $180,000.

Instead of continuing to try to sell the original residence, Dr. Payne converted it to rental property. The basis for cost recovery of the rental property is $180,000 because the fair market value is less than the adjusted basis. The $70,000 decline in value is deemed to be personal (because it occurred while the property was held for personal use by Payne) and therefore nondeductible.

LO.2

Determine the amount of cost recovery under MACRS.

8-2 MODIFIED ACCELERATED COST RECOVERY SYSTEM (MACRS): GENERAL RULES

Under the modified accelerated cost recovery system (MACRS), the cost of an asset is recovered over a predetermined period that generally is shorter than the useful life of the asset or the period that the asset is used to produce income. The MACRS rules were designed to encourage investment, improve productivity, and simplify the pertinent law and its administration.

MACRS provides separate cost recovery syetems for realty and personalty. Based on cost recovery periods (called class lives), methods, and conventions specified in the Internal Revenue Code, the IRS provides tables that identify cost recovery allowances for personalty and for realty. Excerpts from those tables are provided in text Section 8-7d.

Concept Summary 8.2 provides an overview of the class lives, methods, and conventions that apply under MACRS.

Concept Summary 8.2

MACRS: Class Lives, Methods, and Conventions

	Personality	Realty
Class lives	3 to 20 years	Residential: 27.5 years Nonresidential: 39 years
Method	200% declining balance for property with class lives less than 15 years 150% declining balance for property with 15- or 20-year class lives	Straight-line
Convention	Half-year or mid-quarter	Mid-month

8-2a Personalty: Recovery Periods and Methods

Classification of Property

MACRS provides that the cost recovery basis of eligible personalty (and certain realty) is recovered over 3, 5, 7, 10, 15, or 20 years. Property is classified by recovery period under MACRS through the use of Asset Depreciation Range (ADR) midpoint lives issued by the IRS.[4] See Exhibit 8.1 for examples of assets in each class.[5]

Accelerated depreciation is allowed for these six MACRS classes of property. Double declining balance is used for the 3-, 5-, 7-, and 10-year classes, with a switchover to straight-line depreciation when the latter computation yields a larger amount. Cost recovery for the 15- and 20-year classes is based on the 150-percent declining balance method, with an

EXHIBIT 8.1 Cost Recovery Periods: MACRS Personalty

Property Class	Generally Includes Assets with the Following ADR Lives	Examples
3-year	4 years or less	Tractor units for use over-the-road
		A racehorse that is more than 2 years old, or any other horse that is more than 12 years old, at the time it is placed in service
		Special tools used in the manufacturing of motor vehicles, such as dies, fixtures, molds, and patterns
5-year	More than 4 years and less than 10 years	Automobiles and taxis
		Light and heavy general-purpose trucks
		Calculators and copiers
		Computers and peripheral equipment
		Rental appliances, furniture, carpets
7-year	10 years or more and less than 16 years	Office furniture, fixtures, and equipment
		Agricultural machinery and equipment
10-year	16 years or more and less than 20 years	Vessels, barges, tugs, and similar water transportation equipment
		Assets used for petroleum refining or for the manufacture of grain and grain mill products, sugar and sugar products, or vegetable oils and vegetable oil products
		Single-purpose agricultural or horticultural structures
15-year	20 years or more and less than 25 years	Land improvements
		Assets used for industrial steam and electric generation and/or distribution systems
		Assets used in the manufacture of cement
20-year	25 years or more	Farm buildings except single-purpose agricultural and horticultural structures
		Water utilities

---

[4]Personalty is assigned to recovery classes based on asset depreciation range (ADR) midpoint lives (Rev.Proc. 87–56, 1987–2 C.B. 674). ADR lives generally represent estimates of an asset's useful economic life.

[5]§ 168(e).

FINANCIAL DISCLOSURE INSIGHTS **Tax and Book Depreciation**

A common book-tax difference relates to the depreciation amounts that are reported for GAAP and Federal income tax purposes. Typically, tax depreciation deductions are accelerated; that is, they are claimed in earlier reporting periods than is the case for financial accounting purposes.

Almost every tax law change since 1980 has included depreciation provisions that accelerate the related deductions relative to the expenses allowed under GAAP. Accelerated cost recovery deductions represent a means by which the taxing jurisdiction infuses the business with cash flow created by the reduction in the year's tax liabilities.

For instance, recently, about one-quarter of General Electric's deferred tax liabilities related to depreciation differences. For Toyota's and Ford's depreciation differences, that amount was about one-third. And for the trucking firm Ryder Systems, depreciation differences accounted for all but 1 percent of the deferred tax liabilities.

appropriate straight-line switchover.[6] The appropriate computation methods and conventions are built into the tables, so it is not necessary to calculate the appropriate percentages.

To determine the amount of the cost recovery allowance, identify the asset by class and go to the appropriate table for the percentage. The MACRS percentages for personalty appear in Exhibit 8.3 (see text Section 8-7d). Concept Summary 8.3 provides an overview of the various conventions that apply under the MACRS statutory percentage method.

Concept Summary 8.3

Statutory Percentage Method under MACRS

	Personal Property	Real Property*
Convention	Half-year or mid-quarter	Mid-month
Cost recovery deduction in the year of disposition**	Half-year for year of sale or half-quarter for quarter of sale	Half-month for month of sale

*Straight-line method must be used.
**A disposition can include a sale, exchange, abandonment, or retirement. For simplicity, we will assume a sale in this chapter.

Taxpayers may *elect* the straight-line method to compute cost recovery allowances for each of these classes of property. Certain property is not eligible for accelerated cost recovery and must be depreciated under an alternative depreciation system (ADS). Both the straight-line election and ADS are discussed later in the chapter.

MACRS views property as placed in service in the middle of the asset's first year (the **half-year convention**).[7] Thus, for example, the statutory recovery period for property with a life of three years begins in the middle of the year an asset is placed in service and ends three years later. In practical terms, this means that taxpayers must wait an extra year to recover the full cost of depreciable assets. That is, the actual write-offs are claimed over 4, 6, 8, 11, 16, and 21 years. MACRS also allows for a half-year of cost recovery in the year of sale or retirement.

Half-Year Convention

EXAMPLE 3

Kareem acquires a 5-year class asset on April 10, 2016, for $30,000. Kareem's cost recovery deduction for 2016 is computed as follows.

MACRS cost recovery [$30,000 × .20 (Exhibit 8.3)]   <u>$6,000</u>

EXAMPLE 4

Assume the same facts as in Example 3. Kareem sells the asset on March 5, 2018. Kareem's cost recovery deduction for 2018 is $2,880 [$30,000 × $\frac{1}{2}$ × .192 (Exhibit 8.3)].

---

[6]§ 168(b).   [7]§ 168(d)(4)(A).

Mid-Quarter Convention

The half-year convention arises from the simplifying presumption that assets generally are acquired at an even pace throughout the tax year. However, Congress was concerned that taxpayers might defeat that presumption by placing large amounts of property in service towards the end of the taxable year (and, by doing so, receive a half-year's depreciation on those large, end-of-year acquisitions).

To inhibit this behavior, Congress added the **mid-quarter convention** that applies if more than 40 percent of the value of property other than eligible real estate (discussed in a later section) is placed in service during the last quarter of the year.[8] Under this convention, property acquisitions are grouped by the quarter they were acquired for cost recovery purposes. Acquisitions during the first quarter are allowed 10.5 months (three and one-half quarters) of cost recovery; the second quarter, 7.5 months (two and one-half quarters); the third quarter, 4.5 months (one and one-half quarters); and the fourth quarter, 1.5 months (one-half quarter). The percentages are shown in Exhibit 8.4.

<table>
<tr><td colspan="2">Silver Corporation acquires the following new 5-year class property in 2016.</td><td>**EXAMPLE**</td></tr>
<tr><td colspan="2"></td><td>5</td></tr>
</table>

Property Acquisition Dates	Cost
February 15	$ 200,000
July 10	400,000
December 5	600,000
Total	$1,200,000

Under the statutory percentage method, Silver's cost recovery allowances for the first two years are computed below. Because more than 40% ($600,000/$1,200,000 = 50%) of the acquisitions are in the last quarter, the mid-quarter convention applies.

2016

	Mid-Quarter Convention Depreciation (Exhibit 8.4)	Total Depreciation
February 15	$200,000 × .35	$ 70,000
July 10	$400,000 × .15	60,000
December 5	$600,000 × .05	30,000
		$160,000

2017

	Mid-Quarter Convention Depreciation (Exhibit 8.4)	Total Depreciation
February 15	$200,000 × .26	$ 52,000
July 10	$400,000 × .34	136,000
December 5	$600,000 × .38	228,000
		$416,000

Without the mid-quarter convention, Silver's 2016 MACRS deduction would have been $240,000 [$1,200,000 × .20 (Exhibit 8.3)]. The mid-quarter convention slows down the taxpayer's available cost recovery deductions.

When "mid-quarter" property is sold, the property is treated as though it were sold at the midpoint of the quarter. So in the quarter when sold, cost recovery is allowed for one-half of the quarter.

---

[8]§ 168(d)(3).

TAX IN THE NEWS Cost Segregation

Cost segregation identifies certain assets within a commercial property that can qualify for shorter depreciation schedules than the building itself. The identified assets are classified as 5-, 7-, or 15-year property, rather than 39-year property, as part of the building. This allows for greater accelerated depreciation, which reduces taxable income and hence the tax liability.

For instance, a telecommunications system might be segregated from the building in which it is installed. This allows the system to be depreciated over 5 or 7 years, instead of 39 years.

EXAMPLE 6

Assume the same facts as in Example 5, except that Silver Corporation sells the $400,000 asset on November 30, 2017. The cost recovery allowance for 2017 is computed as follows (Exhibit 8.4).

February 15	$200,000 × .26	$ 52,000
July 10	$400,000 × .34 × (3.5/4)	119,000
December 5	$600,000 × .38	228,000
Total		$399,000

The Big Picture

EXAMPLE 7

Return to the facts of *The Big Picture* on p. 8-1. If the placed-in-service date for the office furniture and fixtures and computers and peripheral equipment is September 29 and the placed-in-service date for the dental equipment is October 3, Dr. Payne's total cost recovery is computed as follows.

Office furniture and fixtures:	
MACRS cost recovery $70,000 × .1071 (Exhibit 8.4)	$ 7,497
Computers and peripheral equipment:	
MACRS cost recovery $67,085 × .15 (Exhibit 8.4)	10,063
Dental equipment:	
MACRS cost recovery $475,000 × .0357 (Exhibit 8.4)	16,958
Total cost recovery	$ 34,518

Note the implications of the mid-quarter convention. If the dental equipment had been placed in service before October 1 (the beginning of the fourth quarter), the total cost recovery deduction would have been $91,298 (p. 8-1).

8-2b Realty: Recovery Periods and Methods

Under MACRS, the cost recovery period for residential rental real estate is 27.5 years, and the straight-line method is used. **Residential rental real estate** includes property where 80 percent or more of the gross rental revenues are from residential units (e.g., an apartment building). Hotels, motels, and similar establishments are not residential rental property. Low-income housing is classified as residential rental real estate. Nonresidential real estate uses a recovery period of 39 years; it also is depreciated using the straight-line method.[9]

Some items of real property are not treated as real estate for purposes of MACRS. For example, single-purpose agricultural structures are in the 10-year MACRS class. Land improvements are in the 15-year MACRS class.

All eligible real estate is depreciated using the **mid-month convention**.[10] Regardless of when the property is placed in service, it is deemed to have been placed in service at

---

[9]§§ 168(b), (c), and (e). A 31.5-year life is used for such property placed in service before May 13, 1993.

[10]§ 168(d)(1).

the middle of the month. This allows for one-half month's cost recovery for the month the property is placed in service. If the property is sold before the end of the recovery period, one-half month's cost recovery is permitted for the month of sale (no matter when the property is sold).

Cost recovery is computed by multiplying the applicable rate (Exhibit 8.8) by the cost recovery basis.

Real Estate Cost Recovery

Alec acquired a building on April 1, 1999, for $800,000. If the building is classified as residential rental real estate, the cost recovery deduction for 2016 is $29,088 (.03636 × $800,000).

If the building is sold on October 7, 2016, the cost recovery deduction for 2016 is $23,028 [.03636 × (9.5/12) × $800,000]. (See Exhibit 8.8 for percentage.)

EXAMPLE 8

Jane acquired a building on March 2, 1993, for $1 million. If the building is classified as non-residential real estate, the cost recovery deduction for 2016 is $31,740 (.03174 × $1,000,000).

If the building is sold on January 5, 2016, the cost recovery deduction for 2016 is $1,323 [.03174 × (.5/12) × $1,000,000]. (See Exhibit 8.8 for percentage.)

EXAMPLE 9

Mark acquired a building on November 19, 2016, for $1.2 million. If the building is classified as nonresidential real estate, the cost recovery deduction for 2016 is $3,852 [.00321 × $1,200,000 (Exhibit 8.8)]. The cost recovery deduction for 2017 is $30,768 [.02564 × $1,200,000 (Exhibit 8.8)].

If the building is sold on May 21, 2017, the cost recovery deduction for 2017 is $11,538 [.02564 × (4.5/12) × $1,200,000 (Exhibit 8.8)].

EXAMPLE 10

8-2c **Straight-Line Election**

Although MACRS requires straight-line depreciation for all eligible real estate, the taxpayer may *elect* to use the straight-line method for depreciable personal property.[11] The property is depreciated using the class life (recovery period) of the asset with a half-year convention or a mid-quarter convention, whichever applies. The election is available on a class-by-class and year-by-year basis (see Concept Summary 8.4). The percentages for the straight-line election with a half-year convention appear in Exhibit 8.5.

Concept Summary 8.4

Straight-Line Election under MACRS

	Personal Property	**Real Property***
Convention	Half-year or mid-quarter	Mid-month
Cost recovery deduction in the year of disposition**	Half-year for year of sale or half-quarter for quarter of sale	Half-month for month of sale
Elective or mandatory	Elective	Mandatory
Breadth of election	Class by class	

*Straight-line method must be used.
**A disposition can include a sale, exchange, abandonment, or retirement. For simplicity, we will assume a sale in this chapter.

---

[11]§ 168(b)(5).

The Big Picture

EXAMPLE 11

Return to the facts of *The Big Picture* on p. 8-1. If Dr. Payne elects the straight-line method of cost recovery, his total cost recovery is computed as follows.

Office furniture and fixtures ($70,000 × .0714) (Exhibit 8.5)	$ 4,998
Computers and peripheral equipment ($67,085 × .10) (Exhibit 8.5)	6,709
Dental equipment ($475,000 × .0714) (Exhibit 8.5)	33,915
Total cost recovery	$45,622

If Payne does not elect the straight-line cost recovery method, his cost recovery deduction is $91,298 (as detailed on p. 8-1).

The Big Picture

EXAMPLE 12

Assume the same facts as in Example 11, except that Dr. Payne sells the computers and peripheral equipment on November 21, 2017. His cost recovery deduction for 2017 is $6,709 ($67,085 × .20 × 1/2) (Exhibit 8.5).

8-3 MODIFIED ACCELERATED COST RECOVERY SYSTEM (MACRS): SPECIAL RULES

8-3a Additional First-Year Depreciation

As noted in Chapter 1, Congress uses the tax system to stimulate the economy—especially in challenging economic times. Such is the case with **additional first-year depreciation** (also referred to as bonus depreciation). Under this provision, taxpayers can take an additional 50 percent cost recovery in the year qualified property is placed in service.[12]

The term *qualified property* includes most *new* depreciable assets other than buildings with a recovery period of 20 years or less. The term *new* means the original or first use of the property. Property that is used but "new to the taxpayer" does not qualify.

The additional first-year depreciation is taken in the year in which the qualifying property is placed in service; it may be claimed in addition to the otherwise available depreciation deduction. After the additional first-year depreciation is determined, the standard MACRS cost recovery allowance is calculated by multiplying the cost recovery basis (original cost recovery basis less additional first-year depreciation) by the appropriate MACRS percentage. A taxpayer may elect *not* to take additional first-year depreciation.

Bonus Depreciation

EXAMPLE 13

Morgan acquires, for $50,000, and places in service a 5-year class asset on March 20, 2016. Morgan's total 2016 cost recovery deduction is:

50% additional first-year depreciation ($50,000 × .50)	$25,000
MACRS cost recovery [($50,000 − $25,000) × .20 (Exhibit 8.3)]	5,000
Total cost recovery	$30,000

---

[12]§ 168(k). Additional first-year depreciation is allowed for qualified property placed in service after 2011 and before 2020. The additional first-year depreciation percentage decreases from 50% to 40% in 2018 and then to 30% in 2019. No bonus depreciation is scheduled for tax years after 2019. Different rules applied between 2008 and 2011.

Bonus Depreciation

Assume the same facts as in Example 13. Morgan sells the asset on October 22, 2017. Morgan's 2017 cost recovery deduction for the asset is $4,000 [$25,000 basis for MACRS recovery × ½ year convention × .32 (Exhibit 8.3)].

EXAMPLE
14

The Big Picture

Return to the facts of *The Big Picture* on p. 8-1, and assume that the tax year is 2016. If Dr. Payne takes additional first-year depreciation, his total cost recovery is computed as follows.

EXAMPLE
15

Office furniture and fixtures	
Additional first-year depreciation ($70,000 × .50)	$ 35,000
MACRS cost recovery [($70,000 − $35,000) × .1429 (Exhibit 8.3)]	5,002
Computers and peripheral equipment	
Additional first-year depreciation ($67,085 × .50)	33,543
MACRS cost recovery [($67,085 − $33,543) × .20 (Exhibit 8.3)]	6,708
Dental equipment	
Additional first-year depreciation ($475,000 × .50)	237,500
MACRS cost recovery [($475,000 − $237,500) × .1429 (Exhibit 8.3)]	33,939
Total cost recovery	$351,692

If Payne does not elect additional first-year depreciation, his cost recovery deduction is $91,298 (as detailed on p. 8-1).

No — he must opt-out

8-3b Election to Expense Assets (§ 179)

LO.3

Recognize when and how to make the § 179 expensing election, calculate the amount of the deduction, and apply the effect of the election in making the MACRS calculation.

Section 179 (Election to Expense Certain Depreciable Business Assets) permits the taxpayer to elect to write off up to $500,000 of the acquisition cost of *tangible personal property* used in a trade or business. Amounts that are expensed under § 179 are not eligible for additional first-year depreciation or cost recovery under MACRS.

The **§ 179 expensing** election is an annual election that applies to the acquisition cost of property placed in service that year. The immediate expense election generally is not available for real property or for property used for the production of income.[13]

Any elected § 179 expense is taken *before* additional first-year depreciation is computed. The base for calculating the remaining standard MACRS deduction is net of the § 179 expense and any additional first-year depreciation.

Kelly acquires equipment (5-year class asset) on February 1, 2016, at a cost of $525,000 and elects to expense $500,000 under § 179. Kelly takes the statutory percentage cost recovery for 2016 (see Exhibit 8.3). As a result, the total deduction for the year is calculated as follows.

EXAMPLE
16

§ 179 expense	$500,000
50% additional first-year depreciation [($525,000 − $500,000) × 50%]	12,500
Standard MACRS calculation [($525,000 − $500,000 − $12,500) × .20]	2,500
	$515,000

---

[13]The § 179 amount allowed is per taxpayer, per year. On a joint return, the statutory amount applies to the couple. If the taxpayers are married and file separate returns, each spouse is eligible for 50% of the statutory amount.

The annual expense and phaseout amounts ($500,000 and $2 million, respectively) apply to 2010 and subsequent tax years. These amounts are adjusted for inflation beginning in 2016 and rounded to the nearest $10,000 multiple.

Limited types of "qualified real property," computer software, and heating and air conditioning units also are eligible for expensing.

Annual Limitations

Two additional limitations apply to the amount deductible under § 179. First, the ceiling amount on the deduction ($500,000) is reduced dollar for dollar when § 179 property placed in service during the taxable year exceeds a maximum amount ($2,010,000 in 2016; $2 million in 2015). Second, the § 179 deduction cannot exceed the taxpayer's trade or business taxable income, computed without regard to the § 179 amount.

Any § 179 amount in excess of taxable income is carried forward to future taxable years and added to other amounts eligible for expensing. For 2016, the § 179 amount eligible for expensing in a carryforward year is limited to the *lesser* of (1) the statutory dollar amount ($500,000) reduced by the cost of § 179 property placed in service in excess of $2,010,000 in the carryforward year or (2) business taxable income in the carryforward year.

EXAMPLE 17

Jill owns a computer service and operates it as a sole proprietorship. In 2016, taxable income is $138,000 before considering any § 179 deduction. If Jill spends $2.3 million on new equipment, her § 179 expense deduction for the year is computed as follows.

§ 179 deduction before adjustment	$ 500,000
Less: Dollar limitation reduction ($2,300,000 − $2,010,000)	(290,000)
Remaining § 179 deduction	$ 210,000
Business income limitation	$ 138,000
§ 179 deduction allowed	$ 138,000
§ 179 deduction carryforward ($210,000 − $138,000)	$ 72,000

Effect on Basis

The basis of the property for cost recovery purposes is reduced by the § 179 amount after accounting for the current-year amount of property placed in service in excess of the specified maximum amount ($2,010,000 for 2016). This adjusted amount does not reflect any business income limitation.

Conversion to Personal Use

Conversion of the expensed property to personal use at any time results in recapture income (see Chapter 17). A property is converted to personal use if it is not used predominantly in a trade or business.[14]

ETHICS & EQUITY Section 179 Limitation

Joe Moran worked in the construction business throughout most of his career. In June of the current year, he sold his interest in Ajax Enterprises LLC for a profit of $300,000. Shortly thereafter, Joe started his own business, which involves the redevelopment of distressed residential real estate.

In connection with his new business venture, Joe purchased a dump truck at a cost of $70,000. The new business struggled and showed a net operating loss for the year. Joe is considering expensing the $70,000 cost of the truck under §179 on this year's tax return. Evaluate Joe's plan.

LO.4

Identify listed property and apply the deduction limitations on listed property and on luxury automobiles.

8-3c Business and Personal Use of Automobiles and Other Listed Property

Limits exist on MACRS deductions for automobiles and other listed property that are used for both personal and business purposes.[15] If the listed property is *predominantly used* for business, the taxpayer can use the MACRS tables to recover the cost. In cases where the property is *not predominantly used* for business, the cost is recovered using the *straight-line method*.

---

[14]See Reg. § 1.179–1(e) and related examples.   [15]§ 280F.

Listed property includes:

- Any passenger automobile.
- Any other property used as a means of transportation.
- Any property of a type generally used for purposes of entertainment, recreation, or amusement.
- Any computer or peripheral equipment, with the exception of equipment used exclusively at a regular business establishment, including a qualifying home office.
- Any other property specified in the Regulations.

Automobiles and Other Listed Property Used Predominantly in Business

For listed property to be considered as *predominantly used in business*, its *business usage* must exceed 50 percent.[16] The use of listed property for production of income does not qualify as business use for purposes of the more-than-50% test. However, both production of income and business use percentages are used to compute the cost recovery deduction.

On September 1, 2016, Emma places in service listed 5-year recovery property. The property cost $10,000. She elects not to take any available additional first-year depreciation.

If Emma uses the property 40% for business and 25% for the production of income, the property is not considered as predominantly used for business. The cost is recovered using straight-line cost recovery. Emma's cost recovery allowance for the year is $650 ($10,000 × .10 × 65%).

If, however, Emma uses the property 60% for business and 25% for the production of income, the property is considered as used predominantly for business. Therefore, she may use the statutory percentage method. Emma's cost recovery allowance for the year is $1,700 ($10,000 × .20 × 85%).

EXAMPLE 18

In determining the percentage of business usage for listed property, a mileage-based percentage is used for automobiles. For other listed property, one employs the most appropriate unit of time (e.g., hours) for which the property actually is used (rather than its availability for use).[17]

Limits on Cost Recovery for Automobiles

The law places special limitations on cost recovery deductions for passenger automobiles. These statutory dollar limits were imposed on passenger automobiles because of the belief that the tax system was being used to underwrite automobiles whose cost and luxury far exceeded what was needed for the taxpayer's business use.

A *passenger automobile* is any four-wheeled vehicle manufactured for use on public streets, roads, and highways with an unloaded gross vehicle weight (GVW) rating of 6,000 pounds or less.[18] This definition specifically excludes vehicles used directly in the business of transporting people or property for compensation, such as taxicabs, ambulances, hearses, and trucks and vans as prescribed by the Regulations.

The following "luxury auto" depreciation limits apply.[19]

Date Placed in Service	First Year	Second Year	Third Year	Fourth and Later Years
2015*	$3,160	$5,100	$3,050	$1,875
2012–2014	$3,160	$5,100	$3,050	$1,875
2010–2011	$3,060	$4,900	$2,950	$1,775
2009	$2,960	$4,800	$2,850	$1,775

*Because the 2016 indexed amounts are not yet available, the 2015 amounts are used in the Examples and end-of-chapter problem materials.

---

[16]§ 280F(b)(3).
[17]Reg. § 1.280F–6T(e).

[18]§ 280F(d)(5).
[19]§ 280F(a)(1); Rev.Proc. 2015–19 (2015–8 I.R.B.656).

For an automobile placed in service prior to 2009, the limitation for subsequent years' cost recovery is based on the limits for the year the automobile was placed in service.[20]

In the event a passenger automobile used predominantly for business qualifies for additional first-year depreciation (i.e., new property), the first-year recovery limitation is increased by $8,000.[21] Therefore, for acquisitions made in 2015, the initial-year cost recovery limitation increases from $3,160 to $11,160 ($3,160 + $8,000).

There are also separate cost recovery limitations for trucks and vans and for electric automobiles. Because these limitations are applied in the same manner as those imposed on passenger automobiles, these additional limitations are not discussed further in this chapter.

The luxury auto limits are imposed before any percentage reduction for personal use. In addition, the limitation in the first year includes any amount the taxpayer elects to expense under § 179.[22] If the passenger automobile is used partly for personal use, the personal use percentage is ignored for the purpose of determining the unrecovered cost available for deduction in later years.

On July 1, 2016, Dan places in service a new automobile that cost $40,000. He does not elect § 179 expensing, and he elects not to take any available additional first-year depreciation. The car is used 80% for business and 20% for personal use in each tax year. Dan chooses the MACRS 200% declining-balance method of cost recovery (the auto is a 5-year asset).

The depreciation computation for 2016 through 2021 is summarized in the table below. The cost recovery allowed is the lesser of the MACRS amount or the recovery limitation.

Year	MACRS Amount	Recovery Limitation	Depreciation Allowed
2016	$6,400 ($40,000 × .2000 × 80%)	$2,528 ($3,160 × 80%)	$2,528
2017	$10,240 ($40,000 × .3200 × 80%)	$4,080 ($5,100 × 80%)	$4,080
2018	$6,144 ($40,000 × .1920 × 80%)	$2,440 ($3,050 × 80%)	$2,440
2019	$3,686 ($40,000 × .1152 × 80%)	$1,500 ($1,875 × 80%)	$1,500
2020	$3,686 ($40,000 × .1152 × 80%)	$1,500 ($1,875 × 80%)	$1,500
2021	$1,843 ($40,000 × .0576 × 80%)	$1,500 ($1,875 × 80%)	$1,500

If Dan continues to use the car after 2021, his cost recovery is limited to the lesser of the recoverable basis or the recovery limitation (i.e., $1,875 × business use percentage). For this purpose, the recoverable basis is computed as if the full recovery limitation was allowed even if it was not. Thus, the recoverable basis as of January 1, 2022, is $23,065 ($40,000 − $3,160 − $5,100 − $3,050 − $1,875 − $1,875 − $1,875).

If Dan takes additional first-year depreciation, the calculated amount of additional first-year depreciation is $16,000 ($40,000 × 50% × 80%). However, the deduction would be limited to $8,928 [($8,000 + $3,160) × 80%].

The cost recovery limitations are maximum amounts. If the regular MACRS calculation produces a lesser amount of cost recovery, the lesser amount is used.

On April 2, 2016, Gail places in service a used automobile that cost $10,000. The car is always used 70% for business and 30% for personal use. The cost recovery allowance for 2016 is $1,400 ($10,000 × .20 MACRS table factor × 70%), and not $2,212 ($3,160 passenger auto maximum × 70%).

The luxury auto limitations apply *only* to passenger automobiles and not to other listed property.

---

[20]Cost recovery limitations for years prior to 2009 are found in IRS Publication 463.

[21]§ 168(k)(2)(F). The $8,000 amount will decrease to $6,400 in 2018 and $4,800 in 2019. No increase in the first-year recovery limitation will be allowed after 2019.

[22]§ 280F(d)(1).

Special Limitation

A $25,000 limit applies for the § 179 deduction when the luxury auto limits do not apply. ─SUVs
The limit is in effect for sport utility vehicles (SUVs) with an unloaded GVW rating of
more than 6,000 pounds and not more than 14,000 pounds.[23]

During 2016, Jay acquires and places in service a new SUV that cost $70,000 and has a GVW
of 8,000 pounds. Jay uses the vehicle 100% of the time for business use. The total deduction
for 2016 with respect to the SUV is computed as follows.

§ 179 expense	$25,000
50% additional first-year depreciation [($70,000 − $25,000) × 50%]	22,500
Standard MACRS calculation [($70,000 − $25,000 − $22,500) × .20 (Exhibit 8.3)]	4,500
	$52,000

Automobiles and Other Listed Property Not Used Predominantly in Business

For automobiles and other listed property not used predominantly in business in the
year of acquisition (i.e., 50 percent or less), the straight-line method under the alternative depreciation system is required (see text Section 8-3d).[24] Under this system, the
straight-line recovery period for automobiles is five years. However, the cost recovery
allowance for any passenger automobile cannot exceed the luxury auto amount.

Auto Not Predominantly Used in Business

On July 27, 2016, Fred places in service an automobile that cost $20,000. The auto is used 40% for
business and 60% for personal use. The cost recovery allowance for 2016 is $800 [$20,000 × .10
(Exhibit 8.7) × 40%].

Assume the same facts as in Example 22, except that the automobile cost $50,000. The cost recov-
ery allowance for 2016 is $1,264 [$50,000 × .10 (Exhibit 8.7) = $5,000 (limited to $3,160) × 40%].

The straight-line method is used even if, at some later date, the business usage of the
property increases to more than 50 percent. In that case, the amount of cost recovery
reflects the increase in business usage.

Assume the same facts as in Example 22, except that in 2017, Fred uses the automobile 70% for
business and 30% for personal use. Fred's cost recovery allowance for 2017 is $2,800 [$20,000 ×
.20 (Exhibit 8.7) × 70%], which is less than 70% of the second-year limit.

Change from Predominantly Business Use

If the business use percentage of listed property falls to 50 percent or less after the year
the property is placed in service, the property is subject to *cost recovery recapture*. The
amount required to be recaptured and included in the taxpayer's ordinary income is the
excess cost recovery.

Excess cost recovery is the excess of the cost recovery deduction taken in prior years
using the statutory percentage method over the amount that would have been allowed
if the straight-line method had been used since the property was placed in service.[25]

---

[23]§ 179(b)(6).   [25]§ 280F(b)(2).
[24]§ 280F(b)(1).

EXAMPLE
25

Seth purchased a new car on January 22, 2016, at a cost of $20,000. Business usage was 80% in 2016, 70% in 2017, 40% in 2018, and 60% in 2019. Seth elects not to take any available additional first-year depreciation. Seth's excess cost recovery to be recaptured as ordinary income in 2018 is:

2016	
MACRS [($20,000 × .20 × 80%) (limited to $3,160 × 80%)]	$ 2,528
Straight-line [($20,000 × .10 × 80%) (limited to $3,160 × 80%)]	(1,600)
Excess	$ 928

→ report in 2016
→ this cal later

2017	
MACRS [($20,000 × .32 × 70%) (limited to $5,100 × 70%)]	$ 3,570
Straight-line [($20,000 × .20 × 70%) (limited to $5,100 × 70%)]	(2,800)
Excess	$ 770

2018	
2016 excess	$ 928
2017 excess	770
Ordinary income recapture	$1,698

After the business usage of the listed property drops below the more-than-50% level, the straight-line method is used for the remaining life of the property.

EXAMPLE
26

Assume the same facts as in Example 25. Seth's cost recovery deduction for 2018 and 2019 is:

2018 $1,220 [($20,000 × .20 × 40%) limited to $3,050 × 40%]
2019 $1,125 [($20,000 × .20 × 60%) limited to $1,875 × 60%]

Concept Summary 8.5 illustrates the cost recovery rules for various types of listed property.

Concept Summary 8.5

Listed Property Cost Recovery

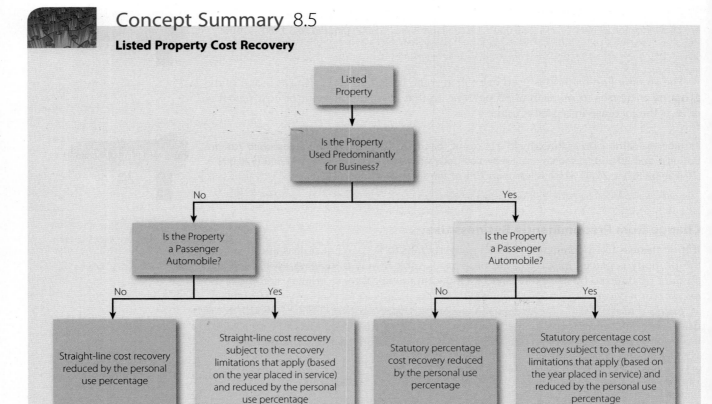

Leased Automobiles

A taxpayer who leases a passenger automobile reports an *inclusion amount* in gross income. The inclusion amount is computed from an IRS table for each taxable year for which the taxpayer leases the automobile. The purpose of this provision is to prevent taxpayers from circumventing the luxury auto and other limitations by leasing, instead of purchasing, an automobile.

The inclusion amount is based on the fair market value of the automobile; it is pro-rated for the number of days the auto is used during the taxable year. The prorated dollar amount then is multiplied by the business and income-producing usage percentage.[26] The taxpayer deducts the lease payments, multiplied by the business and income-producing usage percentage. In effect, the taxpayer's annual deduction for the lease payment is reduced by the inclusion amount.

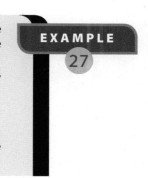

EXAMPLE

27

On April 1, 2016, Jim leases and places in service a passenger automobile worth $52,400. The lease is to be for a period of five years. During the taxable years 2016 and 2017, Jim uses the automobile 70% for business and 30% for personal use.

Assuming that the dollar amounts from the IRS table for 2016 and 2017 are $53 and $115, respectively, Jim includes in gross income:

2016 $53 × (275/366) × 70% = $28
2017 $115 × (365/365) × 70% = $81

In each year, Jim still can deduct 70% of the lease payments made, related to his business use of the auto.

Substantiation Requirements

Listed property is subject to the substantiation requirements of § 274. This means that the taxpayer must prove for any business usage the amount of expense or use, the time and place of use, the business purpose for the use, and the business relationship to the taxpayer of persons using the property.

Substantiation requires adequate records or sufficient evidence corroborating the tax-payer's statement. However, these substantiation requirements do not apply to vehicles that, by reason of their nature, are not likely to be used more than a *de minimis* amount for personal purposes.[27]

8-3d Alternative Depreciation System (ADS)   *Not on Exam*

The **alternative depreciation system (ADS)** must be used:[28]

LO.5

Determine when and how to use the alternative depreciation system (ADS).

- To calculate the portion of depreciation treated as an alternative minimum tax (AMT) adjustment for purposes of the corporate and individual AMT (see Chapters 12 and 20).[29]

- To compute depreciation allowances for property:
  - Used predominantly outside the United States.
  - Leased or otherwise used by a tax-exempt entity.
  - Financed with the proceeds of tax-exempt bonds.
  - Imported from foreign countries that maintain discriminatory trade practices or otherwise engage in discriminatory acts.

- To compute depreciation allowances for earnings and profits purposes (see Chapter 20).

---

[26]Reg. § 1.280F–7(a).
[27]§§ 274(d) and (i).
[28]§ 168(g).

[29]This AMT adjustment applies for real and personal property placed in service before 1999. However, it also applies for personal property placed in service after 1998 if the taxpayer uses the 200% declining-balance method for regular income tax purposes. See Chapter 12.

In general, ADS depreciation is computed using straight-line recovery. However, for purposes of the AMT, depreciation of personal property is computed using the 150 percent declining-balance method with an appropriate switch to the straight-line method.

The taxpayer must use the half-year or the mid-quarter convention, whichever is applicable, for all property other than eligible real estate. The mid-month convention is used for eligible real estate. The applicable ADS rates are found in Exhibits 8.6, 8.7, and 8.9. Generally, personal property is depreciated under the ADS using the appropriate asset class life (e.g., 5- or 7-year) and the 150 percent declining-balance method. ADS uses straight-line depreciation for all realty, over a 40-year class life.[30]

Taxpayers may *elect* to use the 150 percent declining-balance method to compute the regular income tax rather than the 200 percent declining-balance method that is available for personal property. If this election is made, there is no difference between the cost recovery for computing the regular income tax and the AMT.[31]

On March 1, 2016, Abby purchases computer-based telephone central office switching equipment for $80,000. Abby elects not to take any available additional first-year depreciation. If Abby uses statutory percentage cost recovery (assuming no § 179 election), her deduction for 2016 is $16,000 [$80,000 × .20 (Exhibit 8.3, 5-year class property)].

If Abby elects to use ADS 150% declining-balance cost recovery for the regular income tax (assuming no § 179 election), the cost recovery allowance for 2016 is $12,000 [$80,000 × .15 (Exhibit 8.6, 5-year class property)].

Rather than determining depreciation under the regular MACRS method, taxpayers may *elect* straight-line under ADS for property that qualifies for the regular MACRS method. One reason for making this election is to avoid a difference between deductible depreciation and earnings and profits depreciation, thereby reducing the number of cost recovery computations that must be made.[32]

Polly acquires an apartment building on March 17, 2016, for $700,000. She takes the maximum cost recovery allowance for determining taxable income. For 2016, Polly deducts $20,153 [$700,000 × .02879 (Exhibit 8.8)].

However, Polly's cost recovery for computing her earnings and profits is only $13,853 [$700,000 × .01979 (Exhibit 8.9)].

LO.6

Report cost recovery deductions appropriately.

8-4 REPORTING PROCEDURES

Sole proprietors engaged in a business file a Schedule C, Profit or Loss from Business, to accompany Form 1040. A 2015 Schedule C is illustrated, as the 2016 Schedule C was not available on our print date.

The top part of page 1 requests certain key information about the taxpayer (e.g., name, address, Social Security number, principal business activity, and accounting method used). Part I provides for the reporting of items of income. If the business requires the use of inventories and the computation of cost of goods sold (see Chapter 18 for when this is necessary), Part III must be completed and the cost of goods sold amount transferred to line 4 of Part I.

---

[30]The class life for certain properties described in § 168(e)(3) is specially determined under § 168(g)(3)(B).

[31]For personal property placed in service before 1999, taxpayers making the election use the ADS recovery periods in computing cost recovery for the regular income tax. The ADS recovery periods generally are longer than the regular recovery periods under MACRS.

[32]This straight-line election is made on a year-by-year basis. For property other than real estate, the election is made by MACRS class and applies to all assets in that MACRS class. So, for example, the election could be made for 7-year MACRS property and not for 5-year MACRS property placed in service during the same year. For real estate, the election is made on a property-by-property basis.

Part II allows for the reporting of deductions. Some of the deductions discussed in this chapter and their location on the form are depletion (line 12) and depreciation (line 13). Other expenses (line 27) include those items not already covered (see lines 8–26). An example is research and experimental expenditures.

If depreciation is claimed, it should be supported by completing Form 4562. A 2015 Form 4562 is illustrated, as the 2016 Form 4562 is not yet available. The amount listed on line 22 of Form 4562 is transferred to line 13 of Part II of Schedule C.

EXAMPLE

30

Thomas Andrews, Social Security number 111-11-1111, was employed as an accountant until May 2015, when he opened his own practice. His address is 279 Mountain View, Ogden, UT 84201. Andrews keeps his books on the cash basis and reported the following revenue and business expenses in 2015.

a. Revenue from accounting practice, $192,000.
b. Insurance, $5,000.
c. Office supplies, $4,000.
d. Office rent, $16,000.
e. Copier lease payments, $3,000.
f. Licenses, $2,000.
g. New furniture and fixtures were acquired on May 10, for $142,000. Thomas elects § 179 expensing and uses the statutory percentage cost recovery method.

Andrews reports the above information on Schedule C and Form 4562 as illustrated on the following pages.

8-5 **AMORTIZATION**

LO.7

Identify intangible assets that are eligible for amortization and calculate the amount of the deduction.

Taxpayers can claim an **amortization** deduction on intangible assets called "amortizable § 197 intangibles." The amount of the deduction is determined by amortizing the adjusted basis of such intangibles ratably over a 15-year period beginning in the month in which the intangible is acquired.[33]

An *amortizable § 197 intangible* is any § 197 intangible acquired after August 10, 1993, and held in connection with the conduct of a trade or business or for the production of income. Section 197 intangibles include goodwill and going-concern value, franchises, trademarks, and trade names. Covenants not to compete, copyrights, and patents also are included if they are acquired in connection with the acquisition of a business. Generally, self-created intangibles are not § 197 intangibles.

The 15-year amortization period applies regardless of the actual useful life of an amortizable § 197 intangible. No other depreciation or amortization deduction is permitted with respect to any amortizable § 197 intangible except those permitted under the 15-year amortization rules.

EXAMPLE

31

On June 1, 2016, Neil purchased and began operating the Falcon Café. Of the purchase price, $90,000 is allocated to goodwill. The 2016 § 197 amortization deduction is $3,500 [($90,000/15) × (7/12)].

Startup expenditures are partially amortizable by using a § 195 election.[34] A taxpayer must make this election no later than the due date of the return for the taxable year in which the trade or business begins.[35] If no election is made, the startup expenditures are capitalized.[36]

---

[33]§ 197(a).
[34]§ 195(b).
[35]§ 195(d).
[36]§ 195(a).

Form **4562**	**Depreciation and Amortization**	OMB No. 1545-0172
	(Including Information on Listed Property)	**20 15**
Department of the Treasury Internal Revenue Service (99)	▶ Attach to your tax return. ▶ **Information about Form 4562 and its separate instructions is at** *www.irs.gov/form4562.*	Attachment Sequence No. **179**

Name(s) shown on return	Business or activity to which this form relates	Identifying number
Thomas Andrews	*Andrews Accounting Services*	*111-11-1111*

Part I   Election To Expense Certain Property Under Section 179

Note: If you have any listed property, complete Part V before you complete Part I.

1	Maximum amount (see instructions)	**1**	
2	Total cost of section 179 property placed in service (see instructions)	**2**	*142,000*
3	Threshold cost of section 179 property before reduction in limitation (see instructions)	**3**	
4	Reduction in limitation. Subtract line 3 from line 2. If zero or less, enter -0-	**4**	*-0-*
5	Dollar limitation for tax year. Subtract line 4 from line 1. If zero or less, enter -0-. If married filing separately, see instructions	**5**	*142,000*

6	(a) Description of property	(b) Cost (business use only)	(c) Elected cost
	Furniture and Fixtures	*142,000*	*142,000*

7	Listed property. Enter the amount from line 29 . . . . **7**		
8	Total elected cost of section 179 property. Add amounts in column (c), lines 6 and 7	**8**	*142,000*
9	Tentative deduction. Enter the **smaller** of line 5 or line 8	**9**	*142,000*
10	Carryover of disallowed deduction from line 13 of your 2014 Form 4562	**10**	*-0-*
11	Business income limitation. Enter the smaller of business income (not less than zero) or line 5 (see instructions)	**11**	*142,000*
12	Section 179 expense deduction. Add lines 9 and 10, but do not enter more than line 11	**12**	*142,000*
13	Carryover of disallowed deduction to 2016. Add lines 9 and 10, less line 12 ▶ **13**		

Note: Do not use Part II or Part III below for listed property. Instead, use Part V.

Part II   Special Depreciation Allowance and Other Depreciation (Do not include listed property.**)** (See instructions.)

14	Special depreciation allowance for qualified property (other than listed property) placed in service during the tax year (see instructions)	**14**	
15	Property subject to section 168(f)(1) election	**15**	
16	Other depreciation (including ACRS)	**16**	

Part III   MACRS Depreciation (Do not include listed property.**)** (See instructions.)

Section A

17	MACRS deductions for assets placed in service in tax years beginning before 2015	**17**	
18	If you are electing to group any assets placed in service during the tax year into one or more general asset accounts, check here . . . . ▶ ☐		

Section B—Assets Placed in Service During 2015 Tax Year Using the General Depreciation System

(a) Classification of property	(b) Month and year placed in service	(c) Basis for depreciation (business/investment use only—see instructions)	(d) Recovery period	(e) Convention	(f) Method	(g) Depreciation deduction
19a 3-year property						
b 5-year property						
c 7-year property						
d 10-year property						
e 15-year property						
f 20-year property						
g 25-year property			25 yrs.		S/L	
h Residential rental property			27.5 yrs.	MM	S/L	
			27.5 yrs.	MM	S/L	
i Nonresidential real property			39 yrs.	MM	S/L	
				MM	S/L	

Section C—Assets Placed in Service During 2015 Tax Year Using the Alternative Depreciation System

20a Class life					S/L	
b 12-year			12 yrs.		S/L	
c 40-year			40 yrs.	MM	S/L	

Part IV   Summary (See instructions.)

21	Listed property. Enter amount from line 28	**21**	
22	**Total.** Add amounts from line 12, lines 14 through 17, lines 19 and 20 in column (g), and line 21. Enter here and on the appropriate lines of your return. Partnerships and S corporations—see instructions .	**22**	*142,000*
23	For assets shown above and placed in service during the current year, enter the portion of the basis attributable to section 263A costs **23**		

For Paperwork Reduction Act Notice, see separate instructions.   Cat. No. 12906N   Form **4562** (2015)

**SCHEDULE C
(Form 1040)**

Department of the Treasury
Internal Revenue Service (99)

Profit or Loss From Business
(Sole Proprietorship)

▶ Information about Schedule C and its separate instructions is at *www.irs.gov/schedulec.*
▶ Attach to Form 1040, 1040NR, or 1041; partnerships generally must file Form 1065.

OMB No. 1545-0074

2015

Attachment
Sequence No. **09**

Name of proprietor	Social security number (SSN)
Thomas Andrews	*111–11–1111*

A	Principal business or profession, including product or service (see instructions)	B Enter code from instructions ▶

C	Business name. If no separate business name, leave blank. *Andrews Accounting Services*	D Employer ID number (EIN), (see instr.)

E Business address (including suite or room no.) ▶ *279 Mountain View*
City, town or post office, state, and ZIP code   *Ogden, UT 84201*

F Accounting method: (1) ☒ Cash (2) ☐ Accrual (3) ☐ Other (specify) ▶ _____

G Did you "materially participate" in the operation of this business during 2015? If "No," see instructions for limit on losses . ☒ Yes ☐ No

H If you started or acquired this business during 2015, check here . . . . ▶ ☐

I Did you make any payments in 2015 that would require you to file Form(s) 1099? (see instructions) . . . . . . ☐ Yes ☐ No

J If "Yes," did you or will you file required Forms 1099? . . . . ☐ Yes ☐ No

Part I   Income

1	Gross receipts or sales. See instructions for line 1 and check the box if this income was reported to you on Form W-2 and the "Statutory employee" box on that form was checked . . . . ▶ ☐	**1**	*192,000*
2	Returns and allowances	**2**	
3	Subtract line 2 from line 1	**3**	*192,000*
4	Cost of goods sold (from line 42)	**4**	
5	**Gross profit.** Subtract line 4 from line 3	**5**	*192,000*
6	Other income, including federal and state gasoline or fuel tax credit or refund (see instructions) . . .	**6**	
7	**Gross income.** Add lines 5 and 6 . . . . ▶	**7**	*192,000*

Part II   Expenses. Enter expenses for business use of your home **only** on line 30.

8	Advertising	**8**		18	Office expense (see instructions)	**18**	*4,000*
9	Car and truck expenses (see instructions)	**9**		19	Pension and profit-sharing plans .	**19**	
10	Commissions and fees .	**10**		20	Rent or lease (see instructions):		
11	Contract labor (see instructions)	**11**		**a**	Vehicles, machinery, and equipment	**20a**	*3,000*
12	Depletion	**12**		**b**	Other business property . . .	**20b**	*16,000*
13	Depreciation and section 179 expense deduction (not included in Part III) (see instructions)	**13**	*142,000*	21	Repairs and maintenance . . .	**21**	
				22	Supplies (not included in Part III) .	**22**	
				23	Taxes and licenses	**23**	*2,000*
				24	Travel, meals, and entertainment:		
14	Employee benefit programs (other than on line 19) . .	**14**	*5,000*	**a**	Travel	**24a**	
15	Insurance (other than health)	**15**		**b**	Deductible meals and entertainment (see instructions) .	**24b**	
16	Interest:			25	Utilities	**25**	
a	Mortgage (paid to banks, etc.)	**16a**		26	Wages (less employment credits) .	**26**	
b	Other	**16b**		27a	Other expenses (from line 48) . .	**27a**	
17	Legal and professional services	**17**		**b**	**Reserved for future use** . . .	**27b**	

28	**Total expenses** before expenses for business use of home. Add lines 8 through 27a . . . . . . ▶	**28**	*172,000*
29	Tentative profit or (loss). Subtract line 28 from line 7	**29**	*20,000*
30	Expenses for business use of your home. Do not report these expenses elsewhere. Attach Form 8829 unless using the simplified method (see instructions). **Simplified method filers only:** enter the total square footage of: (a) your home: _____ and (b) the part of your home used for business: _____ . Use the Simplified Method Worksheet in the instructions to figure the amount to enter on line 30	**30**	
31	**Net profit or (loss).** Subtract line 30 from line 29. • If a profit, enter on both **Form 1040, line 12** (or **Form 1040NR, line 13**) and on **Schedule SE, line 2.** (If you checked the box on line 1, see instructions). Estates and trusts, enter on **Form 1041, line 3.** • If a loss, you **must** go to line 32.	**31**	*20,000*
32	If you have a loss, check the box that describes your investment in this activity (see instructions). • If you checked 32a, enter the loss on both **Form 1040, line 12,** (or **Form 1040NR, line 13**) and on **Schedule SE, line 2.** (If you checked the box on line 1, see the line 31 instructions. Estates and trusts, enter on **Form 1041, line 3.** • If you checked 32b, you **must** attach **Form 6198.** Your loss may be limited.	32a ☐ All investment is at risk. 32b ☐ Some investment is not at risk.	

For Paperwork Reduction Act Notice, see the separate instructions.   Cat. No. 11334P   Schedule C (Form 1040) 2015

The amortization election for startup expenditures allows the taxpayer to deduct the lesser of (1) the amount of startup expenditures with respect to the trade or business or (2) $5,000, reduced, but not below zero, by the amount by which the startup expenditures exceed $50,000. Any startup expenditures not deducted are amortized ratably over a 180-month period, beginning in the month in which the trade or business begins.[37]

EXAMPLE 32

Startup Expenditures

Green Corporation begins business on August 1, 2016. The corporation incurs startup expenditures of $47,000. If Green elects amortization under § 195, the total startup expenditures that Green may deduct in 2016 is computed as follows.

Deductible amount	$5,000
Amortizable amount {[($47,000 − $5,000)/180] × 5 months}	1,167
Total deduction	$6,167

EXAMPLE 33

Assume the same facts as in Example 32, except that the startup expenditures total $53,000. The 2016 deduction is computed as follows.

Deductible amount [$5,000 − ($53,000 − $50,000)]	$2,000
Amortizable amount {[($53,000 − $2,000)/180] × 5 months}	1,417
Total deduction	$3,417

Amortizable startup expenditures generally must satisfy two requirements.[38] First, the expenditures must be paid or incurred in connection with:

- The creation of an active trade or business,
- The investigation of the creation or acquisition of an active trade or business, or
- Any activity engaged in for profit in anticipation of it becoming an active trade or business.

Second, the expenses must reflect those that could be deducted in an existing trade or business in the same field (see Investigation of a Business, Chapter 6).

The startup costs of creating a new active trade or business could include advertising; salaries and wages; travel and other expenses incurred in lining up prospective distributors, suppliers, or customers; and salaries and fees for executives, consultants, and professional services. Costs that relate to either created or acquired businesses could include expenses incurred for the analysis or survey of potential markets, products, labor supply, transportation facilities, and the like. Startup expenditures do not include allowable deductions for interest, taxes, and research and experimental costs.[39]

Amortization deductions also can be claimed for organizational expenses (see Chapter 20) and research and experimental expenditures (see Chapter 7).

LO.8

Determine the amount of depletion expense, including being able to apply the alternative tax treatments for intangible drilling and development costs.

8-6 DEPLETION

Natural resources (e.g., oil, gas, coal, gravel, and timber) are subject to **depletion**, which can be seen as a form of depreciation applicable to natural resources. Land generally cannot be depleted.

The owner of an interest in the natural resource is entitled to deduct depletion. An owner is one who has an economic interest in the property.[40] An economic interest

---

[37]§§ 195(b)(1)(A) and (B).
[38]§§ 195(c)(1)(A) and (B).

[39]§ 195(c).
[40]Reg. § 1.611–1(b).

requires the acquisition of an interest in the resource in place and the receipt of income from the extraction or severance of that resource. Like depreciation, depletion is a trade or business deduction *for* adjusted gross income.

Although all natural resources are subject to depletion, oil and gas wells are used as an example in the following paragraphs to illustrate the related costs and issues.

In developing an oil or gas well, the producer typically makes four types of expenditures.

- Natural resource costs.
- Intangible drilling and development costs.
- Tangible asset costs.
- Operating costs.

Natural resources are physically limited, and the costs to acquire them (e.g., oil under the ground) are, therefore, recovered through depletion. Costs incurred in making the property ready for drilling, such as the cost of labor in clearing the property, erecting derricks, and drilling the hole, are **intangible drilling and development costs (IDCs)**. These costs generally have no salvage value and are a lost cost if the well is dry.

Costs for tangible assets such as tools, pipes, and engines are capitalized and recovered through depreciation (cost recovery). Costs incurred after the well is producing are operating costs. These costs include expenditures for such items as labor, fuel, and supplies. Operating costs are deductible as trade or business expenses. Depletable costs and intangible drilling and development costs receive different treatment.

8-6a **Intangible Drilling and Development Costs (IDCs)**

Intangible drilling and development costs can be handled in one of two ways at the option of the taxpayer. They can be either charged off as an expense in the year in which they are incurred *or* capitalized and written off through depletion. The taxpayer makes the election in the first year such expenditures are incurred, either by taking a deduction on the return or by adding them to the depletable basis.

Once made, the election is binding on both the taxpayer and the IRS for all such expenditures in the future. If the taxpayer fails to elect to expense IDCs on the original timely filed return for the first year in which such expenditures are incurred, an irrevocable election to capitalize them has been made.

As a general rule, it is more advantageous to expense IDCs. The obvious benefit of an immediate write-off (as opposed to a deferred write-off through depletion) is not the only advantage. Because a taxpayer can use percentage depletion, which is calculated without reference to basis (see Example 35), the IDCs may be completely lost as a deduction if they are capitalized.

8-6b **Depletion Methods**

There are two methods of calculating depletion. *Cost depletion* can be used on any wasting asset (and is the only method allowed for timber). *Percentage depletion* is subject to a number of limitations, particularly for oil and gas deposits. Depletion should be calculated both ways, and the method that results in the larger deduction should be used. The choice between cost depletion and percentage depletion is an annual decision; the taxpayer can use cost depletion in one year and percentage depletion in the following year.

Cost Depletion

Cost depletion is determined by using the adjusted basis of the asset.[41] The basis is divided by the estimated recoverable units of the asset (e.g., barrels and tons) to arrive at the depletion per unit. This amount then is multiplied by the number of units sold (*not* the units produced) during the year to arrive at the cost depletion allowed. Cost depletion, therefore, resembles the units-of-production method of calculating depreciation.

---

[41]§ 612.

TAX IN THE NEWS **Depletion of Air Space**

Landfill operators are allowed a depletion allowance, which is a deduction in computing Federal taxable income. The depletion deduction is the value of the air space that is being filled up. The value of the air space is the product of some of the goodwill costs; some of the land costs; and all of the engineering, siting, and construction costs.

EXAMPLE 34

On January 1, 2016, Pablo purchases the rights to a mineral interest for $1 million. At that time, the remaining recoverable units in the mineral interest are estimated to be 200,000. The depletion per unit is $5 ($1,000,000 adjusted basis ÷ 200,000 estimated recoverable units).

If 60,000 units are mined and 25,000 are sold this year, the cost depletion is $125,000 ($5 depletion per unit × 25,000 units sold).

If the taxpayer later discovers that the original estimate was incorrect, the depletion per unit for future calculations is redetermined, using the revised estimate.[42]

EXAMPLE 35

Assume the same facts as in Example 34. In 2017, Pablo realizes that an incorrect estimate was made as to the capacity of the mine. The remaining recoverable units now are determined to be 400,000. Based on this new information, the revised depletion per unit is $2.1875 ($875,000 adjusted basis ÷ 400,000 estimated recoverable units). The $875,000 adjusted basis is the original cost ($1,000,000) reduced by the depletion claimed in 2016 ($125,000).

If 30,000 units are sold in 2017, the depletion for the year is $65,625 ($2.1875 depletion per unit × 30,000 units sold).

Percentage Depletion

Percentage depletion (also referred to as statutory depletion) uses a specified percentage provided by the Code. The percentage varies according to the type of mineral interest involved. A sample of these percentages is shown in Exhibit 8.2. The rate is applied to the gross income from the property, but in no event may percentage depletion exceed 50 percent of the taxable income from the property before the allowance for depletion.[43]

EXAMPLE 36

CarrollCo reports gross income of $100,000 and other property-related expenses of $60,000 and uses a depletion rate of 22%. CarrollCo's depletion allowance is determined as follows.

Gross income	$100,000
Less: Other expenses	(60,000)
Taxable income before depletion	$ 40,000
Depletion allowance [the lesser of $22,000 (22% × $100,000) or $20,000 (50% × $40,000)]	(20,000)
Taxable income after depletion	$ 20,000

The adjusted basis of CarrollCo's property is reduced by $20,000, the depletion deduction allowed. If the other expenses had been only $55,000, the full $22,000 could have been deducted, and the adjusted basis would have been reduced by $22,000.

Note that percentage depletion is based on a percentage of the gross income from the property and makes no reference to cost. All other deductions detailed in this chapter are

---

[42]§ 611(a).

[43]§ 613(a). Special rules apply for certain oil and gas wells (e.g., the 50% ceiling is replaced with a 100% ceiling, and the percentage depletion may not exceed 65% of the taxpayer's taxable income from all sources before the allowance for depletion). § 613A.

EXHIBIT 8.2	**Sample of Percentage Depletion Rates**

22% Depletion

Cobalt	Sulfur
Lead	Tin

15% Depletion

Copper	Oil, gas, oil shale
Gold	Silver

14% Depletion

Granite	Marble
Limestone	Potash

10% Depletion

Coal	Sodium chloride

5% Depletion

Gravel	Sand

a function of the adjusted basis (cost) of the property. Thus, when percentage depletion is used, it is possible to claim aggregate depletion deductions that exceed the original cost of the property. If percentage depletion is used, however, the adjusted basis of the property (for computing cost depletion in a future tax year) is reduced by any depletion deducted, until the basis reaches zero. See Example 40.

8-7 TAX PLANNING

LO.9

Identify tax planning opportunities for cost recovery, amortization, and depletion.

8-7a **Cost Recovery**

Cost recovery schedules should be reviewed annually for possible retirements, abandonments, and obsolescence.

An examination of the cost recovery schedule of Eagle Company reveals:

- Asset A was abandoned when it was discovered that the cost of repairs would be in excess of the cost of replacement. Asset A had an adjusted basis of $3,000.
- Asset J became obsolete this year, at which point its adjusted basis was $8,000.

Assets A and J should be written off, resulting in deductions of $11,000.

EXAMPLE

37

Because of the deductions for cost recovery, interest, and ad valorem property taxes, investments in real estate can be highly attractive. In examining the economics of such investments, one should take into account any tax savings that result.

The Big Picture

Return to the facts of *The Big Picture* on p. 8-1. In early January 2015, Dr. Payne purchased residential rental property for $170,000 (of which $20,000 was allocated to the land and $150,000 to the building). He made a down payment of $25,000 and assumed the seller's mortgage for the balance. Under the mortgage agreement, monthly payments of $1,000 are required and are applied toward interest, taxes, insurance, and principal.

Because the property was already occupied, Payne continued to receive rent income of $1,200 per month from the tenant. He actively participates in this activity and so comes under the special rule for a rental real estate activity with respect to the limitation on passive activity losses (refer to Chapter 11). He is in the 28% tax bracket.

EXAMPLE

38

continued

For 2016, Payne's expenses were determined to include:

Interest	$10,000
Taxes	800
Insurance	1,000
Repairs and maintenance	2,200
Depreciation ($150,000 × .03636)	5,454
Total expenses	$19,454

The deductible loss from the rental property is:

Rent income ($1,200 × 12 months)	$ 14,400
Less total expenses (see above)	(19,454)
Net loss	($ 5,054)

But what is Dr. Payne's net cash position for the year when the tax benefit of the loss is taken into account?

Intake—		
Rent income	$14,400	
Tax savings [28% (income tax bracket) × $5,054 (loss from the property)]	1,415	$ 15,815
Outlay—		
Mortgage payments ($1,000 × 12 months)	$12,000	
Repairs and maintenance	2,200	(14,200)
Net cash benefit		$ 1,615

Should Payne cease to be an active participant in the rental activity, the passive activity loss rules would apply and he could lose the current period benefit of the loss.

Another consideration when making decisions with respect to cost recovery is whether fast or slow cost recovery will be more beneficial for the taxpayer. If the taxpayer's goal is to recover the cost of fixed assets as quickly as possible, the following strategies should be used.

- When constructing a facility, keep in mind any resulting property tax implications. Refer to the discussion in Chapter 1 (text Section 1-5a).
- When electing § 179 expensing, choose assets with longer lives.
- Choose accelerated cost recovery methods where available.

If a taxpayer has a new business with little income or a business with a net operating loss carryover, the taxpayer's goal may be to slow down cost recovery. In such a situation, the taxpayer should:

- Elect not to take additional first-year depreciation, if available.
- Choose the straight-line cost recovery method.
- Make no election under § 179.
- Defer placing assets in service in the current tax year or postpone capital outlays until future tax years.

Section 179 and the Mid-Quarter Convention

The mid-quarter convention generally results in smaller depreciation deductions in the asset's acquisition year. However, the basis of property used to determine whether the mid-quarter convention applies is derived *after* any § 179 immediate expense election.[44] As a result, a taxpayer may be able to avoid the mid-quarter convention by designating § 179 treatment for assets placed in service during the last quarter of the taxable year.

---

[44]Reg. § 1.168(d)–1(b)(4).

EXAMPLE

39

Dimond Manufacturing places the following assets in service during 2016. All are 5-year class assets, and they are the only assets that Dimond placed in service during the year.

Asset 1 (April 3, 2016)	$ 438,000
Asset 2 (July 17, 2016)	232,000
Asset 3 (October 22, 2016)	580,000
Total	$1,250,000

As Dimond has placed more than 40% of the assets in service during the last quarter of the taxable year, the mid-quarter convention applies ($580,000/$1,250,000 = 46.4%). As a result, Dimond's MACRS deduction for the year is computed as follows (see Exhibit 8.4).

Asset 1	$438,000 × .25	$109,500
Asset 2	$232,000 × .15	34,800
Asset 3	$580,000 × .05	29,000
Total		$173,300

However, if Dimond elects to expense $500,000 of the October 22 acquisition under § 179, the mid-quarter convention would not apply.

Asset 1 (April 3, 2016)	$438,000
Asset 2 (July 17, 2016)	232,000
Asset 3 (October 22, 2016; $580,000 – $500,000)	80,000
Total	$750,000

Now Dimond has placed only 10.7% ($80,000/$750,000) of the assets in service during the last quarter of the taxable year. As a result, the mid-quarter convention does not apply, and Dimond's MACRS deduction for the year (including the § 179 expense election) is:

MACRS depreciation ($750,000 × .20; Exhibit 8.3)	$150,000
Section 179 expense (Asset 3)	500,000
Total	$650,000

As a result of its effective use of § 179, Dimond has increased its 2016 MACRS deduction and simplified its reporting and record keeping related to these assets.

8-7b **Amortization**

When a business is purchased, goodwill and covenants not to compete are both subject to a statutory amortization period of 15 years. Therefore, the purchaser does not derive any tax benefits when part of the purchase price is assigned to a covenant rather than to goodwill.

Thus, from the purchaser's perspective, bargaining for a covenant should be based on legal rather than tax reasons. Note, however, that from the seller's perspective, goodwill is a capital asset, and the covenant is an ordinary income asset.

Because the amortization period for both goodwill and a covenant is 15 years, the purchaser may want to attempt to minimize these amounts if the purchase price can be assigned to assets with shorter lives (e.g., inventory, receivables, and personalty). Conversely, the purchaser may want to attempt to maximize these amounts if part of the purchase price will otherwise be assigned to assets with longer recovery periods (e.g., realty) or to assets not eligible for cost recovery (e.g., land).

8-7c **Depletion**

As long as the basis of a depletable asset remains above zero, cost depletion or percentage depletion, whichever method produces the larger deduction, will be used. When the basis of the asset is exhausted, percentage depletion still can be taken.

EXAMPLE
40

Melissa reports the following related to her sulfur mine.

Remaining depletable basis	$ 11,000
Gross income (10,000 units)	100,000
Expenses (other than depletion)	30,000

Because cost depletion is limited to the remaining depletable basis of $11,000, Melissa would choose percentage depletion of $22,000 (a 22% depletion rate is used for sulfur). Her basis in the mine then becomes zero. In future years, however, she can continue to take percentage depletion; percentage depletion is computed without reference to the remaining basis.

8-7d Cost Recovery Tables

Summary of Tables

Exhibit 8.3	Modified ACRS statutory percentage table for personalty.
	Applicable depreciation methods: 200 or 150 percent declining-balance switching to straight-line.
	Applicable recovery periods: 3, 5, 7, 10, 15, 20 years.
	Applicable convention: half-year.
Exhibit 8.4	Modified ACRS statutory percentage table for personalty.
	Applicable depreciation method: 200 percent declining-balance switching to straight-line.
	Applicable recovery periods: 3, 5, 7 years.
	Applicable convention: mid-quarter.
Exhibit 8.5	Modified ACRS optional straight-line table for personalty.
	Applicable depreciation method: straight-line.
	Applicable recovery periods: 3, 5, 7, 10, 15, 20 years.
	Applicable convention: half-year.
Exhibit 8.6	Alternative minimum tax declining-balance table for personalty.
	Applicable depreciation method: 150 percent declining-balance switching to straight-line.
	Applicable recovery periods: 3, 5, 7, 9.5, 10, 12 years.
	Applicable convention: half-year.
Exhibit 8.7	Alternative depreciation system straight-line table for personalty.
	Applicable depreciation method: straight-line.
	Applicable recovery periods: 5, 10, 12 years.
	Applicable convention: half-year.
Exhibit 8.8	Modified ACRS straight-line table for realty.
	Applicable depreciation method: straight-line.
	Applicable recovery periods: 27.5, 31.5, 39 years.
	Applicable convention: mid-month.
Exhibit 8.9	Alternative depreciation system straight-line table for realty.
	Applicable depreciation method: straight-line.
	Applicable recovery period: 40 years.
	Applicable convention: mid-month.

EXHIBIT 8.3	MACRS Accelerated Depreciation for Personal Property Assuming Half-Year Convention

For Property Placed in Service after December 31, 1986

Recovery Year	3-Year (200% DB)	5-Year (200% DB)	7-Year (200% DB)	10-Year (200% DB)	15-Year (150% DB)	20-Year (150% DB)
1	33.33	20.00	14.29	10.00	5.00	3.750
2	44.45	32.00	24.49	18.00	9.50	7.219
3	14.81*	19.20	17.49	14.40	8.55	6.677
4	7.41	11.52*	12.49	11.52	7.70	6.177
5		11.52	8.93*	9.22	6.93	5.713
6		5.76	8.92	7.37	6.23	5.285
7			8.93	6.55*	5.90*	4.888
8			4.46	6.55	5.90	4.522
9				6.56	5.91	4.462*
10				6.55	5.90	4.461
11				3.28	5.91	4.462
12					5.90	4.461
13					5.91	4.462
14					5.90	4.461
15					5.91	4.462
16					2.95	4.461
17						4.462
18						4.461
19						4.462
20						4.461
21						2.231

*Switchover to straight-line depreciation.

EXHIBIT 8.4	MACRS Accelerated Depreciation for Personal Property Assuming Mid-Quarter Convention

For Property Placed in Service after December 31, 1986 (Partial Table*)

		3-Year		
Recovery Year	First Quarter	Second Quarter	Third Quarter	Fourth Quarter
1	58.33	41.67	25.00	8.33
2	27.78	38.89	50.00	61.11
		5-Year		
Recovery Year	First Quarter	Second Quarter	Third Quarter	Fourth Quarter
1	35.00	25.00	15.00	5.00
2	26.00	30.00	34.00	38.00
		7-Year		
Recovery Year	First Quarter	Second Quarter	Third Quarter	Fourth Quarter
1	25.00	17.85	10.71	3.57
2	21.43	23.47	25.51	27.55

*The figures in this table are taken from the official tables that appear in Rev.Proc. 87–57, 1987–2 C.B. 687. Because of their length, the complete tables are not presented.

EXHIBIT 8.5	MACRS Straight-Line Depreciation for Personal Property Assuming Half-Year Convention*

For Property Placed in Service after December 31, 1986

MACRS Class	% First Recovery Year	Other Recovery Years		Last Recovery Year	
		Years	%	Year	%
3-year	16.67	2–3	33.33	4	16.67
5-year	10.00	2–5	20.00	6	10.00
7-year	7.14	2–7	14.29	8	7.14
10-year	5.00	2–10	10.00	11	5.00
15-year	3.33	2–15	6.67	16	3.33
20-year	2.50	2–20	5.00	21	2.50

*The official table contains a separate row for each year. For ease of presentation, certain years are grouped in this table. In some instances, this will produce a difference of .01 for the last digit when compared with the official table.

EXHIBIT 8.6	Alternative Minimum Tax: 150% Declining-Balance Assuming Half-Year Convention

For Property Placed in Service after December 31, 1986 (Partial Table*)

Recovery Year	3-Year 150%	5-Year 150%	7-Year 150%	9.5-Year 150%	10-Year 150%	12-Year 150%
1	25.00	15.00	10.71	7.89	7.50	6.25
2	37.50	25.50	19.13	14.54	13.88	11.72
3	25.00**	17.85	15.03	12.25	11.79	10.25
4	12.50	16.66**	12.25**	10.31	10.02	8.97
5		16.66	12.25	9.17**	8.74**	7.85
6		8.33	12.25	9.17	8.74	7.33**
7			12.25	9.17	8.74	7.33
8			6.13	9.17	8.74	7.33
9				9.17	8.74	7.33
10				9.16	8.74	7.33
11					4.37	7.32
12						7.33
13						3.66

*The figures in this table are taken from the official table that appears in Rev.Proc. 87–57, 1987–2 C.B. 687. Because of its length, the complete table is not presented.
**Switchover to straight-line depreciation.

EXHIBIT 8.7	ADS Straight-Line for Personal Property Assuming Half-Year Convention

Not on Exam

For Property Placed in Service after December 31, 1986 (Partial Table)*

Recovery Year	5-Year Class	10-Year Class	12-Year Class
1	10.00	5.00	4.17
2	20.00	10.00	8.33
3	20.00	10.00	8.33
4	20.00	10.00	8.33
5	20.00	10.00	8.33
6	10.00	10.00	8.33
7		10.00	8.34
8		10.00	8.33
9		10.00	8.34
10		10.00	8.33
11		5.00	8.34
12			8.33
13			4.17

*The figures in this table are taken from the official table that appears in Rev.Proc. 87–57, 1987–2 C.B. 687. Because of its length, the complete table is not presented. The tables for the mid-quarter convention also appear in Rev.Proc. 87–57.

EXHIBIT 8.8	MACRS Straight-Line Depreciation for Real Property Assuming Mid-Month Convention*

For Property Placed in Service after December 31, 1986: 27.5-Year Residential Real Property

Recovery Year(s)	The Applicable Percentage Is (Use the Column for the Month in the First Year the Property Is Placed in Service):											
	1	2	3	4	5	6	7	8	9	10	11	12
1	3.485	3.182	2.879	2.576	2.273	1.970	1.667	1.364	1.061	0.758	0.455	0.152
2–18	3.636	3.636	3.636	3.636	3.636	3.636	3.636	3.636	3.636	3.636	3.636	3.636
19–27	3.637	3.637	3.637	3.637	3.637	3.637	3.637	3.637	3.637	3.637	3.637	3.637
28	1.970	2.273	2.576	2.879	3.182	3.485	3.636	3.636	3.636	3.636	3.636	3.636
29	0.000	0.000	0.000	0.000	0.000	0.000	0.152	0.455	0.758	1.061	1.364	1.667

For Property Placed in Service after December 31, 1986, and before May 13, 1993: 31.5-Year Nonresidential Real Property

Recovery Year(s)	The Applicable Percentage Is (Use the Column for the Month in the First Year the Property Is Placed in Service):											
	1	2	3	4	5	6	7	8	9	10	11	12
1	3.042	2.778	2.513	2.249	1.984	1.720	1.455	1.190	0.926	0.661	0.397	0.132
2–19	3.175	3.175	3.175	3.175	3.175	3.175	3.175	3.175	3.175	3.175	3.175	3.175
20–31	3.174	3.174	3.174	3.174	3.174	3.174	3.174	3.174	3.174	3.174	3.174	3.174
32	1.720	1.984	2.249	2.513	2.778	3.042	3.175	3.175	3.175	3.175	3.175	3.175
33	0.000	0.000	0.000	0.000	0.000	0.000	0.132	0.397	0.661	0.926	1.190	1.455

For Property Placed in Service after May 12, 1993: 39-Year Nonresidential Real Property

Recovery Year(s)	The Applicable Percentage Is (Use the Column for the Month in the First Year the Property Is Placed in Service):											
	1	2	3	4	5	6	7	8	9	10	11	12
1	2.461	2.247	2.033	1.819	1.605	1.391	1.177	0.963	0.749	0.535	0.321	0.107
2–39	2.564	2.564	2.564	2.564	2.564	2.564	2.564	2.564	2.564	2.564	2.564	2.564
40	0.107	0.321	0.535	0.749	0.963	1.177	1.391	1.605	1.819	2.033	2.247	2.461

*The official tables contain a separate row for each year. For ease of presentation, certain years are grouped in these tables. In some instances, this will produce a difference of .001 for the last digit when compared with the official tables.

EXHIBIT 8.9   ADS Straight-Line for Real Property Assuming Mid-Month Convention

For Property Placed in Service after December 31, 1986

Recovery Year	Month Placed in Service											
	1	**2**	**3**	**4**	**5**	**6**	**7**	**8**	**9**	**10**	**11**	**12**
1	2.396	2.188	1.979	1.771	1.563	1.354	1.146	0.938	0.729	0.521	0.313	0.104
2–40	2.500	2.500	2.500	2.500	2.500	2.500	2.500	2.500	2.500	2.500	2.500	2.500
41	0.104	0.312	0.521	0.729	0.937	1.146	1.354	1.562	1.771	1.979	2.187	2.396

REFOCUS ON THE BIG PICTURE

CALCULATING COST RECOVERY DEDUCTIONS

Regardless of whether the accrual method or the cash method of accounting is used, MACRS must be used in calculating the depreciation expense for fixed assets for tax purposes. Evidently, Dr. Payne's financial reporting system uses MACRS, because $91,298 is the correct amount of depreciation expense. The computers and peripheral equipment are 5-year property. The office furniture and fixtures and the dental equipment are 7-year property.

Based on the IRS cost recovery tables, the following percentages are used in calculating depreciation expense for the first year of each asset's life.

5-year property	20.00%
7-year property	14.29%

Payne can deduct depreciation on the house he converted from personal use to rental use and on the rental house he purchased.

What If?

From a tax planning perspective, what can Dr. Payne do to increase the depreciation deductions associated with the purchase of these fixed assets and thereby reduce the amount of the business net income reported on Schedule C of Form 1040 for his dental practice?

In addition to the standard MACRS deduction using the percentages for 2016, § 179 provides for the limited expensing of fixed assets. This provision applies to personalty, but does not apply to realty (e.g., buildings). In 2016, the maximum amount that can be deducted under this limited expensing provision is subject to several overall limits. First, the total amount deducted cannot exceed $500,000. Second, the $500,000 amount is reduced dollar for dollar for § 179 asset purchases placed in service during the tax year once such purchases exceed $2,010,000. Finally, the § 179 deduction for a tax year cannot exceed the taxable income from the trade or business.

If Payne elects § 179 treatment for some of the fixed asset purchases of his dental practice, he can reduce the Schedule C net income of his dental practice beyond the $91,298 of depreciation expense computed using MACRS to a maximum of $500,000 § 179 expense for 2016.

The remaining amount of the $612,085 purchases of § 179 assets not deducted in the current year are eligible for additional first-year depreciation and MACRS cost recovery.

For future reference associated with similar fixed asset purchases for his business, the sequence of calculating the deduction is as follows.

- § 179 limited expensing.
- Additional first-year depreciation.
- Standard MACRS cost recovery.

Key Terms

Accelerated cost recovery
system (ACRS), 8-2

Additional first-year depreciation, 8-10

Alternative depreciation
system (ADS), 8-17

Amortization, 8-19

Cost depletion, 8-23

Cost recovery, 8-2

Depletion, 8-22

Depreciation, 8-2

Half-year convention, 8-6

Intangible drilling and development costs
(IDCs), 8-23

Listed property, 8-13

Mid-month convention, 8-8

Mid-quarter convention, 8-7

Modified accelerated cost recovery
system (MACRS), 8-2

Percentage depletion, 8-24

Residential rental real estate, 8-8

Section 179 expensing, 8-11

Startup expenditures, 8-19

Discussion Questions

1. **LO.1** Discuss whether property that is classified as personal use is subject to cost recovery.

2. **LO.1** Discuss the difference between personal property and personal use property.

3. **LO.1** Discuss whether land improvements are eligible for cost recovery.

4. **LO.2** At the beginning of the current year, Henry purchased a ski resort for $10 million. Henry does not own the land on which the resort is located. The Federal government owns the land, and Henry has the right to operate the resort on the land pursuant to Special Use Permits, which are terminable at will by the Federal government, and Term Special Use Permits, which allow the land to be used for a fixed number of years.

   In preparing the income tax return for the current year, Henry properly allocated $2 million of the purchase price to the costs of constructing mountain roads, slopes, and trails. Since the acquisition, Henry has spent an additional $1 million on maintaining the mountain roads, slopes, and trails. Identify the relevant tax issues for Henry.

   Issue ID

5. **LO.2** Identify the three factors reflected in the MACRS tables when the amount of cost recovery is determined.

6. **LO.2** Discuss the computation of cost recovery in the year an asset is placed in service when the mid-quarter convention is being used.

7. **LO.2** Discuss the computation of cost recovery in the year of sale of an asset when the mid-quarter convention is being used.

8. **LO.2** Robert purchased and placed in service $100,000 of 7-year class assets on August 10 of the current year. He also purchased and placed in service $500,000 of 5-year class assets on November 15 of the current year. He does not claim any available additional first-year depreciation. If Robert elects to use the MACRS straight-line method of cost recovery on the 7-year class assets, discuss the calculation of cost recovery for the 5-year class assets.

9. **LO.2** Jim owns a very large ranch. A large part of his business is the production and raising of breeding cattle. Jim understands that he is entitled to use MACRS cost recovery on breeding cattle. Identify the relevant tax issues for Jim with respect to taking cost recovery on his self-produced breeding cattle.

   Issue ID

10. **LO.3** Discuss when § 179 expense must be recaptured.

11. **LO.3** Explain how the § 179 limited expensing deduction affects the computation of MACRS cost recovery.

12. **LO.3** Discuss the treatment of a § 179 expensing carryforward.

13. **LO.3** Discuss the definition of *taxable income* as it is used in limiting the § 179 expensing amount.

Issue ID   14. **LO.2, 3** A professional consulting business sells professional tools and equipment and provides associated services, such as repair and maintenance, to its customer base. The company's employees include technicians, who are required to provide and maintain their own tools and equipment for performing the repairs and maintenance work. The company will reimburse a technician for amounts spent to purchase tools and equipment eligible for a § 179 deduction up to a set amount each year. Any costs for tools and equipment that exceed the set amount will not be reimbursed.

    John is a technician for the company. During the current year, he purchased equipment that qualifies for the § 179 deduction. John paid $50,000 for the equipment and was reimbursed the set amount of $40,000. Identify the relevant tax issues for John with respect to § 179 and the computation of his taxable income.

15. **LO.4** Discuss how the limits on cost recovery apply to listed property.

16. **LO.4** Discuss the tax consequences if the business use percentage of listed property falls to 50% or lower after the year the property is placed in service.

17. **LO.7** Explain the amortization period of a § 197 intangible if the actual useful life is less than 15 years.

Issue ID   18. **LO.7** Harold and Bart own 75% of the stock of Orange Motors. The other 25% of the stock is owned by Jeb. Orange Motors entered into an agreement with Harold and Bart to acquire all of their Orange stock.

    In addition, Harold and Bart signed a noncompete agreement with Orange Motors. Under the terms of the noncompete agreement, Orange will pay Harold and Bart $15,000 each per year for four years. Identify the relevant tax issues for Orange Motors.

Issue ID   19. **LO.7** In May 2016, George began searching for a trade or business to acquire. In anticipation of finding a suitable aquisition, George hired an investment banker to evaluate three potential businesses. He also hired a law firm to begin drafting regulatory approval documents for a target company. Eventually, George decided to purchase all of the assets of Brash Corporation. Brash and George entered into an acquisition agreement on December 1, 2016. Identify the relevant tax issues for George.

20. **LO.8** Discuss how the cost of mineral rights enters into the calculation of cost depletion.

Computational Exercises

21. **LO.2** Euclid acquires a 7-year class asset on May 9, 2016, for $80,000. Euclid does not elect immediate expensing under § 179. She does not claim any available additional first-year depreciation. Calculate Euclid's cost recovery deduction for 2016 and 2017.

22. **LO.2** Hamlet acquires a 7-year class asset on November 23, 2016, for $100,000. Hamlet does not elect immediate expensing under § 179. He does not claim any available additional first-year depreciation. Calculate Hamlet's cost recovery deductions for 2016 and 2017.

23. **LO.2** Lopez acquired a building on June 1, 2011, for $1 million. Calculate Lopez's cost recovery deduction for 2016 if the building is:
   a.   Classified as residential rental real estate.
   b.   Classified as nonresidential real estate.

24. **LO.2** Andre acquired a computer on March 3, 2016, for $2,800. He elects the straight-line method for cost recovery. Andre does not elect immediate expensing under § 179. He does not claim any available additional first-year depreciation. Calculate Andre's cost recovery deduction for the computer in 2016 and 2017.

25. **LO.2** Diana acquires, for $65,000, and places in service a 5-year class asset on December 19, 2016. It is the only asset that Diana acquires during 2016. Diana does not elect immediate expensing under § 179. She elects additional first-year deprecation. Calculate Diana's total cost recovery deduction for 2016.

26. **LO.3** McKenzie purchased qualifying equipment for his business that cost $212,000 in 2016. The taxable income of the business for the year is $5,600 before consideration of any § 179 deduction. Calculate McKenzie's § 179 expense deduction for 2016 and any carryover to 2017.

27. **LO.4** On April 5, 2016, Kinsey places in service a new automobile that cost $36,000. He does not elect § 179 expensing, and he elects not to take any available additional first-year depreciation. The car is used 70% for business and 30% for personal use in each tax year.

    Kinsey chooses the MACRS 200% declining-balance method of cost recovery (the auto is a 5-year asset). Assume the following luxury automobile limitations: year 1: $3,160; year 2: $5,100. Compute the total depreciation allowed for 2016 and 2017.

28. **LO.7** On September 30, 2016, Priscilla purchased a business. Of the purchase price, $60,000 is allocated to a patent and $375,000 is allocated to goodwill. Calculate Priscilla's 2016 § 197 amortization deduction.

29. **LO.8** On March 25, 2016, Parscale Company purchases the rights to a mineral interest for $8 million. At that time, the remaining recoverable units in the mineral interest are estimated to be 500,000 tons. If 80,000 tons are mined and 75,000 tons are sold this year, calculate Parscale's cost depletion for 2016.

30. **LO.8** Jebali Company reports gross income of $340,000 and other property-related expenses of $229,000 and uses a depletion rate of 14%. Calculate Jebali's depletion allowance for the current year.

Problems

31. **LO.1, 2** On November 4, 2014, Blue Company acquired an asset (27.5-year residential real property) for $200,000 for use in its business. In 2014 and 2015, respectively, Blue took $642 and $5,128 of cost recovery. These amounts were incorrect; Blue applied the wrong percentages (i.e., those for 39-year rather than 27.5-year assets). Blue should have taken $910 and $7,272 cost recovery in 2014 and 2015, respectively.

    On January 1, 2016, the asset was sold for $180,000. Calculate the gain or loss on the sale of the asset for that year.

32. **LO.1, 2** José purchased a house for $300,000 in 2013. He used the house as his personal residence. In March 2016, when the fair market value of the house was $400,000, he converted the house to rental property. What is José's cost recovery for 2016?

33. **LO.2** Orange Corporation acquired new office furniture on August 15, 2016, for $130,000. Orange does not elect immediate expensing under § 179. Orange claims any available additional first-year depreciation. Determine Orange's cost recovery for 2016.

34. **LO.2** Weston acquires a new office machine (7-year class asset) on November 2, 2015, for $75,000. This is the only asset Weston acquired during the year.

He does not elect immediate expensing under § 179. He claims the maximum additional first-year depreciation deduction. On September 15, 2016, Weston sells the machine.

a. Determine Weston's cost recovery for 2015.

b. Determine Weston's cost recovery for 2016.

35. **LO.2** Juan acquires a new 5-year class asset on March 14, 2016, for $200,000. This is the only asset Juan acquired during the year. He does not elect immediate expensing under § 179. He does not claim any available additional first-year depreciation. On July 15, 2017, Juan sells the asset.

a. Determine Juan's cost recovery for 2016.

b. Determine Juan's cost recovery for 2017.

36. **LO.2** Debra acquired the following new assets during 2016.

Date	Asset	Cost
April 11	Furniture	$40,000
July 28	Trucks	40,000
November 3	Computers	70,000

Determine Debra's cost recovery deductions for the current year. Debra does not elect immediate expensing under § 179. She does not claim any available additional first-year depreciation.

37. **LO.2** On August 2, 2016, Wendy purchased a new office building for $3.8 million. On October 1, 2016, she began to rent out office space in the building. On July 15, 2020, Wendy sold the office building.

a. Determine Wendy's cost recovery deduction for 2016.

b. Determine Wendy's cost recovery deduction for 2020.

38. **LO.2** On April 3, 2016, Terry purchased and placed in service a building that cost $2 million. An appraisal determined that 25% of the total cost was attributed to the value of the land. The bottom floor of the building is leased to a retail business for $32,000. The other floors of the building are rental apartments with an annual rent of $160,000. Determine Terry's cost recovery deduction for 2016.

39. **LO.2** On May 5, 2016, Christy purchased and placed in service a hotel. The hotel cost $10.8 million. Calculate Christy's cost recovery deductions for 2016 and for 2026.

40. **LO.2** Janice acquired an apartment building on June 4, 2016, for $1.6 million. The value of the land is $300,000. Janice sold the apartment building on November 29, 2022.

a. Determine Janice's cost recovery deduction for 2016.

b. Determine Janice's cost recovery deduction for 2022.

Decision Making   41. **LO.2, 3, 9** Lori, who is single, purchased 5-year class property for $200,000 and 7-year class property for $400,000 on May 20, 2016. Lori expects the taxable income derived from her business (without regard to the amount expensed under § 179) to be about $800,000. Lori wants to elect immediate § 179 expensing, but she doesn't know which asset she should expense under § 179. She does not claim any available additional first-year depreciation.

a. Determine Lori's total deduction if the § 179 expense is first taken with respect to the 5-year class asset.

b. Determine Lori's total deduction if the § 179 expense is first taken with respect to the 7-year class asset.

c. What is your advice to Lori?

d. Assume that Lori is in the 25% marginal tax bracket and that she uses § 179 on the 7-year asset. Determine the present value of the tax savings from the depreciation deductions for both assets. See Appendix H for present value factors, and assume a 6% discount rate.

e. Assume the same facts as in (d), except that Lori decides not to use § 179 on either asset. What is the present value of the tax savings generated by using the § 179 deduction on the 7-year asset?

42. **LO.2, 3** Olga is the proprietor of a small business. In 2016, the business's income, before consideration of any cost recovery or § 179 deduction, is $250,000.

Olga spends $600,000 on new 7-year class assets and elects to take the § 179 deduction on them. She does not claim any available additional first-year depreciation. Olga's cost recovery deduction for 2016, except for the cost recovery with respect to the new 7-year assets, is $95,000. Determine Olga's total cost recovery for 2016 with respect to the 7-year class assets and the amount of any § 179 carryforward.

43. **LO.2, 3, 9** On June 5, 2015, Dan purchased and placed in service a 7-year class asset costing $550,000. Determine the maximum deductions that Dan can claim with respect to this asset in 2015 and 2016.

44. **LO.3, 4** Jabari Johnson is considering acquiring an automobile at the beginning of 2016 that he will use 100% of the time as a taxi. The purchase price of the automobile is $35,000. Johnson has heard of cost recovery limits on automobiles and wants to know how much of the $35,000 he can deduct in the first year.

Write a letter to Jabari in which you present your calculations. Also prepare a memo for the tax files, summarizing your analysis. Johnson's address is 100 Morningside, Clinton, MS 39058.

Communications

Letter Writing Assignment

45. **LO.2, 4** On October 15, 2016, Jon purchased and placed in service a used car. The purchase price was $25,000. This was the only business use asset Jon acquired in 2016. He used the car 80% of the time for business and 20% for personal use. Jon used the MACRS statutory percentage method. Calculate the total deduction Jon may take for 2016 with respect to the car.

46. **LO.4** On June 5, 2015, Leo purchased and placed in service a new car that cost $20,000. The business use percentage for the car is always 100%. Leo claims any available additional first-year depreciation. Compute Leo's cost recovery deductions for 2015 and 2016.

47. **LO.2, 3, 4** On March 15, 2016, Helen purchased and placed in service a new Escalade. The purchase price was $62,000, and the vehicle had a rating of 6,500 GVW. The vehicle was used 100% for business. Calculate the maximum total depreciation deduction that Helen may take with respect to the vehicle in 2016.

48. **LO.2, 4** On May 28, 2016, Mary purchased and placed in service a new $20,000 car. The car was used 60% for business, 20% for production of income, and 20% for personal use in 2016. In 2017, the usage changed to 40% for business, 30% for production of income, and 30% for personal use. Mary did not elect immediate expensing under § 179. She did not claim any available additional first-year depreciation. Compute Mary's cost recovery deduction and any cost recovery recapture in 2017.

49. **LO.2, 4, 9** Sally purchased a new computer (5-year property) on June 1, 2016, for $4,000. Sally could use the computer 100% of the time in her business, or she could allow her family to use the computer as well. Sally estimates that if her family uses the computer, the business use will be 45% and the personal use will be 55%.

Determine the tax cost to Sally, in the year of acquisition, of allowing her family to use the computer. Assume that Sally would not elect § 179 limited expensing and that her marginal tax rate is 28%. She does not claim any available additional first-year depreciation.

Decision Making

Decision Making
Communications

50. **LO.2, 4, 9** Dennis Harding is considering acquiring a new automobile that he will use 100% for business. The purchase price of the automobile would be $48,500. If Dennis leased the car for five years, the lease payments would be $375 per month. Dennis will acquire the car on January 1, 2016. The inclusion dollar amounts from the IRS table for the next five years are $47, $103, $153, $183, and $210.

Dennis wants to know the effect on his adjusted gross income of purchasing versus leasing the car for the next five years. He does not claim any available additional first-year depreciation. Write a letter to Dennis, and present your calculations. Also prepare a memo for the tax files. His address is 150 Avenue I, Memphis, TN 38112.

51. **LO.2, 5** In 2016, Muhammad purchased a new computer for $16,000. The computer is used 100% for business. Muhammad did not make a § 179 election with respect to the computer. He does not claim any available additional first-year depreciation. If Muhammad uses the MACRS statutory percentage method, determine his cost recovery deduction for 2016 for computing taxable income and for computing his alternative minimum tax.

Decision Making

52. **LO.2, 5, 9** Jamie purchased $100,000 of new office furniture for her business in June of the current year. Jamie understands that if she elects to use ADS to compute her regular income tax, there will be no difference between the cost recovery for computing the regular income tax and the AMT.

a. Jamie wants to know the present value of the *tax cost*, after three years, of using ADS rather than MACRS. Assume that Jamie does not elect § 179 expensing, she does not claim any additional first-year depreciation, and her marginal tax rate is 28%. See Appendix H for present value factors, and assume a 6% discount rate.

b. What is the present value of the tax savings/costs that result over the life of the asset if Jamie uses MACRS rather than ADS?

Decision Making
Communications

53. **LO.2, 7, 9** Mike Saxon is negotiating the purchase of a business. The final purchase price has been agreed upon, but the allocation of the purchase price to the assets is still being discussed. Appraisals on a warehouse range from $1.2 million to $1.5 million. If a value of $1.2 million is used for the warehouse, the remainder of the purchase price, $800,000, will be allocated to goodwill. If $1.5 million is allocated to the warehouse, goodwill will be $500,000.

Mike wants to know what effect each alternative will have on cost recovery and amortization during the first year. Under the agreement, Mike will take over the business on January 1 of next year. Write a letter to Mike in which you present your calculations and recommendation. Also prepare a memo for the tax files. Mike's address is 200 Rolling Hills Drive, Shavertown, PA 18708.

54. **LO.7** Oleander Corporation, a calendar year entity, begins business on March 1, 2016. The corporation incurs startup expenditures of $64,000. If Oleander elects § 195 treatment, determine the total amount of startup expenditures that it may deduct in 2016.

55. **LO.7** Martha was considering starting a new business. During her preliminary investigations related to the new venture, she incurred the following expenditures.

Salaries	$22,000
Travel	18,000
Interest on short-term note	4,000
Professional fees	13,000

Martha begins the business on July 1 of the current year. If Martha elects § 195 treatment, determine her startup expenditure deduction for the current year.

56. **LO.8** Wes acquired a mineral interest during the year for $10 million. A geological survey estimated that 250,000 tons of the mineral remained in the deposit. During the year, 80,000 tons were mined, and 45,000 tons were sold for $12 million. Other related expenses amounted to $5 million. Assuming that the mineral depletion rate is 22%, calculate Wes's lowest taxable income, after any depletion deductions.

Cumulative Problems

57. Janice Morgan, age 24, is single and has no dependents. She is a freelance writer. In January 2015, Janice opened her own office located at 2751 Waldham Road, Pleasant Hill, NM 88135. She called her business Writers Anonymous. Janice is a cash basis taxpayer. She lives at 132 Stone Avenue, Pleasant Hill, NM 88135. Her Social Security number is 123-45-6789. Janice's parents continue to provide health insurance for her under their policy. Janice wants to contribute to the Presidential Election Campaign Fund.

Tax Return Problem

TAX SOFTWARE

During 2015, Janice reported the following income and expense items connected with her business.

Income from sale of articles	$85,000
Rent	16,500
Utilities	7,900
Supplies	1,800
Insurance	5,000
Travel (including meals of $1,200)	3,500

Janice purchased and placed in service the following fixed assets for her business. Janice wants to elect immediate expensing under § 179.

- Furniture and fixtures (new) costing $21,000 on January 10.
- Computer equipment (new) costing $12,400 on July 28.

Janice's itemized deductions include:

State income tax	$3,000
Home mortgage interest paid to First Bank	6,000
Property taxes on home	1,500
Charitable contributions	1,200

Janice did not keep a record of the sales tax she paid. The pertinent amount from the sales tax table is $437.

Janice reports interest income of $4,000 on certificates of deposit at Second Bank. Janice makes estimated tax payments of $3,000 for 2015.

Compute Janice Morgan's 2015 Federal income tax payable (or refund due). If you use tax forms for your computations, you will need Forms 1040 and 4562 and Schedules A, B, and C. Suggested software: H&R BLOCK Tax Software.

58. John Smith, age 31, is single and has no dependents. At the beginning of 2016, John started his own excavation business and named it Earth Movers. John lives at 1045 Center Street, Lindon, UT, and his business is located at 381 State Street, Lindon, UT. The ZIP Code for both addresses is 84042. John's Social Security number is 111-11-1111, and the business identification number is 11-1111111. John is a cash basis taxpayer. During 2016, John reports the following items in connection with his business.

Tax Computation Problem

Decision Making

Communications

Fee income for services rendered	$912,000
Building rental expense	36,000
Office furniture and equipment rental expense	9,000
Office supplies	2,500
Utilities	4,000
Salary for secretary	34,000
Salary for equipment operators	42,000
Payroll taxes	7,000
Fuel and oil for the equipment	21,000
Purchase of three new front-end loaders on January 15, 2016, for $550,000.	550,000
Purchase of a new dump truck on January 18, 2016	80,000

During 2016, John recorded the following additional items.

Interest income from First National Bank	$10,000
Dividends from ExxonMobil	9,500
Quarterly estimated tax payments	11,500

John makes the election under § 179 on the three front-end loaders purchased in January. John claims any available additional first-year depreciation.

On October 8, 2016, John inherited IBM stock from his Aunt Mildred. John had been her favorite nephew. According to the data provided by the executor of Aunt Mildred's estate, the stock was valued for estate tax purposes at $110,000. John is considering selling the IBM stock for $125,000 on December 29, 2016, and using $75,000 of the proceeds to purchase an Acura ZDX. He would use the car 100% for business. John wants to know what effect these transactions would have on his 2016 adjusted gross income.

Write a letter to John in which you present your calculations, and prepare a memo for the tax files. Ignore any Federal self-employment tax implications.

Research Problems

THOMSON REUTERS
CHECKPOINT®
Student Edition

Note: Solutions to Research Problems can be prepared by using the Checkpoint® Student Edition online research product, which is available to accompany this text. It is also possible to prepare solutions to the Research Problems by using tax research materials found in a standard tax library.

Communications

Research Problem 1. Your client, Dave's Sport Shop, sells sports equipment and clothing in three retail outlets in New York City. During 2016, the CFO decided that keeping track of inventory using a combination of QuickBooks and Excel was not an efficient way to manage the stores' inventories. So Dave's purchased an inventory management system for $9,000 that allowed the entity to keep track of inventory, as well as automate ordering and purchasing, without replacing QuickBooks for its accounting function.

The CFO would like to know whether the cost of the inventory management program can be expensed in the year of purchase. Write a letter to the CFO, Cassandra Martin, that addresses the tax treatment of purchased software. Cassandra's mailing address is 867 Broadway, New York, NY 10003.

Research Problem 2. In 2012, Jed James began planting a vineyard. The costs of the land preparation, labor, rootstock, and planting were capitalized. The land preparation costs do not include any nondepreciable land costs. In 2016, when the plants became viable, Jed placed the vineyard in service. Jed wants to know whether he can claim a deduction under § 179 on his 2016 income tax return for the 2012 costs for planting the vineyard.

Research Problem 3. Juan owns a business that acquires exotic automobiles that are high-tech, state-of-the-art vehicles with unique design features or equipment. The exotic automobiles are not licensed or set up to be used on the road. Rather, the cars are used exclusively for car shows or related promotional photography. With respect to the exotic automobiles, Juan would like to know whether he can take a cost recovery deduction on his Federal income tax return.

Partial list of research aids:
Bruce Selig, 70 TCM 1125, T.C.Memo. 1995–519.

Use the tax resources of the Internet to address the following questions. Do not restrict your search to the Web, but include a review of newsgroups and general reference materials, practitioner sites and resources, primary sources of the tax law, chat rooms and discussion groups, and other opportunities.

Internet Activity

Research Problem 4. Locate a financial calculator program that assesses the wisdom of buying versus leasing a new car. Install the program on your computer, and become familiar with it. Use the program to work through Problem 50 in this chapter.

Research Problem 5. Changes to depreciation systems often are discussed by policymakers and observers of the tax system. Outline the terms and policy objectives of one of the changes currently proposed by the Treasury, a member of Congress, or a tax policy think tank.

Communications

Roger CPA Review Questions

1. Quanti Co., a calendar year taxpayer, purchased small tools for $5,000 on December 21, 2016, representing the company's *only* purchase of tangible personal property that took place during 2016. On its 2016 tax return, how many months of MACRS depreciation may Quanti Co. claim on the tools?

   a. One-and-a-half months   c. Six months
   b. One month   d. None

2. Which of the following is *correct* about depreciation under Federal tax law?

   I.   The recovery period is longer than the useful life of the asset.
   II. There are different recovery periods for new and used property.
   III. Salvage values are ignored.

   a. I and II only   c. III only
   b. II only   d. I, II, and III

3. Joe purchased a van on February 1, 2016, for use in his business, Crew Airport Transport. The van was purchased for $30,000, has an estimated useful life of 10 years, and has a salvage value of $2,000. No other assets were put into service that year. What is Joe's MACRS depreciation for the van in 2016?

   a. $2,567   c. $10,500
   b. $6,000   d. $10,267

4. Dolly purchased and placed into service qualifying depreciable property in 2016 at a total cost of $2,250,000. Dolly has elected to take the § 179 deduction. What is Dolly's § 179 deduction for 2016?

   a. $0   c. $500,000
   b. $260,000   d. $1,750,000

5. In 2016, Christa purchased and placed into service five-year assets at a total cost of $2,250,000. If Christa elects both the § 179 deduction and additional first-year bonus depreciation, but does not elect the straight-line method, what is Christa's depreciation expense for tax purposes for the year, assuming a half-year convention?

   a. $260,000   c. $1,250,000
   b. $500,000   d. $1,454,000

Deductions: Employee and Self-Employed-Related Expenses

LEARNING OBJECTIVES: *After completing Chapter 9, you should be able to:*

LO.1 Distinguish between employee and self-employed (independent contractor) status.

LO.2 Recognize deductible transportation expenses.

LO.3 Describe how travel expenses are treated.

LO.4 Determine the moving expense deduction.

LO.5 Differentiate between deductible and nondeductible education expenses.

LO.6 Explain how entertainment and meal expenses are treated.

LO.7 Identify other employee expenses.

LO.8 Compare various deductions for contributions to retirement accounts.

LO.9 Demonstrate the difference between accountable and nonaccountable employee plans.

LO.10 Apply the limitations on miscellaneous itemized deductions.

LO.11 List and evaluate tax planning ideas related to employee business expenses.

CHAPTER OUTLINE

© ISTOCKPHOTO.COM/SVETIKD

THE BIG PICTURE

THE FIRST JOB

After an extensive search, Morgan, a recent college graduate with a major in finance, has accepted a job with Kite Corporation. The job is in sales and will require travel and some entertainment (i.e., business lunches). She will be based in a major metropolitan area in another state. Kite has no available space in the locale, so Morgan will have to maintain her own work facility. In addition to her salary, Morgan will receive a travel allowance. However, Kite has made it clear that the allowance *will not* cover all of her travel expenses. Kite requires all travel expenses to be documented appropriately (e.g., receipts provided, business purpose explained) and submitted in a timely manner.

Morgan is delighted with the new job because it will enable her to maintain a flexible work schedule. Furthermore, working out of her own apartment avoids a time-consuming and costly commute.

What are some of the income tax problems presented by this situation?

Read the chapter and formulate your response.

9-1

FRAMEWORK 1040   Tax Formula for Individuals

This chapter covers the boldfaced portions of the Tax Formula for Individuals that was introduced in Concept Summary 3.1 on p. 3-3. Below those portions are the sections of Form 1040 where the results are reported.

Income *(broadly defined)*	$xx,xxx
Less: Exclusions	(x,xxx)
Gross income	$xx,xxx
Less: **Deductions** *for* adjusted gross income	(x,xxx)

FORM 1040 (p. 1)

12	Business income or (loss). Attach Schedule C or C-EZ	
23	Educator expenses	**23**
24	Certain business expenses of reservists, performing artists, and fee-basis government officials. Attach Form 2106 or 2106-EZ	**24**
26	Moving expenses. Attach Form 3903	**26**
32	IRA deduction	**32**
34	Tuition and fees. Attach Form 8917	**34**

Adjusted gross income	$xx,xxx
Less: The greater of total **itemized deductions** *or* the standard deduction	(x,xxx)

FORM 1040 (p. 2)

40	**Itemized deductions** (from Schedule A) **or** your **standard deduction**

Personal and dependency exemptions	(x,xxx)
Taxable income	$xx,xxx
Tax on taxable income *(see Tax Tables or Tax Rate Schedules)*	$ x,xxx
Less: Tax credits *(including income taxes withheld and prepaid)*	(xxx)
Tax due (or refund)	$ xxx

C onsidering the large number of taxpayers affected, the tax treatment of job-related expenses is unusually complex. To resolve this matter in a systematic fashion, a number of key questions must be asked:

- Is the taxpayer an *employee* or *self-employed?*
- If an employee, what expenses *qualify* as deductions?
- How are the expenses that qualify *classified* for tax purposes?
- To the extent the expenses are classified as deductions *from* AGI, are they subject to any *limitation?*

Once these questions have been posed and answered, the chapter considers various planning procedures available to maximize the deductibility of employee and self-employed expenses.

LO.1

Distinguish between employee and self-employed (independent contractor) status.

9-1   EMPLOYEE VERSUS INDEPENDENT CONTRACTOR

When one person performs services for another, the person performing the service either is an employee or is self-employed (an **independent contractor**). Failure to recognize a person's work status correctly can have serious tax consequences (in addition to Federal and state labor law consequences). Tax deficiencies as well as interest and penalties may result from improper classification.

Unlike employees, self-employed persons do not have to be included in various fringe benefit programs (e.g., group term life insurance and retirement plans). Because they are not covered by FICA and FUTA (see Chapter 1), these payroll costs are avoided. The IRS is very much aware of the tendency of businesses to wrongly classify workers as self-employed rather than as employees.

In terms of tax consequences, employment status makes a great deal of difference to the persons who perform the services. Expenses of self-employed taxpayers, to the extent allowable, are classified as deductions *for* AGI and are reported on Schedule C (Profit or Loss From Business) of Form 1040.[1] With the exception of reimbursement under an accountable plan (see later in the chapter), expenses of employees are deductions *from* AGI. They are reported on Form 2106 (Employee Business Expenses) and Schedule A (Itemized Deductions) of Form 1040.[2]

Most persons classified as employees are common law employees. The common law employee classification originated in judicial case law and is summarized in various IRS pronouncements.[3] Revenue Ruling 87–41, for example, lists 20 factors that can be used in determining whether a worker is a common law employee or an independent contractor (and, thus, self-employed).[4] The IRS has indicated that these 20 factors can be grouped into three broad categories: behavioral control, financial control, and the relationship of the parties.

A common law employee-employer relationship exists when the employer has the right to specify the end result and the ways and means by which that result is to be attained.[5] An employee is subject to the will and control of the employer with respect not only to what shall be done but also to how it shall be done. If the individual is subject to the direction or control of another only to the extent of the end result but not as to the means of accomplishment, an employee-employer relationship does not exist.

Certain factors indicate a common law employee-employer relationship. These include the performance of the following by the employer:

- Furnishing tools or equipment and a place to work.

- Providing support services, including the hiring of assistants to help do the work.

- Making training available to provide needed job skills.

- Allowing participation in various workplace fringe benefits (e.g., accident and health plans, group life insurance, and retirement plans).

- Paying for services based on time rather than the task performed.

For their part, independent contractors are more likely than employees to have unreimbursed business expenses, a significant investment in tools and work facilities, and less permanency in their business relationships. Independent contractors, moreover, anticipate a profit from their work, make their services available to the relevant marketplace, and are likely to be paid a flat fee on a per-job basis.

In resolving employment status, each case must be tested on its own merits. Keep in mind, however, that the right to control the means and methods of accomplishment is the definitive test that leads to a common law employee result. Concept Summary 9.1 provides an overview of the current IRS position.

Employee *versus* Independent Contractor

Arnold is a lawyer whose major client accounts for 60% of his billings. He does the routine legal work and income tax returns at the client's request. He is paid a monthly retainer in addition to amounts charged for extra work. Arnold is a self-employed individual. Even though most of his income comes from one client, he still has the right to determine how the end result of his work is attained.

EXAMPLE
1

---

[1]In simple situations, a Schedule C–EZ can be used. Also, a Schedule SE (Self-Employment Tax) must be filed.

[2]In simple situations, a Form 2106–EZ (Unreimbursed Employee Business Expenses) can be used.

[3]See, for example, IRS Publication 15–A (*Employer's Supplemental Tax Guide*).

[4]1987–1 C.B. 296. Also see IRS Publication 1779 (*Independent Contractor or Employee*).

[5]Reg. § 31.3401(c)–(1)(b).

Concept Summary 9.1

Employee versus Independent Contractor

Although the 20 factors identified by the Internal Revenue Service in Revenue Ruling 87–41 remain relevant, the IRS has grouped these factors into three broad categories in order to provide some clarity to a difficult area, while acknowledging that the 20 factors are not all-inclusive.

Behavioral Control	**Financial Control**	**The Relationship of the Parties**

• Does the business control (or have the right to control) what the worker does and how the worker does his or her job?
• Facts that show whether the business has **behavioral control** include:
  • *Instructions.* An employee is generally told:
    1. When, where, and how to work.
    2. What equipment, tools, or processes to use.
    3. What workers can be hired to assist with the work.
    4. Where to purchase supplies and services.
    5. What work must be performed by a specified individual.
    6. What order or sequence to follow in performing the work.
  • *Training.* An employee normally receives training to perform work in a particular manner.
	• Are the business aspects of the worker's job controlled by the payer?
	• Facts that show whether the business has **financial control** include:
	  • The extent to which the worker has unreimbursed business expenses.
	  • The extent of the worker's investment.
	  • The extent to which the worker makes services available to a larger market (e.g., is the worker marketing his or her services to multiple businesses?).
	  • How the business pays the worker (is it the same or different from how employees are paid?).
	  • The extent to which the worker can realize a profit or loss.
		• A variety of facts and documents can show the **relationship of the parties**:
		  • Written contracts describing the relationship the parties intended to create.
		  • Whether the worker is provided with employee-type fringe benefits.
		  • The permanency of the relationship (e.g., is the work for a specified period of time or indefinite?).
		  • How integral the services are to the principal activity of the business.

Summary

1. Businesses must weigh all factors when determining whether a worker is an employee or independent contractor. Some factors might indicate that the worker is an employee, while other factors might indicate that the worker is an independent contractor.
2. No set number of factors "makes" the worker an employee or an independent contractor, and no one factor stands alone in making this determination. Also, factors that are relevant in one situation may not be relevant in a different situation.
3. Overall, one must look at the entirety of the relationship, consider the degree or extent of the right to direct and control, and document each of the factors used in coming to a decision.

Employee *versus* Independent Contractor

Ellen is a lawyer hired by Arnold to assist him in the performance of services for the client mentioned in Example 1. Ellen is under Arnold's supervision; he reviews her work and pays her an hourly fee. Ellen is an employee of Arnold.

When one taxpayer holds multiple jobs, it is possible to have dual status as both an employee and an independent contractor (i.e., self-employed).

Dr. Davis, DDS, is a full-time employee at the Robin University Health Center. In the evenings and on weekends, he shares a practice with another dentist who works the Monday through Friday daytime shifts. Dr. Davis is both employed and self-employed.

Certain workers who *are not* common law employees are treated as employees for employment tax purposes. Known as **statutory employees**, this group includes certain drivers (e.g., nondairy beverage distributors and laundry and dry cleaning pickup service), life insurance sales agents, home workers, and other salespersons. These employees are allowed to claim their business-related expenses as deductions *for* AGI by using Schedule C. The wages or commissions paid to statutory employees are not subject to Federal income tax withholding but are subject to Social Security tax.[6]

To avoid the confusion that might otherwise result in their classification, the tax law categorically treats certain categories of workers as independent contractors. Included in this group are licensed real estate agents and direct sellers. Such persons are treated as self-employed for all Federal purposes, including income and employment taxes.[7]

If a taxpayer wants clarification as to whether employee or independent contractor status exists, a ruling from the IRS can be obtained by filing Form SS–8 (Determination of Worker Status for Purposes of Federal Employment Taxes and Income Tax Withholding). An adverse ruling is appealable to the U.S. Tax Court.[8]

9-2 EMPLOYEE EXPENSES—IN GENERAL

Once the employment relationship is established, employee expenses fall into one of the following categories:

- Transportation.
- Travel.
- Moving.
- Education.
- Entertainment.
- Other.

These expenses are discussed below in the order presented.

Keep in mind, however, that these expenses are not necessarily limited to employees. A deduction for business transportation, for example, is equally available to taxpayers who are self-employed.

9-3 TRANSPORTATION EXPENSES

LO.2

Recognize deductible transportation expenses.

9-3a Qualified Expenditures

An employee may deduct unreimbursed employment-related transportation expenses as an itemized deduction *from* AGI. **Transportation expenses** include only the cost of transporting the employee from one place to another in the course of employment when the employee is *not* away from home *in travel status*. Such costs include taxi fares, automobile expenses, tolls, and parking.

Commuting Expenses

Commuting between home and one's place of employment is a personal, nondeductible expense. The fact that one employee drives 30 miles to work and another employee walks six blocks is of no significance.

---

[6]§ 3121(d)(3). See Circular E, *Employer's Tax Guide* (IRS Publication 15), for further discussion of statutory employees.

[7]§ 3508. See *Employer's Supplemental Tax Guide* (IRS Publication 15–A).

[8]§ 7436.

EXAMPLE 4

Geraldo is employed by Sparrow Corporation. He drives 22 miles each way to work. The 44 miles he drives each workday are nondeductible commuting expenses.

The rule that disallows a deduction for commuting expenses has several exceptions. An employee who uses an automobile to transport heavy tools to work and who otherwise would not drive to work is allowed a deduction, but only for the additional costs incurred to transport the work implements. Additional costs are those exceeding the cost of commuting by the same mode of transportation without the tools. For example, the rental of a trailer for transporting tools is deductible, but the expenses of operating the automobile generally are not deductible. The Supreme Court has held that a deduction is permitted only when the taxpayer can show that the automobile would not have been used without the necessity to transport tools or equipment.[9]

Another exception is provided for an employee who has a second job. The expenses of getting from one job to another are deductible. If the employee goes home between jobs, the deduction is based on the distance between jobs.

EXAMPLE 5

In the current year, Cynthia holds two jobs, a full-time job with Blue Corporation and a part-time job with Wren Corporation. Cynthia customarily leaves home at 7:30 A.M. and drives 30 miles to the Blue Corporation plant, where she works until 5:00 P.M. After dinner at a nearby café, Cynthia drives 20 miles to Wren Corporation and works from 7:00 to 11:00 P.M. The distance from the second job to Cynthia's home is 40 miles. Her deduction is based on 20 miles (the distance between jobs).

If the taxpayer is required to incur a transportation expense to travel between workstations, that expense is deductible.

EXAMPLE 6

Norman is the local manager for a national chain of fast-food outlets. Each workday, he drives from his home to his office to handle administrative matters. Most of his day, however, is then spent making the rounds of the retail outlets, after which he drives home. The costs incurred in driving to his office and driving home from the last outlet are nondeductible commuting expenses. The other transportation costs are deductible.

Likewise, the commuting costs from home to a temporary workstation and from the temporary workstation to home are deductible.

EXAMPLE 7

Vivian works for a firm in downtown Denver and commutes to work. She occasionally works in a customer's office. On one such occasion, Vivian drove directly to the customer's office, a round-trip distance from her home of 40 miles. She did not go into her office, which is a 52-mile round-trip. Her mileage for going to and from the temporary workstation is deductible.

Also deductible is the reasonable travel cost between the general working area and a temporary workstation outside that area.

EXAMPLE 8

Sam, a building inspector in Minneapolis, regularly inspects buildings for building code violations for his employer, a general contractor. During one busy season, the St. Paul inspector became ill, and Sam was required to inspect several buildings in St. Paul. The expenses for transportation for the trips to St. Paul are deductible.

---

[9]*Fausner v. Comm.*, 73–2 USTC ¶9515, 32 AFTR 2d 73–5202, 93 S.Ct. 2820 (USSC, 1973).

What constitutes the general working area depends on the facts and circumstances of each situation. Furthermore, if an employee customarily works on several temporary assignments in a localized area, that localized area becomes the regular place of employment. Transportation from home to these locations becomes a personal, non-deductible commuting expense.

If a taxpayer has an office in the home that qualifies as a principal place of business, the transportation between home and various work locations is not a commuting expense.

The Big Picture

Return to the facts of *The Big Picture* on p. 9-1. Because Morgan will have an office in her home, the apartment will be her principal place of business. Thus, any transportation from her home to business sites is *not* a commuting expense.[10]

EXAMPLE

9

9-3b Computation of Automobile Expenses

A taxpayer has two choices in determining automobile expenses: the automatic mileage method and the actual cost method. If a mixed-use automobile is involved, only the expenses attributable to the business use are deductible. The percentage of business use is usually arrived at by comparing the business mileage with total mileage—both business and personal.

Automatic Mileage Method

Also called the standard mileage method, the **automatic mileage method** is convenient in that it simplifies record keeping. The rate allowed per mile takes into account average operating expenses (such as gas and oil, repairs, and depreciation). Consequently, the taxpayer only has to multiply the automatic mileage rate by the miles driven to compute the deduction for business transportation.

For 2016, the deduction is based on 54 cents per mile for business miles.[11] This represents a three and one-half cent decrease from the rate of 57.5 cents applicable to 2015. Although the mileage rate usually remains constant for an entire year, such is not always the case. In the past and due to the extreme variation in the cost of fuel, the IRS has made mid-year changes in the rate. The possibility of such a change makes it important that the taxpayer be able to identify when the mileage took place.

The automatic mileage rate for deductible education expenses is the same as for business; 19 cents per mile is allowed for moving (discussed later in this chapter) and medical purposes, and the rate for the charitable contribution deduction is 14 cents a mile (as to medical and charitable deductions, see Chapter 10). Parking fees and tolls are allowed in addition to expenses computed using the automatic mileage method.

Generally, a taxpayer may elect either method for any particular year. However, the following restrictions apply to the standard mileage method:

- The vehicle must be owned or leased by the taxpayer.
- The vehicle is not used for hire (e.g., taxicab).
- If five or more vehicles are in use (for business purposes) at the *same* time (not alternately), a taxpayer may not use the automatic mileage method.
- A basis adjustment is required if the taxpayer changes from the automatic mileage method to the actual operating cost method. Depreciation is considered allowed for the business miles in accordance with the following schedule for the most recent five years:

---

[10]*Walter K. Strohmalter*, 113 T.C. 106 (1999).

[11]Notice 2016–1, 2016–2 I.R.B. 265 and Rev.Proc. 2010–51, 2010–51 I.R.B.883.

Year	Rate per Mile
2016	24 cents
2015	24 cents
2014	22 cents
2013	23 cents
2012	23 cents

EXAMPLE 10

Tim purchased his automobile in 2013 for $36,000. It is used 90% for business purposes. Tim drove the automobile for 10,000 business miles in 2015, 8,500 business miles in 2014, and 6,000 business miles in 2013. At the beginning of 2016, the basis of the business portion is $26,750.

Depreciable basis ($36,000 × 90%)	$32,400
Less depreciation:	
2015 (10,000 miles × 24 cents)	(2,400)
2014 (8,500 miles × 22 cents)	(1,870)
2013 (6,000 miles × 23 cents)	(1,380)
Adjusted business basis 1/1/2016	$26,750

- Use of the automatic mileage method in the first year the auto is placed in service is considered an election to exclude the auto from the MACRS method of depreciation (discussed in Chapter 8).
- A taxpayer may not switch to the automatic mileage method if the MACRS statutory percentage method or the election to expense under § 179 has been used.

Actual Cost Method

Under this method, the actual cost of operating the automobile is used to compute the deduction. Actual costs include the following expenses:

- Gas and oil, lubrication.
- Depreciation (or lease payments).
- Insurance.
- Dues to auto clubs.
- Repairs.
- Tires and other parts.
- Licenses and registration fees.
- Parking and tolls.

As noted in Chapter 8, the allowance for depreciation (or lease payments) is subject to limitations when mixed-use vehicles are involved. Interest on car loans is not deductible if the taxpayer is an employee, but it can qualify as a business expense if the taxpayer is self-employed. Sales taxes paid on the purchase of a car are added to the cost of the car and recovered by means of the depreciation deduction. In mixed-use situations, the portion of the sales tax attributable to personal use may, in some cases, be claimed as a deduction *from* AGI (see Chapter 10 and the choice required between state and local income and sales taxes).

Except for parking and tolls, none of the expenses noted previously can be separately claimed under the automatic mileage method. A deduction for parking tickets and other traffic violations is not allowed under either method because it is a violation of public policy [§ 162(f); see Chapter 6].

EXAMPLE

11

Return to the facts of *The Big Picture* on p. 9-1. During Morgan's senior year in college, her parents gave her one of the family cars—a 2010 Chevrolet Impala. Morgan has no idea as to the car's original cost or the odometer reading at the time the car was registered in her name. She has, however, kept track of the miles driven for business since she accepted her new job. Morgan should use the automatic mileage method in claiming business use of the car.

9-4 TRAVEL EXPENSES

LO.3

Describe how travel expenses are treated.

9-4a Definition of Travel Expenses

An itemized deduction is allowed for unreimbursed travel expenses related to a taxpayer's employment. **Travel expenses** are more broadly defined in the Code than are transportation expenses. Travel expenses include transportation expenses and meals and lodging while away from home in the pursuit of a trade or business. Meals cannot be lavish or extravagant under the circumstances. Transportation expenses (as previously discussed) are deductible even though the taxpayer is not away from home. A deduction for travel expenses is available only if the taxpayer is away from his or her tax home. Travel expenses also include reasonable laundry and incidental expenses.

9-4b Away-from-Home Requirement

The crucial test for the deductibility of travel expenses is whether the employee is away from home overnight. "Overnight" need not be a 24-hour period, but it must be a period substantially longer than an ordinary day's work and must require rest, sleep, or a relief-from-work period.[12] A one-day business trip is not travel status, and meals and lodging for such a trip are not deductible.

Temporary Assignments

The employee must be away from home for a temporary period. If the taxpayer-employee is reassigned to a new post for an indefinite period of time, that new post becomes his or her tax home. *Temporary* indicates that the assignment's termination is expected within a reasonably short period of time. The position of the IRS is that the tax home is the business location, post, or station of the taxpayer. Thus, travel expenses are not deductible if a taxpayer is reassigned for an indefinite period and does not move his or her place of residence to the new location.

EXAMPLE

12

Malcolm's employer opened a branch office in San Diego. Malcolm was assigned to the new office for three months to train a new manager and to assist in setting up the new office. He tried commuting from his home in Los Angeles for a week and decided that he could not continue driving several hours a day. He rented an apartment in San Diego, where he lived during the week. He spent weekends with his wife and children at their home in Los Angeles.

Malcolm's rent, meals, laundry, incidentals, and automobile expenses in San Diego are deductible. To the extent that Malcolm's transportation expense related to his weekend trips home exceeds what his cost of meals and lodging would have been, the excess is personal and nondeductible.

---

[12]*U.S. v. Correll,* 68–1 USTC ¶9101, 20 AFTR 2d 5845, 88 S.Ct. 445 (USSC, 1967); Rev.Rul. 75–168, 1975–1 C.B. 58.

Temporary Becomes Permanent

EXAMPLE 13

Assume that Malcolm in Example 12 was transferred to the new location to become the new manager permanently. His wife and children continued to live in Los Angeles until the end of the school year.

Malcolm is no longer "away from home" because the assignment is not temporary. His travel expenses are not deductible.

To curtail controversy in this area, the Code specifies that a taxpayer "*shall not* be treated as *temporarily* away from home during any period of employment if such period exceeds 1 year."[13]

Determining the Tax Home

Under ordinary circumstances, determining the location of a taxpayer's tax home does not present a problem. The tax home is the area in which the taxpayer derives his or her source of income.

It is possible for a taxpayer never to be away from his or her tax home. In other words, the tax home follows the taxpayer. Thus, all meals and lodging remain personal and are not deductible.

EXAMPLE 14

Jim is single and works full-time as a long-haul truck driver. He lists his mother's home as his address and stays there during holidays. However, he contributes nothing toward its maintenance.

Because Jim has no regular place of duty or place where he regularly lives, his tax home is where he works (i.e., on the road). As an itinerant (transient), he is never away from home, and all of his meals and lodging while on the road are personal and not deductible.

The result reached in Example 14 is justified on the grounds that there is no duplication of living expenses in the case of itinerant taxpayers.[14]

When a taxpayer has more than one place of business or work, the main one is considered to be the tax home. This is determined by considering the time spent, the level of activity involved, and the income earned at each job.

EXAMPLE 15

Art, a physical therapist, lives with his family in Lancaster, Pennsylvania. For seven months each year, he is employed by the New Orleans Saints football team at a salary of $150,000. During this period, he rents an apartment in New Orleans. In the off-season, he works for the Lancaster YMCA at a salary of $15,000.

Art's tax home is clearly New Orleans and not Lancaster. Consequently, his living expenses while in New Orleans (i.e., food and lodging) are not deductible.

9-4c **Restrictions on Travel Expenses**

The possibility always exists that taxpayers will attempt to treat vacation or pleasure travel as deductible business travel. To prevent such practices, the law contains restrictions on certain travel expenses.

Conventions

For travel expenses to be deductible, a convention must be directly related to the taxpayer's trade or business.[15] Compare Examples 16 and 17.

---

[13]§ 162(a).

[14]Rev.Rul. 73–529, 1973–2 C.B. 37 and *James O. Henderson*, 70 TCM 1407, T.C.Memo. 1995–559, *aff'd* by 98–1 USTC ¶50,375, 81 AFTR 2d 98–1748, 143 F.3d 497 (CA–9, 1998).

[15]§ 274(h)(1).

Dr. Hill, a pathologist who works for a hospital in Ohio, travels to Las Vegas to attend a two-day session on recent developments in estate planning. No deduction is allowed for Dr. Hill's travel expenses.

EXAMPLE 16

Assume the same facts as in Example 16, except that the convention deals entirely with recent developments in pathology. Now a travel deduction is allowed.

EXAMPLE 17

If the proceedings of the convention are videotaped, the taxpayer must attend convention sessions to view the videotaped materials along with other participants. However, a deduction will be allowed for costs (other than travel, meals, and entertainment) of renting or using videotaped materials related to business.

A CPA is unable to attend a convention at which current developments in taxation are discussed. She pays $300 for videotapes of the lectures and views them at home later. The $300 is a miscellaneous itemized deduction if the CPA is an employee. If she is self-employed, the $300 is a deduction *for* AGI.

EXAMPLE 18

The Code places stringent restrictions on the deductibility of travel expenses of the taxpayer's spouse or dependent.[16] Generally, the accompaniment by the spouse or dependent must serve a bona fide business purpose, and the expenses must be otherwise deductible.

Assume the same facts as in Example 17 with the additional fact that Dr. Hill is accompanied by Mrs. Hill. Mrs. Hill is not employed, but possesses secretarial skills and takes notes during the proceedings. No deduction is allowed for Mrs. Hill's travel expenses.

If, however, Mrs. Hill is a nurse trained in pathology and is employed by Dr. Hill as his assistant, her travel expenses become deductible.

EXAMPLE 19

Education

Travel as a form of education is not deductible.[17] If, however, the education qualifies as a deduction, the travel involved is allowed. Compare Examples 20 and 21.

Greta, a German teacher, travels to Germany to maintain general familiarity with the language and culture. No travel expense deduction is allowed.

EXAMPLE 20

Jean-Claude, a scholar of French literature, travels to Paris to do specific library research that cannot be done elsewhere and to take courses that are offered only at the Sorbonne. The travel costs are deductible, assuming that the other requirements for deducting education expenses (discussed later in the chapter) are met.

EXAMPLE 21

9-4d Combined Business and Pleasure Travel

To be deductible, travel expenses need not be incurred in the performance of specific job functions.

---

[16]§ 274(m)(3).   [17]§ 274(m)(2).

Domestic Travel for Business and Pleasure

In order to limit the possibility of a taxpayer claiming a tax deduction for what is essentially a personal vacation, several provisions have been enacted to govern deductions associated with combined business and pleasure trips. If the business/pleasure trip is from one point in the United States to another point in the United States, the transportation expenses are deductible only if the trip is *primarily for business*.[18] Meals, lodging, and other expenses are allocated between business and personal days. If the trip is primarily for pleasure, no transportation expenses qualify as a deduction. Compare Examples 22 and 23.

Meeting the Primary Business Purpose Requirement

EXAMPLE 22

In the current year, Hana travels from Seattle to New York primarily for business. She spends five days conducting business and three days sightseeing and attending shows. Her plane and taxi fare amounts to $1,160. Her meals amount to $200 per day, and lodging and incidental expenses are $350 per day.

She can deduct the transportation charges of $1,160, because the trip is primarily for business (five days of business versus three days of sightseeing). Meals are limited to five days and are subject to the 50% cutback (discussed later in the chapter), for a total of $500 [5 days × ($200 × 50%)], and other expenses are limited to $1,750 (5 days × $350). If Hana is an employee, the unreimbursed travel expenses are miscellaneous itemized deductions.

EXAMPLE 23

Assume that Hana goes to New York for a two-week vacation. While there, she spends several hours renewing acquaintances with people in her company's New York office. Her transportation expenses are not deductible.

Foreign Travel for Business and Pleasure

When the trip is *outside the United States*, special rules apply. Transportation expenses must be allocated between business and personal unless (1) the taxpayer is away from home for seven days or less *or* (2) less than 25 percent of the time was for personal purposes. No allocation is required if the taxpayer has no substantial control over arrangements for the trip or the desire for a vacation is not a major factor in taking the trip. If the trip is primarily for pleasure, no transportation charges are deductible. Days devoted to travel are considered business days. Weekends, legal holidays, and intervening days are considered business days, provided both the preceding and succeeding days were business days.[19] Compare Examples 24 and 25.

The Amount of Nonbusiness Time Permitted

EXAMPLE 24

In the current year, Robert takes a trip from New York to Japan primarily for business purposes. He is away from home from June 10 through June 19. He spends three days vacationing and seven days (including two travel days) conducting business. His airfare is $4,000, his meals amount to $200 per day, and lodging and incidental expenses are $300 per day. Because Robert is away from home for more than seven days and more than 25% of his time is devoted to personal purposes, only 70% (7 days business/10 days total) of the transportation is deductible. His deductions are as follows:

Transportation (70% × $4,000)		$2,800
Lodging ($300 × 7)		2,100
Meals ($200 × 7)	$1,400	
Less: 50% cutback (discussed later)	(700)	700
Total		$5,600

---

[18]Reg. § 1.162–2(b)(1).

[19]§ 274(c) and Reg. § 1.274–4. For purposes of the seven-days-or-less exception, the departure travel day is not counted.

The Amount of Nonbusiness Time Permitted

EXAMPLE
25

Assume the same facts as in Example 24. Robert is gone the same period of time but spends only two days (rather than three) vacationing.

Now no allocation of transportation is required. Because the pleasure portion of the trip is less than 25% of the total, all of the airfare qualifies for the travel deduction.

9-5 MOVING EXPENSES

LO.4
Determine the moving expense deduction.

Moving expenses are deductible for moves in connection with the commencement of work at a new principal workplace.[20] Both employees and self-employed individuals can deduct these expenses. To be eligible for a moving expense deduction, a taxpayer must meet two basic tests: distance and time.

9-5a Distance Test

To meet the distance test, the taxpayer's new job location must be at least 50 miles farther from the taxpayer's old residence than the old residence was from the former place of employment. In this regard, the location of the new residence is not relevant. This eliminates a moving deduction for taxpayers who purchase a new home in the same general area without changing their place of employment. Those who accept a new job in the same general area as the old job location are also eliminated.

Concept Summary 9.2 illustrates what does and does not satisfy the distance test.

Concept Summary 9.2

Meeting and Not Meeting the Distance Test

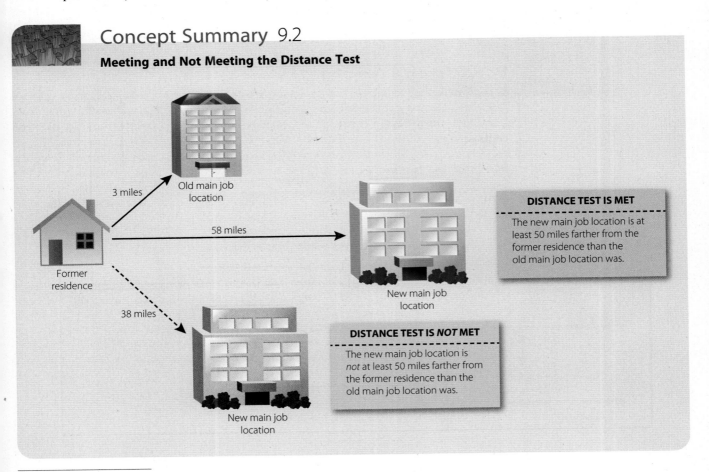

If an individual is not employed before the move, the new job must be at least 50 miles from the former residence.

9-5b Time Test

To meet the time test, an employee must be employed on a full-time basis at the new location for 39 weeks in the 12-month period following the move. If the taxpayer is a self-employed individual, he or she must work in the new location for 78 weeks during the next two years. The first 39 weeks must be in the first 12 months. The time test is disregarded if the taxpayer dies, becomes disabled, or is discharged (other than for willful misconduct) or transferred by the employer.

A taxpayer might not be able to meet the 39-week test by the due date of the tax return for the year of the move. For this reason, two alternatives are allowed. The taxpayer can take the deduction in the year the expenses are incurred, even though the 39-week test has not been met. If the taxpayer later fails to meet the test, either (1) the income of the following year is increased by an amount equal to the deduction previously claimed for moving expenses or (2) an amended return is filed for the year of the move. The second alternative is to wait until the test is met and then file an amended tax return for the year of the move.

These rules are summarized in Concept Summary 9.3. Members of the armed forces are subject to special rules.[21]

Concept Summary 9.3

Qualifying for the Moving Expense Deduction

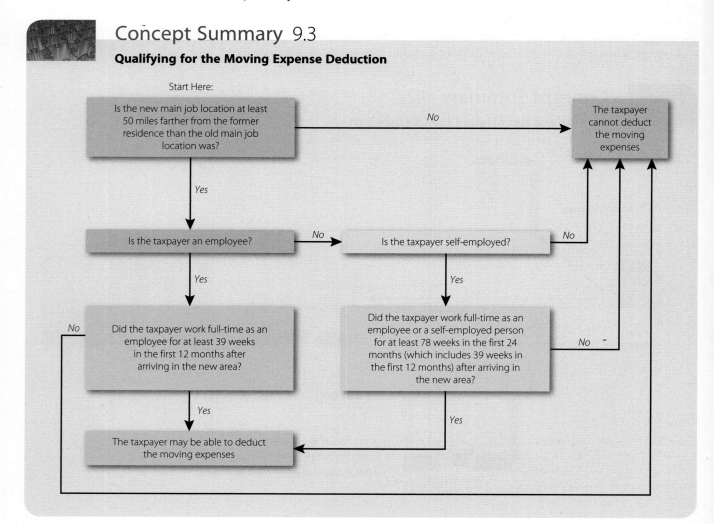

---

[21]See IRS Publication 521 (*Moving Expenses*), pp. 14–15 and § 217.

9-5c Treatment of Moving Expenses

What Is Included

"Qualified" moving expenses include *reasonable* expenses of:

- Moving household goods and personal effects.
- Traveling from the former residence to the new place of residence.

For this purpose, *traveling* includes lodging, but not meals, for the taxpayer and members of the household.[22] The taxpayer can elect to use actual auto expenses (no depreciation is allowed) or the automatic mileage method. In this case, moving expense mileage is limited in 2016 to 19 cents per mile for each car. The automatic mileage rate for 2015 was 23 cents. These expenses are also limited by the reasonableness standard. For example, if one moves from Texas to Florida via Maine and takes six weeks to do so, the transportation and lodging must be allocated between personal and moving expenses.

EXAMPLE 26

Jill is transferred by her employer from the Atlanta office to the San Francisco office. In this connection, she spends the following amounts:

Cost of moving furniture	$4,800
Transportation	700
Meals	450
Lodging	600

Jill's total qualified moving expense is $6,100 ($4,800 + $700 + $600).

The moving expense deduction is allowed regardless of whether the employee is transferred by the existing employer or is employed by a new employer. It is allowed if the employee moves to a new area and obtains employment or switches from self-employed status to employee status (and vice versa). The moving expense deduction is also allowed if an individual is unemployed before obtaining employment in a new area.

What Is Not Included

In addition to meals while en route, the moving expense deduction does *not* include the following costs:

- New car tags and driver's licenses.
- Loss on the sale of a residence or penalty for breaking a lease.
- Forfeiture of security deposits and loss from disposing of club memberships.
- Pre-move house-hunting expenses.
- Temporary living expenses.

Also not deductible are the costs of moving servants and others who are not members of the household.

How Treated

Qualified moving expenses that are paid (or reimbursed) by the employer are not reported as part of the gross income of the employee.[23] Moving expenses that are paid (or reimbursed) by the employer and are not qualified moving expenses are included in the employee's gross income and are not deductible.

---

[22]§ 217(b).

[23]§§ 132(a)(6) and (g).

The employer is responsible for allocating the reimbursement between the qualified and nonqualified moving expenses. Reimbursed qualified moving expenses are separately stated on the Form W–2 given to the employee for the year involved. Qualified moving expenses that are not reimbursed and those of self-employed taxpayers are deductions *for* AGI.[24]

The Big Picture

EXAMPLE 27

Return to the facts of *The Big Picture* on p. 9-1. Even though this is her first job, Morgan will be entitled to a moving expense deduction. This presumes that she is not reimbursed by Kite Corporation for these expenses. She should not forget that the mileage on her auto also is allowed. Her deduction is *for* AGI and can be claimed even if she chooses the standard deduction option.

Form 3903 is used to report the details of the moving expense deduction if the employee is not reimbursed or a self-employed person is involved.

9-6 EDUCATION EXPENSES

LO.5

Differentiate between deductible and nondeductible education expenses.

9-6a General Requirements

An employee can deduct expenses incurred for education (education expenses) as ordinary and necessary business expenses provided the expenses are incurred for either of two reasons:

- To meet the express requirements of the employer or the requirements imposed by law to retain his or her employment status.
- To maintain or improve existing skills required in the present job.

Education expenses are *not* deductible if the education is for either of the following purposes (except as discussed under A Limited Deduction Approach, which follows):

- To meet the minimum educational standards for qualification in the taxpayer's existing job.
- To qualify the taxpayer for a new trade or business.[25]

Fees incurred for professional qualification exams (the bar exam, for example) and fees for review courses (such as a CPA review course) are not deductible.[26] If the education incidentally results in a promotion or raise, the deduction still can be taken as long as the education maintained and improved existing skills and did not qualify a person for a new trade or business. A change in duties is not always fatal to the deduction if the new duties involve the same general work. For example, the IRS has ruled that a practicing dentist's education expenses incurred to become an orthodontist are deductible.[27]

9-6b Requirements Imposed by Law or by the Employer for Retention of Employment

Taxpayers are permitted to deduct education expenses if additional courses are required by the employer or are imposed by law. Many states require a minimum of a bachelor's degree and a specified number of additional courses to retain a teaching job. In addition, some public school systems have imposed a master's degree requirement and require teachers to make satisfactory progress toward a master's degree to keep

---

[24]§ 62(a)(15).
[25]Reg. §§ 1.162–5(b)(2) and (3).

[26]Reg. § 1.212–1(f) and Rev.Rul. 69–292, 1969–1 C.B. 84.
[27]Rev.Rul. 74–78, 1974–1 C.B. 44.

GLOBAL TAX ISSUES **Expatriates and the Moving Expense Deduction**

Expatriates, U.S. persons who accept work assignments overseas, enjoy several favorable tax advantages regarding foreign moves. First, the cost of storing household goods qualifies as a moving expense. This could lead to a major tax saving because expatriates do not ship most of their household effects to the foreign location. Furthermore, the cost of storage, particularly in a climate-controlled facility, is not insignificant.

The second advantage expatriates could enjoy is an exemption from the time test. Those who return to the United States to retire are absolved from the 39-week or 78-week work requirement. Thus, the return home expenses are treated as qualified moving expenses.

Source: Internal Revenue Code § 217(i).

their positions. If the required education is the minimum degree required for the job, no deduction is allowed.

A taxpayer classified as a staff accountant who went back to school to obtain a bachelor's degree in accounting was not allowed to deduct the expenses. Although some courses tended to maintain and improve his existing skills in his entry-level position, the degree was the minimum requirement for his job.[28]

Expenses incurred for education required by law for various professions will also qualify for deduction.

To satisfy the State Board of Public Accountancy rules for maintaining her CPA license, Nancy takes an auditing course sponsored by a local college. The cost of the education is deductible.

**EXAMPLE
28**

9-6c **Maintaining or Improving Existing Skills**

The "maintaining or improving existing skills" requirement in the Code has been difficult for both taxpayers and the courts to interpret. For example, a business executive may be permitted to deduct the costs of obtaining an MBA on the grounds that the advanced management education is undertaken to maintain and improve existing management skills. The executive is eligible to deduct the costs of specialized, nondegree management courses that are taken for continuing education or to maintain or improve existing skills. Expenses incurred by the executive to obtain a law degree are not deductible, however, because the education constitutes training for a new trade or business. The Regulations specifically deny a self-employed accountant a deduction for expenses relating to law school.[29]

The conditions required for the regular education expense deduction are summarized in Concept Summary 9.4.

9-6d **Classification of Specific Items**

Education expenses include books and supplies, tuition, and transportation (e.g., from the office to night school) and travel (e.g., meals and lodging while away from home at summer school).

---

[28]Reg. § 1.162–5(b)(2)(iii) Example (2); *Collin J. Davidson*, 43 TCM 743, T.C.Memo. 1982–119. But see the subsequent discussion of § 222 (i.e., the deduction for higher education qualified tuition and related expenses).

[29]Reg. § 1.162–5(b)(3)(ii) Example (1).

Concept Summary 9.4

Condition for Deducting Regular Education Expenses

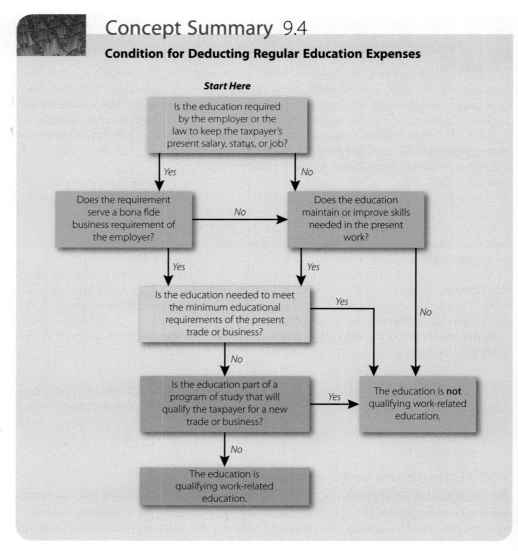

Bill, who holds a bachelor of education degree, is a secondary education teacher in the Charleston school system. The school board recently raised its minimum education requirement for new teachers from four years of college training to five. A grandfather clause allows teachers with only four years of college to continue to qualify if they show satisfactory progress toward a graduate degree. Bill enrolls at the University of South Carolina and takes two graduate courses. His unreimbursed expenses for this purpose are as follows:

Books and tuition	$3,600
Lodging while in travel status (June–August)	2,150
Meals while in travel status	1,100
Laundry while in travel status	220
Transportation	900

Bill has an itemized deduction as follows:

Books and tuition	$3,600
Lodging	2,150
Meals less 50% cutback (see below)	550
Laundry	220
Transportation	900
	$7,420

9-6e A Limited Deduction Approach

One of the major shortcomings of the education deduction, previously discussed, is that it is unavailable for taxpayers obtaining a basic skill (i.e., to meet the minimum standards required for the taxpayer's current job). This shortcoming has been partly resolved with the **deduction for qualified tuition and related expenses**.

A deduction *for* AGI is allowed for qualified tuition and related expenses involving higher education (i.e., postsecondary). The deduction is the lesser of the qualifying amount spent or the maximum amount allowed by § 222. The maximum deductions allowed are shown in Exhibit 9.1. Note that the limitations are based on the taxpayer's MAGI and filing status.[30] Although a phaseout is provided for, note its short and drastic effect. Only two steps are involved ($65,000/$80,000 for single and $130,000/$160,000 for married), and the benefit of § 222 *disappears completely* after the second step. Thus, a married couple with MAGI of $160,000 would lose the entire deduction if they earned an additional $1. The § 222 limitations are not indexed for inflation.[31]

Various aspects of the higher education tuition deduction are summarized below:

- *Qualified tuition and related expenses* include whatever is required for enrollment at the institution. Usually, student activity fees, books, and room and board are not included.[32]

- The expense need not be employment related, although it can be.

- The deduction is available for a taxpayer's spouse or anyone who can be claimed as a dependent and is an eligible student.

- The deduction is not available for married persons who file separate returns.

- To avoid a "double benefit," the deduction must be coordinated with other education provisions (e.g., American Opportunity and lifetime learning credits). Along this same line, no deduction is allowed for a taxpayer who qualifies as another's dependent.[33]

EXHIBIT 9.1	**Limitations for Qualified Tuition Deduction**	
Filing Status	**MAGI Limit**	**Maximum Deduction Allowed**
Single	$ 65,000	$4,000
Married	130,000	
Single	65,001 to 80,000*	2,000
Married	130,001 to 160,000*	2,000

*No deduction at all is available if MAGI exceeds this amount.

---

[30]MAGI is modified adjusted gross income as defined in § 222(b)(2)(C). Examples of some of these modifications include the adding back to regular AGI of the foreign earned income exclusion and the domestic production activities deduction. See IRS Publication 970 (*Tax Benefits for Education*).

[31]Section 222 expires on December 31, 2016.

[32]Section 222(d) refers to § 25A(f), which deals with the American Opportunity and lifetime learning credits (see Chapter 13). Student activity fees and prescribed course-related books may be allowed if they are a condition for enrollment.

[33]§ 222(c).

- The deduction *for* AGI classification avoids the 2%-of-AGI floor on miscellaneous itemized deductions. As noted later in the chapter, this is the fate suffered by other education-related employee expenses.

The deduction for qualified tuition and related expenses can be determined by completing Form 8917 (Tuition and Fees Deduction). The form should be attached to Form 1040 (or Form 1040–A). Beginning in 2016, the taxpayer must have received a Form 1098–T (Tuition Statement) from a higher education institution in order to claim a deduction.

The Big Picture

EXAMPLE

30

Return to the facts of *The Big Picture* on p. 9-1. After starting her new job, Morgan enrolls in the night program of a local law school and begins attending classes. Although Morgan does not plan to practice law, she thinks that a law degree will advance her career.

Although Morgan believes that the law degree would be useful, it is not a requirement of her current employer and it is not needed to maintain or improve existing skills in her current job. As a result, except for the deduction allowed by § 222, none of her expenses relating to the education will be deductible.[34]

9-6f Other Provisions Dealing with Education

Although this chapter deals with employment-related expenses, mention should be made of various other tax provisions that deal with education. Because the encouragement of education is a desirable social goal, Congress continues to enact laws that provide tax incentives. The incentives come in the form of income exclusions, deductions (both *for* AGI and *from* AGI), and various credits.

Concept Summary 9.5 reviews the tax consequences of the various provisions dealing with education and indicates where they are discussed in the text.

LO.6

Explain how entertainment and meal expenses are treated.

9-7 ENTERTAINMENT AND MEAL EXPENSES

Many taxpayers attempt to deduct personal entertainment expenses as business expenses. For this reason, the tax law restricts the deductibility of entertainment expenses. The Code contains strict record-keeping requirements and provides restrictive tests for the deduction of certain types of entertainment expenses.

9-7a Cutback Adjustment

During the administration of President Jimmy Carter, considerable controversy arose regarding the "three martini" business lunch. By virtue of allowing a tax deduction, should the tax law be subsidizing a practice that contained a significant element of personal pleasure? One possible remedy for the situation was to disallow any deduction for business entertainment, but this option was regarded as being too harsh. Instead the *cutback* rule was instituted. Rather than disallowing *all* of the deduction, only a certain percentage would be allowed, and the rest of the expenditure would be cut back. Currently, only 50 percent of meal and entertainment expenses are allowed as a deduction.[35] The limitation applies in the context of both employment and self-employment status. Although the 50 percent cutback can apply to either the employer or the employee, it will not apply twice. The cutback applies to the one who really pays (economically) for the meals or entertainment.

---

[34]*Steven Galligan*, 83 TCM 1859, T.C.Memo. 2002–150.   [35]§ 274(n).

Concept Summary 9.5

Tax Consequences of Provisions Dealing with Education

Provision	Tax Effect	Income Phaseout[a]	Reference Code	Reference Text
Educational savings bonds	*Exclusion* for interest on U.S. Series EE bonds used for higher education	Yes	§ 135	Ch. 5, p. 5-24
Qualified tuition program	No deduction; *exclusion* for distributions	No	§ 529	Ch. 5, p. 5-25
Educational assistance plans	*Exclusion* of up to $5,250 for employer-provided assistance	No[b]	§ 127	Ch. 5, p. 5-16
Scholarships	*Exclusion* allowed for education costs (excluding room and board)	No	§ 117	Ch. 5, p. 5-7
Qualified tuition reduction plan	*Exclusion* as to tuition waivers for employees (and dependents) of nonprofit educational institutions	No[b]	§ 117(d)	Ch. 5, p. 5-7
Coverdell Education Savings Account (CESA)	No deduction ($2,000 maximum annual contribution); *exclusion* for distributions	Yes[c]	§ 530	Ch. 5, p. 5-26
Premature distributions from IRAs	If used for qualified higher education, income recognized but penalty waived	—	§ 72(t)	Ch. 19, p. 19-24
Qualified tuition and related expenses	*Deduction for* AGI; up to $4,000	Yes	§ 222	Ch. 9, p. 9-19
Educator expenses	*Deduction for* AGI; up to $250	No	§ 62(a)(2)(D)	Ch. 9, p. 9-28
Interest on student loans	*Deduction for* AGI; up to $2,500 per year	Yes	§ 221	Ch. 10, p. 10-14
Job-related education expenses	*Deduction from* AGI for an *employee* and subject to 2%-of-AGI floor; *deduction for* AGI for *self-employed*	No	§ 162	Ch. 9, p. 9-16
American Opportunity credit	Formerly the HOPE credit; extended to four years of postsecondary education; up to $2,500 per year	Yes	§ 25A(i)	Ch. 13, p. 13-22
Lifetime learning credit	20% of qualifying expenses (not to exceed $10,000 per year)	Yes	§ 25(A)(c)	Ch. 13, p. 13-22

[a]The phaseout of benefits occurs when income reaches a certain level. The phaseout amounts vary widely, depend on filing status (i.e., single or married filing jointly), and are based on MAGI (modified AGI).
[b]The availability of the benefit cannot be discriminatory (i.e., cannot favor higher-income taxpayers).
[c]The phaseout begins once AGI reaches $190,000 (married taxpayers) or $95,000 (unmarried taxpayers).

EXAMPLE 31

Jane, an employee of Pato Corporation, entertains one of her clients. If Pato Corporation does not reimburse Jane, she is subject to the cutback adjustment. If, however, Pato Corporation reimburses Jane (or pays for the entertainment directly), Pato suffers the cutback.

In certain situations, however, a full 50 percent cutback seems unfair. If, for example, the hours of service are regulated (by the U.S. Department of Transportation) and away-from-home meals are frequent and necessary, the "three martini" business lunch type of abuse is unlikely. Consequently, the cutback rule is mitigated for the following types of employees:

- Certain air transportation employees, such as flight crews, dispatchers, mechanics, and control tower operators.
- Interstate truck and bus drivers.
- Certain railroad employees, such as train crews and dispatchers.
- Certain merchant mariners.

In these situations, 80 percent of the cost of meals is allowed as a deduction.[36]

---

[36]§ 274(n)(3).

What Is Covered

Transportation expenses are not affected by the cutback rule—only meals and entertainment. The cutback also applies to taxes and tips relating to meals and entertainment. Cover charges, parking fees at an entertainment location, and room rental fees for a meal or cocktail party are also subject to the 50 percent rule.

Joe pays a $40 cab fare to meet his client for dinner. The meal costs $150, and Joe leaves a $30 tip. His deduction is $130 [($150 + $30) × 50% + $40 cab fare].

What Is Not Covered

The cutback rule has a number of exceptions. One exception covers the case where the full value of the meals or entertainment is included in the compensation of the employee (or independent contractor).

Myrtle wins an all-expense-paid trip to Europe for selling the most insurance for her company during the year. Her employer treats this trip as additional compensation to Myrtle. The cutback adjustment does not apply to the employer.

Another exception applies to meals and entertainment in a subsidized eating facility or where the *de minimis* fringe benefit rule is met (see Chapter 5).

Exemption from Cutback Rule

General Hospital has an employee cafeteria on the premises for its doctors, nurses, and other employees. The cafeteria operates at cost. The cutback rule does not apply to General Hospital.

Canary Corporation gives a ham, a fruitcake, and a bottle of wine to each employee at year-end. Because the *de minimis* fringe benefit exclusion applies to business gifts of packaged foods and beverages, their *full* cost is deductible by Canary.

A similar exception applies to employer-paid recreational activities for employees (e.g., the annual holiday party or spring picnic).[37]

---

[37]§ 274(e)(4).

9-7b Classification of Expenses

Entertainment expenses are categorized as follows: those *directly related* to business and those *associated with* business.[38] Directly related expenses are related to an actual business meeting or discussion. These expenses are distinguished from entertainment expenses that are incurred to promote goodwill, such as maintaining existing customer relations. To obtain a deduction for directly related entertainment, it is not necessary to show that actual benefit resulted from the expenditure as long as there was a reasonable expectation of benefit. To qualify as directly related, the expense should be incurred in a clear business setting. If there is little possibility of engaging in the active conduct of a trade or business due to the nature of the social facility, it is difficult to qualify the expenditure as directly related to business.

Expenses associated with, rather than directly related to, business entertainment must serve a specific business purpose, such as obtaining new business or continuing existing business. These expenditures qualify only if the expenses directly precede or follow a bona fide business discussion (e.g., taking a client to a sporting event after a business meeting). Entertainment occurring on the same day as the business discussion meets the test.

9-7c Restrictions on Deductibility

Business Meals

Any business meal is deductible only if all of the following are true:[39]

- The meal is directly related to or associated with the active conduct of a trade or business.
- The expense is not lavish or extravagant under the circumstances.
- The taxpayer (or an employee) is present at the meal.

A business meal with a business associate or customer is not deductible unless business is discussed before, during, or after the meal. This requirement is not intended to disallow the deduction for a meal consumed while away from home on business.

Lacy travels to San Francisco for a business convention. She pays for dinner with three colleagues and is not reimbursed by her employer. They do not discuss business. She can deduct 50% of the cost of her meal. However, she cannot deduct the cost of her colleagues' meals.

EXAMPLE 36

The taxpayer or an employee must be present at the business meal for the meal to be deductible.

Lance, a party to a contract negotiation, buys dinner for other parties to the negotiation but does not attend the dinner. No deduction is allowed.

EXAMPLE 37

ETHICS & EQUITY Your Turn or Mine?

Natalie (a CPA), Mathew (an attorney), Jacob (a banker), and Avery (an insurance agent) all live and work in the same community. They have been friends since college. Every Friday, they have lunch together and make it a point to discuss some business matters. They take turns paying for the group's lunches, and each deducts the amount he or she paid for the lunch as an entertainment expense. Presuming that one of the four is audited, do you anticipate any difficulty with the IRS? Explain.

---

[38]§ 274(a)(1)(A).   [39]§ 274(k).

Club Dues

The Code provides: "No deduction shall be allowed ... for amounts paid or incurred for membership in any club organized for business, pleasure, recreation, or other social purpose."[40] Although this prohibition seems quite broad, the IRS does allow a deduction for dues to clubs whose primary purpose is public service and community volunteerism (e.g., Kiwanis, Lions, and Rotary).

Even though dues are not deductible, actual entertainment at a club may qualify.

EXAMPLE 38

During the current year, Vincent spent $1,400 on business lunches at the Lakeside Country Club. The annual membership fee was $6,000, and Vincent used the facility 60% of the time for business. Presuming that the lunches meet the business meal test, Vincent may claim $700 (50% × $1,400) as a deduction. None of the club dues are deductible.

Ticket Purchases for Entertainment

A deduction for the cost of a ticket for an entertainment activity is limited to the face value of the ticket.[41] This limitation is applied before the 50 percent rule. The face value of a ticket includes any tax. Under this rule, the excess payment to a scalper for a ticket is not deductible. Similarly, the fee to a ticket agency for the purchase of a ticket is not deductible.

Expenditures for the rental or use of a luxury skybox at a sports arena in excess of the face value of regular tickets are disallowed as deductions. If a luxury skybox is used for entertainment that is directly related to or associated with business, the deduction is limited to the face value of nonluxury box seats. All seats in the luxury skybox are counted, even when some seats are unoccupied.

The taxpayer may also deduct stated charges for food and beverages under the general rules for business entertainment. The deduction for skybox seats, food, and beverages is limited to 50 percent of cost.

EXAMPLE 39

In the current year, Jay Company pays $12,000 to rent a 10-seat skybox at City Stadium for three football games. Nonluxury box seats at each event range from $55 to $120 a seat. In September, a Jay representative and eight clients use the skybox for the first game. The entertainment follows a bona fide business discussion, and Jay spends $490 for food and beverages during the game. The deduction for the first sports event is as follows:

Food and beverages	$ 490
Deduction for seats ($120 × 10 seats)	1,200
Total entertainment expense	$1,690
50% limitation	× .50
Deduction	$ 845

Business Gifts

Although not subject to a cutback adjustment, business gifts are deductible only to the extent of $25 per donee per year.[42] An exception is made for gifts costing $4 or less (e.g., pens with the employee's or company's name on them) or promotional materials. Such items are not treated as business gifts subject to the $25 limitation. In addition, incidental costs such as engraving of jewelry and nominal charges for gift-wrapping, mailing, and delivery are not included in the cost of the gift in applying the limitation. Gifts to superiors and employers are not deductible.

The $25 limitation on business gifts cannot be circumvented by having the donor's spouse join in the gift or by making multiple gifts that include the customer's family.

Records must be maintained to substantiate business gifts.

---

[40]§ 274(a)(3).
[41]§ 274(l).

[42]§ 274(b)(1).

Record-Keeping/Documentation Requirements

Proper documentation of expenditures is essential because of the strict record-keeping requirements and the restrictive tests that must be met. For example, documentation that consists solely of credit card receipts and canceled checks may be inadequate to substantiate the business purpose and business relationship.[43] Taxpayers should maintain detailed records of amounts, time, place, business purpose, and business relationships. A credit card receipt details the place, date, and amount of the expense. A notation made on the receipt of the names of the person(s) attending, the business relationship, and the topic of discussion should constitute proper documentation.

Associated with or goodwill entertainment is not deductible unless a business discussion is conducted immediately before or after the entertainment. Furthermore, a business purpose must exist for the entertainment. Taxpayers should arrange for a business discussion before or after such entertainment. They must provide documentation of the business purpose, such as obtaining new business from a prospective customer.

9-8 OTHER EMPLOYEE EXPENSES

LO.7

Identify other employee expenses.

9-8a Office in the Home

Employees and self-employed individuals are not allowed a deduction for **office in the home expenses** unless a portion of the residence is used *exclusively* on a *regular basis* as either of the following:

- The principal place of business for any trade or business of the taxpayer.
- A place of business used by clients, patients, or customers.

Employees must meet an additional test: The use must be for the *convenience of the employer* rather than merely being "appropriate and helpful."[44]

The precise meaning of "principal place of business" has been the subject of considerable controversy.[45] Congress ultimately resolved the issue by amending the Code.[46] The term *principal place of business* now includes a place of business that satisfies the following requirements:

- The office is used by the taxpayer to conduct administrative or management activities of a trade or business.
- There is no other fixed location of the trade or business where the taxpayer conducts these activities.

EXAMPLE 40

Dr. Smith is a self-employed anesthesiologist. During the year, he spends 30 to 35 hours per week administering anesthesia and postoperative care to patients in three hospitals, none of which provides him with an office. He also spends two or three hours per day in a room in his home that he uses exclusively as an office. He does not meet patients there, but he performs a variety of tasks related to his medical practice (e.g., contacting surgeons, doing bookkeeping, and reading medical journals). A deduction will be allowed because Dr. Smith uses the office in the home to conduct administrative or management activities of his trade or business and there is no other fixed location where these activities can be carried out.

The exclusive use requirement means that part of the home must be used solely for business purposes. An exception allows mixed use (both business and personal) of the home if a licensed day-care business is involved.

---

[43]*Kenneth W. Guenther*, 54 TCM 382, T.C.Memo. 1987–440.
[44]§ 280A(c)(1).

[45]See the restrictive interpretation arrived at in *Comm. v. Soliman*, 93–1 USTC ¶50,014, 71 AFTR 2d 93–463, 113 S.Ct. 701 (USSC, 1993).
[46]§ 280A(c)(1) as modified by the Tax Reform Act of 1997.

Exclusive Use Requirement

EXAMPLE 41

Troy is self-employed and maintains an office in his home for business purposes. The office is also used by his wife to pay the family bills and by his children to do homework assignments. Troy does not satisfy the exclusive use requirement, and no office in the home deduction is allowed.

EXAMPLE 42

Muriel operates a licensed day-care center in her home. The children use the living room as a play area during the day, and Muriel and her family use it for personal purposes in the evening and on weekends. The mixed use of the living room does not disqualify Muriel from an office in the home deduction.

The office in the home deduction can be determined in either of two ways: the regular (actual expense) method or the simplified (safe harbor) method.

Regular Method

In arriving at the office in the home deduction, relevant expenses are categorized as direct or indirect. Direct expenses benefit only the business part of the home (e.g., the office is repainted) and are deducted in full. Indirect expenses are for maintaining and operating the home. Because they benefit both business and personal use, an allocation between the two is necessary. The allocation is made based on the floor space involved—divide the business area by the total home area to arrive at the business percentage.

The allowable home office expenses cannot exceed the gross income from the business less all other business expenses attributable to the activity. Furthermore, the home office expenses that are allowed as itemized deductions anyway (e.g., mortgage interest and real estate taxes) must be deducted first. All home office expenses of an employee are miscellaneous itemized deductions, except those (such as interest and taxes) that qualify as other personal itemized deductions. Home office expenses of a self-employed individual are trade or business expenses and are deductible *for* AGI.

Any disallowed home office expenses are *carried forward* and used in future years subject to the same limitations.

EXAMPLE 43

Rick is a certified public accountant employed by a regional CPA firm as a tax manager. He operates a separate business in which he refinishes furniture in his home. For this business, he uses two rooms in the basement of his home exclusively and regularly. The floor space of the two rooms is 240 square feet, which constitutes 10% of the total floor space of his 2,400-square-foot residence. Gross income from the business totals $8,000. Expenses of the business (other than home office expenses) are $6,500. Rick incurs the following home office expenses:

Real property taxes on residence	$ 4,000
Interest expense on residence	7,500
Operating expenses of residence (including homeowners insurance)	2,000
Depreciation on residence (based on 10% business use)	350

Rick's deductions are determined as follows:

Business income		$ 8,000
Less: Other business expenses		(6,500)
Net income from the business (before the office in the home deduction)		$ 1,500
Less: Allowable taxes ($4,000 × 10%)	$400	
Allocable interest ($7,500 × 10%)	750	(1,150)
		$ 350
Allocable operating expenses of the residence ($2,000 × 10%)		(200)
		$ 150
Allocable depreciation ($350, limited to remaining income)		(150)
		$ –0–

continued

Rick has a carryover of $200 (the unused excess depreciation). Because he is self-employed, the allocable taxes and interest ($1,150), the other deductible office expenses ($200 + $150), and $6,500 of other business expenses are deductible *for* AGI.

As noted in Example 43, the office in the home deduction includes an allocable portion of the depreciation on the personal residence. To arrive at this depreciation, taxpayers use the MACRS percentage for 39-year nonresidential real property. Except for the first and last years (i.e., 1 and 40), the applicable percentage is 2.564 percent—see Exhibit 8.8 in Chapter 8. Office furnishings are handled separately and are either expensed under § 179 or depreciated in accordance with the rules discussed in Chapter 8—see Exhibits 8.1 and 8.3.

An office in the home deduction is also available to those who rent (rather than own) their home. If the taxpayer does not own the property, the applicable percentage of business use is applied to the rent being paid.

The office in the home deduction as computed under the regular method is claimed using Form 8829 (Expenses for Business Use of Your Home).

Simplified Method

Because of the complexity involved in using the regular method and, in particular, the difficulty in working with Form 8829, the IRS established an optional simplified method for the office in the home deduction.[47] If the simplified method is chosen, Form 8829 is not required. Presuming the taxpayer has met the requirements for the deduction (e.g., business purpose, exclusive use requirements), the amount allowed is $5 per square foot of space devoted to the office. However, as no more than 300 square feet can be counted, the maximum deduction is limited to $1,500. The various rules governing the use of the simplified method are summarized below.

- No depreciation on the residence can be claimed.
- Actual expenses of maintaining and operating the home (e.g., qualified residence interest, property taxes, homeowners insurance, utilities) are ignored. Some of these expenses (e.g., qualified residence interest, property taxes) might otherwise be claimed elsewhere on the return. Further, these expenses can be claimed in full without any reduction due to a home office deduction being claimed.
- No unused deduction (e.g., in excess of the net income from the business) can be carried over to a future year. Nor can an unused deduction from a prior year be carried to a simplified method year.

Taxpayers who claim an office in the home deduction are allowed an annual choice between the regular method and the simplified method. Although the choice of the simplified method once made is binding for that year, it is not binding on future years. Care should be taken in making the choice because the simplified method may yield a smaller deduction.

EXAMPLE

44

Assume the same facts as in Example 43, except that Rick does not choose the regular method for determining the office in the home deduction. He chooses the simplified method with the following results:

Net income from the business (before the office in the home deduction)	$1,500
Simplified office in the home deduction ($5 × 240 square feet)	1,200
Net income from the business	$ 300

[47]Rev.Proc. 2013–13, 2013–6 I.R.B. 478.

In comparing the results of Examples 43 and 44, note that the use of the simplified method left Rick with $500 less in deductions (counting the $200 unused carryover). However, Rick can now restore the nonallocated property taxes ($400) and interest ($750) to his itemized deductions on Schedule A.

9-8b Miscellaneous Employee Expenses

Miscellaneous employee expenses include those costs that are job-related and are not otherwise covered elsewhere. As the focus here is on their deductibility, this discussion presumes that such expenses have not been reimbursed by the employer under an accountable plan arrangement (discussed later in the chapter).

Expenses related to maintaining job status make up a significant category of miscellaneous expenses. They include such costs as union dues, membership dues to professional organizations, subscriptions to trade publications and professional journals, and various license fees paid to government agencies and other regulatory bodies.

Special Clothing

To be deductible, special clothing must be both specifically required as a condition of employment and not adaptable for regular wear. For example, a police officer's uniform must be worn when "on duty" but is not suitable for "off-duty" activities. Its cost, therefore, is deductible. When special clothing qualifies for deductibility, so does the cost of its maintenance (i.e., alterations, laundry, and dry cleaning).

The cost of clothing possessing *safety* features to prevent workplace injuries will qualify. This includes such items as safety glasses, shoes (e.g., "steel-toed"), special gloves, lab coats, and hard hats. The tolerance of the IRS in the area of safety clothing is partially attributable to its lack of suitability for personal use.

Job Hunting

The expenses incurred in seeking employment can be deductible under certain conditions. The search must involve the same trade or business as the taxpayer's current position. No deduction is allowed for the cost of obtaining the first job. In terms of deductibility, it does not matter whether the job search is successful. Nor does a change in jobs have to result. Costs that qualify include job counseling, résumé printing, compilation and distribution of biographical data (such as work history), and unreimbursed travel for job interviews.

The Big Picture

EXAMPLE 45

Return to the facts of *The Big Picture* on p. 9-1. Recall that Morgan conducted an extensive job search before obtaining her position with Kite Corporation. Because this is her first job, the expenses she incurred in the search are not deductible.

Educator Expenses

Many teachers pay for professional development courses or purchase school supplies for classroom use and are not reimbursed by their employer. These out-of-pocket expenses can be deducted only if the teacher itemizes his or her deductions *from* AGI, and even then they are subject to the 2%-of-AGI floor (see later in this chapter). Thus, these restrictions can reduce or eliminate any tax benefit available to the teacher. *Modest* relief is provided for such out-of-pocket expenses by allowing elementary and secondary school teachers to claim up to $250 of these expenses as a deduction *for* AGI.[48] Eligible educators must work at least 900 hours during a school year as a teacher, an instructor, a counselor, a principal, or an aide at either public or private elementary and secondary schools. Covered costs include unreimbursed expenses for professional development courses, books, supplies, computer and other equipment, and supplementary materials used in the classroom.

---

[48]§ 62(a)(2)(D).

Hortense is a full-time teacher at Hoover Elementary. During the year, she spends $1,200 for school supplies for her fourth-grade class. Under an accountable plan (see later in the chapter), Hoover reimburses her for $400 of these supplies. As to the $800 balance, Hortense may claim $250 as a deduction *for* AGI and $550 as a miscellaneous itemized deduction (subject to the 2%-of-AGI floor).

EXAMPLE
46

9-9 CONTRIBUTIONS TO RETIREMENT ACCOUNTS

LO.8

Compare various deductions for contributions to retirement accounts.

Pension considerations are an essential feature of any compensation arrangement. As noted in Chapter 1, providing retirement security for employees can be justified on both economic and social grounds. Because the public sector (i.e., Social Security) will not provide sufficient retirement security for recipients, the private sector must fill the need. Congress has given the private sector the necessary incentive by enacting various measures that provide significant tax advantages for retirement plans. These plans fall into two major classifications: those available to employees and those available to self-employed persons.

9-9a Employee IRAs

Pension plans covering employees follow one of two income tax approaches. Most plans allow an *exclusion* for the contributions the employee makes to the plan. The employee's income tax return shows nothing regarding the contribution—no income, exclusion, or deduction. This is the case even if the contribution is funded entirely (or partially) by means of a salary reduction.[49]

The other income tax approach is followed by the **traditional IRA**. Here, the contributing employee is allowed a deduction *for* AGI. The amount, a maximum of $5,500 in 2016 and 2015 or $6,500 in 2016 and 2015 for those age 50 and older, is reported as a deduction on Form 1040.[50] As with the exclusion variety of pension plan, nothing is taxed to the employee-participant until distributions from the traditional IRA occur. Consequently, all of these types of retirement plans carry the advantage of deferring the taxation of income. As described in Chapter 19, all retirement plans are subject to various rules regarding coverage requirements, degree of vesting, excessive contributions, and premature distributions. Generally, these rules are less stringent for traditional IRAs.

The traditional IRA is to be distinguished from the **Roth IRA**, which takes a radically different tax approach. No tax benefit (i.e., exclusion or deduction) results from the initial contribution to a Roth IRA. Instead, later distributions (including postcontribution earnings) are recovered tax-free.[51]

9-9b Self-Employed Keogh (H.R. 10) Plans

Self-employed taxpayers can also participate in retirement plans with tax-favored benefits. Known as Keogh (or H.R. 10) plans, these arrangements follow the deduction approach of traditional IRAs.[52] The amount contributed under a plan is a deduction *for* AGI and is reported as a deduction on Form 1040. The plan established by a self-employed taxpayer who has employees must meet stringent requirements to ensure that it provides similar retirement benefits for the group. The law is structured to ensure that employees share an owner-employer's ability to defer taxes.

Retirement plans for self-employed taxpayers and other small businesses are not restricted to H.R. 10 plans. Other options include solo or individual § 401(k) plans, simplified employee pension (SEP) plans, and savings incentive match plans for employees (SIMPLEs).[53] The operational rules governing all of these plans are covered in Chapter 19.

---

[49]See, for example, §§ 401(k), 403(b), and 457.

[50]§§ 219 and 408.

[51]§ 408A.

[52]§ 401(c).

[53]Relevant Code Sections are § 408(k) for SEPs and § 408(p) for SIMPLEs.

LO.9
Demonstrate the difference between accountable and nonaccountable employee plans.

9-10 CLASSIFICATION OF EMPLOYEE EXPENSES

The classification of employee expenses depends on whether they are reimbursed by the employer under an accountable plan. If so, they are not reported by the employee at all. In effect, therefore, this result is equivalent to treating the expenses as deductions *for* AGI. If the expenses are reimbursed under a nonaccountable plan or are not reimbursed at all, then they are classified as deductions *from* AGI and can be claimed only if the employee-taxpayer itemizes. An exception is made for moving expenses and the employment-related expenses of a qualified performing artist.[54] Here, deduction *for* AGI classification is allowed.

For classification purposes, therefore, the difference between accountable and nonaccountable plans is significant.

9-10a Accountable Plans

An accountable plan requires the employee to satisfy these two requirements:

- Adequately account for (substantiate) the expenses. An employee renders an *adequate accounting* by submitting a record, with receipts and other substantiation, to the employer.[55]
- Return any excess reimbursement or allowance. An "excess reimbursement or allowance" is any amount the employee does not adequately account for as an ordinary and necessary business expense.

Substantiation

The law provides that no deduction is allowed for any travel, entertainment, business gift, or listed property (automobiles and computers) expenditure unless properly substantiated by adequate records. The records should contain the following information:[56]

- The amount of the expense.
- The time and place of travel or entertainment (or date of gift).
- The business purpose of the expense.
- The business relationship of the taxpayer to the person entertained (or receiving the gift).

This means that the taxpayer must maintain an account book or diary in which the above information is recorded at the time of the expenditure. Documentary evidence, such as itemized receipts, is required to support any expenditure for lodging while traveling away from home and for any other expenditure of $75 or more. If a taxpayer fails to keep adequate records, each expense must be established by a written or oral statement of the exact details of the expense and by other corroborating evidence.[57]

Inadequate Substantiation

EXAMPLE 47

Bertha has travel expenses substantiated only by canceled checks. The checks establish the date, place, and amount of the expenditure. Because neither the business relationship nor the business purpose is established, the deduction is disallowed.[58]

EXAMPLE 48

Dwight has travel and entertainment expenses substantiated by a diary showing the time, place, and amount of the expenditure. His oral testimony provides the business relationship and business purpose. However, because he has no receipts, any expenditures of $75 or more are disallowed.[59]

[54]As defined in § 62(b).
[55]Reg. § 1.162–17(b)(4).
[56]§ 274(d).

[57]Reg. § 1.274–5T(c)(3).
[58]*William T. Whitaker*, 56 TCM 47, T.C.Memo. 1988–418.
[59]*W. David Tyler*, 43 TCM 927, T.C.Memo. 1982–160.

Deemed Substantiation

In lieu of reimbursing actual expenses for travel away from home, many employers reduce their paperwork by adopting a policy of reimbursing employees with a *per diem* allowance, a flat dollar amount per day of business travel. Of the substantiation requirements listed previously, the *amount* of the expense is proved, or *deemed substantiated*, by using such a per diem allowance or reimbursement procedure. The amount of expenses that is deemed substantiated is equal to the lesser of the per diem allowance or the amount of the Federal per diem rate.

The regular Federal per diem rate is the highest amount the Federal government will pay to its employees for lodging, meals, and incidental expenses[60] while in travel status away from home in a particular area. The rates are different for different locations.[61]

The use of the standard Federal per diem rates for meals and incidental expenses constitutes an adequate accounting. Employees and self-employed persons can use these standard allowances instead of deducting the actual cost of daily meals and incidental expenses, even if not reimbursed. There is no standard lodging allowance, however.

Only the amount of the expense is considered substantiated under the deemed substantiated method. The other substantiation requirements must be provided: place, date, business purpose of the expense, and the business relationship of the parties involved.

9-10b Nonaccountable Plans

A **nonaccountable plan** is a plan in which an adequate accounting or return of excess amounts, or both, is not required. All reimbursements of expenses are reported in full as wages on the employee's Form W–2. Any allowable expenses are deductible in the same manner as unreimbursed expenses.

Unreimbursed Employee Expenses

Unreimbursed employee expenses are treated in a straightforward manner. Meals and entertainment expenses are subject to the 50 percent limit. Total unreimbursed employee business expenses are usually reported as miscellaneous itemized deductions subject to the 2%-of-AGI floor (see next page). If the employee could have received, but did not seek, reimbursement for whatever reason, none of the employment-related expenses are deductible.

Failure to Comply with Accountable Plan Requirements

An employer may have an accountable plan and require employees to return excess reimbursements or allowances, but an employee may fail to follow the rules of the plan. In that case, the expenses and reimbursements are subject to nonaccountable plan treatment.

9-10c Reporting Procedures

The reporting requirements range from no reporting at all (accountable plans when all requirements are met) to the use of some or all of the following forms: Form W–2 (Wage and Tax Statement), Form 2106 (Employee Business Expenses) or Form 2106–EZ (Unreimbursed Employee Business Expenses), and Schedule A (Itemized Deductions) for nonaccountable plans and unreimbursed employee expenses. Expenses reimbursed under a nonaccountable plan and unreimbursed expenses are deductible *from* AGI on Schedule A, subject to the 2%-of-AGI floor.

When a reimbursement under an accountable plan is paid in separate amounts relating to designated expenses such as meals or entertainment, no problem arises. The reimbursements and expenses are reported as such on the appropriate forms. If the reimbursement is made in a single amount, an allocation must be made to determine the appropriate portion of the reimbursement that applies to meals and entertainment and to other employee expenses.

---

[60]Incidental expenses include tips and fees to porters, bellhops, hotel maids, etc. For travel away from home, the term does *not* include expenses for laundry and dry cleaning of clothing, lodging taxes, and telephone calls.

[61]*Per Diem Rates* (IRS Publication 1542) contains the list and amounts for the year. This publication is available only on the Internet at **www.irs.gov**. Links to per diem rates can also be found at **www.gsa.gov**.

EXAMPLE

49

Sophia, who is employed by Garnet Company, had AGI of $60,000 during the year. She incurred employment-related expenses as follows: $4,000 (transportation), $3,000 (lodging), $2,000 (meals), and $1,000 (entertainment). Under an accountable plan, Sophia received partial reimbursement from Garnet of $6,000. Because Sophia was not fully reimbursed, she must make an allocation to determine the portion attributable to the expenses subject to the cutback adjustment.

$$\frac{\$2,000 \text{ (meals)} + \$1,000 \text{ (entertainment)}}{\$10,000 \text{ (total expenses)}} = 30\%$$

Thus, 30% of the reimbursement, or $1,800, relates to meals and entertainment, while the balance of $4,200 applies to transportation and lodging. Further computations follow to account for the reimbursement (treated, in effect, as a deduction *for* AGI), apply the cutback adjustment, and deduct the 2% floor.

	No Cutback Adjustment	Cutback Adjustment
Transportation and lodging ($4,000 + $3,000)	$ 7,000	
Meals and entertainment ($2,000 + $1,000)		$ 3,000
Less reimbursement		
(70% × $6,000)	(4,200)	
(30% × $6,000)		(1,800)
	$ 2,800	$ 1,200
Cutback adjustment (50% × $1,200)		(600)
Unreimbursed portion	$ 2,800	$ 600

The unreimbursed portion of $3,400 ($2,800 + $600) is reported on Schedule A and is reduced by 2% of AGI. Thus, $3,400 − $1,200 [2% × $60,000 (AGI)] yields a deduction *from* AGI of $2,200. Sophia does not have to report any of the $6,000 reimbursement.

LO.10

Apply the limitations on miscellaneous itemized deductions.

9-11 **LIMITATIONS ON ITEMIZED DEDUCTIONS**

Many itemized deductions, such as medical expenses and charitable contributions, are subject to limitations expressed as a percentage of AGI. These limitations may be expressed as floors or ceilings and are discussed in Chapter 10.

9-11a **Miscellaneous Itemized Deductions Subject to the 2 Percent Floor**

Certain miscellaneous itemized deductions, including most *unreimbursed employee business expenses*, are aggregated and then reduced by 2 percent of AGI.[62] Expenses subject to the 2 percent floor include the following:

- All § 212 expenses, except expenses of producing rent and royalty income (refer to Chapter 6).
- All unreimbursed employee expenses (after the 50 percent reduction, if applicable), except moving expenses.
- Professional dues and subscriptions.
- Union dues and work uniforms.
- Employment-related education expenses (except § 222 qualified tuition and related expenses).
- Malpractice insurance premiums.

---

[62]§ 67.

- Expenses of job hunting (including employment agency fees and résumé-writing expenses).
- Home office expenses of an employee or outside salesperson.
- Legal, accounting, and tax return preparation fees.
- Hobby expenses (up to hobby income).
- Investment expenses, including investment counsel fees, subscriptions, and safe deposit box rental.
- Custodial fees relating to income-producing property or a traditional IRA or a Keogh plan.
- Any fees paid to collect interest or dividends.
- Appraisal fees establishing a casualty loss or charitable contribution.

9-11b Miscellaneous Itemized Deductions Not Subject to the 2 Percent Floor

Certain miscellaneous itemized deductions, including the following, are not subject to the 2 percent floor:

- Impairment-related work expenses of handicapped individuals.
- Gambling losses to the extent of gambling winnings.
- Certain terminated annuity payments.

EXAMPLE 50

Ted, who has AGI of $40,000, has the following miscellaneous itemized deductions:

Gambling losses (to extent of gains)	$2,200
Tax return preparation fees	500
Unreimbursed employee transportation	600
Professional dues and subscriptions	360
Safe deposit box rental	90

Ted's itemized deductions are as follows:

Deduction not subject to 2% floor (gambling losses)		$2,200
Deductions subject to 2% floor ($500 + $600 + $360 + $90)	$1,550	
Less 2% of AGI	(800)	750
Total miscellaneous itemized deductions		$2,950

If instead Ted's AGI is $80,000, the floor is $1,600 (2% of $80,000); in this case, he can only deduct the $2,200 because his expenses subject to the 2% floor do not exceed $1,600.

9-12 TAX PLANNING

LO.11

List and evaluate tax planning ideas related to employee business expenses.

9-12a Employment Status

When considering the merits of employee or independent contractor status, much depends on which party is involved. If it is the worker, being self-employed carries the obvious advantage of a deduction *for* AGI category of job-related expenses and the avoidance of the 2 percent limitation applicable to any unreimbursed excess.

However, a self-employed individual may have other costs, such as local gross receipts taxes, license fees, franchise fees, personal property taxes, and occupation taxes. In addition, the record-keeping and filing requirements can be quite burdensome.

One of the most expensive considerations is the Social Security tax versus the self-employment tax. For an employee in 2016, for example, the Social Security tax applies at

In two recent cases, the taxpayers sincerely believed that their workers were independent contractors and applied for Section 530 relief (see text discussion) against their reclassification as employees. The relief was denied because they did not file Form 1099–MISC for any of the workers and, therefore, did not meet one of the three requirements.

_____

Sources: *John Keller* (103 TCM 1298, T.C.Memo. 2012–62); *Atlantic Coast Masonry, Inc.* (104 TCM 189, T.C.Memo. 2012–233).

a rate of 6.2 percent on a base amount of wages of $118,500 (the same in 2015) and the Medicare tax applies at a rate of 1.45 percent with no limit on the base amount. Further, a .9 percent additional Medicare tax applies to certain high earners. For self-employed persons, the rate, but not the base amount, for each tax doubles. Even though a deduction *for* AGI is allowed for part of the self-employment tax paid, an employee and a self-employed individual are not in the same tax position on equal amounts of earnings. The self-employment tax is explained in Chapter 13. For the applicability of these taxes to employees, see Chapter 1.

9-12b **Misclassification Danger**

Recently, the Patient Protection and Affordable Care Act, commonly called the Affordable Care Act (ACA), has imposed certain compliance burdens (both financial and reporting) on employers with reference to providing health care coverage for their employees. The rules are complex and vary according to the size of the employer (large or small) and the status of the employee (full- or part-time).[63] Because the ACA does not apply to independent contractors and part-time employees, the misclassification of workers by some employers may be more likely. To discourage such misclassification, penalties will be levied on those employers who wrongfully categorize workers as independent contractors.

There are many other reasons to favor classifying workers as independent contractors rather than as employees. Besides avoiding payroll taxes and income tax withholdings, the employer circumvents a myriad of state and local laws. Examples include vacation pay obligations, unemployment tax and workers' compensation requirements, and overtime and minimum wage restrictions. Because complying with these rules is costly and burdensome, many employers are motivated to misclassify their workers as independent contractors.

In the event of misclassification, two remedies are available regarding Federal employment taxes—one legislative and one administrative. The legislative option, known as Section 530 relief, absolves the employer of the employment taxes that should have been paid.[64] To obtain Section 530 relief, *all* three of the following requirements must be met:

- The employer has a reasonable basis for *not* treating the workers as employees. Reasonable basis means reliance on any of the following:
  - A judicial precedent, a published ruling, or technical advice.
  - A past IRS audit that resulted in no employment tax assessment.
  - A longstanding practice of independent contractor status in the same industry.
- The employer has consistently treated the workers as independent contractors.
- The employer has filed Form 1099–MISC (Miscellaneous Income) for each worker (when such filing was required).

As noted in "Tax in the News" (see above), a common hurdle to securing Section 530 relief is the failure to file the required Forms 1099–MISC.

_____

[63]Large employers are those with 50 or more full-time or full-time equivalent employees. Part-time employees work less than 30 hours per week.

[64]This safe harbor for withholding purposes originated in Section 530 of the Revenue Act of 1978. See IRS *Headliner*, vol. 152 (March 27, 2006).

Section 530 relief does not absolve an employer of any Affordable Care Act (ObamaCare) penalties.

A Federal administrative remedy for employers who are misclassifying workers is the Voluntary Classification Settlement Program (VCSP).[65] A type of amnesty arrangement, the VCSP allows the applicant to be absolved from all employment taxes that should have been paid plus any interest and penalties that would be due. To be accepted, Form 8952 [Application for Voluntary Classification Settlement Program (VCSP)] must be filed with the IRS and certain conditions met.[66] A major condition is the payment of 10 percent of the employment taxes that are usually due when workers are reclassified.

9-12c Improving the Tax Position of Employees

For an employee with job-related expenses who receives reimbursement from the employer, the ideal tax position results from the following arrangement:

- Render an adequate accounting to the employer.
- Be fully reimbursed.
- Return any excess reimbursement.

If these conditions exist, the employee will avoid any cutback adjustment (for meals and entertainment) and will completely eliminate the 2 percent floor on employee expenses. As all of the employee expenses are shifted to the employer, the employee may even be able to claim the standard deduction rather than itemize.

Even if the reimbursement of expenses is partial (not full), some planning is possible. Consider what happens in Example 49 if Garnet's reimbursement states that it specifically covers the $2,000 meals and $1,000 entertainment expenditures. Sophia now has no cutback adjustment, and her deduction is increased.

These considerations should be taken into account when an employee enters into an employment agreement. In some cases, it may even be worthwhile to accept a lower base salary in order to obtain a favorable expense reimbursement arrangement.

9-12d Transportation and Travel Expenses

Adequate detailed records of all transportation and travel expenses should be kept. Because the automatic (standard) mileage allowance often is modest in amount, a new, expensive automobile used primarily for business may generate a higher expense based on actual cost. In using the actual cost method, include the business portion of depreciation, repairs and maintenance, automobile club dues, insurance, gasoline and oil, and other related costs. The cost of gasoline, when coupled with the poor mileage performance of some vehicles, can be a significant factor. If the taxpayer is located in a metropolitan area, automobile insurance is more expensive. For the self-employed taxpayer, the business portion of finance charges (i.e., interest on car loans) can be included under the actual cost method.

Once a method is chosen, a later change may be possible. Conversion from the automatic mileage method to the actual cost method is allowed if a basis adjustment is made for depreciation deemed taken (see Example 10). Conversion from the actual cost method to the automatic mileage method is possible only if the taxpayer has not used the MACRS statutory percentage method or claimed § 179 limited expensing.

If an automobile has mixed use (i.e., both personal and business), the business use portion should be realistic under the circumstances. For example, a 95 percent business use allocation for a one-car family living in the suburbs does not make sense (i.e., does the 5 percent allocated to personal use suffice to cover, for example, trips to the grocery store and mall, soccer practice, and dance lessons?). More likely, the large business use percentage claimed will be an invitation for an IRS audit.

If a taxpayer wants to sightsee or vacation on a business trip, it would be beneficial to schedule business on both a Friday and a Monday to turn the weekend into business

[65]Announcement 2011–64, 2011–4 I.R.B. 503.

[66]The conditions to be met are identified in the instructions for Form 8952. Many of these conditions are the same as those required for Section 530 relief.

days for allocation purposes. It is especially crucial to schedule appropriate business days when foreign travel is involved.

9-12e **Moving Expenses**

Persons who retire and move to a new location incur personal nondeductible moving expenses. If the retired person accepts a full-time job in the new location, the moving expenses are deductible.

EXAMPLE 51

At the time of his retirement from the national office of a major accounting firm, Gordon had an annual salary of $420,000. He moves from New York City to Seattle to retire. To qualify for the moving expense deduction, Gordon accepts a full-time teaching position at a Seattle junior college at an annual salary of $15,000. If Gordon satisfies the 39-week test, his moving expenses are deductible. The disparity between the two salaries (previous and current) is of no consequence.

9-12f **Education Expenses**

Education expenses are treated as nondeductible personal items unless the individual is employed or is engaged in a trade or business. A temporary leave of absence for further education is one way to reasonably ensure that the taxpayer is still qualified, even if a full-time student. An individual was permitted to deduct education expenses even though he resigned from his job, returned to school full-time for two years, and accepted another job in the same field upon graduation. The court held that the student had merely suspended active participation in his field.[67]

If the time away from the field is too long, educational expense deductions will be disallowed. For example, a teacher who left the field for four years to raise her child and curtailed her employment searches and writing activities was denied a deduction. She was not actively engaged in the trade or business of being an educator.[68]

To secure the deduction, an individual should arrange his or her work situation to preserve employee or business status.

The deduction for qualified tuition and related expenses provides some relief from the current restrictions on the deduction of education expenses by employees. First, the education expense does not have to be work-related. Second, it is a deduction *for* (not *from*) AGI. Unfortunately, the deduction possesses severe shortcomings: the annual amount allowed not only is quite modest but also may be unavailable to certain taxpayers. It is not available, for example, to those who exceed an AGI ceiling or to someone who can be claimed as a dependent of another.

Before selecting the § 222 deduction approach, however, consider the possible availability of the American Opportunity (formerly the HOPE) credit or the lifetime learning credit under § 25A.[69] As credits provide a dollar-for-dollar reduction of tax liability, these provisions could yield a greater tax benefit than deductions *for* AGI. But these credits may not be available to higher-income taxpayers.

9-12g **Office in the Home**

The availability of the simplified method under Rev.Proc. 2013–13 presents another decision that a taxpayer will have to make each year. In arriving at which method to use for computing the office in the home deduction, here are some factors to consider:

- The simplified method requires fewer calculations and less record keeping.
- Because no depreciation is allowed, the simplified method will avoid the 25 percent tax on real estate gains (see Chapter 17).

---

[67]*Stephen G. Sherman*, 36 TCM 1191, T.C.Memo. 1977–301.

[68]*Brian C. Mulherin*, 42 TCM 834, T.C.Memo. 1981–454; *George A. Baist*, 56 TCM 778, T.C.Memo. 1988–554.

[69]These credits are briefly mentioned on p. 9-19 and are discussed at greater length in Chapter 13.

- Even though the simplified method frees up certain home-related expenses (e.g., qualified residence interest, property taxes, homeowners insurance, utilities), are these expenses otherwise deductible? Some are (property taxes), and some are not (homeowners insurance). But even the expenses that are deductible (property taxes) may be subject to various limitations placed on itemized deductions (see Chapter 10).

- The simplified method, being limited to a maximum of $1,500, does not offer a very generous result. In most cases, the regular method will yield a larger deduction.

- Unlike the regular method, under the simplified method, a taxpayer is not allowed to carry over unused deductions.

- Once a taxpayer has made a choice for a year, the election is irrevocable and cannot be changed.

EXAMPLE

52

Tyler, a calendar year taxpayer, prepared and filed his own tax return for 2015. Being in a hurry, he chose and used the simplified method of computing his deduction for an office in the home. In March 2017, Tyler seeks tax advice and learns how much he could have saved by using the regular method. Tyler cannot file an amended return for 2015, but he can switch to the regular method for 2016.

REFOCUS ON THE BIG PICTURE

THE FIRST JOB

The first issue that might arise as a result of Morgan's new job is the dependency exemption possibility. If Morgan was living at home and accepted the job late in the year, she could qualify as a dependent of her parents. If so, they might also be able to claim the qualified tuition deduction (or the lifetime learning credit). If, however, her employment began early in the year, she could not be a qualifying child (due to the self-supporting limitation) or a qualifying relative (due to the gross income limitation)—see Chapter 3.

Although Morgan's "extensive search" for employment indicates that she may have incurred job hunting expenses, such expenses are not deductible in a *first job* setting (see Example 45). Her qualified moving expenses, however, are not so restricted. Moving expenses are deductions *for* AGI (see Example 27).

Morgan is justified in claiming an office in the home deduction because its use is for the convenience of her employer. She can use either the regular (actual expense) method or the simplified (safe harbor) method. Under the regular method, the deduction would include a portion of the rent and utilities paid and related maintenance costs (e.g., janitorial service). The safe harbor method would allow Morgan $5 per square foot for business space, but not more than 300 square feet, or $1,500. Under either method, she would also be allowed depreciation (or expensing) of office equipment and furnishings (e.g., computer, copier, desk, file cabinet). She must be careful, however, not to violate the "exclusive use" restriction (see Examples 41, 43, and 44) regardless of which method she uses.

As she is required to travel as part of her job, Morgan will use her car for business. Thus, she will need to make a choice between the automatic mileage method and the actual cost method (see Example 11). Because her tax home is in her apartment, she will have no nondeductible commuting expenses (see Example 9).

continued

Based on the facts, Kite maintains an accountable plan for expense reimbursements. If Morgan renders an adequate accounting (and has to return any excess) to Kite Corporation, then her allowance need not be reported on her Federal income tax return. Nonreimbursed amounts, however, will have to be allocated between meals and entertainment (subject to the 50 percent cutback adjustment) and other employment-related expenses. The balance is an itemized deduction subject to the 2%-of-AGI floor.

If she does not render an adequate accounting, the full allowance is included in her gross income. All of the meals and entertainment expenses are subject to the 50 percent cutback adjustment, and the total of all employment-related expenses is an itemized deduction subject to the 2%-of-AGI floor.

If Morgan started the job with Kite Corporation late in the year, it is unlikely that she will be in a position to itemize her deductions *from* AGI. Instead, she will claim the standard deduction.

Morgan must maintain adequate substantiation regarding all of these employment-related transactions. Detailed records are particularly important in arriving at the office in the home deduction (if the regular method is used) and the business use of an automobile (under the actual cost method). If Morgan does not render an accounting to Kite, records are crucial in supporting the travel and entertainment expenses.

Key Terms

Accountable plan, 9-30

Automatic mileage method, 9-7

Deduction for qualified tuition and related expenses, 9-19

Education expenses, 9-16

Entertainment expenses, 9-20

Independent contractor, 9-2

Moving expenses, 9-13

Nonaccountable plan, 9-31

Office in the home expenses, 9-25

Roth IRA, 9-29

Statutory employees, 9-5

Traditional IRA, 9-29

Transportation expenses, 9-5

Travel expenses, 9-9

Discussion Questions

Issue ID   1.   **LO.1, 9** Sophia and Jacob are married and file a joint return. The return for 2015 included a Form 2106 for each of them. The return for 2016, however, included a Form 2106 and a Schedule C. In terms of employment status, what could have changed?

2.   **LO.1** Mason performs services for Isabella. In determining whether Mason is an employee or an independent contractor, comment on the relevance of each of the factors listed below.

a.   Mason performs services only for Isabella and does not work for anyone else.

b.   Mason sets his own work schedule.

c.   Mason reports his job-related expenses on a Schedule C.

d.   Mason obtained his job skills from Isabella's training program.

e.   Mason performs the services at Isabella's business location.

f.   Mason is paid based on time worked rather than on task performed.

3. **LO.2** Milton is a resident of Mobile (AL) and is employed by Scaup Corporation. Because Scaup closed its Mobile office, Milton no longer has any nondeductible commuting expenses although he continues to work for Scaup. Explain why.   Issue ID

4. **LO.2** In 2014, Emma purchased an automobile, which she uses for both business and personal purposes. Although Emma does not keep records as to operating expenses (e.g., gas, oil, and repairs), she can prove the percentage of business use and the miles driven each year. In March 2016, Emma seeks your advice as to what income tax benefit, if any, she can derive from the use of her automobile. What would you suggest?   Issue ID

5. **LO.3** Dr. Werner is a full-time professor of accounting at Pelican University. During the year, he teaches continuing education programs for CPA groups in several cities. He also serves as an expert witness in numerous lawsuits involving accounting fraud. Comment on the possible tax treatment of Dr. Werner's job-related expenses.   Issue ID

6. **LO.4** To qualify for the moving expense deduction, a taxpayer must satisfy a time test.
   a. What is the time test?
   b. When might the taxpayer be excused from satisfying the time test?
   c. What reporting procedure should be followed when the taxpayer has to file a return *after* the moving expenses have been incurred but *before* the time test requirement is met?
   d. Create a brief PowerPoint presentation (two or three slides) summarizing your solution, and e-mail it to your instructor.

7. **LO.4** Emma, who lives and works in Wisconsin, is planning to retire and move to Costa Rica. She has heard that when you retire and move to a foreign country, all moving expenses are deductible. Does Emma have a correct grasp of the rules involved? Explain.

8. **LO.5, 10** Jamie has an undergraduate degree in finance and is employed full-time by a bank. She is taking courses at a local university leading to an MBA degree.
   a. Is the cost of this education deductible to her?
   b. If so, what limitations are imposed on the deduction?

9. **LO.5, 10** In connection with § 222 (deduction for qualified tuition and related expenses), comment on the relevance of the following:
   a. The standard deduction is claimed.
   b. Enrollment at a college does not require the payment of a student activity fee.
   c. Miscellaneous itemized deductions are less than 2% of AGI.
   d. The taxpayer is married and files a separate return.
   e. A father pays the tuition on behalf of a daughter who does not qualify as his dependent.
   f. The taxpayer is single and has MAGI of $80,001.
   g. The lifetime learning credit is claimed.
   h. The taxpayer, a CPA, pays for tuition and course materials to attend law school.

10. **LO.6** In each of the following situations, indicate whether there is a cutback adjustment.
   a. Each year, the employer awards its top salesperson an all-expense-paid trip to Jamaica.
   b. The employer has a cafeteria for its employees where meals are furnished at cost.
   c. The employer sponsors an annual Labor Day picnic for its employees.
   d. Every Christmas, the employer gives each employee a fruitcake.

e. The taxpayer, an airline pilot, pays for meals and lodging during a layover between flights.

f. The taxpayer pays a cover charge to take key clients to a nightclub.

g. The taxpayer gives business gifts to her clients at Christmas.

h. The taxpayer purchases tickets to take clients to an athletic event.

11. **LO.7** In connection with the office in the home deduction, comment on the following:

a. The exclusive use requirement.

b. The distinction between *direct* and *indirect* expenses.

c. The effect of the taxpayer's work status (i.e., employed or self-employed) on the deduction.

d. The ownership status of the residence (i.e., owned or rented).

e. The tax treatment of office furnishings (e.g., desk, chairs, and file cabinets).

f. The treatment of expenses that exceed the gross income from the business.

12. **LO.7** Review the advantages and disadvantages of the simplified method for determining the office in the home deduction. Create a brief summary of your findings, and e-mail it to your instructor.

Issue ID   13. **LO.4, 7** Trent, a resident of Florida, attends Rice University. After graduation, he moves to Dallas, where he begins a job search. Shortly thereafter, he accepts a position with a local TV station as a reporter. Trent's college degree is in accounting. Presuming no reimbursement, what employment-related expenses might Trent be eligible to deduct?

14. **LO.8** Regarding the tax implications of various retirement plans, comment on the following:

a. The difference between Keogh (H.R. 10) and traditional deductible IRA plans.

b. The difference between traditional IRA and Roth IRA plans.

15. **LO.9** What tax return reporting procedures must be followed by an employee under the following circumstances?

a. Expenses and reimbursements are equal under an accountable plan.

b. Reimbursements at the appropriate Federal per diem rate exceed expenses, and an adequate accounting is made to the employer.

c. Expenses exceed reimbursements under a nonaccountable plan.

Computational Exercises

16. **LO.2** Michael holds a full-time job with Brown Company and a part-time job with Tan Corporation. During a workday, he drives 20 miles to Brown, returns home, has a meal, and then drives 15 miles to Tan. Tan is located 12 miles from Brown. What is Michael's deductible mileage?

17. **LO.2** Lara uses the standard mileage method for determining auto expenses. During 2016, she used her car as follows: 9,000 miles for business, 2,000 miles for personal use, 2,500 miles for a move to a new job, 1,000 miles for charitable purposes, and 500 miles for medical visits. Presuming that all the mileage expenses are allowable (i.e., not subject to percentage limitations), what is Lara's deduction for:

a. Business?

b. Moving?

c. Charitable?

d. Medical?

18. **LO.3** Fred travels from Denver to Miami primarily on business. He spends five days conducting business and two days sightseeing. His expenses are $400 (airfare), $150 per day (meals), and $300 per night (lodging). What are Fred's deductible expenses?

19. **LO.3** Brenda travels from Chicago to Barcelona (Spain) on business. She is gone 10 days (including 2 days of travel) during which time she spends 5 days conducting business and 3 days sightseeing. Her expenses are $1,500 (airfare), $200 per day (meals), and $400 per night (lodging). Because Brenda stayed with relatives while sightseeing, she only paid for 5 nights of lodging. What is Brenda's deduction for:

   a. Airfare?
   b. Meals?
   c. Lodging?

20. **LO.4** After accepting his first job upon graduating from college, Christian has the following moving expenses:

Rental of moving van	$450
Meals	200
Lodging	250

   Presuming no reimbursement, what is Christian's moving expense deduction?

21. **LO.5** Samantha was recently employed by an accounting firm. During the year, she spends $2,500 for a CPA exam review course and begins working on a law degree in night school. Her law school expenses were $4,200 for tuition and $450 for books (which are not a requirement for enrollment in the course). Assuming no reimbursement, how much can Samantha deduct for the:

   a. CPA exam review course?
   b. Law school expenses?

22. **LO.6** Robert entertains four key clients and their spouses at a nightclub. Substantive business discussions occurred over dinner and prior to the entertainment beginning. Expenses were $200 (limo charge), $120 (cover charge), $700 (drinks and dinner), and $140 (tips to servers). If Robert is self-employed, how much can he deduct for this event?

23. **LO.6** The CEO of Crimson, Inc., entertains seven clients at a skybox in Memorial Stadium for an athletic event. Substantive business discussions occurred at various times during the event. The box costs $2,000 per event and seats 10 people. (The cost of a regular seat at Memorial ranges from $55 to $100.) Refreshments served during the event cost $700. How much of these costs may Crimson deduct?

24. **LO.6** Andrew sends Godiva chocolates to 10 of his key clients at Christmas. The chocolates cost $50 a box not including $4 for gift wrapping and shipping. How much can Andrew deduct?

25. **LO.7** Cindy maintains an office in her home that comprises 8% (200 square feet) of total floor space. Gross income for her business is $42,000, and her residence expenses are as follows:

Real property taxes	$2,400
Interest on mortgage	4,000
Operating expenses	2,200
Depreciation (based on 8% business use)	450

   What is Cindy's office in the home deduction based on:

   a. The regular method?
   b. The simplified method?

26. **LO.4, 7** Mason, a licensed pharmacist, has always lived and worked in Boston. When he retires from a national drugstore chain, he conducts an extensive job search for any kind of employment in Florida. He finally moves to Tampa where he is able to obtain a position as a night manager of a motel. In connection with the relocation, he incurs job search expenses of $7,000 and qualified moving expenses of $12,000. How much can Mason deduct?

27. **LO.10** Ava has AGI of $58,000 and the following miscellaneous itemized deductions:

Home office expenses	$1,200
Union dues and work uniforms	350
Unreimbursed employee expenses	415
Gambling losses to the extent of gambling winnings	890

What is Ava's total itemized deduction (after any percentage limit)?

Problems

28. **LO.2, 3** During the year, Olivia holds two jobs. After an eight-hour day at the first job, she works three hours at the second job. On Fridays of each week, she returns home for dinner before going to the second job. On the other days (Monday through Thursday), she goes directly from the first job to the second job, stopping along the way for a meal. The mileage involved is as follows:

Home to first job	15
First job to second job	18
Home to second job	20

a. Assuming that Olivia works 48 weeks during the year, how much of her mileage is deductible?

b. Can Olivia deduct the dinners she purchased? Why or why not?

29. **LO.2, 5** William is employed by an accounting firm and uses his automobile in connection with his work. During the month of October 2016, he works at the office for 3 days and participates in the audit of a key client for 19 days. In the audit situation, William goes directly from his home to the client's office. On all other days, he drives to his employer's office. On four Saturdays in October, he drives from his home to a local university where he attends classes in a part-time MBA program. Relevant mileage is as follows:

Home to office	12
Office to audit client	13
Home to audit client	14
Home to university	10

Using the automatic mileage method, what is William's deduction for the month?

30. **LO.2** Ella is the regional sales manager for a fast-food chain. She starts her work day by driving from home to the regional office, works there for several hours, and then visits the three sales outlets in her region. Relevant mileage is as follows:

Home to regional office	10
Regional office to sales outlet 1	13
Sales outlet 1 to sales outlet 2	11
Sales outlet 2 to sales outlet 3	9
Sales outlet 3 to home	15

If Ella uses the automatic mileage method and works 240 days in 2016, what is her deduction for the year?

31. **LO.2** Jackson uses his automobile 90% for business and during 2016 drove a total of 14,000 business miles. Information regarding his car expenses is listed below.

Business parking	$ 140
Auto insurance	1,300
Auto club dues (includes towing service)	180
Toll road charges (business-related)	200
Oil changes and engine tune-ups	210
Repairs	160
Depreciation allowable	2,850
Fines for traffic violations (incurred during business use)	320
Gasoline purchases	2,800

What is Jackson's deduction in 2016 for the use of his car if he uses:

a. The actual cost method?

b. The automatic mileage method?

c. What records must Jackson maintain?

32. **LO.2** On July 1, 2012, Rex purchases a new automobile for $40,000. He uses the car 80% for business and drives the car as follows: 8,000 miles in 2012, 19,000 miles in 2013, 20,000 miles in 2014, and 15,000 miles in 2015. Determine Rex's basis in the auto as of January 1, 2016, under the following assumptions.

a. Rex uses the automatic mileage method.

b. Rex uses the actual cost method. [Assume that no § 179 expensing is claimed and that 200% declining-balance cost recovery with the half-year convention is used—see Chapter 8. The recovery limitation for an auto placed in service in 2012 is as follows: $3,160 (first year), $5,100 (second year), $3,050 (third year), and $1,875 (fourth year).]

33. **LO.3** Kristen, the regional manager for a national hardware chain, is based in Atlanta. During March and April of this year, she has to replace the district manager in Jackson (Mississippi) temporarily. During this period, Kristen flies to Jackson on Sunday night, spends the week at the district office, and returns home to Atlanta on Friday afternoon. The cost of returning home is $550, while the cost of spending the weekend in Jackson would have been $490.

a. Presuming no reimbursement by her employer, how much, if any, of these weekend expenses may Kristen deduct?

b. Would your answer in (a) change if the amounts involved were reversed (i.e., the trip home would have cost $490; staying in Jackson would have been $550)? Explain.

34. **LO.3, 6** In June of this year, Dr. and Mrs. Bret Spencer traveled to Denver to attend a three-day conference sponsored by the American Society of Implant Dentistry. Bret, a practicing oral surgeon, participated in scheduled technical sessions dealing with the latest developments in surgical procedures. On two days, Mrs. Spencer attended group meetings where various aspects of family tax planning were discussed. On the other day, she went sightseeing. Mrs. Spencer does not work for her husband, but she does their tax returns and handles the family investments. Expenses incurred in connection with the conference are summarized below.

Airfare (two tickets)	$2,000
Lodging (single and double occupancy are the same rate—$250 each day)	750
Meals ($200 × 3 days)*	600
Conference registration fee (includes $120 for Family Tax Planning sessions)	620
Car rental	300

*Split equally between Dr. and Mrs. Spencer.

How much, if any, of these expenses can the Spencers deduct?

35. **LO.1, 3, 6** Kim works for a clothing manufacturer as a dress designer. She travels to New York City to attend five days of fashion shows and then spends three days sightseeing. Her expenses are as follows:

Airfare	$1,500
Lodging (8 nights)	1,920
Meals (8 days)	1,440
Airport transportation	120

[Assume that lodging/meals are the same amount for the business and personal portion of the trip ($240 per day for lodging and $180 per day for meals).]

a. Presuming no reimbursement, how much can Kim deduct as to the trip?

b. Would the tax treatment of Kim's deduction differ if she was an independent contractor (rather than an employee)? Explain.

36. **LO.3** On Thursday, Justin flies from Baltimore (his home office) to Cadiz (Spain). He conducts business on Friday and Tuesday; vacations on Saturday, Sunday, and Monday (a legal holiday in Spain); and returns to Baltimore on Thursday. Justin was scheduled to return home on Wednesday, but all flights were canceled due to bad weather. Therefore, he spent Wednesday watching floor shows at a local casino.

a. For tax purposes, what portion of Justin's trip is regarded as being for business?

b. Suppose Monday was not a legal holiday. Would this change your answer to (a)? Explain.

c. Under either (a) or (b), how much of Justin's airfare qualifies as a deductible business expense?

Decision Making   37. **LO.3** Monica travels from her office in Boston to Lisbon, Portugal, on business. Her absence of 13 days was spent as follows:

Thursday	Depart for and arrive at Lisbon
Friday	Business transacted
Saturday and Sunday	Vacationing
Monday through Friday	Business transacted
Saturday and Sunday	Vacationing
Monday	Business transacted
Tuesday	Depart Lisbon and return to office in Boston

a. For tax purposes, how many days has Monica spent on business?

b. What difference does it make?

c. Could Monica have spent more time than she did vacationing on the trip without loss of existing tax benefits? Explain.

38. **LO.4** Caden, a financial planner, decides to quit his job with an investment bank in Charleston, South Carolina, and establish a private practice in Santa Fe, New Mexico. In connection with the move in 2016, he incurs the following expenses:

Moving van charge	$4,500
Lodging during move	540
Meals during move	410
Loss on sale of residence in Charleston	9,000
Mileage for personal autos	3,500 miles

How much of these expenses, if any, can Caden deduct?

39. **LO.4, 7** Upon losing his job as a plant manager in Quincy, Massachusetts, Anthony incurs $6,200 in job search expenses. Having no success in finding new employment in the same type of work, Anthony moves to Clearwater, Florida, in 2016 and begins a charter boat business. His expenses in connection with the move are summarized below.

Penalty for breaking lease on Quincy rented residence	$2,800
Forfeiture of membership in Quincy Country Club	2,200
Packing and moving van charges	7,100
Lodging during move (3 nights)	380
Meals during move	360
Mileage (for two automobiles)	2,400 miles

How much of these expenses may Anthony deduct?

40. **LO.4** After being downsized by his former employer in November 2015, Wayne moves from Minnesota to Alabama to accept a new job. When filing his Federal income tax return for 2015, Wayne deducts the $14,000 in moving expenses he incurred (none of which were reimbursed by either his former or new employer). On June 6, 2016, Wayne's employment terminates. What are the tax consequences if the termination occurred because:

a. Wayne was killed by a drunk driver?

b. Wayne was downsized by the new employer?

c. Wayne was fired by the new employer because he assaulted a client?

d. Wayne quit because he inherited a large amount of money and decided he did not want to work anymore?

41. **LO.5** Elijah is employed as a full-time high school teacher. The school district where he works recently instituted a policy requiring all of its teachers to start working on a master's degree. Pursuant to this new rule, Elijah spent most of the summer of 2016 taking graduate courses at an out-of-town university. His expenses are as follows:

Tuition	$6,600
Books and course materials	1,500
Lodging	1,700
Meals	2,200
Laundry and dry cleaning	200
Campus parking	300

In addition, Elijah drove his personal automobile 2,200 miles in connection with the education. He uses the automatic mileage method.

a. How much, if any, of these expenses might qualify as deductions *for* AGI?

b. How much, if any, of these expenses might qualify as deductions *from* AGI?

42. **LO.5** In each of the following independent situations, determine how much, if any, qualifies as a deduction *for* AGI under § 222 (qualified tuition and related expenses):

a. Lily is single and is employed as an architect. During 2016, she spends $4,100 in tuition to attend law school at night. Her MAGI is $64,000.

b. Liam is single and is employed as a pharmacist. During 2016, he spends $2,400 ($2,100 for tuition and $300 for books) to take a course in herbal supplements at a local university. His MAGI is $81,000.

c. Hailey is married and is employed as a bookkeeper. She spends $5,200 for tuition and $900 for books and supplies pursuing a bachelor's degree in accounting. Her MAGI is $40,000 on the separate return she files.

d. John spends $6,500 of his savings on tuition to attend Carmine State College. John is claimed as a dependent by his parents.

e. How much, if any, of the above amounts *not allowed under* § 222 might otherwise qualify as a deduction *from* AGI?

43. **LO.6, 9** Eric is a licensed commercial pilot who works for Snipe Charter Jet Service. Typically, Eric, who lives near the airport, flies a charter out of Tupelo, Mississippi, to either Las Vegas or Reno, spends several nights there, and then returns home with the same group. Snipe provides Eric with a travel allowance of $1,800 per month but requires no accountability. For the current calendar year, Eric had the following job-related expenses:

Meals	$ 7,000
Lodging	10,000
Transportation (taxis, limos)	500
Uniforms	1,300
Dry cleaning of uniforms	400
Annual physical exam	1,500

The uniforms are required to be worn on the job. The Federal Aviation Administration requires the annual physical exam for the maintenance of a commercial pilot's license. How may Eric treat these expenses for Federal income tax purposes?

44. **LO.6** Stork Associates paid $60,000 for a 20-seat skybox at Veterans Stadium for eight professional football games. Regular seats to these games range from $80 to $250 each. At one game, an employee of Stork entertained 18 clients. Stork furnished food and beverages for the event at a cost of $1,300. The game was preceded by a bona fide business discussion, and all expenses are adequately substantiated.

   a. How much may Stork deduct for this event?

   b. What if there was no bona fide business discussion either before or after the event?

45. **LO.6** During the current year, Paul, the vice president of a bank, made gifts in the following amounts:

To Sarah (Paul's personal assistant) at Christmas	$36
To Darryl (a key client)—$3 was for gift wrapping	53
To Darryl's wife (a homemaker) on her birthday	20
To Veronica (Paul's boss) at Christmas	30

In addition, on professional assistants' day, Paul takes Sarah to lunch at a cost of $82. Presuming that Paul has adequate substantiation and is not reimbursed, how much can he deduct?

46. **LO.7** Melanie is employed full-time as an accountant for a national hardware chain. She recently started a private consulting practice, which provides tax advice and financial planning to the general public. For this purpose, she maintains an office in her home. Expenses relating to her home for 2016 are as follows:

Real property taxes	$3,600
Interest on home mortgage	3,800
Operating expenses of home	900

Melanie's residence cost $350,000 (excluding land) and has living space of 2,000 square feet, of which 20% (400 square feet) is devoted to business. The office was placed in service in February 2015, and under the regular method, Melanie had an unused office in the home deduction of $800 for 2015. Presuming sufficient net income from her consulting practice, what is Melanie's office in the home deduction under the:

   a. Regular method.

   b. Simplified method.

47. **LO.7** Christine is a full-time teacher of the fourth grade at Vireo Academy. During the current year, she spends $1,400 for classroom supplies. On the submission of adequate substantiation, Vireo reimburses her for $500 of these expenses— the maximum reimbursement allowed for supplies under school policy. [The

reimbursement is not shown as income (Box 1) of Form W–2 given to Christine by Vireo.] What are the income tax consequences of the $1,400 if Christine:

a. Itemizes her deductions *from* AGI?

b. Chooses the standard deduction?

48. **LO.3, 6, 9** Charles has AGI of $94,000 during the year and the following expenses related to his employment:

Lodging while in travel status	$5,000
Meals during travel	4,000
Business transportation	6,000
Entertainment of clients	3,800
Professional dues and subscriptions	800

Charles is reimbursed $14,000 under his employer's accountable plan. What are his deductions *for* and *from* AGI?

49. **LO.3, 6, 9** During the year, Brenda has the following expenses related to her employment: Decision Making

Airfare	$8,500
Meals	4,000
Lodging	4,900
Transportation while in travel status (taxis and limos)	940
Entertainment of clients	8,000

Although Brenda renders an adequate accounting to her employer, she is reimbursed for only $12,000 of the above expenses. What are Brenda's tax consequences based on the following assumptions?

a. The $12,000 reimbursement does not designate which expenses are covered.

b. The reimbursement specifically covers *only* the meals and entertainment expenses.

c. The reimbursement covers any of the expenses *other than* meals and entertainment.

d. If Brenda has a choice of reimbursement procedures [parts (a), (b), or (c) above], which should she select? Why?

50. **LO.6, 9, 10** Audry, age 38 and single, earns a salary of $59,000. She has interest income of $1,600 and has a $2,000 long-term capital loss from the sale of a stock investment. Audry incurs the following employment-related expenses during the year:

Transportation	$5,500
Meals	2,800
Lodging	4,200
Entertainment of clients	2,200
Professional dues and subscriptions	300

Under an accountable plan, Audry receives reimbursements of $4,500 from her employer. Calculate her AGI and itemized employee business expenses.

51. **LO.6, 9, 10, 11** Ava recently graduated from college and is interviewing for a posi-   Decision Making
tion in marketing. Gull Corporation has offered her a job as a sales representative that will require extensive travel and entertainment but provide valuable experience. Under the offer, she has two options: a salary of $53,000 and she absorbs all expenses; a salary of $39,000 and Gull reimburses for all expenses. Gull assures Ava that the $14,000 difference in the two options will be adequate to cover the expenses incurred. What issues should have an impact on Ava's choice?

52. **LO.5, 7, 10** B. J. and Carolyn Grace are full-time employees. B. J. is an elementary school teacher, and Carolyn is a registered nurse at a hospital. During the year, they incur the following employment-related expenses:

School supplies for use in the classroom	$1,400
Emergency room uniforms	800
Union dues (teachers association)	200
Job hunting expenses (Carolyn obtained another nursing position but decided not to change jobs)	1,300
Continuing education correspondence courses (required to maintain nursing license)	380
Professional dues and subscriptions	1,100

None of these expenses are reimbursed by the employers.

For the year, the Graces file a joint return reflecting salary income of $90,000. They also have gambling income of $6,000 and gambling losses of $7,000 (fully substantiated). They pay $400 to have their tax return prepared. They have other itemized deductions (i.e., interest on home mortgage, property taxes on personal residence, state income taxes, and charitable contributions) of $14,500. Determine the total amount of itemized deductions allowed to the Graces.

53. **LO.1, 2, 4, 5, 7, 10** Complete the following table by classifying each of the independent expenditures (assume that no reimbursement takes place).

	Expense Item	Deductible *for* AGI	Deductible *from* AGI	Not Deductible
a.	Moving expense of an employee	_____	_____	_____
b.	Tax return preparation fee incurred by an employed plumber	_____	_____	_____
c.	Safety glasses purchased by an employed pipefitter	_____	_____	_____
d.	Dues to auto club (e.g., AAA) for taxpayer who uses the automatic mileage method	_____	_____	_____
e.	Nursing refresher course for taxpayer who retired from nursing five years ago	_____	_____	_____
f.	Gambling loss *not* in excess of gambling gain by a self-employed architect	_____	_____	_____
g.	Contribution to Roth IRA by a self-employed attorney	_____	_____	_____
h.	Business travel expenses by a statutory employee	_____	_____	_____
i.	Job hunting expense by an elementary school teacher seeking a position as an elementary school principal	_____	_____	_____
j.	Cost of bar exam review course taken by a recent law school graduate	_____	_____	_____

Cumulative Problems

Tax Return Problem

Communications

TAX SOFTWARE

54. David R. and Ella M. Cole (ages 39 and 38, respectively) are husband and wife who live at 1820 Elk Avenue, Denver, CO 80202. David is a regional sales manager for Wren Industries, a national wholesaler of plumbing and heating supplies, and Ella is a part-time dental hygienist for a chain of dental clinics.

- David is classified by Wren as a statutory employee with compensation for 2015 (based on commissions) of $95,000. He is expected to maintain his own office and pay for all business expenses from this amount. Wren does not require him to render any accounting as to the use of these funds. It does not withhold Federal and state income taxes but does withhold and account for the payroll taxes incurred (e.g., Social Security and Medicare). The Coles are adequately covered by Wren's noncontributory medical plan but have chosen not to participate in its § 401(k) retirement plan.

David's employment-related expenses for 2015 are summarized below.

Airfare	$8,800
Lodging	5,000
Meals (during travel status)	4,800
Entertainment	3,600
Ground transportation (e.g., limos, rental cars, and taxis)	800
Business gifts	900
Office supplies (includes postage, overnight delivery, and copying)	1,500

The entertainment involved business meals for purchasing agents, store owners, and building contractors. The business gifts consisted of $50 gift certificates to a national restaurant. These were sent by David during the Christmas holidays to 18 of his major customers.

In addition, David drove his 2013 Ford Expedition 11,000 miles for business and 3,000 for personal use during 2015. He purchased the Expedition on August 15, 2012, and has always used the automatic (standard) mileage method for tax purposes. Parking and tolls relating to business use total $340 in 2015.

- When the Coles purchased their present residence in April 2012, they devoted 450 of the 3,000 square feet of living space to an office for David. The property cost $440,000 ($40,000 of which is attributable to the land) and has since appreciated in value. Expenses relating to the residence in 2015 (except for mortgage interest and property taxes; see below) are as follows:

Insurance	$2,600
Repairs and maintenance	900
Utilities	4,700
Painting office area; area rugs and plants (in the office)	1,800

In terms of depreciation, the Coles use the MACRS percentage tables applicable to 39-year nonresidential real property. As to depreciable property (e.g., office furniture), David tries to avoid capitalization and uses whatever method provides the fastest write-off for tax purposes.

- Ella works part-time as a substitute for whichever hygienist is ill or on vacation or when one of the clinics is particularly busy (e.g., prior to the beginning of the school year). Besides her transportation, she must provide and maintain her own uniforms. Her expenses for 2015 appear below.

Uniforms	$690
State and city occupational licenses	380
Professional journals and membership dues in the American Dental Hygiene Association	340
Correspondence study course (taken online) dealing with teeth whitening procedures	420

Ella's salary for the year is $42,000, and her Form W–2 for the year shows income tax withholdings of $4,000 (Federal) and $1,000 (state) and the proper amount of Social Security and Medicare taxes. Because Ella is a part-time employee, she is not included in her employer's medical or retirement plans.

- Besides the items already mentioned, the Coles had the following receipts during 2015.

Interest income—		
State of Colorado general purpose bonds	$2,500	
IBM bonds	800	
Wells Fargo Bank CD	1,200	$ 4,500
Federal income tax refund for year 2014		510
Life insurance proceeds paid by Eagle Assurance Corporation		200,000
Inheritance of savings account from Sarah Cole		50,000
Sales proceeds from two ATVs		9,000

For several years, the Coles' household has included David's divorced mother, Sarah, who has been claimed as their dependent. In late November 2015, Sarah unexpectedly died of coronary arrest in her sleep. Unknown to Ella and David, Sarah had a life insurance policy and a savings account (with David as the designated beneficiary of each). In 2014, the Coles purchased two ATVs for $14,000. After several near mishaps, they decided that the sport was too dangerous. In 2015, they sold the ATVs to their neighbor.

- Additional expenditures for 2015 include:

Funeral expenses for Sarah		$ 4,500
Taxes—		
Real property taxes on personal residence	$6,400	
Colorado state income tax due (paid in April 2015 for tax year 2014)	310	6,710
Mortgage interest on personal residence		6,600
Paid church pledge		2,400
Contributions to traditional IRAs for Ella and David ($5,500 + $5,500)		11,000

In 2015, the Coles made quarterly estimated tax payments of $1,400 (Federal) and $500 (state) for a total of $5,600 (Federal) and $2,000 (state).

Part 1—Tax Computation

Using the appropriate forms and schedules, compute the Coles' Federal income tax for 2015. Disregard the alternative minimum tax (AMT) and various education credits as these items are not discussed until later in the text (Chapters 12 and 13). Relevant Social Security numbers are:

David Cole	123-45-6788
Ella Cole	123-45-6787
Sarah Cole	123-45-6799

The Coles do not want to contribute to the Presidential Election Campaign Fund. Also, they want any overpayment of tax refunded to them and *not* applied toward next year's tax liability. Suggested software: H&R BLOCK Tax Software.

Part 2—Follow-Up Advice

Ella has always wanted to pursue a career in nursing. To this end, she has earned a substantial number of college credits on a part-time basis. With Sarah no longer requiring home care, Ella believes that she can now complete her degree by attending college on a full-time basis.

David would like to know how Ella's plans will affect their income tax position. Specifically, he wants to know:

- How much Federal income tax they will save if Ella quits her job.
- Any tax benefits that might be available from the cost of the education.

Write a letter to David addressing these concerns. Note: In making your projections, assume that David's salary and expenses remain the same. Also disregard any consideration of the educational tax credits (i.e., American Opportunity and lifetime learning) as they are not discussed until Chapter 13.

55. Addison Parker, single and age 32, lives at 3218 Columbia Drive, Spokane, WA 99210. She is employed as regional sales manager by VITA Corporation, a manufacturer and distributor of vitamins and food supplements. Addison is paid an annual salary of $83,000 and a separate travel allowance of $24,000. As to the travel allowance, VITA does not require any accounting on the part of Addison.

Tax Computation Problem

- Addison participates in VITA's contributory health and § 401(k) plans. During 2016, she paid $3,500 for her share of the medical insurance and contributed $11,000 to the § 401(k) retirement plan.

- Addison uses her automobile 70% for business and 30% for personal. The automobile, a Toyota Avalon, was purchased new on June 30, 2014, for $37,000 (no trade-in was involved). Depreciation has been claimed under MACRS 200% declining balance method, and no § 179 election was made in the year of purchase. (For depreciation information, see the IRS Instructions for Form 4562, Part V). During 2016, Addison drove 15,000 miles and incurred and paid the following expenses relating to the automobile:

Gasoline	$3,100
Insurance	2,900
Auto club dues	240
Interest on car loan	1,100
Repairs and maintenance	1,200
Parking (during business use)	600
Traffic fines (during business use)	500

- Because VITA does not have an office in Spokane, the company expects Addison to maintain one in her home. Out of 1,500 square feet of living space in her apartment, Addison has set aside 300 square feet as an office. Expenses for 2016 relating to the office are listed below.

Rent	$18,000
Utilities	4,000
Insurance (renter's casualty and theft coverage)	1,600
Carpet replacement (office area only)	1,200

- Addison's employment-related expenses (except for the trip to Korea) for 2016 are summarized below.

Airfare	$4,100
Lodging	3,200
Meals	2,800
Entertainment (business lunches)	2,400
Transportation (taxis and airport limos)	300
Business gifts	540
Continuing education	400
Professional journals	140

Most of Addison's business trips involve visits to retail outlets in her region. Store managers and their key employees, as well as some suppliers, were the parties entertained. The business gifts were boxes of candy costing $30 ($25 each plus $5 for wrapping and shipping) sent to 18 store managers at Christmas. The continuing education was a noncredit course dealing with improving management skills that Addison took online.

- In July 2016, Addison traveled to Korea to investigate a new process that is being developed to convert fish parts to a solid consumable tablet form. She spent one week checking out the process and then took a one-week vacation tour of the country. The round-trip airfare was $3,600, while her expenses relating to business were $2,100 for lodging ($300 each night), $1,470 for meals, and $350 for transportation. Upon returning to the United States, Addison sent her findings about the process to her employer. VITA was so pleased with her report that it gave her an employee achievement award of $10,000. The award was sent to Addison in January 2017.

- Addison provides more than 50% of the support of her parents (Gordon and Anita Parker), who live in Seattle. In addition to modest Social Security benefits, her parents receive a small amount of interest on municipal bonds and nontaxable retirement income.

- Besides the items already mentioned, Addison had the following receipts in 2016:

Interest income—		
City of Tacoma general purpose bonds	$ 350	
Olympia State Bank	400	$ 750
Proceeds from property sales—		
City lot	$13,000	
Sailboat	18,000	31,000
Cash found at airport		5,000

Regarding the city lot (located in Vancouver), Addison purchased the property in 2001 for $16,000 and held it as an investment. Unfortunately, the neighborhood where the lot was located deteriorated, and property values declined. In 2016, Addison decided to cut her losses and sold the property for $13,000. The sailboat was used for pleasure and was purchased in 2012 for $16,500. Addison sold the boat because she purchased a new and larger model (see below). While at the Spokane airport, Addison found an unmarked envelope containing $5,000 in $50 bills. As no mention of any lost funds was noted in the media, Addison kept the money.

- Addison's expenditures for 2016 (not previously noted) are summarized below.

Medical (not covered by insurance)	$7,000
State and local general sales tax	3,300
Church pledge (2015 and 2016)	5,600
Fee paid for preparation of 2015 income tax return	500
Contribution to mayor's reelection campaign fund	200
Premiums on life insurance policy	2,100
Contribution to a Coverdell Education Savings account (on behalf of a favorite nephew)	2,000

Most of the medical expenses Addison paid were for her mother's dental implants. Addison keeps careful records regarding sales taxes. In 2016, the sales tax total was unusually high due to the purchase of a new sailboat. In 2016, Addison decided to pay her church pledge for both 2015 and 2016. The insurance premium was on a policy covering her father's life. (Addison is the designated beneficiary under the policy.)

Relevant Social Security numbers are 123-45-6785 (Addison), 123-45-6783 (Gordon), and 123-45-6784 (Anita). Addison's employer withheld $5,600 for Federal income tax purposes, and she applied her $800 overpayment for 2015 toward the 2016 tax liability.

Compute Addison's Federal income tax payable (or refund) for 2016. In making the calculation, use the Tax Rate Schedule and disregard the application of the alternative minimum tax (AMT), which is not discussed until Chapter 12.

Research Problems

Note: Solutions to Research Problems can be prepared by using the Checkpoint® Student Edition online research product, which is available to accompany this text. It is also possible to prepare solutions to the Research Problems by using tax research materials found in a standard tax library.

THOMSON REUTERS
CHECKPOINT
Student Edition

Research Problem 1. Aaron, a resident of Minnesota, has been a driver for Green Delivery Service for the past six years. For this purpose, he leases a truck from Green, and his compensation is based on a percentage of the income resulting from his pickup and delivery services. Green allows its drivers to choose their 10-hour shifts and does not exercise any control on how these services are carried out (e.g., the route to be taken or the order in which parcels are delivered or picked up). Under Green's operating agreement with its drivers, Green can terminate the arrangement after 30 days' notice. In practice, however, Green allows its truckers to quit immediately without giving advance notice. The agreement also labels the drivers as independent contractors. Green maintains no health or retirement plans for its drivers, and each year it reports their income by issuing Forms 1099–MISC (and not Forms W–2). Green requires its drivers to maintain a commercial driver's license and be in good standing with the state highway law enforcement division.

Citing the employment tax Regulations in §§ 31.3121(d)–1(c)(2) and 31.3306(i)–1(b), an IRS agent contends that Aaron is an independent contractor and, therefore, is subject to the self-employment tax. Based on *Peno Trucking, Inc.* (93 TCM 1027, T.C.Memo. 2007–66), Aaron disagrees and contends that he is an employee (i.e., not self-employed). Who is correct? Why?

Research Problem 2. Your client, a large construction firm organized as a C corporation, allows certain employees (including the president of the corporation) to use its company-owned airplane for nonbusiness flights. The employees include the value of the flights in their income. Your client is uncertain about how to treat the expenses related to these nonbusiness flights. In certain situations, the expenses of operating the plane are more than the income imputed to the employees, and in certain circumstances, the expenses are less. In doing some of its own research, your client found *Sutherland Lumber-Southwest, Inc.* [114 T.C. 197 (2000)], which suggests that as long as the employee imputes income, the full amount of the related expenses can be deducted. [The decision in the case was affirmed on appeal, *Sutherland Lumber-Southwest, Inc. v. Comm.*, 2001–2 USTC ¶50,503, 88 AFTR 2d 2001–5026, 255 F.3d 495 (CA–8, 2001).] Should your client follow the approach in *Sutherland?* Explain.

Research Problem 3. Rick Beam has been an independent sales representative for various textile manufacturers for many years. His products consist of soft goods, such as tablecloths, curtains, and drapes. Rick's customers are clothing store chains, department stores, and smaller specialty stores. The employees of these companies who are responsible for purchasing merchandise are known as buyers. These companies generally prohibit their buyers from accepting gifts from manufacturers' sales representatives.

Communications

Each year, Rick gives cash gifts (never more than $25) to most of the buyers who are his customers. Generally, he cashes a large check in November and gives the money personally to the buyers around Christmas. Rick says, "This is one of the ways I maintain my relationship with my buyers." He maintains adequate substantiation of all of the gifts.

Rick's deductions for these gifts have been disallowed by the IRS, based on § 162(c)(2). Rick is confused and comes to you, a CPA, for advice.

a. Write a letter to Rick concerning his tax position on this issue. Rick's address is 948 Octavia Street, Baton Rouge, LA 70821.

b. Prepare a memo for your files supporting the advice you have given.

Internet
Activity

Use the tax resources of the Internet to address the following questions. Do not restrict your search to the Web, but include a review of newsgroups and general reference materials, practitioner sites and resources, primary sources of the tax law, chat rooms and discussion groups, and other opportunities.

Research Problem 4. What are the guidelines regarding the deductibility of luxury water travel (e.g., cruise ships) for business purposes? Refer to Chapter 1 of IRS Publication 463.

Research Problem 5. In reporting the transactions of a self-employed taxpayer, when can a Schedule C–EZ be used instead of the regular Schedule C of Form 1040?

Research Problem 6. Retrieve IRS Form 8919 (Uncollected Social Security and Medicare Tax on Wages). According to the instructions, who should file this form?

Roger CPA Review Questions

1. The following facts pertain to Lewis Productions, a sole proprietorship owned by Lewis, in the current year:

Total cost of holiday gifts given to top 10 clients (each gift identical)	$ 550
Receivable for prior-year purchase from Egan, who declared bankruptcy in the current year	2,500
Lodging costs incurred by Lewis while traveling to client sites	3,000
Meal costs incurred by Lewis only while traveling to and from client sites	1,500
Meal costs incurred by Lewis while entertaining business clients and engaging in some business-related discussion	3,000

Considering only the above facts, what is the total amount of business expenses that Lewis can declare on Schedule C of the current year's tax return?

a. $8,000   c. $6,250
b. $5,500   d. $8,750

2. Pinnacle Productions, Inc., holds a luxury skybox season ticket at a local sporting arena. Pinnacle uses the skybox to entertain clients while holding business meetings. The cost of Pinnacle's luxury skybox season ticket is $25,000; the cost of the most expensive non-luxury season ticket is $15,000. How much of the luxury skybox season ticket cost may Pinnacle deduct from its corporate taxable income?

a. $7,500   c. $10,000
b. $20,000   d. $15,000

3. Betty, a salesperson, is an employee with $52,000 AGI who maintains a home office for the convenience of her employer, Smart Systems. The office takes up 5% of Betty's home and is used exclusively for her job. Smart Systems reimburses all of Betty's direct costs of maintaining the home office. Betty also has the following expenses associated with her home:

Expense	Amount
Real property taxes on residence	$3,500
Interest expense on residence	5,000
Operating expenses on residence	1,800
Depreciation on residence (based on 5% home office use)	150

Considering these facts, how much may Betty deduct *from* AGI on her tax return, assuming she elects to itemize deductions?

a. $0

b. $665

c. $9,410

d. $10,450

4. In 2016, Archer, a single individual, moved from Minneapolis to Phoenix to start a new job with InnoTech, which began February 1, 2016. Archer worked for Inno-Tech until November 15, 2016, when Archer accepted a job offer from InnoTech's Phoenix rival MegaTech. The following 2016 facts apply to Archer:

Income	$75,000
Expenses incurred during Minneapolis–Phoenix move:	
1,000	Moving truck rental
1,000	Packing and unloading costs paid to moving company
1,500	Loss on sale of Minneapolis home
750	Lodging
250	Meals
100	Storage costs in Phoenix prior to move-in to new home

Considering only the above facts, what is Archer's 2016 adjusted gross income?

a. $70,475

b. $70,650

c. $72,150

d. $75,000

5. Which allowable deduction can be claimed in arriving at an individual's adjusted gross income?

a. Half the cost of meals eaten while moving over 50 miles for a new job

b. Alimony paid directly to a college for education expenses, as dictated by divorce decree

c. Home mortgage loan interest, subject to certain limits

d. Medical insurance premiums paid by an employee

Deductions and Losses: Certain Itemized Deductions

LEARNING OBJECTIVES: *After completing Chapter 10, you should be able to:*

LO.1 Distinguish between deductible and nondeductible personal expenses.

LO.2 Define medical expenses and compute the medical expense deduction.

LO.3 Contrast deductible taxes with nondeductible fees, licenses, and other charges.

LO.4 Explain the Federal income tax treatment of state and local income taxes and sales taxes.

LO.5 Distinguish between deductible and nondeductible interest and apply the appropriate limitations to deductible interest.

LO.6 Recognize charitable contributions and identify their related measurement problems and percentage limitations.

LO.7 List the business and personal expenditures that are deductible either as miscellaneous itemized deductions or as other itemized deductions.

LO.8 Recognize the limitation on certain itemized deductions applicable to high-income taxpayers.

LO.9 Identify tax planning strategies that can maximize the benefit of itemized deductions.

CHAPTER OUTLINE

THE BIG PICTURE

IMPACT OF ITEMIZED DEDUCTIONS ON MAJOR PURCHASES

John and Susan Williamson, a young professional couple, have been renting an apartment in Atlanta, Georgia, since they were married. Their income has grown as they've become more established in their careers, and they now believe that the time has come to purchase their own home. In addition, their desire to buy a home now may be coming at a good time, because John's mother, Martha, needs to move in with them due to her declining health and their current apartment is too small to accommodate her. John and Susan's current monthly rent is $2,000, but they are willing to spend $2,500 per month on an after-tax basis if necessary for their first home.

After months of house hunting, they have found the perfect home, but they fear it may be too expensive. If they acquire a standard mortgage to finance the purchase of the home, the total cash outlay during the first year of ownership will be $43,000 ($2,000 principal payments, $37,000 interest payments, and $4,000 real estate taxes). Alternatively, if they use their retirement and taxable investments to secure the home financing, they can qualify for a lower interest rate and thereby reduce the interest charge from $37,000 to $35,000. They expect their Federal AGI to be $200,000, and their taxable income to range between $160,000 and $185,000 for the year. John and Susan have not itemized their deductions in prior years because the amount of their qualifying personal expenditures has fallen just short of the standard deduction amount. Assume that the Williamsons' marginal income tax rate under Georgia law is 6 percent.

Can John and Susan Williamson afford to pursue their dream of home ownership?

Read the chapter and formulate your response.

FRAMEWORK 1040 **Tax Formula for Individuals**

This chapter covers the boldfaced portions of the Tax Formula for Individuals that was introduced in Concept Summary 3.1 on p. 3-3. Below those portions are the sections of Form 1040 where the results are reported.

Income *(broadly defined)*	$xx,xxx
Less: Exclusions	(x,xxx)
Gross income	$xx,xxx
Less: Deductions *for* adjusted gross income	(x,xxx)
Adjusted gross income	$xx,xxx
Less: The greater of total **itemized deductions** *or* the standard deduction	(x,xxx)

FORM 1040 (p. 2)

40   **Itemized deductions** (from Schedule A) **or** your **standard deduction** . . . .

Personal and dependency exemptions	(x,xxx)
Taxable income	$xx,xxx
Tax on taxable income *(see Tax Tables or Tax Rate Schedules)*	$ x,xxx
Less: Tax credits *(including income taxes withheld and prepaid)*	(xxx)
Tax due (or refund)	$ xxx

LO.1

Distinguish between deductible and nondeductible personal expenses.

As a general rule, a deduction for personal expenditures is disallowed by § 262 of the Code. However, Congress has chosen to allow certain personal expenditures to be deducted as itemized deductions. Personal expenditures that are deductible as itemized deductions include medical expenses, certain taxes, mortgage interest, investment interest, and charitable contributions. These expenditures and other personal expenditures that are allowed as itemized deductions are covered in this chapter. Although certain exceptions exist (e.g., alimony and traditional IRA contributions are deductible *for* AGI), personal expenditures not specifically allowed as itemized deductions by the tax law are nondeductible.

Allowable itemized deductions are deductible *from* AGI in arriving at taxable income if the taxpayer elects to itemize. The election to itemize is appropriate when total itemized deductions exceed the standard deduction based on the taxpayer's filing status.[1]

The Big Picture

EXAMPLE

1

Return to the facts of *The Big Picture* on p. 10-1. John and Susan Williamson will discover that with the purchase of a home, they will be able to itemize their deductions for the first time instead of claiming the standard deduction. Assuming that the home mortgage interest expense and real estate taxes meet the requirements discussed in this chapter, they will be deducted *from* AGI because their total would exceed the amount of the standard deduction for a married couple filing a joint return. Further, other qualifying expenditures, such as state income taxes and charitable contributions, likewise will be deductible as itemized deductions, providing an explicit tax benefit to the Williamsons.

---

[1]See §§ 63(c) and (d), respectively, for the definitions of the terms *standard deduction* and *itemized deductions.*

TAX IN THE NEWS   The Debate Continues over the Future of Itemized Deductions

In an era of large government deficits and debt ceiling debates, many have concluded that the Federal government needs to learn to live within its means. In simplest of terms, to bring the government's spending in line with its revenues, more revenues must be raised, expenditures must be decreased, or some combination of the two must occur. During these debates, some continue to argue that "tax reform" should occur simultaneously with the search for increased tax revenues, and such reform should lead to certain tax deductions being either repealed or scaled back. They observe that if the tax code were simplified by no longer allowing certain popular itemized deductions, billions of dollars of additional tax revenue would be collected because taxable income would be higher.

Currently, popular tax deductions "cost" the government billions by virtue of the fact that they reduce taxable income. These deductions are often referred to as "tax expenditures." Recently, the Joint Committee on Taxation estimated the cost during 2016 of allowing the following itemized deductions for individuals:

Deduction	Cost in Billions of Dollars
Medical expenses	$12.4
Mortgage interest on owner-occupied housing	81.6
Interest on student loans	1.9
Charitable contributions	47.0
State and local income, sales, and personal property taxes	63.0
Property tax on real property	36.4

Arguably, by repealing these deductions, government revenues would increase by significant amounts. While repealing all of these deductions may not be feasible for political, economic, or other reasons, be aware that certain politicians or policy wonks will push to reform, limit, or scale back these deductions to all or certain taxpayers in the future.

Source: Joint Committee on Taxation, "Estimates of Federal Tax Expenditures for Fiscal Years 2014–2018," (JCX-97-14), August 5, 2014, Table 1.

10-1   MEDICAL EXPENSES

LO.2

Define medical expenses and compute the medical expense deduction.

Medical expenses paid for the care of the taxpayer, spouse, and dependents are allowed as an itemized deduction to the extent the expenses are not reimbursed. The **medical expense** deduction is limited to the amount by which such expenses *exceed* a threshold percentage of the taxpayer's AGI. Under current law, the threshold percentage is 10 percent for most taxpayers. For taxpayers age 65 and older, however, the threshold is 7.5 percent of AGI until 2017, when it increases to 10 percent.[2]

The Big Picture

Return to the facts of *The Big Picture* on p. 10-1. Because the Williamsons' AGI for the year is $200,000, they must itemize their deductions and have more than $20,000 ($200,000 × 10%) in unreimbursed medical expenses to receive a tax benefit from those expenses.

10-1a   Medical Expenses Defined

The term *medical care* includes expenditures incurred for the "diagnosis, cure, mitigation, treatment, or prevention of disease, or for the purpose of affecting any structure or function of the body."[3] A *partial* list of deductible and nondeductible medical items appears in Exhibit 10.1.

A medical expense does not have to relate to a particular ailment to be deductible. Because the definition of medical care is broad enough to cover preventive measures, the cost of periodic physical and dental exams qualifies even for a taxpayer in good health.

---

[2]Prior to 2013, the percentage threshold for regular income tax purposes was 7.5 percent of AGI for all taxpayers.

[3]§ 213(d)(1)(A).

EXHIBIT 10.1	Examples of Deductible and Nondeductible Medical Expenses Paid by Taxpayer

Deductible	Nondeductible
Medical (including dental, mental, and hospital) care	Funeral, burial, or cremation expenses
Prescription drugs and insulin	Nonprescription drugs (except insulin)
Special equipment	Bottled water
Wheelchairs	Toiletries, cosmetics
Crutches	Diaper service, maternity clothes
Artificial limbs	Programs for the *general* improvement of health
Eyeglasses (including contact lenses)	Weight reduction
Hearing aids	Health spas
Transportation for medical care	Social activities (e.g., dancing and swimming lessons)
Medical and hospital insurance premiums	Unnecessary cosmetic surgery
Long-term care insurance premiums (subject to limitations)	
Cost of alcohol and drug rehabilitation	
Certain costs to stop smoking	
Weight reduction programs related to obesity	

Amounts paid for unnecessary *cosmetic surgery* are not deductible medical expenses. However, if cosmetic surgery is deemed necessary, it is deductible as a medical expense. Cosmetic surgery is necessary when it improves the effects of (1) a deformity arising from a congenital abnormality, (2) a personal injury, or (3) a disfiguring disease.

EXAMPLE 3

Art, age 75, paid $21,000 to a plastic surgeon for a face-lift. Art merely wanted to improve his appearance. The $21,000 does not qualify as a medical expense because the surgery was unnecessary.

In contrast, Marge's face is disfigured as a result of a serious automobile accident. The cost of restorative cosmetic surgery is deductible as a medical expense.

TAX IN THE NEWS   Medical Expense Deductions Are Now Harder to Come By

For taxpayers under age 65, being in a position to claim a medical expense deduction is more challenging than ever because of an increase a few years ago in the AGI threshold that limits a medical expense's deductibility. Currently, the threshold is 10 percent of AGI for most taxpayers, an increase from 7.5 percent under prior law. For example, if a taxpayer's AGI is $100,000, only those medical expenses in excess of $10,000 are deductible ($100,000 × 10%—an increase of $2,500 from the prior threshold).

This means that to protect a medical expense deduction, taxpayers must have a better grasp on what qualifies as a medical expense and do a better job of documenting these costs. IRS Publication 502, *Medical and Dental Expenses*, includes a long list of qualifying expenses as well as expenses that do not qualify.

For example, the travel costs to see a doctor or dentist count, as well as fees paid to a chiropractor or psychologist for medical care. Contact lenses, pregnancy test kits, and even doctor-prescribed weight loss programs may qualify. However, the law is not liberal enough to allow for the deductibility of health club dues or for the purchase of substances that are illegal under Federal law, such as medical marijuana.

The cost of care in a *nursing home or home for the aged*, including meals and lodging, can be included in deductible medical expenses if the primary reason for being in the home is to get medical care. If the primary reason for being there is personal, any costs for medical or nursing care can be included in deductible medical expenses, but the cost of meals and lodging must be excluded.[4]

Norman has a chronic heart ailment. In October, his family decides to place Norman in a nursing home equipped to provide medical and nursing care. Total nursing home expenses amount to $80,000 during the year. Of this amount, $50,000 is directly attributable to medical and nursing care.

Because Norman is in need of significant medical and nursing care and is placed in the facility primarily for this purpose, all $80,000 of the nursing home costs are deductible (subject to the AGI floor, explained earlier).

Tuition expenses of a dependent at a special school may be deductible as a medical expense. The cost of medical care can include the expenses of a special school for a mentally or physically handicapped individual. The deduction is allowed if a principal reason for sending the individual to the school is the school's special resources for alleviating the infirmities. In this case, the cost of meals and lodging, in addition to the tuition, is a proper medical expense deduction.[5]

Jason's daughter Sophia attended public school through the seventh grade. Because Sophia was a poor student, she was examined by a psychiatrist who diagnosed a problem that created a learning disability. Upon the recommendation of the psychiatrist, Sophia is enrolled in a private school so that she can receive individual attention. The school has no special program for students with learning disabilities and does not provide special medical treatment.

The expense related to Sophia's attendance is not deductible as a medical expense. The cost of any psychiatric care, however, qualifies as a medical expense.

Example 5 shows that the recommendation of a physician does not automatically make the expenditure deductible.

10-1b Capital Expenditures for Medical Purposes

When capital expenditures are incurred for medical purposes, they must be deemed medically necessary by a physician, the facility must be used primarily by the patient alone, and the expense must be reasonable. Examples of such expenditures include dust elimination systems,[6] elevators,[7] and vans specially designed for wheelchair-bound taxpayers. Other examples of expenditures that may qualify are swimming pools if the taxpayer does not have access to a neighborhood pool and air conditioners if they do not become permanent improvements (e.g., window units).[8]

Both a capital expenditure for a permanent improvement and expenditures made for the operation or maintenance of the improvement may qualify as medical expenses. The allowable cost of such qualified medical expenditures is deductible in the year incurred. Although depreciation is required for most other capital expenditures, it is not required for those qualifying for medical purposes.

A permanent capital improvement that ordinarily would not have a medical purpose qualifies as a medical expense if it is directly related to prescribed medical care and is deductible to the extent that the expenditure *exceeds* the increase in value of the related property. Appraisal costs related to capital improvements are also deductible, but not as medical expenses. These costs are classified as expenses incurred in the determination of the taxpayer's tax liability.[9]

---

[4]Reg. § 1.213–1(e)(1)(v).

[5]*Donald R. Pfeifer*, 37 TCM 816, T.C.Memo. 1978–189. Also see Rev.Rul. 78–340, 1978–2 C.B. 124.

[6]Ltr.Rul. 7948029.

[7]*Riach v. Frank*, 62–1 USTC ¶9419, 9 AFTR 2d 1263, 302 F.2d 374 (CA–9, 1962).

[8]Reg. § 1.213–1(e)(1)(iii).

[9]§ 212(3).

Fred is afflicted with heart disease. His physician advises him to install an elevator in his residence so that he will not be required to climb the stairs. The cost of installing the elevator is $10,000, and the increase in the value of the residence is determined to be only $4,000.

Therefore, $6,000 ($10,000 − $4,000) is treated as a medical expense. Additional utility costs to operate the elevator and maintenance costs are also medical expenses as long as the medical reason for the capital expenditure continues to exist.

The full cost of certain home-related capital expenditures incurred to enable a *physically handicapped* individual to live independently and productively qualifies as a medical expense. Qualifying costs include expenditures for constructing entrance and exit ramps to the residence, widening hallways and doorways to accommodate wheelchairs, installing support bars and railings in bathrooms and other rooms, and adjusting electrical outlets and fixtures.[10] These expenditures are subject to the AGI percentage limitation only, and the increase in the home's value is deemed to be zero.

10-1c Medical Expenses Incurred for Spouse and Dependents

In computing the medical expense deduction, a taxpayer may include medical expenses for a spouse and for a person who was a dependent at the time the expenses were paid or incurred. Of the requirements that normally apply in determining dependency status,[11] neither the gross income nor the joint return test applies in determining dependency status for medical expense deduction purposes.

William (age 22) is married and a full-time student at a university. During the year, William incurred medical expenses that were paid by Karen (William's mother). She provided more than half of William's support for the year.

Even if William files a joint return with his wife, Karen may claim the medical expenses she paid for him. Karen would combine William's expenses with her own before applying the AGI floor.

For *divorced persons* with children, a special rule applies to the noncustodial parent. The noncustodial parent may claim any medical expenses he or she pays even though the custodial parent claims the children as dependents.

Irv and Joan were divorced last year, and Joan was awarded custody of their child, Keith. During the current year, Irv pays $2,500 of Keith's medical bills. Together, Irv and Joan provide more than half of Keith's support.

Even though Joan claims Keith as a dependent, Irv can combine the $2,500 of medical expenses that he pays for Keith with his own when calculating his medical expense deduction.

10-1d Transportation, Meal, and Lodging Expenses for Medical Treatment

Payments for transportation to and from a point of treatment for medical care are deductible as medical expenses (subject to the AGI floor). These costs include bus, taxi, train, or plane fare; charges for ambulance service; and out-of-pocket expenses for the use of an automobile. A mileage allowance of 19 cents per mile for 2016 may be used instead of actual out-of-pocket automobile expenses.[12] Whether the taxpayer chooses to claim out-of-pocket automobile expenses or the 19 cents per mile automatic mileage option, related parking fees and tolls can also be deducted. Also

---

[10]For a complete list of the items that qualify, see Rev.Rul. 87–106, 1987–2 C.B. 67.

[11]Refer to Chapter 3 for discussion of these requirements.

[12]This amount is adjusted periodically. The allowance was 23 cents per mile for 2015.

included are transportation expenditures for someone such as a parent or nurse who must accompany the patient. The cost of meals while en route to obtain medical care is not deductible.

A deduction is allowable for lodging while away from home for medical care if the following requirements are met:[13]

- The lodging is primarily for and essential to medical care.
- Medical care is provided by a physician in a licensed hospital or a similar medical facility (e.g., a clinic).
- The lodging is not lavish or extravagant under the circumstances.
- There is no significant element of personal pleasure, recreation, or vacation in the travel away from home.

The deduction for lodging expenses included as medical expenses cannot exceed $50 *per* night for *each* person. The deduction is allowed not only for the patient but also for anyone who must travel with the patient.

The Big Picture

EXAMPLE 9

Return to the facts of *The Big Picture* on p. 10-1. John's mother, Martha, eventually moves in with the Williamsons because of her declining health, and she becomes their dependent. John is advised by his family physician that Martha needs specialized treatment for her heart condition. Consequently, John and Martha fly to Cleveland, Ohio, where Martha receives the therapy at a heart clinic on an outpatient basis. Expenses in connection with the trip are as follows:

Round-trip airfare ($250 each)	$500
Lodging in Cleveland for two nights ($120 each per night)	480

Assuming that the Williamsons itemize their deductions (including medical expenses), the medical expense deduction for transportation is $500 and the medical expense deduction for lodging is $200 ($50 per night per person). Because of the severity of Martha's health condition, it is assumed that John's accompanying her is justified.

No deduction is allowed for the cost of meals unless they are part of the medical care and are furnished at a medical facility. When allowable, such meals are not subject to the 50 percent limit applicable to business meals (see Chapter 9).

10-1e Amounts Paid for Medical Insurance Premiums

Medical insurance premiums are included with other medical expenses subject to the AGI floor. Premiums paid by the taxpayer under a group plan or an individual plan are included as medical expenses. If an employer pays all or part of the taxpayer's medical insurance premiums, the amount paid by the employer is not included in gross income by the employee. Likewise, the premiums are not included in the employee's medical expenses. However, the medical insurance premiums paid by the employer are deductible as business expenses on the employer's tax return (see Chapter 6).

If a taxpayer is *self-employed*, insurance premiums paid for medical coverage are deductible as a *business* expense (*for* AGI).[14] The deduction *for* AGI is allowed for premiums paid on behalf of the taxpayer, the taxpayer's spouse, and dependents of the taxpayer. The deduction is not allowed to any taxpayer who is eligible to participate in a subsidized health plan maintained by any employer of the taxpayer or of the taxpayer's spouse.

---

[13]§ 213(d)(2). [14]§ 162(l).

The Big Picture

EXAMPLE 10

Return to the facts of *The Big Picture* on p. 10-1. John Williamson is the sole practitioner in his unincorporated accounting firm. During the year, he paid health insurance premiums of $12,000 for his own coverage and $8,000 for coverage for his wife, Susan. John can deduct $20,000 as a business deduction (*for* AGI) in computing their taxable income.

Taxpayers may also include premiums paid on qualified long-term care insurance contracts in medical expenses, subject to limitations based on the age of the insured. For 2016, the per-person limits range from $390 for taxpayers age 40 and under to $4,870 for taxpayers over age 70. See IRS Publication 502 for details relating to requirements for deducting costs associated with qualified long-term care insurance contracts.[15]

10-1f Year of Deduction

Regardless of a taxpayer's method of accounting, medical expenses are deductible only in the year *paid*. In effect, this places all individual taxpayers on a cash basis as far as the medical expense deduction is concerned. One exception, however, is allowed for deceased taxpayers. If the medical expenses are paid within one year from the day following the day of death, they can be treated as being paid at the time they were *incurred*. Thus, such expenses may be reported on the final income tax return of the decedent or on earlier returns if incurred before the year of death.

No current deduction is allowed for payment for medical care to be rendered in the future unless the taxpayer is under an obligation to make the payment. Whether an obligation to make the payment exists depends upon the policy of the physician or the institution furnishing the medical care.

EXAMPLE 11

Upon the recommendation of his regular dentist, in December 2016, Gary consults Dr. Smith, a prosthodontist, who specializes in crown and bridge work. Dr. Smith tells Gary that he can do the restorative work for $12,000 and that he requires all new patients to prepay 40% of the total cost of the procedure. Accordingly, Gary pays $4,800 in December 2016. The balance of $7,200 is paid when the work is completed in January 2017.

Under these circumstances, the qualifying medical expense deductions are $4,800 for 2016 and $7,200 in 2017. The result would be the same even if Gary prepaid the full $12,000 in 2016.

10-1g Reimbursements

If medical expenses are reimbursed in the same year as paid, no problem arises. The reimbursement merely reduces the amount that would otherwise qualify for the medical expense deduction. But what happens if the reimbursement occurs in a later year than the expenditure? In computing casualty losses, any reasonable prospect of recovery must be considered (refer to Chapter 7). For medical expenses, however, any expected reimbursement is disregarded in measuring the amount of the deduction. Instead, the reimbursement is accounted for separately in the year in which it occurs.

Under the *tax benefit rule*, a taxpayer who receives an insurance reimbursement for medical expenses deducted in a previous year must include the reimbursement in income up to the amount of the deductions that decreased taxable income in the earlier year. A taxpayer who did not itemize deductions in the year the expenses were paid did not receive a tax benefit and is *not* required to include a reimbursement in gross income.

---

[15]The amounts for 2015 were $380 for taxpayers age 40 and under and $4,750 for taxpayers over age 70.

EXAMPLE 12

Daniel (age 50) had AGI of $45,000 for 2016. He was injured in a car accident and paid $4,300 for hospital expenses and $700 for doctor bills. Daniel also incurred medical expenses of $600 for his dependent child. In 2017, Daniel was reimbursed $650 by his insurance company for the medical expenses attributable to the car accident. His deduction for medical expenses in 2016 is computed as follows:

Hospitalization	$ 4,300
Bills for doctor's services	700
Medical expenses for dependent	600
Total	$ 5,600
Less: Medical expense floor (10% of $45,000)	(4,500)
Medical expense deduction (assuming that Daniel itemizes his deductions)	$ 1,100

Assume that Daniel would have elected to itemize his deductions even if he had no medical expenses in 2016. If the reimbursement for medical care had occurred in 2016, the medical expense deduction would have been only $450 [$5,600 (total medical expenses) − $650 (reimbursement) − $4,500 (floor)] and Daniel would have paid more income tax.

Because the reimbursement was made in a subsequent year, Daniel will include $650 in gross income for 2017. If Daniel had not itemized in 2016, he would *not* have included the $650 reimbursement in 2017 gross income because he would have received no tax benefit for the medical expenses in 2016.

10-1h Health Savings Accounts

Qualifying individuals may make deductible contributions to a **Health Savings Account (HSA)**. An HSA is a qualified trust or custodial account administered by a qualified HSA trustee, which can be a bank, an insurance company, or another IRS-approved trustee.[16] A taxpayer can use an HSA in conjunction with a high-deductible medical insurance policy to help reduce the overall cost of medical coverage. Converting from a low-deductible to a high-deductible plan can generally save an individual a considerable amount in premiums. The high-deductible policy provides coverage for extraordinary medical expenses (in excess of the deductible), and expenses not covered by the policy can be paid with funds withdrawn tax-free from the HSA.

EXAMPLE 13

Sanchez, who is married and has three dependent children, carries a high-deductible medical insurance policy with a deductible of $4,400. He establishes an HSA and contributes the maximum allowable amount to the HSA in 2016.

During 2016, the Sanchez family incurs medical expenses of $7,000. The high-deductible policy covers $2,600 of the expenses ($7,000 expenses − $4,400 deductible). Sanchez may withdraw $4,400 from the HSA to pay the medical expenses not covered by the high-deductible policy.

High-Deductible Plans

High-deductible policies are less expensive than low-deductible policies, so taxpayers with low medical costs can benefit from the lower premiums and use funds from the HSA to pay costs not covered by the high-deductible policy. A plan must meet two requirements to qualify as a high-deductible plan.[17]

1. The annual deductible in 2016 is not less than $1,300 for self-only coverage ($2,600 for family coverage).
2. The annual limit in 2016 on total out-of-pocket costs (excluding premiums) under the plan does not exceed $6,550 for self-only coverage ($13,100 for family coverage).

---

[16]§ 223.   [17]§ 223(c)(2).

TAX IN THE NEWS   **Health Savings Accounts Offer Additional Retirement Savings Opportunities**

Many Americans understand that for a financially secure retirement to be possible, a career-long savings and investment habit must be developed. While this may be easier said than done, most people know that IRAs and § 401(k)s are qualified retirement savings vehicles that provide important tax advantages, which can help in the construction of that retirement nest egg. Now an additional option is being discussed, where a Health Savings Account (HSA) is touted as an additional retirement savings vehicle for those who can afford it.

The idea is to make annual tax-deductible contributions to the HSA at the highest amount permissible {$8,750 in 2016 for married couples who are each at least age 55 [$6,750 + ($1,000 × 2)]} and then allow all or part of the account to grow on a tax-deferred basis. As intended by Congress, the account balance can be tapped to pay for medical costs, and such distributions used to pay for medical expenses not covered by the taxpayer's high-deductible policy will be free of income tax. Any remaining amount withdrawn from the HSA once the taxpayer reaches age 65 will be taxed in the same fashion as traditional IRA and § 401(k) distributions, even if the distribution is used for nonmedical purposes.

Sources: Peter S. Green, "Health Savings Accounts Can Double as Shadow IRAs," *Wall Street Journal*, June 2, 2014 and Elizabeth O'Brien, "Health Savings Accounts Gain Acceptance as Retirement Tool," **www.marketwatch.com/story/health-savings-accounts-gain-acceptance-as-retirement-tool-2015-05-28**.

Tax Treatment of HSA Contributions and Distributions

To establish an HSA, a taxpayer contributes funds to a tax-exempt trust.[18] As illustrated in the preceding example, funds can be withdrawn from an HSA to pay medical expenses that are not covered by the high-deductible policy. The following general tax rules apply to HSAs:

1. Contributions made by the taxpayer to an HSA are deductible from gross income to arrive at AGI (deduction *for* AGI). Thus, the taxpayer does not need to itemize to take the deduction.
2. Earnings on HSAs are not subject to taxation unless distributed, in which case taxability depends on the way the funds are used.[19]

   - Distributions from HSAs are excluded from gross income if they are used to pay for medical expenses not covered by the high-deductible policy.

   - Distributions that are not used to pay for medical expenses are included in gross income and are subject to an additional 20 percent penalty if made before age 65, death, or disability. Such distributions made by reason of death or disability and distributions made after the HSA beneficiary becomes eligible for Medicare are taxed but not penalized.

HSAs have at least two other attractive features. First, an HSA is portable. Taxpayers who switch jobs can take their HSAs with them. Second, anyone under age 65 who has a high-deductible plan and is not covered by another policy that is not a high-deductible plan can establish an HSA.

Deductible Amount

The annual deduction for contributions to an HSA is limited to the sum of the monthly limitations. The monthly limitation is calculated for each month the individual is an eligible individual. The monthly deduction is not allowed after the individual becomes eligible for Medicare coverage.

The amount of the monthly limitation for an individual who has self-only coverage in 2016 is one-twelfth of $3,350, while the monthly limitation for an individual who has

---

[18]§ 223(d).   [19]§ 223(f).

family coverage in 2016 is one-twelfth of $6,750. These amounts are subject to annual cost-of-living adjustments.[20] An eligible taxpayer who has attained age 55 by the end of the tax year may make an additional annual contribution in 2016 of up to $1,000. This additional amount is referred to as a *catch-up* contribution.

Determining the Maximum HSA Contribution Deduction

Liu (age 45), who is married and self-employed, carries a high-deductible medical insurance policy with family coverage and an annual deductible of $4,000. In addition, he has established an HSA. Liu's maximum annual deductible contribution to the HSA in 2016 is $6,750.

EXAMPLE
14

During 2016, Adam, who is self-employed, made 12 monthly payments of $1,200 for an HSA contract that provides medical insurance coverage with a $3,600 deductible. The plan covers Adam, his wife, and two children. Of the $1,200 monthly fee, $675 was for the high-deductible policy and $525 was deposited into an HSA. The deductible monthly contribution to the HSA is calculated as follows:

EXAMPLE
15

Maximum annual deduction for family coverage	$ 6,750
Monthly limitation (1/12 of $6,750)	$562.50

Because Adam is *self-employed*, he can deduct $8,100 of the amount paid for the high-deductible policy ($675 per month × 12 months) as a deduction *for* AGI (refer to Example 10 and related discussion). In addition, he can deduct the $6,300 ($525 × 12) paid to the HSA as a deduction *for* AGI. Note that the $6,300 HSA deduction does not exceed the $6,750 ceiling.

10-2 **TAXES**

LO.3

Contrast deductible taxes with nondeductible fees, licenses, and other charges.

A deduction is allowed for certain state and local taxes paid or accrued by a taxpayer.[21] The deduction was created to relieve the burden of multiple taxes upon the same source of revenue.

10-2a **Deductibility as a Tax**

A distinction must be made between a tax and a fee, because fees are not deductible unless incurred as an ordinary and necessary business expense or as an expense in the production of income. The IRS has defined a tax as follows:

> A tax is an enforced contribution exacted pursuant to legislative authority in the exercise of taxing power, and imposed and collected for the purpose of raising revenue to be used for public or governmental purposes, and not as payment for some special privilege granted or service rendered. Taxes are, therefore, distinguished from various other contributions and charges imposed for particular purposes under particular powers or functions of the government. In view of such distinctions, the question whether a particular contribution or charge is to be regarded as a tax depends upon its real nature.[22]

Accordingly, fees for dog licenses, automobile inspections, automobile titles and registration, hunting and fishing licenses, bridge and highway tolls, driver's licenses, parking meter deposits, and postage are not deductible if personal in nature. Deductible and nondeductible taxes are summarized in Exhibit 10.2.

---

[20]§ 223(b)(2). The annual limits were $3,350 and $6,650 in 2015.

[21]Most deductible taxes are listed in § 164, while nondeductible items are included in § 275.

[22]Rev.Rul. 57–345, 1957–2 C.B. 132, and Rev.Rul. 70–622, 1970–2 C.B. 41.

EXHIBIT 10.2	**Deductible and Nondeductible Taxes**
Deductible	**Nondeductible**
State, local, and foreign real property taxes	Federal income taxes
	FICA taxes imposed on employees
State and local personal property taxes	Employer FICA taxes paid on domestic household workers
State and local income taxes *or* sales/use taxes	Estate, inheritance, and gift taxes
Foreign income taxes	Federal, state, and local excise taxes (e.g., gasoline, tobacco, and spirits)
	Foreign income taxes if the taxpayer chooses the foreign tax credit option
	Taxes on real property to the extent such taxes are to be apportioned and treated as imposed on another taxpayer

10-2b **Property Taxes**

State, local, and foreign taxes on real property are generally deductible only by the person upon whom the tax is imposed. Deductible personal property taxes must be *ad valorem* (assessed in relation to the value of the property). Therefore, a motor vehicle tax based on weight, model, year, and horsepower is not an ad valorem tax. However, a tax based on value and other criteria may qualify in part.

The Big Picture

EXAMPLE 16

Return to the facts of *The Big Picture* on p. 10-1. Assuming that the Williamsons proceed with the purchase of a home, the real estate taxes they pay will be deductible *from* AGI because they qualify to itemize their deductions. However, if they also pay a personal property tax on their automobile, the payment may be only partially deductible.

For example, assume that in their state, the government imposes a motor vehicle registration tax on 2% of the value of the vehicle plus 40 cents per hundredweight. The Williamsons own a car having a value of $20,000 and weighing 3,000 pounds. They pay an annual registration tax of $412. Of this amount, $400 (2% × $20,000 of value) is deductible as a personal property tax. The remaining $12, based on the weight of the car, is not deductible.

Assessments for Local Benefits

As a general rule, real property taxes do not include taxes assessed for local benefits because such assessments tend to increase the value of the property (e.g., special assessments for streets, sidewalks, curbing, and other similar improvements). A taxpayer was denied a deduction for the cost of a new sidewalk (relative to a personal residence), even though the construction was required by the city and the sidewalk may have provided an incidental benefit to the public welfare.[23] Such assessments are added to the basis of the taxpayer's property.

Apportionment of Real Property Taxes between Seller and Purchaser

Real estate taxes for the entire year are apportioned between the buyer and seller on the basis of the number of days the property was held by each during the real property

---
[23]*Erie H. Rose*, 31 TCM 142, T.C.Memo. 1972–39; Reg. § 1.164–4(a).

tax year. This apportionment is required whether the tax is paid by the buyer or the seller or is prorated according to the purchase agreement. The apportionment determines who is entitled to deduct the real estate taxes in the year of sale. The required apportionment prevents the shifting of the deduction for real estate taxes from the buyer to the seller, or vice versa. In making the apportionment, the assessment date and the lien date are disregarded.[24]

EXAMPLE 17

A county's real property tax year runs from January 1 to December 31. Abigail, the owner on January 1 of real property located in the county, sells the real property to Bob on June 30 (assume that this year is not a leap year). Bob owns the real property from June 30 through December 31. The tax for the real property tax year, January 1 through December 31, is $3,650.

The portion of the real property tax treated as imposed upon Abigail, the seller, is $1,800 [(180/365) × $3,650, January 1 through June 29], and $1,850 [(185/365) × $3,650, June 30 through December 31] of the tax is treated as imposed upon Bob, the purchaser.

If the actual real estate taxes are not prorated between the buyer and seller as part of the purchase agreement, adjustments are required. The adjustments are necessary to determine the amount realized by the seller and the basis of the property to the buyer. If the buyer pays the entire amount of the tax, he or she has, in effect, paid the seller's portion of the real estate tax and has therefore paid more for the property than the actual purchase price. Thus, the amount of real estate tax that is apportioned to the seller (for Federal income tax purposes) and paid by the buyer is added to the buyer's basis. The seller must increase the amount realized on the sale by the same amount.

EXAMPLE 18

Seth sells real estate on October 3 for $400,000. The buyer, Wilma, pays the real estate taxes of $3,650 for the calendar year, which is the real estate property tax year. Assuming that this is not a leap year, $2,750 (for 275 days) of the real estate taxes is apportioned to and is deductible by the seller, Seth, and $900 (for 90 days) of the taxes is deductible by Wilma. The buyer has, in effect, paid Seth's real estate taxes of $2,750 and has therefore paid $402,750 for the property. Wilma's basis is increased to $402,750, and the amount realized by Seth from the sale is increased to $402,750.

The opposite result occurs if the seller (rather than the buyer) pays the real estate taxes. In this case, the seller reduces the amount realized from the sale by the amount that has been apportioned to the buyer. The buyer is required to reduce his or her basis by a corresponding amount.

10-2c State and Local Income Taxes and Sales Taxes

LO.4

Explain the Federal income tax treatment of state and local income taxes and sales taxes.

The position of the IRS is that state and local income taxes imposed upon an individual are deductible only as itemized deductions, even if the taxpayer's sole source of income is from a business, rents, or royalties.

Cash basis taxpayers are entitled to deduct state income taxes withheld by the employer in the year the taxes are withheld. In addition, estimated state income tax payments are deductible in the year the payment is made by cash basis taxpayers even if the payments relate to a prior or subsequent year.[25] If the taxpayer overpays state income taxes because of excessive withholdings or estimated tax payments, the refund received is included in gross income of the following year to the extent the deduction reduced taxable income in the prior year.

---

[24]For most years, the apportionment is based on a 365-day year. However, in a leap year (i.e., a year that is evenly divisible by 4, such as 2016), the taxes are prorated over 366 days. In making the apportionment, the date of sale counts as a day the property is owned by the buyer.

[25]Rev.Rul. 71–190, 1971–1 C.B. 70. See also Rev.Rul. 82–208, 1982–2 C.B. 58, where a deduction is not allowed when the taxpayer cannot, in good faith, reasonably determine that there is additional state income tax liability.

EXAMPLE 19

Leona, a cash basis, unmarried taxpayer, had $800 of state income tax withheld during 2016. Also in 2016, Leona paid $100 that was due when she filed her 2015 state income tax return and made estimated payments of $300 toward her 2016 state income tax liability. When Leona files her 2016 Federal income tax return in April 2017, she elects to itemize deductions, which amount to $8,500, including the $1,200 of state income tax payments and withholdings, all of which reduce her taxable income.

As a result of overpaying her 2016 state income tax, Leona receives a refund of $200 early in 2017. She will include this amount in her 2017 gross income in computing her Federal income tax. It does not matter whether Leona received a check from the state for $200 or applied the $200 toward her 2017 state income tax.

Itemized Deduction for Sales Taxes Paid

Individuals can elect to deduct either their state and local income taxes or their sales/use taxes paid as an itemized deduction on Schedule A of Form 1040. The annual election can reflect actual sales/use tax payments or an amount from an IRS table (see Appendix A). The amount from the table may be increased by sales tax paid on the purchase of motor vehicles, boats, and other specified items. Most often, the sales tax deduction will be elected by those living in states with no individual income tax.

10-3 INTEREST

LO.5

Distinguish between deductible and nondeductible interest and apply the appropriate limitations to deductible interest.

A deduction for interest has been allowed since the income tax law was enacted in 1913. Despite its long history of congressional acceptance, the interest deduction has been one of the most controversial areas in the tax law. The controversy centered around the propriety of allowing the deduction of interest charges for the purchase of consumer goods and services and interest on borrowings used to acquire investments (investment interest). Currently, personal (consumer) interest is not deductible. This includes credit card interest, interest on car loans, and other types of interest. However, interest on qualified student loans, qualified residence (home mortgage) interest, and investment interest continue to be deductible, subject to the limits discussed on the following pages.

10-3a Allowed and Disallowed Items

The Supreme Court has defined *interest* as compensation for the use or forbearance of money.[26] The general rule permits a deduction for interest paid or accrued within the taxable year on indebtedness.

Interest on Qualified Student Loans

Taxpayers who pay interest on a qualified student loan may be able to deduct the interest as a deduction *for* AGI. The deduction is allowable only to the extent that the proceeds of the loan are used to pay qualified education expenses. Such payments must be made to qualified educational institutions.[27]

The maximum annual deduction for qualified student loan interest is $2,500. However, in 2016, the deduction is phased out for taxpayers with modified AGI (MAGI) between $65,000 and $80,000 ($130,000 and $160,000 on joint returns). The deduction is not allowed for taxpayers who are claimed as dependents or for married taxpayers filing separately.[28]

The numerator in the phaseout computation is equal to MAGI minus the floor of the phaseout range (i.e., $65,000 or $130,000, depending on filing status). The denominator

---

[26]*Old Colony Railroad Co. v. Comm.*, 3 USTC ¶880, 10 AFTR 786, 52 S.Ct. 211 (USSC, 1932).

[27]See IRS Publication 970, *Tax Benefits for Education*, for details.

[28]§ 221. See § 221(b)(2)(C) for the definition of MAGI. For 2015, the MAGI threshold amounts also were $65,000 and $80,000 ($130,000 and $160,000 on joint returns).

is equal to the amount of the phaseout range (e.g., $160,000 − $130,000 = $30,000$ for married taxpayers filing jointly).

EXAMPLE 20

In 2016, Curt and Rita, who are married and file a joint return, paid $3,000 of interest on a qualified student loan. Their MAGI was $137,500. Their maximum potential deduction for qualified student loan interest is $2,500, but it must be reduced by $625 as a result of the phaseout rules.

$$\$2,500 \text{ interest } \times \frac{\$137,500 \text{ (MAGI)} - \$130,000 \text{ (phaseout floor)}}{\$30,000 \text{ (phaseout range)}} = \$625 \text{ reduction}$$

Curt and Rita are allowed a student loan interest deduction of $1,875 ($2,500 maximum deduction − $625 reduction = $1,875 deduction *for* AGI).

Qualified Residence Interest

Qualified residence interest is interest paid or accrued during the taxable year on indebtedness (subject to limitations) *secured* by any property that is a qualified residence of the taxpayer. Qualified residence interest falls into two categories: (1) interest on acquisition indebtedness and (2) interest on home equity loans. Before discussing each of these categories, however, the term *qualified residence* must be defined.

A *qualified residence* includes the taxpayer's principal residence and one other residence of the taxpayer or spouse. The *principal residence* meets the requirement for nonrecognition of gain upon sale under § 121 (see Chapter 15). The *one other residence*, or second residence, is used as a residence if not rented or, if rented, meets the requirements for a personal residence under the rental of vacation home rules (refer to Chapter 6). A taxpayer who has more than one second residence can make the selection each year as to which one is the qualified second residence. A residence includes, in addition to a house in the ordinary sense, cooperative apartments, condominiums, and mobile homes and boats that have living quarters (sleeping accommodations and toilet and cooking facilities).

Although in most cases interest paid on a home mortgage is fully deductible, there are limitations.[29] Interest paid or accrued during the tax year on aggregate **acquisition indebtedness** of $1 million or less ($500,000 for married persons filing separate returns) is deductible as qualified residence interest. *Acquisition indebtedness* refers to amounts incurred in acquiring, constructing, or substantially improving a qualified residence of the taxpayer.

The Big Picture

EXAMPLE 21

Return to the facts of *The Big Picture* on p. 10-1. Given that John and Susan Williamson will need to borrow at least a portion of the purchase price of a new home, a standard mortgage likely will qualify as acquisition indebtedness because the borrowed funds are used to acquire a principal residence. However, the interest on the acquisition indebtedness will be fully deductible only if the amount of the mortgage is $1 million or less (assuming that John and Susan file a joint return) and the mortgage is secured by the home, which is the typical case.

Recall that the Williamsons are also considering what appears to be a less expensive route of using their retirement and taxable investments to secure the debt. If they choose this alternative, the interest will not be deductible as qualified residence interest because the loan would not be acquisition indebtedness (i.e., the loan would not be secured by the home).

Qualified residence interest also includes interest on **home equity loans**. These loans utilize the personal residence of the taxpayer as security, typically in the form of a second mortgage. Because the funds from home equity loans can be used for personal purposes (e.g., auto purchases and medical expenses), what would otherwise have been nondeductible personal interest becomes deductible qualified residence interest.

---

[29]§ 163(h)(3).

However, interest is deductible only on the portion of a home equity loan that does not exceed the *lesser of*:

- The fair market value of the residence, reduced by the acquisition indebtedness, *or*
- $100,000 ($50,000 for married persons filing separate returns).

Larry owns a personal residence with a fair market value of $450,000 and an outstanding first mortgage of $420,000. Therefore, his equity in his home is $30,000 ($450,000 − $420,000). Larry issues a second mortgage on the residence and in return borrows $15,000 to purchase a new family automobile.

All interest on the $435,000 of first and second mortgage debt is treated as qualified residence interest.

Under current law, mortgage insurance premiums paid by the taxpayer on a qualified residence may be deducted (treated as qualified residence interest). However, the deduction begins to phase out for taxpayers with AGI in excess of $100,000 ($50,000 for married taxpayers filing separately). The deduction is fully phased out when AGI exceeds $109,000 ($54,500 for married taxpayers filing separately).[30]

Interest Paid for Services

Mortgage loan companies commonly charge a fee, often called a loan origination fee, for finding, placing, or processing a mortgage loan. Loan origination fees are typically nondeductible amounts included in the basis of the acquired property. Other fees, sometimes called **points** and expressed as a percentage of the loan amount, are paid to reduce the interest rate charged over the term of the loan. Essentially, the payment of points is a prepayment of interest and is considered compensation to a lender solely for the use or forbearance of money. To be deductible, points must be in the nature of interest and cannot be a form of service charge or payment for specific services.[31]

Points must be capitalized and are amortized and deductible ratably over the life of the loan. A special exception, however, permits the purchaser of a principal residence to deduct qualifying points in the year of payment.[32] The exception also covers points paid to obtain funds for home improvements.

Points paid to *refinance* an existing home mortgage cannot be immediately deducted, but must be capitalized and amortized as an interest deduction over the life of the new loan.[33]

Sandra purchased her residence many years ago, obtaining a 30-year mortgage at an annual interest rate of 8%. In the current year, Sandra refinances the mortgage to reduce the interest rate to 4%. To obtain the refinancing, she has to pay points of $2,600.

The $2,600, which is considered prepayment of interest, must be capitalized and amortized over the life of the mortgage.

Points paid by the seller for a buyer are, in effect, treated as an adjustment to the price of the residence, and the buyer is treated as having used cash to pay the points that were paid by the seller. A buyer may deduct seller-paid points in the tax year in which they are paid if certain conditions are met.[34]

Prepayment Penalty

When a mortgage or loan is paid off in full in a lump sum before its term (early), the lending institution may require an additional payment of a certain percentage applied to the unpaid amount at the time of prepayment. This is known as a prepayment penalty and is considered to be interest (e.g., personal, qualified residence, or investment) in the year paid. The general rules for deductibility of interest also apply to prepayment penalties.

---

[30] §§ 163(h)(3)(E)(i) and (ii). This provision is available through December 2016. However, many tax professionals expect that Congress will extend this provision.

[31] Rev.Rul. 69–188, 1969–1 C.B. 54.

[32] § 461(g)(2).

[33] Rev.Rul. 87–22, 1987–1 C.B. 146.

[34] Refer to Revenue Procedure 94–27 for a complete list of these conditions and additional aspects of this arrangement. Rev.Proc. 94–27, 1994–1 C.B. 613.

Interest Paid to Related Parties

Nothing prevents the deduction of interest paid to a related party as long as the payment actually took place and the interest meets the requirements for deductibility. Recall from Chapter 6 that a special rule for related taxpayers applies when the debtor uses the accrual basis and the related creditor is on the cash basis. If this rule is applicable, interest that has been accrued but not paid at the end of the debtor's tax year is not deductible until payment is made and the income is reportable by the cash basis recipient.

Investment Interest

Taxpayers frequently borrow funds they use to acquire investment assets. Congress, however, has limited the deductibility of interest on funds borrowed for the purpose of purchasing or continuing to hold investment property. Under this limitation, the deduction for investment interest expense may not exceed the net investment income for the year. A complete discussion of investment interest occurs in Chapter 11 in the context of the limitations taxpayers face when dealing with assets held for investment purposes.

Tax-Exempt Securities

The tax law provides that no deduction is allowed for interest on debt incurred to purchase or carry tax-exempt securities.[35] A major problem for the courts has been to determine what is meant by the words *to purchase or carry*. Refer to Chapter 6 for a detailed discussion of these issues.

10-3b Restrictions on Deductibility and Timing Considerations

Even if the interest expense qualifies as a type that is deductible (e.g., qualified residence interest), a current deduction still may not be available unless certain additional conditions described below are met.

Taxpayer's Obligation

Allowed interest is deductible if the related debt represents a bona fide obligation for which the taxpayer is liable.[36] Thus, for interest to be deductible, both the debtor and the creditor must intend for the loan to be repaid. Intent of the parties can be especially crucial between related parties such as a shareholder and a closely held corporation. In addition, an individual may not deduct interest paid on behalf of another taxpayer. For example, a shareholder may not deduct interest paid by the corporation on his or her behalf.[37] Likewise, a husband may not deduct interest paid on his wife's property if he files a separate return, except in the case of qualified residence interest. If both husband and wife consent in writing, either the husband or the wife may deduct the allowed interest on the principal residence and one other residence.

Time of Deduction

Generally, interest must be paid to secure a deduction unless the taxpayer uses the accrual method of accounting. Under the accrual method, interest is deductible ratably over the life of the loan.

EXAMPLE

24

On November 1, 2016, Ramon borrows $2,000 to purchase appliances for a rental house. The loan is payable in 90 days at 6% interest. On the due date in late January 2017, Ramon pays the $2,000 note and interest amounting to $30.

Ramon can deduct the accrued portion ($2/3 \times \$30 = \$20$) of the interest in 2016 only if he is an accrual basis taxpayer. Otherwise, the entire amount of interest ($30) is deductible in 2017.

---

[35]§ 265(a)(2).

[36]*Arcade Realty Co.*, 35 T.C. 256 (1960).

[37]*Continental Trust Co.*, 7 B.T.A. 539 (1927).

Prepaid Interest

Accrual method reporting is imposed on cash basis taxpayers for interest prepayments that extend beyond the end of the taxable year.[38] Such payments must be allocated to the tax years to which the interest payments relate. These provisions are intended to prevent cash basis taxpayers from *manufacturing* tax deductions before the end of the year by prepaying interest.

10-3c Classification of Interest Expense

Whether interest is deductible *for* AGI or as an itemized deduction (*from* AGI) depends on whether the indebtedness has a business, investment, or personal purpose. If the indebtedness is incurred in relation to a business (other than performing services as an employee) or for the production of rent or royalty income, the interest is deductible *for* AGI. If the indebtedness is incurred for personal use, such as qualified residence interest, any deduction allowed is taken *from* AGI and is reported on Schedule A of Form 1040 if the taxpayer elects to itemize. Recall, however, that interest on a student loan is a deduction *for* AGI. If the taxpayer is an employee who incurs debt in relation to his or her employment, the interest is considered to be personal, or consumer, interest and is not deductible. Business expenses appear on Schedule C of Form 1040, and expenses related to rents or royalties are reported on Schedule E.

See Concept Summary 10.1 for a summary of the interest deduction rules.

Concept Summary 10.1

Deductibility of Personal, Student Loan, Mortgage, and Investment Interest

Type	Deductible	Comments
Personal (consumer) interest	No	Includes any interest that is not qualified residence interest, qualified student loan interest, investment interest, or business interest. Examples include interest on car loans and credit card debt.
Qualified student loan interest	Yes	Deduction *for* AGI; subject to limitations.
Qualified residence interest on acquisition indebtedness	Yes	Deductible as an itemized deduction; limited to indebtedness of $1 million.
Qualified residence interest on home equity indebtedness	Yes	Deductible as an itemized deduction; limited to indebtedness equal to lesser of $100,000 or FMV of residence minus acquisition indebtedness.
Investment interest (*not* related to rental or royalty property)	Yes	Itemized deduction; limited to net investment income for the year; disallowed interest can be carried over to future years. See Chapter 11 for a complete discussion of investment interest.
Investment interest (related to rental or royalty property)	Yes	Deduction *for* AGI; limited to net investment income for the year; disallowed interest can be carried over to future years. See Chapter 11 for a complete discussion of investment interest.

LO.6

Recognize charitable contributions and identify their related measurement problems and percentage limitations.

10-4 CHARITABLE CONTRIBUTIONS

Section 170 allows individuals and corporations to deduct contributions made to qualified *domestic* organizations. Contributions to qualified charitable organizations serve certain social welfare needs and thus relieve the government of the cost of providing these needed services to the community.

---

[38]§ 461(g)(1).

The charitable contribution provisions are among the most complex in the tax law. To determine the amount deductible as a charitable contribution, several important questions must be answered:

- What constitutes a charitable contribution?
- Was the contribution made to a qualified organization?
- When is the contribution deductible?
- What record-keeping and reporting requirements apply to charitable contributions?
- How is the value of donated property determined?
- What special rules apply to contributions of property that has increased in value?
- What percentage limitations apply to the charitable contribution deduction?
- What rules apply to amounts in excess of percentage limitations (carryovers)?

These questions are addressed in the sections that follow.

10-4a **Criteria for a Gift**

A *charitable contribution* is defined as a gift made to a qualified organization.[39] The major elements needed to qualify a contribution as a gift are a donative intent, the absence of consideration, and acceptance by the donee. Consequently, the taxpayer has the burden of establishing that the transfer was made from motives of *disinterested generosity* as established by the courts.[40] This test is quite subjective and has led to problems of interpretation (refer to the discussion of gifts in Chapter 5).

Benefit Received Rule

When a donor derives a tangible benefit from a contribution, he or she cannot deduct the value of the benefit.

Ralph purchases a ticket at $100 for a special performance of the local symphony (a qualified charity). If the price of a ticket to a symphony concert is normally $35, Ralph is allowed only $65 as a charitable contribution. Even if Ralph does not attend the concert, the deduction is limited to $65.

If, however, Ralph does *not* accept the ticket from the symphony (or returns it prior to the event), he can deduct the full $100.

EXAMPLE 25

An exception to this benefit rule provides for the deduction of an automatic percentage of the amount paid for the right to purchase athletic tickets from colleges and universities.[41] Under this exception, 80 percent of the amount paid to or for the benefit of the institution qualifies as a charitable contribution deduction.

Janet donates $5,000 to State University's athletic department. The payment guarantees that she will have preferred seating on the 50-yard line at football games. Subsequently, Janet buys four $50 game tickets. Under the exception to the benefit rule, she is allowed a $4,000 (80% of $5,000) charitable contribution deduction for the taxable year.

If, however, Janet's $5,000 donation includes four $50 tickets, that portion [$200 ($50 × 4)] and the remaining portion of $4,800 ($5,000 − $200) are treated as separate amounts. Thus, Janet is allowed a charitable contribution deduction of $3,840 (80% of $4,800).

EXAMPLE 26

Contribution of Services

No deduction is allowed for a contribution of one's services to a qualified charitable organization. However, unreimbursed expenses related to the services rendered may

---

[39]§ 170(c). In recent years, easements have become a popular means of claiming a charitable contribution deduction (e.g., for scenic, historical, noncommercial development, or other similar purposes), and many court cases have focused on the valuation of these easements. See Chapter 14 for additional details about easements and their effect on the basis of property.

[40]*Comm. v. Duberstein*, 60–2 USTC ¶9515, 5 AFTR 2d 1626, 80 S.Ct. 1190 (USSC, 1960).

[41]§ 170(l).

be deductible. For example, the cost of a uniform (without general utility) that is required to be worn while performing services may be deductible, as are certain out-of-pocket transportation costs incurred for the benefit of the charity. In lieu of these out-of-pocket costs for an automobile, a standard mileage rate of 14 cents per mile is allowed.[42] Deductions are permitted for transportation, reasonable expenses for lodging, and the cost of meals while away from home that are incurred in performing the donated services. The travel expenses are not deductible if the travel involves a significant element of personal pleasure, recreation, or vacation.[43]

EXAMPLE 27

Grace, a delegate representing her church in Miami, Florida, travels to a two-day national meeting in Denver, Colorado, in February. After the meeting, Grace spends two weeks at a nearby ski resort.

Under these circumstances, none of the transportation, meals, or lodging is deductible because the travel involved a significant element of personal pleasure, recreation, or vacation.

Nondeductible Items

In addition to the benefit received rule and the restrictions placed on contributions of services, the following items may *not* be deducted as charitable contributions:

- Dues, fees, or bills paid to country clubs, lodges, fraternal orders, or similar groups.
- Cost of raffle, bingo, or lottery tickets.
- Cost of tuition.
- Value of blood given to a blood bank.
- Donations to homeowners associations.
- Gifts to individuals.
- Rental value of property used by a qualified charity.

10-4b Qualified Organizations

To be deductible, a contribution must be made to one of the following organizations:[44]

- A state or possession of the United States or any subdivisions thereof.
- A corporation, trust, community chest, fund, or foundation that is situated in the United States and is organized and operated exclusively for religious, charitable, scientific, literary, or educational purposes or for the prevention of cruelty to children or animals.
- A veterans' organization.
- A fraternal organization operating under the lodge system.
- A cemetery company.

The IRS publishes a list of organizations that have applied for and received tax-exempt status under § 501 of the Code.[45] This publication is updated frequently and may be helpful in determining whether a gift has been made to a qualifying charitable organization.

Because gifts made to needy individuals are not deductible, a deduction will not be permitted if a gift is received by a donee in an individual capacity rather than as a representative of a qualifying organization.

---

[42]§ 170(i).

[43]§ 170(j).

[44]§ 170(c).

[45]Although this *Cumulative List of Organizations*, IRS Publication 78, may be helpful, qualified organizations are not required to be listed. Not all organizations that qualify are listed in this publication. The list is also available at **www.irs.gov**.

In July, a plane crashed into a residential community in Middleboro, destroying and damaging many homes. Chloe's church, a qualified charitable organization, initiated a fund-raising drive to help the Middleboro citizens whose homes had been affected. Chloe donated $50,000 to First Middleboro Church and suggested to the pastor that $25,000 of her contribution should be given to her sister, Rebecca, whose home had suffered extensive damage. The pastor appointed a committee to award funds to needy citizens. The committee solicited applications from the community and awarded Rebecca $15,000. Discuss whether Chloe is justified in deducting $50,000 as a charitable contribution.

10-4c **Time of Deduction**

A charitable contribution generally is deducted in the year the payment is made. This rule applies to both cash and accrual basis individuals. A contribution is ordinarily deemed to have been made on the delivery of the property to the donee. For example, if a gift of securities (properly endorsed) is made to a qualified charitable organization, the gift is considered complete on the day of delivery or mailing. However, if the donor delivers the certificate to his or her bank or broker or to the issuing corporation, the gift is considered complete on the date the stock is transferred on the books of the corporation.

A contribution made by check is considered delivered on the date of mailing. Thus, a check mailed on December 31, 2016, is deductible on the taxpayer's 2016 tax return. If the contribution is charged on a credit card, the date the charge is made determines the year of deduction.

10-4d **Record-Keeping and Valuation Requirements**

Recall that income tax deductions allowed by law are a matter of legislative grace, but a taxpayer still bears the burden of showing that he or she is entitled to claim the deduction. Not surprisingly, the IRS provides specific documentation requirements that must be met if a charitable contribution deduction is to be protected.

Record-Keeping Requirements

No deduction is allowed for a charitable contribution made to a qualified organization unless the taxpayer gathers (and, in some cases, supplies to the IRS) the appropriate documentation and substantiation. The specific type of documentation required depends on the amount of the contribution and whether the contribution is made in cash or noncash property.[46] In addition, special rules may apply to gifts of certain types of property (e.g., used automobiles) where Congress has noted taxpayer abuse in the past. Further, for certain gifts of noncash property, Form 8283 (Noncash Charitable Contributions) must be attached to the taxpayer's return.

The required substantiation must be obtained before the earlier of (1) the due date (including extensions) of the return for the year the contribution is claimed or (2) the date the return is filed. Failure to comply with the reporting rules may result in disallowance of the charitable contribution deduction. In addition, significant overvaluation exposes the taxpayer to stringent penalties.

Common documentation and substantiation requirements are summarized in Concept Summary 10.2.

Valuation Requirements

Property donated to a charity is generally valued at fair market value at the time the gift is made. The Code and Regulations give very little guidance on the measurement of the

---

[46]The specific documentation thresholds and requirements are provided in § 170(f).

Concept Summary 10.2

Documentation and Substantiation Requirements for Charitable Contributions

Cash gifts	• A deduction is allowed only if the taxpayer has a proper receipt (e.g., bank record such as a canceled check or written statement from the charity) showing the name of the charitable organization and the date and amount of the contribution.
	• A written statement from the charity is required if a payment is for more than $75 and is partly a contribution and partly for goods or services. The statement must provide an estimate of the value of the goods and services received by the donor.
Noncash gifts (e.g., household items)	• A receipt from the charity must be kept for any gift of property other than money. Clothes or other household items are deductible if they are in "good used condition or better" at the time of the gift.
	• If the items are not in good used condition or better and their value is $500 or more, a deduction is allowed if a "qualified appraisal" is included with the return.
Used automobiles	• The deduction is generally limited to the amount the charity receives on the sale of the car. The taxpayer should obtain a statement from the charity documenting the sales price of the automobile.
Cash or noncash gifts of $250 or more	• Written acknowledgment from the charity (or certain payroll records in the case of gifts made by payroll deductions) is required to deduct a single cash or property contribution of $250 or more. The acknowledgment must include the amount of money and a description of any other property contributed, whether the charity provided any goods or services in return for the contribution, and a description and estimated value of the goods or services provided.
Noncash gifts of more than $500	• Additional substantiation (e.g., how the property was acquired and its basis) is required on the tax return if donated noncash property is valued at more than $500. Qualified appraisals may be required if noncash contributions exceed $5,000 in value.
Antiques, paintings, jewelry, and other "tangible personal property"	• The deduction is equal to the property's appreciated FMV only if the charity puts the property to "a use related to its tax-exempt purpose." Otherwise, the deduction is limited to the property's cost. The taxpayer should obtain a statement from the charity documenting the property's use.

fair market value except to say, "The fair market value is the price at which the property would change hands between a willing buyer and a willing seller, neither being under any compulsion to buy or sell and both having reasonable knowledge of relevant facts."

Generally, charitable organizations do not attest to the fair market value of the donated property. Nevertheless, as noted in Concept Summary 10.2, the taxpayer must maintain reliable written evidence of the donation.

TAX IN THE NEWS   Complying with Documentation Requirements Is Critical, Even for IRS Agents

The income tax law is clear that a taxpayer bears the burden to show that he or she is entitled to claim a deduction for a gift made to a qualified charity. Some may argue that the documentation and substantiation rules written by the IRS are overly strict. Nonetheless, if a taxpayer wants to take a deduction for charitable gifts, the best recommendation would be to follow the rules carefully and be able to provide credible support if requested by the IRS.

One taxpayer, a 28-year employee of the IRS, was denied charitable deductions in two years because she was unable to provide convincing evidence that she had made cash gifts of over $20,000 to a New York church (*Margaret Payne*,

T.C. Summary Opinion 2013–64). The evidence Payne provided to support the deduction, a statement on church letterhead, was characterized as a "cut and paste job" that was apparently signed by one of Payne's children. The Tax Court ultimately denied the deduction stating that the "record was full of inconsistencies, contradicting testimony, fabricated documents, and simple untruths."

So if any lessons can be gleaned from this experience, they may be that tax rules apply equally to IRS agents and regular citizens alike, and if a cash gift is made to one's favorite charity, whether it be for $20,000 or $20, legitimate and convincing documentation must be gathered to support it.

GLOBAL TAX ISSUES **Choose the Charity Wisely**

Maiya, a U.S. citizen of Nepali descent, was distressed by the damage caused by a major earthquake in Nepal. She donated $100,000 to the Earthquake Victims' Relief Fund, a Nepali charitable organization that was set up to help victims of the earthquake. Raju, also a U.S. citizen of Nepali descent, donated $100,000 to help with the relief effort. However, Raju's contribution went to his church, which sent the proceeds of a fund drive to the Earthquake Victims' Relief Fund in Nepal. Maiya's contribution is not deductible, but Raju's is. Why? Contributions to charitable organizations are not deductible unless the organization is a U.S. charity.

10-4e Limitations on Charitable Contribution Deduction

The potential charitable contribution deduction is the total of all donations, both money and property, that qualify for the deduction. After this determination is made, the actual amount of the charitable contribution deduction that is allowed for individuals for the tax year is limited as follows:

- If the qualifying contributions for the year total 20 percent or less of AGI, they are fully deductible.

- If the qualifying contributions are more than 20 percent of AGI, the deductible amount may be limited to 20 percent, 30 percent, or 50 percent of AGI, depending on the type of property given and the type of organization to which the donation is made.

- In any case, the maximum charitable contribution deduction may not exceed 50 percent of AGI for the tax year.

To understand the complex rules for computing the amount of a charitable contribution deduction, it is necessary to understand the distinction between capital gain property and ordinary income property. In addition, it is necessary to understand when the 50 percent, 30 percent, and 20 percent limitations apply. If a taxpayer's contributions for the year exceed the applicable percentage limitations, the excess contributions may be carried forward and deducted during a five-year carryover period. These topics are discussed in the sections that follow.

Ordinary Income Property

Ordinary income property is any property that, if sold, will result in the recognition of ordinary income. The term includes inventory for sale in the taxpayer's trade or business, a work of art created by the donor, and a manuscript prepared by the donor. It also includes, *for purposes of the charitable contribution calculation*, a capital asset held by the donor for less than the required holding period for long-term capital gain treatment (long-term is a period longer than one year). To the extent that a disposition of property results in the recognition of ordinary income due to the depreciation recapture rules (see Chapter 17), it is ordinary income property.[47]

If ordinary income property is contributed, the deduction is equal to the fair market value of the property less the amount of ordinary income that would have been reported if the property were sold. In most instances, the deduction is limited to the adjusted basis of the property to the donor.

---

[47]For a more complete discussion of the difference between ordinary income and capital gain property, see Chapter 16.

EXAMPLE
28

Tim donates stock in White Corporation to a university on May 1, 2016. Tim had purchased the stock for $2,500 on March 3, 2016, and the stock had a value of $3,600 when he made the donation. Because he had not held the property long enough to meet the long-term capital gain requirement, Tim would have recognized a short-term capital gain of $1,100 if he had sold the property.

Because short-term capital gain property is treated as ordinary income property for charitable contribution purposes, Tim's charitable contribution deduction is limited to the property's basis of $2,500 ($3,600 − $1,100).

Assume, instead, that the stock had a fair market value of $2,300 (rather than $3,600) when Tim donated it to the university. Because the fair market value now is less than the basis, the charitable contribution deduction is $2,300.

Capital Gain Property

Capital gain property is any property that would have resulted in the recognition of long-term capital gain or § 1231 gain if the property had been sold by the donor.[48] As a general rule, the deduction for a contribution of capital gain property is equal to the fair market value of the property.

Two common exceptions disallow the deductibility of the appreciation on capital gain property. One exception concerns certain private foundations. Private foundations are organizations that traditionally do not receive their funding from the general public (e.g., the Bill and Melinda Gates Foundation). Generally, foundations fall into two categories: operating and nonoperating. A private *operating* foundation spends substantially all of its income in the active conduct of the charitable undertaking for which it was established. Other private foundations are *nonoperating* foundations. Often, only the private foundation knows its status (operating or nonoperating) for sure, and the status can change from year to year.

If capital gain property is contributed to a private *nonoperating* foundation, the taxpayer must reduce the contribution by the long-term capital gain that would have been recognized if the property had been sold at its fair market value. The effect of this provision is to limit the deduction to the property's adjusted basis.[49]

EXAMPLE
29

Ten years ago, Walter purchased land for $8,000 and has held it as an investment since then. This year, when the land is worth $20,000, he donates it to a private *nonoperating* foundation. Walter's charitable contribution is $8,000 ($20,000 − $12,000), the land's basis.

If, instead, Walter had donated the land to either a public charity or a private *operating* foundation, his charitable contribution would have been $20,000, the fair market value of the land.

A second exception applying to capital gain property relates to *tangible personalty*. Tangible personalty is all property that is not realty (land and buildings) and does not include intangible property such as stock or securities. If tangible personalty is contributed to a public charity such as a museum, church, or university, the charitable deduction may have to be reduced. The amount of the reduction is the long-term capital gain that would have been recognized if the property had been sold for its fair market value. In general, the reduction is required if the property is put to an *unrelated use*. The term *unrelated use* means a use that is unrelated to the exempt purpose or function of the charitable organization. For example, artwork donated to the American Red Cross is unlikely to be put to a related use. Instead, the Red Cross would likely sell the art to generate funds that would then be used to support its mission of providing assistance to individuals who have been struck by disasters.

This reduction generally will not apply if the property is, in fact, not put to an unrelated use or if, at the time of the contribution, it was reasonable to anticipate that the property would not be put to an unrelated use by the donee.[50]

---

[48]See General Scheme of Taxation in Chapter 16 for a discussion of holding periods.

[49]§ 170(e)(1)(B)(ii).

[50]§ 170(e)(1)(B)(i) and Reg. § 1.170A–4(b)(3)(ii)(b).

Emma contributes a Picasso painting, for which she paid $20,000, to a local museum. She had owned the painting for four years. It had a value of $30,000 at the time of the donation. The museum displays the painting for five years and subsequently sells it for $50,000.

The charitable contribution is $30,000. It is not reduced by the unrealized appreciation because the painting is not put to an unrelated use even though it is later sold by the museum.

Fifty Percent Ceiling

Contributions made to public charities may not exceed 50 percent of an individual's AGI for the year. The 50 percent ceiling on contributions applies to public charities such as churches; schools; hospitals; and Federal, state, or local governmental units. The 50 percent ceiling also applies to contributions to private operating foundations and certain private nonoperating foundations.

In the remaining discussion of charitable contributions, public charities and private foundations (both operating and nonoperating) that qualify for the 50 percent ceiling will be referred to as *50 percent organizations*.

Thirty Percent Ceiling

A 30 percent ceiling applies to contributions of cash and ordinary income property to private nonoperating foundations that are not 50 percent organizations. The 30 percent ceiling also applies to contributions of appreciated capital gain property to 50 percent organizations.[51]

In the event the contributions for any one tax year involve both 50 percent and 30 percent property, the allowable deduction comes first from the 50 percent property.

During the year, Lisa makes the following donations to her church: cash of $2,000 and unimproved land worth $30,000. Lisa had purchased the land four years ago for $22,000 and held it as an investment. Therefore, it is capital gain property. Lisa's AGI for the year is $60,000. Disregarding percentage limitations, Lisa's potential deduction is $32,000 [$2,000 (cash) + $30,000 (fair market value of land)].

In applying the percentage limitations, however, the *current* deduction for the land is limited to $18,000 [30% (limitation applicable to capital gain property) × $60,000 (AGI)]. Thus, the total current deduction is $20,000 ($2,000 cash + $18,000 land). Note that the total deduction does not exceed $30,000, which is 50% of Lisa's AGI.

Twenty Percent Ceiling

A 20 percent ceiling applies to contributions of appreciated capital gain property to private nonoperating foundations that are not 50 percent organizations.

Concept Summary 10.3 summarizes limitations on the deductibility of charitable gifts.

Contribution Carryovers

Contributions that exceed the percentage limitations for the current year can be carried over for five years. In the carryover process, such contributions do not lose their identity for limitation purposes. Thus, if the contribution originally involved 30 percent property, the carryover will continue to be classified as 30 percent property in the carryover year.

Assume the same facts as in Example 31. Because only $18,000 of the $30,000 value of the land is deducted in the current year, the balance of $12,000 may be carried over to the following year. But the carryover will still be treated as capital gain property and is subject to the 30%-of-AGI limitation.

---

[51]Under a special election, a taxpayer may choose to permanently forgo a deduction of the appreciation on capital gain property. Referred to as the reduced deduction election, this enables the taxpayer to move from the 30% limitation to the 50% limitation. See § 170(b)(1)(C)(iii).

Concept Summary 10.3

Determining the Deduction for Contributions of Appreciated Property by Individuals

If the Type of Property Contributed Is:	And the Property Is Contributed to:	The Contribution Is Measured by:	But the Deduction Is Limited to:
1. Capital gain property (see Example 31)	A 50% organization	Fair market value of the property	30% of AGI
2. Ordinary income property (see Example 28)	A 50% organization	The basis of the property*	50% of AGI
3. Capital gain property (and the property is tangible personal property put to an unrelated use by the donee; see Example 30)	A 50% organization	The basis of the property*	50% of AGI
4. Capital gain property (see Example 29)	A private nonoperating foundation that is not a 50% organization	The basis of the property*	The lesser of: 1. 20% of AGI 2. 50% of AGI minus other contributions to 50% organizations

* If the fair market value of the property is less than the adjusted basis (i.e., the property has declined in value instead of appreciating), the fair market value is used.

In applying the percentage limitations, current charitable contributions must be claimed first before any carryovers can be considered. If carryovers involve more than one year, they are utilized in a first-in, first-out order.

LO.7

List the business and personal expenditures that are deductible either as miscellaneous itemized deductions or as other itemized deductions.

10-5 MISCELLANEOUS ITEMIZED DEDUCTIONS

In general, no deduction is allowed for personal, living, or family expenses.[52] However, a taxpayer who is an employee, for example, may incur a number of expenditures related to employment. In this situation, if the employee incurs unreimbursed business expenses or expenses that are reimbursed under a *nonaccountable plan*, including travel and transportation, the expenses are deductible as miscellaneous itemized deductions.[53] Importantly, however, some other expenses also fall into the miscellaneous itemized deduction category. These expenses are deductible only if, in total, they exceed 2 percent of the taxpayer's AGI. These miscellaneous itemized deductions that are subject to the 2%-of-AGI limitation include (but are not limited to) the following:

- Professional dues to membership organizations.
- Cost of uniforms or other clothing that cannot be used for normal wear.
- Fees incurred for the preparation of one's tax return or fees incurred for tax litigation before the IRS or the courts.
- Job-hunting costs.
- Fee paid for a safe deposit box used to store papers and documents relating to taxable income-producing investments.
- Investment expenses that are deductible under § 212 as discussed in Chapter 6.

---

[52]§ 262.

[53]Actors and performing artists who meet certain requirements are not subject to this rule. See § 62(a)(2)(B).

- Appraisal fees to determine the amount of a casualty loss or the fair market value of donated property.
- Hobby losses up to the amount of hobby income (refer to Chapter 6).
- Unreimbursed employee expenses (refer to Chapter 9).

Certain employee business expenses that are reimbursed are not itemized deductions, but are deducted *for* AGI. Employee business expenses are discussed in depth in Chapter 9.

10-6 OTHER MISCELLANEOUS DEDUCTIONS

Certain expenses and losses do not fall into any category of itemized deductions already discussed but are nonetheless deductible. The following expenses and losses are deductible on line 28 of Schedule A as Other Miscellaneous Deductions. These are not subject to the 2%-of-AGI floor.

- Gambling losses up to the amount of gambling winnings.
- Impairment-related work expenses of a handicapped person.
- Federal estate tax on income in respect of a decedent.
- Deduction for repayment of amounts under a claim of right (but only if more than $3,000; discussed in Chapter 18).
- The unrecovered investment in an annuity contract when the annuity ceases by reason of death, discussed in Chapter 4.

10-7 COMPREHENSIVE EXAMPLE OF SCHEDULE A

Harry and Jean Brown (ages 42 and 43, respectively), married filing jointly, had the following transactions for 2015:

Medicines that required a prescription	$ 430
Doctor and dentist bills paid and not reimbursed	3,120
Medical insurance premium payments	1,200
Contact lenses	170
Transportation for medical purposes on March 1, 2015 (230 miles × 23 cents/mile + $10.00 parking)	63
State income tax withheld (This amount exceeds the sales tax from the sales tax table)	3,900
Real estate taxes	1,580
Interest paid on qualified residence mortgage	2,340
Qualifying charitable contributions paid by check	860
Transportation in performing charitable services (800 miles × 14 cents/mile + $7.00 parking and tolls)	119
Unreimbursed employee expenses (from Form 2106)	870
Tax return preparation	150
Safe deposit box (used for keeping investment documents and tax records)	170

The Browns' AGI is $40,000. Their completed 2015 Schedule A (on the following page) reports itemized deductions totaling $10,172. A 2015 example (and related illustration using a 2015 Schedule A) is used because the 2016 form is not yet available.

SCHEDULE A **(Form 1040)** Department of the Treasury Internal Revenue Service (99)	**Itemized Deductions** ▶ Information about Schedule A and its separate instructions is at *www.irs.gov/schedulea*. ▶ **Attach to Form 1040.**	OMB No. 1545-0074 **2015** Attachment Sequence No. **07**

Name(s) shown on Form 1040	Your social security number
Harry and Jean Brown	*111-11-1111*

Caution: Do not include expenses reimbursed or paid by others.

Medical and Dental Expenses	**1** Medical and dental expenses (see instructions) . . .	**1**	*4,983*	
	2 Enter amount from Form 1040, line 38 **2** *40,000*			
	3 Multiply line 2 by 10% (.10). But if either you or your spouse was born before January 2, 1951, multiply line 2 by 7.5% (.075) instead	**3**	*4,000*	
	4 Subtract line 3 from line 1. If line 3 is more than line 1, enter -0-		**4**	*983*
Taxes You Paid	**5** State and local **(check only one box):** a ☒ Income taxes, **or** . . . . b ☐ General sales taxes	**5**	*3,900*	
	6 Real estate taxes (see instructions)	**6**	*1,580*	
	7 Personal property taxes	**7**		
	8 Other taxes. List type and amount ▶ _____	**8**		
	9 Add lines 5 through 8		**9**	*5,480*
Interest You Paid **Note:** Your mortgage interest deduction may be limited (see instructions).	**10** Home mortgage interest and points reported to you on Form 1098	**10**	*2,340*	
	11 Home mortgage interest not reported to you on Form 1098. If paid to the person from whom you bought the home, see instructions and show that person's name, identifying no., and address ▶ _____ _____	**11**		
	12 Points not reported to you on Form 1098. See instructions for special rules	**12**		
	13 Mortgage insurance premiums (see instructions)	**13**		
	14 Investment interest. Attach Form 4952 if required. (See instructions.)	**14**		
	15 Add lines 10 through 14		**15**	*2,340*
Gifts to Charity If you made a gift and got a benefit for it, see instructions.	**16** Gifts by cash or check. If you made any gift of $250 or more, see instructions	**16**	*860*	
	17 Other than by cash or check. If any gift of $250 or more, see instructions. You **must** attach Form 8283 if over $500 . . .	**17**	*119*	
	18 Carryover from prior year	**18**		
	19 Add lines 16 through 18		**19**	*979*
Casualty and Theft Losses	**20** Casualty or theft loss(es). Attach Form 4684. (See instructions.)		**20**	
Job Expenses and Certain Miscellaneous Deductions	**21** Unreimbursed employee expenses—job travel, union dues, job education, etc. Attach Form 2106 or 2106-EZ if required. (See instructions.) ▶ _____	**21**	*870*	
	22 Tax preparation fees	**22**	*150*	
	23 Other expenses—investment, safe deposit box, etc. List type and amount ▶ *Safe deposit box* _____	**23**	*170*	
	24 Add lines 21 through 23	**24**	*1,190*	
	25 Enter amount from Form 1040, line 38 **25** *40,000*			
	26 Multiply line 25 by 2% (.02)	**26**	*800*	
	27 Subtract line 26 from line 24. If line 26 is more than line 24, enter -0-		**27**	*390*
Other Miscellaneous Deductions	**28** Other—from list in instructions. List type and amount ▶ _____ _____		**28**	
Total Itemized Deductions	**29** Is Form 1040, line 38, over $154,950? ☒ **No.** Your deduction is not limited. Add the amounts in the far right column for lines 4 through 28. Also, enter this amount on Form 1040, line 40. } . .		**29**	*10,172*
	☐ **Yes.** Your deduction may be limited. See the Itemized Deductions Worksheet in the instructions to figure the amount to enter.			
	30 If you elect to itemize deductions even though they are less than your standard deduction, check here . . . . ▶ ☐			

For Paperwork Reduction Act Notice, see Form 1040 instructions.   Cat. No. 17145C   **Schedule A (Form 1040) 2015**

TAX IN THE NEWS **The First Family and Itemized Deduction Phaseouts**

In 2015, President Barack H. and Michelle L. Obama itemized deductions on their 2014 tax return. Because of their income level, their itemized deductions were reduced by $5,170 as shown in the column to the right.

Because the marginal rate of 33 percent applied to the Obamas' taxable income in 2014, the phaseout of itemized deductions cost them $1,706 in additional Federal income tax ($5,170 reduction × 33% marginal tax rate). Over the years, phaseouts such as this have been a popular way to raise tax revenues without increasing tax rates.

Itemized Deductions	
Taxes	$ 54,390
Interest	39,566
Charitable contributions	70,712
Total itemized deductions	$164,668
Reduction due to phaseout [($477,383 AGI − $305,050) × 3%]	(5,170)
Itemized deductions allowed	$159,498

10-8 OVERALL LIMITATION ON CERTAIN ITEMIZED DEDUCTIONS

LO.8

Recognize the limitation on certain itemized deductions applicable to high-income taxpayers.

Similar in effect to the exemption phaseout described in Chapter 3, high-income taxpayers also are subject to a limitation on the tax benefits from certain itemized deductions. In 2016, the phaseout of itemized deductions (also referred to as a *cutback adjustment*) applies to married taxpayers filing jointly whose AGI exceeds $311,300 ($259,400 for single filers).[54] Phaseouts of this type are sometimes referred to as "stealth taxes." The "Tax in the News" above reports the effect of the limitation on President and Mrs. Obama's 2014 income tax return, which required them to pay $1,706 more in Federal income taxes than they would have paid had their itemized deductions been fully deductible.

The limitation applies to the following frequently encountered itemized deductions:

- Taxes.
- Home mortgage interest, including points.
- Charitable contributions.
- Unreimbursed employee expenses subject to the 2%-of-AGI floor.
- All other expenses subject to the 2%-of-AGI floor.

The following are *not* subject to the limitation on itemized deductions:

- Medical expenses.
- Investment interest expense.
- Nonbusiness casualty and theft losses.
- Gambling losses.

Taxpayers subject to the limitation must reduce itemized deductions by the *lesser* of:

- 3 percent of the amount by which AGI exceeds $311,300 ($259,400 if single).
- 80 percent of itemized deductions that are affected by the limit.

The overall limitation is applied after applying all other limitations to those itemized deductions that are affected by the overall limitation. For example, other limitations apply to charitable contributions, certain meals and entertainment expenses, and certain miscellaneous itemized deductions.

---

[54]§ 68. The AGI thresholds are $285,350 for heads of household and $155,650 for married taxpayers filing separately. In 2015, the phaseouts applied to married taxpayers filing jointly whose AGI exceeded $309,900 ($258,250 for single taxpayers, $284,050 for heads of household, and $154,950 for married taxpayers filing separately).

EXAMPLE 33

Gavin, who is single and age 45, had AGI of $275,000 for 2016. He incurred the following expenses and losses during the year:

Medical expenses before 10%-of-AGI limitation	$29,500
State and local income taxes	3,200
Real estate taxes	2,800
Home mortgage interest	7,200
Charitable contributions	2,000
Casualty loss before 10% limitation (after $100 floor)	29,000
Unreimbursed employee expenses (subject to 2%-of-AGI limitation)	5,800
Gambling losses (Gavin had $3,000 of gambling income)	7,000

Gavin's itemized deductions *before* the overall limitation are computed as follows:

Medical expenses [$29,500 − (10% × $275,000)]	$ 2,000
State and local income taxes	3,200
Real estate taxes	2,800
Home mortgage interest	7,200
Charitable contributions	2,000
Casualty loss [$29,000 − (10% × $275,000)]	1,500
Unreimbursed employee expenses [$5,800 − (2% × $275,000)]	300
Gambling losses ($7,000 loss limited to $3,000 of gambling income)	3,000
Total itemized deductions before overall limitation	$22,000

Gavin's itemized deductions subject to the overall limitation are as follows:

State and local income taxes	$ 3,200
Real estate taxes	2,800
Home mortgage interest	7,200
Charitable contributions	2,000
Unreimbursed employee expenses	300
Total	$15,500

Gavin must reduce the amount by the smaller of the following:

• 3% × ($275,000 AGI − $259,400)	$ 468
• 80% of itemized deductions subject to limitation ($15,500 × .80)	12,400

Therefore, the amount of the reduction is $468, and Gavin has $21,532 of deductible itemized deductions, computed as follows:

Deductible itemized deductions subject to overall limitation ($15,500 − $468)	$15,032
Itemized deductions not subject to overall limitation:	
Medical expenses	2,000
Casualty loss	1,500
Gambling losses	3,000
Deductible itemized deductions	$21,532

LO.9

Identify tax planning strategies that can maximize the benefit of itemized deductions.

10-9 TAX PLANNING

10-9a Effective Utilization of Itemized Deductions

Because an individual may use the standard deduction in one year and itemize deductions in another year, it is frequently possible to obtain maximum benefit by shifting itemized deductions from one year to another. For example, if a taxpayer's itemized deductions and the standard deduction are approximately the same for each year of a two-year period, the taxpayer should use the standard deduction in one year and shift itemized deductions (to the extent permitted by law) to the other year. The individual could, for example, prepay a church pledge for a particular year to shift the deduction to the current year or avoid paying end-of-the-year medical expenses to shift the deduction to the following year.

10-9b Utilization of Medical Deductions

When a taxpayer anticipates that medical expenses will approximate the percentage floor, much might be done to generate a deductible excess. Any of the following procedures can help build a deduction by the end of the year:

- Incur the obligation for needed dental work or have needed work carried out.[55]
- Have elective remedial surgery that may have been postponed from prior years.
- Incur the obligation for capital improvements to the taxpayer's personal residence recommended by a physician (e.g., an air filtration system to alleviate a respiratory disorder).

As an aid to taxpayers who may experience temporary cash-flow problems at the end of the year, the use of credit cards is deemed to be payment for purposes of timing the deductibility of charitable and medical expenses.

On December 13, 2016, Marge (a calendar year taxpayer) purchases two pairs of prescription contact lenses and one pair of prescribed orthopedic shoes for a total of $450. These purchases are separately charged to Marge's credit card. On January 6, 2017, Marge receives her statement containing these charges and makes payment shortly thereafter.

The purchases are deductible as medical expenses in the year charged (2016) and not in the year the account is settled (2017).

EXAMPLE
34

Recognizing which expenditures qualify for the medical deduction also may be crucial to exceeding the percentage limitations.

Ethan employs Lana (an unrelated party) to care for his incapacitated and dependent mother. Lana is not a trained nurse but spends approximately one-half of the time performing nursing duties (e.g., administering injections and providing physical therapy) and the rest of the time doing household chores. An allocable portion of Lana's wages that Ethan pays (including the employer's portion of FICA taxes) qualifies as a medical expense.

EXAMPLE
35

10-9c Timing the Payment of Deductible Taxes

It is sometimes possible to defer or accelerate the payment of certain deductible taxes, such as state income tax, real property tax, and personal property tax. For instance, the final installment of estimated state income tax is generally due after the end of a given tax year. Accelerating the payment of the final installment could result in larger itemized deductions for the current year.

Jenny, who is single, expects to have itemized deductions of $6,000 in 2016 and $4,000 in 2017. She plans to pay $900 as the final installment on her 2016 estimated state income tax, which is due on January 15, 2017. The standard deduction for 2016 is $6,300 for single taxpayers. If Jenny does not pay the final installment until 2017, she will not itemize in either 2016 or 2017.

However, if she pays the final installment in December 2016, her itemized deductions will be $6,900 ($6,000 + $900) in 2016 and she will benefit from itemizing.

EXAMPLE
36

---

[55]Prepayment of medical expenses does not generate a current deduction unless the taxpayer is under an obligation to make the payment.

10-9d **Protecting the Interest Deduction**

Although the deductibility of prepaid interest by a cash basis taxpayer has been severely restricted, a notable exception allows a deduction for points paid by the buyer to obtain financing for the purchase or improvement of a principal residence in the year of payment. However, such points must actually be paid by the taxpayer obtaining the loan and must represent a charge for the use of money. It has been held that points paid from the mortgage proceeds do not satisfy the payment requirement.[56] Also, the portion of the points attributable to service charges does not represent deductible interest.[57] Taxpayers financing home purchases or improvements usually should direct their planning toward avoiding these two hurdles to immediate deductibility.

In rare instances, a taxpayer may find it desirable to forgo the immediate expensing of points in the year paid. Instead, it could prove beneficial to capitalize the points and write them off as interest expense over the life of the mortgage.

EXAMPLE 37

Alexander purchases a home on December 15, 2016, for $380,000 with $120,000 cash and a 15-year mortgage of $260,000 financed by the Greater Metropolis National Bank. Alexander pays two points in addition to interest allocated to the period from December 15 until December 31, 2016, at an annual rate of 4%.

If Alexander does not have enough itemized deductions to exceed the standard deduction for 2016, he should elect to capitalize the points and amortize them over 15 years. In this instance, Alexander would deduct $346.67 for 2017, as part of his qualified residence interest expense [$5,200 (two points) divided by 15 years], if he elects to itemize that year.

Because personal (consumer) interest is not deductible, taxpayers should consider making use of home equity loans. Recall that these loans utilize the personal residence of the taxpayer as security. The funds from these loans can be used for personal purposes (e.g., auto purchases and vacations). By making use of home equity loans, therefore, what would have been nondeductible personal interest becomes deductible qualified residence interest.

10-9e **Ensuring the Charitable Contribution Deduction**

For a charitable contribution deduction to be available, the recipient must be a qualified charitable organization. Sometimes the mechanics of how the contribution is carried out can determine whether a deduction results.

EXAMPLE 38

Fumiko wants to donate $5,000 to her church's mission in Kobe, Japan. In this regard, she considers three alternatives:

1. Send the money directly to the mission.
2. Give the money to her church in Charlotte with the understanding that it is to be passed on to the mission.
3. Give the money directly to the missionary in charge of the mission who is currently in the United States on a fund-raising trip.

If Fumiko wants to obtain a deduction for the contribution, she should choose alternative 2. A direct donation to the mission (alternative 1) is not deductible because the mission is a foreign charity. A direct gift to the missionary (alternative 3) does not comply because an individual cannot be a qualified charity for income tax purposes.[58]

---

[56]*Alan A. Rubnitz*, 67 T.C. 621 (1977). Seller-paid points may also be deductible by the buyer under the provisions of Rev.Proc. 94–27, cited in footnote 34.

[57]*Donald L. Wilkerson*, 70 T.C. 240 (1978).

[58]*Thomas E. Lesslie*, 36 TCM 495, T.C.Memo. 1977–111.

When making noncash donations, the type of property chosen can have decided implications in determining the amount, if any, of the deduction.

EXAMPLE 39

Sam wants to give $60,000 in value to his church in some form other than cash. In this connection, he considers four alternatives:

1. Stock held for two years as an investment with a basis of $100,000 and a fair market value of $60,000.
2. Stock held for five years as an investment with a basis of $10,000 and a fair market value of $60,000.
3. The rent-free use for a year of a building that normally leases for $5,000 a month.
4. A valuable stamp collection held as an investment and owned for 10 years with a basis of $10,000 and a fair market value of $60,000. The church plans to sell the collection if and when it is donated.

Alternative 1 is ill-advised as the subject of the gift. Even though Sam would obtain a deduction of $60,000, he would forgo the potential loss of $40,000 that would be recognized if the property were sold.[59]

Alternative 2 makes good sense because the deduction still is $60,000 and none of the $50,000 of appreciation that has occurred must be recognized as income.

Alternative 3 yields no deduction at all and is not a wise choice.

Alternative 4 involves tangible personalty that the recipient does not plan to use. As a result, the amount of the deduction is limited to $10,000, the stamp collection's basis.[60]

For property transfers (particularly real estate), the ceiling limitations on the amount of the deduction allowed in any one year (50 percent, 30 percent, or 20 percent of AGI, as the case may be) could be a factor to take into account. With proper planning, donations can be controlled to stay within the limitations and therefore avoid the need for a carryover of unused charitable contributions.

EXAMPLE 40

Andrew wants to donate to Eastern University (a qualified charitable organization) a tract of unimproved land held as an investment. The land has been held for six years and has a current fair market value of $300,000 and a basis to Andrew of $50,000. Andrew's AGI for the current year is estimated to be $200,000, and he expects much the same for the next few years. In the current year, he deeds (transfers) an undivided one-fifth interest in the real estate to the university.

What has Andrew in Example 40 accomplished for income tax purposes? In the current year, he will be allowed a charitable contribution deduction of $60,000 ($1/5 \times $300,000), which will be within the applicable limitation of AGI (30% × $200,000). Presuming no other charitable contributions for the year, Andrew has avoided the possibility of a carryover. In future years, Andrew can arrange donations of undivided interests in the real estate to stay within the bounds of the percentage limitations. The only difficulty with this approach is the need to revalue the real estate each year before the donation, because the amount of the deduction is based on the fair market value of the interest contributed at the time of the donation.

---

[59]*LaVar M. Withers*, 69 T.C. 900 (1978).

[60]No reduction of appreciation is necessary in alternative 2 because stock is intangible property and not tangible personalty.

REFOCUS ON THE BIG PICTURE

ITEMIZED DEDUCTIONS CAN REDUCE THE AFTER-TAX COST OF MAJOR PURCHASES

Because the Federal tax law provides that qualified residence interest and real estate taxes are deductible by individual taxpayers, the after-tax cost of a home purchase will be reduced by the tax savings associated with these itemized tax deductions (see Example 1). Given the Williamsons' projected taxable income, they are in the 28 percent Federal income tax bracket and the 6 percent state income tax bracket (i.e., aggregate marginal tax bracket of 34 percent). As a result, the after-tax cost of financing the purchase of the home will be:

Nondeductible principal payments	$ 2,000
Deductible qualified residence interest and real estate taxes	
[($37,000 + $4,000) × (1 − .34)]	27,060
Total	$29,060
After-tax monthly cost ($29,060 ÷ 12)	$ 2,422

Because the Williamsons will be able to itemize their deductions if they purchase a new home and will be able to deduct most of their monthly house payment, the home purchase will be affordable (see Examples 16 and 21).

What If?

What if the Williamsons use the less expensive route to finance the purchase of their home by using their retirement and taxable portfolio as security for the loan? What may at first appear to be a cost-effective approach ends up being more costly when considering the impact of the tax law. With this approach, the interest expense is not deductible because it is not qualified residence interest (see Example 21); further, it is not deductible as investment interest (see Chapter 11). Therefore, the after-tax cost of financing the home using this approach makes the home unaffordable.

Nondeductible principal and interest payments ($2,000 + $35,000)	$37,000
Deductible real estate taxes [$4,000 × (1 − .34)]	2,640
Total	$39,640
After-tax monthly cost ($39,640 ÷ 12)	$ 3,303

Key Terms

Acquisition indebtedness, 10-15

Capital gain property, 10-24

Charitable contribution, 10-19

Health Savings Account (HSA), 10-9

Home equity loans, 10-15

Medical expense, 10-3

Miscellaneous itemized deductions, 10-26

Ordinary income property, 10-23

Points, 10-16

Qualified residence interest, 10-15

Discussion Questions

1. **LO.1, 2** Dan, a self-employed individual taxpayer, prepared his own income tax return for the past year and has asked you to check it for accuracy. Your review indicates that Dan failed to claim certain business entertainment expenses.
   a. Will the correction of this omission affect the amount of medical expenses Dan can deduct? Explain.
   b. Would it matter if Dan were employed rather than self-employed? Explain.

2. **LO.2** Joe was in an accident and required cosmetic surgery for injuries to his nose. He also had the doctor do additional surgery to reshape his chin, which had not been injured. Will the cosmetic surgery to Joe's nose qualify as a medical expense? Will the cosmetic surgery to Joe's chin qualify as a medical expense? Explain.

3. **LO.2, 9** Jerry and Ernie are comparing their tax situations. Both are paying all of the nursing home expenses of their parents. Jerry can include the expenses in computing his medical expense deduction, but Ernie cannot. What explanation can you offer for the difference?

4. **LO.2** Cheryl incurred $8,700 of medical expenses in November 2016. On December 5, the clinic where she was treated mailed her the insurance claim form it had prepared for her with a suggestion that she sign and return the form immediately to receive her reimbursement from the insurance company by December 31. What tax issues should Cheryl consider in deciding whether to sign and return the form in December 2016 or January 2017? Issue ID

5. **LO.2** David, a sole proprietor of a bookstore, pays a $7,500 premium for medical insurance for him and his family. Joan, an employee of a small firm that doesn't provide her with medical insurance, pays medical insurance premiums of $8,000 for herself. How does the tax treatment differ for David and Joan?

6. **LO.2** Jayden, a calendar year taxpayer, paid $16,000 in medical expenses and sustained a $20,000 casualty loss in 2016. He expects $12,000 of the medical expenses and $14,000 of the casualty loss to be reimbursed by insurance companies in 2017. Before considering any limitations on these deductions, how much can Jayden include in determining his itemized deductions for 2016?

7. **LO.2** Jacob, a self-employed taxpayer, is married and has two children. He has asked you to explain the tax and nontax advantages of creating a Health Savings Account (HSA) for him and his family.

8. **LO.5, 9** Diane owns a principal residence in Georgia, a townhouse in San Francisco, and a yacht in Cape Cod. All of the properties have mortgages on which Diane pays interest. What are the limitations on Diane's mortgage interest deduction? What strategy should Diane consider to maximize her mortgage interest deduction? Decision Making

9. **LO.5, 9** Mason Gregg's car was destroyed by a flood. Unfortunately, his insurance had lapsed two days before he incurred the loss. Mason uses his car for both business and personal use. Mason, who is self-employed, does not have adequate savings to replace the car and must borrow money to purchase a new car. He is considering taking out a home equity loan, at a 5% interest rate, to obtain funds for the purchase. Margaret, his wife, would prefer not to do so because they paid off their mortgage recently and she does not want to incur any obligations related to their home. She would prefer to sell some of their stock in Bluebird, Inc., to raise funds to purchase the new car. Mason does not want to sell the stock because it has declined in value since they purchased it and he is convinced that its price will increase in the next two years. Mason has suggested that they obtain conventional financing for the purchase from their bank, which charges 7% interest on Issue ID

car loans. Identify the tax issues related to each of the three alternatives Mason and Margaret are considering.

10. **LO.5** Commercial Bank has initiated an advertising campaign that encourages customers to take out home equity loans to pay for purchases of automobiles. Are there any tax advantages related to this type of borrowing? Explain.

11. **LO.5** Thomas purchased a personal residence from Rachel. To sell the residence, Rachel agreed to pay $5,500 in points related to Thomas's mortgage. Discuss the deductibility of the points.

12. **LO.6** The city of Lawrence recently was hit by a tornado, leaving many families in need of food, clothing, shelter, and other necessities. Betty contributed $500 to a family whose home was completely destroyed by the tornado. Jack contributed $700 to the family's church, which gave the money to the family. Discuss the deductibility of these contributions.

13. **LO.6** Mike purchased four $100 tickets to a fund-raising dinner and dance sponsored by the public library, a qualified charitable organization. In its advertising for the event, the library indicated that the cost of the tickets would be deductible for Federal income tax purposes. Comment on the library's assertion.

Issue ID 14. **LO.6, 9** William, a high school teacher, earns about $50,000 each year. In December 2016, he won $1 million in the state lottery. William plans to donate $100,000 to his church. He has asked you, his tax adviser, whether he should donate the $100,000 in 2016 or 2017. Identify the tax issues related to William's decision.

Computational Exercises

15. **LO.2** Barbara incurred the following expenses during the year: $840 dues at a health club she joined at the suggestion of her physician to improve her general physical condition, $240 for multiple vitamins and antioxidant vitamins, $500 for a smoking cessation program, $250 for nonprescription nicotine gum, $600 for insulin, and $7,200 for funeral expenses for her mother who passed away in June. Before considering the AGI limitation, what amount may Barbara include in computing her medical expense deduction?

16. **LO.3** Tabitha sells real estate on March 2 for $260,000. The buyer, Ramona, pays the real estate taxes of $5,200 for the calendar year, which is the real estate property tax year. Assume that this is not a leap year.

a. Determine the real estate taxes apportioned to and deductible by the seller, Tabitha, and the amount of taxes deductible by Ramona.

b. Calculate Ramona's basis in the property and the amount realized by Tabitha from the sale.

17. **LO.4** Pierre, a cash basis, unmarried taxpayer, had $1,400 of state income tax withheld during 2016. Also in 2016, Pierre paid $455 that was due when he filed his 2015 state income tax return and made estimated payments of $975 toward his 2016 state income tax liability. When Pierre files his 2016 Federal income tax return in April 2017, he elects to itemize deductions, which amount to $10,650, including the state income tax payments and withholdings, all of which reduce his taxable income.

a. What is Pierre's 2016 state income tax deduction?

b. As a result of overpaying his 2016 state income tax, Pierre receives a refund of $630 early in 2017. The standard deduction for single taxpayers for 2016 was $6,300. How much of the $630 will Pierre include in his 2017 gross income?

18. **LO.4** Derek, a cash basis, unmarried taxpayer, had $610 of state income tax withheld during 2016. Also in 2016, Derek paid $50 that was due when he filed his 2015 state income tax return and made estimated payments of $100 toward his 2016 state income tax liability. When Derek files his 2016 Federal income tax return in April 2017, he elects to take the standard deduction, which reduced his taxable income. As a result of overpaying his 2016 state income tax, Derek receives a refund of $435 early in 2017. How much of the $435 will Derek include in his 2017 gross income?

19. **LO.5** Miller owns a personal residence with a fair market value of $195,000 and an outstanding first mortgage of $157,500. Miller gets a second mortgage on the residence and in return borrows $10,000 to purchase new jet skis. How much of the first and second mortgage debt is treated as qualified residence indebtedness?

20. **LO.6** Donna donates stock in Chipper Corporation to the American Red Cross on September 10, 2016. She purchased the stock for $18,100 on December 28, 2015, and it had a fair market value of $27,000 when she made the donation.
    a. What is Donna's charitable contribution deduction?
    b. Assume instead that the stock had a fair market value of $15,000 (rather than $27,000) when it was donated to the American Red Cross. What is Donna's charitable contribution deduction?

21. **LO.7** Issac has AGI of $73,400 and incurred the following expenses. How much of the business and personal expenditures are deductible (after any limitation) either as miscellaneous itemized deductions or as other itemized deductions?

Cost of uniforms	$ 535
Tax return preparation fees	600
Fee paid for a safe deposit box used to store papers and documents relating to taxable income-producing investments	65
Job-hunting costs	1,100

22. **LO.8** Pedro, who is a single taxpayer, had AGI of $328,000 for 2016. He incurred the following expenses during the year:

Medical expenses before 10%-of-AGI limitation	$12,000
State and local income taxes	8,900
Real estate taxes	1,600
Home mortgage interest	16,000
Charitable contributions	2,200
Deductible investment interest expense	1,700

Compute the amount of Pedro's itemized deductions after any applicable reductions.

23. **LO.9** The Wilmoths plan to purchase a house but want to determine the after-tax cost of financing its purchase. Given their projected taxable income, the Wilmoths are in the 28% Federal income tax bracket and the 8% state income tax bracket (i.e., an aggregate marginal tax bracket of 36%). The total cash outlay during the first year of ownership will be $23,400 ($1,200 principal payments, $22,200 qualified residence interest payments). Determine the initial year after-tax cost of financing the purchase of the home.

Problems

Communications   24. **LO.2** Emma Doyle, age 55, is employed as a corporate attorney. For calendar year 2016, she had AGI of $100,000 and paid the following medical expenses:

Medical insurance premiums	$3,700
Doctor and dentist bills for Bob and April (Emma's parents)	6,800
Doctor and dentist bills for Emma	5,200
Prescription medicines for Emma	400
Nonprescription insulin for Emma	350

Bob and April would qualify as Emma's dependents except that they file a joint return. Emma's medical insurance policy does not cover them. Emma filed a claim for reimbursement of $2,800 of her own expenses with her insurance company in December 2016 and received the reimbursement in January 2017. What is Emma's maximum allowable medical expense deduction for 2016? Prepare a memo for your firm's tax files in which you document your conclusions.

25. **LO.2** Reba, who is single and age 45, does a lot of business entertaining at home. Lawrence, Reba's 84-year-old dependent grandfather, lived with Reba until this year, when he moved to Lakeside Nursing Home because he needs medical and nursing care. During the year, Reba made the following payments on behalf of Lawrence:

Room at Lakeside	$11,000
Meals for Lawrence at Lakeside	2,200
Doctor and nurse fees at Lakeside	1,700
Cable TV service for Lawrence's room at Lakeside	380
Total	$15,280

Lakeside has medical staff in residence. Disregarding the 10%-of-AGI floor, how much, if any, of these expenses qualifies for a medical expense deduction by Reba?

26. **LO.2** Paul, age 62, suffers from emphysema and severe allergies and, upon the recommendation of his physician, has a dust elimination system installed in his personal residence. In connection with the system, Paul incurs and pays the following amounts during 2016:

Doctor and hospital bills	$ 2,500
Dust elimination system	10,000
Increase in utility bills due to the system	450
Cost of certified appraisal	300

In addition, Paul pays $750 for prescribed medicines.

The system has an estimated useful life of 20 years. The appraisal was to determine the value of Paul's residence with and without the system. The appraisal states that his residence was worth $350,000 before the system was installed and $356,000 after the installation. Paul's AGI for the year was $50,000. How much of the medical expenses qualify for the medical expense deduction in 2016?

27. **LO.2** For calendar year 2016, Jean was a self-employed consultant with no employees. She had $80,000 of net profit from consulting and paid $7,000 in medical insurance premiums on a policy covering 2016. How much of these premiums may Jean deduct as a deduction *for* AGI? How much may she deduct as an itemized deduction (subject to the AGI floor)?

28. **LO.2** During 2016, Susan, age 49, incurred and paid the following expenses for Beth (her daughter), Ed (her father), and herself:

Surgery for Beth	$4,500
Red River Academy charges for Beth:	
Tuition	5,100
Room, board, and other expenses	4,800
Psychiatric treatment	5,100
Doctor bills for Ed	2,200
Prescription drugs for Susan, Beth, and Ed	780
Insulin for Ed	540
Nonprescription drugs for Susan, Beth, and Ed	570
Charges at Heartland Nursing Home for Ed:	
Medical care	5,000
Lodging	2,700
Meals	2,650

Beth qualifies as Susan's dependent, and Ed would also qualify except that he receives $7,400 of taxable retirement benefits from his former employer. Beth's psychiatrist recommended Red River Academy because of its small classes and specialized psychiatric treatment program that is needed to treat Beth's illness. Ed, who is a paraplegic and diabetic, entered Heartland in October. Heartland offers the type of care that he requires.

Upon the recommendation of a physician, Susan has an air filtration system installed in her personal residence. She suffers from severe allergies. In connection with this equipment, Susan incurs and pays the following amounts during the year:

Filtration system and cost of installation	$6,500
Increase in utility bills due to the system	700
Cost of certified appraisal	360

The system has an estimated useful life of 10 years. The appraisal was to determine the value of Susan's residence with and without the system. The appraisal states that the system increased the value of Susan's residence by $2,200. Ignoring the 10%-of-AGI floor, what is the total of Susan's expenses that qualifies for the medical expense deduction?

29. **LO.2** In May, Rebecca's daughter, Isabella, sustained a serious injury that made it   Issue ID
impossible for her to continue living alone. Isabella, who is a novelist, moved back into Rebecca's home after the accident. Isabella has begun writing a novel based on her recent experiences. To accommodate Isabella, Rebecca incurred significant remodeling expenses (widening hallways, building a separate bedroom and bathroom, and making kitchen appliances accessible to Isabella). In addition, Rebecca had an indoor swimming pool constructed so that Isabella could do rehabilitation exercises prescribed by her physician.

In September, Isabella underwent major reconstructive surgery in Denver. The surgery was performed by Dr. Rama Patel, who specializes in treating injuries of the type sustained by Isabella. Rebecca drove Isabella from Champaign, Illinois, to Denver, a total of 1,100 miles, in Isabella's specially equipped van. They left Champaign on Tuesday morning and arrived in Denver on Thursday afternoon. Rebecca incurred expenses for gasoline, highway tolls, meals, and lodging while traveling to Denver. Rebecca stayed in a motel near the clinic for eight days while Isabella was hospitalized. Identify the relevant tax issues based on this information, and prepare a list of questions you would need to ask Rebecca and Isabella to advise them as to the resolution of any issues you have identified.

30. **LO.2** In the current year, Roger pays a $3,000 premium for high-deductible medical insurance for him and his family. In addition, he contributed $2,600 to a Health Savings Account.

    a. How much may Roger deduct if he is self-employed? Is the deduction *for* AGI or *from* AGI?

    b. How much may Roger deduct if he is an employee? Is the deduction *for* AGI or *from* AGI?

31. **LO.3** Alicia sold her personal residence to Rick on June 30 for $300,000. Before the sale, Alicia paid the real estate tax of $4,380 for the calendar year. For income tax purposes, the deduction is apportioned as follows: $2,160 to Alicia and $2,220 to Rick. What is Rick's basis in the residence?

32. **LO.4** Norma, who is single and uses the cash method of accounting, lives in a state that imposes an income tax. In April 2016, she files her state income tax return for 2015 and pays an additional $1,000 in state income taxes. During 2016, her withholdings for state income tax purposes amount to $7,400, and she pays estimated state income tax of $700. In April 2017, she files her state income tax return for 2016, claiming a refund of $1,800. Norma receives the refund in August 2017.

    a. Assuming that Norma itemized deductions in 2016, how much may she claim as a deduction for state income taxes on her Federal return for calendar year 2016 (filed April 2017)?

    b. Assuming that Norma itemized deductions in 2016 (which totaled $20,000), how will the refund of $1,800 that she received in 2017 be treated for Federal income tax purposes?

    c. Assume that Norma itemized deductions in 2016 (which totaled $20,000) and that she elects to have the $1,800 refund applied toward her 2017 state income tax liability. How will the $1,800 be treated for Federal income tax purposes?

    d. Assuming that Norma did not itemize deductions in 2016, how will the refund of $1,800 received in 2017 be treated for Federal income tax purposes?

33. **LO.5** Ten years ago, Liam, who is single, purchased a personal residence for $340,000 and took out a mortgage of $200,000 on the property. In May of the current year, when the residence had a fair market value of $440,000 and Liam owed $140,000 on the mortgage, he took out a home equity loan for $220,000. He used the funds to purchase a recreational vehicle, which he uses 100% for personal use. What is the maximum amount on which Liam can deduct home equity interest?

34. **LO.5** Malcolm owns 60% and Buddy owns 40% of Magpie Corporation. On July 1, 2016, each lends the corporation $30,000 at an annual interest rate of 10%. Malcolm and Buddy are not related. Both shareholders are on the cash method of accounting, and Magpie Corporation is on the accrual method. All parties use the calendar year for tax purposes. On June 30, 2017, Magpie repays the loans of $60,000 together with the specified interest of $6,000.

    a. How much of the interest can Magpie Corporation deduct in 2016? In 2017?

    b. When is the interest included in Malcolm and Buddy's gross income?

35. **LO.6** Nadia donates $4,000 to Eastern University's athletic department. The payment guarantees that Nadia will have preferred seating near the 50-yard line.

    a. Assume that Nadia subsequently buys four $100 game tickets. How much can she deduct as a charitable contribution to the university's athletic department?

    b. Assume that Nadia's $4,000 donation includes four $100 tickets. How much can she deduct as a charitable contribution to the university's athletic department?

36. **LO.6** Liz had AGI of $130,000 in 2016. She donated Bluebird Corporation stock with a basis of $10,000 to a qualified charitable organization on July 5, 2016.

    a. What is the amount of Liz's deduction assuming that she purchased the stock on December 3, 2015, and the stock had a fair market value of $17,000 when she made the donation?

    b. Assume the same facts as in (a), except that Liz purchased the stock on July 1, 2013.

    c. Assume the same facts as in (a), except that the stock had a fair market value of $7,500 (rather than $17,000) when Liz donated it to the charity.

37. **LO.6** During the year, Ricardo made the following contributions to a qualified public charity:

Cash	$220,000
Stock in Seagull, Inc. (a publicly traded corporation)	280,000

    Ricardo acquired the stock in Seagull, Inc., as an investment five years ago at a cost of $120,000. Ricardo's AGI is $840,000.

    a. What is Ricardo's charitable contribution deduction?

    b. How are excess amounts, if any, treated?

    c. Ricardo expects his taxable income to vacillate over the next several years, and his ability to claim the remaining charitable contribution deduction in those years is uncertain. Calculate the present value of the tax savings from the charitable contribution if the excess contribution deduction is taken in the *third year* following the actual contribution or is taken in the *fifth year* following the contribution. Assume that Ricardo is in the 39.6%, 25%, and 15% tax brackets in the year of contribution, the third year following the contribution, and the fifth year following the contribution, respectively. See Appendix H for the present value factors, and assume a 6% discount rate.

38. **LO.6** Ramon had AGI of $180,000 in 2016. He is considering making a charitable contribution this year to the American Heart Association, a qualified charitable organization. Determine the current allowable charitable contribution deduction in each of the following independent situations, and indicate the treatment for any amount that is not deductible currently.

    Decision Making

    a. A cash gift of $95,000.

    b. A gift of OakCo stock worth $95,000 on the contribution date. Ramon had acquired the stock as an investment two years ago at a cost of $84,000.

    c. A gift of a painting worth $95,000 that Ramon purchased three years ago for $60,000. The charity has indicated that it would sell the painting to generate cash to fund medical research.

39. **LO.6** On December 27, 2016, Roberta purchased four tickets to a charity ball sponsored by the city of San Diego for the benefit of underprivileged children. Each ticket cost $200 and had a fair market value of $35. On the same day as the purchase, Roberta gave the tickets to the minister of her church for personal use by his family. At the time of the gift of the tickets, Roberta pledged $4,000 to the building fund of her church. The pledge was satisfied by a check dated December 31, 2016, but not mailed until January 3, 2017.

    a. Presuming that Roberta is a cash basis and calendar year taxpayer, how much can she deduct as a charitable contribution for 2016?

    b. Would the amount of the deduction be any different if Roberta was an accrual basis taxpayer? Explain.

Decision Making

Communications

40. **LO.6, 9** In December of each year, Eleanor Young contributes 10% of her gross income to the United Way (a 50% organization). Eleanor, who is in the 28% marginal tax bracket, is considering the following alternatives for satisfying the contribution.

	Fair Market Value
(1) Cash donation	$23,000
(2) Unimproved land held for six years ($3,000 basis)	23,000
(3) Blue Corporation stock held for eight months ($3,000 basis)	23,000
(4) Gold Corporation stock held for two years ($28,000 basis)	23,000

Eleanor has asked you to help her decide which of the potential contributions listed above will be most advantageous taxwise. Evaluate the four alternatives, and write a letter to Eleanor to communicate your advice to her. Her address is 2622 Bayshore Drive, Berkeley, CA 94709.

Decision Making

Communications

41. **LO.2, 3, 4, 5, 7, 9** Bart and Elizabeth Forrest, both age 47, are married and have no dependents. They have asked you to advise them whether they should file jointly or separately in 2016. They present you with the following information:

	Bart	Elizabeth	Joint
Salary	$38,000		
Business net income		$110,000	
Interest income	400	1,200	$2,200
Deductions *for* AGI	2,400	14,000	
Medical expenses	10,427	3,358	
State income tax	800	1,800	
Real estate tax			3,800
Mortgage interest			4,200
Unreimbursed employee expenses	1,200		

If they file separately, Bart and Elizabeth will split the real estate tax and mortgage interest deductions equally. Write Bart and Elizabeth a letter in which you make and explain a recommendation on filing status for 2016. Bart and Elizabeth reside at 2003 Highland Drive, Durham, NC 27707.

42. **LO.2, 3, 4, 5, 6, 7, 8** Evan, age 61, is single and has AGI of $277,300 in 2016. His potential itemized deductions before any limitations for the year total $52,300 and consist of the following:

Medical expenses (before the 10%-of-AGI limitation)	$28,000
Interest on home mortgage	8,700
State income taxes	9,500
Real estate taxes	3,600
Charitable contributions	2,500

After all necessary adjustments are made, what is the amount of itemized deductions Evan may claim?

43. **LO.2, 3, 4, 5, 6, 7, 8** Linda, age 37, who files as a single taxpayer, had AGI of $280,000 for 2016. She incurred the following expenses and losses during the year:

Medical expenses (before the 10%-of-AGI limitation)	$33,000
State and local income taxes	4,500
State sales tax	1,300
Real estate taxes	4,000
Home mortgage interest	5,000
Automobile loan interest	750
Credit card interest	1,000
Charitable contributions	7,000
Casualty loss (before 10% limitation but after $100 floor)	34,000
Unreimbursed employee expenses subject to the 2%-of-AGI limitation	7,600

Calculate Linda's allowable itemized deductions for the year.

44. **LO.2, 3, 4, 5, 6, 7, 8** For calendar year 2016, Stuart and Pamela Gibson file a joint return reflecting AGI of $350,000. Their itemized deductions are as follows:

Casualty loss after $100 floor (not covered by insurance)	$48,600
Home mortgage interest	19,000
Credit card interest	800
Property taxes on home	16,300
Charitable contributions	28,700
State income tax	18,000
Tax return preparation fees	1,200

Calculate the amount of itemized deductions the Gibsons may claim for the year.

Cumulative Problems

45. Alice J. and Bruce M. Byrd are married taxpayers who file a joint return. Their Social Security numbers are 123-45-6789 and 111-11-1112, respectively. Alice's birthday is September 21, 1968, and Bruce's is June 27, 1967. They live at 473 Revere Avenue, Lowell, MA 01850. Alice is the office manager for Lowell Dental Clinic, 433 Broad Street, Lowell, MA 01850 (employer identification number 98-7654321). Bruce is the manager of a Super Burgers fast-food outlet owned and operated by Plymouth Corporation, 1247 Central Avenue, Hauppauge, NY 11788 (employer identification number 11-1111111).

Tax Return Problem

Decision Making

TAX SOFTWARE

The following information is shown on their Wage and Tax Statements (Form W–2) for 2015.

Line	Description	Alice	Bruce
1	Wages, tips, other compensation	$58,000	$62,100
2	Federal income tax withheld	4,500	6,300
3	Social Security wages	58,000	62,100
4	Social Security tax withheld	3,596	3,850
5	Medicare wages and tips	58,000	62,100
6	Medicare tax withheld	841	900
15	State	Massachusetts	Massachusetts
16	State wages, tips, etc.	58,000	62,100
17	State income tax withheld	2,950	3,100

The Byrds provide over half of the support of their two children, Cynthia (born January 25, 1991, Social Security number 123-45-6788) and John (born February 7, 1995, Social Security number 123-45-6786). Both children are full-time students and live with the Byrds except when they are away at college. Cynthia earned $4,200 from a summer internship in 2015, and John earned $3,800 from a part-time job.

During 2015, the Byrds provided 60% of the total support of Bruce's widower father, Sam Byrd (born March 6, 1939, Social Security number 123-45-6787). Sam lived alone and covered the rest of his support with his Social Security benefits. Sam died in November, and Bruce, the beneficiary of a policy on Sam's life, received life insurance proceeds of $1,600,000 on December 28.

The Byrds had the following expenses relating to their personal residence during 2015:

Property taxes	$5,000
Qualified interest on home mortgage	8,700
Repairs to roof	5,750
Utilities	4,100
Fire and theft insurance	1,900

The Byrds had the following medical expenses for 2015:

Medical insurance premiums	$4,500
Doctor bill for Sam incurred in 2014 and not paid until 2015	7,600
Operation for Sam	8,500
Prescription medicines for Sam	900
Hospital expenses for Sam	3,500
Reimbursement from insurance company, received in 2015	3,600

The medical expenses for Sam represent most of the 60% that Bruce contributed toward his father's support.

Other relevant information follows:

- When they filed their 2014 state return in 2015, the Byrds paid additional state income tax of $900.
- During 2015, Alice and Bruce attended a dinner dance sponsored by the Lowell Police Disability Association (a qualified charitable organization). The Byrds paid $300 for the tickets. The cost of comparable entertainment would normally be $50.
- The Byrds contributed $5,000 to Lowell Presbyterian Church and gave used clothing (cost of $1,200 and fair market value of $350) to the Salvation Army. All donations are supported by receipts, and the clothing is in very good condition.
- In 2015, the Byrds received interest income of $2,750, which was reported on a Form 1099–INT from Second National Bank.
- Alice's employer requires that all employees wear uniforms to work. During 2015, Alice spent $850 on new uniforms and $566 on laundry charges.
- Bruce paid $400 for an annual subscription to the *Journal of Franchise Management* and $741 for annual membership dues to his professional association.
- Neither Alice's nor Bruce's employer reimburses for employee expenses.
- The Byrds do not keep the receipts for the sales taxes they paid and had no major purchases subject to sales tax.
- All members of the Byrd family had health insurance coverage for all of 2015.
- Alice and Bruce paid no estimated Federal income tax. Neither Alice nor Bruce wants to designate $3 to the Presidential Election Campaign Fund.

Part 1—Tax Computation

Compute net tax payable or refund due for Alice and Bruce Byrd for 2015. If they have overpaid, they want the amount to be refunded to them. If you use tax forms for your computations, you will need Forms 1040 and 2106 and Schedules A and B. Suggested software: H&R BLOCK At Home.

Part 2—Tax Planning

Alice and Bruce are planning some significant changes for 2016. They have provided you with the following information and asked you to project their taxable income and tax liability for 2016.

The Byrds will invest the $1,600,000 of life insurance proceeds in short-term certificates of deposit (CDs) and use the interest for living expenses during 2016. They expect to earn total interest of $32,000 on the CDs.

Bruce has been promoted to regional manager, and his salary for 2016 will be $88,000. He estimates that state income tax withheld will increase by $4,000 and the Social Security tax withheld will be $5,456.

Alice, who has been diagnosed with a serious illness, will take a leave of absence from work during 2016. The estimated cost for her medical treatment is $15,400, of which $6,400 will be reimbursed by their insurance company in 2016. Their medical insurance premiums will increase to $9,769. Property taxes on their residence are expected to increase to $5,100. The Byrds' home mortgage interest expense and charitable contributions are expected to be unchanged from 2015.

John will graduate from college in December 2015 and will take a job in New York City in January 2016. His starting salary will be $46,000.

Assume that all of the information reported in 2015 will be the same in 2016 unless other information has been presented above.

46. Paul and Donna Decker are married taxpayers, ages 44 and 42, respectively, who file a joint return for 2016. The Deckers live at 1121 College Avenue, Carmel, IN 46032. Paul is an assistant manager at Carmel Motor Inn, and Donna is a teacher at Carmel Elementary School. They present you with W–2 forms that reflect the following information:

Tax Computation Problem

	Paul	Donna
Salary	$68,000	$56,000
Federal tax withheld	6,770	6,630
State income tax withheld	900	800
FICA (Social Security and Medicare) withheld	5,202	4,284
Social Security numbers	111-11-1112	123-45-6789

Donna is the custodial parent of two children from a previous marriage who reside with the Deckers through the school year. The children, Larry and Jane Parker, reside with their father, Bob, during the summer. Relevant information for the children follows:

	Larry	Jane
Age	17	18
Social Security numbers	123-45-6788	123-45-6787
Months spent with Deckers	9	9

Under the divorce decree, Bob pays child support of $150 per month per child during the nine months the children live with the Deckers. Bob says that he spends $200 per month per child during the three summer months they reside with him. Donna and Paul can document that they provide $2,000 support per child per year. The divorce decree is silent as to which parent can claim the exemptions for the children.

In August, Paul and Donna added a suite to their home to provide more comfortable accommodations for Hannah Snyder (123-45-6786), Donna's mother, who had moved in with them in February 2015 after the death of Donna's father. Not wanting to borrow money for this addition, Paul sold 300 shares of Acme Corporation stock for $50 per share on May 3, 2016, and used the proceeds of $15,000 to cover construction costs. The Deckers had purchased the stock on April 29, 2011, for $25 per share. They received dividends of $750 on the jointly owned stock a month before the sale.

Hannah, who is 66 years old, received $7,500 in Social Security benefits during the year, of which she gave the Deckers $2,000 to use toward household expenses and deposited the remainder in her personal savings account. The Deckers determine that they have spent $2,500 of their own money for food, clothing, medical expenses, and other items for Hannah. They do not know what the rental value of Hannah's suite would be, but they estimate it would be at least $300 per month.

Interest paid during the year included the following:

Home mortgage interest (paid to Carmel Federal Savings & Loan)	$7,890
Interest on an automobile loan (paid to Carmel National Bank)	1,660
Interest on Citibank Visa card	620

In July, Paul hit a submerged rock while boating. Fortunately, he was uninjured after being thrown from the boat and landing in deep water. However, the boat, which was uninsured, was destroyed. Paul had paid $25,000 for the boat in June 2015, and its value was appraised at $18,000 on the date of the accident.

The Deckers paid doctor and hospital bills of $10,700 and were reimbursed $2,000 by their insurance company. They spent $640 for prescription drugs and medicines and $5,904 for premiums on their health insurance policy. They have filed additional claims of $1,200 with their insurance company and have been told they will receive payment for that amount in January 2017. Included in the amounts paid for doctor and hospital bills were payments of $380 for Hannah and $850 for the children. All members of the Decker family had health insurance coverage for all of 2016.

Additional information of potential tax consequence follows:

Real estate taxes paid	$3,850
Sales taxes paid (per table)	1,379
Contributions to church	1,950
Appraised value of books donated to public library	740
Paul's unreimbursed employee expenses to attend hotel management convention:	
Airfare	340
Hotel	170
Meals	95
Registration fee	340
Refund of state income tax for 2015 (the Deckers itemized on their 2015 Federal tax return)	1,520

Compute net tax payable or refund due for the Deckers for 2016. Ignore the child tax credit in your computations. If the Deckers have overpaid, the amount is to be credited toward their taxes for 2017.

Research Problems

Note: Solutions to Research Problems can be prepared by using the Checkpoint® Student Edition online research product, which is available to accompany this text. It is also possible to prepare solutions to the Research Problems by using tax research materials found in a standard tax library.

Research Problem 1. Jane suffers from a degenerative spinal disorder. Her physician said that swimming could help prevent the onset of permanent paralysis and recommended the installation of a swimming pool at her residence for her use. Jane's residence had a market value of approximately $500,000 before the swimming pool was installed. The swimming pool was built, and an appraiser estimated that the value of Jane's home increased by $98,000 because of the addition.

The pool cost $194,000, and Jane claimed a medical expense deduction of $96,000 ($194,000 − $98,000) on her tax return. Upon audit of the return, the IRS determined that an adequate pool should have cost $70,000 and would increase the value of her home by only $31,000. Thus, the IRS claims that Jane is entitled to a deduction of only $39,000 ($70,000 − $31,000).

a. Is there any ceiling limitation on the amount deductible as a medical expense? Explain.

b. Can capital expenditures be deductible as medical expenses? Explain.

c. What is the significance of a "minimum adequate facility"? Should aesthetic or architectural qualities be considered in the determination? Why or why not?

Research Problem 2. Ken and Mary Jane Blough, your neighbors, have asked you for advice after receiving correspondence in the mail from the IRS. You learn that the IRS is asking for documentation in support of the itemized deductions the Bloughs claimed on a recent tax return. The Bloughs tell you that their income in the year of question was $75,000. Because their record-keeping habits are poor, they felt justified in claiming itemized deductions equal to the amounts that represent the average claimed by other taxpayers in their income bracket. These averages are calculated and reported by the IRS annually based on actual returns filed in an earlier year. Accordingly, they claimed medical expenses of $7,102, taxes of $6,050, interest of $10,659, and charitable contributions of $2,693. What advice do you give the Boughs?

Partial list of research aids:
Cheryl L. de Werff, T.C. Summary Opinion, 2011–29.

Research Problem 3. Marcia, a shareholder in a corporation with stores in five states, donated stock with a basis of $10,000 to a qualified charitable organization in 2015. Although the stock of the corporation was not traded on a public stock exchange, many shares had been sold over the past several years. Based on the average selling price for the stock in 2015, Marcia deducted $95,000 on her 2015 tax return. Marcia received a notice from the IRS that the $95,000 deduction had been reduced to $10,000 because she had not obtained a qualified appraisal or attached a summary of her appraisal to her tax return. Marcia has asked you to advise her on this matter. Write a letter containing your conclusions to Ms. Marcia Meyer, 1311 Santos Court, San Bruno, CA 94066.

Communications

Partial list of research aids:
Reg. § 1.170A–13(c)(2).

Use the tax resources of the Internet to address the following questions. Do not restrict your search to the Web, but include a review of newsgroups and general reference materials, practitioner sites and resources, primary sources of the tax law, chat rooms and discussion groups, and other opportunities.

 Internet Activity

Research Problem 4. The cutback adjustment that limits the amount of itemized deductions for some taxpayers is otherwise known as the Pease limitation. This limitation is named after former Congressman Donald Pease and was first in effect for tax years after December 31, 1990. The purpose of this limitation is to raise additional tax revenue by limiting some popular and common itemized deductions incurred by high-income taxpayers. One such deduction is the charitable contribution deduction. Search Google or a business press database to see what tax law analysts speculated the consequences would be of limiting charitable contribution deductions. Also determine whether such speculation has materialized.

Research Problem 5. Use the IRS's website to determine whether taxpayers who are not U.S. residents can claim itemized deductions when calculating their taxable income.

Roger CPA Review Questions

1. Kellye, a teacher, volunteers for eight hours per week at a school for high-risk children, a qualified charitable organization. Kellye's normal rate for teaching is $30 per hour. Kellye's out-of-pocket costs in 2016 were $250 for supplies, and she spent $20 each week in transportation getting to and from the school. Kellye had no cash contributions to charity in 2016. If Kellye volunteered every week in 2016, what is her charitable contributions deduction?

   a. $0   c. $1,290
   b. $250   d. $13,770

2. Aaron, age 55, has an adjusted gross income in 2016 of $30,000. His expenses are as follows:

Non-prescription medicine	$ 100
Prescription medicine	500
Doctor visits	500
Weekly meal preparation for a diet plan	2,000
Removal of a benign facial mole	400
Contact lenses	500
Eyeglasses	200
Dental services	300

   What is Aaron's itemized deduction for medical expenses?

   a. $0   c. $2,000
   b. $1,500   d. $4,500

3. Which of the following deductions for taxes paid may be taken in the same year?
   a. Real estate taxes, state income taxes, state sales taxes.
   b. Real estate taxes, property taxes, state income taxes.
   c. Property taxes, state income taxes, state sales taxes.
   d. Real estate taxes, property taxes, state income taxes, state sales taxes.

4. Zunilda is 77-year-old individual with an AGI of $25,000 in 2015. She began living in a nursing home in 2015 upon the recommendation of her primary care physician in order to receive medical care for a specific condition. She had the following unreimbursed expenses in 2015:

Expense	Amount
Nursing home health care costs	$5,000
Nursing home meal and lodging costs	8,000
Prescription drugs	1,500

   As a result of these unreimbursed expenses, how much may Zunilda deduct from AGI on her 2015 tax return? Assume Zunilda elects to itemize deductions.

   a. $12,000   c. $12,625
   b. $4,000   d. $4,625

CHAPTER

11

Investor Losses

LEARNING OBJECTIVES: *After completing Chapter 11, you should be able to:*

LO.1 Explain the tax shelter problem and the reasons for at-risk and passive activity loss limitations.

LO.2 Discuss the at-risk limitation.

LO.3 Describe how the passive activity loss rules limit deductions for losses and identify the taxpayers subject to these restrictions.

LO.4 Explore the elements required for an activity to be treated as passive and review the rules for identifying an activity.

LO.5 Identify the tests for material participation.

LO.6 Describe the nature of rental activities under the passive activity loss rules.

LO.7 Determine the relationship between the at-risk and passive activity loss limitations.

LO.8 Recognize the special treatment available to real estate activities.

LO.9 Determine the proper tax treatment upon the disposition of a passive activity.

LO.10 Identify restrictions placed on the deductibility of other investor losses and deductions, including those that apply to investment interest.

LO.11 Suggest tax planning strategies to minimize the effect of the passive activity loss and investment interest limitations and recognize the general impact of the additional tax on net investment income.

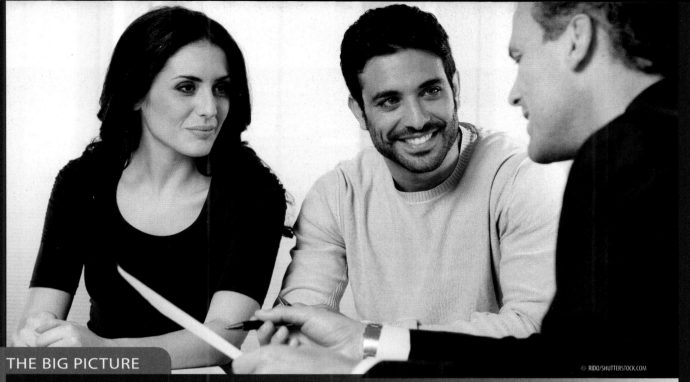

THE BIG PICTURE

INVESTOR LOSS LIMITATIONS AFFECT THE VIABILITY OF CERTAIN INVESTMENT OPPORTUNITIES

Trudy and Jim Reswick are considering ways to enhance their financial security. In fact, they are willing to borrow a substantial sum so that they can make an appropriate investment.

Currently, Trudy and Jim's sole source of income is their salaries, totaling $100,000, from their full-time jobs. Their most significant asset is their personal residence (fair market value of $500,000 with a mortgage of $350,000). The Reswicks' broker suggests that they borrow $100,000 at 8 percent and use the proceeds to make *one* of the following investments:

- A high-growth, low-yield portfolio of marketable securities. The portfolio's value is expected to grow 10 percent each year.

- An interest in a limited partnership that owns and operates orange groves in Florida. The limited partnership interest is expected to generate tax losses of $25,000 in each of the next five years, after which profits are expected. The broker predicts that after taking into account the tax benefit from the losses, the Reswicks would average an annual 10 percent return over a 10-year period.

- An interest in a local limited partnership that owns and rents apartments to college students. This limited partnership interest also would generate losses of $25,000 per year for five years, after which profits would follow. These expected profits and losses would produce an average annual total return of 10 percent over a 10-year period.

Trudy and Jim want to choose the alternative that produces the best after-tax return over a 10-year planning horizon. They are aware, however, that tax restrictions may limit the advantages of some of these investment options. In this connection, evaluate each option.

Read the chapter and formulate your response.

FRAMEWORK 1040 **Tax Formula for Individuals**

This chapter covers the boldfaced portions of the Tax Formula for Individuals that was introduced in Concept Summary 3.1 on p. 3-3. Below those portions are the sections of Form 1040 where the results are reported.

Income *(broadly defined)*	$xx,xxx
Less: Exclusions	(x,xxx)
Gross income	$xx,xxx
Less: Deductions *for* **adjusted gross income**	(x,xxx)

FORM 1040 (p. 1)

12	Business income or (loss). Attach Schedule C or C-EZ	
13	Capital gain or (loss). Attach Schedule D if required. If not required, check here ▶ ☐	
14	Other gains or (losses). Attach Form 4797	
17	Rental real estate, royalties, partnerships, S corporations, trusts, etc. Attach Schedule E	

Adjusted gross income	$xx,xxx
Less: The greater of total **itemized deductions** *or* the standard deduction	(x,xxx)

FORM 1040 (p. 2)

40	**Itemized deductions** (from Schedule A) **or** your **standard deduction**

Personal and dependency exemptions	(x,xxx)
Taxable income	$xx,xxx
Tax on taxable income *(see Tax Tables or Tax Rate Schedules)*	$ x,xxx
Less: Tax credits *(including income taxes withheld and prepaid)*	(xxx)
Tax due (or refund)	$ xxx

A s discussed in Chapter 6, a tax deduction for an expense or a loss is not allowed unless specifically provided for by Congress. For example, losses can be recognized and deducted in the case of certain unprofitable investments only because the Code so provides. Such losses can arise from the operation of an activity or upon its ultimate disposition. For most individual taxpayers, deductible investor losses come within the scope of § 165(c)(2) relating to transactions entered into for profit.[1] But what happens if the investment is mostly motivated by the tax loss it generates and the profit objective is not controlling? Or what if the investment generates expenses that offset ordinary income and it later is expected to produce appreciation taxed at capital gain rates? This chapter addresses these tax minimization strategies and the Code provisions enacted to restrict their use.

Explain the tax shelter problem and the reasons for at-risk and passive activity loss limitations.

11-1 THE TAX SHELTER PROBLEM

Before Congress enacted legislation to reduce their effectiveness, **tax shelters** provided a popular way to avoid or defer taxes, as they could generate deductions and other benefits to offset income from other sources. Because of the tax avoidance potential of many tax shelters, they were attractive to wealthy taxpayers in high-income tax brackets. Many tax shelters merely provided an opportunity for "investors" to buy deductions and credits in ventures that were not expected to generate a profit, even in the long run.

---

[1]If the losses are incurred in connection with a trade or business, § 165(c)(1) applies.

Although it may seem odd that a taxpayer would intentionally invest in an activity that was designed to produce losses, there is a logical explanation. The typical tax shelter operated as a partnership and relied heavily on nonrecourse financing.[2] Accelerated depreciation and interest expense deductions generated large losses in the early years of the activity. At the very least, the tax shelter deductions deferred the recognition of any net income from the venture until the activity was sold. In the best of situations, the investor could realize additional tax savings by offsetting other income (e.g., salary, interest, dividends) with deductions flowing from the tax shelter. Ultimately, the sale of the investment would result in capital gain. The following example illustrates what was possible *before* Congress enacted legislation to curb tax shelter abuses.

> **EXAMPLE 1**
>
> Bob, who earned a salary of $400,000 as a business executive and dividend income of $15,000, invested $20,000 for a 10% interest in a cattle-breeding tax shelter. Through the use of $800,000 of nonrecourse financing and available cash of $200,000, the partnership acquired a herd of an exotic breed of cattle costing $1 million. Depreciation, interest, and other deductions related to the activity resulted in a loss of $400,000, of which Bob's share was $40,000. Bob was allowed to deduct the $40,000 loss even though he had invested and stood to lose only $20,000 if the investment became worthless. The net effect of the $40,000 deduction from the partnership was that a portion of Bob's salary and dividend income was "sheltered," and as a result, he was required to calculate his tax liability on only $375,000 of income [$415,000 (salary and dividends) − $40,000 (deduction)] rather than $415,000. If this deduction were available under current law and if Bob was in a combined Federal and state income tax bracket of 40%, this deduction would generate a tax savings of $16,000 ($40,000 × 40%) in the first year alone!

A review of Example 1 shows that the taxpayer took a *two-for-one* write-off ($40,000 deduction, $20,000 amount invested). In the heyday of these types of tax shelters, promoters often promised tax deductions for the investor well in excess of the amount invested.

The first major provision aimed at tax shelters was the **at-risk limitation**. Its objective is to limit a taxpayer's deductions to the amount "at risk," which is the amount the taxpayer stands to lose if the investment becomes worthless. Thus, in Example 1, the at-risk rule limits Bob's loss to $20,000—the amount at risk.

The second major attack on tax shelters came with the passage of the **passive activity loss** rules. The passive activity loss rules require the taxpayer to segregate all income and losses into three categories: active, portfolio, and passive. (These categories are defined in text Section 11-3.) In general, the passive activity loss limits disallow the deduction of passive activity losses against active or portfolio income even when the taxpayer is at risk to the extent of the loss. In general, passive activity losses can only offset passive activity income.

Thus, in Example 1, the passive activity loss rules disallow a current deduction for any of the loss. The loss from the tax shelter is a passive activity loss because Bob does not materially participate in the activity. Therefore, the $20,000 loss that is allowed under the at-risk rules is disallowed under the passive activity loss rules because Bob does not report any passive activity income for the year—he reports only active and portfolio income. Consequently, Bob's current-year income must reflect his nonpassive activity income of $415,000. As explained later in the chapter, the disallowed $20,000 passive activity loss is suspended and may be deducted in a future year under certain conditions.

The nature of the at-risk limits and the passive activity loss rules and their impact on investors are discussed in the pages that follow. An interesting consequence of these

---

[2]Nonrecourse debt is an obligation for which the borrower is not personally liable. An example of nonrecourse debt is a liability on real estate acquired by a partnership without the partnership or any of the partners assuming any liability for the mortgage. The acquired property generally is pledged as collateral for the loan.

rules is that now investors evaluating potential investments must consider mainly the economics of the venture instead of the tax benefits or tax avoidance possibilities that an investment may generate.

11-2 AT-RISK LIMITS

The at-risk provisions limit the deductibility of losses from business and income-producing activities. These provisions, which apply to individuals and closely held corporations, are designed to prevent taxpayers from deducting losses in excess of their actual economic investment in an activity. In the case of an S corporation or a partnership, the at-risk limits apply at the owner level. Under the at-risk rules, a taxpayer's deductible loss from an activity for any taxable year is limited to the amount the taxpayer has at risk at the end of the taxable year (the amount the taxpayer could actually lose in the activity).

While the amount at risk generally vacillates over time, the initial amount considered at risk consists of the following:[3]

- The amount of cash and the adjusted basis of property contributed to the activity by the taxpayer.
- Amounts borrowed for use in the activity for which the taxpayer is personally liable or has pledged as security property not used in the activity.

This amount generally is increased each year by the taxpayer's share of income and is decreased by the taxpayer's share of deductible losses and withdrawals from the activity. In addition, because general partners are jointly and severally liable for recourse debts of the partnership, their at-risk amounts are increased when the partnership increases its debt and are decreased when the partnership reduces its debt. However, a taxpayer generally is not considered at risk with respect to borrowed amounts if either of the following is true:

- The taxpayer is not personally liable for repayment of the debt (e.g., nonrecourse debt).
- The lender has an interest (other than as a creditor) in the activity.

An important exception provides that in the case of an activity involving the holding of real property, a taxpayer is considered at risk for his or her share of any *qualified nonrecourse financing* that is secured by real property used in the activity.[4]

Subject to the passive activity loss rules discussed later in the chapter, a taxpayer may deduct a loss as long as the at-risk amount is positive. However, once the at-risk amount is exhausted, any remaining loss cannot be deducted until a later year. Any losses disallowed for any given taxable year by the at-risk rules may be deducted in the first succeeding year in which the rules do not prevent the deduction—that is, when there is, and to the extent of, a positive at-risk amount.

The Big Picture

EXAMPLE

2

Return to the facts of *The Big Picture* on p. 11-1. In addition to the three investment options presented to the Reswicks, in 2016, they invest $40,000 in an oil partnership that incurs a first-year net loss, of which $60,000 is their share. Assume that the Reswicks' interest in the partnership is subject to the at-risk limits but is not subject to the passive activity loss limits. Because the Reswicks have only $40,000 of capital at risk, they cannot deduct more than $40,000 against their other income and must reduce their at-risk amount to zero ($40,000 at-risk amount − $40,000 loss deducted). The nondeductible loss of $20,000 ($60,000 loss generated − $40,000 loss allowed) can be carried over to 2017.

---

[3]§ 465(b)(1).

[4]Section 465(b)(6) defines qualified nonrecourse financing.

The Big Picture

EXAMPLE
3

In 2017, the Reswicks in the preceding example have taxable income of $15,000 from the oil partnership and invest an additional $10,000 in the venture. Their at-risk amount is now $25,000 ($0 beginning balance + $15,000 taxable income + $10,000 additional investment). This enables them to deduct the carryover loss and requires them to reduce their at-risk amount to $5,000 ($25,000 at-risk amount − $20,000 carryover loss allowed).

Complicating the at-risk rule is the fact that previously allowed losses must be recaptured to the extent the at-risk amount is reduced below zero.[5] That is, previous losses that were allowed must be offset by the recognition of enough income to bring the at-risk amount up to zero. This rule applies in situations such as those when the amount at risk is reduced below zero by distributions to the taxpayer or when the status of indebtedness changes from recourse to nonrecourse.

Calculation of at-risk amount is reviewed in Concept Summary 11.1.

Concept Summary 11.1

Calculation of At-Risk Amount

Increases to a taxpayer's at-risk amount:	Decreases to a taxpayer's at-risk amount:
• Cash and the adjusted basis of property contributed to the activity.	• Withdrawals from the activity.
• Amounts borrowed for use in the activity for which the taxpayer is personally liable or has pledged as security property not used in the activity.	• Taxpayer's share of the activity's deductible loss.
• Taxpayer's share of amounts borrowed for use in the activity that are qualified nonrecourse financing.	• Taxpayer's share of any reductions of debt for which recourse against the taxpayer exists or any reductions of qualified nonrecourse debt.
• Taxpayer's share of the activity's income.	

11-3 PASSIVE ACTIVITY LOSS LIMITS

LO.3

Describe how the passive activity loss rules limit deductions for losses and identify the taxpayers subject to these restrictions.

This section identifies and explains a number of key issues that are pertinent when applying the passive activity loss limits.

- The limits apply only to passive activity losses incurred by certain types of taxpayers.
- Losses are limited under these rules only if they are generated by a passive activity.
- Special rules exist for interests in real estate activities.
- Benefits may arise when a disposition of a passive activity occurs.

11-3a Classification and Impact of Passive Activity Income and Losses

The passive activity loss rules operate by requiring taxpayers to classify their income and losses into various categories. Then the rules limit the extent to which losses in the passive category can be used to offset income in the other categories.

---

[5]§ 465(e).

TAX IN THE NEWS   "Passive" under the Tax Law May Not Be "Passive" in the Real World

As the real estate market continues to strengthen from the economic depths of several years ago, more Americans are interested in buying and managing rental property as a sideline. Many such investors quickly learn that holding rental property invariably is more involved than simply collecting rent every month.

Managing rental property can be a time-consuming business venture. Screening potential renters, routinely maintaining and upgrading the property, managing the books and accounting records, and responding to calls from the renters at any hour of the day or night concerning property issues are but a few of the tasks that rental property owners face regularly.

Then at the end of the year when the tax preparer mentions to the taxpayer that the rental property is a passive activity, the taxpayer is mystified by the disconnect between reality and the terminology of the tax law. But the more significant sting may arise from the application of the passive activity loss restrictions that apply under the tax law.

Classification

The passive activity loss rules require income and losses to be classified into one of three categories: active, portfolio, or passive. **Active income** includes the following:

- Wages, salary, commissions, bonuses, and other payments for services rendered by the taxpayer.
- Profit from a trade or business in which the taxpayer is a material participant (material participation is described later in the chapter).
- Gain on the sale or other disposition of assets used in an active trade or business.
- Income from intangible property if the taxpayer's personal efforts significantly contributed to the creation of the property.

Portfolio income includes the following:

- Interest, dividends, annuities, and royalties not derived in the ordinary course of a trade or business.
- Gain or loss from the disposition of property that produces portfolio income or is held for investment purposes.

Section 469 provides that passive activity income or loss arises from activities that are treated as passive, which include:

- Any trade or business or income-producing activity in which the taxpayer does not materially participate.
- Subject to certain exceptions (discussed later in the chapter), all rental activities, whether the taxpayer materially participates or not.

General Impact

Losses or expenses generated by passive activities can be deducted only to the extent of income from all of the taxpayer's passive activities. Any excess loss may not be used to offset income from active sources or portfolio income. Instead, any unused passive activity losses are suspended and carried forward to future years to offset passive activity income generated in those years. Otherwise, suspended losses may be used only when a taxpayer disposes of his or her entire interest in an activity. In that event, generally all current and suspended passive activity losses related to the activity may offset active and portfolio income.

The Big Picture

Return to the facts of *The Big Picture* on p. 11-1. In addition to their salaries of $100,000 from full-time jobs, assume that the Reswicks receive $12,000 in dividends and interest from various portfolio investments. Further, assume that they decide to invest $100,000 in the orange grove limited partnership, which produces a $25,000 loss for the Reswicks this year. Because their at-risk basis in the partnership is $100,000, the current $25,000 loss is not limited by the at-risk rules. However, because the loss is a passive activity loss, it is not deductible against their other income. The loss is suspended and carried over to the future. If the Reswicks have passive activity income from this investment or from other passive activities in the future, they can offset the suspended loss against that passive activity income. If they do not have passive activity income to offset this suspended loss in the future, they will be allowed to offset the loss against other types of income when they eventually dispose of their investment in the passive activity.

EXAMPLE

4

Impact of Suspended Losses

When a taxpayer disposes of his or her entire interest in a passive activity, the actual economic gain or loss from the investment, including any suspended losses, can finally be determined. As a result, under the passive activity loss rules described above, upon a fully taxable disposition, any overall loss realized from the taxpayer's activity is recognized and can be offset against any income.

A fully taxable disposition generally involves a sale of the property to a third party at arm's length and thus, presumably, for a price equal to the property's fair market value. As presented in the following example, a gain recognized upon the transfer of an interest in a passive activity generally is treated as passive and is first offset by the suspended passive activity losses from that activity.

Rex sells an apartment building, a passive activity, with an adjusted basis of $100,000 for $180,000. In addition, he has suspended losses of $60,000 associated with the building. His total gain, $80,000, and his taxable gain, $20,000, are calculated as follows:

Net sales price	$ 180,000
Less: Adjusted basis	(100,000)
Total gain	$ 80,000
Less: Suspended losses	(60,000)
Taxable gain (passive)	$ 20,000

EXAMPLE

5

If current and suspended losses of the passive activity exceed the gain realized or if the sale results in a realized loss, the amount of

- any loss from the activity for the tax year (including losses suspended in the activity disposed of)

in excess of

- net income or gain for the tax year from all passive activities (without regard to the activity disposed of)

is treated as a loss that is not from a passive activity. In computing the loss from the activity for the year of disposition, any gain or loss recognized is included.

Dean sells an apartment building, a passive activity, with an adjusted basis of $100,000 for $150,000. In addition, he has current and suspended losses of $60,000 associated with the building and has no other passive activities. His total gain of $50,000 and his deductible loss of $10,000 are calculated as follows:

EXAMPLE

6

continued

Net sales price	$ 150,000
Less: Adjusted basis	(100,000)
Total gain	$ 50,000
Less: Suspended losses	(60,000)
Deductible loss (not passive)	($ 10,000)

The $10,000 deductible loss is offset against Dean's active and portfolio income. Even if the building is sold for a loss (i.e., the adjusted basis exceeds the sales price), the total loss, including the suspended losses, is deductible as a nonpassive activity loss.

Carryovers of Suspended Losses

The preceding examples assumed that the taxpayer had an interest in only one passive activity; as a result, the suspended loss was related exclusively to the activity that was disposed of. However, taxpayers often own interests in more than one activity, in which case any suspended losses must be allocated among those passive activities that generated losses. The allocation to an activity is made by multiplying the disallowed passive activity loss from all activities using the following fraction:

$$\frac{\text{Loss from one passive activity}}{\text{Sum of losses for taxable year from all passive activities having losses}}$$

Diego has investments in three passive activities with the following income and losses for 2015:

Activity A	($30,000)
Activity B	(20,000)
Activity C	25,000
Net passive activity loss	($25,000)
Net passive activity loss of $25,000 allocated to:	
Activity A ($25,000 × $30,000/$50,000)	($15,000)
Activity B ($25,000 × $20,000/$50,000)	(10,000)
Total suspended losses	($25,000)

Suspended losses are carried over indefinitely and are offset in the future first against any passive activity income from the activities to which they relate and then against passive activity income from other passive activities.[6] Taxpayers subject to the passive activity loss limitation rule must maintain records to track the suspended losses and the activities to which they belong.

Assume that the facts are the same as in Example 7 and that in 2016, Activity A produces $10,000 of income. Diego may use $10,000 of Activity A's suspended loss of $15,000 from 2015 to offset the $10,000 income from this activity. If Diego sells Activity A in early 2017, the remaining $5,000 suspended loss is used to offset any income from the activity reported by Diego in 2017 and to determine his final gain or loss.

Passive Activity Credits

Credits (such as the low-income housing credit and rehabilitation credit—discussed in Chapter 13) that arise from passive activities are limited in much the same way as passive activity losses. Passive activity credits can be utilized only against regular tax attributable to passive activity income,[7] which is calculated by comparing the tax on all income (including passive activity income) with the tax on income excluding passive activity income.

Read
Again

---

[6]§ 469(b).

[7]§ 469(d)(2).

Sam owes $50,000 of tax, disregarding net passive activity income, and $80,000 of tax, considering both net passive activity and other taxable income (disregarding the credits in both cases). The amount of tax attributable to the passive activity income is $30,000.

EXAMPLE 9

In the preceding example, Sam can claim a maximum of $30,000 of passive activity credits; the excess credits are carried over. These passive activity credits can be used only against the *regular* tax attributable to passive activity income. If a taxpayer has a net loss from passive activities during a given year, no credits can be used.

← Read Again

Carryovers of Passive Activity Credits

Tax credits attributable to passive activities can be carried forward indefinitely much like suspended passive activity losses. Unlike passive activity losses, however, passive activity credits are lost forever when the activity is disposed of in a taxable transaction where loss is recognized. Credits are allowed on dispositions only when there is sufficient tax on passive activity income to absorb them.

Use of Passive Activity Credits upon Disposition of an Activity

Alicia sells a passive activity for a gain of $10,000. The activity had suspended losses of $40,000 and suspended credits of $15,000. The $10,000 gain is offset by $10,000 of the suspended losses, and the remaining $30,000 of suspended losses is deductible against Alicia's active and portfolio income. The suspended credits are lost forever because the sale of the activity did not generate any tax.

EXAMPLE 10

If Alicia in Example 10 had realized a $100,000 gain on the sale of the passive activity, the suspended credits could have been used to the extent of the regular tax attributable to the net passive activity income.

EXAMPLE 11

Gain on sale	$100,000
Less: Suspended losses	(40,000)
Taxable gain	$ 60,000

If the tax attributable to the taxable gain of $60,000 is $15,000 or more, the entire $15,000 of suspended credits can be used. If the tax attributable to the gain is less than $15,000, the excess of the suspended credits over the tax attributable to the gain is lost forever.

When a taxpayer has sufficient regular tax liability from passive activities to trigger the use of suspended credits, the credits lose their character as passive activity credits. They are reclassified as regular tax credits and made subject to the same limits as other credits (discussed in Chapter 13).

Passive Activity Changes to Active

If a formerly passive activity becomes an active one, suspended losses are allowed to the extent of income from the now active business.[8] If any of the suspended loss remains, it continues to be treated as a loss from a passive activity. The excess suspended loss can be deducted from passive activity income or carried over to the next tax year and deducted to the extent of income from the now active business in the succeeding year(s). The activity must continue to be the same activity.

---

[8]§ 469(f).

EXAMPLE 12

For several years, Rebecca has owned an interest in a passive activity that has produced losses of $80,000 during that period. Because she did not have passive activity income from other sources, she could not deduct any of the activity's passive activity losses. In the current year, she has become a material participant in the activity and her share of the business profits total $25,000. As a result, she may use $25,000 of the suspended passive activity loss to offset the current business profits. Rebecca's remaining suspended passive activity loss from the activity is $55,000 ($80,000 − $25,000), which is carried over to future years and used to offset income from the formerly passive activity or income from other passive activities.

11-3b Taxpayers Subject to the Passive Activity Loss Rules

The passive activity loss rules apply to individuals, estates, trusts, personal service corporations, and closely held C corporations.[9] Passive activity income or loss from investments in partnerships or S corporations (see Chapter 20) flows through to the owners, and the passive activity loss rules are applied at the owner level.

Personal Service Corporations

Application of the passive activity loss limitations to personal service corporations is intended to prevent taxpayers from sheltering personal service income by creating personal service corporations and acquiring passive activities at the corporate level.

EXAMPLE 13

Two tax accountants who earn an aggregate of $200,000 a year in their individual practices agree to work together in a newly formed personal service corporation. Shortly after its formation, the corporation invests in a passive activity that produces a $200,000 loss during the year. Because the passive activity loss rules apply to personal service corporations, the corporation may not deduct the $200,000 passive activity loss against the $200,000 of active income.

Determination of whether a corporation is a **personal service corporation** is based on rather broad definitions. A personal service corporation is a regular (or C) corporation that meets *both* of the following conditions:

- The principal activity is the performance of personal services.
- Such services are substantially performed by employee-owners.

Generally, personal service corporations include those in the fields of health, law, engineering, architecture, accounting, actuarial science, performing arts, and consulting.[10] A corporation is treated as a personal service corporation if more than 10 percent of the stock (by value) is held by employee-owners.[11] An employee is treated as an employee-owner if he or she owns stock on *any day* during the taxable year.[12] For these purposes, shareholder status and employee status do not have to occur on the same day.

Closely Held C Corporations

Application of the passive activity loss rules to closely held (nonpersonal service) C corporations is also intended to prevent individuals from incorporating to avoid the passive activity loss limitations. A corporation is classified as a **closely held corporation** if at any time during the taxable year more than 50 percent of the value of its outstanding stock is owned, directly or indirectly, by or for five or fewer individuals. Closely held C corporations (other than personal service corporations) may use passive activity losses to offset *active* income but not portfolio income.

---

[9]§ 469(a).
[10]§ 448(d)(2)(A).

[11]§ 469(j)(2).
[12]§ 269A(b)(2).

Silver Corporation, a closely held (nonpersonal service) C corporation, has $500,000 of passive activity losses from a rental activity, $400,000 of active income, and $100,000 of portfolio income. The corporation may offset $400,000 of the $500,000 passive activity loss against the $400,000 of active business income but may not offset the remainder against the $100,000 of portfolio income. Thus, $100,000 of the passive activity loss is suspended ($500,000 passive activity loss − $400,000 offset against active income).

Application of the passive activity loss limitations to closely held C corporations prevents taxpayers from transferring their portfolio investments to such corporations to offset passive activity losses against portfolio income.

11-3c **Rules for Determining Passive Activities**

As noted earlier, the following types of activities are treated as passive:

- Any trade or business or income-producing activity in which the taxpayer does not materially participate.
- Subject to certain exceptions pertaining to real estate (discussed later), all rental activities.

To understand the meaning of the term *passive activity* and the impact of the rules, one must address the following issues, each of which is the subject of statutory or administrative guidance:

- What constitutes an activity?
- What is meant by material participation?
- When is an activity a rental activity?

Even though guidance is available to help the taxpayer deal with these issues, their resolution is anything but simple.

LO.4

Explore the elements required for an activity to be treated as passive and review the rules for identifying an activity.

Identification of an Activity

Identifying what constitutes an activity is a necessary first step in applying the passive activity loss limitations. Taxpayers who are involved in complex business operations need to determine whether a given segment of their overall business operations constitutes a separate activity or is to be treated as part of a single activity. Proper treatment is necessary to determine whether income or loss from an activity is active or passive.

Treatment as a Component of an Activity or as a Separate Activity

Ben owns a business with two separate departments. Department A generates net income of $120,000, and Department B generates a net loss of $95,000. Ben participates 700 hours in the operations of Department A and 100 hours in Department B. If Ben is allowed to treat the departments as components of a single activity, he can offset the $95,000 loss from Department B against the $120,000 of income from Department A.

Assume the same facts as in the previous example. If Ben is required to treat each department as a separate activity, the tax result is not as favorable. Because he is a material participant in Department A (having devoted 700 hours to it), the $120,000 profit is active income. Assuming that Ben is not considered a material participant in Department B (100 hours), the $95,000 loss is a passive activity loss. Therefore, Ben cannot offset the $95,000 passive activity loss from Department B against the $120,000 of active income from Department A. (A complete discussion of the material participation rules follows.)

Recall that on the disposition of a passive activity, a taxpayer is allowed to offset suspended losses from the activity against other types of income. Therefore, as illustrated in the next example, identifying what constitutes an activity is of crucial importance for this purpose too.

TAX IN THE NEWS If You Can't Trust Your Tax Preparer, Who Can You Trust?

Many taxpayers choose to remain ignorant of the tax law because they assume that by paying a "professional" to complete their returns, they have shifted all responsibility to someone else. But they do so at their own risk. Failure to have at least a general understanding of the tax rules that apply to one's return can be a big mistake and can lead to various tax penalties.

One such taxpayer invested in several partnerships that engaged in horse activities in California. Being fully employed in New York, he did not participate in the partnerships' activities and had no knowledge of their business operations. When he received the tax information from the partnerships about his investments, he simply turned over the statements to his tax preparer, who included the information on the return filed. Essentially, the tax return reflected the taxpayer's losses from the horse activities even though they are disallowed under the passive activity loss rules.

When the IRS discovered the error, the taxpayer pleaded ignorance and blamed the tax preparer. The taxpayer claimed that he had been "duped by a charlatan" and pleaded for mercy. The Tax Court showed no compassion and held that he owed additional taxes, interest, and penalties (*Ralph P. Cunningham*, 98 TCM 143, T.C.Memo. 2009–194). Perhaps the result would have been different if the taxpayer had had a better understanding of the tax law in general and the passive activity rules in particular. Reliance on a tax preparer is not an excuse for blindly signing a tax return without understanding its content.

EXAMPLE 17

Linda owns a business with two departments. Department A has a net loss of $125,000 in the current year, and Department B has a $70,000 net loss. She disposes of Department B at the end of the year. Assuming that Linda is allowed to treat the two departments as separate passive activities, she can offset the passive activity loss from Department B against other types of income in the following order: gain from disposition of the passive activity, other passive activity income, and nonpassive activity income. This treatment leaves her with a suspended loss of $125,000 from Department A. If Departments A and B are treated as components of the same activity, however, upon the disposal of Department B, its $70,000 net loss would be suspended along with the other $125,000 of suspended loss of the activity.

The rules used to delineate what constitutes an activity for purposes of the passive activity loss limitations are provided in the Regulations.[13] These guidelines state that in general, a taxpayer can treat one or more trade or business activities or rental activities as a single activity if those activities form an *appropriate economic unit* for measuring gain or loss. To determine what ventures form an appropriate economic unit, all of the relevant facts and circumstances must be considered. Taxpayers may use any reasonable method in applying the facts and circumstances. The following example, adapted from the Regulations, illustrates the application of the general rules for grouping activities.[14]

EXAMPLE 18

George owns a men's clothing store and an Internet café in Chicago. He also owns a men's clothing store and an Internet café in Milwaukee. Reasonable methods of applying the facts and circumstances test may result in any of the following groupings:

- All four activities may be grouped into a single activity because of common ownership and control.
- The clothing stores may be grouped into an activity, and the Internet cafés may be grouped into a separate activity.
- The Chicago activities may be grouped into an activity, and the Milwaukee activities may be grouped into a separate activity.
- Each of the four activities may be treated as a separate activity.

---

[13]Reg. § 1.469–4.

[14]Reg. § 1.469–4(c)(3).

Regrouping of Activities Taxpayers should carefully consider all tax factors when deciding how to group their activities. Once activities have been grouped, they cannot be regrouped unless the original grouping was clearly inappropriate or there has been a material change in the facts and circumstances. The Regulations also grant the IRS the right to regroup activities when both of the following conditions exist:[15]

- The taxpayer's grouping fails to reflect one or more appropriate economic units.
- One of the primary purposes of the taxpayer's grouping is to avoid the passive activity loss limitations.

Special Grouping Rules for Rental Activities Two rules deal specifically with the grouping of rental activities. These provisions are designed to prevent taxpayers from grouping rental activities, which are generally passive, with other businesses in a way that would result in a tax advantage. First, a rental activity may be grouped with a trade or business activity only if one activity is insubstantial in relation to the other. That is, the rental activity must be insubstantial in relation to the trade or business activity, or the trade or business activity must be insubstantial in relation to the rental activity. The Regulations provide no clear guidelines as to the meaning of "insubstantial."[16]

[handwritten margin note: One is Insubstantial]

> **EXAMPLE 19**
>
> Schemers, a firm of CPAs, owns a building in downtown Washington, D.C., in which it conducts its public accounting practice. The firm also rents space on the street level of the building to several retail establishments, which generally is considered a passive activity. Of the total revenue generated by the firm, 95% is associated with the public accounting practice and 5% is related to the rental operation. It is likely that the rental activity would be considered insubstantial relative to the accounting practice and the two ventures could be grouped as one nonrental activity. This grouping could be advantageous to the firm, particularly if the rental operation generates a loss! Alternatively, treating the rental operation as a *separate* activity may be advantageous if this operation produces (passive activity) income. The passive activity income could then be used to absorb otherwise nondeductible passive activity losses.

Second, taxpayers generally may not treat an activity involving the rental of real property and an activity involving the rental of personal property as a single activity.

Material Participation

As indicated previously, if an individual taxpayer materially participates in a nonrental trade or business activity, any loss from that activity is treated as an active loss that can offset active or portfolio income. (Participation is defined later in the chapter.) If a taxpayer does not materially participate, however, the loss is treated as a passive activity loss, which can only offset passive activity income. Therefore, controlling whether a particular activity is treated as active or passive is an important part of the tax strategy of a taxpayer who owns an interest in one or more businesses. Consider the following examples.

LO.5

Identify the tests for material participation.

> **Implications of Material Participation Status**
>
> **EXAMPLE 20**
>
> Dewayne, a corporate executive, earns a salary of $600,000 per year. In addition, he owns a separate business in which he participates. The business produces a loss of $100,000 during the year. If Dewayne materially participates in the business, the $100,000 loss is an active loss that may offset his active income from his corporate employer. If he does not materially participate, the loss is passive and is suspended unless he has other passive activity income. Dewayne may use the suspended loss in the future only when he has passive activity income or disposes of the activity.

---

[15]Reg. § 1.469–4(f).　　　　　　　　[16]Reg. § 1.469–4(d).

Implications of Material Participation Status

EXAMPLE

21

Kay, an attorney, earns $350,000 a year in her law practice. In addition, she owns interests in two activities, A and B, in which she participates. Activity A, in which she does *not* materially participate, produces a loss of $50,000. Kay has not yet met the material participation standard, described below, for Activity B, which produces income of $80,000. However, she can meet the material participation standard if she spends an additional 50 hours in Activity B during the year. Should Kay attempt to meet the material participation standard for Activity B? If she continues working in Activity B and becomes a material participant, the $80,000 of income from the activity is *active*, and the $50,000 passive activity loss from Activity A must be suspended. A more favorable tax strategy is for Kay *not to meet* the material participation standard for Activity B, thus making the income from that activity passive. This enables her to offset the $50,000 passive activity loss from Activity A against most of the passive activity income from Activity B.

you want

Profit ⇒ Passive

Loss ⇒ Active

It is possible to devise numerous scenarios in which the taxpayer could control the tax outcome by increasing or decreasing his or her participation in different activities. Examples 20 and 21 demonstrate some of the possibilities. The conclusion reached in most analyses of this type is that taxpayers will benefit by having profitable activities classified as passive so that any passive activity losses can be used to offset that passive activity income. If the activity produces a loss, however, the taxpayer will benefit if it is classified as active so that the loss is not subject to the passive activity loss limitations.

As discussed previously, a nonrental trade or business in which a taxpayer owns an interest must be treated as a passive activity unless the taxpayer materially participates. As the Staff of the Joint Committee on Taxation explained, a material participant is one who has "a significant nontax economic profit motive" for taking on activities and selects them for their economic value. In contrast, a passive investor mainly seeks a return from a capital investment (including a possible reduction in taxes) as a supplement to an ongoing source of livelihood.[17] Even if the concept or the implication of being a material participant is clear, the precise meaning of the term **material participation** can be vague. As enacted, § 469 requires a taxpayer to participate on a *regular, continuous, and substantial* basis to be a material participant. In many situations, however, it is difficult or impossible to gain any assurance that this nebulous standard is met.

In response to this dilemma, Temporary Regulations[18] provide seven tests that serve to determine when material participation is achieved. Material participation is achieved by meeting any *one* of the tests. These tests are listed in Concept Summary 11.2 and can be divided into the following three categories:

- Tests based on current participation.
- Tests based on prior participation.
- Test based on facts and circumstances.

Participation Defined Participation generally includes any work done by an individual in an activity that he or she owns. Participation does not include work if it is of a type not customarily done by owners *and if* one of its principal purposes is to avoid the disallowance of passive activity losses or credits. Also, work done in an individual's capacity as an investor (e.g., reviewing financial reports in a nonmanagerial capacity) is not counted in applying the material participation tests. However, participation by an owner's spouse counts as participation by the owner.[19]

---

[17]*General Explanation of the Tax Reform Act of 1986* ("Blue Book"), prepared by The Staff of the Joint Committee on Taxation, May 4, 1987, H.R. 3838, 99th Cong., p. 212.

[18]Temp.Reg. § 1.469–5T(a). The Temporary Regulations are also Proposed Regulations. Temporary Regulations have the same effect as final Regulations. Refer to Chapter 2 for a discussion of the different categories of Regulations.

[19]§ 469(h)(5) and Temp.Reg. § 1.469–5T(f)(3).

Concept Summary 11.2

Tests to Determine Material Participation

Tests Based on Current Participation

1. The individual participates in the activity for more than 500 hours during the year.

2. The individual's participation in the activity for the taxable year constitutes substantially all of the participation in the activity of all individuals (including nonowner employees) for the year.

3. The individual participates in the activity for more than 100 hours during the year, and this participation is not less than that participation of any other individual (including nonowner employees) for the year.

4. The activity is a **significant participation activity** (where the person's participation *exceeds* 100 hours during the year), and the hours for all significant participation activities during the year is more than 500 hours.

Tests Based on Prior Participation

5. The individual materially participated in the activity for any 5 taxable years during the 10 taxable years that immediately precede the current taxable year.

6. The activity is a personal service activity, and the individual materially participated in the activity for any 3 preceding taxable years.

Test Based on Facts and Circumstances

7. Based on all of the facts and circumstances, the individual participates in the activity on a regular, continuous, and substantial basis during the year.

EXAMPLE 22

Tom, who is a partner in a CPA firm, owns a computer store that operated at a loss during the year. To offset this loss against the income from his CPA practice, Tom would like to avoid having the computer business classified as a passive activity. During the year, he worked 480 hours in the business in management and selling activities and 30 hours doing janitorial chores. In addition, Tom's wife participated 40 hours as a salesperson. It is likely that Tom's 480 hours of participation in management and selling activities will count as participation in work customarily done by owners, but the 30 hours spent doing janitorial chores will not. However, the 40 hours of participation by his wife will count. Assuming that none of the participation's principal purposes is to avoid the disallowance of passive activity losses or credits, Tom will qualify as a material participant under the more-than-500-hour rule (480 + 40 = 520).

Limited Partners A *limited* partner is a partner whose liability to third-party creditors of the partnership is limited to the amount the partner has invested in the partnership. Such a partnership must have at least one *general* partner who is fully liable in an individual capacity for the debts of the partnership to third parties. Generally, a *limited partner* is not considered a material participant unless he or she qualifies under Test 1, 5, or 6 as shown in Concept Summary 11.2. However, a *general partner* may qualify as a material participant by meeting any of the seven tests. If a general partner also owns a limited interest in the same limited partnership, all interests are treated as a general interest.[20]

 — You can do this ?

Rental Activities Defined

LO.6

Describe the nature of rental activities under the passive activity loss rules.

Subject to certain exceptions, all rental activities are to be treated as passive activities.[21] A **rental activity** is defined as any activity where payments are received principally for the use of tangible (real or personal) property.[22] Importantly, an activity that is classified as a rental activity is subject to the passive activity loss rules even if the taxpayer involved is a material participant.

---

[20]§ 469(h)(2) and Temp.Reg. § 1.469–5T(e)(3)(ii). Under Prop.Reg. § 1.469–5, however, material participation status for owners of LLCs and LLPs is dependent on the taxpayer's general involvement in the business.

[21]§ 469(c)(2).

[22]§ 469(j)(8).

EXAMPLE 23

Sarah owns a fleet of automobiles that are held for rent, and she spends an average of 60 hours a week in the activity. Assuming that her automobile business is classified as a rental activity, it is automatically subject to the passive activity rules even though Sarah spends more than 500 hours a year in its operation.

Certain rentals of real and personal property might be classified under the passive activity loss rules as nonrental activities.[23] In these situations, assuming the activity is a trade or business, the material participation tests shown in Concept Summary 11.2 must be applied to determine whether the activity is a passive activity. Consider the following example.

EXAMPLE 24

Dan owns a bicycle rental business at a nearby resort. Because the average period of customer use is seven days or less, Dan's business is not treated as a rental activity.

This exception to the definition of a rental activity is based on the presumption that a person who rents property for seven days or less is generally required to provide significant services to the customer. Providing such services supports a conclusion that the person is engaged in a service business rather than a rental business.

The fact that Dan's business in the previous example is not treated as a rental activity does not necessarily mean that it is classified as a nonpassive activity. Instead, the business is treated as a trade or business activity subject to the material participation standards listed in Concept Summary 11.2. If Dan is a material participant, the business is treated as active. If he is not a material participant, it is treated as a passive activity. For additional discussion of the rental exceptions, see IRS Publication 925 (*Passive Activity and At-Risk Rules*).

11-3d Interaction of the At-Risk and Passive Activity Loss Limits

LO.7

Determine the relationship between the at-risk and passive activity loss limitations.

The determination of whether a loss is suspended under the passive activity loss rules is made *after* application of the at-risk rules, as well as other provisions relating to the measurement of taxable income. A loss that is not allowed for the year because the taxpayer is not at risk with respect to it is suspended under the at-risk provision, not under the passive activity loss rules. Further, a taxpayer's at-risk basis is reduced by the losses (but not below zero) even if the deductions are not currently usable because of the passive activity loss rules. The following examples illustrate these points.

[23]Temp.Reg. § 1.469–1T(e)(3).

At-Risk and Passive Activity Loss Interactions

Jack's adjusted basis in a passive activity is $10,000 at the beginning of 2015. His loss from the activity in 2015 is $4,000. Because Jack has no passive activity income, the $4,000 cannot be deducted. At year-end, Jack has an adjusted basis and an at-risk amount of $6,000 in the activity and a suspended passive activity loss of $4,000.

EXAMPLE 25

Jack in Example 25 has a loss of $9,000 in the activity in 2016. Because the $9,000 exceeds his at-risk amount ($6,000) by $3,000, that $3,000 loss is disallowed by the at-risk rules. If Jack has no passive activity income, the remaining $6,000 is suspended under the passive activity rules. At year-end, he has:

- A $3,000 loss suspended under the at-risk rules.
- $10,000 of suspended passive activity losses ($4,000 from 2015 and $6,000 from 2016).
- An adjusted basis and an at-risk amount in the activity of zero.

EXAMPLE 26

Jack in Example 26 realizes $1,000 of passive activity income from the activity in 2017. Because the $1,000 increases his at-risk amount, $1,000 of the $3,000 unused loss from 2016 is reclassified as a passive activity loss. If he has no other passive activity income, the $1,000 income is offset by $1,000 of suspended passive activity losses. At the end of 2017, Jack has:

- No taxable passive activity income.
- $2,000 ($3,000 − $1,000) of suspended losses under the at-risk rules.
- $10,000 of (reclassified) suspended passive activity losses ($10,000 + $1,000 of reclassified suspended at-risk losses − $1,000 of passive activity losses offset against passive activity income).
- An adjusted basis and an at-risk amount in the activity of zero.

EXAMPLE 27

In 2018, Jack has no gain or loss from the activity in Example 27. He contributes $5,000 more to the passive activity. Because the $5,000 increases his at-risk amount, the $2,000 of losses suspended under the at-risk rules is reclassified as passive. Jack gets no passive activity loss deduction in 2018. At year-end, he has:

- No suspended losses under the at-risk rules.
- $12,000 of suspended passive activity losses ($10,000 + $2,000 of reclassified suspended at-risk losses).
- An adjusted basis and an at-risk amount of $3,000 ($5,000 additional investment − $2,000 of reclassified losses).

EXAMPLE 28

The Big Picture

Return to the facts of *The Big Picture* on p. 11-1. If the Reswicks invest in the orange grove limited partnership, the at-risk rules will not limit the deductibility of the $25,000 losses until after year 4. Ample at-risk basis will exist until the close of that year (i.e., the at-risk basis is reduced from $100,000 by $25,000 over each of the first four years of the investment). However, the passive activity loss rules prohibit deductions for the losses in the first four years of the investment (assuming that the Reswicks do not have passive activity income from other sources). Therefore, based on the facts provided, none of the suspended losses would be deductible until year 6, when the orange grove is expected to begin producing profits.

EXAMPLE 29

See Concept Summary 11.3 where the interactions of the at-risk and passive activity limits are set out.

Concept Summary 11.3

Treatment of Losses Subject to the At-Risk and Passive Activity Loss Limitations

LO.8

Recognize the special treatment available to real estate activities.

11-3e Special Passive Activity Rules for Real Estate Activities

The passive activity loss limits contain two exceptions related to real estate activities. These exceptions allow all or part of real estate rental losses to offset active or portfolio income even though the activity otherwise is defined as a passive activity.

Material Participation in a Real Property Rental Trade or Business

The first exception relates to a special rule for material participation in a real estate rental trade or business. Losses from real estate rental activities are *not* treated as passive activity losses for certain real estate professionals.[24] To qualify for nonpassive treatment, a taxpayer must satisfy both of the following requirements:

- More than half of the personal services that the taxpayer performs in trades or businesses are performed in real property trades or businesses in which the taxpayer materially participates.

- The taxpayer performs more than 750 hours of services in these real property trades or businesses as a material participant.

Taxpayers who do not satisfy the above requirements must continue to treat income and losses from real estate rental activities as passive activity income and losses.

During the current year, Della performs personal service activities as follows: 900 hours as a personal financial planner, 550 hours in a real estate development business, and 600 hours in a real estate rental activity. Any loss Della incurs in either real estate activity will not be subject to the passive activity loss rules. Being a nonrental business, the development business is deemed active under the more-than-500-hour material participation test. The real estate rental activity is active because more than 50% of her personal services are devoted to real property trades or businesses (i.e., the development and rental businesses) and her material participation in those real estate activities exceeds 750 hours. Thus, any losses from either real estate activity can offset active and portfolio sources of income. Likewise, any income from these activities is nonpassive (active) income.

---

[24]§ 469(c)(7).

Full-Time Employees May Face Difficulty Showing Real Estate Professional Status

To qualify as a real estate professional, a taxpayer must devote more than 50 percent of his or her personal services to real property trades or businesses. This requirement typically would make it difficult for a person with a full-time job to qualify for this status because the efforts as an employee likely would comprise the bulk of the taxpayer's labor.

If you were a judge, how reasonable would a taxpayer's assertion be that he worked more time on his real estate properties than his full-time, 40-hour-a-week job? One taxpayer, who faced such a challenge before the Tax Court (*Mohammad Hassanipour* 105 TCM 1542, T.C.Memo. 2013–88), was unable to convince the judge. Consequently, he was required to pay additional taxes and penalties—over

$45,000—for inappropriately claiming deductions as a real estate professional.

Essentially, the taxpayer reported that he worked 1,936 hours for his employer and was not able to persuade the judge that he spent more than this working on his real estate properties. In the end, the Tax Court stated that the taxpayer's testimony was undermined by "his questionable claims about the contemporaneous calendar, and by the vagueness and inherent improbability of his estimates."

A basic premise of tax compliance illustrated by the case is that a taxpayer should never claim a deduction unless he or she is entitled to it and it can be supported with adequate and convincing documentation.

As discussed earlier, a spouse's work is taken into consideration in satisfying the material participation requirement. However, the hours worked by a spouse are *not* taken into account when ascertaining whether a taxpayer has worked for more than 750 hours in real property trades or businesses during a year.[25] Services performed by an employee are not treated as being related to a real estate trade or business unless the employee performing the services owns more than a 5 percent interest in the employer. In addition, a closely held C corporation may also qualify for the passive activity loss relief if more than 50 percent of its gross receipts for the year are derived from real property trades or businesses in which it materially participates.

Punching the Time Clock at Year-End

As the end of the tax year approaches, Ralph, a successful full-time real estate developer and investor, recognizes that his income tax situation for the year could be bleak. Unless he and his wife are able to generate more hours of participation in one of his real estate rental activities, they will not reach the material participation threshold. Consequently, the tax losses from the venture will not be deductible. To ensure deductibility, Ralph suggests the following plan:

- He will document the time he spends "thinking" about his rental activities.

- During the week, his wife will visit the apartment building to oversee (in a management role) the operations of the rentals.

- On weekends, he and his wife will visit the same units to further evaluate the operations.

- Also on the weekends, while they are doing their routine household shopping, they will be on the lookout for other rental properties to buy. Ralph plans to count both his and his wife's weekend hours toward the tally of total participation.

Ralph contends that the law clearly allows the efforts of one's spouse to count for purposes of the material participation tests. Likewise, nothing in the tax law requires taxpayers to be efficient in their hours of participation. How do you react?

Real Estate Rental Activities with Active Participation

The second exception to the passive activity loss limits is more significant in that it is not restricted to real estate professionals. This exception allows individuals to deduct

---

[25]§ 469(c)(7)(B) and Reg. § 1.469–9. In *Frank Aragona Trust*, 142 T.C. 165 (2014), the Tax Court found that a trust also could qualify for the real estate professional rule.

up to $25,000 of losses from real estate rental activities against active and portfolio income.[26] The potential annual $25,000 deduction is reduced by 50 percent of the taxpayer's AGI in excess of $100,000. Thus, the entire deduction is phased out at $150,000 of AGI. If married individuals file separately, the $25,000 deduction is reduced to zero unless they lived apart for the entire year, in which case the loss amount is $12,500 each and the phaseout begins at $50,000 of AGI. AGI for purposes of the phaseout is calculated without regard to IRA deductions, Social Security benefits, interest deductions on education loans, and net losses from passive activities.

To qualify for the $25,000 exception, a taxpayer must meet both of the following requirements:[27]

- Actively participate in the real estate rental activity.
- Own 10 percent or more (in value) of all interests in the activity during the entire taxable year (or shorter period during which the taxpayer held an interest in the activity).

The difference between *active participation* and *material participation* is that the former can be satisfied without regular, continuous, and substantial involvement in operations as long as the taxpayer participates in making management decisions in a significant and bona fide sense. In this context, relevant management decisions include decisions such as approving new tenants, deciding on rental terms, and approving capital or repair expenditures.

The Big Picture

EXAMPLE 31

Return to the facts of *The Big Picture* on p. 11-1. If the Reswicks invest in the apartment rental limited partnership, their $25,000 loss would be deductible under the real estate rental activities exception. This assumes that they actively participate and own at least a 10% interest in the partnership. The loss will be deductible in each of the first four years of their investment before their at-risk basis has been exhausted (as explained earlier, the Reswick's original at-risk basis of $100,000 will be reduced to $0 over four years) even if they do not have passive activity income from other sources.

The $25,000 allowance is available after all active participation rental losses and gains are netted and applied to other passive activity income. If a taxpayer has a real estate rental loss in excess of the amount that can be deducted under the real estate rental exception, that excess is treated as a passive activity loss, usable in future years.

EXAMPLE 32

Brad has $90,000 of AGI before considering rental activities. Brad also has $85,000 of losses from a real estate rental activity in which he actively participates. He also actively participates in another real estate rental activity from which he has $30,000 of income. He has other passive activity income of $36,000. Of the net rental loss of $55,000 ($30,000 − $85,000), $36,000 is absorbed by the passive activity income, leaving $19,000 that can be deducted against active or portfolio income because of the availability of the $25,000 allowance.

The $25,000 offset allowance is an aggregate of both deductions and credits in deduction equivalents. The deduction equivalent of a passive activity credit is the amount of deductions that reduces the tax liability for the taxable year by an amount equal to the credit.[28] A taxpayer with $5,000 of credits and a tax bracket of 25 percent would have a deduction equivalent of $20,000 ($5,000 ÷ 25%).

If the total deduction and deduction equivalent exceed $25,000, the taxpayer must allocate the allowance on a pro rata basis, first among the losses (including real estate rental activity losses suspended in prior years) and then to credits in the following order:

---

[26]§ 469(i).

[27]§ 469(i)(6).

[28]§ 469(j)(5).

(1) credits other than rehabilitation and low-income housing credits, (2) rehabilitation credits, and (3) low-income housing credits.

Deduction Equivalent Considerations

Kevin is an active participant in a real estate rental activity that produces $8,000 of income, $26,000 of deductions, and $1,500 of credits. Kevin, who is in the 25% tax bracket, may deduct the net passive activity loss of $18,000 ($8,000 − $26,000). After deducting the loss, he has an available deduction equivalent of $7,000 ($25,000 − $18,000 passive activity loss). Because the actual credits produce a deduction equivalent ($1,500 ÷ 25% = $6,000) that is less than $7,000, Kevin may claim the entire $1,500 credit.

EXAMPLE 33

Kelly, who is in the 25% tax bracket, is an active participant in three separate real estate rental activities. The relevant tax results for each activity are as follows:

- Activity A: $20,000 of losses.
- Activity B: $10,000 of losses.
- Activity C: $4,200 of credits.

Kelly's deduction equivalent from the credits is $16,800 ($4,200 ÷ 25%). Therefore, the total passive activity deductions and deduction equivalents are $46,800 ($20,000 + $10,000 + $16,800), which exceeds the maximum allowable amount of $25,000. Consequently, Kelly must allocate pro rata first from among losses and then from among credits. Deductions from losses are limited as follows:

- Activity A {$25,000 × [$20,000 ÷ ($20,000 + $10,000)]} = $16,667.
- Activity B {$25,000 × [$10,000 ÷ ($20,000 + $10,000)]} = $8,333.

Because the amount of passive activity deductions exceeds the $25,000 maximum, the deduction balance of $5,000 and passive activity credits of $4,200 must be carried forward. Kelly's suspended losses and credits by activity are as follows:

EXAMPLE 34

	Total	Activity A	Activity B	Activity C
Allocated losses	$ 30,000	$ 20,000	$10,000	$ –0–
Allocated credits	4,200	–0–	–0–	4,200
Utilized losses	(25,000)	(16,667)	(8,333)	–0–
Suspended losses	5,000	3,333	1,667	–0–
Suspended credits	4,200	–0–	–0–	4,200

11-3f Dispositions of Passive Interests

Recall from an earlier discussion that if a taxpayer disposes of an entire interest in a passive activity, any suspended losses (and in certain cases, suspended credits) may be utilized when calculating the final economic gain or loss on the investment. In addition, if a loss ultimately results, that loss can offset other types of income. However, the consequences may differ if the activity is disposed of in a transaction that is other than a fully taxable transaction. The following sections discuss the treatment of suspended passive activity losses in other types of dispositions.

LO.9

Determine the proper tax treatment upon the disposition of a passive activity.

Disposition of a Passive Activity at Death

When a transfer of a taxpayer's interest occurs because of the taxpayer's death, suspended losses are allowed (to the decedent) to the extent they exceed the amount, if any, of the allowed step-up in basis.[29] Suspended losses that are equal to or less than

---

[29]§ 469(g)(2).

the amount of the basis increase are, however, lost. The losses allowed generally are reported on the final return of the deceased taxpayer.

Disposition of Suspended Passive Activity Losses at Death

EXAMPLE 35

Alyson dies with passive activity property having an adjusted basis of $40,000, suspended losses of $10,000, and a fair market value at the date of her death of $75,000. The increase (i.e., step-up) in basis (see Chapter 14) is $35,000 (fair market value at date of death in excess of adjusted basis). None of the $10,000 suspended loss is deductible on Alyson's final return or by the beneficiary. The suspended losses ($10,000) are lost because they do not exceed the step-up in basis ($35,000).

EXAMPLE 36

Assume the same facts as in the previous example except that the property's fair market value at the date of Alyson's death is $47,000. Because the step-up in basis is only $7,000 ($47,000 − $40,000), the suspended losses allowed are limited to $3,000 ($10,000 suspended loss at time of death − $7,000 increase in basis). The $3,000 loss available to Alyson is reported on her final income tax return.

Disposition of a Passive Activity by Gift

In a disposition of a taxpayer's interest in a passive activity by gift, the suspended losses are added to the basis of the property.[30] As such, the suspended losses become permanently nondeductible to both the donor and the donee. Nonetheless, a tax *benefit* may be available to the donee for another reason. Due to the increase in the property's basis, greater depreciation deductions can result, and there will be less gain (or more loss) on a subsequent sale of the property. The side benefits of increased basis do not materialize if the recipient is a charity, as such organizations generally are not subject to income taxation.

EXAMPLE 37

Carlton makes a gift to Yolanda of passive activity property having an adjusted basis of $40,000, suspended losses of $10,000, and a fair market value at the date of the gift of $100,000. Carlton cannot deduct the suspended losses in the year of the disposition. However, the suspended losses transfer with the property and are added to the adjusted basis of the property, thus becoming $50,000 in Yolanda's hands. Assuming that Yolanda is able to sell the property for $105,000 soon after she receives the gift, her taxable gain would be $55,000 ($105,000 − $50,000), which reflects the benefit from the increased basis.

Installment Sale of a Passive Activity

An installment sale of a taxpayer's entire interest in a passive activity triggers recognition of the suspended losses.[31] The losses are allowed each year as payments are received on the installment obligation in the ratio that the gain recognized in each year bears to the total gain on the sale.

EXAMPLE 38

Stan sells his entire interest in a passive activity for $100,000. His adjusted basis in the property is $60,000. If he uses the installment method, his gross profit ratio is 40% ($40,000/$100,000). If Stan receives a $20,000 down payment, he will recognize a gain of $8,000 (40% of $20,000). If the activity has a suspended loss of $25,000, Stan will deduct $5,000 [($8,000 ÷ $40,000) × $25,000] of the suspended loss in the first year.

The general rules relating to passive activity losses are reviewed in Concept Summary 11.4.

---

[30]§ 469(j)(6).

[31]§ 469(g)(3).

Concept Summary 11.4 *PALS need PIGS*

Passive Activity Loss Rules: Key Issues and Answers

What is the fundamental passive activity rule?	Passive activity losses may be deducted only against passive activity income and gains. Losses not allowed are suspended and used in future years.
Who is subject to the passive activity rules?	Individuals.
	Estates.
	Trusts.
	Personal service corporations.
	Closely held C corporations.
What is a passive activity?	Trade or business or income-producing activity in which the taxpayer does not materially participate during the year or rental activities, subject to certain exceptions, regardless of the taxpayer's level of participation.
What is an activity?	One or more trade or business or rental activities that comprise an appropriate economic unit.
How is an appropriate economic unit determined?	Based on a reasonable application of the relevant facts and circumstances.
What is material participation?	In general, the taxpayer participates on a regular, continuous, and substantial basis. More specifically, when the taxpayer meets the conditions of one of the seven tests provided in the Regulations.
What is a rental activity?	In general, an activity where payments are received for the use of tangible property. Special rules apply to rental real estate.

More on a handout

11-4 INVESTMENT INTEREST LIMITATION

LO.10

Identify restrictions placed on the deductibility of other investor losses and deductions, including those that apply to investment interest.

As just described, well-to-do investors tried to use the Code for many years to generate deductible tax losses. As a result, Congress imposed special rules placing limitations on losses where the taxpayer was not at risk or where the losses were from passive activities. Another approach in using the tax law to create wealth involved the use of the interest deduction. By borrowing to purchase investments that would appreciate in the future, the interest on the debt was claimed as an ordinary deduction when paid. Later, when the asset was sold at a gain, only a capital gains tax was due on the appreciation. Thus, today's interest deduction could lead to tomorrow's capital gain.

—Later

11-4a Limitation Imposed

In response, Congress has limited the deductibility of **investment interest**, which is interest paid on debt borrowed for the purpose of purchasing or continuing to hold investment property. The deduction for investment interest allowed during the tax year is limited to the lesser of the investment interest paid or net investment income.[32]

The Big Picture

EXAMPLE
39

Return to the facts of *The Big Picture* on p. 11-1. If the Reswicks invest in the high-growth, low-yield portfolio of marketable securities, most of the investment return will consist of appreciation, which will not be taxed until the securities are sold. Relatively little of the current return will consist of currently taxable interest and dividend income. Assume that the interest and dividend income for the year from these securities equals $500 and that all of it is treated as investment income. If the investment interest expense on the $100,000 loan is $8,000, only $500 of this interest will be deductible this year (i.e., the deduction for the investment interest is limited to the $500 of net investment income).

---

[32]§ 163(d)(1).

Investment Income and Expenses

Net investment income, which serves as the ceiling on the deductibility of investment interest, is the excess of investment income over investment expenses. **Investment income** includes gross income from interest, annuities, and royalties not derived in the ordinary course of a trade or business.[33] However, investment income does not include any income taken into account when calculating income or loss from a passive activity.

Investment expenses are those deductible expenses directly connected with the production of investment income, such as brokerage and investment counsel fees. Investment expenses do not include interest expense.

11-4b Computation of Allowable Deduction

After net investment income is determined, the allowable deductible investment interest expense is calculated.

EXAMPLE 40

Ethan's financial records for the year reflect the following:

Interest income from bank savings account	$10,000
Taxable annuity receipts	5,500
Investment counsel fee	1,100
Safe deposit box rental (to hold annuity documents)	200
Investment interest expense	17,000

Ethan's investment income amounts to $15,500 ($10,000 + $5,500), and investment expenses total $1,300 ($1,100 + $200). Therefore, his net investment income is $14,200 ($15,500 − $1,300). Consequently, the investment interest deduction is limited to $14,200, the lesser of investment interest paid or net investment income.

The amount of investment interest disallowed is carried over to future years. In Example 40, therefore, the amount that is carried over to the following year is $2,800 ($17,000 investment interest expense − $14,200 deduction allowed). No limit is placed on the length of the carryover period.[34] The investment interest expense deduction is determined by completing Form 4952 (Investment Interest Deduction).

11-5 OTHER INVESTMENT LOSSES

The investment activities summarized below are discussed elsewhere in this text as shown in Concept Summary 11.5.

- Sales of securities held as investments for less than basis result in capital losses. These losses can offset capital gains. In the case of individual taxpayers, excess losses are applied against ordinary income up to $3,000 (§ 1211). Any remaining excess capital losses are carried over for use in future years (§ 1212).

- When an activity is classified as a hobby, any losses resulting are limited to the income from the activity [§ 183(b)(2)]. If the activity is not a hobby (i.e., a profit motive controls), however, full deduction of the losses is allowed [§§ 162 and 212(2)].

- Losses on small business stock (i.e., stock that qualifies under § 1244) are treated as ordinary losses up to a maximum of $100,000. Thus, the limitations placed on capital losses (see above) are avoided.

- Vacation homes that are rented for part of the year may generate investment losses depending on the extent of the rental period as compared to time devoted to personal use (§ 280A). If sufficient rental activity takes place, the facility may be treated as rental property. As such, any losses could be subject to the passive activity loss rules.

---

[33]§ 163(d)(4)(B).

[34]§ 163(d)(2).

Concept Summary 11.5

Common Investment Loss Limitation Provisions

Item	Refer to Chapter	General Nature of Limitation
At-risk rules	11	Losses in excess of the at-risk basis are not deducted in the current year. Losses not deducted are suspended and used in future years when the at-risk basis increases.
Capital losses	16	Individuals may offset capital gains by capital losses realized. Up to $3,000 of realized net capital losses may offset ordinary income. Remaining excess capital losses are carried over to future years.
Hobby losses	6	Losses from hobby activities may be deducted to the extent of income from hobby activities. Excess hobby losses are carried forward to future years.
Investment interest	11	The deduction of investment interest is limited to the taxpayer's net investment income. Excess investment interest is deductible in future years.
Passive activity loss limitations	11	Generally, passive activity losses are deducted only to the extent of passive activity income. Excess passive activity losses are suspended and used in future years.
Small business (§ 1244) stock	7	Losses from the disposition of small business stock are given ordinary treatment up to a maximum of $100,000 per year.
Vacation homes	6	The deductibility of losses from vacation homes may be limited, depending on the relative number of rental use days and personal use days of the property.
Worthless securities	7	Losses arising from investment securities that become worthless are treated as occurring on the last day of the tax year.

- Securities held as an investment that become worthless produce capital losses. The losses are usually long term because they are treated as occurring on the last day of the year in which the securities become worthless [§ 165(g)(1)]. Because the securities must be completely worthless, determining the year when this takes place is often difficult.

11-6 TAX PLANNING

11-6a Utilizing Passive Activity Losses

Perhaps the biggest challenge individuals face with the passive activity loss rules is to recognize the potential impact of the rules and then to structure their affairs to minimize this impact. Taxpayers who have passive activity losses (PALs) should adopt a strategy of generating passive activity income that can be sheltered by existing passive activity losses. One approach is to buy an interest in a passive activity that is generating income (referred to as passive income generators, or PIGs). Then the PAL can offset income from the PIG. From a tax perspective, it would be foolish to buy a loss-generating passive activity unless one has other passive activity income to shelter or the activity is rental real estate that can qualify for the $25,000 exception or the exception available to real estate professionals.

If a taxpayer does invest in an activity that produces losses subject to the passive activity loss rules, the following strategies may help minimize the loss of current deductions:

- If money is borrowed to finance the purchase of a passive activity, the associated interest expense is generally treated as part of any passive activity loss. Consequently, by using more available (i.e., not borrowed) cash to purchase the passive investment, the investor will need less debt and will incur less interest expense. By incurring less interest expense, a possible suspended passive activity loss deduction is reduced.

LO.11

Suggest tax planning strategies to minimize the effect of the passive activity loss and investment interest limitations and recognize the general impact of the additional tax on net investment income.

• If the investor does not have sufficient cash readily available for the larger down payment, cash can be obtained by borrowing against the equity in his or her personal residence. The interest expense on such debt will be deductible under the qualified residence interest provisions (see Chapter 10) and will not be subject to the passive activity loss limitations. Thus, the taxpayer avoids the passive activity loss limitation and secures a currently deductible interest expense.

As explained earlier, unusable passive activity losses often accumulate and provide no current tax benefit because the taxpayer has no passive activity income. When the taxpayer disposes of the entire interest in a passive activity, however, any suspended losses from that activity are used to reduce the taxable gain. If any taxable gain still remains, it can be offset by losses from other passive activities. As a result, the taxpayer should carefully select the year in which to dispose of a passive activity. It is to the taxpayer's advantage to wait until sufficient passive activity losses have accumulated to offset any gain recognized on the asset's disposition.

EXAMPLE 41

Bill, a calendar year taxpayer, owns interests in two passive activities: Activity A, which he plans to sell in December of this year at a gain of $100,000, and Activity B, which he plans to keep indefinitely. Current and suspended losses associated with Activity B total $60,000, and Bill expects losses from the activity to be $40,000 next year. If Bill sells Activity A this year, the $100,000 gain can be offset by the current and suspended losses of $60,000 from Activity B, producing a net taxable gain of $40,000. However, if Bill delays the sale of Activity A until January of next year, the $100,000 gain will be fully offset by the $100,000 of losses generated by Activity B ($60,000 current and prior losses + $40,000 next year's loss). Consequently, by postponing the sale by one month, he could avoid recognizing $40,000 of gain that would otherwise result.

Taxpayers with passive activity losses should consider the level of their involvement in all other trades or businesses in which they have an interest. If they show that they do not materially participate in a profitable activity, the activity becomes a passive activity. Any income generated by the profitable business then could be sheltered by current and suspended passive activity losses. Family partnerships in which certain members do not materially participate would qualify. The silent partner in any general partnership engaged in a trade or business would also qualify.

EXAMPLE 42

Gail has an investment in a limited partnership that produces annual passive activity losses of approximately $25,000. She also owns a newly acquired interest in a convenience store where she works. Her share of the store's income is $35,000. If she works enough to be classified as a material participant, her $35,000 share of income is treated as active income. This results in $35,000 being subject to tax every year, while her $25,000 loss is suspended. However, if Gail reduces her involvement at the store so that she is not a material participant, the $35,000 of income receives passive treatment. Consequently, the $35,000 of income can be offset by the $25,000 passive activity loss, resulting in only $10,000 being subject to tax. Thus, by reducing her involvement, Gail ensures that the income from the profitable trade or business receives passive treatment and can then be used to absorb passive activity losses from other passive activities.

The impact of the passive activity loss rules often extend to other seemingly unrelated Code sections. For example, because of the restrictive nature of the passive activity loss rules, it may be advantageous for a taxpayer to use a vacation home enough to convert it to a second residence. This would enable all of the qualified interest and real estate taxes to be deducted without limitation. However, this strategy would lead to the loss of other deductions, such as repairs, maintenance, and insurance. See Examples 26 and 28 and the related discussion in Chapter 6.

As this chapter has shown, the passive activity loss rules can have a dramatic effect on a taxpayer's ability to claim passive activity losses currently. As a result, it is important to keep accurate records of all sources of income and losses, particularly any suspended passive activity losses and credits and the activities to which they relate, so that their potential tax benefit will not be lost.

11-6b **Planning with the Investment Interest Limitation**

The term *investment income* includes net capital gain and qualified dividend income only if the taxpayer *elects* to treat them as such. For this purpose,

- net capital gain includes gain attributable to property held for investment and
- qualified dividend income includes dividends that are taxed at the same marginal rate that is applicable to a net capital gain.

By electing to include net capital gain and qualified dividend income as components of investment income, the amount of investment interest deductible in a particular year likewise increases. Form 4952 is used to make such an election. However, the election comes with a cost and is available only if the taxpayer agrees to reduce amounts qualifying for the preferential tax rates that otherwise apply to net capital gain (see Chapter 16) and qualified dividends (refer to Chapter 4) by an equivalent amount.[35]

EXAMPLE 43

Terry incurred $13,000 of interest expense related to her investments during the year. Her investment income included $4,000 of interest, $2,000 of qualified dividends, and a $5,000 net capital gain on the sale of investment securities. If Terry does not make the election to include the net capital gain and qualified dividends in investment income, her investment income for purposes of computing the investment income limitation is $4,000 (interest income). If she does make the election, her investment income is $11,000 ($4,000 interest + $2,000 qualified dividends + $5,000 net capital gain). In that case, $11,000 of her interest expense, rather than $4,000, is deductible currently.

Should Terry in the previous example make the election to include the additional $7,000 of qualified dividends and net capital gain as investment income? By doing so, the current-year investment interest deduction increases by $7,000, and the investment interest deduction potentially carried forward to future years is reduced by the same amount. That is, the election allows for an acceleration of the investment interest deduction. As Terry evaluates her decision, she should consider the following points:

- The election would make sense only if her marginal ordinary income tax rate exceeds the applicable capital gains rate.
- Using time value of money concepts, she should compare the tax cost of postponing the interest deduction to a subsequent year with the impact of losing the benefit from the preferential capital gains rate. In performing this analysis, consideration should be given to the length of the deferral of the investment interest deduction and the current and future years' tax brackets.

11-6c **Effect of the Additional Tax on Net Investment Income**

As if the passive activity loss and investment interest limitations are not complicated enough, individuals, estates, and trusts also are subject to an additional 3.8 percent tax on net investment income. This tax provision arose as a part of the Federal health care reform enacted in 2010.[36] Net investment income *for this purpose* generally includes amounts such as interest, dividends, long- and short-term capital gains, royalties, rents, and income from passive activities. The tax is levied at the flat 3.8 percent rate on the lesser of the taxpayer's net investment income or the excess of modified AGI over a threshold amount. The threshold amounts for individuals are $250,000 for surviving spouses and taxpayers filing a joint return, $125,000 for married taxpayers filing separate returns, and $200,000 for all other individual taxpayers. As a consequence, this tax is aimed at higher-income taxpayers. Unfortunately, this tax could very well come as a surprise to taxpayers, potentially increasing the marginal capital gain tax rate to 23.8 percent (from 20 percent) and the marginal ordinary income tax bracket to 43.4 percent (from 39.6 percent). See Chapter 13 for a complete discussion of this net investment income tax.

---

[35]Reg. § 1.163(d)–1.   [36]§ 1411.

INVESTOR LOSS LIMITATIONS CAN SIGNIFICANTLY AFFECT INVESTMENT RETURNS

The objective for most investors should be to maximize after-tax wealth from among investment alternatives. This requires an understanding of the relevant tax restrictions that apply to certain expenses and losses arising from various investment choices. The after-tax returns from the three alternatives the Reswicks are considering may be affected by the at-risk, passive activity, and investment interest limitations.

The high-growth, low-yield portfolio is expected to generate very little, if any, current interest and dividend income (i.e., investment income). Nonetheless, if the broker's prediction is correct, the market value of the securities will grow by approximately 10 percent a year. However, the annual $8,000 interest expense on the debt incurred to purchase the securities is not deductible as investment interest to the extent there is no investment income. Unless investment income is generated from this or some other source, the interest will not be deductible until the securities are sold (see Example 39). In addition, to the extent that any capital gain from the portfolio's sale is treated as investment income, the gain will not be subject to preferential capital gains rates (see Example 43). As a result, the net after-tax return will be impaired because of the investment interest limitation.

The net returns from the other two investment choices will be diminished by the at-risk and passive activity loss rules in addition to the investment interest limitation. The projected 10 percent return is apparently contingent on the investor being able to utilize the current tax losses as they arise. These benefits will be deferred because the at-risk and passive activity loss rules delay the timing of the deductions. For example, in the case of the orange grove investment, none of the passive activity losses are deductible until year 6, when the investment is expected to produce passive activity income (see Example 29). In the real estate rental venture, however, the Reswicks could deduct the $25,000 passive activity loss under the exception for rental real estate for the first four years (see Example 31); the at-risk rules would limit any additional losses in year 5 to the at-risk amount. Consequently, because the at-risk and passive activity loss rules limit the tax losses flowing to the Reswicks, the after-tax return will not be nearly as high as their broker predicts.

What If?

If the Reswicks decide that the investment in marketable securities is their best option, could they modify their plan so that they avoid the restriction imposed by the investment interest limitation? The Reswicks' net after-tax return would improve if the interest cost of financing their investment could be deducted as incurred. They could finance their investment by borrowing up to $100,000 against the equity in their home (see Chapter 10). The interest on the home equity loan would be fully deductible; consequently, the after-tax return from their investment would increase. Furthermore, any gain recognition would be deferred until the securities are sold, and the tax on the gain would be subject to the preferential capital gains rate.

Key Terms

Active income, 11-6	Material participation, 11-14	Rental activity, 11-15
At-risk limitation, 11-3	Net investment income, 11-24	Significant participation activity, 11-15
Closely held corporation, 11-10	Passive activity loss, 11-3	Tax shelters, 11-2
Investment income, 11-24	Personal service corporation, 11-10	
Investment interest, 11-23	Portfolio income, 11-6	

Discussion Questions

1. **LO.1, 2, 3** Identify two provisions designed to limit the tax benefits a taxpayer may obtain from a tax shelter investment. Describe how these rules reduce or defer the recognition of tax losses.

2. **LO.2** List some events that increase or decrease an investor's at-risk amount. What are some strategies that a taxpayer can employ to increase the at-risk amount to claim a higher deduction for losses?

3. **LO.2, 3** Roberto invested $18,000 in a chicken production operation. Using nonrecourse notes, the business purchases $120,000 worth of grain to feed the chickens. If Roberto's share of the expense is $26,000, how much can he deduct?

4. **LO.3** Explain the meaning of the terms *active income, portfolio income*, and *passive activity income*.

5. **LO.3** Carlos owns an interest in an activity that produces a $100,000 loss during the year. Would he prefer to have the activity classified as active or passive? Explain.

6. **LO.3** Kim owns an interest in an activity that produces $100,000 of income during the year. Would Kim prefer to have the activity classified as active or passive? Discuss.

7. **LO.3** Upon a taxable disposition of a passive activity, the taxpayer can utilize any suspended losses and credits related to that activity. Do you agree? Explain.

8. **LO.3** Discuss whether the passive activity loss rules apply to the following: individuals, closely held C corporations, S corporations, partnerships, and personal service corporations.

9. **LO.3** Bronze Corporation has $100,000 of active income, $55,000 of portfolio income, and a $55,000 passive activity loss. Under what circumstances is Bronze prohibited from deducting the loss? Allowed to deduct the loss?

10. **LO.4** Discuss what constitutes a passive activity.

11. **LO.5** What is the significance of the term *material participation*? Why is the extent of a taxpayer's participation in an activity important in determining whether a loss from the activity is deductible or nondeductible?

12. **LO.5** How many hours must a participant work in a nonrental activity to be guaranteed material participation status?

13. **LO.5** Suzanne owns interests in a bagel shop, a lawn and garden store, and a convenience store. Several full-time employees work at each of the enterprises. As of the end of November of the current year, Suzanne has worked 150 hours in the bagel shop, 250 hours at the lawn and garden store, and 70 hours at the convenience store. In reviewing her financial records, you learn that she has no passive investments

Decision Making

that are generating income and that she expects these three ventures collectively to produce a loss. What recommendation would you offer Suzanne as she plans her activities for the remainder of the year?

14. **LO.5, 11** John, an engineer, operates a separate business that he acquired eight years ago. If he participates 85 hours in the business and it incurs a loss of $34,000, under what circumstances can John claim an active loss?

Issue ID   15. **LO.2, 3, 5** Rita retired from public accounting after a long and successful career of 45 years. As part of her retirement package, she continues to share in the profits and losses of the firm, albeit at a lower rate than when she was working full-time. Because Rita wants to stay busy during her retirement years, she has invested and works in a local hardware business, operated as a partnership. Unfortunately, the business has recently gone through a slump and has not been generating profits. Identify relevant tax issues for Rita.

16. **LO.5** Some types of work are counted in applying the material participation standards, and some types are not counted. Discuss and give examples of each type.

Issue ID   17. **LO.5** Last year Alan's accountant informed him that he could not claim any of his passive activity losses on his income tax return because of his lack of material participation. To circumvent the tax problem this year, Alan tells his wife that she may have to put in some time at the various businesses. Identify the tax issues that Alan faces.

18. **LO.5** Sean, a limited partner in Ivy Nursery, is informed that his portion of the entity's current loss is $18,000. As a limited partner, can Sean assume that his share of the partnership loss is a passive activity loss? Explain.

19. **LO.6** Explain why some rental activities may not be *treated* as such under the passive activity loss rules.

20. **LO.3, 4, 5, 6** How is *passive activity* defined in the Code? What aspects of the definition have been clarified by final or Temporary Regulations?

21. **LO.8** What is a *real estate professional*? Why could qualifying for this status be beneficial under the passive activity loss rules?

22. **LO.8** Caroline owns a real estate rental activity that produces a loss of $65,000 during the current year. Under what circumstances can Caroline treat the entire loss as nonpassive?

Issue ID   23. **LO.8** Since his college days, Charles has developed an entrepreneurial streak. After working in his family's grocery business, he starts several ventures on his own. Even though Charles is independently wealthy, he is looking forward to working in each of the ventures. He plans to "drop in" on the businesses from time to time between personal trips to Europe and the Caribbean. As of the end of the year, he has established computer software stores in Dayton (Ohio), Austin, and Seattle; bagel bakeries in Albany, Athens (Georgia), and Tallahassee; and mountain bike and ski rental shops in small towns in Vermont, West Virginia, Colorado, and California. Identify the tax issues facing Charles.

24. **LO.8** Brad owns a small townhouse complex that generates a loss during the year. Under what circumstances can Brad deduct a loss from the rental activity? What limitations apply?

25. **LO.8** In connection with passive activities, what is a *deduction equivalent* and how is it computed?

26. **LO.10** What is *investment interest expense*? Describe the basic rules that may limit its deductibility.

Computational Exercises

27. **LO.2** In the current year, Ed invests $30,000 in an oil partnership. He has taxable income for the current year of $2,000 from the oil partnership and withdraws $10,000. What is Ed's at-risk amount at the end of the year?

28. **LO.3** Lucy sells her partnership interest, a passive activity, with an adjusted basis of $305,000 for $330,000. In addition, she has current and suspended losses of $28,000 associated with the partnership and has no other passive activities. Calculate Lucy's total gain and her current deductible loss. Describe the type of income that the deductible loss may offset.

29. **LO.4, 5** Forrester owns a nonrental business with two separate departments. Department A generates net income of $70,000, and Department B generates a net loss of $58,000. Forrester participates 800 hours in the operations of Department A and 300 hours in the operations of Department B. If Forrester is allowed to treat the departments as components of a single activity, calculate the amount of the Department B loss that can be offset against the income from Department A in the current year.

30. **LO.7** Rhonda has an adjusted basis and an at-risk amount of $7,500 in a passive activity at the beginning of the year. She also has a suspended passive activity loss of $1,500 carried over from the prior year. During the current year, she has a loss of $12,000 from the passive activity. Rhonda has no passive activity income from other sources this year. Determine the following items relating to Rhonda's passive activity as of the end of the year.

    a. Adjusted basis and at-risk amount in the passive activity.
    b. Loss suspended under the at-risk rules.
    c. Suspended passive activity loss.

31. **LO.8** Noah, who has $62,000 of AGI before considering rental activities, has $70,000 of losses from a real estate rental activity in which he actively participates. He also actively participates in another real estate rental activity from which he has $33,000 of income. He has other passive activity income of $20,000. What amount of rental loss can Noah use to offset active or portfolio income in the current year?

32. **LO.9** Rose dies with passive activity property having an adjusted basis of $65,000, suspended losses of $13,000, and a fair market value at the date of her death of $90,000. Of the $13,000 suspended loss existing at the time of Rose's death, how much is deductible on her final return or by the beneficiary?

33. **LO.10** Troy's financial records for the year reflect the following:

Interest income from bank savings account	$ 900
Taxable annuity receipts	1,800
Safe deposit box rental (to hold annuity documents)	125
Investment interest expense	3,200

Calculate Troy's net investment income and his current investment interest deduction. Assume that Troy does not itemize his personal deductions. How is any potential excess investment interest deduction treated?

Problems

34. **LO.2** In 2015, Fred invested $50,000 in a general partnership. Fred's interest is not considered to be a passive activity. If his share of the partnership losses is $35,000 in 2015 and $25,000 in 2016, how much can he deduct in each year?

Communications   35. **LO.2** In the current year, Bill Parker (54 Oak Drive, St. Paul, MN 55164) is considering making an investment of $60,000 in Best Choice Partnership. The prospectus provided by Bill's broker indicates that the partnership investment is not a passive activity and that Bill's share of the entity's loss in the current year will likely be $40,000, while his share of the partnership loss next year will probably be $25,000. Write a letter to Bill in which you indicate how the losses would be treated for tax purposes in the current year and the following year.

Decision Making   36. **LO.2, 11** Heather wants to invest $40,000 in a relatively safe venture and has discovered two alternatives that would produce the following reportable ordinary income and loss over the next three years:

Year	Alternative 1 Income (Loss)	Alternative 2 Income (Loss)
1	($20,000)	($48,000)
2	(28,000)	32,000
3	72,000	40,000

She is interested in the after-tax effects of these alternatives over a three-year horizon. Assume that Heather's investment portfolio produces sufficient passive activity income to offset any potential passive activity loss that may arise from these alternatives, that her cost of capital is 6% (see Appendix H for the present value factors), that she is in the 25% tax bracket, that each investment alternative possesses equal growth potential, and that each alternative exposes her to comparable financial risk. In addition, assume that in the loss years for each alternative, there is no cash flow from or to the investment (i.e., the loss is due to depreciation), while in those years when the income is positive, cash flows to Heather equal the amount of the income. Based on these facts, compute the present value of these two investment alternatives and determine which option Heather should choose.

37. **LO.1, 3** Dorothy acquired a 100% interest in two passive activities: Activity A in January 2011 and Activity B in 2012. Through 2014, Activity A was profitable, but it produced losses of $200,000 in 2015 and $100,000 in 2016. Dorothy has passive activity income from Activity B of $20,000 in 2015 and $40,000 in 2016. After offsetting passive activity income, how much of the net losses may she deduct?

38. **LO.1, 3** A number of years ago, Kay acquired an interest in a partnership in which she is not a material participant. Kay's basis in her partnership interest at the beginning of 2015 is $40,000. Kay's share of the partnership loss is $35,000 in 2015, while her share of the partnership income is $15,000 in 2016. How much may Kay deduct in 2015 and 2016, assuming that she owns no other passive activities?

39. **LO.3** Mike, an attorney, earns $200,000 from his law practice and receives $45,000 in dividends and interest during the year. In addition, he incurs a loss of $50,000 from an investment in a passive activity acquired three years ago. What is Mike's net income for the current year after considering the passive investment?

Decision Making   40. **LO.3, 11** Emily has $100,000 that she wants to invest and is considering the following two options:

• Option A: Investment in Redbird Mutual Fund, which is expected to produce interest income of $8,000 per year.

- Option B: Investment in Cardinal Limited Partnership (buys, sells, and operates wine vineyards). Emily's share of the partnership's ordinary income and loss over the next three years would be as follows:

Year	Income (Loss)
1	($ 8,000)
2	(2,000)
3	34,000

Emily is interested in the after-tax effects of these alternatives over a three-year horizon. Assume that Emily's investment portfolio produces ample passive activity income to offset any passive activity losses that may be generated. Her cost of capital is 8% (see Appendix H for the present value factors), and she is in the 28% tax bracket. The two investment alternatives possess equal growth potential and comparable financial risk. Based on these facts, compute the present value of these two investment alternatives and determine which option Emily should choose.

41. **LO.3** Ray acquired an activity several years ago, and in the current year, it generates a loss of $50,000. Ray has AGI of $140,000 before considering the loss from the activity. If the activity is a bakery and Ray is not a material participant, what is his AGI?

42. **LO.3, 11** Jorge owns two passive investments, Activity A and Activity B. He plans to dispose of Activity A in the current year or next year. Juanita has offered to buy Activity A this year for an amount that would produce a taxable passive activity gain to Jorge of $115,000. However, if the sale, for whatever reason, is not made to Juanita, Jorge believes that he could find a buyer who would pay about $7,000 less than Juanita. Passive activity losses and gains generated (and expected to be generated) by Activity B follow:

Decision Making

Two years ago	($35,000)
Last year	(35,000)
This year	(8,000)
Next year	(30,000)
Future years	Minimal profits

All of Activity B's losses are suspended. Should Jorge close the sale of Activity A with Juanita this year, or should he wait until next year and sell to another buyer? Jorge is in the 28% tax bracket.

43. **LO.3** Sarah has investments in four passive activity partnerships purchased several years ago. Last year the income and losses were as follows:

Activity	Income (Loss)
A	$ 30,000
B	(30,000)
C	(15,000)
D	(5,000)

In the current year, she sold her interest in Activity D for a $10,000 gain. Activity D, which had been profitable until last year, had a current loss of $1,500. How will the sale of Activity D affect Sarah's taxable income in the current year?

44. **LO.3** Leon sells his interest in a passive activity for $100,000. Determine the tax effect of the sale based on each of the following independent facts:

a. Adjusted basis in this investment is $35,000. Losses from prior years that were not deductible due to the passive activity loss restrictions total $40,000.

b. Adjusted basis in this investment is $75,000. Losses from prior years that were not deductible due to the passive activity loss restrictions total $40,000.

c. Adjusted basis in this investment is $75,000. Losses from prior years that were not deductible due to the passive activity loss restrictions total $40,000. In addition, suspended credits total $10,000.

45. **LO.3** Ash, Inc., a closely held personal service corporation, has $100,000 of passive activity losses. In addition, Ash has $80,000 of active business income and $20,000 of portfolio income. How much of the passive activity loss may Ash use to offset the other types of income?

46. **LO.3** In the current year, White, Inc., earns $400,000 from operations and receives $36,000 of interest income from various portfolio investments. White also pays $150,000 to acquire a 20% interest in a passive activity that produces a $200,000 loss.

a. Assuming that White is a personal service corporation, how will these transactions affect its taxable income?

b. Same as (a), except that White is closely held but not a personal service corporation.

Decision Making
Communications

47. **LO.2, 3, 7, 11** Kristin Graf (123 Baskerville Mill Road, Jamison, PA 18929) is trying to decide how to invest a $10,000 inheritance. One option is to make an additional investment in Rocky Road Excursions in which she has an at-risk basis of $0, suspended losses under the at-risk rules of $7,000, and suspended passive activity losses of $1,000. If Kristin makes this investment, her share of the expected profits this year will be $8,000. If her investment stays the same, her share of profits from Rocky Road Excursions will be $1,000. Another option is to invest $10,000 as a limited partner in the Ragged Mountain Winery; this investment will produce passive activity income of $9,000. Write a letter to Kristin to review the tax consequences of each alternative. Kristin is in the 28% tax bracket.

Decision Making

48. **LO.2, 3, 7, 11** The end of the year is approaching, and Maxine has begun to focus on ways of minimizing her income tax liability. Several years ago she purchased an investment in Teal Limited Partnership, which is subject to the at-risk and the passive activity loss rules. (Last year Maxine sold a different investment that was subject to these rules and that produced passive activity income.) She believes that her investment in Teal has good long-term economic prospects. However, it has been generating tax losses for several years in a row. In fact, when she was discussing last year's income tax return with her tax accountant, he said that unless "things change" with respect to her investments, she would not be able to deduct losses this year.

a. What was the accountant referring to in his comment?

b. You learn that Maxine's current at-risk basis in her investment is $1,000 and that her share of the current loss is expected to be $13,000. Based on these facts, how will her loss be treated?

c. After reviewing her situation, Maxine's financial adviser suggests that she invest at least an additional $12,000 in Teal to ensure a full loss deduction in the current year. How do you react to his suggestion?

d. What would you suggest Maxine consider as she attempts to maximize her current-year deductible loss?

49. **LO.2, 3, 7** A number of years ago, Lee acquired a 20% interest in the BlueSky Partnership for $60,000. The partnership was profitable through 2015, and Lee's amount at risk in the partnership interest was $120,000 at the beginning of 2016. BlueSky incurred a loss of $400,000 in 2016 and reported income of $200,000 in 2017. Assuming that Lee is not a material participant, how much of his loss from BlueSky Partnership is deductible in 2016 and 2017? Consider the at-risk and passive activity loss rules, and assume that Lee owns no other passive investments.

50. **LO.2, 3, 5, 7** Grace acquired an activity four years ago. The loss from the activity is $50,000 in the current year (at-risk basis of $40,000 as of the beginning of the year). Without considering the loss from the activity, she has gross income of $140,000. If the activity is a convenience store and Grace is a material participant, what is the effect of the activity on her taxable income?

51. **LO.2, 3, 5, 7** Jonathan, a physician, earns $200,000 from his practice. He also receives $18,000 in dividends and interest from various portfolio investments. During the year, he pays $45,000 to acquire a 20% interest in a partnership that produces a $300,000 loss. Compute Jonathan's AGI, assuming that:

a. He does not participate in the operations of the partnership.

b. He is a material participant in the operations of the partnership.

52. **LO.2, 3, 7** Five years ago Gerald invested $150,000 in a passive activity, his sole investment venture. On January 1, 2015, his amount at risk in the activity was $30,000. His shares of the income and losses were as follows:

Year	Income (Loss)
2015	($40,000)
2016	(30,000)
2017	50,000

Gerald holds no suspended at-risk or passive activity losses at the beginning of 2015. How much can Gerald deduct in 2015 and 2016? What is his taxable income from the activity in 2017? Consider the at-risk rules as well as the passive activity loss rules.

53. **LO.3, 8** Several years ago Benny Jackson (125 Hill Street, Charleston, WV 25311) acquired an apartment building that currently generates a loss of $60,000. Benny's AGI is $130,000 before considering the loss. The apartment building is in an exclusive part of the city, and Benny is an active participant. Write a letter to Benny explaining what effect the loss will have on his AGI. **Communications**

54. **LO.3, 5, 8** This year Maria works 1,200 hours as a computer consultant, 320 hours in a real estate development business, and 400 hours in real estate rental activities. Juan, her husband, works 250 hours in the real estate development business and 180 hours in the real estate rental business. Maria earns $60,000 as a computer consultant, while she and Juan lost $18,000 in the real estate development business and $26,000 in the real estate rental business. How should they treat the losses?

55. **LO.3, 8, 11** Bonnie and Jake (ages 35 and 36, respectively) are married with no dependents and live in Montana (not a community property state). Because Jake has large medical expenses, they seek your advice about filing separately to save taxes. Their income and expenses for 2016 are as follows: **Decision Making**

Bonnie's salary	$ 42,500
Jake's salary	26,000
Interest income (joint)	1,500
Rental loss from actively managed rental property	(23,000)
Jake's unreimbursed medical expenses	8,500
All other itemized deductions:*	
Bonnie	9,000
Jake	3,400

*None subject to limitations

Determine whether Bonnie and Jake should file jointly or separately for 2016.

56. **LO.3, 8, 11** Mary and Charles have owned a beach cottage on the New Jersey shore for several years and have always used it as a family retreat. When they acquired the property, they had no intentions of renting it. Because family **Decision Making**

circumstances have changed, they are considering using the cottage for only two weeks a year and renting it for the remainder of the year. Their AGI approximates $80,000 per year, and they are in the 32% tax bracket (combined Federal and state). Interest and real estate taxes total $8,000 per year and are expected to continue at this level in the foreseeable future. If Mary and Charles rent the property, their *incremental* revenue and expenses are projected to be:

Rent income	$ 22,000
Rental commissions	(4,000)
Maintenance expenses	(9,000)
Depreciation expense	(10,000)

If the cottage is converted to rental property, they plan to be actively involved in key rental and maintenance decisions. Given the tax effects of converting the property to rental use, would the cash flow from renting the property be enough to meet the $12,000 annual mortgage payment? Explain.

57. **LO.3, 8** During the current year, Gene, a CPA, performs services as follows: 1,800 hours in his tax practice and 50 hours in an apartment leasing operation in which he has a 15% interest. Because of his oversight duties, Gene is considered to be an active participant. He expects that his share of the loss realized from the apartment leasing operation will be $30,000 and that his tax practice will show a profit of approximately $80,000. Gene is single and has no other income. Discuss the character and treatment of the income and losses generated by these activities.

58. **LO.3, 8** Ida, who has AGI of $80,000 before considering rental activities, is active in three separate real estate rental activities and is in the 28% tax bracket. She has $12,000 of losses from Activity A, $18,000 of losses from Activity B, and income of $10,000 from Activity C. She also has $2,100 of tax credits from Activity A. Calculate the deductions and credits that she is allowed and the suspended losses and credits.

59. **LO.8** Ella has $105,000 of losses from a real estate rental activity in which she actively participates. She has other rental income of $25,000 and other passive activity income of $32,000. Her AGI before considering these items of income and loss is $95,000. How much rental loss can Ella deduct against active and portfolio income (ignoring the at-risk rules)? Does she have any suspended losses to carry over? Explain.

60. **LO.9** At death, Francine owns an interest in a passive activity property (adjusted basis of $160,000, suspended losses of $16,000, and fair market value of $170,000). What is deductible on Francine's final income tax return?

61. **LO.9** In the current year, Abe gives an interest in a passive activity to his daughter, Andrea. The value of the interest at the date of the gift is $25,000, and its adjusted basis to Abe is $13,000. During the time that Abe owned the investment, losses of $3,000 could not be deducted because of the passive activity loss limitations. What is the tax treatment of the suspended passive activity losses to Abe and Andrea?

62. **LO.9** Tonya sells a passive activity in the current year for $150,000. Her adjusted basis in the activity is $50,000, and she uses the installment method of reporting the gain. The activity has suspended losses of $12,000. Tonya receives $60,000 in the year of sale. What is her gain? How much of the suspended losses can she deduct?

Decision Making

Communications

63. **LO.10, 11** In 2016, Kathleen Tweardy incurs $30,000 of interest expense related to her investments. Her investment income includes $7,500 of interest, $6,000 of qualified dividends, and a $12,000 net capital gain on the sale of securities. Kathleen asks you to compute the amount of her deduction for investment interest, taking into consideration any options she might have. In addition, she wants your

suggestions as to any tax planning alternatives that are available. Write a letter to her that contains your advice. Kathleen lives at 11934 Briarpatch Drive, Midlothian, VA 23113.

64. **LO.10** Helen borrowed $150,000 to acquire a parcel of land to be held for investment purposes. During 2016, she paid interest of $12,000 on the loan. She had AGI of $90,000 for the year. Other items related to Helen's investments include the following:

Investment income	$11,000
Long-term capital gain on sale of stock	3,500
Investment counsel fees	200

Helen is unmarried and does not itemize her deductions.

a. Determine Helen's investment interest deduction for 2016.

b. Discuss the treatment of the portion of Helen's investment interest that is disallowed in 2016.

Research Problems

Note: Solutions to Research Problems can be prepared by using the Checkpoint® Student Edition online research product, which is available to accompany this text. It is also possible to prepare solutions to the Research Problems by using tax research materials found in a standard tax library.

THOMSON REUTERS
CHECKPOINT®
Student Edition

Research Problem 1. Carol is a successful physician who owns 100% of her incorporated medical practice. She and her husband, Dick, are considering the purchase of a commercial office building located near the local community hospital. If they purchase the building, Carol will move her medical practice to the new location and rent space for an arm's length price. The rent income Carol and Dick receive will be available to absorb passive activity losses generated by other passive activities they own. The net effect of this arrangement is a reduction in their income tax liability. Will Carol and Dick's plan work? Why or why not?

Research Problem 2. Five years ago Bridget decided to purchase a limited partnership interest in a fast-food restaurant conveniently located near the campus of Southeast State University. The general partner of the restaurant venture promised her that the investment would prove to be a winner. During the process of capitalizing the business, $2 million was borrowed from Northside Bank; however, each of the partners was required to pledge personal assets as collateral to satisfy the bank loan in the event that the restaurant defaulted. Bridget pledged shares of publicly traded stock (worth $200,000, basis of $75,000) to satisfy the bank's requirement.

The restaurant did a good business until just recently, when flagrant health code violations were discovered and widely publicized by the media. As a result, business has declined to a point where the restaurant's continued existence is doubtful. In addition, the $2 million loan is now due for payment. Because the restaurant cannot pay, the bank has called for the collateral provided by the partners to be used to satisfy the debt. Bridget sells the pledged stock for $200,000 and forwards the proceeds to the bank. Bridget believes that her share of the restaurant's current and suspended passive activity losses can offset the $125,000 gain from the stock sale. As a result, after netting the passive activity losses against the gain, none of the gain is subject to tax.

How do you react to Bridget's position?

Research Problem 3. Ida Ross has decided to purchase a new home in a retirement community for $400,000. She has $50,000 in cash for the down payment but needs to borrow the remaining $350,000 to finance the purchase. Her financial adviser, Marc, suggests that rather than seeking a conventional mortgage, she should borrow the funds from State Bank using her portfolio of appreciated securities as collateral. Selling the securities to generate $350,000 in cash would lead to a substantial tax on the capital gain recognized. Therefore, a better strategy would be to borrow against her securities and then claim a deduction for the interest paid on the loan. How do you react to the financial adviser's strategy?

Partial list of research aids:
Temp.Reg. § 1.163–8T(c).

Internet
Activity

Use the tax resources of the Internet to address the following questions. Do not restrict your search to the Web, but include a review of newsgroups and general reference materials, practitioner sites and resources, primary sources of the tax law, chat rooms and discussion groups, and other opportunities.

Research Problem 4. Investment advisers and tax professionals are continuously striving to create sophisticated transactions and investment vehicles (i.e., tax-advantaged investments) that are designed to provide economic benefits to investors by reducing their taxes. These professionals might like to patent such schemes. Identify whether patenting a tax strategy is a legal possibility.

Research Problem 5. Scan the materials offered in several newsgroups frequented by tax advisers and consultants. In what context are "tax shelters" discussed by these professionals? Do these advisers and consultants adequately take into account the rules of §§ 465 and 469?

Research Problem 6. Oil and gas ventures operating as publicly traded partnerships typically attract sophisticated investors who purchase limited partnership interests. Investments in these types of publicly traded partnerships are subject to a restrictive set of passive activity loss rules. Identify three publicly traded oil and gas partnerships that are currently marketed to investors, describe the benefits the promoters claim will result from such investments, and briefly review the basic nature of the unique passive activity loss restrictions placed on such investments.

Roger CPA Review Questions

1. Lee, a married individual, is an employee with three rental properties in which Lee does not actively participate. In 2015, Property 1 had a net loss of $10,000, Property 2 had a net gain of $25,000, and Property 3 had a net loss of $5,000. Lee's W–2 income in 2015 was $110,000. Considering only the foregoing facts, what is Lee's 2015 adjusted gross income?

   a. $120,000   c. $110,000
   b. $125,000   d. $135,000

2. Anscomb is an employee who also solely owns and actively participates in a rental activity which produced a $20,000 loss in the current year. Anscomb's W–2 income in the current year is $115,000. Considering only the foregoing facts, what should Anscomb's adjusted gross income be for the current year?

   a. $97,500   c. $107,500
   b. $115,000   d. $102,500

3. Lewis is not an active participant in three rental activities, which have turned profits in recent years. The following gain and losses apply to the current year for Lewis:

	Gain or (Loss)
Rental Activity 1	($10,000)
Rental Activity 2	12,000
Rental Activity 3	(8,000)
Total	($ 6,000)

What amount of the suspended loss should Lewis allocate to Rental Activity 3?

a. $4,500

b. $2,667

c. $0

d. Suspended losses may be allocated according to the taxpayer's preference

4. Smith bought a rental property in year 1 for $100,000. In year 1, Smith's adjusted gross income (AGI) was $125,000 and Smith sustained a $30,000 loss on the property. In year 2, Smith's AGI was $175,000 and Smith sustained a $20,000 loss on the property. In year 3, Smith sold the property for $155,000. What amount of gain or loss must Smith report on Smith's year 3 tax return as a result of the sale? Assume Smith actively participated in the rental activity in all three years, but is not considered a real estate professional for tax purposes.

a. $17,500 gain   c. $22,500 gain

b. $0 (no gain or loss)   d. $20,000 gain

5. Patel bought a rental property in year 1 for $150,000. In year 1, Patel's adjusted gross income (AGI) was $100,000 and Patel sustained a $15,000 loss on the property. In year 2, Patel's AGI was $140,000 and Patel sustained a $10,000 loss on the property. In year 3, Patel sold the property for $175,000. What amount of gain or loss must Patel report on Patel's year 3 tax return as a result of the sale? Assume Patel did not actively participate in the rental activity in any of the three years.

a. $25,000   c. $5,000

b. $0 (no income or loss) d. $20,000

6. The following chart applies to Bettelli, an investor who owns two rental activities, Property A and Property B, and has no other involvement in passive activities:

	Property	Income (Loss)
Year 1	A	($12,000)
	B	5,000
Year 2	A	(6,000)
	B	1,000

Bettelli met the requirements for active participation in year 1 but not in year 2. Bettelli's AGI in year 1 was $140,000; in year 2, $180,000. In year 3, Bettelli sells Property A for a $15,000 gain. How much of the gain must Bettelli report on Bettelli's year 3 tax return?

a. $0   c. $8,000

b. $3,000   d. $13,000

7. Albert, Berry, and Collins formed ABC Partnership in the current year. Collins, a limited partner, contributed $20,000 in cash to the partnership and also pledged $10,000 of personal property as collateral to meet any partnership debts that may arise. Collins's share of the current ABC Partnership loss is $50,000. How much of the loss is deductible by Collins under the at-risk rules?

a. $0   c. $20,000

b. $10,000   d. $30,000

PART 5

PROPERTY TRANSACTIONS

Part 5 presents the tax treatment of sales, exchanges, and other dispositions of property. Included are the determination of the realized gain or loss and recognized gain or loss, along with the classification of any recognized gain or loss as capital or ordinary. The topic of basis is evaluated both in terms of its effect on the calculation of the gain or loss and in terms of the determination of the basis of any property acquired as part of the transaction.

Property Transactions: Determination of Gain or Loss and Basis Considerations

LEARNING OBJECTIVES: *After completing Chapter 14, you should be able to:*

LO.1 State and explain the computation of realized gain or loss on property dispositions.

LO.2 Distinguish between realized and recognized gain or loss.

LO.3 Review and illustrate how basis is determined for various methods of asset acquisition.

LO.4 Describe various loss disallowance provisions.

LO.5 Identify tax planning opportunities related to selected property transactions.

CHAPTER OUTLINE

PROPOSED SALE OF A HOUSE AND OTHER PROPERTY TRANSACTIONS

Alice owns a house that she received from her mother seven months ago. Her mother's cost for the house was $275,000. Alice is considering selling the house to her favorite nephew, Dan, for $275,000. Alice anticipates that she will have no gain or loss on the transaction. She comes to you for advice.

As Alice's tax adviser, you need answers to the following questions:

- You are aware that Alice's mother died around the time Alice indicates that she received the house from her mother. Did Alice receive the house by gift prior to her mother's death? If so, what was the mother's adjusted basis? Did Alice instead inherit the house from her mother? If so, what was the fair market value of the house on the date of her mother's death?

- Has the house been Alice's principal residence during the period she has owned it? Was it her principal residence before she received it from her mother?

- How long did Alice's mother own the house?

- What is the current fair market value of the house?

- Does Alice intend for the transaction with Dan to be a sale or part sale and part gift?

- What does Alice intend to do with the sale proceeds?

Alice would also like to know the tax consequences of selling her boat, which she purchased for $22,000 four months ago and has used exclusively for personal use. She has been disappointed with its layout and capacity. Because it is a new model, there is significant demand for the boat, and based on listings in her area, she anticipates that she can sell it for $20,000 to $23,000.

In addition, earlier this year, Alice sold some stock at a realized loss and subsequently repurchased some shares of the same stock. She has also asked you about the tax consequences of these transactions.

Once you have more information, you can advise Alice on the tax consequences of these various transactions.

Read the chapter and formulate your response.

FRAMEWORK 1,040   **Tax Formula for Individuals**

This chapter covers the boldfaced portions of the Tax Formula for Individuals that was introduced in Concept Summary 3.1 on p. 3-3. Below those portions are the sections of Form 1040 where the results are reported.

Income *(broadly defined)*	$ xx,xxx
Less: Exclusions	(x,xxx)
Gross income..	**$xx,xxx**

FORM 1040 (p. 1)

12	Business income or (loss). Attach Schedule C or C-EZ	
13	Capital gain or (loss). Attach Schedule D if required. If not required, check here ▶ ☐	
14	Other gains or (losses). Attach Form 4797	

Less: Deductions *for* **adjusted gross income**	(x,xxx)
Adjusted gross income...	$ xx,xxx
Less: The greater of total **itemized deductions** *or* the standard deduction	(x,xxx)
Personal and dependency exemptions	(x,xxx)
Taxable income	**$ xx,xxx**
Tax on taxable income *(see Tax Tables or Tax Rate Schedules)*....................................	$ x,xxx
Less: Tax credits *(including income taxes withheld and prepaid)*	(xxx)
Tax due (or refund)	$ xxx

This chapter and the following three chapters explain the income tax consequences of property transactions (the sale or other disposition of property). Specifically, the following questions are considered:

- Is there a realized gain or loss?
- If so, is the gain or loss recognized?
- If the gain or loss is recognized, is it ordinary or capital?
- What is the basis of any replacement property that is acquired?

Chapters 14 and 15 discuss the determination of realized and recognized gain or loss and the basis of property. Chapters 16 and 17 cover the classification of the recognized gain or loss as ordinary or capital.

LO.1

State and explain the computation of realized gain or loss on property dispositions.

14-1 DETERMINATION OF GAIN OR LOSS

The first step in determining the tax consequences of a property transaction is to determine the gain or loss realized. Then the taxpayer must determine whether the realized gain or loss is recognized. Not all realized gains or losses are recognized for tax purposes.

14-1a **Realized Gain or Loss**

Realized gain or loss is the difference between the amount realized from the sale or other disposition of property and the property's adjusted basis on the date of disposition. If the amount realized exceeds the property's adjusted basis, the result is a **realized gain**. Conversely, if the property's adjusted basis exceeds the amount realized, the result is a **realized loss**.[1]

---

[1] § 1001(a) and Reg. § 1.1001–1(a).

Chapter 14 Property Transactions: Determination of Gain or Loss and Basis Considerations 14-3

Tab sells Swan Corporation stock with an adjusted basis of $3,000 for $5,000. Tab's realized gain is $2,000. If Tab had sold the stock for $2,000, he would have had a realized loss of $1,000.

EXAMPLE 1

Sale or Other Disposition

The term *sale or other disposition* is defined broadly in the tax law and includes virtually any disposition of property. Thus, transactions such as trade-ins, casualties, condemnations, thefts, and bond retirements are treated as dispositions of property. The most common disposition of property is through a sale or exchange. Usually, the key factor in determining whether a disposition has taken place is whether an identifiable event has occurred[2] as opposed to a mere fluctuation in the value of the property.[3]

Lori owns Tan Corporation stock that cost $3,000. The stock has appreciated in value by $2,000 since Lori purchased it. Lori has no realized gain because mere fluctuation in value is not a disposition or an identifiable event for tax purposes. Nor would Lori have a realized loss if the stock declined in value by $2,000.

EXAMPLE 2

Amount Realized

The **amount realized** from a sale or other disposition of property is the sum of any money received plus the fair market value of other property received. The amount realized also includes any real property taxes treated as imposed on the seller that are actually paid by the buyer.[4] The reason for including these taxes in the amount realized is that by paying the taxes, the purchaser is, in effect, paying an additional amount to the seller of the property.

The amount realized also includes any liability on the property disposed of, such as a mortgage debt, if the buyer assumes the mortgage or the property is sold subject to the mortgage.[5] The amount of the liability is included in the amount realized even if the debt is nonrecourse and the amount of the debt is greater than the fair market value of the mortgaged property.[6]

Barry sells property on which there is a mortgage of $20,000 to Cole for $50,000 cash. Barry's amount realized from the sale is $70,000 if Cole assumes the mortgage or takes the property subject to the mortgage.

EXAMPLE 3

The **fair market value** of property received in a sale or other disposition has been defined by the courts as the price at which property will change hands between a willing seller and a willing buyer when neither is compelled to sell or buy.[7] Fair market value is determined by considering the relevant factors in each case.[8] An expert appraiser is often required to evaluate these factors in arriving at fair market value. When the fair market value of the property received cannot be determined, the value of the property given up by the taxpayer may be used.[9]

In calculating the amount realized, selling expenses (such as advertising, commissions, and legal fees) relating to the disposition are deducted. The amount realized is the net amount the taxpayer received directly or indirectly, in the form of cash or anything else of value, from the disposition of the property.

---

[2]Reg. § 1.1001–1(c)(1).

[3]*Lynch v. Turrish*, 1 USTC ¶18, 3 AFTR 2986, 38 S.Ct. 537 (USSC, 1918).

[4]§ 1001(b) and Reg. § 1.1001–1(b). Refer to Chapter 10 and Examples 17 and 18 for a discussion of this subject.

[5]*Crane v. Comm.*, 47–1 USTC ¶9217, 35 AFTR 776, 67 S.Ct. 1047 (USSC, 1947). Although a legal distinction exists between the direct assumption of a mortgage and the taking of property subject to a mortgage, the tax consequences in calculating the amount realized are the same.

[6]*Comm. v. Tufts*, 83–1 USTC ¶9328, 51 AFTR 2d 83–1132, 103 S.Ct. 1826 (USSC, 1983).

[7]*Comm. v. Marshman*, 60–2 USTC ¶9484, 5 AFTR 2d 1528, 279 F.2d 27 (CA–6, 1960).

[8]*O'Malley v. Ames*, 52–1 USTC ¶9361, 42 AFTR 19, 197 F.2d 256 (CA–8, 1952).

[9]*U.S. v. Davis*, 62–2 USTC ¶9509, 9 AFTR 2d 1625, 82 S.Ct. 1190 (USSC, 1962).

Adjusted Basis

The **adjusted basis** of property disposed of is the property's original basis adjusted to the date of disposition.[10] Original basis is the cost or other basis of the property on the date the property is acquired by the taxpayer. Considerations involving original basis are discussed later in this chapter. *Capital additions* increase and *recoveries of capital* decrease the original basis so that on the date of disposition, the adjusted basis reflects the unrecovered cost or other basis of the property.[11] Adjusted basis is determined as follows:

> Cost (or other adjusted basis) on date of acquisition
> + Capital additions
> − Capital recoveries
> = Adjusted basis on date of disposition

Capital Additions

Capital additions include the cost of capital improvements and betterments made to the property by the taxpayer. These expenditures are distinguishable from expenditures for the ordinary repair and maintenance of the property, which are neither capitalized nor added to the original basis (refer to Chapter 6). The latter expenditures are deductible in the current taxable year if they are related to business or income-producing property. Amounts representing real property taxes treated as imposed on the seller but paid or assumed by the buyer are part of the cost of the property.[12] Any liability on property that is assumed by the buyer is also included in the buyer's original basis of the property. The same rule applies if property is acquired subject to a liability. Amortization of the discount on bonds increases the adjusted basis of the bonds.[13]

Capital Recoveries

Capital recoveries decrease the adjusted basis of property. The prominent types of capital recoveries are discussed below.

Depreciation and Cost Recovery Allowances The original basis of depreciable property is reduced by the annual depreciation charges (or cost recovery allowances) while the property is held by the taxpayer. The amount of depreciation that is subtracted from the original basis is the greater of the *allowed* or *allowable* depreciation calculated on an annual basis.[14] In most circumstances, the allowed and allowable depreciation amounts are the same (refer to Chapter 8).

Casualties and Thefts A casualty or theft may result in the reduction of the adjusted basis of property.[15] The adjusted basis is reduced by the amount of the deductible loss. In addition, the adjusted basis is reduced by the amount of insurance proceeds received. However, the receipt of insurance proceeds may result in a recognized gain rather than a deductible loss. The gain increases the adjusted basis of the property.[16]

Capital Recoveries: Casualties and Thefts

EXAMPLE 4

An insured truck that Marvin used in his trade or business is destroyed in an accident. At the time of the accident, the adjusted basis was $8,000, and the fair market value was $6,500. Marvin receives insurance proceeds of $6,500. The amount of the casualty loss is $1,500 ($6,500 insurance proceeds − $8,000 adjusted basis). The truck's adjusted basis is reduced by the $1,500 casualty loss and the $6,500 of insurance proceeds received ($8,000 basis before casualty − $1,500 casualty loss − $6,500 insurance proceeds = $0 adjusted basis).

---

[10]§ 1011(a) and Reg. § 1.1011–1.

[11]§ 1016(a) and Reg. § 1.1016–1.

[12]Reg. §§ 1.1001–1(b)(2) and 1.1012–1(b). Refer to Chapter 10 for a discussion of this subject.

[13]See Chapter 16 for a discussion of bond discount and the related amortization.

[14]§ 1016(a)(2) and Reg. § 1.1016–3(a)(1)(i).

[15]Refer to Chapter 7 for the discussion of casualties and thefts.

[16]Reg. § 1.1016–6(a).

Capital Recoveries: Casualties and Thefts

An insured truck that Marvin used in his trade or business is destroyed in an accident. At the time of the accident, the adjusted basis was $6,500, and the fair market value was $8,000. Marvin receives insurance proceeds of $8,000. The amount of the casualty gain is $1,500 ($8,000 insurance proceeds − $6,500 adjusted basis). The truck's adjusted basis is increased by the $1,500 casualty gain and is reduced by the $8,000 of insurance proceeds received ($6,500 basis before casualty + $1,500 casualty gain − $8,000 insurance proceeds = $0 adjusted basis).

Certain Corporate Distributions A corporate distribution to a shareholder that is not taxable is treated as a return of capital, and it reduces the basis of the shareholder's stock in the corporation.[17] For example, if a corporation makes a cash distribution to its shareholders and has no earnings and profits, the distributions are treated as a return of capital. Once the basis of the stock is reduced to zero, the amount of any subsequent distributions is a capital gain if the stock is a capital asset. These rules are illustrated in Example 25 of Chapter 20.

Amortizable Bond Premium The basis in a bond purchased at a premium is reduced by the amortizable portion of the bond premium.[18] Investors in taxable bonds may *elect* to amortize the bond premium.[19] The amount of the amortized premium on taxable bonds is allowed as an interest deduction. Therefore, the election enables the taxpayer to take an annual interest deduction to offset ordinary income in exchange for a larger capital gain or smaller capital loss on the disposition of the bond. The amortization deduction is allowed for taxable bonds because the premium is viewed as a cost of earning the taxable interest from the bonds. The reason the basis of taxable bonds is reduced is that the amortization deduction is a recovery of the cost or basis of the bonds.

Unlike taxable bonds, the premium on tax-exempt bonds *must be* amortized (and the basis is reduced even though the amortization is not allowed as a deduction). No amortization deduction is permitted on tax-exempt bonds because the interest income is exempt from tax and the amortization of the bond premium merely represents an adjustment of the effective amount of such income.

Antonio purchases Eagle Corporation taxable bonds with a face value of $100,000 for $110,000, thus paying a premium of $10,000. The annual interest rate is 7%, and the bonds mature 10 years from the date of purchase. The annual interest income is $7,000 (7% × $100,000).

If Antonio elects to amortize the bond premium, the $10,000 premium is deducted over the 10-year period. Antonio's basis for the bonds is reduced each year by the amount of the amortization deduction.

If the bonds were tax-exempt, amortization of the bond premium and the basis adjustment would be mandatory. However, no deduction would be allowed for the amortization.

Easements An easement is the legal right to use another's land for a special purpose. Historically, easements were commonly used to obtain rights-of-way for utility lines, roads, and pipelines. In recent years, grants of conservation easements have become a popular means of obtaining charitable contribution deductions and reducing the value of real estate for transfer tax (i.e., estate and gift) purposes. Likewise, scenic easements are used to reduce the value of land as assessed for ad valorem property tax purposes.

The amount received for granting an easement is subtracted from the basis of the property. If the taxpayer does not retain any right to the use of the land, all of the basis is assigned to the easement. However, if the use of the land is only partially restricted, an allocation of some of the basis to the easement is appropriate. If, however, it is impossible or impractical to separate the basis of the part of the property on which the easement is granted, the basis of the whole property is reduced by the amount received. If the amount received for the easement exceeds the basis, a taxable gain results.[20]

---

[17]§ 1016(a)(4) and Reg. § 1.1016–5(a).

[18]§ 1016(a)(5) and Reg. § 1.1016–5(b). The accounting treatment of bond premium amortization is the same as for tax purposes. The amortization results in a decrease in the bond investment account.

[19]§ 171(c).

[20]See Rev.Rul. 68–291, 1968–1 C.B. 351 and Rev.Rul. 77–414, 1977–2 C.B. 299.

LO.2

Distinguish between realized and recognized gain or loss.

14-1b **Recognized Gain or Loss**

Recognized gain is the amount of the realized gain that is included in the taxpayer's gross income.[21] A **recognized loss**, on the other hand, is the amount of a realized loss that is deductible for tax purposes.[22] As a general rule, the entire amount of a realized gain or loss is recognized.[23]

Concept Summary 14.1 summarizes the realized gain or loss and recognized gain or loss concepts.

Concept Summary 14.1

Realized and Recognized Gain or Loss

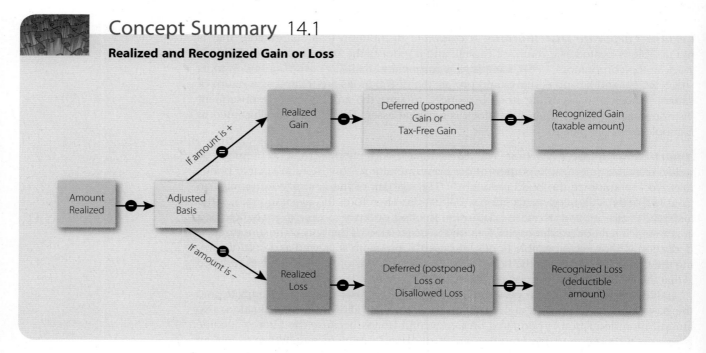

14-1c **Nonrecognition of Gain or Loss**

In certain cases, a realized gain or loss is not recognized upon the sale or other disposition of property. One such case involves nontaxable exchanges, which are covered in Chapter 15. Others include losses realized upon the sale, exchange, or condemnation of personal use assets (as opposed to business or income-producing property) and gains realized upon the sale of a residence (see Chapter 15). In addition, realized losses from the sale or exchange of business or income-producing property between certain related parties are not recognized.[24]

Sale, Exchange, or Condemnation of Personal Use Assets

A realized loss from the sale, exchange, or condemnation of personal use assets (e.g., a personal residence or an automobile not used at all for business or income-producing purposes) is not recognized for tax purposes. An exception exists for casualty or theft losses from personal use assets (see Chapter 7). In contrast, any gain realized from the sale or other disposition of personal use assets is, generally, fully taxable.

The Big Picture

EXAMPLE

7

Return to the facts of *The Big Picture* on p. 14-1. Assume that Alice sells the boat, which she has held exclusively for personal use, for $23,000. Recall that her adjusted basis of the boat is $22,000. Alice has a realized and recognized gain of $1,000.

---

[21]§ 61(a)(3) and Reg. § 1.61–6(a).
[22]§ 165(a) and Reg. § 1.165–1(a).

[23]§ 1001(c) and Reg. § 1.1002–1(a).
[24]§ 267(a)(1).

TAX IN THE NEWS   **Tax Implications of Virtual Currency (Bitcoin)**

In Notice 2014–21 (2014–16 I.R.B. 938), the Internal Revenue Service (IRS), through a series of questions and answers, describes how existing tax principles apply to transactions using virtual currency.

Background. Bitcoin is a decentralized virtual store of value that is beginning to gain greater acceptance as a medium of exchange in the mainstream marketplace. Notice 2014–21 describes virtual currencies such as Bitcoin as follows:

> "[A] digital representation of value that functions as a medium of exchange, a unit of account, and/or a store of value … Virtual currency that has an equivalent value in real currency, or that acts as a substitute for real currency, is referred to as 'convertible' virtual currency. …"

Bitcoin derives value not from governmental backing or a link to an underlying commodity, but purely from its finite nature, the effort required to generate new Bitcoin, and the value its users place on it and its acceptance as a medium of exchange in certain segments of the market. Bitcoin supply is finite (the maximum number of Bitcoin that will ever exist is approximately 21 million). A good summary of fundamental questions and answers surrounding Bitcoin can be found at **https://bitcoin.org/en/faq**.

IRS Guidance. Notice 2014–21 provides answers to frequently asked questions (FAQs) on virtual currency such as Bitcoin. These FAQs provide basic information on the U.S. Federal tax implications of transactions in, or transactions that use, virtual currency. In some environments, virtual currency operates like "real" currency (e.g., the coin and paper money of the United States) but it does not have legal tender status in any jurisdiction.

In its guidance, the IRS indicates that Bitcoin is *not* currency; rather, virtual currency is treated as *property* for U.S. Federal tax purposes. General tax principles that apply to property transactions apply to transactions using virtual currency. Among other things, this means that:

- Wages paid to employees using virtual currency are taxable to the employee, must be reported by an employer on a Form W–2, and are subject to Federal income tax withholding and payroll taxes.

- Payments using virtual currency made to independent contractors and other service providers are taxable, and self-employment tax rules generally apply. Payers are subject to the same information reporting requirements as any other payer (so, for example, a Form 1099–MISC must be issued to an independent contractor if Bitcoin payments exceed $600 per year).

- The character of gain or loss from the sale or exchange of virtual currency depends on whether the virtual currency is a capital asset in the hands of the taxpayer.

- A payment made using virtual currency is subject to information reporting to the same extent as any other payment made in property.

The full set of 16 questions and answers provided by the IRS can be found at **www.irs.gov/pub/irs-drop/n-14-21.pdf**.

The Big Picture

Assume that Alice sells the boat in Example 7 for $20,000. She has a realized loss of $2,000, but the loss is not recognized.

EXAMPLE

8

14-2 BASIS CONSIDERATIONS

LO.3

Review and illustrate how basis is determined for various methods of asset acquisition.

A key element in calculating gain or loss from a property transaction is the asset's basis at the time of the transaction. Various methods for determining basis apply, depending on how the asset was acquired.

14-2a Determination of Cost Basis

As noted earlier, the basis of property is generally the property's cost. Cost is the amount paid for the property in cash or other property.[25] This general rule follows logically from the recovery of capital doctrine; that is, the cost or other basis of property is to be recovered tax-free by the taxpayer.

---

[25]§ 1012 and Reg. § 1.1012–1(a).

A *bargain purchase* of property is an exception to the general rule for determining basis. A bargain purchase may result when an employer transfers property to an employee at less than the property's fair market value (as compensation for services) or when a corporation transfers property to a shareholder at less than the property's fair market value (a dividend). The amount included in income as either compensation for services or dividend income is the difference between the bargain purchase price and the property's fair market value. The basis of property acquired in a bargain purchase is the property's fair market value.[26] If the basis of the property were not increased by the bargain amount, the taxpayer would be taxed on this amount again at disposition.

EXAMPLE 9

Wade buys land from his employer for $10,000 on December 30. The fair market value of the land is $15,000.

Wade must include the $5,000 difference between the cost and the fair market value of the land in gross income for the taxable year. The bargain element represents additional compensation to Wade. His basis for the land is $15,000, the land's fair market value.

Identification Problems

Cost identification problems are frequently encountered in securities transactions. For example, the Regulations require that the taxpayer adequately identify the particular stock that has been sold (specific identification).[27] A problem arises when the taxpayer has purchased separate lots of stock on different dates or at different prices and cannot adequately identify the lot from which a particular sale takes place. In this case, the stock is presumed to come from the first lot or lots purchased (a FIFO presumption).[28] When securities are left in the custody of a broker, it may be necessary to provide specific instructions and receive written confirmation as to which securities are being sold. Brokers and others in similar enterprises are now required to provide investors with an annual report on the cost basis of their stocks sold during the year (to be included on Form 1099–B and reported to the IRS).

EXAMPLE 10

Polly purchases 100 shares of Olive Corporation stock on July 1, 2014, for $5,000 ($50 a share) and another 100 shares of Olive stock on July 1, 2015, for $6,000 ($60 a share). She sells 50 shares of the stock on January 2, 2016.

The cost of the stock sold, assuming that Polly cannot adequately identify the shares, is $50 a share, or $2,500. This is the cost Polly will compare with the amount realized in determining the gain or loss from the sale.

Allocation Problems

When a taxpayer acquires *multiple assets in a lump-sum purchase*, the total cost must be allocated among the individual assets.[29] Allocation is necessary for several reasons:

- Some of the assets acquired may be depreciable (e.g., buildings), while others may not be (e.g., land).
- Only a portion of the assets acquired may be sold.
- Some of the assets may be capital or § 1231 assets that receive special tax treatment upon subsequent sale or other disposition.

The lump-sum cost is allocated on the basis of the fair market values of the individual assets acquired.

---

[26]Reg. §§ 1.61–2(d)(2)(i) and 1.301–1(j). See the discussion in Chapter 5 of the circumstances under which what appears to be a taxable bargain purchase is an excludible qualified employee discount.

[27]Reg. § 1.1012–1(c)(1).

[28]*Kluger Associates, Inc.*, 69 T.C. 925 (1978).

[29]Reg. § 1.61–6(a).

EXAMPLE 11

Harry purchases a building and land for $800,000. Because of the depressed nature of the industry in which the seller was operating, Harry was able to negotiate a very favorable purchase price. Appraisals of the individual assets indicate that the fair market value of the building is $600,000 and that of the land is $400,000.

Harry's basis for the building is $480,000 [($600,000/$1,000,000) × $800,000], and his basis for the land is $320,000 [($400,000/$1,000,000) × $800,000].

If a business is purchased and **goodwill** is involved, a special allocation rule applies. Initially, the purchase price is assigned to the assets, excluding goodwill, to the extent of their total fair market value. This assigned amount is allocated among the assets on the basis of the fair market value of the individual assets acquired. Goodwill is then assigned the residual amount of the purchase price. The resultant allocation is applicable to both the buyer and the seller.[30]

EXAMPLE 12

Rocky sells his business to Paul. They agree that the values of the individual assets are as follows:

Inventory	$ 50,000
Building	500,000
Land	200,000
Goodwill	150,000

After negotiations, Rocky and Paul agree on a sales price of $1 million. Applying the residual method with respect to goodwill results in the following allocation of the $1 million purchase price:

Inventory	$ 50,000
Building	500,000
Land	200,000
Goodwill	250,000

The residual method requires that all of the excess of the purchase price over the fair market value of the assets ($1,000,000 − $900,000 = $100,000) be allocated to goodwill. Without this requirement, the purchaser could allocate the excess pro rata to all of the assets, including goodwill, based on their respective fair market values. This would have resulted in only $166,667 [$150,000 + ($150,000 ÷ $900,000 × $100,000)] being assigned to goodwill.

In the case of *nontaxable stock dividends*, the allocation depends on whether the dividend is a common stock dividend on common stock or a preferred stock dividend on common stock. If the stock dividend is common on common, the cost of the original common shares is allocated to the total shares owned after the dividend.[31]

EXAMPLE 13

Susan owns 100 shares of Sparrow Corporation common stock for which she paid $1,100. She receives a 10% common stock dividend, giving her a new total of 110 shares. Before the stock dividend, Susan's basis was $11 per share ($1,100 ÷ 100 shares). The basis of each share after the stock dividend is $10 ($1,100 ÷ 110 shares).

If the nontaxable stock dividend is preferred stock on common, the cost of the original common shares is allocated between the common and preferred shares on the basis of their relative fair market values on the date of distribution.[32]

---

[30]§ 1060. The classification of the seller's recognized gain associated with the goodwill is discussed in Chapter 16.

[31]§§ 305(a) and 307(a).

[32]Reg. § 1.307–1(a).

Fran owns 100 shares of Cardinal Corporation common stock for which she paid $1,000. She receives a nontaxable stock dividend of 50 shares of preferred stock on her common stock. The fair market values on the date of distribution of the preferred stock dividend are $30 a share for common stock and $40 a share for preferred stock.

Fair market value of common ($30 × 100 shares)	$3,000
Fair market value of preferred ($40 × 50 shares)	2,000
	$5,000
Basis of common: 3/5 × $1,000	$ 600
Basis of preferred: 2/5 × $1,000	$ 400

The basis per share for the common stock is $6 ($600/100 shares). The basis per share for the preferred stock is $8 ($400/50 shares).

The holding period for a nontaxable stock dividend, whether received in the form of common stock or preferred stock, includes the holding period of the original shares.[33] The significance of the holding period for capital assets is discussed in Chapter 16.

14-2b Gift Basis

When a taxpayer receives property as a gift, there is no cost to the donee (recipient). Thus, under the cost basis provision, the donee's basis would be zero. However, this would violate the statutory intent that gifts not be subject to the income tax.[34] With a zero basis, if the donee sold the property, all of the amount realized would be treated as realized gain. Therefore, a basis is assigned to the property received depending on the following:

* The date of the gift.
* The basis of the property to the donor.
* The amount of the gift tax paid.
* The fair market value of the property.

Gift Basis Rules If No Gift Tax Is Paid

Property received by gift can be referred to as *dual basis* property; that is, the basis for gain and the basis for loss might not be the same amount. The present basis rules for gifts of property are as follows:

* If the donee disposes of gift property in a transaction that results in a gain, the basis to the donee is the same as the donor's adjusted basis.[35] The donee's basis in this case is referred to as the *gain basis*. Therefore, a *realized gain* results if the amount realized from the disposition exceeds the donee's gain basis.

Melissa purchased stock in 2015 for $10,000. She gave the stock to her son, Joe, in 2016, when the fair market value was $15,000. No gift tax is paid on the transfer, and Joe subsequently sells the property for $15,000. Joe's basis is $10,000, and he has a realized gain of $5,000.

* If the donee disposes of gift property in a transaction that results in a loss, the basis to the donee is the *lower* of the donor's adjusted basis or the fair market value on the date of the gift. The donee's basis in this case is referred to as the *loss basis*. Therefore, a *realized loss* results if the amount realized from the disposition is less than the donee's loss basis.

---

[33]§ 1223(5) and Reg. § 1.1223–1(e).

[34]§ 102(a).

[35]§ 1015(a) and Reg. § 1.1015–1(a)(1). See Reg. § 1.1015–1(a)(3) for cases in which the facts necessary to determine the donor's adjusted basis are

unknown. Refer to Example 18 for the effect of depreciation deductions by the donee.

EXAMPLE 16

Burt purchased stock in 2015 for $10,000. He gave the stock to his son, Cliff, in 2016, when the fair market value was $7,000. No gift tax is paid on the transfer. Cliff later sells the stock for $6,000.

Cliff's basis is $7,000 (fair market value is less than donor's adjusted basis of $10,000), and the realized loss from the sale is $1,000 ($6,000 amount realized − $7,000 basis).

The amount of the loss basis will *differ* from the amount of the gain basis only if, at the date of the gift, the adjusted basis of the property exceeds the property's fair market value. Note that the loss basis rule prevents the donee from receiving a tax benefit from a decline in value that occurred while the donor held the property.

Therefore, in Example 16, Cliff has a loss of only $1,000 rather than a loss of $4,000 ($6,000 − $10,000). The $3,000 difference represents the decline in value that occurred while Burt held the property. Ironically, however, the gain basis rule may result in the donee being subject to income tax on the appreciation that occurred while the donor held the property, as illustrated in Example 15.

If the amount realized from a sale or other disposition is *between* the basis for loss and the basis for gain, no gain or loss is realized.

EXAMPLE 17

Assume the same facts as in Example 16, except that Cliff sells the stock for $8,000. Application of the gain basis rule produces a loss of $2,000 ($8,000 − $10,000). Application of the loss basis rule produces a gain of $1,000 ($8,000 − $7,000).

Because the amount realized is between the gain basis and the loss basis, Cliff recognizes neither a gain nor a loss.

Adjustment for Gift Tax

Because of the size of the unified estate and gift tax exemption ($5.45 million in 2016), basis adjustments for gift taxes paid are rare. If, however, gift taxes are paid by the donor, the portion of the gift tax paid that is related to any appreciation is taken into account in determining the donee's gain basis.[36]

For *gifts made before 1977*, the full amount of the gift tax paid is added to the donor's basis, with basis capped at the donor's fair market value at the date of the gift.

Holding Period

The **holding period** for property acquired by gift begins on the date the donor acquired the property if the gain basis rule applies.[37] The holding period starts on the date of the gift if the loss basis rule applies.[38] The significance of the holding period for capital assets is discussed in Chapter 16.

Basis for Depreciation

The basis for depreciation on depreciable gift property is the donee's gain basis.[39] This rule is applicable even if the donee later sells the property at a loss and uses the loss basis rule in calculating the amount of the realized loss.

EXAMPLE 18

Vito gave a machine to Tina in 2016. At that time, the adjusted basis was $32,000 (cost of $40,000 − accumulated depreciation of $8,000), and the fair market value was $26,000. No gift tax was paid. Tina's gain basis at the date of the gift is $32,000, and her loss basis is $26,000. During 2016, Tina deducts depreciation (cost recovery) of $6,400 ($32,000 × 20%). (Refer to Chapter 8 for the cost recovery tables.) At the end of 2016, Tina's gain basis and loss basis are calculated as follows:

	Gain Basis	Loss Basis
Donor's basis or fair market value	$32,000	$26,000
Depreciation	(6,400)	(6,400)
	$25,600	$19,600

---

[36]§ 1015(d)(6) and Reg. § 1.1015–5(c)(2). Examples illustrating these rules can be found in Reg. § 1.1015–5(c)(5) and IRS Publication 551 (*Basis of Assets*), p. 9.

[37]§ 1223(2) and Reg. § 1.1223–1(b).

[38]Rev.Rul. 59–86, 1959–1 C.B. 209.

[39]§ 1011 and Reg. §§ 1.1011–1 and 1.167(g)–1.

14-2c **Property Acquired from a Decedent**

Special basis rules apply for a taxpayer who has received property from a decedent (someone who has passed away). Typically, these rules are favorable to the taxpayer receiving such property.

General Rules

The basis of property acquired from a decedent is generally the property's fair market value at the date of death (referred to as the *primary valuation amount*).[40] The property's basis is the fair market value six months after the date of death if the executor or administrator of the estate *elects* the alternate valuation date for estate tax purposes. This amount is referred to as the *alternate valuation amount*.

The Big Picture

EXAMPLE 19

Return to the facts of *The Big Picture* on p. 14-1. Alice and various other family members inherited property from Alice's mother, who died in 2015. At the date of death, the mother's basis for the property Alice inherited—her mother's house—was $275,000. The house's fair market value at the date of death was $475,000. The alternate valuation date was not elected.

Alice's basis for income tax purposes is $475,000. This is commonly referred to as a *stepped-up basis*.

The Big Picture

EXAMPLE 20

Assume the same facts as in Example 19, except that the house's fair market value at the date of the mother's death was $260,000.

Alice's basis for income tax purposes is $260,000. This is commonly referred to as a *stepped-down basis*.

The alternate valuation date and amount are only available to estates for which an estate tax return must be filed [generally, estates with a valuation in excess of $5.45 million in 2016 ($5.43 million in 2015)]. Even if an estate tax return is filed and the executor elects the alternate valuation date, the six months after death date is available only for property that the executor has not distributed before this date.[41]

The alternate valuation date can be elected *only if*, as a result of the election, both the value of the gross estate and the estate tax liability are lower than they would have been if the primary valuation date had been used.[42]

Income in Respect of a Decedent

Income in respect of a decedent (IRD) is income earned by a decedent to the point of death but not reportable on the final income tax return under the method of accounting used. IRD is most frequently applicable to decedents using the cash basis of accounting. IRD also occurs, for example, when a taxpayer at the time of death held installment notes receivable on which the gain has been deferred. For both cash and accrual taxpayers, IRD includes most post-death distributions from retirement plans [e.g., traditional IRA, § 401(k), H.R. 10 (Keogh), § 403(b), and other qualified plans]. With the exception of Roth IRAs, distributions from retirement plans invariably contain an income component that has not yet been subject to income tax.

---

[40]§§ 1014(a) and 1022. See *South-Western Federal Taxation: Corporations, Partnerships, Estates & Trusts*, Chapter 18, for additional information.

[41]§ 2032(a)(1) and Rev.Rul. 56–60, 1956–1 C.B. 443. For any property distributed by the executor during the six-month period preceding the alternate valuation date, the adjusted basis to the beneficiary will equal the fair market value on the date of distribution.

[42]§ 2032(c); this provision prevents the alternate valuation election from being used to increase the basis of the property to the beneficiary for income tax purposes without simultaneously increasing the estate tax liability (because of estate tax deductions or credits).

EXAMPLE

21

George, age 58, was entitled to a salary payment of $18,000 and a bonus of $20,000 at the time of his death. In addition, George had been contributing to a traditional IRA for over 20 years. The IRA has a basis of $83,000 (due to some nondeductible contributions over the years) and a current value of $560,000. George's estate collects the salary and bonus payments, and George's wife (his only beneficiary) cashes in the IRA.

Both the estate and George's wife have income in respect of a decedent (IRD) and must include ordinary income in their computation of taxable income for the year. The estate has IRD of $38,000 (salary of $18,000 plus bonus of $20,000), and George's wife has IRD of $477,000 ($560,000 proceeds less $83,000 basis). A better outcome might be achieved for George's wife if she rolled over the inherited IRA into an IRA in her name and deferred receiving distributions until required. (Note: Only a surviving spouse can roll over an inherited IRA without tax consequences.[43])

IRD is included in the gross estate at its fair market value on the appropriate valuation date. Because IRD is not subject to the step-up or step-down rules applicable to property passed by death, the income tax basis of the decedent transfers to the estate or heirs.[44] Furthermore, the recipient of IRD must classify it in the same manner (e.g., ordinary income or capital gain) as the decedent would have.[45]

Survivor's Share of Property

Both the decedent's share and the survivor's share of *community property* have a basis equal to the fair market value on the date of the decedent's death.[46] This result applies to the decedent's share of the community property because the property is included in the estate and assumes a fair market value basis. Because the surviving spouse's share of the community property is treated as if it is acquired from the decedent, it also has a basis equal to the fair market value.

Community Property

EXAMPLE

22

Floyd and Vera are married and reside in a community property state. They own, as community property, 200 shares of Crow stock acquired in 1991 for $100,000. Floyd dies in 2016, when the securities are valued at $300,000. One-half of the Crow stock is included in Floyd's estate. If Vera inherits Floyd's share of the community property, the basis for gain or loss is $300,000, determined as follows:

Vera's one-half of the community property (stepped up from $50,000 to $150,000 due to Floyd's death)	$150,000
Floyd's one-half of the community property (stepped up from $50,000 to $150,000 due to inclusion in his gross estate)	150,000
Vera's new basis	$300,000

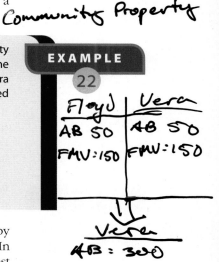

In a *common law* state, only one-half of jointly held property of spouses (tenants by the entirety or joint tenants with rights of survivorship) is included in the estate.[47] In such a case, no adjustment of the basis is permitted for the excluded property interest (the surviving spouse's share).

Common Law

EXAMPLE

23

Assume the same facts as in Example 22, except that the property is jointly held by Floyd and Vera who reside in a common law state. Floyd purchased the property and made a gift of one-half of the property to Vera when the stock was acquired. No gift tax was paid. Only one-half of the Crow stock is included in Floyd's estate. Vera's basis for determining gain or loss in the excluded half is not adjusted upward for the increase in value to date of death. Therefore, Vera's basis is $200,000, determined as follows:

continued

She keeps her old AB of her half.

---

[43]See *South-Western Federal Taxation: Corporations, Partnerships, Estates & Trusts,* Chapter 19, for additional information.

[44]§ 1014(c).

[45]§ 691(a)(3).

[46]§ 1014(b)(6). See the listing of community property states in Chapter 4.

[47]§ 2040(b).

Vera's one-half of the jointly held property (carryover basis of $50,000)	$ 50,000
Floyd's one-half of the jointly held property (stepped up from $50,000 to $150,000 due to inclusion in his gross estate)	150,000
Vera's new basis	$200,000

Holding Period of Property Acquired from a Decedent

The holding period of property acquired from a decedent is *deemed to be long term* (held for the required long-term holding period). This provision applies regardless of whether the property is disposed of at a gain or at a loss.[48]

14-2d **Disallowed Losses**

LO.4

Describe various loss disallowance provisions.

In certain situations, losses that normally would be recognized are disallowed. Transactions between related parties and wash sales are two of these situations.

Related Taxpayers

Section 267 provides that realized losses from sales or exchanges of property, directly or indirectly, between certain related parties are not recognized. This loss disallowance provision applies to several types of related-party transactions. The most common involve (1) members of a family and (2) an individual and a corporation in which the individual owns, directly or indirectly, more than 50 percent in value of the corporation's outstanding stock. Section 707 provides a similar loss disallowance provision where the related parties are a partner and a partnership in which the partner owns, directly or indirectly, more than 50 percent of the capital interests or profits interests in the partnership. The rules governing the relationships covered by § 267 were discussed in Chapter 6. See Chapter 15 for a discussion of the special rules under § 1041 for property transfers between spouses or incident to divorce.

If income-producing or business property is transferred to a related taxpayer and a loss is disallowed, the basis of the property to the recipient is the property's cost to the transferee. However, if a subsequent sale or other disposition of the property by the original transferee results in a realized gain, the amount of gain is reduced by the loss that was previously disallowed.[49] This *right of offset* is not applicable if the original sale involved the sale of a personal use asset (e.g., the sale of a personal residence between related taxpayers). Furthermore, the right of offset is available only to the original transferee (the related-party buyer).[50]

EXAMPLE

24

Pedro sells business property with an adjusted basis of $50,000 to his daughter, Josefina, for its fair market value of $40,000. Pedro's realized loss of $10,000 is not recognized.

- How much gain does Josefina recognize if she sells the property for $52,000? Josefina recognizes a $2,000 gain. Her realized gain is $12,000 ($52,000 less her basis of $40,000), but she can offset Pedro's $10,000 loss against the gain.

- How much gain does Josefina recognize if she sells the property for $48,000? Josefina recognizes no gain or loss. Her realized gain is $8,000 ($48,000 less her basis of $40,000), but she can offset $8,000 of Pedro's $10,000 loss against the gain. Note that Pedro's loss can only offset Josefina's gain. It cannot create a loss for Josefina.

- How much loss does Josefina recognize if she sells the property for $38,000? Josefina recognizes a $2,000 loss, the same as her realized loss ($38,000 less $40,000 basis). Pedro's loss does not increase Josefina's loss. His loss can be offset only against a gain. Because Josefina has no realized gain, Pedro's loss cannot be used and is never recognized. This part of the example assumes that the property is business or income-producing property to Josefina. If not, her $2,000 loss is personal and is not recognized.

---

[48]§ 1223(11).

[49]§ 267(d) and Reg. § 1.267(d)–1(a).

[50]The loss disallowance rules (1) prevent a taxpayer from directly transferring an unrealized loss to a related taxpayer in a higher tax bracket who could receive a greater tax benefit from recognition of the loss and (2) eliminate a substantial administrative burden on the Internal Revenue Service as to the appropriateness of the selling price (i.e., fair market value or not). The loss disallowance rules are applicable even where the selling price is equal to the fair market value and can be validated (e.g., listed stocks).

The holding period of the buyer for the property is not affected by the holding period of the seller. That is, the buyer's *holding period* includes only the period of time he or she has held the property.[51]

Wash Sales

Section 1091 stipulates that in certain cases, a realized loss on the sale or exchange of stock or securities is not recognized. Specifically, if a taxpayer sells or exchanges stock or securities and within 30 days before *or* after the date of the sale or exchange acquires substantially identical stock or securities, any loss realized from the sale or exchange is not recognized because the transaction is a **wash sale** .[52] The term *acquire* means acquire by purchase or in a taxable exchange and includes an option to purchase substantially identical securities. *Substantially identical* means the same in all important particulars. Corporate bonds and preferred stock normally are not considered substantially identical to the corporation's common stock. However, if the bonds and preferred stock are convertible into common stock, they may be considered substantially identical under certain circumstances.[53] Attempts to avoid the application of the wash sales rules by having a related taxpayer repurchase the securities have been unsuccessful.[54] The wash sales provisions do *not* apply to gains. Concept Summary 14.2 provides an overview of the wash sale rules.

Concept Summary 14.2

Wash Sale Rules

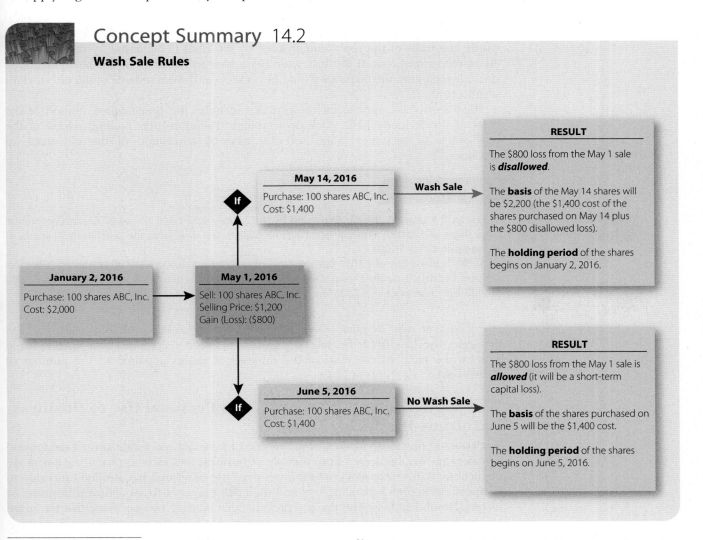

May 14, 2016

Purchase: 100 shares ABC, Inc.
Cost: $1,400

Wash Sale →

RESULT

The $800 loss from the May 1 sale is *disallowed*.

The **basis** of the May 14 shares will be $2,200 (the $1,400 cost of the shares purchased on May 14 plus the $800 disallowed loss).

The **holding period** of the shares begins on January 2, 2016.

January 2, 2016

Purchase: 100 shares ABC, Inc.
Cost: $2,000

May 1, 2016

Sell: 100 shares ABC, Inc.
Selling Price: $1,200
Gain (Loss): ($800)

June 5, 2016

Purchase: 100 shares ABC, Inc.
Cost: $1,400

No Wash Sale →

RESULT

The $800 loss from the May 1 sale is *allowed* (it will be a short-term capital loss).

The **basis** of the shares purchased on June 5 will be the $1,400 cost.

The **holding period** of the shares begins on June 5, 2016.

---

[51]§§ 267(d) and 1223(2) and Reg. § 1.267(d)–1(c)(3).
[52]§ 1091(a) and Reg. §§ 1.1091–1(a) and (f).
[53]Rev.Rul. 56–406, 1956–2 C.B. 523.

[54]*McWilliams v. Comm.*, 47–1 USTC ¶9289, 35 AFTR 1184, 67 S.Ct. 1477 (USSC, 1947).

Although short sales have traditionally involved stocks, today the term *short sale* also refers to the sale of a personal residence by a homeowner who is "underwater," owing more on the home than it is worth. In a short sale, the homeowner sells the residence for its fair market value, which is less than the mortgage (or mortgages) on the property. One possible result of this transaction is that the taxpayer realizes a loss—the selling price is less than his or her basis in the property. Unfortunately, the realized loss cannot be recognized because a residence is a personal use asset. To add to the trauma of losing the home in a nondeductible loss sale, the mortgage company may require the taxpayer to keep paying on the portion of the mortgage still outstanding (i.e., the amount of the mortgage in excess of the net sales price). Thus, the taxpayer has triple misery: no home, a nondeductible loss, and an outstanding debt to pay.

Recognition of the loss is disallowed because the taxpayer is considered to be in substantially the same economic position after the sale and repurchase as before the sale and repurchase. This disallowance rule does not apply to taxpayers engaged in the business of buying and selling securities.[55] Investors, however, are not allowed to create losses through wash sales to offset income for tax purposes.

Realized loss that is not recognized is added to the *basis* of the substantially identical stock or securities whose acquisition resulted in the nonrecognition of loss.[56] In other words, the basis of the replacement stock or securities is increased by the amount of the unrecognized loss. If the loss were not added to the basis of the newly acquired stock or securities, the taxpayer would never recover the entire basis of the old stock or securities.

The basis of the new stock or securities includes the unrecovered portion of the basis of the formerly held stock or securities. Therefore, the *holding period* of the new stock or securities begins on the date of acquisition of the old stock or securities.[57]

The Big Picture

EXAMPLE 25

Return to the facts of *The Big Picture* on p. 14-1. Alice owned 100 shares of Green Corporation stock (basis of $20,000). She sold 50 shares for $8,000. Ten days later, she purchased 50 shares of the same stock for $7,000.

Alice's realized loss of $2,000 ($8,000 amount realized − $10,000 basis of 50 shares) is not recognized because it resulted from a wash sale. Alice's basis in the newly acquired stock is $9,000 ($7,000 purchase price + $2,000 unrecognized loss from the wash sale).

A taxpayer may acquire fewer shares than the number sold in a wash sale. In this case, the loss from the sale is prorated between recognized and unrecognized loss on the basis of the ratio of the number of shares acquired to the number of shares sold.[58]

14-2e Conversion of Property from Personal Use to Business or Income-Producing Use

As discussed previously, losses from the sale of personal use assets are not recognized for tax purposes, but losses from the sale of business and income-producing assets are deductible. Can a taxpayer convert a personal use asset that has declined in value to business or income-producing use and then sell the asset to recognize a business or income-producing loss? The tax law prevents this practice by specifying that the *original basis for loss* on personal use assets converted to business or income-producing use

[55]Reg. § 1.1091–1(a).
[56]§ 1091(d) and Reg. § 1.1091–2(a).
[57]§ 1223(4) and Reg. § 1.1223–1(d).
[58]§ 1091(b) and Reg. § 1.1091–1(c).

is the *lower* of the property's adjusted basis or fair market value on the date of conversion.[59] The *gain basis* for converted property is the property's adjusted basis on the date of conversion. The tax law is not concerned with gains on converted property because gains are recognized regardless of whether property is business, income-producing, or personal use.

Diane's personal residence has an adjusted basis of $175,000 and a fair market value of $160,000. Diane converts the personal residence to rental property. Her basis for loss is $160,000 (lower of $175,000 adjusted basis and fair market value of $160,000). The $15,000 decline in value is a personal loss and can never be recognized for tax purposes. Diane's basis for gain is $175,000.

The basis for loss is also the *basis for depreciating* the converted property.[60] This is an exception to the general rule that the basis for depreciation is the gain basis (e.g., property received by gift). This exception prevents the taxpayer from recovering a personal loss indirectly through depreciation of the higher original basis. After the property is converted, both its basis for loss and its basis for gain are adjusted for depreciation deductions from the date of conversion to the date of disposition. These rules apply only if a conversion from personal to business or income-producing use has actually occurred.

At a time when his personal residence (adjusted basis of $140,000) is worth $150,000, Keith converts one-half of it to rental use. Assume that the property is not MACRS recovery property. At this point, the estimated useful life of the residence is 20 years, and there is no estimated salvage value. After renting the converted portion for five years, Keith sells the property for $144,000. All amounts relate only to the building; the land has been accounted for separately. Keith has a $2,000 realized gain from the sale of the personal use portion of the residence and a $19,500 realized gain from the sale of the rental portion. These gains are computed as follows:

	Personal Use	Rental
Original basis for gain and loss—adjusted basis on date of conversion (fair market value is greater than the adjusted basis)	$70,000	$ 70,000
Depreciation—five years	(–0–)	(17,500)
Adjusted basis—date of sale	$70,000	$ 52,500
Amount realized	72,000	72,000
Realized gain	$ 2,000	$ 19,500

As discussed in Chapter 15, Keith may be able to exclude the $2,000 realized gain from the sale of the personal use portion of the residence under § 121. If the § 121 exclusion applies, only $17,500 (equal to the depreciation deducted) of the $19,500 realized gain from the rental portion is recognized.

Assume the same facts as in Example 27, except that the fair market value on the date of conversion is $130,000 and the sales proceeds are $90,000. Keith has a $25,000 realized loss from the sale of the personal use portion of the residence and a $3,750 realized loss from the sale of the rental portion. These losses are computed as follows:

continued

---

[59]Reg. § 1.165–9(b)(2).   [60]Reg. § 1.167(g)–1.

	Personal Use	Rental
Original basis for loss—fair market value on date of conversion (fair market value is less than the adjusted basis)	*	$ 65,000
Depreciation—five years	(–0–)	(16,250)
Adjusted basis—date of sale	$70,000	$ 48,750
Amount realized	45,000	45,000
Realized loss	($25,000)	($ 3,750)

*Not applicable.

The $25,000 loss from the sale of the personal use portion of the residence is not recognized. The $3,750 loss from the rental portion is recognized.

14-2f Additional Complexities in Determining Realized Gain or Loss

Amount Realized

The calculation of the amount realized may appear to be one of the least complex areas associated with property transactions. However, because numerous positive and negative adjustments may be required, this calculation can be complex and confusing. In addition, determining the fair market value of the items received by the taxpayer can be difficult. The following example provides insight into various items that can affect the amount realized.

EXAMPLE
29

Ridge sells an office building and the associated land on October 1, 2016. Under the terms of the sales contract, Ridge is to receive $600,000 in cash. The purchaser is to assume Ridge's mortgage of $300,000 on the property. To enable the purchaser to obtain adequate financing, Ridge is to pay the $15,000 in points charged by the lender. The broker's commission on the sale is $45,000. The purchaser agrees to pay the $12,000 in property taxes for the entire year. The amount realized by Ridge is determined as follows:

Selling price:		
Cash	$600,000	
Mortgage assumed by purchaser	300,000	
Seller's property taxes paid by purchaser ($12,000 × 9/12)	9,000	$909,000
Less:		
Broker's commission	$ 45,000	
Points paid by seller	15,000	(60,000)
Amount realized		$849,000

Adjusted Basis

Three types of issues tend to complicate the determination of adjusted basis. First, the applicable tax provisions for calculating the adjusted basis depend on how the property was acquired (e.g., purchase, taxable exchange, nontaxable exchange, gift, or inheritance). Second, if the asset is subject to depreciation, cost recovery, amortization, or depletion, adjustments must be made to the basis during the time period the asset is held by the taxpayer. Upon disposition of the asset, the taxpayer's records for both of these items may be deficient. For example, the donee does not know the amount of the donor's basis or the amount of gift tax paid by the donor, or the taxpayer does not know how much depreciation he or she has deducted. Third, the complex positive and negative adjustments encountered in calculating the amount realized are also involved in calculating the adjusted basis.

EXAMPLE

30

Jane purchased a personal residence in 2007. The purchase price and the related closing costs were as follows:

Purchase price	$325,000
Recording costs	140
Title fees and title insurance	815
Survey costs	225
Attorney's fees	750
Appraisal fee	250

Other relevant tax information for the house during the time Jane owned it is as follows:

- Constructed a swimming pool for medical reasons. The cost was $20,000, of which $5,000 was deducted as a medical expense.
- Added a solar heating system. The cost was $18,000.
- Deducted home office expenses of $6,000. Of this amount, $5,200 was for depreciation.

The adjusted basis for the house is calculated as follows:

Purchase price	$325,000
Recording costs	140
Title fees and title insurance	815
Survey costs	225
Attorney's fees	750
Appraisal fee	250
Swimming pool ($20,000 − $5,000)	15,000
Solar heating system	18,000
	$360,180
Less: Depreciation deducted on home office	(5,200)
Adjusted basis	$354,980

14-2g **Summary of Basis Adjustments**

Some of the more common items that either increase or decrease the basis of an asset appear in Concept Summary 14.3.

In discussing the topic of basis, a number of specific techniques for determining basis have been presented. Although the various techniques are responsive to and mandated by transactions occurring in the marketplace, they do possess enough common characteristics to be categorized as follows:

- The basis of the asset may be determined by reference to the asset's cost.
- The basis of the asset may be determined by reference to the basis of another asset.
- The basis of the asset may be determined by reference to the asset's fair market value.
- The basis of the asset may be determined by reference to the basis of the asset to another taxpayer.

14-3 **TAX PLANNING**

LO.5

Identify tax planning opportunities related to selected property transactions.

14-3a **Cost Identification and Documentation Considerations**

When multiple assets are acquired in a single transaction, the contract price must be allocated for several reasons. First, some of the assets may be depreciable, while others are not. From the different viewpoints of the buyer and the seller, this may produce a tax conflict that needs to be resolved. That is, the seller prefers a high allocation for non-depreciable assets, whereas the purchaser prefers a high allocation for depreciable assets (see Chapters 16 and 17). Second, the seller needs to know the amount realized

Concept Summary 14.3

Adjustments to Basis

Item	Effect	Refer to Chapter	Explanation
Amortization of bond discount	Increase	16	Amortization is mandatory for certain taxable bonds and elective for tax-exempt bonds.
Amortization of bond premium	Decrease	14	Amortization is mandatory for tax-exempt bonds and elective for taxable bonds.
Amortization of covenant not to compete	Decrease	8	Covenant must be for a definite and limited time period. The amortization period is a statutory period of 15 years.
Amortization of intangibles	Decrease	8	Intangibles are amortized over a 15-year period.
Assessment for local benefits	Increase	10	To the extent not deductible as taxes (e.g., assessment for streets and sidewalks that increase the value of the property versus one for maintenance or repair or for meeting interest charges).
Bad debts	Decrease	7	Only the specific charge-off method is permitted.
Capital additions	Increase	14	Certain items, at the taxpayer's election, can be capitalized or deducted (e.g., selected medical expenses).
Casualty	Decrease	7	For a casualty loss, the amount of the adjustment is the sum of the deductible loss and the insurance proceeds received. For a casualty gain, the amount of the adjustment is the insurance proceeds received reduced by the recognized gain.
Condemnation	Decrease	15	See casualty explanation.
Cost recovery	Decrease	8	§ 168 is applicable to tangible assets placed in service after 1980 whose useful life is expressed in terms of years.
Depletion	Decrease	8	Use the greater of cost or percentage depletion. Percentage depletion can still be deducted when the basis is zero.
Depreciation	Decrease	8	§ 167 is applicable to tangible assets placed in service before 1981 and to tangible assets not depreciated in terms of years.
Easement	Decrease	14	If the taxpayer does not retain any use of the land, all of the basis is allocable to the easement transaction. However, if only part of the land is affected by the easement, only part of the basis is allocable to the easement transaction.
Improvements by lessee to lessor's property	Increase	5	Adjustment occurs only if the lessor is required to include the fair market value of the improvements in gross income under § 109.
Imputed interest	Decrease	18	Amount deducted is not part of the cost of the asset.
Inventory: lower of cost or market	Decrease	18	Not available if the LIFO method is used.
Limited expensing under § 179	Decrease	8	Occurs only if the taxpayer elects § 179 treatment.
Medical capital expenditure permitted as a medical expense	Decrease	10	Adjustment is the amount of the deduction (the effect on basis is to increase it by the amount of the capital expenditure net of the deduction).
Real estate taxes: apportionment between the buyer and seller	Increase or decrease	10	To the extent the buyer pays the seller's pro rata share, the buyer's basis is increased. To the extent the seller pays the buyer's pro rata share, the buyer's basis is decreased.
Rebate from manufacturer	Decrease		Because the rebate is treated as an adjustment to the purchase price, it is not included in the buyer's gross income.
Stock dividend	Decrease	5	Adjustment occurs only if the stock dividend is nontaxable. While the basis per share decreases, the total stock basis does not change.
Stock rights	Decrease	14	Adjustment to stock basis occurs only for nontaxable stock rights and only if the fair market value of the rights is at least 15% of the fair market value of the stock or, if less than 15%, the taxpayer elects to allocate the basis between the stock and the rights.
Theft	Decrease	7	See casualty explanation.

on the sale of the capital assets and the ordinary income assets so that the recognized gains and losses can be classified as capital or ordinary. For example, an allocation to goodwill or to a covenant not to compete (see Chapters 8, 16, and 17) produces different tax consequences to the seller. Third, the buyer needs the adjusted basis of each asset to calculate the realized gain or loss on a subsequent sale or other disposition of each asset.

14-3b **Selection of Property for Making Gifts**

A donor can achieve several tax advantages by making gifts of appreciated property. The donor avoids income tax on the unrealized gain that would have occurred had the donor sold the property. A portion of this amount can be permanently avoided because the donee's adjusted basis is increased by part or all of any gift tax paid by the donor. Even without this increase in basis, the income tax liability on the sale of the property by the donee can be less than the income tax liability that would have resulted from the donor's sale of the property, if the donee is in a lower tax bracket than the donor. In addition, any subsequent appreciation during the time the property is held by the lower tax bracket donee results in a tax savings on the sale or other disposition of the property. Such gifts of appreciated property can be an effective tool in family tax planning.

Taxpayers should generally not make gifts of depreciated property (property that, if sold, would produce a realized loss) because the donor does not receive an income tax deduction for the unrealized loss element. In addition, the donee receives no benefit from this unrealized loss upon the subsequent sale of the property because of the loss basis rule. The loss basis rule provides that the donee's basis is the lower of the donor's basis or the fair market value at the date of the gift. If the donor anticipates that the donee will sell the property upon receiving it, the donor should sell the property and take the loss deduction, assuming that the loss is deductible. The donor can then give the proceeds from the sale to the donee.

14-3c **Selection of Property for Making Bequests**

A taxpayer should generally make bequests of appreciated property in his or her will. Doing so enables both the decedent and the heir to avoid income tax on the unrealized gain because the recipient takes the fair market value as his or her basis.

Taxpayers generally should not make bequests of depreciated property (property that, if sold, would produce a realized loss) because the decedent does not receive an income tax deduction for the unrealized loss element. In addition, the heir will receive no benefit from this unrealized loss upon the subsequent sale of the property.

EXAMPLE
31

On the date of her death in 2016, Marta owned land held for investment purposes. The land had an adjusted basis of $130,000 and a fair market value of $100,000. If Marta had sold the property before her death, the recognized loss would have been $30,000.

If Roger inherits the property and later sells it for $90,000, the recognized loss is $10,000 (the decline in value since Marta's death). In addition, regardless of the period of time Roger holds the property, the holding period is long term (see Chapter 16).

From an income tax perspective, it is preferable to transfer appreciated property as a bequest rather than as a gift. The reason is that inherited property receives a step-up in basis, whereas property received by gift has a carryover basis to the donee. However, in making this decision, the estate tax consequences of the bequest should also be weighed against the gift tax consequences of the gift.

14-3d Disallowed Losses

Section 267 Disallowed Losses

Taxpayers should be aware of the desirability of avoiding transactions that activate the loss disallowance provisions for related parties. This is so even in light of the provision that permits the related-party buyer to offset his or her realized gain by the related-party seller's disallowed loss. Even with this offset, several inequities exist. First, the tax benefit associated with the disallowed loss ultimately is realized by the wrong party (the related-party buyer rather than the related-party seller). Second, the tax benefit of this offset to the related-party buyer does not occur until the buyer disposes of the property. Therefore, the longer the time period between the purchase and disposition of the property by the related-party buyer, the less the economic benefit. Third, if the property does not appreciate to at least its adjusted basis to the related-party seller during the time period the related-party buyer holds it, part or all of the disallowed loss is permanently lost. Fourth, because the right of offset is available only to the original transferee (the related-party buyer), all of the disallowed loss is permanently lost if the original transferee subsequently transfers the property by gift or bequest.

EXAMPLE 32

Tim sells property with an adjusted basis of $35,000 to Wes, his brother, for $25,000, the fair market value of the property. The $10,000 realized loss to Tim is disallowed by § 267.

If Wes subsequently sells the property to an unrelated party for $37,000, he has a recognized gain of $2,000 (realized gain of $12,000 reduced by disallowed loss of $10,000). Therefore, from the perspective of the family unit, the original $10,000 realized loss ultimately is recognized.

However, if Wes sells the property for $29,000, he has a recognized gain of $0 (realized gain of $4,000 reduced by disallowed loss of $4,000 necessary to offset the realized gain). From the perspective of the family unit, $6,000 of the realized loss of $10,000 is permanently lost ($10,000 realized loss − $4,000 offset permitted).

Wash Sales

The wash sales provisions can be avoided if the security that was sold is replaced within the statutory time period with a similar rather than a substantially identical security. For example, a sale of Dell, Inc. common stock accompanied by a purchase of Hewlett-Packard common stock is not treated as a wash sale. Such a procedure can enable the taxpayer to use an unrealized capital loss to offset a recognized capital gain. The taxpayer can sell the security before the end of the taxable year, offset the recognized capital loss against the capital gain, and invest the sales proceeds in a similar security.

Because the wash sales provisions do not apply to gains, it may be desirable to engage in a wash sale before the end of the taxable year. The recognized capital gain may be used to offset capital losses or capital loss carryovers from prior years. Because the basis of the replacement stock or securities will be the purchase price, the taxpayer in effect has exchanged a capital gain for an increased basis for the stock or securities.

ETHICS & EQUITY   **Washing a Loss Using an IRA**

Sam owns 1,500 shares of Eagle, Inc. stock that he purchased over 10 years ago for $80,000. Although the stock has a current market value of $52,000, Sam still views the stock as a solid long-term investment. He has sold other stock during the year with overall gains of $30,000, so he would like to sell the Eagle stock and offset the $28,000 loss against these gains—but somehow keep his Eagle investment. He has devised a plan to keep his Eagle investment by using funds in his traditional IRA to purchase 1,500 Eagle shares immediately after selling the shares he currently owns. Evaluate Sam's treatment of these stock transactions. Can his plan work?

REFOCUS ON THE BIG PICTURE

PROPOSED SALE OF A HOUSE AND OTHER PROPERTY TRANSACTIONS

Alice's tax adviser asked a number of questions to advise her on her proposed transaction for the house. Alice provided the following answers (refer to Example 19):

- Alice inherited the house from her mother. The fair market value of the house at the date of her mother's death, based on the estate tax return, was $475,000. Based on an appraisal, the house currently is worth $485,000. Alice's mother lived in the house for 38 years. According to the mother's attorney, her adjusted basis for the house was $275,000.

- As a child, Alice lived in the house for 10 years. She has not lived there during the 25 years she has been married.

- The house has been vacant during the seven months Alice has owned it. She has been trying to decide whether she should sell it for its fair market value or sell it to her nephew for $275,000. Alice has suggested a $275,000 price for the sale to Dan because she believes this is the amount at which she will have no gain or loss.

- Alice intends to invest the $275,000 in stock.

You advise Alice that her adjusted basis for the house is the $475,000 fair market value on the date of her mother's death. If Alice sells the house for $485,000 (assuming no selling expenses), she would have a recognized gain of $10,000 ($485,000 amount realized − $475,000 adjusted basis). The house is a capital asset, and Alice's holding period is long term because she inherited the house. Thus, the gain would be classified as a long-term capital gain. If, instead, Alice sells the house to her nephew for $275,000, she will have a part sale and part gift. The realized gain on the sale of $5,670 is recognized.

Amount realized	$ 275,000
Less: Adjusted basis	(269,330)*
Realized gain	$ 5,670
Recognized gain	$ 5,670

*[($275,000/$485,000) × $475,000] = $269,330.

The gain is classified as a long-term capital gain. Alice is then deemed to have made a gift to Dan of $210,000 ($485,000 − $275,000). With this information, Alice can make an informed selection between the two options.

See Examples 7 and 8 for the tax consequences associated with Alice's questions regarding selling the boat. See Example 25 for the tax consequences associated with Alice's questions regarding the wash sale of the stock.

Key Terms

www For the latest in changes to tax legislation, visit www.cengagebrain.com.

Discussion Questions

1. **LO.1** Upon the sale or other disposition of property, what four questions should be considered for income tax purposes?

Decision Making   2. **LO.1** Ivan invests in land, and Grace invests in taxable bonds. The land appreciates by $8,000 each year, and the bonds earn interest of $8,000 each year. After holding the land and bonds for five years, Ivan and Grace sell them. There is a $40,000 realized gain on the sale of the land and no realized gain or loss on the sale of the bonds. Are the tax consequences to Ivan and Grace the same for each of the five years? Explain.

3. **LO.1** Carol and Dave each purchase 100 shares of stock of Burgundy, Inc., a publicly owned corporation, in July for $10,000 each. Carol sells her stock on December 31 for $8,000. Because Burgundy's stock is listed on a national exchange, Dave is able to ascertain that his shares are worth $8,000 on December 31. Does the tax law treat the decline in value of the stock differently for Carol and Dave? Explain.

4. **LO.1** If a taxpayer sells property for cash, the amount realized consists of the net proceeds from the sale. For each of the following, indicate the effect on the amount realized:
   a. The property is sold on credit.
   b. A mortgage on the property is assumed by the buyer.
   c. A mortgage on the property is assumed by the seller.
   d. The buyer acquires the property subject to a mortgage of the seller.
   e. Stock that has a basis to the purchaser of $6,000 and a fair market value of $10,000 is received by the seller as part of the consideration.

Decision Making   5. **LO.1** Taylor is negotiating to buy some land. Under the first option, Taylor will give Ella $150,000 and assume her mortgage on the land for $100,000. Under the second option, Taylor will give Ella $250,000, and she will immediately pay off the mortgage. Taylor wants his basis for the land to be as high as possible. Given this objective, which option should Taylor select?

6. **LO.1** Marge owns land and a building (held for investment) with an adjusted basis of $75,000 and a fair market value of $250,000. The property is subject to a mortgage of $400,000. Because Marge is in arrears on the mortgage payments, the creditor is willing to accept the property in return for canceling the amount of the mortgage.
   a. How can the adjusted basis of the property be less than the amount of the mortgage?
   b. If the creditor's offer is accepted, what are the effects on the amount realized, the adjusted basis, and the realized gain or loss for Marge?
   c. Does it matter in (b) if the mortgage is recourse or nonrecourse? Explain.

7. **LO.1** On July 16, 2016, Logan acquires land and a building for $500,000 to use in his sole proprietorship. Of the purchase price, $400,000 is allocated to the building, and $100,000 is allocated to the land. Cost recovery of $4,708 is deducted in 2016 for the building (nonresidential real estate).
   a. What is the adjusted basis for the land and the building at the acquisition date?
   b. What is the adjusted basis for the land and the building at the end of 2016?

8. **LO.1** Auralia owns stock in Orange Corporation and Blue Corporation. She receives a $10,000 distribution from both corporations. The instructions from Orange state that the $10,000 is a dividend. The instructions from Blue state that the $10,000 is not a dividend. What could cause the instructions to differ as to the tax consequences?

9. **LO.2** Wanda is considering selling two personal use assets that she owns. One has appreciated in value by $20,000, and the other has declined in value by $17,000. Wanda believes that she should sell both assets in the same tax year so that the loss of $17,000 can offset the gain of $20,000.

    a. Advise Wanda regarding the tax consequences of her plan.

    b. Could Wanda achieve better tax results by selling the assets in different tax years? Explain.

Decision Making

10. **LO.2** Ron sold his sailboat for a $5,000 loss in the current year because he was diagnosed with skin cancer. His spouse wants him to sell his Harley-Davidson motorcycle because her brother broke his leg while riding his motorcycle. Because Ron no longer has anyone to ride with, he is seriously considering accepting his wife's advice. Because the motorcycle is a classic, Ron has received two offers. Each offer would result in a $5,000 gain. Joe would like to purchase the motorcycle before Christmas, and Jeff would like to purchase it after New Year's. Identify the relevant tax issues Ron faces in making his decision.

Issue ID

11. **LO.1, 2, 3, 5** Simon owns stock that has declined in value since acquired. He has decided either to give the stock to his nephew, Fred, or to sell it and give Fred the proceeds. If Fred receives the stock, he will sell it to obtain the proceeds. Simon is in the 15% tax bracket, while Fred's bracket is 25%. In either case, the holding period for the stock will be short term. Identify the tax issues relevant to Simon in deciding whether to give the stock or the sale proceeds to Fred.

Issue ID

12. **LO.3** Robin inherits 1,000 shares of Wal-Mart stock from her aunt in 2016. According to the information received from the executor of her aunt's estate, Robin's adjusted basis for the stock is $55,000. Albert, Robin's fiancé, receives 1,000 shares of Wal-Mart stock from his uncle as a gift in 2016. His uncle tells Albert that his adjusted basis for the Wal-Mart stock is $7,000. What could cause the substantial difference in the adjusted basis for Robin's and Albert's respective 1,000 shares of Wal-Mart stock?

13. **LO.3** Thelma inherited land from Sadie on June 7, 2016. The land appreciated in value by 100% during the six months it was owned by Sadie. The value has remained stable during the three months Thelma has owned it, and she expects it to continue to do so in the near future. Although she would like to sell the land now, Thelma has decided to postpone the sale for another three months. The delay is to enable the recognized gain to qualify for long-term capital gain treatment. Evaluate Thelma's understanding of the tax law.

14. **LO.4** Marilyn owns land that she acquired three years ago as an investment for $250,000. Because the land has not appreciated in value as she anticipated, she sells it to her brother, Amos, for its fair market value of $180,000. Amos sells the land two years later for $240,000.

    a. Explain why Marilyn's realized loss of $70,000 ($180,000 amount realized − $250,000 adjusted basis) is disallowed.

    b. Explain why Amos has neither a recognized gain nor a recognized loss on his sale of the land.

    c. Is the family unit treated fairly under the related-party disallowance rule under § 267? Explain.

    d. Which party wins, and which party loses?

    e. How could Marilyn have avoided the loss disallowance on her sale of the land?

Decision Making

15. **LO.4, 5** Comment on the following transactions:

    a. Mort owns 500 shares of Pear, Inc. stock with an adjusted basis of $22,000. On July 28, 2016, he sells 100 shares for $3,000. On August 16, 2016, he purchases another 100 shares for $3,400. Mort's realized loss of $1,400 ($3,000 − $4,400)

Decision Making

on the July 28 sale is not recognized, and his adjusted basis for the 100 shares purchased on August 16 is $4,800. Explain.

b.   How would your answer in (a) change if Mort purchased the 100 shares on December 27, 2016, rather than on August 16, 2016?

Computational Exercises

16. **LO.1** Sally owns real property for which the annual property taxes are $9,000. She sells the property to Shelley on March 1 for $550,000. Shelley pays the real property taxes for the entire year on October 1.

a.   How much of the property taxes can be deducted by Sally and how much by Shelley?

b.   What effect does the property tax apportionment have on Shelley's adjusted basis in the property?

c.   What effect does the apportionment have on Sally's amount realized from the sale?

d.   How would the answers in (b) and (c) differ if the taxes were paid by Sally?

17. **LO.1** Melba purchases land from Adrian. Melba gives Adrian $225,000 in cash and agrees to pay Adrian an additional $400,000 one year later plus interest at 5%.

a.   What is Melba's adjusted basis for the land at the acquisition date?

b.   What is Melba's adjusted basis for the land one year later?

18. **LO.1** On July 1, 2016, Katrina purchased tax-exempt bonds (face value of $75,000) for $82,000. The bonds mature in five years, and the annual interest rate is 6%. The market rate of interest is 2%.

a.   How much interest income and/or interest expense must Katrina report in 2016?

b.   What is Katrina's adjusted basis for the bonds on January 1, 2017?

19. **LO.3** Luciana, a nonshareholder, purchases a condominium from her employer for $85,000. The fair market value of the condominium is $120,000. What is Luciana's basis in the condominium and the amount of any income as a result of this purchase?

20. **LO.3** Sebastian purchases two pieces of equipment for $100,000. Appraisals of the equipment indicate that the fair market value of the first piece of equipment is $72,000 and that of the second piece of equipment is $108,000. What is Sebastian's basis in these two assets?

21. **LO.3** Heather owns 400 shares of Diego Corporation common stock for which she paid $4,000. She receives a nontaxable stock dividend of 20 shares of preferred stock on her common stock. The fair market values on the date of distribution of the preferred stock dividend are $20 a share for common stock and $100 a share for preferred stock. What is Heather's basis in the common and preferred shares?

22. **LO.3** Juliana purchased land in 2013 for $50,000. She gave the land to Tom, her brother, in 2016, when the fair market value was $70,000. No gift tax is paid on the transfer. Tom subsequently sells the property for $63,000.

a.   What is Tom's basis in the land, and what is his realized gain or loss on the sale?

b.   Assume, instead, that the land has a fair market value of $45,000 and that Tom sold the land for $43,000. Now what is Tom's basis in the land, and what is his realized gain or loss on the sale?

23. **LO.3** Ashley inherited all of the property of her aunt, who died in 2016. Her aunt's adjusted basis for the property at the date of death was $1,200,000. The property's fair market value was $4,500,000 at the date of death and $4,800,000 six months after the date of death. What is Ashley's adjusted basis of the property for income tax purposes?

24. **LO.4** Lisa sells business property with an adjusted basis of $130,000 to her son, Alfred, for its fair market value of $100,000.
    a. What is Lisa's realized and recognized gain or loss?
    b. What is Alfred's recognized gain or loss if he subsequently sells the property for $138,000? For $80,000?

25. **LO.4** Juan owned 200 shares of Circle Corporation stock (adjusted basis of $30,000). He sold 100 shares for $12,000. Twenty days later he purchased 100 shares of the same stock for $8,500. What is Juan's realized and recognized loss? What is his basis in the newly acquired shares?

26. **LO.4** Arianna's personal residence has an adjusted basis of $230,000 and a fair market value of $210,000. Arianna converts the personal residence to rental property. What is Arianna's gain basis? What is her loss basis?

27. **LO.4** Peyton sells an office building and the associated land on May 1, 2016. Under the terms of the sales contract, Peyton is to receive $1,600,000 in cash. The purchaser is to assume Peyton's mortgage of $950,000 on the property. To enable the purchaser to obtain adequate financing, Peyton is to pay the $9,000 in points charged by the lender. The broker's commission on the sale is $75,000. The purchaser agrees to pay the $24,000 in property taxes for the entire year. What is Peyton's amount realized?

Problems

28. **LO.1** Anne sold her home for $290,000 in 2016. Selling expenses were $17,400. She purchased it in 2010 for $200,000. During the period of ownership, Anne did the following:
    * Deducted $50,500 office-in-home expenses, which included $4,500 in depreciation. (Refer to Chapter 9.)
    * Deducted a casualty loss in 2012 for residential trees destroyed by a hurricane. The total loss was $19,000 (after the $100 floor and the 10%-of-AGI floor), and Anne's insurance company reimbursed her for $13,500. (Refer to Chapter 7.)
    * Paid street paving assessment of $7,000 and added sidewalks for $8,000.
    * Installed an elevator for medical reasons. The total cost was $20,000, and Anne deducted $13,000 as medical expenses. (Refer to Chapter 10.)

    What is Anne's realized gain?

29. **LO.1** Kareem bought a rental house in March 2011 for $300,000, of which $50,000 is allocated to the land and $250,000 to the building. Early in 2013, he had a tennis court built in the backyard at a cost of $7,500. Kareem has deducted $30,900 for depreciation on the house and $1,300 for depreciation on the court. In January 2016, he sells the house and tennis court for $330,000 cash.
    a. What is Kareem's realized gain or loss?
    b. If an original mortgage of $80,000 is still outstanding and the buyer assumes the mortgage in addition to the cash payment, what is Kareem's realized gain or loss?
    c. If the buyer takes the property subject to the $80,000 mortgage, rather than assuming it, what is Kareem's realized gain or loss?

30. **LO.1** Norm is negotiating the sale of a tract of his land to Pat. Use the following classification scheme to classify each of the items contained in the proposed sales contract:

Legend		
DARN	=	Decreases amount realized by Norm
IARN	=	Increases amount realized by Norm
DABN	=	Decreases adjusted basis to Norm
IABN	=	Increases adjusted basis to Norm
DABP	=	Decreases adjusted basis to Pat
IABP	=	Increases adjusted basis to Pat

a.   Norm is to receive cash of $50,000.

b.   Norm is to receive Pat's note payable for $25,000, payable in three years.

c.   Pat assumes Norm's mortgage of $5,000 on the land.

d.   Pat agrees to pay the realtor's sales commission of $8,000.

e.   Pat agrees to pay the property taxes on the land for the entire year. If each party paid his or her respective share, Norm's share would be $1,000 and Pat's share would be $3,000.

f.   Pat pays legal fees of $500.

g.   Norm pays legal fees of $750.

31. **LO.1** Nissa owns a building (adjusted basis of $600,000 on January 1, 2016) that she rents to Len, who operates a restaurant in the building. The municipal health department closed the restaurant for three months during 2016 because of health code violations. Under MACRS, the cost recovery deduction for 2016 would be $20,500. However, Nissa deducted cost recovery only for the nine months the restaurant was open because she waived the rent income during the three-month period the restaurant was closed.

a.   What is the amount of the cost recovery deduction Nissa should report on her 2016 income tax return?

b.   Calculate the adjusted basis of the building at the end of 2016.

32. **LO.1, 2** Pam owns a personal use boat that has a fair market value of $35,000 and an adjusted basis of $45,000. Pam's AGI is $100,000. Calculate the realized and recognized gain or loss if:

a.   Pam sells the boat for $35,000.

b.   Pam exchanges the boat for another boat worth $35,000.

c.   The boat is stolen and Pam receives insurance proceeds of $35,000.

d.   Would your answer in (a) change if the fair market value and the selling price of the boat were $48,000?

33. **LO.1** Ricky owns stock in Dove Corporation. His adjusted basis for the stock is $90,000. During the year, he receives a distribution from the corporation of $75,000 that is labeled a return of capital (i.e., Dove has no earnings and profits).

a.   Determine the tax consequences to Ricky.

b.   Assume instead that the amount of the distribution is $150,000. Determine the tax consequences to Ricky.

c.   Assume instead in (a) that the $75,000 distribution is labeled a taxable dividend (i.e., Dove has earnings and profits of at least $75,000).

34. **LO.1, 2** Chee purchases Tan, Inc. bonds for $108,000 on January 2, 2016. The face value of the bonds is $100,000; the maturity date is December 31, 2020; and the annual interest rate is 5%. Chee will amortize the premium only if he is required to do so. Chee sells the bonds on July 1, 2018, for $106,000.

a. Determine the interest income Chee should report for 2016.

b. Calculate Chee's recognized gain or loss on the sale of the bonds in 2018.

35. **LO.1, 2** Which of the following results in a recognized gain or loss?

a. Kay sells her vacation cabin (adjusted basis of $100,000) for $150,000.

b. Adam sells his personal residence (adjusted basis of $150,000) for $100,000.

c. Carl's personal residence (adjusted basis of $65,000) is condemned by the city. He receives condemnation proceeds of $55,000.

d. Olga's land is worth $40,000 at the end of the year. She had purchased the land six months earlier for $25,000.

e. Vera's personal vehicle (adjusted basis of $22,000) is stolen. She receives $23,000 from the insurance company and does not plan to replace the automobile.

f. Jerry sells used clothing (adjusted basis of $500) to a thrift store for $50.

36. **LO.1, 2** Yancy's personal residence is condemned as part of an urban renewal project. His adjusted basis for the residence is $480,000. He receives condemnation proceeds of $460,000 and invests the proceeds in stocks and bonds.

a. Calculate Yancy's realized and recognized gain or loss.

b. If the condemnation proceeds are $505,000, what are Yancy's realized and recognized gain or loss?

c. What are Yancy's realized and recognized gain or loss in (a) if the house was rental property?

37. **LO.3** Buddy Morgan is a real estate agent for Coastal Estates, a residential real   Communications
estate development. Because of his outstanding sales performance, Buddy is permitted to buy a lot for $300,000 that normally would sell for $500,000. Buddy is the only real estate agent for Coastal Estates who is permitted to do so.

a. Does Buddy have gross income from the transaction? Explain.

b. What is Buddy's adjusted basis for the land?

c. Write a letter to Buddy informing him of the tax consequences of his acquisition of the lot. His address is 100 Tower Road, San Diego, CA 92182.

38. **LO.1, 2, 3** Karen makes the following purchases and sales of stock:

Transaction	Date	Number of Shares	Company	Price per Share
Purchase	1-1-2014	300	MDG	$ 75
Purchase	6-1-2014	150	GRU	300
Purchase	11-1-2014	60	MDG	70
Sale	12-3-2014	200	MDG	80
Purchase	3-1-2015	120	GRU	375
Sale	8-1-2015	90	GRU	330
Sale	1-1-2016	150	MDG	90
Sale	2-1-2016	75	GRU	500

Assuming that Karen is unable to identify the particular lots that are sold with the original purchase, determine the recognized gain or loss on each type of stock:

a. As of July 1, 2014.

b. As of December 31, 2014.

c. As of December 31, 2015.

d. As of July 1, 2016.

39. **LO.1, 2, 3** Kevin purchases 1,000 shares of Bluebird Corporation stock on October 3, 2016, for $300,000. On December 12, 2016, Kevin purchases an additional 750 shares of Bluebird stock for $210,000. According to market quotations, Bluebird stock is selling for $285 per share on December 31, 2016. Kevin sells 500 shares of Bluebird stock on March 1, 2017, for $162,500.

    a. What is the adjusted basis of Kevin's Bluebird stock on December 31, 2016?

    b. What is Kevin's recognized gain or loss from the sale of Bluebird stock on March 1, 2017, assuming that the shares sold are from the shares purchased on December 12, 2016?

    c. What is Kevin's recognized gain or loss from the sale of Bluebird stock on March 1, 2017, assuming that Kevin cannot adequately identify the shares sold?

Communications   40. **LO.3** Rod Clooney purchases Agnes Mitchell's sole proprietorship for $990,000 on August 15, 2016. The assets of the business are as follows:

Asset	Agnes's Adjusted Basis	FMV
Accounts receivable	$ 70,000	$ 70,000
Inventory	90,000	100,000
Equipment	150,000	160,000
Furniture and fixtures	95,000	130,000
Building	190,000	250,000
Land	25,000	75,000
Total	$620,000	$785,000

    a. Calculate Agnes's realized and recognized gain.

    b. Determine Rod's basis for each of the assets.

    c. Write a letter to Rod informing him of the tax consequences of the purchase. His address is 300 Riverview Drive, Delaware, OH 43015.

41. **LO.3** Donna owns 800 shares of common stock in Macaw Corporation (adjusted basis of $40,000). She receives a 5% stock dividend when the stock is selling for $60 per share.

    a. How much gross income must Donna recognize because of the stock dividend?

    b. What is Donna's basis for her 840 shares of stock?

42. **LO.1, 2, 3** Roberto has received various gifts over the years. He has decided to dispose of the following assets he received as gifts:

    a. In 1951, he received land worth $32,000. The donor's adjusted basis was $35,000. Roberto sells the land for $95,000 in 2016.

    b. In 1956, he received stock in Gold Company. The donor's adjusted basis was $19,000. The fair market value on the date of the gift was $34,000. Roberto sells the stock for $40,000 in 2016.

    c. In 1962, he received land worth $15,000. The donor's adjusted basis was $20,000. Roberto sells the land for $9,000 in 2016.

    d. In 2003, he received stock worth $30,000. The donor's adjusted basis was $42,000. Roberto sells the stock for $38,000 in 2016.

    What is the recognized gain or loss from each of the preceding transactions? Assume for each of the gift transactions that no gift tax was paid.

43. **LO.1, 2, 3** Nicky receives a car from Sam as a gift. Sam paid $48,000 for the car. He had used it for business purposes and had deducted $10,000 for depreciation up to the time he gave the car to Nicky. The fair market value of the car is $33,000.

    a. Assuming that Nicky uses the car for business purposes, what is her basis for depreciation?

b.   Assume that Nicky deducts depreciation of $6,500 and then sells the car for $32,500. What is her recognized gain or loss?

c.   Assume that Nicky deducts depreciation of $6,500 and then sells the car for $20,000. What is her recognized gain or loss?

44. **LO.3** Margo receives a gift of real estate with an adjusted basis of $175,000 and a fair market value of $100,000. The donor paid gift tax of $15,000 on the transfer. If Margo later sells the property for $110,000, what is her recognized gain or loss?

45. **LO.3** On September 18, 2016, Gerald received land and a building from Frank as a gift. Frank's adjusted basis and the fair market value at the date of the gift are as follows:

Asset	Adjusted Basis	FMV
Land	$100,000	$212,000
Building	80,000	100,000

No gift tax was paid on the transfer.

a.   Determine Gerald's adjusted basis for the land and building.

b.   Assume instead that the fair market value of the land was $87,000 and that of the building was $65,000. Determine Gerald's adjusted basis for the land and building.

46. **LO.1, 2, 3, 5** Ira Cook is planning to make a charitable contribution to the Boy Scouts of Crystal, Inc. stock worth $20,000. The stock has an adjusted basis of $15,000. A friend has suggested that Ira sell the stock and contribute the $20,000 in proceeds rather than contribute the stock.

Decision Making

Communications

a.   Should Ira follow the friend's advice? Why or why not?

b.   Assume that the fair market value is only $13,000. In this case, should Ira follow the friend's advice? Why or why not?

c.   Rather than make a charitable contribution to the Boy Scouts, Ira is going to make a gift to Nancy, his niece. Advise Ira regarding (a) and (b).

d.   Write a letter to Ira regarding whether in (a) he should sell the stock and contribute the cash or contribute the stock. He has informed you that he purchased the stock six years ago. Ira's address is 500 Ireland Avenue, DeKalb, IL 60115.

47. **LO.3** As sole heir, Dazie receives all of Mary's property (adjusted basis of $1,400,000 and fair market value of $3,820,000). Six months after Mary's death in 2016, the fair market value is $3,835,000.

a.   Can the executor of Mary's estate elect the alternate valuation date and amount? Explain.

b.   What is Dazie's basis for the property?

c.   Assume instead that the fair market value six months after Mary's death is $3,800,000. Respond to (a) and (b).

48. **LO.3** Dan bought a hotel for $2,600,000 in January 2012. In May 2016, he died and left the hotel to Ed. While Dan owned the hotel, he deducted $289,000 of cost recovery. The fair market value in May 2016 was $2,800,000. The fair market value six months later was $2,850,000.

a.   What is the basis of the property to Ed?

b.   What is the basis of the property to Ed if the fair market value six months later was $2,500,000 (not $2,850,000) and the objective of the executor was to minimize the estate tax liability?

49. **LO.3** Helene and Pauline are twin sisters who live in Louisiana and Mississippi, respectively. Helene is married to Frank, and Pauline is married to Richard. Frank and Richard are killed in an auto accident in 2016 while returning from a sporting event.

    Helene and Frank jointly owned some farmland in Louisiana (value of $940,000, cost of $450,000). Pauline and Richard jointly owned some farmland in Mississippi (value of $940,000, cost of $450,000). Assume that all of Frank's and Richard's property passes to their surviving wives.

    a. Calculate Helene's basis in the land.
    b. Calculate Pauline's basis in the land.
    c. What causes the difference?

50. **LO.3, 4** Sheila sells land to Elane, her sister, for the fair market value of $40,000. Six months later when the land is worth $45,000, Elane gives it to Jacob, her son. (No gift tax resulted.) Shortly thereafter, Jacob sells the land for $48,000.

    a. Assuming that Sheila's adjusted basis for the land is $24,000, what are Sheila's and Jacob's recognized gain or loss on the sales?
    b. Assuming that Sheila's adjusted basis for the land is $60,000, what are Sheila's and Jacob's recognized gain or loss on the sales?

51. **LO.1, 2, 3, 4** Louis owns three pieces of land with an adjusted basis as follows: parcel A, $75,000; parcel B, $125,000; and parcel C, $175,000. Louis sells parcel A to his uncle for $50,000, parcel B to his partner for $120,000, and parcel C to his mother for $150,000.

    a. What is the recognized gain or loss from the sale of each parcel?
    b. If Louis's uncle eventually sells his land for $90,000, what is his recognized gain or loss?
    c. If Louis's partner eventually sells his land for $130,000, what is his recognized gain or loss?
    d. If Louis's mother eventually sells her land for $165,000, what is her recognized gain or loss?

Decision Making   52. **LO.1, 2, 3, 4** Tyneka inherited 1,000 shares of Aqua, Inc. stock from Joe. Joe's basis was $35,000, and the fair market value on July 1, 2016 (the date of death) was $45,000. The shares were distributed to Tyneka on July 15, 2016. Tyneka sold the stock on July 30, 2017, for $33,000. After giving the matter more thought, she decides that Aqua is a good investment and purchases 1,000 shares for $30,000 on August 20, 2017.

    a. What is Tyneka's basis for the 1,000 shares purchased on August 20, 2017?
    b. Could Tyneka have obtained different tax consequences in (a) if she had sold the 1,000 shares on December 27, 2016, and purchased the 1,000 shares on January 5, 2017? Explain.

Decision Making   53. **LO.1, 2, 4** On December 28, 2016, Kramer sells 150 shares of Lavender, Inc. stock for $77,000. On January 10, 2017, he purchases 100 shares of the same stock for $82,000.

    a. Assuming that Kramer's adjusted basis for the stock sold is $65,000, what is his recognized gain or loss? What is his basis for the new shares?
    b. Assuming that Kramer's adjusted basis for the stock sold is $89,000, what is his recognized gain or loss? What is his basis for the new shares?
    c. Advise Kramer on how he can avoid any negative tax consequences encountered in part (b).

54. **LO.1, 2, 4** Abby's home had a basis of $360,000 ($160,000 attributable to the land) and a fair market value of $340,000 ($155,000 attributable to the land)

when she converted 70% of it to business use by opening a bed-and-breakfast. Four years after the conversion, Abby sells the home for $500,000 ($165,000 attributable to the land).

a. Calculate Abby's basis for gain, loss, and cost recovery for the portion of her personal residence that was converted to business use.

b. Calculate the cost recovery deducted by Abby during the four-year period of business use, assuming that the bed-and-breakfast is opened on January 1 of year 1 and the house is sold on December 31 of year 4.

c. What is Abby's recognized gain or loss on the sale of the business use portion?

55. **LO.4, 5** Surendra's personal residence originally cost $340,000 (ignore land). After living in the house for five years, he converts it to rental property. At the date of conversion, the fair market value of the house is $320,000. As to the rental property, calculate Surendra's basis for:

    Decision Making

a. Loss.

b. Depreciation.

c. Gain.

d. Could Surendra have obtained better tax results if he had sold his personal residence for $320,000 and then purchased another house for $320,000 to hold as rental property? Explain.

56. **LO.3, 5** Hun, age 93, has accumulated substantial assets during his life. Among his many assets are the following, which he is considering giving to Koji, his grandson.

    Decision Making

Asset	Adjusted Basis	Fair Market Value
Silver Corporation stock	$900,000	$700,000
Red Corporation stock	70,000	71,000
Emerald Corporation stock	200,000	500,000

Hun has been in ill health for the past five years. His physician has informed him that he probably will not live for more than six months. Advise Hun on which of the stocks should be transferred as gifts and which as bequests.

Cumulative Problems

57. Alton Newman, age 67, is married and files a joint return with his wife, Clair, age 65. Alton and Clair are both retired, and during 2015, they received Social Security benefits of $10,000. Both Alton and Clair are covered by Medicare. Alton's Social Security number is 111-11-1112, and Clair's is 123-45-6789. They reside at 210 College Drive, Columbia, SC 29201.

    Tax Return Problem

Alton, who retired on January 1, 2015, receives benefits from a qualified pension plan of $2,750 a month for life. His total contributions to the plan (none of which were deductible) were $168,250. In January 2015, he received a bonus of $2,000 from his former employer for service performed in 2014. Although the former employer accrued the bonus in 2014, it was not paid until 2015.

Clair, who retired on December 31, 2014, started receiving benefits of $1,400 a month on January 1, 2015. Her contributions to the qualified pension plan (none of which were deductible) were $74,100.

On September 27, 2015, Alton and Clair received a pro rata 10% stock dividend on 600 shares of stock they owned. They had bought the stock on March 5, 2008, for $20 a share. On December 16, 2015, they sold the 60 dividend shares for $55 a share.

On October 10, 2015, Clair sold the car she had used in commuting to and from work for $17,000. She had paid $31,000 for the car in 2009.

On July 14, 2007, Alton and Clair received a gift of 1,000 shares of stock from their son, Thomas. Thomas's basis in the stock was $35 a share (fair market value at the date of gift was $25). No gift tax was paid on the transfer. Alton and Clair sold the stock on October 8, 2015, for $24 a share.

On May 1, 2015, Clair's mother died, and Clair inherited her personal residence. In February 2015, her mother had paid the property taxes for 2015 of $2,100. The residence had a fair market value of $235,000 and an adjusted basis to the mother of $160,000 on the date of her death. Clair listed the house with a real estate agent, who estimated it was worth $240,000 as of December 31, 2015.

Clair received rent income of $6,000 on a beach house she inherited three years ago from her uncle Charles. She had rented the property for one week during the July 4 holiday and one week during the Thanksgiving holidays. Charles's adjusted basis in the beach house was $150,000, and its fair market value on the date of his death was $240,000. Clair and Alton used the beach house for personal purposes for 56 days during the year. Expenses associated with the house were $3,700 for utilities, maintenance, and repairs; $2,200 for property taxes; and $800 for insurance. There are no mortgages on the property.

Clair and Alton paid estimated Federal income tax of $3,100 and had itemized deductions of $6,800 (excluding any itemized deductions associated with the beach house). If they have overpaid their Federal income tax, they want the amount refunded. Both Clair and Alton want $3 to go to the Presidential Election Campaign Fund.

Compute their net tax payable or refund due for 2015. If you use tax forms for your computations, you will need at a minimum Form 1040 and Schedule D. Suggested software: H&R BLOCK Tax Software.

Tax Computation Problem
Decision Making
Communications

58. John Benson, age 40, is single. His Social Security number is 111-11-1111, and he resides at 150 Highway 51, Tangipahoa, LA 70465.

John has a 5-year-old child, Kendra, who lives with her mother, Katy. John pays alimony of $6,000 per year to Katy and child support of $12,000. The $12,000 of child support covers 65% of Katy's costs of rearing Kendra. Kendra's Social Security number is 123-45-6789, and Katy's is 123-45-6788.

John's mother, Sally, lived with him until her death in early September 2016. He incurred and paid medical expenses for her of $12,900 and other support payments of $11,000. Sally's only sources of income were $5,500 of interest income on certificates of deposit and $5,600 of Social Security benefits, which she spent on her medical expenses and on maintenance of John's household. Sally's Social Security number was 123-45-6787.

John is employed by the Highway Department of the State of Louisiana in an executive position. His salary is $95,000. The appropriate amounts of Social Security tax and Medicare tax were withheld. In addition, $9,500 was withheld for Federal income taxes, and $4,000 was withheld for state income taxes.

In addition to his salary, John's employer provides him with the following fringe benefits:

- Group term life insurance with a maturity value of $95,000. The cost of the premiums for the employer was $295.

- Group health insurance plan. John's employer paid premiums of $5,800 for his coverage. The plan paid $2,600 for John's medical expenses during the year.

Upon the death of his aunt Josie in December 2015, John, her only recognized heir, inherited the following assets:

Asset	Josie's Adjusted Basis	FMV at Date of Death
Car	$35,000	$ 19,000
Land—300 acres	90,000	175,000
IBM stock	15,000	40,000
Cash	10,000	10,000

Three months prior to her death, Josie gave John a mountain cabin. Her adjusted basis for the mountain cabin was $120,000, and the fair market value was $195,000. No gift taxes were paid.

During the year, John had the following transactions:

- On February 1, 2016, he sold for $45,000 Microsoft stock that he inherited from his father four years ago. His father's adjusted basis was $49,000, and the fair market value at the date of the father's death was $41,000.

- The car John inherited from Josie was destroyed in a wreck on October 1, 2016. He had loaned the car to Katy to use for a two-week period while the engine in her car was being replaced. Fortunately, neither Katy nor Kendra was injured. John received insurance proceeds of $16,000, the fair market value of the car on October 1, 2016.

- On December 28, 2016, John sold the 300 acres of land to his brother, James, for its fair market value of $160,000. James planned on using the land for his dairy farm.

Other sources of income for John were as follows:

Dividend income (qualified dividends)	$ 3,500
Interest income:	
Guaranty Bank	1,000
City of Kentwood water bonds	2,000
Award from state of Louisiana for outstanding suggestion for highway beautification	10,000

Potential itemized deductions for John, in addition to items already mentioned, were as follows:

Property taxes paid on his residence and cabin	$7,000
Property taxes paid on personalty	3,500
Estimated Federal income taxes paid	3,000
Charitable contributions	4,500
Mortgage interest on his residence	7,200
Orthodontic expenses for Kendra	4,000

Part 1—Tax Computation
Compute John's net tax payable or refund due for 2016.

Part 2—Tax Planning
Assume that rather than selling the land to James, John is considering leasing it to him for $12,000 annually with the lease beginning on October 1, 2016. James would prepay the lease payments through December 31, 2016. Thereafter, he would make monthly lease payments at the beginning of each month. What effect would this have on John's 2016 tax liability? What potential problem might John encounter? Write a letter to John in which you advise him of the tax consequences of leasing versus selling. Also prepare a memo for the tax files.

Research Problems

Note: Solutions to Research Problems can be prepared by using the Checkpoint® Student Edition online research product, which is available to accompany this text. It is also possible to prepare solutions to the Research Problems by using tax research materials found in a standard tax library.

THOMSON REUTERS
CHECKPOINT®
Student Edition

Research Problem 1. Terry owns real estate with an adjusted basis of $600,000 and a fair market value of $1.1 million. The amount of the nonrecourse mortgage on the property is $2.5 million. Because of substantial past and projected future losses associated with the real estate development (occupancy rate of only 37% after three years), Terry deeds the property to the creditor.

a. What are the tax consequences to Terry?

b. Assume that the data are the same, except that the fair market value of the property is $2,525,000. Therefore, when Terry deeds the property to the creditor, she also receives $25,000 from the creditor. What are the tax consequences to Terry?

Research Problem 2. Your client, Jacob, turned 66 years old this year. Jacob has no heirs and has decided that he would like to sell a life insurance policy to fund a trip to Africa that he has wanted to take.

Jacob knew that he could surrender the policy (a whole-life policy) back to the insurance company, but a friend told him he could get more for the policy if he sold it to a life settlement company. A life settlement company buys life insurance policies from policyholders who are not ill and who generally have a life expectancy of between 2 and 15 years. In return, the seller of the policy receives a lump-sum payment. The life settlement company either holds the policy to maturity or resells the policy to an investor.

The lump sum received depends on factors such as age, health, and the terms and conditions of the policy, but is generally more than the policy's cash surrender value (which would be received from the life insurance company upon surrender of the policy).

In November 2016, Jacob (who was not terminally or chronically ill) sold his policy to a life settlement company for $160,000. During the time he owned the policy, Jacob did not borrow against the policy or receive any distributions. Jacob also had paid premiums totaling $122,000 (of which $32,000 was paid for the provision of insurance before the sale of the policy).

How should Jacob calculate his basis in the life insurance policy to determine if he has a realized gain or loss on the surrender of the policy?

Communications **Research Problem 3.** Ruth Ames died on January 10, 2016. In filing the estate tax return, her executor, Melvin Sims, elects the primary valuation date and amount (fair market value on the date of death). On March 12, 2016, Melvin invests $30,000 of cash that Ruth had in her money market account in acquiring 1,000 shares of Orange, Inc. ($30 per share). On January 10, 2016, Orange was selling for $29 per share. The stock is distributed to a beneficiary, Annette Rust, on June 1, 2016, when it is selling for $33 per share. Melvin wants you to determine the amount at which the Orange shares should appear on the estate tax return and the amount of Annette's adjusted basis for the stock. Write a letter to Melvin in which you respond to his inquiry, and prepare a memo for the tax files. His address is 100 Center Lane, Miami, FL 33124.

Internet Activity

Use the tax resources of the Internet to address the following questions. Do not restrict your search to the Web, but include a review of newsgroups and general reference materials, practitioner sites and resources, primary sources of the tax law, chat rooms and discussion groups, and other opportunities.

Communications **Research Problem 4.** Many see the "step-up in basis at death" rule of § 1014 as an expensive tax loophole enjoyed by the wealthy. Find the latest estimates of the revenue loss to the Treasury that is attributable to this rule.

a. How does Canada's tax law determine the basis of property acquired from a decedent?

b. Send an e-mail to a member of the House Ways and Means Committee expressing a preference for the preservation of the current § 1014 rule or the modifications made to it by the Tax Relief Reconciliation Act of 2001 and the Tax Relief Act of 2010.

Research Problem 5. The specific identification method is important when one invests in mutual funds. When taxpayers sell part of their holdings, the basis of the surrendered shares can be difficult to compute. Go to the site of an investment adviser or a mutual fund to find instructions on how to compute the basis of the shares sold. What options are available to the taxpayer according to this information? Illustrate each of the alternatives.

Roger CPA Review Questions

1. Stephen purchased a video game console five years ago for $500. In order to raise money for the "latest and greatest" console, Stephen sold his console for $100. Because of advances in technology, Stephen can purchase the new console for $400. What is the tax treatment of Stephen's sale of his console?
   a. Stephen recognizes a $400 loss.
   b. Stephen does not report the sale.
   c. Stephen recognizes a $300 loss.
   d. Stephen recognizes a $100 gain.

2. Uncle Ubb gave his nephew, Leroy Lamprey, a gift of stock worth $10,000. Uncle Ubb's basis in the stock was $15,000. Leroy sold the stock to an unrelated party for $11,000. What amount of gain or loss should Leroy report as a result of this sale?
   a. $0
   b. $4,000 loss
   c. $200 gain
   d. $1,000 gain

3. On June 1, 2015, Heloise gave Henrietta a gift of stock worth $10,000. Heloise had purchased the stock on January 1, 2015 for $13,000. Henrietta sold the stock to an unrelated party on January 1, 2016 for $13,500. What is the amount and character of Henrietta's gain or loss upon the sale?
   a. $500 short-term capital gain
   b. $3,500 short-term capital gain
   c. $500 long-term capital gain
   d. $3,500 long-term capital gain

4. On July 1, 2015, Penelope gave Peter a gift of stock worth $9,000. Penelope had purchased the stock for $10,000 in 2013. On November 1, 2015, Peter sold the stock to an unrelated party for $8,500. What is the amount and character of Peter's gain or loss upon the sale?
   a. $500 short-term capital loss
   b. $1,500 long-term capital loss
   c. $500 long-term capital loss
   d. $1,500 short-term capital loss

5. On June 1, 2016, Gary gave Gertrude a gift of stock worth $10,000, paying no gift tax on the transaction. Gary had purchased the stock for $7,500 in 2012. On October 1, 2016, Gertrude sold the stock to an unrelated party for $11,000. What is the amount and character of Gertrude's gain upon the sale?
   a. $1,000 short-term capital gain
   b. $3,500 long-term capital gain
   c. $1,000 long-term capital gain
   d. $3,500 short-term capital gain

6. Shomit purchases 100 shares of stock in Classy Corporation for $500 in year 1. On December 20 of year 2, he purchases an additional 100 shares in the company for $400. On December 27 of year 2, Shomit sells the 100 shares acquired in year 1 for $410. What is Shomit's resulting basis in the shares acquired on December 20 of year 2?
   a. $400
   b. $500
   c. $490
   d. $410

7. Helmut purchases 100 shares of stock in Caisson Corporation for $1,000 in year 1. On December 1 of year 2, he purchases an additional 100 shares in the company for $1,500. On December 28 of year 2, Helmut sells the 100 shares acquired in year 1 for

$1,200. What is Helmut's recognized gain or loss from the December 28 sale, and what is his resulting basis in the stock purchased on December 1 of year 2?

	Recognized Gain or Loss on Sale	**Resulting Basis in December 1 Purchase**
a.	$0	$1,800
b.	$0	1,500
c.	$300 loss	1,200
d.	$200 gain	1,500

8. Sengupta died on February 1, 2015, and bequeathed two different assets to a beneficiary, Roberts. Asset One was distributed to Roberts on April 24, 2015; Asset Two was distributed to Roberts on October 25, 2015. The executor of Sengupta's estate makes a qualified alternate valuation date election. The basis of each bequeathed asset will thus be the fair market value on which date?

	Asset One	**Asset Two**
a.	August 1, 2015	August 1, 2015
b.	April 24, 2015	August 1, 2015
c.	April 24, 2015	October 25, 2015
d.	August 1, 2015	October 25, 2015

9. Which of the following answer choices best describes income in respect of a decedent?

   a. Income earned or received by the decedent up to 30 days after the date of death

   b. Income pledged by others to charitable causes out of respect toward a recent decedent's wishes

   c. Income paid to an estate that was earned by the decedent prior to death

   d. Estate income earmarked for the provision of a respectful funeral ceremony for the decedent

CHAPTER 15

Property Transactions: Nontaxable Exchanges

LEARNING OBJECTIVES: *After completing Chapter 15, you should be able to:*

LO.1 State and explain the rationale for nonrecognition (postponement) of gain or loss in certain property transactions.

LO.2 Apply the nonrecognition provisions and basis determination rules for like-kind exchanges.

LO.3 Explain the nonrecognition provisions available on the involuntary conversion of property.

LO.4 Describe the provision for the permanent exclusion of gain on the sale of a personal residence.

LO.5 Identify other nonrecognition provisions contained in the Code.

LO.6 Review and apply various tax planning opportunities related to the nonrecognition provisions discussed in the chapter.

ALTERNATIVE USES OF PROPERTY

Recall the situation introduced in *The Big Picture* in Chapter 14. After 11 months, Alice has changed her mind about selling the house to her nephew for $275,000. As a result of a recent groundbreaking for an upscale real estate development nearby, the appraised value of the house has increased to $600,000. Alice has decided that she needs to do something with the house other than let it remain vacant. She is considering the following options and has come to you for advice.

- Sell the house for approximately $600,000 using the services of a real estate agent. The real estate commission rate is 5 percent, and her inherited basis is $475,000.

- Convert the house to a vacation home (100 percent personal use by Alice and her family); then sell it in two years.

- Convert the house to a vacation home (projected 40 percent rental use and 60 percent personal use); then sell it in two years.

- Sell her current home and move into the inherited house. She has owned and lived in the current home for 15 years, and her gain on the sale would be about $200,000. Because she is nearing retirement, she would live in the inherited house for only the required two-year minimum period and then sell it.

Alice expects the inherited house to continue to appreciate in value by about 5 percent per year. She plans on retiring from her job in two years and moving to a warmer climate. Until then, she is neutral as to which house she lives in. What advice can you offer Alice?

Read the chapter and formulate your response.

This chapter covers the boldfaced portions of the Tax Formula for Individuals that was introduced in Concept Summary 3.1 on p. 3-3. Below those portions are the sections of Form 1040 where the results are reported.

Income *(broadly defined)*	$xx,xxx
Less: Exclusions	(x,xxx)
Gross income	$xx,xxx

FORM 1040 (p. 1)

12	Business income or (loss). Attach Schedule C or C-EZ	
13	Capital gain or (loss). Attach Schedule D if required. If not required, check here ▶ ☐	
14	Other gains or (losses). Attach Form 4797	

Less: Deductions *for* adjusted gross income	(x,xxx)
Adjusted gross income	$xx,xxx
Less: The greater of total **itemized deductions** *or* the standard deduction	(x,xxx)
Personal and dependency exemptions	(x,xxx)
Taxable income	$xx,xxx
Tax on taxable income *(see Tax Tables or Tax Rate Schedules)*	$ x,xxx
Less: Tax credits *(including income taxes withheld and prepaid)*	(xxx)
Tax due (or refund)	$ xxx

C hapter 14 was the first of a four-chapter sequence in Part 5 dealing with property transactions. In Chapter 14, the sale or exchange concept is explained along with how basis is determined. As noted in Concept Summary 14.1, the intermediate result is realized gain or loss. What happens to the realized gain or loss depends on the nature of the sale or exchange. Some or all of the gain or loss may be recognized, deferred, or even avoided. Chapter 15 concentrates on several types of sales or exchanges where the usual result is deferral or avoidance of recognizing realized gain or loss.

LO.1

State and explain the rationale for nonrecognition (postponement) of gain or loss in certain property transactions.

15-1 GENERAL CONCEPT OF A NONTAXABLE EXCHANGE

A taxpayer who is going to replace a productive asset (e.g., machinery) used in a trade or business may structure the transactions as a sale of the old asset and the purchase of a new asset. When this approach is used, any realized gain or loss on the asset sale is recognized. The basis of the new asset is its cost. Alternatively, the taxpayer may be able to trade the old asset for the new asset. This exchange of assets may produce beneficial tax consequences by qualifying for nontaxable exchange treatment.

The tax law recognizes that nontaxable exchanges result in a change in the *form* but not in the *substance* of the taxpayer's relative economic position. The replacement property received in the exchange is viewed as substantially a continuation of the old investment.[1] Additional justification for nontaxable exchange treatment is that this type of transaction does not provide the taxpayer with the wherewithal to pay the tax on any realized gain.

The nonrecognition provisions for nontaxable exchanges do not apply to realized losses from the sale or exchange of personal use assets. Such losses are not recognized (are disallowed) because they are personal in nature and not because of any nonrecognition provision.

---

[1]Reg. § 1.1002–1(c).

In a **nontaxable exchange**, realized gains or losses are not recognized. However, the non-recognition is usually temporary. The recognition of gain or loss is *postponed* (deferred) until the property received in the nontaxable exchange is subsequently disposed of in a taxable transaction. This is accomplished by assigning a carryover basis to the replacement property.

Debra completes a *nontaxable exchange* of property with an adjusted basis of $10,000 and a fair market value of $12,000 for property with a fair market value of $12,000.

Debra has a realized gain of $2,000 ($12,000 amount realized − $10,000 adjusted basis). Her recognized gain is $0. Her basis in the replacement property is a carryover basis of $10,000.

Assume that the replacement property is nondepreciable and that Debra subsequently sells it for $12,000. Her realized and recognized gain will be the $2,000 gain that was postponed (deferred) in the nontaxable transaction. If the replacement property is depreciable, the carryover basis of $10,000 is used in calculating depreciation.

EXAMPLE

1

In some nontaxable exchanges, only part of the property involved in the transaction qualifies for nonrecognition treatment. If the taxpayer receives cash or other nonqualify-ing property, part or all of the realized gain from the exchange is recognized. In these instances, gain is recognized because the taxpayer has changed or improved his or her relative economic position and has the wherewithal to pay income tax to the extent of cash or other property received.

It is important to distinguish between a nontaxable disposition, as the term is used in the statute, and a tax-free transaction. First, a direct exchange is not required in all circumstances (e.g., replacement of involuntarily converted property). Second, as previously mentioned, the term *nontaxable* refers to postponement of recognition via a carryover basis. In a *tax-free* transaction, the nonrecognition is permanent (e.g., see the discussion later in the chapter of the § 121 exclusion of realized gain on the sale of a personal residence). Therefore, the basis of any property acquired in a tax-free transaction does not depend on the basis of the property disposed of by the taxpayer.

15-2 **LIKE-KIND EXCHANGES—§ 1031**

LO.2

Apply the nonrecognition provisions and basis determination rules for like-kind exchanges.

Section 1031 provides for nontaxable exchange treatment if the following requirements are satisfied:[2]

- The form of the transaction is an exchange.
- Both the property transferred and the property received are held either for pro-ductive use in a trade or business or for investment.
- The property is like-kind property.

Like-kind exchanges include business for business, business for investment, invest-ment for business, and investment for investment property. Property held for personal use, inventory, and partnership interests (both limited and general) do not qualify under the like-kind exchange provisions. Securities, even though held for investment, do not qualify for like-kind exchange treatment.

The nonrecognition provision for like-kind exchanges is *mandatory* rather than elec-tive. A taxpayer who wants to recognize a realized gain or loss will have to structure the transaction in a form that does not satisfy the statutory requirements for a like-kind exchange. This topic is discussed further under Tax Planning.

15-2a **Like-Kind Property**

"The words 'like-kind' refer to the nature or character of the property and not to its grade or quality. One kind or class of property may not … be exchanged for property of a different kind or class."[3]

The term *like-kind* is intended to be interpreted very broadly. However, three cate-gories of exchanges are not included. First, livestock of different sexes do not qualify as like-kind property. Second, real estate can be exchanged only for other real estate, and

---

[2]§ 1031(a) and Reg. § 1.1031(a)–1(a).   [3]Reg. § 1.1031(a)–1(b).

personalty can be exchanged only for other personalty. For example, the exchange of a machine (personalty) for an office building (realty) is not a like-kind exchange. *Real estate* (or realty) includes principally rental buildings, office and store buildings, manufacturing plants, warehouses, and land. It is immaterial whether real estate is improved or unimproved. Thus, unimproved land can be exchanged for an apartment house. Personalty includes principally machines, equipment, trucks, automobiles, furniture, and fixtures. Third, real property located in the United States exchanged for foreign real property (and vice versa) does not qualify as like-kind property.

EXAMPLE 2

Wade made the following exchanges during the taxable year:

(a) Inventory for a machine used in business.
(b) Land held for investment for a building used in business.
(c) Stock held for investment for equipment used in business.
(d) A light-duty business truck for a light-duty business truck.
(e) An automobile used for personal transportation for an automobile used in business.
(f) Livestock for livestock of a different sex.
(g) Land held for investment in New York for land held for investment in London.

Exchanges (b), investment real property for business real property, and (d), business personalty for business personalty, qualify as exchanges of like-kind property.

The other exchanges do not qualify because they involve (a), inventory; (c), stock; (e), personal use automobile (not held for business or investment purposes); (f), livestock of different sexes; and (g), U.S. and foreign real estate.

Regulations dealing with § 1031 like-kind exchange treatment provide that if the exchange transaction involves multiple assets of a business (e.g., a television station for another television station), the determination of whether the assets qualify as like-kind property will not be made at the business level.[4] Instead, the underlying assets must be evaluated.

Special Rule for Depreciable Tangible Personal Property

The Regulations also provide for greater specificity in determining whether depreciable tangible personal property is of a like kind or class. Such property held for productive use in a business is of a like class only if the exchanged property is within the same *general business asset class* (as specified by the IRS in Revenue Procedure 87–57 or as subsequently modified) or the same *product class* (as specified by the Department of Commerce). Property included in a general business asset class is evaluated under this system rather than under the product class system.

The following are examples of general business asset classes:

- Office furniture, fixtures, and equipment.
- Information systems (computers and peripheral equipment).
- Airplanes.
- Automobiles and taxis.
- Buses.
- Light general-purpose trucks.
- Heavy general-purpose trucks.

These Regulations have made it more difficult for depreciable tangible personal property to qualify for § 1031 like-kind exchange treatment. For example, the exchange of office equipment for a computer does not qualify as an exchange of like-kind property. Even though both assets are depreciable tangible personal property, they are not like-kind property because they are in different general business asset classes.

15-2b Exchange Requirement

The transaction must involve a direct exchange of property to qualify as a like-kind exchange. The sale of old property and the purchase of new property, even though like

---

[4]Reg. § 1.1031(j)–1.

kind, is generally not an exchange. However, if the two transactions are mutually dependent, the IRS may treat them as a like-kind exchange. For example, if the taxpayer sells an old business machine to a dealer and purchases a new one from the same dealer, like-kind exchange treatment could result.[5]

The taxpayer may want to avoid nontaxable exchange treatment. Recognition of gain gives the taxpayer a higher basis for depreciation (see Example 31). To the extent that such gains would, if recognized, either receive favorable capital gain treatment or be passive activity income that could offset passive activity losses, it might be preferable to avoid the nonrecognition provisions through an indirect exchange transaction. For example, a taxpayer may sell property to one individual, recognize the gain, and subsequently purchase similar property from another individual. The taxpayer may also want to avoid nontaxable exchange treatment so that a realized loss can be recognized.

Time Limitations

Like-kind exchanges—especially those involving real estate—can be complex. Further, it can be extremely difficult to coordinate a simultaneous transaction if the properties being exchanged are located in different counties or states. As a result, delayed (non-simultaneous) exchanges are allowed, but there are time limits on its completion. In a delayed like-kind exchange, one party does not take immediate title to the new property because it has not yet been identified. The Code provides that the delayed swap—often made with the assistance of a qualified intermediary—will qualify as a like-kind exchange if the following requirements are satisfied (see Concept Summary 15.1):

- *Identification period.* The new property must be identified within 45 days of the date when the old property was transferred.
- *Exchange period.* The new property must be received by the earlier of the following:
  - Within 180 days of the date when the old property was transferred.
  - The due date (including extensions) for the tax return covering the year of the transfer.

Concept Summary 15.1

Delayed § 1031 Exchange

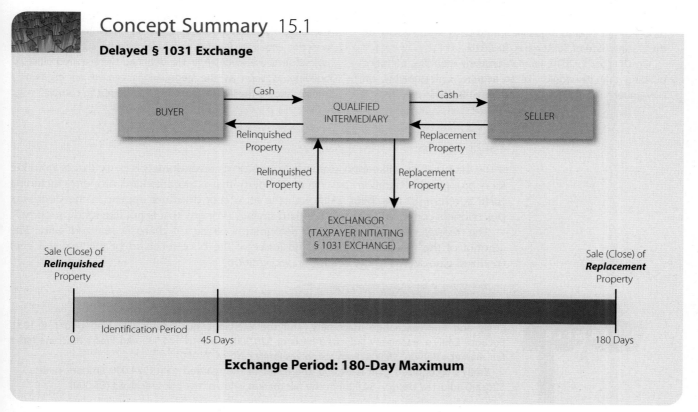

Exchange Period: 180-Day Maximum

---

[5]Rev.Rul. 61–119, 1961–1 C.B. 395.

TAX IN THE NEWS   What Happens to § 1031 Deferral If the Qualified Intermediary Defaults?

Normally, the IRS takes the position that the provisions of § 1031 are to be interpreted narrowly with respect to delayed § 1031 like-kind exchanges. In Revenue Procedure 2010–14, however, the IRS has announced an exception to this strict compliance requirement.

The exception applies if the 180-day time requirement for a delayed § 1031 like-kind exchange is not satisfied

because the qualified intermediary defaults due to a bankruptcy or receivership proceeding. In this situation, no gain is recognized by the taxpayer until a payment is received from the qualified intermediary or the bankruptcy trustee. As payments are received, gain is recognized using the gross profit ratio method.

Are these time limits firm, or can they be extended due to unforeseen circumstances? Indications are that the IRS will allow no deviation from either the identification period or the exchange period even when events outside the taxpayer's control preclude strict compliance. See the exception to strict compliance provided for in Revenue Procedure 2010–14 in the "Tax in the News" above.

ETHICS & EQUITY   A Delayed § 1031 Like-Kind Exchange: If At First You Don't Succeed, Try Again

Randall owns an office building (adjusted basis of $250,000) that he has been renting to a group of physicians. During negotiations over a new seven-year lease, the physicians offer to purchase the building for $900,000. Randall accepts the offer with the stipulation that the sale be structured as a delayed § 1031 transaction. Consequently, the sales proceeds are paid to a qualified third-party intermediary on the closing date of September 30, 2016.

On October 2, 2016, Randall properly identifies an office building that he would like to acquire. Unfortunately, on November 10, 2016, the property Randall selected is

withdrawn from the market. Working with the intermediary, on November 12, 2016, Randall identifies another office building that meets his requirements. The purchase of this property closes on December 15, 2016, and the title is transferred to Randall.

Randall treats the transaction as a § 1031 like-kind exchange. Even though the original office building identified was not acquired, Randall concludes that in substance, he has satisfied the 45-day rule. He identified the acquired office building as soon as the negotiations ceased on his first choice. Should the IRS accept Randall's attempt to comply?

15-2c **Boot**

If the taxpayer in a like-kind exchange gives or receives some property that is not like-kind property, recognition may occur. Property that is not like-kind property, including cash, is referred to as **boot**. Although the term *boot* does not appear in the Code, tax practitioners commonly use it rather than saying "property that is not like-kind property."

The *receipt* of boot will trigger recognition of gain if there is realized gain. The amount of the recognized gain is the *lesser* of the boot received or the realized gain (realized gain serves as the ceiling on recognition).

Implications of Boot Received

EXAMPLE 3

Emily and Fran exchange machinery, and the exchange qualifies as like kind under § 1031. Because Emily's machinery (adjusted basis of $20,000) is worth $24,000 and Fran's machine has a fair market value of $19,000, Fran also gives Emily cash of $5,000.

Emily's recognized gain is $4,000, the lesser of the realized gain ($24,000 amount realized − $20,000 adjusted basis = $4,000) or the fair market value of the boot received ($5,000).

Implications of Boot Received

Assume the same facts as in the previous example, except that Fran's machine is worth $21,000 (not $19,000). Under these circumstances, Fran gives Emily cash of $3,000 to make up the difference.

Emily's recognized gain is $3,000, the lesser of the realized gain of $4,000 ($24,000 amount realized − $20,000 adjusted basis) or the fair market value of the boot received of $3,000.

The receipt of boot does not result in recognition if there is realized loss.

Implications of Boot Received

Assume the same facts as in Example 3, except that the adjusted basis of Emily's machine is $30,000. Emily's realized loss is $6,000 ($24,000 amount realized − $30,000 adjusted basis). The receipt of the boot of $5,000 does not trigger recognition. Therefore, the recognized loss is $0.

The *giving* of boot usually does not trigger recognition. If the boot given is cash, no realized gain or loss is recognized.

Implications of Boot Given

Sarah and Gary exchange equipment in a like-kind exchange. Sarah receives equipment with a fair market value of $75,000 and transfers equipment worth $63,000 (adjusted basis of $45,000) and cash of $12,000.

Sarah's realized gain is $18,000 ($75,000 amount realized − $45,000 adjusted basis − $12,000 cash). However, none of the realized gain is recognized.

If, however, the boot given is appreciated or depreciated property, gain or loss is recognized to the extent of the difference between the adjusted basis and the fair market value of the boot. For this purpose, *appreciated or depreciated property* is defined as property whose adjusted basis is not equal to the fair market value.

Implications of Boot Given

Assume the same facts as in Example 6, except that Sarah transfers equipment worth $30,000 (adjusted basis of $36,000) and boot worth $45,000 (adjusted basis of $27,000). Sarah's net gain on this exchange is $12,000 [$75,000 − adjusted basis of $63,000 ($36,000 + $27,000)]. But she is transferring two pieces of property: equipment (like-kind property) with a built-in realized loss of $6,000 ($30,000 fair market value − $36,000 adjusted basis) and non-like-kind property (boot) with a built-in realized gain of $18,000 ($45,000 fair market value − $27,000 adjusted basis).

In this case, the $6,000 realized loss on the like-kind property is *deferred* (not recognized) and the $18,000 realized gain on the non-like-kind property is recognized. In other words, the realized loss on the like-kind property *cannot* be used to offset the realized gain on the boot given up as part of the transaction.

15-2d **Basis and Holding Period of Property Received**

If an exchange does not qualify as nontaxable under § 1031, gain or loss is recognized and the basis of property received in the exchange is the property's fair market value. If the exchange qualifies for nonrecognition, the basis of property received must be adjusted to reflect any postponed (deferred) gain or loss. The *basis of like-kind property* received in the exchange is the property's fair market value less postponed gain or plus postponed loss. If the exchange partially qualifies for nonrecognition (if recognition is associated with boot), the basis of like-kind property received in the exchange is the property's fair market value less postponed gain or plus postponed loss. The *basis of any boot* received is the boot's fair market value.

If there is a postponed loss, nonrecognition creates a situation in which the taxpayer has recovered *less* than the cost or other basis of the property exchanged in an amount equal to the unrecognized loss. If there is a postponed gain, the taxpayer has recovered *more* than the cost or other basis of the property exchanged in an amount equal to the unrecognized gain.

Basis of Like-Kind Property Received

EXAMPLE 8

Jaime exchanges a building (used in his business) with an adjusted basis of $30,000 and a fair market value of $38,000 for land with a fair market value of $38,000. The land is to be held as an investment. The exchange qualifies as like kind (an exchange of business real property for investment real property).

The basis of the land is $30,000 (land's fair market value of $38,000 − $8,000 postponed gain on the building). If the land is later sold for its fair market value of $38,000, the $8,000 postponed gain is recognized.

EXAMPLE 9

Assume the same facts as in the previous example, except that the building has an adjusted basis of $48,000 and a fair market value of only $38,000.

The basis in the newly acquired land is $48,000 (fair market value of $38,000 + $10,000 postponed loss on the building). If the land is later sold for its fair market value of $38,000, the $10,000 postponed loss is recognized.

The Code provides an alternative approach for determining the basis of like-kind property received:

> Adjusted basis of like-kind property surrendered
> + Adjusted basis of boot given
> + Gain recognized
> − Fair market value of boot received
> − Loss recognized
> = *Basis of like-kind property received*

This approach is logical in terms of the recovery of capital doctrine. That is, the unrecovered cost or other basis is increased by additional cost (boot given) or decreased by cost recovered (boot received). Any gain recognized is included in the basis of the new property. The taxpayer has been taxed on this amount and is now entitled to recover it tax-free. Any loss recognized is deducted from the basis of the new property. The taxpayer has received a tax benefit on that amount.

The holding period of the property surrendered in the exchange carries over and *tacks on* to the holding period of the like-kind property received.[6] The holding period for boot received in a like-kind exchange begins with the date of the exchange. See Chapter 16 for a discussion of the relevance of the holding period.

Depreciation recapture potential carries over to the property received in a like-kind exchange.[7] See Chapter 17 for a discussion of this topic.

The following comprehensive example illustrates the like-kind exchange rules.

EXAMPLE 10

Vicki exchanged the following old machines for new machines in five independent like-kind exchanges:

Exchange	Adjusted Basis of Old Machine	Fair Market Value of Old Machine	Fair Market Value of New Machine	Adjusted Basis of Boot Given	Fair Market Value of Boot Received
1	$4,000	$ 9,000	$9,000	$ −0−	$ −0−
2	4,000	6,000	9,000	3,000	−0−
3	4,000	3,000	9,000	6,000	−0−
4	4,000	12,000	9,000	−0−	3,000
5	4,000	3,800	3,500	−0−	300

continued

---

[6]§ 1223(1) and Reg. § 1.1223–1(a). For this carryover holding period rule to apply to like-kind exchanges after March 1, 1954, the like-kind property surrendered must have been either a capital asset or § 1231 property.

[7]Reg. §§ 1.1245–2(a)(4) and 1.1250–2(d)(1).

Vicki's realized and recognized gains and losses and the basis of each of the like-kind properties received are as follows:

				New Basis Calculation				
Exchange	Realized Gain (Loss)	Recognized Gain (Loss)	Old Adj. Basis +	Boot Given +	Gain Recognized −	Boot Received =	New Basis
1	$ 5,000	$–(0)–	$4,000 +	$ –0– +	$ –0– −	$ –0– =	$ 4,000*
2	2,000	–(0)–	4,000 +	3,000 +	–0– −	–0– =	7,000*
3	(1,000)	–(0)–	4,000 +	6,000 +	–0– −	–0– =	10,000**
4	8,000	3,000	4,000 +	–0– +	3,000 −	3,000 =	4,000*
5	(200)	–(0)–	4,000 +	–0– +	–0– −	300 =	3,700**

*Basis may be determined in gain situations under the alternative method by subtracting the gain not recognized from the fair market value of the new property:
$9,000 − $5,000 = $4,000 for exchange 1.
$9,000 − $2,000 = $7,000 for exchange 2.
$9,000 − $5,000 = $4,000 for exchange 4.
**In loss situations, basis may be determined by adding the loss not recognized to the fair market value of the new property:
$9,000 + $1,000 = $10,000 for exchange 3.
$3,500 + $200 = $3,700 for exchange 5.
The basis of the boot received is the boot's fair market value.

If the taxpayer either assumes a liability or takes property subject to a liability, the amount of the liability is treated as boot given. For the taxpayer whose liability is assumed or whose property is taken subject to the liability, the amount of the liability is treated as boot received. Example 11 illustrates the effect of such a liability. In addition, the example illustrates the tax consequences for both parties involved in the like-kind exchange.

EXAMPLE 11

Jill Saunders and Rick Thompson exchange real estate investments. Jill gives up property with an adjusted basis of $250,000 (fair market value of $420,000) that is subject to a mortgage of $80,000 (assumed by Rick). In return for this property, Jill receives property with a fair market value of $340,000 (Rick's adjusted basis in the property is $200,000). Jill's and Rick's realized and recognized gains and their basis in the like-kind property received are computed as follows:[8]

	Jill	Rick
Compute Realized Gain (Loss)		
FMV of like-kind property received	$ 340,000	$ 420,000
+ FMV of other property received		
+ Cash received		
+ Debt relief	80,000	
− Cash paid		
− Debt assumed		(80,000)
= Net Consideration Received	$ 420,000	$ 340,000
− Adjusted basis of property given	(250,000)	(200,000)
= Realized Gain (Loss)	$ 170,000	$ 140,000
Compute Boot Received		
Debt relief	$ 80,000	$ –0–
+ Cash received		
+ FMV of other property received		
= Boot Received	$ 80,000	$ –0–

continued

---

[8]Example (2) of Reg. § 1.1031(d)–2 illustrates a special situation in which both the buyer and the seller transfer liabilities that are assumed by the other party or both parties acquire property that is subject to a liability.

	Jill	Rick
Compute Recognized Gain		
Lesser of realized gain or boot received	$ 80,000	$ -0-
Compute Basis for New Property (Other Than Cash)		
Adjusted Basis of Property Given	$ 250,000	$ 200,000
+ Boot given (cash paid; debt assumed)	-0-	80,000
+ Gain recognized	80,000	-0-
− Boot received	(80,000)	-0-
= Basis of New Property	$ 250,000	$ 280,000

15-2e Reporting Considerations

Section 1031 transactions are reported on Form 8824 (Like-Kind Exchanges). Part III of Form 8824 has been completed based on the information provided for Jill Saunders's exchange.

This form should be used even though the like-kind exchange transaction results in no recognized gain or loss. It must be filed with the regular return for the tax year in which the taxpayer transfers property in a like-kind exchange.

If the like-kind exchange is with a related party, additional Forms 8824 must be filed for the following two years.

Form 8824 (2015)   Page **2**

Name(s) shown on tax return. Do not enter name and social security number if shown on other side. | Your social security number

Jill Saunders (Example 11)

Part III   Realized Gain or (Loss), Recognized Gain, and Basis of Like-Kind Property Received

Caution: *If you transferred **and** received (a) more than one group of like-kind properties or (b) cash or other (not like-kind) property, see* **Reporting of multi-asset exchanges** *in the instructions.*

Note: *Complete lines 12 through 14 **only** if you gave up property that was not like-kind. Otherwise, go to line 15.*

12	Fair market value (FMV) of other property given up	**12**	
13	Adjusted basis of other property given up	**13**	
14	Gain or (loss) recognized on other property given up. Subtract line 13 from line 12. Report the gain or (loss) in the same manner as if the exchange had been a sale	**14**	
	Caution: *If the property given up was used previously or partly as a home, see* **Property used as home** *in the instructions.*		
15	Cash received, FMV of other property received, plus net liabilities assumed by other party, reduced (but not below zero) by any exchange expenses you incurred (see instructions) . .	**15**	*80,000*
16	FMV of like-kind property you received	**16**	*340,000*
17	Add lines 15 and 16	**17**	*420,000*
18	Adjusted basis of like-kind property you gave up, net amounts paid to other party, plus any exchange expenses **not** used on line 15 (see instructions)	**18**	*250,000*
19	**Realized gain or (loss).** Subtract line 18 from line 17	**19**	*170,000*
20	Enter the smaller of line 15 or line 19, but not less than zero	**20**	*80,000*
21	Ordinary income under recapture rules. Enter here and on Form 4797, line 16 (see instructions)	**21**	*-0-*
22	Subtract line 21 from line 20. If zero or less, enter -0-. If more than zero, enter here and on Schedule D or Form 4797, unless the installment method applies (see instructions)	**22**	*80,000*
23	**Recognized gain.** Add lines 21 and 22	**23**	*80,000*
24	Deferred gain or (loss). Subtract line 23 from line 19. If a related party exchange, see instructions .	**24**	*90,000*
25	**Basis of like-kind property received.** Subtract line 15 from the sum of lines 18 and 23 . .	**25**	*250,000*

15-3 INVOLUNTARY CONVERSIONS—§ 1033

LO.3

Explain the nonrecognition provisions available on the involuntary conversion of property.

Section 1033 provides that a taxpayer who suffers an involuntary conversion of property may postpone recognition of *gain* realized from the conversion. The objective of this provision is to provide relief to the taxpayer who has suffered hardship and does not have the wherewithal to pay the tax on any gain realized from the conversion. Postponement of realized gain is permitted to the extent that the taxpayer *reinvests* the amount realized from the conversion in replacement property. The rules for nonrecognition of gain are as follows:

- If the amount reinvested in replacement property *equals or exceeds* the amount realized, realized gain is *not recognized*.

- If the amount reinvested in replacement property is *less than* the amount realized, realized gain *is recognized* to the extent of the deficiency.

If a *loss* occurs on an involuntary conversion, § 1033 does not modify the normal rules for loss recognition. That is, if a realized loss would otherwise be recognized, § 1033 does not change the result.

15-3a Involuntary Conversion Defined

An **involuntary conversion** results from the destruction (complete or partial), theft, seizure, requisition or condemnation, or sale or exchange under threat or imminence of requisition or condemnation of the taxpayer's property.[9] To prove the existence of a threat or imminence of condemnation, the taxpayer must obtain confirmation that there has been a decision to acquire the property for public use. In addition, the taxpayer must have reasonable grounds to believe the property will be taken.[10] The property does not have to be sold to the authority threatening to condemn it to qualify for § 1033 postponement. If the taxpayer satisfies the confirmation and reasonable grounds requirements, he or she can sell the property to another party.[11] Likewise, the sale of property to a condemning authority by a taxpayer who acquired the property from its former owner with the knowledge that the property was under threat of condemnation also qualifies as an involuntary conversion under § 1033.[12] A voluntary act, such as a taxpayer destroying the property by arson, is not an involuntary conversion.[13]

15-3b Computing the Amount Realized

The amount realized from an involuntary conversion is normally any insurance proceeds received. In the case of the condemnation of property, the amount realized usually includes only the amount received as compensation for the property.[14] Any amount received that is designated as severance damages by both the government and the taxpayer is not included in the amount realized. *Severance awards* usually occur when only a portion of the property is condemned (e.g., a strip of land is taken to build a highway). Severance damages are awarded because the value of the taxpayer's remaining property has declined as a result of the condemnation. Such damages are a tax-free recovery of capital and reduce the basis of the property. However, if either of the following requirements is satisfied, the nonrecognition provision of § 1033 applies to the severance damages:

- The severance damages are used to restore the usability of the remaining property.

- The usefulness of the remaining property is destroyed by the condemnation, and the property is sold and replaced at a cost equal to or exceeding the sum of the condemnation award, severance damages, and sales proceeds.

---

[9]§ 1033(a) and Reg. §§ 1.1033(a)−1(a) and −2(a).
[10]Rev.Rul. 63−221, 1963−2 C.B. 332 and *Joseph P. Balistrieri*, 38 TCM 526, T.C.Memo. 1979−115.
[11]Rev.Rul. 81−180, 1981−2 C.B. 161.

[12]Rev.Rul. 81−181, 1981−2 C.B. 162.
[13]Rev.Rul. 82−74, 1982−1 C.B. 110.
[14]*Pioneer Real Estate Co.*, 47 B.T.A. 886 (1942), *acq.* 1943 C.B. 18.

§ 1033 and Severance Damages

EXAMPLE 12

The government condemns a portion of Ron's farmland to build part of an interstate highway. Because the highway denies his cattle access to a pond and some grazing land, Ron receives severance damages in addition to the condemnation proceeds for the land taken.

Ron must reduce the basis of the property by the amount of the severance damages. If the amount of the severance damages received exceeds the adjusted basis, Ron recognizes gain.

EXAMPLE 13

Assume the same facts as in the previous example, except that Ron uses the proceeds from the condemnation and the severance damages to build another pond and to clear woodland for grazing.

As a result, all of the proceeds are eligible for § 1033 treatment. There is no possibility of gain recognition as the result of the amount of the severance damages received exceeding the adjusted basis.

15-3c Replacement Property

The requirements for replacement property generally are more restrictive than those for like-kind property under § 1031. The basic requirement is that the replacement property be similar or related in service or use to the involuntarily converted property.[15]

Different interpretations of the phrase *similar or related in service or use* apply depending on whether the involuntarily converted property is held by an *owner-user* or by an *owner-investor* (e.g., lessor). A taxpayer who uses the property in his or her trade or business is subject to a more restrictive test in terms of acquiring replacement property. For an owner-investor, the *taxpayer use* test applies, and for an owner-user, the *functional use test* applies. Furthermore, a special test applies in the case of involuntary conversions that result from condemnations.

Taxpayer Use Test

The taxpayer use test for owner-investors provides the taxpayer with more flexibility in terms of what qualifies as replacement property than does the functional use test for owner-users. Essentially, the properties must be used by the taxpayer (the owner-investor) in similar endeavors. For example, rental property held by an owner-investor qualifies if replaced by other rental property, regardless of the type of rental property involved. The test is met when an investor replaces a manufacturing plant with a wholesale grocery warehouse if both properties are held for the production of rent income.[16] The replacement of a rental residence with a personal residence does not meet the test.[17]

Functional Use Test

The functional use test applies to owner-users (e.g., a manufacturer whose manufacturing plant is destroyed by fire is required to replace the plant with another facility of similar functional use). Under this test, the taxpayer's use of the replacement property and of the involuntarily converted property must be the same. Replacing a manufacturing plant with a wholesale grocery warehouse does not meet this test. Replacing a rental residence with a personal residence also does not pass the test.

Special Rule for Condemnations

Under one set of circumstances, the broader replacement rules for like-kind exchanges are substituted for the narrow replacement rules normally used for involuntary conversions. This beneficial provision applies if business real property or investment real property is condemned. This provision gives the taxpayer substantially more flexibility in selecting replacement property. For example, improved real property can be replaced with unimproved real property.

---

[15]§ 1033(a) and Reg. § 1.1033(a)–1.

[16]*Loco Realty Co. v. Comm.*, 62–2 USTC ¶9657, 10 AFTR 2d 5359, 306 F.2d 207 (CA–8, 1962).

[17]Rev.Rul. 70–466, 1970–2 C.B. 165.

The rules concerning the nature of replacement property are illustrated in Concept Summary 15.2.

Concept Summary 15.2
Involuntary Conversions: Replacement Property Tests

[handwritten: Most Restrictive] *[handwritten: Most Lenient]*

Type of Property and User	Taxpayer Use Test	Functional Use Test	Special Rule for Condemnations*
An investor's rented shopping mall is destroyed by fire; the mall may be replaced with other rental properties (e.g., an apartment building). *[handwritten: owner/Investor]*	X		
A manufacturing plant is destroyed by fire; replacement property must consist of another manufacturing plant that is functionally the same as the property converted. *[handwritten: Owner user]*		X	
Personal residence of a taxpayer is condemned by a local government authority; replacement property must consist of another personal residence. *[handwritten: Personal Use + condemned]*		X	
Land used by a manufacturing company is condemned by a local government authority.			X
Apartment and land held by an investor are sold due to the threat or imminence of condemnation. *[handwritten: Both are business or investment · condemned]*			X

*Applies the same test as in the case of like-kind exchanges.

15-3d Time Limitation on Replacement

The taxpayer normally has a two-year period after the close of the taxable year in which gain is realized from an involuntary conversion to replace the property.[18] This rule affords as much as three years from the date of realization of gain to replace the property if the realization of gain took place on the first day of the taxable year.[19]

EXAMPLE 14

Megan's building is destroyed by fire on December 16, 2015. The adjusted basis is $325,000. Megan receives $400,000 from the insurance company on January 10, 2016. She is a calendar year and cash method taxpayer.

The latest date for replacement is December 31, 2018 (the end of the taxable year in which realized gain occurred plus two years). The critical date is not the date the involuntary conversion occurred, but rather the date of gain realization.

In the case of a condemnation of real property used in a trade or business or held for investment, a three-year period is substituted for the normal two-year period. In this case, the taxpayer can actually have as many as four years from the date of realization of gain to replace the property.

EXAMPLE 15

Assume the same facts as in the previous example, except that Megan's building is condemned. Megan receives notification of the future condemnation on November 1, 2015. The condemnation occurs on December 16, 2015, with the condemnation proceeds being received on January 10, 2016.

The latest date for replacement is December 31, 2019 (the end of the taxable year in which realized gain occurred plus three years).

The *earliest date* for replacement typically is the date the involuntary conversion occurs. However, if the property is condemned, it is possible to replace the condemned property before this date. In this case, the earliest date is the date of the threat or

---

[18]§§ 1033(a)(2)(B) and (g)(4) and Reg. § 1.1033(a)–2(c)(3). The two-year period is extended to a four-year period if the property is located in a Presidentially-declared disaster area.

[19]The taxpayer can apply for an extension of this time period anytime before its expiration [Reg. § 1.1033(a)–2(c)(3)]. Also, the period for filing the application for extension can be extended if the taxpayer shows reasonable cause.

imminence of requisition or condemnation of the property. The purpose of this provision is to enable the taxpayer to make an orderly replacement of the condemned property.

EXAMPLE 16

Assume the same facts as in Example 15. The earliest date that Megan can replace the building is November 1, 2015, which is the date of the condemnation of the building.

15-3e Nonrecognition of Gain

Nonrecognition of gain can be either mandatory or elective, depending on whether the conversion is direct (into replacement property) or indirect (into money).

Direct Conversion

If the conversion is directly into replacement property rather than into money, nonrecognition of realized gain is *mandatory*. In this case, the basis of the replacement property is the same as the adjusted basis of the converted property. Direct conversion is rare in practice and usually involves condemnations.

EXAMPLE 17

Lupe's property, with an adjusted basis of $20,000, is condemned by the state. Lupe receives property with a fair market value of $50,000 as compensation for the property taken.

Because the nonrecognition of realized gain is mandatory for direct conversions, Lupe's realized gain of $30,000 is not recognized and the basis of the replacement property is $20,000 (adjusted basis of the condemned property).

Conversion into Money

If the conversion is into money, the realized gain is recognized only to the extent the amount realized from the involuntary conversion exceeds the cost of the qualifying replacement property.[20] This is the usual case, and nonrecognition (postponement) is *elective*. If the election is not made, the realized gain is recognized.

The basis of the replacement property is the property's cost less any postponed (deferred) gain.[21] If the election to postpone gain is made, the holding period of the replacement property includes the holding period of the converted property.

Section 1033 applies *only to gains* and *not to losses*. Losses from involuntary conversions are recognized if the property is held for business or income-producing purposes. Personal casualty losses are recognized, but condemnation losses related to personal use assets (e.g., a personal residence) are neither recognized nor postponed.

Involuntary Conversion Gain or Loss

EXAMPLE 18

Walt's building (used in his trade or business), with an adjusted basis of $50,000, is destroyed by fire on October 5, 2016. Walt is a calendar year taxpayer. On November 17, 2016, he receives an insurance reimbursement of $100,000 for the loss. Walt invests $80,000 in a new building and uses the other $20,000 of insurance proceeds to pay off credit card debt.

- Walt has until December 31, 2018, to make the new investment and qualify for the nonrecognition election.
- Walt's realized gain is $50,000 ($100,000 insurance proceeds received − $50,000 adjusted basis of old building).
- Assuming that the replacement property qualifies as similar or related in service or use, Walt's recognized gain is $20,000. Because he reinvested $20,000 less than the insurance proceeds received ($100,000 proceeds − $80,000 reinvested), his realized gain is recognized to that extent.
- Walt's basis in the new building is $50,000. This is the building's cost of $80,000 less the postponed gain of $30,000 (realized gain of $50,000 − recognized gain of $20,000).

---

[20]§ 1033(a)(2)(A) and Reg. § 1.1033(a)–2(c)(1).   [21]§ 1033(b).

Involuntary Conversion Gain or Loss

Assume the same facts as in the previous example, except that Walt receives only $45,000 of insurance proceeds. He has a realized and recognized loss of $5,000. The basis of the new building is the building's cost of $80,000.

EXAMPLE 19

If the destroyed building in Example 19 had been held for personal use, the recognized loss would have been subject to the following additional limitations.[22] The loss of $5,000 would have been limited to the decline in fair market value of the property, and the amount of the loss would have been reduced first by $100 and then by 10 percent of adjusted gross income (refer to Chapter 7).

15-3f Reporting Considerations

Involuntary conversions from casualty and theft are reported first on Form 4684, Casualties and Thefts. Casualty and theft losses on personal use property for the individual taxpayer are carried from Form 4684 to Schedule A of Form 1040. For other casualty and theft items, the Form 4684 amounts are generally reported on Form 4797, Sales of Business Property, unless Form 4797 is not required. In the latter case, the amounts are reported directly on the tax return involved.

Except for personal use property, recognized gains and losses from involuntary conversions other than by casualty and theft are reported on Form 4797. As stated previously, if the property involved in the involuntary conversion (other than by casualty and theft) is personal use property, any realized loss is not recognized. Any realized gain is treated as gain on a voluntary sale.

What procedure should be followed if the taxpayer intends to acquire qualifying replacement property but has not done so by the time the tax return is filed? The taxpayer should elect § 1033 and report all of the details of the transaction on a statement attached to the return. Although a tax form (Form 8824) is available for § 1031 like-kind exchanges, no special form is provided for § 1033 transactions. When the qualifying replacement property is acquired, the taxpayer should attach a statement to the tax return that contains relevant information on the replacement property.

An amended return must be filed if qualified replacement property is not acquired during the statutory time period allowed. An amended return also is required if the cost of the replacement property is less than the amount realized from the involuntary conversion. In this case, the return would recognize the portion of the realized gain that can no longer be deferred.

15-4 SALE OF A RESIDENCE—§ 121

LO.4

Describe the provision for the permanent exclusion of gain on the sale of a personal residence.

A taxpayer's personal residence is a personal use asset. Therefore, a realized loss from the sale of a personal residence is not recognized.[23]

A realized gain from the sale of a personal residence is subject to taxation. However, favorable relief from recognition of gain is provided in the form of the § 121 exclusion. Under this provision, a taxpayer can exclude up to $250,000 of realized gain on the sale of a taxpayer's principal residence.[24]

15-4a Principal Residence

Whether property is the taxpayer's principal residence "depends upon all of the facts and circumstances in each case."[25] A residence does not have to be a house. For example, a houseboat, a house trailer, or a motor home can qualify.[26] Land, under certain

---

[22]§ 165(c)(3) and Reg. § 1.165–7.
[23]§ 165(c).
[24]§ 121(b).

[25]Regulation § 1.121–1(b)(2) includes factors to be considered in determining a taxpayer's principal residence.
[26]Reg. § 1.1034–1(c)(3)(i).

circumstances, can qualify for exclusion treatment. The lot on which a house is built obviously qualifies. An adjacent lot can qualify if it is regularly used by the owner as part of the residential property. To qualify, the land must be sold along with the residence or within two years before or after the sale of the residence.

Mitch graduates from college and moves to Boston, where he is employed. He decides to rent an apartment in Boston because of its proximity to his place of employment. He purchases a beach condo in the Cape Cod area that he occupies most weekends. Mitch does not intend to live at the beach condo except on weekends. The apartment in Boston is his principal residence.

15-4b **Requirements for Exclusion Treatment**

To qualify for exclusion treatment, at the date of the sale, the residence must have been *owned* and *used* by the taxpayer as the principal residence for at least two years during the five-year period ending on the date of the sale.[27]

Melissa sells her principal residence on September 18, 2016. She had purchased it on July 5, 2014, and lived in it since then. The sale of Melissa's residence qualifies for the § 121 exclusion.

The five-year window enables the taxpayer to qualify for the § 121 exclusion even though the property is not his or her principal residence at the date of the sale.

Benjamin sells his former principal residence on August 16, 2016. He had purchased it on April 1, 2008, and lived in it until July 1, 2015, when he converted it to rental property.

Even though the property is rental property on August 16, 2016, rather than Benjamin's principal residence, the sale qualifies for the § 121 exclusion.[28] During the five-year period from August 16, 2011, to August 16, 2016, Benjamin owned and used the property as his principal residence for at least two years.

Taxpayers might be tempted to make liberal use of the § 121 exclusion as a means of speculating when the price of residential housing is rising. Without any time restriction on its use, § 121 would permit the exclusion of realized gain on multiple sales of principal residences. The Code curbs this approach by denying the application of the § 121 exclusion to sales occurring within two years of its last use.[29]

Mike sells his principal residence (the first residence) in June 2015 for $150,000 (realized gain of $60,000). He then buys and sells the following (all of which qualify as principal residences):

	Date of Purchase	Date of Sale	Amount Involved
Second residence	July 2015		$160,000
Second residence		April 2016	180,000
Third residence	May 2016		200,000

Because multiple sales have taken place within a period of two years, § 121 does not apply to the sale of the second residence. Thus, the realized gain of $20,000 [$180,000 (selling price) − $160,000 (purchase price)] must be recognized.

15-4c **Exceptions to the Two-Year Ownership Rule**

The two-year ownership and use requirement and the "only once every two years" provision could create a hardship for taxpayers in certain situations that are beyond

---

[27]§ 121(a). However, § 121(d)(10) provides that exclusion treatment does not apply if the residence was acquired in a like-kind exchange within the prior five years of the sale of the residence.

[28]However, any realized gain on the sale that is attributable to depreciation is not eligible for the § 121 exclusion. See Example 36.

[29]§ 121(b)(3).

TAX IN THE NEWS **Living in a High-Crime Neighborhood**

Normally, a taxpayer must satisfy the two-year ownership and use requirements and the "only once every two years" provision to be eligible for the § 121 exclusion. However, under the unforeseen circumstances exception, a taxpayer who does not satisfy these three requirements may be eligible for a reduced § 121 exclusion.

In several letter rulings, the IRS has been sympathetic to crime victims. One ruling involved a taxpayer who was accosted leaving his home, driven to several locations, and forced to withdraw money from an ATM. In another ruling, the taxpayers and their son were hospitalized after being assaulted by neighbors. In both cases, the taxpayers sold their homes. Although the taxpayers had not satisfied the three time period requirements, the IRS held that they were eligible for reduced § 121 exclusion treatment under the unforeseen circumstances exception.

their control. As a result, under the following special circumstances, the requirements are waived:[30]

- Change in place of employment.
- Health.
- To the extent provided in the Regulations, other unforeseen circumstances.

These three exceptions have been amplified by Treasury Department Regulations and are discussed in the sections that follow.[31] Each of these exceptions provides a *partial* exclusion. The calculation of the partial exclusion is discussed later in this chapter (see Relief Provision in text Section 15-4d).

Change in Place of Employment

For this exception to apply, the distance requirements applicable to the deductibility of moving expenses must be satisfied (see Chapter 9). Consequently, the location of the taxpayer's new employment must be at least 50 miles further from the old residence than the old residence was from the old job. The house must be used as the principal residence of the taxpayer at the time of the change in the place of employment. Employment includes the commencement of employment with a new employer, the continuation of employment with the same employer, and the commencement or continuation of self-employment.

EXAMPLE 24

Assume the same facts as in the previous example, except that in March 2016, Mike's employer transfers him to a job in another state that is 400 miles away.

As a result, the sale of the second residence and the purchase of the third residence were due to relocation of employment. Consequently, the § 121 exclusion is partially available on the sale of the second residence.

Health Considerations

For the health exception to apply, health must be the primary reason for the sale or exchange of the residence. A sale or exchange that is merely beneficial to the general health or well-being of the individual will not qualify. The health exception can be satisfied under either a general facts and circumstances approach or by a safe harbor established in the Regulations. The safe harbor applies if there is a physician's recommendation for a change of residence (1) to obtain, provide, or facilitate the diagnosis, cure, mitigation, or treatment of disease, illness, or injury or (2) to obtain or provide medical or personal care for an individual suffering from a disease, an illness, or an injury.

---

[30]§ 121(c)(2)(B).

[31]See Reg. § 1.121–3 and IRS Publication 523 (*Selling Your Home*) for further details and illustrations.

Unforeseen Circumstances

For the unforeseen circumstances exception to apply, the primary reason for the sale or exchange of the residence must be an event the taxpayer did not anticipate before purchasing and occupying the residence. This exception can be satisfied under either a general facts and circumstances approach or by a safe harbor established in the Regulations. The safe harbor applies in any of the following instances:

- Involuntary conversion of the residence.
- Natural or human-made disasters or acts of war or terrorism resulting in a casualty to the residence.
- Death of a qualified individual.
- Cessation of employment that results in eligibility for unemployment compensation.
- Change in employment or self-employment that results in the taxpayer being unable to pay housing costs and reasonable basic living expenses for the taxpayer's household.
- Divorce or legal separation.
- Multiple births resulting from the same pregnancy.

EXAMPLE 25

Debra and Roy are engaged and buy a house (sharing the mortgage payments) and live in it as their personal residence. Eighteen months after the purchase, they cancel their wedding plans, and Roy moves out of the house. Because Debra cannot afford to make the payments alone, they sell the house.

While the sale does not fit under the safe harbor, the sale does qualify under the unforeseen circumstances exception.

15-4d Calculation of the Amount of the Exclusion

General Provisions

The amount of the available § 121 exclusion on the sale of a principal residence is $250,000.[32] If the realized gain does not exceed $250,000, there is no recognized gain.

Realized gain is calculated in the normal manner. The *amount realized* is the selling price less the selling expenses, which include items such as the cost of advertising the property for sale, real estate broker commissions, legal fees in connection with the sale, and loan placement fees paid by the taxpayer as a condition of arranging financing for the buyer. Repairs and maintenance performed by the seller to aid in selling the property are treated neither as selling expenses nor as adjustments to the taxpayer's adjusted basis for the residence.

The Big Picture

EXAMPLE 26

Return to the facts of *The Big Picture* on p. 15-1. Recall that one of Alice's options is to sell her current house and move into the inherited house. Assume that Alice, who is single, sells her current personal residence (adjusted basis of $130,000) for $348,000. She has owned and lived in the house for 15 years. Her selling expenses are $18,000. Three weeks prior to the sale, Alice pays a carpenter and a painter $1,000 to make some repairs and paint the two bathrooms. Her recognized gain would be calculated as follows:

Amount realized ($348,000 − $18,000)	$ 330,000
Adjusted basis	(130,000)
Realized gain	$ 200,000
§ 121 exclusion	(200,000)
Recognized gain	$ –0–

Because the available § 121 exclusion of $250,000 would exceed Alice's realized gain of $200,000, her recognized gain would be $0.

---

[32]§ 121(b)(1).

The Big Picture

Continue with *The Big Picture* and the facts of Example 26, except that the selling price is $490,000.

EXAMPLE
27

Amount realized ($490,000 − $18,000)	$ 472,000
Adjusted basis	(130,000)
Realized gain	$ 342,000
§ 121 exclusion	(250,000)
Recognized gain	$ 92,000

Because the realized gain of $342,000 would exceed the § 121 exclusion amount of $250,000, Alice's recognized gain would be $92,000.

Effect on Married Couples

If a married couple files a joint return, the $250,000 amount is increased to $500,000 if the following requirements are satisfied:[33]

- Either spouse meets the at-least-two-years *ownership* requirement.
- Both spouses meet the at-least-two-years *use* requirement.
- Neither spouse is ineligible for the § 121 exclusion on the sale of the current principal residence because of the sale of another principal residence within the prior two years.

Margaret sells her personal residence (adjusted basis of $150,000) for $650,000. She has owned and lived in the residence for six years. Her selling expenses are $40,000. Margaret is married to Ted, and they file a joint return. Ted has lived in the residence since they were married two and one-half years ago.

EXAMPLE
28

Amount realized ($650,000 − $40,000)	$ 610,000
Adjusted basis	(150,000)
Realized gain	$ 460,000
§ 121 exclusion	(460,000)
Recognized gain	$ −0−

Because the realized gain of $460,000 is less than the available § 121 exclusion amount of $500,000, no gain is recognized.

A surviving spouse can continue to use the $500,000 exclusion amount on the sale of a personal residence for the next two years following the deceased spouse's death. If the sale occurs in the year of death, however, a joint return must be filed by the surviving spouse.

Relief Provision

As discussed earlier in Exceptions to the Two-Year Ownership Rule, partial § 121 exclusion treatment may be available when not all of the statutory requirements are satisfied. Under the relief provision, the § 121 exclusion amount ($250,000 or $500,000) is multiplied by a fraction, the numerator of which is the number of qualifying months and the denominator of which is 24 months. The resulting amount is the excluded gain.[34]

On October 1, 2015, Rich and Audrey, who file a joint return and live in Chicago, sell their personal residence, which they have owned and lived in for eight years. The realized gain of $325,000 is excluded under § 121. They purchase another personal residence for $525,000 on October 2, 2015. Audrey's employer transfers her to the Denver office in August 2016. Rich and Audrey sell their Chicago residence on August 2, 2016, and they purchase a residence in Denver shortly thereafter. The realized gain on the sale is $300,000.

EXAMPLE
29

continued

---

[33]§ 121(b)(2).   [34]§ 121(c)(1).

The $325,000 gain on the first Chicago residence is excluded under § 121. The sale of the second Chicago residence is within the two-year window of the prior sale, but because it resulted from a change in employment, Rich and Audrey can qualify for partial § 121 exclusion treatment as follows:

Realized gain	$ 300,000
§ 121 exclusion:	
$\frac{10 \text{ months}}{24 \text{ months}} \times \$500,000$	(208,333)
Recognized gain	$ 91,667

Basis of New Residence

Because § 121 is an exclusion provision rather than a postponement of gain provision, the basis of a new residence is its cost.[35]

15-4e Involuntary Conversion and Using §§ 121 and 1033

A taxpayer can use both the § 121 exclusion of gain provision and the § 1033 postponement of gain provision.[36] The taxpayer initially can elect to exclude realized gain under § 121 to the extent of the statutory amount. Then a qualified replacement of the residence under § 1033 can be used to postpone the remainder of the realized gain. In applying § 1033, the amount of the required reinvestment is reduced by the amount of the § 121 exclusion.

EXAMPLE 30

Angel's principal residence is destroyed by a tornado. Her adjusted basis for the residence is $140,000. She receives insurance proceeds of $480,000.

If Angel does not elect to use the § 121 exclusion, her realized gain on the involuntary conversion of her principal residence is $340,000 ($480,000 amount realized − $140,000 adjusted basis). Thus, to postpone the $340,000 realized gain under § 1033, she would need to acquire qualifying property costing at least $480,000.

Using the § 121 exclusion enables Angel to reduce the amount of the required reinvestment for § 1033 purposes from $480,000 to $230,000. That is, by using § 121 in conjunction with § 1033, the amount realized, for § 1033 purposes, is reduced to $230,000 ($480,000 − $250,000 § 121 exclusion).

Note that if Angel does not acquire qualifying replacement property for § 1033 purposes, her recognized gain is $90,000 ($480,000 − $140,000 adjusted basis − $250,000 § 121 exclusion).

LO.5

Identify other nonrecognition provisions contained in the Code.

15-5 OTHER NONRECOGNITION PROVISIONS

The typical taxpayer experiences the sale of a personal residence or an involuntary conversion more frequently than the other types of nontaxable exchanges. Several less common nonrecognition provisions are treated briefly in the remainder of this chapter.

15-5a Exchange of Stock for Property—§ 1032

Under § 1032, a corporation does not recognize gain or loss on the receipt of money or other property in exchange for its stock (including treasury stock). In other words, a corporation does not recognize gain or loss when it deals in its own stock. This provision is consistent with the accounting treatment of such transactions.

---

[35]§ 1012.

[36]§ 121(d)(5).

15-5b **Certain Exchanges of Insurance Policies—§ 1035**

Under § 1035, no gain or loss is recognized from the exchange of certain insurance contracts or policies. The rules relating to exchanges not solely in kind and the basis of the property acquired are the same as under § 1031. Exchanges qualifying for nonrecognition include the following:

- The exchange of life insurance contracts.
- The exchange of a life insurance contract for an endowment or annuity contract.
- The exchange of an endowment contract for another endowment contract that provides for regular payments beginning at a date not later than the date payments would have begun under the contract exchanged.
- The exchange of an endowment contract for an annuity contract.
- The exchange of annuity contracts.

15-5c **Exchange of Stock for Stock of the Same Corporation—§ 1036**

Section 1036 provides that a shareholder does not recognize gain or loss on the exchange of common stock solely for common stock in the same corporation or from the exchange of preferred stock for preferred stock in the same corporation. Exchanges between individual shareholders as well as between a shareholder and the corporation are included. The rules relating to exchanges not solely in kind and the basis of the property acquired are the same as under § 1031. For example, a nonrecognition exchange occurs when common stock with different rights, such as voting for nonvoting, is exchanged. A shareholder usually recognizes gain or loss from the exchange of common for preferred or preferred for common even though the stock exchanged is in the same corporation.

15-5d **Certain Reacquisitions of Real Property—§ 1038**

Under § 1038, no loss is recognized from the repossession of real property sold on an installment basis. Gain is recognized to a limited extent.

15-5e **Transfers of Property between Spouses or Incident to Divorce—§ 1041**

Section 1041 provides that transfers of property *between spouses or former spouses incident to divorce* are nontaxable transactions. Therefore, the basis to the recipient is a carryover basis. To be treated as incident to the divorce, the transfer must be related to the cessation of marriage or occur within one year after the date on which the marriage ceases.

Section 1041 also provides for nontaxable exchange treatment on property transfers *between spouses during marriage*. The basis to the recipient spouse is a carryover basis.

15-5f **Rollovers into Specialized Small Business Investment Companies—§ 1044**

A postponement opportunity is available for some sellers of publicly traded securities under § 1044. If the amount realized is reinvested in the common stock or partnership interest of a specialized small business investment company (SSBIC), the realized gain is not recognized. Any amount not reinvested will trigger recognition of the realized gain to the extent of the deficiency. The taxpayer must reinvest the proceeds within 60 days of the date of sale to qualify. Various statutory ceilings apply to the amount of realized gain that can be postponed, and time limitations are also imposed.[37]

---

[37]See IRS Publication 550 (*Investment Income and Expenses*), Chapter 4, p. 66.

15-6 **TAX PLANNING**

LO.6

Review and apply various tax planning opportunities related to the nonrecognition provisions discussed in the chapter.

15-6a **Like-Kind Exchanges**

Because application of the like-kind exchange provisions is mandatory rather than elective, in certain instances, it may be preferable to avoid qualifying for § 1031 nonrecognition. To avoid the application of a deferral under § 1031, the taxpayer should structure the transaction so that at least one of the statutory requirements for a § 1031 like-kind exchange is not satisfied. If the like-kind exchange provisions do not apply, the end result may be the recognition of capital gain in exchange for a higher basis in the newly acquired asset. Also, the immediate recognition of gain may be preferable in certain situations. Examples in which immediate recognition is beneficial include the following:

- Taxpayer has unused net operating loss carryovers.
- Taxpayer has unused general business credit carryovers.
- Taxpayer has suspended or current passive activity losses.

Alicia disposes of a machine (used in her business) with an adjusted basis of $3,000 for $4,000. She also acquires a new business machine for $9,000.

If § 1031 applies, the $1,000 realized gain is not recognized and the basis of the new machine is reduced by $1,000 (from $9,000 to $8,000).

If § 1031 does not apply, a $1,000 gain is recognized and may receive favorable capital gain treatment to the extent the gain is not recognized as ordinary income due to the depreciation recapture provisions (see Chapter 17). In addition, the basis for depreciation on the new machine is $9,000 rather than $8,000 because there is no unrecognized gain.

The application of § 1031 nonrecognition treatment should also be avoided when the adjusted basis of the property being disposed of exceeds the fair market value.

Assume the same facts as in the previous example, except that the fair market value of the machine is $2,500. If § 1031 applies, the $500 realized loss is not recognized.

To recognize the loss, Alicia should sell the old machine and purchase the new one. The purchase and sale transactions should be with different taxpayers.

On the other hand, the like-kind exchange procedure can be utilized to control the amount of recognized gain.

Rex has property with an adjusted basis of $40,000 and a fair market value of $100,000. Sandra wants to buy Rex's property, but Rex wants to limit the amount of recognized gain on the proposed transaction. Sandra acquires other like-kind property (from an outside party) for $80,000. She then exchanges this property and $20,000 cash for Rex's property.

Rex has a realized gain of $60,000 ($100,000 amount realized − $40,000 adjusted basis). His recognized gain is only $20,000, the lower of the $20,000 boot received or the $60,000 realized gain. Rex's basis for the like-kind property is $40,000 ($40,000 adjusted basis + $20,000 gain recognized − $20,000 boot received). Further, it is permissible for Rex to identify the like-kind property that he wants Sandra to purchase.[38]

If Rex had sold the property to Sandra for its fair market value of $100,000, the result would have been a $60,000 recognized gain ($100,000 amount realized − $40,000 adjusted basis).

---

[38]*Franklin B. Biggs*, 69 T.C. 905 (1978); Rev.Rul. 73–476, 1973–2 C.B. 300; and *Starker v. U.S.*, 79–2 USTC ¶9541, 44 AFTR 2d 79–5525, 602 F.2d 1341 (CA–9, 1979).

In the present economic environment, however, there is another consideration. The beneficial result of tax deferral of realized gain could be more than offset by future tax rate increases. Some real estate investors who followed this approach, particularly with respect to undeveloped land, planned wisely. They were willing to accept current taxation at 15 percent to avoid the possibility of future taxation at a much higher rate (which turned out to be 20 percent for certain high-income taxpayers). Although turning down a tax deferral may sound like a strange strategy, it fits the notion of "pay a tax today to avoid a higher tax tomorrow."

15-6b Involuntary Conversions

In certain cases, a taxpayer may prefer to recognize gain from an involuntary conversion. Keep in mind that § 1033, unlike § 1031 (dealing with like-kind exchanges), generally is an elective provision.

EXAMPLE 34

Ahmad has a $40,000 realized gain from the involuntary conversion of an office building. He reinvests the entire proceeds of $450,000 in a new office building. He does not elect to postpone gain under § 1033, however, because of an expiring net operating loss carryover that is offset against the gain.

As a result, none of the realized gain of $40,000 is postponed. Because Ahmad did not elect § 1033 postponement, his basis in the replacement property is the property's cost of $450,000 rather than $410,000 ($450,000 reduced by the $40,000 realized gain).

15-6c Sale of a Principal Residence

Election to Forgo

The § 121 exclusion automatically applies if the taxpayer is eligible. That is, the taxpayer does not have to make an election. However, if the taxpayer wants to avoid § 121 exclusion treatment on an otherwise eligible sale, the taxpayer may elect to do so.[39]

EXAMPLE 35

George owns two personal residences that satisfy the two-year ownership and use test with respect to the five-year window. The Elm Street residence has appreciated by $25,000, and the Maple Street residence has appreciated by $230,000. He intends to sell both of them and move into rental property. He sells the Elm Street residence in December 2016 and expects to sell the Maple Street residence early next year.

Unless George elects not to apply the § 121 exclusion to the sale of the Elm Street residence, he will exclude the $25,000 realized gain on that residence in 2016. In 2017, however, he will have a recognized gain of $230,000 on the sale of the Maple Street residence.

If George makes the election to forgo, he will report a recognized gain of $25,000 on the sale of the Elm Street residence in 2016. But by using the § 121 exclusion in 2017, he will eliminate the recognized gain of $230,000 on the sale of the Maple Street residence.

Negative Effect of Renting or Using as a Home Office

The residence does not have to be the taxpayer's principal residence at the date of sale to qualify for the § 121 exclusion. During part of the five-year window, it could have been rental property (e.g., either a vacation home or entirely rental property). In addition, the taxpayer can have used part of the principal residence as a qualifying home office. In either of these circumstances, the taxpayer may claim deductions for the expenses attributable to the rental or business use. But what effect, if any, do such

---

[39]§ 121(f).

deductions have on a later sale of the residence? Will the sales proceeds still qualify for nonrecognition of gain treatment under § 121?

Concern that the § 121 exclusion might be denied may have deterred some taxpayers from claiming legitimate deductions, particularly in the case of an office in the home. As noted below, however, the IRS has clarified its position regarding the effect of any such depreciation.

In either the rental or the home office setting, the taxpayer will have deducted depreciation. Any realized gain on the sale that is attributable to depreciation claimed after May 5, 1997, is not eligible for the § 121 exclusion.[40]

EXAMPLE 36

On December 5, 2016, Amanda sells her principal residence, which qualifies for the § 121 exclusion. Her realized gain is $190,000. From January through November 2015, she was temporarily out of town on a job assignment in another city and rented the residence to a college student. For this period, she deducted MACRS cost recovery of $7,000. Without the depreciation provision, Amanda could exclude the $190,000 realized gain. However, the depreciation taken requires her to recognize $7,000 of the realized gain.

Qualification for § 121 Exclusion

The key requirement for the § 121 exclusion is that the taxpayer must have *owned* and *used* the property as a principal residence for at least two years during the five-year window. As taxpayers advance in age, they quite frequently make decisions such as the following:

- Sell the principal residence and buy a smaller residence or rent the principal residence.
- Sell vacation homes they own.
- Sell homes they are holding as rental property.

These properties may have experienced substantial appreciation during the ownership period. Clearly, the sale of the principal residence is eligible for the § 121 exclusion. Less clear, however, is that proper planning can make it possible for a vacation home or rental property to qualify for the exclusion. Although this strategy may require taxpayers to be flexible about where they live, it can result in substantial tax savings.

EXAMPLE 37

Thelma and David are approaching retirement. They have substantial appreciation on their principal residence and on a house they own at the beach (about two hours away). After retirement, they plan to move to Florida. They have owned and lived in the principal residence for 28 years and have owned the beach house for 9 years.

If they sell their principal residence, it qualifies for the § 121 exclusion. At retirement, they could move into their beach house for two years and make it eligible for the exclusion.

If the beach house were close enough, they could sell the principal residence now and move into the beach house to start the running of the two-year use period. Any realized gain on the beach house attributable to depreciation is not eligible for the § 121 exclusion. In addition, a reduction in the § 121 exclusion for prior use as a vacation home is required.[41]

---

[40]§ 121(d)(6).

[41]Additional information and examples can be found on pp. 3–6 of IRS Publication 523 (*Selling Your Home*).

REFOCUS ON THE BIG PICTURE

ALTERNATIVE USES OF PROPERTY

Alice needs to be aware of the different tax consequences of her proposals and whether there are any limits to these consequences.

- *Sale of the inherited house.* This is by far the simplest transaction for Alice. Based on the facts, her recognized gain would be:

Amount realized ($600,000 − $30,000)	$ 570,000
Adjusted basis	(475,000)
Recognized gain	$ 95,000

Because the sale of the house is not eligible for the § 121 exclusion, the tax liability is $14,250 ($95,000 × 15%). So Alice's net cash flow would be $555,750 ($570,000 − $14,250).

- *Conversion into a vacation home with only personal use.* With this alternative, the only tax benefit Alice would receive is the deduction for property taxes as an itemized deduction. She would continue to incur upkeep costs (e.g., repairs, utilities, and insurance). At the end of the two-year period, the sales results are similar to those of a current sale. The sale of the house would not be eligible for the § 121 exclusion.

- *Conversion into a vacation home with partial personal use and partial rental use.* In this case, Alice would be able to deduct 40 percent of costs such as property taxes, the agent's management fee, depreciation, maintenance and repairs, utilities, and insurance. However, this amount cannot exceed the rent income generated. The remaining 60 percent of the property taxes can be claimed as an itemized deduction.

  At the end of the two-year period, the sales results would be similar to those of a current sale. In determining recognized gain, adjusted basis must be reduced by the amount of the depreciation claimed. The sale of the house would not be eligible for the § 121 exclusion.

- *Current sale of present home with sale of inherited home in two years.* The present sale of her current principal residence and the future sale of her inherited residence would enable Alice to qualify for the § 121 exclusion as to each sale (see Example 26). She would satisfy the two-year ownership requirement, the two-year use requirement, and the allowance of the § 121 exclusion only once every two years. Alice must be careful to occupy the inherited residence for at least two years. Also, the period between the sales of the first and second houses must be greater than two years. Qualifying for the § 121 exclusion of up to $250,000 would allow Alice to avoid any Federal income tax liability.

With this information, Alice can make an informed choice. In all likelihood, she probably will select the strategy of selling her current house now and the inherited house in the future. A noneconomic benefit of this option is that she will have to sell only one house at the time of her retirement.

Key Terms

Discussion Questions

1. **LO.1** In most nontaxable exchanges, is the nonrecognition of the realized gain or loss temporary or permanent? Explain.

2. **LO.1** Distinguish between a loss that is not recognized on a nontaxable exchange and a loss that is not recognized on the sale or exchange of a personal use asset.

3. **LO.2** Karla exchanges personal use property for property to be held for productive use in her business. Can this transaction qualify for like-kind exchange treatment? Explain.

4. **LO.2** Which of the following qualify as like-kind exchanges under § 1031?
   a. Improved for unimproved real estate.
   b. Vending machine (used in business) for inventory.
   c. Rental house for personal residence.
   d. Business equipment for securities.
   e. Warehouse for office building (both used for business).
   f. Truck for computer (both used in business).
   g. Rental house for land (both held for investment).
   h. Ten shares of stock in Blue Corporation for 10 shares of stock in Red Corporation.
   i. Office furniture for office equipment (both used in business).
   j. Unimproved land in Jackson, Mississippi, for unimproved land in Toledo, Spain.
   k. General partnership interest for a general partnership interest.

Issue ID 5. **LO.2** Melissa owns a residential lot in Spring Creek, Louisiana, that has appreciated substantially in value. She holds the lot for investment. She is considering exchanging the lot for a residential lot located in Paris, France, that she also will hold for investment. Identify the relevant tax issues for Melissa.

Issue ID 6. **LO.2** Ross would like to dispose of some land he acquired five years ago because he believes that it will not continue to appreciate. Its value has increased by $50,000 over the five-year period. He also intends to sell stock that has declined in value by $50,000 during the eight-month period he has owned it. Ross has four offers to acquire the stock and land:

Buyer 1:	Exchange land.
Buyer 2:	Purchase land for cash.
Buyer 3:	Exchange stock.
Buyer 4:	Purchase stock for cash.

Identify the tax issues relevant to Ross in disposing of this land and stock.

7. **LO.2** Edith exchanges a machine used in her business for another machine and stock of Teal, Inc. If Edith had sold her machine, she would have had a realized gain. Explain why the new machine will have a different holding period than the stock.

8. **LO.2** Mortgaged real estate may be received in a like-kind exchange. If the taxpayer's mortgage is assumed, what effect does the mortgage have on the recognition of realized gain? On the basis of the real estate received?

9. **LO.3** Sheila's appreciated property is involuntarily converted. She receives insurance proceeds equal to the fair market value of the property. What is the minimum amount Sheila must reinvest in qualifying property to defer recognition of realized gain?

10. **LO.3** Ed receives severance damages from the state government for a public road built across his property. Under what circumstances can the § 1033 involuntary conversion provision apply to prevent the recognition of gain?

11. **LO.3** Vera owns an office building that she leases to tenants. If the building is destroyed by a tornado, is the functional use test or the taxpayer use test applied as to replacement property? Explain the differences between the two tests.

12. **LO.3** Reba, a calendar year taxpayer, owns an office building that she uses in her business. The building is involuntarily converted on November 15, 2016. On January 5, 2017, Reba receives enough proceeds to produce a realized gain. What is the latest date she can replace the building and qualify for § 1033 postponement treatment if the conversion event is:

    a. A flood?

    b. A condemnation?

    c. A tornado?

13. **LO.3** Bob is notified by the city public housing authority on May 3, 2016, that his apartment building is going to be condemned as part of an urban renewal project. On June 1, 2016, Carol offers to buy the building from Bob. Bob sells the building to Carol on June 30, 2016. Condemnation occurs on September 1, 2016, and Carol receives the condemnation proceeds from the city. Assume that both Bob and Carol are calendar year taxpayers.

    a. What is the earliest date on which Bob can dispose of the building and qualify for § 1033 postponement treatment?

    b. Does the sale to Carol qualify as a § 1033 involuntary conversion? Why or why not?

    c. What is the latest date on which Carol can acquire qualifying replacement property and qualify for postponement of the realized gain?

    d. What type of property will be qualifying replacement property?

14. **LO.3** A warehouse owned by Martha and used in her business (i.e., to store inventory) is being condemned by the city to provide a right-of-way for a highway. The warehouse has appreciated by $180,000 based on Martha's estimate of its fair market value. In the negotiations, the city is offering $35,000 less than what Martha believes the property is worth. Alan, a real estate broker, has offered to purchase Martha's property for $20,000 more than the city's offer. Martha plans to invest the proceeds she will receive in an office building she will lease to various tenants.   Issue ID

    a. Identify the relevant tax issues for Martha.

    b. Would the answer in (a) change if Martha's warehouse was property being held for investment rather than being used in her business? Explain.

15. **LO.4** To qualify for exclusion treatment on the sale of a principal residence, the residence must have been owned and used by the taxpayer for at least two years during the five-year period ending on the date of the sale. Are there any exceptions to this provision? Explain.

Computational Exercises

16. **LO.2, 6** Andrew owns a lathe (adjusted basis of $40,000) that he uses in his business. He exchanges the lathe and $20,000 in cash for a new lathe worth $50,000. May Andrew avoid like-kind exchange treatment to recognize his realized loss of $10,000? Explain.

17. **LO.2** Sue exchanges a sport-utility vehicle (adjusted basis of $16,000; fair market value of $19,500) for cash of $2,000 and a pickup truck (fair market value of $17,500). Both vehicles are for business use. Sue believes that her basis for the truck is $17,500. In calculating her basis, what has Sue failed to consider?

18. **LO.2** Logan and Johnathan exchange land, and the exchange qualifies as like kind under § 1031. Because Logan's land (adjusted basis of $85,000) is worth $100,000 and Johnathan's land has a fair market value of $80,000, Johnathan also gives Logan cash of $20,000.

    a. What is Logan's recognized gain?

    b. Assume instead that Johnathan's land is worth $90,000 and he gives Logan $10,000 cash. Now what is Logan's recognized gain?

19. **LO.2** Mandy and Timothy exchange equipment in a like-kind exchange. Mandy receives equipment with a fair market value of $28,000 and transfers equipment worth $20,000 (adjusted basis of $14,000) and cash of $8,000. What is Mandy's realized and recognized gain?

20. **LO.3** On June 5, 2016, Brown, Inc., a calendar year taxpayer, receives cash of $750,000 from the county upon condemnation of its warehouse building (adjusted basis of $500,000 and fair market value of $750,000).

    a. What must Brown do to qualify for § 1033 postponement of gain treatment?

    b. How would your advice to Brown differ if the adjusted basis was $795,000?

21. **LO.3** Camilo's property, with an adjusted basis of $155,000, is condemned by the state. Camilo receives property with a fair market value of $180,000 as compensation for the property taken.

    a. What is Camilo's realized and recognized gain?

    b. What is the basis of the replacement property?

22. **LO.3** On February 24, 2016, Allison's building, with an adjusted basis of $1.3 million (and used in her trade or business), is destroyed by fire. On March 31, 2016, she receives an insurance reimbursement of $1.65 million for the loss. Allison invests $1.55 million in a new building and buys stock with the balance of insurance proceeds. Allison is a calendar year taxpayer.

    a. By what date must Allison make the new investment to qualify for the non-recognition election?

    b. Assuming that the replacement property qualifies as similar or related in service or use, what is Allison's realized gain, recognized gain, and basis in the replacement building?

23. **LO.4** Gary, who is single, sells his principal residence (owned and occupied by him for seven years) in November 2016 for a realized gain of $148,000. He had purchased a more expensive new residence eight months prior to the sale. He anticipates that he will occupy this new house as his principal residence for only about 18 additional months. He expects it to appreciate substantially while he owns it. Gary would like to recognize the realized gain on the 2016 sale to offset a large investment loss from the sale of stock. Can he recognize the realized gain of $148,000 on the sale of his principal residence in 2016? Explain.

24. **LO.4** Arnold, who is single, sold his principal residence on April 10, 2016, and excluded the realized gain under § 121 (exclusion on the sale of a principal residence). On April 12, 2016, he purchased another principal residence, which he sells on January 12, 2017, for a realized gain of $80,000. Can Arnold exclude the $80,000 realized gain on the January 2017 sale if his reason for selling was:

    a. His noisy neighbors? Explain.

    b. A job transfer to another city? Explain.

25. **LO.4** Constanza, who is single, sells her current personal residence (adjusted basis of $165,000) for $450,000. She has owned and lived in the house for 30 years. Her selling expenses are $22,500. What is Constanza's realized and recognized gain?

26. **LO.4** On August 31, 2015, Harvey and Margaret, who file a joint return and live in Charleston, South Carolina, sell their personal residence, which they have owned and lived in for 10 years. The realized gain of $292,000 was excluded under § 121. They purchased another personal residence in Charleston for $480,000 on September 1, 2015. However, in 2016, Harvey's employer transfers him to Houston, Texas. They sell their Charleston home on February 28, 2016, and purchase a new home in Houston. The realized gain on the second sale is $180,000. What is Harvey and Margaret's recognized gain on the second sale?

Problems

27. **LO.2** Katrina owns undeveloped land with an adjusted basis of $300,000. She exchanges it for undeveloped land worth $750,000.
    a. What are Katrina's realized and recognized gain or loss?
    b. What is Katrina's basis in the undeveloped land she receives?
    c. Would the answers in (a) and (b) change if Katrina exchanged the undeveloped land for land and a building? Explain.

28. **LO.2** Kareem owns a pickup truck that he uses exclusively in his business. The adjusted basis is $22,000, and the fair market value is $14,000. Kareem exchanges the truck for another truck that he will use exclusively in his business.
    a. What are Kareem's realized and recognized gain or loss?
    b. What is his basis in the new truck?
    c. What are the tax consequences to Kareem in (a) and (b) if he used the old truck and will use the new truck exclusively for personal purposes?

29. **LO.2** Tanya Fletcher owns undeveloped land (adjusted basis of $80,000 and fair market value of $92,000) on the East Coast. On January 4, 2016, she exchanges it with Lisa Martin (an unrelated party) for undeveloped land on the West Coast and $3,000 cash. Lisa has an adjusted basis of $72,000 for her land, and its fair market value is $89,000. As the real estate market on the East Coast is thriving, on September 1, 2017, Lisa sells the land she acquired for $120,000.

    Decision Making
    Communications

    a. What are Tanya's recognized gain or loss and adjusted basis for the West Coast land on January 4, 2016?
    b. What are Lisa's recognized gain or loss and adjusted basis for the East Coast land on January 4, 2016?
    c. What is Lisa's recognized gain or loss from the September 1, 2017 sale?
    d. What effect does Lisa's 2017 sale have on Tanya?
    e. Write a letter to Tanya advising her of the tax consequences of this exchange. Her address is The Corral, El Paso, TX 79968.

30. **LO.2** Sarah exchanges a yellow bus (used in her business) for Tyler's gray bus and some garage equipment (used in his business). The assets have the following characteristics:

	Adjusted Basis	Fair Market Value
Yellow bus	$6,000	$15,000
Gray bus	3,000	11,000
Equipment	2,000	4,000

    a. What are Sarah's recognized gain or loss and basis for the gray bus and garage equipment?
    b. What are Tyler's recognized gain or loss and basis for the yellow bus?

Decision Making   31. **LO.2, 6** In two unrelated transactions, Laura exchanges property that qualifies for like-kind exchange treatment. In the first exchange, Laura gives up office equipment purchased in May 2014 (adjusted basis of $20,000; fair market value of $17,000) in exchange for new office equipment (fair market value of $15,000) and $2,000 cash. In the second exchange, Laura receives a parking garage (to be used in her business) with a fair market value of $50,000 in exchange for a plot of land she had held for investment. The land was purchased in April 2008 for $12,000 and has a current fair market value of $48,000. In addition to transferring the land, Laura pays an additional $2,000 to the other party.

a. What is Laura's adjusted basis for the new office equipment?

b. When does the holding period begin?

c. What is Laura's adjusted basis for the parking garage?

d. When does the holding period begin?

e. How could Laura structure either of the transactions differently to produce better tax consequences?

32. **LO.2** Susan owns a car that she uses exclusively for personal purposes. Its original cost was $26,000, and the fair market value is $12,000. She exchanges the car and $18,000 cash for a new car.

a. Calculate Susan's realized and recognized gain or loss.

b. Calculate Susan's basis for the new car.

c. Determine when Susan's holding period for the new car begins.

33. **LO.2** Stephanie owns a machine (adjusted basis of $90,000; fair market value of $125,000) that she uses in her business. She exchanges it for another machine (worth $100,000) and stock (worth $25,000). Determine Stephanie's:

a. Realized and recognized gain or loss on the exchange.

b. Basis in the new machine.

c. Basis in the stock she received.

34. **LO.2** Ed owns investment land with an adjusted basis of $35,000. Polly has offered to purchase the land from Ed for $175,000 for use in a real estate development. The amount offered by Polly is $10,000 in excess of what Ed perceives as the fair market value of the land. Ed would like to dispose of the land to Polly but does not want to incur the tax liability that would result. He identifies an office building with a fair market value of $175,000 that he would like to acquire. Polly purchases the office building and then exchanges the office building for Ed's land.

a. Calculate Ed's realized and recognized gain on the exchange and his basis for the office building.

b. Calculate Polly's realized and recognized gain on the exchange and her basis in the land.

35. **LO.2** What is the basis of the new property in each of the following exchanges?

a. Apartment building held for investment (adjusted basis of $145,000) for office building to be held for investment (fair market value of $225,000).

b. Land and building used as a barbershop (adjusted basis of $190,000) for land and building used as a grocery store (fair market value of $350,000).

c. Office building (adjusted basis of $45,000) for bulldozer (fair market value of $42,000), both held for business use.

d. IBM common stock (adjusted basis of $20,000) for ExxonMobil common stock (fair market value of $28,000).

e. Rental house (adjusted basis of $90,000) for mountain cabin to be held for rental use (fair market value of $225,000).

f. General partnership interest (adjusted basis of $400,000) for a limited partnership interest (fair market value of $580,000).

36. **LO.2** Steve owns Machine A (adjusted basis of $12,000 and fair market value of $15,000), which he uses in his business. Steve sells Machine A for $15,000 to Aubry (a dealer) and then purchases Machine B for $15,000 from Joan (also a dealer). Machine B would normally qualify as like-kind property.

    a.   What are Steve's realized and recognized gain on the sale of Machine A?

    b.   What is Steve's basis for Machine B?

    c.   What factors would motivate Steve to sell Machine A and purchase Machine B rather than exchange one machine for the other?

    d.   Assume that the adjusted basis of Machine A is $15,000 and the fair market value of both machines is $12,000. Respond to (a) through (c).

37. **LO.2** Tab exchanges real estate used in his business along with stock for real estate to be held for investment. The stock transferred has an adjusted basis of $45,000 and a fair market value of $50,000. The real estate transferred has an adjusted basis of $85,000 and a fair market value of $190,000. The real estate acquired has a fair market value of $240,000.

    a.   What is Tab's realized gain or loss?

    b.   His recognized gain or loss?

    c.   The basis of the newly acquired real estate?

38. **LO.2, 6** Tom and Frank are brothers. Each owns investment property in the other's hometown. To make their lives easier, they decide to exchange the investment properties legally. Under the terms of the exchange, Frank will transfer realty (adjusted basis of $52,000; fair market value of $80,000) and Tom will exchange realty (adjusted basis of $60,000; fair market value of $92,000). Tom's property is subject to a mortgage of $12,000 that will be assumed by Frank.   *Decision Making*

    a.   What are Frank's and Tom's recognized gains?

    b.   What are their adjusted bases?

    c.   As an alternative, Frank has proposed that rather than assuming the mortgage, he will transfer cash of $12,000 to Tom. Tom would use the cash to pay off the mortgage. Advise Tom on whether this alternative would be beneficial to him from a tax perspective.

39. **LO.2** Determine the realized, recognized, and postponed gain or loss and the new basis for each of the following like-kind exchanges:

	Adjusted Basis of Old Machine	Boot Given	Fair Market Value of New Asset	Boot Received
a.	$ 7,000	$ –0–	$12,000	$4,000
b.	14,000	2,000	15,000	–0–
c.	3,000	7,000	8,000	500
d.	15,000	–0–	29,000	–0–
e.	10,000	–0–	11,000	1,000
f.	17,000	–0–	14,000	–0–

40. **LO.2** Shontelle owns an apartment house that has an adjusted basis of $760,000 but is subject to a mortgage of $192,000. She transfers the apartment house to Dave and receives from him $120,000 in cash and an office building with a fair market value of $780,000 at the time of the exchange. Dave assumes the $192,000 mortgage on the apartment house.

    a.   What is Shontelle's realized gain or loss?

    b.   What is her recognized gain or loss?

    c.   What is the basis of the newly acquired office building?

41. **LO.3** Howard's roadside vegetable stand (adjusted basis of $275,000) is destroyed by a tractor-trailer accident. He receives insurance proceeds of $240,000 ($300,000 fair market value − $60,000 coinsurance). Howard immediately uses the proceeds plus additional cash of $45,000 to build another roadside vegetable stand at the same location. What are the tax consequences to Howard?

42. **LO.3** Albert owns 100 acres of land on which he grows spruce Christmas trees. His adjusted basis for the land is $100,000. He receives condemnation proceeds of $10,000 when the city's new beltway takes 5 acres along the eastern boundary of his property. He also receives a severance award of $6,000 associated with the possible harmful effects of exhaust fumes on his Christmas trees. Albert invests the $16,000 in a growth mutual fund. Determine the tax consequences to Albert of the:
    a. Condemnation proceeds.
    b. Severance award.

43. **LO.3** For each of the following involuntary conversions, indicate whether the property acquired qualifies as replacement property, the recognized gain, and the basis for the property acquired:
    a. Frank owns a warehouse that is destroyed by a tornado. The space in the warehouse was rented to various tenants. The adjusted basis was $470,000. Frank uses all of the insurance proceeds of $700,000 to build a shopping mall in a neighboring community where no property has been damaged by tornadoes. The shopping mall is rented to various tenants.
    b. Ivan owns a warehouse that he uses in his business. The adjusted basis is $300,000. The warehouse is destroyed by fire. Because of economic conditions in the area, Ivan decides not to rebuild the warehouse. Instead, he uses all of the insurance proceeds of $400,000 to build a warehouse to be used in his business in another state.
    c. Ridge's personal residence is condemned as part of a local government project to widen the highway from two lanes to four lanes. The adjusted basis is $170,000. Ridge uses all of the condemnation proceeds of $200,000 to purchase another personal residence.
    d. Juanita owns a building that she uses in her retail business. The adjusted basis is $250,000. The building is destroyed by a hurricane. Because of an economic downturn in the area caused by the closing of a military base, Juanita decides to rent space for her retail outlet rather than replace the building. She uses all of the insurance proceeds of $300,000 to buy a four-unit apartment building in another city. A real estate agent in that city will handle the rental of the apartments for her.
    e. Susan and Rick's personal residence is destroyed by a tornado. They had owned it for 15 months. The adjusted basis was $170,000. Because they would like to travel, they decide not to acquire a replacement residence. Instead, they invest all of the insurance proceeds of $200,000 in a duplex, which they rent to tenants.
    f. Ellen and Harry's personal residence (adjusted basis of $245,000) is destroyed in a flood. They had owned it for 18 months. Of the insurance proceeds of $350,000, they reinvest $342,000 in a replacement residence four months later.

44. **LO.3** Mitchell, a calendar year taxpayer, is the sole proprietor of a fast-food restaurant. His adjusted basis for the building and the related land is $450,000. On March 12, 2016, state authorities notify Mitchell that his property is going to be condemned so that the highway can be widened. On June 20, Mitchell's property is officially condemned, and he receives an award of $625,000. Because Mitchell's business was successful in the past, he would like to reopen the restaurant in a new location.

a. What is the earliest date Mitchell can acquire a new restaurant and qualify for § 1033 postponement?

b. On June 30, Mitchell purchases land and a building for $610,000. Assuming that he elects postponement of gain under § 1033, what is his recognized gain?

c. What is Mitchell's adjusted basis for the new land and building?

d. If he does not elect § 1033, what are Mitchell's recognized gain and adjusted basis?

e. Suppose he invests the $625,000 condemnation proceeds in the stock market on June 30. What is Mitchell's recognized gain?

45. **LO.3** Edith's warehouse (adjusted basis of $450,000) is destroyed by a hurricane in October 2016. Edith, a calendar year taxpayer, receives insurance proceeds of $525,000 in January 2017. Calculate Edith's realized gain or loss, recognized gain or loss, and basis for the replacement property if she:

a. Acquires a new warehouse for $550,000 in January 2017.

b. Acquires a new warehouse for $500,000 in January 2017.

c. Does not acquire replacement property.

46. **LO.3** Cabel's warehouse, which has an adjusted basis of $380,000 and a fair market value of $490,000, is condemned by an agency of the Federal government to make way for a highway interchange. The initial condemnation offer is $425,000. After substantial negotiations, the agency agrees to transfer to Cabel a surplus warehouse that he believes is worth $490,000. Cabel is a calendar year taxpayer. The condemnation and related asset transfer occur during September 2016.   *Decision Making*

a. What are the recognized gain or loss and the basis of the replacement warehouse if Cabel's objective is to recognize as much gain as possible?

b. Advise Cabel regarding what he needs to do by what date to achieve his objective.

47. **LO.3** What are the *maximum* postponed gain or loss and the basis for the replacement property for the following involuntary conversions?

	Property	Type of Conversion	Amount Realized	Adjusted Basis	Amount Reinvested
a.	Drugstore (business)	Casualty	$160,000	$130,000	$110,000
b.	Apartments (investment)	Condemned	100,000	125,000	175,000
c.	Grocery store (business)	Casualty	400,000	300,000	450,000
d.	Residence (personal)	Casualty	16,000	18,000	17,000
e.	Vacant lot (investment)	Condemned	240,000	160,000	220,000
f.	Residence (personal)	Casualty	20,000	18,000	19,000
g.	Residence (personal)	Condemned	18,000	20,000	26,000
h.	Apartments (investment)	Condemned	150,000	100,000	200,000

48. **LO.3, 6** Wanda, a calendar year taxpayer, owned a building (adjusted basis of $250,000) in which she operated a bakery that was destroyed by fire in December 2016. She receives insurance proceeds of $290,000 for the building the following March. Wanda is considering two options regarding the investment of the insurance proceeds. First, she could purchase a local building (suitable for a bakery) that is for sale for $275,000. Second, she could buy a new home for $290,000 and go back to college and finish her degree.   *Decision Making*

a. To minimize her tax liability, which of these alternatives should Wanda choose?

b. What is the latest date on which Wanda can replace the involuntarily converted property to qualify for § 1033?

c. What is the latest date on which Wanda can replace the involuntarily converted property to qualify for § 1033 if the involuntary conversion is a condemnation?

Decision Making   49. **LO.4, 6** Karl purchased his residence on January 2, 2015, for $260,000, after having lived in it during 2014 as a tenant under a lease with an option to buy clause. On August 1, 2016, Karl sells the residence for $315,000. On June 13, 2016, Karl purchases a new residence for $367,000.

a.   What is Karl's recognized gain? His basis for the new residence?

b.   Assume instead that Karl purchased his original residence on January 2, 2014 (rather than January 2, 2015). What is Karl's recognized gain? His basis for the new residence?

c.   In (a), what could Karl do to minimize his recognized gain?

50. **LO.4** Taylor has owned and occupied her personal residence (adjusted basis of $190,000) for four years. In April 2016, she sells the residence for $300,000 (selling expenses are $20,000). On the same day as the sale, Taylor purchases another house for $350,000. Because of noisy neighbors, she sells the new house after just 10 months. The selling price is $483,000 (selling expenses are $18,000).

a.   What is Taylor's recognized gain on the sale of the first residence?

b.   What is Taylor's basis for her second residence?

c.   What is Taylor's recognized gain on the sale of the second residence?

d.   Assume instead that the sale of the second residence was due to Taylor's job transfer to another state. What is her recognized gain on the sale of the second residence?

51. **LO.4** Wesley, who is single, listed his personal residence with a real estate agent on March 3, 2016, at a price of $390,000. He rejected several offers in the $350,000 range during the summer. Finally, on August 16, 2016, he and the purchaser signed a contract to sell for $363,000. The sale (i.e., closing) took place on September 7, 2016. The closing statement showed the following disbursements:

Real estate agent's commission	$ 21,780
Appraisal fee	600
Exterminator's certificate	300
Recording fees	800
Mortgage to First Bank	305,000
Cash to seller	34,520

Wesley's adjusted basis for the house is $200,000. He owned and occupied the house for seven years. On October 1, 2016, Wesley purchases another residence for $325,000.

a.   Calculate Wesley's recognized gain on the sale.

b.   What is Wesley's adjusted basis for the new residence?

c.   Assume instead that the selling price is $800,000. What is Wesley's recognized gain? His adjusted basis for the new residence?

52. **LO.4** Pedro, age 57, is the sole owner of his principal residence, which he has owned and occupied for 10 years. Maria, his spouse, has also lived there 10 years. He sells the house for a realized gain of $340,000.

a.   Can Pedro use the § 121 exclusion if he and Maria file a joint return? If so, what are the available amount of the exclusion and the recognized gain?

b.   Can Pedro use the § 121 exclusion if he files a separate return? If so, what are the available amount of the exclusion and the recognized gain?

c.   Assume instead that the realized gain is $550,000 and a joint return is filed.

d.   Assume instead that the realized gain is $550,000 and separate returns are filed.

e.   Assume instead that Maria and Pedro have been married for only 18 months and that she has lived in his house only since their marriage. They file a joint return.

53. **LO.4** Nell, Nina, and Nora Sanders, who are sisters, sell their principal residence   Communications
    (owned as tenants in common) in which they have lived for the past 25 years.
    The youngest of the sisters is age 60. The selling price is $960,000, selling expenses
    and legal fees are $63,000, and the adjusted basis is $120,000 (the fair market value
    of the residence when inherited from their parents 25 years ago; they made no capi-
    tal improvements during the time they held the residence). Because the sisters are
    going to live in rental housing, they do not plan to acquire another residence. Nell
    has contacted you on behalf of the three sisters regarding the tax consequences of
    the sale.

    a.   Write a letter to Nell advising her of the tax consequences and how taxes can
         be minimized. Nell's address is 100 Oak Avenue, Billings, MT 59101.
    b.   Prepare a memo for the tax files.

54. **LO.4** Lloyd owns a beach house (four years) and a cabin in the mountains (six   Decision Making
    years). His adjusted basis is $300,000 in the beach house and $315,000 in the
    mountain cabin. Llyod also rents a townhouse in the city where he is employed.
    During the year, he occupies each of the three residences as follows:

Townhouse	135 days
Beach house	155 days
Mountain cabin	75 days

    The beach house is close enough to the city that he can commute to work during the
    spring and summer. While this level of occupancy may vary slightly from year to year,
    it is representative during the time period that Lloyd has owned the two residences.
        As Lloyd plans on retiring in several years, he sells both the beach house and the
    mountain cabin. The mountain cabin is sold on March 3, 2016, for $540,000 (related
    selling expenses of $35,000). The beach house is sold on December 10, 2016, for
    $700,000 (related selling expenses of $42,000).

    a.   Calculate Lloyd's lowest recognized gain on the sale of the two residences.
    b.   Assume instead that both residences satisfy the two-year ownership and use
         tests as Lloyd's principal residence. Because the mountain cabin is sold first, is it
         possible for Lloyd to apply the § 121 exclusion to the sale of the beach house?
         Why or why not?

55. **LO.4, 6** Cisco, a calendar year taxpayer who is age 63, owns a residence in which   Decision Making
    he has lived for 21 years. The residence is destroyed by fire on August 8,
    2016. The adjusted basis is $190,000, and the fair market value is $320,000. Cisco
    receives insurance proceeds of $320,000 for the residence on September 1, 2016.
    He is trying to decide whether to purchase a comparable house. He anticipates that
    he will retire in two years and will move to a warmer climate, where he will rent in
    case he decides to live in different places.

    a.   Advise Cisco of the tax consequences of replacing versus not replacing the resi-
         dence.
    b.   Which do you recommend to him?
    c.   How would your answer in (a) change if the fair market value and insurance
         proceeds received were $510,000?

56. **LO.4, 6** Missy, age 30, has owned her principal residence (adjusted basis of   Decision Making
    $225,000) for five years. During the first three years of ownership, she
    occupied it as her principal residence. During the past two years, she was in grad-
    uate school and rented the residence. After graduate school, Missy returned to the
    same location where she previously worked. At this point, she purchased another
    residence for $400,000 and listed her old residence for sale at $340,000. Due to
    a slow real estate market, 11 months later Missy finally receives an offer of
    $330,000.

a.   What is Missy's recognized gain if she immediately accepts the $330,000 offer (i.e., 11 months after the listing date)? Selling expenses are $20,000.

b.   What is Missy's recognized gain if she rejects the $330,000 offer and accepts another offer of $340,000 three months later (i.e., 14 months after the listing date)?

c.   Advise Missy on which offer she should accept (assume that she is in the 28% tax bracket).

Decision Making   57. **LO.5** Roby and James have been married for nine years. Roby sells Plum, Inc. stock that she has owned for four years to James for its fair market value of $180,000. Her adjusted basis is $200,000.

a.   Calculate Roby's recognized gain or recognized loss.

b.   Calculate James's adjusted basis for the stock.

c.   How would the tax consequences in (a) and (b) differ if Roby had made a gift of the stock to James? Which form of the transaction would you recommend?

58. **LO.5** On September 1, 2016, Marsha sells stock in Orange, Inc., for $90,000. The stock is specialized small business investment company (SSBIC) stock and was purchased on August 16, 2015, for $60,000. On September 30, 2016, Marsha purchases $85,000 of Blue, Inc., also SSBIC stock.

a.   What is Marsha's realized and recognized gain (or loss) on the sale of the Orange stock?

b.   What is Marsha's basis in the Blue stock?

Cumulative Problems

Tax Return Problem

TAX SOFTWARE

59. Devon Bishop, age 45, is single. He lives at 1507 Rose Lane, Albuquerque, NM 87131. His Social Security number is 111-11-1112. Devon does not want $3 to go to the Presidential Election Campaign Fund.

Devon's wife, Ariane, passed away in 2011. Devon's son, Tom, who is age 16, resides with Devon. Tom's Social Security number is 123-45-6788.

Devon owns a sole proprietorship for which he uses the accrual method of accounting and maintains no inventory. His revenues and expenses for 2015 are as follows:

Sales revenue	$740,000
Cost of goods sold (based on purchases for the year)	405,000
Salary expense	88,000
Rent expense	30,000
Utilities	8,000
Telephone	6,500
Advertising	4,000
Bad debts	5,000
Depreciation*	21,000
Health insurance**	26,000
Accounting and legal fees	7,000
Supplies	1,000

*New office equipment ($21,000); Devon chose to use the immediate expense election.
**$18,000 for employees and $8,000 for Devon.

Other income received by Devon includes the following:

Dividend income (qualified dividends):	
Swan, Inc.	$10,000
Wren, Inc.	2,000
Interest income:	
First Bank	11,000
Second Bank	2,500
City of Asheville bonds	17,000

During the year, Devon and his sole proprietorship had the following property transactions:

a. Sold Blue, Inc. stock for $45,000 on March 12, 2015. He had purchased the stock on September 5, 2012, for $50,000.

b. Received an inheritance of $300,000 from his uncle, Henry. Devon used $200,000 to purchase Green, Inc. stock on May 15, 2015, and invested $100,000 in Gold, Inc. stock on May 30, 2015.

c. Received Orange, Inc. stock worth $9,500 as a gift from his aunt, Jane, on June 17, 2015. Her adjusted basis for the stock was $5,000. No gift taxes were paid on the transfer. Jane had purchased the stock on April 1, 2009. Devon sold the stock on July 1, 2015, for $22,000.

d. On July 15, 2015, Devon sold one-half of the Green, Inc. stock for $40,000.

e. Devon was notified on August 1, 2015, that Yellow, Inc. stock he purchased from a colleague on September 1, 2014, for $52,500 had become worthless. While he perceived that the investment was risky, he did not anticipate that the corporation would declare bankruptcy.

f. On August 15, 2015, Devon received a parcel of land in Phoenix worth $220,000 in exchange for a parcel of land he owned in Tucson. Because the Tucson parcel was worth $245,000, he also received $25,000 cash. Devon's adjusted basis for the Tucson parcel was $210,000. He originally purchased it on September 18, 2012.

g. On December 1, 2015, Devon sold the condominium in which he had been living for the past 20 years (1844 Lighthouse Lane, Albuquerque, NM 87131) and moved into a rented townhouse. The sales price was $480,000, selling expenses were $28,500, and repair expenses related to the sale were $9,400. Devon purchased the condominium for $180,000.

Devon's potential itemized deductions, exclusive of the aforementioned information, are as follows:

Medical expenses (before the 10% floor)	$ 9,500
Property taxes on residence	5,800
State income taxes	4,000
Charitable contributions	10,000
Mortgage interest on residence	9,900
Sales taxes paid	5,000

During the year, Devon makes estimated Federal income tax payments of $40,000.

Compute Devon's lowest net tax payable or refund due for 2015 assuming that he makes any available elections that will reduce the tax. If you use tax forms for your computations, you will need Forms 1040, 4562, 8824, and 8949 and Schedules A, B, C, D, and SE. Suggested software: H&R BLOCK Tax Software.

60. Tom and Alice Honeycutt, ages 35 and 36, respectively, live at 101 Glass Road, Delton, MI 49046. Tom is a county employee, and Alice is a self-employed accountant. Tom's Social Security number is 111-11-1111; Alice's Social Security number is 123-45-6789. The income and expenses associated with Alice's accounting practice for 2016 are as follows:

Tax Computation Problem
Decision Making
Communications

Revenues (cash receipts during 2016)	$185,000
Expenses	
Salaries	$ 45,000
Office supplies	3,200
Postage	2,900
Depreciation of equipment	42,000
Telephone	800
	$ 93,900

Because Alice is a cash method taxpayer, she does not record her receivables as revenue until she receives cash payment. At the beginning of 2016, her accounts receivable were $48,000, and the balance had decreased to $8,000 by the end of the year.

Alice used one room in their 10-room house as the office for her accounting practice (400 square feet out of a total square footage of 4,000). They paid the following expenses related to the house during 2016:

Utilities	$4,500
Insurance	2,100
Property taxes	5,200
Repairs	3,500

Tom and Alice purchased the house on September 1, 2015, for $400,000 (exclusive of land cost).

Tom and Alice have one child, Connor, age 16. Connor's Social Security number is 123-45-6788.

Tom received a salary of $50,000 during 2016. The appropriate amounts of Social Security tax and Medicare tax were withheld. In addition, $5,000 of Federal income taxes and $2,000 of state income taxes were withheld.

Alice provides part of the support of her father, age 69. Her father's Social Security number is 123-45-6787. The total support in 2016 for her father was as follows:

Social Security benefits	$5,200
From Alice	3,200
From Bob, Alice's brother	2,200
From Susan, Alice's sister	2,300

Bob and Susan have both indicated their willingness to sign a multiple support waiver form if it will benefit Alice.

Tom and Alice's allowable itemized deductions during 2016, excluding any itemized deductions related to the house, were $11,000. They made estimated tax payments of $25,000.

Part 1—Tax Computation
Compute Tom and Alice's lowest net tax payable or refund due for 2016.

Part 2—Tax Planning
Tom and Alice have 30 acres of prime farmland that they inherited from Tom's father several years ago. At that time, the fair market value of the land was $150,000 (which became their basis in the land). The Honeycutts have been holding the land as an investment. The property was recently appraised for $190,000, and there is an outstanding mortgage on the land of $28,000. They are considering trading this land for property in the mountains of southern Colorado. Ultimately, they would like to build a vacation home on the Colorado property. The Colorado property owner—who has significant land holdings in the area—has provided two options to Tom and Alice (in both cases, the Colorado property owner would assume the mortgage as part of the exchange):

1. 15 acres of property with a fair market value of $135,000 plus $27,000 of cash; or
2. 10 acres of property with a fair market value of $160,000 plus $2,000 of cash.

The Honeycutts have come to you for advice, believing either transaction to be a like-kind exchange that will allow them to defer any gain. Assume that Tom and Alice expect their marginal tax rate to remain the same for 2017. Write a letter to Tom and Alice that contains your advice on the proposed transactions. Also prepare a memo for the tax files.

Research Problems

Note: Solutions to Research Problems can be prepared by using the Checkpoint® Student Edition online research product, which is available to accompany this text. It is also possible to prepare solutions to the Research Problems by using tax research materials found in a standard tax library.

Research Problem 1. Charlene and Alton Dutro had lived in their home for two and one-half years when they decided to enlarge and remodel the house. However, their architect advised them that more stringent building and permit restrictions had been imposed since the house was built 10 years earlier. So the Dutros decided to demolish the house and rebuild on the same site. Rather than occupying the new house, however, the Dutros sold it for a realized gain in excess of $500,000.

In calculating the recognized gain on their Federal income tax return, the Dutros reduced the realized gain of more than $500,000 by the $500,000 exclusion of § 121. The IRS has issued an income tax deficiency notice on the grounds that the Dutros did not satisfy the two-out-of-five-years requirement of § 121(a).

Who is correct?

Partial list of research aids:
§ 121(a)(1).
David A. Gates, 135 T.C. 1 (2010).

Research Problem 2. Ted and Marvin Brown purchased an apartment building in 2005 as equal tenants in common. After a hectic decade of co-ownership, the brothers decided that their business association should be terminated. This led to the sale of the apartment building and a division of the proceeds.

The realized gain on the sale of the apartment building for each brother was $350,000. Ted recognized gain on his share and used the net proceeds to invest in stock. Marvin wanted to defer any recognized gain, so he worked with a realtor to identify property that would be eligible for § 1031 like-kind exchange treatment. After one prospect failed, the realtor identified a single-family home on Lake Tahoe that was currently being rented by the owner. Marvin agreed with the choice and acquired the single-family house using the proceeds from the apartment building. Because the single-family house qualified as like-kind property, Marvin deferred all of his realized gain.

After attempting to rent the property for eight months without success, Marvin concluded that he could not continue to make the mortgage payments on his primary residence and this rental property. To ease his financial liquidity problem, Marvin sold his principal residence for a realized gain of $190,000 and moved into the Lake Tahoe house. He reported no recognized gain on the sale of his principal residence as the sale qualified for § 121 exclusion treatment.

The IRS issued a deficiency notice to Marvin associated with the sale of the apartment building. The position of the IRS was that Marvin did not hold the single-family residence for investment purposes as required by § 1031. Instead, his intention was personal—to use it as a replacement for his current residence that he planned on selling.

Who should prevail?

Research Problem 3. Taylor owns a 150-unit motel that was constructed in the late 1960s. It is located on 10 acres on the main highway leading into the city. Taylor renovated the motel three years ago.

Taylor's motel is condemned by the city, which is going to use 2 of the 10 acres for a small park. The other 8 acres are to be sold to a time-share developer who intends to build 400 units on the property. The developer has already secured approval from the city planning commission.

Taylor's attorney advises him not to contest the condemnation of the 2 acres for the park. Under the eminent domain provision, the city does have the right to take "private property for public use." However, the attorney advises Taylor to contest the condemnation of the remaining property. According to the attorney, the city does not have the right to take "private property for private use."

The city's position is that the condemnation will result in a substantial number of new jobs and additional tax revenue for the city.

Will Taylor be successful if he follows his attorney's advice? Explain.

Internet Activity

Use the tax resources of the Internet to address the following questions. Do not restrict your search to the Web, but include a review of newsgroups and general reference materials, practitioner sites and resources, primary sources of the tax law, chat rooms and discussion groups, and other opportunities.

Research Problem 4. Find two newspaper stories about transactions to which you believe the involuntary conversion rules could apply. Do not limit your search to individual taxpayers.

Research Problem 5. In general, the 45-day identification period and the 180-day exchange period for like-kind exchanges cannot be extended. Does this rule change if the like-kind property or the taxpayer involved in the exchange is located in a Presidentially-declared disaster area? Use the IRS's website (**www.irs.gov**) to find the answer.

Roger CPA Review Questions

ROGER
CPA Review

1. Kellye purchased her home in 2011 for $140,000. After living in it for five years, she sold it in 2016 for $170,000, its market value. What is the tax treatment of the sale of Kellye's home?

   a. A $30,000 gain is recognized but not reported.

   b. A $30,000 gain is recognized and reported.

   c. A $30,000 gain is carried forward.

   d. The transaction is not reported.

2. Ike, a single taxpayer, is reassigned for his job and must move to a new state. While searching for a place to live, he encounters a person who is selling her home in order to move to Ike's current city. The two agree to trade their properties to each other without any further consideration. Ike's house has a fair market value of $200,000 and basis of $130,000. He has lived in the house for one year. The house he is acquiring in the trade has a fair market value of $300,000. What gain will Ike recognize for Federal tax purposes?

   a. $50,000   c. $0

   b. $100,000   d. $300,000

3. Kathryn has lived in her house for one year. Her company recently relocated to a city 100 miles away, forcing her to move. She purchased her house a year ago for $400,000 and sold it for $525,000, its current fair market value. What amount of gain will Kathryn recognize for Federal tax purposes?

   a. $0   c. $125,000

   b. $62,500   d. $250,000

4. An office building owned by Milo was destroyed by Hurricane Mel on September 25, 2015. On October 2, 2015, the President of the United States declared the area where the office building was located a federal disaster area. Milo received settlement of his insurance claim for the destruction of his building on January 2, 2016.

In order to qualify for nonrecognition of gain on this involuntary conversion, what is the last date for Milo to acquire qualified replacement property?

   a.   December 31, 2019   c.   December 31, 2020

   b.   October 2, 2019   d.   January 2, 2020

5. Mikhail owns real estate with a basis of $400,000 and a fair market value of $650,000. He exchanges it for other real estate with a fair market value of $480,000. In addition, Mikhail is relieved of a mortgage on the old property of $200,000, assumes a mortgage on the new property of $100,000, and receives $70,000 in cash. Under Code Section 1031, what is Mikhail's recognized gain on the exchange?

   a. $170,000   c. $70,000

   b. $270,000   d. $350,000

Property Transactions: Capital Gains and Losses

LEARNING OBJECTIVES: *After completing Chapter 16, you should be able to:*

LO.1 Explain the general scheme of taxation for capital gains and losses.

LO.2 Distinguish capital assets from ordinary assets.

LO.3 State and explain the relevance of a sale or exchange to classification as a capital gain or loss and apply the special rules for the capital gain or loss treatment of the retirement of corporate obligations, options, patents, franchises, and lease cancellation payments.

LO.4 Determine whether the holding period for a capital asset is long term or short term.

LO.5 Describe the beneficial tax treatment for capital gains and the detrimental tax treatment for capital losses for noncorporate taxpayers.

LO.6 Describe the tax treatment for capital gains and the detrimental tax treatment for capital losses for corporate taxpayers.

LO.7 Identify tax planning opportunities arising from the sale or exchange of capital assets.

CHAPTER OUTLINE

MANAGING CAPITAL ASSET TRANSACTIONS

Maurice has come to you for tax advice regarding his investments. He inherited $500,000 from his uncle, Joe. A financial adviser suggested that he make the following investments, which he did nine months ago.

- $5,000 for 100 shares of Eagle Company stock.

- $50,000 for a 50 percent interest in a patent that Kevin, a college roommate who is an unemployed inventor, obtained for a special battery he developed to power green cars. To date, Kevin has been unable to market the battery to an auto manufacturer or supplier, but he has high hopes of doing so in the future.

- $95,000 to purchase a franchise from Orange, Inc.

- $200,000 in the stock of Purple, a publicly held bank that follows a policy of occasionally paying dividends. At one time, the stock appreciated to $300,000, but now it is worth only $210,000. Maurice is considering unloading this stock.

- $50,000 in tax-exempt bonds. The interest rate on the bonds is only 3 percent. Maurice is considering moving this money into taxable bonds that pay 3.5 percent.

- $100,000 for a 10 percent ownership interest as a limited partner in a real estate development. Lots in the development are selling well.

Maurice read an article that talked about the beneficial tax rates for capital assets and dividends. He really liked the part about "costless" capital gains, although he did not understand it.

Maurice has retained his job as a toll booth supervisor at the municipal airport. His annual compensation is $35,000. He likes the job and has met some interesting people there.

Respond to Maurice's request for tax advice.

Read the chapter and formulate your response.

FRAMEWORK 1040 **Tax Formula for Individuals**

This chapter covers the boldfaced portions of the Tax Formula for Individuals that was introduced in Concept Summary 3.1 on p. 3-3. Below those portions are the sections of Form 1040 where the results are reported.

Income *(broadly defined)*	$ xx,xxx
Less: Exclusions	(x,xxx)
Gross income	$xx,xxx
Less: Deductions *for* adjusted gross income	(x,xxx)

FORM 1040 (p. 1)

12	Business income or (loss). Attach Schedule C or C-EZ	
13	Capital gain or (loss). Attach Schedule D if required. If not required, check here ▶ ☐	
14	Other gains or (losses). Attach Form 4797	

Adjusted gross income	$xx,xxx
Less: The greater of total **itemized deductions** *or* the standard deduction	(x,xxx)
Personal and dependency exemptions	(x,xxx)
Taxable income	$xx,xxx
Tax on taxable income *(see Tax Tables or Tax Rate Schedules)*	$ x,xxx

FORM 1040 (p. 2)

44	**Tax** (see instructions). Check if any from: **a** ☐ Form(s) 8814 **b** ☐ Form 4972 **c** ☐ _____

Less: Tax credits *(including income taxes withheld and prepaid)*	(xxx)
Tax due (or refund)	$ xxx

F ourteen years ago, a taxpayer purchased 100 shares of IBM stock for $17 a share. This year, the taxpayer sells the shares for $152 a share. Should the $135 per-share gain receive any special tax treatment? The $135 gain has built up over 14 years, so it may not be fair to tax it the same as income that was all earned this year.

What if the stock had been purchased for $152 per share and sold for $17 a share? Should the $135 loss be fully deductible? The tax law has an intricate approach to answering these investment activity-related questions.

As you study this chapter, keep in mind that how investment-related gains and losses are taxed can dramatically affect whether taxpayers make investments and which investments are made. Except for a brief discussion in Chapter 3, earlier chapters dwelt on how to determine the amount of gain or loss from a property disposition, but did not discuss the classification of gains and losses. This chapter will focus on that topic.

The tax law requires **capital gains** and **capital losses** to be separated from other types of gains and losses. There are two reasons for this treatment. First, long-term capital gains may be taxed at a lower rate than ordinary gains. The second reason the Code requires separate reporting of gains and losses and a determination of their tax character is that a net capital loss is subject to deduction limitations. For noncorporate taxpayers, a net capital loss is only deductible up to $3,000 per year. Any excess loss over the annual limit carries over and may be deductible in a future tax year.

For these reasons, capital gains and losses must be distinguished from other types of gains and losses. Most of this chapter and the next chapter describe the intricate rules for determining what type of gains and losses the taxpayer has.

As a result of the need to distinguish and separately match capital gains and losses, the individual tax forms include very extensive reporting requirements for capital gains and losses. This chapter explains the principles underlying the forms, which are illustrated with an example at the end of the chapter.

16-1 GENERAL SCHEME OF TAXATION

LO.1

Explain the general scheme of taxation for capital gains and losses.

Recognized gains and losses must be properly classified. Proper classification depends upon three characteristics:

- The tax status of the property.
- The manner of the property's disposition.
- The holding period of the property.

The three possible tax statuses are capital asset, § 1231 asset, and ordinary asset. Property disposition may be by sale, exchange, casualty, theft, or condemnation.

There are two holding periods: short term and long term. The short-term holding period is one year or less. The long-term holding period is more than one year. (More explanation of the holding period is provided later in the chapter.)

The major focus of this chapter is capital gains and losses. Capital gains and losses usually result from the disposition of a capital asset. The most common disposition is a sale of the asset. Capital gains and losses can also result from the disposition of § 1231 assets, which is discussed in Chapter 17.

16-2 CAPITAL ASSETS

LO.2

Distinguish capital assets from ordinary assets.

Personal use assets and investment assets are the most common capital assets owned by individual taxpayers. Personal use assets usually include items such as clothing, recreational equipment, a residence, and automobiles. Investment assets usually include investments in mutual funds, corporate stocks and bonds, government bonds, and vacant land. Remember, however, that losses from the sale or exchange of personal use assets are not recognized. Therefore, the classification of such losses as capital losses can be ignored.

The crux of capital asset determination hinges on whether the asset is held for personal use purposes (capital asset), investment purposes (capital asset), or business purposes (ordinary asset). The taxpayer's use of the property often provides objective evidence.

EXAMPLE

1

David buys an expensive painting.

- If David purchased the painting for personal use (as a decoration in his home) and it is not of investment quality, it is a capital asset; however, any loss on its sale is not usable, whereas gain from its sale is taxable. Investment quality generally means that the painting is expected to appreciate in value.

- If the painting is used to decorate David's business office and is of investment quality, the painting is not depreciable and, therefore, is a capital asset.

- If David's business is buying and selling paintings, the painting is inventory and, therefore, an ordinary asset.

- If the painting is not of investment quality and the business did not purchase it for investment, the painting is an ordinary asset and it is depreciable even though it serves a decorative purpose in David's office.

- If David depreciates the painting, that is objective evidence that the painting is held for use in his business, is not being held for investment or as inventory, and is not a capital asset.

Due to the historical preferential treatment of capital gains, taxpayers have preferred that gains be capital gains rather than ordinary gains. As a result, a great many statutes, cases, and rulings have accumulated in the attempt to define what is and what is not a capital asset.

16-2a **Definition of a Capital Asset (§ 1221)**

Capital assets are not directly defined in the Code. Instead, § 1221(a) defines what is *not* a capital asset. In general, a **capital asset** is property *other than* inventory, accounts and notes receivable, supplies, and most fixed assets of a business.

Specifically, the Code defines a capital asset as property held by the taxpayer (when it is connected with the taxpayer's business) that is *not* any of the following:

- Inventory or property held primarily for sale to customers in the ordinary course of a business. The Supreme Court, in *Malat v. Riddell*, defined *primarily* as meaning "of first importance or principally."[1]

- Accounts and notes receivable acquired from the sale of inventory or acquired for services rendered in the ordinary course of business.

- Depreciable property or real estate used in a business.

- Certain copyrights; literary, musical, or artistic compositions; or letters, memoranda, or similar property held by (1) a taxpayer whose efforts created the property; (2) in the case of a letter, memorandum, or similar property, a taxpayer for whom it was produced; or (3) a taxpayer in whose hands the basis of the property is determined, for purposes of determining gain from a sale or exchange, in whole or in part by reference to the basis of such property in the hands of a taxpayer described in (1) or (2). When a sale or exchange involves musical compositions or copyrights in musical works either (1) created by the taxpayer's personal efforts or (2) having a basis determined by reference to the basis in the hands of a taxpayer whose personal efforts created the compositions or copyrights, the taxpayer may elect to treat the sale or exchange as the disposition of a capital asset.[2]

- U.S. government publications that are (1) received by a taxpayer from the U.S. government other than by purchase at the price at which they are offered for sale to the public or (2) held by a taxpayer whose basis, for purposes of determining gain from a sale or exchange, is determined by reference to a taxpayer described in (1).

- Supplies of a type regularly used or consumed in the ordinary course of a business.

Often, the only business asset that is a capital asset is "self-generated" goodwill (purchased goodwill is a § 1231 asset). The following discussion provides further detail on each part of the capital asset definition.

Inventory

What constitutes inventory is determined by the taxpayer's business.

Inventory Determination

EXAMPLE 2

Green Company buys and sells used cars. Its cars are inventory. Its gains from the sale of the cars are ordinary income.

EXAMPLE 3

Soong sells her personal use automobile at a $500 gain. The automobile is a personal use asset and, therefore, a capital asset. The gain is a capital gain.

No asset is inherently capital or ordinary. If Soong (Example 3) sells her "capital asset" automobile to Green Company (Example 2), that same automobile loses its capital asset status, because it is inventory to Green Company. Whether an asset is capital or ordinary, therefore, depends entirely on the relationship of the asset to the taxpayer who sold it. This classification dilemma is but one feature of capital asset treatment that makes this area so confusing and complicated.

---

[1]66–1 USTC ¶9317, 17 AFTR 2d 604, 86 S.Ct. 1030 (USSC, 1966).   [2]§ 1221(b)(3).

Accounts and Notes Receivable

Collection of an accrual basis account receivable usually does not result in a gain or loss because the amount collected equals the receivable's basis. The sale of an account or note receivable may generate a gain or loss, and the gain or loss is ordinary because the receivable is not a capital asset. The sale of an accrual basis receivable may result in a gain or loss because it will probably be sold for more or less than its basis. A cash basis account receivable has no basis. Sale of such a receivable generates a gain. Collection of a cash basis receivable generates ordinary income rather than a gain. A gain usually requires a sale of the receivable. See the discussion of Sale or Exchange later in this chapter.

EXAMPLE 4

Oriole Company has accounts receivable of $100,000. Because Oriole needs working capital, it sells the receivables for $83,000 to a financial institution.

If Oriole is an *accrual basis taxpayer*, it has a $17,000 ordinary loss. Revenue of $100,000 would have been recorded, and a $100,000 basis would have been established when the receivable was created.

If Oriole is a *cash basis taxpayer*, it has $83,000 of ordinary income because it would not have recorded any revenue earlier; thus, the receivable has no tax basis.

Business Fixed Assets

Depreciable personal property and real estate (both depreciable and nondepreciable) used by a business are not capital assets. Thus, *business fixed assets* are generally not capital assets.

The Code has a very complex set of rules related to this property. One of these rules is discussed later in the chapter [Real Property Subdivided for Sale (§ 1237)]; the remainder of the rules are discussed in Chapter 17. Although business fixed assets are not capital assets, a long-term capital gain can sometimes result from their sale. Chapter 17 discusses the potential capital gain treatment for business fixed assets under § 1231.

Copyrights and Creative Works

Generally, the person whose efforts led to the copyright or creative work has an ordinary asset, not a capital asset. *Creative works* include the works of authors, composers, and artists. Also, the person for whom a letter, a memorandum, or another similar property was created has an ordinary asset. Finally, a person receiving a copyright, creative work, a letter, a memorandum, or similar property by gift from the creator or the person for whom the work was created has an ordinary asset. As mentioned earlier, a taxpayer may elect to treat the sale or exchange of a musical composition or a copyright of a musical work as the disposition of a capital asset. (Patents are subject to special statutory rules discussed later in the chapter.)

Creative Works

EXAMPLE 5

Wanda is a part-time music composer. A music publisher purchases one of her songs for $5,000.

Wanda has a $5,000 ordinary gain from the sale of an ordinary asset unless she elects to treat the gain as a capital gain.

Creative Works

EXAMPLE

6

Ed received a letter from the President of the United States in 1982. In the current year, Ed sells the letter to a collector for $300.

Ed has a $300 ordinary gain from the sale of an ordinary asset (because the letter was created for Ed).

EXAMPLE

7

Isabella gives her son a song she composed. The son sells the song to a music publisher for $5,000.

The son has a $5,000 ordinary gain from the sale of an ordinary asset unless he elects to treat the gain as a capital gain.

If the son inherits the song from Isabella, his basis for the song is its fair market value at Isabella's death. In this situation, the song is a capital asset because the son's basis is not related to Isabella's basis for the song.

ETHICS & EQUITY   Sculpture as a Capital Asset

Cynthia is a successful sculptor who created a work that is now worth $400,000 and has no tax basis. Cynthia forms a corporation and contributes the sculpture to it in exchange for the corporation's shares. Fourteen months later, she sells all the stock for $400,000. She wants to treat the sale of the stock as a long-term capital gain. Evaluate the propriety of Cynthia's actions.

U.S. Government Publications

U.S. government publications received from the U.S. government (or its agencies) for a reduced price are *not* capital assets. This prevents a taxpayer from later donating the publications to charity and claiming a charitable contribution equal to the fair market value of the publications. A charitable contribution of a capital asset generally yields a deduction equal to the fair market value. A charitable contribution of an ordinary asset generally yields a deduction equal to less than the fair market value. If such property is received by gift from the original purchaser, the property is not a capital asset to the donee. (For a more comprehensive explanation of charitable contributions of property, refer to Chapter 10.)

16-2b **Effect of Judicial Action**

Court decisions play an important role in the definition of capital assets. Because the Code only lists categories of what are *not* capital assets, judicial interpretation is sometimes required to determine whether a specific item fits into one of those categories. The Supreme Court follows a literal interpretation of the categories. For instance, corporate stock is not mentioned in § 1221. Thus, corporate stock is *usually* a capital asset. However, what if corporate stock is purchased for resale to customers? Then it is *inventory* and not a capital asset because inventory is one of the categories in § 1221. (See the discussion of Dealers in Securities that follows.)

A Supreme Court decision was required to distinguish between capital asset and non-capital asset status when a taxpayer who normally did not acquire stock for resale to customers acquired stock with the intention of resale.[3] The Court decided that because the stock was not acquired primarily for sale to customers (the taxpayer did not sell the stock to its regular customers), the stock was a capital asset.

Because of the uncertainty associated with capital asset status, Congress has enacted several Code Sections to clarify the definition. These statutory expansions of the capital asset definition are discussed in the following section.

---

[3]*Arkansas Best v. Comm.*, 88–1 USTC ¶9210, 61 AFTR 2d 88–655, 108 S.Ct. 971 (USSC, 1988).

16-2c **Statutory Expansions**

Congress has often expanded the § 1221 general definition of what is *not* a capital asset.

Dealers in Securities

As a general rule, securities (stocks, bonds, and other financial instruments) held by a dealer are considered to be inventory and are, therefore, not subject to capital gain or loss treatment. A *dealer in securities* is a merchant (e.g., a brokerage firm) that regularly engages in the purchase and resale of securities to customers. The dealer must identify any securities being held for investment. Generally, if a dealer clearly identifies certain securities as held for investment purposes by the close of business on the acquisition date, gain from the securities' sale will be capital gain. However, the gain will not be capital gain if the dealer ceases to hold the securities for investment prior to the sale. Losses are capital losses if at any time the securities have been clearly identified by the dealer as held for investment.

EXAMPLE
8

Tracy is a securities dealer. She purchases 100 shares of Swan stock. If Tracy takes no further action, the stock is inventory and an ordinary asset. If she designates in her records that the stock is held for investment, the stock is a capital asset. Tracy must designate the investment purpose by the close of business on the acquisition date. If Tracy maintains her investment purpose and later sells the stock, the gain or loss is capital gain or loss. If Tracy redesignates the stock as held for resale (inventory) and then sells it, any gain is ordinary, but any loss is capital loss.

Real Property Subdivided for Sale (§ 1237)

Substantial real property development activities may result in the owner being considered a dealer for tax purposes. Income from the sale of real estate property lots is treated as the sale of inventory (ordinary income) if the owner is considered to be a dealer. However, § 1237 allows real estate investors capital gain treatment if they engage *only* in *limited* development activities. To be eligible for § 1237 treatment, the following requirements must be met:

- The taxpayer may not be a corporation.
- The taxpayer may not be a real estate dealer.
- No substantial improvements may be made to the lots sold. *Substantial* generally means more than a 10 percent increase in the value of a lot. Shopping centers and other commercial or residential buildings are considered substantial, while filling, draining, leveling, and clearing operations are not.
- The taxpayer must have held the lots sold for at least 5 years, except for inherited property. The substantial improvements test is less stringent if the property is held at least 10 years.

If the preceding requirements are met, all gain is capital gain until the tax year in which the *sixth* lot is sold. Sales of contiguous lots to a single buyer in the same transaction count as the sale of one lot. Beginning with the tax year the *sixth* lot is sold, some of the gain may be ordinary income. Five percent of the revenue from lot sales is potential ordinary income. That potential ordinary income is offset by any selling expenses from the lot sales. Practically, sales commissions often are at least 5 percent of the sales price, so none of the gain is treated as ordinary income.

Section 1237 does not apply to losses. A loss from the sale of subdivided real property is an ordinary loss unless the property qualifies as a capital asset under § 1221. The following example illustrates the application of § 1237.

EXAMPLE

9

Jack owns a large tract of land and subdivides it for sale. Assume that Jack meets all of the requirements of § 1237 and during the tax year sells the first 10 lots to 10 different buyers for $10,000 each. Jack's basis in each lot sold is $3,000, and he incurs total selling expenses of $4,000 on the sales. Jack's gain is computed as follows:

Selling price (10 × $10,000)	$100,000	
Less: Selling expenses (10 × $400)	(4,000)	
Amount realized		$ 96,000
Basis (10 × $3,000)		(30,000)
Realized and recognized gain		$ 66,000
Classification of recognized gain:		
Ordinary income		
Five percent of selling price (5% × $100,000)	$ 5,000	
Less: Selling expenses	(4,000)	
Ordinary gain		1,000
Capital gain		$ 65,000

A portion of the gain is given ordinary treatment because the *sixth* lot is sold in the current year.

Nonbusiness Bad Debts

A loan not made in the ordinary course of business is classified as a nonbusiness receivable. In the year the receivable becomes completely worthless, it is a *nonbusiness bad debt*, and the bad debt is treated as a short-term capital loss. Even if the receivable was outstanding for more than one year, the loss is still a short-term capital loss. Chapter 7 discusses nonbusiness bad debts more thoroughly.

LO.3

State and explain the relevance of a sale or exchange to classification as a capital gain or loss and apply the special rules for the capital gain or loss treatment of the retirement of corporate obligations, options, patents, franchises, and lease cancellation payments.

16-3 SALE OR EXCHANGE

Recognition of capital gain or loss usually requires a sale or exchange of a capital asset. The Code uses the term **sale or exchange**, but does not define it. Generally, a property sale involves the receipt of money by the seller and/or the assumption by the purchaser of the seller's liabilities. An exchange involves the transfer of property for other property. Thus, an involuntary conversion (casualty, theft, or condemnation) is not a sale or exchange. In several situations, the determination of whether a sale or exchange has taken place has been clarified by the enactment of Code Sections that specifically provide for sale or exchange treatment.

Recognized gains or losses from the cancellation, lapse, expiration, or any other termination of a right or an obligation with respect to personal property (other than stock) that is or would be a capital asset in the hands of the taxpayer are capital gains or losses.[4] See the discussion under Options later in the chapter for more details.

16-3a Worthless Securities and § 1244 Stock

Occasionally, securities such as stock and, especially, bonds may become worthless due to the insolvency of their issuer. If such a security is a capital asset, the loss is deemed to have occurred as the result of a sale or exchange on the *last day* of the tax year.[5] This last-day rule may have the effect of converting what otherwise would have been a short-term capital loss into a long-term capital loss. (See Treatment of Net Capital Losses later in this chapter.) Worthless securities are discussed in text Section 7-2a.

Section 1244 allows an ordinary deduction on disposition of stock at a loss. The stock must be that of a small business corporation, and the ordinary deduction is limited to $50,000 ($100,000 for married taxpayers filing jointly) per year. For a more detailed discussion, refer to text Section 7-2b.

---

[4]§ 1234A.   [5]§ 165(g)(1).

During 2009, General Motors went into bankruptcy, was reorganized, and emerged from bankruptcy. However, the common shareholders of the General Motors that went into bankruptcy were not the common shareholders of the General Motors that emerged from bankruptcy. The original common shareholders lost their entire investment because their stock became worthless. The holding period of their stock ended for tax purposes on December 31, 2009, because of the worthless stock rules. They had a capital loss equal to whatever their basis was for the worthless shares. The debtors of General Motors accepted common shares in the General Motors that emerged from bankruptcy. Generally, the exchange of debt for common shares in a bankruptcy reorganization is not a taxable transaction, and the basis of the debt becomes the basis for the shares.

16-3b **Special Rule—Retirement of Corporate Obligations**

A debt obligation (e.g., a bond or note payable) may have a tax basis in excess of or less than its redemption value because it may have been acquired at a premium or discount. Consequently, the collection of the redemption value may result in a loss or gain. Generally, the collection of a debt obligation is *treated* as a sale or exchange.[6] Therefore, any loss or gain can be a capital loss or capital gain because a sale or exchange has taken place.

Fran acquires $1,000 of Osprey Corporation bonds for $980 in the open market. If the bonds are held to maturity, the $20 difference between Fran's collection of the $1,000 redemption value and her cost of $980 is treated as capital gain.

EXAMPLE
10

Original Issue Discount (§§ 1272–1288)

The benefit of the sale or exchange exception that allows a capital gain from the collection of certain obligations is reduced when the obligation has original issue discount. **Original issue discount (OID)** arises when the issue price of a debt obligation is less than the maturity value of the obligation. OID must generally be amortized over the life of the debt obligation using the effective interest method. The OID amortization increases the basis of the bond. Most new publicly traded bond issues do not carry OID because the stated interest rate is set to make the market price on issue the same as the bond's face amount. In addition, even if the issue price is less than the face amount, the difference is not considered to be OID if the difference is less than one-fourth of 1 percent of the redemption price at maturity multiplied by the number of years to maturity.[7]

In the case where OID does exist, it may or may not have to be amortized, depending upon the date the obligation was issued. When OID is amortized, the amount of gain upon collection, sale, or exchange of the obligation is correspondingly reduced. The obligations covered by the OID amortization rules and the method of amortization are presented in §§ 1272–1275. Similar rules for other obligations can be found in §§ 1276–1288.

Jerry purchases $10,000 of newly issued White Corporation bonds for $6,000. The bonds have OID of $4,000. Jerry must amortize the discount over the life of the bonds. The OID amortization *increases* his interest income. (The bonds were selling at a discount because the market rate of interest was greater than the bonds' stated interest rate.) After Jerry has amortized $1,800 of OID, he sells the bonds for $8,000. Jerry has a capital gain of $200 [$8,000 − ($6,000 cost + $1,800 OID amortization)].

The OID amortization rules prevent him from converting ordinary interest income into capital gain. Without the OID amortization, Jerry would have capital gain of $2,000 ($8,000 − $6,000 cost).

EXAMPLE
11

---

[6]§ 1271.

[7]§ 1273(a)(3).

16-3c **Options**

Frequently, a potential buyer of property wants some time to make the purchase decision, but wants to control the sale and/or the sale price in the meantime. **Options** are used to achieve these objectives. The potential purchaser (grantee) pays the property owner (grantor) for an option on the property. The grantee then becomes the option holder. The option, which usually sets a price at which the grantee can buy the property, expires after a specified period of time.

Sale of an Option

A grantee may sell or exchange the option rather than exercising it or letting it expire. Generally, the grantee's sale or exchange of the option results in capital gain or loss if the option property is (or would be) a capital asset to the grantee.[8]

EXAMPLE 12

Rosa wants to buy some vacant land for investment purposes. She cannot afford the full purchase price. Instead, Rosa (grantee) pays the landowner (grantor) $3,000 to obtain an option to buy the land for $100,000 anytime in the next two years. The option is a capital asset for Rosa because if she actually purchased the land, the land would be a capital asset.

Three months after purchasing the option, Rosa sells it for $7,000. She has a $4,000 ($7,000 − $3,000) short-term capital gain on this sale because she held the option for one year or less.

Failure to Exercise Options

If an option holder (grantee) fails to exercise the option, the lapse of the option is considered a sale or exchange on the option expiration date. Thus, the loss is a capital loss if the property subject to the option is (or would be) a capital asset in the hands of the grantee.

The grantor of an option on *stocks, securities, commodities, or commodity futures* receives short-term capital gain treatment upon the expiration of the option. Options on property *other than* stocks, securities, commodities, or commodity futures (for instance, vacant land) result in ordinary income to the grantor when the option expires. For example, an individual investor who owns certain stock (a capital asset) may sell a call option, entitling the buyer of the option to acquire the stock at a specified price higher than the value at the date the option is granted. The writer of the call receives a premium (e.g., 10 percent) for writing the option. If the price of the stock does not increase during the option period, the option will expire unexercised. Upon the expiration of the option, the grantor must recognize short-term capital gain (whereas the grantee recognizes a loss, the character of which depends on the underlying asset). These provisions do not apply to options held for sale to customers (the inventory of a securities dealer).

Exercise of Options by Grantee

If the option is exercised, the amount paid for the option is added to the optioned property's selling price. This increases the gain (or reduces the loss) to the grantor resulting from the sale of the property. The grantor's gain or loss is capital or ordinary depending on the tax status of the property. The grantee adds the cost of the option to the basis of the property purchased.

---

[8]§ 1234(a) and Reg. § 1.1234–1(a)(1). Stock options are discussed in Chapter 19.

The Big Picture

EXAMPLE
13

Return to the facts of *The Big Picture* on p. 16-1. On February 1, 2016, Maurice purchases 100 shares of Eagle Company stock for $5,000. On April 1, 2016, he writes a call option on the stock, giving the grantee the right to buy the stock for $6,000 during the following six-month period. Maurice (the grantor) receives a call premium of $500 for writing the call.

- If the call is exercised by the grantee on August 1, 2016, Maurice has $1,500 ($6,000 + $500 − $5,000) of short-term capital gain from the sale of the stock. The grantee has a $6,500 ($500 option premium + $6,000 purchase price) basis for the stock.
- Investors sometimes get nervous and want to "lock in" gains or losses.
  - Assume that Maurice, prior to exercise of the grantee's call, decides to sell his stock for $6,000 and enters into a closing transaction by purchasing a call on 100 shares of Eagle Company stock for $5,000.
  - Because the Eagle stock is selling for $6,000, Maurice must pay a call premium of $1,000.
  - He recognizes a $500 short-term capital loss [$500 (call premium received) − $1,000 (call premium paid)] on the closing transaction.
  - On the actual sale of the Eagle stock, Maurice has a short-term capital gain of $1,000 [$6,000 (selling price) − $5,000 (cost)].
  - The original grantee is not affected by Maurice's closing transaction. The original option is still in existence, and the grantee's tax consequences depend on what action the grantee takes—exercising the option, letting the option expire, or selling the option.
- Assume that the original option expired unexercised. Maurice has a $500 short-term capital gain equal to the call premium received for writing the option. This gain is not recognized until the option expires. The grantee has a loss from expiration of the option. The nature of the loss will depend upon whether the option was a capital asset or an ordinary asset.

Concept Summary 16.1 summarizes the consequences of various transactions involving options, to both the grantor and grantee.

Concept Summary 16.1

Options: Consequences to the Grantor and Grantee

	Effect on	
Event	**Grantor**	**Grantee**
Option is granted.	Receives value and has a contract obligation (a liability).	Pays value and has a contract right (an asset).
Option expires.	Has a short-term capital gain if the option property is stocks, securities, commodities, or commodity futures. Otherwise, gain is ordinary income.	Has a loss (capital loss if option property would have been a capital asset for the grantee).
Option is exercised.	Amount received for option increases proceeds from sale of the option property.	Amount paid for option becomes part of the basis of the option property purchased.
Option is sold or exchanged by grantee.	Result depends upon whether option later expires or is exercised (see above).	Could have gain or loss (capital gain or loss if option property would have been a capital asset for the grantee).

16-3d Patents

Transfer of a **patent** is treated as the sale or exchange of a long-term capital asset when *all substantial rights* to the patent (or an undivided interest that includes all such rights) are transferred by a *holder*.[9] The transferor/holder may receive payment in virtually any form. Lump-sum or periodic payments are most common. The amount of the payments may also

---

[9]§ 1235.

be contingent on the transferee/purchaser's productivity, use, or disposition of the patent. If the transfer meets these requirements, any gain or loss is *automatically a long-term* capital gain or loss. Whether the asset was a capital asset for the transferor, whether a sale or exchange occurred, and how long the transferor held the patent are not relevant.

Copyrights for authors, composers, and artists are not capital assets, as discussed earlier. Example 14 illustrates the special treatment for patents.

Substantial Rights

As noted previously, to receive favorable capital gain treatment, *all substantial rights* to the patent (or an undivided interest in it) must be transferred. All substantial rights to a patent means all rights (whether then held by the grantor) that are valuable at the time the patent rights (or an undivided interest in the patent) are transferred. All substantial rights have not been transferred when the transfer is limited geographically within the issuing country or when the transfer is for a period less than the remaining life of the patent. The circumstances of the entire transaction, rather than merely the language used in the transfer instrument, are to be considered in deciding whether all substantial rights have been transferred.[10]

The Big Picture

EXAMPLE 14

Return to the facts of *The Big Picture* on p. 16-1. Kevin transfers his remaining 50% share of the rights in the patent to the Green Battery Company, Inc., in exchange for a $1 million lump-sum payment plus $.50 for each battery sold. Assuming that Kevin has transferred all substantial rights, the question of whether the transfer is a sale or exchange of a capital asset is not relevant. Kevin automatically has a long-term capital gain from both the $1 million lump-sum payment and the $.50 per battery royalty to the extent those proceeds exceed his basis for the patent.

Kevin also had an automatic long-term capital gain when he sold the other 50% of his rights in the patent to Maurice, because Kevin transferred an undivided interest that included all substantial rights in the patent.

Whether Maurice gets long-term capital gain treatment depends upon whether Maurice is a holder. See the following discussion and Example 15.

Holder Defined

The *holder* of a patent must be an *individual* and is usually the invention's creator. A holder may also be an individual who purchases the patent rights from the creator before the patented invention is reduced to practice. However, the creator's employer and certain parties related to the creator do not qualify as holders. Thus, in the common situation where an employer has all rights to an employee's inventions, the employer is not eligible for long-term capital gain treatment. More than likely, the employer will have an ordinary asset because the patent was developed as part of its business.

The Big Picture

EXAMPLE 15

Return to the facts of *The Big Picture* on p. 16-1. Continuing with the facts of Example 14, Kevin is clearly a holder of the patent because he is the inventor and was not an employee when he invented the battery. When Maurice purchased a 50% interest in the patent nine months ago, he became a holder if the patent had not yet been reduced to practice. Because the patent apparently was not being utilized in the manufacturing process at the time of the purchase, it had not been reduced to practice.

Consequently, Maurice is also a holder, and he has an automatic long-term capital gain or loss if he transfers all substantial rights in his 50% interest to the Green Battery Company. Maurice's basis for his share of the patent is $50,000, and his proceeds equal $1 million plus $.50 for each battery sold. Thus, Maurice has a long-term capital gain even though he has not held his interest in the patent for more than one year.

---

[10]Reg. § 1.1235–2(b)(1).

16-3e Franchises, Trademarks, and Trade Names (§ 1253)

A mode of operation, a widely recognized brand name (trade name), and a widely known business symbol (trademark) are all valuable assets. These assets may be licensed (commonly known as franchising) by their owner for use by other businesses. Many fast-food restaurants (such as McDonald's and Taco Bell) are franchises. The franchisee usually pays the owner (franchisor) an initial fee plus a contingent fee. The contingent fee is often based upon the franchisee's sales volume.

For Federal income tax purposes, a **franchise** is an agreement that gives the franchisee the right to distribute, sell, or provide goods, services, or facilities within a specified area.[11] A franchise transfer includes the grant of a franchise, a transfer by one franchisee to another person, or the renewal of a franchise.

Section 1253 provides that a transfer of a franchise, trademark, or trade name is not a transfer of a capital asset when the transferor retains any significant power, right, or continuing interest in the property transferred.

Significant Power, Right, or Continuing Interest

Significant powers, rights, or continuing interests include control over assignment, quality of products and services, sale or advertising of other products or services, and the right to require that substantially all supplies and equipment be purchased from the transferor. Also included are the right to terminate the franchise at will and the right to substantial contingent payments. Most franchising operations involve some or all of these powers, rights, or continuing interests.

In the unusual case where no significant power, right, or continuing interest is retained by the transferor, a sale or exchange may occur, and capital gain or loss treatment may be available. For capital gain or loss treatment to be available, the asset transferred must qualify as a capital asset.

The Big Picture

EXAMPLE 16

Return to the facts of *The Big Picture* on p. 16-1. Maurice sells for $210,000 to Mauve, Inc., the franchise purchased from Orange, Inc., nine months ago. The $210,000 received by Maurice is not contingent, and all significant powers, rights, and continuing interests are transferred.

The $115,000 gain ($210,000 proceeds − $95,000 adjusted basis) is a short-term capital gain because Maurice has held the franchise for only nine months.

Noncontingent Payments

When the transferor retains a significant power, right, or continuing interest, the transferee's noncontingent payments to the transferor are ordinary income to the transferor. The franchisee capitalizes the payments and amortizes them over 15 years. If the franchise is sold, the amortization is subject to recapture under § 1245.[12]

EXAMPLE 17

Grey Company signs a 10-year franchise agreement with DOH Donuts. Grey (the franchisee) makes payments of $3,000 per year for the first 8 years of the franchise agreement—a total of $24,000. Grey cannot deduct $3,000 per year as the payments are made. Instead, Grey may amortize the $24,000 total over 15 years. Thus, Grey may deduct $1,600 per year for each of the 15 years of the amortization period.

The same result would occur if Grey made a $24,000 lump-sum payment at the beginning of the franchise period. Assuming that DOH Donuts (the franchisor) retains significant powers, rights, or a continuing interest, it will have ordinary income when it receives the payments from Grey.

---

[11]§ 1253(b)(1).

[12]See Chapter 17 for a discussion of the recapture provisions.

Contingent Payments

The contingent franchise payments are ordinary income for the franchisor and an ordinary deduction for the franchisee when the transferor retains a significant power, right, or continuing interest. For this purpose, a payment qualifies as a contingent payment only if the following requirements are met:

- The contingent amounts are part of a series of payments that are paid at least annually throughout the term of the transfer agreement.
- The payments are substantially equal in amount or are payable under a fixed formula.

EXAMPLE 18

TAK, a spicy chicken franchisor, transfers an eight-year franchise to Otis. TAK retains a significant power, right, or continuing interest. Otis, the franchisee, agrees to pay TAK 15% of sales. This contingent payment is ordinary income to TAK and a business deduction for Otis as the payments are made.

Sports Franchises

Professional sports franchises (e.g., the Detroit Tigers) are subject to § 1253.[13] Player contracts are usually one of the major assets acquired with a sports franchise. These contracts last only for the time stated in the contract. By being classified as § 197 intangibles, the player contracts and other intangible assets acquired in the purchase of the sports franchise are amortized over a statutory 15-year period.[14]

Concept Summary 16.2 reviews the effects of transactions involving franchises on both the franchisor and franchisee.

Concept Summary 16.2

Franchises: Consequences to the Franchisor and Franchisee

Event	Effect on	
	Franchisor	**Franchisee**
Franchisor Retains Significant Powers and Rights		
Noncontingent payment	Ordinary income.	Capitalized and amortized over 15 years as an ordinary deduction; if franchise is sold, amortization is subject to recapture under § 1245.
Contingent payment	Ordinary income.	Ordinary deduction.
Franchisor Does *Not* Retain Significant Powers and Rights		
Noncontingent payment	Ordinary income if franchise rights are an ordinary asset; capital gain if franchise rights are a capital asset (unlikely).	Capitalized and amortized over 15 years as an ordinary deduction; if the franchise is sold, amortization is subject to recapture under § 1245.
Contingent payment	Ordinary income.	Ordinary deduction.

16-3f Lease Cancellation Payments

The tax treatment of payments received for canceling a lease depends on whether the recipient is the **lessor** or the **lessee** and whether the lease is a capital asset.

---

[13]Section 1253(e) previously exempted sports franchises from § 1253, but was repealed for franchises acquired after October 22, 2004.   [14]§ 197(a).

Lessee Treatment

Lease cancellation payments received by a lessee are treated as an exchange.[15] Thus, these payments are capital gains if the lease is a capital asset. Generally, a lessee's lease is a capital asset if the property (either personalty or realty) is used for the lessee's personal use (e.g., his or her residence). A lessee's lease is an ordinary asset if the property is used in the lessee's trade or business and the lease has existed for one year or less when it is canceled. A lessee's lease is a § 1231 asset if the property is used in the lessee's trade or business and the lease has existed for more than a year when it is canceled.[16]

Mark owns an apartment building that he is going to convert into an office building. Vicki is one of the apartment tenants and receives $1,000 from Mark to cancel the lease.

Vicki has a capital gain of $1,000 (which is long term or short term depending upon how long she has held the lease). Mark has an ordinary deduction of $1,000.

Lessor Treatment

Payments received by a lessor for a lease cancellation are always ordinary income because they are considered to be in lieu of rental payments.[17]

Floyd owns an apartment building near a university campus. Hui-Fen is one of the tenants. Hui-Fen is graduating early and offers Floyd $800 to cancel the apartment lease. Floyd accepts the offer.

Floyd has ordinary income of $800. Hui-Fen has a nondeductible payment because the apartment was personal use property.

16-4 HOLDING PERIOD

LO.4

Determine whether the holding period for a capital asset is long term or short term.

Property must be held more than one year to qualify for long-term capital gain or loss treatment.[18] Property not held for the required long-term period results in short-term capital gain or loss. To compute the **holding period**, start counting on the day after the property was acquired and include the day of disposition.

The Big Picture

Return to the facts of *The Big Picture* on p. 16-1. Assume that Maurice purchased the Purple stock on January 15, 2015. If he sells it on January 16, 2016, Maurice's holding period is more than one year and the gain or loss is long term.

If instead Maurice sells the stock on January 15, 2016, the holding period is exactly one year and the gain or loss is short term.

To be held for more than one year, a capital asset acquired on the last day of any month must not be disposed of until on or after the first day of the thirteenth succeeding month.[19]

Leo purchases a capital asset on February 28, 2015. If Leo sells the asset on February 29, 2016, the holding period is one year and Leo will have a short-term capital gain or loss.

If Leo sells the asset on March 1, 2016, the holding period is more than one year and he will have a long-term capital gain or loss.

---

[15]§ 1241 and Reg. § 1.1241–1(a).
[16]Reg. § 1.1221–1(b) and PLR 200045019.
[17]Reg. § 1.61–8(b).

[18]§ 1222(3).
[19]Rev.Rul. 66–7, 1966–1 C.B. 188.

16-4a **Review of Special Holding Period Rules**

There are several special holding period rules.[20] The application of these rules depends upon the type of asset and how it was acquired.

Nontaxable Exchanges

The holding period of property received in a like-kind exchange includes the holding period of the former asset if the property that has been exchanged is a capital asset or a § 1231 asset. In certain nontaxable transactions involving a substituted basis, the holding period of the former property is *tacked on* to the holding period of the newly acquired property.

> **EXAMPLE 23**
>
> On April 22, 2016, Vern exchanges a business truck he acquired on March 15, 2013, for another truck in a qualifying like-kind exchange.
>
> The holding period of the replacement truck begins March 15, 2013, because the holding period of the truck given up in the exchange *tacks* to the holding period of the replacement truck.

Certain Nontaxable Transactions Involving a Carryover of Another Taxpayer's Basis

FMV > Donee's Basis

If a transaction is nontaxable and the former owner's basis carries over to the present owner (e.g., a gift), the former owner's holding period is included in ("tacked on" to) the present owner's holding period. A donor's adjusted basis carries over to the donee when the property's fair market value at the date of the gift is greater than the donor's adjusted basis. These transactions are discussed in Chapter 14.

> **Carryover Basis**
>
> **EXAMPLE 24**
>
> Kareem acquires 100 shares of Robin Corporation stock for $1,000 on December 31, 2012. He transfers the shares by gift to Megan on December 31, 2015, when the stock is worth $2,000. Kareem's basis of $1,000 becomes the basis for determining gain or loss on a subsequent sale by Megan. Megan's holding period begins with the date the stock was acquired by Kareem.

> **EXAMPLE 25**
>
> Assume the same facts as in Example 24, except that the fair market value of the shares is only $800 on the date of the gift. The holding period begins on the date of the gift if Megan sells the stock for a loss. The value of the shares on the date of the gift is used in the determination of her basis for loss. If she sells the shares for $500 on April 1, 2016, Megan has a $300 recognized capital loss and the holding period is from December 31, 2015, to April 1, 2016 (thus, the loss is short term).

Certain Disallowed Loss Transactions

Under several Code provisions, realized losses are disallowed. When a loss is disallowed, there is no carryover of holding period. Losses can be disallowed under § 267 (sale or exchange between related taxpayers) and § 262 (sale or exchange of personal use assets) as well as other Code Sections. Taxpayers who acquire property in a disallowed loss transaction will have a new holding period begin and will have a basis equal to the purchase price.

> **EXAMPLE 26**
>
> Janet sells her personal automobile at a loss. She may not deduct the loss because it arises from the sale of personal use property. Janet purchases a replacement automobile for more than the selling price of her former automobile. Janet has a basis equal to the cost of the replacement automobile, and her holding period begins when she acquires the replacement automobile.

---

[20]§ 1223.

Inherited Property

The holding period for inherited property is treated as long term no matter how long the property is actually held by the heir. The holding period of the decedent or the decedent's estate is not relevant for the heir's holding period.

Shonda inherits Blue Company stock from her father, who died in 2016. She receives the stock on April 1, 2016, and sells it on November 1, 2016. Even though Shonda did not hold the stock more than one year, she receives long-term capital gain or loss treatment on the sale.

EXAMPLE
27

16-4b Special Rules for Short Sales

General

The Code provides special rules for determining the holding period of property sold short.[21] A **short sale** occurs when a taxpayer sells borrowed property and repays the lender with substantially identical property either held on the date of the sale or purchased after the sale. Short sales usually involve corporate stock. The seller's objective is to make a profit in anticipation of a decline in the stock's price. If the price declines, the seller in a short sale recognizes a profit equal to the difference between the sales price of the borrowed stock and the price paid for the replacement stock.

EXAMPLE
28

Chris does not own any shares of Brown Corporation. However, Chris sells 30 shares of Brown. The shares are borrowed from Chris's broker and must be replaced within 45 days. Chris has a short sale because he was short the shares he sold. He will *close* the short sale by purchasing Brown shares and delivering them to his broker.

   If the original 30 shares were sold for $10,000 and Chris later purchases 30 shares for $8,000, he has a gain of $2,000. Chris's hunch that the price of Brown stock would decline was correct. Chris was able to profit from selling high and buying low.

   If Chris had to purchase Brown shares for $13,000 to close the short sale, he would have a loss of $3,000. In this case, Chris would have sold low and bought high—not the result he wanted. Chris would be making a short sale against the box if he borrowed shares from his broker to sell and then closed the short sale by delivering other Brown shares he owned at the time he made the short sale.

A short sale gain or loss is a capital gain or loss to the extent that the short sale property constitutes a capital asset of the taxpayer. The gain or loss is not recognized until the short sale is closed. Generally, the holding period of the short sale property is determined by how long the property used to close the short sale was held. However, when *substantially identical property* (e.g., other shares of the same stock) is held by the taxpayer, the holding period is determined as follows:

- The short sale *gain or loss* is *short term* when, on the short sale date, the substantially identical property has been held *short term* (i.e., for one year or less). (See Examples 29 and 30.)
- The short sale *gain* is *long term* when, on the short sale date, the substantially identical property has been held *long term* (i.e., for more than one year) *and* is used to close the short sale. If the long-term substantially identical property is not used to close the short sale, the short sale gain is *short term*. (See Example 31.)
- The short sale *loss* is *long term* when, on the short sale date, the substantially identical property has been held *long term* (i.e., for more than one year).
- The short sale *gain or loss* is *short term* if the substantially identical property is acquired *after* the short sale date and on or before the closing date. (See Example 32.)

---

[21]§ 1233.

Concept Summary 16.3 summarizes the short sale rules. These rules are intended to prevent the conversion of short-term capital gains into long-term capital gains and long-term capital losses into short-term capital losses.

Concept Summary 16.3

Short Sales of Securities

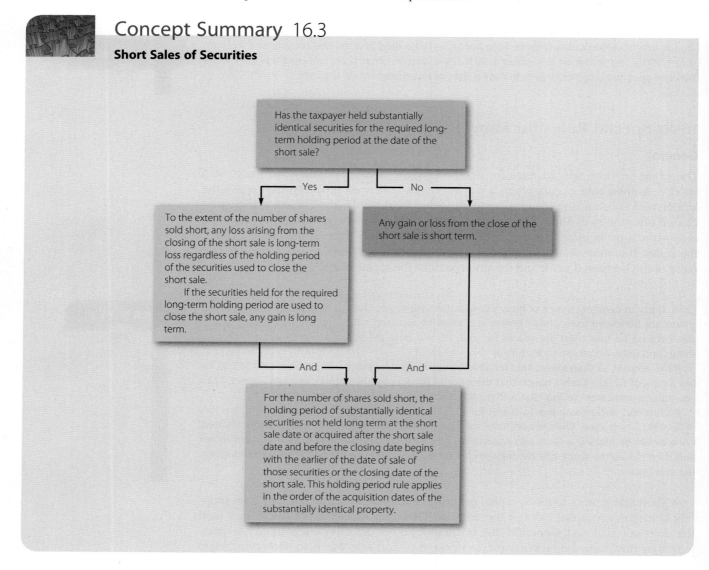

Has the taxpayer held substantially identical securities for the required long-term holding period at the date of the short sale?

Yes — To the extent of the number of shares sold short, any loss arising from the closing of the short sale is long-term loss regardless of the holding period of the securities used to close the short sale.

If the securities held for the required long-term holding period are used to close the short sale, any gain is long term.

No — Any gain or loss from the close of the short sale is short term.

And — For the number of shares sold short, the holding period of substantially identical securities not held long term at the short sale date or acquired after the short sale date and before the closing date begins with the earlier of the date of sale of those securities or the closing date of the short sale. This holding period rule applies in the order of the acquisition dates of the substantially identical property.

Disposition Rules for Short Sales against the Box

A *short sale against the box* occurs when the stock is borrowed from a broker by a seller and the seller already owns the substantially identical securities on the short sale date or acquires them before the closing date.[22] To remove the taxpayer's flexibility as to when the short sale gain must be reported, a constructive sale approach is used. If the taxpayer has not closed the short sale by delivering the short sale securities to the broker *before* January 31 of the year following the short sale, the short sale is deemed to have been closed on the *earlier* of two events:

- On the short sale date if the taxpayer owned substantially identical securities at that time.
- On the date during the year of the short sale that the taxpayer acquired substantially identical securities.[23]

---

[22]The "box" is the safe deposit box stock owners routinely used to keep stock certificates. Although stockbrokers today generally keep stock for their customers, the terminology *short sale against the box* is still used.

[23]§ 1259.

The basis of the shares in the deemed transfer of shares is used to compute the gain or loss on the short sale. As Examples 31 and 32 illustrate, when shares are *actually* transferred to the broker to close the short sale, there may be a gain or loss because the shares transferred will have a basis equal to the short sale date price and the value at the *actual* short sale closing date may be different from the short sale date price.

Illustrations

The following examples illustrate the treatment of short sales and short sales against the box.

Short Sales and Short Sales Against the Box

On January 4, 2016, Donald purchases five shares of Osprey Corporation common stock for $100. On April 14, 2016, he engages in a short sale of five shares of the same stock for $150. On August 15, Donald closes the short sale by repaying the borrowed stock with the five shares purchased on January 4. Because his substantially identical shares were held short term as of the short sale date, Donald's $50 capital gain is short term.

EXAMPLE 29

Assume the same facts as in the previous example, except that Donald closes the short sale on January 28, 2017, by repaying the borrowed stock with five shares purchased on January 27, 2017, for $200. Because Donald's substantially identical property (purchased on January 4, 2016) was short-term property at the April 14, 2016 short sale date, his $50 capital loss ($200 cost of stock purchased on January 27, 2017, and a short sale selling price of $150) is short term.

EXAMPLE 30

On January 18, 2015, Rita purchases 200 shares of Owl Corporation stock for $1,000. On November 11, 2016, she sells short, for $1,300, 200 shares of Owl Corporation stock that she borrows from her broker. On February 10, 2017, Rita closes the short sale by delivering the 200 shares of Owl Corporation stock that she had acquired in 2015. On that date, Owl Corporation stock had a market price of $3 per share.

Because Rita owned substantially identical stock on the date of the short sale and did not close the short sale before January 31, 2017, she is *deemed* to have closed the short sale on November 11, 2016 (the date of the short sale). On her 2016 tax return, she reports a $300 long-term capital gain ($1,300 short sale price − $1,000 basis).

On February 10, 2017, Rita has a $700 short-term capital loss [$600 short sale closing date price (200 shares × $3 per share) − $1,300 basis] because the holding period of the shares used to close the short sale commences with the date of the short sale.

EXAMPLE 31

Assume the same facts as in Example 31, except that Rita did not own any Owl Corporation stock on the short sale date and acquired the 200 shares of Owl Corporation stock for $1,000 on December 12, 2016 (after the November 11, 2016 short sale date).

The *deemed* closing of the short sale is December 12, 2016, because Rita held substantially identical shares at the end of 2016 and did not close the short sale before January 31, 2017. Her 2016 short sale gain is a *short-term* gain of $300 ($1,300 short sale price − $1,000 basis), and she still has a short-term capital loss of $700 on February 10, 2017.

EXAMPLE 32

16-5 TAX TREATMENT OF CAPITAL GAINS AND LOSSES OF NONCORPORATE TAXPAYERS

LO.5

Describe the beneficial tax treatment for capital gains and the detrimental tax treatment for capital losses for noncorporate taxpayers.

All taxpayers net their capital gains and losses. Short-term gains and losses (if any) are netted against one another, and long-term gains and losses (if any) are netted against one another. The results will be net short-term gain or loss and net long-term gain or loss. If these two net positions are of opposite sign (one is a gain and one is a loss), they are netted against each other.

Recently, the term *short sale* has taken on a meaning in real estate transactions that is different from its use with regard to securities transactions. A short sale in real estate takes place when the mortgage on property exceeds the property's fair market value. A property owner in this predicament negotiates with the lender to allow the property to be sold at its fair market value to a third party with the lender accepting the sales price in full satisfaction of the mortgage. Lenders typically will not negotiate with such property owners until the owner has failed to make required mortgage payments and foreclosure by the lender is imminent. If the negotiations are successful, the property owner avoids foreclosure but may have debt cancellation income for the difference between the mortgage and the sales price.

Six possibilities exist for the result after all possible netting has been completed. Three of these final results are gains, and three are losses. One possible result is a net long-term capital gain (NLTCG). Net long-term capital gains of noncorporate taxpayers are eligible for an alternative tax calculation that normally results in a lower tax liability. A second possibility is a net short-term capital gain (NSTCG). Third, the netting may result in both NLTCG and NSTCG. The NLTCG portion of these results is eligible for an alternative tax calculation, which is discussed later in the chapter under Alternative Tax on Net Capital Gain and Qualified Dividend Income.

The last three results of the capital gain and loss netting process are losses. Thus, a fourth possibility is a net long-term capital loss (NLTCL). A fifth result is a net short-term capital loss (NSTCL). Finally, a sixth possibility includes both an NLTCL and an NSTCL. Neither NLTCLs nor NSTCLs are treated as ordinary losses. Treatment as an ordinary loss generally is preferable to capital loss treatment because ordinary losses are deductible in full while the deductibility of capital losses is subject to certain limitations. An individual taxpayer may deduct a maximum of $3,000 of net capital losses for a taxable year.[24]

16-5a **Capital Gain and Loss Netting Process**

Net short-term capital gain is not eligible for any special tax rate. It is taxed at the same rate as the taxpayer's other taxable income.

Net long-term capital gain is eligible for one or more of *five* alternative tax rates: 0 percent, 15 percent, 20 percent, 25 percent, and 28 percent. The 25 percent and 28 percent rates are used only in unique circumstances, so the discussion below concentrates more heavily on the other three rates. The net long-term capital gain components are referred to as the *0%/15%/20% gain*, the *25% gain*, and the *28% gain*.

The *25% gain* is technically called the **unrecaptured § 1250 gain** and is related to gain from disposition of § 1231 assets. Gains and losses from disposition of § 1231 assets are discussed in Chapter 17. In this chapter, the discussion will focus only on how the *25% gain* is taxed and not how it is determined. The *28% gain* relates to collectibles and small business stock gain (both discussed later in this section).

The *0% gain* portion of the *0%/15%/20% gain* applies when the taxable income (before taxing the *0%/15%/20% gain*) does not put the taxpayer out of the 15 percent bracket. Once the taxable income (including any portion of the *0%/15%/20% gain* taxed at 0 percent) puts the taxpayer above the 15 percent bracket, the remaining portion of the *0%/15%/20% gain* is taxed at 15 percent rather than at the regular tax rate until the taxable income reaches the 39.6 percent bracket. Once the taxable income (including any portion of the *0%/15%/20% gain* taxed at 0 percent or 15 percent) puts the taxpayer above the 35 percent bracket, the remaining portion of the *0%/15%/20% gain* is taxed at 20 percent rather than at the 39.6 percent regular tax rate.

When the long-term capital gain exceeds short-term capital loss, a **net capital gain (NCG)** exists.[25] Net capital gain qualifies for beneficial alternative tax treatment (see the coverage later in the chapter).

---

[24]§ 1211(b).

[25]§ 1222(11).

Because there are both short- and long-term capital gains and losses and because the long-term capital gains may be taxed at various rates, an *ordering procedure* is required. The ordering procedure is intended to preserve the lowest long-term capital gain tax rate when there is a net long-term capital gain. This ordering procedure is explained in the following steps and then illustrated by several examples.

Step 1. Group all gains and losses into short term and 28%, 25%, and 0%/15%/20% long term.

Step 2. Net the gains and losses within each group.

Step 3. Offset the net 28% and net 25% amounts if they are of opposite sign.

Step 4. Offset the results after step 3 against the 0%/15%/20% amount if they are of opposite sign. If the 0%/15%/20% amount is a loss, offset it against the *highest-taxed gain first*. After this step, there is a net long-term capital gain or loss. If there is a net long-term capital gain, it may consist of only *28% gain*, only *25% gain*, only *0%/15%/20% gain*, or some combination of all of these gains. If there is a net long-term capital loss, it is simply a net long-term capital loss.

Step 5. Offset the net short-term amount against the results of step 4 if they are of opposite sign. The netting rules offset net short-term capital loss against the *highest-taxed gain first*. Consequently, if there is a net short-term capital loss and a net gain from step 4, the short-term capital loss offsets first the *28% gain*, then the *25% gain*, and finally the *0%/15%/20% gain*.

If the result of step 5 is *only* a short-term capital gain, the taxpayer is not eligible for a reduced tax rate. If the result of step 5 is a loss, the taxpayer may be eligible for a *capital loss deduction* (discussed later in this chapter). If there was no offsetting in step 5 because the short-term and step 4 results were both gains *or* if the result of the offsetting is a long-term gain, a net capital gain exists and the taxpayer may be eligible for a reduced tax rate. The net capital gain may consist of *28% gain, 25% gain*, and/or *0%/15%/20% gain*.

The five steps outlined above can have many unique final results. See Concept Summary 16.5 later in the chapter for a summary of the outcomes of the netting rules and how capital gains and losses are taxed. The following series of examples illustrates the capital gain and loss netting process.

Capital Gain and Loss Netting Process

This example shows how a *net short-term capital gain* may result from the netting process.

EXAMPLE 33

Step	Short Term	Long-Term Gains and Losses 28%	25%	0%/15%/20%	Comment
1	$13,000	$ 12,000		$ 3,000	
	(2,000)	(20,000)			
2	$11,000	($ 8,000)		$ 3,000	
3					No 28%/25% netting because no opposite sign.
4		3,000		(3,000)	Netted because of opposite sign.
		($ 5,000)		$ –0–	
5	(5,000)	5,000			The net short-term capital gain is taxed as ordinary income.
	$ 6,000	$ –0–			
	Net short-term capital gain				

Capital Gain and Loss Netting Process

EXAMPLE 34

This example shows how a *net long-term capital gain* may result from the netting process.

Step	Short Term	Long-Term Gains and Losses 28%	25%	0%/15%/20%	Comment
1	$ 3,000 (5,000)	$15,000 (7,000)	$4,000	$ 3,000 (8,000)	
2	($ 2,000)	$ 8,000	$4,000	($ 5,000)	
3					No 28%/25% netting because no opposite sign.
4		(5,000) $ 3,000	⟵	5,000 $ –0–	Netted because of opposite sign. Net 0%/15%/20% loss is netted against *28% gain* first.
5	2,000 ⟶ $ –0–	(2,000) $ 1,000 Net *28% gain*	$4,000 Net *25% gain*		The net short-term capital loss is netted against *28% gain* first. The net long-term capital gain is $5,000 ($1,000 + $4,000).

EXAMPLE 35

This example shows how a *net long-term capital loss* may result from the netting process.

Step	Short Term	Long-Term Gains and Losses 28%	25%	0%/15%/20%	Comment
1	$ 3,000	$ 1,000		$ 3,000 (8,000)	
2	$ 3,000	$ 1,000		($ 5,000)	
3					No 28%/25% netting because no opposite sign.
4		(1,000) $ –0–	⟶	1,000 ($ 4,000)	Netted because of opposite sign.
5	(3,000) $ –0–	⟶	⟶	3,000 ($ 1,000) Net long-term capital loss	The net short-term capital gain is netted against the net long-term capital loss, and the remaining loss is eligible for the capital loss deduction.

Use of Capital Loss Carryovers

A short-term capital loss carryover to the current year retains its character as short-term and is combined with the short-term items of the current year. A net long-term capital loss carries over as a long-term capital loss and is combined with the current-year long-term items. The long-term loss carryover is first offset with *28% gain* of the current year, then *25% gain*, and then *0%/15%/20% gain* until it is absorbed.

In 2016, Abigail has a $4,000 short-term capital gain, a $36,000 28% long-term capital gain, and a $13,000 0%/15%/20% long-term capital gain. She also has a $3,000 short-term capital loss carryover and a $2,000 long-term capital loss carryover from 2015.

Thus, in 2016, Abigail has a $1,000 net short-term capital gain ($4,000 − $3,000), a $34,000 net 28% long-term capital gain ($36,000 − $2,000), and a $13,000 net 0%/15%/20% long-term capital gain.

Definition of Collectibles

Capital assets that are collectibles, even though they are held long term, are not eligible for the *0%/15%/20%* alternative tax rate. Instead, a 28 percent alternative tax rate applies.

For capital gain or loss purposes, **collectibles** include:[26]

- Any work of art.
- Any rug or antique.
- Any metal or gem.
- Any stamp.
- Any alcoholic beverage.
- Most coins.
- Any historical objects (documents, clothes, etc.).

Small Business Stock

A special *exclusion* is available to noncorporate taxpayers who derive capital gains from the sale or exchange of **qualified small business stock**.[27] Any amount not excluded from income is taxed at a maximum rate of 28 percent (as noted earlier). The exclusion amount varies, depending on when the qualified small business stock was acquired:

- 100 percent of the gain is excluded for qualified stock acquired after September 27, 2010.
- 75 percent of the gain is excluded for qualified stock acquired after February 17, 2009, and before September 28, 2010.
- 50 percent of the gain is excluded for qualified stock acquired before February 18, 2009.

As a result, the maximum effective tax rate on gains from the sale of qualified small business stock is 0 percent (28% × 0%), 7 percent (28% × 25%), or 14 percent (28% × 50%).

Yolanda realized a $100,000 gain on the sale of qualified small business stock that she acquired in 2005. Yolanda is subject to the 33% marginal tax rate without considering this gain. As the stock was acquired before February 18, 2009, $50,000 of this gain (50%) is excluded from gross income, and the other $50,000 is taxed at the maximum rate of 28%. As a result, Yolanda owes Federal income tax of $14,000 on the stock sale ($50,000 × 28%), an effective tax rate of 14% on the entire $100,000 gain.

If, instead, Yolanda acquired the stock in January 2011 and sold it in March 2016, she would exclude 100% of the gain.

Given this very favorable treatment of gains, Congress imposed additional restrictions to ensure that the gain exclusion only applied in very specific situations. These restrictions include the following.

- The stock must have been newly issued *after* August 10, 1993.
- The taxpayer must have held the stock *more than five years.*
- The issuing corporation must use at least 80 percent of its assets, determined by their value, in the *active conduct* of a trade or business.
- When the stock was issued, the issuing corporation's assets must not have exceeded $50 million, at adjusted basis, including the proceeds of the stock issuance.

---

[26]§ 408(m)(2) and Reg. § 1.408–10(b).   [27]§ 1202(a).

- The corporation does not engage in banking, financing, insurance, investing, leasing, farming, mineral extraction, hotel or motel operations, restaurant operations, or any business whose principal asset is the *reputation or skill* of its employees (such as accounting, architecture, health, law, engineering, or financial services).

Even if each of these requirements is met, the amount of gain eligible for the exclusion is limited to the *greater* of 10 times the taxpayer's basis in the stock or $10 million per taxpayer per company,[28] computed on an aggregate basis.

EXAMPLE 38

Vanita purchased $100,000 of qualified small business stock when it was first issued in October 2001. This year, she sold the stock for $4 million. Her gain is $3.9 million ($4,000,000 − $100,000). Although this amount exceeds 10 times her basis ($100,000 × 10 = $1,000,000), it is *less* than $10 million; so the entire $3.9 million gain is eligible for a 50% exclusion.

Transactions that fail to satisfy *any one* of the applicable requirements are taxed as capital gains (and losses) realized by noncorporate taxpayers generally.

Gains are also eligible for *nonrecognition* treatment if the sale proceeds are invested in other qualified small business stock within 60 days.[29] To the extent that the sale proceeds are not so invested, gain is recognized, but the exclusion still applies. To be eligible for this treatment, the stock sold must have been held more than six months.

EXAMPLE 39

Assume the same facts as in the preceding example, except that Vanita sold her stock in January 2017 and used $3.5 million of the sale proceeds to purchase other qualified small business stock one month later. Vanita's gain is recognized to the extent that the sale proceeds were not reinvested—namely, $500,000 ($4,000,000 sale proceeds − $3,500,000 reinvested). A 50% exclusion will apply, however, to the $500,000.

16-5b Qualified Dividend Income

Dividends paid from current or accumulated earnings and profits of domestic and certain foreign corporations are eligible to be taxed at the 0%/15%/20% long-term capital gain rates if they are **qualified dividend income (QDI)**. The question of which dividends constitute qualified dividend income is discussed more fully in Chapter 4. Here the discussion focuses on how the qualified dividend income is taxed.

The Big Picture

EXAMPLE 40

Return to the facts of *The Big Picture* on p. 16-1. After holding the Purple stock for 10 months, Maurice receives $350 of dividends. If Purple is a domestic or qualifying foreign corporation, these are qualified dividends eligible for the 0%/15%/20% tax rate.

After the net capital gain or loss has been determined, the QDI is added to the net long-term capital gain portion of the net capital gain and is taxed as *0%/15%/ 20% gain*. If there is a net capital loss, the net capital loss is still deductible *for* AGI up to $3,000 per year with the remainder of the loss (if any) carrying forward. In this case, the QDI is still eligible to be treated as *0%/15%/20% gain* in the alternative tax calculation (it is *not* offset by the net capital loss).

---

[28]For married persons filing separately, the limitation is $5 million.   [29]§ 1045(a).

Refer to Example 34, but assume that there is qualified dividend income (QDI) of $2,500 in addition to the items shown. The QDI is not netted against the capital gains and losses. Instead, the taxpayer has $1,000 of *28% gain*, $4,000 of *25% gain*, and $2,500 of QDI taxed at 0% / 15% / 20%.

Refer to Example 35, but assume that there is QDI of $2,500 in addition to the items shown. The QDI is not netted against the net capital loss. The taxpayer has a $1,000 capital loss deduction and $2,500 of QDI taxed at 0% / 15% / 20%.

16-5c Alternative Tax on Net Capital Gain and Qualified Dividend Income

Section 1 contains the statutory provisions that enable the *net capital gain* to be taxed at special rates (0, 15, 20, 25, and 28 percent). This calculation is referred to as the **alternative tax** on net capital gain.[30] The alternative tax applies only if taxable income includes some long-term capital gain (there is net capital gain) and/or qualified dividend income (QDI). Taxable income includes *all* of the net capital gain and/or QDI unless taxable income is less than the net capital gain and/or QDI. In addition, the net capital gain and/or QDI is taxed *last*, after other taxable income (including any short-term capital gain).

Joan, an unmarried taxpayer, has taxable income of $118,000, including a $10,000 net capital gain and $2,000 QDI. The last $12,000 of her $118,000 taxable income is the layer related to the net capital gain and/or QDI. The first $106,000 ($118,000 − $12,000) of her taxable income is her other taxable income and is not subject to any special tax rate, so it is taxed using the regular tax rates.

Because the net capital gain and/or QDI may be made up of various *rate layers*, it is important to know in what order those layers are taxed. (Review the five-step ordering procedure discussed on p. 16-21 and the examples that follow the discussion.) For *each* of the layers, the taxpayer compares the regular tax rate on that layer of income and the alternative tax rate on that portion of the net capital gain and/or QDI.

The layers are taxed in the following order:

- Any *25% gain,*
- Any *28% gain,*
- The 0 percent portion of the *0% / 15% / 20% gain* and/or QDI,
- The 15 percent portion of the *0% / 15% / 20% gain* and/or QDI, and then
- The 20 percent portion of the *0% / 15% / 20% gain* and/or QDI.

As a result of this layering:

- The taxpayer benefits from the 0 percent portion of the net capital gain and/or QDI if the taxpayer is still in the 10 percent or 15 percent regular rate bracket after taxing other taxable income and the 25 percent and 28 percent portions of the net capital gain.
- The taxpayer benefits from the 15 percent portion of the net capital gain and/or QDI if the taxpayer is still in the 25 percent, 28 percent, 33 percent, or 35 percent regular rate bracket after taxing other taxable income and the 25 percent, 28 percent, and 0 percent portions of the net capital gain and/or QDI.
- The taxpayer benefits from the 20 percent portion of the net capital gain and/or QDI when taxable income reaches the 39.6 percent regular tax bracket.

---

[30]§ 1(h) Note: Examples 43, 44, and 45 use the 2016 Tax Rate Schedules rather than the 2016 Tax Tables (which are not yet available) to calculate the tax on the non-long-term capital gain portion of taxable income. This approach is used to better illustrate the concepts under discussion. The actual tax on the non-long-term portion of taxable income would be calculated using the Tax Tables because that income is less than $100,000.

Concept Summary 16.4 summarizes the alternative tax computation.

Concept Summary 16.4

Income Layers for Alternative Tax on Capital Gain Computation

Compute tax on:	Other taxable income (including net short-term capital gain) using the regular tax rates.
Compute tax on:	Each of the layers below using the *lower* of the alternative tax rate or the regular tax rate for that layer (or portion of a layer) of taxable income.

+   25% long-term capital gain (unrecaptured § 1250 gain) portion of taxable income

+   28% long-term capital gain

+   0% long-term capital gain (portion of *0%/15%/20% gain* and/or qualified dividend income (QDI) that is taxed at 0%; available only if other taxable income plus 25% and 28% capital gain layers do not put the taxpayer above the 15% regular tax bracket; 0% rate is no longer available once income, including the portion of the gain and/or QDI taxed at 0%, puts the taxpayer out of the 15% regular tax bracket)

+   15% long-term capital gain (portion of *0%/15%/20% gain* and/or QDI that is taxed at 15%; available only if other taxable income plus the 25%, 28%, and 0% layers put the taxpayer above the 15% regular tax bracket and only until other taxable income plus the 25%, 28%, 0%, and 15% layers put the taxpayer above the 35% regular tax bracket)

+   20% long-term capital gain (portion of *0%/15%/20% gain* and/or QDI that is taxed at 20%; available when other taxable income plus the 25%, 28%, 0%, and 15% layers put the taxpayer above the 35% regular tax bracket)

=   Alternative tax on taxable income

Alternative Tax on Net Capital Gain

EXAMPLE 43

Assume that Joan's $10,000 net capital gain in Example 42 is made up of $7,000 *25% gain* and $3,000 *0%/15%/20% gain*. In addition, she has $2,000 of QDI. Examination of the 2016 tax rates reveals that $106,000 ($118,000 − $12,000) of other taxable income for a single individual puts Joan at a marginal tax rate of 28%. Consequently, she uses the alternative tax on the $7,000 gain, the $3,000 gain, and the $2,000 QDI.

Her alternative tax liability for 2016 is $25,217:

$22,717 (normal tax on $106,000 of other taxable income)
+   1,750 ($7,000 × .25; 25% rate on *25% gain*)
+   450 ($3,000 × .15; 15% rate on *0%/15%/20% gain*)
+   300 ($2,000 × .15; 15% rate on QDI)
= $25,217 Alternative Tax Liability

Because the combination of the $106,000 other taxable income and her $7,000 *25% gain* puts her above the 15% regular tax bracket, none of the $3,000 *0%/15%/20% gain* or $2,000 QDI is taxed at 0%.

Her regular tax liability on $118,000 is $26,077. Thus, Joan saves $860 ($26,077 − $25,217) by using the alternative tax calculation. Since none of Joan's taxable income puts her in the 39.6% bracket, none of her *0%/15%/20% gain* or QDI is taxed at the 20% alternative tax rate.

Alternative Tax on Net Capital Gain

EXAMPLE 44

Assume that Joan, an unmarried taxpayer, has 2016 taxable income of $25,000. Of this amount, $11,000 is net capital gain, $1,000 is QDI, and $13,000 is other taxable income. The $11,000 net capital gain is made up of $8,300 of *25% gain* and $2,700 of *0%/15%/20% gain*.

Her alternative tax liability for 2016 is $2,731:

$1,486 (tax on $13,000 of other taxable income)
+ 1,245 (tax on $8,300 *25% gain* at 15%)
+   0 (tax on $2,700 *0%/15%/20% gain* at 0%)
+ _____0 (tax on $1,000 QDI at 0%)
= $2,731 Alternative Tax Liability

Because her marginal rate is still 15% after taxing the $13,000 of other taxable income, she uses the 15% regular tax rate rather than the 25% alternative tax rate on the $8,300 *25% gain*. After taxing the $13,000 and the $8,300, a total of $21,300 of the $25,000 taxable income has been taxed. Because her marginal rate is still 15%, she uses the 0% alternative rate for the $2,700 of *0%/15%/20% gain* and $1,000 QDI.

Joan's regular tax liability on $25,000 is $3,286. Thus, she saves $555 ($3,286 − $2,731) by using the alternative tax calculation.

The alternative tax computation allows the taxpayer to receive the *lower of* the regular tax or the alternative tax on *each layer* of net capital gain and/or QDI or *portion of each layer* of net capital gain and/or QDI.

EXAMPLE 45

Assume the same facts as in Example 44, except that Joan's 2016 taxable income is $40,000, consisting of $11,000 of net capital gain, $1,000 of QDI, and $28,000 of other taxable income.

Not all of the combined *0%/15%/20% gain* and QDI ($3,700; $2,700 + $1,000) is taxed at 0% because Joan's taxable income exceeds $37,650, taking her out of the 15% regular tax bracket. Consequently, the last $2,350 ($40,000 − $37,650) of the $3,700 is taxed at 15% rather than 0%.

Her tax liability using the alternative tax computation is $5,335:

$3,737 (tax on $28,000 of other taxable income)
+ 1,245 (tax on $8,300 *25% gain* at 15%)
+   0 (tax on $1,350 of the $3,700 combined *0%/15%/20% gain* and QDI at 0%)
+ __353_ (tax on $2,350 of the $3,700 combined *0%/15%/20% gain* and QDI at 15%)
= $5,335 Alternative Tax Liability

Joan's regular tax liability on $40,000 is $5,771. Thus, she saves $436 ($5,771 − $5,335) by using the alternative tax calculation.

TAX IN THE NEWS **Losses from Day Trading**

Many investors were caught up with "rising market frenzy" during 2015. One such investor made *15,000* trades during the year. No stock was held more than one year, so each transaction resulted in a short-term capital gain or loss. Each trade had to be documented as to the basis for the stock sold, its holding period, and the selling price net of the sales commission. Unfortunately, there was a $75,000 net short-term capital loss after all transactions were accounted for. Only $3,000 of this loss was deductible in 2015 because the investor had no long-term capital gains to offset against the $75,000 loss, and there is an annual $3,000 capital loss deduction limit. The remaining $72,000 capital loss carries forward and can be used to offset capital gains in later years. In this case, however, the investor had no capital left to invest. Consequently, his annual loss deduction will be limited to $3,000 for many years to come.

16-5d **Treatment of Net Capital Losses**

Computation of Net Capital Loss

A **net capital loss (NCL)** results if capital losses exceed capital gains for the year. An NCL may be all long term, all short term, or part long and part short term.[31] The characterization of an NCL as long or short term is important in determining the capital loss deduction (discussed next).

EXAMPLE 46

Three different individual taxpayers have the following capital gains and losses during the year:

Taxpayer	LTCG	LTCL	STCG	STCL	Result of Netting	Description of Result
Robert	$1,000	($2,800)	$1,000	($ 500)	($1,300)	NLTCL
Carlos	1,000	(500)	1,000	(2,800)	(1,300)	NSTCL
Troy	400	(1,200)	500	(1,200)	(1,500)	NLTCL ($800)
						NSTCL ($700)

Robert's NCL of $1,300 is all long term. Carlos's NCL of $1,300 is all short term. Troy's NCL is $1,500, $800 of which is long term and $700 of which is short term.

Capital Loss Deduction

An NCL is deductible from gross income to the extent of $3,000 per tax year.[32] Although there may or may not be beneficial treatment for capital gains, there is *unfavorable* treatment for capital losses in terms of the $3,000 annual limitation on deducting NCL against ordinary income. If the NCL includes both long-term and short-term capital loss, the short-term capital loss is counted first toward the $3,000 annual limitation.

EXAMPLE 47

Burt has an NCL of $5,500, of which $2,000 is STCL and $3,500 is LTCL. Burt has a capital loss deduction of $3,000 ($2,000 of STCL and $1,000 of LTCL). He has an LTCL carryforward of $2,500 ($3,500 − $1,000).

Carryovers

Taxpayers are allowed to carry over unused capital losses indefinitely. The short-term capital loss (STCL) retains its character as STCL. Likewise, the long-term capital loss retains its character as LTCL.

EXAMPLE 48

In 2016, Mark incurred $1,000 of STCL and $11,000 of LTCL. In 2017, Mark has a $400 LTCG.

- Mark's NCL for 2016 is $12,000. Mark deducts $3,000 ($1,000 STCL and $2,000 LTCL). He has $9,000 of LTCL carried forward to 2017.
- Mark combines the $9,000 LTCL carryforward with the $400 LTCG for 2017. He has an $8,600 NLTCL for 2017. Mark deducts $3,000 of LTCL in 2017 and carries forward $5,600 of LTCL to 2018.

---

[31]Section 1222(10) defines a net capital loss as the net loss after the capital loss deduction. However, that definition confuses the discussion of net capital loss. Therefore, net capital loss is used here to mean the result after netting capital gains and losses and before considering the capital loss deduction. The capital loss deduction is discussed later in this section.

[32]§ 1211(b)(1). Married taxpayers filing separate returns are limited to a $1,500 deduction per tax year.

When a taxpayer has both a capital loss deduction and negative taxable income, a special computation of the capital loss carryover is required.[33] Specifically, the capital loss carryover is the NCL minus the lesser of:

- The capital loss deduction claimed on the return.
- The negative taxable income increased by the capital loss deduction claimed on the return and the personal and dependency exemption deduction.

Without this provision, some of the tax benefit of the capital loss deduction would be wasted when the deduction drives taxable income below zero. However, the capital loss deduction is not reduced if taxable income before the exemption deduction is a positive number or zero. In that situation, it is the exemption deduction, and not the capital loss deduction, that is creating the negative taxable income.

EXAMPLE 49

In 2016, Joanne has a $13,000 NCL (all long-term), a $4,050 personal exemption deduction, and $6,000 negative taxable income. The negative taxable income includes a $3,000 capital loss deduction. The capital loss carryover to 2017 is $11,950, computed as follows:

- The $6,000 negative taxable income is treated as a negative number, but the capital loss deduction and exemption deduction are treated as positive numbers.

- The normal ceiling on the capital loss deduction is $3,000.

- However, if the $3,000 capital loss deduction and the $4,050 exemption deduction are added back to the $6,000 negative taxable income, only $1,050 ($3,000 + $4,050 − $6,000) of the $3,000 capital loss deduction is needed to make taxable income equal to zero.

- Therefore, this special computation results in only $1,050 of the $13,000 NCL being consumed. The LTCL carryforward is $11,950 ($13,000 − $1,050).

Concept Summary 16.5 summarizes the rules for noncorporate taxpayers' treatment of capital gains and losses.

16-5e **Reporting Procedures**

The following example is used to discuss and illustrate the tax forms used for reporting (2015 forms are used because the 2016 tax forms are not yet available).

EXAMPLE 50

During 2015, Joan Rapson (Social Security number 123-45-6789) had the following sales of capital assets. In addition, she has other taxable income of $66,000, including $300 of qualified dividend income. Joan is single and has no dependents.

Description	Acquired On	Date Sold	Sales Price	Tax Basis	Gain or Loss	Character
100 shares Blue stock	1/21/15	11/11/15	$11,000	$17,000	($ 6,000)	STCL
100 shares Yellow stock	9/12/10	10/12/15	36,000	20,000	16,000	LTCG
100 shares Purple stock	3/14/13	10/12/15	14,000	12,000	2,000	LTCG

Joan has a net capital gain of $12,000 ($16,000 *0%/15%/20% gain* + $2,000 *0%/15%/20% gain* − $6,000 short-term capital loss). Consequently, all of the net capital gain is composed of *0%/15%/20% gain*. Joan's $78,000 taxable income includes $65,700 of other taxable income ($78,000 − $12,000 net capital gain − $300 qualified dividend income).

Joan's stockbroker reported total stock sales to her on Form 1099-B, which showed the sales proceeds and adjusted basis of each of her transactions. Following a discussion of the reporting rules, Joan's completed forms and a worksheet are presented.

---

[33]§ 1212(b).

Concept Summary 16.5

Some Possible Final Results of the Capital Gain and Loss Netting Process and How They Are Taxed

Result	Maximum Tax Rate	Comments
Net short-term capital loss	—	Eligible for capital loss deduction ($3,000 maximum per year).
Net long-term capital loss	—	Eligible for capital loss deduction ($3,000 maximum per year).
Net short-term capital loss *and* net long-term capital loss	—	Eligible for capital loss deduction ($3,000 maximum per year). Short-term capital losses are counted first toward the deduction.
Net short-term capital gain	10%–39.6%	Taxed as ordinary income.
Net long-term capital gain	0%–28%	The net long-term capital gain may have as many as five tax rate components: 25%, 28%, and 0% / 15% / 20%.
• The net long-term capital gain is the *last* portion of taxable income.		The components are taxed in the following order: 25%, 28%, 0%, 15%, 20%. They are taxed *after* the non-long-term capital gain portion of taxable income has been taxed. The 0% / 15% / 20% component may include qualified dividend income.
• Each net long-term capital gain component of taxable income is taxed at the *lower* of the regular tax on that component or the alternative tax.		The alternative tax on net long-term capital gain can never increase the tax on taxable income, but it can reduce the tax on taxable income.
Net short-term capital gain *and* net long-term capital gain	10%–39.6% on net short-term capital gain; 0%–28% on net long-term capital gain	The net short-term capital gain is taxed as ordinary income; the net long-term capital gain is taxed as discussed above for just net long-term capital gain.

Capital gains and losses are reported on Schedule D of Form 1040 (Capital Gains and Losses). Part I of Schedule D is used to report short-term capital gains and losses. Part II of Schedule D is used to report long-term capital gains and losses. The information shown in Parts I and II comes from Form 8949 (Sales and Other Dispositions of Assets). Form 8949 is used to accumulate gains and losses from three sources:

- Capital gain and loss transactions for which a Form 1099–B (Proceeds from Broker and Barter Exchange Transactions) has been received and the provider of the form had information on the sales proceeds *and* the tax basis of the assets disposed of.

- Capital gain and loss transactions for which a Form 1099–B has been received and the provider of the form had information on the sales proceeds *but did not* have information on the tax basis of the assets disposed of.

- Capital gain and loss transactions for which a Form 1099–B was not received.

Part III of Form 1040 Schedule D summarizes the results of Parts I and II and indicates whether the taxpayer has a net capital gain or a net capital loss. Part III then helps determine which alternative tax worksheet is used to calculate the alternative tax on long-term capital gains and qualified dividends. If the taxpayer has a net long-term capital gain that does not include any 28% or 25% long-term capital gain, then the alternative tax is calculated using the Qualified Dividends and Capital Gain Worksheet from the Form 1040 instructions. If the taxpayer has a net long-term capital gain that does include either 28% or 25% long-term capital gain, then the alternative tax is calculated using the Schedule D Tax Worksheet from the Schedule D instructions. These worksheets do not have to be filed with the tax return, but are kept for the taxpayer's records.

SCHEDULE D (Form 1040)	**Capital Gains and Losses**	OMB No. 1545-0074

Capital Gains and Losses

► Attach to Form 1040 or Form 1040NR.

► Information about Schedule D and its separate instructions is at *www.irs.gov/scheduled*.

► Use Form 8949 to list your transactions for lines 1b, 2, 3, 8b, 9, and 10.

Department of the Treasury
Internal Revenue Service (99)

20**15**
Attachment
Sequence No. **12**

Name(s) shown on return	Your social security number
Joan Rapson	*123-45-6789*

Part I — Short-Term Capital Gains and Losses—Assets Held One Year or Less

See instructions for how to figure the amounts to enter on the lines below. This form may be easier to complete if you round off cents to whole dollars.	**(d)** Proceeds (sales price)	**(e)** Cost (or other basis)	**(g)** Adjustments to gain or loss from Form(s) 8949, Part I, line 2, column (g)	**(h) Gain or (loss)** Subtract column (e) from column (d) and combine the result with column (g)
1a Totals for all short-term transactions reported on Form 1099-B for which basis was reported to the IRS and for which you have no adjustments (see instructions). However, if you choose to report all these transactions on Form 8949, leave this line blank and go to line 1b .				
1b Totals for all transactions reported on Form(s) 8949 with **Box A** checked	*11,000*	*17,000*		*(6,000)*
2 Totals for all transactions reported on Form(s) 8949 with **Box B** checked				
3 Totals for all transactions reported on Form(s) 8949 with **Box C** checked				

4 Short-term gain from Form 6252 and short-term gain or (loss) from Forms 4684, 6781, and 8824 .	**4**	
5 Net short-term gain or (loss) from partnerships, S corporations, estates, and trusts from Schedule(s) K-1	**5**	
6 Short-term capital loss carryover. Enter the amount, if any, from line 8 of your **Capital Loss Carryover Worksheet** in the instructions	**6** ( )
7 **Net short-term capital gain or (loss).** Combine lines 1a through 6 in column (h). If you have any long-term capital gains or losses, go to Part II below. Otherwise, go to Part III on the back	**7**	*(6,000)*

Part II — Long-Term Capital Gains and Losses—Assets Held More Than One Year

See instructions for how to figure the amounts to enter on the lines below. This form may be easier to complete if you round off cents to whole dollars.	**(d)** Proceeds (sales price)	**(e)** Cost (or other basis)	**(g)** Adjustments to gain or loss from Form(s) 8949, Part II, line 2, column (g)	**(h) Gain or (loss)** Subtract column (e) from column (d) and combine the result with column (g)
8a Totals for all long-term transactions reported on Form 1099-B for which basis was reported to the IRS and for which you have no adjustments (see instructions). However, if you choose to report all these transactions on Form 8949, leave this line blank and go to line 8b .				
8b Totals for all transactions reported on Form(s) 8949 with **Box D** checked	*50,000*	*32,000*		*18,000*
9 Totals for all transactions reported on Form(s) 8949 with **Box E** checked				
10 Totals for all transactions reported on Form(s) 8949 with **Box F** checked.				

11 Gain from Form 4797, Part I; long-term gain from Forms 2439 and 6252; and long-term gain or (loss) from Forms 4684, 6781, and 8824	**11**	
12 Net long-term gain or (loss) from partnerships, S corporations, estates, and trusts from Schedule(s) K-1	**12**	
13 Capital gain distributions. See the instructions	**13**	
14 Long-term capital loss carryover. Enter the amount, if any, from line 13 of your **Capital Loss Carryover Worksheet** in the instructions	**14** ( )
15 **Net long-term capital gain or (loss).** Combine lines 8a through 14 in column (h). Then go to Part III on the back	**15**	*18,000*

For Paperwork Reduction Act Notice, see your tax return instructions.   Cat. No. 11338H   Schedule D (Form 1040) 2015

Part III	**Summary**

16 Combine lines 7 and 15 and enter the result . . . . **16** | 12,000

- If line 16 is a **gain,** enter the amount from line 16 on Form 1040, line 13, or Form 1040NR, line 14. Then go to line 17 below.
- If line 16 is a **loss,** skip lines 17 through 20 below. Then go to line 21. Also be sure to complete line 22.
- If line 16 is **zero,** skip lines 17 through 21 below and enter -0- on Form 1040, line 13, or Form 1040NR, line 14. Then go to line 22.

17 Are lines 15 and 16 **both** gains?
☒ **Yes.** Go to line 18.
☐ **No.** Skip lines 18 through 21, and go to line 22.

18 Enter the amount, if any, from line 7 of the **28% Rate Gain Worksheet** in the instructions . . ▶ **18** | 0

19 Enter the amount, if any, from line 18 of the **Unrecaptured Section 1250 Gain Worksheet** in the instructions . . . . ▶ **19** | 0

20 Are lines 18 and 19 **both** zero or blank?
☒ **Yes.** Complete the **Qualified Dividends and Capital Gain Tax Worksheet** in the instructions for Form 1040, line 44 (or in the instructions for Form 1040NR, line 42). **Do not** complete lines 21 and 22 below.

☐ **No.** Complete the **Schedule D Tax Worksheet** in the instructions. **Do not** complete lines 21 and 22 below.

21 If line 16 is a loss, enter here and on Form 1040, line 13, or Form 1040NR, line 14, the **smaller** of:

- The loss on line 16 or
- ($3,000), or if married filing separately, ($1,500) } . . . . **21** |( )

Note: When figuring which amount is smaller, treat both amounts as positive numbers.

22 Do you have qualified dividends on Form 1040, line 9b, or Form 1040NR, line 10b?

☐ **Yes.** Complete the **Qualified Dividends and Capital Gain Tax Worksheet** in the instructions for Form 1040, line 44 (or in the instructions for Form 1040NR, line 42).

☐ **No.** Complete the rest of Form 1040 or Form 1040NR.

Form **8949**

Department of the Treasury
Internal Revenue Service

Sales and Other Dispositions of Capital Assets

▶ Information about Form 8949 and its separate instructions is at *www.irs.gov/form8949.*
▶ File with your Schedule D to list your transactions for lines 1b, 2, 3, 8b, 9, and 10 of Schedule D.

OMB No. 1545-0074

20**15**

Attachment
Sequence No. **12A**

Name(s) shown on return

Joan Rapson

Social security number or taxpayer identification number

123-45-6789

Before you check Box A, B, or C below, see whether you received any Form(s) 1099-B or substitute statement(s) from your broker. A substitute statement will have the same information as Form 1099-B. Either will show whether your basis (usually your cost) was reported to the IRS by your broker and may even tell you which box to check.

Part I **Short-Term.** Transactions involving capital assets you held 1 year or less are short term. For long-term transactions, see page 2.

Note: You may aggregate all short-term transactions reported on Form(s) 1099-B showing basis was reported to the IRS and for which no adjustments or codes are required. Enter the totals directly on Schedule D, line 1a; you aren't required to report these transactions on Form 8949 (see instructions).

You *must* check Box A, B, *or* C below. Check only one box. If more than one box applies for your short-term transactions, complete a separate Form 8949, page 1, for each applicable box. If you have more short-term transactions than will fit on this page for one or more of the boxes, complete as many forms with the same box checked as you need.

- ☒ **(A)** Short-term transactions reported on Form(s) 1099-B showing basis was reported to the IRS (see **Note** above)
- ☐ **(B)** Short-term transactions reported on Form(s) 1099-B showing basis was **not** reported to the IRS
- ☐ **(C)** Short-term transactions not reported to you on Form 1099-B

1 (a) Description of property (Example: 100 sh. XYZ Co.)	(b) Date acquired (Mo., day, yr.)	(c) Date sold or disposed of (Mo., day, yr.)	(d) Proceeds (sales price) (see instructions)	(e) Cost or other basis. See the **Note** below and see *Column (e)* in the separate instructions	Adjustment, if any, to gain or loss. If you enter an amount in column (g), enter a code in column (f). See the separate instructions. (f) Code(s) from instructions	(g) Amount of adjustment	(h) Gain or (loss). Subtract column (e) from column (d) and combine the result with column (g)
100 Shares Blue Stock	*01/21/15*	*11/11/15*	*11,000*	*17,000*			*(6,000)*
2 Totals. Add the amounts in columns (d), (e), (g), and (h) (subtract negative amounts). Enter each total here and include on your Schedule D, **line 1b** (if **Box A** above is checked), **line 2** (if **Box B** above is checked), or **line 3** (if **Box C** above is checked) ▶			*11,000*	*17,000*			*(6,000)*

Note: If you checked Box A above but the basis reported to the IRS was incorrect, enter in column (e) the basis as reported to the IRS, and enter an adjustment in column (g) to correct the basis. See *Column (g)* in the separate instructions for how to figure the amount of the adjustment.

For Paperwork Reduction Act Notice, see your tax return instructions.   Cat. No. 37768Z   Form **8949** (2015)

Form 8949 (2015)

Name(s) shown on return. Name and SSN or taxpayer identification no. not required if shown on other side	Social security number or taxpayer identification number

Before you check Box D, E, or F below, see whether you received any Form(s) 1099-B or substitute statement(s) from your broker. A substitute statement will have the same information as Form 1099-B. Either will show whether your basis (usually your cost) was reported to the IRS by your broker and may even tell you which box to check.

Part II   **Long-Term.** Transactions involving capital assets you held more than 1 year are long term. For short-term transactions, see page 1.

Note: You may aggregate all long-term transactions reported on Form(s) 1099-B showing basis was reported to the IRS and for which no adjustments or codes are required. Enter the totals directly on Schedule D, line 8a; you aren't required to report these transactions on Form 8949 (see instructions).

You *must* check Box D, E, *or* F below. **Check only one box.** If more than one box applies for your long-term transactions, complete a separate Form 8949, page 2, for each applicable box. If you have more long-term transactions than will fit on this page for one or more of the boxes, complete as many forms with the same box checked as you need.

- ☒ **(D)** Long-term transactions reported on Form(s) 1099-B showing basis was reported to the IRS (see **Note** above)
- ☐ **(E)** Long-term transactions reported on Form(s) 1099-B showing basis was **not** reported to the IRS
- ☐ **(F)** Long-term transactions not reported to you on Form 1099-B

1

(a) Description of property (Example: 100 sh. XYZ Co.)	(b) Date acquired (Mo., day, yr.)	(c) Date sold or disposed of (Mo., day, yr.)	(d) Proceeds (sales price) (see instructions)	(e) Cost or other basis. See the **Note** below and see *Column (e)* in the separate instructions	(f) Code(s) from instructions	(g) Amount of adjustment	(h) Gain or (loss). Subtract column (e) from column (d) and combine the result with column (g)
100 Shares Yellow Stock	*09/12/10*	*10/12/15*	*36,000*	*20,000*			*16,000*
100 Shares Purple Stock	*03/14/13*	*10/12/15*	*14,000*	*12,000*			*2,000*
2 Totals. Add the amounts in columns (d), (e), (g), and (h) (subtract negative amounts). Enter each total here and include on your Schedule D, **line 8b** (if **Box D** above is checked), **line 9** (if **Box E** above is checked), or **line 10** (if **Box F** above is checked) ▶			*50,000*	*32,000*			*18,000*

Note: If you checked Box D above but the basis reported to the IRS was incorrect, enter in column (e) the basis as reported to the IRS, and enter an adjustment in column (g) to correct the basis. See *Column (g)* in the separate instructions for how to figure the amount of the adjustment.

Form **8949** (2015)

Qualified Dividends and Capital Gain Tax Worksheet—Line 44

Keep for Your Records

Before you begin:	✓ See the earlier instructions for line 44 to see if you can use this worksheet to figure your tax.	
	✓ Before completing this worksheet, complete Form 1040 through line 43.	
	✓ If you do not have to file Schedule D and you received capital gain distributions, be sure you checked the box on line 13 of Form 1040.	

1.	Enter the amount from Form 1040, line 43. However, if you are filing Form 2555 or 2555-EZ (relating to foreign earned income), enter the amount from line 3 of the Foreign Earned Income Tax Worksheet ...... **1.**		78,000
2.	Enter the amount from Form 1040, line 9b* ...... **2.**	300	
3.	Are you filing Schedule D?*		
	☒ **Yes.** Enter the **smaller** of line 15 or 16 of Schedule D. If either line 15 or line 16 is blank or a loss, enter -0- } **3.**	12,000	
	☐ **No.** Enter the amount from Form 1040, line 13		
4.	Add lines 2 and 3 .... **4.**	12,300	
5.	If filing Form 4952 (used to figure investment interest expense deduction), enter any amount from line 4g of that form. Otherwise, enter -0- .... **5.**		
6.	Subtract line 5 from line 4. If zero or less, enter -0- .... **6.**		12,300
7.	Subtract line 6 from line 1. If zero or less, enter -0- .... **7.**		65,700
8.	Enter: $37,450 if single or married filing separately, $74,900 if married filing jointly or qualifying widow(er), $50,200 if head of household. } .... **8.**		37,450
9.	Enter the smaller of line 1 or line 8 .... **9.**		37,450
10.	Enter the smaller of line 7 or line 9 .... **10.**		37,450
11.	Subtract line 10 from line 9. This amount is taxed at 0% .... **11.**		0
12.	Enter the smaller of line 1 or line 6 .... **12.**		12,300
13.	Enter the amount from line 11 .... **13.**		0
14.	Subtract line 13 from line 12 .... **14.**		12,300
15.	Enter: $413,200 if single, $232,425 if married filing separately, $464,850 if married filing jointly or qualifying widow(er), $439,000 if head of household. } .... **15.**		413,200
16.	Enter the smaller of line 1 or line 15 .... **16.**		78,000
17.	Add lines 7 and 11 .... **17.**		65,700
18.	Subtract line 17 from line 16. If zero or less, enter -0- .... **18.**		12,300
19.	Enter the smaller of line 14 or line 18 .... **19.**		12,300
20.	Multiply line 19 by 15% (.15) .... **20.**		1,845
21.	Add lines 11 and 19 .... **21.**	12,300	
22.	Subtract line 21 from line 12 .... **22.**	0	
23.	Multiply line 22 by 20% (.20) .... **23.**		0
24.	Figure the tax on the amount on line 7. If the amount on line 7 is less than $100,000, use the Tax Table to figure the tax. If the amount on line 7 is $100,000 or more, use the Tax Computation Worksheet .... **24.**		12,225
25.	Add lines 20, 23, and 24 .... **25.**		14,070
26.	Figure the tax on the amount on line 1. If the amount on line 1 is less than $100,000, use the Tax Table to figure the tax. If the amount on line 1 is $100,000 or more, use the Tax Computation Worksheet .... **26.**		15,300
27.	**Tax on all taxable income.** Enter the **smaller** of line 25 or line 26. Also include this amount on Form 1040, line 44. If you are filing Form 2555 or 2555-EZ, do not enter this amount on Form 1040, line 44. Instead, enter it on line 4 of the Foreign Earned Income Tax Worksheet .... **27.**		14,070

If you are filing Form 2555 or 2555-EZ, see the footnote in the Foreign Earned Income Tax Worksheet before completing this line.

Describe the tax treatment for capital gains and the detrimental tax treatment for capital losses for corporate taxpayers.

16-6 TAX TREATMENT OF CAPITAL GAINS AND LOSSES OF CORPORATE TAXPAYERS

The treatment of a corporation's net capital gain or loss differs from the rules for individuals. Briefly, the differences are as follows:

- There is an NCG alternative tax rate of 35 percent.[34] However, because the maximum corporate tax rate is 35 percent, the alternative tax is not beneficial.
- Capital losses offset only capital gains. No deduction of capital losses is permitted against other taxable income (whereas a $3,000 deduction is allowed to individuals).[35]
- Corporations may carry back net capital losses (whether long-term or short-term) as short-term capital losses for three years; if losses still remain after the carryback, the remaining losses may be carried forward five years.[36] Individuals may carry forward unused capital losses indefinitely, but there is no carryback.

EXAMPLE 51

Sparrow Corporation has a $15,000 NLTCL for the current year and $57,000 of other taxable income. Sparrow may not offset the $15,000 NLTCL against its other income by taking a capital loss deduction.

The $15,000 NLTCL becomes a $15,000 STCL for carryback and carryover purposes. This amount may be offset against capital gains in the three-year carryback period or, if not absorbed there, offset capital gains in the five-year carryforward period. Any amount remaining after this carryforward period expires is permanently lost.

The rules applicable to corporations are discussed in greater detail in Chapter 20.

Identify tax planning opportunities arising from the sale or exchange of capital assets.

16-7 TAX PLANNING

16-7a Importance of Capital Asset Status

Why is capital asset status important? Capital asset status enables the taxpayer to be eligible for the alternative tax on net capital gain. Individuals who receive income in the form of long-term capital gains or qualified dividend income have an advantage over taxpayers who cannot receive income in these forms.

Capital asset status is also important because capital gains must be offset by capital losses. If a net capital loss results, the maximum deduction is $3,000 per year.

Consequently, capital gains and losses must be segregated from other types of gains and losses and must be reported separately on Schedule D of Form 1040.

16-7b Planning for Capital Asset Status

It is important to keep in mind that capital asset status often is a question of objective evidence. Thus, property that is not a capital asset to one party may qualify as a capital asset to another party.

EXAMPLE 52

Diane, a real estate dealer, transfers by gift a tract of land to Jeff, her son. The land was recorded as part of Diane's inventory (it was held for resale) and was therefore not a capital asset to her. Jeff, however, treats the land as an investment. The land is a capital asset in Jeff's hands, and any later taxable disposition of the property by him will yield a capital gain or loss.

If proper planning is carried out, even a dealer may obtain long-term capital gain treatment on the sale of the type of property normally held for resale.

---

[34]§ 1201.

[35]§ 1211(a).

[36]§ 1212(a)(1).

Jim, a real estate dealer, segregates Tract A from the real estate he regularly holds for resale and designates the property as being held for investment purposes. The property is not advertised for sale and is disposed of several years later. The negotiations for the subsequent sale were initiated by the purchaser and not by Jim. Under these circumstances, it would appear that any gain or loss from the sale of Tract A should be a capital gain or loss.[37]

EXAMPLE 53

When a business is being sold, one of the major decisions usually concerns whether a portion of the sales price is for goodwill. For the seller, goodwill generally represents the disposition of a capital asset. Goodwill has no basis and represents a residual portion of the selling price that cannot be allocated reasonably to the known assets. The amount of goodwill thus represents capital gain.

From a legal perspective, the buyer may prefer that the residual portion of the purchase price be allocated to a covenant not to compete (a promise that the seller will not compete against the buyer by conducting a business similar to the one the buyer has purchased). Both purchased goodwill and a covenant not to compete are § 197 intangibles. Thus, both must be capitalized and can be amortized over a 15-year statutory period.

To the seller, a covenant produces ordinary income. Thus, the seller would prefer that the residual portion of the selling price be allocated to goodwill—a capital asset. If the buyer does not need the legal protection provided by a covenant, the buyer is neutral regarding whether the residual amount be allocated to a covenant or to goodwill. Because the seller would receive a tax advantage from labeling the residual amount as goodwill, the buyer should factor this into the negotiation of the purchase price.

Marcia is buying Jack's dry cleaning proprietorship. An appraisal of the assets indicates that a reasonable purchase price would exceed the value of the known assets by $30,000. If the purchase contract does not specify the nature of the $30,000, the amount will be for goodwill and Jack will have a long-term capital gain of $30,000. Marcia will have a 15-year amortizable $30,000 asset.

If Marcia is paying the extra $30,000 to prevent Jack from conducting another dry cleaning business in the area (a covenant not to compete), Jack will have $30,000 of ordinary income. Marcia will have a $30,000 deduction over the statutory 15-year amortization period rather than over the actual life of the covenant (e.g., 5 years).

EXAMPLE 54

16-7c **Effect of Capital Asset Status in Transactions Other Than Sales**

The nature of an asset (capital or ordinary) is important in determining the tax consequences that result when a sale or exchange occurs. It may, however, be just as significant in circumstances other than a taxable sale or exchange. When a capital asset is

---

[37]*Toledo, Peoria & Western Railroad Co.*, 35 TCM 1663, T.C.Memo. 1976–366.

disposed of, the result is not always a capital gain or loss. Rather, in general, the disposition must be a sale or exchange. Collection of a debt instrument having a basis less than the face value results in a capital gain if the debt instrument is a capital asset. The collection is a sale or exchange. Sale of the debt shortly before the due date for collection will produce a capital gain.[38] If selling the debt in such circumstances could produce a capital gain but collecting could not, the consistency of what constitutes a capital gain or loss would be undermined. Another illustration of the sale or exchange principle involves a donation of certain appreciated property to a qualified charity. Recall that in certain circumstances, the measure of the charitable contribution is fair market value when the property, if sold, would have yielded a long-term capital gain (refer to the discussion of contributions of capital gain property in Chapter 10).

Sharon wants to donate a tract of unimproved land (basis of $40,000 and fair market value of $200,000) held for the required long-term holding period to State University (a qualified charitable organization). However, Sharon currently is under audit by the IRS for capital gains she reported on certain real estate transactions during an earlier tax year. Although Sharon is not a licensed real estate broker, the IRS agent conducting the audit is contending that she has achieved dealer status by virtue of the number and frequency of the real estate transactions she has conducted.

Under these circumstances, Sharon would be well advised to postpone the donation to State University until her status is clarified. If she has achieved dealer status, the unimproved land may be inventory (refer to Example 53 for another possible result) and Sharon's charitable contribution deduction would be limited to $40,000. If not and if the land is held as an investment, Sharon's deduction is $200,000 (the fair market value of the property).

16-7d Stock Sales

The following rules apply in determining the date of a stock sale:

- The date the sale is executed is the date of the sale. The execution date is the date the broker completes the transaction on the stock exchange.

- The settlement date is the date the cash or other property is paid to the seller of the stock. This date is *not* relevant in determining the date of sale.

Lupe, a cash basis taxpayer, sells stock that results in a gain. The sale was executed on December 29, 2015. The settlement date is January 2, 2016. The date of sale is December 29, 2015 (the execution date). The holding period for the stock sold ends with the execution date.

16-7e Maximizing Benefits

Ordinary losses generally are preferable to capital losses because of the limitations imposed on the deductibility of net capital losses and the requirement that capital losses be used to offset capital gains. The taxpayer may be able to convert what would otherwise have been capital loss to ordinary loss. For example, business (but not nonbusiness) bad debts, losses from the sale or exchange of small business investment company stock, and losses from the sale or exchange of small business corporation stock all result in ordinary losses.[39]

Although capital losses can be carried over indefinitely, *indefinite* becomes definite when a taxpayer dies. Any loss carryovers not used by the taxpayer are permanently lost. That is, no tax benefit can be derived from the carryovers subsequent to death.[40] Therefore, the potential benefit of carrying over capital losses diminishes when dealing with older taxpayers.

It is usually beneficial to spread gains over more than one taxable year. In some cases, this can be accomplished through the installment sales method of accounting.

---

[38]§ 1271(b).

[39]§§ 166(d), 1242, and 1244. Refer to the discussion in Chapter 7.

[40]Rev.Rul. 74–175, 1974–1 C.B. 52.

16-7f **Year-End Planning**

The following general rules can be applied for timing the recognition of capital gains and losses near the end of a taxable year:

- If the taxpayer already has recognized more than $3,000 of capital loss, sell assets to generate capital gain equal to the excess of the capital loss over $3,000.

- If the taxpayer already has recognized capital gain, sell assets to generate capital loss equal to the capital gain. The gain will not be taxed, and the loss will be fully *deductible* against the gain.
- Generally, if the taxpayer has a choice between recognizing short-term capital gain or long-term capital gain, long-term capital gain should be recognized because it is subject to a lower tax rate.

REFOCUS ON THE BIG PICTURE

MANAGING CAPITAL ASSET TRANSACTIONS

You explain to Maurice that your area of expertise is tax, so you are providing tax advice and not investment advice. From an overall perspective, he is correct that certain capital gains and dividends are eligible for either a 0 percent, a 15 percent, or a 20 percent tax rate rather than the regular income tax rates that go as high as 39.6 percent. You then discuss the potential tax consequences of each of his investments.

- *Purple stock and Eagle stock.* To qualify for the beneficial tax rate, the holding period for the stock must be longer than one year. From a tax perspective, Maurice should retain his stock investments for at least an additional three months and a day. To be eligible for the "costless" capital gains (i.e., capital gains taxed at 0%), his taxable income should not exceed $37,650 for 2016. The dividends received on the Purple stock are "qualified dividends" eligible for the *0%/15%/20%* alternative tax rate.
- *Patent.* Because he is a "holder" of the patent, it will qualify for the beneficial capital gain rate regardless of the holding period if the patent should produce income in excess of his $50,000 investment. However, if he loses money on the investment, he will be able to deduct only $3,000 of the loss per year against his ordinary income (assuming that there are no offsetting capital gains).
- *Tax-exempt bonds.* The after-tax return on the taxable bonds would be less than the 3 percent on the tax-exempt bonds. In addition, the interest on the taxable bonds would increase his taxable income, possibly moving it out of the desired 15 percent marginal tax rate into the 25 percent marginal tax rate.
- *Franchise rights.* The franchise rights purchased from Orange, Inc., probably require the payment of a franchise fee based upon the sales in the franchise business. Maurice should either start such a business or sell the franchise rights.
- *Partnership interest.* Whether Maurice receives capital or ordinary treatment associated with his partnership interest depends on whether he is reporting his share of profits or losses (ordinary income or ordinary loss) or is reporting recognized gain or loss from the sale of his partnership interest (capital gain or capital loss).

You conclude your tax advice to Maurice by telling him that whatever he does regarding his investments should make economic sense. There are no 100 percent tax rates. For example, disposing of the bank stock in the current market could be the wise thing to do.

Key Terms

Alternative tax, 16-25

Capital asset, 16-4

Capital gains, 16-2

Capital losses, 16-2

Collectibles, 16-23

Franchise, 16-13

Holding period, 16-15

Lessee, 16-14

Lessor, 16-14

Net capital gain (NCG), 16-20

Net capital loss (NCL), 16-28

Options, 16-10

Original issue discount (OID), 16-9

Patent, 16-11

Qualified dividend income (QDI), 16-24

Qualified small business stock, 16-23

Sale or exchange, 16-8

Short sale, 16-17

Unrecaptured § 1250 gain, 16-20

Discussion Questions

Issue ID   1. **LO.2, 4, 5** Sheila inherited 300 shares of stock, 100 shares of Magenta and 200 shares of Purple. She has a stockbroker sell the shares for her, uses the proceeds for personal expenses, and thinks nothing further about the transactions. What issues does she face when she prepares her Federal income tax return?

Issue ID   2. **LO.2** An individual taxpayer sells some used assets at a garage sale. Why are none of the proceeds taxable in most situations?

Issue ID   3. **LO.2, 4** Alison owns a painting that she received as a gift from her aunt 10 years ago. The aunt created the painting. Alison has displayed the painting in her home and has never attempted to sell it. Recently, a visitor noticed the painting and offered Alison $5,000 for it. If Alison decides to sell the painting, what tax issues does she face?

4. **LO.2** Is a note receivable that arose in the ordinary course of the taxpayer's retail business a capital asset? Why or why not?

5. **LO.2** Anwar owns vacant land that he purchased many years ago as an investment. After getting approval to subdivide it into 35 lots, he made minimal improvements and then sold the entire property to a real estate developer. Anwar's recognized gain on the sale was $1.2 million. Is this transaction eligible for the "real property subdivided for sale" provisions? Why or why not?

Issue ID   6. **LO.3** Hubert purchases all of the rights in a patent from the inventor who developed the patented product. After holding the patent for two years, Hubert sells all of the rights in the patent for a substantial gain. What issues does Hubert face if he wants to treat the gain as a long-term capital gain?

7. **LO.3** Blue Corporation and Fuchsia Corporation are engaged in a contract negotiation over the use of Blue's trademarked name, DateSiteForSeniors. For a one-time payment of $45,000, Blue licensed Fuchsia to use the name DateSiteForSeniors, and the license requires that Fuchsia pay Blue a royalty every time a new customer signs up on Fuchsia's website. Blue is a developer of "website ideas" that it then licenses to other companies such as Fuchsia. Did Fuchsia purchase a franchise right from Blue, or did Fuchsia purchase the name DateSiteForSeniors from Blue?

8. **LO.4** At the date of a short sale, Sylvia has held substantially identical securities for more than 12 months. What is the nature of any gain or loss from the close of her short sale?

9. **LO.5** After netting all of her short-term and long-term capital gains and losses, Misty has a net short-term capital loss and a net long-term capital loss. Can she net these against each other? Why or why not?

10. **LO.2, 5** Charlie sells his antique farm tractor collection at a loss. He had acquired all of the tractors for his personal pleasure and sold all of them for less than

he paid for them. What is the tax status of the tractors? Is his loss a 28% collectibles loss? Explain.

11. **LO.2, 5, 7** Near the end of 2016, Byron realizes that he has a net short-term capital loss of $13,000 for the year. Byron has taxable income (not including the loss) of $123,000 and is single. He owns numerous stocks that could be sold for a long-term capital gain. What should he do before the end of 2016?

Issue ID

Computational Exercises

12. **LO.2** Dexter owns a large tract of land and subdivides it for sale. Assume that Dexter meets all of the requirements of § 1237 and during the tax year sells the first eight lots to eight different buyers for $22,000 each. Dexter's basis in each lot sold is $15,000, and he incurs total selling expenses of $900 on each sale. What is the amount of Dexter's capital gain and ordinary income?

13. **LO.3** Shelia purchases $50,000 of newly issued Gingo Corporation bonds for $45,000. The bonds have original issue discount (OID) of $5,000. After Sheila amortized $2,300 of OID and held the bonds for four years, she sold the bonds for $48,000. What is the amount and character of her gain or loss?

14. **LO.3** Olivia wants to buy some vacant land for investment purposes. She cannot afford the full purchase price. Instead, Olivia pays the landowner $8,000 to obtain an option to buy the land for $175,000 anytime in the next four years. Fourteen months after purchasing the option, Olivia sells the option for $10,000. What is the amount and character of Olivia's gain or loss?

15. **LO.3** On May 9, 2016, Glenna purchases 500 shares of Ignaz Company stock for $7,500. On June 30, 2016, she writes a call option on the stock, giving the grantee the right to buy the stock for $9,000 during the following 12-month period. Glenna receives a call premium of $750 for writing the call. The call is exercised by the grantee on December 15, 2016.
    a. What is the amount and character of Glenna's gain or loss?
    b. Assume that the original option expired unexercised. What is the amount and character of Glenna's gain or loss?

16. **LO.4** Shen purchased corporate stock for $20,000 on April 10, 2014. On July 14, 2016, when the stock was worth $12,000, Shen died and his son, Mijo, inherited the stock. Mijo sold the stock for $14,200 on November 12, 2016. What is the amount and character of Mijo's gain or loss?

17. **LO.5** Coline has the following capital gain and loss transactions for 2016.

Short-term capital gain	$ 5,000
Short-term capital loss	(2,100)
Long-term capital gain (28%)	6,000
Long-term capital gain (15%)	2,000
Long-term capital loss (28%)	(10,500)

After the capital gain and loss netting process, what is the amount and character of Coline's gain or loss?

18. **LO.5** Elliott has the following capital gain and loss transactions for 2016.

Short-term capital gain	$ 1,500
Short-term capital loss	(3,600)
Long-term capital gain (28%)	12,000
Long-term capital gain (25%)	4,800

Long-term capital gain (15%)	$ 6,000
Long-term capital loss (28%)	(4,500)
Long-term capital loss (15%)	(9,000)

After the capital gain and loss netting process, what is the amount and character of Elliott's gain or loss?

Problems

19. **LO.2** During the year, Eugene had the four property transactions summarized below. Eugene is a collector of antique glassware and occasionally sells a piece to get funds to buy another. What are the amount and nature of the gain or loss from each of these transactions?

Property	Date Acquired	Date Sold	Adjusted Basis	Sales Price
Antique vase	06/18/05	05/23/16	$37,000	$42,000
Blue Growth Fund (100 shares)	12/23/07	11/22/16	22,000	38,000
Orange bonds	02/12/08	04/11/16	34,000	42,000*
Green stock (100 shares)	02/14/16	11/23/16	11,000	13,000

*The sales price included $750 of accrued interest.

Decision Making

20. **LO.2, 5** Rennie owns a video game arcade. He buys vintage video games from estates, often at much less than the retail value of the property. He usually installs the vintage video games in a special section of his video game arcade that appeals to players of "classic" video games. Recently, Rennie sold a classic video game that a customer "just had to have." Rennie paid $11,250 for it, owned it for 14 months, and sold it for $18,000. Rennie had suspected that this particular classic video game would be of interest to collectors; so he had it refurbished, put it on display in his video arcade, and listed it for sale on the Internet. No customers in the arcade had played it other than those testing it before considering it for purchase. Rennie would like the gain on the sale of the classic video game to be a long-term capital gain. Did he achieve that objective? Why or why not?

21. **LO.2** George is the owner of numerous classic automobiles. His intention is to hold the automobiles until they increase in value and then sell them. He rents the automobiles for use in various events (e.g., antique automobile shows) while he is holding them. In 2016, he sold a classic automobile for $1.5 million. He had held the automobile for five years, and it had a tax basis of $750,000. Was the automobile a capital asset? Why or why not?

22. **LO.2, 4** Barbella purchased a wedding ring for $15 at a yard sale in May. She thought the ring was costume jewelry, but it turned out to be a real diamond ring. She is not in the business of buying and selling anything. She researched the ring on the Internet and discovered that it was worth at least $1,000. She sold it on an Internet auction site for $1,100 in July. Was the ring a capital asset? What were the amount and nature of the gain or loss from its sale by Barbella?

23. **LO.2** Puce is a corporation that buys and sells financial assets. It purchases notes receivable from manufacturers that need cash immediately and cannot wait to collect the notes. Puce pays about 88% of the face value of the receivables and then collects them. Because of the quality of the notes, Puce collected less than it paid for some of the notes. Does Puce have a capital loss when it collects the receivables for less than it paid for them? Explain.

24. **LO.2** Faith Godwin is a dealer in securities. She has spotted a fast-rising company   Communications
    and would like to buy and hold its stock for investment. The stock is currently
    selling for $2 per share, and Faith thinks it will climb to $40 a share within two years.
    Faith's coworkers have told her that there is "no way" she can get long-term capital
    gain treatment when she purchases stock because she is a securities dealer. Faith
    has asked you to calculate her potential gain and tell her whether her coworkers are
    right. Draft a letter to Faith responding to her request. Her address is 200 Catamon
    Drive, Great Falls, MT 59406.

25. **LO.2** Maria meets all of the requirements of § 1237 (subdivided realty). In 2016, she
    begins selling lots and sells four separate lots to four different purchasers. She
    also sells two contiguous lots to another purchaser. The sales price of each lot is
    $30,000. Maria's basis for each lot is $15,000. Selling expenses are $500 per lot.
    a. What are the realized and recognized gain?
    b. Explain the nature of the gain (i.e., ordinary income or capital gain).
    c. Would your answers change if, instead, the lots sold to the fifth purchaser were
       not contiguous? If so, how?

26. **LO.2, 3, 5** Melaney has had a bad year with her investments. She lent a friend   Decision Making
    $8,000; the friend did not repay the loan when it was due and then
    declared bankruptcy. The loan is totally uncollectible. Melaney also was notified by
    her broker that the Oak corporate bonds she owned became worthless on October
    13, 2016. She had purchased the bonds for $22,000 on November 10, 2015. Melaney
    also had a $60,000 loss on the disposition of § 1244 corporate stock that she pur-
    chased several years ago. Melaney is single.
    a. What are the nature and amount of Melaney's losses?
    b. What is Melaney's AGI for 2016 assuming that she has $65,000 of ordinary gross
       income from sources other than those discussed?
    c. What are the nature and amount of Melaney's loss carryforwards?

27. **LO.2, 3** Benny purchased $400,000 of Peach Corporation face value bonds for
    $320,000 on November 13, 2015. The bonds had been issued with $80,000
    of original issue discount because Peach was in financial difficulty in 2015. On
    December 3, 2016, Benny sold the bonds for $283,000 after amortizing $1,000 of the
    original issue discount. What are the nature and amount of Benny's gain or loss?

28. **LO.3** Fred is an investor in vacant land. When he thinks he has identified property   Decision Making
    that would be a good investment, he approaches the landowner, pays the
    landowner for a "right of first refusal" to purchase the land, records this right in the
    property records, and then waits to see if the land increases in value. The right of
    first refusal is valid for four years. Fourteen months ago, Fred paid a landowner
    $9,000 for a right of first refusal. The land was selected as the site of a new shopping
    center, and the landowner was offered $1 million for the land. In its title search on
    the land, the buyer discovered Fred's right of first refusal and involved him in the
    purchase negotiations. Ultimately, the landowner paid Fred $220,000 to give up his
    right of first refusal; the landowner then sold the land to the buyer for $4,220,000.
    Fred has a marginal tax rate of 39.6%.
    a. What difference does it make whether Fred treats the right of first refusal as an
       option to purchase the land?
    b. What difference does it make whether Fred is a "dealer" in land?

29. **LO.3** Carla was the owner of vacant land that she was holding for investment. She
    paid $2 million for the land in 2014. Raymond was an investor in vacant land.
    He thought Carla's land might be the site of an exit ramp from a new freeway. Ray-
    mond gave Carla $836,000 for an option on her land in 2015. The option was good
    for two years and gave Raymond the ability to purchase Carla's land for $4,765,000.

The freeway was not approved by the government, and Raymond's option expired in 2016. Does Carla have $836,000 of long-term capital gain upon the expiration of the option? Explain.

30. **LO.3** Hilde purchased all of the rights to a patent on a new garden tool developed by a friend of hers who was an amateur inventor. The inventor had obtained the patent rights, set up a manufacturing company to produce and sell the garden tool, and produced substantial quantities of the tool, but he then became discouraged when no large garden company would agree to distribute the tool for him. Hilde purchased the patent rights (but not the manufacturing company) for $120,000 on October 24, 2015. Hilde had never engaged in such a transaction before, but she is a salesperson in the garden industry and thought she could succeed where her friend had failed. On June 27, 2016, she sold all of the patent rights to Garden Tool Company for $1,233,000. Garden Tool will manufacture the tool in its own factory and sell it to its customers. What is the nature of Hilde's gain from this transaction?

Decision Making   31. **LO.3, 4, 7** Mac, an inventor, obtained a patent on a chemical process to clean old aluminum siding so that it can be easily repainted. Mac has a $50,000 tax basis in the patent. Mac does not have the capital to begin manufacturing and selling this product, so he has done nothing with the patent since obtaining it two years ago. Now a group of individuals has approached him and offered two alternatives. Under one alternative, they will pay Mac $600,000 (payable evenly over the next 15 years) for the exclusive right to manufacture and sell the product. Under the other, they will form a business and contribute capital to it to begin manufacturing and selling the product; Mac will receive 20% of the company's shares of stock in exchange for all of his patent rights. Discuss which alternative is better for Mac.

32. **LO.3** Freys, Inc., sells a 12-year franchise to Reynaldo. The franchise contains many restrictions on how Reynaldo may operate his store. For instance, Reynaldo cannot use less than Grade 10 Idaho potatoes; must fry the potatoes at a constant 410 degrees; must dress store personnel in Freys-approved uniforms; and must have a Freys sign that meets detailed specifications on size, color, and construction. When the franchise contract is signed, Reynaldo makes a noncontingent $160,000 payment to Freys. During the same year, Reynaldo pays Freys $300,000—14% of Reynaldo's sales. How does Freys treat each of these payments? How does Reynaldo treat each of the payments?

Issue ID   33. **LO.3** Angie owns numerous strip malls. A major tenant of one of the strip malls wanted to cancel its lease because it was moving to another city. After lengthy negotiations, the tenant paid Angie $60,000 to cancel its obligations under the lease. If the tenant had fulfilled the lease terms, Angie would have received rent of $700,000. What factors should Angie consider to determine the amount and character of her income from these circumstances?

34. **LO.3** Consuela was a tenant in a campus apartment. She is a student at State University. Her lease began on August 1, 2016, and was due to expire on July 31, 2017. However, her landlord sold the building, and the new owner wanted to demolish it to build a retail building. Consuela's landlord paid her $1,000 to cancel the lease. Consuela received the $1,000 on November 30, 2016; moved out; and rented another apartment. How should Consuela treat the $1,000?

35. **LO.4** Maria held vacant land that qualified as an investment asset. She purchased the vacant land on April 10, 2012. She exchanged the vacant land for a rental house in a qualifying like-kind exchange on January 22, 2016. Maria was going to hold the house for several years and then sell it. However, she got an "offer she

could not refuse" and sold it on November 22, 2016, for a substantial gain. What was Maria's holding period for the house?

36. **LO.4** Roger inherited 100 shares of Periwinkle stock when his mother, Emily, died. Emily had acquired the stock for a total of $60,000 on November 15, 2012. She died on August 10, 2016, and the shares were worth a total of $55,000 at that time. Roger sold the shares for $36,000 on December 22, 2016. How much gain or loss does Roger recognize? What is the nature of that gain or loss?

37. **LO.4** Sarah received a gift of farmland from her father. The land was worth $4 million at the date of the gift, had been farmed by her father for 40 years, and had a tax basis for her father of $30,000. Sarah never farmed the land and sold it eight months after receiving it from her father for $4.2 million. What is Sarah's holding period for the farmland? What is the nature of the gain from its disposition?

38. **LO.4** Dennis sells short 100 shares of ARC stock at $20 per share on January 15, 2016. He buys 200 shares of ARC stock on April 1, 2016, at $25 per share. On May 2, 2016, he closes the short sale by delivering 100 of the shares purchased on April 1.
    a. What are the amount and nature of Dennis's loss upon closing the short sale?
    b. When does the holding period for the remaining 100 shares begin?
    c. If Dennis sells (at $27 per share) the remaining 100 shares on January 20, 2017, what will be the nature of his gain or loss?

39. **LO.5** Elaine Case (single with no dependents) has the following transactions in 2016: *Communications*

AGI (exclusive of capital gains and losses)	$240,000
Long-term capital gain	22,000
Long-term capital loss	(8,000)
Short-term capital gain	19,000
Short-term capital loss	(23,000)

What is Elaine's net capital gain or loss? Draft a letter to Elaine describing how the net capital gain or loss will be treated on her tax return. Assume that Elaine's income from other sources puts her in the 39.6% bracket. Elaine's address is 300 Ireland Avenue, Shepherdstown, WV 25443.

40. **LO.3, 5** In 2016, Bertha Jarow (head of household with three dependents) had a *Communications*
$28,000 loss from the sale of a personal residence. She also purchased from an individual inventor for $7,000 (and resold in two months for $18,000) a patent on a rubber bonding process. The patent had not yet been reduced to practice. Bertha purchased the patent as an investment. In addition, she had the following capital gains and losses from stock transactions:

Long-term capital loss	($ 6,000)
Long-term capital loss carryover from 2015	(12,000)
Short-term capital gain	21,000
Short-term capital loss	(7,000)

What is Bertha's net capital gain or loss? Draft a letter to Bertha explaining the tax treatment of the sale of her personal residence. Assume that Bertha's income from other sources puts her in the 28% bracket. Bertha's address is 1120 West Street, Ashland, OR 97520.

41. **LO.2, 4, 5** Bridgette is known as the "doll lady." She started collecting dolls as a *Issue ID*
child, always received one or more dolls as gifts on her birthday, never sold any dolls, and eventually owned 600 dolls. She is retiring and moving to a small apartment and has decided to sell her collection. She lists the dolls on an Internet

auction site and, to her great surprise, receives an offer from another doll collector of $45,000 for the entire collection. Bridgette sells the entire collection, except for five dolls she purchased during the last year. She had owned all of the dolls sold for more than a year. What tax factors should Bridgette consider in deciding how to report the sale?

42. **LO.5** Phil and Susan are married taxpayers filing a joint return. The couple have two dependent children. Susan has wages of $34,000 in 2016. Phil does not work due to a disability, but he is a buyer and seller of stocks on the Internet. He generally buys and holds for long-term gain, but occasionally gets in and out of a stock quickly. The couple's 2016 stock transactions are detailed below. In addition, they have $2,300 of qualifying dividends. What is Phil and Susan's AGI?

Item	Date Acquired	Date Sold	Cost	Sales Price
Blue stock	11/10/15	03/12/16	$ 3,000	$ 6,000
Puce stock	12/13/14	05/23/16	36,000	32,000
Beige stock	12/14/11	07/14/16	13,000	14,500
Red stock	06/29/15	05/18/16	26,000	27,000
Black stock	05/15/15	10/18/16	67,000	67,800
Gray stock	04/23/14	10/18/16	89,000	88,200

43. **LO.5** Paul has the following long-term capital gains and losses for 2016: $62,000 28% gain, $21,000 28% loss, $18,000 25% gain, and $64,000 0%/15%/20% gain. He also has a $53,000 short-term loss and a $5,000 short-term gain. What is Paul's AGI from these transactions? If he has a net long-term capital gain, what is its makeup in terms of the alternative tax rates?

44. **LO.5** Helena has the following long-term capital gains and losses for 2016: $65,000 28% gain, $53,000 28% loss, $28,000 25% gain, and $24,000 0%/15%/20% loss. She also has a $33,000 short-term loss and a $65,000 short-term gain. What is Helena's AGI from these transactions? If she has a net long-term capital gain, what is its makeup in terms of the alternative tax rates?

45. **LO.5** For 2016, Ashley has gross income of $8,350 and a $5,000 long-term capital loss. She claims the standard deduction. Ashley is 35 years old and unmarried with two dependent children. How much of Ashley's $5,000 capital loss carries over to 2017?

46. **LO.5** Jane and Blair are married taxpayers filing jointly and have 2016 taxable income of $97,000. The taxable income includes $5,000 of gain from a capital asset held five years, $2,100 of gain from a capital asset held seven months, and $13,000 of gain from a capital asset held four years. All of the capital assets were stock in publicly traded corporations. Jane and Blair also have qualified dividend income of $3,000. What is the couple's tax on taxable income?

47. **LO.5** For 2016, Wilma has properly determined taxable income of $36,000, including $3,000 of unrecaptured § 1250 gain and $8,200 of 0%/15%/20% gain. Wilma qualifies for head-of-household filing status. Compute Wilma's tax liability and the tax savings from the alternative tax on net capital gain.

48. **LO.5** Asok's AGI for 2016 is $133,050. Included in this AGI is a $45,000 25% long-term capital gain and a $13,000 0%/15%/20% long-term capital gain. Asok is single, uses the standard deduction, and has only his personal exemption. Compute his taxable income, the tax liability, and the tax savings from the alternative tax on net capital gain.

49. **LO.6** Gray, Inc., a C corporation, has taxable income from operations of $1,452,000 for 2016. It also has a net long-term capital loss of $355,000 from the sale of a subsidiary's stock. The year 2016 is the first year in the last 10 years that Gray has not had at least $500,000 per year of net long-term capital gains. What is Gray's 2016 taxable income? What, if anything, can it do with any unused capital losses?

50. **LO.2, 3, 7** Harriet, who is single, is the owner of a sole proprietorship. Two years ago, Harriet developed a process for preserving doughnuts that gives the doughnut a much longer shelf life. The process is not patented or copyrighted, and only Harriet knows how it works. Harriet has been approached by a company that would like to buy the process. Harriet insists that she receive a long-term employment contract with the acquiring company as well as be paid for the rights to the process. The acquiring company offers Harriet a choice of two options: (1) $650,000 in cash for the process and a 10-year covenant not to compete at $65,000 per year or (2) $650,000 in cash for a 10-year covenant not to compete and $65,000 per year for 10 years in payment for the process. Which option should Harriet accept? What is the tax effect on the acquiring company of each approach?

Decision Making

Cumulative Problems

Tax Return Problem

TAX SOFTWARE

51. Ashley Panda lives at 1310 Meadow Lane, Wayne, OH 43466, and her Social Security number is 123-45-6789. Ashley is single and has a 20-year-old son, Bill. His Social Security number is 111-11-1112. Bill lives with Ashley, and she fully supports him. Bill spent 2015 traveling in Europe and was not a college student. He had gross income of $4,655 in 2015.

Ashley owns Panda Enterprises, LLC sole proprietorship, a data processing service (98-7654321), which is located at 456 Hill Street, Wayne, OH 43466. The business activity code is 514210. Her 2015 Form 1040, Schedule C for Panda Enterprises shows revenues of $315,000, office expenses of $66,759, employee salary of $63,000, employee payroll taxes of $4,820, meals and entertainment expenses (before the 50% reduction) of $22,000, and rent expense of $34,000. The rent expense includes payments related to renting an office ($30,000) and payments related to renting various equipment ($4,000). There is no depreciation because all depreciable equipment owned has been fully depreciated in previous years. No fringe benefits are provided to the employee. Ashley personally purchases health insurance on herself and Bill. The premiums are $23,000 per year.

Ashley has an extensive stock portfolio and has prepared the following analysis:

Stock	Number of Shares	Date Purchased	Date Sold	Per-Share Cost	Per-Share Selling Price	Total Dividends
Beige	10	10/18/14	10/11/15	$80	$ 74	$30
Garland	30	10/11/08	10/11/15	43	157	70
Puce	15	3/10/15	8/11/15	62	33	45

NOTE: Ashley received a Form 1099–B from her stockbroker that included the adjusted basis and sales proceeds for each of her stock transactions. The per-share cost includes commissions, and the per-share selling price is net of commissions. Also, the dividends are the actual dividends received in 2015, and these are both ordinary dividends and qualified dividends.

Ashley had $800 of interest income from State of Ohio bonds and $600 of interest income on her Wayne Savings Bank account. She paid $25,000 of alimony to her former husband. His Social Security number is 123-45-6788.

Ashley itemizes her deductions and had the following items, which may be relevant to her return:

Item	Amount	Comment
Unreimbursed medical expenses for Ashley (all for visits to doctors)	$1,786	Does not include health insurance premiums.
State income taxes paid	1,830	
Real property taxes on personal residence	3,230	
Interest paid on home mortgage (Form 1098)	8,137	The loan is secured by the residence and was incurred when the home was purchased.
Charitable contributions	940	Cash paid to Ashley's church.
Sales taxes	619	Amount per sales tax table.

Ashley made a $30,000 estimated Federal income tax payment, does not want any of her taxes to finance presidential elections, has no foreign bank accounts or trusts, and wants any refund to be applied against her 2016 taxes.

Compute Ashley's net tax payable or refund due for 2015. If you use tax forms for your computations, you will need Form 1040 and its Schedules A, C, D, and SE and Form 8949. Suggested software: H&R BLOCK Tax Software.

Tax Computation Problem

Communications

52. Paul Barrone is a graduate student at State University. His 10-year-old son, Jamie, lives with him, and Paul is Jamie's sole support. Paul's wife died in 2015, and Paul has not remarried. Paul received $320,000 of life insurance proceeds (related to his wife's death) in early 2016 and immediately invested the entire amount as shown below:

Item	Date Acquired	Cost	Date Sold	Selling Price	Dividends/ Interest
1,000 shares Blue	01/23/16	$ 14,000	12/03/16	$ 3,500	None
400 shares Magenta	01/23/16	23,000			$750
600 shares Orange	01/23/16	230,000			$2,300
100 shares Brown	06/23/10	2,800	01/23/16	14,000	None
Green bonds	01/23/16	23,000			$1,200
Gold money market account	01/23/16	30,000			$600

Paul had $42,000 of taxable graduate assistant earnings from State University and received a $10,000 scholarship. He used $8,000 of the scholarship to pay his tuition and fees for the year and $2,000 for Jamie's day care. Jamie attended Little Kids Daycare Center, a state-certified child care facility. Paul received a statement related to the Green bonds saying that there was $45 of original issue discount amortization during 2016. Paul maintains the receipts for the sales taxes he paid of $735.

Paul lives at 1610 Cherry Lane, Bradenton, FL 34212, and his Social Security number is 111-11-1111. Jamie's Social Security number is 123-45-6789. The university withheld $3,000 of Federal income tax from Paul's salary. Paul is not itemizing his deductions.

Part 1—Tax Computation
Compute Paul's lowest tax liability for 2016.

Part 2—Tax Planning
Paul is concerned because the Green bonds were worth only $18,000 at the end of 2016, $5,000 less than he paid for them. He is an inexperienced investor and wants to know if this $5,000 is deductible. The bonds had original issue discount of $2,000 when he purchased them, and he is curious about how that affects his investment in the bonds. The bonds had 20 years left to maturity when he purchased them. Draft a brief letter to Paul explaining how to handle these items. Also prepare a memo for Paul's tax file.

Research Problems

THOMSON REUTERS
CHECKPOINT
Student Edition

Note: Solutions to Research Problems can be prepared by using the Checkpoint® Student Edition online research product, which is available to accompany this text. It is also possible to prepare solutions to the Research Problems by using tax research materials found in a standard tax library.

Research Problem 1. Ali owns 100 shares of Brown Corporation stock. He purchased the stock at five different times and at five different prices per share as indicated:

Share Block	Number of Shares	Per-Share Price	Purchase Date
A	10	$60	10/10/99
B	20	20	8/11/00
C	15	15	10/24/01
D	35	30	4/23/02
E	20	25	7/28/02

On April 28, 2016, Ali will sell 40 shares of Brown stock for $40 per share. All of Ali's shares are held by his stockbroker. The broker's records track when the shares were purchased. May Ali designate the shares he sells? If so, which shares should he sell? Assume that Ali wants to maximize his gain because he has a capital loss carryforward.

Research Problem 2. Clyde had worked for many years as the chief executive of Red Industries, Inc., and had been a major shareholder. Clyde and the company had a falling out, and Clyde was terminated. Clyde and Red executed a document under which Clyde's stock in Red would be redeemed and Clyde would agree not to compete against Red in its geographic service area. After extensive negotiations between the parties, Clyde agreed to surrender his Red stock in exchange for $600,000. Clyde's basis in his shares was $143,000, and he had held the shares for 17 years. The agreement made no explicit allocation of any of the $600,000 to Clyde's agreement not to compete against Red. How should Clyde treat the $600,000 payment on his 2016 tax return?

Research Problem 3. Siva Nathaniel owns various plots of land in Fulton County, Georgia. He acquired the land at various times during the last 20 years. About every fourth year, Siva subdivides into lots one of the properties he owns. He then has water, sewer, natural gas, and electricity hookups put in each lot and paves new streets. Siva has always treated his sales of such lots as sales of capital assets. His previous tax returns were prepared by an accountant whose practice you recently purchased. Has the proper tax treatment been used on the prior tax returns? Explain

Partial list of research aids:
§§ 1221 and 1237 and *Jesse W. and Betty J. English*, 65 TCM 2160, T.C.Memo. 1993–111.

Use the tax resources of the Internet to address the following questions. Do not restrict your search to the Web, but include a review of newsgroups and general reference materials, practitioner sites and resources, primary sources of the tax law, chat rooms and discussion groups, and other opportunities.

Internet Activity

Research Problem 4. Perform a Google search to find information about capital gains tax rates worldwide (and across U.S. states). Try searching for "capital gains rate by country (state)." What jurisdiction has the highest capital gains tax rate? What U.S. states have high capital gains tax rates?

Research Problem 5. Find a website, other than the IRS website, that discusses the taxation of short sales of securities.

Roger CPA Review Questions

 ROGER CPA Review

1. Identify which of the following is a capital asset:

   I.   A canvas painting of a portrait client, in the painter's hands
   II. Depreciable fixtures in a business parking lot
   III. Office supplies held by a business

   a.   II only
   b.   II and III only
   c.   III only
   d.   None of the above

2. On January 15 of the current year, Kreutzer, an individual, received as an inheritance from Gladstone's estate shares of stock worth $25,000. Gladstone had purchased the shares in June of the previous year for $20,000, and the shares were worth $25,000 at Gladstone's date of death in November of the previous year. The executor of Gladstone's estate did not elect to use the alternate valuation date. In March of the current year, Kreutzer sold the shares for $27,000. As a result of the sale, what is the amount and type of gain reported by Kreutzer?

   a. $7,000 long-term capital gain
   b. $2,000 short-term capital gain
   c. $7,000 short-term capital gain
   d. $2,000 long-term capital gain

3. The following facts apply to Collins, an individual:

   In February of the current year, Hodge, who had owed a $5,000 personal debt to Collins for the past three years, declared bankruptcy.

   Collins sold land held for investment for a $10,000 gain. The land had been purchased by Collins five years prior.

   In July of the current year, Collins received shares of stock as a gift from Bellamy. Bellamy had purchased the shares in January of the current year. In November, Collins sold the stock for a gain of $3,000.

   Considering only the above facts, what will Collins report on the current year tax return?

   a. $2,000 long-term capital gain
   b. $8,000 long-term capital gain
   c. $10,000 ordinary income and $2,000 short-term capital loss
   d. $10,000 long-term capital gain and $3,000 short-term capital gain

4. In 2016 Colossus Corporation incurred a net capital loss in the amount of $25,000. Colossus had the following net capital gains in the previous five years:

   2015: $7,000
   2014: $2,000
   2013: $5,000
   2012: $4,000
   2011: $3,000

   How much of the 2016 net capital loss may Colossus carry over to 2017?

   a. $0
   b. $25,000
   c. $11,000
   d. $4,000

5. The following facts apply to Eliot, an individual, in the current year:

April 2: Sold shares of stock, purchased on April 1 of the previous year, for a $2,000 gain.

May 15: Sold equipment used in Eliot's business, which had been purchased in July of the previous year, for a $2,000 gain.

July 12: Sold shares of stock, purchased in February of the previous year, for a $7,000 gain.

November 3: Sold equipment used in Eliot's business, which had been purchased in January of the current year, for a $1,000 loss.

December 9: Sold shares of stock, purchased on February 22 of the current year, for a $3,000 loss.

Considering only the above facts, what is Eliot's net capital gain for the current year?

a. $7,000 long-term capital gain
b. $9,000 long-term capital gain
c. $5,000 long-term capital gain
d. $6,000 long-term capital gain

Property Transactions: § 1231 and Recapture Provisions

LEARNING OBJECTIVES: *After completing Chapter 17, you should be able to:*

LO.1 State the rationale for and the nature and treatment of gains and losses from the disposition of business assets.

LO.2 Distinguish § 1231 assets from ordinary assets and capital assets and calculate the § 1231 gain or loss.

LO.3 Determine when § 1245 recapture applies and how it is computed.

LO.4 Determine when § 1250 recapture applies.

LO.5 Identify considerations common to §§ 1245 and 1250.

LO.6 Apply the special recapture provisions for related parties and intangible drilling costs (IDCs) and be aware of the special recapture provision for corporations.

LO.7 Describe and apply the reporting procedures for §§ 1231, 1245, and 1250.

LO.8 Identify tax planning opportunities associated with §§ 1231, 1245, and 1250.

CHAPTER OUTLINE

DEPRECIATION RECAPTURE

Hazel Brown (a sole proprietor filing a Form 1040 Schedule C) owns and operates a retail arts and crafts store. She has some 15-year-old snow removal equipment with a $1,000 tax basis. Next to her store is a small lot that she bought several years ago for $15,000 to expand the store's parking lot. In 2013, she remodeled the store and replaced the store's equipment (counters, display racks, etc.), at a cost of $450,000, with used equipment that she bought from a competitor. The equipment is 7-year MACRS property. That year, she claimed $250,000 of § 179 expense on it and depreciated the balance. She did not expense the entire $450,000 (the maximum § 179 deduction in 2013 was $500,000) because she expected to be in a higher tax bracket in later years and wanted to "save" some of the depreciation. As of June 30, 2016, the equipment has an adjusted basis of $74,960 ($450,000 cost − $250,000 § 179 expense − $125,040 of regular MACRS depreciation). Now Hazel is again planning to replace the store's equipment, and she has determined that she can sell all of the existing equipment for $128,000.

If Hazel completes this transaction, what will be the impact on her 2016 tax return?

Read the chapter and formulate your response.

FRAMEWORK 1040 **Tax Formula for Individuals**

This chapter covers the boldfaced portions of the Tax Formula for Individuals that was introduced in Concept Summary 3.1 on p. 3-3. Below those portions are the sections of Form 1040 where the results are reported.

Income *(broadly defined)*	$xx,xxx
Less: Exclusions	(x,xxx)
Gross income	**$xx,xxx**
Less: Deductions *for* adjusted gross income	**(x,xxx)**

FORM 1040 (p. 1)

12	Business income or (loss). Attach Schedule C or C-EZ	
13	Capital gain or (loss). Attach Schedule D if required. If not required, check here ▶	☐
14	Other gains or (losses). Attach Form 4797	

Adjusted gross income	$xx,xxx
Less: The greater of total itemized deductions *or* the standard deduction	(x,xxx)
Personal and dependency exemptions	(x,xxx)
Taxable income	**$xx,xxx**
Tax on taxable income *(see Tax Tables or Tax Rate Schedules)*	**$ x,xxx**

FORM 1040 (p. 2)

44	**Tax** (see instructions). Check if any from: **a** ☐ Form(s) 8814 **b** ☐ Form 4972 **c** ☐ _____

Less: Tax credits *(including income taxes withheld and prepaid)*	(xxx)
Tax due (or refund)	$ xxx

G eneric Manufacturing LLC (a limited liability company) sold machinery, office furniture, and unneeded production plants for $100 million last year. The company's disposition of these assets resulted in $60 million of gains and $13 million of losses. How are these gains and losses treated for tax purposes? Do any special tax rules apply? Could any of the gains and losses receive capital gain or loss treatment? This chapter answers these questions by explaining how to *classify* gains and losses from the disposition of assets that are used in the business rather than held for resale. Chapter 8 discussed how to *depreciate* such assets. Chapters 14 and 15 discussed how to determine the *adjusted basis* and the *amount* of gain or loss from their disposition.

A long-term capital gain was defined in Chapter 16 as the recognized gain from the sale or exchange of a capital asset held for the required long-term holding period.[1] Long-term capital assets are capital assets held more than one year.

This chapter is concerned with classification under § 1231, which applies to the sale or exchange of business properties and to certain involuntary conversions. Section 1221(a)(2) provides that such properties are not capital assets because they are depreciable and/or real property used in business or for the production of income. Nonetheless, these business properties may be held for long periods of time and may be sold at a gain.

Congress decided many years ago that such assets deserved *limited* capital gain-type treatment, which sometimes gives too much tax advantage when assets are eligible for depreciation (or cost recovery). Thus, certain recapture rules may prevent the capital gain treatment when depreciation is taken. This chapter covers the recapture provisions that tax as ordinary income certain gains that might otherwise qualify for long-term capital gain treatment.

---

[1] § 1222(3). To be eligible for any beneficial tax treatment, the holding period must be more than one year.

TAX IN THE NEWS Investment Confusion

Over the past few years, many newspaper articles have discussed the investment opportunities available to taxpayers who purchase foreclosed real estate, fix it up, and then either sell the property for a capital gain or rent it to people who can no longer afford to purchase a home.

However, some of these articles are misleading because this property is *not* a capital asset. If it is held for resale in the ordinary course of business, it is an ordinary asset. If it is held more than a year and rented to others, it is a § 1231 asset. In either case, the asset is *not* a capital asset.

17-1 SECTION 1231 ASSETS

17-1a Relationship to Capital Assets

Because depreciable property and real property used in business are not capital assets,[2] the recognized gains from the disposition of this property would appear to be ordinary income rather than capital gain. Due to § 1231, however, *net gain* from the disposition of this property is sometimes *treated* as *long-term capital gain.* A long-term holding period requirement must be met; the disposition must generally be from a sale, exchange, or involuntary conversion; and certain recapture provisions must be satisfied for this result to occur. Section 1231 may also apply to involuntary conversions of capital assets even though such a disposition, which is not a sale or exchange, normally would not result in a capital gain.

If the disposition of depreciable property and real property used in business results in a *net loss*, § 1231 *treats* the *loss* as an *ordinary loss* rather than as a capital loss. Ordinary losses are fully deductible *for* adjusted gross income (AGI). Capital losses are offset by capital gains, and if any loss remains, the loss is deductible to the extent of $3,000 per year for individuals and currently is not deductible at all by regular corporations. It seems, therefore, that § 1231 provides the *best* of both potential results: net gain may be treated as long-term capital gain, and net loss is treated as ordinary loss.

LO.1

State the rationale for and the nature and treatment of gains and losses from the disposition of business assets.

The Big Picture

EXAMPLE

1

Return to the facts of *The Big Picture* on p. 17-1. If Hazel sells the parking lot for $18,000, she will have disposed of a § 1231 asset because it was property used in a trade or business and held for the long-term holding period (more than one year).

Hazel's gain will be $3,000 ($18,000 selling price − $15,000 adjusted basis). Because the asset is a § 1231 asset, all of the gain is § 1231 gain, and it *may* be treated as long-term capital gain (depending on its netting with any other § 1231 gains or losses during the year).

The Big Picture

EXAMPLE

2

Return to the facts of *The Big Picture* on p. 17-1. Assume that Hazel sells the snow removal equipment for $100, generating a $900 loss and the parking lot for $15,700, generating a $700 gain.

Both properties were held for use in her business for the long-term holding period and, therefore, are § 1231 assets. Hazel's net § 1231 loss is $200, and that net loss is an ordinary loss.

The rules regarding § 1231 treatment do *not* apply to *all* business property. Important in this regard are the holding period requirements and the fact that the property must be either depreciable property or real estate used in business. Nor is § 1231 necessarily limited to business property. Transactions involving certain capital assets may fall into the § 1231 category. Thus, § 1231 singles out only some types of business property.

---

[2]§ 1221(a)(2).

As discussed in Chapter 16, long-term capital gains receive beneficial tax treatment. Section 1231 requires netting of **§ 1231 gains and losses**. If the result is a gain, it may be treated as a long-term capital gain. The net gain is added to the "real" long-term capital gains (if any) and netted with capital losses (if any). Thus, the net § 1231 gain may eventually be eligible for beneficial capital gain treatment or help avoid the unfavorable net capital loss result. As noted earlier, if the § 1231 gain and loss netting results in a loss, it is an ordinary loss. Finally, § 1231 assets are treated the same as capital assets for purposes of the appreciated property charitable contribution provisions (refer to Chapter 10).

17-1b Justification for Favorable Tax Treatment

The favorable capital gain/ordinary loss treatment sanctioned by § 1231 can be explained by examining several historical developments. Before 1938, business property had been included in the definition of capital assets. Thus, if such property was sold for a loss (not an unlikely possibility during the depression years of the 1930s), a capital loss resulted. If, however, the property was depreciable and could be retained for its estimated useful life, much (if not all) of its costs could be recovered in the form of depreciation. Because the allowance for depreciation was fully deductible whereas capital losses were not, the tax law favored those who did not dispose of an asset. Congress recognized this inequity when it removed business property from the capital asset classification. During the period 1938–1942, therefore, all such gains and losses were ordinary gains and losses.

With the advent of World War II, two developments in particular forced Congress to reexamine the situation regarding business assets. First, the sale of business assets at a gain was discouraged because the gain would be ordinary income. Gains were common because the war effort had inflated prices. Second, taxpayers who did not want to sell their assets often were required to because the government acquired them through condemnation. Often, as a result of the condemnation awards, taxpayers who were forced to part with their property experienced large gains and were deprived of the benefits of future depreciation deductions. Of course, the condemnations constituted involuntary conversions, so taxpayers could defer the gain by timely reinvestment in property that was "similar or related in service or use." But where was such property to be found in view of wartime restrictions and other governmental condemnations? The end result did not seem equitable: a large ordinary gain due to government action and no possibility of deferral due to government restrictions.

In recognition of these conditions, in 1942, Congress eased the tax bite on the disposition of some business property by allowing preferential capital gain treatment. Thus, the present scheme of § 1231 and the dichotomy of capital gain/ordinary loss treatment evolved from a combination of economic considerations existing in 1938 and 1942.

17-1c Property Included

LO.2

Distinguish § 1231 assets from ordinary assets and capital assets and calculate the § 1231 gain or loss.

Section 1231 property generally includes the following assets if they are held for more than one year:

- Depreciable or real property used in business or for the production of income (principally machinery and equipment, buildings, and land).
- Timber, coal, or domestic iron ore to which § 631 applies.
- Livestock held for draft, breeding, dairy, or sporting purposes.
- Unharvested crops on land used in business.
- Certain *purchased* intangible assets (such as patents and goodwill) that are eligible for amortization.

These assets are ordinary assets until they have been held for more than one year. Only then do they become § 1231 assets.

17-1d **Property Excluded**

Section 1231 property generally does *not* include the following:

- Property not held for the long-term holding period. Because the benefit of § 1231 is long-term capital gain treatment, the holding period must correspond to the more-than-one-year holding period that applies to capital assets. Livestock must be held at least 12 months (24 months in some cases). Unharvested crops do not have to be held for the required long-term holding period, but the land must be held for the long-term holding period.

- Nonpersonal use property where casualty losses exceed casualty gains for the taxable year. If a taxpayer has a net casualty loss, the individual casualty gains and losses are treated as ordinary gains and losses.

- Inventory and property held primarily for sale to customers.

- Copyrights; literary, musical, or artistic compositions, etc.; and certain U.S. government publications.

- Accounts receivable and notes receivable arising in the ordinary course of the trade or business.

17-1e **Special Rules for Certain § 1231 Assets**

A rather diverse group of assets is included under § 1231. The following discussion summarizes the special rules for some of those assets.

Timber

Congress has provided preferential treatment relative to the natural growth value of timber, which takes a relatively long time to mature. Congress believed that this preferential treatment would encourage reforestation of timber lands. A taxpayer disposing of timber held for the long-term holding period has a long-term capital gain or loss if the timber was held for investment, has a § 1231 gain or loss if the timber was used in a trade or business, but, without special statutory treatment, would have ordinary income or loss if the timber was held as inventory. Section 631(a) allows the taxpayer to *elect* to treat the cutting of timber as a sale or exchange and, if the election is made, to treat the sale as the disposition of a § 1231 asset.[3]

The recognized § 1231 gain or loss is determined at the time the timber is cut and is equal to the difference between the timber's fair market value as of the *first day* of the taxable year and the adjusted basis for depletion. If a taxpayer sells the timber for more or less than the fair market value as of the first day of the taxable year in which it is cut, the difference is ordinary income or loss.

Several years ago, Tom, a timber dealer, purchased a tract of land with a substantial stand of trees on it. The land cost $40,000, and the timber cost $100,000. On the first day of 2016, the timber was appraised at $250,000. In August 2016, Tom cut the timber and sold it for $265,000. Tom elects to treat the cutting as a sale or exchange under § 1231. He has a $150,000 § 1231 gain ($250,000 − $100,000) and a $15,000 ordinary gain ($265,000 − $250,000).

What if the timber had been sold for $235,000? Tom would still have a $150,000 § 1231 gain, but he would also have a $15,000 ordinary loss. The price for computing § 1231 gain is the price at the beginning of the tax year. Any difference between that price and the sales price is ordinary gain or loss. Here, because the price declined by $15,000, Tom has an ordinary loss in that amount.

EXAMPLE 3

Livestock

Cattle and horses must be held 24 months or more and other livestock must be held 12 months or more to qualify under § 1231.[4] The primary reason for enacting this

---

[3]§ 631(a) and Reg. § 1.631–1. To receive § 631 treatment, the holding period for the timber must be greater than one year.

[4]Note that the holding period is "12 months or more" and not "more than 12 months."

provision was the considerable amount of litigation over the character of livestock [whether livestock was held primarily for sale to customers (ordinary income) or for use in a trade or business (§ 1231 property)]. Poultry is not livestock for purposes of § 1231.

Section 1231 Assets Disposed of by Casualty or Theft

When § 1231 assets are disposed of by casualty or theft, a special netting rule is applied. For simplicity, the term *casualty* is used to mean both casualty and theft dispositions. First, the casualty gains and losses from § 1231 assets *and* the casualty gains and losses from **long-term nonpersonal use capital assets** are determined. A nonpersonal use capital asset might be art held as an investment or a baseball card collection held by a nondealer.

Next, the § 1231 asset casualty gains and losses and the nonpersonal use capital asset casualty gains and losses are netted together (see Concept Summary 17.1 later in the chapter). If the result is a *net loss*, the § 1231 casualty gains and the nonpersonal use capital asset casualty gains are treated as ordinary gains, the § 1231 casualty losses are deductible *for* AGI, and the nonpersonal use capital asset casualty losses are deductible *from* AGI subject to the 2%-of-AGI limitation.

If the result of the netting is a *net gain*, the net gain is treated as a § 1231 gain. Thus, a § 1231 asset disposed of by casualty may or may not get § 1231 treatment, depending on whether the netting process results in a gain or a loss. Also, a nonpersonal use capital asset disposed of by casualty may get § 1231 treatment or ordinary treatment, but it will not get capital gain or loss treatment.

Personal use property casualty gains and losses are not subject to the § 1231 rules. If the result of netting these gains and losses is a gain, the net gain is a capital gain. If the netting results in a loss, the net loss is a deduction *from* AGI to the extent it exceeds 10 percent of AGI.

Casualties, thefts, and condemnations are *involuntary conversions*. Involuntary conversion gains may be deferred if conversion proceeds are reinvested; involuntary conversion losses are recognized currently (refer to Chapter 15) regardless of whether the conversion proceeds are reinvested. Thus, the special netting process discussed previously for casualties and thefts would not include gains that are not currently recognizable because the insurance proceeds are reinvested.

The special netting process for casualties and thefts also does not include condemnation gains and losses. Consequently, a § 1231 asset disposed of by condemnation will receive § 1231 treatment. This variation between recognized casualty and condemnation gains and losses sheds considerable light on what § 1231 is all about. Section 1231 has no effect on whether *realized* gain or loss is recognized. Instead, § 1231 merely dictates how such *recognized* gain or loss is *classified* (ordinary, capital, or § 1231) under certain conditions.

Personal use property condemnation gains and losses are not subject to the § 1231 rules. The gains are capital gains (because personal use property is a capital asset), and the losses are nondeductible because they arise from the disposition of personal use property.

17-1f General Procedure for § 1231 Computation

The tax treatment of § 1231 gains and losses depends on the results of a rather complex *netting* procedure. The steps in this netting procedure are as follows.

Step 1: Casualty Netting

Net all recognized long-term gains and losses from casualties of § 1231 assets and nonpersonal use capital assets. Casualty gains result when insurance proceeds exceed the adjusted basis of the property. This casualty netting is beneficial because if there is a net gain, the gain may receive long-term capital gain treatment. If there is a net loss, it receives ordinary loss treatment.

a. If the casualty gains exceed the casualty losses, add the excess to the other § 1231 gains for the taxable year.
b. If the casualty losses exceed the casualty gains, exclude all casualty losses and gains from further § 1231 computation. If this is the case, all casualty gains are ordinary income. Section 1231 asset casualty losses are deductible *for* AGI. Other casualty losses are deductible *from* AGI.

Step 2: § 1231 Netting

After adding any net casualty gain from step 1a to the other § 1231 gains and losses (including recognized § 1231 asset condemnation gains and losses), net all § 1231 gains and losses.

a. If the gains exceed the losses, the net gain is offset by the "lookback" nonrecaptured § 1231 losses (see step 3).
b. If the losses exceed the gains, all gains are ordinary income. Section 1231 asset losses are deductible *for* AGI. Other casualty losses are deductible *from* AGI.

Step 3: § 1231 Lookback Provision

The net § 1231 gain from step 2a is offset by the nonrecaptured net § 1231 losses for the five preceding taxable years (the § 1231 lookback provision). For transactions in 2016, the lookback years are 2011, 2012, 2013, 2014, and 2015.

a. To the extent of the nonrecaptured net § 1231 loss, the current-year net § 1231 gain is ordinary income. The *nonrecaptured* net § 1231 losses are losses that have not already been used to offset net § 1231 gains.
b. Only the net § 1231 gain exceeding this net § 1231 loss carryforward is given long-term capital gain treatment.

Concept Summary 17.1 summarizes the § 1231 computation procedure. Examples 4 through 7 illustrate its application without the § 1231 lookback provision. Examples 6 and 7 illustrate its application with the § 1231 lookback provision.

Concept Summary 17.1

Section 1231 Netting Procedure

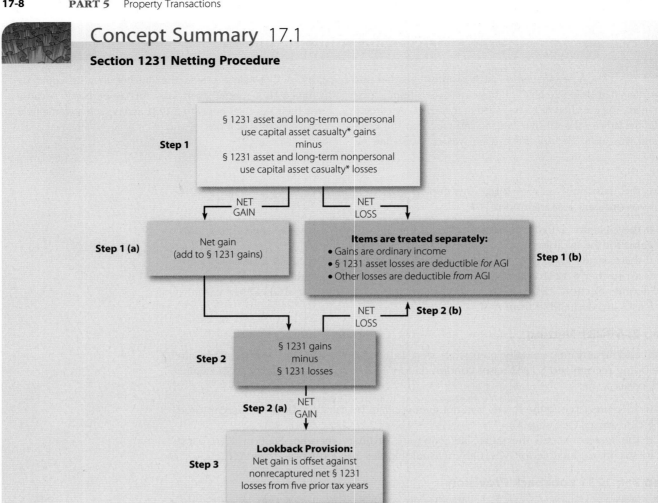

*Includes casualties and thefts.

Section 1231 Computations

EXAMPLE 4

During 2016, Ross had $125,000 of AGI before considering the following recognized gains and losses:

Capital Gains and Losses	
Long-term capital gain	$3,000
Long-term capital loss	(400)
Short-term capital gain	1,000
Short-term capital loss	(200)

continued

Casualties	
Theft of diamond ring (owned four months)	($800)*
Fire damage to personal residence (owned 10 years)	(400)*
Gain from insurance recovery on fire loss to business building (owned two years)	200
§ 1231 Gains and Losses from Depreciable Business Assets Held Long Term	
Asset A	$ 300
Asset B	1,100
Asset C	(500)
Gains and Losses from Sale of Depreciable Business Assets Held Short Term	
Asset D	$ 200
Asset E	(300)

*As adjusted for the $100 floor on personal casualty losses.

Ross had no net § 1231 losses in tax years before 2016.

Disregarding the recapture of depreciation (discussed later in the chapter), Ross's gains and losses receive the following tax treatment:

- The diamond ring and the residence are personal use assets. Therefore, these casualties are not § 1231 transactions. The $800 (ring) plus $400 (residence) losses are potentially deductible *from* AGI. However, the total loss of $1,200 does not exceed 10% of AGI.

- **Step 1:** Only the business building (a § 1231 asset) casualty gain remains. The netting of the § 1231 asset and nonpersonal use capital asset casualty gains and losses contains only one item—the $200 gain from the business building. Consequently, there is a net gain, and that gain is treated as a § 1231 gain (and added to the § 1231 gains).

- **Step 1 (a):** The gains from § 1231 transactions (Assets A and B and the § 1231 asset casualty gain) exceed the losses (Asset C) by $1,100 ($1,600 − $500). This excess is a long-term capital gain and is added to Ross's other long-term capital gains.

- **Step 2:** Ross's net long-term capital gain is $3,700 ($3,000 + $1,100 from § 1231 transactions − $400 long-term capital loss). Ross's net short-term capital gain is $800 ($1,000 − $200). The result is capital gain net income of $4,500. The $3,700 net long-term capital gain portion is eligible for beneficial capital gain treatment [assume that all of the gain is *0%/15%/20% gain* (see the discussion in Chapter 16)]. The $800 net short-term capital gain is subject to tax as ordinary income.[5]

- Ross treats the gain and loss from Assets D and E (depreciable business assets held for less than the long-term holding period) as ordinary gain and loss.

Results of the Gains and Losses on Ross's Tax Computation	
NLTCG	$ 3,700
NSTCG	800
Ordinary gain from sale of Asset D	200
Ordinary loss from sale of Asset E	(300)
AGI from other sources	125,000
AGI	$129,400

- Ross will have personal use property casualty losses of $1,200 [$800 (diamond ring) + $400 (personal residence)]. A personal use property casualty loss is deductible only to the extent it exceeds 10% of AGI. Thus, none of the $1,200 is deductible ($129,400 × 10% = $12,940).

---

[5]Ross's taxable income (unless his itemized deductions and the personal and dependency exemptions are extremely large) will put him in at least the 28% bracket. Thus, the alternative tax computation will yield a lower tax. See Example 43 in Chapter 16.

Section 1231 Computations

EXAMPLE

5

Assume the same facts as in Example 4, except that the loss from Asset C was $1,700 instead of $500.

- The treatment of the casualty losses is the same as in Example 4.
- **Step 1 (b):** The losses from § 1231 transactions now exceed the gains by $100 ($1,700 − $1,600). As a result, the gains from Assets A and B and the § 1231 asset casualty gain are ordinary income, and the loss from Asset C is a deduction *for* AGI (a business loss). The same result can be achieved by simply treating the $100 net loss as a deduction *for* AGI.
- Capital gain net income is $3,400 ($2,600 long term + $800 short term). The $2,600 net long-term capital gain portion is eligible for beneficial capital gain treatment, and the $800 net short-term capital gain is subject to tax as ordinary income.

Results of the Gains and Losses on Ross's Tax Computation	
NLTCG	$ 2,600
NSTCG	800
Net ordinary loss on Assets A, B, and C and § 1231 casualty gain	(100)
Ordinary gain from sale of Asset D	200
Ordinary loss from sale of Asset E	(300)
AGI from other sources	125,000
AGI	$128,200

- None of the personal use property casualty losses will be deductible because $1,200 does not exceed 10% of $128,200.

EXAMPLE

6

Assume the same facts as in Example 4, except that Ross has a $700 nonrecaptured net § 1231 loss from 2015.

- The treatment of the casualty losses is the same as in Example 4.
- **Step 3 (a):** The 2016 net § 1231 gain of $1,100 is treated as ordinary income to the extent of the 2015 nonrecaptured § 1231 loss of $700.
- **Step 3 (b):** The remaining $400 net § 1231 gain is a long-term capital gain and is added to Ross's other long-term capital gains.
- Ross's net long-term capital gain is $3,000 ($3,000 + $400 from § 1231 transactions − $400 long-term capital loss). Ross's net short-term capital gain is still $800 ($1,000 − $200). The result is capital gain net income of $3,800. The $3,000 net long-term capital gain portion is eligible for beneficial capital gain treatment, and the $800 net short-term capital gain is subject to tax as ordinary income.

Results of the Gains and Losses on Ross's Tax Computation	
NLTCG	$ 3,000
NSTCG	800
Ordinary gain from recapture of § 1231 losses	700
Ordinary gain from sale of Asset D	200
Ordinary loss from sale of Asset E	(300)
AGI from other sources	125,000
AGI	$129,400

- None of the personal use property casualty losses will be deductible because $1,200 does not exceed 10% of $129,400.

> ### Section 1231 Computations
>
> Assume the same facts as in Example 4, except that Ross had a net § 1231 loss of $2,700 in 2014 and a net § 1231 gain of $300 in 2015.
>
> - The treatment of the casualty losses is the same as in Example 4.
> - **Step 3 (a):** The 2014 net § 1231 loss of $2,700 will have carried over to 2015 and been offset against the 2015 net § 1231 gain of $300. Thus, the $300 gain will have been classified as ordinary income, and $2,400 of nonrecaptured 2014 net § 1231 loss will carry over to 2016. The 2016 net § 1231 gain of $1,100 will be offset against this loss, resulting in $1,100 of ordinary income. The nonrecaptured net § 1231 loss of $1,300 ($2,400 − $1,100) carries over to 2017.
> - Capital gain net income is $3,400 ($2,600 net long-term capital gain + $800 net short-term capital gain). The $2,600 net long-term capital gain portion is eligible for beneficial capital gain treatment, and the $800 net short-term capital gain is subject to tax as ordinary income.
>
> **Results of the Gains and Losses on Ross's Tax Computation**
>
> | | |
> |---|---:|
> | NLTCG | $ 2,600 |
> | NSTCG | 800 |
> | Ordinary gain from recapture of § 1231 losses | 1,100 |
> | Ordinary gain from sale of Asset D | 200 |
> | Ordinary loss from sale of Asset E | (300) |
> | AGI from other sources | 125,000 |
> | AGI | $129,400 |
>
> - None of the personal use property casualty losses will be deductible because $1,200 does not exceed 10% of $129,400.

EXAMPLE 7

17-2 SECTION 1245 RECAPTURE

LO.3

Determine when § 1245 recapture applies and how it is computed.

Now that the basic rules of § 1231 have been introduced, it is time to add some complications. The Code contains two major *recapture* provisions—§§ 1245 and 1250. These provisions cause *gain* to be treated *initially* as ordinary gain. Thus, what may appear to be a § 1231 gain is ordinary gain instead. This recapture phenomenon applies exclusively to § 1231 gains; § 1231 assets generating losses are unaffected by these recapture provisions.

These recapture provisions may also cause a gain in a nonpersonal use casualty to be *initially* ordinary gain rather than casualty gain. Classifying gains (and losses) properly initially is important because improper initial classification may lead to incorrect mixing and matching of gains and losses. This section discusses the § 1245 recapture rules, and the next section discusses the § 1250 recapture rules.

Section 1245 requires taxpayers to treat all gain as ordinary gain unless the property is disposed of for more than its original cost. This result is accomplished by requiring that all gain be treated as ordinary gain to the extent of the depreciation taken on the property disposed of. The excess of the sales price over the original cost is § 1231 gain. Section 1245 applies *primarily* to non-real-estate property such as machinery, trucks, and office furniture. Section 1245 does not apply if property is disposed of at a loss. Generally, the loss will be a § 1231 loss unless the form of the disposition is a casualty.

> ### The Big Picture
>
> Refer to the facts of *The Big Picture* on p. 17-1. Hazel purchased the equipment for $450,000 and has deducted $375,040 of depreciation ($250,000 § 179 expense + $125,040 regular MACRS depreciation). As a result, the equipment's adjusted basis is $74,960.
>
> If Hazel sells the equipment for $128,000, she will have a gain of $53,040 ($128,000 − $74,960). If it were not for § 1245, the $53,040 gain would be § 1231 gain. Section 1245 prevents this potentially favorable result by treating as ordinary income (not as § 1231 gain) any gain to the extent of depreciation taken. In this example, the entire $53,040 gain would be ordinary income.

EXAMPLE 8

continued

If, instead, Hazel sold the equipment for $485,000, she would have a gain of $410,040 ($485,000 − $74,960 adjusted basis). The § 1245 gain would be $375,040 (equal to the depreciation taken), and the § 1231 gain would be $35,000 (equal to the excess of the sales price over the $450,000 original cost).

Section 1245 recapture provides, in general, that the portion of recognized gain from the sale or other disposition of § 1245 property that represents depreciation [including § 167 depreciation, § 168 cost recovery, § 179 immediate expensing, § 168(k) additional first-year depreciation, and § 197 amortization] is *recaptured* as ordinary income. Thus, in Example 8, $53,040 of the $375,040 depreciation taken is recaptured as ordinary income when the business equipment is sold for $128,000. Only $53,040 is recaptured rather than $375,040 because Hazel is only required to recognize § 1245 recapture ordinary gain equal to the *lower* of the depreciation taken or the gain recognized.

The method of depreciation (e.g., accelerated or straight-line) does not matter. All depreciation taken is potentially subject to recapture. Thus, § 1245 recapture is often referred to as *full recapture*. Any remaining gain after subtracting the amount recaptured as ordinary income will usually be § 1231 gain. If the property is disposed of in a casualty event, however, the remaining gain will be casualty gain. If the business equipment in Example 8 had been disposed of by casualty and the $128,000 received had been an insurance recovery, Hazel would still have a gain of $53,040 and the gain would still be recaptured by § 1245 as ordinary gain. The § 1245 recapture rules apply before there is any casualty gain. Because all of the $53,040 gain is recaptured, no casualty gain arises from the casualty.

The following examples illustrate the general application of § 1245.

Section 1245 Recapture Computations

EXAMPLE 9

In the current year, Gary sold for $13,000 a machine acquired several years ago for $12,000. He had taken $10,000 of depreciation on the machine.

- The recognized gain from the sale is $11,000. This is the amount realized of $13,000 less the adjusted basis of $2,000 ($12,000 cost − $10,000 depreciation taken).
- Depreciation taken is $10,000. Therefore, because § 1245 recapture gain is the lower of depreciation taken or gain recognized, $10,000 of the $11,000 recognized gain is ordinary income, and the remaining $1,000 gain is § 1231 gain.
- The § 1231 gain of $1,000 is also equal to the excess of the sales price over the original cost of the property ($13,000 − $12,000 = $1,000 § 1231 gain).

EXAMPLE 10

Assume the same facts as in the previous example, except that the asset is sold for $9,000 instead of $13,000.

- The recognized gain from the sale is $7,000. This is the amount realized of $9,000 less the adjusted basis of $2,000.
- Depreciation taken is $10,000. Therefore, because the $10,000 depreciation taken exceeds the recognized gain of $7,000, the entire $7,000 recognized gain is ordinary income.
- The § 1231 gain is zero. There is no § 1231 gain because the selling price ($9,000) does not exceed the original purchase price ($12,000).

EXAMPLE 11

Assume the same facts as in Example 9, except that the asset is sold for $1,500 instead of $13,000.

- The recognized loss from the sale is $500. This is the amount realized of $1,500 less the adjusted basis of $2,000.
- Because there is a loss, there is no depreciation recapture. All of the loss is § 1231 loss.

If § 1245 property is disposed of in a transaction other than a sale, exchange, or involuntary conversion, the maximum amount recaptured is the excess of the property's fair market value over its adjusted basis. See the discussion under Considerations Common to §§ 1245 and 1250 in text Section 17-4.

17-2a Section 1245 Property

Generally, § 1245 property includes all depreciable personal property (e.g., machinery and equipment), including livestock. Buildings and their structural components generally are not § 1245 property. The following property is *also* subject to § 1245 treatment:

- Amortizable personal property such as goodwill, patents, copyrights, and lease-holds of § 1245 property.

- Professional baseball and football player contracts.

- Expensed costs to remove architectural and transportation barriers that restrict the handicapped and/or elderly.

- Immediately expensed depreciable tangible personal property costs under § 179.

- Certain depreciable tangible real property (other than buildings and their structural components) employed as an integral part of certain activities such as manufacturing and production. For example, a natural gas storage tank where the gas is used in the manufacturing process is § 1245 property.

- Pollution control facilities, railroad grading and tunnel bores, on-the-job training, and child care facilities on which amortization is taken.

- Single-purpose agricultural and horticultural structures and petroleum storage facilities (e.g., a greenhouse or silo).

- Fifteen-year, 18-year, and 19-year nonresidential real estate for which accelerated cost recovery is used is subject to the § 1245 recapture rules, although it is technically not § 1245 property. This property, known as ACRS property, would have been placed in service after 1980 and before 1987.

put in service

EXAMPLE

12

Steve acquired nonresidential real estate on December 1, 1986, for $100,000. He used the required ACRS accelerated method to compute the cost recovery. He sells the asset on January 15, 2016, for $120,000. The amount and nature of Steve's gain are computed as follows:

Amount realized		$120,000
Adjusted basis		
Cost	$ 100,000	
Less cost recovery: 1986–2005	(100,000)	
2006–2016	(–0–)	
January 15, 2016 adjusted basis		(–0–)
Gain realized and recognized		$120,000

The gain of $120,000 is treated as ordinary income to the extent of *all* depreciation taken because the property is 19-year nonresidential real estate for which accelerated depreciation was used. Thus, Steve reports ordinary income of $100,000 and § 1231 gain of $20,000 ($120,000 − $100,000).

What is he used S/L? He'd use 1250, not 1231

I think that's what Al said. It is.

In notebook

17-2b Observations on § 1245

- In most instances, the total depreciation taken will exceed the recognized gain. Therefore, the disposition of § 1245 property usually results in ordinary income rather than § 1231 gain. Thus, generally, no § 1231 gain will occur unless the § 1245 property is disposed of for more than its original cost. Refer to Examples 9 and 10.

- Recapture applies to the total amount of depreciation allowed or allowable regardless of the depreciation method used.

- Recapture applies regardless of the holding period of the property. Of course, the entire recognized gain would be ordinary income if the property were held for less than the long-term holding period because § 1231 would not apply.

- Section 1245 does not apply to losses, which receive § 1231 treatment.
- Gains from the disposition of § 1245 assets may also be treated as passive activity gains (see Chapter 11).

Determine when § 1250 recapture applies.

17-3 **SECTION 1250 RECAPTURE**

Generally, **§ 1250 property** is depreciable real property (principally buildings and their structural components) that is not subject to § 1245.[6] Intangible real property, such as leaseholds of § 1250 property, is also included.

Section 1250 recapture rarely applies because only the amount of *additional depreciation* is subject to recapture. To have additional depreciation, accelerated depreciation must have been taken on the asset. Straight-line depreciation is not recaptured (except for property held one year or less). Because depreciable real property placed in service after 1986 can generally only be depreciated using the straight-line method, there will usually be *no § 1250 depreciation recapture* on such property. Finally, § 1250 does not apply if the real property is sold at a loss.

It is important to know what assets are defined as § 1250 property because even when there is no additional depreciation, the gain from such property may be subject to a special 25 percent tax rate. See the discussion of Unrecaptured § 1250 Gain (Real Estate 25% Gain) in text Section 17-3b.

EXAMPLE 13

Sanjay acquires a residential rental building on January 1, 2015, for $300,000. He receives an offer of $450,000 for the building in 2016 and sells it on December 23, 2016.

- Sanjay takes $20,909 {($300,000 × .03485) + [$300,000 × .03636 × (11.5/12)] = $20,909} of total depreciation for 2015 and 2016, and the adjusted basis of the property is $279,091 ($300,000 − $20,909).
- Sanjay's recognized gain is $170,909 ($450,000 − $279,091).
- All of the gain is § 1231 gain.

17-3a **Section 1250 Recapture Situations**

In addition to residential real estate acquired before 1987 and nonresidential real estate acquired before 1981, accelerated depreciation may be taken on other types of real property. The § 1250 recapture rules apply to the following property for which accelerated depreciation was used:

- Additional first-year depreciation [§ 168(k)] exceeding straight-line depreciation taken on leasehold improvements, qualified restaurant property, and qualified retail improvement property.
- Immediate expense deduction [§ 179(f)] exceeding straight-line depreciation taken on leasehold improvements, qualified restaurant property, and qualified retail improvement property.
- Real property used predominantly outside the United States.
- Certain government-financed or low-income housing.[7]

Concept Summary 17.2 compares and contrasts the § 1245 and § 1250 depreciation recapture rules.

---

[6]As noted above, in one limited circumstance, § 1245 does apply to nonresidential real estate. If the nonresidential real estate was placed in service after 1980 and before 1987 and accelerated depreciation was used, the § 1245 recapture rules apply (rather than the § 1250 recapture rules).

[7]Described in § 1250(a)(1)(B).

Concept Summary 17.2

Comparison of § 1245 and § 1250 Depreciation Recapture

	§ 1245	§ 1250
Property affected	All depreciable personal property, but also nonresidential real property acquired after December 31, 1980, and before January 1, 1987, for which accelerated cost recovery was used. Also includes miscellaneous items such as § 179 expense and § 197 amortization of intangibles such as goodwill, patents, and copyrights.	Nonresidential real property acquired after December 31, 1969, and before January 1, 1981, on which accelerated depreciation was taken. Residential rental real property acquired after December 31, 1975, and before January 1, 1987, on which accelerated depreciation was taken.
Depreciation recaptured	Potentially all depreciation taken. If the selling price is greater than or equal to the original cost, all depreciation is recaptured. If the selling price is between the adjusted basis and the original cost, only some depreciation is recaptured.	Normally, there is no depreciation recapture, but in the special situations listed above, there can be § 1250 depreciation recapture of additional depreciation (the excess of accelerated cost recovery over straight-line cost recovery or the excess of accelerated depreciation over straight-line depreciation).
Limit on recapture	Lower of depreciation taken or gain recognized.	Lower of additional depreciation or gain recognized.
Treatment of gain exceeding recapture gain	Usually § 1231 gain.	Usually § 1231 gain.
Treatment of loss	No depreciation recapture; loss is usually § 1231 loss.	No depreciation recapture; loss is usually § 1231 loss.

17-3b **Unrecaptured § 1250 Gain (Real Estate 25% Gain)**

Any **unrecaptured § 1250 gain** is subject to a 25 percent tax rate. This gain, which relates to the sale of depreciable real estate, is used in the alternative tax computation for net capital gain discussed in Chapter 16. Unrecaptured § 1250 gain (*25% gain*) is some or all of the § 1231 gain that is treated as long-term capital gain.

The maximum amount of this *25% gain* is the depreciation taken on real property sold at a recognized gain. That maximum amount is computed in one or more of the following ways:

- The recognized gain from disposition is more than the depreciation taken. The *25% gain* is equal to the depreciation taken. Refer to Example 13. The depreciation taken was $20,909, but the recognized gain was $170,909. Consequently, *some* of the recognized gain is potential *25%* § 1231 gain.

- The recognized gain from disposition is less than or equal to the depreciation taken. In this case, the *25% gain* is all of the recognized gain. Refer to Example 13, but assume that the building sales price is $285,000. The recognized gain is $5,909 ($285,000 − $279,091), all of this gain is a § 1231 gain, and it is entirely a *25%* § 1231 gain.

- There is § 1245 depreciation recapture because the property is nonresidential real estate acquired in 1981–1986 on which accelerated depreciation was taken. No *25%* § 1231 gain will be left because § 1245 will recapture all of the depreciation or the recognized gain, whichever is less. Refer to Example 12. Depreciation of $100,000 was taken, but all of it was recaptured as ordinary income by § 1245. Thus, there is no remaining potential *25%* § 1231 gain. The entire $20,000 § 1231 gain in Example 12 is potential *0%/15%/20% gain*.

- Section 1231 loss from disposition of other § 1231 assets held long term reduces the gain from real estate.

- Section 1231 lookback losses convert some or all of the potential *25%* § 1231 gain to ordinary income.

TAX IN THE NEWS   Building or Tangible Personal Property?

Many taxpayers have "cost-segregated" their buildings. This means that an engineering study is done to determine whether some of a building's cost can be segregated into tangible personal property (generally a 5-year or 7-year MACRS life with accelerated depreciation) rather than real property (a 27.5-year or 39-year MACRS life with straight-line depreciation). The faster depreciation for the tangible personal property yields significant tax savings. However, there is a downside. When the property is sold, the tangible personal property gains are taxable as ordinary income due to § 1245 depreciation recapture, whereas the gain from the sale of the building is not subject to recapture, is a § 1231 gain, and may receive long-term capital gain treatment.

Special 25% Gain Netting Rules

Where there is a § 1231 gain from real estate and that gain includes both potential *25% gain* and potential *0%/15%/20% gain*, any § 1231 loss from disposition of other § 1231 assets *first offsets* the *0%/15%/20%* portion of the § 1231 gain and then offsets the *25% gain* portion of the § 1231 gain. Also, any § 1231 lookback loss *first recharacterizes* the *25% gain* portion of the § 1231 gain and then recharacterizes the *0%/15%/20%* portion of the § 1231 gain as ordinary income.

Net § 1231 Gain Limitation

The amount of unrecaptured § 1250 gain may not exceed the net § 1231 gain that is eligible to be treated as long-term capital gain. The unrecaptured § 1250 gain is the *lesser of* the unrecaptured § 1250 gain or the net § 1231 gain that is treated as capital gain. Thus, if there is a net § 1231 gain but it is all converted to ordinary income by the five-year § 1231 lookback loss provision, there is no surviving § 1231 gain or unrecaptured § 1250 gain.

Refer to Example 6. There was $200 of § 1231 gain from the building fire that would also be potential *25% gain* if at least $200 of depreciation was taken. The net § 1231 gain was $1,100 including the $200 building gain. (The $500 loss from Asset C would offset the potential *0%/15%/20%* § 1231 gain and not the potential *25% gain*, so all of the potential *25% gain* of $200 is in the $1,100 net § 1231 gain.) However, the $700 of § 1231 lookback losses would *first* absorb the $200 building gain, so the $400 of § 1231 gain that is treated as long-term capital gain includes no *25% gain*.

Section 1250 Property for Purposes of the Unrecaptured § 1250 Gain

Section 1250 property includes any real property (other than § 1245 property) that is or has been depreciable. Land is *not* § 1250 property because it is not depreciable.

EXAMPLE 14

Bill is a single taxpayer with 2016 taxable income of $120,000 composed of:

- $100,000 ordinary taxable income,
- $3,000 short-term capital loss,
- $15,000 long-term capital gain from sale of stock, and
- $8,000 § 1231 gain that is all unrecaptured § 1250 gain (the actual unrecaptured gain was $11,000, but net § 1231 gain is only $8,000).

Bill's net capital gain is $20,000 ($15,000 long-term capital gain + $8,000 unrecaptured § 1250 gain/net § 1231 gain − $3,000 short-term capital loss). The $3,000 short-term capital loss is offset against the $8,000 unrecaptured § 1250 gain, reducing that gain to $5,000 (see the discussion in Chapter 16 concerning netting of capital losses). Bill's adjusted net capital gain is $15,000 ($20,000 net capital gain − $5,000 unrecaptured § 1250 gain).

Bill's total tax (using the alternative tax calculation discussed in Chapter 16) is $24,537 [$21,037 (tax on $100,000 other taxable income) + $1,250 ($5,000 unrecaptured § 1250 gain × 25%) + $2,250 ($15,000 adjusted net capital gain × 15%)].

ETHICS & EQUITY   The Sale of a "Cost-Segregated" Building

Many taxpayers have "cost-segregated" their buildings. This means that an engineering study is done to determine whether some of a building's cost can be segregated into tangible personal property (generally a 5-year or 7-year MACRS life with accelerated depreciation) rather than real property (a 27.5-year or 39-year MACRS life with straight-line depreciation). The faster depreciation for the tangible personal property yields significant tax savings. A CPA is determining the gain or loss from disposition of an office building. A sale document details the selling price of the land and building. However, the building was cost-segregated and the CPA finds records of cost and related depreciation for the tangible personal property that was part of the cost segregation. No mention of this tangible personal property was made in the sale agreement, but the building and all of its contents were sold. What should the CPA do?

17-4 CONSIDERATIONS COMMON TO §§ 1245 AND 1250

LO.5

Identify considerations common to §§ 1245 and 1250.

17-4a Exceptions

Gifts

Depreciation recapture potential carries over to the donee.[8]

EXAMPLE 15

Wade gives his daughter, Helen, § 1245 property with an adjusted basis of $1,000. The amount of recapture potential is $700. Helen uses the property in her business and claims further depreciation of $100 before selling it for $1,900.

Helen's recognized gain is $1,000 ($1,900 amount realized − $900 adjusted basis), of which $800 is recaptured as ordinary income ($100 depreciation taken by Helen + $700 recapture potential carried over from Wade). The remaining gain of $200 is § 1231 gain. Even if Helen used the property for personal purposes, the $700 recapture potential would still be carried over.

Death

Although not a very attractive tax planning approach, death eliminates all recapture potential.[9] In other words, any depreciation recapture potential does not carry over from a decedent to an estate or heir.

EXAMPLE 16

Assume the same facts as in Example 15, except that Helen receives the property as a result of Wade's death. The $700 recapture potential from Wade is extinguished. Helen has a basis for the property equal to the property's fair market value at Wade's death (assume that the FMV is $1,700).

Helen will have a $300 gain when the property is sold because the selling price ($1,900) exceeds the property's adjusted basis of $1,600 ($1,700 original basis to Helen − $100 depreciation) by $300. Because of § 1245, $100 is ordinary income. The remaining gain of $200 is § 1231 gain.

Charitable Transfers

Depreciation recapture potential reduces the amount of the charitable contribution deduction under § 170.[10]

The Big Picture

EXAMPLE 17

Return to the facts of *The Big Picture* on p. 17-1. If instead of selling the old equipment Hazel gives it to a charity, her charitable contribution will be zero.

The potential § 1245 recapture on the equipment is $375,040 (the depreciation taken). When that amount is subtracted from the equipment's $128,000 fair market value, the result is zero because the charitable contribution cannot be less than zero.

---

[8]§§ 1245(b)(1) and 1250(d)(1) and Reg. §§ 1.1245–4(a)(1) and 1.1250–3(a)(1).

[9]§§ 1245(b)(2) and 1250(d)(2).

[10]§ 170(e)(1)(A) and Reg. § 1.170A–4(b)(1). In certain circumstances, § 1231 gain also reduces the amount of the charitable contribution. See § 170(e)(1)(B).

Certain Nontaxable Transactions

In certain transactions, the transferor's adjusted basis of property carries over to the transferee.[11] If this is the case, the depreciation recapture potential also carries over to the transferee.[12] Included in this category are the following transfers of property:

- Nontaxable incorporations under § 351.
- Certain liquidations of subsidiary companies under § 332.
- Nontaxable contributions to a partnership under § 721.
- Nontaxable reorganizations.

Gain may be recognized in these transactions if boot is received. If gain is recognized, it is treated as ordinary income to the extent of the recapture potential or recognized gain, whichever is lower.[13]

Like-Kind Exchanges (§ 1031) and Involuntary Conversions (§ 1033)

Realized gain will be recognized to the extent of boot received under § 1031. Realized gain also will be recognized to the extent the proceeds from an involuntary conversion are not reinvested in similar property under § 1033. Such recognized gain is subject to recapture as ordinary income under §§ 1245 and 1250. The remaining recapture potential, if any, carries over to the property received in the exchange. Realized losses are not recognized in like-kind exchanges, but are recognized in involuntary conversions (see Chapter 15).

The Big Picture

EXAMPLE 18

Refer to the facts of *The Big Picture* on p. 17-1. Rather than sell the equipment, Hazel could exchange it. If the equipment received in the exchange is worth $150,000, Hazel would have to pay $22,000 ($150,000 − the $128,000 fair market value of the equipment given up in the exchange) and would have a § 1031 like-kind exchange.

Her realized gain is $53,040 ($128,000 fair market value of the equipment given up − $74,960 adjusted basis of the equipment given up), but the gain is not recognized because boot was given (the $22,000 cash) and not received. The $375,040 of depreciation taken on the equipment given up carries over to the replacement equipment as potential § 1245 depreciation recapture.

17-4b Other Applications

Sections 1245 and 1250 apply notwithstanding any other provisions in the Code.[14] That is, the recapture rules under these Sections *override* all other Sections. Special applications include installment sales and property dividends.

Installment Sales

Recapture gain is recognized in the year of the sale regardless of whether gain is otherwise recognized under the installment method.[15] All gain is ordinary income until the recapture potential is fully absorbed. Nonrecapture (§ 1231) gain is recognized under the installment method as cash is received.

Gain is also recognized on installment sales in the year of the sale in an amount equal to the § 179 (immediate expensing) deduction taken with respect to the property sold.

---

[11]§§ 1245(b)(3) and 1250(d)(3) and Reg. §§ 1.1245–4(c) and 1.1250–3(c).

[12]Reg. §§ 1.1245–2(a)(4) and −2(c)(2) and 1.1250–2(d)(1) and (3) and −3(c)(3).

[13]§§ 1245(b)(3) and 1250(d)(3) and Reg. §§ 1.1245–4(c) and 1.1250–3(c). Some of these special corporate problems are discussed in Chapter 20. Partnership contributions are also discussed in Chapter 20.

[14]§§ 1245(d) and 1250(i).

[15]§ 453(i). The installment method of reporting gains on the sale of property is discussed in Chapter 18.

Return to the facts of *The Big Picture* on p. 17-1. Assume that Hazel could sell the used equipment for $28,000 down, with the $100,000 balance received in five yearly installments of $20,000 plus interest.

Helen would have to recognize her entire $53,040 gain ($128,000 sales price − $74,960 adjusted basis) in 2016. All of the gain is § 1245 depreciation recapture gain because the $375,040 depreciation taken exceeds the $53,040 recognized gain.

Property Dividends

A corporation generally recognizes gain if it distributes appreciated property as a dividend. Recapture under §§ 1245 and 1250 applies to the extent of the *lower* of the recapture potential or the excess of the property's fair market value over the adjusted basis.[16]

Emerald Corporation distributes § 1245 property as a dividend to its shareholders. The amount of the recapture potential is $300, and the excess of the property's fair market value over the adjusted basis is $800. Emerald recognizes $300 of ordinary income and $500 of § 1231 gain.

Concept Summary 17.3 integrates the depreciation recapture rules with the § 1231 netting process. It is an expanded version of Concept Summary 17.1.

17-5 SPECIAL RECAPTURE PROVISIONS

LO.6

Apply the special recapture provisions for related parties and intangible drilling costs (IDCs) and be aware of the special recapture provision for corporations.

17-5a Special Recapture for Corporations

Corporations selling depreciable real estate may have ordinary income in addition to that required by § 1250.[17] Under this provision, corporations selling depreciable real property are required to recapture as ordinary income the smaller of two amounts: (1) 20 percent of the recognized gain or (2) 20 percent of the depreciation taken. See the discussion of this topic in Chapter 20.

17-5b Gain from Sale of Depreciable Property between Certain Related Parties

When the sale or exchange of property, which in the hands of the *transferee* is depreciable property (principally machinery, equipment, and buildings, but not land), is between certain related parties, any gain recognized is ordinary income.[18] This provision applies to both direct and indirect sales or exchanges. A **related party** is defined as an individual and his or her controlled corporation or partnership or a taxpayer and any trust in which the taxpayer (or the taxpayer's spouse) is a beneficiary.

Isabella sells a personal use automobile (therefore nondepreciable) to her controlled corporation. The automobile, which was purchased two years ago, originally cost $5,000 and is sold for $7,000. The automobile is to be used in the corporation's business. If the related-party provision did not exist, Isabella would realize a $2,000 long-term capital gain. The income tax consequences would be favorable because Isabella's controlled corporation is entitled to depreciate the automobile based upon the purchase price of $7,000. Under the related-party provision, Isabella's $2,000 gain is ordinary income.

---

[16]§ 311(b) and Reg. §§ 1.1245–1(c) and −6(b) and 1.1250–1(a)(4), −1(b)(4), and −1(c)(2).

[17]§ 291(a)(1).

[18]§ 1239.

GLOBAL TAX ISSUES   **Depreciation Recapture in Other Countries**

The rules for dispositions of depreciated property are more complex in the United States than in any other country. Most countries treat the gain or loss from the disposition of business depreciable assets as ordinary income or loss. Consequently, although the U.S. rules are more complex, they can be more beneficial than those of other countries because at least some gains from the disposition of depreciable business property may be taxed at the lower capital gain rates.

Concept Summary 17.3

Depreciation Recapture and § 1231 Netting Procedure

*Includes casualties and thefts.

17-5c **Intangible Drilling Costs**

Taxpayers may elect to either *expense or capitalize* intangible drilling and development costs for oil, gas, or geothermal properties.[19] **Intangible drilling and development costs (IDCs)** include operator (one who holds a working or operating interest in any tract or parcel of land) expenditures for wages, fuel, repairs, hauling, and supplies. These expenditures must be incident to and necessary for the drilling of wells and preparation of wells for production. In most instances, taxpayers elect to expense IDCs to maximize tax deductions during drilling.

Intangible drilling and development costs are subject to § 1254 recapture when the property is disposed of. The gain on the disposition of the property is subject to recapture as ordinary income.

17-6 **REPORTING PROCEDURES**

Describe and apply the reporting procedures for §§ 1231, 1245, and 1250.

Noncapital gains and losses are reported on Form 4797 (Sales of Business Property). However, before Form 4797 is filled out, Part B of Form 4684 (Casualties and Thefts) must be completed to determine whether any casualties will enter into the § 1231 computation procedure. Recall that recognized gains from § 1231 asset casualties may be recaptured by § 1245 or § 1250. These gains will not appear on Form 4684. The § 1231 gains and nonpersonal use long-term capital gains are netted against § 1231 losses and nonpersonal use long-term capital losses on Form 4684 to determine if there is a net gain to transfer to Form 4797, Part I.

Because 2016 tax forms are not yet available, 2015 tax forms are used for the remainder of the discussion.

Form 4797 is divided into four parts, summarized as follows:

Part	Function
I	To report regular § 1231 gains and losses [including recognized gains and losses from certain involuntary conversions (condemnations)].
II	To report ordinary gains and losses.
III	To determine the portion of the gain that is subject to recapture (e.g., §§ 1245 and 1250 gain).
IV	Computation of recapture amounts under §§ 179 and 280F when business use of depreciable property drops to 50% or less.

Generally, the best approach to completing Form 4797 is to start with Part III. Once the recapture amount has been determined, it is transferred to Part II. The balance of any gain remaining after the recapture has been accounted for is transferred from Part III to Part I. Also transferred to Part I is any net gain from certain casualties and thefts as reported on Form 4684, Part B (refer to the beginning of this section and Chapter 15). If the netting process in Form 4797, Part I, results in a gain, it is reduced by the nonrecaptured net § 1231 losses from prior years (line 8 of Part I). Any remaining gain is shifted to Schedule D (Capital Gains and Losses), of Form 1040. If the netting process in Part I of Form 4797 results in a loss, it goes to Part II to be treated as an ordinary loss.

The complex rules for the alternative tax on net capital gain for individuals, estates, and trusts affect the reporting of gains and losses from the disposition of business and rental assets. S corporations, partnerships, individuals, estates, and trusts that use Form 4797 must provide information sufficient to determine what portion of the gain surviving Form 4797, Part I (the gain that goes to Schedule D), is *28% gain*, *25% gain*, or *0%/15%/20% gain*.

The process explained below is based upon an analysis of Form 1040, Schedule D, and Form 4797 and their instructions. One key point to remember is that all of the gains and losses that end up being treated as ordinary gains and losses (and therefore end up in Part II of Form 4797) are not eligible for any of the special tax rates for net capital gain. Another key point is that the net § 1231 gain goes from Part I of Form 4797 to line 11 of Schedule D (as a long-term capital gain).

---

[19]§ 263(c).

The *25% gain* (if any) from Form 4797 is part of the Schedule D, line 11, gain. *Nothing on the face of Form 4797 or Schedule D identifies this gain.* Only when the alternative tax on net capital gain is computed is the *25% gain* portion of the Form 4797 net gain specifically mentioned (see Schedule D, line 19).

Also remember that § 1231 assets are assets held more than one year. Therefore, no gain or loss is reportable on Form 4797, Part I or Part III, unless that holding period requirement is satisfied.

EXAMPLE 22

For 2015, Troy Williams, a single taxpayer (Social Security number 111-11-1111), has taxable income of $133,000 *including* the following recognized gains and losses (assume that Troy has no nonrecaptured § 1231 losses from prior years):

Sale of Depreciable Business Assets Held Long Term

Asset A (Note 1)	$36,500
Asset B (Note 2)	20,126
Asset C (Note 3)	(880)

Sale of Depreciable Business Assets Held Short Term

Asset D (Note 4)	($ 600)

Capital Assets

Long-term gain (Note 5)	$3,000
Short-term loss (Note 6)	(200)

Note 1.   Asset A was acquired on June 23, 2012, for $50,000. It was 5-year MACRS property, and four years' cost recovery totaled $38,480. The property was sold for $48,020 on August 31, 2015.

Note 2.   Asset B was purchased on May 10, 2005, for $37,000. It was 27.5-year residential rental real estate, and straight-line depreciation totaled $14,126. Asset B was sold for $43,000 on November 10, 2015.

Note 3.   Asset C was purchased on December 9, 2012, for $16,000. It was 5-year MACRS property, and four years' cost recovery totaled $12,314. The property was sold for $2,806 on December 30, 2015.

Note 4.   Asset D was purchased for $7,000 on July 27, 2015. It was 5-year MACRS property but proved unsuitable to Troy's business. Troy sold it for $6,400 on November 3, 2015.

Note 5.   The LTCG resulted from the sale of 100 shares of Orange Corporation stock purchased for $10,000 on April 5, 2013. The shares were sold on October 21, 2015, for $13,223. Expenses of sale were $223.

Note 6.   The STCL resulted from the sale of 50 shares of Blue Corporation stock purchased for $350 on March 14, 2015. The shares were sold for $170 on August 20, 2015. Expenses of sale were $20.

Reporting Consequences

Form 4797

Part III. The sales of Assets A and B are reported here because both generated gains.

- **Asset A (§ 1245 Recapture Potential).** The sale of Asset A results in the recapture of cost recovery (depreciation) deductions. Here, the depreciation recapture potential ($38,480) is greater than the realized gain. So all of the gain will be treated as depreciation recaptured under § 1245 (and ordinary income). That recapture is shown on line 25b and is carried to line 31.

- **Asset B (§ 1250 Recapture Potential).** As straight-line cost recovery was used on Asset B, there is no § 1250 recapture. The $20,126 gain from the sale of Asset B is included on lines 30 and 32 and then is carried from line 32 to Part I, line 6.

Part I. Gains and losses from § 1231 assets not appearing in Part III are reported here. In addition, the § 1231 netting process occurs here (on lines 7 to 9).

- **Asset C.** The loss from Asset C is reported on line 2.

- **§ 1231 Netting.** The § 1231 gains and losses are netted and appear on line 7. Given that Troy has no nonrecaptured net § 1231 losses from prior years (these would be reported on line 8), the net gain on line 7 is transferred to Schedule D, line 11.

continued

Part II. Any ordinary gains and losses are accumulated here.

- *Asset D.* The loss from Asset D is reported on line 10.

- The depreciation recapture from Part III, line 31 appears on line 13.

- The net gain on line 18 is ordinary income and is transferred to Form 1040, line 14.

Schedule D (Form 1040)

Part I. Short-Term Capital Gains and Losses.

- *Blue Corporation Stock.* The short-term capital loss from the Blue Corporation stock is reported on line 1a. It is assumed that the sale of the Blue Corporation stock was reported to Troy on a Form 1099–B that showed the adjusted basis and selling price of the stock. If not, a Form 8949 would be required.

Part II. Long-Term Capital Gains and Losses.

- *Orange Corporation Stock.* The long-term capital gain from the Orange Corporation stock is reported on line 8a. It is assumed that the sale of the Orange Corporation stock was reported to Troy on a Form 1099–B that showed the adjusted basis and selling price of the stock. If not, a Form 8949 would be required.

- *Net § 1231 Gain.* The net § 1231 gain transferred from Form 4797 appears on line 11.

Part III. Summary.

- The combination of short-term and long-term capital gains and losses appears on line 16. In this case, the amount is a *net capital gain*. The net capital gain is then carried to line 13 of Form 1040.

Tax Computation

- In 2015, five alternative tax rates applied: 25%, 28%, and 0%/15%/20%.

- On Form 4797, Part III, the $20,126 § 1231 gain from Asset B is made up of $14,126 of potential *25% gain* (equal to the depreciation taken) and $6,000 of potential *0%/15%/20% gain*.

  - The $880 § 1231 loss from Form 4797, Part I, line 2 offsets the potential *0%/15%/20%* portion of the $20,126 § 1231 gain on Form 4797, Part I, line 6.

  - Consequently, the $19,246 § 1231 gain that goes from Form 4797, Part I, line 7 to Schedule D, line 11 is made up of (1) $14,126 *25% gain* and (2) $5,120 *0%/15%/20% gain*.

- Schedule D, Part III, line 19 shows an unrecaptured § 1250 gain of $13,926. A worksheet in the Form 1040 Schedule D instructions must be used to determine this amount. This gain results from the $14,126 *25% gain* being reduced by the $200 short-term capital loss from Schedule D, line 7.

- Troy's 2015 tax liability is $28,804, computed as follows:

$ 24,104	Tax on other taxable income of $110,954
	($133,000 taxable income − $22,046 net long-term capital gain)
+ 3,482	Tax on the *25% gain* ($13,926 × .25)
+ 1,218	Tax on the *0%/15%/20% gain* ($8,120 × .15)
$ 28,804	

The 2015 tax form solution for Example 22 appears on the following pages.

ETHICS & EQUITY Incorrect Depreciation and Recognized Gain

A staff accountant for a large international company is calculating the tax gain from a disposition of business equipment. The equipment was 7-year MACRS property and has been fully depreciated for tax purposes. The staff accountant notices that the equipment was used in Germany, not the United States, although it is listed as an asset of the U.S. company for which the staff accountant works. Because the property was used outside the United States, it should have been depreciated using straight-line over a nine-year life. Consequently, the tax depreciation has been overstated, and the tax basis should be greater than zero, causing a smaller gain. What should the staff accountant do?

Form **4797**

Department of the Treasury
Internal Revenue Service

Sales of Business Property
**(Also Involuntary Conversions and Recapture Amounts
Under Sections 179 and 280F(b)(2))**

► Attach to your tax return.

► Information about Form 4797 and its separate instructions is at *www.irs.gov/form4797.*

OMB No. 1545-0184

2015

Attachment
Sequence No. **27**

Name(s) shown on return	Identifying number
Troy Williams	*111 - 11 - 1111*

1 Enter the gross proceeds from sales or exchanges reported to you for 2015 on Form(s) 1099-B or 1099-S (or substitute statement) that you are including on line 2, 10, or 20 (see instructions) . . . . | **1** |

Part I   Sales or Exchanges of Property Used in a Trade or Business and Involuntary Conversions From Other Than Casualty or Theft—Most Property Held More Than 1 Year (see instructions)

2	(a) Description of property	(b) Date acquired (mo., day, yr.)	(c) Date sold (mo., day, yr.)	(d) Gross sales price	(e) Depreciation allowed or allowable since acquisition	(f) Cost or other basis, plus improvements and expense of sale	(g) Gain or (loss) Subtract (f) from the sum of (d) and (e)
	Asset C	*12/09/12*	*12/30/15*	*2,806*	*12,314*	*16,000*	*(880)*

3	Gain, if any, from Form 4684, line 39	**3**	
4	Section 1231 gain from installment sales from Form 6252, line 26 or 37	**4**	
5	Section 1231 gain or (loss) from like-kind exchanges from Form 8824	**5**	
6	Gain, if any, from line 32, from other than casualty or theft.	**6**	*20,126*
7	Combine lines 2 through 6. Enter the gain or (loss) here and on the appropriate line as follows:	**7**	*19,246*

Partnerships (except electing large partnerships) and S corporations. Report the gain or (loss) following the instructions for Form 1065, Schedule K, line 10, or Form 1120S, Schedule K, line 9. Skip lines 8, 9, 11, and 12 below.

Individuals, partners, S corporation shareholders, and all others. If line 7 is zero or a loss, enter the amount from line 7 on line 11 below and skip lines 8 and 9. If line 7 is a gain and you did not have any prior year section 1231 losses, or they were recaptured in an earlier year, enter the gain from line 7 as a long-term capital gain on the Schedule D filed with your return and skip lines 8, 9, 11, and 12 below.

8	Nonrecaptured net section 1231 losses from prior years (see instructions)	**8**	
9	Subtract line 8 from line 7. If zero or less, enter -0-. If line 9 is zero, enter the gain from line 7 on line 12 below. If line 9 is more than zero, enter the amount from line 8 on line 12 below and enter the gain from line 9 as a long-term capital gain on the Schedule D filed with your return (see instructions)	**9**	

Part II   Ordinary Gains and Losses (see instructions)

10 Ordinary gains and losses not included on lines 11 through 16 (include property held 1 year or less):

	Asset D	*07/27/15*	*11/03/15*	*6,400*	*0*	*7,000*	*(600)*

11	Loss, if any, from line 7	**11** ( )
12	Gain, if any, from line 7 or amount from line 8, if applicable	**12**	
13	Gain, if any, from line 31	**13**	*36,500*
14	Net gain or (loss) from Form 4684, lines 31 and 38a	**14**	
15	Ordinary gain from installment sales from Form 6252, line 25 or 36	**15**	
16	Ordinary gain or (loss) from like-kind exchanges from Form 8824.	**16**	
17	Combine lines 10 through 16	**17**	*35,900*

18 For all except individual returns, enter the amount from line 17 on the appropriate line of your return and skip lines a and b below. For individual returns, complete lines a and b below:

a If the loss on line 11 includes a loss from Form 4684, line 35, column (b)(ii), enter that part of the loss here. Enter the part of the loss from income-producing property on Schedule A (Form 1040), line 28, and the part of the loss from property used as an employee on Schedule A (Form 1040), line 23. Identify as from "Form 4797, line 18a." See instructions . . | **18a** | |

b Redetermine the gain or (loss) on line 17 excluding the loss, if any, on line 18a. Enter here and on Form 1040, line 14 | **18b** | *35,900* |

For Paperwork Reduction Act Notice, see separate instructions.   Cat. No. 13086I   Form **4797** (2015)

Form 4797 (2015) Page **2**

Part III Gain From Disposition of Property Under Sections 1245, 1250, 1252, 1254, and 1255 (see instructions)

19	(a) Description of section 1245, 1250, 1252, 1254, or 1255 property:	(b) Date acquired (mo., day, yr.)	(c) Date sold (mo., day, yr.)
A	*Asset A*	*06/23/12*	*08/31/15*
B	*Asset B*	*05/10/05*	*11/10/15*
C			
D			

These columns relate to the properties on lines 19A through 19D. ▶		**Property A**	**Property B**	**Property C**	**Property D**
20	Gross sales price (**Note:** *See line 1 before completing.*) .	**20**	*48,020*	*43,000*		
21	Cost or other basis plus expense of sale	**21**	*50,000*	*37,000*		
22	Depreciation (or depletion) allowed or allowable. . .	**22**	*38,480*	*14,126*		
23	Adjusted basis. Subtract line 22 from line 21. . . .	**23**	*11,520*	*22,874*		
24	Total gain. Subtract line 23 from line 20	**24**	*36,500*	*20,126*		
25	**If section 1245 property:**					
a	Depreciation allowed or allowable from line 22 . . .	**25a**	*38,480*			
b	Enter the **smaller** of line 24 or 25a	**25b**	*36,500*			
26	**If section 1250 property:** If straight line depreciation was used, enter -0- on line 26g, except for a corporation subject to section 291.					
a	Additional depreciation after 1975 (see instructions) .	**26a**				
b	Applicable percentage multiplied by the **smaller** of line 24 or line 26a (see instructions)	**26b**				
c	Subtract line 26a from line 24. If residential rental property **or** line 24 is not more than line 26a, skip lines 26d and 26e	**26c**				
d	Additional depreciation after 1969 and before 1976. .	**26d**				
e	Enter the **smaller** of line 26c or 26d	**26e**				
f	Section 291 amount (corporations only)	**26f**				
g	Add lines 26b, 26e, and 26f.	**26g**		*0*		
27	**If section 1252 property:** Skip this section if you did not dispose of farmland or if this form is being completed for a partnership (other than an electing large partnership).					
a	Soil, water, and land clearing expenses	**27a**				
b	Line 27a multiplied by applicable percentage (see instructions)	**27b**				
c	Enter the **smaller** of line 24 or 27b	**27c**				
28	**If section 1254 property:**					
a	Intangible drilling and development costs, expenditures for development of mines and other natural deposits, mining exploration costs, and depletion (see instructions)	**28a**				
b	Enter the **smaller** of line 24 or 28a	**28b**				
29	**If section 1255 property:**					
a	Applicable percentage of payments excluded from income under section 126 (see instructions)	**29a**				
b	Enter the **smaller** of line 24 or 29a (see instructions) .	**29b**				

Summary of Part III Gains. Complete property columns A through D through line 29b before going to line 30.

30	Total gains for all properties. Add property columns A through D, line 24	**30**	*56,626*
31	Add property columns A through D, lines 25b, 26g, 27c, 28b, and 29b. Enter here and on line 13	**31**	*36,500*
32	Subtract line 31 from line 30. Enter the portion from casualty or theft on Form 4684, line 33. Enter the portion from other than casualty or theft on Form 4797, line 6	**32**	*20,126*

Part IV Recapture Amounts Under Sections 179 and 280F(b)(2) When Business Use Drops to 50% or Less (see instructions)

			(a) Section 179	(b) Section 280F(b)(2)
33	Section 179 expense deduction or depreciation allowable in prior years.	**33**		
34	Recomputed depreciation (see instructions)	**34**		
35	Recapture amount. Subtract line 34 from line 33. See the instructions for where to report . .	**35**		

Form **4797** (2015)

SCHEDULE D	Capital Gains and Losses	OMB No. 1545-0074

SCHEDULE D
(Form 1040)

Department of the Treasury
Internal Revenue Service (99)

Capital Gains and Losses

► **Attach to Form 1040 or Form 1040NR.**
► **Information about Schedule D and its separate instructions is at** *www.irs.gov/scheduled*.
► **Use Form 8949 to list your transactions for lines 1b, 2, 3, 8b, 9, and 10.**

OMB No. 1545-0074

20 15

Attachment
Sequence No. **12**

Name(s) shown on return	Your social security number
Troy Williams	*111-11-1111*

Part I Short-Term Capital Gains and Losses—Assets Held One Year or Less

See instructions for how to figure the amounts to enter on the lines below. This form may be easier to complete if you round off cents to whole dollars.	**(d)** Proceeds (sales price)	**(e)** Cost (or other basis)	**(g)** Adjustments to gain or loss from Form(s) 8949, Part I, line 2, column (g)	**(h) Gain or (loss)** Subtract column (e) from column (d) and combine the result with column (g)
1a Totals for all short-term transactions reported on Form 1099-B for which basis was reported to the IRS and for which you have no adjustments (see instructions). However, if you choose to report all these transactions on Form 8949, leave this line blank and go to line 1b .	*170*	*370*		*(200)*
1b Totals for all transactions reported on Form(s) 8949 with **Box A** checked				
2 Totals for all transactions reported on Form(s) 8949 with **Box B** checked				
3 Totals for all transactions reported on Form(s) 8949 with **Box C** checked				

4 Short-term gain from Form 6252 and short-term gain or (loss) from Forms 4684, 6781, and 8824 .	**4**	
5 Net short-term gain or (loss) from partnerships, S corporations, estates, and trusts from Schedule(s) K-1	**5**	
6 Short-term capital loss carryover. Enter the amount, if any, from line 8 of your **Capital Loss Carryover Worksheet** in the instructions	**6** ( )
7 **Net short-term capital gain or (loss).** Combine lines 1a through 6 in column (h). If you have any long-term capital gains or losses, go to Part II below. Otherwise, go to Part III on the back	**7**	*(200)*

Part II Long-Term Capital Gains and Losses—Assets Held More Than One Year

See instructions for how to figure the amounts to enter on the lines below. This form may be easier to complete if you round off cents to whole dollars.	**(d)** Proceeds (sales price)	**(e)** Cost (or other basis)	**(g)** Adjustments to gain or loss from Form(s) 8949, Part II, line 2, column (g)	**(h) Gain or (loss)** Subtract column (e) from column (d) and combine the result with column (g)
8a Totals for all long-term transactions reported on Form 1099-B for which basis was reported to the IRS and for which you have no adjustments (see instructions). However, if you choose to report all these transactions on Form 8949, leave this line blank and go to line 8b .	*13,223*	*10,223*		*3,000*
8b Totals for all transactions reported on Form(s) 8949 with **Box D** checked				
9 Totals for all transactions reported on Form(s) 8949 with **Box E** checked				
10 Totals for all transactions reported on Form(s) 8949 with **Box F** checked.				

11 Gain from Form 4797, Part I; long-term gain from Forms 2439 and 6252; and long-term gain or (loss) from Forms 4684, 6781, and 8824	**11**	*19,246*
12 Net long-term gain or (loss) from partnerships, S corporations, estates, and trusts from Schedule(s) K-1	**12**	
13 Capital gain distributions. See the instructions	**13**	
14 Long-term capital loss carryover. Enter the amount, if any, from line 13 of your **Capital Loss Carryover Worksheet** in the instructions	**14** ( )
15 **Net long-term capital gain or (loss).** Combine lines 8a through 14 in column (h). Then go to Part III on the back	**15**	*22,246*

For Paperwork Reduction Act Notice, see your tax return instructions.   Cat. No. 11338H   **Schedule D (Form 1040) 2015**

Part III	Summary

16   Combine lines 7 and 15 and enter the result **16**   *22,046*

- If line 16 is a **gain,** enter the amount from line 16 on Form 1040, line 13, or Form 1040NR, line 14. Then go to line 17 below.
- If line 16 is a **loss,** skip lines 17 through 20 below. Then go to line 21. Also be sure to complete line 22.
- If line 16 is **zero,** skip lines 17 through 21 below and enter -0- on Form 1040, line 13, or Form 1040NR, line 14. Then go to line 22.

17   Are lines 15 and 16 **both** gains?
   ☒ **Yes.** Go to line 18.
   ☐ **No.** Skip lines 18 through 21, and go to line 22.

18   Enter the amount, if any, from line 7 of the **28% Rate Gain Worksheet** in the instructions   . . ▶   **18**   *0*

19   Enter the amount, if any, from line 18 of the **Unrecaptured Section 1250 Gain Worksheet** in the instructions   . . . . ▶   **19**   *13,926*

20   Are lines 18 and 19 **both** zero or blank?
   ☐ **Yes.** Complete the **Qualified Dividends and Capital Gain Tax Worksheet** in the instructions for Form 1040, line 44 (or in the instructions for Form 1040NR, line 42). **Do not** complete lines 21 and 22 below.

   ☒ **No.** Complete the **Schedule D Tax Worksheet** in the instructions. **Do not** complete lines 21 and 22 below.

21   If line 16 is a loss, enter here and on Form 1040, line 13, or Form 1040NR, line 14, the **smaller** of:

- The loss on line 16 or
- ($3,000), or if married filing separately, ($1,500)   } . . . .   **21** (   )

   Note: When figuring which amount is smaller, treat both amounts as positive numbers.

22   Do you have qualified dividends on Form 1040, line 9b, or Form 1040NR, line 10b?

   ☐ **Yes.** Complete the **Qualified Dividends and Capital Gain Tax Worksheet** in the instructions for Form 1040, line 44 (or in the instructions for Form 1040NR, line 42).

   ☐ **No.** Complete the rest of Form 1040 or Form 1040NR.

LO.8
Identify tax planning opportunities associated with §§ 1231, 1245, and 1250.

17-7 **TAX PLANNING**

17-7a **Timing of § 1231 Gain**

Although §§ 1245 and 1250 recapture much of the gain from the disposition of business property, sometimes § 1231 gain is still substantial. For instance, land held as a business asset will generate either § 1231 gain or § 1231 loss. If the taxpayer already has a capital loss for the year, the sale of land at a gain should be postponed so that the net § 1231 gain is not netted against the capital loss. The capital loss deduction will therefore be maximized for the current tax year, and the capital loss carryforward (if any) may be offset against the gain when the land is sold. If the taxpayer already has a § 1231 loss, § 1231 gains might be postponed to maximize the ordinary loss deduction this year. However, the carryforward of unrecaptured § 1231 losses will make some or all of the § 1231 gain next year an ordinary gain.

In the examples below, the 2016 and 2017 long-term capital gain rates are assumed to be the same.

Section 1231 Planning

EXAMPLE 23

Mark has a $2,000 net STCL for 2016. He could sell business land held 27 months for a $3,000 § 1231 gain. He will have no other capital gains and losses or § 1231 gains and losses in 2016 or 2017. He has no nonrecaptured § 1231 losses from prior years. Mark is in the 28% tax bracket in 2016 and will be in the 25% bracket in 2017. If he sells the land in 2016, he will have a $1,000 net LTCG ($3,000 § 1231 gain − $2,000 STCL) and will pay a tax of $150 ($1,000 × 15%).

If Mark sells the land in 2017, he will have a 2016 tax savings of $560 ($2,000 capital loss deduction × 28% tax rate on ordinary income). In 2017, he will pay tax of $450 ($3,000 × 15%).

By postponing the sale by a year, Mark gets the use of $710 ($560 + $150) of tax savings until he has to pay $450 in 2017, for a net savings of $260 between the two years without considering the time value of money and other factors.

EXAMPLE 24

Beth has a $15,000 § 1231 loss in 2016. She could sell business equipment held 30 months for a $20,000 § 1231 gain and a $12,000 § 1245 gain. Beth is in the 28% tax bracket in 2016 and will be in the 25% bracket in 2017. She has no nonrecaptured § 1231 losses from prior years. If she sold the equipment in 2016, she would have a $5,000 net § 1231 gain and $12,000 of ordinary gain. Her tax would be $4,110 [($5,000 § 1231 gain × 15%) + ($12,000 ordinary gain × 28%)].

If Beth postponed the equipment sale until 2017, she would have a 2016 ordinary loss of $15,000 and tax savings of $4,200 ($15,000 × 28%). In 2017, she would have $5,000 of § 1231 gain (the 2016 § 1231 loss carries over and recaptures $15,000 of the 2017 § 1231 gain as ordinary income) and $27,000 of ordinary gain. Her tax would be $7,500 [($5,000 § 1231 gain × 15%) + ($27,000 ordinary gain × 25%)].

By postponing the sale of the § 1231 property until 2017, Beth gets the use of $8,310 ($4,200 + $4,110) of tax savings until she has to pay $7,500 in 2017, for a net savings of $810 between the two years without considering the time value of money and other factors.

17-7b **Timing of Recapture**

Because recapture is usually not triggered until the property is sold or disposed of, it may be possible to plan for recapture in low-bracket or loss years. If a taxpayer has net operating loss (NOL) carryovers that are about to expire, the recognition of ordinary income from recapture may be advisable to absorb the loss carryovers.

EXAMPLE 25

Ahmad has a $15,000 NOL carryover that will expire this year. He owns a machine that he plans to sell in the early part of next year. The expected gain of $17,000 from the sale of the machine will be recaptured as ordinary income under § 1245. Ahmad sells the machine before the end of this year and uses the $15,000 NOL carryover to offset $15,000 of the ordinary income.

17-7c **Postponing and Shifting Recapture**

It is also possible to postpone recapture or to shift the burden of recapture to others. For example, recapture is avoided upon the disposition of a § 1231 asset if the taxpayer replaces the property by entering into a like-kind exchange. In this instance, recapture potential is merely carried over to the newly acquired property (refer to Example 18).

Recapture can be shifted to others through the gratuitous transfer of § 1245 or § 1250 property to family members. A subsequent sale of such property by the donee will trigger recapture to the donee rather than the donor (refer to Example 15). This procedure would be advisable only if the donee was in a lower income tax bracket compared with the donor.

17-7d **Avoiding Recapture**

The immediate expensing election (§ 179) is subject to § 1245 recapture. If the election is not made, the § 1245 recapture potential will accumulate more slowly (refer to Chapter 8). Because using the immediate expense deduction complicates depreciation and book accounting for the affected asset, not taking the deduction may make sense even though the time value of money might indicate that it should be taken.

REFOCUS ON THE BIG PICTURE

DEPRECIATION RECAPTURE

© RL PRODUCTIONS/DIGITALVISION/GETTY IMAGES

Even though Hazel did not maximize her depreciation deductions when she acquired the store equipment in 2013, she still has ordinary income when she sells the equipment in 2016. She has a basis lower than the store equipment's value due to the § 179 immediate expense deduction she took and the rapid 7-year MACRS depreciation. Section 1245 "recaptures" this gain as ordinary income.

One way Hazel could avoid currently recognizing the $53,040 gain ($128,000 sales price − $74,960 adjusted basis) would be to do a like-kind exchange of the equipment acquired in 2013 for the replacement equipment to be acquired in 2016 (see Example 18). She would likely have to give up the 2013 equipment plus cash to acquire the replacement equipment. Thus, there would be no "boot received" and, therefore, no current gain recognized. However, the depreciation recapture potential on the 2013 equipment would carry over to the replacement equipment.

Key Terms

Discussion Questions

Issue ID   1. **LO.1, 2** Harriet, an organic farmer, has owned depreciable farm equipment for several years. Is the equipment a capital asset? Why or why not?

2. **LO.1** If there is a net loss from the sale of depreciable business property held long term, what is the character of the loss? How is it deducted (*for* or *from* AGI)?

Issue ID   3. **LO.1, 2** Bernice, a sole proprietor, sold two business assets during the year. As a result, she has an ordinary loss and a § 1231 gain. The loss asset was office furniture that was held for eight months, and the gain asset is land that was held for five years. Why doesn't the ordinary loss offset the § 1231 gain?

Issue ID   4. **LO.1, 2** Hakim's rental building was not insured when it was destroyed by a hurricane. His adjusted basis for the building was substantial, but was less than he had paid for the building in 2012. The building was Hakim's only asset that was damaged by the hurricane. How should Hakim handle this situation?

5. **LO.2** An individual taxpayer had a net § 1231 loss in 2016. Could any of this loss be treated as a long-term capital loss? Why or why not?

Issue ID   6. **LO.2** Steven established a sole proprietorship in 2011. He sold § 1231 assets at a loss in 2014 and 2015. He had only sold § 1231 assets at a gain before 2014. In 2016, he could sell a § 1231 asset at a gain and would like to have the gain taxed as a long-term capital gain. What issue is Steven facing?

7. **LO.2** Review Examples 4 and 6 in the text. In both examples, the taxpayer's AGI is $129,400 even though in Example 6 there is $700 of nonrecaptured § 1231 loss from 2015. Explain why the two AGI amounts are the same.

8. **LO.3** A depreciable business dump truck has been owned for four years and is no longer useful to the taxpayer. What would have to be true for the disposition of the dump truck to generate at least some § 1231 loss?

9. **LO.1, 3** If depreciable equipment used in a business is sold at a recognized gain on July 10, 2016, and it was purchased on August 21, 2015, does § 1245 depreciation recapture apply to the asset? Explain.

Issue ID   10. **LO.3** A professional football player's contract is sold at a gain after it has been held for two years. What issues should the team consider in determining the nature of this gain?

11. **LO.3** A retailer's store is destroyed by a tornado, but is insured for its replacement cost. Consequently, the retailer has a $40,000 gain after receiving the insurance proceeds. The store is not replaced because the retailer spends the insurance proceeds on additional inventory. What is the nature of the gain if the store originally cost $100,000 three years ago and had an adjusted basis of $82,000 at the time of its destruction?

12. **LO.4** In the current year, an individual taxpayer has net long-term capital gain from disposition of capital assets and has unrecaptured § 1250 gain. What would the circumstances have to be for the unrecaptured § 1250 gain to be taxed at 25%?

13. **LO.3, 5** Mary receives tangible personal property as a gift. The property was depreciated by the donor, and Mary will also depreciate it. At the date of the gift, the property was worth more than the donor's adjusted basis. What is the impact of these facts on Mary when she sells the property at a gain several years after she acquired it?

14. **LO.3, 5** Thomas receives tangible personal property as an inheritance from a decedent who died in 2016. The property was depreciated by the deceased, and Thomas will also depreciate it. At the date of the deceased's death, the property was worth more than the deceased's adjusted basis. What is the impact of these facts on Thomas when he sells the property at a gain several years after he acquired it?

15. **LO.3, 5** Dino contributes to charity some tangible personal property that he had used in his business and depreciated. At the date of the donation, the property has a fair market value greater than its adjusted basis, but less than the original cost. What is the impact of these facts on Dino's charitable contribution?

16. **LO.3, 5** A corporation distributes a truck it has owned for three years to its sole shareholder. The shareholder will use the truck for personal use activity. The truck's fair market value at the time of the distribution is greater than its adjusted basis, but less than its original cost. Does the corporation recognize a gain? If so, what is the character of the gain?

17. **LO.6** A corporation distributes a truck it has owned for three years to its sole shareholder. The shareholder will use the truck for business activity. The truck's fair market value at the time of the distribution is greater than its adjusted basis, but less than its original cost. Does the corporation recognize a gain? If so, what is the character of the gain?

18. **LO.6** Complete the following statements regarding special recapture provisions.
    a. Corporations selling depreciable real property are required to recapture as ordinary income the _____ of two amounts: (1) _____% of the recognized gain or (2) _____% of the depreciation taken.
    b. When the sale or exchange of property, which in the hands of the transferee is depreciable property, is between certain related parties, _____ recognized is ordinary income.
    c. Intangible drilling and development costs are subject to _____ recapture when the property is disposed of.

19. **LO.7** Refer to Form 4797 near the end of this chapter. Where would a § 1231 loss be entered on the form?

20. **LO.7** Refer to Form 4797 near the end of this chapter. Where would a § 1231 gain on the disposition of business land be entered on the form?

Computational Exercises

21. **LO.1** Lena is a sole proprietor. In April of this year, she sold equipment purchased four years ago for $26,000 with an adjusted basis of $15,500 for $17,000. Later in the year, Lena sold another piece of equipment purchased two years ago with an adjusted basis of $8,200 for $5,500. What is the amount and character of Lena's gain or loss?

22. **LO.2** Several years ago, Nicolas, a timber dealer, purchased a tract of land with a substantial stand of trees on it. The land cost $8,000, and the timber cost $250,000. On the first day of 2016, the timber was appraised at $325,000. In August 2016, Nicolas cut the timber and sold it for $360,000. Nicolas elects to treat the cutting as a sale or exchange under § 1231. What is the amount and character of Nicolas's gain or loss?

23. **LO.3** Renata Corporation purchased equipment in 2014 for $180,000 and has taken $83,000 of regular MACRS depreciation. Renata Corporation sells the equipment in 2016 for $110,000. What is the amount and character of Renata's gain or loss?

24. **LO.3** Jacob purchased business equipment for $56,000 in 2013 and has taken $35,000 of regular MACRS depreciation. Jacob sells the equipment in 2016 for $26,000. What is the amount and character of Jacob's gain or loss?

25. **LO.1, 2, 3** Sissie owns two items of business equipment. Both were purchased in 2012 for $100,000, both have a 7-year MACRS recovery period, and both have an adjusted basis of $37,490. Sissie is considering selling these assets in 2016. One of them is worth $60,000, and the other is worth $23,000. Because both items were used in her business, Sissie simply assumes that the loss on one will be offset against the gain from the other and that the net gain or loss will increase or reduce her business income. What is the amount and character of Sissie's gain or loss?

26. **LO.4** An apartment building was acquired in 2007. The depreciation taken on the building was $123,000, and the building was sold for a $34,000 gain. What is the maximum amount of *25% gain*?

27. **LO.4** An individual taxpayer has $25,000 of § 1231 gain from the disposition of non-residential real estate. Straight-line depreciation of $43,000 was deducted on the real estate. The taxpayer also has a § 1231 loss of $56,000 from the sale of equipment. How much of the § 1231 gain is taxed as unrecaptured § 1250 gain?

28. **LO.4** Enzo is a single taxpayer with the following gains and losses for 2016:

- $2,100 short-term capital loss.
- $24,000 long-term capital gain from sale of stock.
- $14,000 § 1231 gain that is all unrecaptured § 1250 gain.

What is the amount and character of Enzo's gain or loss?

29. **LO.5** In a § 1031 like-kind exchange, Rafael exchanges a piece of equipment that originally cost $200,000. On the date of the exchange, the equipment given up has an adjusted basis of $85,000 and a fair market value of $110,000. Rafael pays $15,000 and receives equipment with a fair market value of $125,000. What is the amount and character of Rafael's gain or loss?

30. **LO.5** Gaston Corporation distributes § 1245 property as a dividend to its shareholders. The property's fair market value is $580,000, and the adjusted basis is $560,000. In addition, the amount of the recapture potential is $55,000. What is the amount and character of Gaston's gain or loss?

Problems

31. **LO.1, 2** Jenny purchased timber on a 100-acre tract of land in South Dakota in March 2014 for $100,000. On January 1, 2016, the timber had a fair market value of $145,000. Because of careless cutting in November 2016, when the fair market value was $158,000, the wood was sold on January 30, 2017, for $98,000.
    a. What gain (loss) was recognized in 2015, 2016, and 2017 if Jenny elected to treat the cutting as a sale?
    b. What was the nature of the gains (losses) in (a)?
    c. Does the answer change if the timber was sold in December 2016? Why or why not?
    d. If the timber was worth only $58,000 on January 1, 2016, was cut in November when it was worth $33,000, and was sold in December for $59,000, how would the answers to (a) and (b) change?

32. **LO.2** Bob owns a farming sole proprietorship. During the year, Bob sold a milk cow that he had owned for 15 months and a workhorse that he had owned for 66 months. The cow had an adjusted basis of $38,000 and was sold for $55,000. The horse had an adjusted basis of $750 and was sold for $4,000. Bob also has a $200 long-term capital loss from the sale of corporate stock. He has $55,000 of other AGI (not associated with the items above) for the year. He has $4,000 non-recaptured § 1231 losses from the previous five years. What is the nature of the gains or losses from the disposition of the farm animals? What is Bob's AGI for the year?

33. **LO.2** A sculpture that Korliss Kane held for investment was destroyed in a flood. The sculpture was insured, and Korliss had a $60,000 gain from this casualty. He also had a $17,000 loss from an uninsured antique vase that was destroyed by the flood. The vase was also held for investment. Korliss had no other property transactions during the year and has no nonrecaptured § 1231 losses from prior years. Both the sculpture and the vase had been held more than one year when the flood occurred. Compute Korliss's net gain or loss, and identify how it would be treated. Also write a letter to Korliss, explaining the nature of the gain or loss. Korliss's address is 2367 Meridian Road, Hannibal, MO 63401.

Communications

34. **LO.2** Keshara has the following net § 1231 results for each of the years shown. What would be the nature of the net gains in 2015 and 2016?

Tax Year	Net § 1231 Loss	Net § 1231 Gain
2011	$18,000	
2012	33,000	
2013	42,000	
2014		$41,000
2015		30,000
2016		41,000

35. **LO.2, 8** Jinjie owns two parcels of business land (§ 1231 assets). One parcel can be sold at a loss of $60,000, and the other parcel can be sold at a gain of $70,000. Jinjie has no nonrecaptured § 1231 losses from prior years. The parcels could be sold at any time because potential purchasers are abundant. Jinjie has a $35,000 short-term capital loss carryover from a prior tax year and no capital assets that could be sold to generate long-term capital gains. Both land parcels have been held more than one year. What should Jinjie do based upon these facts? (Assume that tax rates are constant, and ignore the present value of future cash flow.)

Decision Making

36. **LO.1, 2, 3** Siena Industries (a sole proprietorship) sold three § 1231 assets during 2016. Data on these property dispositions are as follows:

Asset	Cost	Acquired	Depreciation	Sold for	Sold on
Rack	$100,000	10/10/12	$62,000	$85,000	10/10/16
Forklift	35,000	10/16/13	23,000	5,000	10/10/16
Bin	87,000	03/12/15	34,000	60,000	10/10/16

a. Determine the amount and the character of the recognized gain or loss from the disposition of each asset.
b. Assuming that Siena has no nonrecaptured net § 1231 losses from prior years, how much of the 2016 recognized gains is treated as capital gains?

37. **LO.2, 3** Amber Industries (a sole proprietorship) sold three § 1231 assets during 2016. Data on these property dispositions are as follows:

Asset	Cost	Acquired	Depreciation	Sold for	Sold on
Rack	$100,000	10/10/12	$100,000	$145,000	10/10/16
Forklift	35,000	10/16/13	23,000	3,000	10/10/16
Bin	87,000	03/12/15	31,000	60,000	10/10/16

a. Determine the amount and the character of the recognized gain or loss from the disposition of each asset.
b. Assuming that Amber has $5,000 nonrecaptured net § 1231 losses from the five prior years, how much of the 2016 recognized gains is treated as capital gains?

38. **LO.2, 3** Copper Industries (a sole proprietorship) sold three § 1231 assets during 2016. Data on these property dispositions are as follows:

Asset	Cost	Acquired	Depreciation	Sold for	Sold on
Rack	$110,000	10/10/13	$70,000	$55,000	10/10/16
Forklift	45,000	10/16/12	21,000	15,000	10/10/16
Bin	97,000	03/12/15	31,000	60,000	10/10/16

a. Determine the amount and the character of the recognized gain or loss from the disposition of each asset.

b. Assuming that Copper has $6,000 nonrecaptured net § 1231 losses from prior years, how much of the 2016 recognized gains is treated as capital gains?

Communications   39. **LO.2, 3** On December 1, 2014, Lavender Manufacturing Company (a corporation) purchased another company's assets, including a patent. The patent was used in Lavender's manufacturing operations; $49,500 was allocated to the patent, and it was amortized at the rate of $275 per month. On July 30, 2016, Lavender sold the patent for $95,000. Twenty months of amortization had been taken on the patent. What are the amount and nature of the gain Lavender recognizes on the disposition of the patent? Write a letter to Lavender, discussing the treatment of the gain. Lavender's address is 6734 Grover Street, Boothbay Harbor, ME 04538. The letter should be addressed to Bill Cubit, Controller.

40. **LO.2, 4** On June 1, 2012, Skylark Enterprises (not a corporation) acquired a retail store building for $500,000 (with $100,000 being allocated to the land). The store building was 39-year real property, and the straight-line cost recovery method was used. The property was sold on June 21, 2016, for $385,000.

a. Compute the cost recovery and adjusted basis for the building using Exhibit 8.8 from Chapter 8.

b. What are the amount and nature of Skylark's gain or loss from disposition of the building? What amount, if any, of the gain is unrecaptured § 1250 gain?

41. **LO.2, 3, 4** On May 2, 1987, Hannah acquired residential rental real estate for $450,000. Of the cost, $100,000 was allocated to the land and $350,000 to the building. On August 20, 2016, the building, which then had an adjusted basis of $0, was sold for $545,000 and the land for $200,000.

a. Determine the amount and character of the recognized gain from the sale of the building.

b. Determine the amount and character of the recognized gain from the sale of the land.

42. **LO.2, 3, 4** Larry is the sole proprietor of a trampoline shop. During 2016, the following transactions occurred:

- Unimproved land adjacent to the store was condemned by the city on February 1. The condemnation proceeds were $15,000. The land, acquired in 1985, had an allocable basis of $40,000. Larry has additional parking across the street and plans to use the condemnation proceeds to build his inventory.

- A truck used to deliver trampolines was sold on January 2 for $3,500. The truck was purchased on January 2, 2012, for $6,000. On the date of sale, the adjusted basis was zero.

- Larry sold an antique rowing machine at an auction. Net proceeds were $4,900. The rowing machine was purchased as used equipment 17 years ago for $5,200 and is fully depreciated.

- Larry sold an apartment building for $300,000 on September 1. The rental property was purchased on September 1, 2013, for $150,000 and was being depreciated over a 27.5-year life using the straight-line method. At the date of sale, the adjusted basis was $124,783.

- Larry's personal yacht was stolen on September 5. The yacht had been purchased in August at a cost of $25,000. The fair market value immediately preceding the theft was $19,600. Larry was insured for 50% of the original cost, and he received $12,500 on December 1.
- Larry sold a Buick on May 1 for $9,600. The vehicle had been used exclusively for personal purposes. It was purchased on September 1, 2012, for $20,800.
- Larry's trampoline stretching machine (owned two years) was stolen on May 5, but the business's insurance company will not pay any of the machine's value because Larry failed to pay the insurance premium. The machine had a fair market value of $8,000 and an adjusted basis of $6,000 at the time of theft.
- Larry had AGI of $102,000 from sources other than those described above.
- Larry has no nonrecaptured § 1231 lookback losses.

a. For each transaction, what are the amount and nature of recognized gain or loss?

b. What is Larry's 2016 AGI?

43. **LO.2, 4** On January 1, 2007, Stephanie Bridges acquired depreciable real property for $50,000. She used straight-line depreciation to compute the asset's cost recovery. The asset was sold for $96,000 on January 3, 2016, when its adjusted basis was $38,000.

Communications

a. What are the amount and nature of the gain if the real property was residential?

b. Stephanie is curious about how the recapture rules differ for tangible personal property and for residential rental real estate acquired in 1987 and thereafter. Write a letter to Stephanie, explaining the differences. Her address is 2345 Westridge Street #23, Edna, KS 67342.

44. **LO.2, 3, 5, 8** Joanne is in the 28% tax bracket and owns depreciable business equipment that she purchased several years ago for $135,000. She has taken $100,000 of depreciation on the equipment, and it is worth $55,000. Joanne's niece, Susan, is starting a new business and is short of cash. Susan has asked Joanne to gift the equipment to her so that Susan can use it in her business. Joanne no longer needs the equipment. Identify the alternatives available to Joanne if she wants to help Susan and the tax effects of those alternatives. (Assume that all alternatives involve the business equipment in one way or another, and ignore the gift tax.)

Decision Making

45. **LO.2, 3, 5** Anna received tangible personal property with a fair market value of $65,000 as a gift in 2014. The donor had purchased the property for $77,000 and had taken $77,000 of depreciation. Anna used the property in her business. Anna sells the property for $23,000 in 2016. What are the tax status of the property and the nature of the recognized gain when she sells the property?

46. **LO.2, 3, 5** Miguel receives tangible personal property as an inheritance in 2014. The property was depreciated by the deceased (Miguel's father), and Miguel will also depreciate it. At the date of the deceased's death, the property was worth $532,000. The deceased had purchased it for $900,000 and had taken $523,000 of depreciation on the property. Miguel takes $223,000 of depreciation on the property before selling it for $482,000 in 2016. What are the tax status of the property and the nature of the recognized gain when Miguel sells the property?

47. **LO.5** David contributes to charity some tangible personal property that he had used in his business and depreciated. At the date of the donation, the property has a fair market value of $233,000 and an adjusted basis of zero; it was originally acquired for $400,000. What is the amount of David's charitable contribution?

48. **LO.2, 3, 5** Dedriea contributes to her wholly owned corporation some tangible personal property that she had used in her sole proprietorship business and depreciated. She had acquired the property for $566,000 and had taken $431,000 of depreciation on it before contributing it to the corporation. At the date of the contribution, the property had a fair market value of $289,000. The corporation took $100,000 of depreciation on the property and then sold it for $88,000 in 2016. What are the tax status of the property to the corporation and the nature of the recognized gain or loss when the corporation sells the property?

49. **LO.2, 3, 6** Tan Corporation purchased depreciable tangible personal property for $100,000 in 2014 and immediately expensed the entire cost under § 179. In 2016, when the property was worth $80,000, Tan distributed it as a dividend to the corporation's sole shareholder. What was the tax status of this property for Tan? What is the nature of the recognized gain or loss from the distribution of the property?

50. **LO.5** Jasmine owned rental real estate that she sold to her tenant in an installment sale. Jasmine acquired the property in 2004 for $400,000; took $178,000 of depreciation on it; and sold it for $210,000, receiving $25,000 immediately and the balance (plus interest at a market rate) in equal payments of $18,500 for 10 years. What is the nature of the recognized gain or loss from this transaction?

51. **LO.4, 7** Sasha and Tara are married, filing jointly. Their correctly determined 2016 taxable income is $127,000. This taxable income includes a $5,000 § 1231 gain from the sale of business land that was included in their $22,000 of net long-term capital gain. None of the net long-term capital gain was from collectibles.

    a. In addition to their Form 1040, what tax forms related to their property transactions would the couple include in their income tax return?

    b. Calculate the couple's tax on taxable income using the alternative tax on net capital gain method.

52. **LO.7** On August 10, 2014, Jasper purchased business equipment for $40,000. On his 2014 tax return, $40,000 of § 179 immediate expense was taken on the equipment. On July 14, 2015, Jasper sold the equipment for $12,000. What is the nature of disposition gain or loss? Where is it reported on the 2015 Form 4797?

53. **LO.7** Adrian has a 2015 Form 4797, line 9 gain of $56,000. He also has one transaction on his 2015 Form 1040 Schedule D, Part I—a loss of $58,000. What is Adrian's AGI from these events?

54. **LO.7** Theresa has a 2015 Form 1040 Schedule D, line 16 gain of $45,000. There is also a $45,000 gain on the form's line 19. What is the nature of the gain? What alternative tax rate applies to it?

Decision Making   55. **LO.3, 8** Jay sold three items of business equipment for a total of $300,000. None of the equipment was appraised to determine its value. Jay's cost and adjusted basis for the assets are as follows:

Asset	Cost	Adjusted Basis
Skidder	$230,000	$ 40,000
Driller	120,000	60,000
Platform	620,000	–0–
Total	$970,000	$100,000

Jay has been unable to establish the fair market values of the three assets. All he can determine is that combined they were worth $300,000 to the buyer in this arm's length transaction. How should Jay allocate the sales price and figure the gain or loss on the sale of the three assets?

Cumulative Problems

56. Justin Stone was an employee of DataCare Services, Inc. His salary was $45,000 through November 10, 2015, when he was laid off. DataCare Services provided medical insurance for Justin and his family during his employment and agreed to continue this coverage through the end of 2015. He received $7,000 of unemployment compensation from November 11, 2015, through December 31, 2015. FICA withholdings were as follows: Social Security of $2,790 ($45,000 × 6.2%) and Medicare of $653 ($45,000 × 1.45%). Justin lives at 112 Green Road, Crown City, OH 45623. His Social Security number is 111-11-1112. Justin owned an apartment building until November 22, 2015, when he sold it for $200,000 (the apartment building's address is 4826 Orange Street, Crown City, OH 45623). For 2015, he had rent revenue of $33,000. He incurred and paid expenses as follows: $4,568 of repairs, $22,000 of mortgage interest, and $1,000 of miscellaneous expenses. He purchased the building on January 2, 2009, for $125,000. The building generated an operating profit each year that Justin owned it.

Tax Return Problem

TAX SOFTWARE

   Other information follows:

- On November 22, 2015, Justin sold for $3,500 equipment that had been used for repairing various items in the apartments. The equipment was purchased for $25,000 on July 10, 2008, and was fully depreciated prior to 2015.

- Justin has $3,000 of unrecaptured § 1231 losses from prior years.

- Justin is age 38; is single; is divorced; and has custody of his 9-year-old son, Flint. Justin provides more than 50% of Flint's support. Flint's Social Security number is 123-45-6789.

- Justin had $1,000 interest income from Blue Corporation bonds.

- Justin had $1,500 interest income from a State Bank certificate of deposit.

- Justin had a $2,000 *0%/15%/20%* long-term capital gain distribution from the Brown Stock Investment Fund.

- Justin had the following itemized deductions: $4,600 real estate taxes on his home; $8,900 mortgage interest on his home; $4,760 charitable contributions (all in cash, all properly documented, and no single contribution exceeding $25); $4,300 state income tax withholding during 2015; $2,000 state estimated income tax payments during 2015; $2,600 sales taxes paid.

- Justin does not want to donate to the Presidential Election Campaign Fund.

- He had $12,000 of Federal income tax withholding during 2015 and made total Federal estimated income tax payments of $14,000 during 2015.

   Compute Justin's 2015 net tax payable or refund due. If you use tax forms for your computations, you will need Form 1040 and Schedules A, B, D, and E. You will also need Form 4797. Suggested software: H&R BLOCK Tax Software.

57. Glen and Diane Okumura (both age 48) are married, file a joint return, and live at 39 Kaloa Street, Honolulu, HI 96815. Glen's Social Security number is 111-11-1111, and Diane's is 123-45-6789. The Okumuras have two dependent children, Amy (age 15) and John (age 9). Amy's Social Security number is 123-45-6788, and John's Social Security number is 123-45-6787. Glen works for the Hawaii Public Works Department, and Diane works in a retail dress shop. Glen's employer provided medical insurance to Glen and his family during 2016. The Okumuras had the following transactions during 2016:

Tax Computation Problem

Communications

a. Glen earned $57,000 in wages and had Federal income tax withholding of $2,000.

b. Diane earned $38,000 in wages from the dress shop and had Federal income tax withholding of $1,000.

c. The Okumuras sold a small apartment building for $89,980 on November 15, 2016. The building was acquired in October 2010 for $200,000; cost recovery was $66,820.

d. The Okumuras received $3,000 in qualified dividends on various domestic corporation stocks that they own.

e.   The Okumuras sold stock on November 5 for a $23,000 long-term capital gain and other stock on December 10 at a $2,000 short-term capital loss.

f.   The Okumuras had the following itemized deductions: $12,895 unreimbursed medical expenses, $10,500 personal use real property taxes, $7,000 qualified residence interest, $1,500 of Glen's unreimbursed employee business expenses, $535 of investment-related expenses, $2,700 of state income taxes paid, and $1,061 of sales taxes from the sales tax table.

g.   The Okumuras spent $3,000 on qualifying child care expenses during the year.

Compute the Okumuras' 2016 net tax payable or refund due. Also write a letter to the Okumuras, describing how the sale of the apartment building affects their return.

Research Problems

Note: Solutions to Research Problems can be prepared by using the Checkpoint® Student Edition online research product, which is available to accompany this text. It is also possible to prepare solutions to the Research Problems by using tax research materials found in a standard tax library.

Research Problem 1. Walter is both a real estate developer and the owner and manager of residential rental real estate. Walter is retiring and is going to sell both the land he is holding for future development and the rental properties he owns. Straight-line depreciation was used to depreciate the rental real estate. The rental properties will be sold at a substantial loss, and the development property will be sold at a substantial gain. What is the nature of these gains and losses?

Partial list of research aids:
§§ 1221 and 1231.
Zane R. Tollis, 65 TCM 1951, T.C.Memo. 1993–63.

Research Problem 2. Your client, Alternate Fuel, Inc. (a regular corporation), owns three sandwich shops in the Philadelphia area. In 2013, the year Alternate Fuel incorporated, it acquired land on the outskirts of Philadelphia with the hope of someday farming the land to cultivate humanely harvested meat and grow organic fruits and vegetables to use in its sandwich shops. In 2015, Alternate Fuel drew up plans for the farm and began consulting with agricultural experts about the best locations for crops and the number of animals that could be sustained on the acreage. After reviewing those plans, Alternate Fuel's CEO decided that the plans are not currently financially feasible and would like to sell the land in 2016. The land has appreciated substantially in value, and the company could use the cash infusion. Given that the land has not been used in the business, will any gain realized be categorized as a § 1231 gain or as a long-term capital gain? Explain.

Internet Activity

Use the tax resources of the Internet to address the following questions. Do not restrict your search to the Web, but include a review of newsgroups and general reference materials, practitioner sites and resources, primary sources of the tax law, chat rooms and discussion groups, and other opportunities.

Research Problem 3. Search for the phrase "mortgage and real estate fraud" on the IRS's website (**www.irs.gov**). Read the articles you find, and explain why this type of fraud is often unearthed by the IRS.

Research Problem 4. Find a state website that has tax forms and instructions for the state. Call that state "X." Find a discussion in those sources that reveals whether state X taxes gains from the sale of real estate that is located in state Y when the taxpayer is an individual and is a full-time resident of state X.

Roger CPA Review Questions

1. Joe purchased a van for $30,000 on February 1, 2014, for use with his business, Crew Airport Transport. Joe elected to take the § 179 deduction for the entire cost. On January 1, 2016, Joe sold the van for $20,000. What were the tax effects of this transaction?

   a. $10,000 loss

   b. $20,000 capital gain

   c. $20,000 ordinary gain

   d. $10,000 capital gain, $10,000 ordinary gain

2. In year 1, Gardner used funds earmarked for use in Gardner's business to make a personal loan to Carson. In year 3, Carson declared bankruptcy, having paid off only $500 of the loan at that time. In year 1, Gardner purchased equipment for use in Gardner's business. In year 3, Gardner sold the equipment at a $5,000 loss. In January of year 3, Gardner received shares of stock as a gift from Smith; the shares had been purchased by Smith in year 1. In November of year 3, Gardner sold the shares of stock for a $5,000 gain.

   Which of the above transactions will Gardner report as long-term capital gains or losses for year 3?

   I.   The bad debt write-off
   II. The sale of equipment
   III. The sale of shares

   a. II and III only

   c. III only

   b. I only

   d. None of the above

3. On March 1 of the current year, Reiter, an individual, sold an office building for $300,000 that had an adjusted basis of $220,000, resulting in a gain of $80,000. Reiter had purchased the building for $260,000 on April 1 of the previous year, and $30,000 of the total depreciation taken took advantage of a special tax incentive program Reiter qualified for. How should Reiter report this gain on the current year tax return?

   a. $80,000 ordinary gain

   b. $30,000 ordinary gain and $50,000 long-term capital gain

   c. $50,000 ordinary gain and $30,000 long-term capital gain

   d. $40,000 ordinary gain and $40,000 short-term capital gain

4. In year 3, Daniels, an individual, sold depreciable equipment for $21,000 that had an adjusted basis of $12,000, resulting in a $9,000 gain. The property had cost Daniels $20,000 when purchased in year 1, and $8,000 of MACRS depreciation had been taken. How should Daniels report the gain on Daniels' year 3 tax return?

   a. As a long-term capital gain of $9,000

   b. As an ordinary gain of $1,800 and a § 1231 gain of $7,200

   c. As an ordinary gain of $8,000 and a § 1231 gain of $1,000

   d. As an ordinary gain of $7,200 and a § 1231 gain of $1,800

5. Cowabunga Corp. had a highly profitable year 4, during which it purchased $1,000,000 in tangible personal property and elected to claim the highest depreciation expense allowed for tax purposes under Code § 179. In year 6 Cowabunga sells the tangible personal property, which now has an adjusted basis of $200,000 as a result of the heavy depreciation taken in years 4 and 5. Had only MACRS depreciation been taken on the property, its adjusted basis at the time of sale would have been $800,000. At a sales price of $930,000, how much of the $730,000 realized gain must be reported as ordinary gain for tax purposes?

   a. $720,000

   c. $0

   b. $600,000

   d. $730,000

Appendix A

Tax Rate Schedules and Tables

(The 2016 Tax Tables and 2016 Sales Tax Tables can be accessed at the IRS website when released: **www.irs.gov**)

2015 Tax Rate Schedules

Single—Schedule X

If taxable income is: Over—	But not over—	The tax is:	of the amount over—
$ 0	$ 9,225	.........10%	$ 0
9,225	37,450	$ 922.50 + 15%	9,225
37,450	90,750	5,156.25 + 25%	37,450
90,750	189,300	18,481.25 + 28%	90,750
189,300	411,500	46,075.25 + 33%	189,300
411,500	413,200	119,401.25 + 35%	411,500
413,200	....	119,996.25 + 39.6%	413,200

Head of household—Schedule Z

If taxable income is: Over—	But not over—	The tax is:	of the amount over—
$ 0	$ 13,150	.........10%	$ 0
13,150	50,200	$ 1,315.00 + 15%	13,150
50,200	129,600	6,872.50 + 25%	50,200
129,600	209,850	26,722.50 + 28%	129,600
209,850	411,500	49,192.50 + 33%	209,850
411,500	439,000	115,737.00 + 35%	411,500
439,000	....	125,362.00 + 39.6%	439,000

Married filing jointly or Qualifying widow(er)—Schedule Y–1

If taxable income is: Over—	But not over—	The tax is:	of the amount over—
$ 0	$ 18,450	.........10%	$ 0
18,450	74,900	$ 1,845.00 + 15%	18,450
74,900	151,200	10,312.50 + 25%	74,900
151,200	230,450	29,387.50 + 28%	151,200
230,450	411,500	51,577.50 + 33%	230,450
411,500	464,850	111,324.00 + 35%	411,500
464,850	....	129,996.50 + 39.6%	464,850

Married filing separately—Schedule Y–2

If taxable income is: Over—	But not over—	The tax is:	of the amount over—
$ 0	$ 9,225	.........10%	$ 0
9,225	37,450	$ 922.50 + 15%	9,225
37,450	75,600	5,156.25 + 25%	37,450
75,600	115,225	14,693.75 + 28%	75,600
115,225	205,750	25,788.75 + 33%	115,225
205,750	232,425	55,662.00 + 35%	205,750
232,425	....	64,998.25 + 39.6%	232,425

2016 Tax Rate Schedules

Single—Schedule X

If taxable income is: Over—	But not over—	The tax is:	of the amount over—
$ 0	$ 9,275	.........10%	$ 0
9,275	37,650	$ 927.50 + 15%	9,275
37,650	91,150	5,183.75 + 25%	37,650
91,150	190,150	18,558.75 + 28%	91,150
190,150	413,350	46,278.75 + 33%	190,150
413,350	415,050	119,934.75 + 35%	413,350
415,050	....	120,529.75 + 39.6%	415,050

Head of household—Schedule Z

If taxable income is: Over—	But not over—	The tax is:	of the amount over—
$ 0	$ 13,250	.........10%	$ 0
13,250	50,400	$ 1,325.00 + 15%	13,250
50,400	130,150	6,897.50 + 25%	50,400
130,150	210,800	26,835.00 + 28%	130,150
210,800	413,350	49,417.00 + 33%	210,800
413,350	441,000	116,258.50 + 35%	413,350
441,000	....	125,936.00 + 39.6%	441,000

Married filing jointly or Qualifying widow(er)—Schedule Y–1

If taxable income is: Over—	But not over—	The tax is:	of the amount over—
$ 0	$ 18,550	.........10%	$ 0
18,550	75,300	$ 1,855.00 + 15%	18,550
75,300	151,900	10,367.50 + 25%	75,300
151,900	231,450	29,517.50 + 28%	151,900
231,450	413,350	51,791.50 + 33%	231,450
413,350	466,950	111,818.50 + 35%	413,350
466,950	....	130,578.50 + 39.6%	466,950

Married filing separately—Schedule Y–2

If taxable income is: Over—	But not over—	The tax is:	of the amount over—
$ 0	$ 9,275	.........10%	$ 0
9,275	37,650	$ 927.50 + 15%	9,275
37,650	75,950	5,183.75 + 25%	37,650
75,950	115,725	14,758.75 + 28%	75,950
115,725	206,675	25,895.75 + 33%	115,725
206,675	233,475	55,909.25 + 35%	206,675
233,475	....	65,289.25 + 39.6%	233,475

2015 Tax Table

See the instructions for line 44 to see if you must use the Tax Table below to figure your tax.

Example. Mr. and Mrs. Brown are filing a joint return. Their taxable income on Form 1040, line 43, is $25,300. First, they find the $25,300-25,350 taxable income line. Next, they find the column for married filing jointly and read down the column. The amount shown where the taxable income line and filing status column meet is $2,876. This is the tax amount they should enter on Form 1040, line 44.

Sample Table

At Least	But Less Than	Single	Married filing jointly*	Married filing separately	Head of a household
			Your tax is—		
25,200	25,250	3,323	2,861	3,323	3,126
25,250	25,300	3,330	2,869	3,330	3,134
25,300	25,350	3,338	2,876	3,338	3,141
25,350	25,400	3,345	2,884	3,345	3,149

If line 43 (taxable income) is—		And you are—			
At least	But less than	Single	Married filing jointly *	Married filing separately	Head of a household
			Your tax is—		
0	5	0	0	0	0
5	15	1	1	1	1
15	25	2	2	2	2
25	50	4	4	4	4
50	75	6	6	6	6
75	100	9	9	9	9
100	125	11	11	11	11
125	150	14	14	14	14
150	175	16	16	16	16
175	200	19	19	19	19
200	225	21	21	21	21
225	250	24	24	24	24
250	275	26	26	26	26
275	300	29	29	29	29
300	325	31	31	31	31
325	350	34	34	34	34
350	375	36	36	36	36
375	400	39	39	39	39
400	425	41	41	41	41
425	450	44	44	44	44
450	475	46	46	46	46
475	500	49	49	49	49
500	525	51	51	51	51
525	550	54	54	54	54
550	575	56	56	56	56
575	600	59	59	59	59
600	625	61	61	61	61
625	650	64	64	64	64
650	675	66	66	66	66
675	700	69	69	69	69
700	725	71	71	71	71
725	750	74	74	74	74
750	775	76	76	76	76
775	800	79	79	79	79
800	825	81	81	81	81
825	850	84	84	84	84
850	875	86	86	86	86
875	900	89	89	89	89
900	925	91	91	91	91
925	950	94	94	94	94
950	975	96	96	96	96
975	1,000	99	99	99	99

1,000

If line 43 (taxable income) is—		And you are—			
At least	But less than	Single	Married filing jointly *	Married filing separately	Head of a household
			Your tax is—		
1,000	1,025	101	101	101	101
1,025	1,050	104	104	104	104
1,050	1,075	106	106	106	106
1,075	1,100	109	109	109	109
1,100	1,125	111	111	111	111
1,125	1,150	114	114	114	114
1,150	1,175	116	116	116	116
1,175	1,200	119	119	119	119
1,200	1,225	121	121	121	121
1,225	1,250	124	124	124	124
1,250	1,275	126	126	126	126
1,275	1,300	129	129	129	129
1,300	1,325	131	131	131	131
1,325	1,350	134	134	134	134
1,350	1,375	136	136	136	136
1,375	1,400	139	139	139	139
1,400	1,425	141	141	141	141
1,425	1,450	144	144	144	144
1,450	1,475	146	146	146	146
1,475	1,500	149	149	149	149
1,500	1,525	151	151	151	151
1,525	1,550	154	154	154	154
1,550	1,575	156	156	156	156
1,575	1,600	159	159	159	159
1,600	1,625	161	161	161	161
1,625	1,650	164	164	164	164
1,650	1,675	166	166	166	166
1,675	1,700	169	169	169	169
1,700	1,725	171	171	171	171
1,725	1,750	174	174	174	174
1,750	1,775	176	176	176	176
1,775	1,800	179	179	179	179
1,800	1,825	181	181	181	181
1,825	1,850	184	184	184	184
1,850	1,875	186	186	186	186
1,875	1,900	189	189	189	189
1,900	1,925	191	191	191	191
1,925	1,950	194	194	194	194
1,950	1,975	196	196	196	196
1,975	2,000	199	199	199	199

2,000

If line 43 (taxable income) is—		And you are—			
At least	But less than	Single	Married filing jointly *	Married filing separately	Head of a household
			Your tax is—		
2,000	2,025	201	201	201	201
2,025	2,050	204	204	204	204
2,050	2,075	206	206	206	206
2,075	2,100	209	209	209	209
2,100	2,125	211	211	211	211
2,125	2,150	214	214	214	214
2,150	2,175	216	216	216	216
2,175	2,200	219	219	219	219
2,200	2,225	221	221	221	221
2,225	2,250	224	224	224	224
2,250	2,275	226	226	226	226
2,275	2,300	229	229	229	229
2,300	2,325	231	231	231	231
2,325	2,350	234	234	234	234
2,350	2,375	236	236	236	236
2,375	2,400	239	239	239	239
2,400	2,425	241	241	241	241
2,425	2,450	244	244	244	244
2,450	2,475	246	246	246	246
2,475	2,500	249	249	249	249
2,500	2,525	251	251	251	251
2,525	2,550	254	254	254	254
2,550	2,575	256	256	256	256
2,575	2,600	259	259	259	259
2,600	2,625	261	261	261	261
2,625	2,650	264	264	264	264
2,650	2,675	266	266	266	266
2,675	2,700	269	269	269	269
2,700	2,725	271	271	271	271
2,725	2,750	274	274	274	274
2,750	2,775	276	276	276	276
2,775	2,800	279	279	279	279
2,800	2,825	281	281	281	281
2,825	2,850	284	284	284	284
2,850	2,875	286	286	286	286
2,875	2,900	289	289	289	289
2,900	2,925	291	291	291	291
2,925	2,950	294	294	294	294
2,950	2,975	296	296	296	296
2,975	3,000	299	299	299	299

* This column must also be used by a qualifying widow(er).

(Continued)

2015 Tax Table—*Continued*

If line 43 (taxable income) is—		And you are—				If line 43 (taxable income) is—		And you are—				If line 43 (taxable income) is—		And you are—			
At least	But less than	Single	Married filing jointly *	Married filing separately	Head of a household	At least	But less than	Single	Married filing jointly *	Married filing separately	Head of a household	At least	But less than	Single	Married filing jointly *	Married filing separately	Head of a household
		Your tax is—						Your tax is—						Your tax is—			
3,000						**6,000**						**9,000**					
3,000	3,050	303	303	303	303	6,000	6,050	603	603	603	603	9,000	9,050	903	903	903	903
3,050	3,100	308	308	308	308	6,050	6,100	608	608	608	608	9,050	9,100	908	908	908	908
3,100	3,150	313	313	313	313	6,100	6,150	613	613	613	613	9,100	9,150	913	913	913	913
3,150	3,200	318	318	318	318	6,150	6,200	618	618	618	618	9,150	9,200	918	918	918	918
3,200	3,250	323	323	323	323	6,200	6,250	623	623	623	623	9,200	9,250	923	923	923	923
3,250	3,300	328	328	328	328	6,250	6,300	628	628	628	628	9,250	9,300	930	928	930	928
3,300	3,350	333	333	333	333	6,300	6,350	633	633	633	633	9,300	9,350	938	933	938	933
3,350	3,400	338	338	338	338	6,350	6,400	638	638	638	638	9,350	9,400	945	938	945	938
3,400	3,450	343	343	343	343	6,400	6,450	643	643	643	643	9,400	9,450	953	943	953	943
3,450	3,500	348	348	348	348	6,450	6,500	648	648	648	648	9,450	9,500	960	948	960	948
3,500	3,550	353	353	353	353	6,500	6,550	653	653	653	653	9,500	9,550	968	953	968	953
3,550	3,600	358	358	358	358	6,550	6,600	658	658	658	658	9,550	9,600	975	958	975	958
3,600	3,650	363	363	363	363	6,600	6,650	663	663	663	663	9,600	9,650	983	963	983	963
3,650	3,700	368	368	368	368	6,650	6,700	668	668	668	668	9,650	9,700	990	968	990	968
3,700	3,750	373	373	373	373	6,700	6,750	673	673	673	673	9,700	9,750	998	973	998	973
3,750	3,800	378	378	378	378	6,750	6,800	678	678	678	678	9,750	9,800	1,005	978	1,005	978
3,800	3,850	383	383	383	383	6,800	6,850	683	683	683	683	9,800	9,850	1,013	983	1,013	983
3,850	3,900	388	388	388	388	6,850	6,900	688	688	688	688	9,850	9,900	1,020	988	1,020	988
3,900	3,950	393	393	393	393	6,900	6,950	693	693	693	693	9,900	9,950	1,028	993	1,028	993
3,950	4,000	398	398	398	398	6,950	7,000	698	698	698	698	9,950	10,000	1,035	998	1,035	998
4,000						**7,000**						**10,000**					
4,000	4,050	403	403	403	403	7,000	7,050	703	703	703	703	10,000	10,050	1,043	1,003	1,043	1,003
4,050	4,100	408	408	408	408	7,050	7,100	708	708	708	708	10,050	10,100	1,050	1,008	1,050	1,008
4,100	4,150	413	413	413	413	7,100	7,150	713	713	713	713	10,100	10,150	1,058	1,013	1,058	1,013
4,150	4,200	418	418	418	418	7,150	7,200	718	718	718	718	10,150	10,200	1,065	1,018	1,065	1,018
4,200	4,250	423	423	423	423	7,200	7,250	723	723	723	723	10,200	10,250	1,073	1,023	1,073	1,023
4,250	4,300	428	428	428	428	7,250	7,300	728	728	728	728	10,250	10,300	1,080	1,028	1,080	1,028
4,300	4,350	433	433	433	433	7,300	7,350	733	733	733	733	10,300	10,350	1,088	1,033	1,088	1,033
4,350	4,400	438	438	438	438	7,350	7,400	738	738	738	738	10,350	10,400	1,095	1,038	1,095	1,038
4,400	4,450	443	443	443	443	7,400	7,450	743	743	743	743	10,400	10,450	1,103	1,043	1,103	1,043
4,450	4,500	448	448	448	448	7,450	7,500	748	748	748	748	10,450	10,500	1,110	1,048	1,110	1,048
4,500	4,550	453	453	453	453	7,500	7,550	753	753	753	753	10,500	10,550	1,118	1,053	1,118	1,053
4,550	4,600	458	458	458	458	7,550	7,600	758	758	758	758	10,550	10,600	1,125	1,058	1,125	1,058
4,600	4,650	463	463	463	463	7,600	7,650	763	763	763	763	10,600	10,650	1,133	1,063	1,133	1,063
4,650	4,700	468	468	468	468	7,650	7,700	768	768	768	768	10,650	10,700	1,140	1,068	1,140	1,068
4,700	4,750	473	473	473	473	7,700	7,750	773	773	773	773	10,700	10,750	1,148	1,073	1,148	1,073
4,750	4,800	478	478	478	478	7,750	7,800	778	778	778	778	10,750	10,800	1,155	1,078	1,155	1,078
4,800	4,850	483	483	483	483	7,800	7,850	783	783	783	783	10,800	10,850	1,163	1,083	1,163	1,083
4,850	4,900	488	488	488	488	7,850	7,900	788	788	788	788	10,850	10,900	1,170	1,088	1,170	1,088
4,900	4,950	493	493	493	493	7,900	7,950	793	793	793	793	10,900	10,950	1,178	1,093	1,178	1,093
4,950	5,000	498	498	498	498	7,950	8,000	798	798	798	798	10,950	11,000	1,185	1,098	1,185	1,098
5,000						**8,000**						**11,000**					
5,000	5,050	503	503	503	503	8,000	8,050	803	803	803	803	11,000	11,050	1,193	1,103	1,193	1,103
5,050	5,100	508	508	508	508	8,050	8,100	808	808	808	808	11,050	11,100	1,200	1,108	1,200	1,108
5,100	5,150	513	513	513	513	8,100	8,150	813	813	813	813	11,100	11,150	1,208	1,113	1,208	1,113
5,150	5,200	518	518	518	518	8,150	8,200	818	818	818	818	11,150	11,200	1,215	1,118	1,215	1,118
5,200	5,250	523	523	523	523	8,200	8,250	823	823	823	823	11,200	11,250	1,223	1,123	1,223	1,123
5,250	5,300	528	528	528	528	8,250	8,300	828	828	828	828	11,250	11,300	1,230	1,128	1,230	1,128
5,300	5,350	533	533	533	533	8,300	8,350	833	833	833	833	11,300	11,350	1,238	1,133	1,238	1,133
5,350	5,400	538	538	538	538	8,350	8,400	838	838	838	838	11,350	11,400	1,245	1,138	1,245	1,138
5,400	5,450	543	543	543	543	8,400	8,450	843	843	843	843	11,400	11,450	1,253	1,143	1,253	1,143
5,450	5,500	548	548	548	548	8,450	8,500	848	848	848	848	11,450	11,500	1,260	1,148	1,260	1,148
5,500	5,550	553	553	553	553	8,500	8,550	853	853	853	853	11,500	11,550	1,268	1,153	1,268	1,153
5,550	5,600	558	558	558	558	8,550	8,600	858	858	858	858	11,550	11,600	1,275	1,158	1,275	1,158
5,600	5,650	563	563	563	563	8,600	8,650	863	863	863	863	11,600	11,650	1,283	1,163	1,283	1,163
5,650	5,700	568	568	568	568	8,650	8,700	868	868	868	868	11,650	11,700	1,290	1,168	1,290	1,168
5,700	5,750	573	573	573	573	8,700	8,750	873	873	873	873	11,700	11,750	1,298	1,173	1,298	1,173
5,750	5,800	578	578	578	578	8,750	8,800	878	878	878	878	11,750	11,800	1,305	1,178	1,305	1,178
5,800	5,850	583	583	583	583	8,800	8,850	883	883	883	883	11,800	11,850	1,313	1,183	1,313	1,183
5,850	5,900	588	588	588	588	8,850	8,900	888	888	888	888	11,850	11,900	1,320	1,188	1,320	1,188
5,900	5,950	593	593	593	593	8,900	8,950	893	893	893	893	11,900	11,950	1,328	1,193	1,328	1,193
5,950	6,000	598	598	598	598	8,950	9,000	898	898	898	898	11,950	12,000	1,335	1,198	1,335	1,198

* This column must also be used by a qualifying widow(er).

(Continued)

2015 Tax Table—*Continued*

12,000

At least	But less than	Single	Married filing jointly *	Married filing separately	Head of a household
12,000	12,050	1,343	1,203	1,343	1,203
12,050	12,100	1,350	1,208	1,350	1,208
12,100	12,150	1,358	1,213	1,358	1,213
12,150	12,200	1,365	1,218	1,365	1,218
12,200	12,250	1,373	1,223	1,373	1,223
12,250	12,300	1,380	1,228	1,380	1,228
12,300	12,350	1,388	1,233	1,388	1,233
12,350	12,400	1,395	1,238	1,395	1,238
12,400	12,450	1,403	1,243	1,403	1,243
12,450	12,500	1,410	1,248	1,410	1,248
12,500	12,550	1,418	1,253	1,418	1,253
12,550	12,600	1,425	1,258	1,425	1,258
12,600	12,650	1,433	1,263	1,433	1,263
12,650	12,700	1,440	1,268	1,440	1,268
12,700	12,750	1,448	1,273	1,448	1,273
12,750	12,800	1,455	1,278	1,455	1,278
12,800	12,850	1,463	1,283	1,463	1,283
12,850	12,900	1,470	1,288	1,470	1,288
12,900	12,950	1,478	1,293	1,478	1,293
12,950	13,000	1,485	1,298	1,485	1,298

13,000

At least	But less than	Single	Married filing jointly *	Married filing separately	Head of a household
13,000	13,050	1,493	1,303	1,493	1,303
13,050	13,100	1,500	1,308	1,500	1,308
13,100	13,150	1,508	1,313	1,508	1,313
13,150	13,200	1,515	1,318	1,515	1,319
13,200	13,250	1,523	1,323	1,523	1,326
13,250	13,300	1,530	1,328	1,530	1,334
13,300	13,350	1,538	1,333	1,538	1,341
13,350	13,400	1,545	1,338	1,545	1,349
13,400	13,450	1,553	1,343	1,553	1,356
13,450	13,500	1,560	1,348	1,560	1,364
13,500	13,550	1,568	1,353	1,568	1,371
13,550	13,600	1,575	1,358	1,575	1,379
13,600	13,650	1,583	1,363	1,583	1,386
13,650	13,700	1,590	1,368	1,590	1,394
13,700	13,750	1,598	1,373	1,598	1,401
13,750	13,800	1,605	1,378	1,605	1,409
13,800	13,850	1,613	1,383	1,613	1,416
13,850	13,900	1,620	1,388	1,620	1,424
13,900	13,950	1,628	1,393	1,628	1,431
13,950	14,000	1,635	1,398	1,635	1,439

14,000

At least	But less than	Single	Married filing jointly *	Married filing separately	Head of a household
14,000	14,050	1,643	1,403	1,643	1,446
14,050	14,100	1,650	1,408	1,650	1,454
14,100	14,150	1,658	1,413	1,658	1,461
14,150	14,200	1,665	1,418	1,665	1,469
14,200	14,250	1,673	1,423	1,673	1,476
14,250	14,300	1,680	1,428	1,680	1,484
14,300	14,350	1,688	1,433	1,688	1,491
14,350	14,400	1,695	1,438	1,695	1,499
14,400	14,450	1,703	1,443	1,703	1,506
14,450	14,500	1,710	1,448	1,710	1,514
14,500	14,550	1,718	1,453	1,718	1,521
14,550	14,600	1,725	1,458	1,725	1,529
14,600	14,650	1,733	1,463	1,733	1,536
14,650	14,700	1,740	1,468	1,740	1,544
14,700	14,750	1,748	1,473	1,748	1,551
14,750	14,800	1,755	1,478	1,755	1,559
14,800	14,850	1,763	1,483	1,763	1,566
14,850	14,900	1,770	1,488	1,770	1,574
14,900	14,950	1,778	1,493	1,778	1,581
14,950	15,000	1,785	1,498	1,785	1,589

15,000

At least	But less than	Single	Married filing jointly *	Married filing separately	Head of a household
15,000	15,050	1,793	1,503	1,793	1,596
15,050	15,100	1,800	1,508	1,800	1,604
15,100	15,150	1,808	1,513	1,808	1,611
15,150	15,200	1,815	1,518	1,815	1,619
15,200	15,250	1,823	1,523	1,823	1,626
15,250	15,300	1,830	1,528	1,830	1,634
15,300	15,350	1,838	1,533	1,838	1,641
15,350	15,400	1,845	1,538	1,845	1,649
15,400	15,450	1,853	1,543	1,853	1,656
15,450	15,500	1,860	1,548	1,860	1,664
15,500	15,550	1,868	1,553	1,868	1,671
15,550	15,600	1,875	1,558	1,875	1,679
15,600	15,650	1,883	1,563	1,883	1,686
15,650	15,700	1,890	1,568	1,890	1,694
15,700	15,750	1,898	1,573	1,898	1,701
15,750	15,800	1,905	1,578	1,905	1,709
15,800	15,850	1,913	1,583	1,913	1,716
15,850	15,900	1,920	1,588	1,920	1,724
15,900	15,950	1,928	1,593	1,928	1,731
15,950	16,000	1,935	1,598	1,935	1,739

16,000

At least	But less than	Single	Married filing jointly *	Married filing separately	Head of a household
16,000	16,050	1,943	1,603	1,943	1,746
16,050	16,100	1,950	1,608	1,950	1,754
16,100	16,150	1,958	1,613	1,958	1,761
16,150	16,200	1,965	1,618	1,965	1,769
16,200	16,250	1,973	1,623	1,973	1,776
16,250	16,300	1,980	1,628	1,980	1,784
16,300	16,350	1,988	1,633	1,988	1,791
16,350	16,400	1,995	1,638	1,995	1,799
16,400	16,450	2,003	1,643	2,003	1,806
16,450	16,500	2,010	1,648	2,010	1,814
16,500	16,550	2,018	1,653	2,018	1,821
16,550	16,600	2,025	1,658	2,025	1,829
16,600	16,650	2,033	1,663	2,033	1,836
16,650	16,700	2,040	1,668	2,040	1,844
16,700	16,750	2,048	1,673	2,048	1,851
16,750	16,800	2,055	1,678	2,055	1,859
16,800	16,850	2,063	1,683	2,063	1,866
16,850	16,900	2,070	1,688	2,070	1,874
16,900	16,950	2,078	1,693	2,078	1,881
16,950	17,000	2,085	1,698	2,085	1,889

17,000

At least	But less than	Single	Married filing jointly *	Married filing separately	Head of a household
17,000	17,050	2,093	1,703	2,093	1,896
17,050	17,100	2,100	1,708	2,100	1,904
17,100	17,150	2,108	1,713	2,108	1,911
17,150	17,200	2,115	1,718	2,115	1,919
17,200	17,250	2,123	1,723	2,123	1,926
17,250	17,300	2,130	1,728	2,130	1,934
17,300	17,350	2,138	1,733	2,138	1,941
17,350	17,400	2,145	1,738	2,145	1,949
17,400	17,450	2,153	1,743	2,153	1,956
17,450	17,500	2,160	1,748	2,160	1,964
17,500	17,550	2,168	1,753	2,168	1,971
17,550	17,600	2,175	1,758	2,175	1,979
17,600	17,650	2,183	1,763	2,183	1,986
17,650	17,700	2,190	1,768	2,190	1,994
17,700	17,750	2,198	1,773	2,198	2,001
17,750	17,800	2,205	1,778	2,205	2,009
17,800	17,850	2,213	1,783	2,213	2,016
17,850	17,900	2,220	1,788	2,220	2,024
17,900	17,950	2,228	1,793	2,228	2,031
17,950	18,000	2,235	1,798	2,235	2,039

18,000

At least	But less than	Single	Married filing jointly *	Married filing separately	Head of a household
18,000	18,050	2,243	1,803	2,243	2,046
18,050	18,100	2,250	1,808	2,250	2,054
18,100	18,150	2,258	1,813	2,258	2,061
18,150	18,200	2,265	1,818	2,265	2,069
18,200	18,250	2,273	1,823	2,273	2,076
18,250	18,300	2,280	1,828	2,280	2,084
18,300	18,350	2,288	1,833	2,288	2,091
18,350	18,400	2,295	1,838	2,295	2,099
18,400	18,450	2,303	1,843	2,303	2,106
18,450	18,500	2,310	1,849	2,310	2,114
18,500	18,550	2,318	1,856	2,318	2,121
18,550	18,600	2,325	1,864	2,325	2,129
18,600	18,650	2,333	1,871	2,333	2,136
18,650	18,700	2,340	1,879	2,340	2,144
18,700	18,750	2,348	1,886	2,348	2,151
18,750	18,800	2,355	1,894	2,355	2,159
18,800	18,850	2,363	1,901	2,363	2,166
18,850	18,900	2,370	1,909	2,370	2,174
18,900	18,950	2,378	1,916	2,378	2,181
18,950	19,000	2,385	1,924	2,385	2,189

19,000

At least	But less than	Single	Married filing jointly *	Married filing separately	Head of a household
19,000	19,050	2,393	1,931	2,393	2,196
19,050	19,100	2,400	1,939	2,400	2,204
19,100	19,150	2,408	1,946	2,408	2,211
19,150	19,200	2,415	1,954	2,415	2,219
19,200	19,250	2,423	1,961	2,423	2,226
19,250	19,300	2,430	1,969	2,430	2,234
19,300	19,350	2,438	1,976	2,438	2,241
19,350	19,400	2,445	1,984	2,445	2,249
19,400	19,450	2,453	1,991	2,453	2,256
19,450	19,500	2,460	1,999	2,460	2,264
19,500	19,550	2,468	2,006	2,468	2,271
19,550	19,600	2,475	2,014	2,475	2,279
19,600	19,650	2,483	2,021	2,483	2,286
19,650	19,700	2,490	2,029	2,490	2,294
19,700	19,750	2,498	2,036	2,498	2,301
19,750	19,800	2,505	2,044	2,505	2,309
19,800	19,850	2,513	2,051	2,513	2,316
19,850	19,900	2,520	2,059	2,520	2,324
19,900	19,950	2,528	2,066	2,528	2,331
19,950	20,000	2,535	2,074	2,535	2,339

20,000

At least	But less than	Single	Married filing jointly *	Married filing separately	Head of a household
20,000	20,050	2,543	2,081	2,543	2,346
20,050	20,100	2,550	2,089	2,550	2,354
20,100	20,150	2,558	2,096	2,558	2,361
20,150	20,200	2,565	2,104	2,565	2,369
20,200	20,250	2,573	2,111	2,573	2,376
20,250	20,300	2,580	2,119	2,580	2,384
20,300	20,350	2,588	2,126	2,588	2,391
20,350	20,400	2,595	2,134	2,595	2,399
20,400	20,450	2,603	2,141	2,603	2,406
20,450	20,500	2,610	2,149	2,610	2,414
20,500	20,550	2,618	2,156	2,618	2,421
20,550	20,600	2,625	2,164	2,625	2,429
20,600	20,650	2,633	2,171	2,633	2,436
20,650	20,700	2,640	2,179	2,640	2,444
20,700	20,750	2,648	2,186	2,648	2,451
20,750	20,800	2,655	2,194	2,655	2,459
20,800	20,850	2,663	2,201	2,663	2,466
20,850	20,900	2,670	2,209	2,670	2,474
20,900	20,950	2,678	2,216	2,678	2,481
20,950	21,000	2,685	2,224	2,685	2,489

* This column must also be used by a qualifying widow(er).

(Continued)

2015 Tax Table—*Continued*

If line 43 (taxable income) is—		And you are—			
At least	But less than	Single	Married filing jointly *	Married filing separately	Head of a household
		Your tax is—			

21,000

At least	But less than	Single	Married filing jointly *	Married filing separately	Head of a household
21,000	21,050	2,693	2,231	2,693	2,496
21,050	21,100	2,700	2,239	2,700	2,504
21,100	21,150	2,708	2,246	2,708	2,511
21,150	21,200	2,715	2,254	2,715	2,519
21,200	21,250	2,723	2,261	2,723	2,526
21,250	21,300	2,730	2,269	2,730	2,534
21,300	21,350	2,738	2,276	2,738	2,541
21,350	21,400	2,745	2,284	2,745	2,549
21,400	21,450	2,753	2,291	2,753	2,556
21,450	21,500	2,760	2,299	2,760	2,564
21,500	21,550	2,768	2,306	2,768	2,571
21,550	21,600	2,775	2,314	2,775	2,579
21,600	21,650	2,783	2,321	2,783	2,586
21,650	21,700	2,790	2,329	2,790	2,594
21,700	21,750	2,798	2,336	2,798	2,601
21,750	21,800	2,805	2,344	2,805	2,609
21,800	21,850	2,813	2,351	2,813	2,616
21,850	21,900	2,820	2,359	2,820	2,624
21,900	21,950	2,828	2,366	2,828	2,631
21,950	22,000	2,835	2,374	2,835	2,639

22,000

At least	But less than	Single	Married filing jointly *	Married filing separately	Head of a household
22,000	22,050	2,843	2,381	2,843	2,646
22,050	22,100	2,850	2,389	2,850	2,654
22,100	22,150	2,858	2,396	2,858	2,661
22,150	22,200	2,865	2,404	2,865	2,669
22,200	22,250	2,873	2,411	2,873	2,676
22,250	22,300	2,880	2,419	2,880	2,684
22,300	22,350	2,888	2,426	2,888	2,691
22,350	22,400	2,895	2,434	2,895	2,699
22,400	22,450	2,903	2,441	2,903	2,706
22,450	22,500	2,910	2,449	2,910	2,714
22,500	22,550	2,918	2,456	2,918	2,721
22,550	22,600	2,925	2,464	2,925	2,729
22,600	22,650	2,933	2,471	2,933	2,736
22,650	22,700	2,940	2,479	2,940	2,744
22,700	22,750	2,948	2,486	2,948	2,751
22,750	22,800	2,955	2,494	2,955	2,759
22,800	22,850	2,963	2,501	2,963	2,766
22,850	22,900	2,970	2,509	2,970	2,774
22,900	22,950	2,978	2,516	2,978	2,781
22,950	23,000	2,985	2,524	2,985	2,789

23,000

At least	But less than	Single	Married filing jointly *	Married filing separately	Head of a household
23,000	23,050	2,993	2,531	2,993	2,796
23,050	23,100	3,000	2,539	3,000	2,804
23,100	23,150	3,008	2,546	3,008	2,811
23,150	23,200	3,015	2,554	3,015	2,819
23,200	23,250	3,023	2,561	3,023	2,826
23,250	23,300	3,030	2,569	3,030	2,834
23,300	23,350	3,038	2,576	3,038	2,841
23,350	23,400	3,045	2,584	3,045	2,849
23,400	23,450	3,053	2,591	3,053	2,856
23,450	23,500	3,060	2,599	3,060	2,864
23,500	23,550	3,068	2,606	3,068	2,871
23,550	23,600	3,075	2,614	3,075	2,879
23,600	23,650	3,083	2,621	3,083	2,886
23,650	23,700	3,090	2,629	3,090	2,894
23,700	23,750	3,098	2,636	3,098	2,901
23,750	23,800	3,105	2,644	3,105	2,909
23,800	23,850	3,113	2,651	3,113	2,916
23,850	23,900	3,120	2,659	3,120	2,924
23,900	23,950	3,128	2,666	3,128	2,931
23,950	24,000	3,135	2,674	3,135	2,939

24,000

At least	But less than	Single	Married filing jointly *	Married filing separately	Head of a household
24,000	24,050	3,143	2,681	3,143	2,946
24,050	24,100	3,150	2,689	3,150	2,954
24,100	24,150	3,158	2,696	3,158	2,961
24,150	24,200	3,165	2,704	3,165	2,969
24,200	24,250	3,173	2,711	3,173	2,976
24,250	24,300	3,180	2,719	3,180	2,984
24,300	24,350	3,188	2,726	3,188	2,991
24,350	24,400	3,195	2,734	3,195	2,999
24,400	24,450	3,203	2,741	3,203	3,006
24,450	24,500	3,210	2,749	3,210	3,014
24,500	24,550	3,218	2,756	3,218	3,021
24,550	24,600	3,225	2,764	3,225	3,029
24,600	24,650	3,233	2,771	3,233	3,036
24,650	24,700	3,240	2,779	3,240	3,044
24,700	24,750	3,248	2,786	3,248	3,051
24,750	24,800	3,255	2,794	3,255	3,059
24,800	24,850	3,263	2,801	3,263	3,066
24,850	24,900	3,270	2,809	3,270	3,074
24,900	24,950	3,278	2,816	3,278	3,081
24,950	25,000	3,285	2,824	3,285	3,089

25,000

At least	But less than	Single	Married filing jointly *	Married filing separately	Head of a household
25,000	25,050	3,293	2,831	3,293	3,096
25,050	25,100	3,300	2,839	3,300	3,104
25,100	25,150	3,308	2,846	3,308	3,111
25,150	25,200	3,315	2,854	3,315	3,119
25,200	25,250	3,323	2,861	3,323	3,126
25,250	25,300	3,330	2,869	3,330	3,134
25,300	25,350	3,338	2,876	3,338	3,141
25,350	25,400	3,345	2,884	3,345	3,149
25,400	25,450	3,353	2,891	3,353	3,156
25,450	25,500	3,360	2,899	3,360	3,164
25,500	25,550	3,368	2,906	3,368	3,171
25,550	25,600	3,375	2,914	3,375	3,179
25,600	25,650	3,383	2,921	3,383	3,186
25,650	25,700	3,390	2,929	3,390	3,194
25,700	25,750	3,398	2,936	3,398	3,201
25,750	25,800	3,405	2,944	3,405	3,209
25,800	25,850	3,413	2,951	3,413	3,216
25,850	25,900	3,420	2,959	3,420	3,224
25,900	25,950	3,428	2,966	3,428	3,231
25,950	26,000	3,435	2,974	3,435	3,239

26,000

At least	But less than	Single	Married filing jointly *	Married filing separately	Head of a household
26,000	26,050	3,443	2,981	3,443	3,246
26,050	26,100	3,450	2,989	3,450	3,254
26,100	26,150	3,458	2,996	3,458	3,261
26,150	26,200	3,465	3,004	3,465	3,269
26,200	26,250	3,473	3,011	3,473	3,276
26,250	26,300	3,480	3,019	3,480	3,284
26,300	26,350	3,488	3,026	3,488	3,291
26,350	26,400	3,495	3,034	3,495	3,299
26,400	26,450	3,503	3,041	3,503	3,306
26,450	26,500	3,510	3,049	3,510	3,314
26,500	26,550	3,518	3,056	3,518	3,321
26,550	26,600	3,525	3,064	3,525	3,329
26,600	26,650	3,533	3,071	3,533	3,336
26,650	26,700	3,540	3,079	3,540	3,344
26,700	26,750	3,548	3,086	3,548	3,351
26,750	26,800	3,555	3,094	3,555	3,359
26,800	26,850	3,563	3,101	3,563	3,366
26,850	26,900	3,570	3,109	3,570	3,374
26,900	26,950	3,578	3,116	3,578	3,381
26,950	27,000	3,585	3,124	3,585	3,389

27,000

At least	But less than	Single	Married filing jointly *	Married filing separately	Head of a household
27,000	27,050	3,593	3,131	3,593	3,396
27,050	27,100	3,600	3,139	3,600	3,404
27,100	27,150	3,608	3,146	3,608	3,411
27,150	27,200	3,615	3,154	3,615	3,419
27,200	27,250	3,623	3,161	3,623	3,426
27,250	27,300	3,630	3,169	3,630	3,434
27,300	27,350	3,638	3,176	3,638	3,441
27,350	27,400	3,645	3,184	3,645	3,449
27,400	27,450	3,653	3,191	3,653	3,456
27,450	27,500	3,660	3,199	3,660	3,464
27,500	27,550	3,668	3,206	3,668	3,471
27,550	27,600	3,675	3,214	3,675	3,479
27,600	27,650	3,683	3,221	3,683	3,486
27,650	27,700	3,690	3,229	3,690	3,494
27,700	27,750	3,698	3,236	3,698	3,501
27,750	27,800	3,705	3,244	3,705	3,509
27,800	27,850	3,713	3,251	3,713	3,516
27,850	27,900	3,720	3,259	3,720	3,524
27,900	27,950	3,728	3,266	3,728	3,531
27,950	28,000	3,735	3,274	3,735	3,539

28,000

At least	But less than	Single	Married filing jointly *	Married filing separately	Head of a household
28,000	28,050	3,743	3,281	3,743	3,546
28,050	28,100	3,750	3,289	3,750	3,554
28,100	28,150	3,758	3,296	3,758	3,561
28,150	28,200	3,765	3,304	3,765	3,569
28,200	28,250	3,773	3,311	3,773	3,576
28,250	28,300	3,780	3,319	3,780	3,584
28,300	28,350	3,788	3,326	3,788	3,591
28,350	28,400	3,795	3,334	3,795	3,599
28,400	28,450	3,803	3,341	3,803	3,606
28,450	28,500	3,810	3,349	3,810	3,614
28,500	28,550	3,818	3,356	3,818	3,621
28,550	28,600	3,825	3,364	3,825	3,629
28,600	28,650	3,833	3,371	3,833	3,636
28,650	28,700	3,840	3,379	3,840	3,644
28,700	28,750	3,848	3,386	3,848	3,651
28,750	28,800	3,855	3,394	3,855	3,659
28,800	28,850	3,863	3,401	3,863	3,666
28,850	28,900	3,870	3,409	3,870	3,674
28,900	28,950	3,878	3,416	3,878	3,681
28,950	29,000	3,885	3,424	3,885	3,689

29,000

At least	But less than	Single	Married filing jointly *	Married filing separately	Head of a household
29,000	29,050	3,893	3,431	3,893	3,696
29,050	29,100	3,900	3,439	3,900	3,704
29,100	29,150	3,908	3,446	3,908	3,711
29,150	29,200	3,915	3,454	3,915	3,719
29,200	29,250	3,923	3,461	3,923	3,726
29,250	29,300	3,930	3,469	3,930	3,734
29,300	29,350	3,938	3,476	3,938	3,741
29,350	29,400	3,945	3,484	3,945	3,749
29,400	29,450	3,953	3,491	3,953	3,756
29,450	29,500	3,960	3,499	3,960	3,764
29,500	29,550	3,968	3,506	3,968	3,771
29,550	29,600	3,975	3,514	3,975	3,779
29,600	29,650	3,983	3,521	3,983	3,786
29,650	29,700	3,990	3,529	3,990	3,794
29,700	29,750	3,998	3,536	3,998	3,801
29,750	29,800	4,005	3,544	4,005	3,809
29,800	29,850	4,013	3,551	4,013	3,816
29,850	29,900	4,020	3,559	4,020	3,824
29,900	29,950	4,028	3,566	4,028	3,831
29,950	30,000	4,035	3,574	4,035	3,839

* This column must also be used by a qualifying widow(er).

(Continued)

2015 Tax Table—*Continued*

If line 43 (taxable income) is—		And you are—			
At least	But less than	Single	Married filing jointly *	Married filing separately	Head of a household
		Your tax is—			

30,000

At least	But less than	Single	MFJ*	MFS	HoH
30,000	30,050	4,043	3,581	4,043	3,846
30,050	30,100	4,050	3,589	4,050	3,854
30,100	30,150	4,058	3,596	4,058	3,861
30,150	30,200	4,065	3,604	4,065	3,869
30,200	30,250	4,073	3,611	4,073	3,876
30,250	30,300	4,080	3,619	4,080	3,884
30,300	30,350	4,088	3,626	4,088	3,891
30,350	30,400	4,095	3,634	4,095	3,899
30,400	30,450	4,103	3,641	4,103	3,906
30,450	30,500	4,110	3,649	4,110	3,914
30,500	30,550	4,118	3,656	4,118	3,921
30,550	30,600	4,125	3,664	4,125	3,929
30,600	30,650	4,133	3,671	4,133	3,936
30,650	30,700	4,140	3,679	4,140	3,944
30,700	30,750	4,148	3,686	4,148	3,951
30,750	30,800	4,155	3,694	4,155	3,959
30,800	30,850	4,163	3,701	4,163	3,966
30,850	30,900	4,170	3,709	4,170	3,974
30,900	30,950	4,178	3,716	4,178	3,981
30,950	31,000	4,185	3,724	4,185	3,989

31,000

At least	But less than	Single	MFJ*	MFS	HoH
31,000	31,050	4,193	3,731	4,193	3,996
31,050	31,100	4,200	3,739	4,200	4,004
31,100	31,150	4,208	3,746	4,208	4,011
31,150	31,200	4,215	3,754	4,215	4,019
31,200	31,250	4,223	3,761	4,223	4,026
31,250	31,300	4,230	3,769	4,230	4,034
31,300	31,350	4,238	3,776	4,238	4,041
31,350	31,400	4,245	3,784	4,245	4,049
31,400	31,450	4,253	3,791	4,253	4,056
31,450	31,500	4,260	3,799	4,260	4,064
31,500	31,550	4,268	3,806	4,268	4,071
31,550	31,600	4,275	3,814	4,275	4,079
31,600	31,650	4,283	3,821	4,283	4,086
31,650	31,700	4,290	3,829	4,290	4,094
31,700	31,750	4,298	3,836	4,298	4,101
31,750	31,800	4,305	3,844	4,305	4,109
31,800	31,850	4,313	3,851	4,313	4,116
31,850	31,900	4,320	3,859	4,320	4,124
31,900	31,950	4,328	3,866	4,328	4,131
31,950	32,000	4,335	3,874	4,335	4,139

32,000

At least	But less than	Single	MFJ*	MFS	HoH
32,000	32,050	4,343	3,881	4,343	4,146
32,050	32,100	4,350	3,889	4,350	4,154
32,100	32,150	4,358	3,896	4,358	4,161
32,150	32,200	4,365	3,904	4,365	4,169
32,200	32,250	4,373	3,911	4,373	4,176
32,250	32,300	4,380	3,919	4,380	4,184
32,300	32,350	4,388	3,926	4,388	4,191
32,350	32,400	4,395	3,934	4,395	4,199
32,400	32,450	4,403	3,941	4,403	4,206
32,450	32,500	4,410	3,949	4,410	4,214
32,500	32,550	4,418	3,956	4,418	4,221
32,550	32,600	4,425	3,964	4,425	4,229
32,600	32,650	4,433	3,971	4,433	4,236
32,650	32,700	4,440	3,979	4,440	4,244
32,700	32,750	4,448	3,986	4,448	4,251
32,750	32,800	4,455	3,994	4,455	4,259
32,800	32,850	4,463	4,001	4,463	4,266
32,850	32,900	4,470	4,009	4,470	4,274
32,900	32,950	4,478	4,016	4,478	4,281
32,950	33,000	4,485	4,024	4,485	4,289

33,000

At least	But less than	Single	MFJ*	MFS	HoH
33,000	33,050	4,493	4,031	4,493	4,296
33,050	33,100	4,500	4,039	4,500	4,304
33,100	33,150	4,508	4,046	4,508	4,311
33,150	33,200	4,515	4,054	4,515	4,319
33,200	33,250	4,523	4,061	4,523	4,326
33,250	33,300	4,530	4,069	4,530	4,334
33,300	33,350	4,538	4,076	4,538	4,341
33,350	33,400	4,545	4,084	4,545	4,349
33,400	33,450	4,553	4,091	4,553	4,356
33,450	33,500	4,560	4,099	4,560	4,364
33,500	33,550	4,568	4,106	4,568	4,371
33,550	33,600	4,575	4,114	4,575	4,379
33,600	33,650	4,583	4,121	4,583	4,386
33,650	33,700	4,590	4,129	4,590	4,394
33,700	33,750	4,598	4,136	4,598	4,401
33,750	33,800	4,605	4,144	4,605	4,409
33,800	33,850	4,613	4,151	4,613	4,416
33,850	33,900	4,620	4,159	4,620	4,424
33,900	33,950	4,628	4,166	4,628	4,431
33,950	34,000	4,635	4,174	4,635	4,439

34,000

At least	But less than	Single	MFJ*	MFS	HoH
34,000	34,050	4,643	4,181	4,643	4,446
34,050	34,100	4,650	4,189	4,650	4,454
34,100	34,150	4,658	4,196	4,658	4,461
34,150	34,200	4,665	4,204	4,665	4,469
34,200	34,250	4,673	4,211	4,673	4,476
34,250	34,300	4,680	4,219	4,680	4,484
34,300	34,350	4,688	4,226	4,688	4,491
34,350	34,400	4,695	4,234	4,695	4,499
34,400	34,450	4,703	4,241	4,703	4,506
34,450	34,500	4,710	4,249	4,710	4,514
34,500	34,550	4,718	4,256	4,718	4,521
34,550	34,600	4,725	4,264	4,725	4,529
34,600	34,650	4,733	4,271	4,733	4,536
34,650	34,700	4,740	4,279	4,740	4,544
34,700	34,750	4,748	4,286	4,748	4,551
34,750	34,800	4,755	4,294	4,755	4,559
34,800	34,850	4,763	4,301	4,763	4,566
34,850	34,900	4,770	4,309	4,770	4,574
34,900	34,950	4,778	4,316	4,778	4,581
34,950	35,000	4,785	4,324	4,785	4,589

35,000

At least	But less than	Single	MFJ*	MFS	HoH
35,000	35,050	4,793	4,331	4,793	4,596
35,050	35,100	4,800	4,339	4,800	4,604
35,100	35,150	4,808	4,346	4,808	4,611
35,150	35,200	4,815	4,354	4,815	4,619
35,200	35,250	4,823	4,361	4,823	4,626
35,250	35,300	4,830	4,369	4,830	4,634
35,300	35,350	4,838	4,376	4,838	4,641
35,350	35,400	4,845	4,384	4,845	4,649
35,400	35,450	4,853	4,391	4,853	4,656
35,450	35,500	4,860	4,399	4,860	4,664
35,500	35,550	4,868	4,406	4,868	4,671
35,550	35,600	4,875	4,414	4,875	4,679
35,600	35,650	4,883	4,421	4,883	4,686
35,650	35,700	4,890	4,429	4,890	4,694
35,700	35,750	4,898	4,436	4,898	4,701
35,750	35,800	4,905	4,444	4,905	4,709
35,800	35,850	4,913	4,451	4,913	4,716
35,850	35,900	4,920	4,459	4,920	4,724
35,900	35,950	4,928	4,466	4,928	4,731
35,950	36,000	4,935	4,474	4,935	4,739

36,000

At least	But less than	Single	MFJ*	MFS	HoH
36,000	36,050	4,943	4,481	4,943	4,746
36,050	36,100	4,950	4,489	4,950	4,754
36,100	36,150	4,958	4,496	4,958	4,761
36,150	36,200	4,965	4,504	4,965	4,769
36,200	36,250	4,973	4,511	4,973	4,776
36,250	36,300	4,980	4,519	4,980	4,784
36,300	36,350	4,988	4,526	4,988	4,791
36,350	36,400	4,995	4,534	4,995	4,799
36,400	36,450	5,003	4,541	5,003	4,806
36,450	36,500	5,010	4,549	5,010	4,814
36,500	36,550	5,018	4,556	5,018	4,821
36,550	36,600	5,025	4,564	5,025	4,829
36,600	36,650	5,033	4,571	5,033	4,836
36,650	36,700	5,040	4,579	5,040	4,844
36,700	36,750	5,048	4,586	5,048	4,851
36,750	36,800	5,055	4,594	5,055	4,859
36,800	36,850	5,063	4,601	5,063	4,866
36,850	36,900	5,070	4,609	5,070	4,874
36,900	36,950	5,078	4,616	5,078	4,881
36,950	37,000	5,085	4,624	5,085	4,889

37,000

At least	But less than	Single	MFJ*	MFS	HoH
37,000	37,050	5,093	4,631	5,093	4,896
37,050	37,100	5,100	4,639	5,100	4,904
37,100	37,150	5,108	4,646	5,108	4,911
37,150	37,200	5,115	4,654	5,115	4,919
37,200	37,250	5,123	4,661	5,123	4,926
37,250	37,300	5,130	4,669	5,130	4,934
37,300	37,350	5,138	4,676	5,138	4,941
37,350	37,400	5,145	4,684	5,145	4,949
37,400	37,450	5,153	4,691	5,153	4,956
37,450	37,500	5,163	4,699	5,163	4,964
37,500	37,550	5,175	4,706	5,175	4,971
37,550	37,600	5,188	4,714	5,188	4,979
37,600	37,650	5,200	4,721	5,200	4,986
37,650	37,700	5,213	4,729	5,213	4,994
37,700	37,750	5,225	4,736	5,225	5,001
37,750	37,800	5,238	4,744	5,238	5,009
37,800	37,850	5,250	4,751	5,250	5,016
37,850	37,900	5,263	4,759	5,263	5,024
37,900	37,950	5,275	4,766	5,275	5,031
37,950	38,000	5,288	4,774	5,288	5,039

38,000

At least	But less than	Single	MFJ*	MFS	HoH
38,000	38,050	5,300	4,781	5,300	5,046
38,050	38,100	5,313	4,789	5,313	5,054
38,100	38,150	5,325	4,796	5,325	5,061
38,150	38,200	5,338	4,804	5,338	5,069
38,200	38,250	5,350	4,811	5,350	5,076
38,250	38,300	5,363	4,819	5,363	5,084
38,300	38,350	5,375	4,826	5,375	5,091
38,350	38,400	5,388	4,834	5,388	5,099
38,400	38,450	5,400	4,841	5,400	5,106
38,450	38,500	5,413	4,849	5,413	5,114
38,500	38,550	5,425	4,856	5,425	5,121
38,550	38,600	5,438	4,864	5,438	5,129
38,600	38,650	5,450	4,871	5,450	5,136
38,650	38,700	5,463	4,879	5,463	5,144
38,700	38,750	5,475	4,886	5,475	5,151
38,750	38,800	5,488	4,894	5,488	5,159
38,800	38,850	5,500	4,901	5,500	5,166
38,850	38,900	5,513	4,909	5,513	5,174
38,900	38,950	5,525	4,916	5,525	5,181
38,950	39,000	5,538	4,924	5,538	5,189

* This column must also be used by a qualifying widow(er).

(Continued)

2015 Tax Table—*Continued*

If line 43 (taxable income) is—		And you are—			
At least	But less than	Single	Married filing jointly *	Married filing separately	Head of a household
		Your tax is—			

39,000

At least	But less than	Single	MFJ *	MFS	HoH
39,000	39,050	5,550	4,931	5,550	5,196
39,050	39,100	5,563	4,939	5,563	5,204
39,100	39,150	5,575	4,946	5,575	5,211
39,150	39,200	5,588	4,954	5,588	5,219
39,200	39,250	5,600	4,961	5,600	5,226
39,250	39,300	5,613	4,969	5,613	5,234
39,300	39,350	5,625	4,976	5,625	5,241
39,350	39,400	5,638	4,984	5,638	5,249
39,400	39,450	5,650	4,991	5,650	5,256
39,450	39,500	5,663	4,999	5,663	5,264
39,500	39,550	5,675	5,006	5,675	5,271
39,550	39,600	5,688	5,014	5,688	5,279
39,600	39,650	5,700	5,021	5,700	5,286
39,650	39,700	5,713	5,029	5,713	5,294
39,700	39,750	5,725	5,036	5,725	5,301
39,750	39,800	5,738	5,044	5,738	5,309
39,800	39,850	5,750	5,051	5,750	5,316
39,850	39,900	5,763	5,059	5,763	5,324
39,900	39,950	5,775	5,066	5,775	5,331
39,950	40,000	5,788	5,074	5,788	5,339

40,000

At least	But less than	Single	MFJ *	MFS	HoH
40,000	40,050	5,800	5,081	5,800	5,346
40,050	40,100	5,813	5,089	5,813	5,354
40,100	40,150	5,825	5,096	5,825	5,361
40,150	40,200	5,838	5,104	5,838	5,369
40,200	40,250	5,850	5,111	5,850	5,376
40,250	40,300	5,863	5,119	5,863	5,384
40,300	40,350	5,875	5,126	5,875	5,391
40,350	40,400	5,888	5,134	5,888	5,399
40,400	40,450	5,900	5,141	5,900	5,406
40,450	40,500	5,913	5,149	5,913	5,414
40,500	40,550	5,925	5,156	5,925	5,421
40,550	40,600	5,938	5,164	5,938	5,429
40,600	40,650	5,950	5,171	5,950	5,436
40,650	40,700	5,963	5,179	5,963	5,444
40,700	40,750	5,975	5,186	5,975	5,451
40,750	40,800	5,988	5,194	5,988	5,459
40,800	40,850	6,000	5,201	6,000	5,466
40,850	40,900	6,013	5,209	6,013	5,474
40,900	40,950	6,025	5,216	6,025	5,481
40,950	41,000	6,038	5,224	6,038	5,489

41,000

At least	But less than	Single	MFJ *	MFS	HoH
41,000	41,050	6,050	5,231	6,050	5,496
41,050	41,100	6,063	5,239	6,063	5,504
41,100	41,150	6,075	5,246	6,075	5,511
41,150	41,200	6,088	5,254	6,088	5,519
41,200	41,250	6,100	5,261	6,100	5,526
41,250	41,300	6,113	5,269	6,113	5,534
41,300	41,350	6,125	5,276	6,125	5,541
41,350	41,400	6,138	5,284	6,138	5,549
41,400	41,450	6,150	5,291	6,150	5,556
41,450	41,500	6,163	5,299	6,163	5,564
41,500	41,550	6,175	5,306	6,175	5,571
41,550	41,600	6,188	5,314	6,188	5,579
41,600	41,650	6,200	5,321	6,200	5,586
41,650	41,700	6,213	5,329	6,213	5,594
41,700	41,750	6,225	5,336	6,225	5,601
41,750	41,800	6,238	5,344	6,238	5,609
41,800	41,850	6,250	5,351	6,250	5,616
41,850	41,900	6,263	5,359	6,263	5,624
41,900	41,950	6,275	5,366	6,275	5,631
41,950	42,000	6,288	5,374	6,288	5,639

42,000

At least	But less than	Single	MFJ *	MFS	HoH
42,000	42,050	6,300	5,381	6,300	5,646
42,050	42,100	6,313	5,389	6,313	5,654
42,100	42,150	6,325	5,396	6,325	5,661
42,150	42,200	6,338	5,404	6,338	5,669
42,200	42,250	6,350	5,411	6,350	5,676
42,250	42,300	6,363	5,419	6,363	5,684
42,300	42,350	6,375	5,426	6,375	5,691
42,350	42,400	6,388	5,434	6,388	5,699
42,400	42,450	6,400	5,441	6,400	5,706
42,450	42,500	6,413	5,449	6,413	5,714
42,500	42,550	6,425	5,456	6,425	5,721
42,550	42,600	6,438	5,464	6,438	5,729
42,600	42,650	6,450	5,471	6,450	5,736
42,650	42,700	6,463	5,479	6,463	5,744
42,700	42,750	6,475	5,486	6,475	5,751
42,750	42,800	6,488	5,494	6,488	5,759
42,800	42,850	6,500	5,501	6,500	5,766
42,850	42,900	6,513	5,509	6,513	5,774
42,900	42,950	6,525	5,516	6,525	5,781
42,950	43,000	6,538	5,524	6,538	5,789

43,000

At least	But less than	Single	MFJ *	MFS	HoH
43,000	43,050	6,550	5,531	6,550	5,796
43,050	43,100	6,563	5,539	6,563	5,804
43,100	43,150	6,575	5,546	6,575	5,811
43,150	43,200	6,588	5,554	6,588	5,819
43,200	43,250	6,600	5,561	6,600	5,826
43,250	43,300	6,613	5,569	6,613	5,834
43,300	43,350	6,625	5,576	6,625	5,841
43,350	43,400	6,638	5,584	6,638	5,849
43,400	43,450	6,650	5,591	6,650	5,856
43,450	43,500	6,663	5,599	6,663	5,864
43,500	43,550	6,675	5,606	6,675	5,871
43,550	43,600	6,688	5,614	6,688	5,879
43,600	43,650	6,700	5,621	6,700	5,886
43,650	43,700	6,713	5,629	6,713	5,894
43,700	43,750	6,725	5,636	6,725	5,901
43,750	43,800	6,738	5,644	6,738	5,909
43,800	43,850	6,750	5,651	6,750	5,916
43,850	43,900	6,763	5,659	6,763	5,924
43,900	43,950	6,775	5,666	6,775	5,931
43,950	44,000	6,788	5,674	6,788	5,939

44,000

At least	But less than	Single	MFJ *	MFS	HoH
44,000	44,050	6,800	5,681	6,800	5,946
44,050	44,100	6,813	5,689	6,813	5,954
44,100	44,150	6,825	5,696	6,825	5,961
44,150	44,200	6,838	5,704	6,838	5,969
44,200	44,250	6,850	5,711	6,850	5,976
44,250	44,300	6,863	5,719	6,863	5,984
44,300	44,350	6,875	5,726	6,875	5,991
44,350	44,400	6,888	5,734	6,888	5,999
44,400	44,450	6,900	5,741	6,900	6,006
44,450	44,500	6,913	5,749	6,913	6,014
44,500	44,550	6,925	5,756	6,925	6,021
44,550	44,600	6,938	5,764	6,938	6,029
44,600	44,650	6,950	5,771	6,950	6,036
44,650	44,700	6,963	5,779	6,963	6,044
44,700	44,750	6,975	5,786	6,975	6,051
44,750	44,800	6,988	5,794	6,988	6,059
44,800	44,850	7,000	5,801	7,000	6,066
44,850	44,900	7,013	5,809	7,013	6,074
44,900	44,950	7,025	5,816	7,025	6,081
44,950	45,000	7,038	5,824	7,038	6,089

45,000

At least	But less than	Single	MFJ *	MFS	HoH
45,000	45,050	7,050	5,831	7,050	6,096
45,050	45,100	7,063	5,839	7,063	6,104
45,100	45,150	7,075	5,846	7,075	6,111
45,150	45,200	7,088	5,854	7,088	6,119
45,200	45,250	7,100	5,861	7,100	6,126
45,250	45,300	7,113	5,869	7,113	6,134
45,300	45,350	7,125	5,876	7,125	6,141
45,350	45,400	7,138	5,884	7,138	6,149
45,400	45,450	7,150	5,891	7,150	6,156
45,450	45,500	7,163	5,899	7,163	6,164
45,500	45,550	7,175	5,906	7,175	6,171
45,550	45,600	7,188	5,914	7,188	6,179
45,600	45,650	7,200	5,921	7,200	6,186
45,650	45,700	7,213	5,929	7,213	6,194
45,700	45,750	7,225	5,936	7,225	6,201
45,750	45,800	7,238	5,944	7,238	6,209
45,800	45,850	7,250	5,951	7,250	6,216
45,850	45,900	7,263	5,959	7,263	6,224
45,900	45,950	7,275	5,966	7,275	6,231
45,950	46,000	7,288	5,974	7,288	6,239

46,000

At least	But less than	Single	MFJ *	MFS	HoH
46,000	46,050	7,300	5,981	7,300	6,246
46,050	46,100	7,313	5,989	7,313	6,254
46,100	46,150	7,325	5,996	7,325	6,261
46,150	46,200	7,338	6,004	7,338	6,269
46,200	46,250	7,350	6,011	7,350	6,276
46,250	46,300	7,363	6,019	7,363	6,284
46,300	46,350	7,375	6,026	7,375	6,291
46,350	46,400	7,388	6,034	7,388	6,299
46,400	46,450	7,400	6,041	7,400	6,306
46,450	46,500	7,413	6,049	7,413	6,314
46,500	46,550	7,425	6,056	7,425	6,321
46,550	46,600	7,438	6,064	7,438	6,329
46,600	46,650	7,450	6,071	7,450	6,336
46,650	46,700	7,463	6,079	7,463	6,344
46,700	46,750	7,475	6,086	7,475	6,351
46,750	46,800	7,488	6,094	7,488	6,359
46,800	46,850	7,500	6,101	7,500	6,366
46,850	46,900	7,513	6,109	7,513	6,374
46,900	46,950	7,525	6,116	7,525	6,381
46,950	47,000	7,538	6,124	7,538	6,389

47,000

At least	But less than	Single	MFJ *	MFS	HoH
47,000	47,050	7,550	6,131	7,550	6,396
47,050	47,100	7,563	6,139	7,563	6,404
47,100	47,150	7,575	6,146	7,575	6,411
47,150	47,200	7,588	6,154	7,588	6,419
47,200	47,250	7,600	6,161	7,600	6,426
47,250	47,300	7,613	6,169	7,613	6,434
47,300	47,350	7,625	6,176	7,625	6,441
47,350	47,400	7,638	6,184	7,638	6,449
47,400	47,450	7,650	6,191	7,650	6,456
47,450	47,500	7,663	6,199	7,663	6,464
47,500	47,550	7,675	6,206	7,675	6,471
47,550	47,600	7,688	6,214	7,688	6,479
47,600	47,650	7,700	6,221	7,700	6,486
47,650	47,700	7,713	6,229	7,713	6,494
47,700	47,750	7,725	6,236	7,725	6,501
47,750	47,800	7,738	6,244	7,738	6,509
47,800	47,850	7,750	6,251	7,750	6,516
47,850	47,900	7,763	6,259	7,763	6,524
47,900	47,950	7,775	6,266	7,775	6,531
47,950	48,000	7,788	6,274	7,788	6,539

* This column must also be used by a qualifying widow(er).

(Continued)

2015 Tax Table—*Continued*

If line 43 (taxable income) is— At least	But less than	Single	Married filing jointly *	Married filing separately	Head of a house-hold	If line 43 (taxable income) is— At least	But less than	Single	Married filing jointly *	Married filing separately	Head of a house-hold	If line 43 (taxable income) is— At least	But less than	Single	Married filing jointly *	Married filing separately	Head of a house-hold
					Your tax is—						Your tax is—						Your tax is—

48,000 / 51,000 / 54,000

At least	But less than	Single	MFJ *	MFS	HoH	At least	But less than	Single	MFJ *	MFS	HoH	At least	But less than	Single	MFJ *	MFS	HoH
48,000	48,050	7,800	6,281	7,800	6,546	51,000	51,050	8,550	6,731	8,550	7,079	54,000	54,050	9,300	7,181	9,300	7,829
48,050	48,100	7,813	6,289	7,813	6,554	51,050	51,100	8,563	6,739	8,563	7,091	54,050	54,100	9,313	7,189	9,313	7,841
48,100	48,150	7,825	6,296	7,825	6,561	51,100	51,150	8,575	6,746	8,575	7,104	54,100	54,150	9,325	7,196	9,325	7,854
48,150	48,200	7,838	6,304	7,838	6,569	51,150	51,200	8,588	6,754	8,588	7,116	54,150	54,200	9,338	7,204	9,338	7,866
48,200	48,250	7,850	6,311	7,850	6,576	51,200	51,250	8,600	6,761	8,600	7,129	54,200	54,250	9,350	7,211	9,350	7,879
48,250	48,300	7,863	6,319	7,863	6,584	51,250	51,300	8,613	6,769	8,613	7,141	54,250	54,300	9,363	7,219	9,363	7,891
48,300	48,350	7,875	6,326	7,875	6,591	51,300	51,350	8,625	6,776	8,625	7,154	54,300	54,350	9,375	7,226	9,375	7,904
48,350	48,400	7,888	6,334	7,888	6,599	51,350	51,400	8,638	6,784	8,638	7,166	54,350	54,400	9,388	7,234	9,388	7,916
48,400	48,450	7,900	6,341	7,900	6,606	51,400	51,450	8,650	6,791	8,650	7,179	54,400	54,450	9,400	7,241	9,400	7,929
48,450	48,500	7,913	6,349	7,913	6,614	51,450	51,500	8,663	6,799	8,663	7,191	54,450	54,500	9,413	7,249	9,413	7,941
48,500	48,550	7,925	6,356	7,925	6,621	51,500	51,550	8,675	6,806	8,675	7,204	54,500	54,550	9,425	7,256	9,425	7,954
48,550	48,600	7,938	6,364	7,938	6,629	51,550	51,600	8,688	6,814	8,688	7,216	54,550	54,600	9,438	7,264	9,438	7,966
48,600	48,650	7,950	6,371	7,950	6,636	51,600	51,650	8,700	6,821	8,700	7,229	54,600	54,650	9,450	7,271	9,450	7,979
48,650	48,700	7,963	6,379	7,963	6,644	51,650	51,700	8,713	6,829	8,713	7,241	54,650	54,700	9,463	7,279	9,463	7,991
48,700	48,750	7,975	6,386	7,975	6,651	51,700	51,750	8,725	6,836	8,725	7,254	54,700	54,750	9,475	7,286	9,475	8,004
48,750	48,800	7,988	6,394	7,988	6,659	51,750	51,800	8,738	6,844	8,738	7,266	54,750	54,800	9,488	7,294	9,488	8,016
48,800	48,850	8,000	6,401	8,000	6,666	51,800	51,850	8,750	6,851	8,750	7,279	54,800	54,850	9,500	7,301	9,500	8,029
48,850	48,900	8,013	6,409	8,013	6,674	51,850	51,900	8,763	6,859	8,763	7,291	54,850	54,900	9,513	7,309	9,513	8,041
48,900	48,950	8,025	6,416	8,025	6,681	51,900	51,950	8,775	6,866	8,775	7,304	54,900	54,950	9,525	7,316	9,525	8,054
48,950	49,000	8,038	6,424	8,038	6,689	51,950	52,000	8,788	6,874	8,788	7,316	54,950	55,000	9,538	7,324	9,538	8,066

49,000 / 52,000 / 55,000

At least	But less than	Single	MFJ *	MFS	HoH	At least	But less than	Single	MFJ *	MFS	HoH	At least	But less than	Single	MFJ *	MFS	HoH
49,000	49,050	8,050	6,431	8,050	6,696	52,000	52,050	8,800	6,881	8,800	7,329	55,000	55,050	9,550	7,331	9,550	8,079
49,050	49,100	8,063	6,439	8,063	6,704	52,050	52,100	8,813	6,889	8,813	7,341	55,050	55,100	9,563	7,339	9,563	8,091
49,100	49,150	8,075	6,446	8,075	6,711	52,100	52,150	8,825	6,896	8,825	7,354	55,100	55,150	9,575	7,346	9,575	8,104
49,150	49,200	8,088	6,454	8,088	6,719	52,150	52,200	8,838	6,904	8,838	7,366	55,150	55,200	9,588	7,354	9,588	8,116
49,200	49,250	8,100	6,461	8,100	6,726	52,200	52,250	8,850	6,911	8,850	7,379	55,200	55,250	9,600	7,361	9,600	8,129
49,250	49,300	8,113	6,469	8,113	6,734	52,250	52,300	8,863	6,919	8,863	7,391	55,250	55,300	9,613	7,369	9,613	8,141
49,300	49,350	8,125	6,476	8,125	6,741	52,300	52,350	8,875	6,926	8,875	7,404	55,300	55,350	9,625	7,376	9,625	8,154
49,350	49,400	8,138	6,484	8,138	6,749	52,350	52,400	8,888	6,934	8,888	7,416	55,350	55,400	9,638	7,384	9,638	8,166
49,400	49,450	8,150	6,491	8,150	6,756	52,400	52,450	8,900	6,941	8,900	7,429	55,400	55,450	9,650	7,391	9,650	8,179
49,450	49,500	8,163	6,499	8,163	6,764	52,450	52,500	8,913	6,949	8,913	7,441	55,450	55,500	9,663	7,399	9,663	8,191
49,500	49,550	8,175	6,506	8,175	6,771	52,500	52,550	8,925	6,956	8,925	7,454	55,500	55,550	9,675	7,406	9,675	8,204
49,550	49,600	8,188	6,514	8,188	6,779	52,550	52,600	8,938	6,964	8,938	7,466	55,550	55,600	9,688	7,414	9,688	8,216
49,600	49,650	8,200	6,521	8,200	6,786	52,600	52,650	8,950	6,971	8,950	7,479	55,600	55,650	9,700	7,421	9,700	8,229
49,650	49,700	8,213	6,529	8,213	6,794	52,650	52,700	8,963	6,979	8,963	7,491	55,650	55,700	9,713	7,429	9,713	8,241
49,700	49,750	8,225	6,536	8,225	6,801	52,700	52,750	8,975	6,986	8,975	7,504	55,700	55,750	9,725	7,436	9,725	8,254
49,750	49,800	8,238	6,544	8,238	6,809	52,750	52,800	8,988	6,994	8,988	7,516	55,750	55,800	9,738	7,444	9,738	8,266
49,800	49,850	8,250	6,551	8,250	6,816	52,800	52,850	9,000	7,001	9,000	7,529	55,800	55,850	9,750	7,451	9,750	8,279
49,850	49,900	8,263	6,559	8,263	6,824	52,850	52,900	9,013	7,009	9,013	7,541	55,850	55,900	9,763	7,459	9,763	8,291
49,900	49,950	8,275	6,566	8,275	6,831	52,900	52,950	9,025	7,016	9,025	7,554	55,900	55,950	9,775	7,466	9,775	8,304
49,950	50,000	8,288	6,574	8,288	6,839	52,950	53,000	9,038	7,024	9,038	7,566	55,950	56,000	9,788	7,474	9,788	8,316

50,000 / 53,000 / 56,000

At least	But less than	Single	MFJ *	MFS	HoH	At least	But less than	Single	MFJ *	MFS	HoH	At least	But less than	Single	MFJ *	MFS	HoH
50,000	50,050	8,300	6,581	8,300	6,846	53,000	53,050	9,050	7,031	9,050	7,579	56,000	56,050	9,800	7,481	9,800	8,329
50,050	50,100	8,313	6,589	8,313	6,854	53,050	53,100	9,063	7,039	9,063	7,591	56,050	56,100	9,813	7,489	9,813	8,341
50,100	50,150	8,325	6,596	8,325	6,861	53,100	53,150	9,075	7,046	9,075	7,604	56,100	56,150	9,825	7,496	9,825	8,354
50,150	50,200	8,338	6,604	8,338	6,869	53,150	53,200	9,088	7,054	9,088	7,616	56,150	56,200	9,838	7,504	9,838	8,366
50,200	50,250	8,350	6,611	8,350	6,879	53,200	53,250	9,100	7,061	9,100	7,629	56,200	56,250	9,850	7,511	9,850	8,379
50,250	50,300	8,363	6,619	8,363	6,891	53,250	53,300	9,113	7,069	9,113	7,641	56,250	56,300	9,863	7,519	9,863	8,391
50,300	50,350	8,375	6,626	8,375	6,904	53,300	53,350	9,125	7,076	9,125	7,654	56,300	56,350	9,875	7,526	9,875	8,404
50,350	50,400	8,388	6,634	8,388	6,916	53,350	53,400	9,138	7,084	9,138	7,666	56,350	56,400	9,888	7,534	9,888	8,416
50,400	50,450	8,400	6,641	8,400	6,929	53,400	53,450	9,150	7,091	9,150	7,679	56,400	56,450	9,900	7,541	9,900	8,429
50,450	50,500	8,413	6,649	8,413	6,941	53,450	53,500	9,163	7,099	9,163	7,691	56,450	56,500	9,913	7,549	9,913	8,441
50,500	50,550	8,425	6,656	8,425	6,954	53,500	53,550	9,175	7,106	9,175	7,704	56,500	56,550	9,925	7,556	9,925	8,454
50,550	50,600	8,438	6,664	8,438	6,966	53,550	53,600	9,188	7,114	9,188	7,716	56,550	56,600	9,938	7,564	9,938	8,466
50,600	50,650	8,450	6,671	8,450	6,979	53,600	53,650	9,200	7,121	9,200	7,729	56,600	56,650	9,950	7,571	9,950	8,479
50,650	50,700	8,463	6,679	8,463	6,991	53,650	53,700	9,213	7,129	9,213	7,741	56,650	56,700	9,963	7,579	9,963	8,491
50,700	50,750	8,475	6,686	8,475	7,004	53,700	53,750	9,225	7,136	9,225	7,754	56,700	56,750	9,975	7,586	9,975	8,504
50,750	50,800	8,488	6,694	8,488	7,016	53,750	53,800	9,238	7,144	9,238	7,766	56,750	56,800	9,988	7,594	9,988	8,516
50,800	50,850	8,500	6,701	8,500	7,029	53,800	53,850	9,250	7,151	9,250	7,779	56,800	56,850	10,000	7,601	10,000	8,529
50,850	50,900	8,513	6,709	8,513	7,041	53,850	53,900	9,263	7,159	9,263	7,791	56,850	56,900	10,013	7,609	10,013	8,541
50,900	50,950	8,525	6,716	8,525	7,054	53,900	53,950	9,275	7,166	9,275	7,804	56,900	56,950	10,025	7,616	10,025	8,554
50,950	51,000	8,538	6,724	8,538	7,066	53,950	54,000	9,288	7,174	9,288	7,816	56,950	57,000	10,038	7,624	10,038	8,566

* This column must also be used by a qualifying widow(er).

(Continued)

2015 Tax Table—*Continued*

57,000

At least	But less than	Single	Married filing jointly *	Married filing separately	Head of a household
57,000	57,050	10,050	7,631	10,050	8,579
57,050	57,100	10,063	7,639	10,063	8,591
57,100	57,150	10,075	7,646	10,075	8,604
57,150	57,200	10,088	7,654	10,088	8,616
57,200	57,250	10,100	7,661	10,100	8,629
57,250	57,300	10,113	7,669	10,113	8,641
57,300	57,350	10,125	7,676	10,125	8,654
57,350	57,400	10,138	7,684	10,138	8,666
57,400	57,450	10,150	7,691	10,150	8,679
57,450	57,500	10,163	7,699	10,163	8,691
57,500	57,550	10,175	7,706	10,175	8,704
57,550	57,600	10,188	7,714	10,188	8,716
57,600	57,650	10,200	7,721	10,200	8,729
57,650	57,700	10,213	7,729	10,213	8,741
57,700	57,750	10,225	7,736	10,225	8,754
57,750	57,800	10,238	7,744	10,238	8,766
57,800	57,850	10,250	7,751	10,250	8,779
57,850	57,900	10,263	7,759	10,263	8,791
57,900	57,950	10,275	7,766	10,275	8,804
57,950	58,000	10,288	7,774	10,288	8,816

58,000

At least	But less than	Single	Married filing jointly *	Married filing separately	Head of a household
58,000	58,050	10,300	7,781	10,300	8,829
58,050	58,100	10,313	7,789	10,313	8,841
58,100	58,150	10,325	7,796	10,325	8,854
58,150	58,200	10,338	7,804	10,338	8,866
58,200	58,250	10,350	7,811	10,350	8,879
58,250	58,300	10,363	7,819	10,363	8,891
58,300	58,350	10,375	7,826	10,375	8,904
58,350	58,400	10,388	7,834	10,388	8,916
58,400	58,450	10,400	7,841	10,400	8,929
58,450	58,500	10,413	7,849	10,413	8,941
58,500	58,550	10,425	7,856	10,425	8,954
58,550	58,600	10,438	7,864	10,438	8,966
58,600	58,650	10,450	7,871	10,450	8,979
58,650	58,700	10,463	7,879	10,463	8,991
58,700	58,750	10,475	7,886	10,475	9,004
58,750	58,800	10,488	7,894	10,488	9,016
58,800	58,850	10,500	7,901	10,500	9,029
58,850	58,900	10,513	7,909	10,513	9,041
58,900	58,950	10,525	7,916	10,525	9,054
58,950	59,000	10,538	7,924	10,538	9,066

59,000

At least	But less than	Single	Married filing jointly *	Married filing separately	Head of a household
59,000	59,050	10,550	7,931	10,550	9,079
59,050	59,100	10,563	7,939	10,563	9,091
59,100	59,150	10,575	7,946	10,575	9,104
59,150	59,200	10,588	7,954	10,588	9,116
59,200	59,250	10,600	7,961	10,600	9,129
59,250	59,300	10,613	7,969	10,613	9,141
59,300	59,350	10,625	7,976	10,625	9,154
59,350	59,400	10,638	7,984	10,638	9,166
59,400	59,450	10,650	7,991	10,650	9,179
59,450	59,500	10,663	7,999	10,663	9,191
59,500	59,550	10,675	8,006	10,675	9,204
59,550	59,600	10,688	8,014	10,688	9,216
59,600	59,650	10,700	8,021	10,700	9,229
59,650	59,700	10,713	8,029	10,713	9,241
59,700	59,750	10,725	8,036	10,725	9,254
59,750	59,800	10,738	8,044	10,738	9,266
59,800	59,850	10,750	8,051	10,750	9,279
59,850	59,900	10,763	8,059	10,763	9,291
59,900	59,950	10,775	8,066	10,775	9,304
59,950	60,000	10,788	8,074	10,788	9,316

60,000

At least	But less than	Single	Married filing jointly *	Married filing separately	Head of a household
60,000	60,050	10,800	8,081	10,800	9,329
60,050	60,100	10,813	8,089	10,813	9,341
60,100	60,150	10,825	8,096	10,825	9,354
60,150	60,200	10,838	8,104	10,838	9,366
60,200	60,250	10,850	8,111	10,850	9,379
60,250	60,300	10,863	8,119	10,863	9,391
60,300	60,350	10,875	8,126	10,875	9,404
60,350	60,400	10,888	8,134	10,888	9,416
60,400	60,450	10,900	8,141	10,900	9,429
60,450	60,500	10,913	8,149	10,913	9,441
60,500	60,550	10,925	8,156	10,925	9,454
60,550	60,600	10,938	8,164	10,938	9,466
60,600	60,650	10,950	8,171	10,950	9,479
60,650	60,700	10,963	8,179	10,963	9,491
60,700	60,750	10,975	8,186	10,975	9,504
60,750	60,800	10,988	8,194	10,988	9,516
60,800	60,850	11,000	8,201	11,000	9,529
60,850	60,900	11,013	8,209	11,013	9,541
60,900	60,950	11,025	8,216	11,025	9,554
60,950	61,000	11,038	8,224	11,038	9,566

61,000

At least	But less than	Single	Married filing jointly *	Married filing separately	Head of a household
61,000	61,050	11,050	8,231	11,050	9,579
61,050	61,100	11,063	8,239	11,063	9,591
61,100	61,150	11,075	8,246	11,075	9,604
61,150	61,200	11,088	8,254	11,088	9,616
61,200	61,250	11,100	8,261	11,100	9,629
61,250	61,300	11,113	8,269	11,113	9,641
61,300	61,350	11,125	8,276	11,125	9,654
61,350	61,400	11,138	8,284	11,138	9,666
61,400	61,450	11,150	8,291	11,150	9,679
61,450	61,500	11,163	8,299	11,163	9,691
61,500	61,550	11,175	8,306	11,175	9,704
61,550	61,600	11,188	8,314	11,188	9,716
61,600	61,650	11,200	8,321	11,200	9,729
61,650	61,700	11,213	8,329	11,213	9,741
61,700	61,750	11,225	8,336	11,225	9,754
61,750	61,800	11,238	8,344	11,238	9,766
61,800	61,850	11,250	8,351	11,250	9,779
61,850	61,900	11,263	8,359	11,263	9,791
61,900	61,950	11,275	8,366	11,275	9,804
61,950	62,000	11,288	8,374	11,288	9,816

62,000

At least	But less than	Single	Married filing jointly *	Married filing separately	Head of a household
62,000	62,050	11,300	8,381	11,300	9,829
62,050	62,100	11,313	8,389	11,313	9,841
62,100	62,150	11,325	8,396	11,325	9,854
62,150	62,200	11,338	8,404	11,338	9,866
62,200	62,250	11,350	8,411	11,350	9,879
62,250	62,300	11,363	8,419	11,363	9,891
62,300	62,350	11,375	8,426	11,375	9,904
62,350	62,400	11,388	8,434	11,388	9,916
62,400	62,450	11,400	8,441	11,400	9,929
62,450	62,500	11,413	8,449	11,413	9,941
62,500	62,550	11,425	8,456	11,425	9,954
62,550	62,600	11,438	8,464	11,438	9,966
62,600	62,650	11,450	8,471	11,450	9,979
62,650	62,700	11,463	8,479	11,463	9,991
62,700	62,750	11,475	8,486	11,475	10,004
62,750	62,800	11,488	8,494	11,488	10,016
62,800	62,850	11,500	8,501	11,500	10,029
62,850	62,900	11,513	8,509	11,513	10,041
62,900	62,950	11,525	8,516	11,525	10,054
62,950	63,000	11,538	8,524	11,538	10,066

63,000

At least	But less than	Single	Married filing jointly *	Married filing separately	Head of a household
63,000	63,050	11,550	8,531	11,550	10,079
63,050	63,100	11,563	8,539	11,563	10,091
63,100	63,150	11,575	8,546	11,575	10,104
63,150	63,200	11,588	8,554	11,588	10,116
63,200	63,250	11,600	8,561	11,600	10,129
63,250	63,300	11,613	8,569	11,613	10,141
63,300	63,350	11,625	8,576	11,625	10,154
63,350	63,400	11,638	8,584	11,638	10,166
63,400	63,450	11,650	8,591	11,650	10,179
63,450	63,500	11,663	8,599	11,663	10,191
63,500	63,550	11,675	8,606	11,675	10,204
63,550	63,600	11,688	8,614	11,688	10,216
63,600	63,650	11,700	8,621	11,700	10,229
63,650	63,700	11,713	8,629	11,713	10,241
63,700	63,750	11,725	8,636	11,725	10,254
63,750	63,800	11,738	8,644	11,738	10,266
63,800	63,850	11,750	8,651	11,750	10,279
63,850	63,900	11,763	8,659	11,763	10,291
63,900	63,950	11,775	8,666	11,775	10,304
63,950	64,000	11,788	8,674	11,788	10,316

64,000

At least	But less than	Single	Married filing jointly *	Married filing separately	Head of a household
64,000	64,050	11,800	8,681	11,800	10,329
64,050	64,100	11,813	8,689	11,813	10,341
64,100	64,150	11,825	8,696	11,825	10,354
64,150	64,200	11,838	8,704	11,838	10,366
64,200	64,250	11,850	8,711	11,850	10,379
64,250	64,300	11,863	8,719	11,863	10,391
64,300	64,350	11,875	8,726	11,875	10,404
64,350	64,400	11,888	8,734	11,888	10,416
64,400	64,450	11,900	8,741	11,900	10,429
64,450	64,500	11,913	8,749	11,913	10,441
64,500	64,550	11,925	8,756	11,925	10,454
64,550	64,600	11,938	8,764	11,938	10,466
64,600	64,650	11,950	8,771	11,950	10,479
64,650	64,700	11,963	8,779	11,963	10,491
64,700	64,750	11,975	8,786	11,975	10,504
64,750	64,800	11,988	8,794	11,988	10,516
64,800	64,850	12,000	8,801	12,000	10,529
64,850	64,900	12,013	8,809	12,013	10,541
64,900	64,950	12,025	8,816	12,025	10,554
64,950	65,000	12,038	8,824	12,038	10,566

65,000

At least	But less than	Single	Married filing jointly *	Married filing separately	Head of a household
65,000	65,050	12,050	8,831	12,050	10,579
65,050	65,100	12,063	8,839	12,063	10,591
65,100	65,150	12,075	8,846	12,075	10,604
65,150	65,200	12,088	8,854	12,088	10,616
65,200	65,250	12,100	8,861	12,100	10,629
65,250	65,300	12,113	8,869	12,113	10,641
65,300	65,350	12,125	8,876	12,125	10,654
65,350	65,400	12,138	8,884	12,138	10,666
65,400	65,450	12,150	8,891	12,150	10,679
65,450	65,500	12,163	8,899	12,163	10,691
65,500	65,550	12,175	8,906	12,175	10,704
65,550	65,600	12,188	8,914	12,188	10,716
65,600	65,650	12,200	8,921	12,200	10,729
65,650	65,700	12,213	8,929	12,213	10,741
65,700	65,750	12,225	8,936	12,225	10,754
65,750	65,800	12,238	8,944	12,238	10,766
65,800	65,850	12,250	8,951	12,250	10,779
65,850	65,900	12,263	8,959	12,263	10,791
65,900	65,950	12,275	8,966	12,275	10,804
65,950	66,000	12,288	8,974	12,288	10,816

* This column must also be used by a qualifying widow(er).

(Continued)

2015 Tax Table—*Continued*

66,000

If line 43 (taxable income) is— At least	But less than	Single	Married filing jointly *	Married filing separately	Head of a household
		Your tax is—			
66,000	66,050	12,300	8,981	12,300	10,829
66,050	66,100	12,313	8,989	12,313	10,841
66,100	66,150	12,325	8,996	12,325	10,854
66,150	66,200	12,338	9,004	12,338	10,866
66,200	66,250	12,350	9,011	12,350	10,879
66,250	66,300	12,363	9,019	12,363	10,891
66,300	66,350	12,375	9,026	12,375	10,904
66,350	66,400	12,388	9,034	12,388	10,916
66,400	66,450	12,400	9,041	12,400	10,929
66,450	66,500	12,413	9,049	12,413	10,941
66,500	66,550	12,425	9,056	12,425	10,954
66,550	66,600	12,438	9,064	12,438	10,966
66,600	66,650	12,450	9,071	12,450	10,979
66,650	66,700	12,463	9,079	12,463	10,991
66,700	66,750	12,475	9,086	12,475	11,004
66,750	66,800	12,488	9,094	12,488	11,016
66,800	66,850	12,500	9,101	12,500	11,029
66,850	66,900	12,513	9,109	12,513	11,041
66,900	66,950	12,525	9,116	12,525	11,054
66,950	67,000	12,538	9,124	12,538	11,066

67,000

At least	But less than	Single	Married filing jointly *	Married filing separately	Head of a household
67,000	67,050	12,550	9,131	12,550	11,079
67,050	67,100	12,563	9,139	12,563	11,091
67,100	67,150	12,575	9,146	12,575	11,104
67,150	67,200	12,588	9,154	12,588	11,116
67,200	67,250	12,600	9,161	12,600	11,129
67,250	67,300	12,613	9,169	12,613	11,141
67,300	67,350	12,625	9,176	12,625	11,154
67,350	67,400	12,638	9,184	12,638	11,166
67,400	67,450	12,650	9,191	12,650	11,179
67,450	67,500	12,663	9,199	12,663	11,191
67,500	67,550	12,675	9,206	12,675	11,204
67,550	67,600	12,688	9,214	12,688	11,216
67,600	67,650	12,700	9,221	12,700	11,229
67,650	67,700	12,713	9,229	12,713	11,241
67,700	67,750	12,725	9,236	12,725	11,254
67,750	67,800	12,738	9,244	12,738	11,266
67,800	67,850	12,750	9,251	12,750	11,279
67,850	67,900	12,763	9,259	12,763	11,291
67,900	67,950	12,775	9,266	12,775	11,304
67,950	68,000	12,788	9,274	12,788	11,316

68,000

At least	But less than	Single	Married filing jointly *	Married filing separately	Head of a household
68,000	68,050	12,800	9,281	12,800	11,329
68,050	68,100	12,813	9,289	12,813	11,341
68,100	68,150	12,825	9,296	12,825	11,354
68,150	68,200	12,838	9,304	12,838	11,366
68,200	68,250	12,850	9,311	12,850	11,379
68,250	68,300	12,863	9,319	12,863	11,391
68,300	68,350	12,875	9,326	12,875	11,404
68,350	68,400	12,888	9,334	12,888	11,416
68,400	68,450	12,900	9,341	12,900	11,429
68,450	68,500	12,913	9,349	12,913	11,441
68,500	68,550	12,925	9,356	12,925	11,454
68,550	68,600	12,938	9,364	12,938	11,466
68,600	68,650	12,950	9,371	12,950	11,479
68,650	68,700	12,963	9,379	12,963	11,491
68,700	68,750	12,975	9,386	12,975	11,504
68,750	68,800	12,988	9,394	12,988	11,516
68,800	68,850	13,000	9,401	13,000	11,529
68,850	68,900	13,013	9,409	13,013	11,541
68,900	68,950	13,025	9,416	13,025	11,554
68,950	69,000	13,038	9,424	13,038	11,566

69,000

At least	But less than	Single	Married filing jointly *	Married filing separately	Head of a household
69,000	69,050	13,050	9,431	13,050	11,579
69,050	69,100	13,063	9,439	13,063	11,591
69,100	69,150	13,075	9,446	13,075	11,604
69,150	69,200	13,088	9,454	13,088	11,616
69,200	69,250	13,100	9,461	13,100	11,629
69,250	69,300	13,113	9,469	13,113	11,641
69,300	69,350	13,125	9,476	13,125	11,654
69,350	69,400	13,138	9,484	13,138	11,666
69,400	69,450	13,150	9,491	13,150	11,679
69,450	69,500	13,163	9,499	13,163	11,691
69,500	69,550	13,175	9,506	13,175	11,704
69,550	69,600	13,188	9,514	13,188	11,716
69,600	69,650	13,200	9,521	13,200	11,729
69,650	69,700	13,213	9,529	13,213	11,741
69,700	69,750	13,225	9,536	13,225	11,754
69,750	69,800	13,238	9,544	13,238	11,766
69,800	69,850	13,250	9,551	13,250	11,779
69,850	69,900	13,263	9,559	13,263	11,791
69,900	69,950	13,275	9,566	13,275	11,804
69,950	70,000	13,288	9,574	13,288	11,816

70,000

At least	But less than	Single	Married filing jointly *	Married filing separately	Head of a household
70,000	70,050	13,300	9,581	13,300	11,829
70,050	70,100	13,313	9,589	13,313	11,841
70,100	70,150	13,325	9,596	13,325	11,854
70,150	70,200	13,338	9,604	13,338	11,866
70,200	70,250	13,350	9,611	13,350	11,879
70,250	70,300	13,363	9,619	13,363	11,891
70,300	70,350	13,375	9,626	13,375	11,904
70,350	70,400	13,388	9,634	13,388	11,916
70,400	70,450	13,400	9,641	13,400	11,929
70,450	70,500	13,413	9,649	13,413	11,941
70,500	70,550	13,425	9,656	13,425	11,954
70,550	70,600	13,438	9,664	13,438	11,966
70,600	70,650	13,450	9,671	13,450	11,979
70,650	70,700	13,463	9,679	13,463	11,991
70,700	70,750	13,475	9,686	13,475	12,004
70,750	70,800	13,488	9,694	13,488	12,016
70,800	70,850	13,500	9,701	13,500	12,029
70,850	70,900	13,513	9,709	13,513	12,041
70,900	70,950	13,525	9,716	13,525	12,054
70,950	71,000	13,538	9,724	13,538	12,066

71,000

At least	But less than	Single	Married filing jointly *	Married filing separately	Head of a household
71,000	71,050	13,550	9,731	13,550	12,079
71,050	71,100	13,563	9,739	13,563	12,091
71,100	71,150	13,575	9,746	13,575	12,104
71,150	71,200	13,588	9,754	13,588	12,116
71,200	71,250	13,600	9,761	13,600	12,129
71,250	71,300	13,613	9,769	13,613	12,141
71,300	71,350	13,625	9,776	13,625	12,154
71,350	71,400	13,638	9,784	13,638	12,166
71,400	71,450	13,650	9,791	13,650	12,179
71,450	71,500	13,663	9,799	13,663	12,191
71,500	71,550	13,675	9,806	13,675	12,204
71,550	71,600	13,688	9,814	13,688	12,216
71,600	71,650	13,700	9,821	13,700	12,229
71,650	71,700	13,713	9,829	13,713	12,241
71,700	71,750	13,725	9,836	13,725	12,254
71,750	71,800	13,738	9,844	13,738	12,266
71,800	71,850	13,750	9,851	13,750	12,279
71,850	71,900	13,763	9,859	13,763	12,291
71,900	71,950	13,775	9,866	13,775	12,304
71,950	72,000	13,788	9,874	13,788	12,316

72,000

At least	But less than	Single	Married filing jointly *	Married filing separately	Head of a household
72,000	72,050	13,800	9,881	13,800	12,329
72,050	72,100	13,813	9,889	13,813	12,341
72,100	72,150	13,825	9,896	13,825	12,354
72,150	72,200	13,838	9,904	13,838	12,366
72,200	72,250	13,850	9,911	13,850	12,379
72,250	72,300	13,863	9,919	13,863	12,391
72,300	72,350	13,875	9,926	13,875	12,404
72,350	72,400	13,888	9,934	13,888	12,416
72,400	72,450	13,900	9,941	13,900	12,429
72,450	72,500	13,913	9,949	13,913	12,441
72,500	72,550	13,925	9,956	13,925	12,454
72,550	72,600	13,938	9,964	13,938	12,466
72,600	72,650	13,950	9,971	13,950	12,479
72,650	72,700	13,963	9,979	13,963	12,491
72,700	72,750	13,975	9,986	13,975	12,504
72,750	72,800	13,988	9,994	13,988	12,516
72,800	72,850	14,000	10,001	14,000	12,529
72,850	72,900	14,013	10,009	14,013	12,541
72,900	72,950	14,025	10,016	14,025	12,554
72,950	73,000	14,038	10,024	14,038	12,566

73,000

At least	But less than	Single	Married filing jointly *	Married filing separately	Head of a household
73,000	73,050	14,050	10,031	14,050	12,579
73,050	73,100	14,063	10,039	14,063	12,591
73,100	73,150	14,075	10,046	14,075	12,604
73,150	73,200	14,088	10,054	14,088	12,616
73,200	73,250	14,100	10,061	14,100	12,629
73,250	73,300	14,113	10,069	14,113	12,641
73,300	73,350	14,125	10,076	14,125	12,654
73,350	73,400	14,138	10,084	14,138	12,666
73,400	73,450	14,150	10,091	14,150	12,679
73,450	73,500	14,163	10,099	14,163	12,691
73,500	73,550	14,175	10,106	14,175	12,704
73,550	73,600	14,188	10,114	14,188	12,716
73,600	73,650	14,200	10,121	14,200	12,729
73,650	73,700	14,213	10,129	14,213	12,741
73,700	73,750	14,225	10,136	14,225	12,754
73,750	73,800	14,238	10,144	14,238	12,766
73,800	73,850	14,250	10,151	14,250	12,779
73,850	73,900	14,263	10,159	14,263	12,791
73,900	73,950	14,275	10,166	14,275	12,804
73,950	74,000	14,288	10,174	14,288	12,816

74,000

At least	But less than	Single	Married filing jointly *	Married filing separately	Head of a household
74,000	74,050	14,300	10,181	14,300	12,829
74,050	74,100	14,313	10,189	14,313	12,841
74,100	74,150	14,325	10,196	14,325	12,854
74,150	74,200	14,338	10,204	14,338	12,866
74,200	74,250	14,350	10,211	14,350	12,879
74,250	74,300	14,363	10,219	14,363	12,891
74,300	74,350	14,375	10,226	14,375	12,904
74,350	74,400	14,388	10,234	14,388	12,916
74,400	74,450	14,400	10,241	14,400	12,929
74,450	74,500	14,413	10,249	14,413	12,941
74,500	74,550	14,425	10,256	14,425	12,954
74,550	74,600	14,438	10,264	14,438	12,966
74,600	74,650	14,450	10,271	14,450	12,979
74,650	74,700	14,463	10,279	14,463	12,991
74,700	74,750	14,475	10,286	14,475	13,004
74,750	74,800	14,488	10,294	14,488	13,016
74,800	74,850	14,500	10,301	14,500	13,029
74,850	74,900	14,513	10,309	14,513	13,041
74,900	74,950	14,525	10,319	14,525	13,054
74,950	75,000	14,538	10,331	14,538	13,066

* This column must also be used by a qualifying widow(er).

(Continued)

2015 Tax Table—*Continued*

75,000

At least	But less than	Single	Married filing jointly *	Married filing separately	Head of a household
				Your tax is—	
75,000	75,050	14,550	10,344	14,550	13,079
75,050	75,100	14,563	10,356	14,563	13,091
75,100	75,150	14,575	10,369	14,575	13,104
75,150	75,200	14,588	10,381	14,588	13,116
75,200	75,250	14,600	10,394	14,600	13,129
75,250	75,300	14,613	10,406	14,613	13,141
75,300	75,350	14,625	10,419	14,625	13,154
75,350	75,400	14,638	10,431	14,638	13,166
75,400	75,450	14,650	10,444	14,650	13,179
75,450	75,500	14,663	10,456	14,663	13,191
75,500	75,550	14,675	10,469	14,675	13,204
75,550	75,600	14,688	10,481	14,688	13,216
75,600	75,650	14,700	10,494	14,701	13,229
75,650	75,700	14,713	10,506	14,715	13,241
75,700	75,750	14,725	10,519	14,729	13,254
75,750	75,800	14,738	10,531	14,743	13,266
75,800	75,850	14,750	10,544	14,757	13,279
75,850	75,900	14,763	10,556	14,771	13,291
75,900	75,950	14,775	10,569	14,785	13,304
75,950	76,000	14,788	10,581	14,799	13,316

76,000

At least	But less than	Single	Married filing jointly *	Married filing separately	Head of a household
76,000	76,050	14,800	10,594	14,813	13,329
76,050	76,100	14,813	10,606	14,827	13,341
76,100	76,150	14,825	10,619	14,841	13,354
76,150	76,200	14,838	10,631	14,855	13,366
76,200	76,250	14,850	10,644	14,869	13,379
76,250	76,300	14,863	10,656	14,883	13,391
76,300	76,350	14,875	10,669	14,897	13,404
76,350	76,400	14,888	10,681	14,911	13,416
76,400	76,450	14,900	10,694	14,925	13,429
76,450	76,500	14,913	10,706	14,939	13,441
76,500	76,550	14,925	10,719	14,953	13,454
76,550	76,600	14,938	10,731	14,967	13,466
76,600	76,650	14,950	10,744	14,981	13,479
76,650	76,700	14,963	10,756	14,995	13,491
76,700	76,750	14,975	10,769	15,009	13,504
76,750	76,800	14,988	10,781	15,023	13,516
76,800	76,850	15,000	10,794	15,037	13,529
76,850	76,900	15,013	10,806	15,051	13,541
76,900	76,950	15,025	10,819	15,065	13,554
76,950	77,000	15,038	10,831	15,079	13,566

77,000

At least	But less than	Single	Married filing jointly *	Married filing separately	Head of a household
77,000	77,050	15,050	10,844	15,093	13,579
77,050	77,100	15,063	10,856	15,107	13,591
77,100	77,150	15,075	10,869	15,121	13,604
77,150	77,200	15,088	10,881	15,135	13,616
77,200	77,250	15,100	10,894	15,149	13,629
77,250	77,300	15,113	10,906	15,163	13,641
77,300	77,350	15,125	10,919	15,177	13,654
77,350	77,400	15,138	10,931	15,191	13,666
77,400	77,450	15,150	10,944	15,205	13,679
77,450	77,500	15,163	10,956	15,219	13,691
77,500	77,550	15,175	10,969	15,233	13,704
77,550	77,600	15,188	10,981	15,247	13,716
77,600	77,650	15,200	10,994	15,261	13,729
77,650	77,700	15,213	11,006	15,275	13,741
77,700	77,750	15,225	11,019	15,289	13,754
77,750	77,800	15,238	11,031	15,303	13,766
77,800	77,850	15,250	11,044	15,317	13,779
77,850	77,900	15,263	11,056	15,331	13,791
77,900	77,950	15,275	11,069	15,345	13,804
77,950	78,000	15,288	11,081	15,359	13,816

78,000

At least	But less than	Single	Married filing jointly *	Married filing separately	Head of a household
				Your tax is—	
78,000	78,050	15,300	11,094	15,373	13,829
78,050	78,100	15,313	11,106	15,387	13,841
78,100	78,150	15,325	11,119	15,401	13,854
78,150	78,200	15,338	11,131	15,415	13,866
78,200	78,250	15,350	11,144	15,429	13,879
78,250	78,300	15,363	11,156	15,443	13,891
78,300	78,350	15,375	11,169	15,457	13,904
78,350	78,400	15,388	11,181	15,471	13,916
78,400	78,450	15,400	11,194	15,485	13,929
78,450	78,500	15,413	11,206	15,499	13,941
78,500	78,550	15,425	11,219	15,513	13,954
78,550	78,600	15,438	11,231	15,527	13,966
78,600	78,650	15,450	11,244	15,541	13,979
78,650	78,700	15,463	11,256	15,555	13,991
78,700	78,750	15,475	11,269	15,569	14,004
78,750	78,800	15,488	11,281	15,583	14,016
78,800	78,850	15,500	11,294	15,597	14,029
78,850	78,900	15,513	11,306	15,611	14,041
78,900	78,950	15,525	11,319	15,625	14,054
78,950	79,000	15,538	11,331	15,639	14,066

79,000

At least	But less than	Single	Married filing jointly *	Married filing separately	Head of a household
79,000	79,050	15,550	11,344	15,653	14,079
79,050	79,100	15,563	11,356	15,667	14,091
79,100	79,150	15,575	11,369	15,681	14,104
79,150	79,200	15,588	11,381	15,695	14,116
79,200	79,250	15,600	11,394	15,709	14,129
79,250	79,300	15,613	11,406	15,723	14,141
79,300	79,350	15,625	11,419	15,737	14,154
79,350	79,400	15,638	11,431	15,751	14,166
79,400	79,450	15,650	11,444	15,765	14,179
79,450	79,500	15,663	11,456	15,779	14,191
79,500	79,550	15,675	11,469	15,793	14,204
79,550	79,600	15,688	11,481	15,807	14,216
79,600	79,650	15,700	11,494	15,821	14,229
79,650	79,700	15,713	11,506	15,835	14,241
79,700	79,750	15,725	11,519	15,849	14,254
79,750	79,800	15,738	11,531	15,863	14,266
79,800	79,850	15,750	11,544	15,877	14,279
79,850	79,900	15,763	11,556	15,891	14,291
79,900	79,950	15,775	11,569	15,905	14,304
79,950	80,000	15,788	11,581	15,919	14,316

80,000

At least	But less than	Single	Married filing jointly *	Married filing separately	Head of a household
80,000	80,050	15,800	11,594	15,933	14,329
80,050	80,100	15,813	11,606	15,947	14,341
80,100	80,150	15,825	11,619	15,961	14,354
80,150	80,200	15,838	11,631	15,975	14,366
80,200	80,250	15,850	11,644	15,989	14,379
80,250	80,300	15,863	11,656	16,003	14,391
80,300	80,350	15,875	11,669	16,017	14,404
80,350	80,400	15,888	11,681	16,031	14,416
80,400	80,450	15,900	11,694	16,045	14,429
80,450	80,500	15,913	11,706	16,059	14,441
80,500	80,550	15,925	11,719	16,073	14,454
80,550	80,600	15,938	11,731	16,087	14,466
80,600	80,650	15,950	11,744	16,101	14,479
80,650	80,700	15,963	11,756	16,115	14,491
80,700	80,750	15,975	11,769	16,129	14,504
80,750	80,800	15,988	11,781	16,143	14,516
80,800	80,850	16,000	11,794	16,157	14,529
80,850	80,900	16,013	11,806	16,171	14,541
80,900	80,950	16,025	11,819	16,185	14,554
80,950	81,000	16,038	11,831	16,199	14,566

81,000

At least	But less than	Single	Married filing jointly *	Married filing separately	Head of a household
				Your tax is—	
81,000	81,050	16,050	11,844	16,213	14,579
81,050	81,100	16,063	11,856	16,227	14,591
81,100	81,150	16,075	11,869	16,241	14,604
81,150	81,200	16,088	11,881	16,255	14,616
81,200	81,250	16,100	11,894	16,269	14,629
81,250	81,300	16,113	11,906	16,283	14,641
81,300	81,350	16,125	11,919	16,297	14,654
81,350	81,400	16,138	11,931	16,311	14,666
81,400	81,450	16,150	11,944	16,325	14,679
81,450	81,500	16,163	11,956	16,339	14,691
81,500	81,550	16,175	11,969	16,353	14,704
81,550	81,600	16,188	11,981	16,367	14,716
81,600	81,650	16,200	11,994	16,381	14,729
81,650	81,700	16,213	12,006	16,395	14,741
81,700	81,750	16,225	12,019	16,409	14,754
81,750	81,800	16,238	12,031	16,423	14,766
81,800	81,850	16,250	12,044	16,437	14,779
81,850	81,900	16,263	12,056	16,451	14,791
81,900	81,950	16,275	12,069	16,465	14,804
81,950	82,000	16,288	12,081	16,479	14,816

82,000

At least	But less than	Single	Married filing jointly *	Married filing separately	Head of a household
82,000	82,050	16,300	12,094	16,493	14,829
82,050	82,100	16,313	12,106	16,507	14,841
82,100	82,150	16,325	12,119	16,521	14,854
82,150	82,200	16,338	12,131	16,535	14,866
82,200	82,250	16,350	12,144	16,549	14,879
82,250	82,300	16,363	12,156	16,563	14,891
82,300	82,350	16,375	12,169	16,577	14,904
82,350	82,400	16,388	12,181	16,591	14,916
82,400	82,450	16,400	12,194	16,605	14,929
82,450	82,500	16,413	12,206	16,619	14,941
82,500	82,550	16,425	12,219	16,633	14,954
82,550	82,600	16,438	12,231	16,647	14,966
82,600	82,650	16,450	12,244	16,661	14,979
82,650	82,700	16,463	12,256	16,675	14,991
82,700	82,750	16,475	12,269	16,689	15,004
82,750	82,800	16,488	12,281	16,703	15,016
82,800	82,850	16,500	12,294	16,717	15,029
82,850	82,900	16,513	12,306	16,731	15,041
82,900	82,950	16,525	12,319	16,745	15,054
82,950	83,000	16,538	12,331	16,759	15,066

83,000

At least	But less than	Single	Married filing jointly *	Married filing separately	Head of a household
83,000	83,050	16,550	12,344	16,773	15,079
83,050	83,100	16,563	12,356	16,787	15,091
83,100	83,150	16,575	12,369	16,801	15,104
83,150	83,200	16,588	12,381	16,815	15,116
83,200	83,250	16,600	12,394	16,829	15,129
83,250	83,300	16,613	12,406	16,843	15,141
83,300	83,350	16,625	12,419	16,857	15,154
83,350	83,400	16,638	12,431	16,871	15,166
83,400	83,450	16,650	12,444	16,885	15,179
83,450	83,500	16,663	12,456	16,899	15,191
83,500	83,550	16,675	12,469	16,913	15,204
83,550	83,600	16,688	12,481	16,927	15,216
83,600	83,650	16,700	12,494	16,941	15,229
83,650	83,700	16,713	12,506	16,955	15,241
83,700	83,750	16,725	12,519	16,969	15,254
83,750	83,800	16,738	12,531	16,983	15,266
83,800	83,850	16,750	12,544	16,997	15,279
83,850	83,900	16,763	12,556	17,011	15,291
83,900	83,950	16,775	12,569	17,025	15,304
83,950	84,000	16,788	12,581	17,039	15,316

* This column must also be used by a qualifying widow(er).

(Continued)

2015 Tax Table—Continued

84,000

If line 43 (taxable income) is— At least	But less than	Single	Married filing jointly *	Married filing separately	Head of a household
84,000	84,050	16,800	12,594	17,053	15,329
84,050	84,100	16,813	12,606	17,067	15,341
84,100	84,150	16,825	12,619	17,081	15,354
84,150	84,200	16,838	12,631	17,095	15,366
84,200	84,250	16,850	12,644	17,109	15,379
84,250	84,300	16,863	12,656	17,123	15,391
84,300	84,350	16,875	12,669	17,137	15,404
84,350	84,400	16,888	12,681	17,151	15,416
84,400	84,450	16,900	12,694	17,165	15,429
84,450	84,500	16,913	12,706	17,179	15,441
84,500	84,550	16,925	12,719	17,193	15,454
84,550	84,600	16,938	12,731	17,207	15,466
84,600	84,650	16,950	12,744	17,221	15,479
84,650	84,700	16,963	12,756	17,235	15,491
84,700	84,750	16,975	12,769	17,249	15,504
84,750	84,800	16,988	12,781	17,263	15,516
84,800	84,850	17,000	12,794	17,277	15,529
84,850	84,900	17,013	12,806	17,291	15,541
84,900	84,950	17,025	12,819	17,305	15,554
84,950	85,000	17,038	12,831	17,319	15,566

85,000

At least	But less than	Single	Married filing jointly *	Married filing separately	Head of a household
85,000	85,050	17,050	12,844	17,333	15,579
85,050	85,100	17,063	12,856	17,347	15,591
85,100	85,150	17,075	12,869	17,361	15,604
85,150	85,200	17,088	12,881	17,375	15,616
85,200	85,250	17,100	12,894	17,389	15,629
85,250	85,300	17,113	12,906	17,403	15,641
85,300	85,350	17,125	12,919	17,417	15,654
85,350	85,400	17,138	12,931	17,431	15,666
85,400	85,450	17,150	12,944	17,445	15,679
85,450	85,500	17,163	12,956	17,459	15,691
85,500	85,550	17,175	12,969	17,473	15,704
85,550	85,600	17,188	12,981	17,487	15,716
85,600	85,650	17,200	12,994	17,501	15,729
85,650	85,700	17,213	13,006	17,515	15,741
85,700	85,750	17,225	13,019	17,529	15,754
85,750	85,800	17,238	13,031	17,543	15,766
85,800	85,850	17,250	13,044	17,557	15,779
85,850	85,900	17,263	13,056	17,571	15,791
85,900	85,950	17,275	13,069	17,585	15,804
85,950	86,000	17,288	13,081	17,599	15,816

86,000

At least	But less than	Single	Married filing jointly *	Married filing separately	Head of a household
86,000	86,050	17,300	13,094	17,613	15,829
86,050	86,100	17,313	13,106	17,627	15,841
86,100	86,150	17,325	13,119	17,641	15,854
86,150	86,200	17,338	13,131	17,655	15,866
86,200	86,250	17,350	13,144	17,669	15,879
86,250	86,300	17,363	13,156	17,683	15,891
86,300	86,350	17,375	13,169	17,697	15,904
86,350	86,400	17,388	13,181	17,711	15,916
86,400	86,450	17,400	13,194	17,725	15,929
86,450	86,500	17,413	13,206	17,739	15,941
86,500	86,550	17,425	13,219	17,753	15,954
86,550	86,600	17,438	13,231	17,767	15,966
86,600	86,650	17,450	13,244	17,781	15,979
86,650	86,700	17,463	13,256	17,795	15,991
86,700	86,750	17,475	13,269	17,809	16,004
86,750	86,800	17,488	13,281	17,823	16,016
86,800	86,850	17,500	13,294	17,837	16,029
86,850	86,900	17,513	13,306	17,851	16,041
86,900	86,950	17,525	13,319	17,865	16,054
86,950	87,000	17,538	13,331	17,879	16,066

87,000

At least	But less than	Single	Married filing jointly *	Married filing separately	Head of a household
87,000	87,050	17,550	13,344	17,893	16,079
87,050	87,100	17,563	13,356	17,907	16,091
87,100	87,150	17,575	13,369	17,921	16,104
87,150	87,200	17,588	13,381	17,935	16,116
87,200	87,250	17,600	13,394	17,949	16,129
87,250	87,300	17,613	13,406	17,963	16,141
87,300	87,350	17,625	13,419	17,977	16,154
87,350	87,400	17,638	13,431	17,991	16,166
87,400	87,450	17,650	13,444	18,005	16,179
87,450	87,500	17,663	13,456	18,019	16,191
87,500	87,550	17,675	13,469	18,033	16,204
87,550	87,600	17,688	13,481	18,047	16,216
87,600	87,650	17,700	13,494	18,061	16,229
87,650	87,700	17,713	13,506	18,075	16,241
87,700	87,750	17,725	13,519	18,089	16,254
87,750	87,800	17,738	13,531	18,103	16,266
87,800	87,850	17,750	13,544	18,117	16,279
87,850	87,900	17,763	13,556	18,131	16,291
87,900	87,950	17,775	13,569	18,145	16,304
87,950	88,000	17,788	13,581	18,159	16,316

88,000

At least	But less than	Single	Married filing jointly *	Married filing separately	Head of a household
88,000	88,050	17,800	13,594	18,173	16,329
88,050	88,100	17,813	13,606	18,187	16,341
88,100	88,150	17,825	13,619	18,201	16,354
88,150	88,200	17,838	13,631	18,215	16,366
88,200	88,250	17,850	13,644	18,229	16,379
88,250	88,300	17,863	13,656	18,243	16,391
88,300	88,350	17,875	13,669	18,257	16,404
88,350	88,400	17,888	13,681	18,271	16,416
88,400	88,450	17,900	13,694	18,285	16,429
88,450	88,500	17,913	13,706	18,299	16,441
88,500	88,550	17,925	13,719	18,313	16,454
88,550	88,600	17,938	13,731	18,327	16,466
88,600	88,650	17,950	13,744	18,341	16,479
88,650	88,700	17,963	13,756	18,355	16,491
88,700	88,750	17,975	13,769	18,369	16,504
88,750	88,800	17,988	13,781	18,383	16,516
88,800	88,850	18,000	13,794	18,397	16,529
88,850	88,900	18,013	13,806	18,411	16,541
88,900	88,950	18,025	13,819	18,425	16,554
88,950	89,000	18,038	13,831	18,439	16,566

89,000

At least	But less than	Single	Married filing jointly *	Married filing separately	Head of a household
89,000	89,050	18,050	13,844	18,453	16,579
89,050	89,100	18,063	13,856	18,467	16,591
89,100	89,150	18,075	13,869	18,481	16,604
89,150	89,200	18,088	13,881	18,495	16,616
89,200	89,250	18,100	13,894	18,509	16,629
89,250	89,300	18,113	13,906	18,523	16,641
89,300	89,350	18,125	13,919	18,537	16,654
89,350	89,400	18,138	13,931	18,551	16,666
89,400	89,450	18,150	13,944	18,565	16,679
89,450	89,500	18,163	13,956	18,579	16,691
89,500	89,550	18,175	13,969	18,593	16,704
89,550	89,600	18,188	13,981	18,607	16,716
89,600	89,650	18,200	13,994	18,621	16,729
89,650	89,700	18,213	14,006	18,635	16,741
89,700	89,750	18,225	14,019	18,649	16,754
89,750	89,800	18,238	14,031	18,663	16,766
89,800	89,850	18,250	14,044	18,677	16,779
89,850	89,900	18,263	14,056	18,691	16,791
89,900	89,950	18,275	14,069	18,705	16,804
89,950	90,000	18,288	14,081	18,719	16,816

90,000

At least	But less than	Single	Married filing jointly *	Married filing separately	Head of a household
90,000	90,050	18,300	14,094	18,733	16,829
90,050	90,100	18,313	14,106	18,747	16,841
90,100	90,150	18,325	14,119	18,761	16,854
90,150	90,200	18,338	14,131	18,775	16,866
90,200	90,250	18,350	14,144	18,789	16,879
90,250	90,300	18,363	14,156	18,803	16,891
90,300	90,350	18,375	14,169	18,817	16,904
90,350	90,400	18,388	14,181	18,831	16,916
90,400	90,450	18,400	14,194	18,845	16,929
90,450	90,500	18,413	14,206	18,859	16,941
90,500	90,550	18,425	14,219	18,873	16,954
90,550	90,600	18,438	14,231	18,887	16,966
90,600	90,650	18,450	14,244	18,901	16,979
90,650	90,700	18,463	14,256	18,915	16,991
90,700	90,750	18,475	14,269	18,929	17,004
90,750	90,800	18,488	14,281	18,943	17,016
90,800	90,850	18,502	14,294	18,957	17,029
90,850	90,900	18,516	14,306	18,971	17,041
90,900	90,950	18,530	14,319	18,985	17,054
90,950	91,000	18,544	14,331	18,999	17,066

91,000

At least	But less than	Single	Married filing jointly *	Married filing separately	Head of a household
91,000	91,050	18,558	14,344	19,013	17,079
91,050	91,100	18,572	14,356	19,027	17,091
91,100	91,150	18,586	14,369	19,041	17,104
91,150	91,200	18,600	14,381	19,055	17,116
91,200	91,250	18,614	14,394	19,069	17,129
91,250	91,300	18,628	14,406	19,083	17,141
91,300	91,350	18,642	14,419	19,097	17,154
91,350	91,400	18,656	14,431	19,111	17,166
91,400	91,450	18,670	14,444	19,125	17,179
91,450	91,500	18,684	14,456	19,139	17,191
91,500	91,550	18,698	14,469	19,153	17,204
91,550	91,600	18,712	14,481	19,167	17,216
91,600	91,650	18,726	14,494	19,181	17,229
91,650	91,700	18,740	14,506	19,195	17,241
91,700	91,750	18,754	14,519	19,209	17,254
91,750	91,800	18,768	14,531	19,223	17,266
91,800	91,850	18,782	14,544	19,237	17,279
91,850	91,900	18,796	14,556	19,251	17,291
91,900	91,950	18,810	14,569	19,265	17,304
91,950	92,000	18,824	14,581	19,279	17,316

92,000

At least	But less than	Single	Married filing jointly *	Married filing separately	Head of a household
92,000	92,050	18,838	14,594	19,293	17,329
92,050	92,100	18,852	14,606	19,307	17,341
92,100	92,150	18,866	14,619	19,321	17,354
92,150	92,200	18,880	14,631	19,335	17,366
92,200	92,250	18,894	14,644	19,349	17,379
92,250	92,300	18,908	14,656	19,363	17,391
92,300	92,350	18,922	14,669	19,377	17,404
92,350	92,400	18,936	14,681	19,391	17,416
92,400	92,450	18,950	14,694	19,405	17,429
92,450	92,500	18,964	14,706	19,419	17,441
92,500	92,550	18,978	14,719	19,433	17,454
92,550	92,600	18,992	14,731	19,447	17,466
92,600	92,650	19,006	14,744	19,461	17,479
92,650	92,700	19,020	14,756	19,475	17,491
92,700	92,750	19,034	14,769	19,489	17,504
92,750	92,800	19,048	14,781	19,503	17,516
92,800	92,850	19,062	14,794	19,517	17,529
92,850	92,900	19,076	14,806	19,531	17,541
92,900	92,950	19,090	14,819	19,545	17,554
92,950	93,000	19,104	14,831	19,559	17,566

* This column must also be used by a qualifying widow(er).

(Continued)

2015 Tax Table—*Continued*

If line 43 (taxable income) is—		And you are—			
At least	But less than	Single	Married filing jointly *	Married filing separately	Head of a household
		Your tax is—			

93,000

At least	But less than	Single	MFJ*	MFS	HoH
93,000	93,050	19,118	14,844	19,573	17,579
93,050	93,100	19,132	14,856	19,587	17,591
93,100	93,150	19,146	14,869	19,601	17,604
93,150	93,200	19,160	14,881	19,615	17,616
93,200	93,250	19,174	14,894	19,629	17,629
93,250	93,300	19,188	14,906	19,643	17,641
93,300	93,350	19,202	14,919	19,657	17,654
93,350	93,400	19,216	14,931	19,671	17,666
93,400	93,450	19,230	14,944	19,685	17,679
93,450	93,500	19,244	14,956	19,699	17,691
93,500	93,550	19,258	14,969	19,713	17,704
93,550	93,600	19,272	14,981	19,727	17,716
93,600	93,650	19,286	14,994	19,741	17,729
93,650	93,700	19,300	15,006	19,755	17,741
93,700	93,750	19,314	15,019	19,769	17,754
93,750	93,800	19,328	15,031	19,783	17,766
93,800	93,850	19,342	15,044	19,797	17,779
93,850	93,900	19,356	15,056	19,811	17,791
93,900	93,950	19,370	15,069	19,825	17,804
93,950	94,000	19,384	15,081	19,839	17,816

94,000

At least	But less than	Single	MFJ*	MFS	HoH
94,000	94,050	19,398	15,094	19,853	17,829
94,050	94,100	19,412	15,106	19,867	17,841
94,100	94,150	19,426	15,119	19,881	17,854
94,150	94,200	19,440	15,131	19,895	17,866
94,200	94,250	19,454	15,144	19,909	17,879
94,250	94,300	19,468	15,156	19,923	17,891
94,300	94,350	19,482	15,169	19,937	17,904
94,350	94,400	19,496	15,181	19,951	17,916
94,400	94,450	19,510	15,194	19,965	17,929
94,450	94,500	19,524	15,206	19,979	17,941
94,500	94,550	19,538	15,219	19,993	17,954
94,550	94,600	19,552	15,231	20,007	17,966
94,600	94,650	19,566	15,244	20,021	17,979
94,650	94,700	19,580	15,256	20,035	17,991
94,700	94,750	19,594	15,269	20,049	18,004
94,750	94,800	19,608	15,281	20,063	18,016
94,800	94,850	19,622	15,294	20,077	18,029
94,850	94,900	19,636	15,306	20,091	18,041
94,900	94,950	19,650	15,319	20,105	18,054
94,950	95,000	19,664	15,331	20,119	18,066

95,000

At least	But less than	Single	MFJ*	MFS	HoH
95,000	95,050	19,678	15,344	20,133	18,079
95,050	95,100	19,692	15,356	20,147	18,091
95,100	95,150	19,706	15,369	20,161	18,104
95,150	95,200	19,720	15,381	20,175	18,116
95,200	95,250	19,734	15,394	20,189	18,129
95,250	95,300	19,748	15,406	20,203	18,141
95,300	95,350	19,762	15,419	20,217	18,154
95,350	95,400	19,776	15,431	20,231	18,166
95,400	95,450	19,790	15,444	20,245	18,179
95,450	95,500	19,804	15,456	20,259	18,191
95,500	95,550	19,818	15,469	20,273	18,204
95,550	95,600	19,832	15,481	20,287	18,216
95,600	95,650	19,846	15,494	20,301	18,229
95,650	95,700	19,860	15,506	20,315	18,241
95,700	95,750	19,874	15,519	20,329	18,254
95,750	95,800	19,888	15,531	20,343	18,266
95,800	95,850	19,902	15,544	20,357	18,279
95,850	95,900	19,916	15,556	20,371	18,291
95,900	95,950	19,930	15,569	20,385	18,304
95,950	96,000	19,944	15,581	20,399	18,316

96,000

At least	But less than	Single	MFJ*	MFS	HoH
96,000	96,050	19,958	15,594	20,413	18,329
96,050	96,100	19,972	15,606	20,427	18,341
96,100	96,150	19,986	15,619	20,441	18,354
96,150	96,200	20,000	15,631	20,455	18,366
96,200	96,250	20,014	15,644	20,469	18,379
96,250	96,300	20,028	15,656	20,483	18,391
96,300	96,350	20,042	15,669	20,497	18,404
96,350	96,400	20,056	15,681	20,511	18,416
96,400	96,450	20,070	15,694	20,525	18,429
96,450	96,500	20,084	15,706	20,539	18,441
96,500	96,550	20,098	15,719	20,553	18,454
96,550	96,600	20,112	15,731	20,567	18,466
96,600	96,650	20,126	15,744	20,581	18,479
96,650	96,700	20,140	15,756	20,595	18,491
96,700	96,750	20,154	15,769	20,609	18,504
96,750	96,800	20,168	15,781	20,623	18,516
96,800	96,850	20,182	15,794	20,637	18,529
96,850	96,900	20,196	15,806	20,651	18,541
96,900	96,950	20,210	15,819	20,665	18,554
96,950	97,000	20,224	15,831	20,679	18,566

97,000

At least	But less than	Single	MFJ*	MFS	HoH
97,000	97,050	20,238	15,844	20,693	18,579
97,050	97,100	20,252	15,856	20,707	18,591
97,100	97,150	20,266	15,869	20,721	18,604
97,150	97,200	20,280	15,881	20,735	18,616
97,200	97,250	20,294	15,894	20,749	18,629
97,250	97,300	20,308	15,906	20,763	18,641
97,300	97,350	20,322	15,919	20,777	18,654
97,350	97,400	20,336	15,931	20,791	18,666
97,400	97,450	20,350	15,944	20,805	18,679
97,450	97,500	20,364	15,956	20,819	18,691
97,500	97,550	20,378	15,969	20,833	18,704
97,550	97,600	20,392	15,981	20,847	18,716
97,600	97,650	20,406	15,994	20,861	18,729
97,650	97,700	20,420	16,006	20,875	18,741
97,700	97,750	20,434	16,019	20,889	18,754
97,750	97,800	20,448	16,031	20,903	18,766
97,800	97,850	20,462	16,044	20,917	18,779
97,850	97,900	20,476	16,056	20,931	18,791
97,900	97,950	20,490	16,069	20,945	18,804
97,950	98,000	20,504	16,081	20,959	18,816

98,000

At least	But less than	Single	MFJ*	MFS	HoH
98,000	98,050	20,518	16,094	20,973	18,829
98,050	98,100	20,532	16,106	20,987	18,841
98,100	98,150	20,546	16,119	21,001	18,854
98,150	98,200	20,560	16,131	21,015	18,866
98,200	98,250	20,574	16,144	21,029	18,879
98,250	98,300	20,588	16,156	21,043	18,891
98,300	98,350	20,602	16,169	21,057	18,904
98,350	98,400	20,616	16,181	21,071	18,916
98,400	98,450	20,630	16,194	21,085	18,929
98,450	98,500	20,644	16,206	21,099	18,941
98,500	98,550	20,658	16,219	21,113	18,954
98,550	98,600	20,672	16,231	21,127	18,966
98,600	98,650	20,686	16,244	21,141	18,979
98,650	98,700	20,700	16,256	21,155	18,991
98,700	98,750	20,714	16,269	21,169	19,004
98,750	98,800	20,728	16,281	21,183	19,016
98,800	98,850	20,742	16,294	21,197	19,029
98,850	98,900	20,756	16,306	21,211	19,041
98,900	98,950	20,770	16,319	21,225	19,054
98,950	99,000	20,784	16,331	21,239	19,066

99,000

At least	But less than	Single	MFJ*	MFS	HoH
99,000	99,050	20,798	16,344	21,253	19,079
99,050	99,100	20,812	16,356	21,267	19,091
99,100	99,150	20,826	16,369	21,281	19,104
99,150	99,200	20,840	16,381	21,295	19,116
99,200	99,250	20,854	16,394	21,309	19,129
99,250	99,300	20,868	16,406	21,323	19,141
99,300	99,350	20,882	16,419	21,337	19,154
99,350	99,400	20,896	16,431	21,351	19,166
99,400	99,450	20,910	16,444	21,365	19,179
99,450	99,500	20,924	16,456	21,379	19,191
99,500	99,550	20,938	16,469	21,393	19,204
99,550	99,600	20,952	16,481	21,407	19,216
99,600	99,650	20,966	16,494	21,421	19,229
99,650	99,700	20,980	16,506	21,435	19,241
99,700	99,750	20,994	16,519	21,449	19,254
99,750	99,800	21,008	16,531	21,463	19,266
99,800	99,850	21,022	16,544	21,477	19,279
99,850	99,900	21,036	16,556	21,491	19,291
99,900	99,950	21,050	16,569	21,505	19,304
99,950	100,000	21,064	16,581	21,519	19,316

$100,000 or over use the Tax Computation Worksheet

* This column must also be used by a qualifying widow(er).

2015 OPTIONAL SALES TAX TABLES

When Used

The election to deduct state and local general sales taxes requires that the taxpayer forgo any deduction for state and local income taxes. Whether this is advisable or not depends on a comparison of the amounts involved. In making the choice, however, the outcome could be influenced by the additional sales tax incurred due to certain "big ticket" purchases that were made. For example, a taxpayer who chose to deduct state and local income taxes for 2014 might well prefer the sales tax deduction in 2015 if a new boat was purchased or home improvements were made during the year. To make the sales tax election, the taxpayer must enter the amount on Schedule A, line 5, and check box b.

If the sales tax election is made, the amount of the deduction can be determined by use of the *actual expense method* or the *optional sales tax tables* issued by the IRS. The actual expense method can be used only when the taxpayer has actual receipts to support the deduction claimed. In the absence of receipts, the usual case with most taxpayers, resorting to the optional sales tax tables is necessary. Under neither method, however, is the purchase of items used in a taxpayer's trade or business to be considered.

Adjustments Necessary

The optional sales tax tables are based on a number of assumptions that require adjustments to be made. As the starting point for the use of the tables is AGI, nontaxable receipts have not been included. Examples of receipts that should be added include: tax-exempt interest, veterans' benefits, nontaxable combat pay, public assistance payments, workers' compensation, nontaxable Social Security, and other retirement benefits. They do not include any large nontaxable items that are not likely to be spent. For example, a $100,000 inheritance should not be added if it was invested in a certificate of deposit.

The tables represent the sales tax on the average (and recurring) expenditures based on level of income by family size and do not include exceptional purchases. Therefore, add to the table amount any sales taxes on major purchases (such as motor vehicles, aircraft, boats, and home building materials, etc.).

When the optional sales tax tables are utilized, special adjustments may be needed when a taxpayer has lived in more than one taxing jurisdiction (e.g., state, county, city) during the year. The adjustments involve apportionment of taxes based on days involved and are illustrated in Instructions for Schedule A (Form 1040), pages A-3 to A-6.

Local Sales Taxes

Local sales taxes (i.e., those imposed by counties, cities, transit authorities) may or may not require a separate determination. In those states where they are not imposed, no further computations are necessary. This is also the case where the local taxes are uniform and are incorporated into the state sales tax table. In other situations, another step is necessary to arrive at the optional sales tax table deduction. Depending on where the taxpayer lives, one of two procedures needs to be used. In one procedure, the local sales tax is arrived at by using the **state table** amount—see Example 1 and the related worksheet. In the other procedure, special **local tables** issued by the IRS for specified state and local jurisdictions are modified (if necessary) and used—see Example 2 and the related worksheet.

Use Illustrated

EXAMPLE 1 The Archers file a joint return for 2015 reflecting AGI of $88,000 and claiming three exemptions. They have tax-exempt interest of $3,000, and during the year they incurred sales tax of $1,650 on the purchase of an automobile for their dependent teenage son. They live in Bellaire, Texas, where the general sales tax rates are 6.25% for state and 2% for local. Since the IRS *has not issued* optional local sales tax tables for Texas, use the Worksheet below to arrive at the Archers' general sales tax deduction of $3,025.

Sales Tax Deduction Worksheet
(To be used when *no* IRS Optional Local Sales Tax Table Available)

Adjusted Gross Income (AGI) as listed on line 38 of Form 1040		$88,000
Add nontaxable items		3,000
Table income to be used for purposes of line 1 below		$91,000
1. Use table income to determine table amount—go to state of residence and find applicable range of table income and exemption column* for *state* sales tax		$ 1,042
2a. Enter local general sales tax rate	2.00	
2b. Enter state general sales tax rate	6.25	
2c. Divide 2a by 2b	0.32	
2d. Multiply line 1 by line 2c for the local sales tax		333
3. Enter general sales tax on large purchases		1,650
4. Deduction for general sales tax (add lines 1 + 2d + 3) and report on line 5 of Schedule A of Form 1040		$ 3,025

*Use total of personal and dependency exemptions as reported in item 6d of Form 1040.

EXAMPLE 2 The Hardys file a joint return for 2015, reporting AGI of $42,000 and claiming four exemptions (two personal and two dependency). They received $30,000 in nontaxable pension benefits. Although the Hardys do not keep sales tax receipts, they can prove that they paid $4,800 in sales tax on the purchase of a new boat in 2015. The Hardys are residents of Georgia and live in a jurisdiction that imposes a 2% local sales tax. Since the IRS *has issued* optional local sales tax tables for Georgia, use the Worksheet below to arrive at the Hardys' general sales tax deduction of $5,647.

Sales Tax Deduction Worksheet
(To be used for Alaska, Arizona, Arkansas,
Colorado, Georgia, Illinois, Louisiana, Missouri, New York,
North Carolina, South Carolina, Tennessee, Utah, and Virginia)

Adjusted Gross Income (AGI) as listed on line 38 of Form 1040		$42,000
Add nontaxable income		30,000
Table income to be used for purposes of line 1 below		$72,000
1. Use the table income to determine *state* sales tax amount—go to table for state of residence and find applicable income range and exemption column*		$ 523
2a. Enter local general sales tax rate	2.0	
2b. Enter IRS *local* sales tax table amount (based on a 1% tax rate)	$162	
2c. Multiply line 2b by 2a for the local sales tax		324
3. Enter general sales tax on large purchases		4,800
4. Deduction for general sales tax (add lines 1 + 2c + 3) and report on line 5 of Schedule A of Form 1040		$ 5,647

*Use total of personal and dependency exemptions as reported in item 6d of Form 1040.

2015 Optional State Sales Tax Tables *(State Sales Tax Rate Shown Next to State Name)*

Income At least	But less than	Alabama 1 — 4.0000% 1	2	3	4	5	Over 5	Arizona 2 — 5.6000% 1	2	3	4	5	Over 5	Arkansas 2 — 6.5000% 1	2	3	4	5	Over 5
$0	$20,000	215	255	284	306	325	352	198	220	234	245	254	267	283	318	340	358	372	392
$20,000	$30,000	318	376	417	449	476	514	333	369	393	412	427	448	458	514	551	579	602	634
$30,000	$40,000	372	439	485	522	553	597	409	453	482	505	523	549	554	621	665	699	727	766
$40,000	$50,000	418	492	544	585	619	668	477	528	562	588	610	640	639	716	767	806	838	883
$50,000	$60,000	459	540	596	641	678	732	540	597	635	665	689	723	715	802	859	902	938	988
$60,000	$70,000	496	583	643	691	731	788	597	661	703	735	762	799	786	880	943	991	1030	1085
$70,000	$80,000	531	622	686	737	780	840	651	720	766	802	831	871	851	954	1022	1074	1116	1176
$80,000	$90,000	563	659	726	780	825	889	702	777	826	864	896	939	913	1023	1095	1151	1197	1261
$90,000	$100,000	593	694	764	820	867	934	751	831	883	924	958	1004	971	1088	1165	1225	1273	1341
$100,000	$120,000	633	739	814	873	923	994	817	903	961	1005	1041	1092	1050	1176	1260	1324	1376	1449
$120,000	$140,000	685	799	879	942	996	1072	905	1000	1063	1112	1152	1208	1153	1292	1384	1454	1512	1592
$140,000	$160,000	733	854	939	1006	1063	1144	988	1091	1160	1214	1257	1318	1251	1401	1500	1576	1639	1726
$160,000	$180,000	778	906	995	1066	1125	1210	1066	1177	1252	1309	1356	1422	1341	1502	1609	1691	1758	1851
$180,000	$200,000	820	954	1047	1121	1184	1273	1140	1259	1339	1400	1451	1521	1428	1599	1713	1800	1871	1971
$200,000	$225,000	865	1004	1102	1179	1245	1338	1219	1346	1431	1497	1550	1625	1519	1701	1822	1914	1990	2096
$225,000	$250,000	912	1058	1160	1242	1310	1407	1305	1441	1531	1601	1659	1739	1617	1811	1940	2038	2119	2231
$250,000	$275,000	957	1109	1215	1300	1371	1473	1387	1531	1627	1701	1762	1847	1711	1916	2052	2156	2241	2360
$275,000	$300,000	999	1157	1268	1356	1430	1535	1466	1618	1720	1798	1862	1952	1801	2016	2159	2269	2359	2484
$300,000	or more	1254	1445	1579	1685	1775	1903	1951	2152	2286	2390	2475	2594	2345	2625	2811	2953	3070	3233

Income At least	But less than	California 3 — 7.5000% 1	2	3	4	5	Over 5	Colorado 2 — 2.9000% 1	2	3	4	5	Over 5	Connecticut 4 — 6.3500% 1	2	3	4	5	Over 5
$0	$20,000	271	298	316	329	340	356	104	115	122	127	132	138	247	272	289	301	311	325
$20,000	$30,000	446	489	518	540	558	583	167	184	195	204	211	220	406	447	474	494	511	533
$30,000	$40,000	543	595	630	656	678	708	202	222	235	245	253	265	493	543	576	601	621	649
$40,000	$50,000	629	689	729	760	785	819	232	255	270	281	291	304	570	628	666	695	718	751
$50,000	$60,000	707	775	820	854	882	921	259	285	301	314	325	340	641	706	749	781	808	844
$60,000	$70,000	780	854	903	940	971	1014	285	312	330	345	356	372	706	778	825	860	889	929
$70,000	$80,000	847	927	980	1021	1054	1100	308	338	358	373	385	402	766	845	896	934	966	1009
$80,000	$90,000	911	997	1054	1097	1133	1182	330	362	383	399	412	431	824	908	963	1004	1038	1085
$90,000	$100,000	972	1063	1123	1170	1208	1260	351	385	407	424	438	458	878	968	1026	1070	1107	1156
$100,000	$120,000	1054	1152	1217	1267	1308	1365	380	415	439	458	473	494	951	1048	1112	1160	1199	1253
$120,000	$140,000	1162	1270	1341	1396	1441	1504	417	456	482	502	518	541	1047	1155	1225	1278	1321	1380
$140,000	$160,000	1264	1381	1458	1518	1567	1634	452	494	522	543	561	586	1138	1255	1331	1389	1436	1501
$160,000	$180,000	1359	1485	1568	1632	1684	1756	485	529	559	582	601	627	1224	1349	1431	1493	1543	1613
$180,000	$200,000	1451	1584	1673	1740	1796	1873	516	563	595	619	639	667	1305	1439	1526	1592	1646	1721
$200,000	$225,000	1547	1689	1783	1855	1914	1996	548	599	632	658	679	708	1391	1533	1626	1697	1755	1834
$225,000	$250,000	1651	1802	1902	1979	2042	2129	584	637	672	699	722	753	1483	1636	1735	1810	1872	1956
$250,000	$275,000	1751	1910	2016	2097	2164	2256	618	673	710	739	763	796	1571	1733	1838	1918	1983	2073
$275,000	$300,000	1847	2014	2126	2211	2281	2378	650	708	747	777	802	836	1656	1827	1938	2022	2091	2185
$300,000	or more	2431	2649	2793	2904	2995	3121	846	920	970	1008	1040	1083	2173	2398	2544	2654	2744	2869

Income At least	But less than	District of Columbia 4 — 5.7500% 1	2	3	4	5	Over 5	Florida 1 — 6.0000% 1	2	3	4	5	Over 5	Georgia 2 — 4.0000% 1	2	3	4	5	Over 5
$0	$20,000	168	181	190	197	203	211	230	253	268	280	289	302	143	158	169	176	183	192
$20,000	$30,000	279	302	316	328	337	350	381	418	443	462	477	499	231	255	271	284	294	308
$30,000	$40,000	341	369	387	400	412	427	464	510	540	563	582	608	279	308	327	342	354	372
$40,000	$50,000	397	428	449	465	478	496	539	591	626	653	674	704	321	355	377	394	408	427
$50,000	$60,000	448	483	506	524	539	559	607	666	705	735	759	793	360	397	422	440	456	478
$60,000	$70,000	494	533	559	579	595	618	669	734	777	810	837	874	396	436	463	483	500	524
$70,000	$80,000	538	580	608	630	647	672	728	799	845	881	910	950	429	472	501	523	542	567
$80,000	$90,000	579	625	655	678	697	723	783	859	909	947	979	1022	460	506	537	561	580	608
$90,000	$100,000	619	667	699	724	744	772	836	917	970	1011	1044	1090	489	538	571	596	617	646
$100,000	$120,000	672	725	759	786	808	838	907	994	1052	1096	1132	1182	529	582	617	644	666	697
$120,000	$140,000	742	800	839	868	892	926	1001	1097	1160	1209	1249	1304	582	639	677	707	731	765
$140,000	$160,000	809	872	914	946	972	1008	1090	1194	1263	1316	1359	1419	631	693	734	766	793	829
$160,000	$180,000	871	939	984	1018	1046	1086	1173	1285	1359	1416	1462	1526	677	743	787	821	850	889
$180,000	$200,000	931	1003	1051	1088	1118	1160	1252	1372	1451	1511	1561	1629	721	791	838	874	904	945
$200,000	$225,000	994	1071	1122	1161	1193	1238	1336	1463	1547	1612	1664	1738	767	842	891	929	961	1005
$225,000	$250,000	1063	1145	1199	1241	1275	1322	1427	1562	1652	1721	1777	1855	817	896	949	989	1023	1069
$250,000	$275,000	1128	1215	1272	1316	1353	1403	1513	1657	1752	1825	1884	1967	865	948	1003	1046	1081	1131
$275,000	$300,000	1191	1282	1343	1390	1428	1481	1596	1748	1848	1925	1988	2075	911	998	1056	1101	1138	1189
$300,000	or more	1576	1696	1775	1837	1887	1956	2106	2304	2435	2536	2618	2732	1189	1300	1374	1432	1479	1545

Income At least	But less than	Hawaii 1,6 — 4.0000% 1	2	3	4	5	Over 5	Idaho 1 — 6.0000% 1	2	3	4	5	Over 5	Illinois 2 — 6.2500% 1	2	3	4	5	Over 5
$0	$20,000	241	280	306	327	344	367	321	381	422	454	481	520	230	257	275	290	302	319
$20,000	$30,000	373	433	473	504	530	567	482	568	627	674	713	769	364	405	433	455	473	500
$30,000	$40,000	444	514	562	599	629	672	566	665	734	788	834	898	437	485	518	544	565	596
$40,000	$50,000	505	585	638	680	715	764	639	749	826	886	937	1009	501	554	592	621	646	681
$50,000	$60,000	560	648	708	754	792	846	704	824	908	974	1029	1108	559	618	659	691	719	757
$60,000	$70,000	610	706	770	821	862	921	762	892	982	1053	1112	1197	612	675	720	755	785	827
$70,000	$80,000	656	759	828	882	927	990	816	954	1050	1125	1189	1279	661	729	777	815	846	891
$80,000	$90,000	699	808	882	940	987	1054	867	1012	1113	1193	1260	1355	708	779	830	870	904	951
$90,000	$100,000	740	855	933	994	1044	1115	914	1067	1172	1256	1326	1426	751	827	880	923	958	1008
$100,000	$120,000	794	918	1002	1067	1120	1196	978	1139	1251	1340	1415	1521	810	891	948	993	1031	1085
$120,000	$140,000	865	1000	1091	1161	1220	1302	1060	1234	1354	1450	1530	1644	887	975	1036	1085	1127	1185
$140,000	$160,000	932	1076	1174	1250	1313	1401	1137	1322	1450	1552	1637	1758	960	1053	1119	1172	1216	1279
$160,000	$180,000	994	1147	1251	1331	1398	1493	1209	1403	1539	1646	1736	1863	1028	1127	1197	1253	1299	1366
$180,000	$200,000	1052	1214	1324	1409	1480	1579	1276	1480	1622	1734	1829	1963	1092	1196	1270	1329	1379	1449
$200,000	$225,000	1113	1284	1400	1490	1565	1670	1347	1560	1709	1827	1926	2067	1160	1269	1347	1409	1461	1536
$225,000	$250,000	1179	1360	1482	1577	1656	1767	1422	1646	1802	1926	2030	2177	1233	1348	1430	1496	1551	1629
$250,000	$275,000	1241	1431	1560	1660	1743	1859	1494	1727	1890	2019	2128	2282	1302	1423	1509	1578	1635	1718
$275,000	$300,000	1300	1499	1634	1738	1825	1947	1562	1805	1974	2109	2221	2382	1369	1495	1585	1656	1717	1803
$300,000	or more	1655	1907	2076	2209	2318	2472	1969	2266	2473	2637	2775	2971	1772	1928	2040	2130	2205	2313

(Continued)

2015 Optional State Sales Tax Tables *(Continued)*

Income At least	But less than	Indiana			**4**	**7.0000%**		Iowa			**1**	**6.0000%**		Kansas			**1**	**6.3264%**	
		1	2	3	4	5	Over 5	1	2	3	4	5	Over 5	1	2	3	4	5	Over 5
$0	$20,000	271	301	320	335	347	364	237	263	280	294	305	320	357	422	467	503	532	574
$20,000	$30,000	429	476	506	530	549	575	392	436	465	488	506	531	542	639	706	759	803	865
$30,000	$40,000	514	570	607	635	657	689	479	533	568	596	618	649	639	753	831	893	944	1018
$40,000	$50,000	589	652	694	726	752	788	556	619	660	692	717	753	722	850	939	1008	1066	1149
$50,000	$60,000	656	727	774	809	838	878	626	697	744	779	809	849	797	938	1035	1111	1175	1265
$60,000	$70,000	718	795	846	885	916	960	691	769	821	860	893	937	865	1017	1122	1204	1273	1371
$70,000	$80,000	775	858	913	955	989	1036	751	837	893	936	971	1020	927	1090	1202	1290	1364	1468
$80,000	$90,000	828	918	976	1020	1057	1107	809	901	961	1008	1046	1098	985	1158	1276	1370	1448	1559
$90,000	$100,000	879	974	1035	1082	1121	1174	863	962	1026	1076	1116	1172	1040	1221	1346	1445	1527	1644
$100,000	$120,000	947	1049	1115	1166	1207	1264	936	1044	1114	1168	1212	1273	1113	1306	1440	1545	1632	1757
$120,000	$140,000	1036	1147	1220	1275	1320	1383	1034	1152	1230	1289	1338	1405	1208	1417	1561	1675	1770	1904
$140,000	$160,000	1120	1239	1318	1377	1426	1494	1126	1255	1340	1404	1457	1531	1296	1520	1674	1796	1897	2041
$160,000	$180,000	1198	1325	1409	1472	1524	1597	1212	1351	1442	1512	1569	1648	1378	1615	1779	1907	2015	2167
$180,000	$200,000	1272	1407	1495	1563	1618	1694	1294	1443	1541	1615	1676	1761	1455	1705	1877	2013	2126	2287
$200,000	$225,000	1349	1492	1586	1658	1716	1797	1381	1540	1644	1724	1789	1880	1536	1799	1980	2123	2242	2411
$225,000	$250,000	1433	1585	1684	1760	1822	1907	1475	1645	1757	1842	1912	2008	1622	1900	2090	2241	2366	2544
$250,000	$275,000	1512	1672	1777	1857	1922	2012	1565	1745	1864	1954	2028	2131	1704	1994	2194	2352	2483	2670
$275,000	$300,000	1588	1756	1866	1949	2018	2113	1651	1842	1967	2063	2141	2249	1782	2085	2294	2458	2595	2790
$300,000	or more	2045	2260	2400	2508	2595	2716	2180	2432	2598	2725	2829	2972	2245	2622	2882	3086	3257	3500

Income At least	But less than	Kentucky			**4**	**6.0000%**		Louisiana			**2**	**4.0000%**		Maine			**4**	**5.5000%**	
		1	2	3	4	5	Over 5	1	2	3	4	5	Over 5	1	2	3	4	5	Over 5
$0	$20,000	220	243	259	271	281	295	155	170	180	188	194	202	164	178	188	195	201	209
$20,000	$30,000	355	392	417	436	451	473	257	282	298	310	320	334	271	293	308	319	328	341
$30,000	$40,000	429	473	503	526	544	570	314	343	363	378	390	407	329	356	374	388	399	414
$40,000	$50,000	494	545	579	605	626	656	364	398	421	438	452	472	382	412	433	449	461	479
$50,000	$60,000	554	610	648	676	700	733	410	449	474	493	509	531	429	464	487	504	518	538
$60,000	$70,000	608	670	711	742	768	804	452	495	523	544	561	585	473	511	536	555	571	592
$70,000	$80,000	659	725	769	803	831	870	492	538	568	591	610	636	514	555	582	603	620	643
$80,000	$90,000	707	778	825	861	891	932	529	579	611	636	657	685	553	596	625	648	666	691
$90,000	$100,000	752	827	877	915	947	991	565	618	652	679	700	730	590	636	667	690	710	736
$100,000	$120,000	813	894	947	989	1023	1070	613	670	708	736	760	792	639	689	722	748	769	798
$120,000	$140,000	894	982	1040	1085	1123	1174	676	739	781	812	838	874	705	760	796	824	847	878
$140,000	$160,000	969	1064	1127	1176	1216	1272	736	805	850	884	912	951	767	826	865	895	920	955
$160,000	$180,000	1040	1141	1209	1261	1304	1363	793	866	914	951	981	1023	825	888	930	962	989	1026
$180,000	$200,000	1108	1215	1287	1342	1387	1450	846	925	976	1015	1047	1092	880	948	992	1027	1055	1094
$200,000	$225,000	1179	1292	1368	1427	1475	1542	903	986	1041	1083	1117	1165	939	1010	1058	1094	1124	1166
$225,000	$250,000	1256	1376	1456	1518	1569	1640	964	1053	1112	1156	1193	1243	1002	1078	1128	1167	1199	1243
$250,000	$275,000	1329	1455	1540	1605	1659	1734	1023	1117	1179	1226	1265	1318	1063	1143	1196	1237	1270	1317
$275,000	$300,000	1399	1532	1621	1689	1746	1824	1079	1178	1244	1294	1334	1391	1121	1205	1261	1304	1339	1388
$300,000	or more	1825	1995	2109	2197	2269	2369	1424	1554	1639	1705	1758	1832	1476	1584	1656	1712	1758	1821

Income At least	But less than	Maryland			**4**	**6.0000%**		Massachusetts			**4**	**6.2500%**		Michigan			**4**	**6.0000%**	
		1	2	3	4	5	Over 5	1	2	3	4	5	Over 5	1	2	3	4	5	Over 5
$0	$20,000	203	226	241	254	264	279	195	210	219	227	233	241	212	235	249	261	270	283
$20,000	$30,000	333	368	393	413	429	452	312	335	350	361	371	384	341	376	399	416	431	451
$30,000	$40,000	404	447	476	500	520	547	375	402	420	434	445	460	411	452	480	501	518	542
$40,000	$50,000	467	516	550	577	599	631	431	462	482	498	510	528	473	520	551	575	595	622
$50,000	$60,000	525	579	617	647	672	708	482	516	538	556	570	589	529	581	616	643	665	695
$60,000	$70,000	578	637	679	712	739	778	528	565	590	608	624	645	581	637	675	704	728	761
$70,000	$80,000	628	691	736	772	801	843	571	611	638	658	674	697	629	690	730	762	787	823
$80,000	$90,000	675	743	790	828	860	905	611	654	682	704	721	746	674	739	782	816	843	881
$90,000	$100,000	719	791	842	882	916	964	650	695	725	747	766	792	717	786	831	867	896	936
$100,000	$120,000	779	856	911	954	991	1042	701	750	782	806	826	853	774	848	897	935	966	1010
$120,000	$140,000	858	943	1002	1050	1090	1146	769	822	857	883	905	935	850	930	984	1025	1059	1107
$140,000	$160,000	933	1024	1089	1140	1183	1244	833	890	927	955	979	1011	922	1008	1066	1110	1147	1198
$160,000	$180,000	1003	1100	1169	1224	1270	1335	892	953	992	1023	1048	1082	988	1080	1142	1189	1228	1283
$180,000	$200,000	1070	1173	1246	1304	1353	1422	949	1013	1055	1087	1113	1150	1052	1149	1214	1264	1306	1363
$200,000	$225,000	1140	1249	1327	1388	1440	1514	1008	1076	1120	1154	1182	1220	1118	1222	1290	1343	1387	1448
$225,000	$250,000	1216	1332	1414	1480	1535	1613	1072	1144	1191	1227	1256	1297	1191	1300	1373	1429	1475	1540
$250,000	$275,000	1289	1411	1498	1567	1625	1707	1133	1208	1258	1296	1327	1369	1259	1374	1451	1510	1559	1627
$275,000	$300,000	1359	1487	1578	1650	1711	1797	1192	1271	1322	1362	1394	1439	1325	1445	1526	1588	1639	1710
$300,000	or more	1785	1949	2065	2158	2237	2348	1546	1646	1711	1762	1803	1860	1725	1878	1980	2059	2124	2215

Income At least	But less than	Minnesota			**1**	**6.8750%**		Mississippi			**2**	**7.0000%**		Missouri			**2**	**4.2250%**	
		1	2	3	4	5	Over 5	1	2	3	4	5	Over 5	1	2	3	4	5	Over 5
$0	$20,000	243	261	272	281	288	298	404	472	519	556	586	629	158	180	195	206	216	230
$20,000	$30,000	399	429	448	463	475	491	618	722	792	848	893	958	256	290	314	332	348	369
$30,000	$40,000	485	522	546	563	578	597	731	853	936	1001	1055	1131	309	351	379	401	420	445
$40,000	$50,000	562	605	632	653	669	692	829	967	1061	1134	1195	1281	357	404	437	462	483	512
$50,000	$60,000	632	680	711	734	753	778	917	1069	1172	1253	1320	1415	400	453	489	517	540	573
$60,000	$70,000	696	749	783	809	830	858	997	1161	1273	1361	1433	1536	440	497	537	567	593	629
$70,000	$80,000	756	814	851	879	901	932	1071	1247	1366	1460	1538	1648	476	539	581	614	642	681
$80,000	$90,000	813	875	915	945	969	1002	1139	1326	1453	1553	1636	1752	511	578	623	659	688	730
$90,000	$100,000	866	933	976	1008	1034	1069	1204	1401	1535	1640	1727	1850	544	615	663	701	732	776
$100,000	$120,000	939	1011	1057	1092	1120	1159	1290	1501	1644	1756	1849	1981	589	665	716	757	791	838
$120,000	$140,000	1035	1114	1166	1204	1235	1278	1403	1631	1786	1908	2009	2151	647	730	787	831	868	920
$140,000	$160,000	1125	1212	1268	1310	1343	1390	1508	1752	1919	2049	2157	2310	702	792	853	901	941	997
$160,000	$180,000	1210	1303	1363	1408	1445	1495	1605	1864	2041	2179	2295	2457	754	850	915	966	1009	1069
$180,000	$200,000	1290	1390	1455	1503	1542	1595	1697	1971	2157	2303	2424	2595	803	905	974	1028	1074	1137
$200,000	$225,000	1375	1482	1551	1602	1644	1701	1793	2082	2278	2432	2560	2740	855	963	1036	1094	1142	1209
$225,000	$250,000	1468	1582	1655	1710	1754	1815	1896	2200	2408	2570	2705	2895	911	1025	1103	1164	1215	1287
$250,000	$275,000	1555	1676	1754	1812	1859	1924	1993	2313	2531	2701	2842	3042	964	1085	1167	1231	1285	1360
$275,000	$300,000	1640	1768	1850	1911	1961	2029	2086	2420	2648	2826	2974	3182	1015	1142	1228	1296	1352	1431
$300,000	or more	2155	2324	2432	2513	2579	2669	2640	3059	3344	3567	3753	4014	1327	1489	1600	1687	1759	1861

2015 Optional State Sales Tax Tables

Nebraska 5.5000%

At least	But less than	1	2	3	4	5	Over 5
$0	$20,000	217	240	256	267	276	289
$20,000	$30,000	360	398	423	443	458	480
$30,000	$40,000	439	486	517	540	559	586
$40,000	$50,000	509	564	600	627	649	680
$50,000	$60,000	573	635	675	706	731	766
$60,000	$70,000	632	701	745	779	807	845
$70,000	$80,000	688	762	810	847	878	919
$80,000	$90,000	740	820	872	912	944	989
$90,000	$100,000	790	875	931	973	1008	1056
$100,000	$120,000	857	949	1010	1056	1094	1146
$120,000	$140,000	945	1048	1115	1166	1207	1265
$140,000	$160,000	1029	1141	1214	1269	1315	1378
$160,000	$180,000	1107	1228	1307	1366	1415	1483
$180,000	$200,000	1182	1311	1395	1459	1512	1584
$200,000	$225,000	1261	1399	1489	1557	1613	1690
$225,000	$250,000	1347	1494	1590	1663	1723	1805
$250,000	$275,000	1429	1585	1687	1764	1828	1915
$275,000	$300,000	1507	1672	1780	1862	1929	2021
$300,000	or more	1988	2206	2349	2457	2545	2668

Nevada 6.8500%

At least	But less than	1	2	3	4	5	Over 5
$0	$20,000	248	274	292	305	316	332
$20,000	$30,000	395	435	462	483	500	523
$30,000	$40,000	475	523	554	579	599	627
$40,000	$50,000	545	599	635	663	686	717
$50,000	$60,000	608	668	708	739	764	799
$60,000	$70,000	666	732	775	808	836	874
$70,000	$80,000	721	790	837	873	902	943
$80,000	$90,000	771	846	895	933	965	1008
$90,000	$100,000	819	898	950	990	1024	1070
$100,000	$120,000	884	968	1024	1067	1103	1152
$120,000	$140,000	969	1060	1121	1168	1207	1261
$140,000	$160,000	1049	1147	1213	1263	1304	1362
$160,000	$180,000	1124	1228	1297	1351	1395	1457
$180,000	$200,000	1195	1305	1378	1435	1482	1547
$200,000	$225,000	1269	1385	1463	1523	1572	1641
$225,000	$250,000	1350	1472	1555	1618	1670	1743
$250,000	$275,000	1426	1555	1641	1708	1763	1839
$275,000	$300,000	1500	1634	1725	1794	1852	1932
$300,000	or more	1944	2114	2228	2316	2388	2490

New Jersey 7.0000%

At least	But less than	1	2	3	4	5	Over 5
$0	$20,000	245	262	273	281	288	298
$20,000	$30,000	405	433	451	465	476	492
$30,000	$40,000	493	528	550	567	581	600
$40,000	$50,000	572	612	638	657	673	695
$50,000	$60,000	644	689	718	740	758	782
$60,000	$70,000	711	760	792	816	836	863
$70,000	$80,000	773	826	861	887	908	938
$80,000	$90,000	831	889	926	954	977	1009
$90,000	$100,000	887	948	988	1018	1043	1076
$100,000	$120,000	962	1028	1071	1104	1131	1167
$120,000	$140,000	1062	1134	1182	1218	1247	1288
$140,000	$160,000	1156	1235	1286	1325	1357	1401
$160,000	$180,000	1244	1329	1384	1426	1460	1508
$180,000	$200,000	1328	1418	1478	1522	1559	1609
$200,000	$225,000	1416	1513	1576	1624	1663	1716
$225,000	$250,000	1512	1615	1683	1734	1775	1832
$250,000	$275,000	1604	1713	1784	1838	1882	1943
$275,000	$300,000	1692	1807	1882	1939	1986	2050
$300,000	or more	2231	2382	2480	2555	2616	2700

New Mexico 5.1250%

At least	But less than	1	2	3	4	5	Over 5
$0	$20,000	236	256	268	277	284	295
$20,000	$30,000	383	415	434	449	461	478
$30,000	$40,000	464	502	526	544	558	578
$40,000	$50,000	535	579	606	627	644	667
$50,000	$60,000	600	649	680	703	722	747
$60,000	$70,000	659	713	747	772	793	821
$70,000	$80,000	714	772	809	837	859	890
$80,000	$90,000	766	829	868	898	922	954
$90,000	$100,000	816	882	924	956	981	1016
$100,000	$120,000	882	954	999	1033	1061	1098
$120,000	$140,000	970	1048	1098	1136	1166	1207
$140,000	$160,000	1052	1137	1192	1232	1265	1310
$160,000	$180,000	1129	1220	1279	1322	1357	1405
$180,000	$200,000	1202	1300	1362	1408	1445	1496
$200,000	$225,000	1279	1383	1449	1498	1538	1592
$225,000	$250,000	1363	1473	1543	1596	1638	1696
$250,000	$275,000	1442	1558	1633	1688	1733	1794
$275,000	$300,000	1518	1641	1719	1777	1825	1889
$300,000	or more	1980	2140	2242	2318	2379	2463

New York 4.0000%

At least	But less than	1	2	3	4	5	Over 5
$0	$20,000	143	153	160	166	170	176
$20,000	$30,000	235	252	264	272	279	289
$30,000	$40,000	286	307	321	331	340	351
$40,000	$50,000	331	355	371	383	393	407
$50,000	$60,000	372	400	417	431	442	457
$60,000	$70,000	410	440	460	475	487	503
$70,000	$80,000	446	478	499	515	529	547
$80,000	$90,000	479	514	537	554	568	588
$90,000	$100,000	511	548	572	591	606	626
$100,000	$120,000	554	594	620	640	656	679
$120,000	$140,000	610	655	683	705	723	748
$140,000	$160,000	664	712	743	767	786	813
$160,000	$180,000	714	765	799	824	845	874
$180,000	$200,000	762	816	852	879	902	932
$200,000	$225,000	812	870	908	937	961	994
$225,000	$250,000	867	929	969	1000	1025	1060
$250,000	$275,000	918	984	1027	1060	1086	1123
$275,000	$300,000	969	1038	1083	1117	1145	1184
$300,000	or more	1273	1363	1423	1467	1504	1555

North Carolina 4.7500%

At least	But less than	1	2	3	4	5	Over 5
$0	$20,000	216	248	269	286	299	318
$20,000	$30,000	342	391	424	450	471	501
$30,000	$40,000	409	468	508	538	564	599
$40,000	$50,000	468	535	580	615	644	685
$50,000	$60,000	521	596	646	685	717	762
$60,000	$70,000	570	651	706	748	783	833
$70,000	$80,000	615	703	762	807	845	898
$80,000	$90,000	657	751	814	863	903	959
$90,000	$100,000	697	796	863	915	957	1017
$100,000	$120,000	751	857	929	984	1030	1094
$120,000	$140,000	821	937	1015	1076	1126	1196
$140,000	$160,000	887	1012	1096	1162	1216	1291
$160,000	$180,000	948	1082	1172	1241	1299	1379
$180,000	$200,000	1006	1148	1243	1317	1378	1463
$200,000	$225,000	1067	1217	1318	1396	1461	1551
$225,000	$250,000	1132	1292	1399	1482	1550	1646
$250,000	$275,000	1195	1362	1475	1562	1635	1736
$275,000	$300,000	1254	1430	1548	1640	1716	1822
$300,000	or more	1613	1838	1989	2106	2202	2338

North Dakota 5.0000%

At least	But less than	1	2	3	4	5	Over 5
$0	$20,000	178	199	213	224	234	247
$20,000	$30,000	283	314	336	353	367	388
$30,000	$40,000	340	377	402	423	439	463
$40,000	$50,000	390	431	460	483	502	529
$50,000	$60,000	435	481	513	538	559	589
$60,000	$70,000	476	526	561	588	611	643
$70,000	$80,000	514	568	605	634	659	694
$80,000	$90,000	550	607	647	678	704	741
$90,000	$100,000	585	644	686	719	746	785
$100,000	$120,000	630	694	739	774	803	845
$120,000	$140,000	690	760	808	846	878	924
$140,000	$160,000	747	821	873	914	948	997
$160,000	$180,000	800	878	933	977	1014	1065
$180,000	$200,000	850	933	991	1037	1075	1130
$200,000	$225,000	902	990	1051	1100	1140	1198
$225,000	$250,000	959	1051	1116	1167	1210	1271
$250,000	$275,000	1013	1110	1178	1231	1277	1341
$275,000	$300,000	1065	1166	1237	1293	1340	1407
$300,000	or more	1378	1504	1593	1664	1723	1808

Ohio 5.7500%

At least	But less than	1	2	3	4	5	Over 5
$0	$20,000	223	244	258	268	277	289
$20,000	$30,000	367	400	423	440	454	473
$30,000	$40,000	446	487	514	534	551	574
$40,000	$50,000	516	563	594	618	637	664
$50,000	$60,000	581	633	668	694	716	746
$60,000	$70,000	640	697	735	765	788	821
$70,000	$80,000	695	757	799	830	856	892
$80,000	$90,000	747	814	858	892	920	958
$90,000	$100,000	796	868	915	951	980	1021
$100,000	$120,000	863	940	991	1030	1062	1106
$120,000	$140,000	951	1036	1092	1134	1169	1218
$140,000	$160,000	1035	1126	1187	1233	1271	1324
$160,000	$180,000	1113	1211	1276	1325	1366	1422
$180,000	$200,000	1187	1292	1361	1413	1457	1517
$200,000	$225,000	1265	1377	1450	1506	1552	1616
$225,000	$250,000	1350	1469	1547	1606	1655	1723
$250,000	$275,000	1431	1556	1639	1702	1754	1826
$275,000	$300,000	1509	1641	1728	1794	1849	1924
$300,000	or more	1984	2155	2268	2355	2425	2524

Oklahoma 4.5000%

At least	But less than	1	2	3	4	5	Over 5
$0	$20,000	239	279	308	330	348	375
$20,000	$30,000	368	428	471	504	532	572
$30,000	$40,000	436	507	557	596	629	675
$40,000	$50,000	496	576	631	675	712	765
$50,000	$60,000	550	637	698	747	787	845
$60,000	$70,000	598	693	759	811	855	918
$70,000	$80,000	643	744	815	871	918	985
$80,000	$90,000	686	792	867	926	976	1047
$90,000	$100,000	725	838	916	979	1031	1106
$100,000	$120,000	778	898	982	1049	1105	1185
$120,000	$140,000	848	977	1068	1140	1201	1287
$140,000	$160,000	913	1051	1148	1225	1290	1383
$160,000	$180,000	973	1119	1222	1304	1373	1471
$180,000	$200,000	1030	1184	1293	1379	1451	1554
$200,000	$225,000	1090	1252	1366	1457	1533	1642
$225,000	$250,000	1154	1325	1445	1541	1621	1735
$250,000	$275,000	1215	1394	1520	1620	1704	1824
$275,000	$300,000	1273	1460	1591	1695	1783	1908
$300,000	or more	1622	1853	2016	2146	2256	2412

Pennsylvania 6.0000%

At least	But less than	1	2	3	4	5	Over 5
$0	$20,000	197	214	225	234	241	251
$20,000	$30,000	318	345	363	377	388	404
$30,000	$40,000	385	417	439	455	468	487
$40,000	$50,000	443	480	505	524	539	560
$50,000	$60,000	496	538	565	586	603	627
$60,000	$70,000	545	590	620	643	662	688
$70,000	$80,000	590	639	671	696	716	744
$80,000	$90,000	633	685	720	746	768	798
$90,000	$100,000	673	729	765	793	816	848
$100,000	$120,000	728	787	827	857	882	916
$120,000	$140,000	799	865	908	941	968	1005
$140,000	$160,000	867	937	984	1020	1049	1089
$160,000	$180,000	929	1005	1055	1093	1124	1168
$180,000	$200,000	989	1069	1122	1163	1196	1242
$200,000	$225,000	1052	1137	1194	1237	1272	1321
$225,000	$250,000	1120	1211	1270	1316	1353	1405
$250,000	$275,000	1185	1280	1343	1391	1431	1486
$275,000	$300,000	1247	1347	1413	1464	1506	1563
$300,000	or more	1624	1752	1838	1903	1956	2031

Rhode Island 7.0000%

At least	But less than	1	2	3	4	5	Over 5
$0	$20,000	252	272	285	295	303	314
$20,000	$30,000	406	439	460	476	488	506
$30,000	$40,000	490	529	555	574	589	611
$40,000	$50,000	564	609	638	660	678	703
$50,000	$60,000	631	682	714	739	759	787
$60,000	$70,000	692	748	784	811	833	863
$70,000	$80,000	749	810	849	878	902	935
$80,000	$90,000	803	868	910	941	967	1002
$90,000	$100,000	854	923	967	1001	1028	1065
$100,000	$120,000	922	997	1045	1081	1110	1150
$120,000	$140,000	1013	1094	1147	1187	1219	1263
$140,000	$160,000	1097	1186	1243	1286	1321	1369
$160,000	$180,000	1176	1271	1332	1378	1416	1467
$180,000	$200,000	1251	1352	1418	1467	1506	1561
$200,000	$225,000	1330	1438	1507	1559	1602	1660
$225,000	$250,000	1416	1530	1604	1659	1704	1766
$250,000	$275,000	1497	1618	1696	1754	1802	1867
$275,000	$300,000	1575	1702	1784	1846	1896	1964
$300,000	or more	2046	2211	2318	2398	2463	2552

South Carolina 6.0000%

At least	But less than	1	2	3	4	5	Over 5
$0	$20,000	234	258	274	285	295	308
$20,000	$30,000	381	420	445	464	480	501
$30,000	$40,000	462	509	539	562	581	607
$40,000	$50,000	533	587	622	649	670	700
$50,000	$60,000	598	658	698	728	752	785
$60,000	$70,000	657	724	767	800	827	863
$70,000	$80,000	713	785	832	867	896	936
$80,000	$90,000	765	843	893	931	962	1005
$90,000	$100,000	815	897	951	991	1024	1070
$100,000	$120,000	881	970	1028	1072	1108	1157
$120,000	$140,000	969	1067	1131	1179	1218	1272
$140,000	$160,000	1052	1158	1227	1280	1322	1381
$160,000	$180,000	1129	1243	1318	1374	1419	1482
$180,000	$200,000	1203	1325	1404	1463	1512	1579
$200,000	$225,000	1280	1410	1494	1558	1610	1681
$225,000	$250,000	1364	1502	1592	1660	1715	1791
$250,000	$275,000	1444	1590	1685	1757	1815	1896
$275,000	$300,000	1521	1674	1774	1850	1911	1996
$300,000	or more	1986	2187	2317	2416	2496	2607

Income At least	But less than	South Dakota 1	2	3	1	5 4.0000%	Over 5	Tennessee 1	2	3	2	5 7.0000%	Over 5	Texas 1	2	3	1	5 6.2500%	Over 5
$0	$20,000	227	266	293	315	332	357	350	404	441	469	493	527	243	272	291	306	318	335
$20,000	$30,000	351	412	453	485	512	550	551	634	690	735	771	823	399	447	479	503	523	551
$30,000	$40,000	417	489	537	576	608	653	659	757	824	877	920	981	486	544	583	613	637	671
$40,000	$50,000	475	556	611	654	690	741	753	865	941	1000	1050	1119	562	630	675	710	738	777
$50,000	$60,000	527	616	677	724	764	821	839	962	1046	1112	1167	1244	632	709	759	798	830	874
$60,000	$70,000	573	670	736	788	832	893	917	1051	1142	1214	1273	1357	697	781	837	879	914	963
$70,000	$80,000	617	721	792	847	894	960	989	1133	1231	1308	1372	1462	757	848	909	955	994	1047
$80,000	$90,000	657	768	843	903	952	1022	1057	1210	1315	1396	1464	1560	813	912	977	1027	1068	1125
$90,000	$100,000	696	812	892	955	1007	1080	1121	1283	1393	1480	1552	1653	867	972	1042	1095	1139	1200
$100,000	$120,000	747	871	957	1024	1080	1159	1206	1380	1499	1591	1668	1777	940	1054	1129	1187	1235	1301
$120,000	$140,000	813	949	1042	1115	1175	1261	1319	1508	1637	1738	1821	1939	1036	1161	1245	1309	1361	1434
$140,000	$160,000	876	1021	1121	1199	1264	1356	1424	1628	1766	1875	1965	2092	1126	1263	1354	1423	1480	1560
$160,000	$180,000	934	1088	1194	1278	1347	1445	1522	1739	1886	2002	2098	2233	1211	1358	1456	1530	1592	1677
$180,000	$200,000	988	1152	1264	1352	1425	1529	1616	1845	2001	2123	2224	2367	1292	1449	1553	1633	1698	1790
$200,000	$225,000	1046	1218	1337	1429	1507	1616	1713	1955	2120	2249	2356	2507	1377	1545	1656	1741	1811	1908
$225,000	$250,000	1107	1290	1415	1513	1594	1710	1819	2074	2249	2385	2499	2658	1469	1648	1767	1858	1932	2036
$250,000	$275,000	1166	1357	1489	1591	1677	1799	1919	2187	2371	2514	2633	2802	1557	1747	1872	1969	2048	2158
$275,000	$300,000	1221	1422	1559	1667	1757	1884	2014	2296	2488	2638	2763	2939	1641	1842	1974	2076	2160	2276
$300,000	or more	1555	1807	1981	2116	2230	2390	2591	2947	3190	3380	3538	3761	2157	2420	2595	2729	2839	2992

Income At least	But less than	Utah 1	2	3	2	5 4.7000%	Over 5	Vermont 1	2	3	1	5 6.0000%	Over 5	Virginia 1	2	3	2	5 4.3000%	Over 5
$0	$20,000	230	265	288	306	321	342	160	168	173	176	179	183	168	192	208	220	230	245
$20,000	$30,000	363	416	451	479	502	535	249	261	268	273	277	283	266	301	325	344	359	381
$30,000	$40,000	434	497	539	572	599	638	297	310	318	325	330	337	318	359	388	410	428	454
$40,000	$50,000	497	568	616	653	684	728	338	353	363	370	375	383	364	411	443	468	489	518
$50,000	$60,000	553	632	685	726	761	809	375	392	402	410	416	425	405	457	492	520	543	575
$60,000	$70,000	604	690	748	793	830	883	409	427	438	447	454	463	443	499	538	568	593	628
$70,000	$80,000	652	744	806	855	895	951	440	459	472	481	488	498	479	539	580	612	639	676
$80,000	$90,000	697	795	861	912	955	1016	469	490	503	513	520	531	512	576	619	653	682	722
$90,000	$100,000	739	842	912	967	1012	1076	497	519	532	542	551	562	543	610	656	692	722	764
$100,000	$120,000	796	907	982	1040	1089	1157	534	557	572	582	591	603	585	657	706	745	777	822
$120,000	$140,000	870	991	1072	1136	1189	1263	582	607	623	635	644	657	640	718	772	813	848	897
$140,000	$160,000	940	1070	1157	1226	1283	1363	627	654	671	684	694	708	692	776	833	878	915	967
$160,000	$180,000	1005	1143	1236	1309	1370	1455	669	698	716	729	740	755	740	829	890	937	977	1033
$180,000	$200,000	1067	1212	1311	1389	1453	1543	709	739	758	772	784	799	786	880	944	994	1036	1095
$200,000	$225,000	1132	1285	1390	1471	1539	1634	750	782	802	817	829	846	835	933	1001	1054	1098	1160
$225,000	$250,000	1201	1364	1475	1561	1632	1733	795	828	850	865	878	895	887	991	1062	1118	1164	1230
$250,000	$275,000	1268	1438	1555	1645	1721	1827	837	872	895	911	925	943	936	1045	1120	1179	1228	1296
$275,000	$300,000	1331	1510	1632	1727	1806	1916	878	914	938	955	969	988	984	1098	1176	1237	1288	1360
$300,000	or more	1713	1939	2094	2214	2314	2454	1120	1166	1195	1217	1234	1258	1271	1413	1511	1588	1652	1742

Income At least	But less than	Washington 1	2	3	1	5 6.5000%	Over 5	West Virginia 1	2	3	1	5 6.0000%	Over 5	Wisconsin 1	2	3	1	5 5.0000%	Over 5
$0	$20,000	247	273	290	304	315	330	239	265	282	295	306	321	203	224	238	248	257	268
$20,000	$30,000	413	456	484	506	525	550	395	438	467	488	506	531	333	368	390	407	421	440
$30,000	$40,000	505	558	593	620	642	672	481	534	569	596	617	647	405	447	474	495	512	535
$40,000	$50,000	588	649	689	720	746	782	558	620	660	691	716	751	469	517	549	573	592	619
$50,000	$60,000	664	732	778	813	842	882	628	698	743	778	806	846	527	581	617	644	666	696
$60,000	$70,000	733	809	859	898	930	974	693	770	820	858	889	933	580	640	679	709	733	766
$70,000	$80,000	799	881	936	978	1012	1060	754	837	891	933	967	1015	630	695	737	770	796	832
$80,000	$90,000	861	949	1008	1053	1090	1142	811	900	959	1004	1041	1092	677	747	792	827	855	894
$90,000	$100,000	920	1014	1077	1125	1165	1220	865	961	1023	1071	1111	1165	721	796	844	881	912	953
$100,000	$120,000	999	1101	1170	1222	1265	1325	938	1042	1110	1162	1205	1264	781	862	915	955	987	1033
$120,000	$140,000	1105	1217	1293	1350	1398	1464	1035	1150	1225	1282	1329	1395	860	949	1007	1052	1088	1137
$140,000	$160,000	1204	1327	1409	1472	1524	1596	1127	1251	1333	1396	1447	1518	935	1032	1095	1143	1182	1236
$160,000	$180,000	1298	1430	1518	1586	1642	1719	1212	1347	1435	1502	1558	1634	1005	1109	1177	1228	1271	1329
$180,000	$200,000	1388	1529	1623	1695	1754	1837	1294	1438	1532	1604	1663	1745	1072	1183	1255	1310	1355	1417
$200,000	$225,000	1482	1633	1733	1810	1873	1962	1380	1534	1634	1711	1774	1861	1142	1260	1337	1396	1444	1510
$225,000	$250,000	1585	1746	1853	1935	2003	2097	1474	1638	1745	1827	1895	1988	1218	1344	1426	1489	1540	1611
$250,000	$275,000	1683	1853	1967	2054	2126	2226	1563	1737	1851	1938	2009	2108	1290	1424	1511	1577	1632	1706
$275,000	$300,000	1778	1957	2077	2169	2245	2350	1649	1832	1953	2045	2120	2224	1360	1501	1593	1663	1720	1799
$300,000	or more	2357	2593	2751	2872	2972	3111	2173	2415	2574	2696	2795	2933	1784	1969	2090	2181	2256	2360

Income At least	But less than	Wyoming 1	2	3	1	5 4.0000%	Over 5
$0	$20,000	156	171	181	189	195	203
$20,000	$30,000	257	281	298	310	320	334
$30,000	$40,000	312	342	362	377	389	407
$40,000	$50,000	362	397	419	437	451	471
$50,000	$60,000	407	446	472	491	507	529
$60,000	$70,000	449	492	520	541	558	583
$70,000	$80,000	488	534	564	588	607	633
$80,000	$90,000	525	574	607	632	652	680
$90,000	$100,000	560	612	647	674	695	725
$100,000	$120,000	607	664	701	730	753	786
$120,000	$140,000	669	732	773	805	830	866
$140,000	$160,000	728	796	841	875	903	942
$160,000	$180,000	783	856	904	941	971	1012
$180,000	$200,000	835	913	964	1004	1036	1080
$200,000	$225,000	891	974	1028	1070	1104	1151
$225,000	$250,000	951	1039	1097	1142	1178	1228
$250,000	$275,000	1008	1101	1163	1210	1248	1302
$275,000	$300,000	1063	1161	1226	1276	1316	1372
$300,000	or more	1399	1527	1612	1677	1730	1803

Note: Residents of **Alaska** do not have a state sales tax, but should follow the instructions on the next page to determine their local sales tax amount.

1 Use the Ratio Method to determine your local sales tax deduction, then add that to the appropriate amount in the state table. Your state sales tax rate is provided next to the state name.
2 Follow the instructions on the next page to determine your local sales tax deduction, then add that to the appropriate amount in the state table.
3 The California table includes the 1.25% uniform local sales tax rate in addition to the 6.25% state sales tax rate for a total of 7.50%. Some California localities impose a larger local sales tax. Taxpayers who reside in those jurisdictions should use the Ratio Method to determine their local sales tax deduction, then add that to the appropriate amount in the state table. The denominator of the correct ratio is 7.50%, and the numerator is the total sales tax rate minus 7.50%.
4 This state does not have a local general sales tax, so the amount in the state table is the only amount to be deducted.
5 The Nevada table includes the 2.25% uniform local sales tax rate in addition to the 4.6000% state sales tax rate for a total of 6.85%. Some Nevada localities impose a larger local sales tax. Taxpayers who reside in those jurisdictions should use the Ratio Method to determine their local sales tax deduction, then add that to the appropriate amount in the state table. The denominator of the correct ratio is 6.85%, and the numerator is the total sales tax rate minus 6.85%.
6 The 4.0% rate for Hawaii is actually an excise tax but is treated as a sales tax for purpose of this deduction.

Which Optional Local Sales Tax Table Should I Use?

IF you live in the state of...	AND you live in...	THEN use Local Table...
Alaska	Any locality	C
Arizona	Chandler, Glendale, Gilbert, Mesa, Peoria, Phoenix, Scottsdale, Tempe, Tucson, Yuma, or any other locality	B
Arkansas	Any Locality	B
Colorado	Adams County, Arapahoe County, Boulder County, Centennial, Colorado Springs, Denver City/Denver County, El Paso County, Larimer County, Pueblo County, or any other locality	A
	Aurora, Boulder, Fort Collins, Greeley, Jefferson County, Lakewood, Longmont or Pueblo City.	B
	Arvada, Thornton or Westminster	C
Georgia	Any locality	B
Illinois	Any locality	A
Louisiana	Ascension Parish, Bossier Parish, Caddo Parish, Calcasieu Parish, East Baton Rouge Parish, Iberia Parish, Jefferson Parish, Lafayette Parish, Lafourche Parish, Livingston Parish, Orleans Parish, Ouachita Parish, Rapides Parish, St. Bernard Parish, St. Landry Parish, St. Tammany Parish, Tangipahoa Parish or Terrebonne Parish	C
	Any other locality	B
Mississippi	Cities of Jackson and Tupelo only	B
Missouri	Any locality	B
New York	Counties: Albany, Allegany, Broome, Cattaraugus, Cayuga, Chemung, Clinton, Cortland, Dutchess, Erie, Essex, Franklin, Fulton, Genesee, Herkimer, Jefferson, Lewis, Livingston, Madison, Monroe, Montgomery, Nassau, Niagara, Oneida, Onondaga, Ontario, Orange, Orleans, Oswego, Otsego, Putnam, Rensselaer, Rockland, St. Lawrence, Saratoga, Schenectady, Schoharie, Schuyler, Seneca, Steuben, Suffolk, Sullivan, Tompkins, Ulster, Warren, Washington, Westchester, Wyoming or Yates	B
	Counties: Chautauqua, Chenango, Columbia, Delaware, Greene, Hamilton, Tioga, Wayne, New York City or Norwich City	A
	Any other locality	D*
North Carolina	Any locality	A
South Carolina	Aiken County, Anderson County, Georgetown County, Horry County, Lexington County, Newberry County, Orangeburg County, York County or Myrtle Beach	A
	Bamberg County, Charleston County, Cherokee County, Chesterfield County, Darlington County, Dillon County, Florence County, Hampton County, Jasper County, Lee County, Marion County, Marlboro County or Any other locality	B
Tennessee	Any locality	B
Utah	Any locality	A
Virginia	Any locality	B

* Note: Local Table D is just 25% of the NY State table.

2015 Optional Local Sales Tax Tables

Income		Exemptions						Exemptions						Exemptions						Exemptions					
At least	But less than	1	2	3	4	5	Over 5	1	2	3	4	5	Over 5	1	2	3	4	5	Over 5	1	2	3	4	5	Over 5
		Local Table A						Local Table B						Local Table C						Local Table D					
$0	$20,000	35	39	42	43	45	47	44	52	56	60	63	68	55	64	70	75	79	85	36	38	40	42	43	44
20,000	30,000	56	62	66	69	71	75	69	80	87	93	98	104	86	99	108	116	121	130	59	63	66	68	70	72
30,000	40,000	68	74	79	82	85	89	82	95	103	110	116	124	102	118	128	137	144	154	72	77	80	83	85	88
40,000	50,000	78	85	90	94	98	102	93	108	117	125	131	140	116	134	146	155	163	174	83	89	93	96	98	102
50,000	60,000	87	95	101	105	109	114	104	119	130	139	146	155	128	148	162	172	181	193	93	100	104	108	111	114
60,000	70,000	95	104	110	115	119	125	113	130	142	151	158	169	140	161	176	187	197	210	103	110	115	119	122	126
70,000	80,000	103	113	119	124	129	135	122	140	152	162	170	182	150	173	189	201	211	225	112	120	125	129	132	137
80,000	90,000	110	120	128	133	137	144	130	149	162	173	181	194	160	185	201	214	225	240	120	129	134	139	142	147
90,000	100,000	117	128	135	141	146	153	137	158	172	183	192	205	169	195	213	226	238	254	128	137	143	148	152	157
100,000	120,000	126	138	146	152	157	164	148	169	184	196	206	219	182	209	228	243	255	272	139	149	155	160	164	170
120,000	140,000	139	151	160	166	172	180	161	185	201	213	224	239	198	228	248	264	277	296	153	164	171	176	181	187
140,000	160,000	150	163	173	180	186	194	174	199	216	230	241	257	213	245	267	284	298	318	166	178	186	192	197	203
160,000	180,000	161	175	185	193	199	208	185	212	230	245	257	274	228	261	285	303	318	339	179	191	200	206	211	219
180,000	200,000	171	186	196	204	211	221	196	224	244	259	272	290	241	277	301	320	336	358	191	204	213	220	226	233
200,000	225,000	181	197	208	217	224	234	208	238	258	274	287	306	255	293	318	338	355	379	203	218	227	234	240	249
225,000	250,000	193	210	221	231	238	249	220	252	273	290	304	324	270	310	337	358	376	400	217	232	242	250	256	265
250,000	275,000	204	222	234	243	251	262	232	265	288	305	320	341	284	326	354	377	395	421	230	246	257	265	272	281
275,000	300,000	214	233	246	256	264	276	243	278	301	320	335	357	298	342	371	394	414	441	242	260	271	279	286	296
300,000	or more	278	301	317	330	340	355	311	354	384	407	426	454	380	434	471	501	525	559	318	341	356	367	376	389

Appendix B

Tax Forms

(Tax forms can be obtained from the IRS website: **www.irs.gov**)

Form **1040**	Department of the Treasury—Internal Revenue Service **(99)**			

U.S. Individual Income Tax Return **2015** OMB No. 1545-0074 | IRS Use Only—Do not write or staple in this space.

For the year Jan. 1–Dec. 31, 2015, or other tax year beginning , 2015, ending , 20 | **See separate instructions.**

Your first name and initial | Last name | **Your social security number**

If a joint return, spouse's first name and initial | Last name | **Spouse's social security number**

Home address (number and street). If you have a P.O. box, see instructions. | Apt. no. | ▲ **Make sure the SSN(s) above and on line 6c are correct.**

City, town or post office, state, and ZIP code. If you have a foreign address, also complete spaces below (see instructions).

Presidential Election Campaign
Check here if you, or your spouse if filing jointly, want $3 to go to this fund. Checking a box below will not change your tax or refund. ☐ You ☐ Spouse

Foreign country name | Foreign province/state/county | Foreign postal code

Filing Status

Check only one box.

1 ☐ Single
2 ☐ Married filing jointly (even if only one had income)
3 ☐ Married filing separately. Enter spouse's SSN above and full name here. ▶
4 ☐ Head of household (with qualifying person). (See instructions.) If the qualifying person is a child but not your dependent, enter this child's name here. ▶
5 ☐ Qualifying widow(er) with dependent child

Exemptions

6a ☐ **Yourself.** If someone can claim you as a dependent, **do not** check box 6a . . . . .
  b ☐ **Spouse** . . . .

c Dependents:		(2) Dependent's social security number	(3) Dependent's relationship to you	(4) ✓ if child under age 17 qualifying for child tax credit (see instructions)
(1) First name Last name				☐
				☐
				☐
				☐

If more than four dependents, see instructions and check here ▶ ☐

Boxes checked on 6a and 6b
No. of children on 6c who:
• lived with you
• did not live with you due to divorce or separation (see instructions)
Dependents on 6c not entered above
Add numbers on lines above ▶

d Total number of exemptions claimed . . . .

Income

Attach Form(s) W-2 here. Also attach Forms W-2G and 1099-R if tax was withheld.

If you did not get a W-2, see instructions.

7	Wages, salaries, tips, etc. Attach Form(s) W-2	7	
8a	**Taxable** interest. Attach Schedule B if required	8a	
b	**Tax-exempt** interest. **Do not** include on line 8a . . .	8b	
9a	Ordinary dividends. Attach Schedule B if required	9a	
b	Qualified dividends	9b	
10	Taxable refunds, credits, or offsets of state and local income taxes	10	
11	Alimony received	11	
12	Business income or (loss). Attach Schedule C or C-EZ	12	
13	Capital gain or (loss). Attach Schedule D if required. If not required, check here ▶ ☐	13	
14	Other gains or (losses). Attach Form 4797	14	
15a	IRA distributions .	15a		b Taxable amount . . .	15b	
16a	Pensions and annuities	16a		b Taxable amount . . .	16b	
17	Rental real estate, royalties, partnerships, S corporations, trusts, etc. Attach Schedule E	17	
18	Farm income or (loss). Attach Schedule F	18	
19	Unemployment compensation	19	
20a	Social security benefits	20a		b Taxable amount . . .	20b	
21	Other income. List type and amount _____	21	
22	Combine the amounts in the far right column for lines 7 through 21. This is your **total income** ▶	22	

Adjusted Gross Income

23	Educator expenses	23		
24	Certain business expenses of reservists, performing artists, and fee-basis government officials. Attach Form 2106 or 2106-EZ	24		
25	Health savings account deduction. Attach Form 8889 .	25		
26	Moving expenses. Attach Form 3903	26		
27	Deductible part of self-employment tax. Attach Schedule SE .	27		
28	Self-employed SEP, SIMPLE, and qualified plans . .	28		
29	Self-employed health insurance deduction	29		
30	Penalty on early withdrawal of savings	30		
31a	Alimony paid b Recipient's SSN ▶	31a		
32	IRA deduction	32		
33	Student loan interest deduction	33		
34	Tuition and fees. Attach Form 8917	34		
35	Domestic production activities deduction. Attach Form 8903	35		
36	Add lines 23 through 35	36	
37	Subtract line 36 from line 22. This is your **adjusted gross income** . . . . . ▶	37	

For Disclosure, Privacy Act, and Paperwork Reduction Act Notice, see separate instructions. Cat. No. 11320B   Form **1040** (2015)

Form 1040 (2015) Page **2**

Tax and Credits	38	Amount from line 37 (adjusted gross income)	38	
	39a	Check if: ☐ **You** were born before January 2, 1951, ☐ Blind. ☐ **Spouse** was born before January 2, 1951, ☐ Blind. } Total boxes checked ▶ 39a		
	b	If your spouse itemizes on a separate return or you were a dual-status alien, check here ▶ 39b ☐		
Standard Deduction for— • People who check any box on line 39a or 39b **or** who can be claimed as a dependent, see instructions. • All others: Single or Married filing separately, $6,300 Married filing jointly or Qualifying widow(er), $12,600 Head of household, $9,250	40	**Itemized deductions** (from Schedule A) **or** your **standard deduction** (see left margin) . .	40	
	41	Subtract line 40 from line 38	41	
	42	**Exemptions.** If line 38 is $154,950 or less, multiply $4,000 by the number on line 6d. Otherwise, see instructions	42	
	43	**Taxable income.** Subtract line 42 from line 41. If line 42 is more than line 41, enter -0- . .	43	
	44	**Tax** (see instructions). Check if any from: **a** ☐ Form(s) 8814 **b** ☐ Form 4972 **c** ☐	44	
	45	**Alternative minimum tax** (see instructions). Attach Form 6251	45	
	46	Excess advance premium tax credit repayment. Attach Form 8962	46	
	47	Add lines 44, 45, and 46 . . . . ▶	47	
	48	Foreign tax credit. Attach Form 1116 if required	48	
	49	Credit for child and dependent care expenses. Attach Form 2441	49	
	50	Education credits from Form 8863, line 19	50	
	51	Retirement savings contributions credit. Attach Form 8880	51	
	52	Child tax credit. Attach Schedule 8812, if required . . .	52	
	53	Residential energy credits. Attach Form 5695	53	
	54	Other credits from Form: **a** ☐ 3800 **b** ☐ 8801 **c** ☐	54	
	55	Add lines 48 through 54. These are your **total credits**	55	
	56	Subtract line 55 from line 47. If line 55 is more than line 47, enter -0- . . . . . ▶	56	
Other Taxes	57	Self-employment tax. Attach Schedule SE	57	
	58	Unreported social security and Medicare tax from Form: **a** ☐ 4137 **b** ☐ 8919	58	
	59	Additional tax on IRAs, other qualified retirement plans, etc. Attach Form 5329 if required . .	59	
	60a	Household employment taxes from Schedule H	60a	
	b	First-time homebuyer credit repayment. Attach Form 5405 if required	60b	
	61	Health care: individual responsibility (see instructions) Full-year coverage ☐	61	
	62	Taxes from: **a** ☐ Form 8959 **b** ☐ Form 8960 **c** ☐ Instructions; enter code(s)	62	
	63	Add lines 56 through 62. This is your **total tax** . . . . ▶	63	
Payments If you have a qualifying child, attach Schedule EIC.	64	Federal income tax withheld from Forms W-2 and 1099 . .	64	
	65	2015 estimated tax payments and amount applied from 2014 return	65	
	66a	**Earned income credit (EIC)**	66a	
	b	Nontaxable combat pay election 66b		
	67	Additional child tax credit. Attach Schedule 8812	67	
	68	American opportunity credit from Form 8863, line 8 . . .	68	
	69	Net premium tax credit. Attach Form 8962	69	
	70	Amount paid with request for extension to file	70	
	71	Excess social security and tier 1 RRTA tax withheld . . .	71	
	72	Credit for federal tax on fuels. Attach Form 4136 . . .	72	
	73	Credits from Form: **a** ☐ 2439 **b** ☐ Reserved **c** ☐ 8885 **d** ☐	73	
	74	Add lines 64, 65, 66a, and 67 through 73. These are your **total payments** . . . . . ▶	74	
Refund Direct deposit? See instructions.	75	If line 74 is more than line 63, subtract line 63 from line 74. This is the amount you **overpaid**	75	
	76a	Amount of line 75 you want **refunded to you.** If Form 8888 is attached, check here . ▶ ☐	76a	
	▶ b	Routing number		▶ c Type: ☐ Checking ☐ Savings
	▶ d	Account number		
	77	Amount of line 75 you want **applied to your 2016 estimated tax** ▶ 77		
Amount You Owe	78	**Amount you owe.** Subtract line 74 from line 63. For details on how to pay, see instructions ▶	78	
	79	Estimated tax penalty (see instructions) 79		

Third Party Designee

Do you want to allow another person to discuss this return with the IRS (see instructions)? ☐ **Yes.** Complete below. ☐ **No**

Designee's name ▶	Phone no. ▶	Personal identification number (PIN) ▶

Sign Here

Joint return? See instructions.
Keep a copy for your records.

Under penalties of perjury, I declare that I have examined this return and accompanying schedules and statements, and to the best of my knowledge and belief, they are true, correct, and complete. Declaration of preparer (other than taxpayer) is based on all information of which preparer has any knowledge.

Your signature	Date	Your occupation	Daytime phone number
Spouse's signature. If a joint return, **both** must sign.	Date	Spouse's occupation	If the IRS sent you an Identity Protection PIN, enter it here (see inst.)

Paid Preparer Use Only

Print/Type preparer's name	Preparer's signature	Date	Check ☐ if self-employed	PTIN
Firm's name ▶			Firm's EIN ▶	
Firm's address ▶			Phone no.	

SCHEDULE A
(Form 1040)

Department of the Treasury
Internal Revenue Service (99)

Itemized Deductions

▶ Information about Schedule A and its separate instructions is at *www.irs.gov/schedulea*.
▶ Attach to Form 1040.

OMB No. 1545-0074

20**15**

Attachment
Sequence No. **07**

Name(s) shown on Form 1040

Your social security number

Medical and Dental Expenses		**Caution:** Do not include expenses reimbursed or paid by others.	
	1	Medical and dental expenses (see instructions) **1**	
	2	Enter amount from Form 1040, line 38 **2**	
	3	Multiply line 2 by 10% (.10). But if either you or your spouse was born before January 2, 1951, multiply line 2 by 7.5% (.075) instead **3**	
	4	Subtract line 3 from line 1. If line 3 is more than line 1, enter -0-	**4**
Taxes You Paid	5	State and local (**check only one box**): a ☐ Income taxes, **or** b ☐ General sales taxes **5**	
	6	Real estate taxes (see instructions) **6**	
	7	Personal property taxes **7**	
	8	Other taxes. List type and amount ▶ _____ **8**	
	9	Add lines 5 through 8	**9**
Interest You Paid **Note:** Your mortgage interest deduction may be limited (see instructions).	10	Home mortgage interest and points reported to you on Form 1098 **10**	
	11	Home mortgage interest not reported to you on Form 1098. If paid to the person from whom you bought the home, see instructions and show that person's name, identifying no., and address ▶ _____ _____ **11**	
	12	Points not reported to you on Form 1098. See instructions for special rules **12**	
	13	Mortgage insurance premiums (see instructions) **13**	
	14	Investment interest. Attach Form 4952 if required. (See instructions.) **14**	
	15	Add lines 10 through 14	**15**
Gifts to Charity If you made a gift and got a benefit for it, see instructions.	16	Gifts by cash or check. If you made any gift of $250 or more, see instructions . . . **16**	
	17	Other than by cash or check. If any gift of $250 or more, see instructions. You **must** attach Form 8283 if over $500 . . . **17**	
	18	Carryover from prior year **18**	
	19	Add lines 16 through 18	**19**
Casualty and Theft Losses	20	Casualty or theft loss(es). Attach Form 4684. (See instructions.)	**20**
Job Expenses and Certain Miscellaneous Deductions	21	Unreimbursed employee expenses—job travel, union dues, job education, etc. Attach Form 2106 or 2106-EZ if required. (See instructions.) ▶ _____ **21**	
	22	Tax preparation fees **22**	
	23	Other expenses—investment, safe deposit box, etc. List type and amount ▶ _____ _____ **23**	
	24	Add lines 21 through 23 . . . . **24**	
	25	Enter amount from Form 1040, line 38 **25**	
	26	Multiply line 25 by 2% (.02) **26**	
	27	Subtract line 26 from line 24. If line 26 is more than line 24, enter -0-	**27**
Other Miscellaneous Deductions	28	Other—from list in instructions. List type and amount ▶ _____ _____	**28**
Total Itemized Deductions	29	Is Form 1040, line 38, over $154,950? ☐ **No.** Your deduction is not limited. Add the amounts in the far right column for lines 4 through 28. Also, enter this amount on Form 1040, line 40. ⎱ ☐ **Yes.** Your deduction may be limited. See the Itemized Deductions Worksheet in the instructions to figure the amount to enter. ⎰	**29**
	30	If you elect to itemize deductions even though they are less than your standard deduction, check here . . . . ▶ ☐	

For Paperwork Reduction Act Notice, see Form 1040 instructions.   Cat. No. 17145C   Schedule A (Form 1040) 2015

SCHEDULE B
(Form 1040A or 1040)

Department of the Treasury
Internal Revenue Service (99)

Interest and Ordinary Dividends

▶ **Attach to Form 1040A or 1040.**
▶ **Information about Schedule B and its instructions is at** *www.irs.gov/scheduleb.*

OMB No. 1545-0074

2015

Attachment
Sequence No. **08**

Name(s) shown on return

Your social security number

Part I

Interest

(See instructions on back and the instructions for Form 1040A, or Form 1040, line 8a.)

Note: If you received a Form 1099-INT, Form 1099-OID, or substitute statement from a brokerage firm, list the firm's name as the payer and enter the total interest shown on that form.

		Amount
1	List name of payer. If any interest is from a seller-financed mortgage and the buyer used the property as a personal residence, see instructions on back and list this interest first. Also, show that buyer's social security number and address ▶	
	---	**1**
2	Add the amounts on line 1	**2**
3	Excludable interest on series EE and I U.S. savings bonds issued after 1989. Attach Form 8815	**3**
4	Subtract line 3 from line 2. Enter the result here and on Form 1040A, or Form 1040, line 8a . . . . ▶	**4**

Note: If line 4 is over $1,500, you must complete Part III.

Part II

Ordinary Dividends

(See instructions on back and the instructions for Form 1040A, or Form 1040, line 9a.)

Note: If you received a Form 1099-DIV or substitute statement from a brokerage firm, list the firm's name as the payer and enter the ordinary dividends shown on that form.

		Amount
5	List name of payer ▶	
	---	**5**
6	Add the amounts on line 5. Enter the total here and on Form 1040A, or Form 1040, line 9a . . . . ▶	**6**

Note: If line 6 is over $1,500, you must complete Part III.

Part III
Foreign Accounts and Trusts

(See instructions on back.)

You must complete this part if you **(a)** had over $1,500 of taxable interest or ordinary dividends; **(b)** had a foreign account; or **(c)** received a distribution from, or were a grantor of, or a transferor to, a foreign trust.

		Yes	No
7a	At any time during 2015, did you have a financial interest in or signature authority over a financial account (such as a bank account, securities account, or brokerage account) located in a foreign country? See instructions		
	If "Yes," are you required to file FinCEN Form 114, Report of Foreign Bank and Financial Accounts (FBAR), to report that financial interest or signature authority? See FinCEN Form 114 and its instructions for filing requirements and exceptions to those requirements		
b	If you are required to file FinCEN Form 114, enter the name of the foreign country where the financial account is located ▶		
8	During 2015, did you receive a distribution from, or were you the grantor of, or transferor to, a foreign trust? If "Yes," you may have to file Form 3520. See instructions on back		

For Paperwork Reduction Act Notice, see your tax return instructions.   Cat. No. 17146N   **Schedule B (Form 1040A or 1040) 2015**

SCHEDULE C
(Form 1040)

Department of the Treasury
Internal Revenue Service (99)

Profit or Loss From Business
(Sole Proprietorship)

▶ Information about Schedule C and its separate instructions is at *www.irs.gov/schedulec*.
▶ Attach to Form 1040, 1040NR, or 1041; partnerships generally must file Form 1065.

OMB No. 1545-0074

2015

Attachment
Sequence No. **09**

Name of proprietor	Social security number (SSN)

A	Principal business or profession, including product or service (see instructions)	**B** Enter code from instructions ▶

C	Business name. If no separate business name, leave blank.	**D** Employer ID number (EIN), (see instr.)

E   Business address (including suite or room no.) ▶
City, town or post office, state, and ZIP code

F   Accounting method: **(1)** ☐ Cash   **(2)** ☐ Accrual   **(3)** ☐ Other (specify) ▶

G   Did you "materially participate" in the operation of this business during 2015? If "No," see instructions for limit on losses   ☐ Yes ☐ No

H   If you started or acquired this business during 2015, check here   ▶ ☐

I   Did you make any payments in 2015 that would require you to file Form(s) 1099? (see instructions)   ☐ Yes ☐ No

J   If "Yes," did you or will you file required Forms 1099?   ☐ Yes ☐ No

Part I   Income

1	Gross receipts or sales. See instructions for line 1 and check the box if this income was reported to you on Form W-2 and the "Statutory employee" box on that form was checked ▶ ☐	1	
2	Returns and allowances	2	
3	Subtract line 2 from line 1	3	
4	Cost of goods sold (from line 42)	4	
5	**Gross profit.** Subtract line 4 from line 3	5	
6	Other income, including federal and state gasoline or fuel tax credit or refund (see instructions)	6	
7	**Gross income.** Add lines 5 and 6 ▶	7	

Part II   Expenses. Enter expenses for business use of your home **only** on line 30.

8	Advertising	8			18	Office expense (see instructions)	18	
9	Car and truck expenses (see instructions)	9			19	Pension and profit-sharing plans	19	
10	Commissions and fees	10			20	Rent or lease (see instructions):		
11	Contract labor (see instructions)	11			a	Vehicles, machinery, and equipment	20a	
12	Depletion	12			b	Other business property	20b	
13	Depreciation and section 179 expense deduction (not included in Part III) (see instructions)	13			21	Repairs and maintenance	21	
					22	Supplies (not included in Part III)	22	
					23	Taxes and licenses	23	
					24	Travel, meals, and entertainment:		
14	Employee benefit programs (other than on line 19)	14			a	Travel	24a	
15	Insurance (other than health)	15			b	Deductible meals and entertainment (see instructions)	24b	
16	Interest:				25	Utilities	25	
a	Mortgage (paid to banks, etc.)	16a			26	Wages (less employment credits)	26	
b	Other	16b			27a	Other expenses (from line 48)	27a	
17	Legal and professional services	17			b	**Reserved for future use**	27b	

28	**Total expenses** before expenses for business use of home. Add lines 8 through 27a ▶	28	
29	Tentative profit or (loss). Subtract line 28 from line 7	29	
30	Expenses for business use of your home. Do not report these expenses elsewhere. Attach Form 8829 unless using the simplified method (see instructions).
Simplified method filers only: enter the total square footage of: (a) your home: _____ and (b) the part of your home used for business: _____ . Use the Simplified Method Worksheet in the instructions to figure the amount to enter on line 30	30	
31	**Net profit or (loss).** Subtract line 30 from line 29.
• If a profit, enter on both **Form 1040, line 12** (or **Form 1040NR, line 13**) and on **Schedule SE, line 2**. (If you checked the box on line 1, see instructions). Estates and trusts, enter on **Form 1041, line 3.**
• If a loss, you **must** go to line 32.	31	

32   If you have a loss, check the box that describes your investment in this activity (see instructions).

• If you checked 32a, enter the loss on both **Form 1040, line 12,** (or **Form 1040NR, line 13**) and on **Schedule SE, line 2.** (If you checked the box on line 1, see the line 31 instructions). Estates and trusts, enter on **Form 1041, line 3.**

• If you checked 32b, you **must** attach **Form 6198.** Your loss may be limited.

32a ☐ All investment is at risk.
32b ☐ Some investment is not at risk.

For Paperwork Reduction Act Notice, see the separate instructions.   Cat. No. 11334P   Schedule C (Form 1040) 2015

Schedule C (Form 1040) 2015 Page **2**

| Part III | **Cost of Goods Sold** (see instructions) |

33 Method(s) used to
value closing inventory: **a** ☐ Cost **b** ☐ Lower of cost or market **c** ☐ Other (attach explanation)

34 Was there any change in determining quantities, costs, or valuations between opening and closing inventory?
If "Yes," attach explanation . . . . ☐ Yes ☐ No

35	Inventory at beginning of year. If different from last year's closing inventory, attach explanation . . .	35	
36	Purchases less cost of items withdrawn for personal use	36	
37	Cost of labor. Do not include any amounts paid to yourself	37	
38	Materials and supplies	38	
39	Other costs	39	
40	Add lines 35 through 39	40	
41	Inventory at end of year	41	
42	**Cost of goods sold.** Subtract line 41 from line 40. Enter the result here and on line 4	42	

| Part IV | **Information on Your Vehicle.** Complete this part **only** if you are claiming car or truck expenses on line 9 and are not required to file Form 4562 for this business. See the instructions for line 13 to find out if you must file Form 4562. |

43 When did you place your vehicle in service for business purposes? (month, day, year) ▶ _____ / _____ / _____

44 Of the total number of miles you drove your vehicle during 2015, enter the number of miles you used your vehicle for:

a Business _____ **b** Commuting (see instructions) _____ **c** Other _____

45 Was your vehicle available for personal use during off-duty hours? . . . . ☐ Yes ☐ No

46 Do you (or your spouse) have another vehicle available for personal use? . . . . ☐ Yes ☐ No

47a Do you have evidence to support your deduction? . . . . ☐ Yes ☐ No

b If "Yes," is the evidence written? . . . . ☐ Yes ☐ No

| Part V | **Other Expenses.** List below business expenses not included on lines 8–26 or line 30. |

_____		
_____		
_____		
_____		
_____		
_____		
_____		
_____		
_____		
48	**Total other expenses.** Enter here and on line 27a	48	

Schedule C (Form 1040) 2015

SCHEDULE D
(Form 1040)

Department of the Treasury
Internal Revenue Service (99)

Capital Gains and Losses

► **Attach to Form 1040 or Form 1040NR.**
► **Information about Schedule D and its separate instructions is at** *www.irs.gov/scheduled*.
► **Use Form 8949 to list your transactions for lines 1b, 2, 3, 8b, 9, and 10.**

OMB No. 1545-0074

2015

Attachment
Sequence No. **12**

Name(s) shown on return

Your social security number

Part I   Short-Term Capital Gains and Losses—Assets Held One Year or Less

See instructions for how to figure the amounts to enter on the lines below. This form may be easier to complete if you round off cents to whole dollars.	(d) Proceeds (sales price)	(e) Cost (or other basis)	(g) Adjustments to gain or loss from Form(s) 8949, Part I, line 2, column (g)	(h) Gain or (loss) Subtract column (e) from column (d) and combine the result with column (g)
1a Totals for all short-term transactions reported on Form 1099-B for which basis was reported to the IRS and for which you have no adjustments (see instructions). However, if you choose to report all these transactions on Form 8949, leave this line blank and go to line 1b .				
1b Totals for all transactions reported on Form(s) 8949 with **Box A** checked				
2 Totals for all transactions reported on Form(s) 8949 with **Box B** checked				
3 Totals for all transactions reported on Form(s) 8949 with **Box C** checked				

4 Short-term gain from Form 6252 and short-term gain or (loss) from Forms 4684, 6781, and 8824 .	**4**	
5 Net short-term gain or (loss) from partnerships, S corporations, estates, and trusts from Schedule(s) K-1	**5**	
6 Short-term capital loss carryover. Enter the amount, if any, from line 8 of your **Capital Loss Carryover Worksheet** in the instructions	**6**	( )
7 **Net short-term capital gain or (loss).** Combine lines 1a through 6 in column (h). If you have any long-term capital gains or losses, go to Part II below. Otherwise, go to Part III on the back	**7**	

Part II   Long-Term Capital Gains and Losses—Assets Held More Than One Year

See instructions for how to figure the amounts to enter on the lines below. This form may be easier to complete if you round off cents to whole dollars.	(d) Proceeds (sales price)	(e) Cost (or other basis)	(g) Adjustments to gain or loss from Form(s) 8949, Part II, line 2, column (g)	(h) Gain or (loss) Subtract column (e) from column (d) and combine the result with column (g)
8a Totals for all long-term transactions reported on Form 1099-B for which basis was reported to the IRS and for which you have no adjustments (see instructions). However, if you choose to report all these transactions on Form 8949, leave this line blank and go to line 8b .				
8b Totals for all transactions reported on Form(s) 8949 with **Box D** checked				
9 Totals for all transactions reported on Form(s) 8949 with **Box E** checked				
10 Totals for all transactions reported on Form(s) 8949 with **Box F** checked.				

11 Gain from Form 4797, Part I; long-term gain from Forms 2439 and 6252; and long-term gain or (loss) from Forms 4684, 6781, and 8824	**11**	
12 Net long-term gain or (loss) from partnerships, S corporations, estates, and trusts from Schedule(s) K-1	**12**	
13 Capital gain distributions. See the instructions	**13**	
14 Long-term capital loss carryover. Enter the amount, if any, from line 13 of your **Capital Loss Carryover Worksheet** in the instructions	**14**	( )
15 **Net long-term capital gain or (loss).** Combine lines 8a through 14 in column (h). Then go to Part III on the back	**15**	

For Paperwork Reduction Act Notice, see your tax return instructions.   Cat. No. 11338H   Schedule D (Form 1040) 2015

| **Part III** | **Summary** |

16 Combine lines 7 and 15 and enter the result **16**

> - If line 16 is a **gain,** enter the amount from line 16 on Form 1040, line 13, or Form 1040NR, line 14. Then go to line 17 below.
> - If line 16 is a **loss,** skip lines 17 through 20 below. Then go to line 21. Also be sure to complete line 22.
> - If line 16 is **zero,** skip lines 17 through 21 below and enter -0- on Form 1040, line 13, or Form 1040NR, line 14. Then go to line 22.

17 Are lines 15 and 16 **both** gains?
☐ **Yes.** Go to line 18.
☐ **No.** Skip lines 18 through 21, and go to line 22.

18 Enter the amount, if any, from line 7 of the **28% Rate Gain Worksheet** in the instructions . . ▶ **18**

19 Enter the amount, if any, from line 18 of the **Unrecaptured Section 1250 Gain Worksheet** in the instructions . . . . ▶ **19**

20 Are lines 18 and 19 **both** zero or blank?
☐ **Yes.** Complete the **Qualified Dividends and Capital Gain Tax Worksheet** in the instructions for Form 1040, line 44 (or in the instructions for Form 1040NR, line 42). **Do not** complete lines 21 and 22 below.

☐ **No.** Complete the **Schedule D Tax Worksheet** in the instructions. **Do not** complete lines 21 and 22 below.

21 If line 16 is a loss, enter here and on Form 1040, line 13, or Form 1040NR, line 14, the **smaller** of:

- The loss on line 16 or
- ($3,000), or if married filing separately, ($1,500) . . . . **21** ( )

Note: When figuring which amount is smaller, treat both amounts as positive numbers.

22 Do you have qualified dividends on Form 1040, line 9b, or Form 1040NR, line 10b?

☐ **Yes.** Complete the **Qualified Dividends and Capital Gain Tax Worksheet** in the instructions for Form 1040, line 44 (or in the instructions for Form 1040NR, line 42).

☐ **No.** Complete the rest of Form 1040 or Form 1040NR.

SCHEDULE E (Form 1040)	Supplemental Income and Loss	OMB No. 1545-0074

SCHEDULE E
(Form 1040)

Department of the Treasury
Internal Revenue Service (99)

Supplemental Income and Loss
(From rental real estate, royalties, partnerships, S corporations, estates, trusts, REMICs, etc.)
► **Attach to Form 1040, 1040NR, or Form 1041.**
► **Information about Schedule E and its separate instructions is at** *www.irs.gov/schedulee.*

OMB No. 1545-0074

2015

Attachment
Sequence No. **13**

Name(s) shown on return | Your social security number

Part I **Income or Loss From Rental Real Estate and Royalties** **Note:** If you are in the business of renting personal property, use **Schedule C** or **C-EZ** (see instructions). If you are an individual, report farm rental income or loss from **Form 4835** on page 2, line 40.

A Did you make any payments in 2015 that would require you to file Form(s) 1099? (see instructions) ☐ Yes ☐ No
B If "Yes," did you or will you file required Forms 1099? ☐ Yes ☐ No

1a Physical address of each property (street, city, state, ZIP code)
A
B
C

1b	Type of Property (from list below)	2	For each rental real estate property listed above, report the number of fair rental and personal use days. Check the **QJV** box only if you meet the requirements to file as a qualified joint venture. See instructions.		Fair Rental Days	Personal Use Days	QJV
A				A			☐
B				B			☐
C				C			☐

Type of Property:
1 Single Family Residence
2 Multi-Family Residence
3 Vacation/Short-Term Rental
4 Commercial
5 Land
6 Royalties
7 Self-Rental
8 Other (describe)

Income:	Properties:		A		B		C	
3 Rents received		3						
4 Royalties received		4						
Expenses:								
5 Advertising		5						
6 Auto and travel (see instructions)		6						
7 Cleaning and maintenance		7						
8 Commissions		8						
9 Insurance		9						
10 Legal and other professional fees		10						
11 Management fees		11						
12 Mortgage interest paid to banks, etc. (see instructions)		12						
13 Other interest		13						
14 Repairs		14						
15 Supplies		15						
16 Taxes		16						
17 Utilities		17						
18 Depreciation expense or depletion		18						
19 Other (list) ► _____		19						
20 Total expenses. Add lines 5 through 19		20						
21 Subtract line 20 from line 3 (rents) and/or 4 (royalties). If result is a (loss), see instructions to find out if you must file **Form 6198**		21						
22 Deductible rental real estate loss after limitation, if any, on **Form 8582** (see instructions)		22	(	) (		) (		)

23a	Total of all amounts reported on line 3 for all rental properties	23a	
b	Total of all amounts reported on line 4 for all royalty properties	23b	
c	Total of all amounts reported on line 12 for all properties	23c	
d	Total of all amounts reported on line 18 for all properties	23d	
e	Total of all amounts reported on line 20 for all properties	23e	
24	**Income.** Add positive amounts shown on line 21. **Do not** include any losses	24	
25	**Losses.** Add royalty losses from line 21 and rental real estate losses from line 22. Enter total losses here	25	( )
26	**Total rental real estate and royalty income or (loss).** Combine lines 24 and 25. Enter the result here. If Parts II, III, IV, and line 40 on page 2 do not apply to you, also enter this amount on Form 1040, line 17, or Form 1040NR, line 18. Otherwise, include this amount in the total on line 41 on page 2	26	

For Paperwork Reduction Act Notice, see the separate instructions.   Cat. No. 11344L   Schedule E (Form 1040) 2015

Name(s) shown on return. Do not enter name and social security number if shown on other side. | Your social security number

Caution. The IRS compares amounts reported on your tax return with amounts shown on Schedule(s) K-1.

Part II Income or Loss From Partnerships and S Corporations
Note: If you report a loss from an at-risk activity for which **any** amount is **not** at risk, you **must** check the box in column **(e)** on line 28 and attach **Form 6198**. See instructions.

27 Are you reporting any loss not allowed in a prior year due to the at-risk, excess farm loss, or basis limitations, a prior year unallowed loss from a passive activity (if that loss was not reported on Form 8582), or unreimbursed partnership expenses? If you answered "Yes," see instructions before completing this section.   ☐ **Yes**   ☐ **No**

28	(a) Name	(b) Enter **P** for partnership; **S** for S corporation	(c) Check if foreign partnership	(d) Employer identification number	(e) Check if any amount is not at risk
A			☐		☐
B			☐		☐
C			☐		☐
D			☐		☐

	Passive Income and Loss		Nonpassive Income and Loss		
	(f) Passive loss allowed (attach **Form 8582** if required)	(g) Passive income from **Schedule K-1**	(h) Nonpassive loss from **Schedule K-1**	(i) Section 179 expense deduction from **Form 4562**	(j) Nonpassive income from **Schedule K-1**
A					
B					
C					
D					
29a Totals					
b Totals					

30	Add columns (g) and (j) of line 29a	30	
31	Add columns (f), (h), and (i) of line 29b	31	( )
32	**Total partnership and S corporation income or (loss).** Combine lines 30 and 31. Enter the result here and include in the total on line 41 below	32	

Part III Income or Loss From Estates and Trusts

33	(a) Name	(b) Employer identification number
A		
B		

	Passive Income and Loss		Nonpassive Income and Loss	
	(c) Passive deduction or loss allowed (attach **Form 8582** if required)	(d) Passive income from **Schedule K-1**	(e) Deduction or loss from **Schedule K-1**	(f) Other income from **Schedule K-1**
A				
B				
34a Totals				
b Totals				

35	Add columns (d) and (f) of line 34a	35	
36	Add columns (c) and (e) of line 34b	36	( )
37	**Total estate and trust income or (loss).** Combine lines 35 and 36. Enter the result here and include in the total on line 41 below	37	

Part IV Income or Loss From Real Estate Mortgage Investment Conduits (REMICs)—Residual Holder

38	(a) Name	(b) Employer identification number	(c) Excess inclusion from **Schedules Q,** line 2c (see instructions)	(d) Taxable income (net loss) from **Schedules Q,** line 1b	(e) Income from **Schedules Q,** line 3b

39	Combine columns (d) and (e) only. Enter the result here and include in the total on line 41 below	39	

Part V Summary

40	Net farm rental income or (loss) from **Form 4835**. Also, complete line 42 below	40	
41	**Total income or (loss).** Combine lines 26, 32, 37, 39, and 40. Enter the result here and on Form 1040, line 17, or Form 1040NR, line 18 ▶	41	

42	**Reconciliation of farming and fishing income.** Enter your **gross** farming and fishing income reported on Form 4835, line 7; Schedule K-1 (Form 1065), box 14, code B; Schedule K-1 (Form 1120S), box 17, code V; and Schedule K-1 (Form 1041), box 14, code F (see instructions) . .	42	
43	**Reconciliation for real estate professionals.** If you were a real estate professional (see instructions), enter the net income or (loss) you reported anywhere on Form 1040 or Form 1040NR from all rental real estate activities in which you materially participated under the passive activity loss rules . .	43	

SCHEDULE SE
(Form 1040)

Department of the Treasury
Internal Revenue Service (99)

Self-Employment Tax

▶ Information about Schedule SE and its separate instructions is at *www.irs.gov/schedulese.*

▶ **Attach to Form 1040 or Form 1040NR.**

OMB No. 1545-0074

2015

Attachment
Sequence No. **17**

Name of person with **self-employment** income (as shown on Form 1040 or Form 1040NR)	Social security number of person with **self-employment** income ▶

Before you begin: To determine if you must file Schedule SE, see the instructions.

May I Use Short Schedule SE or Must I Use Long Schedule SE?

Note. Use this flowchart **only if** you must file Schedule SE. If unsure, see *Who Must File Schedule SE* in the instructions.

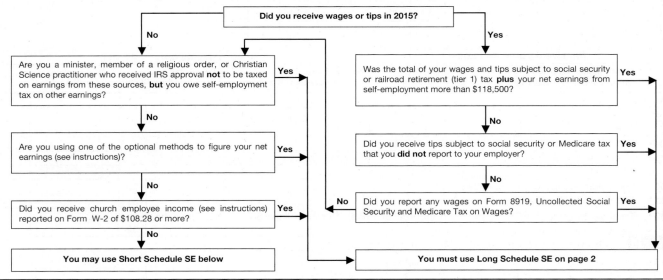

Section A—Short Schedule SE.   Caution.   Read above to see if you can use Short Schedule SE.

1a	Net farm profit or (loss) from Schedule F, line 34, and farm partnerships, Schedule K-1 (Form 1065), box 14, code A	**1a**		
b	If you received social security retirement or disability benefits, enter the amount of Conservation Reserve Program payments included on Schedule F, line 4b, or listed on Schedule K-1 (Form 1065), box 20, code Z	**1b**	(	)
2	Net profit or (loss) from Schedule C, line 31; Schedule C-EZ, line 3; Schedule K-1 (Form 1065), box 14, code A (other than farming); and Schedule K-1 (Form 1065-B), box 9, code J1. Ministers and members of religious orders, see instructions for types of income to report on this line. See instructions for other income to report	**2**		
3	Combine lines 1a, 1b, and 2	**3**		
4	Multiply line 3 by 92.35% (.9235). If less than $400, you do not owe self-employment tax; **do not** file this schedule unless you have an amount on line 1b . . . . ▶	**4**		
	Note. If line 4 is less than $400 due to Conservation Reserve Program payments on line 1b, see instructions.			
5	**Self-employment tax.** If the amount on line 4 is: • $118,500 or less, multiply line 4 by 15.3% (.153). Enter the result here and on **Form 1040, line 57,** or **Form 1040NR, line 55** • More than $118,500, multiply line 4 by 2.9% (.029). Then, add $14,694 to the result. Enter the total here and on **Form 1040, line 57,** or **Form 1040NR, line 55**	**5**		
6	**Deduction for one-half of self-employment tax.** Multiply line 5 by 50% (.50). Enter the result here and on **Form 1040, line 27,** or **Form 1040NR, line 27**	**6**		

For Paperwork Reduction Act Notice, see your tax return instructions.   Cat. No. 11358Z   **Schedule SE (Form 1040) 2015**

Schedule SE (Form 1040) 2015   Attachment Sequence No. **17**   Page **2**

| Name of person with **self-employment** income (as shown on Form 1040 or Form 1040NR) | Social security number of person with **self-employment** income ▶ | |

Section B—Long Schedule SE

Part I   Self-Employment Tax

Note. If your only income subject to self-employment tax is **church employee income,** see instructions. Also see instructions for the definition of church employee income.

A   If you are a minister, member of a religious order, or Christian Science practitioner **and** you filed Form 4361, but you had $400 or more of **other** net earnings from self-employment, check here and continue with Part I . . . . ▶ ☐

1a	Net farm profit or (loss) from Schedule F, line 34, and farm partnerships, Schedule K-1 (Form 1065), box 14, code A. **Note.** Skip lines 1a and 1b if you use the farm optional method (see instructions)	**1a**		
b	If you received social security retirement or disability benefits, enter the amount of Conservation Reserve Program payments included on Schedule F, line 4b, or listed on Schedule K-1 (Form 1065), box 20, code Z	**1b**	(	)
2	Net profit or (loss) from Schedule C, line 31; Schedule C-EZ, line 3; Schedule K-1 (Form 1065), box 14, code A (other than farming); and Schedule K-1 (Form 1065-B), box 9, code J1. Ministers and members of religious orders, see instructions for types of income to report on this line. See instructions for other income to report. **Note.** Skip this line if you use the nonfarm optional method (see instructions)	**2**		
3	Combine lines 1a, 1b, and 2	**3**		
4a	If line 3 is more than zero, multiply line 3 by 92.35% (.9235). Otherwise, enter amount from line 3	**4a**		
	Note. If line 4a is less than $400 due to Conservation Reserve Program payments on line 1b, see instructions.			
b	If you elect one or both of the optional methods, enter the total of lines 15 and 17 here . .	**4b**		
c	Combine lines 4a and 4b. If less than $400, **stop;** you do not owe self-employment tax. **Exception.** If less than $400 and you had **church employee income,** enter -0- and continue ▶	**4c**		
5a	Enter your **church employee income** from Form W-2. See instructions for definition of church employee income . . . **5a**			
b	Multiply line 5a by 92.35% (.9235). If less than $100, enter -0-	**5b**		
6	Add lines 4c and 5b	**6**		
7	Maximum amount of combined wages and self-employment earnings subject to social security tax or the 6.2% portion of the 7.65% railroad retirement (tier 1) tax for 2015	**7**	118,500	00
8a	Total social security wages and tips (total of boxes 3 and 7 on Form(s) W-2) and railroad retirement (tier 1) compensation. If $118,500 or more, skip lines 8b through 10, and go to line 11 **8a**			
b	Unreported tips subject to social security tax (from Form 4137, line 10) **8b**			
c	Wages subject to social security tax (from Form 8919, line 10) **8c**			
d	Add lines 8a, 8b, and 8c	**8d**		
9	Subtract line 8d from line 7. If zero or less, enter -0- here and on line 10 and go to line 11 . ▶	**9**		
10	Multiply the **smaller** of line 6 or line 9 by 12.4% (.124)	**10**		
11	Multiply line 6 by 2.9% (.029)	**11**		
12	**Self-employment tax.** Add lines 10 and 11. Enter here and on **Form 1040, line 57,** or **Form 1040NR, line 55**	**12**		
13	**Deduction for one-half of self-employment tax.** Multiply line 12 by 50% (.50). Enter the result here and on **Form 1040, line 27,** or **Form 1040NR, line 27** **13**			

Part II   Optional Methods To Figure Net Earnings   (see instructions)

Farm Optional Method. You may use this method **only** if **(a)** your gross farm income[1] was not more than $7,320, **or (b)** your net farm profits[2] were less than $5,284.

14	Maximum income for optional methods	**14**	4,880	00
15	Enter the **smaller** of: two-thirds (²/₃) of gross farm income[1] (not less than zero) **or** $4,880. Also include this amount on line 4b above	**15**		

Nonfarm Optional Method. You may use this method **only** if **(a)** your net nonfarm profits[3] were less than $5,284 and also less than 72.189% of your gross nonfarm income,[4] **and (b)** you had net earnings from self-employment of at least $400 in 2 of the prior 3 years. **Caution.** You may use this method no more than five times.

16	Subtract line 15 from line 14	**16**		
17	Enter the **smaller** of: two-thirds (²/₃) of gross nonfarm income[4] (not less than zero) **or** the amount on line 16. Also include this amount on line 4b above	**17**		

[1] From Sch. F, line 9, and Sch. K-1 (Form 1065), box 14, code B.
[2] From Sch. F, line 34, and Sch. K-1 (Form 1065), box 14, code A—minus the amount you would have entered on line 1b had you not used the optional method.
[3] From Sch. C, line 31; Sch. C-EZ, line 3; Sch. K-1 (Form 1065), box 14, code A; and Sch. K-1 (Form 1065-B), box 9, code J1.
[4] From Sch. C, line 7; Sch. C-EZ, line 1; Sch. K-1 (Form 1065), box 14, code C; and Sch. K-1 (Form 1065-B), box 9, code J2.

Schedule SE (Form 1040) 2015

Form **8949**

Department of the Treasury
Internal Revenue Service

Sales and Other Dispositions of Capital Assets

▶ Information about Form 8949 and its separate instructions is at *www.irs.gov/form8949.*

▶ File with your Schedule D to list your transactions for lines 1b, 2, 3, 8b, 9, and 10 of Schedule D.

OMB No. 1545-0074

2015

Attachment
Sequence No. **12A**

Name(s) shown on return

Social security number or taxpayer identification number

Before you check Box A, B, or C below, see whether you received any Form(s) 1099-B or substitute statement(s) from your broker. A substitute statement will have the same information as Form 1099-B. Either will show whether your basis (usually your cost) was reported to the IRS by your broker and may even tell you which box to check.

Part I   **Short-Term.** Transactions involving capital assets you held 1 year or less are short term. For long-term transactions, see page 2.

Note: You may aggregate all short-term transactions reported on Form(s) 1099-B showing basis was reported to the IRS and for which no adjustments or codes are required. Enter the totals directly on Schedule D, line 1a; you aren't required to report these transactions on Form 8949 (see instructions).

You *must* check Box A, B, *or* C below. **Check only one box.** If more than one box applies for your short-term transactions, complete a separate Form 8949, page 1, for each applicable box. If you have more short-term transactions than will fit on this page for one or more of the boxes, complete as many forms with the same box checked as you need.

- ☐ **(A)** Short-term transactions reported on Form(s) 1099-B showing basis was reported to the IRS (see **Note** above)
- ☐ **(B)** Short-term transactions reported on Form(s) 1099-B showing basis was **not** reported to the IRS
- ☐ **(C)** Short-term transactions not reported to you on Form 1099-B

1 (a) Description of property (Example: 100 sh. XYZ Co.)	(b) Date acquired (Mo., day, yr.)	(c) Date sold or disposed of (Mo., day, yr.)	(d) Proceeds (sales price) (see instructions)	(e) Cost or other basis. See the **Note** below and see *Column (e)* in the separate instructions	Adjustment, if any, to gain or loss. If you enter an amount in column (g), enter a code in column (f). See the separate instructions. (f) Code(s) from instructions	(g) Amount of adjustment	(h) Gain or (loss). Subtract column (e) from column (d) and combine the result with column (g)
2 Totals. Add the amounts in columns (d), (e), (g), and (h) (subtract negative amounts). Enter each total here and include on your Schedule D, **line 1b** (if **Box A** above is checked), **line 2** (if **Box B** above is checked), or **line 3** (if **Box C** above is checked) ▶							

Note: If you checked Box A above but the basis reported to the IRS was incorrect, enter in column (e) the basis as reported to the IRS, and enter an adjustment in column (g) to correct the basis. See *Column (g)* in the separate instructions for how to figure the amount of the adjustment.

For Paperwork Reduction Act Notice, see your tax return instructions.   Cat. No. 37768Z   Form **8949** (2015)

Form 8949 (2015)   Attachment Sequence No. **12A**   Page **2**

Name(s) shown on return. Name and SSN or taxpayer identification no. not required if shown on other side	Social security number or taxpayer identification number

Before you check Box D, E, or F below, see whether you received any Form(s) 1099-B or substitute statement(s) from your broker. A substitute statement will have the same information as Form 1099-B. Either will show whether your basis (usually your cost) was reported to the IRS by your broker and may even tell you which box to check.

Part II **Long-Term.** Transactions involving capital assets you held more than 1 year are long term. For short-term transactions, see page 1.

Note: You may aggregate all long-term transactions reported on Form(s) 1099-B showing basis was reported to the IRS and for which no adjustments or codes are required. Enter the totals directly on Schedule D, line 8a; you aren't required to report these transactions on Form 8949 (see instructions).

You *must* check Box D, E, *or* F below. Check only one box. If more than one box applies for your long-term transactions, complete a separate Form 8949, page 2, for each applicable box. If you have more long-term transactions than will fit on this page for one or more of the boxes, complete as many forms with the same box checked as you need.

☐ **(D)** Long-term transactions reported on Form(s) 1099-B showing basis was reported to the IRS (see **Note** above)
☐ **(E)** Long-term transactions reported on Form(s) 1099-B showing basis was **not** reported to the IRS
☐ **(F)** Long-term transactions not reported to you on Form 1099-B

1 (a) Description of property (Example: 100 sh. XYZ Co.)	(b) Date acquired (Mo., day, yr.)	(c) Date sold or disposed of (Mo., day, yr.)	(d) Proceeds (sales price) (see instructions)	(e) Cost or other basis. See the **Note** below and see *Column (e)* in the separate instructions	Adjustment, if any, to gain or loss. If you enter an amount in column (g), enter a code in column (f). **See the separate instructions.** (f) Code(s) from instructions	(g) Amount of adjustment	(h) Gain or (loss). Subtract column (e) from column (d) and combine the result with column (g)

2 Totals. Add the amounts in columns (d), (e), (g), and (h) (subtract negative amounts). Enter each total here and include on your Schedule D, **line 8b** (if **Box D** above is checked), **line 9** (if **Box E** above is checked), or **line 10** (if **Box F** above is checked) ▶

Note: If you checked Box D above but the basis reported to the IRS was incorrect, enter in column (e) the basis as reported to the IRS, and enter an adjustment in column (g) to correct the basis. See *Column (g)* in the separate instructions for how to figure the amount of the adjustment.

Form **8949** (2015)

Form **8958**
(Rev. November 2014)
Department of the Treasury
Internal Revenue Service (99)

Allocation of Tax Amounts Between
Certain Individuals in Community Property States
▶ Attach to Form 1040.
▶ **Information about Form 8958 and its instructions is at** *www.irs.gov/form8958*.

OMB No. 1545-0074

Attachment
Sequence No. **63**

Your first name and initial	Your last name	Your social security number
Spouse's or partner's first name and initial	Spouse's or partner's last name	**Spouse's or partner's social security number**

	A Total Amount	B Allocated to Spouse or RDP SSN _____ - ___ - _____	C Allocated to Spouse or RDP SSN _____ - ___ - _____
1 Wages (each employer)			
2 Interest Income (each payer)			
3 Dividends (each payer)			
4 State Income Tax Refund			
5 Self-Employment Income (See instructions)			
6 Capital Gains and Losses			
7 Pension Income			
8 Rents, Royalties, Partnerships, Estates, Trusts			

For Paperwork Reduction Act Notice, see your tax return instructions.   Cat. No. 37779G   Form **8958** (Rev. 11-2014)

Form 8958 (Rev. 11-2014) Page **2**

	A Total Amount	B Allocated to Spouse or RDP SSN _____ - ___ - _____	C Allocated to Spouse or RDP SSN _____ - ___ - _____
9 Deductible part of Self-Employment Tax (See instructions)			
10 Self-Employment Tax (See instructions)			
11 Taxes Withheld			
12 Other items such as: Social Security Benefits, Unemployment Compensation, Deductions, Credits, etc.			

Form **8958** (Rev. 11-2014)

Form **8959**

Department of the Treasury
Internal Revenue Service

Additional Medicare Tax

▶ **If any line does not apply to you, leave it blank. See separate instructions.**
▶ **Attach to Form 1040, 1040NR, 1040-PR, or 1040-SS.**
▶ **Information about Form 8959 and its instructions is at** *www.irs.gov/form8959.*

OMB No. 1545-0074

2015

Attachment
Sequence No. **71**

Name(s) shown on return

Your social security number

Part I	**Additional Medicare Tax on Medicare Wages**		
1	Medicare wages and tips from Form W-2, box 5. If you have more than one Form W-2, enter the total of the amounts from box 5	**1**	
2	Unreported tips from Form 4137, line 6	**2**	
3	Wages from Form 8919, line 6	**3**	
4	Add lines 1 through 3	**4**	
5	Enter the following amount for your filing status: Married filing jointly. . . . . $250,000 Married filing separately . . . . $125,000 Single, Head of household, or Qualifying widow(er) $200,000	**5**	
6	Subtract line 5 from line 4. If zero or less, enter -0-	**6**	
7	Additional Medicare Tax on Medicare wages. Multiply line 6 by 0.9% (.009). Enter here and go to Part II	**7**	
Part II	**Additional Medicare Tax on Self-Employment Income**		
8	Self-employment income from Schedule SE (Form 1040), Section A, line 4, or Section B, line 6. If you had a loss, enter -0- (Form 1040-PR and Form 1040-SS filers, see instructions.)	**8**	
9	Enter the following amount for your filing status: Married filing jointly. . . . . $250,000 Married filing separately . . . . $125,000 Single, Head of household, or Qualifying widow(er) $200,000	**9**	
10	Enter the amount from line 4	**10**	
11	Subtract line 10 from line 9. If zero or less, enter -0- . . .	**11**	
12	Subtract line 11 from line 8. If zero or less, enter -0-	**12**	
13	Additional Medicare Tax on self-employment income. Multiply line 12 by 0.9% (.009). Enter here and go to Part III	**13**	
Part III	**Additional Medicare Tax on Railroad Retirement Tax Act (RRTA) Compensation**		
14	Railroad retirement (RRTA) compensation and tips from Form(s) W-2, box 14 (see instructions)	**14**	
15	Enter the following amount for your filing status: Married filing jointly. . . . . $250,000 Married filing separately . . . . $125,000 Single, Head of household, or Qualifying widow(er) $200,000	**15**	
16	Subtract line 15 from line 14. If zero or less, enter -0-	**16**	
17	Additional Medicare Tax on railroad retirement (RRTA) compensation. Multiply line 16 by 0.9% (.009). Enter here and go to Part IV	**17**	
Part IV	**Total Additional Medicare Tax**		
18	Add lines 7, 13, and 17. Also include this amount on Form 1040, line 62, (Form 1040NR, 1040-PR, and 1040-SS filers, see instructions) and go to Part V	**18**	
Part V	**Withholding Reconciliation**		
19	Medicare tax withheld from Form W-2, box 6. If you have more than one Form W-2, enter the total of the amounts from box 6	**19**	
20	Enter the amount from line 1	**20**	
21	Multiply line 20 by 1.45% (.0145). This is your regular Medicare tax withholding on Medicare wages	**21**	
22	Subtract line 21 from line 19. If zero or less, enter -0-. This is your Additional Medicare Tax withholding on Medicare wages	**22**	
23	Additional Medicare Tax withholding on railroad retirement (RRTA) compensation from Form W-2, box 14 (see instructions)	**23**	
24	**Total Additional Medicare Tax withholding.** Add lines 22 and 23. Also include this amount with federal income tax withholding on Form 1040, line 64 (Form 1040NR, 1040-PR, and 1040-SS filers, see instructions)	**24**	

For Paperwork Reduction Act Notice, see your tax return instructions.   Cat. No. 59475X   Form **8959** (2015)

Form **8960**

Department of the Treasury
Internal Revenue Service (99)

**Net Investment Income Tax—
Individuals, Estates, and Trusts**
▶ Attach to your tax return.
▶ **Information about Form 8960 and its separate instructions is at** *www.irs.gov/form8960.*

OMB No. 1545-2227

20**15**

Attachment
Sequence No. **72**

Name(s) shown on your tax return

Your social security number or EIN

Part I   Investment Income   ☐ Section 6013(g) election (see instructions)
☐ Section 6013(h) election (see instructions)
☐ Regulations section 1.1411-10(g) election (see instructions)

1	Taxable interest (see instructions)	**1**	
2	Ordinary dividends (see instructions)	**2**	
3	Annuities (see instructions)	**3**	
4a	Rental real estate, royalties, partnerships, S corporations, trusts, etc. (see instructions)	**4a**	
b	Adjustment for net income or loss derived in the ordinary course of a non-section 1411 trade or business (see instructions)	**4b**	
c	Combine lines 4a and 4b	**4c**	
5a	Net gain or loss from disposition of property (see instructions) .	**5a**	
b	Net gain or loss from disposition of property that is not subject to net investment income tax (see instructions)	**5b**	
c	Adjustment from disposition of partnership interest or S corporation stock (see instructions)	**5c**	
d	Combine lines 5a through 5c	**5d**	
6	Adjustments to investment income for certain CFCs and PFICs (see instructions)	**6**	
7	Other modifications to investment income (see instructions)	**7**	
8	Total investment income. Combine lines 1, 2, 3, 4c, 5d, 6, and 7	**8**	

Part II   Investment Expenses Allocable to Investment Income and Modifications

9a	Investment interest expenses (see instructions)	**9a**	
b	State, local, and foreign income tax (see instructions)	**9b**	
c	Miscellaneous investment expenses (see instructions)	**9c**	
d	Add lines 9a, 9b, and 9c	**9d**	
10	Additional modifications (see instructions)	**10**	
11	Total deductions and modifications. Add lines 9d and 10	**11**	

Part III   Tax Computation

12	Net investment income. Subtract Part II, line 11 from Part I, line 8. Individuals complete lines 13–17. Estates and trusts complete lines 18a–21. If zero or less, enter -0-	**12**	
	Individuals:		
13	Modified adjusted gross income (see instructions)	**13**	
14	Threshold based on filing status (see instructions)	**14**	
15	Subtract line 14 from line 13. If zero or less, enter -0-	**15**	
16	Enter the smaller of line 12 or line 15	**16**	
17	Net investment income tax for individuals. Multiply line 16 by 3.8% (.038). **Enter here and include on your tax return** (see instructions)	**17**	
	Estates and Trusts:		
18a	Net investment income (line 12 above)	**18a**	
b	Deductions for distributions of net investment income and deductions under section 642(c) (see instructions)	**18b**	
c	Undistributed net investment income. Subtract line 18b from 18a (see instructions). If zero or less, enter -0-	**18c**	
19a	Adjusted gross income (see instructions)	**19a**	
b	Highest tax bracket for estates and trusts for the year (see instructions)	**19b**	
c	Subtract line 19b from line 19a. If zero or less, enter -0- . . .	**19c**	
20	Enter the smaller of line 18c or line 19c	**20**	
21	Net investment income tax for estates and trusts. Multiply line 20 by 3.8% (.038). **Enter here and include on your tax return** (see instructions)	**21**	

For Paperwork Reduction Act Notice, see your tax return instructions.   Cat. No. 59474M   Form **8960** (2015)

Form **8962**

Department of the Treasury
Internal Revenue Service

Premium Tax Credit (PTC)

▶ Attach to Form 1040, 1040A, or 1040NR.
▶ **Information about Form 8962 and its separate instructions is at *www.irs.gov/form8962*.**

OMB No. 1545-0074

2015

Attachment
Sequence No. **73**

Name shown on your return

Your social security number

You cannot claim the PTC if your filing status is married filing separately unless you are eligible for an exception (see instructions). If you qualify, check the box. ☐

Part I	**Annual and Monthly Contribution Amount**

1 Tax family size. Enter the number of exemptions from Form 1040 or Form 1040A, line 6d, or Form 1040NR, line 7d   **1**

2a Modified AGI. Enter your modified AGI (see instructions) . . . . . **2a**   **b** Enter the total of your dependents' modified AGI (see instructions) . . .   **2b**

3 Household income. Add the amounts on lines 2a and 2b **3**

4 Federal poverty line. Enter the federal poverty line amount from Table 1-1, 1-2, or 1-3 (see instructions). Check the appropriate box for the federal poverty table used. **a** ☐ Alaska   **b** ☐ Hawaii   **c** ☐ Other 48 states and DC   **4**

5 Household income as a percentage of federal poverty line (see instructions) . . . .   **5**   %

6 Did you enter 401% on line 5? (See instructions if you entered less than 100%.)

☐ **No.** Continue to line 7.

☐ **Yes.** You are not eligible to receive PTC. If advance payment of the PTC was made, see the instructions for how to report your excess advance PTC repayment amount.

7 Applicable Figure. Using your line 5 percentage, locate your "applicable figure" on the table in the instructions . .   **7**

8a Annual contribution amount. Multiply line 3 by line 7 . . . . **8a**   **b** Monthly contribution amount. Divide line 8a by 12. Round to whole dollar amount . .   **8b**

Part II	**Premium Tax Credit Claim and Reconciliation of Advance Payment of Premium Tax Credit**

9 Are you allocating policy amounts with another taxpayer or do you want to use the alternative calculation for year of marriage (see instructions)?

☐ **Yes.** Skip to Part IV, Shared Policy Allocation, or Part V, Alternative Calculation for Year of Marriage.   ☐ **No.** Continue to line 10.

10 See the instructions to determine if you can use line 11 or must complete lines 12 through 23.

☐ **Yes.** Continue to line 11. Compute your annual PTC. Then skip lines 12–23 and continue to line 24.   ☐ **No.** Continue to lines 12–23. Compute your monthly PTC and continue to line 24.

Annual Calculation	(a) Annual enrollment premiums (Form(s) 1095-A, line 33A)	(b) Annual applicable SLCSP premium (Form(s) 1095-A, line 33B)	(c) Annual contribution amount (line 8a)	(d) Annual maximum premium assistance (subtract (c) from (b), if zero or less, enter -0-)	(e) Annual premium tax credit allowed (smaller of (a) or (d))	(f) Annual advance payment of PTC (Form(s) 1095-A, line 33C)
11 Annual Totals						

Monthly Calculation	(a) Monthly enrollment premiums (Form(s) 1095-A, lines 21–32, column A)	(b) Monthly applicable SLCSP premium (Form(s) 1095-A, lines 21–32, column B)	(c) Monthly contribution amount (amount from line 8b or alternative marriage monthly contribution)	(d) Monthly maximum premium assistance (subtract (c) from (b), if zero or less, enter -0-)	(e) Monthly premium tax credit allowed (smaller of (a) or (d))	(f) Monthly advance payment of PTC (Form(s) 1095-A, lines 21–32, column C)
12 January						
13 February						
14 March						
15 April						
16 May						
17 June						
18 July						
19 August						
20 September						
21 October						
22 November						
23 December						

24 Total premium tax credit. Enter the amount from line 11(e) or add lines 12(e) through 23(e) and enter the total here   **24**

25 Advance payment of PTC. Enter the amount from line 11(f) or add lines 12(f) through 23(f) and enter the total here   **25**

26 Net premium tax credit. If line 24 is greater than line 25, subtract line 25 from line 24. Enter the difference here and on Form 1040, line 69; Form 1040A, line 45; or Form 1040NR, line 65. If you elected the alternative calculation for marriage, enter zero. If line 24 equals line 25, enter zero. Stop here. If line 25 is greater than line 24, leave this line blank and continue to line 27 .   **26**

Part III	**Repayment of Excess Advance Payment of the Premium Tax Credit**

27 Excess advance payment of PTC. If line 25 is greater than line 24, subtract line 24 from line 25. Enter the difference here   **27**

28 Repayment limitation (see instructions) **28**

29 Excess advance premium tax credit repayment. Enter the smaller of line 27 or line 28 here and on Form 1040, line 46; Form 1040A, line 29; or Form 1040NR, line 44 . . . .   **29**

For Paperwork Reduction Act Notice, see your tax return instructions.   Cat. No. 37784Z   Form **8962** (2015)

Form 8962 (2015)   Page **2**

Part IV Shared Policy Allocation

Complete the following information for up to four shared policy allocations. See instructions for allocation details.

Shared Policy Allocation 1

30	**(a)** Policy Number (Form 1095-A, line 2)	**(b)** SSN of other taxpayer	**(c)** Allocation start month	**(d)** Allocation stop month

Allocation percentage applied to monthly amounts	**(e)** Premium Percentage	**(f)** SLCSP Percentage	**(g)** Advance Payment of the PTC Percentage

Shared Policy Allocation 2

31	**(a)** Policy Number (Form 1095-A, line 2)	**(b)** SSN of other taxpayer	**(c)** Allocation start month	**(d)** Allocation stop month

Allocation percentage applied to monthly amounts	**(e)** Premium Percentage	**(f)** SLCSP Percentage	**(g)** Advance Payment of the PTC Percentage

Shared Policy Allocation 3

32	**(a)** Policy Number (Form 1095-A, line 2)	**(b)** SSN of other taxpayer	**(c)** Allocation start month	**(d)** Allocation stop month

Allocation percentage applied to monthly amounts	**(e)** Premium Percentage	**(f)** SLCSP Percentage	**(g)** Advance Payment of the PTC Percentage

Shared Policy Allocation 4

33	**(a)** Policy Number (Form 1095-A, line 2)	**(b)** SSN of other taxpayer	**(c)** Allocation start month	**(d)** Allocation stop month

Allocation percentage applied to monthly amounts	**(e)** Premium Percentage	**(f)** SLCSP Percentage	**(g)** Advance Payment of the PTC Percentage

34   Have you completed shared policy allocation information for all allocated Forms 1095-A?

☐ **Yes.** Multiply the amounts on Form 1095-A by the allocation percentages entered by policy. Add allocated amounts across all allocated policies with amounts for non-allocated policies from Forms 1095-A, if any, to compute a combined total for each month. Enter the combined total for each month on lines 12–23, columns (a), (b), and (f). Compute the amounts for lines 12–23, columns (c)–(e), and continue to line 24.

☐ **No.** See the instructions to report additional shared policy allocations.

Part V Alternative Calculation for Year of Marriage

Complete line(s) 35 and/or 36 to elect the alternative calculation for year of marriage. For eligibility to make the election, see the instructions for line 9. To complete line(s) 35 and/or 36 and compute the amounts for lines 12–23, see the instructions for this Part V.

35	**Alternative entries for your SSN**	**(a)** Alternative family size	**(b)** Monthly contribution	**(c)** Alternative start month	**(d)** Alternative stop month
36	**Alternative entries for your spouse's SSN**	**(a)** Alternative family size	**(b)** Monthly contribution	**(c)** Alternative start month	**(d)** Alternative stop month

Form **8962** (2015)

Appendix C

Glossary

The key terms in this glossary have been defined to reflect their conventional use in the field of taxation. The definitions may therefore be incomplete for other purposes.

A

AAA bypass election. In the context of a distribution by an S corporation, an election made by the entity to designate that the distribution is first from accumulated earnings and profits (AEP) and only then from the accumulated adjustments account (AAA).

Abandoned spouse. The abandoned spouse provision enables a married taxpayer with a dependent child whose spouse did not live in the taxpayer's home during the last six months of the tax year to file as a head of household rather than as married filing separately.

Accelerated cost recovery system (ACRS). A method in which the cost of tangible property is recovered (depreciated) over a prescribed period of time. This depreciation approach disregards salvage value, imposes a period of cost recovery that depends upon the classification of the asset into one of various recovery periods, and prescribes the applicable percentage of cost that can be deducted each year. A modified system is currently the default cost recovery method; it is referred to as MACRS. § 168.

Accelerated death benefits. The amount received from a life insurance policy by the insured who is terminally ill or chronically ill. Any realized gain may be excluded from the gross income of the insured if the policy is surrendered to the insurer or is sold to a licensed viatical settlement provider. § 101(g).

Acceleration rule. Treatment of an intercompany transaction on a consolidated return, when a sold asset leaves the group.

Accident and health benefits. Employee fringe benefits provided by employers through the payment of health and accident insurance premiums or the establishment of employer-funded medical reimbursement plans. Employers generally are entitled to a deduction for such payments, whereas employees generally exclude such fringe benefits from gross income. §§ 105 and 106.

Accident and health insurance benefits. See *accident and health benefits*.

Accountable plan. A type of expense reimbursement plan that requires an employee to render an adequate accounting to the employer and return any excess reimbursement or allowance. If the expense qualifies, it will be treated as a deduction *for* AGI.

Accounting income. The accountant's concept of income is generally based upon the realization principle. Financial accounting income may differ from taxable income (e.g., accelerated depreciation might be used for Federal income tax and straight-line depreciation for financial accounting purposes). Differences are included in a reconciliation of taxable and accounting income on Schedule M–1 or Schedule M–3 of Form 1120 for corporations.

Accounting method. The method under which income and expenses are determined for tax purposes. Important accounting methods include the cash basis and the accrual basis. Special methods are available for the reporting of gain on installment sales, recognition of income on construction projects (the completed contract and percentage of completion methods), and the valuation of inventories (last-in, first-out and first-in, first-out). §§ 446–474.

Accounting period. The period of time, usually a year, used by a taxpayer for the determination of tax liability. Unless a fiscal year is chosen, taxpayers must determine and pay their income tax liability by using the calendar year (January 1 through December 31) as the period of measurement. An example of a fiscal year is July 1 through June 30. A change in accounting period (e.g., from a calendar year to a fiscal year) generally requires the consent of the IRS. Usually, taxpayers are free to select either an initial calendar or a fiscal year without the consent of the IRS. §§ 441–444.

Accrual method. A method of accounting that reflects expenses incurred and income earned for any one tax year. In contrast to the cash basis of accounting, expenses need not be paid to be deductible, nor need income be received to be taxable. Unearned income (e.g., prepaid interest and rent) generally is taxed in the year of receipt regardless of the method of accounting used by the taxpayer. § 446(c)(2).

Accumulated adjustments account (AAA). An account that aggregates an S corporation's post-1982 income, loss, and deductions for the tax year (including nontaxable income and nondeductible losses and expenses). After the year-end income and expense adjustments are made, the account is reduced by distributions made during the tax year.

Accumulated E & P. See *accumulated earnings and profits (AEP)*.

Accumulated earnings and profits (AEP). Net undistributed tax-basis earnings of a corporation aggregated from March 1, 1913, to the end of the prior tax year. Used to determine the amount of dividend income associated with a distribution to shareholders. § 316 and Reg. § 1.316–2.

Accumulated earnings credit. A reduction allowed in arriving at accumulated taxable income, in determining the accumulated earnings tax.

Accumulated earnings tax. A special tax imposed on C corporations that accumulate (rather than distribute) their earnings beyond the reasonable needs of the business. The accumulated earnings tax and related interest are imposed on accumulated taxable income in addition to the corporate income tax. §§ 531–537.

Accumulated taxable income (ATI). The base upon which the accumulated earnings tax is imposed. Generally, it is the taxable income of the corporation as adjusted for certain items (e.g., the Federal income tax, excess charitable contributions, the dividends received deduction) less the dividends paid deduction and the accumulated earnings credit. § 535.

Accuracy-related penalties. Major civil taxpayer penalties relating to the accuracy of tax return data, including misstatements stemming from taxpayer negligence and improper valuation of income and deductions, are coordinated under this umbrella term. The penalty usually equals 20 percent of the understated tax liability.

ACE adjustment. An adjustment in computing corporate alternative minimum taxable income (AMTI), computed at 75 percent of the excess of adjusted current earnings (ACE) over unadjusted AMTI. ACE computations reflect longer and slower cost recovery deductions and other restrictions on the timing of certain recognition events. Exempt interest, life insurance proceeds, and other receipts that are included in earnings and profits but not in taxable income also increase the ACE adjustment. If unadjusted AMTI exceeds ACE, the ACE adjustment is negative. The negative adjustment is limited to the aggregate of the positive adjustments under ACE for prior years, reduced by any previously claimed negative adjustments.

Acquiescence. Agreement by the IRS on the results reached in certain judicial decisions; sometimes abbreviated *Acq.* or *A.*

Acquisition indebtedness. Debt incurred in acquiring, constructing, or substantially improving a qualified residence of the taxpayer. The interest on such loans is deductible as qualified residence interest. However, interest on such debt is deductible only on the portion of the indebtedness that does not exceed $1,000,000 ($500,000 for married persons filing separate returns). § 163(h)(3).

Active income. Wages, salary, commissions, bonuses, profits from a trade or business in which the taxpayer is a material participant, gain on the sale or other disposition of assets used in an active trade or business, and income from intangible property if the taxpayer's personal efforts significantly contributed to the creation of the property. The passive activity loss rules require classification of income and losses into three categories with active income being one of them.

Ad valorem taxes. A tax imposed on the value of property. The most common ad valorem tax is that imposed by states, counties, and cities on real estate. Ad valorem taxes can be imposed on personal property as well.

Additional first-year depreciation. This provision, effective for property acquired after December 31, 2011, and placed in service before January 1, 2020, provides for an additional cost recovery deduction of 50 percent in the tax year the qualified property is placed in service. (The bonus depreciation percentage is reduced to 40 percent in 2018 and 30 percent in 2019.) Qualified property includes most types of new property other than buildings. The taxpayer can elect to forgo this bonus depreciation. Different rules applied between 2008 and 2011.

Adjusted basis. The cost or other basis of property reduced by depreciation allowed or allowable and increased by capital improvements. Other special adjustments are provided in § 1016 and the related Regulations.

Adjusted current earnings (ACE). Used to determine an adjustment in computing corporate alternative minimum taxable income (AMTI). ACE reflects restrictions on the timing of certain recognition events. Exempt interest, life insurance proceeds, and other receipts that are included in earnings and profits but not in taxable income also increase ACE.

Adjustments. See *AMT adjustments*.

Adoption expenses credit. A provision intended to assist taxpayers who incur nonrecurring costs directly associated with the adoption process, such as legal costs, social service review costs, and transportation costs. Up to $13,460 of costs incurred to adopt an eligible child qualify for the credit (unique rules apply when adopting a special needs child). A taxpayer may claim the credit in the year qualifying expenses are paid or incurred if the expenses are paid during or after the year in which the adoption is finalized. For qualifying expenses paid or incurred in a tax year prior to the year the adoption is finalized, the credit must be claimed in the tax year following the tax year during which the expenses are paid or incurred. § 23.

Affiliated group. A parent-subsidiary group of corporations that is eligible to elect to file on a consolidated basis. Eighty percent ownership of the voting power and value of all of the corporations must be achieved every day of the tax year, and an identifiable parent corporation must exist (i.e., it must own at least 80 percent of another group member without applying attribution rules).

Aggregate (or conduit) concept. The theory of partnership taxation under which, in certain cases, a partnership is treated as a mere collection of the activities of each partner. See also *entity concept*.

Alimony and separate maintenance payments. Alimony deductions result from the payment of a legal obligation arising from the termination of a marital relationship.

Payments designated as alimony generally are included in the gross income of the recipient and are deductible *for* AGI by the payor.

Alimony recapture. The amount of alimony that previously has been included in the gross income of the recipient and deducted by the payor that now is deducted by the recipient and included in the gross income of the payor as the result of front-loading. § 71(f).

All events test. For accrual method taxpayers, income is earned when (1) all of the events have occurred that fix the right to receive the income and (2) the amount can be determined with reasonable accuracy. Accrual of income cannot be postponed simply because a portion of the income may have to be returned in a subsequent period. The all events test also is utilized to determine when expenses can be deducted by an accrual basis taxpayer. The application of the test could cause a variation between the treatment of an item for accounting and for tax purposes. For example, a reserve for warranty expense may be properly accruable under Generally Accepted Accounting Principles but not be deductible under the Federal income tax law. Because of the application of the all events test, the deduction becomes available in the year the warranty obligation becomes fixed and the amount is determinable with reasonable certainty. Reg. §§ 1.446–1(c)(1)(ii) and 1.461–1(a)(2).

Allocate. The assignment of income for various tax purposes. A multistate corporation's nonbusiness income usually is allocated to the state where the nonbusiness assets are located; it is not apportioned with the rest of the entity's income. The income and expense items of an estate or a trust are allocated between income and corpus components. Specific items of income, expense, gain, loss, and credit can be allocated to specific partners if a substantial economic nontax purpose for the allocation is established.

Alternate valuation date. Property passing from a decedent by death may be valued for estate tax purposes as of the date of death or the alternate valuation date. The alternate valuation date is six months after the date of death or the date the property is disposed of by the estate, whichever comes first. To use the alternate valuation date, the executor or administrator of the estate must make an affirmative election. Election of the alternate valuation date is not available unless it decreases the amount of the gross estate and reduces the estate tax liability.

Alternative depreciation system (ADS). A cost recovery system that produces a smaller deduction than would be calculated under ACRS or MACRS. The alternative system must be used in certain instances and can be elected in other instances. § 168(g).

Alternative minimum tax (AMT). The AMT is a fixed percentage of alternative minimum taxable income (AMTI). AMTI generally starts with the taxpayer's adjusted gross income (for individuals) or taxable income (for other taxpayers). To this amount, the taxpayer (1) adds designated preference items (e.g., tax-exempt interest income on private activity bonds), (2) makes other specified adjustments (e.g., to reflect a longer, straight-line cost recovery deduction), (3) adjusts certain AMT itemized deductions for individuals (e.g., interest incurred on housing but not

taxes paid), and (4) subtracts an exemption amount. The taxpayer must pay the greater of the resulting AMT (reduced for larger corporations by only the foreign tax credit) or the regular income tax (reduced by all allowable tax credits). The AMT does not apply at all to certain small C corporations. AMT preferences and adjustments are assigned to partners, LLC members, and S corporation shareholders.

Alternative minimum tax credit. The AMT can result from timing differences that give rise to positive adjustments in calculating the AMT base. To provide equity for the taxpayer when these timing differences reverse, the regular tax liability may be reduced by a tax credit for a prior year's minimum tax liability attributable to timing differences. § 53.

Alternative minimum taxable income (AMTI). The base (prior to deducting the exemption amount) for computing a taxpayer's alternative minimum tax. This consists of the taxable income for the year modified for AMT adjustments and AMT preferences. § 55(b)(2).

Alternative tax. An option that is allowed in computing the tax on net capital gain. For the corporate taxpayer, the rate is 35 percent (the same as the highest regular corporate tax rate). Thus, for corporate taxpayers, the alternative tax does not produce a beneficial result. For noncorporate taxpayers, the rate is usually 15 percent (but is 25 percent for unrecaptured § 1250 gain and 28 percent for collectibles and § 1202 gain). However, if the noncorporate taxpayer is in either the 10 percent or the 15 percent tax bracket, the alternative tax rate is 0 percent (rather than 15 percent). Certain high-income taxpayers (i.e., in the 39.6 percent tax bracket) have an alternative tax rate of 20 percent. §§ 1(h) and 1201.

Alternative tax NOL deduction (ATNOLD). In calculating the AMT, the taxpayer is allowed to deduct NOL carryovers and carrybacks. However, for this purpose, a special calculation is required that is referred to as the ATNOLD. The regular income tax is modified for AMT adjustments and preferences to produce the ATNOLD. § 56(d).

American Opportunity credit. This credit replaces the HOPE scholarship credit for years after 2008 and applies for qualifying expenses for the first four years of postsecondary education. Qualified expenses include tuition and related expenses and books and other course materials. Room and board are ineligible for the credit. The maximum credit available per student is $2,500 (100 percent of the first $2,000 of qualified expenses and 25 percent of the next $2,000 of qualified expenses). Eligible students include the taxpayer, taxpayer's spouse, and taxpayer's dependents. To qualify for the credit, a student must take at least one-half of the full-time course load for at least one academic term at a qualifying educational institution. The credit is phased out for higher-income taxpayers. § 25A.

Amortization. The tax deduction for the cost or other basis of an intangible asset over the asset's estimated useful life. Examples of amortizable intangibles include patents, copyrights, and leasehold interests. Most purchased intangible assets (e.g., goodwill) can be amortized for income tax purposes over a 15-year period.

Amount realized. The amount received by a taxpayer upon the sale or exchange of property. Amount realized is the sum of the cash and the fair market value of any property or services received by the taxpayer plus any related debt assumed by the buyer. Determining the amount realized is the starting point for arriving at realized gain or loss. § 1001(b).

AMT adjustments. In calculating AMTI, certain adjustments are added to or deducted from taxable income. These adjustments generally reflect timing differences. § 56.

AMT exemption. An amount deducted from alternative minimum taxable income in deriving alternative minimum tax base. The exemption amount is phased out when AMTI exceeds specified threshold amounts.

AMT preferences. In calculating alternative minimum taxable income (AMTI), certain preference items are added to taxable income. AMT preferences generally reflect differences between the regular tax and the alternative minimum tax (AMT) computational bases. For instance, interest income from certain state and local bonds may be an AMT preference item.

Annual exclusion. In computing the taxable gifts for the year, each donor excludes the first $14,000 (for 2016) of a gift to each donee. Usually, the annual exclusion is not available for gifts of future interests. § 2503(b).

Annuity. A fixed sum of money payable to a person at specified times for a specified period of time or for life. If the party making the payment (i.e., the obligor) is regularly engaged in this type of business (e.g., an insurance company), the arrangement is classified as a commercial annuity. A so-called private annuity involves an obligor that is not regularly engaged in selling annuities (e.g., a charity or family member).

Apportion. The assignment of the business income of a multistate corporation to specific states for income taxation. Usually, the apportionment procedure accounts for the property, payroll, and sales activity levels of the various states, and a proportionate assignment of the entity's total income is made using a three-factor apportionment formula. These activities indicate the commercial domicile of the corporation relative to that income. Some states exclude nonbusiness income from the apportionment procedure; they allocate nonbusiness income to the states where the nonbusiness assets are located.

Appreciated inventory. In partnership taxation, appreciated inventory is a hot asset, and a partner's share of its ordinary income potential must be allocated. If a partner sells an interest in the partnership, ordinary income is recognized to the extent of the partner's share in the partnership's inventory and unrealized receivables. The definition of "inventory" here is broad enough to include any accounts receivable, including unrealized receivables.

Arm's length. See *arm's length price.*

Arm's length price. The standard under which unrelated parties would determine an exchange price for a transaction. Suppose, for example, Cardinal Corporation sells property to its sole shareholder for $10,000. In testing whether the $10,000 is an "arm's length" price, one would ascertain the price that would have been negotiated between the corporation and an unrelated party in a bargained exchange.

ASC 740 (SFAS 109). Under Generally Accepted Accounting Principles, the rules for the financial reporting of the tax expense of an enterprise. Permanent differences affect the enterprise's effective tax rate. Temporary differences create a deferred tax asset or a deferred tax liability on the balance sheet.

ASC 740-10 (FIN 48). An interpretation by the Financial Accounting Standards Board. When an uncertain tax return position exists, this interpretation is used to determine the financial reporting treatment, if any, for the taxpayer. If it is more likely than not (i.e., a greater than 50 percent probability) that the uncertain return position will be sustained (e.g., by the courts) on its technical merits, it must be reported on the financial statements. The amount to be reported then is computed based on the probabilities of the outcome of the technical review, and the amounts at which the dispute would be resolved. If the more-likely-than-not test is failed, no current financial disclosure of the results of the return position is required.

ASC 740-30 (APB 23). Under Generally Accepted Accounting Principles, the rules for the financial reporting of the tax expense relative to a U.S. corporation's non-U.S. subsidiary. If the parent documents that it is permanently reinvesting the non-U.S. earnings of a non-U.S. subsidiary, the parent does not record as an expense any U.S. income tax the parent might pay on such earnings (i.e., the book tax expense is deferred until such earnings are, if ever, repatriated to the United States).

Asset use test. In the context of a corporate reorganization, a means by which to determine if the continuity of business enterprise requirement is met. The acquiring corporation must continue to use the target entity's assets in the acquiror's business going forward; if this is not the case, the requirement is failed.

Assignment of income. A taxpayer attempts to avoid the recognition of income by assigning to another the property that generates the income. Such a procedure will not avoid income recognition by the taxpayer making the assignment if the income was earned at the point of the transfer. In this case, the income is taxed to the person who earns it.

At-risk limitation. Generally, a taxpayer can deduct losses related to a trade or business, S corporation, partnership, or investment asset only to the extent of the at-risk amount. The taxpayer has an amount at risk in a business or investment venture to the extent that personal assets have been subjected to the risks of the business. Typically, the taxpayer's at-risk amount includes (1) the amount of money or other property that the investor contributed to the venture for the investment, (2) the amount of any of the entity's liabilities for which the taxpayer personally is liable and that relate to the investment, and (3) an allocable share of nonrecourse debts incurred by the venture from third parties in arm's length transactions for real estate investments.

Attribution. Under certain circumstances, the tax law applies attribution (constructive ownership) rules to assign to one taxpayer the ownership interest of another taxpayer. If, for example, the stock of Gold Corporation is held 60 percent by Marsha and 40 percent by Sidney, Marsha may be deemed to own 100 percent of Gold Corporation if Marsha and Sidney are mother and child. In that case, the stock owned by Sidney is attributed to Marsha. Stated differently, Marsha has a 60 percent direct and a 40 percent indirect interest in Gold Corporation. It can also be said that Marsha is the constructive owner of Sidney's interest.

Automatic mileage method. Automobile expenses are generally deductible only to the extent the automobile is used in business or for the production of income. Personal commuting expenses are not deductible. The taxpayer may deduct actual expenses (including depreciation and insurance), or the standard (automatic) mileage rate may be used (54 cents per mile for 2016 and 57.5 cents per mile for 2015). Automobile expenses incurred for medical purposes or in connection with job-related moving expenses are deductible to the extent of actual out-of-pocket expenses or at the rate of 19 cents per mile for 2016 and 23 cents per mile for 2015. For charitable activities, the rate is 14 cents per mile.

B

Bad debt. A deduction is permitted if a business account receivable subsequently becomes partially or completely worthless, providing the income arising from the debt previously was included in income. Available methods are the specific charge-off method and the reserve method. However, except for certain financial institutions, TRA of 1986 repealed the use of the reserve method for 1987 and thereafter. If the reserve method is used, partially or totally worthless accounts are charged to the reserve. A nonbusiness bad debt deduction is allowed as a short-term capital loss if the loan did not arise in connection with the creditor's trade or business activities. Loans between related parties (family members) generally are classified as nonbusiness. § 166.

Balance sheet approach. The process under ASC 740 (SFAS 109) by which an entity's deferred tax expense or deferred tax benefit is determined as a result of the reporting period's changes in the balance sheet's deferred tax asset and deferred tax liability accounts.

Basis in partnership interest. The acquisition cost of the partner's ownership interest in the partnership. Includes purchase price and associated debt acquired from other partners and in the course of the entity's trade or business.

Benchmarking. The tax professional's use of two or more entities' effective tax rates and deferred tax balance sheet accounts. Used chiefly to compare the effectiveness of the entities' tax planning techniques, and to suggest future tax-motivated courses of action.

Blockage rule. A factor to be considered in valuing a large block of corporate stock. Application of this rule generally justifies a discount in the asset's fair market value, because the disposition of a large amount of stock at any one time may depress the value of the shares in the marketplace.

Boot. Cash or property of a type not included in the definition of a tax-deferred exchange. The receipt of boot causes an otherwise tax-deferred transfer to become immediately taxable to the extent of the lesser of the fair market value of the boot or the realized gain on the transfer. For example, see transfers to controlled corporations under § 351(b), reorganizations under § 368, and like-kind exchanges under § 1031(b).

Branch profits tax. A tax on the effectively connected earnings and profits of the U.S. branch of a foreign corporation. The tax is levied in addition to the usual § 11 tax in an amount equal to 30 percent of the dividend equivalent amount. Treaties can override the tax or reduce the withholding percentage. Earnings reinvested in the U.S. operations of the entity are not subject to the tax until repatriation.

Built-in gains tax. A penalty tax designed to discourage a shift of the incidence of taxation on unrealized gains from a C corporation to its shareholders, via an S election. Under this provision, any recognized gain during the first 10 (or seven or five) years of S status generates a corporate-level tax on a base not to exceed the aggregate untaxed built-in gains brought into the S corporation upon its election from C corporation taxable years.

Built-in loss property. Property contributed to a corporation under § 351 or as a contribution to capital that has a basis in excess of its fair market value. An adjustment is necessary to step down the basis of the property to its fair market value. The adjustment prevents the corporation and the contributing shareholder from obtaining a double tax benefit. The corporation allocates the adjustment proportionately among the assets with the built-in loss. As an alternative to the corporate adjustment, the shareholder may elect to reduce the basis in the stock.

Business bad debt. A tax deduction allowed for obligations obtained in connection with a trade or business that have become either partially or completely worthless. In contrast to nonbusiness bad debts, business bad debts are deductible as business expenses. § 166.

Business purpose. A justifiable business reason for carrying out a transaction. Mere tax avoidance is not an acceptable business purpose. The presence of a business purpose is crucial in the area of corporate reorganizations and certain liquidations.

Buy-sell agreement. An arrangement, particularly appropriate in the case of a closely held corporation or a partnership, whereby the surviving owners (shareholders or partners) or the entity agrees to purchase the interest of a withdrawing owner. The buy-sell agreement provides for an orderly disposition of an interest in a business and may aid in setting the value of the interest for estate tax purposes.

Bypass amount. The amount that can be transferred by gift or at death free of any unified transfer tax. For 2016, the bypass amount is $5.45 million for estate tax and $5.45 million for gift tax.

Bypass election. In the context of a distribution by an S corporation, an election made by the entity to designate that the distribution is first from accumulated earnings and profits and only then from the accumulated adjustments account (AAA).

C

C corporation. A separate taxable entity subject to the rules of Subchapter C of the Code. This business form may create a double taxation effect relative to its shareholders. The entity is subject to the regular corporate tax and a number of penalty taxes at the Federal level.

Cafeteria benefit plans. See *cafeteria plan*.

Cafeteria plan. An employee benefit plan under which an employee is allowed to select from among a variety of employer-provided fringe benefits. Some of the benefits may be taxable, and some may be statutory nontaxable benefits (e.g., health and accident insurance and group term life insurance). The employee is taxed only on the taxable benefits selected. A cafeteria benefit plan is also referred to as a flexible benefit plan. § 125.

Capital account. The financial accounting analog of a partner's tax basis in the entity.

Capital asset. Broadly speaking, all assets are capital except those specifically excluded from that definition by the Code. Major categories of noncapital assets include property held for resale in the normal course of business (inventory), trade accounts and notes receivable, and depreciable property and real estate used in a trade or business (§ 1231 assets). § 1221.

Capital contribution. Various means by which a shareholder makes additional funds available to the corporation (placed at the risk of the business), sometimes without the receipt of additional stock. If no stock is received, the contributions are added to the basis of the shareholder's existing stock investment and do not generate gross income to the corporation. § 118.

Capital gains. The gain from the sale or exchange of a capital asset.

Capital gain property. Property contributed to a charitable organization that if sold rather than contributed, would have resulted in long-term capital gain to the donor.

Capital interest. Usually, the percentage of the entity's net assets that a partner would receive on liquidation. Typically determined by the partner's capital sharing ratio.

Capital losses. The loss from the sale or exchange of a capital asset.

Capital sharing ratio. A partner's percentage ownership of the entity's capital.

Cash balance plan. A hybrid form of pension plan similar in some aspects to a defined benefit plan. Such a plan is funded by the employer, and the employer bears the investment risks and rewards. But like defined contribution plans, a cash balance plan establishes allocations to individual employee accounts, and the payout for an employee depends on investment performance.

Cash method. See *cash receipts method.*

Cash receipts method. A method of accounting that reflects deductions as paid and income as received in any one tax year. However, deductions for prepaid expenses that benefit more than one tax year (e.g., prepaid rent and prepaid interest) usually are spread over the period benefited rather than deducted in the year paid. § 446(c)(1).

Casualty loss. A casualty is defined as "the complete or partial destruction of property resulting from an identifiable event of a sudden, unexpected or unusual nature" (e.g., floods, storms, fires, auto accidents). Individuals may deduct a casualty loss only if the loss is incurred in a trade or business or in a transaction entered into for profit or arises from fire, storm, shipwreck, or other casualty or from theft. Individuals usually deduct personal casualty losses as itemized deductions subject to a $100 nondeductible amount and to an annual floor equal to 10 percent of adjusted gross income that applies after the $100 per casualty floor has been applied. Special rules are provided for the netting of certain casualty gains and losses.

Certiorari. Appeal from a U.S. Court of Appeals to the U.S. Supreme Court is by Writ of Certiorari. The Supreme Court does not have to accept the appeal and usually does not (*cert. den.*) unless there is a conflict among the lower courts that needs to be resolved or a constitutional issue is involved.

Charitable contribution. Contributions are deductible (subject to various restrictions and ceiling limitations) if made to qualified nonprofit charitable organizations. A cash basis taxpayer is entitled to a deduction solely in the year of payment. Accrual basis corporations may accrue contributions at year-end if payment is properly authorized before the end of the year and payment is made within two and one-half months after the end of the year. § 170.

Check-the-box Regulations. By using the check-the-box rules prudently, an entity can select the most attractive tax results offered by the Code, without being bound by legal forms. By default, an unincorporated entity with more than one owner is taxed as a partnership; an unincorporated entity with one owner is a disregarded entity, taxed as a sole proprietorship or corporate division. No action is necessary by the taxpayer if the legal form or default status is desired. Form 8832 is used to "check a box" and change the tax status. Not available if the entity is incorporated under state law.

Child tax credit. A tax credit based solely on the number of qualifying children under age 17. The maximum credit available is $1,000 per child. A qualifying child must be claimed as a dependent on a parent's tax return to qualify for the credit. Taxpayers who qualify for the child tax credit may also qualify for a supplemental credit. The supplemental credit is treated as a component of the earned income credit and is therefore refundable. The credit is phased out for higher-income taxpayers. § 24.

Circuit Court of Appeals. Any of 13 Federal courts that consider tax matters appealed from the U.S. Tax Court, a U.S. District Court, or the U.S. Court of Federal Claims. Appeal from a U.S. Court of Appeals is to the U.S. Supreme Court by Certiorari.

Circular 230. A portion of the Federal tax Regulations that describes the levels of conduct at which a tax preparer must operate. Circular 230 dictates, for instance, that a tax preparer may not charge an unconscionable fee or delay the execution of a tax audit with inappropriate delays. Circular 230 requires that there be a reasonable basis for a tax return position and that no frivolous returns be filed.

Citator. A tax research resource that presents the judicial history of a court case and traces the subsequent references to the case. When these references include the citating cases' evaluations of the cited case's precedents, the research can obtain some measure of the efficacy and reliability of the original holding.

Claim of right doctrine. A judicially imposed doctrine applicable to both cash and accrual basis taxpayers that holds that an amount is includible in income upon actual or constructive receipt if the taxpayer has an unrestricted claim to the payment. For the tax treatment of amounts repaid when previously included in income under the claim of right doctrine, see § 1341.

Closely held C corporation. A regular corporation (i.e., the S election is not in effect) for which more than 50 percent of the value of its outstanding stock is owned, directly or indirectly, by five or fewer individuals at any time during the tax year. The term is relevant in identifying C corporations that are subject to the passive activity loss provisions. § 469.

Closely held corporation. A corporation where stock ownership is not widely dispersed. Rather, a few shareholders are in control of corporate policy and are in a position to benefit personally from that policy.

Closing agreement. In a tax dispute, the parties sign a closing agreement to spell out the terms under which the matters are settled. The agreement is binding on both the Service and the taxpayer.

Collectibles. A special type of capital asset, the gain from which is taxed at a maximum rate of 28 percent if the holding period is more than one year. Examples include art, rugs, antiques, gems, metals, stamps, some coins and bullion, and alcoholic beverages held for investment.

Combined return. In multistate taxation, a group of unitary corporations may elect or be required to file an income tax return that includes operating results for all of the affiliates, not just those with nexus in the state. Thus, apportionment data is reported for the group's worldwide or water's-edge operations.

Community property. Louisiana, Texas, New Mexico, Arizona, California, Washington, Idaho, Nevada, and Wisconsin have community property systems. Alaska residents can elect community property status for assets. The rest of the states are common law property jurisdictions. The difference between common law and community property systems centers around the property rights possessed by married persons. In a common law system, each spouse owns whatever he or she earns. Under a community property system, one-half of the earnings of each spouse is considered owned by the other spouse. Assume, for example, that Jeff and Alice are husband and wife and that their only income is the $50,000 annual salary Jeff receives. If they live in New York (a common law state), the $50,000 salary belongs to Jeff. If, however, they live in Texas (a community property state), the $50,000 salary is owned one-half each by Jeff and Alice.

Compensatory damages. Damages received or paid by the taxpayer can be classified as compensatory damages or as punitive damages. Compensatory damages are paid to compensate one for harm caused by another. Compensatory damages are excludible from the recipient's gross income.

Complete termination redemption. Sale or exchange treatment is available relative to this type of redemption. The shareholder must retire all of his or her outstanding shares in the corporation (ignoring family attribution rules) and cannot hold an interest, other than that of a creditor, for the 10 years following the redemption. § 302(b)(3).

Completed contract method. A method of reporting gain or loss on certain long-term contracts. Under this method of accounting, all gross income and expenses are recognized in the tax year in which the contract is completed. Reg. § 1.451–3.

Complex trust. Not a simple trust. Such trusts may have charitable beneficiaries, accumulate income, and distribute corpus. §§ 661–663.

Composite return. In multistate taxation, an S corporation may be allowed to file a single income tax return that assigns pass-through items to resident and nonresident shareholders. The composite or "block" return allows the entity to remit any tax that is attributable to the nonresident shareholders.

Conduit concept. An approach assumed by the tax law in the treatment of certain entities and their owners. Specific tax characteristics pass through the entity without losing their identity. For example, items of income and expense, capital gains and losses, tax credits, etc., realized by a partnership pass through the partnership (a conduit) and are subject to taxation at the partner level. Also, in an S corporation, certain items pass through and are reported on the returns of the shareholders.

Conservation easements. An interest in real property that maintains its natural or pristine condition. Most often it restricts the development of the property. Properly structured, the grant of such an easement can generate an income tax deduction for the donor. If the grant takes place after the owner's death, a § 2055 charitable contribution deduction results, and a portion of the property's value is excluded from the gross estate. § 2031(c).

Conservatism principle. The theory behind much of Generally Accepted Accounting Principles, under which assurance is provided that an entity's balance sheet assets are not overstated, nor liabilities understated. For instance, under ASC 740 (SFAS 109), a deferred tax asset is not recorded until it is more likely than not that the future tax benefit will be realized.

Consolidated returns. A procedure whereby certain affiliated corporations may file a single return, combine the tax transactions of each corporation, and arrive at a single income tax liability for the group. The election to file a consolidated return usually is binding on future years. §§ 1501–1505 and related Regulations.

Consolidation. The combination of two or more corporations into a newly created corporation. Thus, Black Corporation and White Corporation combine to form Gray Corporation. A consolidation may qualify as a nontaxable reorganization if certain conditions are satisfied. §§ 354 and 368(a)(1)(A).

Constructive dividend. A taxable benefit derived by a shareholder from his or her corporation that is not actually initiated by the board of directors as a dividend. Examples include unreasonable compensation, excessive rent payments, bargain purchases of corporate property, and shareholder use of corporate property. Constructive dividends generally are found in closely held corporations.

Constructive liquidation scenario. The means by which recourse debt is shared among partners in basis determination.

Constructive receipt. If income is unqualifiedly available although not physically in the taxpayer's possession, it still is subject to the income tax. An example is accrued interest on a savings account. Under the constructive receipt concept, the interest is taxed to a depositor in the year available, rather than the year actually withdrawn. The fact that the depositor uses the cash basis of accounting for tax purposes is irrelevant. See Reg. § 1.451–2.

Continuity of business enterprise. In a tax-favored reorganization, the acquiring corporation must continue the historic business of the target or use a significant portion of the target's assets in the new business.

Continuity of interest. In a tax-favored reorganization, a shareholder or corporation that has substantially the same investment after an exchange as before should not be taxed on the transaction. Specifically, the seller must acquire an equity interest in the acquiring corporation equal in value to at least 40 percent of all the outstanding stock of the target entity.

Control. Holding a specified level of stock ownership in a corporation. For § 351, the new shareholder(s) must hold at least 80 percent of the total combined voting power of all voting classes of stock and at least 80 percent of the shares of all nonvoting classes. Other tax provisions require different levels of control to bring about desired effects, such as 50 or 100 percent.

Controlled foreign corporation (CFC). A non-U.S. corporation in which more than 50 percent of the total combined voting power of all classes of stock entitled to vote or the total value of the stock of the corporation is owned by U.S. shareholders on any day during the taxable year of the foreign corporation. For purposes of this definition, a U.S. shareholder is any U.S. person who owns, or is considered to own, 10 percent or more of the total combined voting power of all classes of voting stock of the foreign corporation. Stock owned directly, indirectly, and constructively is used in this measure. See *U.S. shareholder.*

Controlled group. A controlled group of corporations is required to share the lower corporate tax rates and various other tax benefits among the members of the group. A controlled group may be either a brother-sister or a parent-subsidiary group.

Corporate liquidation. Occurs when a corporation distributes its net assets to its shareholders and ceases to be a going concern. Generally, a shareholder recognizes capital gain or loss upon the liquidation of the entity, regardless of the corporation's balance in its earnings and profits account. The liquidating corporation recognizes gain and loss on assets that it sells during the liquidation period and on assets that it distributes to shareholders in kind.

Corpus. The body or principal of a trust. Suppose, for example, Grant transfers an apartment building into a trust, income payable to Ruth for life, remainder to Shawn upon Ruth's death. Corpus of the trust is the apartment building.

Correspondence audit. An audit conducted by the IRS by the U.S. mail. Typically, the IRS writes to the taxpayer requesting the verification of a particular deduction or exemption. The remittance of copies of records or other support is requested of the taxpayer.

Cost depletion. Depletion that is calculated based on the adjusted basis of the asset. The adjusted basis is divided by the expected recoverable units to determine the depletion per unit. The depletion per unit is multiplied by the units sold during the tax year to calculate cost depletion.

Cost recovery. The system established in the Internal Revenue Code used to recover the cost of an asset using specific lives, methods, and conventions. Cost recovery methods include MACRS (generally, assets placed in service after 1986) and ACRS (generally, assets placed in service after 1980 and before 1987). § 168.

Court of Federal Claims. A trial court (court of original jurisdiction) that decides litigation involving Federal tax matters. Appeal from this court is to the Court of Appeals for the Federal Circuit.

Court of original jurisdiction. The Federal courts are divided into courts of original jurisdiction and appellate courts. A dispute between a taxpayer and the IRS is first considered by a court of original jurisdiction (i.e., a trial court). The four Federal courts of original jurisdiction are the U.S. Tax Court, the U.S. District Court, the Court of Federal Claims, and the Small Cases Division of the U.S. Tax Court.

Coverdell education savings account (§ 530 plan). Coverdell education savings account exempts from tax the earnings on amounts placed in a qualified account for the education expenses of a named beneficiary. Contributions are limited to $2,000 per year per beneficiary and the proceeds can be withdrawn without tax provided the funds are used to pay qualified educational expenses for primary, secondary, or higher education. The account is named for the late Senator Paul Coverdell (R-GA), who sponsored the legislation in Congress. § 530.

Credit for certain retirement plan contributions. A nonrefundable credit is available based on eligible contributions of up to $2,000 to certain qualified retirement plans, such as traditional and Roth IRAs and § 401(k) plans. The benefit provided by this credit is in addition to any deduction or exclusion that otherwise is available resulting from the qualifying contribution. The amount of the credit depends on the taxpayer's AGI and filing status. § 25B.

Credit for child and dependent care expenses. A tax credit ranging from 20 percent to 35 percent of employment-related expenses (child and dependent care expenses) for amounts of up to $6,000 is available to individuals who are employed (or deemed to be employed) and maintain a household for a dependent child under age 13, disabled spouse, or disabled dependent. § 21.

Credit for employer-provided child care. A nonrefundable credit is available to employers who provide child care facilities to their employees during normal working hours. The credit, limited to $150,000, is comprised of two components. The portion of the credit for qualified child care expenses is equal to 25 percent of these expenses, while the portion of the credit for qualified child care resource and referral services is equal to 10 percent of these expenses. Any qualifying expenses otherwise deductible by the taxpayer must be reduced by the amount of the credit. In addition, the taxpayer's basis for any property used for qualifying purposes is reduced by the amount of the credit. § 45F.

Credit for small employer pension plan startup costs. A nonrefundable credit available to small businesses based on administrative costs associated with establishing and maintaining certain qualified plans. While such qualifying costs generally are deductible as ordinary and necessary business expenses, the availability of the credit is intended to lower the costs of starting a qualified retirement program and therefore encourage qualifying businesses to establish retirement plans for their employees. The credit is available for eligible employers at the rate of 50 percent of qualified startup costs. The maximum credit is $500 (based on a maximum $1,000 of qualifying expenses). § 45E.

Crop insurance proceeds. The proceeds received when an insured crop is destroyed. Section 451(d) permits the farmer to defer reporting the income from the insurance proceeds until the tax year following the taxable year of the destruction.

Crop method. A method of accounting for agricultural crops that are planted in one year but harvested in a subsequent year. Under this method, the costs of raising the crop are accumulated as inventory and are deducted when the income from the crop is realized.

Cross-purchase buy-sell agreement. Under this arrangement, the surviving owners of the business agree to buy out the withdrawing owner. Assume, for example, Ron and Sara are equal shareholders in Tip Corporation. Under a cross-purchase buy-sell agreement, Ron and Sara would contract to purchase the other's interest, should that person decide to withdraw from the business.

Current E & P. Net tax-basis earnings of a corporation aggregated during the current tax year. A corporate distribution is deemed to be first from the entity's current earnings and profits and then from accumulated earnings and profits. Shareholders recognize dividend income to the extent of the earnings and profits of the corporation. A dividend results to the extent of current earnings and profits, even if there is a larger negative balance in accumulated earnings and profits.

Current tax expense. Under ASC 740 (SFAS 109), the book tax expense that relates to the current reporting period's net income and is actually payable (or creditable) to the appropriate governmental agencies for the current period. Also known as "cash tax" or "tax payable."

D

De minimis **fringe.** Benefits provided to employees that are too insignificant to warrant the time and effort required to account for the benefits received by each employee and the value of those benefits. Such amounts are excludible from the employee's gross income. § 132.

De minimis **fringe benefits.** See *de minimis fringe.*

Death benefits. A payment made by an employer to the beneficiary or beneficiaries of a deceased employee on account of the death of the employee.

Debt-financed income. Included in computations of the unrelated business income of an exempt organization, the gross income generated from debt-financed property.

Deceased spouse's unused exclusion (DSUE). In computing the Federal estate tax, the decedent uses the exclusion amount to shelter an amount of the gross estate from taxation. When the first spouse to die fails to use a portion of his/her exclusion amount, the unused portion is "portable," and becomes available to the surviving spouse. The surviving spouse can use the DSUE only of his/her last spouse to predecease.

Deduction for qualified tuition and related expenses. Taxpayers are allowed a deduction of up to $4,000 for higher education expenses. Certain taxpayers are not eligible for the deduction: those whose gross AGI exceeds a specified amount and those who can be claimed as a dependent by another taxpayer. These expenses are classified as a deduction *for* AGI, and they need not be employment-related. § 222.

Deductions *for* adjusted gross income. The Federal income tax is not imposed upon gross income. Rather, it is imposed upon taxable income. Congressionally identified deductions for individual taxpayers are subtracted either from gross income to arrive at adjusted gross income or from adjusted gross income to arrive at the tax base, taxable income.

Deductions *from* adjusted gross income. See *deductions for adjusted gross income.*

Deductions in respect of a decedent. Deductions accrued at the moment of death but not recognizable on the final income tax return of a decedent because of the method of accounting used. Such items are allowed as deductions on the estate tax return and on the income tax return of the estate (Form 1041) or the heir (Form 1040). An example of a deduction in respect of a decedent is interest expense accrued to the date of death by a cash basis debtor.

Deemed-paid credit. A foreign tax credit allowed to a U.S. taxpayer that has received an actual or constructive dividend from a non-U.S. corporation that has paid foreign income taxes. The credit is computed using the proportion of foreign income taxes paid by the payor corporation to its post-1986 undistributed earnings. Under § 78, the U.S. taxpayer claiming a deemed-paid credit includes the same amount in gross income for the tax year.

Deferred compensation. Compensation that will be taxed when received or upon the removal of certain restrictions on receipt and not when earned. Contributions by an employer to a qualified pension or profit sharing plan on behalf of an employee are an example. The contributions will not be taxed to the employee until the funds are made available or distributed to the employee (e.g., upon retirement).

Deferred tax asset. Under ASC 740 (SFAS 109), an item created on an enterprise's balance sheet by a temporary book-tax difference, such that a tax benefit is not recognized until a later date, although it already has been reported in the financial statements (e.g., the carryforward of a disallowed deduction).

Deferred tax benefit. Under ASC 740 (SFAS 109), a reduction in the book tax expense that relates to the current reporting period's net income but will not be realized until a future reporting period. Creates or adds to the entity's deferred tax asset balance sheet account. For instance, the carryforward of a net operating loss is a deferred tax benefit.

Deferred tax expense. Under ASC 740 (SFAS 109), a book tax expense that relates to the current reporting period's net income but will not be realized until a future reporting period. Creates or adds to the entity's deferred tax liability balance sheet account. For instance, a deferred tax expense is created when tax depreciation deductions for the period are "accelerated" and exceed the corresponding book depreciation expense.

Deferred tax liability. As determined under the rules of ASC 740 (SFAS 109), an item created on an enterprise's balance sheet by a temporary book-tax difference, such that a tax benefit is recognized earlier for tax purposes than it is in the financial accounting records (e.g., the use of an accelerated cost recovery deduction).

Defined benefit plan. Qualified plans can be dichotomized into defined benefit plans and defined contribution plans. Under a defined benefit plan, a formula defines the benefits employees are to receive. The formula usually includes years of service, employee compensation, and some stated percentage. The employer must make annual contributions based on actuarial computations that will be sufficient to pay the vested retirement benefits.

Defined contribution pension plan. Qualified plans can be dichotomized into defined benefit plans and defined contribution plans. Under a defined contribution plan, a separate account is maintained for each covered employee. The employee's benefits under the plan are based solely on (1) the amount contributed and (2) income from the fund that accrues to the employee's account. The plan defines the amount the employer is required to contribute (e.g., a flat dollar amount, an amount based on a special formula, or an amount equal to a certain percentage of compensation).

Dependency exemption. See *personal and dependency exemptions.*

Depletion. The process by which the cost or other basis of a natural resource (e.g., an oil or gas interest) is recovered upon extraction and sale of the resource. The two ways to determine the depletion allowance are the cost and percentage (or statutory) methods. Under cost depletion, each unit of production sold is assigned a portion of the cost or other basis of the interest. This is determined by dividing the cost or other basis by the total units expected to be recovered. Under percentage (or statutory) depletion, the tax law provides a special percentage factor for different types of minerals and other natural resources. This percentage is multiplied by the gross income from the interest to arrive at the depletion allowance. §§ 613 and 613A.

Depreciation. The deduction for the cost or other basis of a tangible asset over the asset's estimated useful life. Typically used for financial reporting purposes and for tax purposes if assets were placed in service prior to 1981 (for assets placed in service after 1980, cost recovery is used for tax purposes).

Determination letter. Upon the request of a taxpayer, the IRS will comment on the tax status of a completed transaction. Determination letters frequently are used to determine whether a retirement or profit sharing plan qualifies under the Code, and to determine the tax-exempt status of certain nonprofit organizations.

Disabled access credit. A tax credit designed to encourage small businesses to make their facilities more accessible to disabled individuals. The credit is equal to 50 percent of the eligible expenditures that exceed $250 but do not exceed $10,250. Thus, the maximum amount for the credit is $5,000. The adjusted basis for depreciation is reduced by the amount of the credit. To qualify, the facility must have been placed in service before November 6, 1990. § 44.

Disaster area losses. A casualty sustained in an area designated as a disaster area by the president of the United States. In such an event, the disaster loss may be treated as having occurred in the taxable year immediately preceding the year in which the disaster actually occurred. Thus, immediate tax benefits are provided to victims of a disaster. § 165(i).

Disclaimer. Rejections, refusals, or renunciations of claims, powers, or property. Section 2518 sets forth the conditions required to avoid gift tax consequences as the result of a disclaimer.

Disguised sale. When a partner contributes property to the entity and soon thereafter receives a distribution from the partnership, the transactions are collapsed and the distribution is seen as a purchase of the asset by the partnership. § 707(a)(2)(B).

Disproportionate distribution. A distribution from a partnership to one or more of its partners in which at least one partner's interest in partnership hot assets is increased or decreased. For example, a distribution of cash to one partner and hot assets to another changes both partners' interest in hot assets and is disproportionate. The intent of rules for taxation of disproportionate distributions is to ensure that each partner eventually recognizes his or her proportionate share of partnership ordinary income.

Disproportionate redemption. Sale or exchange treatment is available relative to this type of redemption. After the exchange, the shareholder owns less than 80 percent of his or her pre-redemption interest in the corporation and only a minority interest in the entity. § 302(b)(2).

Disregarded entity. The Federal income tax treatment of business income usually follows the legal form of the taxpayer (i.e., an individual's sole proprietorship is reported on the Form 1040); a C corporation's taxable income is computed on Form 1120. The check-the-box Regulations are used if the unincorporated taxpayer wants to use a different tax regime. Under these rules, a disregarded entity is taxed as an individual or a corporate division; other tax regimes are not available. For instance, a one-member limited liability company is a disregarded entity.

Distributable net income (DNI). The measure that determines the nature and amount of the distributions from estates and trusts that the beneficiaries must include in income. DNI also limits the amount that estates and trusts can claim as a deduction for such distributions. § 643(a).

District Court. See *Federal District Court.*

Dividend. A nondeductible distribution to the shareholders of a corporation. A dividend constitutes gross income to the recipient if it is paid from the current or accumulated earnings and profits of the corporation.

Dividend equivalent amount (DEA). The amount subject to the branch profits tax, it is equal to the effectively connected E & P of the U.S. branch of a foreign corporation, reduced/ (increased) by an increase/(reduction) in U.S. net equity.

Dividends received deduction. A deduction allowed a shareholder that is a corporation for dividends received from a domestic corporation. The deduction usually is 70 percent of the dividends received, but it could be 80 or 100 percent depending upon the ownership percentage held by the recipient corporation. §§ 243–246.

Divisive reorganization. A "Type D" spin-off, split-off, or split-up, reorganization in which the original corporation divides its active business (in existence for at least five years) assets among two or more corporations. The stock received by the original corporation shareholders must be at least 80 percent of the other corporations.

Dock sales. A purchaser uses its owned or rented vehicles to take possession of the product at the seller's shipping dock. In most states, the sale is apportioned to the operating state of the purchaser, rather than the seller. See also *apportion* and *sales factor.*

Dollar-value LIFO. An inventory technique that focuses on the dollars invested in the inventory rather than the particular items on hand each period. Each inventory item is assigned to a pool. A pool is a collection of similar items and is treated as a separate inventory. At the end of the period, each pool is valued in terms of prices at the time LIFO was adopted (base period prices), whether or not the particular items were actually on hand in the year LIFO was adopted, to compare with current prices to determine if there has been an increase or decrease in inventories.

Domestic production activities deduction (DPAD). A deduction based on 9 percent of the lesser of qualified production activities income (QPAI) or taxable income (for a corporate taxpayer). The deduction is further limited to 50 percent of the W–2 production wages paid. In the case of an individual taxpayer, modified adjusted gross income is substituted for taxable income. § 199.

Domestic production gross receipts (DPGR). A key component in computing the domestic production activities deduction (DPAD). Includes receipts from the sale and other disposition of qualified production property produced in significant part within the United States. DPGR is defined in § 199(c)(4).

E

Earned income credit. A tax credit designed to provide assistance to certain low-income individuals who generally have a qualifying child. This is a refundable credit. To receive the most beneficial treatment, the taxpayer must have qualifying children. However, it is possible to qualify for the credit without having a child. See the text chapter on credits for the computation procedure required in order to determine the amount of the credit allowed.

Earnings and profits (E & P). Measures the economic capacity of a corporation to make a distribution to shareholders that is not a return of capital. Such a distribution results in dividend income to the shareholders to the extent of the corporation's current and accumulated earnings and profits.

Economic effect test. Requirements that must be met before a special allocation may be used by a partnership. The premise behind the test is that each partner who receives an allocation of income or loss from a partnership bears the economic benefit or burden of the allocation.

Economic income. The change in the taxpayer's net worth, as measured in terms of market values, plus the value of the assets the taxpayer consumed during the year. Because of the impracticality of this income model, it is not used for tax purposes.

Economic performance test. One of the requirements that must be satisfied for an accrual basis taxpayer to deduct an expense. The accrual basis taxpayer first must satisfy the all events test. That test is not deemed satisfied until economic performance occurs. This occurs when property or services are provided to the taxpayer, or in the case in which the taxpayer is required to provide property or services, whenever the property or services are actually provided by the taxpayer.

Education expenses. Employees may deduct education expenses that are incurred either (1) to maintain or improve existing job-related skills or (2) to meet the express requirements of the employer or the requirements imposed by law to retain employment status. The expenses are not deductible if the education is required to meet the minimum educational standards for the taxpayer's job or if the education qualifies the individual for a new trade or business. Reg. § 1.162–5.

Educational savings bonds. U.S. Series EE bonds whose proceeds are used for qualified higher educational expenses for the taxpayer, the taxpayer's spouse, or a dependent. The interest may be excluded from gross income, provided the taxpayer's adjusted gross income does not exceed certain amounts. § 135.

Effective tax rate. The financial statements for an entity include several footnotes, one of which reconciles the expected (statutory) income tax rate (e.g., 35 percent for a C corporation) with the effective tax rate (i.e., total tax expense as a percentage of book income). The reconciliation often is done in dollar and/or percentage terms.

Effectively connected income. Income of a nonresident alien or foreign corporation that is attributable to the operation of a U.S. trade or business under either the asset-use or the business-activities test.

E-file. The electronic filing of a tax return. The filing is either direct or indirect. As to direct, the taxpayer goes online using a computer and tax return preparation software. Indirect filing occurs when a taxpayer utilizes an authorized IRS e-file provider. The provider often is the tax return preparer.

E-filing. See *e-file*.

Employment taxes. Taxes that an employer must pay on account of its employees. Employment taxes include FICA (Federal Insurance Contributions Act) and FUTA (Federal Unemployment Tax Act) taxes. Employment taxes are paid to the IRS in addition to income tax withholdings at specified intervals. Such taxes can be levied on the employees, the employer, or both.

Energy credits. See *energy tax credits*.

Energy tax credits. Various tax credits are available to those who invest in certain energy property. The purpose of the credit is to create incentives for conservation and to develop alternative energy sources.

Enrolled agents (EAs). A tax practitioner who has gained admission to practice before the IRS by passing an IRS examination and maintaining a required level of continuing professional education.

Entertainment expenses. Expenses that are deductible only if they are directly related to or associated with a trade or business. Various restrictions and documentation requirements have been imposed upon the deductibility of entertainment expenses to prevent abuses by taxpayers. See, for example, the provision contained in § 274(n) that disallows 50 percent (20 percent prior to 1994) of entertainment expenses. § 274.

Entity accounting income. Entity accounting income is not identical to the taxable income of a trust or estate, nor is it determined in the same manner as the entity's financial accounting income would be. The trust document or will determines whether certain income, expenses, gains, or losses are allocated to the corpus of the entity or to the entity's income beneficiaries. Only the items that are allocated to the income beneficiaries are included in entity accounting income.

Entity buy-sell agreement. An arrangement whereby the entity is to purchase a withdrawing owner's interest. When the entity is a corporation, the agreement generally involves a stock redemption on the part of the withdrawing shareholder. See also *buy-sell agreement* and *cross-purchase buy-sell agreement.*

Entity concept. The theory of partnership taxation under which a partnership is treated as a separate and distinct entity from the partners and has its own tax attributes.

Equity method. Under Generally Accepted Accounting Principles, the method of financial reporting for the operations of a subsidiary when the parent corporation owns between 20 and 50 percent of the subsidiary's stock. Creates a book-tax difference, as the two entities' operating results are combined for book purposes, but a Federal income tax consolidated return cannot be filed.

Estate freeze. Procedures directed toward fixing and stabilizing the value of an interest retained in a business, while transferring the growth portion to family members. In the case of a closely held corporation, the estate freeze usually involves keeping the preferred stock and giving away the common stock. The ultimate objective is to reduce estate value when the original owner-donor dies.

Estate tax. A tax imposed on the right to transfer property by death. Thus, an estate tax is levied on the decedent's estate and not on the heir receiving the property.

Estimated tax. The amount of tax (including alternative minimum tax and self-employment tax) a taxpayer expects to owe for the year after subtracting tax credits and income tax withheld. The estimated tax must be paid in installments at designated intervals (e.g., for the individual taxpayer, by April 15, June 15, September 15, and January 15 of the following year).

Excess lobbying expenditures. An excise tax is applied on otherwise tax-exempt organizations with respect to the excess of total lobbying expenditures over grass roots lobbying expenditures for the year.

Excess loss account. When a subsidiary has generated more historical losses than its parent has invested in the entity, the parent's basis in the subsidiary is zero, and the parent records additional losses in an excess loss account. This treatment allows the parent to continue to deduct losses of the subsidiary, even where no basis reduction is possible, while avoiding the need to show a negative stock basis on various financial records. If the subsidiary stock is sold while an excess loss account exists, capital gain income usually is recognized to the extent of the balance in the account.

Excise taxes. A tax on the manufacture, sale, or use of goods; on the carrying on of an occupation or activity; or on the transfer of property. Thus, the Federal estate and gift taxes are, theoretically, excise taxes.

Exclusion amount. The value of assets that is exempt from transfer tax due to the credit allowed for gifts or transfers by death. For gifts and deaths in 2016, the exclusion amount is $5.45 million. An exclusion amount unused by a deceased spouse may be used by the surviving spouse. See also *exemption equivalent amount.*

Exempt organizations. An organization that is either partially or completely exempt from Federal income taxation. § 501.

Exemption amount. See *AMT exemption.*

Exemption equivalent. The maximum value of assets that can be transferred to another party without incurring any Federal gift or estate tax because of the application of the unified tax credit. See also *exemption equivalent amount.*

Exemption equivalent amount. The nontaxable amount (in 2016, $5.45 million for gift tax and estate tax) that is the equivalent of the unified transfer tax credit allowed.

Expanded affiliated group (EAG). For purposes of the domestic production activities deduction (DPAD), all members of an expanded affiliated group (EAG) are treated as a single corporation. Thus, the activities of any member of the group are attributed to the other members. An EAG must meet the requirements for filing a consolidated return with ownership levels lowered to 50 percent. § 199(d)(4)(B).

F

Fair market value. The amount at which property would change hands between a willing buyer and a willing seller, neither being under any compulsion to buy or to sell and both having reasonable knowledge of the relevant facts. Reg. §§ 1.1001–1(a) and 20.2031–1(b).

Farm price method. A method of accounting for agricultural crops. The inventory of crops is valued at its market price less the estimated cost of disposition (e.g., freight and selling expense).

FDAP. Income of a nonresident alien or non-U.S. corporation that is received in the form of dividends, interest, rents, royalties, certain compensation, premiums, annuities, and other "fixed, determinable, annual, or periodic" forms. FDAP income usually is subject to U.S. income taxation at a flat 30 percent tax rate.

Federal District Court. A trial court for purposes of litigating Federal tax matters. It is the only trial court in which a jury trial can be obtained.

Feeder organization. An entity that carries on a trade or business for the benefit of an exempt organization. However, such a relationship does not result in the feeder organization itself being tax-exempt. § 502.

FICA tax. An abbreviation that stands for Federal Insurance Contributions Act, commonly referred to as the Social Security tax. The FICA tax is comprised of the Social Security tax (old age, survivors, and disability insurance) and the Medicare tax (hospital insurance) and is imposed on both employers and employees. The employer is responsible for withholding from the employee's wages the Social Security tax at a rate of 6.2 percent on a maximum wage base and the Medicare tax at a rate of 1.45 percent (no maximum wage base). The maximum Social Security wage base for 2016 is $118,500 and for 2015 is $118,500.

Field audit. An audit conducted by the IRS on the business premises of the taxpayer or in the office of the tax practitioner representing the taxpayer.

Filing status. Individual taxpayers are placed in one of five filing statuses each year (single, married filing jointly, married filing separately, surviving spouse, or head of household). Marital status and household support are key determinants. Filing status is used to determine the taxpayer's filing requirements, standard deduction, eligibility for certain deductions and credits, and tax liability.

Final Regulations. See *finalized Regulations*.

Finalized Regulations. The U.S. Treasury Department Regulations (abbreviated Reg.) represent the position of the IRS as to how the Internal Revenue Code is to be interpreted. Their purpose is to provide taxpayers and IRS personnel with rules of general and specific application to the various provisions of the tax law. Regulations are published in the *Federal Register* and in all tax services.

Financial Accounting Standards Board (FASB). See *Generally Accepted Accounting Principles (GAAP)*.

Fiscal year. A 12-month period ending on the last day of a month other than December. In certain circumstances, a taxpayer is permitted to elect a fiscal year instead of being required to use a calendar year.

Flat tax. In its pure form, a flat tax would eliminate all exclusions, deductions, and credits and impose a one-rate tax on gross income.

Flexible spending plans. An employee benefit plan that allows the employee to take a reduction in salary in exchange for the employer paying benefits that can be provided by the employer without the employee being required to recognize income (e.g., medical and child care benefits).

Flow-through entity. The entity is a tax reporter rather than a taxpayer. The owners are subject to tax. Examples are partnerships, S corporations, and limited liability companies.

Foreign earned income exclusion. The Code allows exclusions for earned income generated outside the United States to alleviate any tax base and rate disparities among countries. In addition, the exclusion is allowed for housing expenditures incurred by the taxpayer's employer with respect to the non-U.S. assignment, and self-employed individuals can deduct foreign housing expenses incurred in a trade or business. The exclusion is limited to $101,300 per year for 2016 ($100,800 in 2015). § 911.

Foreign Investment in Real Property Tax Act (FIRPTA). Under the Foreign Investment in Real Property Tax Act, gains or losses realized by nonresident aliens and non-U.S. corporations on the disposition of U.S. real estate creates U.S. source income and are subject to U.S. income tax.

Foreign tax credit (FTC). A U.S. citizen or resident who incurs or pays income taxes to a foreign country on income subject to U.S. tax may be able to claim some of these taxes as a credit against the U.S. income tax. §§ 27 and 901–905.

Franchise. An agreement that gives the transferee the right to distribute, sell, or provide goods, services, or facilities within a specified area. The cost of obtaining a franchise may be amortized over a statutory period of 15 years. In general, the franchisor's gain on the sale of franchise rights is an ordinary gain because the franchisor retains a significant power, right, or continuing interest in the subject of the franchise. §§ 197 and 1253.

Franchise tax. A tax levied on the right to do business in a state as a corporation. Although income considerations may come into play, the tax usually is based on the capitalization of the corporation.

Fraud. Tax fraud falls into two categories: civil and criminal. Under civil fraud, the IRS may impose as a penalty an amount equal to as much as 75 percent of the underpayment [§ 6651(f)]. Fines and/or imprisonment are prescribed for conviction of various types of criminal tax fraud (§§ 7201–7207). Both civil and criminal fraud involve a specific intent on the part of the taxpayer to evade the tax; mere negligence is not enough. Criminal fraud requires the additional element of willfulness (i.e., done deliberately and with evil purpose). In practice, it becomes difficult to distinguish between the degree of intent necessary to support criminal, rather than civil, fraud. In either situation, the IRS has the burden of proof to show the taxpayer committed fraud.

Fringe benefits. Compensation or other benefit received by an employee that is not in the form of cash. Some fringe benefits (e.g., accident and health plans, group term life insurance) may be excluded from the employee's gross income and therefore are not subject to the Federal income tax.

Frivolous return. A tax return that included a position that has no more than a 5 percent chance of being sustained upon review. Taxpayer and tax preparer penalties are assessed if a frivolous position is included in a filed tax return.

Fruit and tree metaphor. The courts have held that an individual who earns income from property or services cannot assign that income to another. For example, a father cannot assign his earnings from commissions to his child and escape income tax on those amounts.

Functional currency. The currency of the economic environment in which the taxpayer carries on most of its activities and in which the taxpayer transacts most of its business.

FUTA tax. An employment tax levied on employers. Jointly administered by the Federal and state governments, the tax provides funding for unemployment benefits. FUTA applies at a rate of 6.0 percent on the first $7,000 of covered wages paid during the year for each employee in 2016. The Federal government allows a credit for FUTA paid (or allowed under a merit rating system) to the state. The credit cannot exceed 5.4 percent of the covered wages.

Future interest. An interest that will come into being at some future time. It is distinguished from a present interest, which already exists. Assume that Dan transfers securities to a newly created trust. Under the terms of the trust instrument, income from the securities is to be paid each year to Wilma for her life, with the securities passing to Sam upon Wilma's death. Wilma has a present interest in the trust because she is entitled to current income distributions. Sam has a future interest because he must wait for Wilma's death to benefit from the trust. The annual exclusion of $14,000 (in 2016) is not allowed for a gift of a future interest. § 2503(b).

G

General business credit. The summation of various nonrefundable business credits, including the tax credit for rehabilitation expenditures, business energy credit, work opportunity credit, research activities credit, low-income housing credit, and disabled access credit. The amount of general business credit that can be used to reduce the tax liability is limited to the taxpayer's net income tax reduced by the greater of (1) the tentative minimum tax or (2) 25 percent of the net regular tax liability that exceeds $25,000. Unused general business credits can be carried back one year and forward 20 years. § 38.

General partners. A partner who is fully liable in an individual capacity for the debts of the partnership to third parties. A general partner's liability is not limited to the investment in the partnership. See also *limited partner.*

General partnership (GP). A partnership that is owned by one or more general partners. Creditors of a general partnership can collect amounts owed them from both the partnership assets and the assets of the partners individually.

Generally Accepted Accounting Principles (GAAP). Guidelines relating to how to construct the financial statements of enterprises doing business in the United States. Promulgated chiefly by the Financial Accounting Standards Board (FASB).

Gift tax. A tax imposed on the transfer of property by gift. The tax is imposed upon the donor of a gift and is based on the fair market value of the property on the date of the gift.

Golden parachute payments. A severance payment to employees that meets the following requirements: (1) the payment is contingent on a change of ownership of a corporation through a stock or asset acquisition and (2) the aggregate present value of the payment equals or exceeds three times the employee's average annual compensation. To the extent the severance payment meets these conditions, a deduction is disallowed to the employer for the excess of the payment over a statutory base amount (a five-year average of compensation if the taxpayer was an employee for the entire five-year period). In addition, a 20 percent excise tax is imposed on the employee who receives the excess severance pay. §§ 280G and 4999.

Goodwill. The reputation and built-up business of a company. For accounting purposes, goodwill has no basis unless it is purchased. In the purchase of a business, goodwill generally is the difference between the purchase price and the fair market value of the assets acquired. The intangible asset goodwill can be amortized for tax purposes over a 15-year period. Reg. § 1.167(a)–3.

Grantor. A transferor of property. The creator of a trust is usually referred to as the grantor of the entity.

Grantor trust. A trust under which the grantor retains control over the income or corpus (or both) to such an extent that he or she is treated as the owner of the property and its income for income tax purposes. Income from a grantor trust is taxable to the grantor and not to the beneficiary who receives it. §§ 671–679.

Grass roots expenditures. Exempt organizations are prohibited from engaging in political activities, but spending incurred to influence the opinions of the general public relative to specific legislation is permitted by the law.

Gross estate. The property owned or previously transferred by a decedent that is subject to the Federal estate tax. The gross estate can be distinguished from the probate estate, which is property actually subject to administration by the administrator or executor of an estate. §§ 2031–2046.

Gross income. Income subject to the Federal income tax. Gross income does not include all economic income. That is, certain exclusions are allowed (e.g., interest on municipal bonds).

For a manufacturing or merchandising business, gross income usually means gross profit (gross sales or gross receipts less cost of goods sold). § 61 and Reg. § 1.61–3(a).

Group term life insurance. Life insurance coverage provided by an employer for a group of employees. Such insurance is renewable on a year-to-year basis, and typically no cash surrender value is built up. The premiums paid by the employer on the insurance are not taxed to the employees on coverage of up to $50,000 per person. § 79 and Reg. § 1.79–1(b).

Guaranteed payments. Payments made by a partnership to a partner for services rendered or for the use of capital to the extent the payments are determined without regard to the income of the partnership. The payments are treated as though they were made to a nonpartner and thus are deducted by the entity.

H

H.R. 10 plans. See *Keogh plans.*

Half-year convention. A cost recovery convention that assumes that all property is placed in service at mid-year and thus provides for a half-year's cost recovery for that year.

Head of household. An unmarried individual who maintains a household for another and satisfies certain conditions set forth in § 2(b). This status enables the taxpayer to use a set of income tax rates that are lower than those applicable to other unmarried individuals but higher than those applicable to surviving spouses and married persons filing a joint return.

Health Savings Account (HSA). A medical savings account created in legislation enacted in December 2003 that is designed to replace and expand Archer Medical Savings Accounts.

Highly compensated employee. The employee group is generally divided into two categories for fringe benefit (including pension and profit sharing plans) purposes. These are (1) highly compensated employees and (2) non-highly compensated employees. For most fringe benefits, if the fringe benefit plan discriminates in favor of highly compensated employees, it will not be a qualified plan with respect, at a minimum, to the highly compensated employees.

Historic business test. In a corporate reorganization, a means by which to determine if the continuity of business enterprise requirement is met. The acquiring corporation must continue to operate the target entity's existing business(es) going forward; if this is not the case, the requirement is failed.

Hobby losses. Losses from an activity not engaged in for profit. The Code restricts the amount of losses that an individual can deduct for hobby activities so that these transactions cannot be used to offset income from other sources. § 183.

Holding period. The period of time during which property has been held for income tax purposes. The holding period is significant in determining whether gain or loss from the sale or exchange of a capital asset is long or short term. § 1223.

Home equity loans. Loans that utilize the personal residence of the taxpayer as security. The interest on such loans is deductible as qualified residence interest. However, interest is deductible only on the portion of the loan that does not exceed the lesser of (1) the fair market value of the residence, reduced by the acquisition indebtedness, or (2) $100,000 ($50,000 for married persons filing separate returns). A major benefit of a home equity loan is that there are no tracing rules regarding the use of the loan proceeds. § 163(h)(3).

Hot assets. Unrealized receivables and substantially appreciated inventory under § 751. When hot assets are present, the sale of a partnership interest or the disproportionate distribution of the assets can cause ordinary income to be recognized.

Hybrid method. A combination of the accrual and cash methods of accounting. That is, the taxpayer may account for some items of income on the accrual method (e.g., sales and cost of goods sold) and other items (e.g., interest income) on the cash method.

I

Imputed interest. For certain long-term sales of property, the IRS can convert some of the gain from the sale into interest income if the contract does not provide for a minimum rate of interest to be paid by the purchaser. The seller recognizes less long-term capital gain and more ordinary income (interest income). § 483 and the related Regulations.

Inbound taxation. U.S. tax effects when a non-U.S. person begins an investment or business activity in the United States.

Incentive stock options (ISOs). A type of stock option that receives favorable tax treatment. If various qualification requirements can be satisfied, there are no recognition tax consequences when the stock option is granted. However, the spread (the excess of the fair market value at the date of exercise over the option price) is a tax preference item for purposes of the alternative minimum tax. The gain on disposition of the stock resulting from the exercise of the stock option will be classified as long-term capital gain if certain holding period requirements are met (the employee must not dispose of the stock within two years after the option is granted or within one year after acquiring the stock). § 422.

Income. For tax purposes, an increase in wealth that has been realized.

Income in respect of a decedent (IRD). Income earned by a decedent at the time of death but not reportable on the final income tax return because of the method of accounting that appropriately is utilized. Such income is included in the gross estate and is taxed to the eventual recipient (either the estate or heirs). The recipient is, however, allowed an income tax deduction for the estate tax attributable to the income. § 691.

Income tax provision. Under ASC 740 (SFAS 109), a synonym for the book tax expense of an entity for the financial reporting period. Following the "matching principle," all book tax expense that relates to the net income for the reporting period is reported on that period's financial statements, including not only the current tax expense, but also any deferred tax expense and deferred tax benefit.

Income tax treaties. See *tax treaty*.

Independent contractor. A self-employed person as distinguished from one who is employed as an employee.

Indexation. A procedure whereby adjustments are made by the IRS to key tax components (e.g., standard deduction, tax brackets, personal and dependency exemptions) to reflect inflation. The adjustments usually are made annually and are based on the change in the consumer price index.

Individual Retirement Account (IRA). A type of retirement plan to which an individual with earned income can contribute a statutory maximum of $5,500 in 2016. IRAs can be classified as traditional IRAs or Roth IRAs. With a traditional IRA, an individual can contribute and deduct a maximum of $5,500 per tax year in 2016. The deduction is a deduction *for* AGI. However, if the individual is an active participant in another qualified retirement plan, the deduction is phased out proportionally between certain AGI ranges (note that the phaseout limits the amount of the deduction and not the amount of the contribution). With a Roth IRA, an individual can contribute a maximum of $5,500 per tax year in 2016. No deduction is permitted. However, if a five-year holding period requirement is satisfied and if the distribution is a qualified distribution, the taxpayer can make tax-free withdrawals from a Roth IRA. The maximum annual contribution is phased out proportionally between certain AGI ranges. §§ 219 and 408A.

Individual Shared Responsibility Payment (ISRP). A mandate or penalty tax that individuals owe starting in 2014 for any month in which they do not have health coverage and do not qualify for an exemption. This mandate was created as part of the Affordable Care Act to encourage individuals to obtain health care coverage. If owed, the penalty is the greater of a "flat dollar amount" or a percentage of household income less the filing threshold. When fully in effect in 2016, the flat dollar amount is $695 and the percent applied to household income is 2.5 percent. For a family, the flat dollar amount cannot exceed three times the flat dollar amount. After 2016, the $695 amount is adjusted annually. The overall cap on the penalty is the national average cost of a bronze level plan (this amount is published by the IRS). Worksheets for computing the penalty are included in the instructions to Form 8965 (Health Coverage Exemptions). § 5000A.

Inheritance tax. A tax imposed on the right to receive property from a decedent. Thus, theoretically, an inheritance tax is imposed on the heir. The Federal estate tax is imposed on the estate.

Inside basis. A partnership's basis in the assets it owns.

Installment method. A method of accounting enabling certain taxpayers to spread the recognition of gain on the sale of property over the collection period. Under this procedure, the seller arrives at the gain to be recognized by computing the gross profit percentage from the sale (the gain divided by the contract price) and applying it to each payment received. § 453.

Intangible drilling and development costs (IDCs). Taxpayers may elect to expense or capitalize (subject to amortization) intangible drilling and development costs. However, ordinary income recapture provisions apply to oil and gas properties on a sale or other disposition if the expense method is elected. §§ 263(c) and 1254(a).

Intermediate sanctions. The IRS can assess excise taxes on disqualified persons and organization management associated with so-called public charities engaging in excess benefit transactions. An excess benefit transaction is one in which a disqualified person engages in a non-fair market value transaction with the exempt organization or receives unreasonable compensation. Prior to the idea of intermediate sanctions, the only option available to the IRS was to revoke the organization's exempt status.

International Accounting Standards Board (IASB). The body that promulgates International Financial Reporting Standards (IFRS). Based in London, representing accounting standard setting bodies in over 100 countries, the IASB develops accounting standards that can serve as the basis for harmonizing conflicting reporting standards among nations.

International Financial Reporting Standards (IFRS). Produced by the International Accounting Standards Board (IASB), guidelines developed since 2001 as to revenue recognition, accounting for business combinations, and a conceptual framework for financial reporting. IFRS provisions are designed so that they can be used by all entities, regardless of where they are based or conduct business. IFRS have gained widespread acceptance throughout the world, and the SEC is considering how to require U.S. entities to use IFRS in addition to, or in lieu of, the accounting rules of the Financial Accounting Standards Board.

Interpretive Regulations. A Regulation issued by the Treasury Department that purports to explain the meaning of a particular Code Section. An interpretive Regulation is given less deference than a legislative Regulation.

Investment income. Consisting of virtually the same elements as portfolio income, a measure by which to justify a deduction for interest on investment indebtedness.

Investment interest. Payment for the use of funds used to acquire assets that produce investment income. The deduction for investment interest is limited to net investment income for the tax year.

Investor loss. Losses on stock and securities. If stocks and bonds are capital assets in the hands of the holder, a capital loss materializes as of the last day of the taxable year in which the stocks or bonds become worthless. Under certain circumstances involving stocks and bonds of affiliated corporations, an ordinary loss is permitted upon worthlessness.

Involuntary conversion. The loss or destruction of property through theft, casualty, or condemnation. Gain realized on an involuntary conversion can, at the taxpayer's election, be deferred for Federal income tax purposes if the owner reinvests the proceeds within a prescribed period of time in property that is similar or related in service or use. § 1033.

Itemized deductions. Personal and employee expenditures allowed by the Code as deductions from adjusted gross income. Examples include certain medical expenses, interest on home mortgages, state income taxes, and charitable contributions. Itemized deductions are reported on Schedule A of Form 1040. Certain miscellaneous itemized deductions are reduced by 2 percent of the taxpayer's adjusted gross income. In addition, a taxpayer whose adjusted gross income exceeds a certain level (indexed annually) must reduce the itemized deductions by 3 percent of the excess of adjusted gross income over that level. Medical, casualty and theft, and investment interest deductions are not subject to the 3 percent reduction. The 3 percent reduction may not reduce itemized deductions that are subject to the reduction to below 20 percent of their initial amount.

J

Joint tenants. Two or more persons having undivided ownership of property with the right of survivorship. Right of survivorship gives the surviving owner full ownership of the property. Suppose Bob and Tami are joint tenants of a tract of land. Upon Bob's death, Tami becomes the sole owner of the property. For the estate tax consequences upon the death of a joint tenant, see § 2040.

K

Keogh plans. Retirement plans available to self-employed taxpayers. They are also referred to as H.R. 10 plans. Under such plans, a taxpayer may deduct each year up to 100 percent of net earnings from self-employment or $53,000 for 2016, whichever is less. If the plan is a profit sharing plan, the percentage is 25 percent.

Kiddie tax. Passive income, such as interest and dividends, that is recognized by a child under age 19 (or under age 24 if a full-time student) is taxed to him or her at the rates that would have applied had the income been incurred by the child's parents, generally to the extent the income exceeds $2,100 for 2016. The additional tax is assessed regardless of the source of the income or the income's underlying property. If the child's parents are divorced, the custodial parent's rates are used. The parents' rates reflect any applicable alternative minimum tax and the phaseouts of lower tax brackets and other deductions. § 1(g).

L

Least aggregate deferral method. An algorithm set forth in the Regulations to determine the tax year for a partnership or an S corporation with owners whose tax years differ. The tax year selected is the one that produces the least aggregate deferral of income for the owners.

Least aggregate deferral rule. See *least aggregate deferral method.*

Legislative Regulations. Some Code Sections give the Secretary of the Treasury or his delegate the authority to prescribe Regulations to carry out the details of administration or to otherwise complete the operating rules. Regulations issued pursuant to this type of authority truly possess the force and effect of law. In effect, Congress is almost delegating its legislative powers to the Treasury Department.

Lessee. One who rents property from another. In the case of real estate, the lessee is also known as the tenant.

Lessor. One who rents property to another. In the case of real estate, the lessor is also known as the landlord.

Letter ruling. The written response of the IRS to a taxpayer's request for interpretation of the revenue laws with respect to a proposed transaction (e.g., concerning the tax-free status of a reorganization). Not to be relied on as precedent by other than the party who requested the ruling.

Liabilities in excess of basis. On the contribution of capital to a corporation, an investor recognizes gain on the exchange to the extent contributed assets carry liabilities with a face amount in excess of the tax basis of the contributed assets.

This rule keeps the investor from holding the investment asset received with a negative basis. § 357(c).

Life insurance proceeds. A specified sum (the face value or maturity value of the policy) paid to the designated beneficiary of the policy by the life insurance company upon the death of the insured.

Lifetime learning credit. A tax credit for qualifying expenses for taxpayers pursuing education beyond the first two years of postsecondary education. Individuals who are completing their last two years of undergraduate studies, pursuing graduate or professional degrees, or otherwise seeking new job skills or maintaining existing job skills are all eligible for the credit. Eligible individuals include the taxpayer, taxpayer's spouse, and taxpayer's dependents. The maximum credit is 20 percent of the first $10,000 of qualifying expenses and is computed per taxpayer. The credit is phased out for higher-income taxpayers. § 25A.

Like-kind exchanges. An exchange of property held for productive use in a trade or business or for investment (except inventory and stocks and bonds) for other investment or trade or business property. Unless non-like-kind property (boot) is received, the exchange is fully tax-deferred. § 1031.

Limited liability company (LLC). A legal entity allowed by all of the states. The entity is subject to Federal income tax treatment as though it were a partnership in which all members or owners of the LLC are treated much like limited partners. There are no restrictions on ownership, all members may participate in management, and none has personal liability for the entity's debts.

Limited liability limited partnership (LLLP). A limited partnership for which the general partners are also protected from entity liabilities. An LLLP—or "triple LP"—can be formed in about 20 states. In those states, a limited partnership files with the state to adopt LLLP status.

Limited liability partnership (LLP). A legal entity allowed by many of the states, where a general partnership registers with the state as an LLP. Owners are general partners, but a partner is not liable for any malpractice committed by other partners. The personal assets of the partners are at risk for the entity's contractual liabilities, such as accounts payable. The personal assets of a specific partner are at risk for his or her own professional malpractice and tort liability and for malpractice and torts committed by those whom he or she supervises.

Limited partners. A partner whose liability to third-party creditors of the partnership is limited to the amounts invested in the partnership. See also *general partner* and *limited partnership*.

Limited partnership (LP). A partnership in which some of the partners are limited partners. At least one of the partners in a limited partnership must be a general partner.

Liquidating distribution. A distribution by a partnership or corporation that is in complete liquidation of the entity's trade or business activities. Typically, such distributions generate capital gain or loss to the investors without regard, for instance, to the earnings and profits of the corporation or to the partnership's basis in the distributed property. They can, however, lead to recognized gain or loss at the corporate level.

Listed property. Property that includes (1) any passenger automobile; (2) any other property used as a means of transportation; (3) any property of a type generally used for purposes of entertainment, recreation, or amusement; (4) any computer or peripheral equipment (with an exception for exclusive business use); (5) any cellular telephone (or other similar telecommunications equipment); and (6) any other property of a type specified in the Regulations. If listed property is predominantly used for business, the taxpayer is allowed to use the statutory percentage method of cost recovery. Otherwise, the straight-line cost recovery method must be used. § 280F.

Living trust. A revocable trust. Often touted as a means of avoiding some probate costs.

Lobbying expenditures. An expenditure made for the purpose of influencing legislation. Such payments can result in the loss of the exempt status of, and the imposition of Federal income tax on, an exempt organization.

Long-term care insurance. Insurance that helps pay the cost of care when the insured is unable to care for himself or herself. Such insurance is generally thought of as insurance against the cost of an aged person entering a nursing home. The employer can provide the insurance, and the premiums may be excluded from the employee's gross income. § 7702B.

Long-term contract. A building, installation, construction, or manufacturing contract that is entered into but not completed within the same tax year. A manufacturing contract is a long-term contract only if the contract is to manufacture (1) a unique item not normally carried in finished goods inventory or (2) items that normally require more than 12 calendar months to complete. The two available methods to account for long-term contracts are the percentage of completion method and the completed contract method. The completed contract method can be used only in limited circumstances. § 460.

Long-term nonpersonal use capital assets. Includes investment property with a long-term holding period. Such property disposed of by casualty or theft may receive § 1231 treatment.

Long-term tax-exempt rate. Used in deriving the yearly limitation on net operating loss and other tax benefits that carry over from the target to the acquiring when there is an equity structure shift. The highest of the Federal long-term interest rates in effect for any of the last three months. § 382.

Lower of cost or market (replacement cost). An elective inventory method, whereby the taxpayer may value inventories at the lower of the taxpayer's actual cost or the current replacement cost of the goods. This method cannot be used in conjunction with the LIFO inventory method.

Low-income housing credit. Beneficial treatment to owners of low-income housing is provided in the form of a tax credit. The calculated credit is claimed in the year the building is placed in service and in the following nine years. § 42.

Lump-sum distribution. Payment of the entire amount due at one time rather than in installments. Such distributions often occur from qualified pension or profit sharing plans upon the retirement or death of a covered employee. The recipient of a lump-sum distribution may recognize both long-term capital gain and ordinary income upon the receipt of the distribution. The ordinary income portion may be subject to a special 10-year income averaging provision. § 402(e).

M

Majority interest partners. Partners who have more than a 50 percent interest in partnership profits and capital, counting only those partners who have the same taxable year. The term is of significance in determining the appropriate taxable year of a partnership. § 706(b).

Marital deduction. A deduction allowed against the taxable estate or taxable gifts upon the transfer of property from one spouse to another.

Marriage penalty. The additional tax liability that results for a married couple when compared with what their tax liability would be if they were not married and filed separate returns.

Matching rule. Treatment of an intercompany transaction on a consolidated return, when a sold asset remains within the group.

Material participation. If an individual taxpayer materially participates in a nonrental trade or business activity, any loss from that activity is treated as an active loss that can be offset against active income. Material participation is achieved by meeting any one of seven tests provided in the Regulations. § 469(h).

Meaningful reduction test. A decrease in the shareholder's voting control. Used to determine whether a stock redemption qualifies for sale or exchange treatment.

Medical expenses. Medical expenses of an individual, a spouse, and dependents are allowed as an itemized deduction to the extent such amounts (less insurance reimbursements) exceed 10 percent (or 7.5 percent if at least age 65) of adjusted gross income. § 213.

Merger. The absorption of one corporation by another with the corporation being absorbed losing its legal identity. Flow Corporation is merged into Jobs Corporation, and the shareholders of Flow receive stock in Jobs in exchange for their stock in Flow. After the merger, Flow ceases to exist as a separate legal entity. If a merger meets certain conditions, it is not currently taxable to the parties involved. § 368(a)(1).

Mid-month convention. A cost recovery convention that assumes that property is placed in service in the middle of the month that it is actually placed in service.

Mid-quarter convention. A cost recovery convention that assumes that property placed in service during the year is placed in service at the middle of the quarter in which it is actually placed in service. The mid-quarter convention applies if more than 40 percent of the value of property (other than eligible real estate) is placed in service during the last quarter of the year.

Minimum tax credit. See *alternative minimum tax credit.*

Miscellaneous itemized deductions. A special category of itemized deductions that includes expenses such as professional dues, tax return preparation fees, job-hunting costs, unreimbursed employee business expenses, and certain investment expenses. Such expenses are deductible only to the extent they exceed 2 percent of adjusted gross income. § 67.

Modified accelerated cost recovery system (MACRS). A method in which the cost of tangible property is recovered over a prescribed period of time. Enacted by the Economic Recovery Tax Act (ERTA) of 1981 and substantially modified by the Tax Reform Act (TRA) of 1986 (the modified system is referred to as MACRS), the approach disregards salvage value, imposes a period of cost recovery that depends upon the classification of the asset into one of various recovery periods, and prescribes the applicable percentage of cost that can be deducted each year. § 168.

Modified adjusted gross income. A key determinant in computing the domestic production activities deduction (DPAD) and certain other tax provisions (e.g., deduction for higher education tuition, exclusion of interest on education savings bonds). §§ 135, 144, and 199.

Moving expenses. A deduction *for* AGI is permitted to employees and self-employed individuals provided certain tests are met. The taxpayer's new job must be at least 50 miles farther from the old residence than the old residence was from the former place of work. In addition, an employee must be employed on a full-time basis at the new location for 39 weeks in the 12-month period following the move. Deductible moving expenses include the cost of moving the household and personal effects, transportation, and lodging expenses during the move. The cost of meals during the move is not deductible. Qualified moving expenses that are paid (or reimbursed) by the employer can be excluded from the employee's gross income. In this case, the related deduction by the employee is not permitted. §§ 62(a)(15), 132(a)(6), and 217.

Multiple support agreement. To qualify for a dependency exemption, the support test must be satisfied. This requires that over 50 percent of the support of the potential dependent be provided by the taxpayer. Where no one person provides more than 50 percent of the support, a multiple support agreement enables a taxpayer to still qualify for the dependency exemption. Any person who contributed more than 10 percent of the support is entitled to claim the exemption if each person in the group who contributed more than 10 percent files a written consent (Form 2120). Each person who is a party to the multiple support agreement must meet all of the other requirements for claiming the dependency exemption. § 152(c).

Multistate Tax Commission (MTC). A regulatory body of the states that develops operating rules and regulations for the implementation of the UDITPA and other provisions that assign the total taxable income of a multistate corporation to specific states.

N

National sales tax. Intended as a replacement for the current Federal income tax. Unlike a value added tax (VAT), which is levied on the manufacturer, it would be imposed on the consumer upon the final sale of goods and services. To keep the tax from being regressive, low-income taxpayers would be granted some kind of credit or exemption.

Negligence. Failure to exercise the reasonable or ordinary degree of care of a prudent person in a situation that results in harm or damage to another. A penalty is assessed on taxpayers who exhibit negligence or intentional disregard of rules and Regulations with respect to the underpayment of certain taxes.

Net capital gain (NCG). The excess of the net long-term capital gain for the tax year over the net short-term capital loss.

The net capital gain of an individual taxpayer is eligible for the alternative tax. § 1222(11).

Net capital loss (NCL). The excess of the losses from sales or exchanges of capital assets over the gains from sales or exchanges of such assets. Up to $3,000 per year of the net capital loss may be deductible by noncorporate taxpayers against ordinary income. The excess net capital loss carries over to future tax years. For corporate taxpayers, the net capital loss cannot be offset against ordinary income, but it can be carried back three years and forward five years to offset net capital gains. §§ 1211, 1212, and 1221(10).

Net investment income. The excess of investment income over investment expenses. Investment expenses are those deductible expenses directly connected with the production of investment income. Investment expenses do not include investment interest. The deduction for investment interest for the tax year is limited to net investment income. § 163(d).

Net operating loss (NOL). To mitigate the effect of the annual accounting period concept, § 172 allows taxpayers to use an excess loss of one year as a deduction for certain past or future years. In this regard, a carryback period of two (or more) years and a carryforward period of 20 years currently are allowed.

Nexus. The degree of activity that must be present before a taxing jurisdiction has the right to impose a tax on an out-of-state entity. The rules for income tax nexus are not the same as for sales tax nexus.

Ninety-day letter. This notice is sent to a taxpayer upon request, upon the expiration of the 30-day letter, or upon exhaustion by the taxpayer of his or her administrative remedies before the IRS. The notice gives the taxpayer 90 days in which to file a petition with the U.S. Tax Court. If a petition is not filed, the IRS will demand payment of the assessed deficiency. §§ 6211–6216.

No-additional-cost service. Services the employer may provide the employee at no additional cost to the employer. Generally, the benefit is the ability to utilize the employer's excess capacity (e.g., vacant seats on an airliner). Such amounts are excludible from the recipient's gross income.

Nonaccountable plan. An expense reimbursement plan that does not have an accountability feature. The result is that employee expenses must be claimed as deductions *from* AGI. An exception is moving expenses that are deductions *for* AGI.

Nonacquiescence. Disagreement by the IRS on the result reached in certain judicial decisions. *Nonacq.* or *NA*.

Nonbusiness bad debt. A bad debt loss that is not incurred in connection with a creditor's trade or business. The loss is classified as a short-term capital loss and is allowed only in the year the debt becomes entirely worthless. In addition to family loans, many investor losses are nonbusiness bad debts. § 166(d).

Nonliquidating distribution. A payment made by a partnership or corporation to the entity's owner when the entity's legal existence does not cease thereafter. If the payor is a corporation, such a distribution can result in dividend income to the shareholders. If the payor is a partnership, the partner usually assigns a basis in the distributed property that is equal to the lesser of the partner's basis in the partnership interest or the basis of the distributed asset to the partnership. In this regard, the partner first assigns basis to any cash that he or she receives in the distribution. The partner's remaining basis, if any, is assigned to the noncash assets according to their relative bases to the partnership.

Nonqualified deferred compensation (NQDC). Compensation arrangements that are frequently offered to executives. Such plans may include stock options, restricted stock, etc. Often, an executive may defer the recognition of taxable income. The employer, however, does not receive a tax deduction until the employee is required to include the compensation in income.

Nonqualified stock option (NQSO). A type of stock option that does not satisfy the statutory requirements of an incentive stock option. If the NQSO has a readily ascertainable fair market value (e.g., the option is traded on an established exchange), the value of the option must be included in the employee's gross income at the date of the grant. Otherwise, the employee does not recognize income at the grant date. Instead, ordinary income is recognized in the year of exercise of the option.

Nonrecourse debt. Debt secured by the property that it is used to purchase. The purchaser of the property is not personally liable for the debt upon default. Rather, the creditor's recourse is to repossess the related property. Nonrecourse debt generally does not increase the purchaser's at-risk amount.

Nonrefundable credits. A credit that is not paid if it exceeds the taxpayer's tax liability. Some nonrefundable credits qualify for carryback and carryover treatment.

Nonresident alien (NRA). An individual who is neither a citizen nor a resident of the United States. Citizenship is determined under the immigration and naturalization laws of the United States. Residency is determined under § 7701(b) of the Internal Revenue Code.

Nontaxable exchange. A transaction in which realized gains or losses are not recognized. The recognition of gain or loss is postponed (deferred) until the property received in the nontaxable exchange is subsequently disposed of in a taxable transaction. Examples are § 1031 like-kind exchanges and § 1033 involuntary conversions.

Not essentially equivalent redemption. Sale or exchange treatment is given to this type of redemption. Although various safe-harbor tests are failed, the nature of the redemption is such that dividend treatment is avoided, because it represents a meaningful reduction in the shareholder's interest in the corporation. § 302(b)(1).

O

Occupational fee. A tax imposed on various trades or businesses. A license fee that enables a taxpayer to engage in a particular occupation.

Occupational taxes. See *occupational fee*.

Offer in compromise. A settlement agreement offered by the IRS in a tax dispute, especially where there is doubt as to the collectibility of the full deficiency. Offers in compromise can include installment payment schedules, as well as reductions in the tax and penalties owed by the taxpayer.

Office audit. An audit conducted by the IRS in the agent's office.

Office in the home expenses. Employment and business-related expenses attributable to the use of a residence (e.g., den or office) are allowed only if the portion of the residence is exclusively used on a regular basis as a principal place of business of the taxpayer or as a place of business that is used by patients, clients, or customers. If the expenses are incurred by an employee, the use must be for the convenience of the employer as opposed to being merely appropriate and helpful. In computing the office in the home expenses, a taxpayer can use either the regular method or simplified method. As a general rule, the regular method requires more effort and recordkeeping but results in a larger deduction. § 280A.

One-year rule for prepaid expenses. Taxpayers who use the cash method are required to use the accrual method for deducting certain prepaid expenses (i.e., must capitalize the item and can deduct only when used). If a prepayment will not be consumed or expire by the end of the tax year following the year of payment, the prepayment must be capitalized and prorated over the benefit period. Conversely, if the prepayment will be consumed by the end of the tax year following the year of payment, it can be expensed when paid. To obtain the current deduction under the one-year rule, the payment must be a required payment rather than a voluntary payment.

Operating agreement. The governing document of a limited liability company. This document is similar in structure, function, and purpose to a partnership agreement.

Optional adjustment election. See *Section 754 election*.

Options. The sale or exchange of an option to buy or sell property results in capital gain or loss if the property is a capital asset. Generally, the closing of an option transaction results in short-term capital gain or loss to the writer of the call and the purchaser of the call option. § 1234.

Ordinary and necessary. An ordinary expense is common and accepted in the general industry or type of activity in which the taxpayer is engaged. It comprises one of the tests for the deductibility of expenses incurred or paid in connection with a trade or business; for the production or collection of income; for the management, conservation, or maintenance of property held for the production of income; or in connection with the determination, collection, or refund of any tax. §§ 162(a) and 212. A necessary expense is appropriate and helpful in furthering the taxpayer's business or income-producing activity. §§ 162(a) and 212.

Ordinary income property. Property contributed to a charitable organization that, if sold rather than contributed, would have resulted in other than long-term capital gain to the donor (i.e., ordinary income property and short-term capital gain property). Examples are inventory and capital assets held for less than the long-term holding period.

Organizational costs. See *organizational expenditures*.

Organizational expenditures. Items incurred early in the life of a corporation or partnership that are eligible for a $5,000 limited expensing (subject to phaseout) and an amortization of the balance over 180 months. Organizational expenditures exclude those incurred to obtain capital (underwriting fees) or assets (subject to cost recovery).

Typically, eligible expenditures include legal and accounting fees and state incorporation payments. Such items must be incurred by the end of the entity's first tax year. §§ 248 and 709(b).

Original issue discount (OID). The difference between the issue price of a debt obligation (e.g., a corporate bond) and the maturity value of the obligation when the issue price is less than the maturity value. OID represents interest and must be amortized over the life of the debt obligation using the effective interest method. The difference is not considered to be original issue discount for tax purposes when it is less than one-fourth of 1 percent of the redemption price at maturity multiplied by the number of years to maturity. §§ 1272 and 1273(a)(3).

Other adjustments account (OAA). Used in the context of a distribution from an S corporation. The net accumulation of the entity's exempt income (e.g., municipal bond interest).

Other property. In a corporate reorganization, any property in the exchange that is not stock or securities, such as cash or land. This amount constitutes boot. This result is similar to that in a like-kind exchange.

Outbound taxation. U.S. tax effects when a U.S. person begins an investment or business activity outside the United States.

Outside basis. A partner's basis in his or her partnership interest.

Ownership change. An event that triggers a § 382 limitation for the acquiring corporation.

P

Parent-subsidiary controlled group. A controlled or affiliated group of corporations where at least one corporation is at least 80 percent owned by one or more of the others. The affiliated group definition is more difficult to meet.

Partial liquidation. A stock redemption where noncorporate shareholders are permitted sale or exchange treatment. In certain cases, an active business must have existed for at least five years. Only a portion of the outstanding stock in the entity is retired.

Partnership. For income tax purposes, a partnership includes a syndicate, group, pool, or joint venture, as well as ordinary partnerships. In an ordinary partnership, two or more parties combine capital and/or services to carry on a business for profit as co-owners. § 7701(a)(2).

Partnership agreement. The governing document of a partnership. A partnership agreement should describe the rights and obligations of the partners; the allocation of entity income, deductions, and cash flows; initial and future capital contribution requirements; conditions for terminating the partnership; and other matters.

Passive activity loss. Any loss from (1) activities in which the taxpayer does not materially participate or (2) rental activities (subject to certain exceptions). Net passive losses cannot be used to offset income from nonpassive sources. Rather, they are suspended until the taxpayer either generates net passive income (and a deduction of such losses is allowed) or disposes of the underlying property (at which time the loss deductions are allowed in full). One relief provision allows landlords who actively participate in the rental activities to deduct up to $25,000 of passive losses annually. However, a phaseout of the $25,000 amount commences when the landlord's AGI exceeds $100,000. Another relief provision applies for material participation in a real estate trade or business.

Passive investment company. A means by which a multistate corporation can reduce the overall effective tax rate by isolating investment income in a low- or no-tax state.

Passive investment income (PII). Gross receipts from royalties, certain rents, dividends, interest, annuities, and gains from the sale or exchange of stock and securities. When earnings and profits (E & P) also exists, if the passive investment income of an S corporation exceeds 25 percent of the corporation's gross receipts for three consecutive years, S status is lost.

Patent. An intangible asset that may be amortized over a statutory 15-year period as a § 197 intangible. The sale of a patent usually results in favorable long-term capital gain treatment. §§ 197 and 1235.

Payroll factor. The proportion of a multistate corporation's total payroll that is traceable to a specific state. Used in determining the taxable income that is to be apportioned to that state.

Pension plan. A type of deferred compensation arrangement that provides for systematic payments of definitely determinable retirement benefits to employees who meet the requirements set forth in the plan.

Percentage depletion. Depletion based on a statutory percentage applied to the gross income from the property. The taxpayer deducts the greater of cost depletion or percentage depletion. § 613.

Percentage of completion method. A method of reporting gain or loss on certain long-term contracts. Under this method of accounting, the gross contract price is included in income as the contract is completed. Reg. § 1.451–3.

Permanent and total disability. A person is considered permanently and totally disabled if he or she is unable to engage in any substantial gainful activity due to a physical or mental impairment. In addition, this impairment must be one that can be expected to result in death or that has lasted or can be expected to last for a continuous period of not less than 12 months. The taxpayer generally must provide the IRS a physician's statement documenting this condition.

Permanent differences. Under ASC 740 (SFAS 109), tax-related items that appear in the entity's financial statements or its tax return but not both. For instance, interest income from a municipal bond is a permanent book-tax difference.

Permanent establishment (PE). A level of business activity, as defined under an income tax treaty, that subjects the taxpayer to taxation in a country other than that in which the taxpayer is based. Often evidenced by the presence of a plant, an office, or other fixed place of business. Inventory storage and temporary activities do not rise to the level of a PE. PE is the treaty's equivalent to nexus.

Permanently reinvesting. Under ASC 740-30 (APB 23) of Generally Accepted Accounting Principles, a special rule that relates to the book tax expense of non-U.S. subsidiaries. If a parent corporation documents that it is permanently reinvesting the non-U.S. earning of a non-U.S. subsidiary, the parent does not record as an expense any U.S. income tax that the parent might pay on such earnings, i.e., the book tax expense is deferred until such earnings are (if ever) repatriated to the United States.

Personal and dependency exemptions. The tax law provides an exemption for each individual taxpayer and an additional exemption for the taxpayer's spouse if a joint return is filed. An individual may also claim a dependency exemption for each dependent, provided certain tests are met. The amount of the personal and dependency exemptions is $4,050 in 2016 ($4,000 in 2015). The exemption is subject to phaseout once adjusted gross income exceeds certain statutory threshold amounts.

Personal casualty gain. The recognized gain from any involuntary conversion of personal use property arising from fire, storm, shipwreck, or other casualty, or from theft.

Personal casualty loss. The recognized loss from any involuntary conversion of personal use property arising from fire, storm, shipwreck, or other casualty, or from theft.

Personal exemptions. See *personal and dependency exemptions.*

Personal holding company tax. A penalty tax imposed on certain closely held corporations with excessive investment income. Assessed at the top individual tax rate on personal holding company income, reduced by dividends paid and other adjustments. § 541.

Personal residence. If a residence has been owned and used by the taxpayer as the principal residence for at least two years during the five-year period ending on the date of sale, up to $250,000 of realized gain is excluded from gross income. For a married couple filing a joint return, the $250,000 is increased to $500,000 if either spouse satisfies the ownership requirement and both spouses satisfy the use requirement. § 121.

Personal service corporation (PSC). A corporation whose principal activity is the performance of personal services (e.g., health, law, engineering, architecture, accounting, actuarial science, performing arts, or consulting) and where such services are substantially performed by the employee-owners. The 35 percent statutory income tax rate applies to PSCs.

Personalty. All property that is not attached to real estate (realty) and is movable. Examples of personalty are machinery, automobiles, clothing, household furnishings, and personal effects.

Points. Loan origination fees that may be deductible as interest by a buyer of property. A seller of property who pays points reduces the selling price by the amount of the points paid for the buyer. While the seller is not permitted to deduct this amount as interest, the buyer may do so.

Portfolio income. Income from interest, dividends, rentals, royalties, capital gains, or other investment sources. Net passive losses cannot be used to offset net portfolio income.

Power of appointment. A legal right granted to someone by a will or other document that gives the holder the power to dispose of property or the income from property. When the holder may appoint the property to his or her own benefit, the power usually is called a general power of appointment. If the holder cannot benefit himself or herself but may only appoint to certain other persons, the power is a special power of appointment. Assume Gary places

$500,000 worth of securities in trust granting Donna the right to determine each year how the trustee is to divide the income between Ann and Babs. Under these circumstances, Donna has a special power of appointment. If Donna had the further right to appoint the income to herself, she probably possesses a general power of appointment. For the estate tax and gift tax effects of powers of appointment, see §§ 2041 and 2514.

Precedents. A previously decided court decision that is recognized as authority for the disposition of future decisions.

Precontribution gain or loss. Partnerships allow for a variety of special allocations of gain or loss among the partners, but gain or loss that is "built in" on an asset contributed to the partnership is assigned specifically to the contributing partner. § 704(c)(1)(A).

Preferences. See *AMT preferences.*

Preferred stock bailout. A process where a shareholder used the issuance and sale, or later redemption, of a preferred stock dividend to obtain long-term capital gains, without any loss of voting control over the corporation. In effect, the shareholder received corporate profits without suffering the consequences of dividend income treatment. This procedure led Congress to enact § 306, which, if applicable, converts the prior long-term capital gain on the sale or redemption of the tainted stock to dividend income.

Premium Tax Credit (PTC). A tax credit that is refundable and available in advance of filing a return for the year. The PTC serves to reduce the cost of health coverage obtained on the Marketplace (Exchange). A PTC is available to individuals who purchase coverage on the Exchange and have household income equal to or greater than 100 percent of the Federal poverty line (FPL) and no greater than 400 percent of the FPL. Also, an individual must not have been able to obtain affordable coverage from his or her employer. If obtained in advance, the PTC is given to the insurance provider to lower the monthly premium cost to the individual. The PTC is reconciled on Form 8962 (Premium Tax Credit) filed with Form 1040 or 1040-A (not Form 1040-EZ). Individuals who obtain insurance through the Marketplace receive Form 1095-A (Health Insurance Marketplace Statement) by January 31 of the following year. This form provides information necessary to claim or reconcile the PTC, including the monthly cost of premiums and the amount of PTC received in advance each month. § 36B.

Previously taxed income (PTI). Under prior law, the undistributed taxable income of an S corporation was taxed to the shareholders as of the last day of the corporation's tax year and usually could be withdrawn by the shareholders without tax consequences at some later point in time. The role of PTI has been taken over by the accumulated adjustments account. See also *accumulated adjustments account (AAA).*

Principal partner. A partner with a 5 percent or greater interest in partnership capital or profits. § 706(b)(3).

Private activity bonds. Interest on state and local bonds is excludible from gross income. § 103. Certain such bonds are labeled private activity bonds. Although the interest on such bonds is excludible for regular income tax purposes, it is treated as a tax preference in calculating the AMT.

Private foundations. An exempt organization that is subject to additional statutory restrictions on its activities and on contributions made to it. Excise taxes may be levied on certain prohibited transactions, and the Code places more stringent restrictions on the deductibility of contributions to private foundations. § 509.

Probate costs. The costs incurred in administering a decedent's estate.

Probate estate. The property of a decedent that is subject to administration by the executor or administrator of an estate.

Procedural Regulations. A Regulation issued by the Treasury Department that is a housekeeping-type instruction indicating information that taxpayers should provide the IRS as well as information about the internal management and conduct of the IRS itself.

Profit and loss sharing ratios. Specified in the partnership agreement and used to determine each partner's allocation of ordinary taxable income and separately stated items. Profits and losses can be shared in different ratios. The ratios can be changed by amending the partnership agreement or by using a special allocation. § 704(a).

Profit sharing plan. A deferred compensation plan established and maintained by an employer to provide for employee participation in the company's profits. Contributions are paid from the employer's current or accumulated profits to a trustee. Separate accounts are maintained for each participant employee. The plan must provide a definite, predetermined formula for allocating the contributions among the participants. It also must include a definite, predetermined formula for distributing the accumulated funds after a fixed number of years, on the attainment of a stated age, or on the occurrence of certain events such as illness, layoff, or retirement.

Profits (loss) interest. The extent of a partner's entitlement to an allocation of the partnership's operating results. This interest is measured by the profit and loss sharing ratios.

Property. Assets defined in the broadest legal sense. Property includes the unrealized receivables of a cash basis taxpayer, but not services rendered. § 351.

Property dividend. Generally treated in the same manner as a cash distribution, measured by the fair market value of the property on the date of distribution. Distribution of appreciated property causes the distributing C or S corporation to recognize gain. The distributing corporation does not recognize loss on property that has depreciated in value.

Property factor. The proportion of a multistate corporation's total property that is traceable to a specific state. Used in determining the taxable income that is to be apportioned to that state.

Proportionate distribution. A distribution in which each partner in a partnership receives a pro rata share of hot assets being distributed. For example, a distribution of $10,000 of hot assets equally to two 50 percent partners is a proportionate distribution.

Proposed Regulations. A Regulation issued by the Treasury Department in proposed, rather than final, form. The interval between the proposal of a Regulation and its finalization permits taxpayers and other interested parties to comment on the propriety of the proposal.

Proprietorship. A business entity for which there is a single owner. The net profit of the entity is reported on the owner's Federal income tax return (Schedule C of Form 1040).

Public Law 86–272. A congressional limit on the ability of the state to force a multistate corporation to assign taxable income to that state. Under P.L. 86–272, where orders for tangible personal property are both filled and delivered outside the state, the entity must establish more than the mere solicitation of such orders before any income can be apportioned to the state.

Punitive damages. Damages received or paid by the taxpayer can be classified as compensatory damages or as punitive damages. Punitive damages are those awarded to punish the defendant for gross negligence or the intentional infliction of harm. Such damages are includible in gross income. § 104.

Q

Qualified ABLE program. A state program that allows funds to be set aside for the benefit of an individual who became disabled or blind before age 26. Cash may be put into the fund annually up to the annual gift tax exclusion amount. Distributions to the designated beneficiary are not taxable provided they do not exceed qualified disability expenses for the year. § 529A.

Qualified business unit (QBU). A subsidiary, branch, or other business entity that conducts business using a currency other than the U.S. dollar.

Qualified dividend income (QDI). See *qualified dividends*.

Qualified dividends. Distributions made by domestic (and certain non-U.S.) corporations to noncorporate shareholders that are subject to tax at the same rates as those applicable to net long-term capital gains (i.e., 0 percent, 15 percent, or 20 percent). The 20 percent rate applies to certain high-income taxpayers (i.e., whose tax bracket is 39.6 percent). The dividend must be paid out of earnings and profits, and the shareholders must meet certain holding period requirements as to the stock. §§ 1(h)(1) and (11).

Qualified employee discount. Discounts offered employees on merchandise or services that the employer ordinarily sells or provides to customers. The discounts must be generally available to all employees. In the case of property, the discount cannot exceed the employer's gross profit (the sales price cannot be less than the employer's cost). In the case of services, the discounts cannot exceed 20 percent of the normal sales price. § 132.

Qualified joint venture. At the election of the taxpayers, certain joint ventures between spouses can avoid partnership classification. Known as a qualified joint venture, the spouses generally report their share of the business activities from the venture as sole proprietors (using two Schedule C forms). This would be reported on Schedule E if the venture relates to a rental property. § 761(f).

Qualified nonrecourse debt. Debt issued on realty by a bank, retirement plan, or governmental agency. Included in the at-risk amount by the investor. § 465(b)(6).

Qualified production activities income (QPAI). A key determinant in computing the domestic production activities deduction (DPAD). It consists of domestic production gross receipts (DPGR) reduced by cost of goods sold and other assignable expenses. Thus, QPAI represents the profit derived from domestic production activities. § 199.

Qualified real property business indebtedness. Indebtedness that was incurred or assumed by the taxpayer in connection with real property used in a trade or business and is secured by such real property. The taxpayer must not be a C corporation. For qualified real property business indebtedness, the taxpayer may elect to exclude some or all of the income realized from cancellation of debt on qualified real property. If the election is made, the basis of the property must be reduced by the amount excluded. The amount excluded cannot be greater than the excess of the principal amount of the outstanding debt over the fair market value (net of any other debt outstanding on the property) of the property securing the debt. § 108(c).

Qualified residence interest. A term relevant in determining the amount of interest expense the individual taxpayer may deduct as an itemized deduction for what otherwise would be disallowed as a component of personal interest (consumer interest). Qualified residence interest consists of interest paid on qualified residences (principal residence and one other residence) of the taxpayer. Debt that qualifies as qualified residence interest is limited to $1 million of debt to acquire, construct, or substantially improve qualified residences (acquisition indebtedness) plus $100,000 of other debt secured by qualified residences (home equity indebtedness). The home equity indebtedness may not exceed the fair market value of a qualified residence reduced by the acquisition indebtedness for that residence. § 163(h)(3).

Qualified small business corporation. For purposes of computing an exclusion upon the sale of qualified small business stock, a C corporation that has aggregate gross assets not exceeding $50 million and that is conducting an active trade or business. § 1202.

Qualified small business stock. Stock in a qualified small business corporation, purchased as part of an original issue after August 10, 1993. The shareholder may exclude from gross income 50 (or 75 or 100) percent of the realized gain on the sale of the stock if he or she held the stock for more than five years. § 1202.

Qualified terminable interest property (QTIP). Generally, the marital deduction (for gift and estate tax purposes) is not available if the interest transferred will terminate upon the death of the transferee spouse and pass to someone else. Thus, if Jim (the husband) places property in trust, life estate to Mary (the wife), and remainder to their children upon Mary's death, this is a terminable interest that will not provide Jim (or Jim's estate) with a marital deduction. If, however, the transfer in trust is treated as qualified terminable interest property (the QTIP election is made), the terminable interest restriction is waived and the marital deduction becomes available. In exchange for this deduction, the surviving spouse's gross estate must include the value of the QTIP election assets, even though he or she has no control over the ultimate disposition of the asset. Terminable interest property qualifies for this election if the donee (or heir) is the only beneficiary of the asset during his or her lifetime and receives income distributions relative to the property at least annually. For gifts, the donor spouse is the one who makes the QTIP election. For property transferred by death, the executor of the estate of the deceased spouse makes the election. §§ 2056(b)(7) and 2523(f).

Qualified transportation fringes. Transportation benefits provided by the employer to the employee. Such benefits include (1) transportation in a commuter highway vehicle between the employee's residence and the place of employment, (2) a transit pass, and (3) qualified parking. Qualified transportation fringes are excludible from the employee's gross income to the extent categories (1) and (2) above do not exceed $255 per month in 2016 and category (3) does not exceed $255 per month in 2016. These amounts are indexed annually for inflation. § 132.

Qualified tuition program. A program that allows college tuition to be prepaid for a beneficiary. When amounts in the plan are used, nothing is included in gross income provided they are used for qualified higher education expenses. § 529.

Qualifying child. An individual who, as to the taxpayer, satisfies the relationship, abode, and age tests. To be claimed as a dependent, such individual must also meet the citizenship and joint return tests and not be self-supporting. §§ 152(a)(1) and (c).

Qualifying relative. An individual who, as to the taxpayer, satisfies the relationship, gross income, support, citizenship, and joint return tests. Such an individual can be claimed as a dependent of the taxpayer. §§ 152(a)(2) and (d).

R

Rate reconciliation. Under Generally Accepted Accounting Principles, a footnote to the financial statements often includes a table that accounts for differences in the statutory income tax rate that applies to the entity (say, 35 percent) and the higher or lower effective tax rate that the entity realized for the reporting period. The rate reconciliation includes only permanent differences between the book tax expense and the entity's income tax provision. The rate reconciliation table often is expressed in dollar and/or percentage terms.

Realized gain. See *realized gain or loss.*

Realized gain or loss. The difference between the amount realized upon the sale or other disposition of property and the adjusted basis of the property. § 1001.

Realized loss. See *realized gain or loss.*

Realty. Real estate.

Reasonable cause. Relief from taxpayer and preparer penalties often is allowed where reasonable cause is found for the taxpayer's actions. For example, reasonable cause for the late filing of a tax return might be a flood that damaged the taxpayer's record-keeping systems and made a timely completion of the return difficult.

Reasonable needs of the business. A means of avoiding the penalty tax on an unreasonable accumulation of earnings. In determining the base for this tax (accumulated taxable income), § 535 allows a deduction for "such part of earnings and profits for the taxable year as are retained for the reasonable needs of the business." § 537.

Reasonableness. See *reasonableness requirement.*

Reasonableness requirement. The Code includes a reasonableness requirement with respect to the deduction of salaries and other compensation for services. What constitutes reasonableness is a question of fact. If an expense is unreasonable, the amount that is classified as unreasonable is not allowed as a deduction. The question of reasonableness generally arises with respect to closely held corporations where there is no separation of ownership and management. § 162(a)(1).

Recapitalization. A "Type E" reorganization, constituting a major change in the character and amount of outstanding equity of a corporation. Tax-free are stock for stock, bonds for bonds, and bonds for stock. For example, common stock exchanged for preferred stock can qualify as a tax-free "Type E" reorganization.

Recognized gain. See *recognized gain or loss.*

Recognized gain or loss. The portion of realized gain or loss subject to income taxation.

Recognized loss. See *recognized gain or loss.*

Recourse debt. Debt for which the lender may both foreclose on the property and assess a guarantor for any payments due under the loan. A lender also may make a claim against the assets of any general partner in a partnership to which debt is issued, without regard to whether the partner has guaranteed the debt.

Recovery of capital doctrine. When a taxable sale or exchange occurs, the seller may be permitted to recover his or her investment (or other adjusted basis) in the property before gain or loss is recognized.

Redemption to pay death taxes. Sale or exchange treatment is available relative to this type of stock redemption, to the extent of the proceeds up to the total amount paid by the estate or heir for estate/inheritance taxes and administration expenses. The stock value must exceed 35 percent of the value of the decedent's adjusted gross estate. In meeting this test, shareholdings in corporations where the decedent held at least 20 percent of the outstanding shares are combined.

Refundable credits. A credit that is paid to the taxpayer even if the amount of the credit (or credits) exceeds the taxpayer's tax liability.

Regular corporations. See *C corporation.*

Rehabilitation expenditures credit. A credit that is based on expenditures incurred to rehabilitate industrial and commercial buildings and certified historic structures. The credit is intended to discourage businesses from moving from older, economically distressed areas to newer locations and to encourage the preservation of historic structures. § 47.

Rehabilitation expenditures credit recapture. When property that qualifies for the rehabilitation expenditures credit is disposed of or ceases to be used in the trade or business of the taxpayer, some or all of the tax credit claimed on the property may be recaptured as additional tax liability. The amount of the recapture is the difference between the amount of the credit claimed originally and what should have been claimed in light of the length of time the property was actually held or used for qualifying purposes. § 50.

Related party. Various Code Sections define related parties and often include a variety of persons within this (usually detrimental) category. Generally, related parties are accorded different tax treatment from that applicable to other taxpayers who enter into similar transactions. For instance, realized losses that are generated between related parties are not recognized in the year of the loss. However, these deferred losses can be used to offset recognized gains that occur upon the subsequent sale of the asset to a nonrelated party. Other uses of a related-party definition include the conversion of gain upon the sale of a depreciable asset into all ordinary income (§ 1239) and the identification of constructive ownership of stock relative to corporate distributions, redemptions, liquidations, reorganizations, and compensation.

Related-party transactions. The tax law places restrictions upon the recognition of gains and losses between related parties because of the potential for abuse. For example, restrictions are placed on the deduction of losses from the sale or exchange of property between related parties. In addition, under certain circumstances, related-party gains that would otherwise be classified as capital gain are classified as ordinary income. §§ 267, 707(b), and 1239.

Rental activity. Any activity where payments are received principally for the use of tangible property is a rental activity. Temporary Regulations provide that in certain circumstances, activities involving rentals of real and personal property are not to be treated as rental activities. The Temporary Regulations list six exceptions.

Reorganization. Occurs, among other instances, when one corporation acquires another, a single corporation divides into two or more entities, a corporation makes a substantial change in its capital structure, a corporation undertakes a change in its legal name or domicile, or a corporation goes through a bankruptcy proceeding and continues to exist. The exchange of stock and other securities in a corporate reorganization can be effected favorably for tax purposes if certain statutory requirements are followed strictly. Tax consequences include the nonrecognition of any gain that is realized by the shareholders except to the extent of boot received. § 368.

Required taxable year. A partnership or limited liability company must use a required tax year as its tax accounting period, or one of three allowable alternative tax year-ends. The required tax year is determined using the least aggregate deferral rule. But if there is a common tax year used by owners holding a majority of the entity's capital or profits interests, or used by all of the owners who hold 5 percent or more of the capital or profits interests, then that tax year-end is used by the entity.

Research activities credit. A tax credit whose purpose is to encourage research and development. It consists of three components: the incremental research activities credit, the basic research credit, and the energy credit. The incremental research activities credit is equal to 20 percent of the excess qualified research expenditures over the base amount. The basic research credit is equal to 20 percent of the excess of basic research payments over the base amount. § 41.

Research and experimental expenditures. The Code provides three alternatives for the tax treatment of research and experimentation expenditures. They may be expensed in the year paid or incurred, deferred subject to amortization, or capitalized. If the taxpayer does not elect to expense such costs or to defer them subject to amortization (over 60 months), the expenditures must be capitalized. § 174. Three types of research activities credits are available: the basic research credit, the incremental research activities credit, and the energy credit. The rate for each type is 20 percent. § 41.

Reserve method. A method of accounting whereby an allowance is permitted for estimated uncollectible accounts. Actual write-offs are charged to the reserve, and recoveries of amounts previously written off are credited to the reserve. The Code permits only certain financial institutions to use the reserve method. § 166.

Residential rental real estate. Buildings for which at least 80 percent of the gross rents are from dwelling units (e.g., an apartment building). This type of building is distinguished from nonresidential (commercial or industrial) buildings in applying the recapture of depreciation provisions. The term also is relevant in distinguishing between buildings that are eligible for a 27.5-year life versus a 39-year life for MACRS purposes. Generally, residential buildings receive preferential treatment.

Restricted property plan. An arrangement whereby an employer transfers property (usually stock) to an employee at a bargain price (for less than the fair market value). If the transfer is accompanied by a substantial risk of forfeiture and the property is not transferable, no compensation results to the employee until the restrictions disappear. An example of a substantial risk of forfeiture would be a requirement that the employee return the property if his or her employment is terminated within a specified period of time. § 83.

Revenue Agent's Report (RAR). A Revenue Agent's Report (RAR) reflects any adjustments made by the agent as a result of an audit of the taxpayer. The RAR is mailed to the taxpayer along with the 30-day letter, which outlines the appellate procedures available to the taxpayer.

Revenue neutrality. A description that characterizes tax legislation when it neither increases nor decreases the total revenue collected by the taxing jurisdiction. Thus, any tax revenue losses are offset by tax revenue gains.

Revenue Procedures. A matter of procedural importance to both taxpayers and the IRS concerning the administration of the tax laws is issued as a Revenue Procedure (abbreviated Rev.Proc.). A Revenue Procedure is published in an *Internal Revenue Bulletin* (I.R.B.).

Revenue Rulings. A Revenue Ruling (abbreviated Rev.Rul.) is issued by the National Office of the IRS to express an official interpretation of the tax law as applied to specific transactions. It is more limited in application than a Regulation. A Revenue Ruling is published in an *Internal Revenue Bulletin* (I.R.B.).

Reversionary interest. The trust property that reverts to the grantor after the expiration of an intervening income interest. Assume that Phil places real estate in trust with income to Junior for 11 years, and upon the expiration of this term, the property returns to Phil. Under these circumstances, Phil holds a reversionary interest in the property. A reversionary interest is the same as a remainder interest, except that, in the latter case, the property passes to someone other than the original owner (e.g., the grantor of a trust) upon the expiration of the intervening interest.

Roth IRA. See *Individual Retirement Account (IRA)*.

S

S corporation. The designation for a small business corporation. See also *Subchapter S*.

Sale or exchange. A requirement for the recognition of capital gain or loss. Generally, the seller of property must receive money or relief from debt to have sold the property. An exchange involves the transfer of property for other property. Thus, collection of a debt is neither a sale nor an exchange. The term *sale or exchange* is not defined by the Code.

Sales factor. The proportion of a multistate corporation's total sales that is traceable to a specific state. Used in determining the taxable income that is to be apportioned to that state.

Sales tax. A state- or local-level tax on the retail sale of specified property. Generally, the purchaser pays the tax, but the seller collects it, as an agent for the government. Various taxing jurisdictions allow exemptions for purchases of specific items, including certain food, services, and manufacturing equipment. If the purchaser and seller are in different states, a use tax usually applies.

Schedule K–1. A tax information form prepared for each partner in a partnership, each shareholder of an S corporation, and some beneficiaries of certain trusts. The Schedule K–1 reports the owner's share of the entity's ordinary income or loss from operations, as well as the owner's share of separately stated items.

Schedule M–1. On the Form 1120, a reconciliation of book net income with Federal taxable income. Accounts for temporary and permanent differences in the two computations, such as depreciation differences, exempt income, and nondeductible items. On Forms 1120S and 1065, the Schedule M–1 reconciles book income with the owners' aggregate ordinary taxable income.

Schedule M–3. An *expanded* reconciliation of book net income with Federal taxable income (see *Schedule M–1*). Required of C and S corporations and partnerships/LLCs with total assets of $10 million or more.

Scholarship. Scholarships are generally excluded from the gross income of the recipient unless the payments are a disguised form of compensation for services rendered. However, the Code imposes restrictions on the exclusion. The recipient must be a degree candidate. The excluded amount is limited to amounts used for tuition, fees, books, supplies, and equipment required for courses of instruction. Amounts received for room and board are not eligible for the exclusion. § 117.

Section 121 exclusion. If a residence has been owned and used by the taxpayer as the principal residence for at least two years during the five-year period ending on the date of sale, up to $250,000 of realized gain is excluded from gross income. For a married couple filing a joint return, the $250,000 is increased to $500,000 if either spouse satisfies the ownership requirement and both spouses satisfy the use requirement.

Section 179 expensing. The ability to deduct a capital expenditure in the year an asset is placed in service rather than over the asset's useful life or cost recovery period. The annual ceiling on the deduction is $500,000 in 2015 and 2016. However, the deduction is reduced dollar for dollar when § 179 property placed in service during the taxable year exceeds $2,010,000 ($2 million in 2015). In addition, the amount expensed under § 179 cannot exceed the aggregate amount of taxable income derived from the conduct of any trade or business by the taxpayer.

Section 179 expensing election. See *Section 179 expensing*.

Section 338 election. When a corporation acquires at least 80 percent of a subsidiary within a 12-month period, it can elect to treat the acquisition of such stock as an asset purchase. The acquiring corporation's basis in the subsidiary's assets then is the cost of the stock. The subsidiary is deemed to have sold its assets for an amount equal to the grossed-up basis in its stock.

Section 382 limitation. When one corporation acquires another, the acquiring corporation's ability to use the loss and credit carryovers of the target may be limited, in an anti-abuse provision specified in the Code. Generally, for instance, the maximum NOL deduction available to the acquiring is the value of the target when acquired times the long-term tax-exempt interest rate on that date.

Section 401(k) plan. A cash or deferred arrangement plan that allows participants to elect to receive up to $18,000 in 2016 in cash (taxed currently) or to have a contribution made on their behalf to a profit sharing or stock bonus plan (excludible from gross income). The plan may also be in the form of a salary reduction agreement between the participant and the employer.

Section 754 election. An election that may be made by a partnership to adjust the basis of partnership assets to reflect a purchasing partner's outside basis in interest or to reflect a gain, loss, or basis adjustment of a partner receiving a distribution from a partnership. The intent of the election is to maintain the equivalence between outside and inside basis for that partner. Once the election is made, the partnership must make basis adjustments for all future transactions, unless the IRS consents to revoke the election.

Section 1231 gains and losses. If the combined gains and losses from the taxable dispositions of § 1231 assets plus the net gain from business involuntary conversions (of both § 1231 assets and long-term capital assets) is a gain, the gains and losses are treated as long-term capital gains and losses. In arriving at § 1231 gains, however, the depreciation recapture provisions (e.g., § 1245) are applied first to produce ordinary income. If the net result of the combination is a loss, the gains and losses from § 1231 assets are treated as ordinary gains and losses. § 1231(a).

Section 1231 lookback. For gain to be classified as § 1231 gain, the gain must survive the § 1231 lookback. To the extent of nonrecaptured § 1231 losses for the five prior tax years, the gain is classified as ordinary income. § 1231(c).

Section 1231 property. Depreciable assets and real estate used in trade or business and held for the required long-term holding period. § 1231(b).

Section 1244 stock. Stock issued under § 1244 by qualifying small business corporations. If § 1244 stock becomes worthless, the shareholders may claim an ordinary loss rather than the usual capital loss, within statutory limitations.

Section 1245 property. Property that is subject to the recapture of depreciation under § 1245. For a definition of § 1245 property, see § 1245(a)(3).

Section 1245 recapture. Upon a taxable disposition of § 1245 property, all depreciation claimed on the property is recaptured as ordinary income (but not to exceed any recognized gain from the disposition).

Section 1250 property. Real estate that is subject to the recapture of depreciation under § 1250. For a definition of § 1250 property, see § 1250(c).

Section 1250 recapture. Upon a taxable disposition of § 1250 property, accelerated depreciation or cost recovery claimed on the property may be recaptured as ordinary income.

Securities. Generally, stock, debt, and other financial assets. To the extent securities other than the stock of the transferee corporation are received in a § 351 exchange, the new shareholder recognizes a gain. For purposes of corporate reorganizations, generally, debt with terms longer than 10 years. To the extent stock and securities are transferred in a corporate reorganization under § 368, no gain or loss is recognized.

Self-employment tax. A tax of 12.4 percent is levied on individuals with net earnings from self-employment (up to $118,500 in 2016) to provide Social Security benefits (i.e., the old age, survivors, and disability insurance portion) for such individuals. In addition, a tax of 2.9 percent is levied on individuals with net earnings from self-employment (with no statutory ceiling) to provide Medicare benefits (i.e., the hospital insurance portion) for such individuals. If a self-employed individual also receives wages from an employer that are subject to FICA, the self-employment tax will be reduced. A partial deduction is allowed in calculating the self-employment tax. Individuals with net earnings of $400 or more from self-employment are subject to this tax. §§ 1401 and 1402.

Separate foreign tax credit income categories. The foreign tax credit of a taxpayer is computed for each of several types of income sources, as specified by the Code to limit the results of tax planning. FTC income "baskets" include general and passive. The FTC for the year is the sum of the credits as computed within all of the taxpayer's separate FTC baskets used for the tax year.

Separate return limitation year (SRLY). A series of rules limits the amount of an acquired corporation's net operating loss carryforwards that can be used by the acquiror. Generally, a consolidated return can include the acquiree's net operating loss carryforward only to the extent of the lesser of the subsidiary's (1) current-year or (2) cumulative positive contribution to consolidated taxable income.

Separately stated items. Any item of a partnership or an S corporation that might be taxed differently to any two owners of the entity. These amounts are not included in the ordinary income of the entity, but are instead reported separately to the owners; tax consequences are determined at the owner level.

Severance taxes. A tax imposed upon the extraction of natural resources.

Short period. See *short taxable year.*

Short sale. A sale that occurs when a taxpayer sells borrowed property (usually stock) and repays the lender with substantially identical property either held on the date of the short sale or purchased after the sale. No gain or loss is rec-

ognized until the short sale is closed, and such gain or loss is generally short-term. § 1233.

Short taxable year. A tax year that is less than 12 months. A short taxable year may occur in the initial reporting period, in the final tax year, or when the taxpayer changes tax years.

Significant participation activity. Seven tests determine whether an individual has achieved material participation in an activity, one of which is based on more than 500 hours of participation in significant participation activities. A significant participation activity is one in which the individual's participation exceeds 100 hours during the year. Temp.Reg. § 1.469–5T.

Simple trust. Trusts that are not complex trusts. Such trusts may not have a charitable beneficiary, accumulate income, or distribute corpus.

Simplified employee pension (SEP) plans. An employer may make contributions to an employee's IRA in amounts not exceeding the lesser of 15 percent of compensation or $53,000 per individual in 2016. These employer-sponsored simplified employee pensions are permitted only if the contributions are nondiscriminatory and are made on behalf of all employees who have attained age 21 and have worked for the employer during at least three of the five preceding calendar years. § 219(b).

Small business corporation. A corporation that satisfies the definition of § 1361(b), § 1244(c), or both. Satisfaction of § 1361(b) permits an S election, and satisfaction of § 1244 enables the shareholders of the corporation to claim an ordinary loss on the worthlessness of stock.

Small business stock (§ 1244 stock). See *Section 1244 stock.*

Small Cases Division. A division within the U.S. Tax Court where jurisdiction is limited to claims of $50,000 or less. There is no appeal from this court.

Solicitation. A level of activity brought about by the taxpayer within a specific state. Under Public Law 86-272, certain types of solicitation activities do not create nexus with the state. Exceeding mere solicitation, though, creates nexus.

Special allocation. Any amount for which an agreement exists among the partners of a partnership outlining the method used for spreading the item among the partners.

Special use value. Permits the executor of an estate to value, for estate tax purposes, real estate used in a farming activity or in connection with a closely held business at its current use value rather than at its most suitable or optimal use value. Under this option, a farm is valued for farming purposes even though, for example, the property might have a higher potential value as a shopping center. For the executor of an estate to elect special use valuation, the conditions of § 2032A must be satisfied.

Specific charge-off method. A method of accounting for bad debts in which a deduction is permitted only when an account becomes partially or completely worthless.

Spin-off. A type of reorganization where, for example, Apple Corporation transfers some assets to Core Corporation in exchange for Core stock representing control. Apple then distributes the Core stock to its shareholders.

Split-off. A type of reorganization where, for example, Apple Corporation transfers some assets to Core Corporation in exchange for Core stock representing control. Apple then distributes the Core stock to its shareholders in exchange for some of their Apple stock. Not all shareholders need to exchange stock.

Split-up. A type of reorganization where, for example, Firefly Corporation transfers some assets to Fire Corporation and the remainder to Fly Corporation. In return, Firefly receives enough Fire and Fly stock representing control of each corporation. Firefly then distributes the Fire and Fly stock to its shareholders in return for all of their Firefly stock. Firefly then liquidates, and its shareholders now have control of Fire and Fly.

Sprinkling trust. When a trustee has the discretion to either distribute or accumulate the entity accounting income of the trust and to distribute it among the trust's income beneficiaries in varying magnitudes. The trustee can "sprinkle" the income of the trust.

Standard deduction. The individual taxpayer can either itemize deductions or take the standard deduction. The amount of the standard deduction depends on the taxpayer's filing status (single, head of household, married filing jointly, surviving spouse, or married filing separately). For 2016, the amount of the standard deduction ranges from $6,300 (for single) to $12,600 (for married, filing jointly). Additional standard deductions of either $1,250 (for married taxpayers) or $1,550 (for single taxpayers) are available if the taxpayer is blind or age 65 or over. Limitations exist on the amount of the standard deduction of a taxpayer who is another taxpayer's dependent. The standard deduction amounts are adjusted for inflation each year. § 63(c).

Startup expenditures. Expenditures paid or incurred prior to the beginning of the business that would have been deductible as an ordinary and necessary business expense if business operations had begun. Examples of such expenditures include advertising; salaries and wages; travel and other expenses incurred in lining up prospective distributors, suppliers, or customers; and salaries and fees to executives, consultants, and professional service providers. A taxpayer will immediately expense the first $5,000 (subject to phaseout) of startup expenditures and amortize the balance over a period of 180 months, unless the taxpayer elects to not do so.

Statute of limitations. Provisions of the law that specify the maximum period of time in which action may be taken concerning a past event. Code §§ 6501–6504 contain the limitation periods applicable to the IRS for additional assessments, and §§ 6511–6515 relate to refund claims by taxpayers.

Statutory employees. Statutory employees are considered self-employed independent contractors for purposes of reporting income and expenses on their tax returns. Generally, a statutory employee must meet three tests:

- It is understood from a service contract that the services will be performed by the person.

- The person does not have a substantial investment in facilities (other than transportation used to perform the services).

- The services involve a continuing relationship with the person for whom they are performed.

For further information on statutory employees, see Circular E, *Employer's Tax Guide* (IRS Publication 15).

Step transaction. Disregarding one or more transactions to arrive at the final result. Assume, for example, Beta Corporation creates Alpha Corporation by transferring assets desired by Beta's sole shareholder, Carl. Carl then causes Alpha to liquidate to obtain the assets. Under these circumstances, the IRS may contend that the creation and liquidation of Alpha be disregarded. What really happened was a dividend distribution from Beta to Carl.

Step-down in basis. A reduction in the tax basis of property.

Step-up in basis. An increase in the income tax basis of property. A step-up in basis occurs when a decedent dies owning appreciated property. Since the estate or heir acquires a basis in the property equal to the property's fair market value on the date of death (or alternate valuation date if available and elected), any appreciation is not subject to the income tax. Thus, a step-up in basis is the result, with no immediate income tax consequences.

Stock bonus plan. A type of deferred compensation plan in which the employer establishes and maintains the plan and contributes employer stock to the plan for the benefit of employees. The contributions need not be dependent on the employer's profits. Any benefits of the plan are distributable in the form of employer stock, except that distributable fractional shares may be paid in cash.

Stock dividend. Not taxable if pro rata distributions of stock or stock rights on common stock. Section 305 governs the taxability of stock dividends and sets out five exceptions to the general rule that stock dividends are nontaxable.

Stock option. The right to purchase a stated number of shares of stock from a corporation at a certain price within a specified period of time. §§ 421 and 422.

Stock redemption. A corporation buys back its own stock from a specified shareholder. Typically, the corporation recognizes any realized gain on the noncash assets that it uses to effect a redemption, and the shareholder obtains a capital gain or loss upon receipt of the purchase price.

Stock rights. Assets that convey to the holder the power to purchase corporate stock at a specified price, often for a limited period of time. Stock rights received may be taxed as a distribution of earnings and profits. After the right is exercised, the basis of the acquired share includes the investor's purchase price or gross income, if any, to obtain the right. Disposition of the right also can be taxable.

Subchapter S. Sections 1361–1379 of the Internal Revenue Code. An elective provision permitting certain small business corporations (§ 1361) and their shareholders (§ 1362) to elect to be treated for income tax purposes in accordance with the operating rules of §§ 1363–1379. However, some S corporations usually avoid the corporate income tax, and corporate losses can be claimed by the shareholders.

Subpart F. Identifies the current tax treatment of income earned by a controlled foreign corporation. Certain types of income are included in U.S. gross income by U.S. shareholders of such an entity as they are generated, not when they are repatriated.

Subpart F income. See *Subpart F.*

Substance over form. A standard used when one must ascertain the true reality of what has occurred. Suppose, for example, a father sells stock to his daughter for $1,000. If the stock is really worth $50,000 at the time of the transfer, the substance of the transaction is probably a gift to her of $49,000.

Substantial authority. Taxpayer and tax preparer understatement penalties are waived where substantial authority existed for the disputed position taken on the return.

Substantial risk of forfeiture (SRF). A term that is associated with a restricted property plan. Generally, an employee who receives property (e.g., stock of the employer-corporation) from the employer at a bargain price or at no cost must include the bargain element in gross income. However, the employee currently does not have to do so if there is a substantial risk of forfeiture. A substantial risk of forfeiture exists if a person's rights to full enjoyment of property are conditioned upon the future performance, or the refraining from the performance, of substantial services by the individual. § 83.

Sunset provision. A provision attached to new tax legislation that will cause such legislation to expire at a specified date. Sunset provisions are attached to tax cut bills for long-term budgetary reasons to make their effect temporary. Once the sunset provision comes into play, the tax cut is rescinded and former law is reinstated. An example of a sunset provision is contained in the Tax Relief Reconciliation Act of 2001 that related to the estate tax. After the estate tax was phased out in 2010, a sunset provision called for the reinstatement of the estate tax as of January 1, 2011.

Supreme Court. See *U.S. Supreme Court.*

Surviving spouse. When a husband or wife predeceases the other spouse, the survivor is known as a surviving spouse. Under certain conditions, a surviving spouse may be entitled to use the income tax rates in § 1(a) (those applicable to married persons filing a joint return) for the two years after the year of death of his or her spouse. § 2. With respect to the Federal estate tax, this term describes the second spouse to die of a married couple, for the period between the two dates of death.

Syndication costs. Incurred in promoting and marketing partnership interests for sale to investors. Examples include legal and accounting fees, printing costs for prospectus and placement documents, and state registration fees. These items are capitalized by the partnership as incurred, with no amortization thereof allowed.

T

Tax avoidance. The minimization of one's tax liability by taking advantage of legally available tax planning opportunities. Tax avoidance can be contrasted with tax evasion, which entails the reduction of tax liability by illegal means.

Tax benefit rule. A provision that limits the recognition of income from the recovery of an expense or a loss properly deducted in a prior tax year to the amount of the deduction that generated a tax saving. Assume that last year Gary had medical expenses of $4,000 and adjusted gross income of $30,000. Because of the AGI limitation, Gary could deduct only $1,000 of these expenses [$4,000 − (10% × $30,000)]. If this year Gary is reimbursed in full by his insurance company for the $4,000 of expenses, the tax benefit rule limits the amount of income from the reimbursement to $1,000 (the amount previously deducted with a tax saving).

Tax Court. See *U.S. Tax Court.*

Tax credit for the elderly or disabled. An elderly (age 65 and over) or disabled taxpayer may receive a tax credit amounting to 15 percent of $5,000 ($7,500 for qualified married individuals filing jointly). This amount is reduced by Social Security benefits, excluded pension benefits, and one-half of the taxpayer's adjusted gross income in excess of $7,500 ($10,000 for married taxpayers filing jointly). § 22.

Tax credits. Amounts that directly reduce a taxpayer's tax liability. The tax benefit received from a tax credit is not dependent on the taxpayer's marginal tax rate, whereas the benefit of a tax deduction or exclusion is dependent on the taxpayer's tax bracket.

Tax evasion. The reduction of taxes by the use of subterfuge or fraud or other nonlegal means. For example, a cash basis taxpayer tries to increase his or her charitable contribution deduction by prepaying next year's church pledge with a pre-dated check issued in the following year.

Tax haven. A country in which either locally sourced income or residents of the country are subject to a low rate of taxation.

Tax preferences items. See *AMT preferences.*

Tax preparer. One who prepares tax returns for compensation. A tax preparer must register with the IRS and receive a special ID number to practice before the IRS and represent taxpayers before the agency in tax audit actions. The conduct of a tax preparer is regulated under Circular 230. Tax preparers also are subject to penalties for inappropriate conduct when working in the tax profession.

Tax Rate Schedules. Rate schedules that are used by upper-income taxpayers and those not permitted to use the tax table. Separate rate schedules are provided for married individuals filing jointly, heads of households, single taxpayers, estates and trusts, and married individuals filing separate returns. § 1.

Tax research. The method used to determine the best available solution to a situation that possesses tax consequences. Both tax and nontax factors are considered.

Tax shelters. The typical tax shelter generated large losses in the early years of the activity. Investors would offset these losses against other types of income and therefore avoid paying income taxes on this income. These tax shelter investments could then be sold after a few years and produce capital gain income, which is taxed at a lower rate compared to ordinary income. The passive activity loss rules and the at-risk rules now limit tax shelter deductions.

Tax Table. A table that is provided for taxpayers with less than $100,000 of taxable income. Separate columns are provided for single taxpayers, married taxpayers filing jointly, heads of households, and married taxpayers filing separately. § 3.

Tax treaties. An agreement between the U.S. Department of State and another country designed to alleviate double taxation of income and asset transfers and to share administrative information useful to tax agencies in both countries. The United States has income tax treaties with almost 70 countries and transfer tax treaties with about 20.

Taxable estate. The taxable estate is the gross estate of a decedent reduced by the deductions allowed by §§ 2053–2057 (e.g., administration expenses, marital and charitable deductions). The taxable estate is subject to the unified transfer tax at death. § 2051.

Taxable gift. The amount of a gift that is subject to the unified transfer tax. Thus, a taxable gift has been adjusted by the annual exclusion and other appropriate deductions (e.g., marital and charitable). § 2053.

Taxable year. The annual period over which income is measured for income tax purposes. Most individuals use a calendar year, but many businesses use a fiscal year based on the natural business year.

Technical Advice Memoranda (TAM). TAMs are issued by the IRS in response to questions raised by IRS field personnel during audits. They deal with completed rather than proposed transactions and are often requested for questions related to exempt organizations and employee plans.

Technical termination of a partnership. The entity is treated for tax purposes as though it has terminated, even though it continues its activities. When there has been a sale or exchange of more than 50 percent of the capital interests of the partnership within 12 months, the partnership is deemed to have terminated when the 50 percent threshold is crossed. A new partnership immediately is formed through asset contributions by the partners. These activities can affect the entity's tax year and its bases in the assets it holds.

Temporary differences. Under ASC 740 (SFAS 109), tax-related items that appear in the entity's financial statements and its tax return, but in different time periods. For instance, doubtful accounts receivable often create a temporary book-tax difference, as a bad debt reserve is used to compute an expense for financial reporting purposes, but a bad debt often is deductible only under the specific write-off rule for tax purposes, and the difference observed for the current period creates a temporary difference.

Temporary Regulations. A Regulation issued by the Treasury Department in temporary form. When speed is critical, the Treasury Department issues Temporary Regulations that take effect immediately. These Regulations have the same authoritative value as Final Regulations and may be cited as precedent for three years. Temporary Regulations are also issued as proposed Regulations.

Tenants by the entirety. Essentially, a joint tenancy between husband and wife.

Tenants in common. A form of ownership where each tenant (owner) holds an undivided interest in property. Unlike a joint tenancy or a tenancy by the entirety, the interest of a tenant in common does not terminate upon that individual's death (there is no right of survivorship). Assume that Tim and Cindy acquire real estate as equal tenants in common. Upon Tim's death, his one-half interest in the property passes to his estate or heirs, not automatically to Cindy.

Terminable interests. An interest in property that terminates upon the death of the holder or upon the occurrence of some other specified event. The transfer of a terminable in-

terest by one spouse to the other may not qualify for the marital deduction. §§ 2056(b) and 2523(b).

Theft losses. A loss from larceny, embezzlement, or robbery. It does not include misplacement of items.

Thin capitalization. When debt owed by a corporation to the shareholders becomes too large in relation to the corporation's capital structure (i.e., stock and shareholder equity), the IRS may contend that the corporation is thinly capitalized. In effect, some or all of the debt is reclassified as equity. The immediate result is to disallow any interest deduction to the corporation on the reclassified debt. To the extent of the corporation's earnings and profits, interest payments and loan repayments on the reclassified debt are treated as dividends to the shareholders.

Thirty-day letter. A letter that accompanies an RAR (Revenue Agent's Report) issued as a result of an IRS audit of a taxpayer (or the rejection of a taxpayer's claim for refund). The letter outlines the taxpayer's appeal procedure before the IRS. If the taxpayer does not request any such procedures within the 30-day period, the IRS issues a statutory notice of deficiency (the 90-day letter).

Throwback rule. If there is no income tax in the state to which a sale otherwise would be apportioned, the sale essentially is exempt from state income tax, even though the seller is domiciled in a state that levies an income tax. Nonetheless, if the seller's state has adopted a throwback rule, the sale is attributed to the seller's state and the transaction is subjected to a state-level tax.

Traditional IRA. See *Individual Retirement Account (IRA).*

Transfer pricing. The process of setting internal prices for transfers of goods and services among related taxpayers. For example, what price should be used when Subsidiary purchases management services from Parent? The IRS can adjust transfer prices when it can show that the taxpayers were attempting to avoid tax by, say, shifting losses, deductions, or credits from low-tax to high-tax entities or jurisdictions.

Transportation expenses. Transportation expenses for an employee include only the cost of transportation (e.g., taxi fares and automobile expenses) in the course of employment when the employee is not away from home in travel status. Commuting expenses are not deductible.

Travel expenses. Expenses that include meals (generally subject to a 50 percent disallowance) and lodging and transportation expenses while away from home in the pursuit of a trade or business (including that of an employee).

Treaty shopping. An international investor attempts to use the favorable aspects of a tax treaty to his or her advantage, often elevating the form of the transaction over its substance (e.g., by establishing only a nominal presence in the country offering the favorable treaty terms).

U

UDITPA. The Uniform Division of Income for Tax Purposes Act has been adopted in some form by many of the states. The Act develops criteria by which the total taxable income of a multistate corporation can be assigned to specific states.

Unclaimed property. A U.S. state may have the right to acquire property that has been made available to an individual or legal entity for a fixed period of time, where the claimant has not taken possession of the property after a notice period. Examples of such property that a state could acquire are an uncashed payroll check, or an unused gift card.

Undistributed PHCI. The tax base for the personal holding company tax. § 545.

Unearned income. Income received but not yet earned. Normally, such income is taxed when received, even for accrual basis taxpayers.

Unified transfer tax. Rates applicable to transfers by gift and death made after 1976. § 2001(c).

Unified transfer tax credit. A credit allowed against any unified transfer tax. §§ 2010 and 2505.

Uniform capitalization (UNICAP) rules. Under § 263A, the Regulations provide a set of rules that all taxpayers (regardless of the particular industry) can use to determine the items of cost (and means of allocating those costs) that must be capitalized with respect to the production of tangible property.

Unitary approach. See *unitary theory*.

Unitary theory. Sales, property, and payroll of related corporations are combined for nexus and apportionment purposes, and the worldwide income of the unitary entity is apportioned to the state. Subsidiaries and other affiliated corporations found to be part of the corporation's unitary business (because they are subject to overlapping ownership, operation, or management) are included in the apportionment procedure. This approach can be limited if a water's-edge election is in effect.

Unit-livestock-price method. A method of accounting for the cost of livestock. The livestock are valued using a standard cost of raising an animal with the characteristics of the animals on hand to the same age as those animals.

Unrealized receivables. Amounts earned by a cash basis taxpayer but not yet received. Because of the method of accounting used by the taxpayer, these amounts have a zero income tax basis. When unrealized receivables are distributed to a partner, they generally convert a transaction from nontaxable to taxable or an otherwise capital gain to ordinary income (i.e., as a "hot asset").

Unreasonable compensation. A deduction is allowed for "reasonable" salaries or other compensation for personal services actually rendered. To the extent compensation is "excessive" ("unreasonable"), the distribution could be treated as a dividend, such that no deduction is allowed. The problem of unreasonable compensation usually is limited to closely held corporations, where the motivation is to pay out profits in some form that is deductible to the corporation.

Unreasonable position. A tax preparer penalty is assessed regarding the understatement of a client's tax liability due to a tax return position that is found to be too aggressive. The penalty is avoided if there is substantial authority for the position or if the position is disclosed adequately on the tax return. The penalty equals the greater of $1,000 or one-half of the tax preparer's fee that is traceable to the aggressive position.

Unrecaptured § 1250 gain. Gain from the sale of depreciable real estate held more than one year. The gain is equal to or less than the depreciation taken on such property and is reduced by § 1245 and § 1250 gain.

Unrelated business income (UBI). Income recognized by an exempt organization that is generated from activities not related to the exempt purpose of the entity. For instance, the gift shop located in a hospital may generate unrelated business income. § 511.

Unrelated business income tax (UBIT). Levied on the unrelated business income of an exempt organization.

U.S. Court of Federal Claims. A trial court (court of original jurisdiction) that decides litigation involving Federal tax matters. Appeal from this court is to the Court of Appeals for the Federal Circuit.

U.S. shareholder. For purposes of classification of an entity as a controlled foreign corporation, a U.S. person who owns, or is considered to own, 10 percent or more of the total combined voting power of all classes of voting stock of a foreign corporation. Stock owned directly, indirectly, and constructively is counted for this purpose.

U.S. Supreme Court. The highest appellate court or the court of last resort in the Federal court system and in most states. Only a small number of tax decisions of the U.S. Courts of Appeal are reviewed by the U.S. Supreme Court under its certiorari procedure. The Supreme Court usually grants certiorari to resolve a conflict among the Courts of Appeal (e.g., two or more appellate courts have assumed opposing positions on a particular issue) or when the tax issue is extremely important (e.g., size of the revenue loss to the Federal government).

U.S. Tax Court. One of four trial courts of original jurisdiction that decides litigation involving Federal income, death, or gift taxes. It is the only trial court where the taxpayer must not first pay the deficiency assessed by the IRS. The Tax Court will not have jurisdiction over a case unless a statutory notice of deficiency (90-day letter) has been issued by the IRS and the taxpayer files the petition for hearing within the time prescribed.

U.S. trade or business. A set of activities that is carried on in a regular, continuous, and substantial manner. A non-U.S. taxpayer is subject to U.S. tax on the taxable income that is effectively connected with a U.S. trade or business.

Use tax. A sales tax that is collectible by the seller where the purchaser is domiciled in a different state.

V

Vacation homes. The Code places restrictions upon taxpayers who rent their residences or vacation homes for part of the tax year. The restrictions may result in a scaling down of expense deductions for the taxpayers. § 280A.

Valuation allowance. Under ASC 740 (SFAS 109), a tax-related item is reported for book purposes only when it is more likely than not that the item actually will be realized. When the "more likely than not" test is failed, a contra-asset account is created to offset some or all of the related deferred tax asset. For instance, if the entity projects that it will not be able to use all of its net operating loss carryforward due to a lack of future taxable income, a valuation allowance is created to reduce the net deferred tax asset that corresponds to the carryforward. If income projections later change and it appears that the carryforward will be used, the valuation allowance is reversed or "released." Creation of a valuation allowance usually increases the current tax expense and thereby reduces current book income, and its release often increases book income in the later reporting period.

Value added tax (VAT). A national sales tax that taxes the increment in value as goods move through the production process. A VAT is much used in other countries but has not yet been incorporated as part of the U.S. Federal tax structure.

Vesting requirements. A qualified deferred compensation arrangement must satisfy a vesting requirement. Under this provision, an employee's right to accrued plan benefits derived from employer contributions must be nonforfeitable in accordance with one of two vesting time period schedules (or two required alternate vesting schedules for certain employer matching contributions).

Voluntary revocation. The owners of a majority of shares in an S corporation elect to terminate the S status of the entity as of a specified date. The day on which the revocation is effective is the first day of the corporation's C tax year.

W

W–2 wages. The domestic production activities deduction (DPAD) cannot exceed 50 percent of the W–2 wages paid for any particular year. Prop.Reg. § 199–2(f)(2) provides several methods for calculating the W–2 wages, but the payments must involve common law employees. To qualify, employees need to be involved in the production process. § 199.

Wash sale. A loss from the sale of stock or securities that is disallowed because the taxpayer, within 30 days before or after the sale, has acquired stock or securities substantially identical to those sold. § 1091.

Water's edge. A limitation on the worldwide scope of the unitary theory. If a corporate water's-edge election is in effect, the state can consider in the apportionment procedure only the activities that occur within the boundaries of the United States.

Water's-edge election. See *water's edge.*

Wherewithal to pay. This concept recognizes the inequity of taxing a transaction when the taxpayer lacks the means with which to pay the tax. Under it, there is a correlation between the imposition of the tax and the ability to pay the tax. It is particularly suited to situations in which the taxpayer's economic position has not changed significantly as a result of the transaction.

Whistleblower Program. An IRS initiative that offers special rewards to informants who provide evidence regarding tax evasion activities of businesses or high-income individuals. More than $2 million of tax, interest, and penalty must be at stake. The reward can reach 30 percent of the tax recovery that is attributable to the whistleblower's information.

Withholding allowances. The number of withholding allowances serves as the basis for determining the amount of income taxes withheld from an employee's salary or wages. The more withholding allowances claimed, the less income tax withheld by an employer. An employee may claim withholding allowances for personal exemptions for self and spouse (unless claimed as a dependent of another person), dependency exemptions, and special withholding allowances.

Work opportunity tax credit. Employers are allowed a tax credit equal to 40 percent of the first $6,000 of wages (per eligible employee) for the first year of employment. Eligible employees include certain hard-to-employ individuals (e.g., qualified ex-felons, high-risk youth, food stamp recipients, and veterans). The employer's deduction for wages is reduced by the amount of the credit taken. For qualified summer youth employees, the 40 percent rate is applied to the first $3,000 of qualified wages.

Working condition fringes. A type of fringe benefit received by the employee that is excludible from the employee's gross income. It consists of property or services provided (paid or reimbursed) by the employer for which the employee could take a tax deduction if the employee had paid for them. § 132.

Worthless securities. A loss (usually capital) is allowed for a security that becomes worthless during the year. The loss is deemed to have occurred on the last day of the year. Special rules apply to securities of affiliated companies and small business stock. § 165.

Writ of Certiorari. Appeal from a U.S. Court of Appeals to the U.S. Supreme Court is by Writ of Certiorari. The Supreme Court need not accept the appeal, and it usually does not (*cert. den.*) unless a conflict exists among the lower courts that must be resolved or a constitutional issue is involved.

Appendix D-1

Table of Code Sections Cited

[See Title 26 U.S.C.A.]

Appendix D-2

Table of Regulations Cited

Treasury Regulations

Treasury Regulations

Appendix D-3

Table of Revenue Procedures and Revenue Rulings Cited

Appendix E

Practice Set Assignments—Comprehensive Tax Return Problems

PROBLEM 1

David R. and Sheri N. Johnson (ages 45 and 46) are married and live at 641 Cody Way, Casper, WY 82609. David is a consulting engineer, while Sheri is a paralegal. They file a joint return and use the cash basis for tax purposes.

1. Trained as a mining engineer, David has developed considerable expertise in the treatment and disposition of waste material. He is also well-versed in the Federal and state requirements for land reclamation projects. David maintains a consulting practice through which he advises clients on these matters. David's business activity code is 541990. Most of his clients are small and medium-size mine owner/operators located in Wyoming and contiguous states (e.g., Montana, Idaho, Utah). Usually, David is retained by a client on a contract fee basis and is reimbursed for all out-of-pocket expenses. In performing his services, David usually visits the job site and later submits his recommendations in a written report along with a statement for his services and expenses. David received the following amounts from his consulting business in 2015:

Fees for services rendered		$ 92,800
Expense reimbursements:		
Airfare	$8,200	
Meals	6,100	
Lodging	5,200	
Transportation (taxis, airport limos, car rentals)	920	
Subtotal for expense reimbursement		20,420
Total received		$113,220

2. The following fees for rendered services are not included in the receipts listed in item 1 above:

Echo Mining: Payment received January 2016; work done December 2015	$5,100
Sesa Mining: Payment received January 2015; work done December 2014	4,400
Cormorant Mining: No payment received; work done March 2015	3,700

David did not incur travel expenses in any of these engagements (i.e., the work was done in his office). As Cormorant Mining is in bankruptcy, David does not expect to collect any of this fee.

3. Other expenses paid by David in 2015 relating to his practice are listed below.

Contribution to H.R. 10 (Keogh) retirement plan	$9,000
Premiums on medical insurance (covering self, spouse, and dependents)	3,800
Landscape models purchased from topographer for reclamation projects	3,200
Advertising in trade journals	2,400
Office supplies (including drafting materials)	1,200
Business phone and Internet service	860
State occupation license	300
Subscriptions to trade journals	240
Membership dues to trade associations	180

4. David operates his consulting business out of an office in his home. Twenty percent of the 3,000-square-foot living area is devoted to the office. David inherited the home on Cody Way from his father, who died on June 6, 2006, when it had a fair market value of $400,000 ($40,000 of which was allocated to the land). The Johnsons moved into the home in 2006, and David began using his home office in the same year. The home's current fair market value is $500,000 ($50,000 allocated to the land). County land records reflect that David's father bought the land in 1969 for $6,000 and built the house in 1973 at a cost of $60,000. David depreciates the business use of his home using MACRS, treating the home as 39-year nonresidential reality.

Additional information regarding the property for 2015 follows:

Utilities	$4,800
Repairs and maintenance	2,900
Property/casualty insurance	2,300

The property taxes and mortgage interest paid in 2015 on the home are listed in item 15 below. In addition to the repairs and maintenance noted above, David had the office repainted at a cost of $1,200. The furniture in the office, including business equipment (e.g., computer, fax machine, copier), was properly expensed in the year bought and has a zero basis. However, on March 5, 2015, David purchased a heavy-duty, fire-resistant file cabinet with security-vault features for $4,800. He made the acquisition to safeguard and maintain the privacy of client data. If possible, David prefers to avoid capitalizing and depreciating the cabinet.

5. On February 4, 2014, David paid $41,000 (including sales tax) for a used Infiniti crossover SUV (gross weight under 6,000 pounds), which he uses 90% of the time for business. No trade-in was involved, and he did not claim any § 179 expensing of the cost. Last year, David elected to use the actual operating cost method to compute deductible expenses for his business use of the Infiniti. Under this method, he depreciates the SUV using MACRS (half-year convention). (*Hint:* See Table 3 in the Instructions to Form 4562.) His operating expenses for the Infiniti for 2015 are as follows:

Gasoline	$3,300
Auto insurance	1,600
Repairs	240
Auto club dues	180
Oil changes and lubrication	120
License and registration	60

During business use, David received three moving traffic violations (total fines of $680) and incurred tolls and parking charges of $440. The Infiniti was driven a total of 14,500 miles during 2015 (mileage was incurred evenly during the year).

6. Sheri is a licensed paralegal and is employed on a part-time basis by several local attorneys. She commuted to work using the family Suburban for a total of 813 miles and paid parking fees of $310. Her earnings and job-related expenses are summarized below.

Salary (from four employers)	$38,000
Laptop computer	1,200
Subscriptions and dues to professional organizations	180
Continuing education correspondence course	120
Occupational license fee	80

Sheri purchased the laptop computer on March 12 and uses it 80% of the time for business. The correspondence course is required continuing education so she can retain her license.

Sheri is considering going to law school, so she attended a series of LSAT preparation sessions at a cost of $350. Because Sheri is a part-time employee, she is not covered by any of her employers' medical or retirement plans. Sheri is covered under David's insurance, and during 2015, she contributed $5,000 to a traditional IRA that she established several years ago. The Johnsons use the automatic mileage method to calculate any tax deductions that they are entitled to for use of the Suburban.

7. With funds received from the settlement of his father's estate, David purchased rental property at 4620 Cottonwood Lane, Casper, WY 82609. Of the $250,000 purchase price, $30,000 was allocated to the land. After an $80,000 renovation to the house (e.g., new flooring, roof, heating unit), the property was rented beginning February 1, 2009. In 2013, the Johnsons decided that their investment would be more marketable if the house was rented as furnished. Consequently, in May of that year, they spent $38,000 on new furniture (including drapes, carpeting, and appliances). Under the current lease agreement, the property rents for $2,200 a month (payable at the beginning of each month) with utilities not included. Information regarding the property for 2015 appears below.

Rent received	$28,600
Property/casualty insurance premiums paid	3,100
Property taxes paid	2,400
Yard maintenance paid	1,200
Repairs	800

The rent received includes $2,200 for January 2016. The tenants prepaid the rent in mid-December because they went on vacation during the Christmas/New Year holidays. In addition to the property taxes listed above, David paid a special tax assessment of $2,400 to the city of Casper for repaving the street in front of the property. The Johnsons use MACRS to depreciate the rental home and the furnishings within it (assume half-year convention for the personalty).

8. The Johnsons acquired 1,000 shares of common stock in Cormorant Mining on March 7, 2014, to hold for investment purposes. David performed services for the company in late 2013, submitting a bill for $3,900. Because Cormorant was experiencing cash-flow problems at the time, David accepted the stock as payment for his services. Unfortunately, Cormorant is currently in bankruptcy (see item 2 above), and expectations are that the shareholders will not recover anything on their stock investments. The stock is not publicly traded.

9. On March 10, 1997, David's father gave the Johnsons a plot of land located in Teton County as an anniversary present. It had a value of $150,000 at the time of the gift (no gift tax was due on the transfer). The land had been purchased by David's father on June 1, 1987, for $50,000. In December 2014, a real estate developer contacted the Johnsons and offered $800,000 for the property. After considerable negotiation, the following transaction took place on March 4, 2015: the Johnsons transferred the Teton plot in return for $8,000 in cash and four city lots in

Laramie (WY) worth $792,000. The Johnsons considered the city lots to be a good investment because they are located near the state university. All closing costs and legal fees were absorbed by the real estate developer.

10. David inherited an antique gun collection from his father when he died—mainly large caliber rifles used for buffalo hunting. Although David has no idea what his father's cost basis was in these guns, the collection had a date-of-death value of $22,000. Concerned about the maintenance and security of the collection, David sold it to a dealer for $29,000 on July 10, 2015.

11. On July 12, 2001, using $50,000 of funds she had received from an aunt's life insurance policy, Sheri purchased grazing land in Converse County (WY). On August 2, 2014, she sold the land to a local rancher for $75,000. Under the terms of the sale, Sheri received a down payment of $15,000 and 10 annual notes of $6,000 each. Sheri is also to receive simple interest of 8% on the outstanding principle balance each year. On August 4, 2015, Sheri collected $10,800 ($6,000 on the note and interest of $4,800) on the maturity of the first note.

12. Although the Johnsons had several Schedule D transactions during 2014, they ended up with a net short-term capital loss of $7,000. Of this loss, $3,000 was deducted in 2014, and $4,000 carried over to 2015.

13. For several years, Sheri's widowed mother, Vivian Olson, has lived with the Johnsons and has been claimed by them as a dependent. On December 30, 2014, Vivian suffered a heart attack. After six days in the ICU of a local hospital, Vivian died. In early February 2015, the Johnsons paid the following expenses related to Vivian:

Burial expenses	$4,400
Medical expenses incurred in 2014	4,200
Medical expenses incurred in 2015	3,100
Remainder of church pledge for 2015	600

Fortunately, the balance of Vivian's medical expenses ($11,900) was covered by insurance. Besides personal and household effects, Vivian's major asset was life insurance. As the designated beneficiary of the policy, Sheri received $20,000 of death benefits on March 13, 2015.

14. Besides the items already mentioned, the Johnsons had the following receipts during 2015:

Interest income:	
City of Cheyenne general purpose bonds	$1,900
CD at Wells Fargo Bank	1,100
Money market account at Bank of America	400
Yard (garage) sale	950
Qualified dividends on Meadowlark Corporation common stock	700
Jury duty fees	420

The yard sale involved used furniture, appliances, books, toys, and other household goods having an estimated original cost value of $1,800. In connection with her jury duty assignment in June, Sheri drove the Suburban 40 miles and incurred expenses of $30 for parking and $45 for meals.

15. In addition to the items already noted, the Johnsons had the following expenditures for 2015:

Interest on home equity loan used to finance the purchase of personal items (e.g., camper)	$4,400
Charitable contributions (not including Vivian's pledge)	3,200
Ad valorem property taxes on personal residence	3,100
Medical and dental bills (including prescription drugs of $400) other than those relating to Vivian (see item 13)	4,800

The Johnsons drove the Suburban 420 miles to various medical and dental appointments. Wyoming has no state or local income tax but does impose a general sales tax. The county in which they live imposes an additional local sales tax of 1%. Although they do not keep track of their sales taxes, they purchased a camper for $40,000 in May 2015. The sales tax on this purchase was $1,600.

16. Besides Vivian (see item 13), the Johnsons' household includes two daughters, Meredith (age 19) and Kirby (age 18), and one son, Toby (age 17). Kirby and Toby are full-time students in high school. Meredith graduated a year ago and earned $9,000 working part time during 2015. She deposited these earnings in a savings account, hoping someday to attend college.

17. For tax year 2014, the Johnsons had an overpayment of $150, which they applied toward their 2015 income tax. Sheri's income tax withholdings for the year are $5,100, and the Johnsons made Federal quarterly tax payments totaling $16,000 ($4,000 each installment).

18. Relevant Social Security numbers are noted below.

Name	Social Security Number
David Johnson	111-11-1112
Sheri Johnson	123-45-6785
Vivian Olson	123-45-6786
Meredith Johnson	123-45-6787
Kirby Johnson	123-45-6788
Toby Johnson	123-45-6789

Requirements

Prepare an income tax return (with appropriate supporting forms and schedules) for the Johnsons for 2015. In doing this, follow these guidelines:

- Make necessary assumptions for information not given but needed to complete the return.
- The taxpayers are preparing their own return (i.e., no preparer is involved).
- The taxpayers have the necessary written substantiation (e.g., records, receipts) to support the transactions involved.
- If any refund is due, apply it toward next year's taxes.
- The Johnsons do not wish to contribute to the Presidential Election Campaign Fund.

PROBLEM 2

Carrie A. Morgan, age 45, is single and lives with her dependent mother at 426 Grouse Avenue, Allentown, PA 18105. Her Social Security number is 111-11-1112.

1. Carrie is a licensed hairstylist and operates her own business. Located at 480 Laurel Street, Allentown, PA 18105, the business is conducted under the name of "Carrie's Coiffures." Carrie's business activity code is 812112. In addition to 10 workstations (i.e., stylist chairs) and a small reception area, the shop has display and storage areas for the products she sells (see item 2 below). During the year, Carrie leased nine of the stations to other hairstylists. As is common practice in similar businesses in the area, the other stylists are considered to be self-employed. In fact, the IRS sanctioned the self-employment classification for the stylists in an audit of one of Carrie's prior tax returns. Each stylist pays Carrie a fixed rent for the use of a workstation, resulting in $68,000 of rents received during 2015. From her own station, Carrie earned $44,000 (including tips of $12,000) for the styling services she provided to her own clients.

2. Carrie's Coiffures is the local distributor for several beauty products (e.g., conditioners, shampoos) that cannot be purchased anywhere else. Carrie buys these items from the manufacturers and sells them to regular patrons, walk-in customers, and other beauticians (including those who lease chairs from her). Carrie's Coiffures is also known for the selection and quality of its hairpieces (i.e., wigs, toupees). Through the shop, Carrie made the following sales during the year:

Hairpieces and wigs	$69,000
Beauty products	48,000

Although Carrie operates her business on a cash basis, she maintains inventory accounts for the items she sells as required by law. So, she uses the hybrid method of accounting for tax reporting purposes. Relevant information about the inventories (based on lower of cost or market) is summarized below.

	12/31/14	12/31/15
Hairpieces and wigs	$10,700	$12,600
Beauty products	11,400	9,900

Carrie's purchases for 2015 were $30,500 of hairpieces and wigs and $26,100 of beauty products.

Carrie's Coiffures had the following operating expenses for 2015:

Utilities (i.e., gas, electric, telephone)		$12,900
Ad valorem property taxes:		
On realty (e.g., shop building and land)	$4,200	
On personalty (e.g., equipment, inventory)	1,800	6,000
Styling supplies (e.g., rinses, dyes, gels, hair spray)		5,700
Fire and casualty insurance		4,100
Liability insurance		4,000
Accounting services		3,800
Janitorial services		2,400
Sewer service, garbage pickup		2,300
Water		2,200
Occupation licenses (city and state)		1,500
Waiting room supplies (e.g., magazines, coffee)		1,300

As Carrie prefers to avoid employer-employee arrangements and the payroll tax complexities, she retains outside agencies to handle her accounting and janitorial needs.

3. In early 2015, Carrie decided to renovate the waiting room. On May 10, she spent $10,400 for new chairs, a sofa, various lamps, coffee bar, etc. Carrie follows a policy of claiming as much depreciation as soon as possible. The old furnishings were thrown away or given to customers. For tax purposes, the old furnishings had a zero basis.

4. Carrie's Coiffures is located in a building Carrie had constructed at 480 Laurel Street in March 2001. The shop was built for a cost of $300,000 on a lot she purchased earlier for $35,000. Except for a down payment from savings, the cost was financed by a 20-year mortgage. For tax purposes, MACRS depreciation is claimed on the building. During 2015, the following expenses were attributable to the property:

Repainting (both exterior and interior)	$8,000
Repairs (plumbing and electrical)	1,900

In May (after her accident settlement discussed in item 10 below), Carrie paid the balance due on the business mortgage. To do so, she incurred a prepayment penalty of $4,400. Prior to paying off the mortgage, she paid regular interest on the mortgage in 2015 of $6,000.

5. In February 2015, Carrie's Coiffures was cited by the city for improper disposal of certain waste chemicals. Carrie questioned the propriety of the proposed fine of $2,000 and retained an attorney to represent her at the hearing. By pleading *nolo contendere*, the attorney was able to get the fine reduced to $500. Carrie paid both the fine of $500 and the attorney's fee of $600 in 2015.

6. In August 2015, Carrie saw an ad in a trade publication that attracted her attention. The owner of a well-respected styling salon in Reading (PA) had died, and his estate was offering the business for sale. Carrie traveled to Reading, spent several days looking over the business (including books and financial results), and met with the executor. Carried treated the executor to dinner and a music concert. Immediately after the concert, Carrie made an offer for the business, but the executor rejected her offer. Her expenses in connection with this trip were as follows:

Car rental	$140
Entertainment of executor (dinner and concert)	280
Motel (August 6–7)	220
Personal meals	110

7. In March 2014, Joan Myers, one of Carrie's best stylists, left town to get away from a troublesome ex-husband. In order to help Joan establish a business elsewhere, Carrie loaned her $7,000. Joan signed a note dated March 3, 2014, that was payable in one year with 6% interest. On December 30, 2015, Carrie learned that Joan had been declared bankrupt and was awaiting trial on felony theft charges. Carrie never received payment from Joan, nor did she receive any interest on the loan.

8. At Christmas, Carrie gave each of her 35 best customers a large bottle of body lotion. Each bottle had a wholesale cost to Carrie of $12 but a retail price of $24. Carrie also spent $3 to have each bottle gift wrapped. (*Note:* The lotion was special order merchandise and was not part of the business's inventory or purchases for the year—see item 2 above.) She also gave each of the nine stylists who leased chairs from her a fruit basket that cost $30 (not including a $5 delivery cost).

9. In March 2015, the Pennsylvania Department of Revenue audited Carrie's state income tax returns for 2012 and 2013. She was assessed additional state income tax of $340 for these years. Surprisingly, no interest was included in the assessment. Carrie paid the back taxes promptly.

10. On a morning walk in November 2014, Carrie was injured when she was side-swiped by a delivery truck. Carrie was hospitalized for several days, and the driver of the truck was ticketed and charged with DUI. The owner of the truck, a national parcel delivery service, was concerned that further adverse publicity might result if the matter went to court. Consequently, the owner offered Carrie a settlement if she would sign a release. Under the settlement, her medical expenses were paid and she would receive a cash award of $200,000. The award specified that the entire amount was for physical pain and suffering. Since she suffered no permanent injury as a result of the mishap, she signed the release in April 2015 and received the $200,000 settlement.

11. In January 2015, Carrie was contacted by the state of Pennsylvania regarding a tract of land she owned in York County. The state intended to convert the property into a district headquarters, barracks, and training center for its highway patrol. Carrie had inherited the property from her father when he died on August 11, 2014. The property had a value of $140,000 on that date and had been purchased by her father on March 3, 1980, for $30,000. On July 25, 2015, after considerable negotiation and after the state threatened to initiate condemnation proceedings, she sold the tract to the state for $158,000. Since Carrie is not comfortable with real estate investments, she does not plan to reinvest any of the proceeds received in another piece of realty.

12. When her father died in 2014, Carrie did not know that he had an insurance policy on his life (maturity value of $50,000) in which she was named the beneficiary. When her mother told her about the policy in July 2015, Carrie filed a claim with the carrier, Falcon Life Insurance Company. In August 2015, she received a check from Falcon for $51,500 (including $1,500 interest).

13. Upon the advice of a client, who is a respected broker, Carrie purchased 1,000 shares of common stock in Grosbeak Exploration for $40,000 on March 4, 2015. In the months following her purchase, the share value of Grosbeak plummeted. Disgusted with the unexpected erosion in the value of her investment, Carrie sold the stock for $28,000 on December 23, 2015.

14. While on her way to work in 2014, Carrie was rear-ended by a hit-and-run driver. Thankfully, she was not injured in the accident. The damage to her Lexus was covered by her insurance company, General Casualty, except for the $1,000 deductible she was required to pay. In 2015, the insurance company located the driver who caused the accident and was reimbursed by his insurer. Consequently, Carrie received a $1,000 refund check from General Casualty in May 2015 to reimburse her for the $1,000 deductible.

15. After her father's death, Carrie's mother (Mildred Morgan, Social Security number 123-45-6789) moved in with her. Mildred's persistent back trouble made it difficult for her to climb the stairs to the second-floor bedrooms in Carrie's house. So, Carrie had an elevator installed in her personal residence at a cost of $12,000 in January 2015. A qualified appraiser determined that the elevator increased the value of the personal residence by $5,000. The appraisal cost $400. The operation of the elevator during 2015 increased Carrie's electric bill by $300.

16. As a favor to a long-time client who is a drama professor at a local state university, Carrie spent a weekend as a stylist for the key actresses in the annual Theater Department fund-raising event. The drama professor provided all of the resources that Carrie needed to provide her services. Carrie estimates that she would have charged $800 for the services she donated to this charitable event.

17. In addition to the items already mentioned, Carrie had the following receipts during 2015:

Interest income:		
CD at Scranton First National Bank	$900	
City of Lancaster general purpose bonds	490	
Money market account at Allentown State Bank	340	$1,730
Qualified dividends on stock investments:		
General Motors	$470	
AT&T common	380	850
Federal income tax refund (for tax year 2014)		791
Pennsylvania state income tax refund (for tax year 2014)		205

18. Expenditures for 2015, not previously noted, are summarized below.

Contribution to pension plan		$10,000
Medical:		
Premiums on medical insurance	$4,800	
Dental bills	1,400	6,200
Property taxes on personal residence		3,800
Interest on home mortgage		3,200
Professional expenses:		
Subscriptions to trade journals	$ 180	
Dues to beautician groups	140	320

The $10,000 contribution to the pension plan is to a § 401(k) type of plan she established in 2015. Previously, she had contributed to an H.R. 10 (Keogh) plan but found that the § 401(k) retirement arrangement provides more flexibility and is less complex. The medical insurance policy covers Carrie and her dependents and was issued in the name of the business (i.e., "Carrie's Coiffures"). It does not cover dental work or capital modifications to a residence (see item 15 above).

19. During 2015, Carrie made total estimated tax payments with respect to her 2015 tax returns of:

Federal estimated income tax payments	$20,800
Pennsylvania estimated income tax payments	2,400
Allentown City estimated income tax payments	800

Requirements

Prepare an income tax return (with appropriate schedules) for Carrie for 2015. In doing this, use the following guidelines:

- Make necessary assumptions for information not given in the problem.
- Carrie has itemized deductions ever since she became a homeowner many years ago.
- The sales tax option was not chosen in 2014, and Carrie had no major purchases that qualify for the sales tax deduction in 2015.
- Carrie has substantiation (e.g., records, receipts) to support the transactions involved.
- If a refund results, Carrie wants it sent to her.
- Carrie is preparing her own return (i.e., no preparer is involved).
- Carrie does not wish to contribute to the Presidential Election Campaign Fund.

Appendix F

Table of Cases Cited

Appendix G

Tax Formulas

2015 Tax Rate Schedules

Single—Schedule X

If taxable income is: Over—	But not over—	The tax is:	of the amount over—
$ 0	$ 9,225	.........10%	$ 0
9,225	37,450	$ 922.50 + 15%	9,225
37,450	90,750	5,156.25 + 25%	37,450
90,750	189,300	18,481.25 + 28%	90,750
189,300	411,500	46,075.25 + 33%	189,300
411,500	413,200	119,401.25 + 35%	411,500
413,200	....	119,996.25 + 39.6%	413,200

Head of household—Schedule Z

If taxable income is: Over—	But not over—	The tax is:	of the amount over—
$ 0	$ 13,150	.........10%	$ 0
13,150	50,200	$ 1,315.00 + 15%	13,150
50,200	129,600	6,872.50 + 25%	50,200
129,600	209,850	26,722.50 + 28%	129,600
209,850	411,500	49,192.50 + 33%	209,850
411,500	439,000	115,737.00 + 35%	411,500
439,000	....	125,362.00 + 39.6%	439,000

Married filing jointly or Qualifying widow(er)—Schedule Y–1

If taxable income is: Over—	But not over—	The tax is:	of the amount over—
$ 0	$ 18,450	.........10%	$ 0
18,450	74,900	$ 1,845.00 + 15%	18,450
74,900	151,200	10,312.50 + 25%	74,900
151,200	230,450	29,387.50 + 28%	151,200
230,450	411,500	51,577.50 + 33%	230,450
411,500	464,850	111,324.00 + 35%	411,500
464,850	....	129,996.50 + 39.6%	464,850

Married filing separately—Schedule Y–2

If taxable income is: Over—	But not over—	The tax is:	of the amount over—
$ 0	$ 9,225	.........10%	$ 0
9,225	37,450	$ 922.50 + 15%	9,225
37,450	75,600	5,156.25 + 25%	37,450
75,600	115,225	14,693.75 + 28%	75,600
115,225	205,750	25,788.75 + 33%	115,225
205,750	232,425	55,662.00 + 35%	205,750
232,425	....	64,998.25 + 39.6%	232,425

2016 Tax Rate Schedules

Single—Schedule X

If taxable income is: Over—	But not over—	The tax is:	of the amount over—
$ 0	$ 9,275	.........10%	$ 0
9,275	37,650	$ 927.50 + 15%	9,275
37,650	91,150	5,183.75 + 25%	37,650
91,150	190,150	18,558.75 + 28%	91,150
190,150	413,350	46,278.75 + 33%	190,150
413,350	415,050	119,934.75 + 35%	413,350
415,050	....	120,529.75 + 39.6%	415,050

Head of household—Schedule Z

If taxable income is: Over—	But not over—	The tax is:	of the amount over—
$ 0	$ 13,250	.........10%	$ 0
13,250	50,400	$ 1,325.00 + 15%	13,250
50,400	130,150	6,897.50 + 25%	50,400
130,150	210,800	26,835.00 + 28%	130,150
210,800	413,350	49,417.00 + 33%	210,800
413,350	441,000	116,258.50 + 35%	413,350
441,000	....	125,936.00 + 39.6%	441,000

Married filing jointly or Qualifying widow(er)—Schedule Y–1

If taxable income is: Over—	But not over—	The tax is:	of the amount over—
$ 0	$ 18,550	.........10%	$ 0
18,550	75,300	$ 1,855.00 + 15%	18,550
75,300	151,900	10,367.50 + 25%	75,300
151,900	231,450	29,517.50 + 28%	151,900
231,450	413,350	51,791.50 + 33%	231,450
413,350	466,950	111,818.50 + 35%	413,350
466,950	....	130,578.50 + 39.6%	466,950

Married filing separately—Schedule Y–2

If taxable income is: Over—	But not over—	The tax is:	of the amount over—
$ 0	$ 9,275	.........10%	$ 0
9,275	37,650	$ 927.50 + 15%	9,275
37,650	75,950	5,183.75 + 25%	37,650
75,950	115,725	14,758.75 + 28%	75,950
115,725	206,675	25,895.75 + 33%	115,725
206,675	233,475	55,909.25 + 35%	206,675
233,475	....	65,289.25 + 39.6%	233,475

Tax Formula for Individuals

Income (broadly defined)	$xx,xxx
Less: Exclusions	(x,xxx)
Gross income	$xx,xxx
Less: Deductions *for* adjusted gross income	(x,xxx)
Adjusted gross income	$xx,xxx
Less: The greater of—	
Total itemized deductions	
or standard deduction	(x,xxx)
Less: Personal and dependency exemptions	(x,xxx)
Taxable income	$xx,xxx
Tax on taxable income	$ x,xxx
Less: Tax credits (including Federal income tax	
withheld and prepaid)	(xxx)
Tax due (or refund)	$ xxx

Basic Standard Deduction Amounts

	Standard Deduction Amount	
Filing Status	**2015**	**2016**
Single	$ 6,300	$ 6,300
Married, filing jointly	12,600	12,600
Surviving spouse	12,600	12,600
Head of household	9,250	9,300
Married, filing separately	6,300	6,300

Amount of Each Additional Standard Deduction

Filing Status	**2015**	**2016**
Single	$1,550	$1,550
Married, filing jointly	1,250	1,250
Surviving spouse	1,250	1,250
Head of household	1,550	1,550
Married, filing separately	1,250	1,250

Personal and Dependency Exemption

2015	2016
$4,000	$4,050

AMT Formula for Individuals

Taxable income (increased by any standard deduction and personal or dependency exemptions)

Plus or minus: Adjustments

Plus: Preferences

Equals: Alternative minimum taxable income (AMTI)

Minus: Exemption

Equals: Alternative minimum tax (AMT) base

Multiplied by: 26% or 28% rate

Equals: Tentative minimum tax before foreign tax credit

Minus: AMT foreign tax credit

Equals: Tentative minimum tax (TMT)

Minus: Regular tax liability (less any foreign tax credit)

Equals: AMT (if TMT > regular tax liability)

AMT Exemption Phaseout for Individuals for 2016

| | | Phaseout | |
Filing Status	Exemption	Begins at	Ends at
Married, filing jointly	$83,800	$159,700	$494,900
Single or head of household	53,900	119,700	335,300
Married, filing separately	41,900	79,850	247,450

AMT Formula for Corporations

Taxable income prior to any regular tax NOL deduction

Plus or minus: Adjustments

Plus: Preferences

Equals: Pre-ACE alternative minimum taxable income (AMTI)

Plus or minus: ACE adjustment

Equals: AMTI before ATNOLD

Minus: ATNOLD (limited to 90% of AMTI before ATNOLD)

Equals: AMTI

Minus: Exemption

Equals: Alternative minimum tax (AMT) base

Multiplied by: 20%

Equals: Tentative minimum tax before AMT foreign tax credit

Minus: AMT foreign tax credit

Equals: Tentative minimum tax (TMT)

Minus: Regular tax liability (less any foreign tax credit)

Equals: AMT (if TMT > regular tax liability)

Income Tax Rates—Corporations

Taxable Income	Tax Rate
Not over $50,000	15%
Over $50,000 but not over $75,000	25%
Over $75,000 but not over $100,000	34%
Over $100,000 but not over $335,000	39%*
Over $335,000 but not over $10,000,000	34%
Over $10,000,000 but not over $15,000,000	35%
Over $15,000,000 but not over $18,333,333	38%**
Over $18,333,333	35%

* Five percent of this rate represents a phaseout of the benefits of the lower tax rates on the first $75,000 of taxable income.

**Three percent of this rate represents a phaseout of the benefits of the lower tax rate (34% rather than 35%) on the first $10 million of taxable income.

Appendix H

Present Value and Future Value Tables

Present Value of $1

N/R	1%	2%	3%	4%	5%	6%	7%	8%	9%	10%	11%	12%
1	0.9901	0.9804	0.9709	0.9615	0.9524	0.9434	0.9346	0.9259	0.9174	0.9091	0.9009	0.8929
2	0.9803	0.9612	0.9426	0.9246	0.9070	0.8900	0.8734	0.8573	0.8417	0.8264	0.8116	0.7972
3	0.9706	0.9423	0.9151	0.8890	0.8638	0.8396	0.8163	0.7938	0.7722	0.7513	0.7312	0.7118
4	0.9610	0.9238	0.8885	0.8548	0.8227	0.7921	0.7629	0.7350	0.7084	0.6830	0.6587	0.6355
5	0.9515	0.9057	0.8626	0.8219	0.7835	0.7473	0.7130	0.6806	0.6499	0.6209	0.5935	0.5674
6	0.9420	0.8880	0.8375	0.7903	0.7462	0.7050	0.6663	0.6302	0.5963	0.5645	0.5346	0.5066
7	0.9327	0.8706	0.8131	0.7599	0.7107	0.6651	0.6227	0.5835	0.5470	0.5132	0.4817	0.4523
8	0.9235	0.8535	0.7894	0.7307	0.6768	0.6274	0.5820	0.5403	0.5019	0.4665	0.4339	0.4039
9	0.9143	0.8368	0.7664	0.7026	0.6446	0.5919	0.5439	0.5002	0.4604	0.4241	0.3909	0.3606
10	0.9053	0.8203	0.7441	0.6756	0.6139	0.5584	0.5083	0.4632	0.4224	0.3855	0.3522	0.3220
11	0.8963	0.8043	0.7224	0.6496	0.5847	0.5268	0.4751	0.4289	0.3875	0.3505	0.3173	0.2875
12	0.8874	0.7885	0.7014	0.6246	0.5568	0.4970	0.4440	0.3971	0.3555	0.3186	0.2858	0.2567
13	0.8787	0.7730	0.6810	0.6006	0.5303	0.4688	0.4150	0.3677	0.3262	0.2897	0.2575	0.2292
14	0.8700	0.7579	0.6611	0.5775	0.5051	0.4423	0.3878	0.3405	0.2992	0.2633	0.2320	0.2046
15	0.8613	0.7430	0.6419	0.5553	0.4810	0.4173	0.3624	0.3152	0.2745	0.2394	0.2090	0.1827
16	0.8528	0.7284	0.6232	0.5339	0.4581	0.3936	0.3387	0.2919	0.2519	0.2176	0.1883	0.1631
17	0.8444	0.7142	0.6050	0.5134	0.4363	0.3714	0.3166	0.2703	0.2311	0.1978	0.1696	0.1456
18	0.8360	0.7002	0.5874	0.4936	0.4155	0.3503	0.2959	0.2502	0.2120	0.1799	0.1528	0.1300
19	0.8277	0.6864	0.5703	0.4746	0.3957	0.3305	0.2765	0.2317	0.1945	0.1635	0.1377	0.1161
20	0.8195	0.6730	0.5537	0.4564	0.3769	0.3118	0.2584	0.2145	0.1784	0.1486	0.1240	0.1037

Present Value of an Ordinary Annuity of $1

N/R	1%	2%	3%	4%	5%	6%	7%	8%	9%	10%	11%	12%
1	0.9901	0.9804	0.9709	0.9615	0.9524	0.9434	0.9346	0.9259	0.9174	0.9091	0.9009	0.8929
2	1.9704	1.9416	1.9135	1.8861	1.8594	1.8334	1.8080	1.7833	1.7591	1.7355	1.7125	1.6901
3	2.9410	2.8839	2.8286	2.7751	2.7232	2.6730	2.6243	2.5771	2.5313	2.4869	2.4437	2.4018
4	3.9020	3.8077	3.7171	3.6299	3.5460	3.4651	3.3872	3.3121	3.2397	3.1699	3.1024	3.0373
5	4.8534	4.7135	4.5797	4.4518	4.3295	4.2124	4.1002	3.9927	3.8897	3.7908	3.6959	3.6048
6	5.7955	5.6014	5.4172	5.2421	5.0757	4.9173	4.7665	4.6229	4.4859	4.3553	4.2305	4.1114
7	6.7282	6.4720	6.2303	6.0021	5.7864	5.5824	5.3893	5.2064	5.0330	4.8684	4.7122	4.5638
8	7.6517	7.3255	7.0197	6.7327	6.4632	6.2098	5.9713	5.7466	5.5348	5.3349	5.1461	4.9676
9	8.5660	8.1622	7.7861	7.4353	7.1078	6.8017	6.5152	6.2469	5.9952	5.7590	5.5370	5.3282
10	9.4713	8.9826	8.5302	8.1109	7.7217	7.3601	7.0236	6.7101	6.4177	6.1446	5.8892	5.6502
11	10.3676	9.7868	9.2526	8.7605	8.3064	7.8869	7.4987	7.1390	6.8052	6.4951	6.2065	5.9377
12	11.2551	10.5753	9.9540	9.3851	8.8633	8.3838	7.9427	7.5361	7.1607	6.8137	6.4924	6.1944
13	12.1337	11.3484	10.6350	9.9856	9.3936	8.8527	8.3577	7.9038	7.4869	7.1034	6.7499	6.4235
14	13.0037	12.1062	11.2961	10.5631	9.8986	9.2950	8.7455	8.2442	7.7862	7.3667	6.9819	6.6282
15	13.8651	12.8493	11.9379	11.1184	10.3797	9.7122	9.1079	8.5595	8.0607	7.6061	7.1909	6.8109
16	14.7179	13.5777	12.5611	11.6523	10.8378	10.1059	9.4466	8.8514	8.3126	7.8237	7.3792	6.9740
17	15.5623	14.2919	13.1661	12.1657	11.2741	10.4773	9.7632	9.1216	8.5436	8.0216	7.5488	7.1196
18	16.3983	14.9920	13.7535	12.6593	11.6896	10.8276	10.0591	9.3719	8.7556	8.2014	7.7016	7.2497
19	17.2260	15.6785	14.3238	13.1339	12.0853	11.1581	10.3356	9.6036	8.9501	8.3649	7.8393	7.3658
20	18.0456	16.3514	14.8775	13.5903	12.4622	11.4699	10.5940	9.8181	9.1285	8.5136	7.9633	7.4694

Future Value of $1

N/R	1%	2%	3%	4%	5%	6%	7%	8%	9%	10%	11%	12%
1	1.0100	1.0200	1.0300	1.0400	1.0500	1.0600	1.0700	1.0800	1.0900	1.1000	1.1100	1.1200
2	1.0201	1.0404	1.0609	1.0816	1.1025	1.1236	1.1449	1.1664	1.1881	1.2100	1.2321	1.2544
3	1.0303	1.0612	1.0927	1.1249	1.1576	1.1910	1.2250	1.2597	1.2950	1.3310	1.3676	1.4049
4	1.0406	1.0824	1.1255	1.1699	1.2155	1.2625	1.3108	1.3605	1.4116	1.4641	1.5181	1.5735
5	1.0510	1.1041	1.1593	1.2167	1.2763	1.3382	1.4026	1.4693	1.5386	1.6105	1.6851	1.7623
6	1.0615	1.1262	1.1941	1.2653	1.3401	1.4185	1.5007	1.5869	1.6771	1.7716	1.8704	1.9738
7	1.0721	1.1487	1.2299	1.3159	1.4071	1.5036	1.6058	1.7138	1.8280	1.9487	2.0762	2.2107
8	1.0829	1.1717	1.2668	1.3686	1.4775	1.5938	1.7182	1.8509	1.9926	2.1436	2.3045	2.4760
9	1.0937	1.1951	1.3048	1.4233	1.5513	1.6895	1.8385	1.9990	2.1719	2.3579	2.5580	2.7731
10	1.1046	1.2190	1.3439	1.4802	1.6289	1.7908	1.9672	2.1589	2.3674	2.5937	2.8394	3.1058
11	1.1157	1.2434	1.3842	1.5395	1.7103	1.8983	2.1049	2.3316	2.5804	2.8531	3.1518	3.4785
12	1.1268	1.2682	1.4258	1.6010	1.7959	2.0122	2.2522	2.5182	2.8127	3.1384	3.4985	3.8960
13	1.1381	1.2936	1.4685	1.6651	1.8856	2.1329	2.4098	2.7196	3.0658	3.4523	3.8833	4.3635
14	1.1495	1.3195	1.5126	1.7317	1.9799	2.2609	2.5785	2.9372	3.3417	3.7975	4.3104	4.8871
15	1.1610	1.3459	1.5580	1.8009	2.0789	2.3966	2.7590	3.1722	3.6425	4.1772	4.7846	5.4736
16	1.1726	1.3728	1.6047	1.8730	2.1829	2.5404	2.9522	3.4259	3.9703	4.5950	5.3109	6.1304
17	1.1843	1.4002	1.6528	1.9479	2.2920	2.6928	3.1588	3.7000	4.3276	5.0545	5.8951	6.8660
18	1.1961	1.4282	1.7024	2.0258	2.4066	2.8543	3.3799	3.9960	4.7171	5.5599	6.5436	7.6900
19	1.2081	1.4568	1.7535	2.1068	2.5270	3.0256	3.6165	4.3157	5.1417	6.1159	7.2633	8.6128
20	1.2202	1.4859	1.8061	2.1911	2.6533	3.2071	3.8697	4.6610	5.6044	6.7275	8.0623	9.6463

Future Value of an Ordinary Annuity of $1

N/R	1%	2%	3%	4%	5%	6%	7%	8%	9%	10%	11%	12%
1	1.0000	1.0000	1.0000	1.0000	1.0000	1.0000	1.0000	1.0000	1.0000	1.0000	1.0000	1.0000
2	2.0100	2.0200	2.0300	2.0400	2.0500	2.0600	2.0700	2.0800	2.0900	2.1000	2.1100	2.1200
3	3.0301	3.0604	3.0909	3.1216	3.1525	3.1836	3.2149	3.2464	3.2781	3.3100	3.3421	3.3744
4	4.0604	4.1216	4.1836	4.2465	4.3101	4.3746	4.4399	4.5061	4.5731	4.6410	4.7097	4.7793
5	5.1010	5.2040	5.3091	5.4163	5.5256	5.6371	5.7507	5.8666	5.9847	6.1051	6.2278	6.3528
6	6.1520	6.3081	6.4684	6.6330	6.8019	6.9753	7.1533	7.3359	7.5233	7.7156	7.9129	8.1152
7	7.2135	7.4343	7.6625	7.8983	8.1420	8.3938	8.6540	8.9228	9.2004	9.4872	9.7833	10.0890
8	8.2857	8.5830	8.8923	9.2142	9.5491	9.8975	10.2598	10.6366	11.0285	11.4359	11.8594	12.2997
9	9.3685	9.7546	10.1591	10.5828	11.0266	11.4913	11.9780	12.4876	13.0210	13.5795	14.1640	14.7757
10	10.4622	10.9497	11.4639	12.0061	12.5779	13.1808	13.8164	14.4866	15.1929	15.9374	16.7220	17.5487
11	11.5668	12.1687	12.8078	13.4864	14.2068	14.9716	15.7836	16.6455	17.5603	18.5312	19.5614	20.6546
12	12.6825	13.4121	14.1920	15.0258	15.9171	16.8699	17.8885	18.9771	20.1407	21.3843	22.7132	24.1331
13	13.8093	14.6803	15.6178	16.6268	17.7130	18.8821	20.1406	21.4953	22.9534	24.5227	26.2116	28.0291
14	14.9474	15.9739	17.0863	18.2919	19.5986	21.0151	22.5505	24.2149	26.0192	27.9750	30.0949	32.3926
15	16.0969	17.2934	18.5989	20.0236	21.5786	23.2760	25.1290	27.1521	29.3609	31.7725	34.4054	37.2797
16	17.2579	18.6393	20.1569	21.8245	23.6575	25.6725	27.8881	30.3243	33.0034	35.9497	39.1899	42.7533
17	18.4304	20.0121	21.7616	23.6975	25.8404	28.2129	30.8402	33.7502	36.9737	40.5447	44.5008	48.8837
18	19.6147	21.4123	23.4144	25.6454	28.1324	30.9057	33.9990	37.4502	41.3013	45.5992	50.3959	55.7497
19	20.8109	22.8406	25.1169	27.6712	30.5390	33.7600	37.3790	41.4463	46.0185	51.1591	56.9395	63.4397
20	22.0190	24.2974	26.8704	29.7781	33.0660	36.7856	40.9955	45.7620	51.1601	57.2750	64.2028	72.0524

Index

T

AMT Formula for Individuals

Taxable income (increased by any standard deduction and personal or dependency exemptions)

Plus or minus: Adjustments

Plus: Preferences

Equals: Alternative minimum taxable income (AMTI)

Minus: Exemption

Equals: Alternative minimum tax (AMT) base

Multiplied by: 26% or 28% rate

Equals: Tentative minimum tax before foreign tax credit

Minus: AMT foreign tax credit

Equals: Tentative minimum tax (TMT)

Minus: Regular tax liability (less any foreign tax credit)

Equals: AMT (if TMT > regular tax liability)

AMT Exemption Phaseout for Individuals for 2016

Filing Status	Exemption	Phaseout Begins at	Ends at
Married, filing jointly	$83,800	$159,700	$494,900
Single or head of household	53,900	119,700	335,300
Married, filing separately	41,900	79,850	247,450